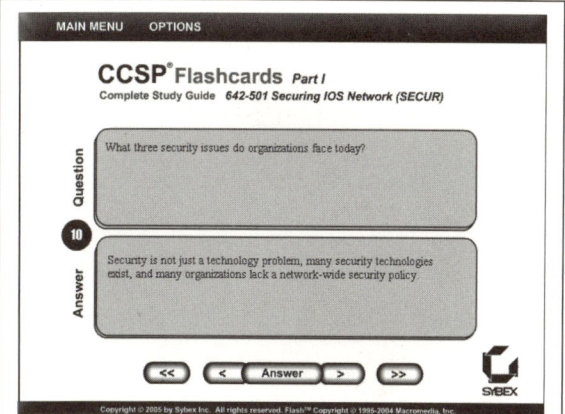

Reinforce understanding of key topics with flashcards for your PC, Pocket PC, or Palm handheld!

- Contains over 500 flashcard questions.
- Runs on multiple platforms for usability and portability.
- Quiz yourself anytime, anywhere!

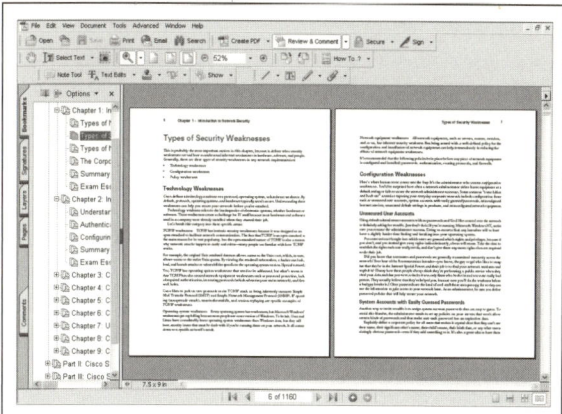

Access the entire book in PDF!

- Full search capabilities let you quickly find the information you need
- Complete with tables and illustrations
- Adobe Acrobat Reader with Search included

CCSP
Complete Study Guide
(642-501, 642-511, 642-521, 642-531, 642-541)

CCSP®
Complete Study Guide
(642-501, 642-511, 642-521, 642-531, 642-541)

Wade Edwards, CCIE
Todd Lammle
Tom Lancaster, CCIE
Justin Menga
Eric Quinn
Jason Rohm, CCIE
Carl Timm, CCIE
Bryant Tow

San Francisco • London

Publisher: Neil Edde
Acquisitions Editor: Heather O'Connor
Developmental Editor: Jeff Kellum
Production Editor: Lori Newman
Technical Editor: Dan Aguilera
Copy Editor: Tiffany Taylor
Compositor: Laurie Stewart, Happenstance Type-O-Rama
Graphic Illustrator: Jeffrey Wilson, Happenstance Type-O-Rama
CD Coordinator: Dan Mummert
CD Technician: Kevin Ly
Proofreaders: Jim Brook, Candace English, Jennifer Larsen, Nancy Riddiough
Indexer: Ted Laux
Book Designer: Bill Gibson, Judy Fung
Cover Designer: Archer Design
Cover Illustrator/Photographer: Photodisc and Victor Arre

Copyright © 2005 SYBEX Inc., 1151 Marina Village Parkway, Alameda, CA 94501. World rights reserved. The author(s) created reusable code in this publication expressly for reuse by readers. Sybex grants readers limited permission to reuse the code found in this publication or its accompanying CD-ROM so long as the author(s) are attributed in any application containing the reusable code and the code itself is never distributed, posted online by electronic transmission, sold, or commercially exploited as a stand-alone product. Aside from this specific exception concerning reusable code, no part of this publication may be stored in a retrieval system, transmitted, or reproduced in any way, including but not limited to photocopy, photograph, magnetic, or other record, without the prior agreement and written permission of the publisher.

Portions of this book were published under the titles:

CCSP Securing Cisco IOS Networks Study Guide © 2003 SYBEX Inc., *CCSP Secure PIX and Secure VPN Study Guide* © 2004 SYBEX Inc., and *CCSP Secure Intrusion Detection and SAFE Implementation* © 2004 SYBEX Inc.

Library of Congress Card Number: 2005920776

ISBN: 0-7821-4422-5

SYBEX and the SYBEX logo are either registered trademarks or trademarks of SYBEX Inc. in the United States and/or other countries.

Screen reproductions produced with FullShot 99. FullShot 99 © 1991–1999 Inbit Incorporated. All rights reserved.

FullShot is a trademark of Inbit Incorporated.

The CD interface was created using Macromedia Director, COPYRIGHT 1994, 1997–1999 Macromedia Inc. For more information on Macromedia and Macromedia Director, visit http://www.macromedia.com.

This study guide and/or material is not sponsored by, endorsed by or affiliated with Cisco Systems, Inc. Cisco®, Cisco Systems®, CCDA™, CCNA™, CCDP™, CCSP™, CCIP™, BSCI™, CCNP™, CCIE™, CCSI™, the Cisco Systems logo, and the CCIE logo are trademarks or registered trademarks of Cisco Systems, Inc. in the United States and certain other countries. All other trademarks are trademarks of their respective owners.

TRADEMARKS: SYBEX has attempted throughout this book to distinguish proprietary trademarks from descriptive terms by following the capitalization style used by the manufacturer.

The author and publisher have made their best efforts to prepare this book, and the content is based upon final release software whenever possible. Portions of the manuscript may be based upon pre-release versions supplied by software manufacturer(s). The author and the publisher make no representation or warranties of any kind with regard to the completeness or accuracy of the contents herein and accept no liability of any kind including but not limited to performance, merchantability, fitness for any particular purpose, or any losses or damages of any kind caused or alleged to be caused directly or indirectly from this book.

Manufactured in the United States of America

10 9 8 7 6 5 4 3 2 1

To Our Valued Readers:

Thank you for looking to Sybex for your CCSP exam prep needs. Cisco developed the CCSP certification to validate expertise in designing and implementing secure Cisco internetworking solutions, and it is currently one of the most highly sought after IT certifications. Just as Cisco is committed to establishing measurable standards for certifying those professionals who work in the field of internetworking, Sybex is committed to providing those professionals with the information they need to excel.

We at Sybex are proud of our reputation for providing certification candidates with the practical knowledge and skills needed to succeed in the highly competitive IT marketplace. This five-in-one CCSP Complete Study Guide reflects our commitment to provide CCSP candidates with the most up-to-date, accurate, and economical instructional material on the market.

The authors and the editors have worked hard to ensure that the book you hold in your hands is comprehensive, in-depth, and pedagogically sound. We're confident that this book will exceed the demanding standards of the certification marketplace and help you, the CCSP certification candidate, succeed in your endeavors.

As always, your feedback is important to us. If you believe you've identified an error in the book, please send a detailed e-mail to support@sybex.com. And if you have general comments or suggestions, feel free to drop me a line directly at nedde@sybex.com. At Sybex we're continually striving to meet the needs of individuals preparing for certification exams.

Good luck in pursuit of your CCSP certification!

Neil Edde
Publisher—Certification
Sybex, Inc.

Software License Agreement: Terms and Conditions

The media and/or any online materials accompanying this book that are available now or in the future contain programs and/or text files (the "Software") to be used in connection with the book. SYBEX hereby grants to you a license to use the Software, subject to the terms that follow. Your purchase, acceptance, or use of the Software will constitute your acceptance of such terms.

The Software compilation is the property of SYBEX unless otherwise indicated and is protected by copyright to SYBEX or other copyright owner(s) as indicated in the media files (the "Owner(s)"). You are hereby granted a single-user license to use the Software for your personal, noncommercial use only. You may not reproduce, sell, distribute, publish, circulate, or commercially exploit the Software, or any portion thereof, without the written consent of SYBEX and the specific copyright owner(s) of any component software included on this media.

In the event that the Software or components include specific license requirements or end-user agreements, statements of condition, disclaimers, limitations or warranties ("End-User License"), those End-User Licenses supersede the terms and conditions herein as to that particular Software component. Your purchase, acceptance, or use of the Software will constitute your acceptance of such End-User Licenses.

By purchase, use or acceptance of the Software you further agree to comply with all export laws and regulations of the United States as such laws and regulations may exist from time to time.

Reusable Code in This Book

The author(s) created reusable code in this publication expressly for reuse by readers. Sybex grants readers limited permission to reuse the code found in this publication, its accompanying CD-ROM or available for download from our website so long as the author(s) are attributed in any application containing the reusable code and the code itself is never distributed, posted online by electronic transmission, sold, or commercially exploited as a stand-alone product.

Software Support

Components of the supplemental Software and any offers associated with them may be supported by the specific Owner(s) of that material, but they are not supported by SYBEX. Information regarding any available support may be obtained from the Owner(s) using the information provided in the appropriate read.me files or listed elsewhere on the media.

Should the manufacturer(s) or other Owner(s) cease to offer support or decline to honor any offer, SYBEX bears no responsibility. This notice concerning support for the Software is provided for your information only. SYBEX is not the agent or principal of the Owner(s), and SYBEX is in no way responsible for providing any support for the Software, nor is it liable or responsible for any support provided, or not provided, by the Owner(s).

Warranty

SYBEX warrants the enclosed media to be free of physical defects for a period of ninety (90) days after purchase. The Software is not available from SYBEX in any other form or media than that enclosed herein or posted to www.sybex.com. If you discover a defect in the media during this warranty period, you may obtain a replacement of identical format at no charge by sending the defective media, postage prepaid, with proof of purchase to:

SYBEX Inc.
Product Support Department
1151 Marina Village Parkway
Alameda, CA 94501
Web: http://www.sybex.com

After the 90-day period, you can obtain replacement media of identical format by sending us the defective disk, proof of purchase, and a check or money order for $10, payable to SYBEX.

Disclaimer

SYBEX makes no warranty or representation, either expressed or implied, with respect to the Software or its contents, quality, performance, merchantability, or fitness for a particular purpose. In no event will SYBEX, its distributors, or dealers be liable to you or any other party for direct, indirect, special, incidental, consequential, or other damages arising out of the use of or inability to use the Software or its contents even if advised of the possibility of such damage. In the event that the Software includes an online update feature, SYBEX further disclaims any obligation to provide this feature for any specific duration other than the initial posting.

The exclusion of implied warranties is not permitted by some states. Therefore, the above exclusion may not apply to you. This warranty provides you with specific legal rights; there may be other rights that you may have that vary from state to state. The pricing of the book with the Software by SYBEX reflects the allocation of risk and limitations on liability contained in this agreement of Terms and Conditions.

Shareware Distribution

This Software may contain various programs that are distributed as shareware. Copyright laws apply to both shareware and ordinary commercial software, and the copyright Owner(s) retains all rights. If you try a shareware program and continue using it, you are expected to register it. Individual programs differ on details of trial periods, registration, and payment. Please observe the requirements stated in appropriate files.

Copy Protection

The Software in whole or in part may or may not be copy-protected or encrypted. However, in all cases, reselling or redistributing these files without authorization is expressly forbidden except as specifically provided for by the Owner(s) therein.

Acknowledgments

We would like to thank Neil Edde, Heather O'Connor, and Jeff Kellum for giving us the opportunity to update this Study Guide. We would also like to take a moment to thank everyone else involved in the creation of this book, including Production Editor Lori Newman, Technical Editor Dan Aguilera, Copy Editor Tiffany Taylor, Proofreaders Jim Brook, Candace English, Jennifer Larsen, and Nancy Riddiough, and the CD Team of Dan Mummert and Kevin Ly. Without the help of this wonderful team this book would have never made it to a bookshelf.

Contents at a Glance

Introduction   *xxvii*

Securing Cisco IOS Networks Assessment Test 1   *lii*

Cisco Secure PIX Firewall Advanced Assessment Test 2   *lxiii*

Cisco Secure Virtual Private Networks Assessment Test 3   *lxviii*

Cisco Secure Intrusion Detection Systems Assessment Test 4   *lxxi*

Cisco SAFE Implementation Assessment Test 5   *lxxvii*

Part I	**Securing Cisco IOS Networks (SECUR)**	**1**
Chapter 1	Introduction to Network Security	3
Chapter 2	Introduction to AAA Security	23
Chapter 3	Configuring Cisco Secure ACS and TACACS+	51
Chapter 4	Cisco Perimeter Router Problems and Solutions	83
Chapter 5	Context-Based Access Control Configuration	101
Chapter 6	Cisco IOS Firewall Authentication and Intrusion Detection	121
Chapter 7	Understanding Cisco IOS IPSec Support	149
Chapter 8	Cisco IOS IPSec Pre-shared Keys and Certificate Authority Support	167
Chapter 9	Cisco IOS Remote Access Using Cisco Easy VPN	209
Part II	**Cisco Secure PIX Firewall Advanced**	**219**
Chapter 10	PIX Firewall Basics	221
Chapter 11	PIX Firewall Configuration	257
Chapter 12	ACLs, Filtering, Object Grouping, and AAA	307
Chapter 13	Advanced Protocol Handling, Attack Guards, and Intrusion Detection	341
Chapter 14	Firewall Failover and PDM	371
Chapter 15	VPNs and the PIX Firewall	405

Part III — Cisco Secure Virtual Private Networks — 463

Chapter 16	Introduction to Virtual Private Networks	465
Chapter 17	Introduction to Cisco VPN Devices	493
Chapter 18	Configuring the VPN Concentrator	533
Chapter 19	Managing the VPN Concentrator	597

Part IV — Cisco Secure Intrusion Detection Systems — 627

Chapter 20	Introduction to Intrusion Detection and Protection	629
Chapter 21	Installing Cisco Secure IDS Sensors and IDSMs	683
Chapter 22	Configuring the Network to Support Cisco Secure IDS Sensors	735
Chapter 23	Configuring Cisco Secure IDS Sensors Using the IDS Device Manager	783
Chapter 24	Configuring Signatures and Using the IDS Event Viewer	865
Chapter 25	Enterprise Cisco Secure IDS Management	941
Chapter 26	Enterprise Cisco Secure IDS Monitoring	1017

Part V — Cisco SAFE Implementation — 1065

Chapter 27	Security Fundamentals	1067
Chapter 28	The Cisco Security Portfolio	1093
Chapter 29	SAFE Small and Medium Network Designs	1111
Chapter 30	SAFE Remote Access Network Design	1141

Index — *1161*

Contents

Introduction	*xxvii*
Securing Cisco IOS Networks Assessment Test 1	*lii*
Cisco Secure PIX Firewall Advanced Assessment Test 2	*lxiii*
Cisco Secure Virtual Private Networks Assessment Test 3	*lxviii*
Cisco Secure Intrusion Detection Systems Assessment Test 4	*lxxi*
Cisco SAFE Implementation Assessment Test 5	*lxxvii*

Part I		**Securing Cisco IOS Networks (SECUR)**	**1**
Chapter	**1**	**Introduction to Network Security**	**3**
		Types of Network Security Threats	5
		Types of Security Weaknesses	6
		Technology Weaknesses	6
		Configuration Weaknesses	7
		Policy Weaknesses	9
		Types of Network Attacks	10
		Eavesdropping	12
		Denial-of-Service Attacks	14
		Unauthorized Access	15
		WareZ	16
		Masquerade Attack (IP Spoofing)	16
		Session Hijacking or Replaying	16
		Rerouting Attacks	17
		Repudiation	17
		Smurfing Attacks	17
		Password Attacks	18
		Man-in-the-Middle Attacks	18
		Application-Layer Attacks	18
		Trojan Horse Programs, Viruses, and Worms	19
		HTML Attacks	19
		The Corporate Security Policy	19
		Summary	20
		Exam Essentials	21

Chapter	**2**	**Introduction to AAA Security**	**23**
		Understanding Network Access Server and Cisco AAA	24
		Authentication Methods	26
		Windows Authentication	28
		Security Server Authentication	28
		PAP and CHAP Authentication	30
		PPP Callback	32
		Configuring the NAS for AAA	35
		Securing Access to the Exec Mode	35
		Enabling AAA Locally on the NAS	38
		Configuring Authentication on the NAS	39
		Configuring Authorization on the NAS	41
		Configuring Accounting on the NAS	44
		Verifying the NAS Configuration	46
		Troubleshooting AAA on the Cisco NAS	47
		Summary	49
		Exam Essentials	50
Chapter	**3**	**Configuring Cisco Secure ACS and TACACS+**	**51**
		Introduction to the Cisco Secure ACS	52
		Using User Databases for Authentication	54
		Populating the User Database	55
		New ACS Features	56
		Installing Cisco Secure ACS 3.0	57
		Administering Cisco Secure ACS	64
		TACACS+ Overview	71
		Configuring TACACS+	72
		Using RADIUS	74
		Cisco Secure User Database NAS Configuration for RADIUS	74
		Verifying TACACS+	78
		Summary	81
		Exam Essentials	81
Chapter	**4**	**Cisco Perimeter Router Problems and Solutions**	**83**
		Solving Eavesdropping and Session Replay Problems	85
		Defending Against Unauthorized Access, Data Manipulation, and Malicious Destruction	86
		Solving Lack of Legal IP Addresses Problems	88
		Fighting Rerouting Attacks	88
		Fighting Denial-of-Service Attacks	90

		Turning Off and Configuring Network Services	92
		Blocking SNMP Packets	92
		Disabling Echo	92
		Turning Off BOOTP and Auto-Config	93
		Disabling the HTTP Interface	93
		Disabling IP Source Routing	94
		Disabling Proxy ARP	94
		Disabling Redirect Messages	94
		Disabling the Generation of ICMP Unreachable Messages	94
		Disabling Multicast Route Caching	95
		Disabling the Maintenance Operation Protocol	95
		Turning Off the X.25 PAD Service	95
		Enabling the Nagle TCP Congestion Algorithm	95
		Logging Every Event	96
		Disabling Cisco Discovery Protocol	96
		Configuring SNMP	96
		Configuring Exec Timeout Values	97
		Disabling the Default Forwarded UDP Protocols	97
	Summary		99
	Exam Essentials		99
Chapter	**5**	**Context-Based Access Control Configuration**	**101**
		Understanding the Cisco IOS Firewall	102
		Authentication Proxy and IDS	103
		Context-Based Access Control	103
		CBAC Compared to ACLs	103
		CBAC-Supported Protocols	106
		Introduction to CBAC Configuration	107
		Using Audit Trails and Alerts	108
		Configuring Global Timeouts and Thresholds	108
		Configuring PAM	110
		Defining Inspection Rules	114
		Applying Inspection Rules and ACLs to Router Interfaces	116
		Configuring IP ACLs at the Interface	117
		Testing and Verifying CBAC	117
	Summary		119
	Exam Essentials		120
Chapter	**6**	**Cisco IOS Firewall Authentication and Intrusion Detection**	**121**
		Introduction to the Cisco IOS Firewall Authentication Proxy	123
		Configuring the AAA Server	125
		Configuring AAA	128

	Configuring the Authentication Proxy	132
	Testing and Verifying Your Configuration	133
Introduction to the Cisco IOS Firewall IDS		135
	Initializing the Cisco IOS Firewall IDS	137
	Configuring, Disabling, and Excluding Signatures	137
Creating and Applying Audit Rules		139
	Setting Default Actions	139
	Creating an Audit Rule	141
	Applying the Audit Rule	142
Verifying the Configuration		143
Stopping the IOS Firewall IDS		145
Summary		146
Exam Essentials		147

Chapter 7   Understanding Cisco IOS IPSec Support   149

What Is a Virtual Private Network?   150
Introduction to Cisco IOS IPSec   151
    IPSec Transforms   152
    IPSec Operation   154
The Components of IPSec   157
    IPSec Encapsulation   157
    Internet Key Exchange (IKE)   159
Summary   165
Exam Essentials   165

Chapter 8   Cisco IOS IPSec Pre-shared Keys and Certificate Authority Support   167

Configuring Cisco IOS IPSec for Pre-shared Keys Site-to-Site   168
    Preparing for IKE and IPSec   169
    Configuring IKE   169
    Configuring IPSec   175
    Testing and Verifying IPSec   184
Configuring IPSec Manually   186
    Configuring IPSec for RSA-Encrypted Nonces   187
Configuring Cisco IOS IPSec Certificate Authority Support
   Site-to-Site   192
    Configuring CA Support Tasks   193
    Preparing for IKE and IPSec   193
    Configuring CA Support   193
    Configuring IKE Using CA   198
    Configuring IPSec for CA   198
    Testing and Verifying IPSec for CA   205
Summary   206
Exam Essentials   206

Chapter	9	**Cisco IOS Remote Access Using Cisco Easy VPN**	**209**

Configuring IOS Remote Access Using Cisco Easy VPN 210
Introduction to Cisco Easy VPN 210
The Easy VPN Server 211
Introduction to the Cisco VPN Software Client 213
Easy VPN Server Configuration Tasks 215
Preconfiguring the Cisco VPN Software Client 216
Router and Security Device Manager Overview 216
Summary 217
Exam Essentials 218

Part II		**Cisco Secure PIX Firewall Advanced**	**219**
Chapter	10	**PIX Firewall Basics**	**221**

Understanding a Firewall's Role in Network Security 222
What Is a Firewall? 222
What Are the Potential Threats? 224
Reviewing Firewall Technologies 224
Dual-Homed Gateways 225
Packet-Filtering Firewalls 225
Stateful Firewalls 226
Firewall Technology Combinations 227
Hardware and Software Components of the Cisco Secure
PIX Firewall 230
PIX Firewall Features 230
PIX Firewall Components 231
PIX Firewall Operation 237
NAT Mechanisms 237
Packet Processing 238
The Adaptive Security Algorithm and Security Levels 239
Working with the Firewall Services Module 241
Overview of Configuration 241
Configuring an IOS Switch 242
Configuring a CatOS Switch 244
Connecting to the Module 244
Configuring the FWSM 245
Using the PIX Firewall CLI 246
CLI Access Methods 246
CLI Modes 247
Editing in the CLI 248
Basic Commands 249
Summary 255
Exam Essentials 256

Chapter	**11**	**PIX Firewall Configuration**	**257**
		Preparing for Firewall Configuration	258
		Using Common Global Configuration Commands	259
		The Remote Access Commands	259
		The *clock* Command	261
		The *ntp* Command	262
		The *domain-name* and *hostname* Commands	263
		The *name/names* Commands	264
		The *dhcpd* Command	264
		The *logging* Command	266
		Configuring PIX Firewall Interfaces	267
		Naming an Interface and Assigning a Security Level	267
		Setting Interface Properties and Shutting Down the Interface	269
		Assigning an IP Address	271
		Setting the Maximum Transfer Unit	272
		Configuring NAT and PAT	273
		Understanding Address Translation	273
		NAT, PAT, and Security	276
		Configuring NAT	277
		Configuring PAT	286
		Configuring NAT on Multiple Interfaces	290
		Configuring Routing	298
		Configuring Dynamic Routing	299
		Configuring Static Routing	301
		Configuring Multicast Routing	304
		Summary	306
		Exam Essentials	306
Chapter	**12**	**ACLs, Filtering, Object Grouping, and AAA**	**307**
		Using PIX Firewall ACLs	308
		Creating a PIX ACL	309
		Applying a PIX ACL	310
		Converting Conduits to ACLs	311
		URL Filtering	312
		How Does URL Filtering Work?	312
		Configuring the PIX Firewall for URL Filtering	313
		PPPoE and the PIX Firewall	315
		Configuring the PPPoE Client Username and Password	316
		Enabling PPPoE on the PIX Firewall	317
		Verifying PPPoE Operation	318
		Object Groups	319
		Configuring Object Groups	320
		Using Object Groups	323

		Authentication, Authorization, and Accounting (AAA) Services	324
		Installing Cisco Secure ACS for Windows 2000/NT	324
		Implementing AAA on the PIX Firewall	330
		Downloadable PIX ACLs	337
		Summary	338
		Exam Essentials	339
Chapter	**13**	**Advanced Protocol Handling, Attack Guards, and Intrusion Detection**	**341**
		Advanced Protocol Handling	342
		Special Protocol Support Basics	343
		File Transfer Protocol	345
		Remote Shell	348
		SQL*Net	349
		Multimedia Support	350
		Alternative Solutions to Problem Protocols	352
		Attack Guards	353
		AAA Flood Guard	353
		SYN Flood Guard	354
		Mail Guard	355
		IP Fragmentation Guard	359
		DNS Guard	362
		Intrusion Detection	362
		IP Audit	362
		Shunning	369
		Summary	370
		Exam Essentials	370
Chapter	**14**	**Firewall Failover and PDM**	**371**
		Fault-Tolerance Concepts	372
		Points of Failure	372
		Fault-Tolerant Strategies	376
		PIX Firewall Failover	377
		PIX Firewall Failover Features	377
		PIX Firewall Failover Requirements	378
		How PIX Firewall Failover Works	378
		Stateful Failover	385
		Basic Failover Configuration	386
		Cisco PIX Device Manager (PDM)	390
		PDM Overview	390
		Operating Requirements	391

	Preparing for PDM	392
	Using PDM to Configure the PIX Firewall	394
	Summary	403
	Exam Essentials	403

Chapter 15   VPNs and the PIX Firewall   405

Preparing to Configure VPN support	406
Configuring IKE on a Firewall	407
Enabling IKE	407
Configuring the IKE Policy	407
Configuring Pre-shared Keys	409
Configuring the Use of Certificate Authorities (CAs) on a Firewall	410
Configuring IPSec on a Firewall	415
Creating Crypto ACLs	415
Creating and Configuring Transform Sets	416
Setting the Tunnel Lifetime	418
Creating Crypto Maps	419
Verifying and Troubleshooting IPSec Configuration on a Firewall	422
Viewing Configuration Information	422
Understanding Error and Status Messages	426
Debugging	426
Understanding Remote Access VPN	426
Extended Authentication (Xauth)	426
IKE Mode Config for Dynamic Addressing	427
Pushing Additional Attributes to the VPN Client	428
Common Commands	429
Installing and Configuring the Cisco VPN Client	432
Deploying the VPN Client	433
Using PDM to Create VPNs	439
Setting Up a Site-to-Site VPN	441
Setting Up a Remote Access VPN	446
Enterprise PIX Firewall Management and Maintenance	451
Cisco Secure Policy Manager (CSPM)	452
PIX Management Center (MC)	453
Auto Update Server (AUS)	456
Summary	460
Exam Essentials	460

Part III — Cisco Secure Virtual Private Networks — 463

Chapter 16 — Introduction to Virtual Private Networks — 465

- VPN Basics — 466
  - Major Types of VPNs — 466
  - VPN Devices — 467
- Introducing IPSec — 470
  - IPSec Services — 471
  - IPSec Building Blocks: AH and ESP — 471
  - Hashing — 476
  - Encryption — 476
  - Diffie-Hellman Key Exchange — 477
  - Internet Key Exchange — 478
  - Transform Sets — 481
  - IPSec Security Associations — 483
- How IPSec Works — 484
  - Defining Interesting Traffic — 485
  - IKE Phase 1 — 486
  - IKE Phase 2 — 487
  - IPSec Task Flow — 488
- IPSec Troubleshooting — 490
  - Traffic Delay Problems — 490
  - Filtering Problems — 490
  - NAT Problems — 491
  - ACL Problems — 491
- Summary — 491
- Exam Essentials — 492

Chapter 17 — Introduction to Cisco VPN Devices — 493

- Introducing the VPN 3000 Concentrators — 494
  - Overview of the VPN 3005 Concentrator — 495
  - Overview of VPN 3015 through 3080 Concentrators — 497
  - VPN Concentrator Client Support — 499
- Introducing the 3002 VPN Hardware Client — 500
  - Configuring the 3002 CLI Quick Configuration Utility — 501
  - Configuring the Hardware Client with the Quick Configuration Utility — 505
  - Managing the Hardware Client — 513
  - Additional VPN 3002 Client Features — 514
- Introducing the VPN Software Clients — 520
  - Configuring the Connection — 521
  - Setting Authentication Properties — 521

		Setting Connection Properties	523
		Installing a Certificate	523
		Preconfiguring the VPN Client	526
		Overview of the Cisco VPN Software Client Auto-Initiation	529
		Summary	531
		Exam Essentials	532
Chapter	18	**Configuring the VPN Concentrator**	**533**
		Using the CLI for Initial Configuration	536
		Starting the CLI	536
		Using Web Quick Configuration Mode	543
		Configuring Physical Interfaces	545
		Setting System Information	545
		Setting the Tunnel-Creation Method	546
		Setting the Address Assignment	546
		Configuring Authentication	547
		Setting a Group Name	548
		Changing the *admin* Password	549
		Configuring User and Policy Management	549
		Navigating the GUI	550
		Setting Up Groups	550
		Setting Up Users	559
		Configuring an Authentication Server	559
		Configuring Access Hours and Filters	560
		Configuring Backup on the Hardware Client	563
		Configuring Load Balancing	564
		Configuring LAN-to-LAN IPSec	566
		Updating Clients Automatically	568
		Setting Up the Stateful Firewall	571
		Configuring the Use of IPSec Digital Certificates	574
		Introducing the Public Key Infrastructure	574
		Requesting and Installing Concentrator Certificates	575
		Requesting and Installing Client Certificates	583
		Firewall Feature Set for the IPSec Software Client	586
		Software Client's Are You There Feature	587
		Software Client's Stateful Firewall Feature	587
		Software Client's Central Policy Protection Feature	587
		Client Firewall Statistics	588
		Customizing Firewall Policy	590
		Configuring the VPN 3000 Concentrator for IPSec over UDP and IPSec over TCP	591
		Overview of Port Address Translation	592
		Configuring IPSec over UDP	592

		Configuring NAT-Transversal	594
		Configuring IPSec over TCP	594
		Summary	595
		Exam Essentials	595
Chapter	**19**	**Managing the VPN Concentrator**	**597**
		Monitoring the VPN Concentrator	598
		Viewing Concentrator Monitoring Information	599
		Configuring Logging and SNMP Traps	609
		Administering the VPN Concentrator	616
		Configuring Access Rights	616
		Administering Sessions	620
		Administering File Management	620
		Updating Software	623
		Pinging Devices	624
		Summary	624
		Exam Essentials	625
Part IV		**Cisco Secure Intrusion Detection Systems**	**627**
Chapter	**20**	**Introduction to Intrusion Detection and Protection**	**629**
		Understanding Security Threats	630
		Hacker Characteristics	631
		Attack Types	632
		Implementing Network Security	646
		Securing the Network	646
		Monitoring Network Security	655
		Testing Network Security	656
		Improving Network Security	657
		Understanding Intrusion Detection Basics	658
		Triggers	658
		IDS System Location	661
		IDS Evasive Techniques	664
		Cisco Secure Intrusion Protection	665
		Introduction to Cisco Secure IDS	667
		Cisco Secure IDS Features	668
		Cisco Secure Sensor Platforms	672
		Cisco Secure IDS Management Platforms	676
		Cisco Host IDS Platforms	678
		Summary	681
		Exam Essentials	682

Chapter	21	**Installing Cisco Secure IDS Sensors and IDSMs**	**683**
		Deploying Cisco Secure IDS	684
		Sensor Selection Considerations	684
		Sensor Deployment Considerations	688
		Installing and Configuring Cisco Secure IDS Sensors	693
		Planning the Installation	694
		Physically Installing the Sensor	695
		Gaining Initial Management Access	704
		Logging In to the Sensor	708
		Configuring the Sensor for the First Time	710
		Administering the Sensor	724
		Cisco Secure IDS Architecture	728
		Summary	732
		Exam Essentials	733
Chapter	22	**Configuring the Network to Support Cisco Secure IDS Sensors**	**735**
		Capturing Traffic	736
		Configuring Traffic Capture for the 4200 Series Sensors	737
		Configuring Traffic Capture Using SPAN	743
		Configuring Traffic Capture Using RSPAN	750
		Configuring Traffic Capture for the IDSM	761
		Configuring SPAN for the IDSM-2	765
		Configuring Traffic Capture Using VACLs	767
		Configuring Traffic Capture using the *mls ip ids* Command	774
		Configuring the Sensing Interface to Control Trunk Traffic	776
		Restricting VLANs on CatOS	777
		Restricting VLANs on Cisco IOS	778
		Assigning the Command-and-Control Port VLAN	778
		Configuring the Command-and-Control VLAN on CatOS	779
		Configuring the Command-and-Control VLAN on Cisco IOS	779
		Configuring Traffic Capture for the NM-CIDS	779
		Summary	781
		Exam Essentials	781
Chapter	23	**Configuring Cisco Secure IDS Sensors Using the IDS Device Manager**	**783**
		IDS Device Manager Introduction	784
		IDM Components and System Requirements	784
		Accessing the IDM for the First Time	785
		Navigating the IDM	788

		Configuring Cisco Secure IDS Sensors Using the IDM	790
		Performing Sensor Setup Using the IDM	790
		Configuring Intrusion Detection Using the IDM	796
		Configuring Blocking Using the IDM	813
		Configuring Auto Update Using the IDM	837
		Administering and Monitoring Cisco Secure IDS Sensors Using the IDM	840
		IDM Administration	841
		IDM Monitoring	854
		Summary	861
		Exam Essentials	862
Chapter	**24**	**Configuring Signatures and Using the IDS Event Viewer**	**865**
		Cisco Secure IDS Signatures	866
		Cisco Secure IDS Signature Engines	868
		Signature Engine Parameters	873
		Configuring Cisco Secure IDS Signatures	884
		Configuring Signatures Using the IDM	884
		Configuring Signatures Using the CLI	893
		Introduction to the IDS Event Viewer	898
		Installing the IEV	900
		Accessing the IEV for the First Time	901
		Configuring the IEV	903
		Adding Sensors to the IEV	903
		Configuring Filters and Views	907
		Creating a View	914
		Configuring Application Settings and Preferences	921
		Administering the IEV Database	924
		Summary	938
		Exam Essentials	939
Chapter	**25**	**Enterprise Cisco Secure IDS Management**	**941**
		Introduction to CiscoWorks VMS	942
		CiscoWorks VMS Components	942
		CiscoWorks VMS System Requirements	944
		Installing CiscoWorks VMS	948
		Installing CiscoWorks Common Services	948
		Installing the IDS Management Center and Security Monitoring Center	952
		Starting the CiscoWorks Desktop	956
		Adding Users	959
		Licensing CiscoWorks VMS Components	960

	Configuring IDS Sensors Using the IDS MC	962
	IDS Management Center Architecture	963
	Starting the IDS Management Center	964
	Configuring Sensor Groups	966
	Adding Sensors to the IDS MC	968
	Configuring Sensors Using the IDS MC	971
	Saving, Generating, Approving, and Deploying Sensor Configurations	996
	Updating Cisco Secure IDS Sensors	1003
	Administering the IDS MC	1006
	Configuring System Configuration Settings	1006
	Configuring Database Rules	1007
	Configuring Report Settings	1011
	Summary	1014
	Exam Essentials	1014
Chapter 26	**Enterprise Cisco Secure IDS Monitoring**	**1017**
	Introduction to the Security Monitor	1018
	Security Monitor Features	1018
	Supported Devices for the Security Monitor	1019
	Accessing the Security Monitor for the First Time	1020
	Configuring the Security Monitor	1023
	Configuring Sensors to Support the Security Monitor	1023
	Defining Devices to Monitor	1023
	Verifying Sensor Connection Status	1029
	Working with Events	1030
	Viewing Events	1030
	Defining Notifications Using Event Rules	1045
	Administering the Security Monitoring Center	1052
	Configuring System Configuration Settings	1053
	Configuring Database Rules	1056
	Configuring Reports	1057
	Summary	1061
	Exam Essentials	1062
Part V	**Cisco SAFE Implementation**	**1065**
Chapter 27	**Security Fundamentals**	**1067**
	Identifying the Need for Network Security	1068
	Network Attack Taxonomy	1071
	Application Layer Attacks	1072
	Denial of Service (DOS) or Distributed Denial of Service (DDOS)	1072

	IP Weaknesses	1073
	Man-in-the-Middle Attacks	1074
	Network Reconnaissance	1074
	Packet Sniffers	1075
	Password Attacks	1076
	Port Redirection	1077
	Trojan Horse	1077
	Trust Exploitation	1077
	Unauthorized Access	1078
	Virus	1078
Network Security Policies		1079
Management Protocols and Functions		1079
	Configuration Management	1080
	SNMP	1080
	Syslog	1081
	TFTP	1081
	NTP	1081
SAFE Architectural Overview		1082
	SAFE SMR Design Fundamentals	1084
	SAFE SMR Architecture	1084
SAFE Axioms		1085
	Routers Are Targets	1086
	Switches Are Targets	1087
	Hosts Are Targets	1087
	Networks Are Targets	1088
	Applications Are Targets	1088
	Intrusion Detection Systems Mitigate Attacks	1088
	Secure Management and Reporting Mitigate Attacks	1089
Identifying the Security Wheel		1089
Summary		1091
Exam Essentials		1091

Chapter 28 The Cisco Security Portfolio 1093

Cisco Security Portfolio Overview		1094
Secure Connectivity: Virtual Private Network Solutions		1095
	Site-to-Site VPN Solution	1097
	Remote Access VPN Solution	1099
	Firewall-Based VPN Solution and Perimeter Security	1101
Understanding Intrusion Protection		1102
	IDS	1103
Secure Scanner		1104
Understanding Identity		1105
	Cisco Secure Access Control Server (ACS)	1106

		Understanding Security Management	1107
		Cisco AVVID	1107
		Summary	1109
		Exam Essentials	1109
Chapter	29	**SAFE Small and Medium Network Designs**	**1111**
		Small Network Design Overview	1112
		Corporate Internet Module	1112
		Campus Module	1115
		Medium Network Design Overview	1117
		Corporate Internet Module	1118
		Campus Module	1120
		WAN Module	1122
		Implementation of Key Devices	1123
		NIDS and HIDS	1123
		Implementing the ISP Router	1123
		Implementing the IOS-based Firewall	1127
		Implementing the PIX Firewall	1134
		Summary	1138
		Exam Essentials	1138
Chapter	30	**SAFE Remote Access Network Design**	**1141**
		Remote Access Network Design Overview	1142
		Key Devices	1143
		Implementing the Remote Access Devices	1144
		Software Access Option	1144
		Remote Site Firewall Option	1149
		VPN Hardware Client Option	1151
		Remote Site Router Option	1156
		Summary	1159
		Exam Essentials	1159
		Index	*1161*

Introduction

This Study Guide is an introduction to the Cisco Certified Security Professional (CCSP) certification track. It will help improve your Cisco security skills so that you can have more opportunities for a better job or job security. Security experience has been the buzzword and it will continue to be because networks need security.

Cisco has been pushing further into the security market, and having a Cisco security certification will greatly expand your opportunities. Let this Study Guide be not only your resource for the Securing Cisco IOS Networks, Cisco Secure PIX Firewall Advanced, Cisco Security Intrusion Detection Systems, Cisco Secure VPN, and Cisco SAFE Implementation exams but also an aid when you're gaining hands-on experience in the field.

Not only will this Study Guide help with your pursuit of you CCSP, but it will improve your understanding of everything related to security internetworking, which is relevant to much more than Cisco products. You'll have a solid knowledge of network security and how different technologies work together to form a secure network. Even if you don't plan on becoming a security professional, the concepts covered in this Study Guide are beneficial to every networking professional. Employees with a Cisco security certification are in high demand, even at companies with only a few Cisco devices. Since you have decided to become Cisco security–certified, this Study Guide will put you way ahead on the path to that goal.

The CCSP reach is beyond the popular certifications such as the CCNA/CCDA and CCNP/CCDP to provide you with a greater understanding of today's secure network, with insight into the Cisco secure world of internetworking.

You might be thinking, "Why are networks so vulnerable to security breaches? Why can't the operating systems provide protection?" The answer is straightforward: Users want lots of features, and software vendors give the users what they want because features sell. Capabilities such as sharing files and printers and logging in to the corporate infrastructure from the Internet aren't just desired, they're expected. The new corporate battle cry is, "Give us complete corporate access from the Internet and make it super fast and easy—but make sure it's really secure!"

Are software developers to blame? There are just too many security issues for any one company to be at fault. But it's true that providing all the features that any user could possibly want on a network at the click of a mouse creates some major security issues. It's also true that we didn't have the types of hackers we have today until we accidentally opened the door for them. To become truly capable of defending yourself, you must understand the vulnerabilities of a plethora of technologies and networking equipment.

So, our goal is twofold: First, we're going to give you the information you need to understand all those vulnerabilities; and second, we're going to show you how to create a single, network-wide security policy. Before we do so, there are two key questions behind most security issues on the Internet:

- How do you protect confidential information but still allow access by the corporate users who need to get to that information?

- How do you protect your network and its resources from unknown or unwanted users outside your network?

If you're going to protect something, you have to know where it is, right? Where important/confidential information is stored is key for any network administrator concerned with security. You'll find the goods in two places: physical storage media (such as hard drives and RAM) and in transit across a network in the form of packets. This book's focus is mainly on network security issues pertaining to the transit of confidential information across a network. But it's important to remember that both physical media and packets need to be protected from intruders within your network and outside it. TCP/IP is used in all the examples in this book because it's the most popular protocol suite these days and also because it has some inherent security weaknesses.

From there, we'll look beyond TCP/IP to help you understand how both operating systems and network equipment come with their own vulnerabilities that you must address as well. If you don't have passwords and authentication properly set on your network equipment, you're in obvious trouble. If you don't understand your routing protocols and, especially, how they advertise throughout your network, you might as well leave the building unlocked at night. Furthermore, how much do you know about your firewall? Do you have one? If so, where are its weak spots? If you don't cover all these bases, your equipment will be your network's Achilles heel.

What Is Good Security?

Now you have a good idea of what you're up against to provide security for your network. To stay competitive in this game, you need to have a sound security policy that is both monitored and used regularly. Good intentions won't stop the bad guys from getting you. Planning and foresight will save your neck. All possible problems need to be considered, written down, discussed, and addressed with a solid action plan.

You also need to communicate your plan clearly and concisely to management, providing solid policy so that they can make informed decisions. With knowledge and careful planning, you can balance security requirements with user-friendly access and approach. And you can accomplish all of it at an acceptable level of operational cost. As with many truly valuable things, however, this won't be easy to attain.

First-class security solutions should allow network managers to offer improved services to their corporate clients, both internally and externally, and save the company a nice chunk of change at the same time. If you can do this, odds are good that you'll end up with a nice chunk of change too. Everybody but the bad guys gets to win!

If you can understand security well, and if you figure out how to effectively provide network services without spending the entire IT budget, you'll enjoy a long, illustrious, and lucrative career in the IT world. You must be able to:

- Enable new networked applications and services.
- Reduce the costs of implementation and operations of the network.
- Make the Internet a global, low-cost access medium.

It's also good to remember that people who make really difficult, complicated things simpler and more manageable tend to be honored, respected, and generally very popular—in other words, in demand and employed. One way to simplify the complex is to break a large, multifaceted thing down into manageable chunks. To do this, you need to classify each network into one of the three types of network security classifications: trusted networks, untrusted networks, and unknown networks. You should know a little about these before you begin reading this book:

Trusted networks *Trusted networks* are the networks you want to protect, and they populate the zone known as the *security perimeter*. The security perimeter is connected to a firewall server through network adapter cards. Virtual private networks (VPNs) are also considered trusted networks, but they send data across untrusted networks. So, they're special: They create special circumstances and require special considerations when you're establishing a security policy for them. The packets transmitted on a VPN are established on a trusted network, so the firewall server needs to authenticate the origin of those packets, check for data integrity, and provide for any other security needs of the corporation.

Untrusted networks *Untrusted networks* are those found outside the security perimeters and not controlled by you or your administrators, such as the Internet and the corporate ISP. These are the networks you're trying to protect yourself from while still allowing access to and from them.

Unknown networks Because you can't categorize something you don't know, *unknown networks* are described as neither trusted or untrusted. This type of mystery network doesn't tell the firewall if it's an inside (trusted) network or outside (untrusted) network.

Cisco Security Certifications

There are quite a few new Cisco security certifications to be had, but the good news is that this book, which covers the all five of the CCSP exams, is the prerequisite for all Cisco security certifications. All these new Cisco security certifications also require a valid CCNA certification.

Cisco Certified Security Professional (CCSP)

You have to pass five exams to get your CCSP certification. The pivotal one is the SECUR exam. Here are the exams you must pass to call that CCSP yours:

- Securing Cisco IOS Networks (642-501 SECUR)
- Cisco Secure PIX Firewall Advanced (642-521 CSPFA)
- Cisco Secure Virtual Private Networks (642-511 CSVPN)
- Cisco Secure Intrusion Detection Systems (642-531 CSIDS)
- Cisco SAFE Implementation (642-541 CSI)

This Study Guide will help you pass all five of these exams.

Cisco Security Specializations

In addition, Cisco offers a number of security specialization tracks, including the following:

Cisco Firewall Specialist Cisco security certifications focus on the growing need for knowledgeable network professionals who can implement complete security solutions. Cisco Firewall

Specialists focus on securing network access using Cisco IOS Software and Cisco PIX firewall technologies.

The two exams you must pass to achieve the Cisco Firewall Specialist certification are Securing Cisco IOS Networks (642-501 SECUR) and Cisco Secure PIX Firewall Advanced (642-521 CSPFA).

Cisco VPN Specialist   Cisco VPN Specialists can configure VPNs across shared public networks using Cisco IOS Software and Cisco VPN 3000 Series Concentrator technologies.

The two exams you must pass to achieve the Cisco VPN Specialist certification are Securing Cisco IOS Networks (642-501 SECUR) and Cisco Secure Virtual Networks (642-511 CSVPN).

Cisco IDS Specialist   Cisco IDS Specialists can both operate and monitor Cisco IOS software and IDS technologies to detect and respond to intrusion activities.

The two exams you must pass to achieve the Cisco IDS Specialist certification are Securing Cisco IOS Networks (642-501 SECUR) and CSIDS (642-531).

Cisco Network Support Certifications

Initially, to secure the coveted Cisco Certified Internetwork Expert (CCIE), you took only one test, and then you were faced with a nearly impossible lab—an all-or-nothing approach that made it tough to succeed. In response, Cisco created a series of new certifications to help you acquire the coveted CCIE and aid prospective employers in measuring skill levels. With these new certifications, which definitely improved the ability of mere mortals to prepare for that almighty lab, Cisco has opened doors that few were allowed through before. What are these stepping-stone certifications, and how do they help you get your CCIE?

Cisco Certified Network Associate (CCNA)

The CCNA certification was the first in the new line of Cisco certifications and was the precursor to all current Cisco certifications. With the new certification programs, Cisco has created a stepping-stone approach to CCNA certification.

And you don't have to stop there. You can choose to continue your studies and achieve a higher certification called the Cisco Certified Network Professional (CCNP). Someone with a CCNP has all the skills and knowledge they need to attempt the CCIE lab. However, because no textbook can take the place of practical experience, we'll discuss what else you need to be ready for the CCIE lab shortly. The first step to becoming a CCNA is, depending on what path you take, to pass one or two exams: either Interconnecting Networking Devices (640-811 ICND) and the INTRO (640-821 INTRO), or the CCNA (640-801).

 Both paths test on the same topics. The only difference is that the CCNA exam is one 90-minute exam, whereas ICND and INTRO are 60 and 90 minutes, respectively.

We can't stress this enough: It's critical that you have some hands-on experience with Cisco routers to prepare for your CCNA certification (as well as your other Cisco certifications). If you can get hold of some Cisco 2500 or 2600 series routers, you're set. Also, you should pick up the best-selling *CCNA: Cisco Certified Network Associate Study Guide, 5th ed.* (Sybex, 2005), which covers all the exam objectives. In addition, the *CCNA: Cisco Certified Network Associate Study Guide, Deluxe Edition* (Sybex 2005) also contains the *CCNA: Virtual Lab Gold Edition*, a comprehensive router simulator.

Sybex also offers a more comprehensive version of the Virtual Lab, the *CCNA Virtual Lab, Platinum Edition.*

Information about Sybex's CCNA offerings can be found at www.sybex.com.

Cisco Certified Network Professional (CCNP)

So you're thinking, "Great, what do I do after passing the CCNA exam?" Well, if you want to become a CCIE in Routing and Switching (the most popular Cisco certification), understand that there's more than one path to that much-coveted CCIE certification. One way is to continue studying and become a CCNP, which means four more tests, in addition to the CCNA certification.

The CCNP program will prepare you to understand and comprehensively tackle the internetworking issues of today and beyond—and it isn't limited to the Cisco world. You'll undergo an immense metamorphosis, vastly increasing your knowledge and skills through the process of obtaining these certifications.

You don't need to be a CCNP or even a CCNA to take the CCIE lab, but it's extremely helpful if you already have these certifications. After becoming a CCNA, the four exams you must take to get your CCNP are as follows:

Exam 642-801: Building Scalable Cisco Internetworks (BSCI)   This exam continues to build on the fundamentals learned in the CCNA course. It focuses on large multiprotocol internetworks and how to manage them with access lists, queuing, tunneling, route distribution, route maps, BGP, EIGRP, OSPF, and route summarization.

Exam 642-811: Building Cisco Multilayer Switched Networks (BCMSN)   This exam tests your knowledge of creating and deploying a global intranet and implementing basic troubleshooting techniques in environments that use Cisco multilayer switches for client hosts and services.

Exam 642-621: Building Cisco Remote Access Networks (BCRAN)   This exam determines whether you can describe, configure, operate, and troubleshoot WAN and remote access solutions.

Exam 642-831: Cisco Internetwork Troubleshooting (CIT)   This exam tests you extensively on troubleshooting suboptimal performance in a converged network environment.

Again, hands-on knowledge is pertinent to prepare for the CCSP exams. But you will also need to know the focus the exams. Also see Sybex's *CCNP Complete Study Guide* (2005).

www.routersim.com has a Cisco router simulator for use in preparing for all of the CCNP exams.

If you hate tests, you can take fewer of them by taking the BCRAN and CIT exams and then taking just one more long exam called the Composite exam (642-891). Doing this also gives you your CCNP, but beware: It's a really long test that fuses all the material from the BSCI and BCMSN exams into one exam.

Remember that test objectives and tests can change any time without notice. Always check the Cisco website for the most up-to-date information (www.cisco.com).

Cisco Certified Internetwork Expert (CCIE)

You've become a CCNP, and now your sights are fixed on getting your CCIE. What do you do next? Cisco recommends a *minimum* of two years of on-the-job experience before taking the CCIE lab. After jumping those hurdles, you then have to pass the written CCIE Exam Qualification before taking the actual lab.

There are four CCIE certifications, and you must pass a written exam for each one of them before attempting the hands-on lab:

CCIE Routing and Switching The CCIE Routing and Switching exam covers IP and IP routing, non-IP desktop protocols such as IPX, and bridge- and switch-related technologies. This is by far Cisco's most popular CCIE track. The *CCIE: Cisco Certified Internetwork Expert Study Guide, 2nd ed.* (Sybex, 2003) is a superb Study Guide that covers both the qualification and lab portions of this track.

CCIE Security The CCIE Security exam covers IP and IP routing as well as specific security components.

CCIE Service Provider The CCIE Service Provider (formerly called Communications and Services) exam covers topics related to networking in service provider environments.

CCIE Voice The CCIE Voice exam covers the technologies and applications that make up a Cisco Enterprise VoIP solution.

CCIE Storage Networking The CCIE Storage Networking exam covers storage solutions running on an extended network infrastructure.

To become a CCIE, Cisco recommends you do the following:

1. Attend a CCIE hands-on training lab program from a Cisco training partner.

2. Pass the written exam. This costs $300 per exam. See the upcoming "Where Do You Take the Exams?" section for more information.

3. Pass the one-day, hands-on lab at Cisco. This costs $1250 per lab, and many people fail it two or more times. Some people never make it through—it's very difficult. Cisco has both added and deleted sites lately for the CCIE lab, so it's best to check the Cisco website for the most current information. Take into consideration that you might need to add travel costs to that $1250.

Cisco Network Design Certifications

In addition to the network support certifications, Cisco has created another certification track for network designers. The two certifications within this track are the Cisco Certified Design Associate and Cisco Certified Design Professional. If you're reaching for the CCIE stars, we highly recommend the CCNP and CCDP certifications before you attempt the lab (or attempt to advance your career).

These certifications will give you the knowledge you need to design routed LAN, routed WAN, and switched LAN and ATM LANE networks.

Cisco Certified Design Associate (CCDA)

To become a CCDA, you must pass the Designing for Cisco Internetwork Solutions exam (640-861 DESGN). To pass this test, you must understand how to do the following:

- Identify the customer's business needs and internetworking requirements.
- Assess the customer's existing network, and identify the potential issues.
- Design the network solution that suits the customer's needs.
- Explain the network design to the customer and network engineers.
- Plan the implementation of the network design.
- Verify the implementation of the network design.

The *CCDA: Cisco Certified Design Associate Study Guide, 2nd ed.* (Sybex, 2003) is the most cost-effective way to study for and pass your CCDA exam.

Cisco Certified Design Professional (CCDP)

If you're already a CCNP and want to get your CCDP, you can take the Designing Cisco Network Service Architectures exam (642-871 ARCH). If you're not yet a CCNP, you must take the CCDA, CCNA, BSCI, BCMSN, and ARCH exams.

You can also take the Composite exam (642-891) and the ARCH exam.

CCDP certification skills include the following:

- Designing complex routed LAN, routed WAN, and switched LAN and ATM LANE networks
- Building on the base level of the CCDA technical knowledge

CCDPs must also demonstrate proficiency in the following:

- Network-layer addressing in a hierarchical environment
- Traffic management with access lists
- Hierarchical network design
- VLAN use and propagation
- Performance considerations: required hardware and software; switching engines; memory, cost, and minimization

How to Use This Book

If you want a solid foundation for the serious effort of preparing for the CCSP, then look no further. We've put this book together in a way that will thoroughly equip you with everything you need to pass these exams as well as teach you how to completely configure security on many Cisco platforms.

This book is loaded with valuable information. You'll get the most out of your study time if you tackle it like this:

1. Take the assessment tests immediately following this introduction. (The answers are at the end of the tests, so no cheating.) It's okay if you don't know any of the answers—that's why you bought this book! But you do need to carefully read over the explanations for any question you get wrong and make note of which chapters the material is covered in. This will help you plan your study strategy. Again, don't be disheartened if you don't know any answers—just think instead of how much you're about to learn.

2. Study each chapter carefully, making sure that you fully understand the information and the test objectives listed at the beginning of each chapter. Zero in on any chapter or part of a chapter that deals with areas where you missed questions in the assessment tests.

3. Take the time to complete the Written Lab for each chapter, which are available on the accompanying CD. Do *not* skip this! It directly relates to the exams and the relevant information you must glean from the chapter you just read. So, no skimming! Make sure you really, *really* understand the reason for each answer.

4. Answer all the review questions related to that chapter, also found on the CD. While you're going through the questions, jot down any questions that trouble you and study those sections of the book again. Don't throw away your notes; go over the questions that were difficult for you again before you take the exam. Seriously: Don't just skim these questions! Make sure you completely understand the reason for each answer, because the questions were written strategically to help you master the material that you must know before taking the exams.

5. Complete all the Hands-on Labs on the CD, referring to the relevant chapter material so that you understand the reason for each step you take. If you don't happen to have a bunch of Cisco equipment lying around to practice on, be sure to study the examples extra carefully.
6. Try your hand at the bonus exams on the CD. Testing yourself will give you a clear overview of what you can expect to see on the real thing.
7. Answer all the flashcard questions on the CD. The flashcard program will help you prepare completely for the exams.

> The electronic flashcards can be used on your Windows computer, Pocket PC, or Palm device.

8. Make sure you read the Exam Essentials at the end of the chapters and are intimately familiar with the information in those sections.

Try to set aside the same time every day to study, and select a comfortable, quiet place to do so. Pick a distraction-free time and place where you can be sharp and focused. If you work hard, you'll get it all down, probably faster than you expect.

This book covers everything you need to know to pass the CCSP exams. If you follow the preceding eight steps; really study; and practice the review questions, bonus exams, electronic flashcards, and Written and Hands-on Labs; and practice with routers, a PIX firewall, VPN Concentrators, Cisco Secure IDS sensors, or a router simulator, it will be diamond-hard to fail the CSIDS and CSI exams.

What Does This Book Cover?

Here's the information you need to know for the CCSP exams—the goods that you'll learn in this book. This book is broken into five parts:

- Part I—Chapters 1 through 9—focuses on the SECUR exam.
- Part II—Chapters 10 through 15—focuses on the CSPFA exam.
- Part III—Chapters 16 through 19—focuses on the CSVPN exam.
- Part IV—Chapters 20 through 26—focuses on the CSIDS exam.
- Part V—Chapters 27 through 30—focuses on the CSI exam.

Chapter 1, "Introduction to Network Security," introduces you to network security and the basic threats you need to be aware of. Chapter 1 also describes the types of weaknesses that might exist on your network. All organizations must have a well-documented policy; this chapter explains how to develop a solid corporate network security policy and outlines what guidelines it should include.

Chapter 2, "Introduction to AAA Security," is an introduction to the Cisco Network Access Server (NAS) and AAA security. Chapter 2 explains how to configure a Cisco NAS router for authentication, authorization, and accounting.

Chapter 3, "Configuring Cisco Secure ACS and TACACS+," explains how to install, configure, and administer the Cisco Secure ACS on Windows 2000 and Windows NT servers. (Chapter 3 also briefly describes the Cisco Secure ACS on Unix servers.) In addition, this chapter describes how the NAS can use either TACACS+ or RADIUS to communicate user access requests to the ACS.

Chapter 4, "Cisco Perimeter Router Problems and Solutions," introduces you to the Cisco perimeter router and the problems that can occur from hackers to a perimeter router on your network. This chapter also describes how you can implement solutions to these problems.

Chapter 5, "Context-Based Access Control Configuration," introduces you to the Cisco IOS Firewall and one of its main components, Context-Based Access Control (CBAC). Chapter 5 explains how CBAC is both different and better than just running static ACLs when it comes to protecting your network.

Chapter 6, "Cisco IOS Firewall Authentication and Intrusion Detection," discusses the IOS Firewall Authentication Proxy, which allows you to create and apply access control policies to individuals rather than to addresses. In addition, this chapter also explains the IOS Firewall Intrusion Detection System (IDS), which allows your IOS router to act as a Cisco Secure IDS sensor would, spotting and reacting to potentially inappropriate or malicious packets.

Chapter 7, "Understanding Cisco IOS IPSec Support," introduces the concept of virtual private networks (VPNs) and explains the solutions to meet your company's off-site network access needs. Chapter 7 also describes how VPNs use IP Security (IPSec) to provide secure communications over public networks.

Chapter 8, "Cisco IPSec Pre-shared Keys and Certificate Authority Support," explains how to configure IPSec for pre-shared keys—the easiest of all the IPSec implementations—and how to configure site-to-site IPSec for certificate authority support.

Chapter 9, "Cisco IOS Remote Access Using Cisco Easy VPN," covers a cool development in VPN technology—Cisco Easy VPN. Cisco Easy VPN is a new feature in IOS that allows any capable IOS router to act as a VPN server.

Chapter 10, "PIX Firewall Basics," introduces you to the basics of firewall technology and how they mitigate security threats. Chapter 10 also describes the types of PIX firewalls and licensing options available. We also discuss the Firewall Service Module (FWSM) and some basic commands on the command-line interface (CLI).

Chapter 11, "PIX Firewall Configuration," is an introduction to how to configure the Cisco PIX firewall. The chapter explains how to configure DHCP server and client services; NAT and PAT concepts and configurations; and static, dynamic, and multicast routing on the PIX firewall.

Chapter 12, "ACLs, Filtering, Object Grouping, and AAA," explains how to configure access control lists (ACLs) on the PIX firewall and how object grouping can make ACLs easier to configure and modify. We also cover how to configure URL filtering using Websense and N2H2 servers. Finally, we discuss how to install, configure, and administer the Cisco Secure ACS on Windows 2000 and Windows NT servers plus how to implement AAA services on a PIX firewall.

Chapter 13, "Advanced Protocol Handling, Attack Guards, and Intrusion Detection," introduces you to the advanced protocol-handling features of the Cisco PIX firewall and how it can be configured to guard against various denial of service (DoS) attacks. This chapter also describes how you can implement the intrusion detections feature and how to stop attacks.

Chapter 14, "Firewall Failover and PDM," introduces you to the failover features of the PIX firewall and how to configure it for stateful failover operation. Chapter 14 explains how to use the Java-based PIX Device Manager to configure the PIX firewall using a generally available web browser.

Chapter 15, "VPNs and the PIX Firewall," discusses how to implement site-to-site and remote access VPNs on the PIX firewall using the CLI and PDM and how to scale the VPN support using digital certificates. This chapter also addresses how to configure and maintain multiple PIX firewalls in an enterprise using CiscoWorks2000 components and the PIX Cisco Secure Policy Manager.

Chapter 16, "Introduction to Virtual Private Networks," provides a high-level overview of VPN technologies and the complex group of protocols that are collectively known as IPSec. Chapter 16 also identifies the key Cisco product offerings for the VPN market.

Chapter 17, "Introduction to Cisco VPN Devices," briefly describes the VPN 3000 Concentrator products. This chapter also explains how to set up the Cisco VPN 3000 series hardware and software clients for a number of common VPN configurations. Information on preparing the client for mass rollout is also included.

Chapter 18, "Configuring the VPN Concentrator," explains how to prepare the VPN Concentrator for use. This chapter includes basic setup as well as more complex features such as load balancing and automatic software updates. Security features such as client firewalls and protocol filters are also covered.

Chapter 19, "Managing the VPN Concentrator," covers the many tools for monitoring concentrator usage and troubleshooting problems. The chapter discusses a number of protocols that can be used to remotely monitor, configure, and troubleshoot the system. Chapter 19 also explains the tools available to control access to the administrative interfaces.

Chapter 20, "Introduction to Intrusion Detection and Protection," is an introduction to the concepts of intrusion detection and provides an overview of the Cisco Secure IDS intrusion detection and protection solution. In this chapter, you'll learn about the different types of security threats and attacks and how the Security Wheel can be applied to successfully ensure the ongoing security of your network. You'll also be introduced to the different types of intrusion detection systems and learn about Cisco Secure IDS.

Chapter 21, "Installing Cisco Secure IDS Sensors and IDSMS," focuses on the different Cisco Secure IDS sensor platforms and how to install them on the network. We'll look at the 4200 series of sensor appliances, the Catalyst 6000/6500 IDS module, and the IDS network module for the Cisco 2600/3600/3700 series routers. You'll be introduced to the sensor CLI and learn about the underlying architecture of the sensor operating system and applications.

Chapter 22, "Configuring the Network to Support Cisco Secure IDS Sensors," focuses on the devices and configuration tasks required to successfully capture all traffic from the network segments that you wish to monitor to your sensors. You'll learn how to configure traffic-capture features on the various Cisco Catalyst switch platforms available and how to enable sensing interfaces on each sensor platform.

Chapter 23, "Configuring Cisco Secure IDS Sensors Using the IDS Device Manager," introduces the IDS Device Manager (IDM), which is used to configure sensors via a web-based graphical interface. In this chapter, you'll learn how to perform common configuration tasks using the IDM, and you'll also learn how to perform the equivalent configuration using the sensor command-line interface.

Chapter 24, "Configuring Signatures and Using the IDS Event Viewer," describes the signature engines included within Cisco Secure IDS and how to tune built-in signatures and create custom signatures. You'll learn how to use the IDS Event Viewer (IEV), which is a Java-based application that can monitor alarms generated by up to five sensors and is suitable for small deployments of Cisco Secure IDS sensors.

Chapter 25, "Enterprise Cisco Secure IDS Management," talks about enterprise management of Cisco Secure IDS sensors using the CiscoWorks VPN/Security Management Solution (VMS) product. In this chapter, you'll learn about the CiscoWorks VMS architecture, common components of CiscoWorks VMS, and how to install CiscoWorks VMS. You'll then learn how to install and use the IDS Management Center (IDS MC) to configure and manage up to 300 sensors.

Chapter 26, "Enterprise Cisco Secure IDS Monitoring," talks about enterprise monitoring of Cisco Secure IDS sensors using the CiscoWorks VPN/Security Management Solution (VMS) product. In this chapter, you'll learn how to install and use the Security Monitoring Center (Security MC), which is an application within the CiscoWorks VMS suite that provides monitoring of alarms generated by up to 300 sensors.

Chapter 27, "Security Fundamentals," is an introduction to the world of SAFE. In this chapter, you'll learn about the different types of network attacks and how to mitigate them. You'll also be introduced to the SAFE SMR Network Design.

Chapter 28, "The Cisco Security Portfolio," focuses on the Cisco products available for implementing a secure environment. We'll look at the different Cisco routers that support the IOS Firewall Feature Set, PIX firewall, VPN concentrator, IDS, and Cisco Secure ACS. This chapter concludes with an overview of the Cisco AVVID framework.

Chapter 29, "SAFE Small and Medium Network Designs," focuses on the details involved in utilizing the Small and Medium Network Design approaches. You'll learn about the different modules of each design as well as the devices involved and attacks they are prone to, and how to mitigate against the attacks. After learning the theory behind this design, you'll learn how to implement the Cisco products that will make this design a reality.

Chapter 30, "SAFE Remote Access Network Design," explores one of the most widely used network designs, the Remote Access Network Design. In this chapter, you'll learn about the different options available for implementing a secure remote access design. We'll also look at the Cisco products involved and how to configure these products.

Appendix A, "Introduction to the PIX Firewall," found on the accompanying CD, describes the features and basic configuration of the Cisco PIX firewall.

The Glossary on the CD is a handy resource for Cisco terms. It's a great reference tool for understanding some of the more obscure terms used in this book.

Most chapters include Written Labs, Hands-on Labs, and plenty of review questions on the CD to make sure you've mastered the material. Again, don't skip these tools. They're invaluable to your success.

What's on the CD?

We've provided some cool tools to help you with your certification process. All the following gear should be loaded on your workstation when you're studying for the test:

The Sybex Test Engine The test preparation software, developed by the experts at Sybex, prepares you to pass the CCSP exams. In this test engine, you'll find review and assessment questions from each chapter of the book, plus five bonus exams. You can take the assessment tests, test yourself by chapter, or take the bonus exams. Your scores will show how well you did on each exam objective.

Electronic Flashcards for PC and Palm Devices We've included more than 500 flashcard questions that can be read on your PC, Palm, or Pocket PC device. These are short questions and answers designed to test you on the most important topics needed to pass the exams.

Glossary of Terms Knowing the definitions of key terms is important in your studies. Therefore, we have provided an exhaustive list of terms and their definitions.

Written Labs In addition to review questions, we feel it's important to be able to answer questions on your own. The Written Labs are short question/answers. If you can answer these with no problem, you are very familiar with the contents of this book.

Hands-on Labs These are designed to give you the hands on you need to not only prepare for the exams, but also to prepare you for the real world. Ideally, you should have your own home lab, or access to the Cisco technologies on which you are being tested. With these at your fingertips, and the labs we provide, you should be able to perform tasks Cisco expects its CCSPs to perform.

CCSP Complete Study Guide Sybex offers the *CCSP Complete Study Guide* in PDF format on the CD so you can read the book on your PC or laptop if you travel and don't want to carry a book, or if you just like to read from the computer screen. In addition, we have included an Appendix A, "Introduction to the PIX Firewall." Acrobat is also included on the CD.

Where Do You Take the Exams?

You may take the exams at any of the more than 800 Thomson Prometric Authorized Testing Centers around the world; find out more at www.2test.com or (800) 204-EXAM (3926). You can also register and take the exams at a Pearson VUE authorized center—www.vue.com; (877) 404-EXAM (3926).

To register for a Cisco certification exam:

1. Determine the number of the exam you want to take. The exams discussed in this book are numbered as follows:
   - SECUR (642-501)
   - CSPFA (642-521)
   - CSVPN (642-511)
   - CSIDS (643-531)
   - CSI (642-541)

2. Register with the nearest Thomson Prometric Registration Center or Pearson VUE testing center. You'll be asked to pay in advance for the exam. At the time of this writing, the exams are $125 each and must be taken within one year of payment. You may schedule an exam up to six weeks in advance or as late as the same day you want to take it. If you fail a Cisco exam, you must wait 72 hours before you get another shot at taking it. If something comes up and you need to cancel or reschedule your exam appointment, contact Thomson Prometric or Pearson VUE at least 24 hours in advance.

3. When you schedule the exam, you'll get instructions regarding all appointment and cancellation procedures, the ID requirements, and information about the testing-center location.

Tips for Taking Your Exams

The CCSP exams are multiple choice, and depending on which exam you take contain between 55 and 75 questions, and must be completed in 75 or 90 minutes.

Many questions on the exam have answer choices that at first glance look a lot alike, especially the syntax questions (see the sidebar). Remember to read through the choices carefully, because close doesn't cut it. If you get commands in the incorrect order or forget one measly character, you'll get the question wrong. So, to practice, do the Hands-on Labs provided with this book over and over again until they feel natural to you.

Also, never forget that the right answer is the Cisco answer. In many cases, more than one appropriate answer is presented, but the *correct* answer is the one that Cisco recommends.

Here are some general tips for exam success:

- Arrive early at the exam center so you can relax and review your study materials.
- Read the questions *carefully*. Don't jump to conclusions. Make sure you're clear about *exactly* what each question asks.
- When answering multiple-choice questions that you're not sure about, use the process of elimination to discard the obviously incorrect answers first. Doing this greatly improves your odds if you need to make an educated guess.
- You can no longer move forward and backward through the Cisco exams. Double-check your answer before pressing Next, because you can't change your mind.

Watch That Syntax!

Unlike Microsoft or other IT certification tests, the Cisco exams have answer choices that are syntactically similar. Although some syntax is dead wrong, it's usually just *subtly* wrong. Some other choices might be syntactically correct, but they're shown in the wrong order. Cisco does split hairs, and it's not at all averse to giving you classic trick questions. Here's an example:

True or False: `access-list 101 deny ip any any eq 23` denies Telnet access to all systems.

This statement looks correct because most people refer to the port number (23) and think, "Yes, that's the port used for Telnet." The catch is that you can't filter IP on port numbers (only TCP and UDP).

After you complete an exam, you'll get immediate, online notification—a printed Examination Score Report that indicates your pass or fail status and your exam results by section. The test administrator will give you that report. Test scores are automatically forwarded to Cisco within five working days after you take the test, so you don't need to send in your score. If you pass the exam, you'll usually receive confirmation from Cisco within four weeks.

The CCSP Exam Objectives

> **Note:** At the beginning of each chapter in this book, we have included the listing of the exam objectives covered in the chapter. These are provided for easy reference and to assure you that you are on track with the objectives. Exam objectives are subject to change at any time without prior notice and at Cisco's sole discretion. Please visit the CCSP page of Cisco's website (http://www.cisco.com/en/US/learning/le3/le2/le37/le54/learning_certification_type_home.html) for the most current listing of exam objectives.

Securing Cisco IOS Networks

To pass this exam, you'll need to master the following subject areas:

  Basic Cisco Router Security

   Secure administrative access for Cisco routers

   Describe the components of a basic AAA implementation

   Test the perimeter router AAA implementation using applicable debug commands

  Advanced AAA Security for Cisco Router Networks

   Describe the features and architecture of CSACS 3.0 for Windows

   Configure the perimeter router to enable AAA processes to use a TACACS remote service

  Cisco Router Threat Mitigation

   Disable unused router services and interfaces

   Use access lists to mitigate common router security threats

  Cisco IOS Firewall CBAC Configuration

   Define the Cisco IOS Firewall and CBAC

   Configure CBAC

  Cisco IOS Firewall Authentication Proxy Configuration

   Describe how authentication proxy technology works

   Configure AAA on a Cisco IOS Firewall

  Cisco IOS Firewall IDS Configuration

   Name the two types of signature implementations used by the Cisco IOS Firewall IDS

   Initialize a Cisco IOS Firewall IDS router

Building Basic IPSec Using Cisco Routers
    Configure a Cisco router for IPSec using pre-shared keys
    Verify the IKE and IPSec configuration
    Explain the issues regarding configuring IPSec manually and using RSA encrypted nonces

Building Advanced IPSec VPNs Using Cisco Routers and Certificate Authorities
    Advanced IPSec VPNs using Cisco Routers and CAs

Configuring Cisco Remote Access IPSec VPNs
    Describe the Easy VPN Server

Managing Enterprise VPN Routers
    Managing Enterprise VPN Routers

Cisco Secure PIX Firewall Advanced

To pass this exam, you'll need to master the following subject areas:

Cisco PIX Firewall Technology and Features
    Firewalls
    PIX Firewall models

Cisco PIX Firewall Family
    PIX Firewall models
    PIX services module
    PIX Firewall licensing

Getting Started with the Cisco PIX Firewall
    User interface
    Examining the PIX Firewall status
    ASA security levels
    Basic PIX Firewall configuration
    Syslog configuration
    DHCP server configuration
    PPPoE and the PIX Firewall

Translations and Connections
    Transport Protocols
    Network Address Translation
    Configuring DNS Support
    Port Address Translations

Access Control Lists and Content Filtering
    ACLS
    Converting Conduits to ACLS
    Using ACLS

Object Grouping
    Overview of object grouping
    Getting started with object groups
    Configuring object groups
    Nested object groups

Advanced Protocol Handling
    Advanced protocols
    Multimedia support

Attack Guards, Intrusion Detection, and Shunning
    Attack guards
    Intrusion detection

Authentication, Authorization, and Accounting
    Introduction
    Installation of CSACS for Windows NT
    Authentication configuration
    Downloadable ACLS

Failover
    Understanding failover
    Serial failover configuration
    LAN-based failover configuration

Virtual Private Networks
    PIX Firewall enables a secure VPN
    Prepare to configure VPN support
    Configure IKE parameter
    Configure IPSec parameters
    Test and verify VPN configuration
    Cisco VPN Client
    Scale PIX Firewall VPNs

System Maintenance
    Remote access
    Command authorization
Cisco PIX Device Manager
    PDM overview
    Prepare for PDM
    Using PDM to configure the PIX Firewall
    Using PDM to create a site-to-site VPN
    Using PDM to create a remote access VPN
Enterprise PIX Firewall Management
    Configuring access and translation rules
    Reporting, tools, and administration
Enterprise PIX Firewall Maintenance
    Introduction to the auto update server
    PIX Firewall and AUS communication settings
    Devices, images, and assignments
    Reports and administration
Firewall Services Module
    FWSM overview
    Using PDM with the FWSM

Cisco Secure Virtual Private Networks

To pass this exam, you'll need to master the following subject areas:

Overview of Virtual Private Networks and IPSec Technologies
    Cisco products enable a secure VPN
    IPSec overview
    IPSec protocol framework
    How IPSec works
Cisco Virtual Private Network 3000 Concentrator Series Hardware
    Overview of the Cisco VPN 3000 Concentrator Series
    Cisco VPN 3000 Concentrator
    Cisco VPN 3000 Concentrator Series Client support

Configuring the Cisco VPN 3000 Series Concentrator for Remote Access Using Pre-shared Keys
- Overview of remote access using pre-shared keys
- Initial configuration of the Cisco VPN 3000 Concentrator Series for remote access
- Browser configuration of the Cisco VPN 3000 Series Concentrator
- Configure users and groups
- More in-depth configuration information
- Configure the Cisco Windows VPN Software Client

Configure Cisco Virtual Private Network 3000 Series Concentrator for Remote Access Using Digital Certificates
- CA support overview
- Certificate generation
- Validating certificates
- Configuring the Cisco VPN 3000 Concentrator Series for CA support

Configure the Cisco Virtual Private Network Firewall Feature for IPSec Software Client
- Overview of software client's firewall feature
- Software Client's Are You There feature
- Software Client's Central Policy Protection feature
- Software Client's firewall statistics
- Customizing firewall policy

Configure the Cisco Virtual Private Network Client Auto-Initiation Feature
- Overview of the Cisco VPN Software Client auto-initiation
- Configure the Cisco VPN Software Client auto-initiation

Monitor and Administer Cisco VPN 3000 Remote Access Networks
- Monitoring
- Administration
- Bandwidth Management

Configure the Cisco VPN 3002 Hardware Client for Remote Access
- Cisco VPN 3002 Hardware client remote access with pre-shared keys

Configure the Cisco Virtual Private Network 3002 Hardware Client
- Overview of the Hardware Client interactive unit and user authentication features
- Configuring the Hardware Client interactive unit authentication feature
- Configuring the Hardware Client user authentication feature
- Monitoring the Hardware Client user statistics

Configure the Cisco Virtual Private Network Client Backup Server and Load Balancing
    Configuring the Cisco VPN Client backup server feature
    Configuring the Cisco VPN Client load balancing feature
    Overview of the Cisco VPN Client Reverse Route Injection feature

Configure the Virtual Private Network 3002 Hardware Client for Software Auto-Update
    Overview and configuration of the VPN 3002 Hardware Client software auto-update feature
    Monitoring the Cisco VPN 3002 Hardware Client software auto-update feature

Configure the Cisco Virtual Private Network 3000 Series Concentrator for the IPSec Over UDP and IPSec Over TCP
    Overview of Port Address Translation
    Configuring IPSec over UDP
    Configuring NAT-Transversal
    Configuring IPSec over TCP

Cisco Virtual Private Network 3000 Series Concentrator LAN-to-LAN with Pre-shared Keys
    Cisco VPN 3000 Series Concentrator IPSec LAN-to-LAN
    LAN-to-LAN configuration

Cisco Virtual Private Network 3000 Series Concentrator LAN-to-LAN with NAT
    LAN-to-LAN overview
    Configuring the Concentrator LAN-LAN NAT feature

Cisco Virtual Private Network 3000 Series Concentrator LAN-to-LAN Using Digital Certificates
    Root certificate installation

Identify certificate installation

Cisco Secure Intrusion Detection Systems

To pass this exam, you'll need to master the following subject areas:

    Describe and explain the various intrusion detection technologies and evasive techniques
        Define intrusion detection
        Explain the difference between true and false, and positive and negative alarms
        Describe the relationship between vulnerabilities and exploits
        Explain the difference between HIP and NIDS
        Describe the various techniques used to evade intrusion detection

Design a Cisco IDS protection solution for small, medium, and enterprise customers
    List the network devices involved in capturing traffic for intrusion detection analysis
    Describe the traffic flows for each of the network devices
    Explain the features and benefits of IDM
    Identify the requirements for IDM
    Configure Cisco Catalyst switches to capture network traffic for intrusion detection analysis

Identify the Cisco IDS Sensor platforms and describe their features
    Describe the features of the various IDS Sensor appliance models

Install and configure a Cisco IDS Sensor including a network appliance and IDS module

Identify the interfaces and ports on the various Sensors
    Distinguish between the functions of the various Catalyst IDS Module ports
    Initialize a Catalyst IDS Module
    Verify the Catalyst 6500 switch and Catalyst IDSM configurations
    Install the Sensor software image
    Install the Sensor appliance on the network
    Obtain management access on the Sensor
    Initialize the Sensor
    Describe the various command line modes
    Navigate the CLI
    Apply configuration changes made via the CLI
    Create user accounts via the CLI
    Configure Sensor communication properties
    Configure Sensor logging properties
    Perform a configuration backup via the CLI
    Setting up Sensors and Sensor Groups
    Sensor Communications Sensor Logging

Tune and customize Cisco IDS signatures to work optimally in specific environments
    Configure the Sensor's sensing parameters
    Configure a signature's enable status, severity level, and action
    Create signature filters to exclude or include a specific signature or list of signatures
    Tune a signature to perform optimally based on a network's characteristics
    Create a custom signature given an attack scenario

Configure a Cisco IDS Sensor to perform device management of supported blocking devices

Describe the device management capability of the Sensor and how it is used to perform blocking with a Cisco device

Design a Cisco IDS solution using the blocking feature, including the ACL placement considerations, when deciding where to apply Sensor-generated ACLs

Configure a Sensor to perform blocking with a Cisco IDS device

Configure a Sensor to perform blocking through a Master Blocking Sensor

Describe the Cisco IDS signatures and determine the immediate threat posed to the network

Explain the Cisco IDS signature features

Select the Cisco IDS signature engine to create a custom signature

Explain the global Cisco IDS signature parameters

Explain the engine-specific signature parameters

Perform maintenance operations such as signature updates, software upgrades, data archival and license updates

Identify the correct IDS software update files for a Sensor and an IDSM

Install IDS signature updates and service packs

Upgrade a Sensor and an IDSM to an IDS major release version

Describe the Cisco IDS architecture including supporting services and configuration files

Explain the Cisco IDS directory structure

Explain the communication infrastructure of the Cisco IDS

Locate and identify the Cisco IDS log and error files

List the Cisco IDS services and their associated configuration files

Describe the Cisco IDS configuration files and their function

Monitor a Cisco IDS protection solution for small and medium networks

Explain the features and benefits of IEV

Identify the requirements for IEV

Install the IEV software and configure it to monitor IDS devices

Create custom IEV views and filters

Navigate IEV to view alarm details

Perform IEV database administration functions

Configure IEV application settings and preferences

Manage a large scale deployment of Cisco IDS Sensors with Cisco IDS Management software

 Define features and key concepts of the IDS MC

 Install the IDS MC

 Generate, approve, and deploy sensor configuration files

 Administer the IDS MC Server

 Use the IDS MC to set up Sensors

 Use the IDS MC to configure Sensor communication properties

 Use the IDS MC to configure Sensor logging properties

Monitor a large scale deployment of Cisco IDS Sensors with Cisco IDS Monitoring software

 Define features and key concepts of the Security Monitor

 Install and verify the Security Monitor functionality

 Monitor IDS devices with the Security Monitor

 Administer Security Monitor event rules

 Create alarm exceptions to reduce alarms and possible false positives

 Use the reporting features of the Security Monitor

 Administer the Security Monitor server

Cisco SAFE Implementation

To pass this exam, you'll need to master the following subject areas:

 Security Fundamentals

  Need for network security

  Network attack taxonomy

  Network security policy

  Management protocols and functions

 Architectural Overview

  Overview

  Design fundamentals

  Safe axioms

  Security wheel

I Introduction

Cisco Security Portfolio
    Overview
    Secure connectivity—Virtual Private Network solutions
    Secure connectivity—the 3000 Concentrator series
    Secure connectivity—Cisco VPN optimized routers
    Perimeter security firewalls—Cisco PIX and Cisco IOS Firewall
    Intrusion protection—IDS and Cisco secure scanner
    Identity—access control solutions
    Security management—VMS and CSPM
    Cisco AVVID

SAFE Small Network Design
    Overview
    Small network corporate Internet module
    Small network campus module
    Implementation—ISP router
    Implementation—IOS Firewall features and configuration
    Implementation—PIX Firewall

SAFE Medium Network Design
    Medium network corporate Internet module
    Mediumnetwork corporate Internet module design guidelines
    Medium network campus module
    Medium network campus module design guidelines
    Medium network WAN module
    Implementation—ISP router
    Implementation—edge router
    Implementation—IOS Firewall
    Implementation—PIX Firewall
    Implementation—NIDS
    Implementation—HIDS
    Implementation—VPN Concentrator
    Implementation—layer 3 switch

SAFE Remote—User Network Implementation
  Overview
  Key devices
  Threat mitigation
  Software access option
  Remote site firewall option
  Hardware VPN Client option
  Remote site router option

How to Contact the Authors

You can reach Wade Edwards at `ccie7009@hotmail.com`, where you can ask questions relating to his books. You can reach Todd Lammle through Globalnet Training Solutions, Inc. (`www.globalnettraining.com`), his training company in Dallas, or at RouterSim, LLC (`www.routersim.com`), his software company in Denver. You can reach Justin Menga at `jmenga@hotmail.com`, Carl Timm at `carl_timm@hotmail.com`, and Jason Rohm at `jasonrohm@athenet.net`.

Securing Cisco IOS Networks Assessment Test 1

1. Which of the following commands trace AAA packets and monitor their activities? (Choose all that apply.)
    A. `debug aaa authentication`
    B. `debug aaa authorization`
    C. `debug aaa all`
    D. `debug aaa accounting`

2. What is the last header you can read in clear text when a packet has been encrypted using IPSec?
    A. Physical
    B. Data Link
    C. Network
    D. Transport

3. Which of the following is an example of a configuration weakness?
    A. Old software
    B. No written security policy
    C. Unsecured user accounts
    D. No monitoring of the security

4. Which IOS feature best prevents DoS SYN flood attacks?
    A. IPSec
    B. TCP Intercept
    C. MD5 authentication
    D. ACLs

5. RSA digital signatures and _____ are IPSec authentication types supported by the Cisco Easy VPN Server.
    A. Pre-shared keys
    B. LSA analog signatures
    C. DSS
    D. DES
    E. 3DES

6. Which of the following commands do you use to change the maximum number of half-open TCP connections per minute to 100?
   A. `ip inspect tcp synwait-time 100`
   B. `ip inspect tcp idle-time 100`
   C. `ip inspect max-incomplete high 100`
   D. `ip inspect one-minute high 100`
   E. `ip inspect tcp max-incomplete host 100`

7. IP spoofing, man-in-the-middle, and session replaying are examples of what type of security weakness?
   A. Configuration weakness
   B. TCP/IP weakness
   C. Policy weakness
   D. User password weakness

8. Alert is the _____ for attack signatures in the IOS Firewall IDS.
   A. Default action
   B. Nondefault action
   C. Exclusionary rule
   D. Inclusionary rule
   E. Configured action

9. If you want to make sure you have the most secure authentication method, what should you use?
   A. Windows username/password
   B. Unix username/password
   C. Token cards/soft tokens
   D. TACACS+

10. Which of the following are considered typical weaknesses in any network implementation? (Choose all that apply.)
    A. Policy weaknesses
    B. Technology weaknesses
    C. Hardware weaknesses
    D. Configuration weaknesses

11. What are RSA-encrypted nonces?
    A. Manually generated/exchanged public keys
    B. Automatically generated/exchanged public keys
    C. Manually generated/exchanged private keys
    D. Automatically generated/exchanged private keys

12. What function does the `clear crypto isakmp *` command perform?
    A. It resets all LDPM SAs configured on a device.
    B. It resets all IKE RSAs configured on a device.
    C. It resets all IKE SAs configured on a device.
    D. It resets the crypto settings for a configured peer.

13. Which component of AAA provides for the login, password, messaging, and encryption of users?
    A. Accounting
    B. Authorization
    C. Authentication
    D. Administration

14. Which of the following commands do you use to change the maximum time CBAC waits before closing idle TCP connections to 10 minutes?
    A. `ip inspect tcp synwait-time 600`
    B. `ip inspect tcp idle-time 600`
    C. `ip inspect max-incomplete high 600`
    D. `ip inspect one-minute high 600`
    E. `ip inspect tcp max-incomplete host 600`

15. Which of the following are examples of policy weaknesses? (Choose all that apply.)
    A. Absence of a proxy server
    B. No trusted networks
    C. Misconfigured network equipment
    D. No disaster recovery plan
    E. Technical support personnel continually changing

16. The ESP protocol provides which service not provided by the AH protocol?
    A. Data confidentiality
    B. Authentication services
    C. Tamper detection
    D. Anti-replay detection

17. Which of the following are valid methods for populating the Cisco Secure User Database? (Choose all that apply.)
    A. Manually
    B. Novell NDS
    C. Windows NT
    D. Database Replication utility
    E. Database Import utility

18. What does the command `aaa new-model` do?
    A. It creates a new AAA server on the NAS.
    B. It deletes the router's configuration and works the same as `erase startup-config`.
    C. It disables AAA services on the router.
    D. It enables AAA services on the router.

19. A connection that has failed to reach an established state is known as _____.
    A. Full-power
    B. Half-baked
    C. Half-open
    D. Chargen

20. Which of the following security database protocols can be used between the NAS and CSNT? (Choose all that apply.)
    A. NTLM
    B. SNA
    C. TACACS+
    D. Clear text
    E. RADIUS

21. Which of the following are examples of a TCP/IP weakness? (Choose all that apply.)
    A. Trojan horse
    B. HTML attack
    C. Session replaying
    D. Application layer attack
    E. SNMP
    F. SMTP

22. You have just configured IPSec encryption. Which problem are you trying to solve?
    A. Denial-of-service (DoS) attacks
    B. Rerouting
    C. Lack of legal IP addresses
    D. Eavesdropping

23. You have just configured MD5 authentication for BGP. Which type of attack are you trying to prevent?
    A. DoS
    B. Rerouting
    C. Hijacking of legal IP addresses
    D. Eavesdropping

24. Using your web browser, which port do you go to (by default) to access the CSNT web server?
    A. 80
    B. 202
    C. 1577
    D. 2002
    E. 8000

25. To help you both set up and configure CBACs, Cisco has defined six steps for configuring CBAC. What is the correct order for the six steps?
    A. Define Port-to-Application Mapping (PAM).
    B. Set audit trails and alerts.
    C. Test and verify CBAC.
    D. Set global timeouts and thresholds.
    E. Apply inspection rules and ACLs to interfaces.
    F. Define inspection rules.

26. What port does ISAKMP use for communications?
    A. TCP 50
    B. UDP 50
    C. TCP 500
    D. UDP 500

27. Policy weaknesses, technology weaknesses, and configuration weaknesses are examples of what type of implementation weakness? (Choose all that apply.)
    A. Policy implementation
    B. Network implementation
    C. Hardware implementation
    D. Software implementation

28. The _____ implement(s) software to protect TCP server from TCP SYN flood attacks.
    A. Cisco access control lists (ACLs)
    B. TCP Intercept feature
    C. Cisco queuing methods
    D. Cisco CBACS

29. Which of the following do *not* participate in the Cisco IOS Cryptosystem? (Choose all that apply.)
   A. DH
   B. MD5
   C. ESP
   D. DES
   E. BPR

30. The `ip inspect tcp max-incomplete host 100` command performs what function when invoked?
   A. It has no known effect on the router.
   B. It sets the total number of TCP connections per host to 1000.
   C. It sets the total number of TCP connections per host to 100.
   D. It changes the maximum number of half-open TCP connections per host to 1000.
   E. It changes the maximum number of half-open TCP connections per host to 100.

31. What key does Diffie-Hellman (DH) create during IKE phase 1?
   A. Xa
   B. Bx
   C. Xor
   D. NorX

32. Which of the following authentication methods is *not* supported by Cisco Secure ACS 3.0 for Windows NT/2000? (Choose all that apply.)
   A. Novell NDS
   B. Banyan StreetTalk
   C. DNS
   D. POP
   E. ODBC
   F. MS Directory Services

33. The `ip inspect max-incomplete high 1000` command changes what setting?
   A. It changes the maximum number of half-open TCP connections to 100.
   B. It changes the minimum number of half-open TCP connections to 1000.
   C. It changes the maximum number of half-open TCP connections to 1000.
   D. It changes the IP inspect idle timer to 1000 seconds.
   E. It changes the IP inspect idle timer to 100 seconds.

34. Which of the following statements about CS ACS 3.0 token-card server support are true? (Choose all that apply.)
    A. Microsoft is supported with service pack 6.0a.
    B. AXENT is natively supported.
    C. CryptoCard is natively supported.
    D. Novell NDS v4.*x* or higher is supported.
    E. ODBC with 6.0.1.1a service pack is supported.

35. IOS version 12.2(8)T is the minimum version required in order to run _____.
    A. LPDM
    B. Windows NT Terminal Services
    C. IOS Easy VPN Server
    D. sRAS (Secure RAS) or sDNS (Secure Domain Name Service)

36. Memory usage and _____ are two issues to consider when implementing the IOS Firewall IDS.
    A. User knowledge
    B. Signature coverage
    C. User address space
    D. TACACS+ server type

37. What does the `aaa authentication login default tacacs+ none` command instruct the router to do? (Choose all that apply.)
    A. No authentication is required to log in.
    B. TACACS+ is the default login method for all authentication.
    C. If the TACACS+ process is unavailable, no access is permitted.
    D. RADIUS is the default login method for all authentication.
    E. If the TACACS+ process is unavailable, no login is required.
    F. If the RADIUS process is unavailable, no login is required.

38. _____ and _____ are both supported by Cisco Easy VPN Server.
    A. Authentication using DSS
    B. DH1
    C. DH2
    D. Manual keys
    E. Perfect forward secrecy (PFS)
    F. DH5

39. What does an atomic signature trigger on?

   A. Single packet

   B. Duplex packet

   C. Atomic packet

   D. Two-way packet

40. Which of these statements are true regarding the following debug output? (Choose all that apply.)

```
01:41:50: AAA/AUTHEN: free_user (0x81420624) user='todd' ruser=''
port='tty0' rem_addr='async/' authen_type=ASCII service=LOGIN priv=101:42:12:
AAA/AUTHEN/CONT (864264997): Method=LOCAL
```

   A. This debug output shows that the user is using a remote database for authenticating the user **todd**.

   B. This is a debug output from the authorization component of AAA.

   C. This is a debug output from the authentication component of AAA.

   D. The password will be checked against the local line password.

Answers to Securing Cisco IOS Networks Assessment Test 1

1. A, B, D. The debug commands debug aaa authentication, debug aaa authorization, and debug aaa accounting can be used to help you trace AAA packets and monitor the AAA activities on the NAS. See Chapter 2 for more information.

2. C. IPSec encrypts all headers (including the data payload) after the Network layer header. See Chapter 7 for more information.

3. C. Unsecured user accounts are considered a weakness in configuration. See Chapter 1 for more information.

4. B. TCP Intercept can protect against DoS SYN flood attacks. See Chapter 4 for more information.

5. A. Pre-shared keys and RSA digital signatures are supported authentication types. DSS is not supported. DES and 3DES are encryption algorithms, not authentication types. See Chapter 9 for more information.

6. D. The ip inspect one-minute high 100 command sets the maximum number of half-open TCP connections per minute to 100. See Chapter 5 for more information.

7. B. TCP/IP has some inherent weaknesses. IP spoofing, man-in-the-middle attacks, and session replaying are some examples of attacks that take advantage of TCP/IP weaknesses. See Chapter 1 for more information.

8. A. The default action for attack signatures is to alert. See Chapter 6 for more information.

9. C. Token cards/soft tokens are the most secure method of user authentication. See Chapter 2 for more information.

10. A, B, D. Policy, technology, and configuration weaknesses are the three typical weaknesses in any network implementation. See Chapter 1 for more information.

11. A. The first step in using RSA-encrypted nonces requires the user to manually generate the keys. The user must then manually enter the public key created on each device into the device they wish to peer with. See Chapter 7 for more information.

12. C. To reset all active IKE SAs on a device, use the * keyword with the clear crypto isakmp command. If you just want to reset a particular IKE SA, use the clear crypto isakmp conn-id command. See Chapter 8 for more information.

13. C. Authentication identifies a user, including login, password, messaging, and encryption. See Chapter 2 for more information.

14. B. The ip inspect tcp idle-time 600 command sets the idle time on TCP connections to 10 minutes (600 seconds). See Chapter 5 for more information.

15. D, E. Cisco describes the absence of a disaster recovery plan and a high turnover rate in the technical support department as policy weaknesses. See Chapter 1 for more information.

16. A. ESP provides for data confidentiality (encryption). AH does not provide encryption. See Chapter 7 for more information.

17. A, D, E. You can populate the Cisco Secure User Database in only three ways: manually, using the Database Replication utility, or using the Database Import utility. CSNT can authenticate to external user databases such as Novell NDS or Windows NT, but it does not import these databases. See Chapter 3 for more information.

18. D. To start AAA on an NAS, use the global configuration command aaa new-model. The new-model keyword reflects changes from the initial implementation, which is no longer supported. See Chapter 2 for more information.

19. C. CBAC defines a half-open connection as any connection that fails to reach an established state. See Chapter 5 for more information.

20. C, E. CSNT supports TACACS+ and RADIUS communication with the NAS. See Chapter 3 for more information.

21. C, E, F. There are many problems with the IP stack, especially in Microsoft products. Session replaying is a weakness that is found in TCP. Both SNMP and SMTP are identified by Cisco as inherently insecure protocols in the TCP/IP stack. See Chapter 1 for more information.

22. D. IPSec and encryption are used to prevent eavesdropping. See Chapter 4 for more information.

23. B. MD5 authentication can be used to secure against rerouting attacks. See Chapter 4 for more information.

24. D. The CSNT web server listens on TCP port 2002. See Chapter 3 for more information.

25. B, D, A, F, E, C. The six steps to configure CBACs are as follows: set audit trails and alerts, set global timeouts and thresholds, define Port-to-Application Mapping, define inspection rules, apply inspection rules and ACLs to interfaces, and finally, test and verify CBAC. See Chapter 5 for more information.

26. D. ISAKMP uses UDP port 500 for communications. See Chapter 7 for more information.

27. B. Policy, technology, and configuration weaknesses are the three typical weaknesses in any network implementation. See Chapter 1 for more information.

28. B. The TCP Intercept feature implements software to protect TCP servers from TCP SYN flood attacks, which are a type of denial-of-service attack. See Chapter 4 for more information.

29. C, E. The Cisco IOS Cryptosystem consists of DES, MD5, DSS, and DH. See Chapter 7 for more information.

30. E. The ip inspect tcp max-incomplete host 100 command sets the maximum number of half-open TCP connections to a single host to 100. See Chapter 5 for more information.

31. A. During IKE phase 1, DH is used to create the private keys, Xa and Xb, and the public keys, Ya and Yb. DH then uses these keys to create the shared secret key ZZ, which is used to encrypt the DES and MD5 keys. So, answer A is correct. See Chapter 7 for more information.

32. B, C, D. The authentication methods supported by Cisco Secure 3.0 include Windows NT/2000, Novell Directory Services (NDS), Directory Services (DS), Token Server, ACS Databases, Microsoft Commercial Internet System Lightweight Directory Access Protocol (MCIS LDAP), and Open Database Connectivity (ODBC). See Chapter 3 for more information.

33. C. The `ip inspect max-incomplete high 1000` command sets the maximum number (regardless of the destination host) of half-open TCP connections to a single host to 1000. See Chapter 5 for more information.

34. B, C. CS ACS supports token-card servers from CryptoCard, ActivCard, Vasco, RSA ACE/Server, Secure Computing SafeWord, and AXENT Defender. See Chapter 3 for more information.

35. C. You must have at least 12.2(8)T to run the IOS Easy VPN Server. See Chapter 9 for more information.

36. B. Both memory usage and signature coverage are issues to consider when planning an IOS Firewall IDS implementation. Performance impact is a third issue to consider. See Chapter 6 for more information.

37. B, E. This command specifies to use the default list against the TACACS+ server and that TACACS+ is the default login method for all authentications. The **none** keyword at the end means that if the TACACS+ process is unavailable, no login is required. See Chapter 3 for more information.

38. C, F. DH groups 2 and 5 are supported by Cisco Easy VPN Server. DSS, DH1, PFS, and manual keys are not supported. See Chapter 9 for more information.

39. A. Atomic signatures trigger on a single packet. See Chapter 6 for more information.

40. C, D. The text after AAA/AUTHEN means that this is from the authentication component of AAA. Method=LOCAL means that the local line will be used for authentication. See Chapter 2 for more information.

Cisco Secure PIX Firewall Advanced Assessment Test 2

1. You enter `enable password abcdefg encrypted` from the Privileged mode prompt. Is this a valid command? (Choose all that apply.)
   A. Yes, it is a valid command.
   B. No, you must enter that command from the Configuration mode prompt.
   C. No, encrypted passwords must be exactly 16 characters.
   D. No, the password must be enclosed in quotation marks.

2. How many VLAN interfaces can be defined on the Firewall Services Module?
   A. 10
   B. 50
   C. 100
   D. There is no limit to the number of VLAN interfaces.

3. Which keyword is used to identify DNS traffic (TCP port 53) through the PIX firewall?
   A. `dns`
   B. `dnsix`
   C. `domain`
   D. `names`

4. When the PIX firewall redirects you to another server for authentication, how do you get back to the original URL?
   A. You are automatically redirected back to your original URL after authentication.
   B. You have to reenter the URL after authentication.
   C. There is a link to get back to the original URL on the redirect page.
   D. There is no redirection; you are sent to the entered URL.

5. Which protocol can be used for command authorization?
   A. RADIUS
   B. TACACS+
   C. RADIUS
   D. None of the above

6. What feature is especially challenging about the RTSP protocol?
   A. It s connectionless.
   B. It uses all multicast addresses.
   C. It can use almost any TCP or UDP port, RTP, HTTP, or the control session for transport.
   D. It does not have a control session for the PIX firewall to monitor.

7. Which of the following actions can be tied to an attack signature class?
   A. Alarm
   B. Drop
   C. Reset
   D. All the above

8. How many poll intervals must pass without receiving a hello packet for a PIX firewall to begin the failover sequence?
   A. One
   B. Two
   C. Three
   D. Four

9. What does it mean if the secondary PIX firewall is also the active PIX?
   A. A failover has occurred.
   B. This cannot happen.
   C. This is the normal status.
   D. You have misconfigured the secondary PIX firewall.

10. Which of the following commands contains the appropriate syntax for configuring the inside interface with IP address 10.1.1.1?
    A. `interface ip (inside) 10.1.1.1 255.255.255.0`
    B. `ip address (inside) 10.1.1.1 255.255.255.0`
    C. `ip address 10.1.1.1 255.255.255.0`
    D. `ip address inside 10.1.1.1 255.255.255.0`

11. What command is used to see the public key of the local device?
    A. `show crypto ca mypubkey rsa`
    B. `show ca mypubkey rsa`
    C. `show crypto pubkey-chain rsa`
    D. `show ca pubkey-chain rsa`

12. Which attack guard feature is not enabled by default?
    A. Fragmentation guard
    B. Flood guard
    C. DNS guard
    D. Mail guard

13. The PIX Management Center uses which port to communicate to the PIX firewall?
   A. UDP/1024 or above
   B. UDP/23
   C. TCP/80
   D. TCP/443
   E. TCP/21

14. When using certificates, NTP should be used. What is NTP?
   A. Network Test Packet
   B. Network Time Packet
   C. Novell Test Packet
   D. Network Time Protocol

15. The interfaces `dmz` and `isp1` have both been set with a security level of 20. What traffic will the PIX firewall allow between these interfaces?
   A. Hosts on the `isp1` network can create a translation slot to the `dmz` network, but hosts on the `dmz` network cannot create a translation slot to hosts on the `isp1` network.
   B. Hosts on the `dmz` network can create a translation slot to the `isp1` network, but hosts on the `isp1` network cannot create a translation slot to the hosts on the `dmz` network.
   C. Hosts on either network can create a translation slot to the other network.
   D. No direct connectivity is allowed between hosts on the `dmz` and `isp1` networks.

16. Which command sets the password for Telnet access to the PIX firewall?
   A. `enable telnet`
   B. `telnet password`
   C. `passwd`
   D. `login password`

17. Which type of object group can be nested within a network object group? (Choose all that apply.)
   A. Network
   B. Service
   C. ICMP
   D. Protocol

18. What username do you use to log in to the PDM when you are *not* using AAA?
   A. `pix`
   B. `enable`
   C. A blank username
   D. Any of the above will work with the proper enable password.

Answers to Cisco Secure PIX Firewall Advanced Assessment Test 2

1. B, C. Passwords are configured from the Configuration mode, and an encrypted string must be exactly 16 characters long. It would be okay to enter **abcdefg** as an unencrypted password, but once the PIX firewall encrypts it, the encrypted string will always be exactly 16 characters long. See Chapter 10 for more information.

2. C. Every PIX firewall is shipped with a 56-bit DES license, but you can upgrade to the 168-bit 3DES license. See Chapter 10 for more information.

3. C. The **dns** keyword describes the **dnsix** port, and **names** and **dnsix** are not valid keywords. See Chapter 11 for more information.

4. A. You will be automatically redirected back to the original URL after authentication. See Chapter 12.

5. B. TACACS+ is the only protocol that can be used to authorize commands using AAA. See Chapter 12.

6. C. RTSP can use other protocols such as RTP or HTTP or even its own control session for transport, and it can use a wide range of TCP and UDP ports. See Chapter 13.

7. D. You can tie all of these actions to either an attack or informational signature class. See Chapter 13.

8. C. The PIX firewall will wait for three failover intervals. See Chapter 14 for more information.

9. A. The secondary PIX firewall will become the active PIX firewall after a failover. See Chapter 14 for more information.

10. D. The command does not use parentheses, but it does require the interface name. See Chapter 11 for more information.

11. B. The command **show ca mypubkey rsa** is used to view the firewall's public key. For more information, see Chapter 15.

12. A. The Fragmentation Guard must be enabled manually. The others are on by default. See Chapter 13.

13. D. The PIX MC uses the Secure Sockets Layer protocol on TCP port 443 for secure communications with the PIX firewall. For more information, see Chapter 15.

14. D. Network Time Protocol allows for accurate time to be kept by configuring the firewall to communicate with a timeserver. For more information, see Chapter 15.

15. D. No connectivity is allowed between equal interfaces. See Chapter 11 for more information.

16. C. The `passwd` command is the only valid command listed here. See Chapter 10 for more information.

17. A. Only like object types can be nested within each other. See Chapter 12.

18. C. When you're *not* using AAA, the username must be left blank and the enable password used at the login prompt. See Chapter 14 for more information.

Cisco Secure Virtual Private Networks Assessment Test 3

1. What is the name of the VPN software client's global configuration file?
   A. vpnclient.ini
   B. oemsetup.inf
   C. ipsecdlr.ini
   D. vpnclient.pcf

2. How many groups are configured on a VPN 3000 Concentrator by default?
   A. 0
   B. 1
   C. 2
   D. 15

3. Which type of VPN is typically used by a mobile sales force?
   A. Intranet VPN
   B. Extranet VPN
   C. Access VPN
   D. Transit VPN

4. Which RFC defines the Encapsulating Security Payload (ESP) header?
   A. 1918
   B. 1826
   C. 2402
   D. 2406

5. Which of the following protocols allows for the generation of a shared secret over an insecure connection?
   A. Message-Digest 5 (MD5)
   B. Diffie-Hellman (DH)
   C. Internet Key Exchange (IKE)
   D. Security Parameter Index (SPI)

6. Which feature is used to provide for multiple VPN clients when the tunnels pass through a firewall or router using Port Address Translation (PAT)?
   A. NAT-Transversal
   B. IPSec over UDP
   C. IPSec over TCP
   D. LAN-to-LAN NAT

7. When the VPN 3000 configuration is saved, what is the previous configuration file renamed?
    A. VPN3000.RST
    B. CONFIG.BAK
    C. SHADOW
    D. FILE000.CHK

8. How many users can be supported by a VPN 3002 Hardware Client?
    A. 10
    B. 50
    C. 100
    D. 253

9. When a VPN concentrator or hardware client is initially set up, it prompts the administrator for basic information. What is this feature called?
    A. Initial Setup Wizard
    B. Quick Configuration mode
    C. Bootstrap script
    D. Initialization dialog

10. Which Cisco VPN 3000 series model includes two Scalable Encryption Processing (SEP) modules?
    A. 3015
    B. 3030
    C. 3060
    D. 3080

11. What feature/service must be used when you need to collect more than 256 log entries on a VPN 3005 Concentrator?
    A. Automatic log filtering
    B. Flash compression
    C. SNMP traps
    D. Syslog server

12. Which of the following is a valid authentication protocol when using encryption with PPTP?
    A. Password Authentication Protocol (PAP)
    B. Challenge-Handshake Authentication Protocol (CHAP)
    C. Microsoft CHAP (MS-CHAP)
    D. Shiva Password Authentication Protocol (SPAP)

Answers to Cisco Secure Virtual Private Networks Assessment Test 3

1. A. The Cisco Unified Client saves its global configuration settings in a standard Windows .ini file called vpnclient.ini. For more information, see Chapter 17.

2. B. The VPN 3000 series has one built-in group called the base_group. The base group cannot be disabled or deleted. For more information, see Chapter 19.

3. C. Cisco distinguishes between access, intranet, and extranet VPNs. The access VPN type is the most common VPN type and applies to any part-time single-user connection. For more information, see Chapter 16.

4. D. The IPSec standards are defined in a number of request for comments (RFC) documents. The Authentication Header (AH) is primarily defined in 1826 and 2402. ESP is defined as RFC 2406. For more information, see Chapter 16.

5. B. Diffie-Hellman key exchange uses mathematical associations to generate an encryption key known as a shared secret. Since the key is generated on each end, it is known only to the exchange partners and is never sent over the network. For more information, see Chapter 16.

6. C. Only IPSec over TCP supports multiple clients through a firewall or router using PAT. For more information, see Chapter 18.

7. B. The primary configuration file is called CONFIG; when the configuration is saved, a backup copy named CONFIG.BAK is saved to flash. For more information, see Chapter 19.

8. D. The hardware client supports up to 253 users, but it's recommended only for 50 or less. For more information, see Chapter 17.

9. B. The initial configuration is done using Quick Configuration mode. For more information, see Chapter 18.

10. C. Models 3015 through 3080 are upgradeable to four SEP modules. Only model 3060 includes two of these as part of the standard bundle. For more information, see Chapter 17.

11. D. The VPN 3000 series has a limited amount of space for log storage. If you need more storage or a historical database, you need to send those logs to a Syslog server. For more information, see Chapter 19.

12. C. Encryption is supported with Point to Point Tunneling Protocol only when MS-CHAP is used as the password protocol. For more information, see Chapter 18.

Cisco Secure Intrusion Detection Systems Assessment Test 4

1. TCP reassembly is a technique used by sensors to counter which of the following IDS evasive techniques?
   A. Obfuscation
   B. Encryption
   C. Flooding
   D. Fragmentation

2. NMAP is an example of a utility that performs which of the following type of attack?
   A. Access
   B. DoS
   C. Distributed DoS
   D. Reconnaissance

3. Cisco Secure IDS sensors fit into which phase of the security wheel?
   A. Secure
   B. Monitor
   C. Test
   D. Improve

4. What is the performance of the IDS-4215 sensor?
   A. 10Mbps
   B. 45Mbps
   C. 80Mbps
   D. 120Mbps

5. What is the minimum BIOS revision level required for IDS-4235 and IDS-4250 sensors to run Cisco Secure IDS 4.x software?
   A. A01
   B. A02
   C. A03
   D. A04

6. What are the sensing interfaces on an IDS-4215-4FE sensor?
   A. int0
   B. int1
   C. int0, int1, int2, int3, int4
   D. int0, int2, int3, int4, int5

7. You define an action of TCP Reset for a signature, but whenever the signature is fired, TCP Resets are never received at the source or destination of the packet that fired the signature. Which of the following is the best explanation for why this is happening?
   A. The source or path to the source is down.
   B. The source or path to the destination is down.
   C. Packets are being sent with a destination TCP port that is not configured to be analyzed by the signature.
   D. The SPAN port on the switch connecting the sensing interface of the sensor isn't configured to accept incoming packets.

8. What is the destination entity for an RSPAN source session?
   A. A destination port
   B. The sensor sensing interface
   C. An RSPAN VLAN
   D. A destination trunk

9. Which of the following variables defines networks internal to an organization?
   A. IN
   B. INSIDE
   C. OUT
   D. OUTSIDE

10. What protocol is used to issue blocking requests from a blocking forwarding sensor to a master blocking sensor?
    A. SSH
    B. Telnet
    C. FTP
    D. RDEP

11. What type of update file is the file IDS-K9-min-4.1-1-S47.rpm.pkg?
    A. Major update
    B. Minor update
    C. Signature update
    D. Service pack

12. Which of the following is *not* an intrusion protection feature?
    A. Block connection
    B. Block host
    C. Log
    D. Reset

13. Which of the following does the regular expression ba(na)+ match? (Choose all that apply.)
    A. ba
    B. bana
    C. banana
    D. bananas

14. Which of the following can you specify in an IDS Event Viewer view? (Choose all that apply.)
    A. Grouping style
    B. Data source
    C. Columns initially shown on the Alarm Information dialog
    D. Columns initially shown on the Drill Down dialog

15. You wish to install a single server that will manage and monitor 50 Cisco Secure IDS sensors. Which of the following products do you install? (Choose all that apply.)
    A. CiscoWorks Common Services
    B. IDS Device Manager
    C. IDS Management Center
    D. IDS Event Viewer
    E. Security Monitoring Center

16. What protocol is used by the IDS MC to manage Cisco Secure IDS sensors?
    A. HTTP
    B. Telnet
    C. SSH
    D. PostOffice

17. You attempt to generate a configuration after making changes in the IDS MC, but the attempt fails. What must you do first to be able to generate the configuration?
    A. Approve the configuration.
    B. Deploy the configuration.
    C. Save the pending configuration.
    D. Rollback the configuration.

18. What protocol is used by the Security MC to import sensor configurations from the IDS MC?
    A. HTTP
    B. HTTPS
    C. Telnet
    D. SSH

19. How do you view events using the Security MC?
    A. Select View ➢ Events.
    B. Select View ➢ Connections.
    C. Select Monitor ➢ Events.
    D. Select Monitor ➢ Connections.

20. What is the maximum number of events that can be displayed in a security MC event viewer grid by default?
    A. 10,000
    B. 25,000
    C. 50,000
    D. 100,000

21. What command is used to configure RSPAN on Cisco IOS?
    A. monitor session
    B. monitor rsession
    C. set span
    D. set rspan

Answers to Cisco Secure Intrusion Detection Systems Assessment Test 4

1. D. TCP Reassembly is used to reassemble TCP segments that are split or fragmented across multiple TCP packets. For more information, see Chapter 20.

2. D. NMAP is a port scanning and operating system fingerprinting utility, used for reconnaissance when an attacker is attempting to find some weakness in a target system or network. For more information, see Chapter 20.

3. B. Cisco Secure IDS sensors are monitoring devices that monitor network segments for intrusive activity. For more information, see Chapter 20.

4. C. The IDS-4215 can analyze up to 80Mbps of traffic for intrusive activity. For more information, see Chapter 21.

5. D. A BIOS revision level of A04 or higher is required for upgrading the IDS-4235 and IDS-4250 sensors to version 4.x. For more information, see Chapter 21.

6. D. The IDS-4215-4FE includes six interfaces, of which the sensing interfaces are int0, int2, int3, int4 and int5. For more information, see Chapter 21.

7. D. The sensing interface on a sensor generates TCP reset packets, so the sensing interface must be connected to a switch port that accepts incoming packets. For more information, see Chapter 22.

8. C. An RSPAN sources session specifies an RSPAN VLAN as the destination out which traffic captured should be sent. This allows propagation of SPAN traffic to multiple switches that understand the RSPAN protocol. For more information, see Chapter 22.

9. A. The IN variable defines internal networks. For more information, see Chapter 23.

10. D. RDEP messages are used to issue blocking requests, which are sent over an HTTP or HTTPS transport. For more information, see Chapter 23.

11. B. The min portion of the filename indicates the file is a minor update. For more information, see Chapter 23.

12. C. The log response provides further information about an attack, but it doesn't provide the intrusion protection features that the block and reset responses provide. For more information, see Chapter 24.

13. B, C. The + metacharacter matches one or more occurrences of the text specified in the brackets. For more information, see Chapter 24.

14. A, B, C. A view allows you to specify grouping style, data source, filter, columns initially shown on the alarm information dialog table, columns initially shown on the alarm aggregation table, and secondary sort order column. For more information, see Chapter 24.

15. A, C, E. To manage and monitor more than five sensors, CiscoWorks VMS is required. All CiscoWorks VMS servers require common services to be installed, whereas the IDS management center provides management and the security monitoring center provides monitoring. For more information, see Chapter 25.

16. C. The IDS MC uses SSH to manage sensors. For more information, see Chapter 25.

17. C. After making configuration changes, you must browse to the Configuration ➤ Pending page and save your configuration changes. You can then generate, approve, and deploy configurations. For more information, see Chapter 25.

18. B. HTTPS is used by the Security MC to connect to the IDS MC and import sensor configurations. For more information, see Chapter 26.

19. C. Selecting the Monitor tab and then selecting the Events option lets you view events using the security MC event viewer. For more information, see Chapter 26.

20. C. By default, the security MC event viewer displays a maximum of 50,000 events in a single grid. This can be modified to any value between 0 and 250,000. For more information, see Chapter 26.

21. A. The `monitor session` command configures both SPAN and RSPAN sessions on Cisco IOS. For more information, see Chapter 22.

Cisco SAFE Implementation Assessment Test 5

1. What is the most secure form of management?
   A. In-band
   B. Network
   C. Device
   D. Out-of-band

2. An attack packet sniffer contains which of the following characteristics? (Choose all that apply.)
   A. It's unable to capture TCP packets.
   B. It captures login sessions.
   C. It captures the first 300 to 400 bytes.
   D. It can decipher encrypted traffic.

3. Which of the following would you use for identity?
   A. ACS
   B. VPN
   C. PIX
   D. TACACS+

4. Which location is it best suited when you're using a Cisco 1700 router?
   A. Central office
   B. Remote office
   C. Medium office
   D. SOHO

5. Which type of VPN solution supports QoS?
   A. Remote access
   B. Firewall-based
   C. Site-to-site
   D. None of the above

6. Which of the following are key devices of the corporate Internet module of the SAFE SMR Small Network Design?
   A. Management server
   B. Firewall
   C. ISP router
   D. Layer 2 switch

7. Which of the following are not modules of the SAFE SMR Small Network Design? (Choose all that apply.)
   A. Campus module
   B. Internet module
   C. Corporate Internet module
   D. Enterprise module

8. In the campus module of the SAFE SMR Small Network Design, where would you want to install HIDS? (Choose all that apply.)
   A. Management servers
   B. Public servers
   C. User workstations
   D. Corporate servers

9. Which of the following options provides stateful packet filtering? (Choose all that apply.)
   A. Remote site router option
   B. VPN Hardware Client option
   C. Software access option
   D. Remote site firewall option

10. When you're using the software access option, when is split tunneling disabled?
    A. Never
    B. Always
    C. When the VPN is operational
    D. When the VPN is non-operational

11. Remote users are prone to which of the following attacks? (Choose all that apply.)
    A. Man-in-the middle
    B. DoS
    C. IP spoofing
    D. Unauthorized access

12. Which of the following are attack mitigation roles of the software access option? (Choose all that apply.)
    A. DoS
    B. Authentication
    C. IP spoofing
    D. Terminate IPSec

Answers to Cisco SAFE Implementation Assessment Test 5

1. **D.** Although SAFE SMR specifies that in-band management be used to save cost, out-of-band management is the most secure. For more information, see Chapter 27.

2. **B, C.** Attack packet sniffers typically are used to capture login sessions. They will capture the first 300 to 400 bytes of traffic. However, they can capture TCP packets and can't decipher encrypted traffic. For more information, see Chapter 27.

3. **A.** The Cisco Secure ACS is used for the purpose of identity. It accomplishes this task through the use of AAA. The PIX and VPN can use the ACS for identity however they don't provide identity. TACACS+ is a protocol that is used for AAA, not a product. For more information, see Chapter 28.

4. **B.** Cisco 1700 series routers are best suited for a remote office. Cisco 7100 and 7200 series routers are best suited for a central office. Cisco 800 and 900 series routers are best suited for a SOHO. Cisco 2600 and 3600 series routers are best suited for medium offices. For more information, see Chapter 28.

5. **C.** Routers are used to provide QoS. In a site-to-site VPN solution, routers are utilized. For more information, see Chapter 28.

6. **B, D.** The corporate Internet module is made up of a layer 2 switch for connectivity, public servers to provide public information about the company, and a firewall to provide protection to the Internal network. So, the correct answers are A and C. For more information, see Chapter 29.

7. **A, C.** The SAFE SMR Small Network Design consists of two modules: the corporate Internet module and the campus module. So, the correct answers are A and C. For more information, see Chapter 29.

8. **A, D.** In the campus module of the SAFE SMR Small Network Design the key devices are management servers, corporate servers, user workstations, and a layer 2 switch. HIDS should be installed on the corporate and management servers. So, the correct answers are A and D. For more information, see Chapter 29.

9. **A, D.** The remote site firewall and router options both provide stateful packet filtering. The other two options require the installation of a personal firewall on your PC. For more information, see Chapter 30.

10. **C.** If your choice for remote access is the software access option, split tunneling will be disabled whenever your VPN is operational. For more information, see Chapter 30.

11. **A, C, D.** Remote users are prone to unauthorized access, network reconnaissance, virus and Trojan horse attacks, IP spoofing, and man-in-the-middle attacks. For more information, see Chapter 30.

12. **B, D.** The software access option provides mitigation by supporting authentication, termination of IPSec tunnels, and the use of personal firewalls and virus scanning for local attack mitigation. For more information, see Chapter 30.

PART I

Securing Cisco IOS Networks (SECUR)

Chapter 1

Introduction to Network Security

THE FOLLOWING SECUR EXAM TOPICS ARE COVERED IN THIS CHAPTER:

- ✓ Introduction to network security
- ✓ Creating a security policy
- ✓ Reasons for creating a security policy
- ✓ Security issues
- ✓ Security threats

In a perfect world, network security would be as simple as installing some cool hardware or software onto your network, and voila! Your network is now Fort Knox. In the real world, you do this and then brace yourself so you don't make too much of a scene when the inevitable corporate security breach occurs. Frustrated, you say to yourself, "I really thought I took the necessary precautions—I did everything I could!" This chapter will help you understand that there's more to network security than technology. Real network security requires understanding the inherent people and corporate policy issues as well.

News and stories about Internet identity theft, hackers jacking sensitive corporate information, and new viruses vaporizing hard drives left and right are definitely the hot topics du jour. Countless shadowy Internet users are spreading havoc from their computers, and it's really difficult—sometimes impossible—to track them down. So how do you protect yourself? Well, to begin addressing this problem, let's take a look at what Cisco says are the three main security issues that a corporate network faces today:

- Security is not just a technology problem. Administrators and users are the cause of many corporate security problems.

- Vast quantities of security technologies exist. Too many network administrators buy technology from a random advertisement they happen to read in a networking magazine. But simply throwing money at your security problems usually isn't the best solution. Predictably, many vendors would absolutely love it if they could succeed in making you believe otherwise!

- Many organizations lack a single, well-defined network-wide security policy. Some corporations don't even have a security policy—no lie! Or worse, even if they do, each department has created its own security policy independently of the others. This is highly ineffective because it creates a myriad of security holes, leaving the network wide open to attacks in a number of places.

Anyone reading this book should be concerned with network security and interested in how a network can become truly secure using proper network policy. An effective network security policy involves a strategic combination of both hardware implementation and the proper corporate handling of information. This chapter will discuss the reasons for creating a corporate security policy. Understanding these reasons will provide you with a solid grasp of the Cisco SECUR exam objectives.

Let's move on to discuss the specific types of threats to which your network may be vulnerable.

Types of Network Security Threats

Sadly, human nature has a nasty side. And unfortunately, its lust for power, money, and revenge is sometimes aimed straight at your data. Although most of us aren't twisted, depraved, and ethically challenged, our fellow humans can and often do present serious threats to our network data. You must realize that you need to protect it. And you can—but before you begin to secure your data, you must understand the different types of threats looming out there, just waiting for the opportunity to strike. Four primary threats to network security define the type of attacker you could be dealing with some day:

Unstructured threats   Unstructured threats typically originate from curious people who have downloaded information from the Internet and want to feel the sense of power this provides them. Sure, some of these folks—commonly referred to as *Script Kiddies*—can be pretty nasty, but most of them are just doing it for the rush and for bragging rights. They're untalented, inexperienced hackers, and they're motivated by the thrill of seeing what they can do.

Structured threats   Hackers who create structured threats are much more sophisticated than Script Kiddies. They're technically competent and calculating in their work, they usually understand network system design, and they're well versed in how to exploit routing and network vulnerabilities. They can and often do create hacking scripts that allow them to penetrate deep into a network's systems at will. They tend to be repeat offenders. Both structured and unstructured threats typically come from the Internet.

External threats   External threats typically come from people on the Internet or from someone who has found a hole in your network from the outside. These serious threats have become ubiquitous in the last six to seven years, during which time most companies began to show their presence on the Internet. External threats generally make their insidious way into your network via the Internet or via a dial-up server, where they try to gain access to your computer systems or network.

Internal threats   Internal threats come from users on your network, typically employees. These are probably the scariest of all threats because they're extremely tough to both catch and stop. And because these hackers are authorized to be on the network, they can do serious damage in less time because they're already in and they know their way around.

Plus, the profile of an internal threat is that of the disgruntled, angry, vengeful former or current employee, or even a contractor who wants nothing more than to cause real pain and suffering. Although most users know this type of activity is illegal, some users also know it's fairly easy to cause a lot of damage—fast—and that they have a shake at getting away with it. That can be a huge, irresistible temptation to those with the right modus operandi or the wrong temperament.

Types of Security Weaknesses

This is probably the most important section in this chapter, because it defines what security weaknesses are and how to understand inherent weaknesses in hardware, software, and people. Generally, there are three types of security weaknesses in any network implementation:

- Technology weaknesses
- Configuration weaknesses
- Policy weaknesses

Technology Weaknesses

Cisco defines a *technology weakness* as a protocol, operating system, or hardware weakness. By default, protocols, operating systems, and hardware typically aren't secure. Understanding their weaknesses can help you secure your network before you're attacked.

Technology weakness refers to the inadequacies of electronic systems, whether hardware or software. These weaknesses create a challenge for IT staff because most hardware and software used in a company were already installed when they started their job.

Let's break this category into three specific areas:

TCP/IP weaknesses TCP/IP has intrinsic security weaknesses because it was designed as an open standard to facilitate network communication. The fact that TCP/IP is an open standard is the main reason for its vast popularity, but the open-standard nature of TCP/IP is also a reason why network attacks happen so easily and often—many people are familiar with how TCP/IP works.

For example, the original Unix sendmail daemon allows access to the Unix root, which, in turn, allows access to the entire Unix system. By viewing the sendmail information, a hacker can lock, load, and launch attacks on vulnerabilities specific to the operating system version. (Special torture!)

Yes, TCP/IP has operating system weaknesses that need to be addressed, but what's worse is that TCP/IP has also created network equipment weaknesses such as password protection, lack of required authentication, its routing protocols (which advertise your entire network), and firewall holes.

Cisco likes to pick on two protocols in the TCP/IP stack as being inherently insecure: Simple Mail Transfer Protocol (SMTP) and Simple Network Management Protocol (SNMP). IP spoofing (masquerade attack), man-in-the-middle, and session replaying are specific examples of TCP/IP weaknesses.

Operating system weaknesses Every operating system has weaknesses, but Microsoft Windows' weaknesses get top billing because most people use some version of Windows. To be fair, Unix and Linux have considerably fewer operating system weaknesses than Windows does, but they still have security issues that must be dealt with if you're running them on your network. It all comes down to a specific network's needs.

Network equipment weaknesses All network equipment, such as servers, routers, switches, and so on, has inherent security weakness. But being armed with a well-defined policy for the configuration and installation of network equipment can help tremendously in reducing the effects of network equipment weaknesses.

It's recommended that the following policies be in place before any piece of network equipment is configured and installed: passwords, authentication, routing protocols, and firewalls.

Configuration Weaknesses

Here's where human error comes into the fray: It's the administrator who creates *configuration weaknesses*. You'd be surprised how often a network administrator either leaves equipment at a default setting or fails to secure the network administrator accounts. Some common "come hither and hack me" scenarios exposing your everyday corporate network include configuration flaws such as unsecured user accounts, system accounts with easily guessed passwords, misconfigured Internet services, unsecured default settings in products, and misconfigured network equipment.

Unsecured User Accounts

Using default administrator accounts with no passwords and God-like control over the network is definitely asking for trouble. Just don't do it! If you're running Microsoft Windows NT, make sure you rename the administrator account. Doing so ensures that any intruders will at least have a slightly harder time finding and breaking into your operating system.

Put some serious thought into which users are granted which rights and privileges, because if you don't, and you instead give away rights indiscriminately, chaos will ensue. Take the time to establish the rights each user really needs, and don't give them any more rights than are required to do their job.

Did you know that usernames and passwords are generally transmitted insecurely across the network? Ever hear of the Reconnaissance intruder—you know, the guy or gal who likes to imagine that they're in the Internet Special Forces and their job is to find your network weakness and exploit it? (Funny how these people always think they're performing a public service when they steal your data and that you were *so* lucky it was only them who broke in and not some really bad person. They actually believe that they've helped you, because now you'll fix the weakness before a bad guy breaks in.) Clear passwords are the kind of cool stuff these snoopers spy for so they can use the information to gain access to your network later. As an administrator, be sure you define password policies that will help secure your network.

System Accounts with Easily Guessed Passwords

Another way to invite trouble is to assign system account passwords that are easy to guess. To avoid this blunder, the administrator needs to set up policies on your servers that won't allow certain kinds of passwords and that make sure each password has an expiration date.

Explicitly define a corporate policy for all users that makes it crystal clear that they can't use their name, their significant other's name, their child's name, their birth date, or any other excruciatingly obvious password—even if they add something to it. It's also a great idea to have them mix lowercase and uppercase letters, numbers, and special characters into their passwords. Doing so helps defend your network against brute-force attacks that use dictionary files to guess passwords.

Misconfigured Internet Services

I know it's hard to believe, but some companies still use routable IP addresses on their network to address their hosts and servers. With the Network Address Translation (NAT) and Port Address Translation (PAT) services that are available now, there is absolutely no reason to use real IP addresses.

But you can use *private IP addresses*. These allow corporations—and even single homes—to use an IP address range that's blocked on the Internet. Doing so provides some security for corporations, whose real IP addresses on the border router allow routing from the Internet.

This isn't a magical cure, though. Ports need to be open on the router connecting the router interface to the Internet in order to allow users access to and from the Internet. This is the very hole in a firewall that attackers can and do exploit.

Don't get me wrong: By putting up a firewall—the Cisco Secure Private Internet Exchange (PIX) Firewall is one of the best—you can provide good security for your network by using *conduits* (which are basically secure connections) to open ports from the Internet to your servers. Is this bulletproof security? No, that doesn't exist; but the PIX box is good—really good.

Another potential source of trouble and exposure is that some network administrators enable Java and JavaScript in their web browsers. Doing this makes it possible for hackers to attack you with hostile Java applets.

Unsecured Default Settings in Products

Tangling things further is the fact that many hardware products either ship with no password at all or make the password available so that the administrator can easily configure the device. On one hand, this really does make life easier—some devices are meant to be plug-and-play. For example, Cisco switches are plug-and-play because Cisco wants you to be able to replace your hubs and instantly make your network better. (And it works, too.) But you definitely need to put a password on that switch, or an attacker could easily break in.

Cisco gave this issue some thought and is a step ahead in solving the problem. Cisco routers and switches won't allow Telnet sessions into them without some type of login configuration on the device. But this cool feature does nothing to guard against other types of break-in attempts, such as what the "Internet Special Forces" are trying to "protect" you from.

This is one reason why it's a good idea to establish a configuration security policy on each device before any new equipment is installed on your network.

Misconfigured Network Equipment

Misconfigured network equipment is another exploitable flaw. Weak passwords, no security policy, and unsecured user accounts can all be part of misconfigured network equipment policies.

Hardware and the protocols that run on it can also create security holes in your network. If you don't have a policy that describes the hardware and the protocols that run on each piece of equipment, hackers could be breaking in without your being aware that you've been attacked until it's too late.

Here's a huge problem: If you use SNMP default settings, tons of information about your network can be deciphered simply and quickly. So, make sure you either disable SNMP or change the default SNMP community strings. These strings are basically passwords for gathering SNMP data.

Policy Weaknesses

You know by now that your corporate network security policy describes how and where security will be implemented within your network. And you understand that your policy should include information about how those configuration policies will be or have been initiated—right?

Let's take a moment to clarify solid security policy by identifying the characteristics that contaminate bad policies.

Absence of a Written Security Policy

If a network administrator (or anyone else around) doesn't understand what's expected of them from the start, they'll make things up as they go along. This is a very bad idea, and it's a good way to create the kind of chaos that will leave your network wide open to bad guys. Start your written security policy by first describing users, passwords, and Internet access. Then describe your network's hardware configuration, including all devices—PCs, servers, routers, and switches—and the security that's required to protect them.

Organization Politics

You thought I was kidding? No way. Office politics absolutely play a leading role in each and every part of the corporate security policy. Understanding the power plays that occur continuously within the annals of upper management (they *are* happening—just pay attention for about five minutes to get the dynamics right) is very important. What does each member of the upper management team envision and expect for the corporation's security? Does one manager have one goal and another manager have a different goal? The answer is always yes. You'll need to find a common ground if you want to get anything done.

Lack of Business Continuity

Here's another hard-to-believe fact: Just about every corporate network is pretty much slapped together with the thought of "doing it right later." And now you're stuck with the mess. Unless you find yourself in the enviable position of being able to move into a new building and design the network from the ground up, you'll be hard-pressed to create a single streamlined corporate security policy that you can implement evenly throughout the organization. Even then, layoffs and constant turnover in the IT department cause security nightmares—in such cases, all passwords for the equipment, servers, and so on must be changed. Sometimes corporate restructuring makes this process nasty and overwhelming, so administrators perform tasks and configure settings hastily just to keep up. Improper and/or incomplete change control on the network can expose ugly policy weaknesses.

> **Note:** If your technical support staff is continually changing, be sure you understand that this can create a security weakness in your policies.

Lax Security Administration

Creating a fabulous corporate security policy, including monitoring and auditing your network's security, is hard work. It can be upsetting when no one cares about your efforts. "Why implement this? They'll just tell me to change it next week!" That's probably true, but you need to try to provide a solid, well-defined security policy that is also well monitored. Think of this as a policy within the policy, because if no one is monitoring or auditing company resources, those resources can and certainly will be wasted. This has potentially catastrophic implications, because that type of lax security administration could easily end up exposing the corporation to legal action.

Installation and Changes That Do Not Follow the Stated Policy

Making sure all software and hardware installations follow the stated installation policy is part of monitoring that policy. And monitoring these installations is integral to the policy's integrity. I know this is difficult and tedious, and it seems as though I'm telling you that you don't get to have a life, but it's very important—really. If you have no installation or configuration policy to adhere to, then unauthorized changes to the network's topology or unapproved application installations can quickly create holes in your network's security.

No Disaster Recovery Plan

Disasters? Those only happen somewhere else, right? But they might happen, and they can even happen to you. So for your network's sake, earthquakes, fires, vandalism, hardware failure, vicious cord-eating rats, and even—God forbid—Internet access failure should all be things that you have a strategy for dealing with in your disaster recovery plan. Your gleaming, brilliant disaster recovery plan should describe your answer to every one of these woes. If you don't do this in times of peace before you experience a meltdown, you'll experience chaos, panic, and total confusion when something really does go down. And certain types of people tend to take advantage of situations like that, don't they? 'Nuf said.

Types of Network Attacks

Okay, you know your enemy and your weaknesses. But what exactly is that enemy up to, and what are they going to do to take advantage of your vulnerabilities? It's extremely important for you to understand this, so you can be prepared for what an attacker may throw at you. Most network attacks fall into these three categories:

Reconnaissance attacks *Reconnaissance attacks* are unauthorized familiarization sessions that a hacker uses to find out what can be attacked on your network. An attacker on reconnaissance is out for discovery—mapping the network and its resources, systems, and vulnerabilities. This is often just a preliminary task. The information gathered is frequently used to attack the network later.

Access attacks   *Access attacks* are waged against networks or systems to retrieve data, gain access, or escalate access privileges. This can be as easy as finding network shares with no passwords. Such attacks aren't always serious—many access attacks are performed out of curiosity or for the intellectual challenge. But beware: Some access attacks are done to nick stuff, whereas other hackers perform access attacks because they want to play with your toys or use you to camouflage their identity in order to make their dirty work look as though it came from your network.

Denial-of-service (DoS) attacks   *Denial-of-service (DoS) attacks* are always nasty. Their sole purpose is to disable or corrupt network services. A DoS attack usually either crashes a system or slows it down to the point that it's rendered useless. DoS attacks are usually aimed at web servers and are surprisingly easy to perform. (The next section discusses DoS attacks in more detail.)

There are many ways—most of them fairly common—to gather information about a network and to compromise corporate information, and even to cause the destruction of a corporate web server and services. In particular, the three network attacks we just discussed can cause the most trouble in your system.

TCP/IP teams up with your operating system to provide many weak, exploitable spots (if not outright invitations) in a corporation's network. TCP/IP and operating system weaknesses are probably the two greatest technology-oriented weaknesses facing corporations today.

Here is a list of the most common attacks that your network may experience:

- Eavesdropping
- DoS attacks
- Unauthorized access
- WareZ
- Masquerade attack (IP spoofing)
- Session hijacking or replaying
- Rerouting
- Repudiation
- Smurfing
- Password attacks
- Man-in-the-middle attacks
- Application-layer attacks
- Trojan horse programs, viruses, and worms
- HTML attacks

When protecting your information from these attacks, it's your job to prevent theft, destruction, corruption, and the introduction of information that can cause irreparable damage to sensitive and confidential data on your network.

Eavesdropping

Eavesdropping, also known in the industry as *network snooping* or *packet sniffing*, is the act of a hacker listening in to your system. A cool product called (surprise!) a *packet sniffer* enables its user to read packets of information sent across a network. Because a network's packets aren't encrypted by default, they can be processed and understood by the sniffer. You can imagine how helpful this capability is to the network administrator trying to optimize or troubleshoot a network. But it's not exactly a stretch to visualize an evil hacker—packet sniffer in hand—using it to break into a network to gather sensitive corporate information.

And gather they can. Did you know that some applications send all information across the network in clear text? This is especially convenient for the hacker who's striving to snag usernames and passwords and use them to gain access to corporate resources. All bad guys need to do is jack the right account information, and they've got the run of your network. Worse, if a hacker manages to gain admin or root access, they can create a new user ID to use at any time as a back door into your network and its resources. Then your network belongs to the hacker—kiss it goodbye.

Even more insidious, eavesdropping is also used for information theft. Imagine the intruder hacking into a financial institution and sneaking credit card numbers, account information, and other personal data from one of the institution's network computers or from the data crossing its network. The hacker now has everything they need for serious identity theft.

Is there anything you can do about this threat? Yes. Again, it comes down to a nice, tight network security policy. To counteract eavesdropping, you need to create a policy forbidding the use of protocols with known susceptibilities to eavesdropping, and you should make sure all important, sensitive network traffic is encrypted.

Real World Scenario

Simple Eavesdropping

Here is an example of simple eavesdropping that I encountered when I was checking my e-mail. This shows how easy it can be to find usernames and passwords.

Notice in this example that the EtherPeek network analyzer I'm using shows that the first packet has the username in clear text:

```
TCP - Transport Control Protocol
    Source Port:         3207
    Destination Port:    110  pop3
    Sequence Number:     1904801173
    Ack Number:          1883396251
    Offset:              5 (20 bytes)
    Reserved:            %000000
    Flags:               %011000
                         0. .... (No Urgent pointer)
```

```
                          .1 .... Ack
                          .. 1... Push
                          .. .0.. (No Reset)
                          .. ..0. (No SYN)
                          .. ...0 (No FIN)
    Window:               64166
    Checksum:             0x078F
    Urgent Pointer:       0
    No TCP Options
  POP - Post Office Protocol
    Line 1:               USER tlammle1<CR><LF>
  FCS - Frame Check Sequence
    FCS (Calculated):     0x0CFCA80E
```

The next packet has the password. Everything seen in this packet (an e-mail address and a username/password) can be used to break into the system:

```
  TCP - Transport Control Protocol
    Source Port:          3207
    Destination Port:     110  pop3
    Sequence Number:      1904801188
    Ack Number:           1883396256
    Offset:               5 (20 bytes)
    Reserved:             %000000
    Flags:                %011000
                          0. .... (No Urgent pointer)
                          .1 .... Ack
                          .. 1... Push
                          .. .0.. (No Reset)
                          .. ..0. (No SYN)
                          .. ...0 (No FIN)
    Window:               64161
    Checksum:             0x078F
    Urgent Pointer:       0
    No TCP Options
  POP - Post Office Protocol
    Line 1:               PASS secretpass<CR><LF>
```

The username is tlammle1, and the password is secretpass—all nice and clear for everyone's viewing pleasure.

Denial-of-Service Attacks

Denial-of-service (DoS) attacks are by far the most debilitating of attacks. Even if there was only one type of DoS attack, these attacks would still be devastating; but they come in a variety of hideous flavors. DoS attacks can bring a corporation to its knees by crippling its ability to conduct business. A common type of DoS attack effectively renders a corporate website useless by making it impossible for legitimate users to gain access to a web server or other available Internet service provided by the victimized corporation.

It sounds complicated, but DoS attacks are alarmingly simple in design. Basically, the idea is to keep open all the available connections supported by the main server, which, in return, locks out any valid attempts to access that server or its services. Legitimate users (customers and employees) are thereby left out in the cold—they can't access the site because all of the targeted site's services and bandwidth are used up. Think about the kind of impact this type of attack could have: It could quickly turn a financially stable company into one that's in trouble.

DoS attacks are most often implemented using common Internet protocols such as TCP and ICMP—TCP/IP weaknesses for which, at present, Cisco has some promising and effective solutions. But, if the truth be told, there isn't anything right now that you could call bulletproof to protect your network from DoS attacks.

Hackers execute TCP attacks by opening more sessions than the victimized server can handle. It's a simple technique, but it's also very effective because it makes that server totally inaccessible to anyone else.

ICMP attacks are known as *The Ping of Death*. Attackers execute them using one of two techniques. The first technique is to send millions of pings to a corporation's server, keeping it occupied with the pings instead of what it's supposed to be doing. The second technique is deployed by modifying the IP portion of a header, which makes the server believe the packet contains more data than it really does. This can ultimately make the server crash if enough of these modified packets are sent.

Here are some other kinds of DoS attacks. Remember these when you're studying for the SECUR exam:

Chargen   In a character generation (Chargen) attack, massive amounts of User Datagram Protocol (UDP) packets are sent to a device, resulting in tremendous congestion on the network.

SYN flood   A SYN flood randomly opens many TCP ports, tying up the network equipment with bogus requests and thereby denying sessions to real users.

Packet fragmentation and reassembly   A packet fragmentation and reassembly attack exploits the buffer overrun bug in hosts or internetwork equipment.

WinNuke   A WinNuke attack uses the infamous port 139 on Windows devices to bring systems resources to their knees.

Accidental   Accidental DoS attacks can happen when legitimate users use misconfigured network devices.

E-mail bombs Many free programs exist that allow users to send bulk e-mail to individuals, groups, lists, or domains, taking up all their e-mail service bandwidth.

Land.c A land.c attack uses the TCP SYN packet that specifies the target host's address as both the source and destination. Land.c also uses the same port on the target host as both the source and destination, which can cause the target host to crash.

The Cisco IOS provides some firewall features that help stop DoS attacks; but at present, you can't stop them completely without cutting off legitimate users. Those firewall features include the following:

Context-Based Access Control (CBAC) CBAC provides advanced traffic-filtering functionality and can be used as an integral part of your network's firewall.

Java blocking Cisco's Java-blocking capability helps stop hostile Java applet attacks.

DoS detection and monitoring If DoS detection and monitoring is used as a strong firewall feature, you'll prevent both attackers and legitimate users from gaining access to the network. You have to weigh the pros and cons of installing a DoS-monitoring system and understand what kind of protection you need versus the capabilities and ease of use that your users can live with.

Audit trails Audit trails work well to keep track of who is attacking you, which can be cool because you can send the logs to the FBI. (In case you don't remember or aren't aware of it, attacking a website is against the law!)

Real-time alerts log Keeping a log of attacks in real time is helpful in case of DoS attacks or other preconfigured conditions.

> The Cisco TCP Intercept feature implements software to protect TCP servers from TCP SYN-flooding attacks, which is a type of DoS attack.

Unauthorized Access

I'm sure that by now you have a clear understanding of why a network intruder would want to gain access to the root in a Unix box or to the administrator function of a Windows host. By doing so, an unauthorized guest can get to the /etc/password file on the Unix host to access important passwords, or add another user on an NT host with administrative privileges and be free to move about within the network at will. Sometimes hackers do this because their goal is to steal software and distribute it if possible (more on that in a bit). Other times, hackers gain access into a network so they can place unauthorized files or resources on another system for ready access by other intruders.

The Cisco IOS offers you some protection with features such as Lock-and-Key; a Terminal Access Controller Access Control System (TACACS+) server; a remote authentication server; and Challenge Handshake Authentication Protocol (CHAP), an authentication protocol. These features provide additional security against unauthorized access attempts.

In addition to a TACACS+ server and CHAP, you can provide a mechanism that authenticates a user beyond an IP network address. It supports features such as password token cards and creates other challenges to gaining access to network resources. This mechanism also requires remote reauthorization after a period of inactivity—another safeguard.

WareZ

The term *WareZ* refers to unauthorized distribution of software. It's not an actual attack on a corporate network or website; its motivation is to sell someone else's software or to distribute the unlicensed versions of software for free on the Internet. This is sometimes initiated by a company's present or former employees, or it can be done by anyone on the Internet with a cracked version of the software. As you can imagine, WareZ is a huge problem for software companies.

There are many ways to provide free software on the Internet, and many servers in the Far East blatantly provide downloads of free software because they know there is nothing anyone can do about it. The only thing that can protect you from WareZ is to provide some type of licensing on your software that stops illegal use.

Masquerade Attack (IP Spoofing)

Masquerading or *IP spoofing* is fairly easy to stop once you understand how it works. An IP spoofing attack happens when someone outside your network pretends to be a trusted computer user by using an IP address that's within the range of your network's IP addresses. The attacker's plan is to steal an IP address from a trusted source for use in gaining access to network resources. (A *trusted computer* is either one that you have administrative control over or one that you've made a decision to trust on your network.)

You can head off this attack by placing an *access control list (ACL)* on the corporate router's interface to the Internet and then denying access to your internal network IP addresses from that interface. This works effectively and easily stops IP spoofing, but only if the attacker is truly coming in from outside the network.

In order to spoof a network ID, a hacker needs to change the routing tables in your router in order to receive any packets. Once they do that, the odds are good that they'll gain access to user accounts and passwords. If your hacker understands messaging protocols, they may add a twist and send e-mail messages from an employee's company e-mail account to other users in the company; that way, it looks as if that user sent the messages. Many hackers get a kick out of embarrassing corporate users, and IP spoofing helps them achieve that goal.

Session Hijacking or Replaying

When two hosts communicate, they typically use the TCP protocol at the Transport layer to set up a reliable session. This session can be *hijacked* by making the hosts believe that they're sending packets to a valid host, when in fact they're delivering their packets to a hijacker.

You don't see this type of attack as much anymore because it's no longer necessary: A network sniffer can gather much more information. But it still happens now and then, so you should be aware of it. You can protect yourself from *session hijacking* or *session replaying* by using a strongly authenticated, encrypted management protocol.

Rerouting Attacks

A *rerouting attack* is launched by a hacker who understands IP routing. The hacker breaks into the corporate router and then changes the routing table to alter the course of IP packets so they'll go to the attacker's unauthorized destination instead. Some types of cookies and Java or ActiveX scripts can also be used to manipulate routing tables on hosts.

To stop a rerouting attack, you should use routing protocols that support route authentication, such as Routing Information Protocol version 2 (RIPv2), Open Shortest Path First (OSPF), Enhanced Internal Gateway Routing Protocol (EIGRP), and Border Gateway Protocol (BGP). You might also think about using static routes.

Repudiation

Repudiation is a denial of a transaction so that no communications can be traced. Doing this can prevent a third party from being able to prove that a communication between two other parties ever took place. *Nonrepudiation* is the opposite—a third party can prove that a communication between two other parties took place. Because you generally want the ability to trace your communications and to prove that they did take place, nonrepudiation is the preferred transaction.

Attackers who want to create a repudiation attack can use Java or ActiveX scripts to do so. They can also use scanning tools that confirm TCP ports for specific services, the network or system architecture, and the operating system. Once information is obtained, the attacker tries to find vulnerabilities associated with those entities.

To stop repudiation, set your browser security setting to high. You can also block any corporate access to public e-mail sites. In addition, add access control and authentication on your network. Nonrepudiation can be used with digital signatures, which are discussed in Chapter 7, "Understanding Cisco IOS IPSec Support."

Smurfing Attacks

The latest trend in the attacker game is the *smurf attack*. This attack sends a large amount of Internet Control Message Protocol (ICMP) echo (ping) traffic to IP broadcast addresses from a supposedly valid host that is traceable. The framed host then gets blamed for the attack.

Smurf attacks send a layer 2 (Data Link layer) broadcast. Most hosts on the attacked IP network respond to each ICMP echo request with an echo reply, multiplying the traffic by the number of hosts responding. This eats up bandwidth and results in a denial of service to valid users because the network traffic is so high.

The smurf attack's cousin is called *fraggle*, and it uses UDP echo packets in the same fashion as the ICMP echo packets. Fraggle is a simple rewrite of smurf to use a layer 4 (Transport layer) broadcast.

To stop a smurf attack, all networks should perform filtering either at the edge of the network where customers connect (the Access layer) or at the edge of the network with connections to the upstream providers. Your goal is to prevent source address–spoofed packets from entering from downstream networks or leaving for upstream ones.

Password Attacks

These days, it's a rare user who isn't aware of password issues; but you can still depend on the user to pick the name of their dog, significant other, or child for their password because those strings are so easy to remember. But you're wise and have defined policies to stop these easy-to-guess passwords, so you have no worries—right?

Well, almost. You've definitely saved yourself a good bit of grief by educating your users. It's just that even if your users pick great passwords, programs that record a username and password can still be used to gather them. When a hacker uses a program that repeatedly attempts to identify a user account and/or password, it's called a *brute-force attack*. If it's successful, the hacker gains access to all the resources the stolen username and password usually provides to the now ripped-off corporate user. It's an especially dark day when the bad guy manages to jack the username and password of an administrator account.

Man-in-the-Middle Attacks

A *man-in-the-middle attack* is just that—a host between you and the network you're connected to. This host is sitting there just waiting to gather all the data you send and receive. For a man-in-the-middle attack to be possible, the attacker must have access to the packets traveling across the networks. This means your middleman could be an internal user, or even someone who works for an Internet service provider (ISP). Man-in-the-middle attacks are usually implemented by using network packet sniffers, routing protocols, or Transport-layer protocols.

Your middleman attacker's goal is any or all of the following:

- Theft of information
- Hijacking of an ongoing session to gain access to your internal network resources
- Traffic analysis to derive information about your network and its users
- Denial of service
- Corruption of transmitted data
- Introduction of new information into network sessions

Application-Layer Attacks

An *Application-layer attack* involves an application with well-known weaknesses that can be easily exploited. PostScript, sendmail, and FTP are a few really good examples of these types of applications. The goal is to gain access to a computer with the permissions of the account running the application, which is usually a privileged, system-level account.

Trojan Horse Programs, Viruses, and Worms

The Trojan horse attack creates a substitute for a common program, duping users into thinking they're in a valid program when they aren't. They're actually in the *Trojan horse*, which gives the attacker the power to monitor login attempts and to capture user account and password information. This attack can even mix it up a notch and allow the horse's rider to modify application behavior so that the attacker receives all your corporate e-mail messages instead of you.

Both worms and viruses spread and infect multiple systems. The difference between the two is that viruses require some form of human intervention to spread, and worms do that on their own. Because viruses, Trojan horses, and worms are conceptually alike, they're all considered to be the same form of attack: software programs created for and aimed at destroying your data. Some variants of these weapons can also deny legitimate users access to resources and consume bandwidth, memory, disk space, and CPU cycles.

So be smart—use an antivirus program on your network, and update it regularly.

HTML Attacks

Another type of attack on the Internet scene exploits several new technologies: the Hypertext Markup Language (HTML) specification, web browser functionality, and HTTP.

HTML attacks can include Java applets and ActiveX controls. Their modus operandi is to pass destructive programs across the network and load them through a user's browser.

Microsoft promotes an Authenticode technology for ActiveX only, but it doesn't do much except to provide a false sense of security to users. This is the case because attackers can use a properly signed and bug-free ActiveX control to create a Trojan horse.

This particular approach is unique because it involves teamwork between the attacker and you. Part one of this attack—the attacker's part—is to modify a program and set it up so that you, the user, initiate the attack when you either start the program or choose a function within it. And these attacks aren't hardware dependent; they're very flexible because of the portability of the programs.

The Corporate Security Policy

Now that you understand the problems associated with equipment, networks, and people, what do you do with all this information? The first step is to begin protecting your corporate network by creating and deploying a security policy that includes each and every way that you and everyone else in the company will guard your oh-so-sensitive data.

RFC 2196 states that a *security policy* is a formal statement of the rules by which people who are given access to an organization's technology and information assets must abide. A corporate security policy is basically a document that summarizes how the company will use and protect its computing and network resources.

When you're creating a security policy, it's important to be ever mindful of that fine balancing act between ease of use and the level of security needed to adequately protect corporate network services. You do a disservice to the client by locking everything down as tightly as possible and/or spending too much money on a network that doesn't need 007-level security.

A security policy defines the following criteria:

- What's important to the enterprise
- What the company is willing to spend (in terms of dollars, personnel, and time) to protect what it has deemed important
- What level of risk it's willing to tolerate

Sounds good, but do you really need to bother with a security policy? Is creating a security policy worth the time, money, and effort required? Absolutely! Here's a short list of why Cisco says doing so is such a good idea. A corporate security policy

- Provides a process to audit existing network security.
- Defines which behavior is and is not allowed.
- Provides a general security framework for implementing network security.
- Often determines which tools and procedures are needed for the organization.
- Communicates consensus among a group of key decision-makers and defines the responsibilities of users and administrators.
- Defines a process for handling network security incidents.
- Enables global security implementation and enforcement. Computer security is now an enterprise-wide issue, and computing sites are expected to conform to the network security policy.
- Creates a basis for legal action if necessary.

Now that you know the basics of creating and implementing a formal security policy in your company, where do you get the rest of the information you need so that you can implement it properly? Good question. This book will seriously strengthen your security grip by showing you how to configure Cisco hardware—a crucial capability you can't do without today.

Summary

A corporate security policy is a declaration of the systems and rules needed to have a secure IT structure. Various weaknesses, holes, and chinks are typically found in the armor of security policies and in the network's security itself. These vulnerabilities fall into three major categories: technology weaknesses, configuration weaknesses, and policy weaknesses.

It's very important to understand the fundamentals and characteristics of all the different weaknesses inherent to a security policy. There are specific protocols for dealing with each special type of weakness, so you should develop solid solutions to secure your system from those vulnerabilities.

Creating a corporate security policy isn't easy, and implementing one is even harder. However, a solid security policy is something your organization can't live without. Hackers have many different types of attacks in their arsenal; eavesdropping and denial-of-service attacks are just two of the most popular types of attacks for people who want to steal from your network and cause problems for your organization.

You can develop and implement strategies to guard against these attacks with a PIX firewall or the Cisco IOS Firewall Feature Set. By combining this understanding with your newfound appreciation of corporate security policies, you'll be empowered to create and maintain a sturdy, intelligent, and cost-effective policy that's tailor-made to meet the needs of your company and its network.

In the next chapter, you'll learn how to configure Authentication, Authorization, and Accounting (AAA) services as part of the Cisco NAS interface.

Exam Essentials

Understand the three typical types of weaknesses in any network implementation. The three typical types of weaknesses found in a network implementation are technology, configuration, and policy weaknesses.

Know which attacks can occur because of TCP/IP's weaknesses. Many attacks can occur because of TCP/IP's inherent weaknesses. The most important attacks to remember are IP spoofing, man-in-the-middle, and session replaying.

Remember the different problems described as configuration weaknesses. Understand the difference between configuration weaknesses and policy weaknesses. Configuration weaknesses include problems such as unsecured user accounts, system accounts with easily guessed passwords, misconfigured Internet services, unsecured default settings in products, and misconfigured network equipment.

Understand what types of issues are considered policy weaknesses. Policy weaknesses involve problems with the corporate security policy such as the absence of a written security policy, organization politics, lack of business continuity, lax security administration, software and hardware that's installed without following the stated installation policy, and the absence of a disaster recovery plan.

Chapter 2

Introduction to AAA Security

THE FOLLOWING SECUR EXAM TOPICS ARE COVERED IN THIS CHAPTER:

- ✓ Securing network access using AAA
- ✓ Authentication methods
- ✓ Configuring local AAA
- ✓ Verifying AAA

In only a few short years, network security has grown from a consideration into a vital and critically important essential for network administrators. In an age of increasing dependence on and use of the Internet, nearly everyone—from individuals and small businesses to huge corporations, institutions, and worldwide organizations—is now a potential victim of hackers and e-crime. Although the defense techniques continue to improve with time, so do the sophistication and weaponry used by the bad guys. Today's tightest security will be laughably transparent three years from now, making it necessary for an administrator to keep current with the industry's quickly evolving security trends.

Solid security hasn't just become a valuable requirement; it's also becoming increasingly complex and multitiered. Cisco continues to develop and extend its features to meet these demands by providing you with sharp tools like the *Network Access Server (NAS)*. The NAS isn't a real physical server; it's a platform created to connect an interface between the packet world and the circuit world.

Authentication, authorization, and accounting (AAA) services are part of the Cisco NAS interface. This technology gives you substantial control over users and what those users are permitted to do inside your networks. And there are more tools in the shed; RADIUS and TACACS+ security servers help you implement a centralized security plan by recording network events to the security server or to a Syslog server via logging.

I know this sounds complicated, and, truthfully, it is. But that's why I'm devoting an entire chapter to explaining these things to you.

I'll start with a brief introduction to Cisco NAS and AAA security. Because it's so important to understand how to properly authenticate users on a network, I'll discuss the various ways (good and bad) to do that. Then I'll cover the ins and outs (pun intended, sorry) of granting permissions and recording activity. Finally, I'll get you into the real goods by describing the more advanced aspects of Cisco NAS and AAA, including how to configure them.

Understanding Network Access Server and Cisco AAA

Before I explain AAA, it's important for you to understand and remember that Cisco's NAS isn't an actual physical server. It's a router with a database; the server is configured and exists within that router's database. This feature—this configuration—gives you the ability to add authentication, authorization, and accounting services to your router so you can provide and apply security where and how you need it. Okay, great. You're asking, "So how do you configure NAS commands on a Cisco router?" I'll explain how to do this and show you how to provide local (AAA) security for an NAS router.

One of the things that's so sweet about AAA architecture is that it enables systematic access security both locally and remotely. AAA technologies work within the remote client system, the NAS, and the security server to secure dial-up access. Here's a definition of each of the As in AAA:

Authentication   *Authentication* requires users to prove that they are who they say they are in one of these three ways:

- Name and password
- Challenge and response
- Token cards

Authorization   *Authorization* takes place only after authentication has validated the user. Authorization provides the needed resources specifically allowed to the user and permits the operations that the user is allowed to perform.

Accounting   AAA's *accounting* and auditing function records what users do on the network and which resources they access. It also keeps track of how much time they spend using network resources for accounting and auditing purposes.

The most common form of router authentication is known as *line authentication*, also known as *character-mode access*. Line authentication uses different passwords to authenticate users, depending on the line the user is connecting through.

You can protect character-mode access to network equipment through a Cisco router as described in Table 2.1.

TABLE 2.1   Local Line Types

Line Type	Description
AUX	Auxiliary EIA/TIA-232 DTE port on Cisco routers and Ethernet switches. Used for modem-supported remote control and asynchronous routing up to 38.4Kbps.
Console	Console EIA/TIA-232 DCE port on Cisco routers and Ethernet switches. Used for asynchronous access to device configuration modes.
TTY	Standard EIA/TIA-232 DTE asynchronous line on an NAS.
VTY	Virtual terminal line and interface terminating incoming character streams that don't have a physical connection to the access server or the router.

In practice, line authentication is limited because all users need to know the same password to authenticate. But the commands to configure line authentication are easy:

```
Todd(config)#line con 0
Todd(config-line)#login
Todd(config-line)#password cisco
Todd(config-line)#line vty 0 4
Todd(config-line)#password lammle
Todd(config-line)#line aux 0
Todd(config-line)#password todd
```

In this example, a user who connects directly to a router console port needs to submit the password `cisco` to be allowed access. Alternatively, a user connecting via a Telnet (`vty`) application needs to provide the password `lammle`. Finally, a user connecting to the auxiliary (`aux`) port (such as over a modem connection) needs to provide the password `todd`.

It's pretty straightforward. The only subtlety you probably noticed is the `login` command under the console configuration. The `login` command instructs the router to check for a line password, and it's enabled by default on Telnet and auxiliary lines. This means that if you don't set a password for the `vty` lines, the default setting won't allow users to telnet into the router.

You might wonder why I'm showing you line authentication when I just told you its use is limited. Line authentication is most effective in environments with few administrators and routers. If one administrator leaves the group, all passwords should be changed on all routers (for obvious security reasons). All current administrators must be aware of the new passwords.

Once the passwords have been set, any administrator attaching to a line will be prompted for a user-mode password. Here's an example that demonstrates an attachment to the console line:

```
Todd con0 is now available

Press RETURN to get started.
User Access Verification

Password:(does not show in output)
Todd>enable
Todd#
```

Authentication Methods

With a terminal server configuration, a router authenticates a user coming in on it by ensuring that the person attempting to connect is valid and is truly permitted access. The most common way the router determines this is by using either a password or a username/password combination. First, the user submits the needed information to the router. Then the router checks to see if that information is correct. If so, the user is authenticated.

But that's only one way for a router to authenticate users from outside its boundaries. You can apply several different authentication methods to your end that involve the operating system, the security server, *Password Authentication Protocol (PAP)*, and *Challenge Handshake Authentication Protocol (CHAP)* authentication. I'll explain all of these techniques shortly; but first, I want to go into more detail about the way authentication is achieved most often—via usernames and passwords.

Username/password methods range from weak to strong in their authentication power; it depends on how vigilant you want to be. A database of usernames and passwords is employed at the simpler and least secure end of the range, whereas more advanced methods utilize one-time passwords. The following list begins with the least secure authentication method and progresses to the most secure method:

No username or password   Obviously, this is the least secure authentication method. It provides ease of connectivity but absolutely no security for network equipment or network resources. An attacker just has to find the server or network address to gain access.

Username/password (static)   This authentication method is set up by a network administrator and remains in place and unchanged until the network administrator changes it. It's better than nothing, but as we discussed in Chapter 1, "Introduction to Network Security," hackers can easily decipher usernames and passwords using snooping devices.

Aging username/password   This authentication method configures passwords that expire after a set time (usually between 30 and 90 days) and must be reset—most often, by the user (the administrator configures the expiration time). This method is tighter than the static username/password method, but it's still susceptible to playback attacks, eavesdropping, theft, and password cracking.

One-time passwords (OTPs)   This is the most secure username/password authentication method. Most OTP systems are based on a secret passphrase that is used to generate a list of passwords. They're good for only one login, so they're useless to anyone who manages to eavesdrop and capture them. A list of accessible passwords is typically generated by S/KEY server software and then distributed to users.

Token cards/soft tokens   This is the most secure authentication method that uses OTP. An administrator passes out a token card and a personal identification number (PIN) to each user. Token cards are typically the size of a credit card and are provided by a vendor to the administrator when they buy a token card server. This type of security usually consists of a remote client computer, an NAS, and a security server running token security software. Token cards and servers generally work as follows:

- An OTP is generated by the user with the token card using a security algorithm.
- The user enters this password into the authentication screen generated on the client.
- The password is sent to the token server via the network and an NAS.
- On the token server, an algorithm is used (the same algorithm that runs on the client) to verify the password and authenticate the user.

The network security policy you create provides you with the guidelines you need to determine the kind of authentication method you choose to implement on your network.

Windows Authentication

Everyone knows that Microsoft graciously includes many captivating bugs and flaws with its operating system, but at least it manages to provide an initial authentication screen. As you probably know, users need to authenticate to log in to Windows. If those users are local, they log in to the device via the Windows logon dialog box. If they're remote, they log in to the Windows remote dialog box using Point-to-Point Protocol (PPP) and TCP/IP over the communication line to the security server. Generally, that security server is responsible for authenticating users, but it doesn't have to be. A user's identity (username and password) can also be validated using an AAA security server.

Security Server Authentication

Cisco AAA access control gives you two options for authentication by a security server: It provides either a local security database or a remote one. Your Cisco NAS runs the local database for a small group of users, and if you have a simple network with one or two NASs, you can opt for local authentication through it. All of the remote security data is on a separate server that runs the AAA security protocol, and that's what provides services for both network equipment and a large group of users.

It's true that local authentication and line security can provide you with an adequate level of security. However, you're better off going there if you have fairly small network, because local authentication and line security require a great deal of administration.

Picture this: a really huge network with, say, 300 routers. Every time a password needs to be changed, the entire roost of routers must be modified *individually* to reflect that change. By the administrator—you! This is exactly why it's so much wiser to use security servers if your network is even somewhat large.

Security servers provide centralized management of usernames and passwords. Here's how they work: When a router wants to authenticate a user, it collects the username and password information from them and submits that information to the security server. The security server then compares the information it's been given to the user database to see if the user should be allowed access to the router. All usernames and passwords are stored centrally on the single security server. With administration consolidated on a single device like this, managing millions of users is like spending a day at the beach.

Cisco routers support three types of security servers: RADIUS, TACACS+, and Kerberos. Let's look at each of them.

RADIUS

Remote Authentication Dial-In User Service (RADIUS) was developed by the Internet Engineering Task Force (IETF) and is basically a security system that works to guard the network against unauthorized access. RADIUS is an open standard implemented by most major vendors, and it's one of the most popular types of security servers.

RADIUS implements a client/server architecture, where the typical client is a router and the typical server is a Windows or Unix device running RADIUS software.

The authentication process has three stages:

1. The user is prompted for a username and password.
2. The username and encrypted password are sent over the network to the RADIUS server.
3. The RADIUS server replies with one of the following:

Response	Meaning
Accept	The user has been successfully authenticated.
Reject	The username and password aren't valid.
Challenge	The RADIUS server requests additional information.
Change Password	The user should select a new password.

TACACS+

Terminal Access Controller Access Control System (TACACS+) is also a security server. It's similar in many ways to RADIUS, except that TACACS+ does all that RADIUS does and more.

TACACS+ was developed by Cisco Systems, so it's specifically designed to interact with Cisco's AAA services. If you're using TACACS+, you have the entire menu of AAA features available to you—and it handles each security aspect separately:

- Authentication includes messaging support in addition to login and password functions.
- Authorization enables explicit control over user capabilities.
- Accounting supplies detailed information about user activities.

Kerberos

Kerberos is an authentication and encryption method that Cisco routers can use to ensure that data can't be "sniffed" off the network. Kerberos was developed at the Massachusetts Institute of Technology (MIT) and is designed to provide you with some hefty security using the Data Encryption Standard (DES) cryptographic algorithm.

Kerberos authenticates users in a manner similar to RADIUS or TACACS+; but after a user is authenticated with Kerberos, they're granted something called an *admission ticket*. This ticket gives the user access to other resources on the network without their having to resubmit their password across the network. These tickets are nontransferable and nonrefundable and have a limited life span—they're good for only one ride. When the ticket expires, the user has to renew it to be able to access resources again.

Cisco routers also support Kerberos for Telnet, rlogin, rsh, and rcp. These Kerberized sessions allow encrypted communication between the end station and the router. This kind of encryption support is especially wonderful for administrators who configure routers, since Telnet data is normally sent in cleartext.

Because it's included with Windows 2000, Kerberos will no doubt continue to gain in popularity. It's currently one of the most secure methods for authenticating a user.

PAP and CHAP Authentication

One of the key benefits of PPP is the ability to add authentication services provided by PAP or CHAP. Although you should be familiar with what PAP is and how it works, you should opt for CHAP because it's the more secure of the two protocols. If your server authenticates based on a Windows NT user database, you have to use PAP or MS-CHAP (a Microsoft proprietary version of the CHAP protocol).

PAP

Password Authentication Protocol (PAP) provides only basic security authentication for connections. It offers a simple way for the remote client to establish its identity using a two-way handshake that happens only after the initial PPP link is established.

That sounds good, but the username and password information is transmitted in cleartext; and as you know by now, that opens up a world of opportunities for a hacker to find ways into your network. The bad news is that a few older systems support only PAP—not the more secure CHAP.

> **WARNING** PAP usernames and passwords are transmitted in cleartext, reducing the security benefits of the protocol. Use CHAP instead whenever possible.

PAP works by first establishing a connection and then checking the username and password information. After this link-establishment phase is complete, a username/password pair is repeatedly sent by the peer system to the authenticator until authentication is acknowledged or the connection is terminated. If the username and password information matches, an OK message is returned, and the session is allowed to proceed. Figure 2.1 illustrates how PAP performs authentication.

To configure PAP, you have to establish both the service and a database of usernames and passwords, as follows:

```
encapsulation ppp
ppp authentication {chap | chap pap | pap chap |
   pap} [if-needed][list-name | default] [callin]
```

FIGURE 2.1 PAP authentication

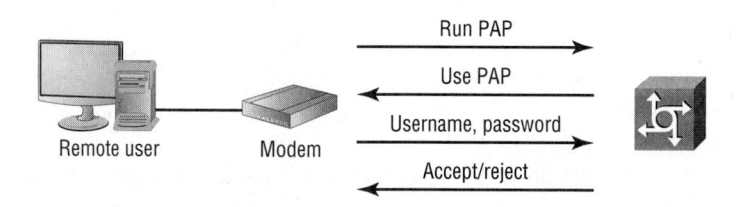

Usernames and passwords are addressed to the router with the `username` *name* `password` *secret* command.

That's pretty much it—there isn't much more to PAP. It works with a minimal amount of configuration mostly because of its lack of security. Be familiar with it, and be aware of it, but don't use this protocol in current designs. PAP is defined in RFC 1334.

CHAP

Challenge Handshake Authentication Protocol (CHAP) is much more secure than PAP, mostly because of the mechanism it uses to transfer the username and password. CHAP periodically verifies the identity of the peer using a three-way handshake that initially occurs upon link establishment and is repeated any time after the link has been established.

CHAP protects against *playback hacking*—resending the packet as part of an attack—by using a hash value that's valid only for that transaction. If a hacker captures the CHAP session and replays the dialogue in an attempt to access the network, the hash method prevents the connection. The password is also hidden from the attacker because it's never sent over the circuit. The hash is valid for a relatively short period of time, and no hacker-enabling unencrypted information is sent over the link. Figure 2.2 illustrates how CHAP performs authentication.

CHAP's configuration commands are a lot like PAP's configuration commands, except that instead of selecting PAP in the `ppp authentication` command, you use the `chap` keyword. The following commands are used to enable PPP (a requirement for CHAP) and to configure the router for CHAP authentication:

```
Encapsulation ppp
ppp authentication {chap | chap pap | pap chap |
    pap} [if-needed][list-name | default] [callin]
```

Notice that you get two additional options here: `chap pap` and `pap chap`. These keywords give you a way to select both protocols to be attempted in exactly that order; `chap pap` tries to authenticate via the CHAP protocol first. Why would you want to do this? You would use this configuration option only during a transitional phase when moving from PAP to CHAP.

Usernames and passwords are added to the router with the `username` *name* `password` *secret* command.

FIGURE 2.2 CHAP authentication

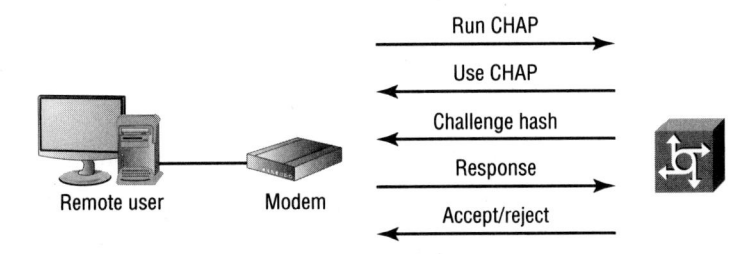

If you use the `debug ppp authentication` command to debug PPP authentication, you'll see output like the following when you connect:

```
1d16h: %LINK-0-UPDOWN: Interface Serial0,
changed state to up
*Oct 17 11:22:15.297: Se0 PPP: Treating connection
as a dedicated line
*Oct 17 11:22:15.441: Se0 PPP: Phase is AUTHENTICATING,
 by this end
*Oct 17 11:22:15.445: Se0 CHAP: O CHALLENGE id 7
len 29 from *NASx
```

You can see that this connection is established on serial interface 0 and that the user is authenticating using CHAP.

In the Windows networking environment, you're given the choice to select password encryption, which works as long as you haven't set PAP to be the only authentication method on your router. Your Windows clients will try to connect with MS-CHAP; but if the box that designates that the password must be encrypted is checked, either PAP or CHAP will be used instead.

MS-CHAP Authentication

Microsoft Challenge Handshake Authentication Protocol (MS-CHAP) is Microsoft's version of CHAP. It enables PPP authentication between a PC using Microsoft Windows and an NAS.

MS-CHAP differs from standard CHAP in these ways:

- MS-CHAP is enabled while the remote client and the NAS negotiate PPP parameters after link establishment.
- The MS-CHAP Response packet is in a format designed for compatibility with Microsoft's Windows networking products.
- MS-CHAP enables the network security server (authenticator) to control retry and password-changing mechanisms. MS-CHAP allows the remote client to change the MS-CHAP password.
- MS-CHAP defines a set of reason-for-failure codes returned to the remote client by the NAS.

PPP Callback

It's always great to have tricks up your sleeve for tightening your security. With PPP, you can beef up security by using a feature called *PPP callback*. PPP callback commands the access server to disconnect the incoming connection and re-establish the connection via outbound dialing. In addition, PPP callback demands that the caller be in a single physical location, so if a username and password happen to get nicked by bad guys, the damage they can do is greatly diminished. You can also use the PPP callback feature to control costs, because all connections appear to be from the remote-access server (read: volume-based discounts). RFC 1570 documents PPP callback.

Configuring Your Corporate Network

This section presents the network diagram of devices you'll be working with and configuring. Take some time to study it carefully. While you're doing that, imagine that you're an expert consultant who's been hired to set up secure administrative and remote access to the NAS routers using the AAA best practices. You'll be configuring Phase 1 of the project in this chapter.

During Phase 1, you'll configure basic AAA services on the NAS using local databases. (During Phase 2, you'll migrate the local AAA database to a Cisco Secure *Access Control System*. But that will happen in Chapter 3, "Configuring Cisco Secure ACS and TACACS+.")

The following graphic illustrates the network you've been hired to secure:

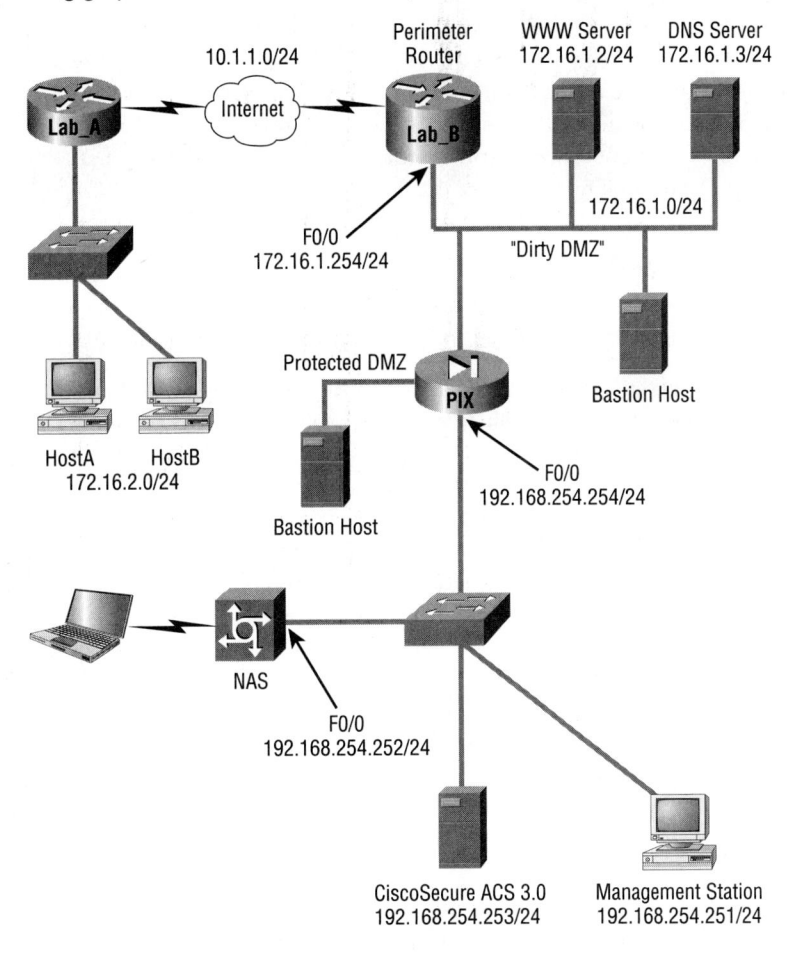

> Let's go over a few of the terms in this diagram.
>
> The *bastion host* is a computer that plays a crucial part in implementing your network security policy (a fact you can guess from its name). The word *bastion* refers to the well-armed defenses stationed around the perimeter of medieval castles. Think of them as the first line of defense—front-line soldiers that you have to ensure are tightly secured because of their exposed position. They are the computers between you and the untrusted or unknown networks that hackers will most often use to get to you and to break into your network. It's common to find bastion hosts multitasking by providing things such as web services and public access systems.
>
> Sometimes people call bastions *sacrificial hosts* because the odds are so good that they'll be attacked. If you're thinking that it might be a good idea to offer the bastion host a little backup, you're on the right track. Because they have only one network interface card (NIC), bastion hosts are vulnerable to IP spoofing attacks. But if you put a bastion host between two routers, you can configure it so that one router filters requests from untrusted networks while the other router filters requests coming in from trusted networks, thus preventing spoofed packets from reaching your bastion host. Your routers verify that any network traffic traveling between them is addressed only to the bastion host. Most of the time, you'll find all-purpose operating systems such as Windows NT, Unix, or VMS running on a bastion host.
>
> Here's another term—the *dirty DMZ*. It's basically a LAN inside your network that uses real Internet IP addresses. Don't confuse a dirty DMZ with a protected DMZ LAN. A DMZ LAN is connected to the inside of the Private Internet Exchange (PIX) and uses private IP addresses instead.
>
> I know it's different, but in the example in the preceding graphic, the dirty DMZ has private IP addresses. That's only because it makes illustrating this configuration easier for the purposes of this book. Just know that your real-world dirty DMZ would have real IP addresses and would be much more vulnerable to attacks than a protected DMZ would be.

The snag here concerns your mobile users. Callback to a hotel room would require repeated configuration and a mechanism to deal with extensions. But some callback solutions allow the remote user to enter the callback number, which removes the physical location restrictions and enhances mobility.

> **NOTE** Cisco's PPP callback feature doesn't permit remote users to dynamically enter the callback number.

Consider the security you get using a callback configuration:

- The remote client (the user) must connect into the remote-access server.
- Using an authentication protocol such as CHAP, the user must authenticate.

- If authentication is successful, the session terminates, and the remote-access server calls the remote client back. If the authentication fails, the connection terminates.
- Upon callback, the client and server can again perform a password verification.

Clearly, these extra steps are worth your effort.

To configure callback, use the `ppp callback accept` command on the interface that receives the inbound call.

> **WARNING** PPP callback won't make repeated retries to establish a return connection. This means that a busy signal or other impediment will require the client side to re-request the session.

Let's move on to look at the corporate network you'll configure with NAS.

Configuring the NAS for AAA

Keeping in mind all you've learned so far, it's time to show you how to configure the NAS to perform AAA using a local database. If you consider that every router is a target, then you must also understand that all interfaces on the NAS are at risk.

Here are the steps you must take to configure the NAS for AAA:

- Secure access to the exec mode with your character-mode passwords.
- Enable AAA locally on the NAS.
- Configure authentication on the NAS.
- Configure authorization on the NAS.
- Configure accounting on the NAS.
- Verify your NAS configuration.
- Troubleshoot AAA on the Cisco NAS.

Securing Access to the Exec Mode

To secure access to the exec modes, set your character-mode passwords first. Keep in mind that there are two access modes to consider when configuring the NAS: *character-mode access* and *packet-mode access*. Table 2.2 lists the different access modes, the port types, and the AAA commands.

TABLE 2.2 NAS Character and Packet Modes

Access Type	Modes	Network Access Server Port	AAA Command Element
Remote management	Character mode (line/exec mode)	TTY, VTY, AUX, and CTY	Login, exec NASI connection, ARAP, and enable
Remote network access	Packet mode (interface mode)	Async, group-async BRI, and serial (PRI)	PPP, network, and ARAP

Earlier in this chapter, you learned how to set your line passwords on the console, VTY, and AUX ports, but you still need to set your enable password. This is done using the following commands:

```
Todd#config t
Enter configuration commands, one per line.  End with CNTL/Z.
Todd(config)#enable secret globalnet
Todd(config)#enable password globalnet
The enable password you have chosen is the same as your enable secret.
This is not recommended.  Re-enter the enable password.
Todd(config)#enable password routersim
Todd(config)#
```

The best command for this task is `enable secret` because it automatically encrypts the password and supercedes the enable password. The two passwords can't be the same.

In addition to adding the character-mode passwords, you can set a username and password for each user by using the `username` command as follows:

```
Todd(config)#username todd password lammle
Todd(config)#line con 0
Todd(config-line)#login local
Todd(config-line)#line aux 0
Todd(config-line)#login local
Todd(config-line)#line vty 0 4
Todd(config-line)#login local
```

The router will now prompt for a username and password when a login attempt is made:

```
Todd con0 is now available
Press RETURN to get started.
```

```
User Access Verification

Username: todd
Password: (not displayed)
Todd>en
Password: (not displayed)
Todd#
```

You can now set up access for each user individually and define different levels of access for each user.

Password Encryption

Because the enable password isn't encrypted by default, it's best to use the enable secret command. By default, those line passwords aren't encrypted either.

Use the following command to encrypt your router passwords:

```
Todd(config)#service password-encryption
Todd(config)#^Z (Ctrl+Z)
Todd#show running-config

Current configuration:
!
hostname Todd
!
enable secret 5 $1$Qrnt$AmoVOSoe/ImPuv6jN9PeL.
enable password 7 06140034584B1B0A0C1A
!
[output cut]
line con 0
 password 7 104D000A0618
 login
 transport input none
line aux 0
 password 7 0958410D1D
 login
line vty 0 4
 password 7 082D4D43041500
 login
```

> Once you've turned on this command, you need to exit from the global configuration mode and enter the show running-config command to see that the passwords are now encrypted.
>
> At this point, turn off the service password-encryption command by using the no service-password encryption command as follows. You do so because the service password-encryption command is still running in the background, and no one needs any extra threads taking up CPU cycles:
>
> ```
> Todd#config t
> Enter configuration commands, one per line.  End with CNTL/Z.
> Todd(config)#no service password-encryption
> Todd(config)#^Z
> Todd#
> ```

Enabling AAA Locally on the NAS

You can also set up AAA on the router, which we'll call an NAS from here on out. After you set the character-mode passwords to secure access to the exec mode, you then need to enable AAA globally on the NAS. It's a simple process:

```
Todd#config t
Enter configuration commands, one per line.  End with CNTL/Z.
Todd(config)#aaa ?
  new-model  Enable NEW access control commands and functions.(Disables OLD
             commands.)
Todd(config)#aaa new-model
Todd(config)#aaa ?
  accounting      Accounting configurations parameters.
  authentication  Authentication configurations parameters.
  authorization   Authorization configurations parameters.
  configuration   Authorization configuration parameters.
  dnis            Associate certain AAA parameters to a specific DNIS number
  nas             NAS specific configuration
  new-model       Enable NEW access control commands and functions.(Disables OLD
                  commands.)
  processes       Configure AAA background processes
  route           Static route downloading
```

And presto—that's it! Well, at least that's it for getting *started* with NAS configuration. Did you notice that once the command aaa new-model was entered, the accounting, authentication, and authorization parameters became available? And did you see that the login local command is no longer available under the line commands? I'll show you the new commands to use shortly.

Although AAA was designed to centralize access control, it still demands configuration on each and every network device. The good news is that once you've configured AAA, you'll rarely find yourself having to alter it. You might need to modify your AAA configuration by changing the encryption key, but other than such minor alterations, all changes—including those for user accounts—are invoked at your security server.

Configuring Authentication on the NAS

Now you're ready for the next step. This section explains how to configure AAA services on the Todd NAS router using a local database.

Authentication is configured differently on Cisco IOS-based and set-based devices, but the general parameters are similar. In broad terms, you must first instruct the device to use an authentication protocol and then provide the IP address for communications.

After you enable the NAS with AAA, you have to configure the authentication method lists and apply them to the lines and interfaces of the NAS. Here are the possible commands to be specified:

```
Todd(config)#aaa authentication ?
    arap        Set authentication lists for arap.
    banner      Message to use when starting login/authentication
    enable      Set authentication list for enable
    fail-message    Message to use for failed    login/authentication
    login       Set authentication lists for logins.
    nasi        Set authentication lists for NASI.
    password-prompt    Text to use when prompting for a password
    ppp         Set authentication lists for ppp.
    username-prompt    Text to use when prompting for a username
```

To configure authentication, first specify the service of PPP, AppleTalk Remote Access Protocol (ARAP), and NetWare Access Server Interface (NASI), or login authentication. For now though, you're interested only in PPP.

First, you need to identify a list name or default. The list name can be any alphanumeric string you choose. Depending on your needs, you can then assign different authentication methods to each named list.

Finally, you need to specify the method used for authentication and designate how the router should handle any response for the various methods you've chosen. Once the lists have been created, you apply them to either the router lines or the interfaces.

The `aaa authentication login` command is used to define the type of authentication protocol you want to use. This command has two options and many variables. Here's one example:

```
Todd(config)#aaa authentication login ?
    WORD      Named authentication list.
    default   The default authentication list.
```

You can create a named list or use the default. The `default` argument gives you quite a few options:

```
Todd(config)#aaa authentication login default ?
  enable      Use enable password for authentication.
  line        Use line password for authentication.
  local       Use local username authentication.
  local-case  Use case-sensitive local username authentication.
  none        NO authentication.
  radius      Use RADIUS authentication.
  tacacs+     Use TACACS+ authentication.

Todd(config)#aaa authentication login default local
```

Look at the preceding command. The `login default local` command tells the router to authenticate using the local username and password, which can then be placed under the console, VTY, and AUX lines with the following commands:

```
Todd(config)#line console 0
Todd(config-line)#login authentication ?
  WORD     Use an authentication list with this name.
  default  Use the default authentication list.

Todd(config-line)#login authentication default
Todd(config-line)#line aux 0
Todd(config-line)#login authentication default
Todd(config-line)#line vty 0 4
Todd(config-line)#login authentication default
Todd(config-line)#
```

The following example illustrates how to use the `login` command with a named authentication list that I'll call `dial-in`. This example puts the authentication list on the `bri0/0` interface of the router:

```
Todd(config)#aaa authentication login ?
  WORD     Named authentication list.
  default  The default authentication list.

Todd(config)#aaa authentication login dial-in ?
  enable      Use enable password for authentication.
  line        Use line password for authentication.
  local       Use local username authentication.
  local-case  Use case-sensitive local username authentication.
```

```
none        NO authentication.
radius      Use RADIUS authentication.
tacacs+     Use TACACS+ authentication.
```

Todd(config)#**aaa authentication login dial-in local**

The `local` keyword at the end of the command tells the router to use the local username and password for authentication.

You still need to set up PPP authentication for the list `dial-in` using the following command:

Todd(config)#**aaa authentication ppp dial-in local**

The authentication method for PPP can be a default or a named list. The preceding example uses a named list.

Now place the authentication method under the interface using the following commands:

Todd(config)#**int bri0/0**
Todd(config-if)#**ppp encapsulation**
Todd(config-if)#**ppp authentication chap dial-in**

Here's another example. Instead of the `login` command, you can use the `enable default` command. Doing this specifies whether a user can access the privileged level of a router. Some options are available with this command, as shown next:

Todd(config)#**aaa authentication enable default ?**
```
enable      Use enable password for authentication.
line        Use line password for authentication.
none        NO authentication.
radius      Use RADIUS authentication.
tacacs+     Use TACACS+ authentication.
```

The `enable` keyword allows the local enable password to be used if network connectivity between the server and router is lost. You could consider this a security risk, but it's not a major one because an attacker would need to either physically access the router or compromise the internal network enough to change routes or block packets. Choosing the `line` command designates the local line passwords for authentication. The `radius` and `tacacs+` commands elect a remote server for authentication. Chapter 3 describes this more completely.

Configuring Authorization on the NAS

It's undoubtedly clear to you by now that authorization is what defines the network services that are available to an individual or group. It also provides an easy means of allowing privileged mode (enable mode) access while restricting the commands that can be executed.

This is a useful option because you might want to restrict most `enable` commands to be used only by a single administrator or manager and at the same time allow operators to perform limited diagnostic functions. You may want your more experienced operators to be granted higher levels of authorization. For example, they could be permitted to shut down an interface. The unrestricted privileged–mode is required in order for the administrator to be able to perform additional functions.

> **WARNING** Use care in restricting administrative rights to the router. This is a helpful option when you're allocating rights to vendors and other parties, but too restrictive a policy can lead to the distribution of the unrestricted account information and create an increased security risk.

Use the following parameters to restrict user access on a network:

```
Todd(config)#aaa authorization ?
  commands         For exec (shell) commands.
  config-commands  For configuration mode commands.
  configuration    For downloading configurations from AAA server
  exec             For starting an exec (shell).
  ipmobile         For Mobile IP services.
  network          For network services. (PPP, SLIP, ARAP)
  reverse-access   For reverse access connections
```

The `commands` command allows authorization for various levels. It's defined by the administrator, who must provide the various commands that each individual user can operate. Levels 1 and 15 are defined by default on all Cisco devices, with level 1 having only viewing access and level 15 having "God-like" access. Here are the available levels:

```
Todd(config)#aaa authorization commands ?
  <0-15>  Enable level

Todd(config)#aaa authorization commands 1 ?
  WORD     Named authorization list.
  default  The default authorization list.
```

The preceding command sets up a level-1 access, and the command string shown next describes how that access will be authorized. I'll name it `begin`:

```
Todd(config)#aaa authorization commands 1 begin ?
  if-authenticated  Succeed if user has authenticated.
  local             Use local database.
  none              No authorization (always succeeds).
  radius            Use RADIUS data for authorization.
  tacacs+           Use TACACS+.

Todd(config)#aaa authorization commands 1 begin local
```

This `begin local` command designates the local username database for authorizing the use of all level 1 commands.

Next, let's set a level-15 access list named `end`. Remember that if you set any access other than level 1 or 15, you have to define each command that can be used at each level:

Todd(config)#**aaa authorization commands 15 end local**

This `end local` command sets the use of the local database to authorize the use of all level-15 commands.

Here's another example of how you can configure AAA authorization on your NAS. Use the following command to run authorization for all network-related service requests. The list name is `admin`:

Todd(config)#**aaa authorization network ?**
  WORD   Named authorization list.
  default The default authorization list.
Todd(config)#**aaa authorization network admin local none**

The preceding command designates the use of the local database to authorize access to all network services such as Serial Line IP (SLIP), PPP, and AppleTalk Remote Access Protocol (ARAP). But if the local server doesn't respond, the user will be able to use all network services by default.

Remember that authorization is the AAA process responsible for granting permission to access particular components in the network. You have to define these permissions based on corporate policy and user privileges.

The commands associated with authorization include parameters for the protocols you'll use. You use these commands to specify what happens after the authentication phase of AAA. Table 2.3 lists and describes these commands.

TABLE 2.3 AAA Authorization Commands

Command	Description
aaa authorization commands level 15	Allows all exec commands at the specified level (0–15). In this example, this is level 15, which is regarded as full authorization and is normally associated with enable mode.
aaa authorization config-commands	Uses AAA authorization for configuration-mode commands.
aaa authorization configuration	Allows you to download the configuration from an AAA server.
aaa authorization exec	Authorizes the exec process with AAA.

TABLE 2.3 AAA Authorization Commands *(continued)*

Command	Description
aaa authorization ipmobile	Allows you to configure Mobile IP services.
aaa authorization network	Performs authorization security on all network services, including SLIP, PPP, and ARAP.
aaa authorization reverse-access	Uses AAA authorization for reverse Telnet connections.

Configuring Accounting on the NAS

AAA's accounting function records who did what and for how long. The accounting function relies on the authentication process to provide part of the audit trail. This is why it's a good idea to establish accounts with easily identified usernames—typically a last-name, first-initial configuration.

The configuration of accounting in AAA is fairly simple, but you do have a few choices to consider:

```
Todd(config)#aaa accounting ?
  commands    For exec (shell) commands.
  connection  For outbound connections. (telnet, rlogin)
  exec        For starting an exec (shell).
  nested      When starting PPP from EXEC, generate NETWORK records before
              EXEC-STOP record.
  network     For network services. (PPP, SLIP, ARAP)
  send        Send records to accounting server.
  suppress    Do not generate accounting records for a specific type of user.
  system      For System events.
  update      Enable accounting update records.
```

The preceding output lists the current AAA accounting commands available from global configuration mode. This section will focus on the **network** command for now.

The aaa accounting network command allows you to configure either a named list or the default:

```
Todd(config)#aaa accounting network ?
  WORD     Named Accounting list.
  default  The default accounting list.

Todd(config)#aaa accounting network default ?
  none     No accounting.
```

```
start-stop    Record start and stop without waiting.
stop-only     Record stop when service terminates.
wait-start    Same as start-stop but wait for start-record commit.

Todd(config)#aaa accounting network default start-stop ?
  radius    Use RADIUS for Accounting.
  tacacs+   Use TACACS+.
```

The **default** keyword lets you record the start and stop times of a user's session on the network. But you've got to have a RADIUS or TACACS+ server for that, so you'll learn more about this configuration in Chapter 3.

For now, check out Table 2.4, which lists the more commonly used commands for configuring AAA accounting. The trick for deciding which command to use is to balance your need for obtaining complete accounting records against the overhead incurred by recording those records.

TABLE 2.4   AAA Accounting Commands

Command	Description
aaa accounting commands level	Audits all commands. If specified, only commands at the specified privilege level (0–15) are included.
aaa accounting connection	Audits all outbound connections, including Telnet and rlogin.
aaa accounting exec	Audits the exec process.
aaa accouting nested	Used when PPP authentication is used to record activity before the start-stop times are recorded.
aaa accounting network	Audits network service requests, including SLIP, PPP, and ARAP requests.
aaa accounting send	Documents the start and stop of a session. Audit information is sent in the background, so there is no delay for the user.
aaa accounting suppress	Sends a stop accounting notice at the end of a user process.
aaa accounting system	Audits system-level events. This includes reload, for example. Because a router reload is one of the ultimate DoS attacks, it would be useful to know the user identification that issues the command.
aaa accounting update	Enables TACACS+ or RADIUS accounting.

> **TIP** One area in which AAA accounting transcends security is charge-back. If accurate start and stop times are well recorded, a company could charge users for their time spent on the system to offset the costs of running the system. ISPs have long considered this as an alternative to the flat-rate model currently used in the United States.

Verifying the NAS Configuration

The following output is from the configuration file of the Todd NAS router. It highlights the commands used for the AAA authentication and authorization configuration:

```
Todd#sh run
Building configuration...

Current configuration:
!
version 12.0
service timestamps debug uptime
service timestamps log uptime
no service password-encryption
!
hostname Todd
!
aaa new-model
aaa authentication login default local
aaa authentication login dial-in local
aaa authentication ppp dial-in local
aaa authorization commands 1 begin local
aaa authorization commands 15 end local
aaa authorization network admin local none
enable secret 5 $1$Qrnt$AmoVOSoe/ImPuv6jN9PeL.
enable password 7 06140034584B1B0A0C1A
!
username todd password 0 lammle
ip subnet-zero
!
 isdn switch-type basic-ni
!
[output cut]
```

The preceding output starts the AAA service and establishes authentication services for both the login default and the dial-in processes. The `aaa authorization` commands provide level-1 and level-15 access to network resources. You'll learn about the accounting commands in Chapter 3.

Troubleshooting AAA on the Cisco NAS

Everything's gone well so far, but for the darker days, let's look at some commands that help you with troubleshooting AAA configurations. You can use these three debugging commands to trace AAA packets and monitor their activities:

- debug aaa authentication
- debug aaa authorization
- debug aaa accounting

The following output results from executing the `debug aaa authentication` command. You can use this information to troubleshoot console logins:

```
Todd#debug aaa authentication
Todd#exit
01:41:50: AAA/AUTHEN: free_user (0x81420624) user='todd' ruser='' port='tty0' rem_addr='async/' authen_type=ASCII service=LOGIN priv=1
01:41:51: AAA: parse name=tty0 idb type=-1 tty=-1
01:41:51: AAA: name=tty0 flags=0x11 type=4 shelf=0 slot=0 adapter=0 port=0 channel=0
01:41:51: AAA/AUTHEN: create_user (0x81420624) user='' ruser='' port='tty0' rem_addr='async/' authen_type=ASCII service=LOGIN priv=1
01:41:51: AAA/AUTHEN/START (864264997): port='tty0' list='' action=LOGIN service=LOGIN
01:41:51: AAA/AUTHEN/START (864264997): using "default" list
01:41:51: AAA/AUTHEN/START (864264997): Method=LOCAL
01:41:51: AAA/AUTHEN (864264997): status = GETUSER
User Access Verification
username:todd
Password: (not shown)
Todd>
01:42:12: AAA/AUTHEN/CONT (864264997): continue_login (user='(undef)')
01:42:12: AAA/AUTHEN (864264997): status = GETUSER
01:42:12: AAA/AUTHEN/CONT (864264997): Method=LOCAL
01:42:12: AAA/AUTHEN (864264997): status = GETPASS
01:42:14: AAA/AUTHEN/CONT (864264997): continue_login (user='todd')
01:42:14: AAA/AUTHEN (864264997): status = GETPASS
01:42:14: AAA/AUTHEN/CONT (864264997): Method=LOCAL
01:42:14: AAA/AUTHEN (864264997): status = PASS
```

The preceding output shows the user-mode access on the NAS (priv=1), that the username is todd, and that the method is local authentication. The following output is the enable access, which is shown as priv=15, meaning level-15 access.

```
Todd>enable
Password: (not shown)
01:42:46: AAA/AUTHEN: dup_user (0x8147DFC4) user='todd' ruser='' port='tty0' rem
_addr='async/' authen_type=ASCII service=ENABLE priv=15 source='AAA dup enable'
01:42:46: AAA/AUTHEN/START (3721425915): port='tty0' list='' action=LOGIN service
=ENABLE
01:42:46: AAA/AUTHEN/START (3721425915): console enable - default to enable pass
word (if any)
01:42:46: AAA/AUTHEN/START (3721425915): Method=ENABLE
01:42:46: AAA/AUTHEN (3721425915): status = GETPASS
Todd#
01:42:50: AAA/AUTHEN/CONT (3721425915): continue_login (user='(undef)')
01:42:50: AAA/AUTHEN (3721425915): status = GETPASS
01:42:50: AAA/AUTHEN/CONT (3721425915): Method=ENABLE
01:42:50: AAA/AUTHEN (3721425915): status = PASS
01:42:50: AAA/AUTHEN: free_user (0x8147DFC4) user='' ruser='' port='tty0' rem_
addr='async/' authen_type=ASCII service=ENABLE priv=15
```

Use the no debug aaa authentication form of the command to disable this debug mode, as follows:

```
Todd#no debug aaa authentication
AAA Authentication debugging is off
Todd#
```

The next output shows a successful AAA authorization:

```
Todd# debug aaa authorization
1:21:23: AAA/AUTHOR (0): user='Todd'
1:21:23: AAA/AUTHOR (0): send AV service=shell
1:21:23: AAA/AUTHOR (0): send AV cmd*
1:21:23: AAA/AUTHOR (342885561): Method=Local
1:21:23: AAA/AUTHOR/TAC+ (342885561): user=Todd
1:21:23: AAA/AUTHOR/TAC+ (342885561): send AV service=shell
1:21:23: AAA/AUTHOR/TAC+ (342885561): send AV cmd*
1:21:23: AAA/AUTHOR (342885561): Post authorization status = PASS
```

You can see here that the username is Todd. The second and third lines show that the attribute value (AV) pairs are authorized. The next line shows the method used for authorizing, and the final line gives you the status of the authorization.

The following output shows output from the `debug aaa accounting` command, which displays information on accountable events as they occur. Chapter 3 covers this topic more thoroughly:

```
Todd# debug aaa accounting
1:09:41: AAA/ACCT: EXEC acct start, line 10
1:09:52: AAA/ACCT: Connect start, line 10, glare
1:09:07: AAA/ACCT: Connection acct stop:
task_id=60 service=exec port=10 protocol=telnet address=172.31.3.78 cmd=glare
bytes_in=308 bytes_out=76 paks_in=45 paks_out=54 elapsed_time=14
```

Remember that the protocol used to transfer the accounting information to a server is independent of the information displayed. In addition to the `debug aaa accounting` command, you can use the `debug tacacs` and `debug radius` commands to examine the specific protocol information. Again, Chapter 3 provides more detail on these commands.

If you are configured for AAA accounting, you can use the `show accounting` command to see all the active sessions and to print accounting records. It's also useful to know that if you activate the `debug aaa accounting` command, the `show accounting` command displays additional data on the internal state of the AAA security system.

Summary

As security needs become more complex in your networking environments, Cisco continues to extend its features to meet demands. Cisco's AAA (authentication, authorization, and accounting) services provide control over user access, manage what those users are permitted to do once they're authorized to get into your network, and record the tasks they perform during their sessions. AAA provides great techniques for network authentication, granting permissions (authorization), and keeping records of activity (accounting).

In addition, RADIUS and TACACS+ security servers allow you to implement a centralized security plan.

The configuration of AAA on the Cisco NAS (Network Access Server) using a local database is important for smaller networks. In Chapter 3, you'll learn how to move the local database to a Cisco NAS.

Exam Essentials

Remember which authentication method is the most secure. Token cards/soft tokens are the most secure method of authentication.

Know what the AAA command wait-start radius provides. The `wait-start radius` command means that a requested service can't start until the acknowledgment has been received from the RADIUS server.

Be able to read the output of a debug aaa authentication command. In the `debug aaa authentication` output, you need to find the username and the method, and see if it was successful.

Be able to read the output of a debug ppp authentication command. In the `debug ppp authentication` output, you need to understand what interface the challenge is coming from.

Remember the command to enable AAA globally on the NAS. The `aaa new-model` command is used to start AAA on the NAS.

Chapter 3

Configuring Cisco Secure ACS and TACACS+

THE FOLLOWING SECUR EXAM TOPICS ARE COVERED IN THIS CHAPTER:

- ✓ Cisco Secure ACS for Windows NT or Windows 2000
- ✓ Installing Cisco Secure ACS 3.0 for Windows NT or Windows 2000
- ✓ Configuring Cisco Secure ACS for Windows 2000
- ✓ Administering and troubleshooting Cisco Secure ACS for Windows NT or Windows 2000
- ✓ Cisco Secure ACS 2.3 for Unix (Solaris)
- ✓ Understanding and configuring TACACS+
- ✓ Verifying TACACS+

Now that you've been introduced to the authentication, authorization, and accounting (AAA) interface, and you're familiar with the configuration of a Network Access Server (NAS) for AAA using the local database, you're ready to put these great tools to use.

And that's exactly where we're going in this chapter. I'll guide you through configuring AAA using a TACACS+ or RADIUS-enabled security server as a centralized database. I'll also explain how to use the Access Control Servers (ACSs) that support this centralized security process.

This chapter begins by looking at Cisco's ACS product on the Microsoft Windows NT/2000 platform, zooming in on how efficient the Cisco Secure ACS 3.0 for Windows NT or Windows 2000 technology can be when it's placed between the NAS and one of several existing user databases. Doing this facilitates AAA without requiring yet another user database—one that you'll have to take the time to configure and maintain. It's a very cool strategy! Next, you'll get a quick tour through Cisco Secure ACS 2.3 for Unix (CSU), an enterprise product that runs on the Solaris platform.

This chapter wraps up by discussing the communication between the NAS and ACS. You'll see that Cisco has provided all that's needed for both TACACS+ and RADIUS communications between the NAS and ACS. So roll up your sleeves, and let's get started.

Introduction to the Cisco Secure ACS

As is true with life, change on your network is inevitable. This is a good thing—it keeps you employed! Products that are adaptable can minimize cost while giving you the options you need to meet changing business requirements with speed and agility. So, the built-in capacity for growth and change is something you love to see in a product. Think chameleon. And Cisco Secure (CS) ACS 3.0 for Windows NT (CSNT) or Windows 2000 is that product: It blends in and works well with any network access device. It can be used with dial-up NASs and firewalls, or it can be used to manage access to switches and routers. The NAS can be literally any device capable of using the TACACS+ or RADIUS protocol—a beautiful chameleon indeed.

Let's look at how Cisco Secure ACS 3.0 for Windows NT or Windows 2000 works in a simple example. Suppose that you have a network such as the one introduced in the last chapter, illustrated in the following graphic:

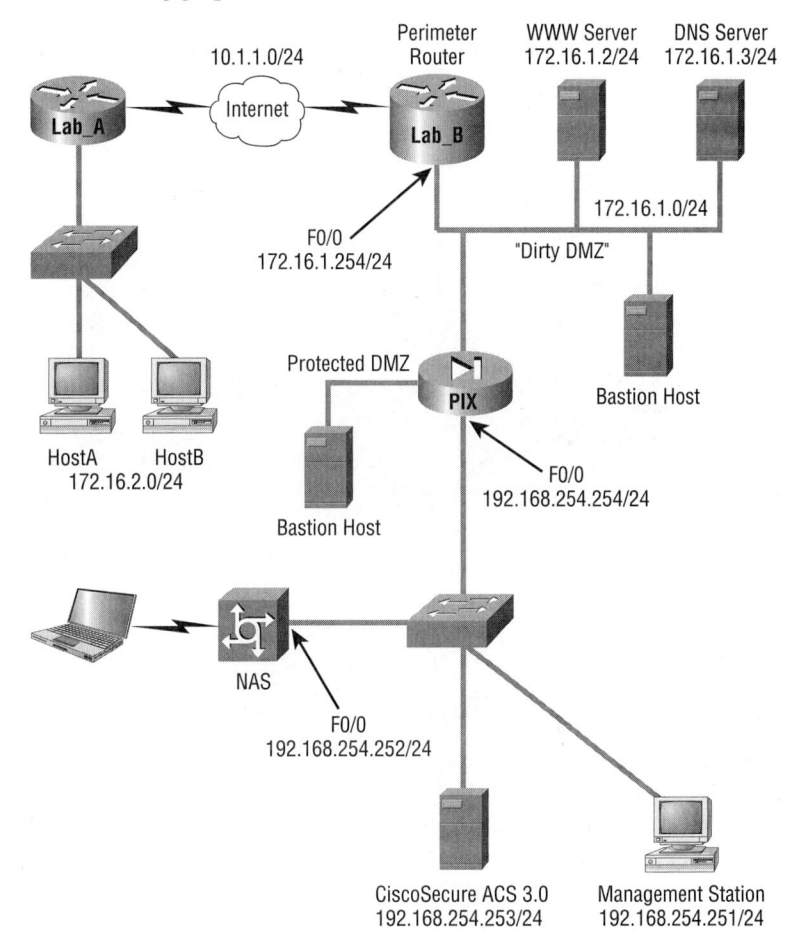

The NAS must be configured so that the user access request is redirected to CS ACS for authentication and authorization rather than checking local user databases for authentication. The NAS uses either the RADIUS or TACACS+ protocol to send the authentication request to CS ACS. CS ACS then verifies the username and password (I'll discuss that process shortly) and replies to the NAS. Once the user has been authenticated, CS ACS sends a set of authorization attributes to the NAS. Finally, if configured, the NAS accounting functions can take effect.

This can be an advantage in situations where you have multiple NASs. Check out the network in Figure 3.1.

In Figure 3.1, multiple NASs are configured using TACACS+ or RADIUS to send their user access requests to a single CS ACS server.

Let's move on to discuss the database used for authentication on the Cisco Secure ACS.

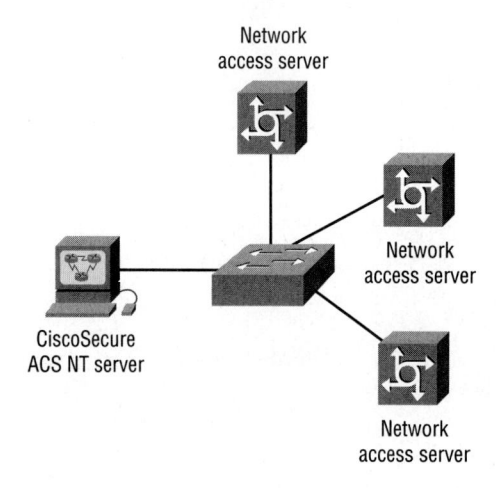

FIGURE 3.1   A network with multiple NAS devices

Using User Databases for Authentication

Cisco Secure ACS 3.0 for Windows NT or Windows 2000 maintains its own database called the *Cisco Secure User Database*. When a user access request arrives at Cisco Secure ACS 3.0 for Windows NT or Windows 2000, it goes to that database first to check for information regarding that user.

If no matching information is found in the Cisco Secure User Database, Cisco Secure ACS 3.0 for Windows NT or Windows 2000 can be configured to check a number of additional user databases—a fine example of that wonderful flexibility—including the following options:

- Windows NT/2000
- Novell Directory Services (NDS)
- Directory Services (DS)
- Token Server
- Microsoft Commercial Internet System Lightweight Directory Access Protocol (MCIS LDAP)
- Open Database Connectivity (ODBC)

The Cisco Secure ACS 3.0 for Windows NT or Windows 2000 can use any of the following *token-card servers* (the most secure method) for authentication:

- ActivCard
- CRYPTOCard
- Vasco
- RSA ACE/Server
- Secure Computing SafeWord
- AXENT Defender

CS ACS for NT or Windows 2000 supports the following authentication protocols:

- ASCII/PAP
- CHAP
- MS-CHAP
- LEAP
- EAP-CHAP
- EAP-TLS
- EAP-MD5
- ARAP

Populating the User Database

Your options don't end with authentication. To provide you with even more flexibility, the Cisco Secure User Database can be populated in a number of ways:

- Manually
- With the Database Replication utility
- With the Database Import utility

Manual population really means "by hand." Unless you're bored, you'll want to avoid all this work by using the replication and import utilities provided with the Cisco ACS.

The Database Replication utility provides fault tolerance and redundancy of your Cisco Secure User Database by allowing several independent CS ACS servers to synchronize their data. This means you can introduce a new CS ACS server that's configured for database replication to the network and can be populated with a replica of the existing Cisco Secure User Database.

If you have an existing ODBC-compliant database, you can also use the included Database Import utility `CSUtil.exe` to import user information from that database. (Refer to Cisco's documentation for formatting and import syntax.)

CS ACS supports data importing from ODBC-compliant databases such as Microsoft Access or Oracle. You use a single table to import user and group information into one or more ACS servers.

> **NOTE** The *CSAccupdate service* processes the ODBC import tables and updates local and remote Cisco Secure ACS installations.

New ACS Features

I've already pointed out some cool capabilities that CS ACS has to offer, but that isn't the end to the goods. It has a rich set of features that allow you to customize and control the AAA process, which is your goal. Being a control freak in issues concerning network security can save your bacon. And, after all, isn't the whole point of security to keep out those who have no good reason to be there in the first place? The following list of CS ACS features is by no means comprehensive, but it includes some of the highlights:

- Password aging
- User-changeable passwords
- Multilevel administration
- Group administration of users
- User and group MaxSessions
- Ability to disable an account on a specific date
- Time-of-day and day-of-week access restrictions
- Ability to disable an account after a certain number of failed attempts, as specified by the administrator
- Ability to see logged-on users and to view detailed information for each user
- Per-user TACACS+ or RADIUS attributes
- Support for Voice over IP (VoIP)
- Differing privilege levels for remote administrators
- Windows NT Performance Monitor support for real-time statistics viewing
- Configurable accounting and auditing information stored in comma-separated values (CSV) format
- Authentication forwarding
- Relational database management system (RDBMS) synchronization

- Database replication
- Scheduled ACS system backup and the ability to restore from the backup file

These and other features give you totally granular control over the AAA process, putting the matter of user access in your hands. In addition, CSNT provides the tools you need to completely monitor the CSNT server and manipulate the user database.

CS ACS 3.0.2 also has the following features and capabilities:

- 802.1x support
- Lightweight and Efficient Application Protocol (LEAP) support
- Extensible Authentication Protocol (EAP) support (EAP-MD5, EAP-TLS)
- Command authorization sets
- Microsoft Challenge Handshake Authentication Protocol (MS-CHAP) version 2 support
- Per-user access control lists
- Shared network access restrictions (NARs)
- Wildcards in NARs
- Multiple devices per AAA client configuration
- Multiple LDAP lookups and LDAP failover
- User-defined RADIUS vendor-specific attributes (VSAs)

Installing Cisco Secure ACS 3.0

The CS ACS installation can be condensed into the following steps:

1. Verify that the NAS and the Windows server can communicate over a LAN using TCP/IP. Ping will work fine for this job.
2. Install the ACS 3.0 ACS on the Windows 2000 server platform. Although this supposedly works with Windows NT 4.0, it's recommended that you use a Windows 2000 server.
3. Disable Internet Access Service (IAS) on the Windows 2000 server (if it's running), or the Cisco RADIUS server will not work.
4. Bring up the web browser interface of the ACS server.
5. Configure the NAS for AAA using TACACS+ and/or RADIUS.
6. Verify the installation and operation of the NAS and ACS server.

Exercise 3.1 assumes that step 1 has been completed and gets right into the installation of the ACS software.

EXERCISE 3.1

Cisco Secure ACS 3.0 Installation

After you bring up and test network connectivity between the Windows server and the NAS server, install the ACS on the Windows server using the following steps:

1. Once you click the Setup file, the ACS program displays the Before You Begin screen:

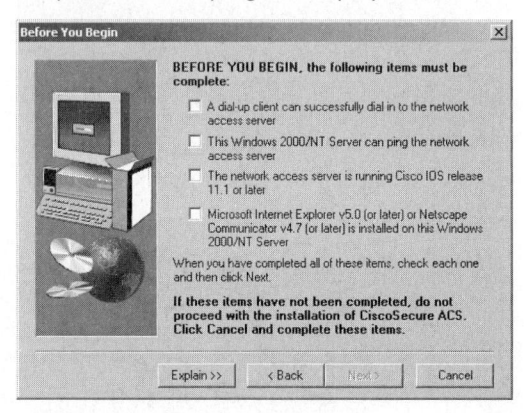

   This screen asks you to verify that you have some basic configuration on the NAS before the ACS is installed. Be sure you don't miss the note about the minimum IOS version on the NAS—especially if you're studying for your SECUR exam.

2. After you've completed the basic configuration needed to install the ACS, click Next. The Authentication Database Configuration screen appears:

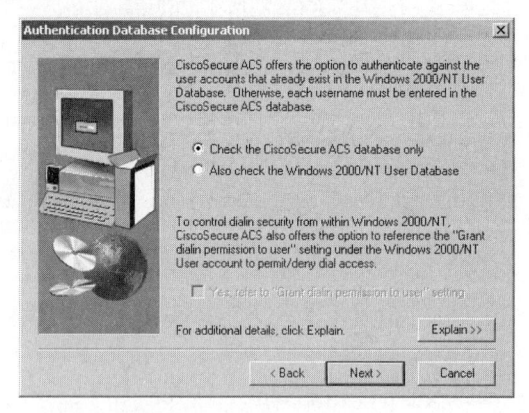

   This is where you choose to use a local database on the ACS server or use the Windows server database.

Installing Cisco Secure ACS 3.0

EXERCISE 3.1 *(continued)*

3. You're prompted to configure the ACS to talk to the NAS on the CiscoSecure ACS Network Access Server Details screen:

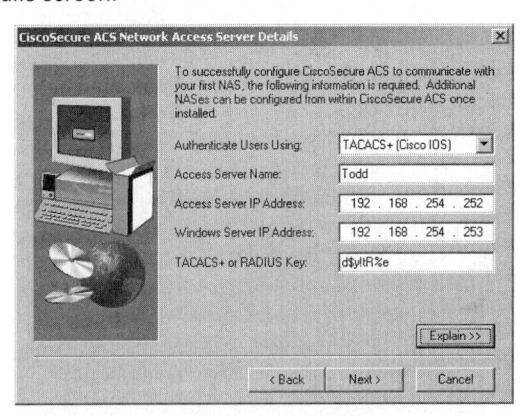

   Look at the lower-right corner of the screen. If you click Explain, an Explanation Of Cisco-Secure ACS Network Access Server Details screen appears:

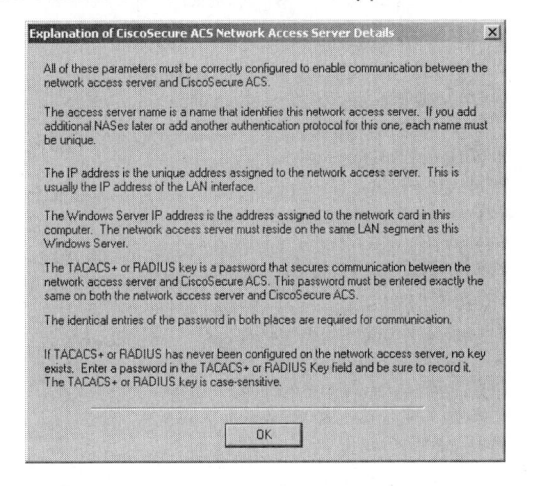

   This screen can be unbelievably helpful. Read this information, and you'll learn what each file in the Details screen requires. On the CiscoSecure ACS Network Access Server Details screen, I entered the name of the NAS and the IP address of the NAS F0/0 interface. For the key, I made up a key that's unique and extremely hard to break.

EXERCISE 3.1 *(continued)*

4. The next screen, Advanced Options, asks you to enter any advanced information to be displayed when using the ACS user interface:

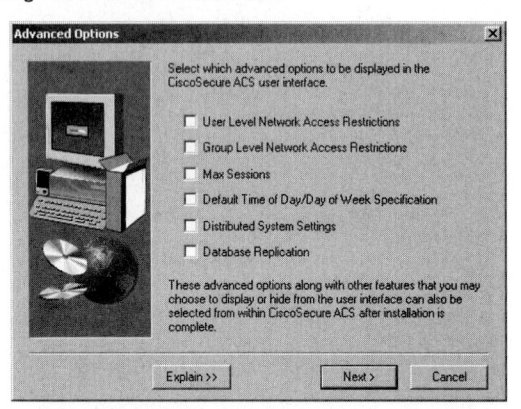

   Advanced Options

   Select which advanced options to be displayed in the CiscoSecure ACS user interface.

   ☐ User Level Network Access Restrictions
   ☐ Group Level Network Access Restrictions
   ☐ Max Sessions
   ☐ Default Time of Day/Day of Week Specification
   ☐ Distributed System Settings
   ☐ Database Replication

   These advanced options along with other features that you may choose to display or hide from the user interface can also be selected from within CiscoSecure ACS after installation is complete.

   [Explain >>] [Next >] [Cancel]

   Again, to find out why you would choose each option, click the Explain button. The Explanation Of Advanced Options Configuration screen appears:

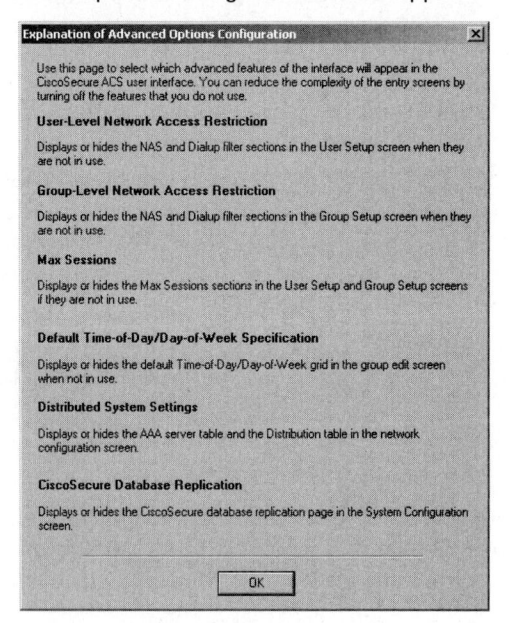

   Explanation of Advanced Options Configuration

   Use this page to select which advanced features of the interface will appear in the CiscoSecure ACS user interface. You can reduce the complexity of the entry screens by turning off the features that you do not use.

   User-Level Network Access Restriction

   Displays or hides the NAS and Dialup filter sections in the User Setup screen when they are not in use.

   Group-Level Network Access Restriction

   Displays or hides the NAS and Dialup filter sections in the Group Setup screen when they are not in use.

   Max Sessions

   Displays or hides the Max Sessions sections in the User Setup and Group Setup screens if they are not in use.

   Default Time-of-Day/Day-of-Week Specification

   Displays or hides the default Time-of-Day/Day-of-Week grid in the group edit screen when not in use.

   Distributed System Settings

   Displays or hides the AAA server table and the Distribution table in the network configuration screen.

   CiscoSecure Database Replication

   Displays or hides the CiscoSecure database replication page in the System Configuration screen.

   [OK]

EXERCISE 3.1 (continued)

5. The next screen, Active Service Monitoring, gives you an opportunity to configure monitoring on the ACS, as shown here:

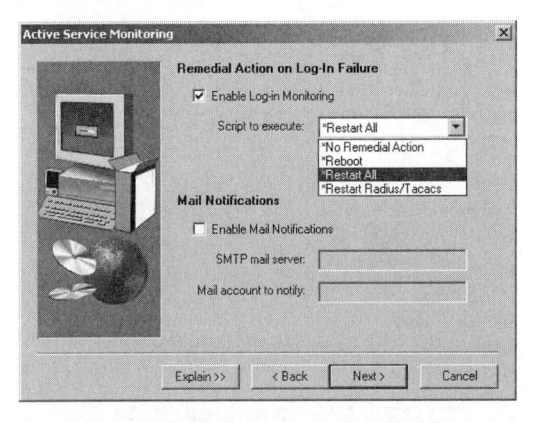

   This screen provides a great way to set up your e-mail notification in case of failure. Clicking Explain provides a description of the options, but you probably won't need to go there because they're self-explanatory.

6. The Network Access Server Configuration screen allows you to configure the ACS so that it configures the NAS server. This is much easier than the local authentication configuration you did in the last chapter:

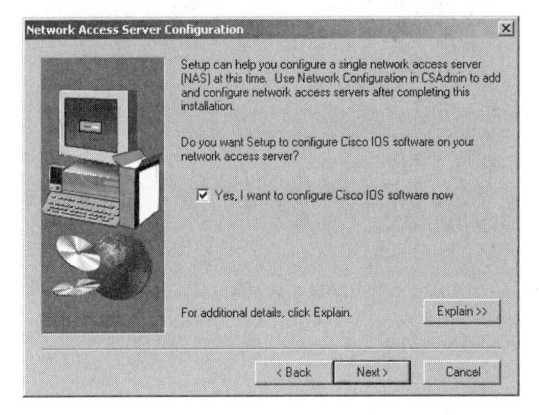

EXERCISE 3.1 *(continued)*

Again, clicking Explain displays additional information:

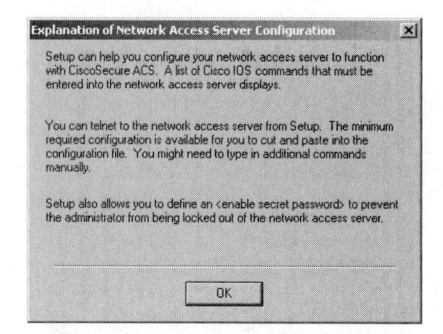

Explanation of Network Access Server Configuration

Setup can help you configure your network access server to function with CiscoSecure ACS. A list of Cisco IOS commands that must be entered into the network access server displays.

You can telnet to the network access server from Setup. The minimum required configuration is available for you to cut and paste into the configuration file. You might need to type in additional commands manually.

Setup also allows you to define an <enable secret password> to prevent the administrator from being locked out of the network access server.

[OK]

7. Next you'll see the Enable Secret Password screen. It asks you for the enable secret password of the NAS and explains what the ACS installation is trying to accomplish:

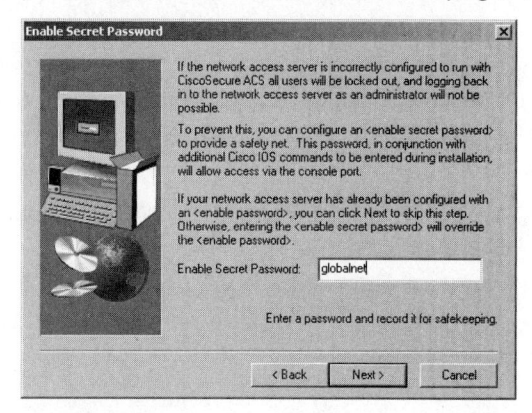

Enable Secret Password

If the network access server is incorrectly configured to run with CiscoSecure ACS all users will be locked out, and logging back in to the network access server as an administrator will not be possible.

To prevent this, you can configure an <enable secret password> to provide a safety net. This password, in conjunction with additional Cisco IOS commands to be entered during installation, will allow access via the console port.

If your network access server has already been configured with an <enable password>, you can click Next to skip this step. Otherwise, entering the <enable secret password> will override the <enable password>.

Enable Secret Password: globalnet

Enter a password and record it for safekeeping.

[< Back] [Next >] [Cancel]

8. The next screen, Access Server Configuration, tells you that the ACS will show you how to configure the NAS, step by step:

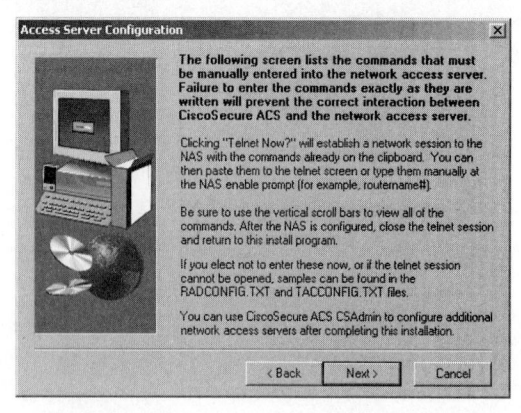

Access Server Configuration

The following screen lists the commands that must be manually entered into the network access server. Failure to enter the commands exactly as they are written will prevent the correct interaction between CiscoSecure ACS and the network access server.

Clicking "Telnet Now?" will establish a network session to the NAS with the commands already on the clipboard. You can then paste them to the telnet screen or type them manually at the NAS enable prompt (for example, routername#).

Be sure to use the vertical scroll bars to view all of the commands. After the NAS is configured, close the telnet session and return to this install program.

If you elect not to enter these now, or if the telnet session cannot be opened, samples can be found in the RADCONFIG.TXT and TACCONFIG.TXT files.

You can use CiscoSecure ACS CSAdmin to configure additional network access servers after completing this installation.

[< Back] [Next >] [Cancel]

EXERCISE 3.1 (continued)

9. Click Next to see the configuration you need to type into the NAS on the NAS Configuration screen:

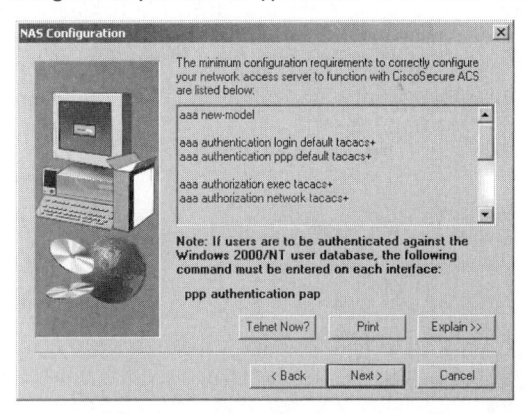

   NAS Configuration

   The minimum configuration requirements to correctly configure your network access server to function with CiscoSecure ACS are listed below:

   ```
   aaa new-model
   aaa authentication login default tacacs+
   aaa authentication ppp default tacacs+
   aaa authorization exec tacacs+
   aaa authorization network tacacs+
   ```

   Note: If users are to be authenticated against the Windows 2000/NT user database, the following command must be entered on each interface:

   ppp authentication pap

10. Keep scrolling down, and you can see the entire configuration you need to configure on the NAS. The last two configuration screens appear as follows:

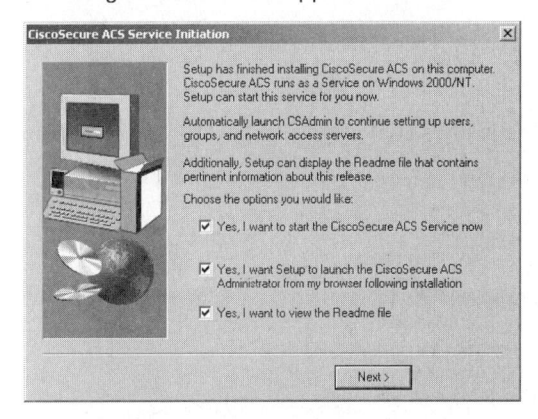

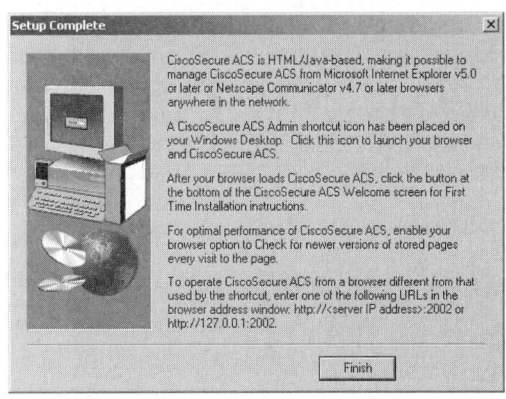

    CiscoSecure ACS Service Initiation

    Setup has finished installing CiscoSecure ACS on this computer. CiscoSecure ACS runs as a Service on Windows 2000/NT. Setup can start this service for you now.

    Automatically launch CSAdmin to continue setting up users, groups, and network access servers.

    Additionally, Setup can display the Readme file that contains pertinent information about this release.

    Choose the options you would like:

    ☑ Yes, I want to start the CiscoSecure ACS Service now

    ☑ Yes, I want Setup to launch the CiscoSecure ACS Administrator from my browser following installation

    ☑ Yes, I want to view the Readme file

    Setup Complete

    CiscoSecure ACS is HTML/Java-based, making it possible to manage CiscoSecure ACS from Microsoft Internet Explorer v5.0 or later or Netscape Communicator v4.7 or later browsers anywhere in the network.

    A CiscoSecure ACS Admin shortcut icon has been placed on your Windows Desktop. Click this icon to launch your browser and CiscoSecure ACS.

    After your browser loads CiscoSecure ACS, click the button at the bottom of the CiscoSecure ACS Welcome screen for First Time Installation instructions.

    For optimal performance of CiscoSecure ACS, enable your browser option to Check for newer versions of stored pages every visit to the page.

    To operate CiscoSecure ACS from a browser different from that used by the shortcut, enter one of the following URLs in the browser address window: http://<server IP address>:2002 or http://127.0.0.1:2002.

It can't get much easier than that. Notice that the Setup Complete screen tells you how to get into the ACS admin screen through a browser, http://127.0.0.1:2002. The 127.0.0.1 address is considered the internal loopback or diagnostic IP address of the local machine. You use it to verify that IP is running properly on a host. In this case, the IP address 127.0.0.1 also tells the browser that you mean "this host." The 2002 is the default port that makes a system call to the CS ACS application.

In a minute, I'll go through the configuration of the NAS, but first let's look at the ACS configuration. (If you want, this is a great time to take a short break and digest what you've just done before moving on.)

Administering Cisco Secure ACS

The CS ACS web browser interface makes the administration of AAA features pretty easy. The installation places an ACS Admin icon on the desktop of the server; when you double-click it, you end up on the ACS Administration page, as illustrated in Figure 3.2.

FIGURE 3.2 ACS administration session

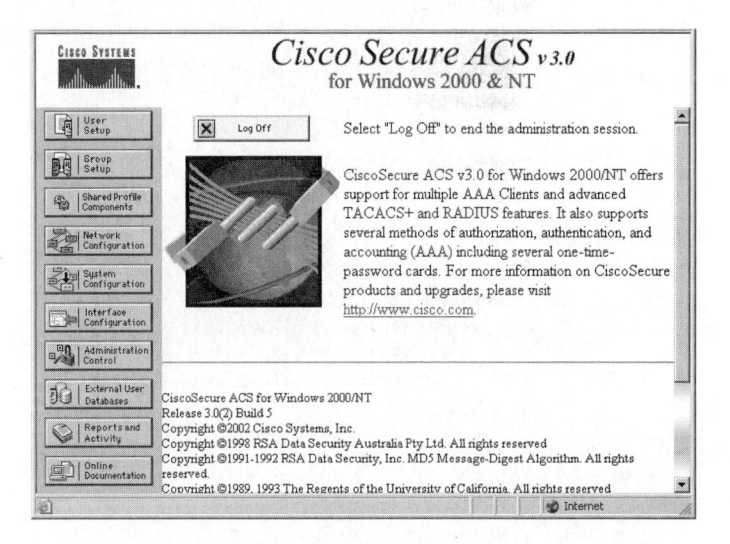

Each button on the navigation bar represents a particular area or function that you can configure. You typically don't need to configure all of the areas; nevertheless, you'll go through them all in Exercise 3.2.

> **NOTE** If you're studying for the exam, you don't have to memorize the fields in this area. Just use this information for documentation purposes.

In this exercise, you'll walk through the ACS administration process step by step in the Windows environment. Then, I'll explain what Unix administration is like.

EXERCISE 3.2

Cisco Secure ACS for Windows Administration

This exercise provides you with step-by-step instructions on how to use the Cisco Secure Administration tool. Follow these steps:

1. Click the User Setup button to begin configuring the Cisco Secure software. This is where you add, edit, or delete user accounts and list users in databases:

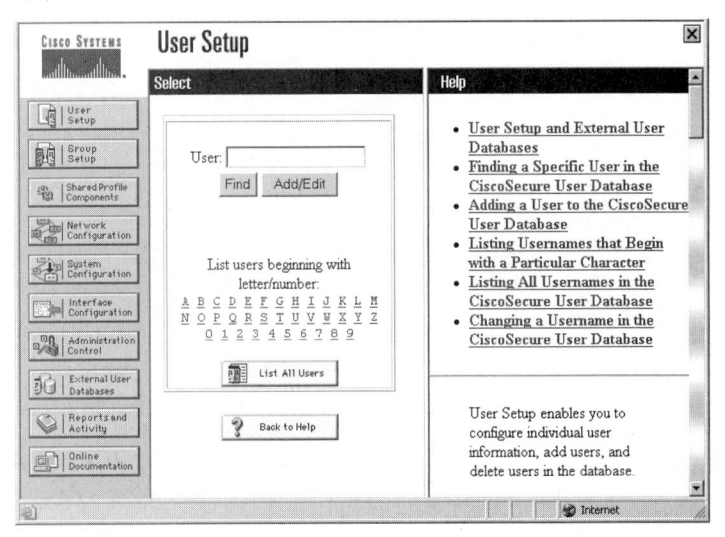

2. When you're done setting up individual users, click the Group Setup button. The Group Setup screen lets you create, edit, and rename groups and list all users in a group:

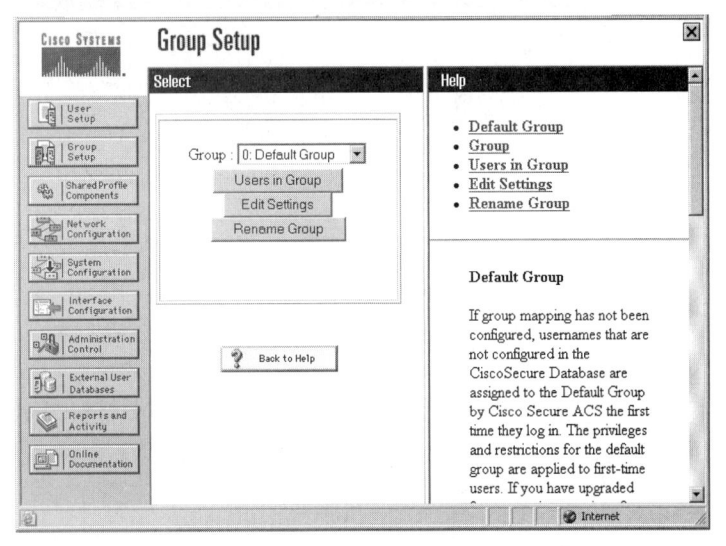

66 Chapter 3 · Configuring Cisco Secure ACS and TACACS+

EXERCISE 3.2 *(continued)*

3. The Shared Profile Components screen allows you to configure command authorization sets, which are configurable sets of authorization rules for device commands:

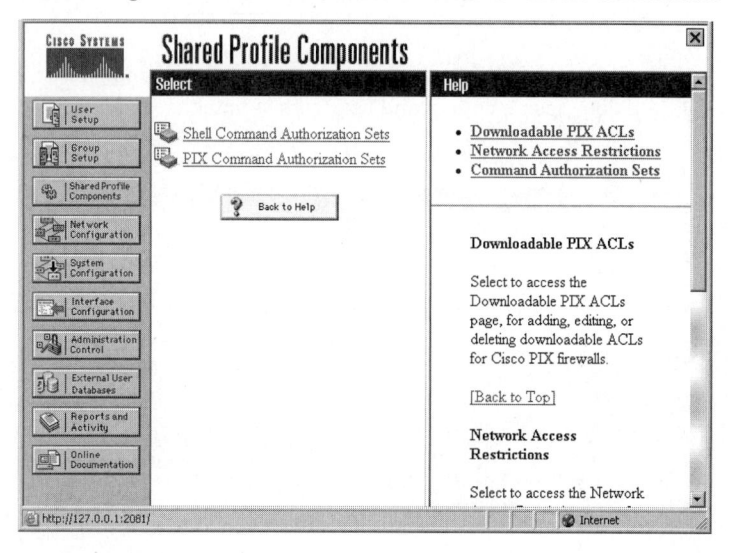

4. The Network Configuration button takes you to a screen where you configure and edit network access server parameters, add and delete network access servers, and configure AAA server distribution parameters:

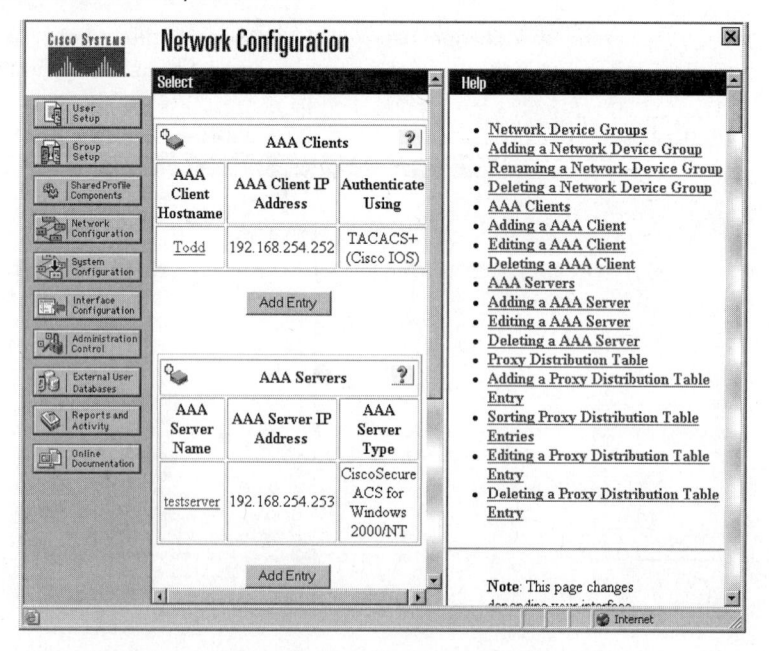

EXERCISE 3.2 *(continued)*

5. In the System Configuration screen, you can start and stop CS ACS services, configure logging, control database replication, and control RDBMS synchronization:

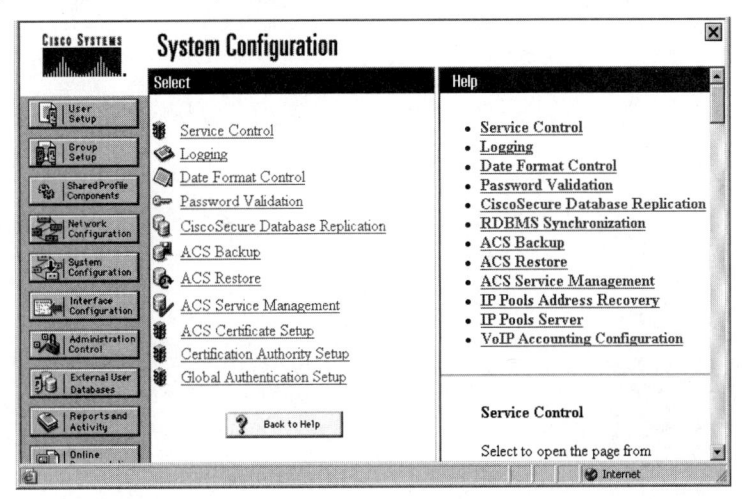

6. The Interface Configuration button takes you to a screen where you can configure user-defined fields that will be recorded in accounting logs, configure TACACS+ and RADIUS options, and control the display of options in the user interface:

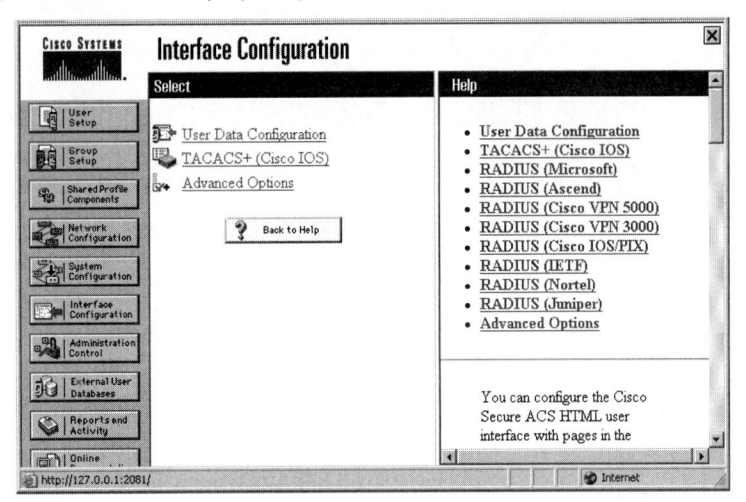

EXERCISE 3.2 *(continued)*

7. The Administration Control screen lets you control the administration of CS ACS from any workstation on the network so you don't have to run all over the building (if you think you need the exercise, don't configure it!):

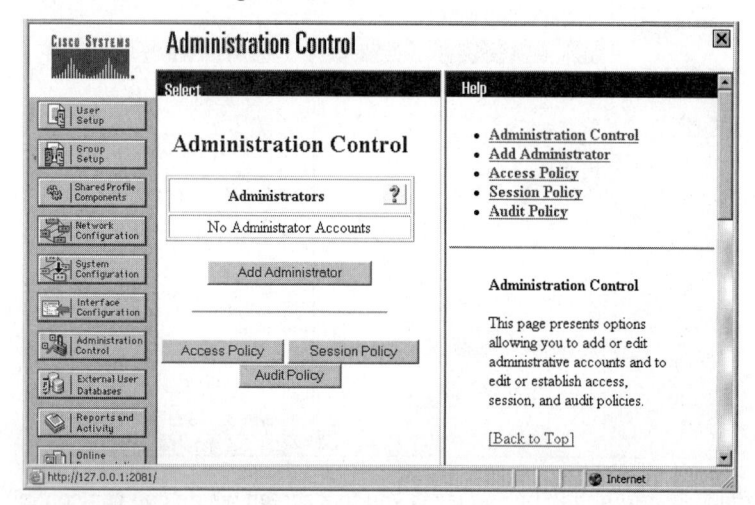

8. The External User Databases button gives you access to two screens where you configure the unknown user policy, configure authorization privileges for unknown users, and configure external database types:

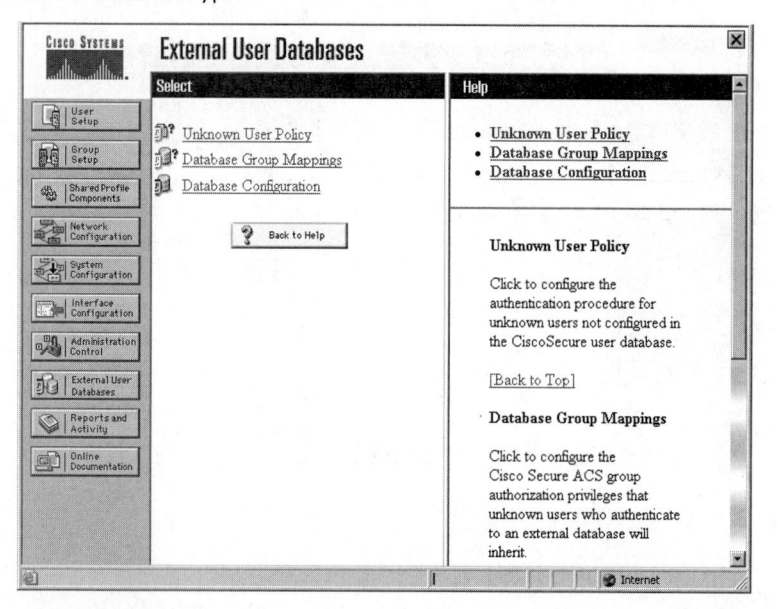

EXERCISE 3.2 *(continued)*

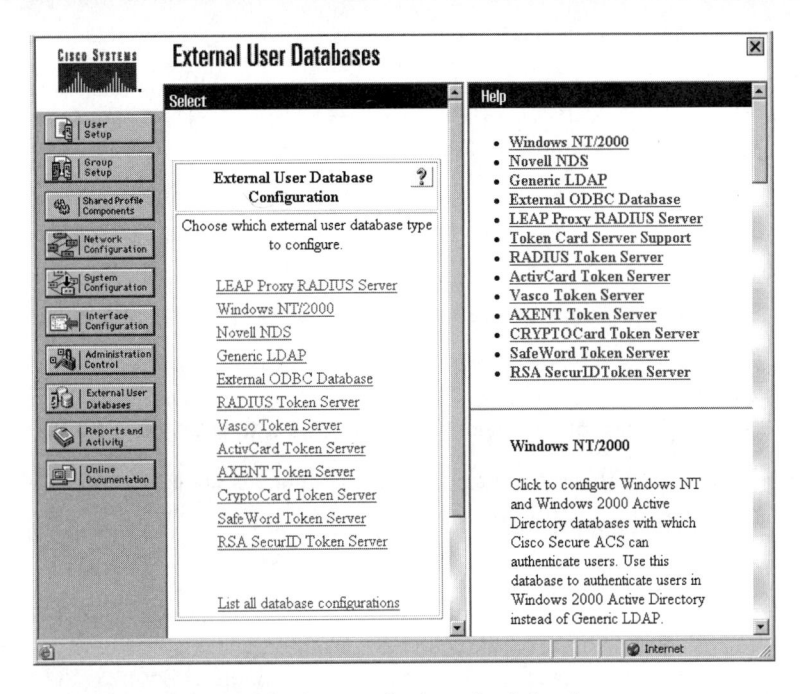

9. Clicking the Reports And Activity button displays the following screen:

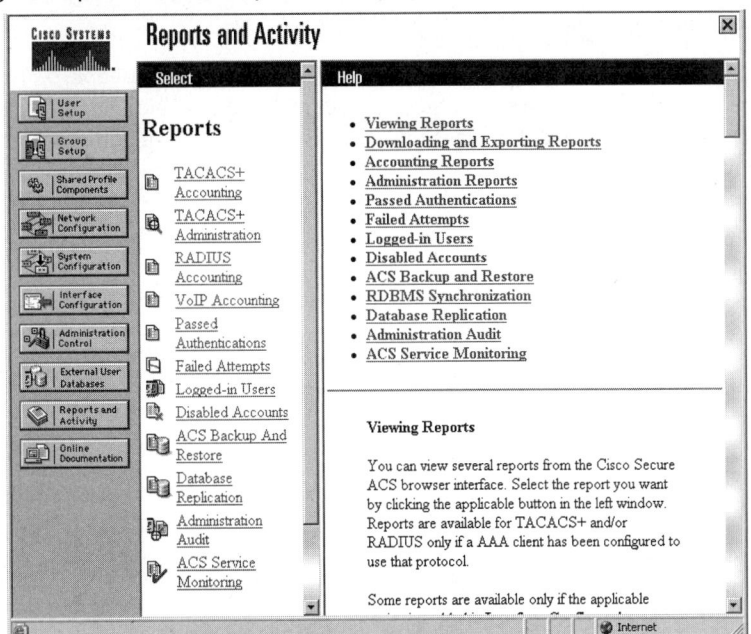

> **EXERCISE 3.2 *(continued)***
>
> On this screen, you can view the following reports:
>
> TACACS+ Accounting: These reports record when sessions stop and start, record network access server messages with usernames, provide caller line identification information, and record the duration of each session.
>
> RADIUS Accounting: These reports record when sessions stop and start, record network access server messages with usernames, provide caller line identification information, and record the duration of each session.
>
> Failed Attempts: This report lists authentication and authorization failures with an indication of the cause.
>
> Logged-in Users: This report lists all users currently receiving services for a single network access server or all network access servers with access to CS ACS.
>
> Disabled Accounts: This report lists all user accounts that are currently disabled.
>
> Admin Accounting reports: These reports list the configuration commands entered on a TACACS+ (Cisco) network access server.
>
> You can import these files into most database and spreadsheet applications. This information is invaluable in helping you profile potentially problematic users by monitoring unusual activity. After you see these reports often enough, you'll spot potential bad guys in a snap. Of course, for that to happen, you or someone on your security team needs to review these reports on a regular basis.
>
> I'll say this again: You can have top-of-the-line products and great people on your team, but if your security policies aren't tight, your security won't be, either. If you've got the goods, make sure policies are in place that guarantee the best use of the technology and personnel you've invested in.
>
> 10. The Online Documentation button provides more detailed information about the configuration, operation, and concepts of CS ACS.

Maybe you're not using Windows. Maybe you've got a Unix server set up. Cisco Secure ACS 2.3 for Unix (CSU) offers the same basic functions as Cisco Secure ACS for Windows, discussed previously in Exercise 3.2:

- CSU accepts user access requests from an NAS using TACACS+ or RADIUS.
- CSU can be used as a centralized database for AAA, working with NASs from a variety of vendors.
- CSU has a web-based administration tool.

CSU offers relational database support for three databases: Sybase, Oracle, and SQL Anywhere (included).

Let's get into TACACS+ and how it can be used to create a more secure network.

TACACS+ Overview

Now that you've met Cisco's ACSs, let's take a second to review how the ACS and the NAS communicate. The NAS can use either TACACS+ or RADIUS to communicate user access requests to the ACS. Each of these two methods of communication has its individual strengths and purposes.

Table 3.1 summarizes the key differences between TACACS+ and RADIUS. I'll go over these in more detail shortly.

As you can see, TACACS+ has many advantages over RADIUS. For this reason, Cisco strongly encourages the use of TACACS+. TACACS+ is a better tool to use when you can, but you may need to use RADIUS, or both TACACS+ and RADIUS in a mixed-vendor network.

Because TACACS+ is a Cisco proprietary authentication scheme, its use in the Cisco AAA process has a number of distinct advantages. My goal here isn't to dissect TACACS+. Instead, I want you to understand its benefits. (RFC 1492 documents Cisco's proprietary TACACS+.)

TACACS+ conforms to the AAA model—it treats authentication, authorization, and accounting as distinct and separate roles (as discussed in Chapter 2, "Introduction to AAA Security"). This means TACACS+ has mechanisms to support each of these services, giving the security administrator much more granular control and latitude in both defining and, more importantly, implementing a security policy.

TABLE 3.1 TACACS+ and RADIUS Comparison

TACACS+	RADIUS
Transport: TCP (connection)	Transport: UDP (no connection)
Bidirectional CHAP	Unidirectional CHAP
Multiprotocol support	No ARA and no NetBEUI
Encrypts the entire packet	Encrypts only passwords
Independent AAA architecture	Authentication and authorization combined
Best choice for router management	Industry standard

TACACS+ uses TCP as a transport protocol. I'm sure you remember that TCP opens a connection and verifies delivery of each segment. TACACS+ then encrypts the *entire contents* of each TCP segment, so anyone listening on the wire won't be able to snag information. TACACS+ supports PAP and CHAP, as well as PPP callback and per-user ACLs—all features covered in Chapter 2.

TACACS+ can be used between the NAS and ACS to control dial-in access and other access into the network. It can also be used between the network devices (routers and switches) and ACS to control authentication and authorization in the management of network devices.

Let's head into configuring TACACS+ on your NAS.

Configuring TACACS+

Think back to Chapter 2 for a second. Remember the discussion about configuring the NAS to use the AAA process to authenticate users to a local database? As you recall, you can configure authentication and authorization for local users with the `username` command. Let's try this out now:

```
Todd(config)#username todd password lammle
Todd(config)#line con 0
Todd(config-line)#login local
Todd(config-line)#line aux 0
Todd(config-line)#login local
Todd(config-line)#line vty 0 4
Todd(config-line)#login local
```

This configuration allows user `todd` to access the configured lines as long as Todd knows their passwords.

In a medium-to-large network, there are significant advantages to using TACACS+ (or other) centralized authentication services instead of local databases.

A common problem for many network administrators is the number of unsynchronized accounts a network user has. How often has a new employee been given 7, 8, or even 10 separate accounts, all with unique passwords, just to access the resources the individual needs? Multiply that by a horde of employees, and you can watch the stress levels build in your organization. Everyone is affected—from frustrated users trying to remember all their passwords on up to senior managers dealing with the boatload of complaints these circumstances create.

But a local database is just that—local to the NAS it resides on. If you have a single NAS, a local database may be fine. But if you have many NASs, do you really want more unsynchronized user databases?

The whole idea behind Cisco Secure ACS 3.0 for Windows NT or Windows 2000 is to allow multiple NASs to use a *single* database for AAA. That way, there is a *single* account database to be administered for each user instead of many.

Just being able to use a single database for AAA is a huge improvement over using local databases on NASs. But Cisco ACS takes it one step further. Let's assume you have an existing network—you probably already have several user databases in existence. If you're running Microsoft

Windows NT/2000 servers anywhere, you have users who have accounts in domains. If you have any Novell NetWare servers that use Novell Directory Services (NDS), you have user accounts there as well. Maybe all of your user information is in an ODBC database.

Cisco Secure ACS 3.0 for Windows NT or Windows 2000 lets you use any of these existing user databases in AAA. This means that instead of creating a new user database exclusively for AAA, you can adopt an existing database from one of these other sources. Now you not only have fewer user databases to maintain, but you also bypass the work of setting up a new one.

This capability to use existing user databases for AAA means that even if you have a single NAS, Cisco Secure ACS 3.0 for Windows NT or Windows 2000 is likely to be a good solution for your company or client.

Suppose you already have more than 1,000 users in your NT domain. And let's just say (okay, this is a stretch) that each of these users needs access to your NAS. Do you really want to create a local database (as outlined in Chapter 2) with those 1,000 user accounts? I'm fairly certain you don't want to do the following:

```
Todd(config)#username user1 password pass1
Todd(config)#username user2 password pass2
Todd(config)#username user3 password pass3
Todd(config)#username user4 password pass4
Todd(config)#username user5 password pass5
Todd(config)#username user6 password pass6
Todd(config)#username user7 password pass7
Todd(config)#username user8 password pass8
Todd(config)#username user9 password pass9
Todd(config)#username user10 password pass10
Todd(config)#username user11 password pass11
Todd(config)#username user12 password pass12
Todd(config)#username user13 password pass13
Todd(config)#username user14 password pass14
Todd(config)#username user15 password pass15
Todd(config)#username user16 password pass16
```

And so on, through `user1000`.

Do you want to maintain those passwords? Of course not! Consider employee turnover. You can't save these tasks for a once-a-week update; new users need computer access immediately, and former employees ideally should be deleted as their shoes pass through the door for the last time due to their potential security risk. So, you'd spend a part of every day maintaining passwords. Don't forget to add the time wasted with the HR department, trying to get an accurate list of people/passwords to add and delete. And how much aggravation would occur if—because you were trying to get this done before a noon meeting—you accidentally deleted, say, a senior vice president and weren't around until after 2 p.m. (because lunch went late) to fix that problem? Scared yet? No worries—Cisco Secure ACS 3.0 for Windows NT or Windows 2000 solves your problem.

What you want to do now is use the corporate network example that you'll be configuring throughout this part of the book and create a TACACS+ centralized database instead of using a single database on the NAS. This allows you more flexibility in your network configuration because you can create one database and use it repeatedly without having to update the database on individual NAS devices.

If you don't want to use the Cisco proprietary TACACS+, you can use the industry-standard RADIUS server. The configuration is pretty similar, and I'll show you how to perform account authorization with RADIUS after you go through the TACACS+ configurations.

> **WARNING** Be sure to first enter the `tacacs-server`'s IP address and key. Otherwise, you can easily lock yourself out of the router once the authorization takes over and for some reason can't reach a server.

Using RADIUS

Unlike TACACS+, which is Cisco proprietary, RADIUS is not proprietary. It's important that you understand the difference between the two remote servers.

Livingston Enterprises, now part of Lucent Technologies, developed RADIUS. Like TACACS+, it's a security database protocol designed for use between an NAS and ACS, except that RADIUS is an industry standard that's supported by many third-party devices. It uses UDP/IP for communications and supports authentication but only supports authentication through passwords. RADIUS can be used for AAA, but it treats authentication and authorization as the same process, and so it combines them—a big disadvantage over TACACS+.

Cisco Secure User Database NAS Configuration for RADIUS

The following example shows the same Cisco 2600 router used in the previous section's example configured to use RADIUS against an NAS server using the Cisco Secure User Database:

```
Todd(config)#aaa new-model
Todd(config)#aaa authentication login default radius
Todd(config)#aaa authentication ppp default radius
Todd(config)#aaa authorization exec radius
Todd(config)#aaa authorization network radius
Todd(config)#aaa accounting network start-stop radius
Todd(config)#aaa accounting exec start-stop radius
Todd(config)#aaa accounting network wait-start radius
Todd(config)#radius-server host 172.16.10.5
```

Our Corporate Network Example

Using the same network you've seen previously, I'll walk you through changing the corporate network example from using a local AAA database residing on the NAS server to using centralized database on a Cisco Secure ACS. Here's our corporate network again:

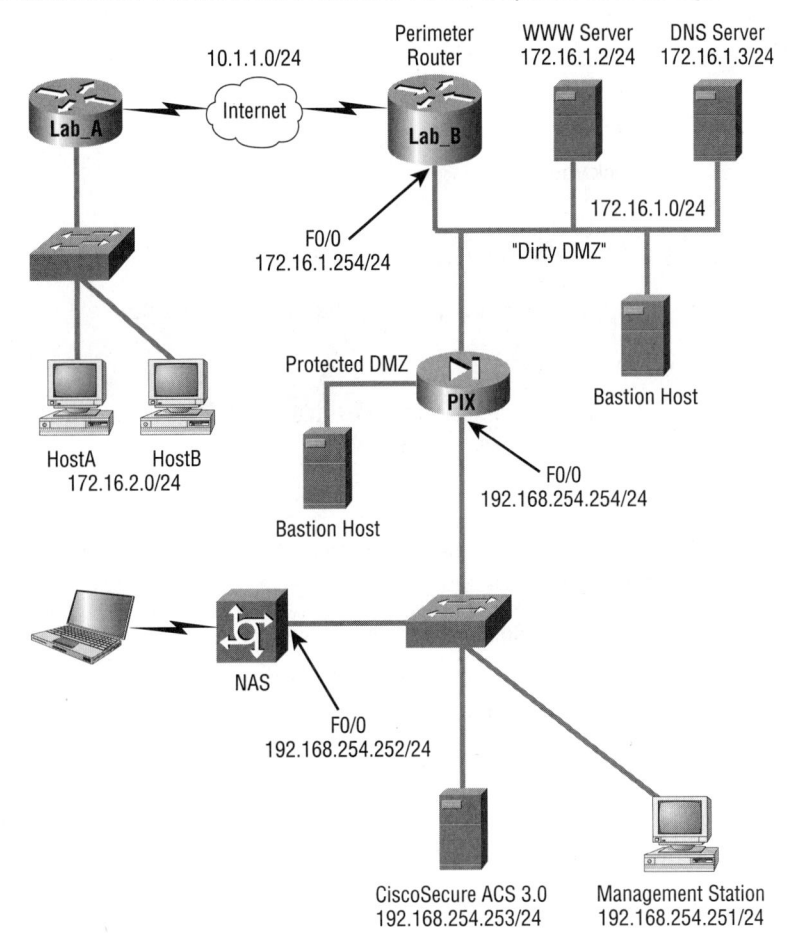

The goal is to install and configure the Cisco Secure ACS on the NAS server to run remote RADIUS and TACACS+ authentication, authorization, and accounting features, as well as to also configure the NAS to use the ACS server for authentication.

The following example shows a configuration using TACACS+ on the Cisco 2600 Todd NAS router, configured in Chapter 2, to now authenticate against a Cisco Secure ACS user database instead:

```
User Access Verification

Username: todd
Password:

Todd>en
Password:
Todd#config t
Enter configuration commands, one per line.  End with CNTL/Z.
```

First, enable AAA by using the aaa new-model global configuration command:

```
Todd(config)#aaa new-model
```

The next command specifies to use the default list against the TACACS+ server and that TACACS+ is the default login method for all authentication:

```
Todd(config)#aaa authentication login default tacacs+
```

You can add the command none at the end of the command, which means that if the TACACS+ process is unavailable, no login is required.

The next command sets the AAA authentication for PPP connection using the default list against the TACACS+ database:

```
Todd(config)#aaa authentication ppp default tacacs+
```

The next authorization command determines if the user is allowed to run an EXEC shell on the NAS against the TACTACS+ database:

```
Todd(config)#aaa authorization exec tacacs+
```

The next command sets AAA authorization for all network-related service requests, including Serial Line IP (SLIP), Point-to-Point Protocol (PPP), PPP NCPs, and AppleTalk Remote Access (ARA) protocol against the TACACS+ database:

```
Todd(config)#aaa authorization network tacacs+
```

The following AAA accounting command sets the EXEC process on the NAS to record the start and stop time of the session against the TACACS+ database:

```
Todd(config)#aaa accounting network start-stop tacacs+
```

This next command sets AAA accounting for EXEC processes on the NAS to record the start and stop time of the session against the TACACS+ database:

Todd(config)#`aaa accounting exec start-stop tacacs+`

The `tacacs-server host` command specifies the IP address of the host name of the remote TACACS+ server host:

Todd(config)#`tacacs-server host 192.168.254.253 single`

The `tacacs-server key` command specifies a shared secret text string used between the access server and the TACACS+ server. The access server and TACACS+ server use this text string to encrypt passwords and exchange responses:

Todd(config)#`tacacs-server key d$y!tR%e`

The next command sets AAA authentication at login to use the enable password for authentication:

Todd(config)#`aaa authentication login no_tacacs enable`

Choose the console 0 line:

Todd(config)#`line console 0`

Finally, specify that the AAA authentication list called no-tacacs is to be used on the console line:

Todd(config-line)#`login authentication no_tacacs`

Todd(config)#`radius-server key d$y!tR%e`
Todd(config)#`enable secret todd`
Todd(config)#`aaa authentication login no_radius enable`
Todd(config)#`line con 0`
Todd(config-line)#`login authentication no_radius`

On each interface that services dial-in users, issue the following command to tell the interface to use PPP CHAP authentication:

Todd(config-if)#`ppp authentication chap`

The only command different from the TACACS+ configuration is this one:

Todd(config)#`aaa accounting network wait-start radius`

As when using the `start-stop` keyword, the preceding command sends both a start and a stop accounting record to the accounting server, a RADIUS server in this example. If you use the `wait-start` keyword, however, the requested service can't start until the acknowledgment has been received from the RADIUS server. A stop-accounting record for network service requests is sent to the RADIUS server.

Basically, the rest of the commands are the same as those used in the TACACS+ configuration, so no additional command explanations are necessary at this point.

Verifying TACACS+

It's imperative that you can verify your configuration, so here are two debugging commands you can use on the NAS to trace TACACS+ packets:

- debug tacacs
- debug tacacs events

However, in addition, you can still use the debug aaa commands you learned about in Chapter 2 to see the output for a TACACS+ login attempt:

```
Todd#debug tacacs
TACACS access control debugging is on
Todd#exit
Todd con0 is now available
Press RETURN to get started.
04:56:38: TAC+: Opened 192.168.254.253 index=1
04:56:38: TAC+: 192.168.254.253 (185613193) ACCT/REQUEST/STOP queued
04:56:38: TAC+: (185613193) ACCT/REQUEST/STOP processed
04:56:38: TAC+: (185613193): received acct response status = SUCCESS
User Access Verification
Password:
Todd>
04:56:43: TAC+: Using default tacacs server list.
04:56:43: TAC+: 192.168.254.253 (2537319283) ACCT/REQUEST/START queued
04:56:43: TAC+: (2537319283) ACCT/REQUEST/START processed
04:56:43: TAC+: (2537319283): received acct response status = SUCCESS

Todd#undebug all
All possible debugging has been turned off
```

More information is displayed with the debug tacacs events command than with just the debug tacacs command:

```
Todd#debug tacacs events
TACACS+ events debugging is on
Todd#exit
```

Verifying TACACS+

```
Todd con0 is now available
Press RETURN to get started.


User Access Verification
Password:
05:01:08: TAC+: periodic timer started
05:01:08: TAC+: 192.168.254.253 req=81490CCC id=3169020093 ver=192 handle=0x0
    (NONE) expire=4 ACCT/REQUEST/STOP queued
05:01:08: TAC+: 192.168.254.253 ESTAB 81490CCC wrote 156 of 156 bytes
05:01:09: TAC+: 192.168.254.253 ESTAB read=12 wanted=12 alloc=17 got=12
05:01:09: TAC+: 192.168.254.253 ESTAB read=17 wanted=17 alloc=17 got=5
05:01:09: TAC+: 192.168.254.253 received 17 byte reply for 81490CCC
05:01:09: TAC+: req=81490CCC id=3169020093 ver=192 handle=0x0 (NONE) expire=4
    ACCT/REQUEST/STOP processed
05:01:09: TAC+: periodic timer stopped (queue empty)
Todd>en
Password:
05:01:55: TAC+: periodic timer started
05:01:55: TAC+: 192.168.254.253 req=81491914 id=3481072133 ver=192 handle=0x0
    (NONE) expire=5 ACCT/REQUEST/START queued
05:01:55: TAC+: 192.168.254.253 ESTAB 81491914 wrote 68 of 68 bytes
05:01:55: TAC+: 192.168.254.253 ESTAB read=12 wanted=12 alloc=17 got=12
05:01:55: TAC+: 192.168.254.253 ESTAB read=17 wanted=17 alloc=17 got=5
05:01:55: TAC+: 192.168.254.253 received 17 byte reply for 81491914
05:01:55: TAC+: req=81491914 id=3481072133 ver=192 handle=0x0 (NONE) expire=4
    ACCT/REQUEST/START processed
05:01:55: TAC+: periodic timer stopped (queue empty)
```

The following is an example of the **debug aaa authentication** command:

```
Todd#un all
All possible debugging has been turned off
Todd#
Todd#debug aaa authentication
AAA Authentication debugging is on
Todd#exit


User Access Verification

Password:
05:05:35: AAA/AUTHEN: free_user (0x81420624) user='' ruser='' port='tty0'
    rem_addr='async/' authen_type=ASCII service=LOGIN priv=1
```

```
05:05:36: AAA: parse name=tty0 idb type=-1 tty=-1
05:05:36: AAA: name=tty0 flags=0x11 type=4 shelf=0 slot=0 adapter=0 port=0
    channel=0
05:05:36: AAA/AUTHEN: create_user (0x81420624) user='' ruser='' port='tty0'
    rem_addr='async/' authen_type=ASCII service=LOGIN priv=1
05:05:36: AAA/AUTHEN/START (2124362753): port='tty0' list='no_tacacs'
    action=LOGIN service=LOGIN
05:05:36: AAA/AUTHEN/START (2124362753): found list no_tacacs
05:05:36: AAA/AUTHEN/START (2124362753): Method=ENABLE
05:05:36: AAA/AUTHEN (2124362753): status = GETPASS
Todd>: AAA/AUTHEN/START (3168314283): found list no_tacacs
05:05:58: AAA/AUTHEN/START (3168314283): Method=ENABLE
05:05:58: AAA/AUTHEN (3168314283): status = GETPASS
05:06:00: AAA/AUTHEN/CONT (3168314283): continue_login (user='(undef)')
05:06:00: AAA/AUTHEN (3168314283): status = GETPASS
05:06:00: AAA/AUTHEN/CONT (3168314283): Method=ENABLE
05:06:00: AAA/AUTHEN (3168314283): status = PASS
Todd>en
Password:
05:06:06: AAA/AUTHEN: dup_user (0x814909F8) user='' ruser='' port='tty0'
    rem_addr='async/' authen_type=ASCII service=ENABLE priv=15 source='AAA
    dup enable'
05:06:06: AAA/AUTHEN/START (338074629): port='tty0' list='' action=LOGIN
    service=ENABLE
05:06:06: AAA/AUTHEN/START (338074629): console enable - default to enable
    password (if any)
05:06:06: AAA/AUTHEN/START (338074629): Method=ENABLE
05:06:06: AAA/AUTHEN (338074629): status = GETPASS
Todd#
05:06:08: AAA/AUTHEN/CONT (338074629): continue_login (user='(undef)')
05:06:08: AAA/AUTHEN (338074629): status = GETPASS
05:06:08: AAA/AUTHEN/CONT (338074629): Method=ENABLE
05:06:08: AAA/AUTHEN (338074629): status = PASS
05:06:08: AAA/AUTHEN: free_user (0x814909F8) user='' ruser='' port='tty0'
    rem_addr='async/' authen_type=ASCII service=ENABLE priv=15
```

The preceding output from the **debug aaa authentication** command shows that the method was TACACS+, and that it was successful.

Summary

Cisco offers an excellent Access Control Server (ACS) that's available on a number of platforms. You learned about both the Cisco Secure ACS 3.0 for Windows NT (CSNT) or Windows 2000 and Cisco Secure ACS 2.3 for Unix (CSU) products.

The ACS will be an important element in your overall network security plan, and it can greatly simplify the task of managing user accounts.

As your network grows in complexity and size and you include Network Access Servers (NASs) from multiple vendors, the ACS will scale and continue to both simplify administration and improve security. This chapter provided the information you need to understand the role of the ACS and the communication between the NAS and ACS.

Exam Essentials

Remember the ways to get user information onto the Cisco Secure User Database. There are three ways to populate the Cisco Secure User Database: manually, through the Database Replication utility, and through the Database Import utility.

Know how to access the CS ACS web-based administration utility. To bring up the web-based administration tool using a web browser, go to the IP address of the CS ACS server, port 2002.

Remember which third-party user databases CS ACS supports. Cisco Secure ACS supports Microsoft Windows NT, Novell NDS, Directory Services, MCIS LDAP, and ODBC databases.

Remember which relational databases CSU supports. Cisco Secure ACS 2.3 for Unix (CSU) supports Sybase, Oracle, and SQL Anywhere databases.

Know the advantages of TACACS+ over RADIUS. The advantages of TACACS+ include encrypted packets versus encrypted passwords in RADIUS and the use of TCP rather than UDP. TACACS+ also treats authentication, authorization, and accounting as separate roles; RADIUS combines authentication and authorization.

Understand how to set an encryption key on the NAS. To set the encryption key on a TACACS+ server, use the following commands:

    Todd(config)#tacacs-server host 192.168.254.253
    Todd(config)#tacacs-server key d$y!tR%e

The `tacacs-server host` *hostname* | *ip address* command specifies the IP address or the host name of the remote TACACS+ server host. The `tacacs-server key` *key* command specifies a shared secret text string used between the access server and the TACACS+ server. You can use the same commands for a RADIUS server; just exchange the keyword `tacacs-server` for `radius-server`.

Chapter 4

Cisco Perimeter Router Problems and Solutions

THE FOLLOWING SECUR EXAM TOPICS ARE COVERED IN THIS CHAPTER:

- ✓ Identifying perimeter security problems and implementing solutions
- ✓ Identifying and overcoming eavesdropping and session replay
- ✓ Identifying and solving unauthorized access, data manipulation, and malicious destruction problems
- ✓ Solving lack of legal IP address problems
- ✓ Defending against rerouting attacks
- ✓ Defending against denial-of-service attacks

By definition, *perimeter routers* are really the boundary between your network and someone else's network—or pretty much everyone else's networks if you're talking about the Internet. This makes perimeter routers your first line of defense. If your perimeter router can prevent any nasty things from getting through in the first place, you clearly won't have to deal with them later.

As I'm sure you can imagine, Internet access into the perimeter router in your network exposes you to some serious security risks. But the Cisco IOS Firewall software is a powerful defense. It equips you with effective security and firewall features that are needed to guard against increasingly sophisticated attacks. Even better, Cisco is working constantly to improve and enhance these features and to develop new ones.

Cisco perimeter routers provide you with your first line of defense for Internet connections. They also define the demilitarized zone (DMZ) and are used to protect the bastion hosts residing there. You can also use perimeter routers to prevent the Private Internet Exchange (PIX) from being vulnerable to a direct attack. They can even provide an alarm system for you if anyone does try to break into your network via a perimeter router.

I've listed five different types of attacks you'll experience that can and do seriously compromise your network security:

- Eavesdropping and session replay
- Unauthorized access, data manipulation, and malicious destruction
- Lack of legal IP addresses
- Rerouting attacks
- Denial-of-service (DoS) attacks

Unfortunately, it seems these attacks are occurring more and more frequently with each passing day. If your defenses aren't in order to prevent their success, your network (and probably your job) can be in serious trouble. Consider each of these problems when you configure your Cisco perimeter router(s). And don't stop there—understand the solutions for them, too.

Some of these attacks should be familiar to you because we talked about them in Chapter 1, "Introduction to Network Security." This chapter will look at them again in more detail and explain how you can use the Cisco IOS Firewall to solve these problems.

Solving Eavesdropping and Session Replay Problems

Remember, *eavesdropping* is when a hacker is listening in and reading your data. *Session replay* happens when a sequence of packets or application commands is captured, manipulated, and replayed by bad guys with the intent of causing harm. You obviously need a solution for these ugly problems; but first let's use the corporate network example, illustrated in the following graphic, as an example of how eavesdropping and session replay can be a problem.

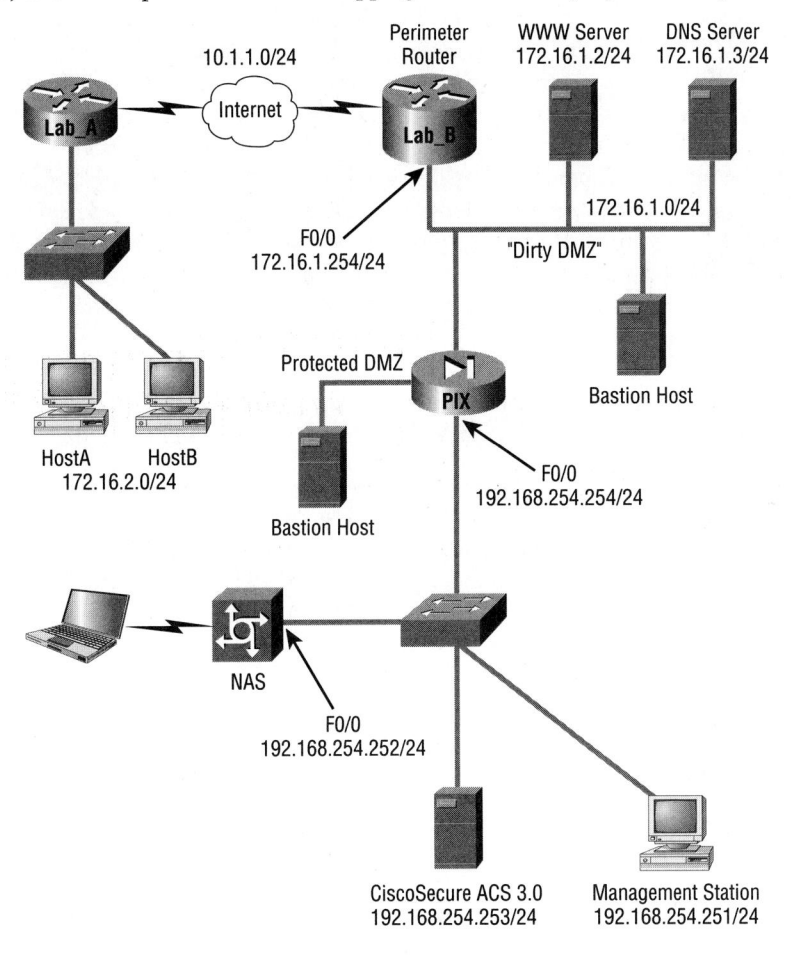

HostA needs to communicate to the bastion host in the dirty DMZ. (Recall that a *dirty DMZ* is defined as the part of a network that's using real Internet IP addresses.)

You have a client machine that must cross an unknown network to reach the bastion host. As you learned in Chapter 1, it's possible for someone in this unknown network who's using a protocol analyzer to capture the conversation between the client and server by eavesdropping. If the hacker is successful, your data can be compromised and the session can be replayed back to the server. Your problem is that you have unencrypted data crossing an unknown network. Unencrypted data—any guesses as to what the solution to this problem could be?

Yes—*encryption*. Of course you'll use encryption to protect the data. In our corporate network example, you can configure the Lab_A router at the remote site to encrypt the data traveling between the client and the bastion host. The perimeter router at the corporate site will also be configured for this same operation. Those two routers will then encrypt all data passing between these two hosts. Any intermediate routers between them can still route the traffic (network headers aren't encrypted). Traffic between the client and the bastion host doesn't need to be encrypted unless you really want it to be. You can control the encryption based on network, subnet, port, or protocol.

The best solution for eavesdropping and session replay is IP Security (IPSec), an open standards framework that ensures private communications over an IP network; it's used and recommended by Cisco as a tool for encryption. Most of the time, the best place to use IPSec is across a public IP network. This not only ensures confidentiality, it also ensures data integrity and authenticity. IPSec is configured between two routers, and it does its work at the Network layer.

Before IPSec was introduced, lots of people used the Secure Sockets Layer (SSL) to provide application encryption for web browsers and other applications. The problem with SSL is that the configuration is on an application-by-application basis, so only applications configured to use SSL are encrypted. By using IPSec, all data at the Network layer is encrypted.

> **NOTE** Cisco suggests that IPSec encryption, virtual private networks (VPNs), and digital certificates are all viable solutions to eavesdropping and session replay problems. Chapter 7, "Understanding Cisco IOS IPSec Support," and Chapter 8, "Cisco IOS IPSec Pre-Shared Keys and Certificate Authority Support," look more closely at IPSec.

Defending Against Unauthorized Access, Data Manipulation, and Malicious Destruction

Think back and picture the perimeter router in the corporate network firewall example illustrated earlier in this chapter. It connects the DMZ to the Internet, which, as you recall, is a potential source of problems. Assuming that this connection is necessary for business purposes, how can you ensure that traffic to and from the Internet is good and legitimate and not the communications equivalent of Stephen King's evil Christine?

Honestly, you can't always be sure, but you can stop most of the nasty stuff using a simple tool: access control lists (ACLs). No doubt you've used these in the past, but ACLs can do a number of tasks for you at the perimeter to significantly beef up your security.

With your perimeter router in mind, here's a list of various packets you probably don't want to allow into your network from the Internet:

- Private address as the source IP address
- One of your internal IP addresses as the source IP address
- Bootstrap Protocol (BOOTP), Trivial File Transfer Protocol (TFTP), and traceroute packets
- TCP connections to servers not in the DMZ
- Dynamic Host Configuration Protocol (DHCP) reserved range
- Loopback addresses

All of these packets can be stopped with inbound ACLs on a perimeter router. Here's an example of an access list on the perimeter router stopping the dirty DMZ IP addresses from being used as source addresses from an outside intruder:

```
Lab_B(config)#access-list 110 deny ip 172.16.1.0 0.0.0.255 any
Lab_B(config)#interface s0/0
Lab_B(config-if)#access-group 110 in
```

Do you remember from your ACL studies that you also need to have a `permit` statement included in your list to make it work? It's the same here—this is just an example.

Here's another example of using a simple ACL to implement network security. These commands prevent a SYN packet from coming into the inside network from the outside network:

```
Lab_B(config)#access-list 110 deny tcp any any established
Lab_B(config)#access-list 110 permit tcp any any
Lab_B(config)#interface s0/0
Lab_B(config-if)#access-group 110 in
```

Doing this allows a SYN packet out, but it won't let anyone "SYN" in. No one from the outside network can create a session to a host on the inside network. A host on the inside network can both send out and receive an ACK so those packets are allowed to enter the DMZ.

These are two types of packets you don't want leaving your network:

- Source address not in your internal IP address space
- Source address of any machine that isn't allowed Internet access by policy

And again, you can prevent that from happening by using fairly simple ACLs.

These simple examples demonstrate how efficient ACLs can be for preventing inappropriate access. If you make the functions we've discussed off-limits to bad guys, you've denied them access to some of the most common techniques that they use to exploit networks.

> **Tip:** ACLs are a great weapon for guarding your network against unauthorized access, data manipulation, and malicious destruction.

Solving Lack of Legal IP Addresses Problems

Let's say you have 500 machines to connect to the Internet, and you have 254 legal IP addresses. This could definitely be a problem; but if you use Network Address Translation (NAT), you can use a pool of IP addresses to meet the needs of a large number of clients. Even better, NAT gives you some additional security benefits beyond extending IP address space.

NAT hides your internal addressing scheme from the external network. The only device that the external network will be able to see is your NAT device; everything behind it is essentially invisible. So, if you configure NAT on your perimeter router, you get to hide all of your addressing.

A subset of NAT called Port Address Translation (PAT) extends NAT functionality by using TCP and UDP ports for address translation. Doing this allows a single Internet IP address to support up to 64,000 hosts, but Cisco recommends that you don't support more than 4,000 per address. (Even so, that's pretty impressive.)

> **Tip:** When your problem is the lack of legal IP addresses, your solution is to use NAT.

Fighting Rerouting Attacks

Let's suppose a bad guy could modify your routing table. Would that make you nervous? It should! The best-case scenario is that the attacker simply breaks into your network. The worst-case scenario is, well, destruction, corruption, and malfunction. Breaking your routing can cause all kinds of security problems, and there are a number of ways for the bad guys to do it. The most obvious way is to somehow gain access to a router, but that's not always necessary.

Let's take a look at the corporate network illustrated earlier in this chapter and use routers Lab_A and Lab_B, which are connected on the same network, for an example. Let's also assume that they're communicating using some routing protocol—say, Enhanced Internal Gateway Routing Protocol (EIGRP). You know that if router Lab_A learns about a new path to a network, it'll dutifully inform router Lab_B using EIGRP.

Router Lab_B may change its routing table to take advantage of this new information. Router Lab_A doesn't log in to router Lab_B, but it's able to change router Lab_B's routing table by just sending an EIGRP update to Lab_B. This is a simple example of dynamic routing, but look again. It also demonstrates how a network can be exposed to a potential security attack.

How? Suppose there's a bad guy between routers Lab_A and Lab_B, listening to their conversations. What if that bad guy builds an EIGRP update and sends it to router Lab_B, claiming that it's from router Lab_A? Router Lab_B gets the update, processes it, and maybe even changes its routing table. This approach does work sometimes—an attacker can introduce a routing update to the network that the receiving router acts on because it has no way of knowing that the update isn't valid. This is a prime example of what's known as a *rerouting attack*.

The fundamental problem here is that the receiving router can't verify that the update was truly sent by the sending router. You can solve this problem by giving the receiving router the ability to verify that the source of the updates it's getting is in fact the router that the updates are supposed to be coming from. You can make this happen by enabling *MD5 authentication* on both routers.

> **NOTE** It's also possible to use distribution lists to address the rerouting problem.

With MD5 authentication enabled, the routers receive a common key that's configured by the administrator. The routers then use that key to sign the routing updates they send and to verify the updates they receive. Any updates without matching keys won't be considered valid updates and therefore won't be acted upon. And since invaders can't extract the key from the update, they can't reproduce it to fake an update.

The following routing protocols can use MD5 authentication:

- Routing Information Protocol version 2 (RIPv2)
- Open Shortest Path First (OSPF)
- Border Gateway Protocol (BGP)
- Enhanced Internet Gateway Routing Protocol (EIGRP)

It's a good idea to deny routing protocol packets at your network's entry points, because you shouldn't see any routing protocols coming in except BGP. If you're not using BGP, it's another good reason to just use static routes to and from the Internet.

Let's look at a configuration example that shows some of these technologies at work. IPSec is covered in Chapter 7, and NAT configuration isn't part of the SECUR exam, so I won't include them here. Instead, this example focuses on enabling MD5 authentication and adding it into your routing process on the Lab_B router, whose EIGRP neighbor is out S0/0:

```
Lab_B#conf t
Lab_B(config)#router eigrp 100
Lab_B(config-router)#network 10.0.0.0
Lab_B(config-router)#network 172.16.0.0
Lab_B(config)#exit
Lab_B(config)#int s0/0
```

```
Lab_B(config-if)#ip authentication mode eigrp 100 md5
Lab_B(config-if)#ip authentication key-chain eigrp 100 toddkey
Lab_B(config-if)#exit
Lab_B(config)#key chain toddkey
Lab_B(config-key)#key 1
Lab_B(config-key)#key-string 4444444444
Lab_B(config-key)#^Z
Lab_B#
```

Of course, the neighbor router Lab_A needs to be configured as well.

> **TIP** When your problem is rerouting attacks, Cisco says your solution is to use MD5 authentication.

Fighting Denial-of-Service Attacks

I first brought up denial-of-service (DoS) attacks back in Chapter 1, so let's take a second for a short review. These are the steps that occur in a normal TCP three-way handshake:

- The first host sends a request to speak (SYN).
- The receiving host responds by acknowledging the request and allocating resources for the conversation (SYN-ACK).
- The first host recognizes the acknowledgment (ACK).

These two hosts have established a TCP connection and can now exchange data.

One type of DoS attack is called a *SYN flood attack*. Let's say I send your server a SYN request with a make-believe source address. What do you think your server will do? It will probably respond to my request with a SYN-ACK and allocate resources for this conversation. Nothing is ever free, so a small amount of RAM on your server has now been consumed. No worries, right? But what if I send your server 100 bogus SYN requests from 100 fake addresses? Your server will send out 100 SYN-ACKs and allocate enough resources for 100 conversations. What if I send 100 more SYN requests, all from fake addresses, *per second*? How about 1,000 per second? Now how is your server doing? My guess is, not well. The server has probably run out of resources and either has crashed or is hanging there, overwhelmed and exhausted. As a result, it could very well be open to exploitation.

In addition, you can't stop me from sending SYN requests to your server unless you don't want the server available for legitimate use. Even finding me is difficult, because I always lie about my origin address. But there is hope for you: *TCP Intercept*.

TCP Intercept on a perimeter router running Cisco IOS Firewall software can run in two modes: intercept and monitor. In intercept mode, the router doesn't immediately forward a SYN request to the server; instead, it proxy-answers the request (SYN-ACK) to verify that the request is valid. If the requesting host doesn't ACK back, the router never notifies the server of the connection attempt. Requests proven to be genuine are eventually handed off to the server. So if a bad guy sends hundreds or thousands of SYN requests per second, it won't matter, because your server won't see any of them. DoS attack thwarted!

When running in monitor mode, TCP Intercept forwards and monitors these TCP three-way handshakes. When it sees one that's poking along beyond an administrator-defined interval, TCP Intercept intervenes and closes that connection. This means that the server won't leave resources open and hanging while waiting for the final ACK to come back.

When enabling TCP Intercept, you use an access list to define the connections to which TCP Intercept will be applied. Suppose that you want to use TCP intercept to protect a server in your DMZ at IP address 172.16.10.25. The configuration commands look like this:

```
Lab_B#config t
Lab_B(config)#access-list 151 permit tcp any host 172.16.10.25
Lab_B(config)#ip tcp intercept list 151
Lab_B(config)#ip tcp intercept mode intercept
Lab_B(config)#^Z
Lab_B#
```

> If your problem is fighting DoS attacks, your solution is to use TCP Intercept.

Real World Scenario

TCP Intercept in Action

Bob is the network administrator for company XYZ. Last night, Bob noticed that the processor utilization on his Cisco 7200 was extremely high. After further investigation, he realized that his router had a tremendous number of half-open TCP sessions. Bob pondered this for a moment and remembered that this type of attack is called a TCP DoS attack. Thinking back to his studies for the CCSP, Bob remembered that he could use TCP Intercept to resolve this problem. Without further ado, Bob implemented TCP Intercept on his Cisco 7200. He let it work for a while and then checked the router's processor performance. Lo and behold, the router's processor utilization had dramatically decreased, and operation was back to normal.

Turning Off and Configuring Network Services

Besides encryption, ACLs, and authorization, there are additional commands you can configure on your perimeter router to limit access to it. By default, the Cisco IOS runs some services that are unnecessary to its normal operation, and if you don't disable them, they can be easy targets for DoS attacks and break-in attempts.

Plus, if you just use a Cisco router's default settings, it won't check routing paths to stop illegitimate traffic, and ARP traffic will be allowed to pass through its interfaces. We'll now look at how to turn off these unneeded services.

Blocking SNMP Packets

The Cisco IOS default configurations permit remote access from any source, so unless you're either way too trusting or insane, it should be obvious to you that those configurations need a bit of attention. You've got to restrict them. If you don't, the router will be an easy target for an attacker who wants to log in to it. This is where access lists come into the game—they can protect you.

If you place the following command on the serial0/0 interface of the perimeter router, it will stop any Simple Network Management Protocol (SNMP) packets from entering the router or the DMZ. (You'd need to have a `permit` command along with this list to make it work, but this is just an example.)

```
Lab_B(config)#access-list 110 deny udp any any eq snmp
Lab_B(config)#interface s0/0
Lab_B(config-if)#access-group 110 in
```

Disabling Echo

In case you don't know this already, *small services* are servers (daemons) running in the router that are useful for diagnostics. And here we go again—by default, the Cisco router has a series of diagnostic ports enabled for certain UDP and TCP services, including echo, chargen, and discard.

When a host attaches to those ports, a small amount of CPU is consumed to service these requests. All a single attacking device needs to do is send a whole slew of requests with different, random, phony source IP addresses to overwhelm the router, making it slow down or even fail. You can use the no version of these commands to stop a chargen attack:

```
Lab_B(config)#no service tcp-small-servers
Lab_B(config)#no service udp-small-servers
```

Finger is a utility program designed to allow users of Unix hosts on the Internet to get information about each other:

```
Lab_B(config)#no service finger
```

This matters because the `finger` command can be used to find information about all users on the network and/or the router. This is also why you should disable it. The `finger` command is equivalent to issuing the `show users` command on the router.

Here are the TCP small services:

Echo   Echoes back whatever you type. Type the command `telnet x.x.x.x echo ?` to see the options.

Chargen   Generates a stream of ASCII data. Type the command `telnet x.x.x.x chargen ?` to see the options.

Discard   Throws away whatever you type. Type the command `telnet x.x.x.x discard ?` to see the options.

Daytime   Returns the system date and time, if correct. It's correct if you're running Network Time Protocol (NTP) or have set the date and time manually from the exec level. Type the command `telnet x.x.x.x daytime ?` to see the options.

The UDP small services are as follows:

Echo   Echoes the payload of the datagram you send.

Discard   Silently pitches the datagram you send.

Chargen   Pitches the datagram you send and responds with a 72-character string of ASCII characters terminated with a CR+LF.

Turning Off BOOTP and Auto-Config

Again, by default, the Cisco router offers async line BOOTP service as well as remote auto-configuration. To disable these functions on your Cisco router, use the following commands:

```
Lab_B(config)#no ip boot server
Lab_B(config)#no service config
```

Disabling the HTTP Interface

The `ip http server` command may be useful for configuring and monitoring the router, but the clear-text nature of HTTP can obviously be a security risk. To disable the HTTP process on your router, use the following command:

```
Lab_B(config)#no ip http server
```

To enable an HTTP server on a router for authentication, authorization, and accounting (AAA), use the global configuration command `ip http server`.

Disabling IP Source Routing

The IP header source-route option allows the source IP host to set a packet's route through the IP network. With IP source routing enabled, packets containing the source-route option are forwarded to the router addresses specified in the header. Use the following command to disable any processing of packets with source-routing header options:

Lab_B(config)#**no ip source-route**

Disabling Proxy ARP

Proxy ARP is the technique in which one host—usually a router—answers ARP requests intended for another machine. By faking its identity, the router accepts responsibility for getting those packets to the real destination. Proxy ARP can help machines on a subnet reach remote subnets without configuring routing or a default gateway. The following command disables proxy ARP:

Lab_B(config)#**interface s0/0**
Lab_B(config-if)#**no ip proxy-arp**

Apply this command to all your router's interfaces.

Disabling Redirect Messages

Internet Control Message Protocol (ICMP) redirect messages are used by routers to notify hosts on the data link that a better route is available for a particular destination. To disable the redirect messages so bad people can't draw out your network topology with this information, use the following command:

Lab_B(config)#**interface s0/0**
Lab_B(config-if)#**no ip redirects**

Apply this command to all your router's interfaces.

Disabling the Generation of ICMP Unreachable Messages

The no ip unreachables command prevents the perimeter router from divulging topology information by telling external hosts which subnets aren't configured. This command is used on a router's interface that is connected to an outside network:

Lab_B(config)#**interface s0/0**
Lab_B(config-if)#**no ip unreachables**

Again, apply this to all the interfaces of your router.

Disabling Multicast Route Caching

The multicast route cache lists multicast routing cache entries. These packets can be read, so they create a security problem. To disable multicast route caching, use the following command:

Lab_B(config)#**interface s0/0**
Lab_B(config-if)#**no ip mroute-cache**

Apply this command to all the interfaces of your router.

Disabling the Maintenance Operation Protocol

The Maintenance Operation Protocol (MOP) works at the Data Link and Network layers in the DECnet protocol suite and is used for utility services such as uploading and downloading system software, remote testing, and problem diagnosis. So, who uses DECnet? Anyone with their hands up? I didn't think so. To disable this service, use the following command:

Lab_B(config)#**interface s0/0**
Lab_B(config-if)#**no mop enabled**

Apply this command to all the interfaces of your router.

Turning Off the X.25 PAD Service

Packet assembler/disassembler (PAD) connects asynchronous devices such as terminals, IC-card readers, and computers to public/private X.25 networks. Since every computer in the world is pretty much IP savvy, and X.25 has gone the way of the dodo bird, there is no reason to leave this service running. Use the following command to disable the PAD service:

Lab_B(config)#**no service pad**

Enabling the Nagle TCP Congestion Algorithm

The Nagle TCP congestion algorithm is useful for small-packet congestion, but if you're using a higher setting than the default MTU of 1500 bytes, it can create an above-average traffic load. To enable this service, use the following command:

Lab_B(config)#**service nagle**

It's important to understand that the Nagle congestion service can break X Window connections to an X server, so don't use it if you're using X Window.

Logging Every Event

Using the Cisco ACS server as a Syslog server can log events for you to verify. Use the `logging trap` debugging command and the `logging ip_address` command to turn on this feature:

```
Lab_B(config)#logging trap debugging
Lab_B(config)#logging 192.168.254.251
Lab_B(config)#exit
Lab_B#sh logging
Syslog logging: enabled (0 messages dropped, 0 flushes, 0 overruns)
    Console logging: level debugging, 15 messages logged
    Monitor logging: level debugging, 0 messages logged
    Buffer logging: disabled
    Trap logging: level debugging, 19 message lines logged
        Logging to 192.168.254.251, 1 message lines logged
```

The `show logging` command provides you with statistics of the log on the router.

Disabling Cisco Discovery Protocol

Cisco Discovery Protocol (CDP) does just that—it's a Cisco proprietary protocol that discovers Cisco devices on the network. But because it's a Data Link–layer protocol, it can't find Cisco devices on the other side of a router. Plus, by default, Cisco switches don't forward CDP packets, so you can't see Cisco devices attached to any other port on a switch.

When you're bringing up your network for the first time, CDP can be a helpful protocol for verifying your network. But because you're going to be thorough and document your network, you don't need the CDP after that. And because CDP does discover Cisco routers and switches on your network, you should disable it. You do that in global configuration mode, which turns off CDP completely for your router or switch:

```
Lab_B(config)#no cdp run
```

Or you can turn off CDP on each individual interface using the following command:

```
Lab_B(config-if)#no cdp enable
```

Configuring SNMP

Simple Network Management Protocol (SNMP) (161) uses two default community strings, *public* and *private*. If you don't want network management information sent from your perimeter router, you can disable SNMP by issuing the following command:

```
RouterA(config)# no snmp-server
```

Turning Off and Configuring Network Services

But if you do want to send out management information, then you'd better change up the default community strings using the following IOS command:

RouterA(config)# **snmp-server community** *string*

Configuring Exec Timeout Values

It can be annoying to have your command line suddenly suspend on you and log you out. But, Cisco has automatically implemented this security feature for us. By default, lines have a default exec-timeout value of 10 minutes.

If you want to increase or decrease this timeout value, you must issue the following command in the line configuration mode:

RouterA(config-line)# **exec-timeout** *value*

Disabling the Default Forwarded UDP Protocols

When you use the `ip helper-address` command as follows on an interface, your router will forward UDP broadcasts to the listed server or servers:

Lab_B(config)#**interface f0/0**
Lab_B(config-if)#**ip helper-address 192.168.254.251**

You'll generally use the `ip helper-address` command when you want to forward DHCP client requests to a DHCP server. The problem is, not only does this forward port 67 (BOOTP server request), it also forwards seven other ports as well. To disable the unused ports, use the following commands:

Lab_B(config)#**no ip forward-protocol udp 69**
Lab_B(config)#**no ip forward-protocol udp 53**
Lab_B(config)#**no ip forward-protocol udp 37**
Lab_B(config)#**no ip forward-protocol udp 137**
Lab_B(config)#**no ip forward-protocol udp 138**
Lab_B(config)#**no ip forward-protocol udp 68**
Lab_B(config)#**no ip forward-protocol udp 49**

Now, only the BOOTP server request (67) will be forwarded to the DHCP server. If you want to forward a certain port, say TACACS+, use the following command:

Lab_B(config)#**ip forward-protocol udp 49**

On the next page, you'll find a list of available ports that you can opt to forward from the router, as well as the ports that are forwarded by default if you use the `ip helper-address` command.

Port or Protocol	Meaning	On by Default
<0–65535>	Port number (create your own)	
biff	Biff (mail notification, comsat, 512)	
bootpc	Bootstrap Protocol (BOOTP) client (68)	X
bootps	Bootstrap Protocol (BOOTP) server (67)	X
discard	Discard (9)	
dnsix	DNSIX security protocol auditing (195)	
domain	Domain Name Service (DNS) (53)	X
echo	Echo (7)	
isakmp	Internet Security Association and Key Management Protocol (ISAKMP) (500)	
mobile-ip	Mobile IP registration (434)	
nameserver	IEN116 name service (obsolete, 42)	
netbios-dgm	NetBios datagram service (138)	X
netbios-ns	NetBios name service (137)	X
netbios-ss	NetBios session service (139)	
ntp	Network Time Protocol (NTP) (123)	
pim-auto-rp	PIM Auto-RP (496)	
rip	Routing Information Protocol (RIP) (router, in.routed, 520)	
snmp	Simple Network Management Protocol (SNMP) (161)	
snmptrap	SNMP traps (162)	
sunrpc	Sun Remote Procedure Call (111)	
syslog	System Logger (514)	
tacacs	TAC access control system (49)	X
talk	Talk (517)	
tftp	Trivial File Transfer Protocol (TFTP) (69)	X
time	Time (37)	X
who	Who service (rwho, 513)	
xdmcp	X Display Manager Control Protocol (XDMCP) (177)	

Summary

You're now familiar with the Cisco IOS Firewall software and some of its features, and you're aware of the dangers lurking at the perimeter of your network. You've also learned about ways to keep your network and its data safe using features built into the Cisco IOS Firewall.

By matching each problem with a specific solution, you're now equipped with strategies that you can use against those attacks. Remember that the solution for eavesdropping and session replay is using encryption schemes such as IPSec. To stop unauthorized users from accessing your network, simple access control lists work fine. To provide relief from an IP address shortage, use NAT on the perimeter router to conserve subnets. The best solution for rerouting attacks is to configure MD5 authentication on your router. And finally, the solution for DoS attacks is to use the TCP Intercept feature.

If you configure these features at the perimeter of your network, you're good and safe to go. A router running the Cisco IOS Firewall software can do all of this for you.

Exam Essentials

Know the solution to eavesdropping. Eavesdropping occurs when someone intercepts traffic that isn't theirs and reads it. To prevent eavesdropping, use IPSec encryption.

Know the commands to stop a chargen attack. The following two commands can stop a chargen attack:

```
Lab_B(config)#no service tcp-small-servers
Lab_B(config)#no service udp-small-servers
```

Know how to prevent unauthorized access, data manipulation, and malicious destruction. To prevent certain inbound and outbound packets, use ACLs. ACLs can be used to prevent traffic based upon numerous options, such as source address, destination address, and traffic type.

Know the solution to the lack of legal IP addresses problem. If you don't have enough legal IP addresses, use NAT and PAT. When you're using NAT, you have a choice between static or dynamic NAT.

Know how to prevent rerouting attacks. A hacker can use a rerouting attack to direct your traffic to them. To secure your network against rerouting attacks, enable MD5 authentication.

Know how to prevent DoS attacks. DoS attacks are used to bring down a needed service. To prevent DoS attacks, enable TCP Intercept.

Chapter 5

Context-Based Access Control Configuration

THE FOLLOWING SECUR EXAM TOPICS ARE COVERED IN THIS CHAPTER:

- ✓ Understanding the Cisco IOS Firewall
- ✓ Configuring Context-Based Access Control
- ✓ Establishing global timeouts and thresholds
- ✓ Implementing Port-to-Application Mapping
- ✓ Defining inspection rules
- ✓ Defining inspection rules and ACLs applied to router interfaces
- ✓ Verifying the Cisco IOS Firewall

Do you have a firewall on every Internet-connected site in your organization? Tell the truth. I'm sure some of you can honestly answer yes, but I'm also sure a lot of you can't. Firewalls are expensive—expensive to buy, expensive to install, and expensive to maintain. People who configure them are expensive, too.

Although it may be true that entities such as huge financial institutions and other large corporations with deep pockets are willing to pony up the kind of cash that it takes to have a firewall guarding every Internet connection in their enterprise, public school districts, nontechnical businesses, small offices, and other organizations often can't.

In this chapter, I'll introduce you to the Cisco IOS Firewall. You'll learn how it's configured so that you can work with it in both your home and your business and save some cash, too. This chapter also explores Context-Based Access Control (CBAC) and explains the ways it can work for you in your internetwork. I'll show you how CBAC is both different and better at protecting your network than running static access control lists (ACLs).

Understanding the Cisco IOS Firewall

The Cisco IOS Firewall is a software firewall that runs on the Internetwork Operating System (IOS) on your Cisco router—a feature you buy that augments the standard IOS and utilizes your existing hardware. You must, of course, have sufficient flash and RAM at your disposal for the IOS Firewall image. Some of you may be thinking that you can just use access control lists (ACLs) on your router and mimic a lot of the functionality of a firewall, and you're right, you can—but only to a degree.

The Cisco IOS Firewall consists of three main components:

- Authentication Proxy
- Intrusion Detection System (IDS)
- Context-Based Access Control (CBAC)

Although I'll cover each of these components, this chapter's main focus will be on CBAC. Both the Authentication Proxy and Intrusion Detection System are topics you'll study thoroughly in Chapter 6, "Cisco IOS Firewall Authentication and Intrusion Detection." For now, I'll give you an overview of each of these powerful tools and then move right into CBAC.

Authentication Proxy and IDS

Have you ever been frustrated—maybe even nervous—because you're creating access policies based on IP addresses when what you really need to control is users? Most network engineers have. You can lock down a PC based on its IP address—that'll show 'em, right? Wrong. You can't prevent someone from getting around that by using another machine.

But armed with the Authentication Proxy, you can create policies based on users rather than IP addresses. You can configure specific user-based access such as HTTP access to the Internet, because the policy follows the user instead of being tied to a single PC. No matter where your user actually is, when they attempt to access resources through the firewall, they're forced to authenticate to the firewall, and so their policy follows them. You give each user their own personal access profile that can be stored on a Cisco Secure ACS or other TACACS+ or RADIUS server.

The IOS Firewall now offers an Intrusion Detection System (IDS) option on mid- to high-range router platforms. This option is particularly valuable at perimeter points within the network or at peering points between networks. The IDS includes profiles or *signatures* for 59 common attacks that run the gamut from the breach-of-security types to information-gathering attacks. When a packet matches one of these signatures, the IDS can react with an alarm (CIDS or Syslog server), it can drop the packet, or it can reset the TCP session.

Context-Based Access Control

The Cisco IOS Firewall Context-Based Access Control (CBAC) engine provides secure, per-application access control across network boundaries. CBAC enhances security for applications that use TCP and UDP well-known ports. It provides this service by scrutinizing source and destination addresses. I'll show you how CBAC is both different and better at protecting your network than just running static ACLs. To give CBAC a proper introduction, I need to make sure you're crystal clear about how different it is from an ACL—both in its operation and in its capabilities.

CBAC Compared to ACLs

There are many differences between ACLs and CBAC, but at a high level, the main distinctions are that CBAC is stateful, dynamic, and can look farther into packets.

In addition, CBAC is application aware—ACLs aren't. In terms of OSI, this means that whereas ACLs make their decisions based on layers 3 and 4 data, CBAC can look at Application-layer information. This capability makes it possible for CBAC to detect problems such as illegal or inappropriate Simple Mail Transfer Protocol (SMTP) commands, whereas an ACL can only permit or block the Transport-layer port.

> ### Real World Scenario
>
> **CBAC in Action**
>
> The Internet can be the ultimate source of grief, pain, and destruction, but don't assume that CBAC doesn't have applications that can protect you elsewhere as well.
>
> Lots of organizations need internal security and controls as much as they need external security (well, almost as much). You can apply CBAC anywhere you could use a firewall, internally or externally.
>
> For instance, let's say your company needs a cheap and easy alternative to purchasing and maintaining a firewall. CBAC can come to the rescue because it's part of the package when you purchase the Cisco IOS Firewall set.
>
> Instead of buying separate hardware for individual security problems, the Cisco IOS Firewall provides great value for an all-in-one product. This can give you flexibility in your multiprotocol networks, as well as perimeter security, intrusion detection, and VPN connections, including IP Security (IPSec), Layer 2 Tunneling Protocol (L2TP), and quality of service (QoS).
>
> Because the Cisco IOS is always being maintained and updated, the CBAC configuration that can be used with a Cisco router will provide many years of investment protection.

CBAC keeps state tables where session information is stored and can dynamically create and modify ACLs to control traffic. It can also recognize and help prevent certain types of DoS attacks.

To begin, let's look at how an ACL works:

1. A packet arrives at an interface with an inbound ACL configured on the router.
2. The packet is compared to successive lines of the ACL, starting with the first line, until a match is made.
3. If a match is made, the packet is acted upon based on the action defined by that line of the ACL.
4. If a match isn't made, the packet is dropped.

    If we were discussing ACLs, we could stop here. But if we did, you'd miss an important distinction between a firewall and a router. So, let's continue with the next packet:

5. Another packet arrives at an interface with an inbound ACL configured on the router.
6. The packet is compared to successive lines of the ACL, starting with the first line, until a match is made.
7. If a match is made, the packet is acted upon based on the action defined by that line of the ACL.
8. If a match isn't made, the packet is dropped.

Okay, this sounds familiar to our understanding of access lists. Let's continue with one more packet:

9. Another packet arrives at an interface with an inbound ACL configured on the router.
10. The packet is compared to successive lines of the ACL, starting with the first line, until a match is made.
11. If a match is made, the packet is acted upon based on the action defined by that line of the ACL.
12. If a match isn't made, the packet is dropped.

What's up with this? Why we are doing this redundant review of how an ACL works? The answer—and a key distinction between a firewall (CBAC) and a simple ACL—lies in this question: What effect does the first packet through the ACL have on the third packet through the ACL? The answer clarifies why CBAC is a much more powerful guardian for your network.

When a router runs with ACLs, every packet arrives fresh at the router: Each packet is subject to the exact same set of rules. A traditional ACL is static—that is, every packet is treated equally, regardless of any other packets that have preceded it through the router. That's the point I was making with the preceding steps—each packet arrives individually at the ACL, and each packet is evaluated and either permitted or denied without any regard to any packet that preceded it. Not so with CBAC; CBAC is smarter than that.

With CBAC, the rules for packets passing through the router can change depending on what has already happened; the fate of a packet can depend on what previous packets have done. This is what I mean when I say that CBAC is *stateful*. Think *state-dependent* if it helps.

CBAC monitors the state of network connections and traffic by keeping a state table of all inspected traffic; CBAC changes the access rules based on this data. An ACL can evaluate only one packet at a time, whereas a firewall (or CBAC) can evaluate *trends* of packets and respond appropriately to the type of trend it has identified. So with CBAC, what happens to the third packet through the router depends on what the two preceding packets did.

Clearly, this means that CBAC can identify and respond to problems that ACLs could never hope to—such as DoS attacks. An ACL can permit or deny TCP SYN requests, but CBAC can count the number of half-open TCP connections and make decisions about any new SYN requests dynamically. Plus, CBAC can evaluate Application-layer information by monitoring control channels and Application-layer conversations, so it can detect inappropriate commands. It literally parses the Application-layer header to extract this information. ACLs can't do that.

All this discussion isn't intended to make you think that ACLs are useless and that if you use them, you might as well put your data out on a public FTP server. I'm not telling you this to convince you to dump your ACLs; I'm just explaining how very different a stateful firewall is from an ACL. ACLs certainly have their place—they're included in standard IOS. CBAC will definitely cost you more for IOS images.

CBAC-Supported Protocols

CBAC is a strong tool and can help you monitor and log sessions created and used with many protocols. You can use several protocols with CBAC to monitor and log sessions.

CBAC can be configured to inspect either all TCP or UDP conversations or to focus on specific protocols. In operation, CBAC sits behind the ACLs and lets the ACL do its work first; so, if a packet is dropped by an ACL, it's never inspected by CBAC. Packets that do pass through are inspected, and CBAC makes necessary changes to the state table for TCP and UDP sessions. The information in the state table is then used to make temporary modifications to ACLs that will serve to permit return traffic, or perhaps additional connections associated with a particular protocol—for example, FTP data connections. These temporary openings in the firewall are removed when they're no longer needed and are never saved to NVRAM.

The choice is yours—you get to decide whether to have CBAC inspect specific protocols or have it examine all TCP and/or UDP traffic. You also get to pick the interface and direction where the inspection will be applied to the protocols you've selected. Once CBAC monitors a protocol, it only allows return traffic to permissible sessions already in the state table.

Some protocols (such as FTP) use two channels when they communicate: one for control information and one for data exchange. CBAC monitors only the control channel. It reads the actual Application-layer commands and their responses so it can protect against certain types of Application-layer attacks. CBAC also tracks TCP sequence numbers, guarding against the types of attacks that manipulate them.

You can tell CBAC to inspect all TCP or UDP sessions, or you can get specific and configure it to act as a watchdog for any of these protocols:

- Remote Procedure Call (RPC)
- Microsoft RPC
- File Transfer Protocol (FTP)
- Trivial File Transfer Protocol (TFTP)
- Unix R-commands (Rlogin, Rsh)
- SMTP
- Java
- SQL*Net
- Real-Time Streaming Protocol (RTSP)
- H.323
- Microsoft NetShow
- StreamWorks
- VDOLive

Introduction to CBAC Configuration

To help you set up and configure CBACs, Cisco has defined these six steps:

1. Set audit trails and alerts.
2. Set global timeouts and thresholds.
3. Define Port-to-Application Mapping (PAM).
4. Define inspection rules.
5. Apply inspection rules and ACLs to interfaces.
6. Test and verify CBAC.

You'll learn about each of these steps in detail throughout the rest of this chapter. The following graphic illustrates the network you'll be working with and configuring:

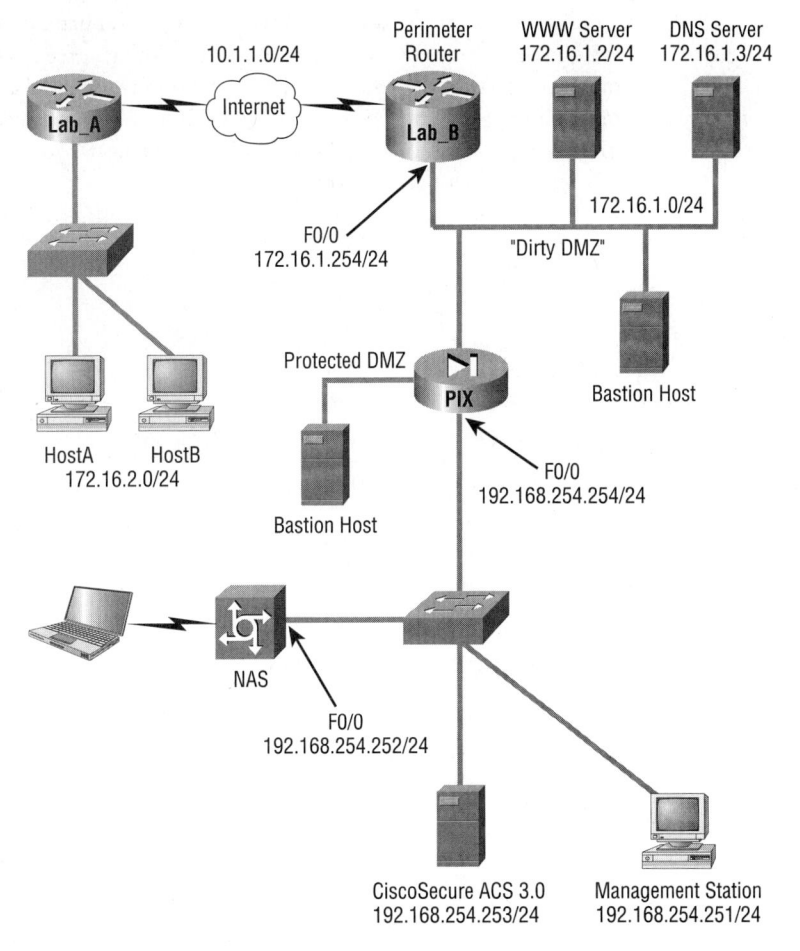

First, you need to understand the configuration and the order of the steps you'll take to build CBAC on the Lab_B router as you work through the examples in the rest of this chapter.

You'll be configuring the border router Lab_B with CBAC to protect the internal network, and you'll need to provide full access to both the web server and the DNS server from the Internet. You'll also allow all general TCP and UDP traffic out to the Internet from your internal hosts, but not anything else.

The next section describes how to set up auditing and real-time alerts from routers running CBAC.

Using Audit Trails and Alerts

If you need it to, CBAC can generate real-time alerts and audit trails through the use of a Syslog server. This is an especially useful feature if you have multiple routers running CBAC, because it lets you monitor all enterprise alerts and even audit trails at a single, centralized location.

Alerts are triggered when CBAC discovers any suspicious activity. They're reported as Syslog error messages to the central Syslog server that you've specified. Alerts provide a record of suspected problems, and they can be used to trigger other real-time events on the Syslog server.

You can use audit trails to create a log of all inspected activities. Think of this as a record of any and all accesses, whether they're a problem or not. Audit trails are useful if your security policy identifies a need to keep a record of all network traffic.

The following example shows how both audit trails and alerts would be configured on your Lab_B router, assuming that your Syslog server is at 192.168.254.251:

```
Lab_B#conf t
Lab_B(config)#logging on
Lab_B(config)#logging 192.168.254.251
Lab_B(config)#ip inspect audit-trail
Lab_B(config)#no ip inspect alert-off
```

The no version of the `ip inspect alert-off` command enables alerts. Removing the no disables alerts. Likewise, the no version of the `ip inspect audit-trail` command disables the audit trail.

You're now logging both alerts and audit trails to your Syslog server. The next step is to configure global timeouts and thresholds.

Configuring Global Timeouts and Thresholds

CBAC uses global timeouts and thresholds to determine how long to preserve state information for all sessions, established or otherwise. You can use the defaults—and you need to know what these are—or you can modify them to meet your individual needs. If you're going to change them, do it now before proceeding with any further CBAC configuration tasks.

Table 5.1 lists the commands you use to modify the default values and then describes the timeout or threshold and its default value. Once set, these values can be restored to their default values by using the no form of the command, as in the following example:

Lab_B#**conf t**
Lab_B(config)#**ip inspect tcp synwait-time 60**

The default time of 30 seconds has been changed to 60 seconds.

Lab_B(config)#**no ip inspect tcp synwait-time 60**

The default of 30 seconds has now been restored.

TABLE 5.1 Some Commands for Changing CBAC Timeouts and Thresholds

Command	Description
ip inspect tcp synwait-time	Sets how long CBAC will wait for a TCP session to be established before dropping the session. The default is 30 seconds.
ip inspect tcp finwait-time	Sets how long CBAC will wait after a TCP FIN before dropping the session. The default is 5 seconds.
ip inspect tcp idle-time	Sets how long CBAC will maintain an idle TCP connection. The default is 1 hour (3,600 seconds).
ip inspect udp idle-time	Sets how long CBAC will maintain idle UDP sessions. The default is 30 seconds.
ip inspect dns-timeout	Sets how long CBAC will maintain an idle DNS name lookup session. The default is 5 seconds.
ip inspect max-incomplete high	Sets the maximum number of half-opened connections that CBAC will allow before it starts deleting them. The default is 500.
ip inspect max-incomplete low	Sets the number below which CBAC stops deleting half-open connections, once it starts deleting these connections. The default is 400.
ip inspect one-minute high	Sets the rate of new, half-open connections that triggers CBAC to start deleting them. The default is 500 per minute.

TABLE 5.1 Some Commands for Changing CBAC Timeouts and Thresholds *(continued)*

Command	Description
ip inspect one-minute low	Sets the rate below which CBAC stops deleting half-open connections, once it starts deleting these connections. The default is 400 per minute.
ip inspect tcp max-incomplete host	Sets the maximum number of half-open connections to the same host that CBAC will allow before starting to drop them. The default is 50.

Most of these commands should be familiar to you, but two deserve special mention:

ip inspect max-incomplete   These values can monitor both TCP and UDP sessions. *Incomplete TCP sessions* are sessions where the three-way handshake hasn't been completed. *Incomplete UDP sessions* are sessions where no return traffic has been detected. Once the maximum number of incomplete sessions is reached, CBAC begins deleting half-open sessions until their numbers total less than the minimum value.

ip inspect one-minute   These commands are similar in operation, but instead of monitoring the total number of incomplete TCP or UDP sessions, they monitor the *rate* at which incomplete TCP or UDP sessions are being established. A sudden surge in incomplete sessions can trigger CBAC to aggressively close them, which it does until the low threshold is reached.

Let's leave the defaults on the Lab_B router and continue on to the Port-to-Application Mapping section.

Configuring PAM

You ask, and Cisco delivers. Previous versions of CBAC assumed that applications were always hosted on the same well-known port. In the real world, this isn't always the case. Haven't you set up a rogue web server on some obscure port? Port-to-Application Mapping (PAM) lets you modify the default values of well-known ports and thus teach CBAC how to recognize these familiar apps in their new homes. Check out the default PAM mappings in Table 5.2.

These are the defaults. But what if you have an HTTP server running on port 8000? That's where PAM comes in. PAM allows you to map these applications or services to the ports you're really using and still get to enjoy all of CBAC's capabilities. The available options in your configuration look like this:

```
Lab_B#conf t
Lab_B(config)#ip port-map ?
  cuseeme        CUSeeMe Protocol
```

```
  dns          Domain Name Server
  exec         Remote Process Execution
  finger       Finger
  ftp          File Transfer Protocol
  gopher       Gopher
  h323         H.323 Protocol (e.g, MS NetMeeting, Intel Video Phone)
  http         Hypertext Transfer Protocol
  imap         Internet Message Access Protocol
  kerberos     Kerberos
  ldap         Lightweight Directory Access Protocol
  login        Remote login
  lotusnote    Lotus Note
  mgcp         Media Gateway Control Protocol
  ms-sql       Microsoft SQL
  msrpc        Microsoft Remote Procedure Call
  netshow      Microsoft NetShow
  nfs          Network File System
  nntp         Network News Transfer Protocol
  pop2         Post Office Protocol - Version 2
  pop3         Post Office Protocol - Version 3
  realmedia    RealNetwork's Realmedia Protocol
  rtsp         Real Time Streaming Protocol
  sap          SAP
  shell        Remote command
  sip          Session Initiation Protocol
  smtp         Simple Mail Transfer Protocol
  snmp         Simple Network Management Protocol
  sql-net      SQL-NET
  streamworks  StreamWorks Protocol
  sunrpc       SUN Remote Procedure Call
  sybase-sql   Sybase SQL
  tacacs       Login Host Protocol (TACACS)
  telnet       Telnet
  tftp         Trivial File Transfer Protocol
  vdolive      VDOLive Protocol
Lab_B(config)#ip port-map http port 8000
```

TABLE 5.2 Default Application Mappings

Application	Port
CUseeMe	7648
Exec	512
FTP	21
HTTP	80
H.323	1720
Login	513
MGCP	2427
MSRPC	135
NetShow	1755
RealMedia	7070
RTSP	554
RTSP	8554
Shell	514
SIP	5060
SMTP	25
SQL*Net	1521
StreamWorks	1558
SunRPC	111
Telnet	23
TFTP	69
VDOLive	7000

Configuring options such as these modifies the default port-mapping of HTTP. You can create multiple ports for the same application, but you'll receive a warning if you try to map an application to the well-known port of another application. You can use the no version of the ip port-map command to remove the configuration, and you can use the show ip port-map command to review the changes and current PAM settings:

```
Lab_B(config)#^Z
Lab_B#show ip port-map
Default mapping: vdolive        port 7000       system defined
Default mapping: sunrpc         port 111        system defined
Default mapping: netshow        port 1755       system defined
Default mapping: cuseeme        port 7648       system defined
Default mapping: tftp           port 69         system defined
Default mapping: rtsp           port 8554       system defined
Default mapping: realmedia      port 7070       system defined
Default mapping: streamworks    port 1558       system defined
Default mapping: ftp            port 21         system defined
Default mapping: telnet         port 23         system defined
Default mapping: rtsp           port 554        system defined
Default mapping: h323           port 1720       system defined
Default mapping: sip            port 5060       system defined
Default mapping: smtp           port 25         system defined
Default mapping: http           port 80         system defined
Default mapping: msrpc          port 135        system defined
Default mapping: exec           port 512        system defined
Default mapping: login          port 513        system defined
Default mapping: sql-net        port 1521       system defined
Default mapping: shell          port 514        system defined
Default mapping: mgcp           port 2427       system defined
Default mapping: http           port 8000       user defined
Lab_B#
```

Did you notice that the HTTP mapping on port 8000 is user-defined, but all the other ports are system-defined? You can set additional parameters for this command to get more than one application or port, as follows:

```
Lab_B#show ip port-map http
Default mapping: http           port 80         system defined
Default mapping: http           port 8000       user defined
Lab_B#show ip port-map port 8000
Default mapping: http           port 8000       user defined
Lab_B#
```

Defining Inspection Rules

You use *inspection rules* to define the applications and traffic types that you want to be inspected. Basically, this comes down to a named list that can have multiple lines, similar to an ACL. Most of the time, you configure only a single inspection rule on a router; but if you're applying CBAC in two directions, you have to create two inspection rules. You'll create a single inspection rule and apply it in a single direction for our corporate network example.

You should list all the applications that you want CBAC to monitor in the inspection rule. Generic TCP or UDP traffic is also allowed here. I've named the inspection rule IOSFW. Here it is on the Lab_B router:

```
Lab_B#conf t
Lab_B(config)#ip inspect name IOSFW ?
  cuseeme      CUSeeMe Protocol
  fragment     IP fragment inspection
  ftp          File Transfer Protocol
  h323         H.323 Protocol (e.g, MS NetMeeting, Intel Video Phone)
  http         HTTP Protocol
  netshow      Microsoft NetShow Protocol
  rcmd         R commands (r-exec, r-login, r-sh)
  realaudio    Real Audio Protocol
  rpc          Remote Prodedure Call Protocol
  rtsp         Real Time Streaming Protocol
  smtp         Simple Mail Transfer Protocol
  sqlnet       SQL Net Protocol
  streamworks  StreamWorks Protocol
  tcp          Transmission Control Protocol
  tftp         TFTP Protocol
  udp          User Datagram Protocol
  vdolive      VDOLive Protocol
Lab_B(config)#ip inspect name IOSFW ftp
Lab_B(config)#ip inspect name IOSFW h323
Lab_B(config)#ip inspect name IOSFW http
Lab_B(config)#ip inspect name IOSFW tcp
Lab_B(config)#ip inspect name IOSFW udp
Lab_B(config)#^Z
Lab_B#
```

You can see that this inspection rule is configured to inspect three protocols—FTP, H.323, and HTTP—plus all generic TCP and UCP traffic. If you want, you can include parameters for each protocol that control alerts, audit trails, and timeouts, as in the following example:

```
Lab_B#conf t
Lab_B(config)#ip inspect name IOSFW http ?
  alert        Turn on/off alert
  audit-trail  Turn on/off audit trail
  java-list    Specify a standard access-list to apply the Java blocking.
               If specified, MUST appear directly after option "http"
  timeout      Specify the inactivity timeout time
  <cr>
Lab_B(config)#ip inspect name IOSFW http alert ?
  off  Turn off alert
  on   Turn on alert
Lab_B(config)#ip inspect name IOSFW http alert on ?
  audit-trail  Turn on/off audit trail
  timeout      Specify the inactivity timeout time
  <cr>
Lab_B(config)#ip inspect name IOSFW http alert on audit-trail ?
  off  Turn off audit trail
  on   Turn on audit trail
Lab_B(config)#ip inspect name IOSFW http alert on audit-trail on
Lab_B(config)#^Z
Lab_B#
```

The ability to define inspection rules is important because several types of applications have special inspection features. For example, when you're configuring Java applet filtering, you can use ACLs to specify trusted applet sources such as these:

```
Lab_B#conf t
Lab_B(config)#ip inspect name IOSFW http java-list 10 alert on
Lab_B(config)#access-list 10 permit 172.16.2.0 0.0.0.255
Lab_B(config)#access-list 10 permit deny any
Lab_B(config)#^Z
Lab_B#
```

If the applet comes from a trusted site, as specified by the ACL, CBAC allows it through. If not, the applet is stripped. There are also specific inspection rules for IP packet fragmentation, RPC, and SMTP that you can apply to prevent certain types of attacks.

You're almost there! With the inspection rules defined, you're ready for the second-to-last step: applying the inspection rules and ACLs to interfaces.

Applying Inspection Rules and ACLs to Router Interfaces

Let's review what you set out to accomplish in the corporate network example and check your progress. You have a perimeter router (Lab_B) that you've been placing CBAC on, and you've configured alerts and audit trails, global timeouts, PAM, and an inspection rule. But you still need to allow access from the external network to the web server and the DNS server on appropriate ports. In addition, you need to let your internal users access the protocols you configured into your inspection rule, as well as give them general TCP and UDP services.

CBAC must be used in conjunction with ACLs. Remember, your inspection rule was to permit your internal clients dynamic access to specified protocols and to generic TCP and UDP services on the external network, while protecting them from any unwanted attacks. Cisco recommends the following guidelines for applying rules and ACLs to interfaces:

- On the interface where traffic initiates (in the corporate network example, the dirty DMZ):
  - Apply an ACL inward that permits only wanted traffic.
  - Apply the CBAC inspection rule in the inward direction that inspects wanted traffic.
- On all other interfaces:
  - Apply an ACL in the inward direction that denies all other traffic except traffic types not inspected by CBAC, such as Internet Control Message Protocol (ICMP).

Let's do this on the Lab_B router using the following commands:

```
Lab_B#conf t
Lab_B(config)#access-list 150 permit ip 172.16.1.0 0.0.0.255 any
Lab_B(config)#access-list 150 deny ip any any
Lab_B(config)#int f0/0
Lab_B(config-if)#ip inspect IOSFW in
Lab_B(config-if)#ip access-group 150 in
Lab_B(config-if)#^Z
Lab_B#
```

So far, so good. You've defined an access list for the interface where traffic initiates that permits wanted traffic (the internal 172.16.1.0 network addresses—you're assuming that the firewall is NATing other internal traffic). You've applied this ACL inbound on the internal interface and applied the CBAC inspection rule inbound on this same interface. Now let's protect that external interface using the following commands:

```
Lab_B#conf t
Lab_B(config)#access-list 151 permit tcp any host 172.16.1.2 eq www
Lab_B(config)#access-list 151 permit udp any host 172.16.1.3 eq domain
Lab_B(config)#access-list 151 deny ip any any
Lab_B(config)#int s1/0
```

```
Lab_B(config-if)#ip access-group 151 in
Lab_B(config-if)#^Z
Lab_B#
```

If you aren't familiar with CBAC, you might not like the looks of this—didn't you just block everything coming in from the Internet except requests to the web server and the DNS server? The `access-list 151` certainly makes it look as if you did. But remember that CBAC is listening to all incoming traffic on F0/0. So, when user requests to the Internet arrive there, CBAC, knowing those requests require responses, temporarily changes the ACL (151) to permit conversation between the local hosts and the Internet host. Once the conversation is over (or times out), CBAC removes the changes.

Suppose that a host on the Internet tries to access a local machine other than the web server or the DNS server. The request arrives at interface S1/0; but CBAC has no record of an open session between an internal host and that particular Internet host, so it hasn't changed the ACL. That packet is denied because the only exceptions to the ACL that will be allowed are those entered by CBAC. If bad guys try to make it seem as though they have an established TCP connection when they don't, their packets will be dropped.

The only items allowed in from the Internet are those allowed by ACL 151, which by default allows access to the web server and the DNS server. CBAC adds entries so that servers contacted by your internal users can respond to user requests. But when your internal users aren't accessing Internet services, CBAC leaves your network locked up tight.

Did I mention that it's possible to configure both internal and external CBAC on the same router? Cool, huh?

Configuring IP ACLs at the Interface

For CBAC to work properly, you must have an ACL in place. Because CBAC dynamically makes changes to the ACL to permit the specific conversations it sees—you can see them too with the `show ip access list` command—the ACL needs to be an extended ACL. In the preceding example, you used `access-list 151`. You may need to have additional permit entries to allow traffic types that CBAC can't predict, such as ICMP, for example.

Testing and Verifying CBAC

As with most IOS commands, a set of `show` and `debug` commands lets you test and verify the operation of CBAC. You can use the following commands to display CBAC operation.

The `show ip inspect config` command displays information about the entire global timeouts and thresholds configuration for CBAC as well as the inspection rule configuration, excluding interface information:

```
Lab_B#show ip inspect config
Session audit trail is enabled
```

```
Session alert is enabled
one-minute (sampling period) thresholds are [400:500] connections
max-incomplete sessions thresholds are [400:500]
max-incomplete tcp connections per host is 50. Block-time 0 minute.
tcp synwait-time is 30 sec -- tcp finwait-time is 5 sec
tcp idle-time is 3600 sec -- udp idle-time is 30 sec
dns-timeout is 5 sec
Inspection Rule Configuration
 Inspection name IOSFW
    ftp alert is on audit-trail is on timeout 3600
    h323 alert is on audit-trail is on timeout 3600
    http java-list 10 alert is on audit-trail is on timeout 3600
    tcp alert is on audit-trail is on timeout 3600
    udp alert is on audit-trail is on timeout 30
```

The show ip inspect interfaces command displays information about the interface configuration:

```
Lab_B#show ip inspect interfaces
Interface Configuration
 Interface FastEthernet0/0
  Inbound inspection rule is IOSFW
    ftp alert is on audit-trail is on timeout 3600
    h323 alert is on audit-trail is on timeout 3600
    http java-list 10 alert is on audit-trail is on timeout 3600
    tcp alert is on audit-trail is on timeout 3600
    udp alert is on audit-trail is on timeout 30
  Outgoing inspection rule is not set
  Inbound access list is 150
  Outgoing access list is not set
```

The show ip inspect name command displays information about the inspection rule configuration:

```
Lab_B#show ip inspect name IOSFW
Inspection name IOSFW
    ftp alert is on audit-trail is on timeout 3600
    h323 alert is on audit-trail is on timeout 3600
    http java-list 10 alert is on audit-trail is on timeout 3600
    tcp alert is on audit-trail is on timeout 3600
    udp alert is on audit-trail is on timeout 30
Lab_B#
```

And you can remove any and all CBAC by doing the following:

```
Lab_B#conf t
Lab_B(config)#no ip inspect
Lab_B(config)#^Z
Lab_B#show ip inspect interfaces
Lab_B#
```

If you do this, you'll wipe out all dynamic ACLs, reset all global timeouts, and delete all existing sessions—so be careful!

Summary

By now, I'm sure you can see that CBAC offers you much tighter security than you can hope to get through the use of ACLs. It can operate like a stateful firewall, keeping track of sessions and dynamically changing access lists to allow the passage of appropriate traffic.

The six steps that Cisco has defined to help you configure CBAC are as follows:

1. Set audit trails and alerts.
2. Set global timeouts and thresholds.
3. Define Port-to-Application Mapping (PAM).
4. Define inspection rules.
5. Apply inspection rules and ACLs to interfaces.
6. Test and verify CBAC.

By using these steps as outlined in this chapter, you can create and maintain a secure and cost-effective internetwork.

Because CBAC is so versatile, it can also be used to prevent certain types of DoS attacks, and it offers you many fine-tuning options, as well as lots of settings for values and timeouts to use to determine appropriate thresholds for your networks. Typically, you'd have to buy more hardware to provide these services, but not with CBAC.

Another example of CBAC's versatility is Port-to-Application Mapping (PAM), which allows you to modify the default values of well-known ports and teach CBAC how to recognize these applications.

And if you need it to, CBAC can generate real-time alerts and audit trails through the use of a Syslog server. This lets you monitor all enterprise alerts and audit trails at a single, centralized location.

To test and verify the operation of CBAC, use the command `show ip inspect config` to enable the session audit trail and the command `show ip inspect interfaces` to see the CBAC interface configuration.

Exam Essentials

Make sure you know the six steps for configuring CBAC. Cisco has outlined six steps for CBAC configuration:

1. Set audit trails and alerts.
2. Set global timeouts and thresholds.
3. Define Port-to-Application Mapping (PAM).
4. Define inspection rules.
5. Apply inspection rules and ACLs to interfaces.
6. Test and verify CBAC.

Be sure you know the global timeouts and thresholds and the commands for changing them. You need to know the commands for changing the global timeouts and thresholds, as well as the default values. Refer to Table 5.1 for a listing of all global timeouts and thresholds and how to change them.

Make sure you know the rules for applying ACLs in conjunction with CBAC. Know that CBAC needs an extended ACL to modify for return traffic. Here is what else you must know:

- On the interface where traffic initiates (in the corporate network example, the dirty DMZ), apply inward an ACL that permits only wanted traffic, and apply inward the CBAC inspection rule that inspects wanted traffic.
- On all other interfaces, apply inward an ACL that denies all other traffic except traffic types not inspected by CBAC (such as ICMP).

Be sure to review the commands to test CBAC, and know the command to disable it. There are three `show ip inspect` commands:

- The `show ip inspect config` command displays information about the entire global timeouts and thresholds configuration for CBAC as well as the inspection rule configuration, excluding interface information.
- The `show ip inspect interfaces` command displays information about the interface configuration.
- The `show ip inspect name` command displays information about the inspection rule configuration.

The `no ip inspect` command in global configuration mode disables all CBAC.

Chapter 6

Cisco IOS Firewall Authentication and Intrusion Detection

THE FOLLOWING SECUR EXAM TOPICS ARE COVERED IN THIS CHAPTER:

- ✓ Understanding the Cisco IOS Firewall Authentication Proxy
- ✓ Configuring the AAA server
- ✓ Configuring AAA
- ✓ Configuring the Authentication Proxy
- ✓ Verifying the Cisco IOS Firewall
- ✓ Understanding IOS Firewall IDS
- ✓ Initializing Cisco IOS Firewall IDS
- ✓ Configuring, disabling, and excluding signatures
- ✓ Creating and applying audit rules

Picture this: You're the networking/security guru working for a company located in the trendiest part of town—you know, where all the old, industrial brick buildings have been converted to cool lofts and chic, pricey offices with gourmet shops, martini bars, and art galleries at street level. Congrats—only, there's a catch. Although snappy and stylish, that edgy design house aesthetic spawned an office environment without cubes, doors, or privacy, where all the desks are out in one big open, collaborative, synergetic space. Said another way, every PC is physically accessible to any user who waits for the office to empty out at lunch or after work to do whatever they please on someone else's computer.

Of course, you have many different levels of employees in this office, and each one requires specific kinds of access to external networks, including the Internet. Assuming that you can't just give everyone full access to all external resources, how do you deal with this nightmare and configure (implement) access controls?

You could sit down, figure out who sits where, and scribble out some access control lists (ACLs). It will then take a half-nanosecond for your users to realize, "@#%&! I can't get to the Web from my PC. But if I wait for someone whose machine can get to the Internet to leave, I've got web access!"

What's your next move? Password-protect the machines? Implement policies about locking screensavers? Those strategies might help a bit, but do you think you'll really be able to get Mr. Know-It-All-VP, who doesn't know diddly about computers, to buy in? And what about shared machines—especially when users sharing the same machine have different security policies? Can you solve that one with an ACL?

All of this highlights a critical issue that you didn't have an effective solution for in the past. Tying ACLs to devices (IP addresses) was pretty much it; but doing that didn't help a lot, because you need to control organic life forms. How would you like to be able to attach an ACL to the user rather than to the resource? Well, now you can—that's the objective of the IOS Firewall Authentication Proxy, which we'll cover in the first part of this chapter.

But the Authentication Proxy is only a partial solution, because once you've got your users squared away, you still have to keep out spam e-mail, viruses, worms, hackers, and deranged former employees seeking to sabotage the company's business processes. It's idealistic to think that you can protect yourself from everyone or everything bent on seriously messing with your system, but there is a powerful tool that can help. The IOS Firewall intrusion detection system

(IDS) gives you more bang for your buck by allowing your IOS router to act as a Cisco Secure IDS sensor would; it can spot and react to potentially inappropriate or malicious packets. It can even be added into the CSIDS Director or Cisco VMS for inclusion in a centralized IDS monitoring system. I won't get into the whole should-you-or-shouldn't-you-profile debate; just know that in network security, you profile suspicious elements. It doesn't make sense to pat down a Mother Teresa packet while the shoe-bomber packet breezes through unquestioned.

The IOS Firewall IDS bases its profiling capabilities on IDS signatures that delineate the types of traffic that may be nasty. You, as the administrator, get to choose which signatures to deploy and how you want to react when patterns of network traffic match the signature. These IDS protections can be used against internal or external attacks and can be executed in conjunction with the other IOS Firewall features we've been discussing.

I'll show you how to configure the IOS Firewall IDS, but first, I'll start by giving you a brief operational overview and pointing out a few other IDS considerations. Then, I'll take you through the process of enabling the IOS Firewall IDS and manipulating the various available signatures. Finally, I'll show you how to create audit rules and verify your configuration.

Introduction to the Cisco IOS Firewall Authentication Proxy

Back in Chapter 1, "Introduction to Network Security," I stressed how important it is that you create a solid security policy to protect your network (and your job). This is because the IOS Firewall Authentication Proxy allows you to create and apply access control policies to *individuals* instead of to *addresses*. When your users move around, their access policies follow them, regardless of which IP address they happen to be using at any given moment. This technology helps you permit Sales Exec A to use the same username and password to log on to the docked laptop at her desk or to dial up from home or anywhere else. Unless Sales Exec A gives away her username and password, no one else gets to log in and pretend to be her or access her individual rights.

With the IOS Firewall Authentication Proxy in place, users are forced to authenticate before access through the IOS Firewall is granted. When a user attempts to initiate communications through the IOS Firewall, they're queried for a username and password, which are then sent to an external authentication, authorization, and accounting (AAA) server running either TACACS+ or RADIUS. The server responds to the firewall's request with a user profile that defines the specific rights and limitations for that individual user's access and is adopted by the firewall for the duration of the communication.

In order to authenticate to the firewall, users must initiate an HTTP session through it. When they do that, an HTTP window appears that's used for authentication, such as the one you see in Figure 6.1.

Users must initiate HTTP and successfully authenticate before other traffic types will be allowed—no HTTP first, no Telnet. After authentication, the user's profile dynamically modifies ACLs on the router to allow the user the specified access. If the user exceeds the idle timer (60 minutes by default), they have to reauthenticate and establish a new HTTP session before they can continue. Remember Sales Exec A? Let's say she took her work home, logged onto the Internet, and left the room before the idle time default elapsed. Now suppose she has a daughter who wanders into the room, sits down at her mom's computer, and accesses a chat room that way, as well. This could be a problem, right? The good news is that you can change that default setting. I'll show you how later in this chapter.

FIGURE 6.1 User authentication screen

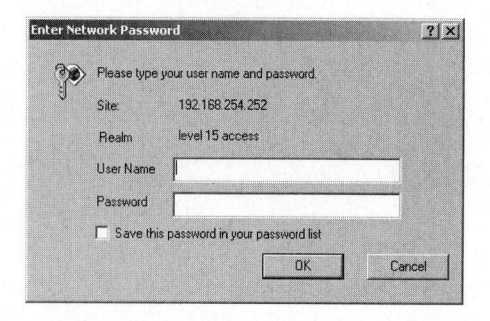

There are four easy steps to setting up the IOS Firewall Authentication Proxy:

1. Configure the AAA server (CSACS, and so on).
2. Configure AAA on the router.
3. Configure the IOS Firewall Authentication Proxy on the router.
4. Test and verify functionality.

As you can see, the first two steps merely get AAA up and running on the router and server. Once you do that, you add the IOS Firewall Authentication Proxy configuration to the router; then you test and verify its functionality. Like I said, it's easy.

Let's walk through these four steps, once again using the setup for the corporate network that you've been using so far in this book, which is illustrated in the following graphic.

In order to understand this chapter's material, you'll configure the CSACS server at 192.168.254.253 and configure the Lab_B perimeter router.

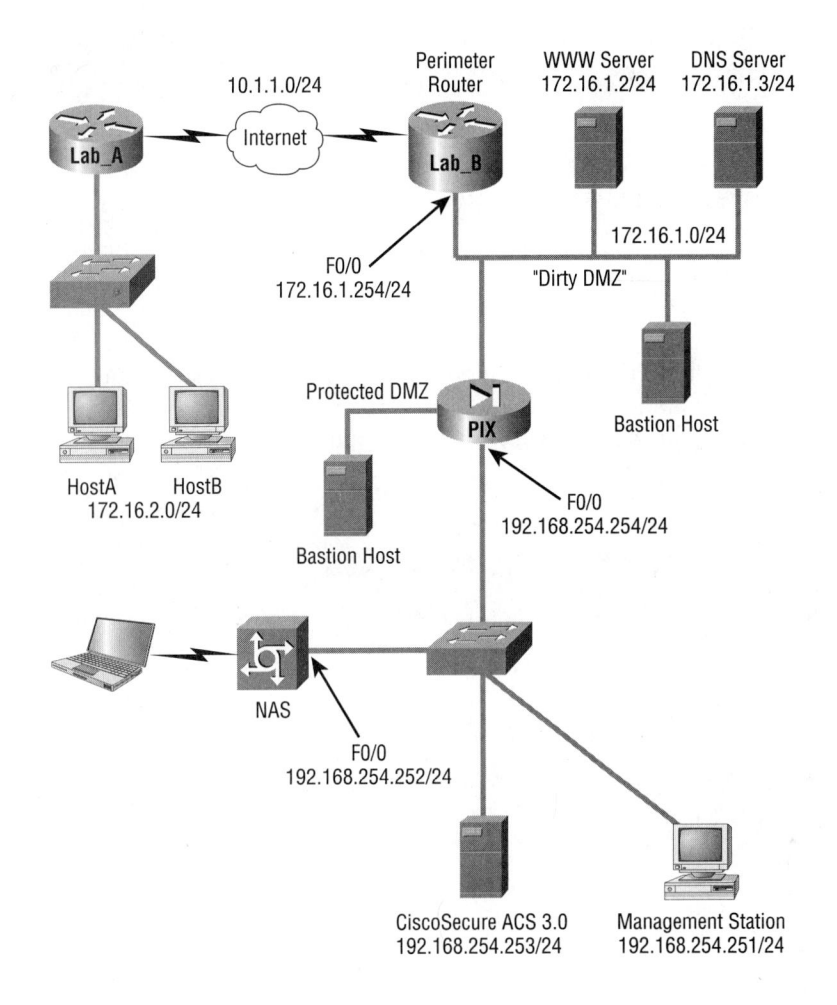

Configuring the AAA Server

As I said, the AAA server can be either a TACACS+ or a RADIUS server—you have lots of options. The IOS Firewall Authentication Proxy supports the following TACACS+ servers:

- CSACS for Windows 2000
- CSACS for Unix
- TACACS+ freeware

The IOS Firewall Authentication Proxy also supports the following RADIUS servers:

- CSACS for Windows 2000
- CSACS for Unix
- Lucent
- Other standard RADIUS servers

The first step in setting up the IOS Firewall Authentication Proxy is to configure the AAA server to support it. You'll use the CSACS for Windows server from the corporate network example to do that. Begin by selecting Interface Configuration from the navigation bar to configure TACACS+, as illustrated in Figure 6.2.

Next, select Group Setup from the navigation bar and edit the settings for your group. Select the Auth-Proxy and Custom Attributes check boxes, and then add your ACL using the appropriate syntax (I'll cover that in a minute), as shown in Figure 6.3.

FIGURE 6.2 Interface configuration for TACACS+

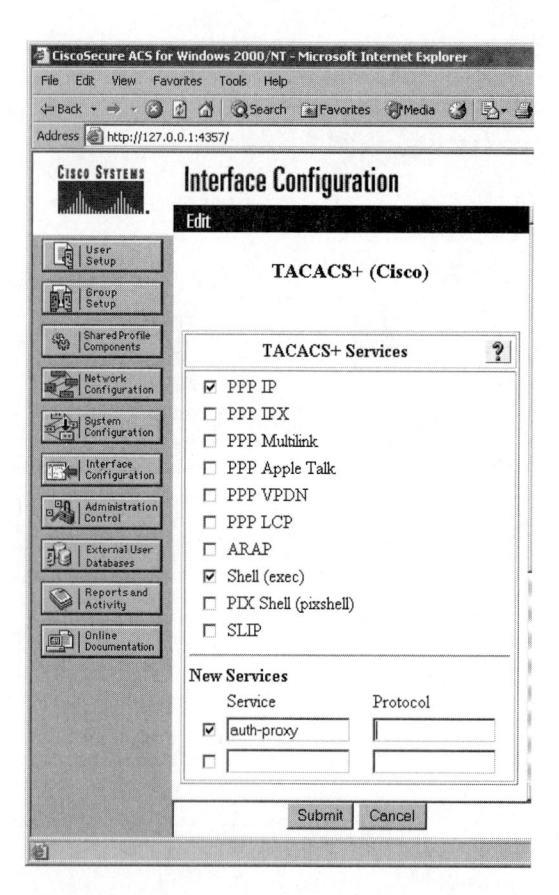

When configuring the ACLs in the AAA server, you use syntax that's similar but not identical to what you use in a router. The similarities make the configuration almost intuitive, but it's also easy to make a mistake if you're not careful. For instance, the following output shows an example of an ACL that allows all traffic after authentication:

```
proxyacl#1=permit ip any any
priv-lvl=15
```

Here's an even more specific example:

```
proxyacl#1=permit tcp any any eq www
proxyacl#2=permit tcp any any eq ftp
proxyacl#3=permit tcp any host 192.168.55.3 eq smtp
priv-lvl=15
```

FIGURE 6.3 Group setup for TACACS+

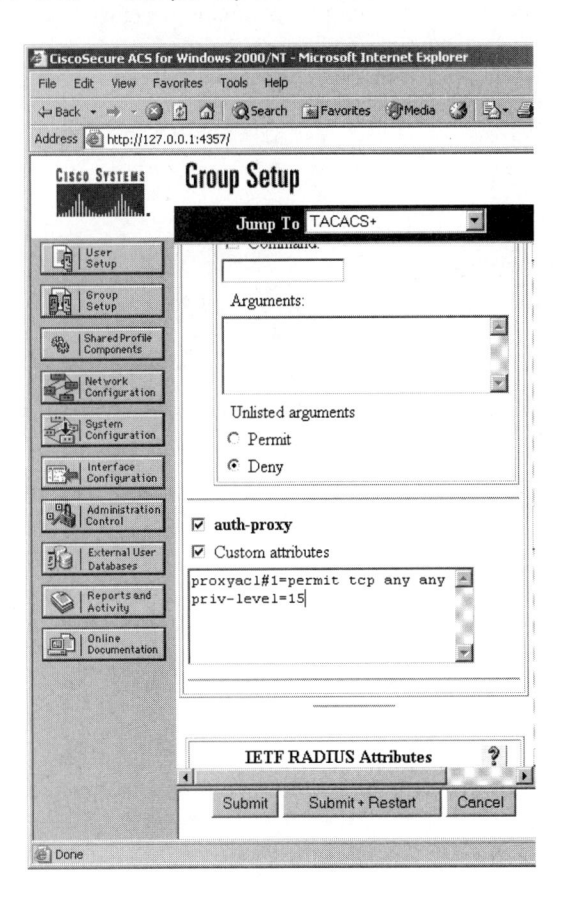

Combining both of these examples with your past experience with ACLs in the Cisco IOS should help you get the syntax down. Here are a few general rules to keep in mind:

- Only use `permit` statements—no `deny` statements.
- The source address must be set to `any`. These addresses will be dynamically replaced with actual source addresses in operation.
- End each list by setting the privilege level to 15.

At this point, the configuration of the AAA server is complete, but you still have to configure AAA on the router and then configure the Authentication Proxy before you can validate your work here.

Configuring AAA

Now that the CSACS server is configured, let's move on to configuring the router that will act as the IOS Firewall Authentication Proxy. First, you enable AAA on the router in preparation for configuring the IOS Firewall Authentication Proxy by following these six steps:

1. Enable AAA.
2. Configure the authentication protocol.
3. Configure the authorization protocol.
4. Specify the TACACS+ server and key.
5. Create an ACL to allow AAA traffic to the router.
6. Enable the router's HTTP server to use AAA.

I'll go over each of these steps separately while you configure the Lab_B router.

Enabling AAA

You enable AAA by using the `aaa new-model` command in global configuration mode:

```
Lab_B#conf t
Lab_B(config)#aaa new-model
Lab_B(config)#^Z
Lab_B#
```

The router is now prepared for further AAA configuration. (Remember, if you want to remove AAA from the router, you can use the `no aaa new-model` command in global configuration mode.)

Configuring the Authentication Protocol

Next, enable AAA authentication. You can do this several different ways, and you can also specify multiple methods if you want. Here's the configuration on the Lab_B router:

```
Lab_B#conf t
Lab_B(config)#aaa authentication ?
  arap           Set authentication lists for arap.
```

```
attempts         Set the maximum number of authentication attempts
banner           Message to use when starting login/authentication.
enable           Set authentication list for enable.
fail-message     Message to use for failed login/authentication.
login            Set authentication lists for logins.
nasi             Set authentication lists for NASI.
password-prompt  Text to use when prompting for a password
ppp              Set authentication lists for ppp.
username-prompt  Text to use when prompting for a username

Lab_B(config)#aaa authentication login ?
  WORD     Named authentication list.
  default  The default authentication list.

Lab_B(config)#aaa authentication login default ?
  enable      Use enable password for authentication.
  group       Use Server-group
  line        Use line password for authentication.
  local       Use local username authentication.
  local-case  Use case-sensitive local username authentication.
  none        NO authentication.

Lab_B(config)#aaa authentication login default group ?
  WORD     Server-group name
  radius   Use list of all Radius hosts.
  tacacs+  Use list of all Tacacs+ hosts.

Lab_B(config)#aaa authentication login default group tacacs+
Lab_B(config)#^Z
Lab_B#
```

In this example, you specify the server-group authentication using a TACACS+ server. If necessary, you could specify an additional authentication method besides TACACS+.

Configuring the Authorization Protocol

As with the authentication protocol, a number of choices are available for specifying the authorization protocol for AAA. In this case, specify the authorization for the IOS Firewall Authentication Proxy service, which is reflected in the command syntax. Here's how the Lab_B router configuration looks now:

```
Lab_B#conf t
Lab_B(config)#aaa authorization ?
```

```
auth-proxy          For Authentication Proxy Services
cache               For AAA cache configuration
commands            For exec (shell) commands.
config-commands     For configuration mode commands.
configuration       For downloading configurations from AAA server
exec                For starting an exec (shell).
network             For network services. (PPP, SLIP, ARAP)
reverse-access      For reverse access connections
```

```
Lab_B(config)#aaa authorization auth-proxy ?
  default  The default authorization list.

Lab_B(config)#aaa authorization auth-proxy default ?
  group  Use server-group.

Lab_B(config)#aaa authorization auth-proxy default group ?
  WORD     Server-group name
  radius   Use list of all Radius hosts.
  tacacs+  Use list of all Tacacs+ hosts.

Lab_B(config)#aaa authorization auth-proxy default group tacacs+
Lab_B(config)#^Z
Lab_B#
```

As with the authentication protocol, you're using TACACS+, but you could specify multiple authorization protocols if necessary.

Specifying the TACACS+ Server and Key

The router certainly needs a TACACS+ server and server key configured, and you can even configure multiple TACACS+ servers. The IOS Firewall Authentication Proxy will query them in the order you enter them. The no tacacs-server host command removes individual servers from the list. Remember, you've designated the CSACS server at 192.168.254.253 in the corporate network example. Here's the Lab_B router configuration:

```
Lab_B#conf t
Lab_B(config)#tacacs-server host 192.168.254.253
Lab_B(config)#tacacs-server key todd
Lab_B(config)#^Z
Lab_B#
```

Creating an ACL to Allow AAA Traffic to the Router

Now you'll create an access list that will allow incoming TACACS+ traffic from the CSACS box to the router. You'll also permit all Internet Control Message Protocol (ICMP) traffic but deny everything else. Here's how Lab_B's output looks now:

```
Lab_B#conf t
Lab_B(config)#access-list 155 permit tcp host 192.168.254.253 eq tacacs host 172.16.1.254
Lab_B(config)#access-list 155 permit icmp any any
Lab_B(config)#access-list 155 deny ip any any
Lab_B(config)#int fast0/0
Lab_B(config-if)#ip access-group 155 in
Lab_B(config)#^Z
Lab_B#
```

Does it seem as though what you just did totally screwed things up? No worries. Remember, just as with CBAC, this ACL won't be what it looks like right off the bat. In a second, when you apply the IOS Firewall Authentication Proxy to this interface, all appropriate network traffic will flow, and all will be well. But even so, there are a few important things to keep in mind when creating this ACL. First, the source address in the first line is the CSACS server, so you have to be sure to allow traffic types that are consistent with the authentication and authorization methods specified earlier (TACACS+ and/or RADIUS). Second, the destination will be the IP address of the interface closest to the CSACS server. And finally, don't forget to explicitly deny all other IP traffic!

Enabling the Router's HTTP Server to Use AAA

You've enabled the HTTP server on the router and told it to use AAA for authentication. Check out the configuration on Lab_B now:

```
Lab_B#conf t
Lab_B(config)#ip http server
Lab_B(config)#ip http ?
  access-class    Restrict access by access-class
  authentication  Set http authentication method
  path            Set base path for HTML
  port            HTTP port
  server          Enable HTTP server

Lab_B(config)#ip http authentication ?
  aaa     Use AAA access control methods
  enable  Use enable passwords
  local   Use local username and passwords
```

```
path    Set base path for HTML
tacacs  Use tacacs to authorize user
```

```
Lab_B(config)#ip http authentication aaa
Lab_B(config)#^Z
Lab_B#
```

Now that Lab B's AAA configuration is complete, the foundation is in place for the IOS Firewall Authentication Proxy configuration. If you need a break, now's a great time to take one.

Configuring the Authentication Proxy

With the AAA configuration in place, the Authentication Proxy configuration is a breeze. The first thing to do is to specify the Authentication Proxy idle timeout value. This is the amount of time in minutes that idle connections will be maintained by the Authentication Proxy. The default value is 60 minutes, which may or may not work for you. Remember the earlier example of the Sales Exec and her daughter? Let's cut that default time in half. Here's the Lab_B router's output:

```
Lab_B#conf t
Lab_B(config)#ip auth-proxy auth-cache-time 30
Lab_B(config-if)#^Z
Lab_B#
```

You can reset this to the default by using the `no ip auth-proxy auth-cache-time` command in global configuration mode.

Next, create an Authentication Proxy rule and name it `toddlock`:

```
Lab_B#conf t
Lab_B(config)#ip auth-proxy name toddlock ?
  http  HTTP Protocol
  <cr>

Lab_B(config)#ip auth-proxy name toddlock http
Lab_B(config)#^Z
Lab_B#
```

Now apply the Authentication Proxy rule to an interface—Fast Ethernet 0/0 on Lab_B:

```
Lab_B#conf t
Lab_B(config)#int fast0/0
Lab_B(config-if)#ip auth-proxy ?
  WORD  Name of authenticaion proxy rule
```

```
Lab_B(config-if)#ip auth-proxy toddlock
Lab_B(config-if)#^Z
Lab_B#
```

You could use an ACL to control which devices can use the IOS Firewall Authentication Proxy: The command `ip auth-proxy name toddlock http list 50` creates an Authentication Proxy rule. The additional `list 50` parameter refers to the standard IP access list 50 to determine which source addresses can be authenticated. You didn't add that, so in the preceding configuration, all hosts are prompted for authentication. If you want to limit hosts that have the ability to authenticate out, you can do so using this ACL parameter.

Now that you're through, it's time to see if everything's working. Next, you'll learn about testing and verification commands.

Testing and Verifying Your Configuration

There are several commands for troubleshooting and validating the operation of the IOS Firewall Authentication Proxy. The syntax of these commands is pretty typical, so if you've made it this far in the book, you could probably guess most, if not all, of the commands. But just in case, I'll briefly explain in this section the **show** commands, the **debug** commands, and the commands for clearing the cache.

show Commands

You need to know three primary **show** commands for checking the contents of the IOS Firewall Authorization Proxy cache, the global configuration parameters, and statistics. Here are some examples demonstrated on the Lab_B router:

```
Lab_B#show ip auth-proxy cache
Authentication Proxy Cache
 Client IP 172.16.1.100 Port 2326, timeout 30, state HTTP_INIT

Lab_B#show ip auth-proxy configuration
Authentication global cache time is 30 minutes
Authentication Proxy Rule Configuration
 Auth-proxy name toddlock
    http list not specified auth-cache-time 30 minutes

Lab_B#show ip auth-proxy statistics
Authentication Proxy Statistics
    proxied client number 1
Lab_B#
```

debug Commands

The number of debug commands available varies a bit as you change IOS versions. The following is a demonstration of the debug ip auth-proxy function-trace command from the previous example that hit Cisco's website (represented here by 1.1.1.1):

```
Lab_B#debug ip auth-proxy ?
  function-trace    Auth-Proxy function trace
  object-creation   Authentication Proxy object creations
  object-deletion   Authentication Proxy object deletions
  timers            Authentication Proxy timer related events

Lab_B#debug ip auth-proxy function-trace
AUTH-PROXY Function Trace debugging is on
Lab_B#
00:55:43: AUTH-PROXY FUNC: auth_proxy_fast_path
00:55:43: AUTH-PROXY auth_proxy_find_conn_info :
    find srcaddr - 172.16.1.100, dstaddr - 1.1.1.1
       ip-srcaddr 172.16.1.100
       pak-srcaddr 0.0.0.0


00:55:43: AUTH-PROXY FUNC: auth_proxy_process_path
00:55:43:   SYN SEQ 537346255 LEN 0
00:55:43: dst_addr 3473868035 src_addr 2886730084 dst_port 80 src_port 2328
00:55:43: AUTH-PROXY auth_proxy_find_conn_info :
    find srcaddr - 172.16.1.100, dstaddr - 1.1.1.1
       ip-srcaddr 172.16.1.100
       pak-srcaddr 0.0.0.0


00:55:43: clientport 2327 state 0
00:55:43: AUTH-PROXY FUNC: auth_proxy_fast_path
00:55:43: AUTH-PROXY auth_proxy_find_conn_info :
    find srcaddr - 172.16.1.100, dstaddr - 1.1.1.1
       ip-srcaddr 172.16.1.100
       pak-srcaddr 0.0.0.0


00:55:43: AUTH-PROXY FUNC: auth_proxy_fast_path
00:55:43: AUTH-PROXY auth_proxy_find_conn_info :
    find srcaddr - 172.16.1.100, dstaddr - 1.1.1.1
```

```
        ip-srcaddr 172.16.1.100
        pak-srcaddr 0.0.0.0
Lab_B#
```

Clearing the Cache

Finally, you need to know the commands for maintaining and clearing the cache. Earlier, you set a timeout parameter for inactive sessions, so these sessions will time out on their own eventually; but there may be times when you want to clear some or all of the connections and force users to reauthenticate. The following output includes the command-line help and an example of clearing all connections:

```
Lab_B#clear ip auth-proxy ?
  cache  Delete auth-proxy cache entries

Lab_B#clear ip auth-proxy cache ?
  *        Delete all auth-proxy cache
  A.B.C.D  Address to delete

Lab_B#clear ip auth-proxy cache *
Lab_B#
```

Your users are now happily typing in usernames and passwords to access external resources, and you've risen above the challenge described at the beginning of this chapter. Now all you have left to do is check each monitor and look under all the keyboards for those little stickies with usernames and passwords scribbled on them, and you're good to go!

Introduction to the Cisco IOS Firewall IDS

Let's make sure you've got the terminology specific to the IOS Firewall IDS straight. I mentioned that the intrusion detection system (IDS) functions on *signatures*. Each signature profiles a specific type of attack or potential problem.

> **NOTE** For specific information on signatures and their descriptions, see www.cisco.com or your CSIDS Director documentation.

Let's begin with the two types of signature implementations:

- *Atomic signatures* trigger based on a single packet.
- *Compound signatures* trigger based on multiple packets.

Atomic signatures are much easier to support for the router because they can evaluate each packet independently. Compound signatures work by buffering previous packets for comparison against current packets to see if traffic trends match their signature, which means that they cost more memory.

Signature types are defined as follows:

- *Info signatures* are informational—they notice when an information-gathering activity such as a port scan is underway.
- *Attack signatures* represent malicious activities such as DoS attacks or inappropriate Application-layer calls.

So, you end up with four types of signatures:

- Info atomic
- Info compound
- Attack atomic
- Attack compound

Although you definitely want to defend your network against attacks, you don't need a nuclear device to kill a mouse in your house; nothing's free, and every precaution you take costs you something. The key issues to consider when deploying the IOS Firewall IDS are

- Memory usage
- Performance impact
- Signature coverage

I'm bringing this up because the IOS Firewall IDS can have a seriously significant impact on router memory and performance. Some signatures have the capability to monitor not just Layer 3 or Layer 4 functions, but application-level functioning as well. Realize that with such signatures enabled, each packet traversing the router must be inspected (potentially up to the Application layer), and decoding all those headers tends to guzzle resources. The more signatures that are enabled, the worse your mileage will be; and with signatures for 59 common attacks currently included with the IOS Firewall IDS, you can imagine the potential impact. And that's nothing—the CSIDS Sensor includes over 300 signatures!

The IOS Firewall IDS is an inline IDS and has a number of options available as reactions to signature matches, so it offers a good bit of flexibility for you in deciding what you want it to do when it sees a problem. Basically, you get three self-explanatory choices of action, which can also be used in combination with one another:

- *Alarm* means to (surprise) generate an alarm to either a CSIDS Director or a Syslog server.
- *Reset* sends a TCP reset to both session participants if the packet used TCP.
- *Drop* means to immediately drop the packet.

Reset doesn't imply drop—it will still forward the packet. For this reason, reset and drop are often used together.

With these preliminaries out of the way, let's add the IOS Firewall IDS configuration to your trusty Lab_B router.

Initializing the Cisco IOS Firewall IDS

The first thing you'll do is configure the IOS Firewall IDS to notify the Syslog server at 172.16.1.200. Remember that you have the choice of notifying either a Syslog server or a CSIDS Director, and you can see that choice in the following output. Configure it to notify the Syslog server:

```
Lab_B#conf t
Lab_B(config)#ip audit notify ?
  log          Send events as syslog messages
  nr-director  Send events to the nr-director

Lab_B(config)#ip audit notify log
Lab_B(config)#logging 172.16.1.200
Lab_B(config)#^Z
Lab_B#
```

And yes—the no form of the ip audit notify command removes event notifications from the router.

Configuring, Disabling, and Excluding Signatures

Only the acutely disturbed like getting spam e-mail. The rest of us tolerate the pain and hope/pray/chant/scream for the day when every router in the world runs an IOS Firewall IDS with spam protection enabled.

Want to put that spam back in the can? Here's how! In the following example, you can see how to limit the number of Simple Mail Transfer Protocol (SMTP) destination addresses using the IOS Firewall IDS:

```
Lab_B#conf t
Lab_B(config)#ip audit ?
  attack     Specify default action for attack signatures
  info       Specify default action for informational signatures
  name       Specify an IDS audit rule
  notify     Specify the notification mechanisms (nr-director or log) for the
               alarms
  po         Specify nr-director's PostOffice information (for sending events
               to the nr-directors)
  protected  Specify addresses that are on a protected network
  signature  Add a policy to a signature
  smtp       Specify SMTP Mail spam threshold

Lab_B(config)#ip audit smtp ?
```

```
   spam     Specify the threshold for spam signature
   <cr>

Lab_B(config)#ip audit smtp spam ?
   <1-65535>  Threshold of correspondents to trigger alarm

Lab_B(config)#ip audit smtp spam 100
Lab_B(config)#^Z
Lab_B#
```

By following the context-sensitive help, you can see the parameter definitions in the final `ip audit smtp spam 100` command. The default maximum number of recipients is 250; here, you change it to 100. If only everyone on the Internet would do this, we could realize the dream of a spamless Internet utopia.

Disabling Signatures

As I said, running signatures noshes resources, so you probably don't want to run every signature available. You probably won't need them all anyway, so let's disable signature 3102 on the Lab_B router.

> **Note:** Signature 3102 is an attack compound signature. It's a Sendmail Invalid Sender signature that triggers when the From: field is a pipe (|) symbol.

Here's the command syntax for removing this signature:

```
Lab_B#conf t
Lab_B(config)#ip audit signature ?
   <1-65535>  Signature to be configured

Lab_B(config)#ip audit signature 3102 ?
   disable  Disable the specified signature
   list     Specify a standard access list to match
   <cr>

Lab_B(config)#ip audit signature 3102 disable
Lab_B(config)#^Z
Lab_B#
```

But what if you decide that you need the signature back? You use the **no** form of the command to restore it:

```
Lab_B#conf t
Lab_B(config)#no ip audit signature 3102 disable
```

```
Lab_B(config)#^Z
Lab_B#
```

Excluding Signatures by Host or Network

Suppose you want to get surgical and apply a signature *selectively* instead of completely disabling it. You can do that by using an ACL to pick and choose specific hosts and/or networks that you don't want a given signature to apply to. Here's an example:

```
Lab_B#conf t
Lab_B(config)#ip audit signature 3102 ?
  disable  Disable the specified signature
  list     Specify a standard access list to match
  <cr>

Lab_B(config)#ip audit signature 3102 list 75
Lab_B(config)#access-list 75 deny host 172.16.1.50
Lab_B(config)#access-list 75 deny 192.160.1.0 0.0.0.255
Lab_B(config)#access-list 75 permit any
Lab_B(config)#^Z
Lab_B#
```

This kind of ACL includes `deny` statements for hosts or networks to exclude them from the signature. It must end with a `permit any` command to indicate that all other networks and hosts should still be subjected to it.

Creating and Applying Audit Rules

Let's begin tackling this section by defining default actions for both info and attack signature types and then creating an *audit rule*. Then you'll apply the audit rule to an interface and specify a direction.

Setting Default Actions

Recall the three possible actions the IOS Firewall IDS can take when a signature is matched: alarm, reset, or drop. You can use any one or any combination of these actions, but the default is to alarm:

```
Lab_B#conf t
Lab_B(config)#ip audit ?
  attack   Specify default action for attack signatures
  info     Specify default action for informational signatures
```

```
  name       Specify an IDS audit rule
  notify     Specify the notification mechanisms (nr-director or log) for the
               alarms
  po         Specify nr-director's PostOffice information (for sending events to
               the nr-directors
  protected  Specify addresses that are on a protected network
  signature  Add a policy to a signature
  smtp       Specify SMTP Mail spam threshold

Lab_B(config)#ip audit info ?
  action  Specify the actions

Lab_B(config)#ip audit info action ?
  alarm  Generate events for matching signatures
  drop   Drop packets matching signatures
  reset  Reset the connection (if applicable)
Lab_B(config)#ip audit info action alarm
```

This takes care of the info signatures, leaving them set to the default action of alarm. To change the action for attack signatures to both drop and reset in addition to alarm, check out the following example:

```
Lab_B(config)#ip audit attack ?
  action  Specify the actions

Lab_B(config)#ip audit attack action ?
  alarm  Generate events for matching signatures
  drop   Drop packets matching signatures
  reset  Reset the connection (if applicable)

Lab_B(config)#ip audit attack action alarm ?
  drop   Drop packets matching signatures
  reset  Reset the connection (if applicable)
  <cr>

Lab_B(config)#ip audit attack action alarm drop ?
  reset  Reset the connection (if applicable)
  <cr>

Lab_B(config)#ip audit attack action alarm drop reset ?
  <cr>
```

```
Lab_B(config)#ip audit attack action alarm drop reset
Lab_B(config)#^Z
Lab_B#
```

Look at the context-sensitive help offered in the preceding example, and note that after setting the alarm action, you still have the option to drop and/or reset. Also, the option <cr> becomes available only after you add all three actions.

Creating an Audit Rule

With the default settings out of the way, you're ready to create an audit rule and give it a name. A little later, you'll apply it to an interface. As with the default actions you just ran through, you can specify a list of actions for the audit rule based on both info and action signatures. Replicating what you did with these two signatures previously and naming your audit rule `toddaudit`, this configuration on the Lab_B router looks like the following:

```
Lab_B#conf t
Lab_B(config)#ip audit name ?
  WORD  Name of audit specfication

Lab_B(config)#ip audit name toddaudit ?
  attack  All attack signatures
  info    All informational signatures

Lab_B(config)#ip audit name toddaudit info ?
  action  Specify action(s) for matching signatures
  list    Specify a standard access list
  <cr>

Lab_B(config)#ip audit name toddaudit info action ?
  alarm  Generate events for matching signatures
  drop   Drop packets matching signatures
  reset  Reset the connection (if applicable)

Lab_B(config)#ip audit name toddaudit info action alarm
Lab_B(config)#ip audit name toddaudit ?
  attack  All attack signatures
  info    All informational signatures

Lab_B(config)#ip audit name toddaudit attack ?
  action  Specify action(s) for matching signatures
  list    Specify a standard access list
  <cr>
```

```
Lab_B(config)#ip audit name toddaudit attack action ?
  alarm  Generate events for matching signatures
  drop   Drop packets matching signatures
  reset  Reset the connection (if applicable)

Lab_B(config)#ip audit name toddaudit attack action alarm ?
  drop   Drop packets matching signatures
  reset  Reset the connection (if applicable)
  <cr>

Lab_B(config)#ip audit name toddaudit attack action alarm drop ?
  reset  Reset the connection (if applicable)
  <cr>

Lab_B(config)#ip audit name toddaudit attack action alarm drop reset ?
  <cr>

Lab_B(config)#ip audit name toddaudit attack action alarm drop reset
Lab_B(config)#^Z
Lab_B#
```

Again, the context-sensitive help demonstrates the ways you can further define the available parameters.

Applying the Audit Rule

Now that you've created the audit rule, it's time to apply it to an interface. The following example applies the toddaudit audit rule to the fast0/1 interface on the Lab_B router:

```
Lab_B#conf t
Lab_B(config)#int fast0/1
Lab_B(config-if)#ip audit ?
  WORD  Name of audit defined

Lab_B(config-if)#ip audit toddaudit ?
  in   Inbound audit
  out  Outbound audit

Lab_B(config-if)#ip audit toddaudit in ?
  <cr>
```

```
Lab_B(config-if)#ip audit toddaudit in
Lab_B(config-if)#^Z
Lab_B#
```

The direction in which you apply the audit rule makes a huge difference in the function of the IOS Firewall IDS. If you choose inbound on an interface, packets are audited before any ACLs are applied. But if you opt for outbound, packets may be discarded by inbound ACLs on other interfaces before the IOS Firewall IDS has a chance to evaluate them. This could be bad—it means that precious alerts and resets could be missed because the IDS is never even given a chance to see these packets. Personally, I like the option of evaluating all packets that try to attack, because doing so helps me refine my security policy and plug any holes. That's why you see the IOS Firewall IDS applied inbound on the Lab_B router in the preceding example.

With everything in place so far, it's time to define which network is to be protected by the router. Here's the `ip audit` command on the Lab_B router:

```
Lab_B#conf t
Lab_B(config)#ip audit po protected 172.16.1.1 to 172.16.1.254
Lab_B(config-if)#^Z
Lab_B#
```

Realize that once the audit rule is in place, several—even many—signatures may be scrutinizing packets. The different modules are evaluated in the following order:

1. IP
2. ICMP (if applicable)
3. TCP or UDP
4. Application-level protocol

If a signature match is made, the appropriate action is taken.

Verifying the Configuration

It's not a perfect world, and not everything runs smoothly the first time, right? As you might expect, several **show** commands are available to you for verifying and troubleshooting the IOS Firewall IDS. Here's the output from the most useful **show** command:

```
Lab_B#show ip audit ?
  all            IDS all available information
  configuration  IDS configuration
  interfaces     IDS interfaces
  name           IDS name
  sessions       IDS sessions
  statistics     IDS statistics
```

```
Lab_B#show ip audit statistics
Interfaces configured for audit 1
Session creations since subsystem startup or last reset 0
Current session counts (estab/half-open/terminating) [0:0:0]
Maxever session counts (estab/half-open/terminating) [0:0:0]
Last session created never
Last statistic reset never

Post Office is not enabled - No connections are active

Lab_B#show ip audit configuration
Event notification through syslog is enabled
Event notification through Net Director is disabled
Default action(s) for info signatures is alarm
Default action(s) for attack signatures is alarm drop reset
Default threshold of recipients for spam signature is 100
Signature 3102 list 75
PostOffice:HostID:0 OrgID:0 Msg dropped:0
     :Curr Event Buf Size:0  Configured:100
Post Office is not enabled - No connections are active
Audit Rule Configuration
 Audit name toddaudit
    info actions alarm
    attack actions alarm drop reset

Lab_B#show ip audit interface
Interface Configuration
 Interface FastEthernet0/1
  Inbound IDS audit rule is toddaudit
    info actions alarm
    attack actions alarm drop reset
  Outgoing IDS audit rule is not set
Lab_B#
```

The preceding statistics indicate a largely idle network, but the configuration and interface output points to the work you've done so far and checks out. There are also several **debug** command options available:

```
Lab_B#debug ip audit ?
   detailed         Audit Detailed debug records
   ftp-cmd          Audit FTP commands and responses
   ftp-token        Audit FTP tokens
```

```
function-trace     Audit function trace
icmp               Audit ICMP packets
ip                 Audit IP packets
object-creation    Audit Object Creations
object-deletion    Audit Object Deletions
rpc                Audit RPC
smtp               Audit SMTP
tcp                Audit TCP
tftp               Audit TFTP
timers             Audit Timer related events
udp                Audit UDP

Lab_B#
```

Stopping the IOS Firewall IDS

Sometimes you just have to pull the plug, and in order to pull it, you have to know where it is. If you need to kill the IOS Firewall IDS lights, there are several steps to take. First, let's start with the `show ip audit configuration` screen again to verify that the configuration is still in place:

```
Lab_B#show ip audit configuration
Event notification through syslog is enabled
Event notification through Net Director is disabled
Default action(s) for info signatures is alarm
Default action(s) for attack signatures is alarm drop reset
Default threshold of recipients for spam signature is 100
Signature 3102 list 75
PostOffice:HostID:0 OrgID:0 Msg dropped:0
    :Curr Event Buf Size:0  Configured:100
Post Office is not enabled - No connections are active
Audit Rule Configuration
 Audit name toddaudit
    info actions alarm
    attack actions alarm drop reset
```

Yup—it's there.

Next, use the `clear ip audit configuration` command to disable IDS, remove all IDS configuration, and release all dynamic resources:

```
Lab_B#clear ip audit configuration
```

And finally (as always), you must verify that it did what it was supposed to do. Look at the output from the `show ip audit configuration` command:

```
Lab_B#show ip audit configuration
Event notification through syslog is enabled
Event notification through Net Director is disabled
Default action(s) for info signatures is alarm
Default action(s) for attack signatures is alarm
Default threshold of recipients for spam signature is 250
PostOffice:HostID:0 OrgID:0 Msg dropped:0
     :Curr Event Buf Size:0  Configured:100
Post Office is not enabled - No connections are active
Lab_B#
```

It's good to go—all values have been reset to the defaults.

Summary

The IOS Firewall was introduced in Chapter 5, "Context-Based Access Control Configuration," which explained CBAC, but this chapter covered two of its critically important additional capabilities:

- Authentication Proxy
- Intrusion detection system (IDS)

The IOS Firewall Authentication Proxy bestows upon the networking world the ability to control user access based on *users* rather than on IP addresses or other device information. In the IOS Firewall world, users are forced to authenticate before accessing external resources. Their now-personalized access policies are retrieved from centralized AAA servers and follow them wherever they roam on the network.

Add to the Authentication Proxy the IOS Firewall IDS—a capable guard with the ability to alert, reset, and drop when security signatures are matched—and you can select which signatures to deactivate, or you can selectively apply signatures using ACLs.

Exam Essentials

Remember the two types of AAA servers you can use for the IOS Authentication Proxy. TACACS+ and RADIUS are the two types of AAA servers you can use for Authentication Proxy.

Know the default idle time for the IOS Firewall Authentication Proxy. The default idle time for the Authentication Proxy is 60 minutes.

Know the different types of signatures for the IOS Firewall IDS. The four types of signatures are info atomic, info compound, attack atomic, and attack compound.

Be familiar with the *show* and *debug* commands for both the IOS Firewall Authentication Proxy and the IOS Firewall IDS. For the IOS Firewall Authentication Proxy, the commands are show ip auth-proxy and debug ip auth-proxy. For the IOS Firewall IDS, the commands are show ip audit and debug ip audit.

Remember the three actions that the IOS Firewall IDS can take when a signature is matched. The three actions the IOS Firewall IDS can take when a signature is matched are alert, reset, and drop.

Chapter 7

Understanding Cisco IOS IPSec Support

THE FOLLOWING SECUR EXAM TOPICS ARE COVERED IN THIS CHAPTER:

- ✓ Understanding Cisco IOS IPSec technologies
- ✓ Using key exchange mechanisms
- ✓ Understanding the Cisco IOS Cryptosystem
- ✓ Establishing IPSec support in Cisco systems products
- ✓ Using tunneling protocols
- ✓ Using virtual private networks

Technology changes things—the way you live, work, communicate—your very needs. The standard 9-to-5 job, with everyone at one location, needed a type of network that is now for the most part obsolete because of current trends such as telecommuting and video conferencing. These business requirements have exponentially increased the demand for users to access secure communications over public networks. Companies now need communications technology such as distributed and virtual private networks to stay competitive—if they want to stay in business now and in the future, that is.

This chapter introduces you to the concept of virtual private networks (VPNs) and describes the solutions you need to meet your company's off-site network access needs. You'll get an in-depth look at how these networks utilize IP Security (IPSec) to provide secure communications over a public network such as the Internet. The chapter concludes with a discussion of the devices that Cisco provides to implement these solutions and an introduction to the Cisco IOS Cryptosystem.

This chapter is *very* theory intensive. If you feel lost after reading a section, take a moment to go back and review the material. Don't rush or skim over sections you don't really understand. You need a thorough knowledge of this content to provide the best service to your employer or clients.

Chapter 8, "Cisco IOS IPSec Pre-Shared Keys and Certificate Authority Support," will demonstrate how to implement the solutions discussed in this chapter. So, let's begin the introduction to VPNs.

What Is a Virtual Private Network?

I'd be willing to bet you've heard the term VPN more than once before. Maybe you even know what one is; but just in case you don't, a virtual private network (VPN) allows for the creation of private networks across the Internet, enabling privacy and tunneling of non-TCP/IP protocols. VPNs are used daily to give remote users and disjointed networks connectivity over a public medium such as the Internet instead of using more expensive permanent means.

The types of VPNs are named based on the role they play in a business environment. There are three different categories of VPNs:

Remote access VPNs   Remote access VPNs allow remote users like telecommuters to securely access the corporate network whenever and from wherever they need to.

Site-to-site VPNs   A site-to-site VPN, also called an *intranet VPN*, allows a company to connect its remote sites to the corporate backbone securely over a public medium such as the Internet instead of requiring more expensive WAN connections like Frame Relay.

Extranet VPNs   Extranet VPNs allow an organization's suppliers, partners, and customers to be connected to the corporate network in a limited way for business-to-business (B2B) communications.

There's more than one way to bring a VPN into being. The first approach uses IPSec to create authentication and encryption services between endpoints on an IP network. The second way is accomplished via tunneling protocols, allowing you to establish a tunnel between endpoints on a network. The tunnel itself is a means for data or protocols to be encapsulated inside another protocol—clean!

I'll go over the first way to create a VPN (using IPSec) shortly; but first, I want to describe four of the most common tunneling protocols in use:

Layer 2 Forwarding (L2F)   Layer 2 Forwarding (L2F) is a Cisco Proprietary tunneling protocol. It was Cisco's initial tunneling protocol, and it was created for virtual private dial-up networks (VPDNs). VPDNs let a device use a dial-up connection to create a secure connection to a corporate network. L2F was later replaced by Layer 2 Tunneling Protocol (L2TP), which is backward compatible with L2F.

Point-to-Point Tunneling Protocol (PPTP)   Point-to-Point Tunneling Protocol (PPTP) was created by Microsoft to allow the secure transfer of data from remote networks to the corporate network.

Layer 2 Tunneling Protocol (L2TP)   Layer 2 Tunneling Protocol (L2TP) was created by Cisco and Microsoft to replace L2F and PPTP. L2TP merged the capabilities of both L2F and PPTP into one tunneling protocol.

Generic routing encapsulation (GRE)   Generic Routing Encapsulation (GRE) is another Cisco Proprietary tunneling protocol. It forms virtual point-to-point links, allowing for a variety of protocols to be encapsulated in IP tunnels.

Now that you're clear on exactly what a VPN is and the various types of VPNs available, it's time to dive into IPSec.

Introduction to Cisco IOS IPSec

Here's the $64,000 question: What is IP Security (IPSec)? No, it doesn't have anything to do with an airport screener. Simply put, IPSec is an industry-wide standard suite of protocols and algorithms that allows for secure data transmission over an IP-based network, and it functions at Layer 3 (the Network layer) of the OSI model.

Did you notice I said, "IP-based network?" That's important, because by itself, IPSec can't be used to encrypt non-IP traffic. This means that if you run into a situation where you have to encrypt non-IP traffic, you'll need to create a GRE tunnel for it and then use IPSec to encrypt that tunnel.

IPSec runs by utilizing transforms such as protocols and algorithms that give IPSec its direction. There are five steps to IPSec operation. This section will discuss the IPSec transforms and how IPSec works.

> **Real World Scenario**
>
> **IPSec Support in Cisco Systems Products**
>
> Numerous Cisco devices can be utilized in the creation of IPSec VPNs. You can use Cisco routers to create router-to-router VPN solutions and client VPN solutions. When you're attempting to configure IPSec VPNs on routers, you should be sure you have the correct feature set. The Cisco Secure VPN Concentrator series can be used for remote-user VPN access to your network. The PIX Firewall (discussed in the appendix, "Introduction to the PIX Firewall," on the CD accompanying this book) can be used as an endpoint for VPN connections and provide you with the protection of a firewall.

IPSec Transforms

An IPSec transform specifies a single security protocol with its corresponding security algorithm; without these transforms, IPSec wouldn't be able to give you its encryption technologies. It's important to be familiar with these technologies, so let me take a second to define the security protocols and briefly introduce the supporting encryption and hashing algorithms that IPSec relies on.

Security Protocols

The two primary security protocols used by IPSec are Authentication Header (AH) and Encapsulating Security Payload (ESP).

The AH protocol provides authentication for the data and IP header of a packet using a one-way hash for packet authentication. It works like this: The sender generates a one-way hash, and then the receiver generates the same one-way hash. If the packet has changed in any way, it won't be authenticated, so it's dropped. Basically, IPSec relies on AH to guarantee authenticity. AH checks the entire packet, but it doesn't offer any encryption services.

No, ESP won't tell you when the NASDAQ's going to bounce back. But it does provide confidentiality, data origin authentication, connectionless integrity, anti-replay service, and limited traffic-flow confidentiality by defeating traffic-flow analysis (which is almost as good).

ESP has four components:

Confidentiality Confidentiality is provided through the use of symmetric encryption algorithms such as Data Encryption Standard (DES) or Triple DES (3DES). Confidentiality can be selected separately from all other services, but the confidentiality selected must be the same on all endpoints of your VPN.

Data origin authentication and connectionless integrity Data origin authentication and connectionless integrity are joint services offered as an option in conjunction with the likewise optional confidentiality.

Anti-replay service You can only use the anti-replay service if data origin authentication is selected. Anti-replay election is based on the receiver, meaning that the service is effective only if the receiver checks the sequence number. In case you were wondering, a replay attack occurs when an attacker snags a copy of an authenticated packet and later transmits it to the intended destination. When the duplicate, authenticated IP packet gets to the destination, it can disrupt services or cause other ugly consequences. The Sequence Number field is designed to foil this type of attack.

Traffic flow For traffic flow confidentiality to work, you have to have tunnel mode selected. Tunnel mode is most effective if it's implemented at a security gateway where tons of traffic amass—a condition that can mask the true source-destination patterns of bad guys trying to breach your network's security.

> **NOTE** Although both confidentiality and authentication are optional, at least one of them must be selected.

Encryption and Hashing Algorithms

Encryption algorithms are used to encrypt and decrypt data, and many encryption and hashing algorithms are available for IPSec. A *hashing algorithm* is used to create a (surprise) *hash*—a one-way encryption algorithm that takes an input message of random length and creates a fixed-length output message.

Cisco uses a hash variant known as Hashed Message Authentication Code (HMAC), which provides an extra level of hashing. This section will discuss Data Encryption Standard (DES), Triple DES, and some variations on the HMAC algorithms.

Data Encryption Standard (DES)

Data Encryption Standard (DES) is known as a *symmetric key algorithm*, meaning that a single key is used to encrypt and decrypt data. DES utilizes cipher block chaining (CBC) to connect a series of cipher blocks for encrypting data. It uses a 64-bit fixed-length cipher block and a 56-bit key, stored as a 64-bit (eight-octet) quantity with the least significant bit of each octet used as a parity bit. The key used by DES is the same on both sides of the connection. DES functions as follows:

1. The data to be encrypted arrives at the device.
2. DES uses its 56-bit key to encrypt the data.
3. The encrypted data is transmitted to its destination.
4. The encrypted data is received by the decrypting device.
5. The decrypting device uses its 56-bit DES key to decrypt the data.

Triple DES (3DES)

Do you need more security muscle? For a bigger bouncer, try Triple DES (3DES). It's a much beefier version of DES; the main difference is in how traffic encryption takes place. Instead of encrypting data only once before sending it, 3DES does the following:

1. 3DES encrypts the traffic using one 56-bit key.
2. 3DES decrypts the traffic using another 56-bit key.
3. 3DES then encrypts the traffic once more with another 56-bit key and finally sends the traffic to its destination.

So basically, it's the number of times that 3DES encrypts and decrypts traffic before sending it that makes it such a force, and so much stronger than DES.

Hashed Message Authentication Code-Message Digest 5 (HMAC-MD5)

Hashed Message Authentication Code-Message Digest 5 (HMAC-MD5), also known as HMAC-MD5-96, is a hashing algorithm that creates a 128-bit secret key. It works by producing a 128-bit authentication value that is truncated using the first 96 bits—hence the name HMAC-MD5-96. This truncated value is inserted into the authenticator field of AH or ESP and sent to the peer. The peer then computes its own 128-bit authentication value and compares the first 96 bits of it to the truncated value stored in the authenticator field of the packet it just received. If the values match, the device is authenticated.

Hashed Message Authentication Code-Secure Hash Algorithm-1 (HMAC-SHA-1)

Hashed Message Authentication Code-Secure Hash Algorithm-1 (HMAC-SHA-1), also known as HMAC-SHA-1-96, is HMAC-MD5's big brother. It's a stronger hashing algorithm that creates a 160-bit authenticator value, which is truncated at 96 bits. It works similarly to HMAC-MD5 in that the truncated value is stored in the AH or ESP authenticator field of the packet and sent to the peer. The peer then computes its own 160-bit authenticator value and compares the first 96 bits of it to the truncated value stored in the authenticator field of the packet it has just received. If the values match, the device is authenticated.

IPSec Operation

I'll go into greater detail about all the components of IPSec in a bit. For now, understand that the operation of IPSec can be broken down into five steps:

1. IPSec process initiation
2. IKE phase 1
3. IKE phase 2
4. Data transfer
5. IPSec tunnel termination

IPSec Process Initiation

IPSec process initiation does pretty much what the name implies—it initiates the operation of IPSec. It works a lot like making a phone call. First, you decide *who* you're going to call, and then you look up that person's *phone number*. With IPSec, *who* is the traffic that needs to be encrypted, and the *phone number* is where that traffic encryption needs to take place. Once those decisions have been made, a policy specifying the traffic to encrypt needs to be manually created and then applied to the devices that will form the VPN and encrypt the traffic. These devices are known as *IPSec peers*. What happens after the policy has been implemented? The answer is simple—when traffic that needs to be encrypted is detected on one of the IPSec peers, IKE phase 1 negotiation begins.

IKE Phase 1

Right now, all you need to know about Internet Key Exchange (IKE) is that it's used to form the IPSec encrypted tunnel. I'll discuss IKE in much more detail later in this chapter. *IKE phase 1* is the term used to describe the process of determining your IKE policy. During this second step of IPSec operation, the goal is to authenticate IPSec peers and to form the IKE tunnel.

What's actually happening in IKE phase 1? Well, first, IKE *security associations (SAs)* are negotiated on the IPSec peers. The IKE SAs are used to specify the type of peer authentication and which Diffie-Hellman (DH) group to use.

Next, an authenticated Diffie-Hellman Key Agreement (discussed later in this chapter) of matching keys is used to authenticate and protect the identities of IPSec peers. Finally, the IKE tunnel is formed for IKE phase 2 negotiation.

It's also worth mentioning that IKE can use either *main mode* or *aggressive mode* for phase 1 negotiation:

Main mode In this mode, IKE uses three two-way handshakes for phase 1 negotiation:

1. During the first exchange, the security algorithms IKE will use are decided on for the IKE SAs. The security algorithms are specified in the IKE policy that has been configured on the IPSec peers. (Chapter 8 discusses the configuration of IKE policies.)
2. During the second exchange, the Diffie-Hellman Key Agreement is used to generate the shared keying information, which is then used to generate the shared secret keys. Finally, the shared secret keys are used to validate the IPSec peers' identities.
3. During the third exchange, the peer device's identity is verified.

Aggressive mode Aggressive mode is faster than main mode because it uses only the following two exchanges:

1. During the first exchange, aggressive mode performs both steps 1 and 2 of main mode.
2. During the second exchange, the receiving peer sends back information that is needed to complete the exchange. Finally, the initiator sends back a confirmation.

As you can see, IPSec peer authentication is a priority of IKE phase 1. The completion of IKE phase 1 signals the beginning of the next step, IKE phase 2.

IKE Phase 2

The third step in the IPSec operation is called *IKE phase 2*, which is the process of creating the IPSec policy. The final outcome of IKE phase 2 is the negotiation of IPSec SAs. An IPSec SA is a unidirectional connection established between IPSec peers and is used to determine the IPSec services that will be offered. To say this another way, the IPSec SA specifies the type of encryption and IPSec services that are offered in one direction. Because an IPSec SA is unidirectional, two SAs must be set up: one from the sender to the receiver and one from the receiver to the sender. The IPSec SAs operate over the secure IKE tunnel that was set up in IKE phase 1.

Figure 7.1 illustrates two devices setting up SAs with one another.

FIGURE 7.1 Two devices setting up security associations

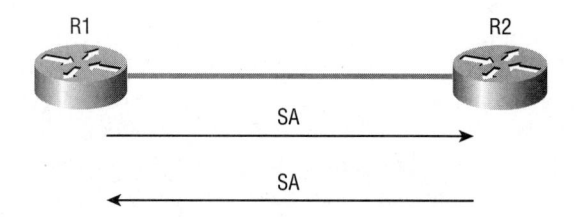

Let me explain the process illustrated in Figure 7.1:

1. R1 sends an SA to R2.
2. R2 accepts the SA.
3. R2 sends the SA back to R1.
4. Two unidirectional SAs are set up.

It's important to remember that a device has an SA for every IPSec device it peers with. These SAs are stored in the devices' security association database (SAD) and are indexed by their Security Parameter Index (SPI).

The SPI is a unique identification mechanism for each SA on a device. When an IPSec packet arrives, the device checks the SPI contained in the packet and compares the SPI in the packet to the SPIs in the device's SAD to determine which IPSec policy is in effect.

Also, make note of the fact that each SA has a unique triple identity consisting of an SPI, an IP destination address, and a security protocol (AH or ESP) identifier. The completion of this step is marked by the formation of an IPSec tunnel. The IPSec tunnel is then used to transport the encrypted traffic.

Data Transfer

Finally, we've reached the step in which traffic will begin to flow. Once the IPSec SAs have been negotiated and the IPSec tunnel has been formed, traffic can begin passing over the IPSec tunnel. The traffic that's allowed to enter the IPSec tunnel is encrypted and decrypted based on the information contained within the IPSec SA.

IPSec Tunnel Termination

IPSec tunnel termination can occur for one of two reasons: the tunnel is deleted, or the IPSec SA lifetime expires. When an IPSec SA lifetime expires, IKE phase 2 negotiation begins again and, if needed, so does IKE phase 1 negotiation.

It's about time you started learning about the different IPSec components, but before moving on, you might want to go back and review anything that's still unclear. It would be great if I could show you how to create a tunnel between this book and your brain so that all this data could just flow into it without studying, huh? Maybe someday; but for now, you'll have to deal with the grind. So take a break if you need to, and then let's get into IPSec components.

The Components of IPSec

You've just learned about how IPSec operates and about IKE. With that foundation in place, you're ready to take a detailed look at the encapsulations that make IPSec possible and at the IKE components.

IPSec Encapsulation

IPSec handles packet encapsulation through the use of ESP and/or AH. ESP encrypts the payload of a packet, whereas AH provides protection to the entire datagram by embedding the header in the data and verifying the integrity of the IP datagram.

IPSec can encapsulate data by one of two methods: transport mode or tunnel mode.

Transport Mode Encapsulation

Transport mode encapsulation uses the original IP header and inserts the header for ESP and/or AH. In transport mode, the original IP header must contain a routable IP address.

Figure 7.2 illustrates the format of a packet using ESP in transport mode.
Figure 7.3 illustrates the format of a packet using AH in transport mode.
Figure 7.4 illustrates the format of a packet using ESP and AH in transport mode.
With transport mode down, let's look at tunnel mode.

FIGURE 7.2 Packet format using ESP in transport mode

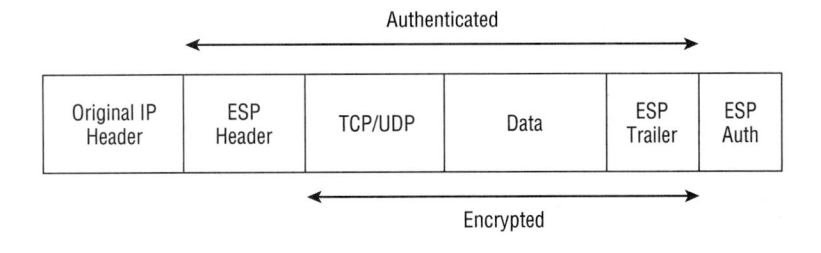

| Original IP Header | ESP Header | TCP/UDP | Data | ESP Trailer | ESP Auth |

Authenticated: Original IP Header through ESP Trailer
Encrypted: ESP Header through ESP Trailer

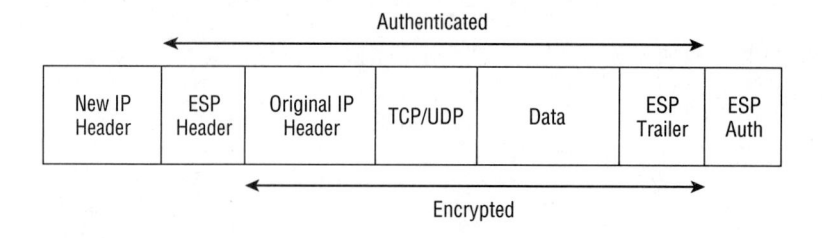

FIGURE 7.3 Packet format using AH in transport mode

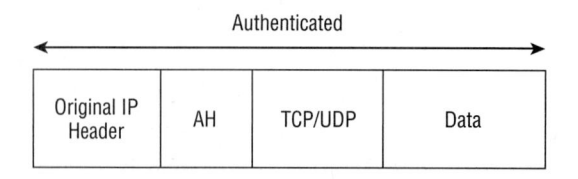

```
         <---------- Authenticated ---------->
      +-------------+-----+---------+---------+
      | Original IP |  AH | TCP/UDP |  Data   |
      |   Header    |     |         |         |
      +-------------+-----+---------+---------+
```

FIGURE 7.4 Packet format using ESP and AH in transport mode

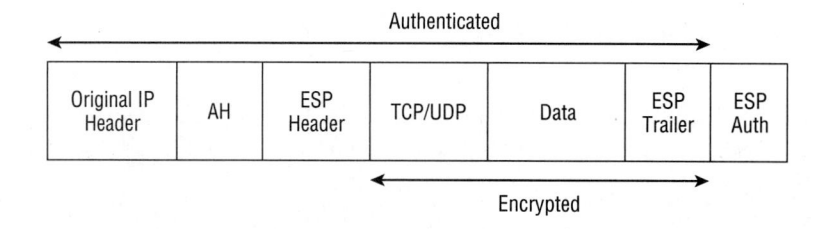

```
        <--------------- Authenticated --------------->
   +-----------+----+--------+--------+------+-------+------+
   |Original IP| AH |  ESP   |TCP/UDP | Data |  ESP  | ESP  |
   |  Header   |    | Header |        |      |Trailer| Auth |
   +-----------+----+--------+--------+------+-------+------+
                             <------ Encrypted ----->
```

Tunnel Mode Encapsulation

When you use *tunnel mode* encapsulation, the original IP header doesn't transport the packet. Instead, a new IP header is created using the IP addresses of the IPSec peers as the source and destination of the packet. This mode works great when you're creating a VPN across the Internet because the addresses of the originating devices can be private, so they're less vulnerable to unwanted access. As with transport mode, tunnel mode uses ESP and/or AH.

Figure 7.5 illustrates the format of a packet using ESP in tunnel mode.

Figure 7.6 illustrates the format of a packet using AH in tunnel mode.

Figure 7.7 illustrates the format of a packet using ESP and AH in tunnel mode.

FIGURE 7.5 Packet format using ESP in tunnel mode

```
         <--------------- Authenticated --------------->
   +--------+--------+-----------+--------+------+-------+------+
   | New IP |  ESP   |Original IP|TCP/UDP | Data |  ESP  | ESP  |
   | Header | Header |  Header   |        |      |Trailer| Auth |
   +--------+--------+-----------+--------+------+-------+------+
                     <------------ Encrypted ----------->
```

FIGURE 7.6   Packet format using AH in tunnel mode

← Authenticated →

New IP Header	AH	Original IP Header	TCP/UDP	Data

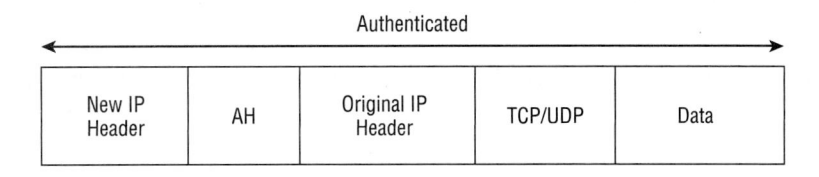

FIGURE 7.7   Packet format using ESP and AH in tunnel mode

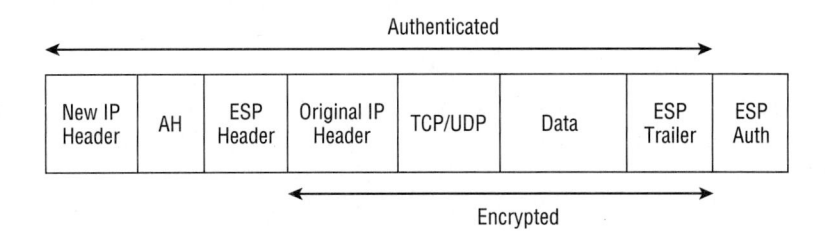

← Authenticated →

New IP Header	AH	ESP Header	Original IP Header	TCP/UDP	Data	ESP Trailer	ESP Auth

← Encrypted →

Internet Key Exchange (IKE)

IPSec can be configured with or without Internet Key Exchange (IKE), but it's a better idea to use IKE. IKE enhances IPSec by providing additional features, flexibility, and ease of configuration for the IPSec standard. It's a hybrid protocol that implements the OAKLEY key exchange and SKEME key exchange inside the Internet Security Association and Key Management Protocol (ISAKMP) framework.

Now's a good time to define some of the terms I just threw at you:

ISAKMP   Internet Security Association and Key Management Protocol (ISAKMP) is a protocol framework that defines the payload format, the mechanics of implementing a key exchange protocol, and the negotiation of an SA.

OAKLEY   OAKLEY is a key exchange protocol that defines how to derive authenticated keying material.

SKEME   SKEME is a key exchange protocol that defines how to derive authenticated keying material with rapid key refreshment.

Now that you're clear on the terminology, let's get back into the discussion. IKE gives us the goods in the following six ways:

- It eliminates the need to manually specify all the IPSec security parameters in the crypto maps at both peers.

- It allows you to specify a lifetime for the IPSec security SA.
- It allows encryption keys to change during IPSec sessions.
- It allows IPSec to provide anti-replay services.
- It permits certification authority (CA) support for a manageable, scalable IPSec implementation.
- It allows dynamic authentication of peers.

IKE consists of the two phases mentioned earlier in this chapter: IKE phase 1 and IKE phase 2. During phase 1, IKE negotiates the IKE SAs and authenticates the IPSec peers. During phase 2, IKE negotiates the IPSec SAs and creates the IPSec tunnel.

IKE relies heavily on Diffie-Hellman during phase 1, so let's take a closer look at that feature.

Diffie-Hellman Key Agreement

The *Diffie-Hellman (DH) Agreement* is a means for two parties to agree on a shared secret number that is then used to encrypt secret keys for other algorithms such as DES and MD5. DH occurs in phase 1 of IKE negotiation.

> **NOTE** The process of DH occurs over unsecured lines.

Before we dive into how DH works, here's a list of keys you need to understand:

P P is a randomly generated prime integer.

G G is a primitive root of P.

Xa Xa is a private key generated by the formula (G mod P).

Xb Xb is a private key generated by the formula (G mod P).

Ya Ya is a public key generated by the formula ((G to the power of Xa) mod P).

Yb Yb is a public key generated by the formula ((G to the power of Xb) mod P).

ZZ ZZ is a shared secret key generated by the formula ((Yb to the power of Xa) mod P) on one device and the formula ((Ya to the power of Xb) mod P) on the other device.

> **NOTE** *Mod* stands for a modulus or division.

With the terminology and formulas out of the way, you're ready to get into the six-step process DH goes through in the creation of ZZ. Use the network in Figure 7.8 for reference in this discussion of DH.

FIGURE 7.8 A Diffie-Hellman network

1. The first step of DH uses the generated P value on each device to create the G value. The following steps are what the devices in Figure 7.8 go through:
   a. Both R1 and R2 generate a P value.
   b. R1 transmits its P value to R2, and R2 transmits its P value to R1.
   c. Both R1 and R2 use the two P values to create G.
2. The second step of DH uses G and P on each device to generate Xa on one device and Xb on the other device. The routers in Figure 7.8 go through the following process:
   a. R1 uses the formula (G mod P) to create its private key Xa.
   b. R2 uses the formula (G mod P) to create its private key Xb.
3. Now it's time to generate each device's public key. To generate the public keys for R1 and R2, the devices in Figure 7.8 go through the following process:
   a. Using the formula ((G to the power of Xa) mod P), R1 creates its public key Ya.
   b. Using the formula ((G to the power of Xb) mod P), R2 creates its public key Yb.
4. The devices now exchange their public keys. R1 sends its public key, Ya, to R2, and R2 sends its public key, Yb, to R1.
5. R1 and R2 generate the secret shared key ZZ. R1 uses the formula ((Yb to the power of Xa) mod P) to create ZZ, and R2 uses the formula ((Ya to the power of Xb) mod P) to create ZZ.
6. On each device, ZZ encrypts the key that will be used by DES or MD5 for the purpose of encrypting data.

Once this last step has been completed, DH is finished with its initial function. But DH can be used later in IKE phase 2 to generate new keying material for IPSec SAs.

Now you understand how DH is used with IKE. Let's look at some of the authentication mechanisms available to IKE during phase 1 that it can use to authenticate a peer's identity.

Authentication

I've mentioned authentication several times in this chapter, but I've never gone into any detail. That's what I'll do here. Any of the following three authentication types can be used for IKE:

- Pre-shared keys
- RSA-encrypted nonces
- RSA signatures and digital certificates

Pre-shared Keys

Pre-shared keys must be configured on each IPSec peer, and any keys used must be the same on each peer. This is the case because IKE peers authenticate each other by creating and sending a keyed hash that includes the pre-shared key. Once the receiving peer receives the hash, it attempts to create the same hash by using its configured pre-shared key. Needless to say, the peer is authenticated only if the hashes match.

RSA-Encrypted Nonces

RSA-encrypted nonces are a type of public/private key cryptography that is very secure but not very scalable. A *nonce* is a pseudo-random number. RSA-encrypted nonces can be used to authenticate the IKE exchange and the Diffie-Hellman Key Agreement.

Let's look at how RSA-encrypted nonces work. This section could get a little confusing, so I'll use an example.

Suppose you have two devices you want to peer using RSA-encrypted nonces: R1 and R2. You have to manually generate a public key on both R1 and R2 and then manually enter the public key generated by R1 into R2 and vice versa.

Next, R1 generates a nonce that it then encrypts along with its IKE identity using RSA encryption and the public key that was manually entered. R1 transmits the cipher text to R2. While R1 is doing this, R2 is doing the same using the public key that you manually entered into it.

Once R1 receives the encrypted packet from R2, it decrypts the packet using its own private RSA key. After the packet has been decrypted, R1 removes both the nonce and R2's IKE identity. R1 then hashes R2's nonce and IKE identity and sends the hash back to R2. R2 is performing all these same functions simultaneously.

After both R1 and R2 receive their respective hash, each device then hashes its own nonce and IKE identity. With that done, each device compares the hash it received with the hash it just generated to determine if they match. If they do, authentication has occurred.

RSA-encrypted nonces aren't very scalable because of the fact that you must both manually generate and then exchange public keys. Even so, RSA signatures do scale the best.

RSA Signatures and Digital Certificates

RSA signatures rely on digital signatures—something I'll get to in a second. Through the use of digital signatures, RSA signatures overcome the scalability limitations of RSA-encrypted nonces.

You still need to manually generate the public/private key pair on each device when you use RSA signatures. Once you've done that, you have to register each peer with a *certificate authority (CA)*. When you register a device with the CA, it also registers the public key you've just generated. The CA then issues a signed digital certificate to you, validating that you really are who you say you are. Each peer absolutely must have a signed digital certificate before RSA can be used.

Once each device has a signed digital certificate, they send it, along with their IKE identities, to the other device. The IKE exchange is authenticated by the signed digital certificate.

This is good because using digital certificates eliminates the need to manually enter a device's generated public key in each and every device that it needs to peer with. It's a significant advantage because it allows for greater scalability.

Now it's time to talk in depth about digital certificates. They contain device-specific information such as the device's name and IP address, as well as its generated public key. This is why a digital certificate can be used in place of manually entering public keys for IKE authentication.

How does this work? First, the CA you're using needs to be trusted by the devices that you want to be able to peer with. This occurs when the device first begins talking to the CA. The following are the steps required for a device to receive a signed digital signature from a CA:

1. You must manually generate the public/private key pair on the device.
2. The device requests the specified CA's public key.
3. The CA sends its public key to the device.
4. The device requests a signed digital certificate from the CA. In that request, the device includes device-specific information and its public key.
5. The CA generates the digital signature, incorporating both the device's public key and the CA's private key.
6. The CA sends the signed digital signature back to the device.

So, after a device receives its signed digital signature, it offers it to all the devices it wants to peer with. A peer device trusts the device's public key once it verifies the device's signature using the public key from the CA. This entire process is a type of Digital Signature Standard (DSS) encryption.

> **NOTE** DSS encryption is a mechanism that uses digital signatures to protect data.

Cisco fully supports the use of digital certificates by IKE and implements the following standards:

X.509v3   The standard certificate format. X.509v3 specifies how to form a certificate.

CRLv2   The certificate revocation list (CRL), version 2. CRLv2 is a list of revoked certificates, that is, certificates that should no longer be trusted. The CRL database is queried for revoked certificates by using the certificates unique serial number.

Certificate Enrollment Protocol (CEP)   A certificate management protocol jointly developed by Cisco Systems and VeriSign, Inc. CEP is an early implementation of Certificate Request Syntax (CRS), a standard proposed to the Internet Engineering Task Force (IETF). CEP specifies how a device communicates with a CA, including how to retrieve the CA's public key, how to enroll a device with the CA, and how to retrieve a CRL. CEP uses RSA's Public-Key Cryptography Standards (PKCS) 7 and 10 as key component technologies. The IETF's Public Key Infrastructure (PKI) Working Group is moving forward to standardize a protocol for these functions, either CRS or an equivalent. When an IETF standard is stable, Cisco will add support for it.

IKE Mode Configuration

IKE mode configuration allows IKE to scale an IPSec policy out to remote users. This is accomplished by permitting a gateway to download an IP address and other network-level configuration through Dynamic Host Configuration Protocol (DHCP) to a client during IKE negotiation. Afterward, this address is used as the inner IP address to be encapsulated under IPSec and can then be matched against an IPSec policy.

The last IKE feature I need to describe is IKE's extended authentication capabilities.

IKE Extended Authentication (XAuth)

Until the advent of IKE extended authentication (XAuth), IKE was able to support authentication of the device, but not of the user. XAuth introduced a way for IKE to use AAA to authenticate the user after it has authenticated the device, adding an extra level of security to the network.

That's all there is to understanding IPSec. The sidebar "Cisco IOS Cryptosystem" explores Cisco's IOS Cryptosystem and goes further into the encryption and hash algorithms described earlier.

Cisco IOS Cryptosystem

To put it simply, a *cryptosystem* is a combination of encryption technologies, working in harmony, that are used to encrypt data so that only the intended receiver can decrypt it. Cisco uses the following four technologies to create its IOS Cryptosystem:

- Digital Encryption Standard (DES)
- Message Digest 5 (MD5)
- Digital Signature Standard (DSS)
- Diffie-Hellman Key Agreement

These four technologies perform the following tasks in Cisco's cryptosystem:

- DES encrypts data.
- MD5 creates a message hash.
- DSS verifies peers by exchanging public keys.
- Diffie-Hellman establishes private and public keys that encrypt the keys used by DES and MD5.

When all of these items work together as a team, they create a very secure environment for transmitting data.

Summary

This chapter introduced you to many new concepts. VPNs are growing in demand, and if you want to remain relevant in today's competitive marketplace, you positively must understand their terms and processes.

Cisco utilizes IPSec VPNs to provide a secure connection over a public network—connections that can be designed based on the business needs of your company. You can use remote-access solutions for telecommuters, site-to-site solutions for remote offices that need access to the corporate network, and extranet solutions to provide your customers and partners with the limited information they need.

Cisco provides a number of products to meet your IPSec needs. Cisco routers, Cisco Secure VPN Concentrators, and PIX Firewalls can all be used to create VPN solutions for your specific situation.

You must have a thorough understanding of the concepts discussed in this chapter before proceeding to Chapter 8. So, if you feel shaky on anything covered here, take the time you need to go back and review.

Exam Essentials

Be able to explain virtual private networks. You must be able to explain how VPNs are used in the creation of secure networks. You need to understand the three different types of VPNs: site-to-site, extranet, and remote access.

Be sure you can list and explain the different tunneling technologies. The tunneling protocols currently available are GRE, L2F, L2TP, and PPTP.

Be able to explain IPSec operation. You need a solid understanding of the five steps of IPSec operation: how an IPSec process initiates, IKE phase 1, IKE phase 2, data transfer, and IPSec tunnel termination.

Understand the different key exchange methods. The key exchange methods are as follows: pre-shared keys, RSA-encrypted nonces, and RSA signatures. You need to explain how each one operates and when each should be used.

Be sure you can explain the Cisco IOS Cryptosystem. A cryptosystem is a combination of encryption technologies, working in harmony, that are used to encrypt data so that only the intended receiver can decrypt it. The Cisco IOS Cryptosystem uses DES, MD5, DSS, and DH.

Be able to list the Cisco equipment available for IPSec. Cisco uses their routers, VPN Concentrators, and the PIX Firewalls for IPSec VPN solutions.

Chapter 8

Cisco IOS IPSec Pre-shared Keys and Certificate Authority Support

THE FOLLOWING SECUR EXAM TOPICS ARE COVERED IN THIS CHAPTER:

- ✓ Configuring IPSec encryption tasks
- ✓ Preparing for IKE and IPSec
- ✓ Configuring IKE
- ✓ Configuring IPSec
- ✓ Configuring transform set suites
- ✓ Configuring global IPSec Security Association (SA) lifetimes
- ✓ Creating crypto ACLs
- ✓ Creating crypto maps
- ✓ Applying crypto maps to interfaces
- ✓ Testing and verifying IPSec
- ✓ Configuring IPSec manually
- ✓ Configuring IPSec for RSA-encrypted nonces
- ✓ Configuring CA support tasks
- ✓ Understanding CA support
- ✓ Configuring CA support

In another life, I was a professional musician and played guitar in a band. I didn't study a lot of music theory, but I did know a lot about making music and performing it live. In the last chapter, I went over all the theory behind Internet Key Exchange (IKE) and IP Security (IPSec) with you. Now, I'll build on that material by showing you what to do with it. In this chapter, you'll learn how to configure IKE and IPSec, because while understanding theory is good, you'd better know how to implement it when show time comes.

Everybody has different strengths and weaknesses. Some people struggle with the theory part of this material but fly through the application, whereas others experience the opposite. Some of you are loving every minute of it, handling both the concepts and their implementation with ease. But no matter which category you fall into, the fact remains that you have to know this stuff—both in theory and in practice—if you want to pass the test and be capable of working with the technologies competently.

That's the goal of this chapter—to pull together theory and execution and integrate them into one tight package. I've got to be honest with you, though; achieving this goal will take a while. This chapter is one of the longest in this book.

Configuring Cisco IOS IPSec for Pre-shared Keys Site-to-Site

IPSec for pre-shared keys is the easiest of all the IPSec implementations. Implementing IPSec requires that you configure an IKE policy, pre-shared keys, and IPSec, but it's not very scalable because you have to manually configure the pre-shared keys on the devices, plus manage them. This can become tangled and messy in large networks. Hear that sucking sound? Those are the man-hours being consumed if you use IPSec for pre-shared keys on a large network. It's not exactly cost-effective—go for another option in a larger environment. In the next section, you'll learn the configuration tasks for IPSec and how to plan your approach to implementing IPSec so you can configure it correctly the first time.

Configuring IPSec for pre-shared keys requires you to do these four tasks:

- Prepare for IKE and IPSec.
- Configure IKE.
- Configure IPSec.
- Test and verify IPSec.

By the time you're done with this section, you'll be able to implement site-to-site IPSec for pre-shared keys, so let's get going.

Preparing for IKE and IPSec

Before you get into configuring IPSec utilizing pre-shared keys, you need to plan your approach. Think of it as a football game—you don't just show up at the field and play. You show up with a decided strategy to win the game, complete with a book of plays you plan to use depending on the circumstances and your opponent. You've also done your research, so you're packing detailed notes on all the other team's codes and signs. It's pretty much the same thing for IPSec. You don't start configuring IPSec without first coming up with a solid plan of attack.

Here are five questions you need to answer that will help you develop a plan:

- Can the devices you want to peer already ping each other? If not, you need to verify network connectivity. If yes, move on to the next question.
- Does existing packet filtering currently allow IPSec traffic? If not, update the access lists to allow IPSec traffic. If yes, move on to the next question.
- What's the current configuration of the device? Knowing this will allow you to establish two things: the crypto map name already in use and which interfaces currently have crypto maps applied to them. Time to move on to the next question.
- What IKE policy do you want to enforce between the devices you're going to peer? Asking yourself this question will make you think about the message-encryption and hash algorithms, the authentication method, and the key exchange parameters. These decisions should directly correspond with what you've outlined in your corporate security policy. That done, you're ready for the next question.
- What type of IPSec policy do you want to enforce between the devices with which you wish to peer? To answer this one, you'll have to think about two factors: the IPSec mode you're going to use and which IPSec transforms to use.

Now that you've answered these questions (and documented your answers, of course), you're ready to go. The first step in configuring IPSec utilizing pre-shared keys is to configure IKE on each device.

Configuring IKE

Once your IKE policy has been identified, configuring IKE is relatively simple. Configuring IKE with pre-shared keys is a four-step process:

1. Enable IKE.
2. Create the IKE policy.
3. Configure the IKE identity and pre-shared keys.
4. Verify IKE operation.

Enabling IKE

To configure IKE, it must first be enabled. You enable IKE by entering the following command in global configuration mode:

`crypto isakmp enable`

Once the preceding command has been entered, IKE will be enabled on the device. If you ever need to disable it, enter the following command, also in global configuration mode:

`no crypto isakmp enable`

> **WARNING** Don't use the no `crypto isakmp enable` command lightly—disabling all IKE operation on a device can have serious ramifications.

Creating the IKE Policy

With IKE enabled, you now need to create the IKE policy. Doing this requires you to have already answered the following questions:

- What priority will you give the policy? Lower numbers indicate a higher priority in the policy and vice versa. This is critical when a device has multiple IKE policies configured.
- What type of message encryption will you use? The default is Data Encryption Standard (DES), but you can change it to Triple DES (3DES) if you have the right feature set.
- What message hash will you use? The default is Secure Hash Algorithm (SHA), but you can change it to Message Digest 5 (MD5).
- What authentication method do you want to use? The default is rsa-sig, but it can be changed to pre-shared or rsa-encr. The example in this book uses pre-shared keys.
- What Diffie-Hellman group do you want to use? The default is 1, but it can be changed to 2. Group 1 is 768-bit Diffie-Hellman; group 2 is 1024-bit Diffie-Hellman.
- What lifetime would you like to set for the IKE security association (SA)? The default is 86,400, but that can be changed.

Don't forget that the policy you have set on one device must be the same as the policy you set on the devices you wish to peer with. The exceptions are: first, the priority given to the policy, which is locally significant; and second, the lifetime that's negotiated during IKE phase 1.

To create the IKE policy, enter the following command in global configuration mode, where *priority* is a value between 1 and 10,000.

`crypto isakmp policy priority`

Once you enter this command, the IKE policy is created with all the default values, and the router is placed in IKE policy configuration mode. All the configuration in this section is accomplished while in this mode.

Next, you need to specify which message-encryption algorithm to use by entering the following command:

encryption {des | 3des}

After configuring the message-encryption algorithm, you configure the message hash by entering this command:

hash {sha | md5}

Now you configure the authentication method by entering the following command:

authentication {rsa-sig | rsa-encr | pre-share}

Because this section discusses only pre-shared keys, you need to use the `pre-share` keyword.

Next, you configure the Diffie-Hellman group by entering this command:

group {1 | 2}

To finish this off, you configure the IKE SA lifetime by entering the following command, where *seconds* is a value between 60 and 86,400:

lifetime *seconds*

> **NOTE**
> Entering the commands discussed in this section is all you need to do if you want to change the default value or change a value that's already been configured. To create a new IKE policy or enter IKE policy configuration mode, you have to enter the `crypto isakmp policy priority` command.

Configuring the IKE Identity and Pre-shared Keys

Your IKE policy has been created and configured on all of the devices. Now it's time to set the IKE identity and configure the pre-shared key that is used during IKE negotiations to authenticate peers.

Because you're reading this book, you probably know that a device can use either the router's IP address or the router's hostname for its identity. By default, devices use their IP address as their IKE identity. This is important because unless you want to set the device to use its hostname instead, or the device is already using the hostname and you want to change it back to use the device's IP address, you don't need to configure a thing. To accomplish one of these tasks, just enter the following command in global configuration mode:

crypto isakmp identity {*address* | *hostname*}

> **WARNING**
> If you choose to use a device's hostname for IKE identity, make sure a DNS server is available for name resolution. Your other option is to manually enter the hostname of the device in the hostname table of all devices you wish to peer with.

Once you've nailed the IKE identity, it's time to configure the pre-shared key. But first, you need to determine which pre-shared key to use on all the devices you wish to peer. When you've made your decision, enter the following command in global configuration mode on each device, where *keystring* is the pre-shared key you want to use, *peer-address* is the IP address of the remote device, and *peer-hostname* is the hostname of the remote device:

crypto isakmp key *keystring* {**address** *peer-address* | **hostname** *peer-hostname*}

This command needs to be entered on a device for each device it wishes to peer with.

> **NOTE** Use the address keyword if the remote peer is using an IKE identity of the address. Use the hostname keyword if the remote peer is using an IKE identity of the hostname.

That was a ton of input, so let's take a second to put it all together visually. The following graphic illustrates a potential network for setting up a VPN. Remember our corporate network example? You'll be using it again for Exercise 8.1.

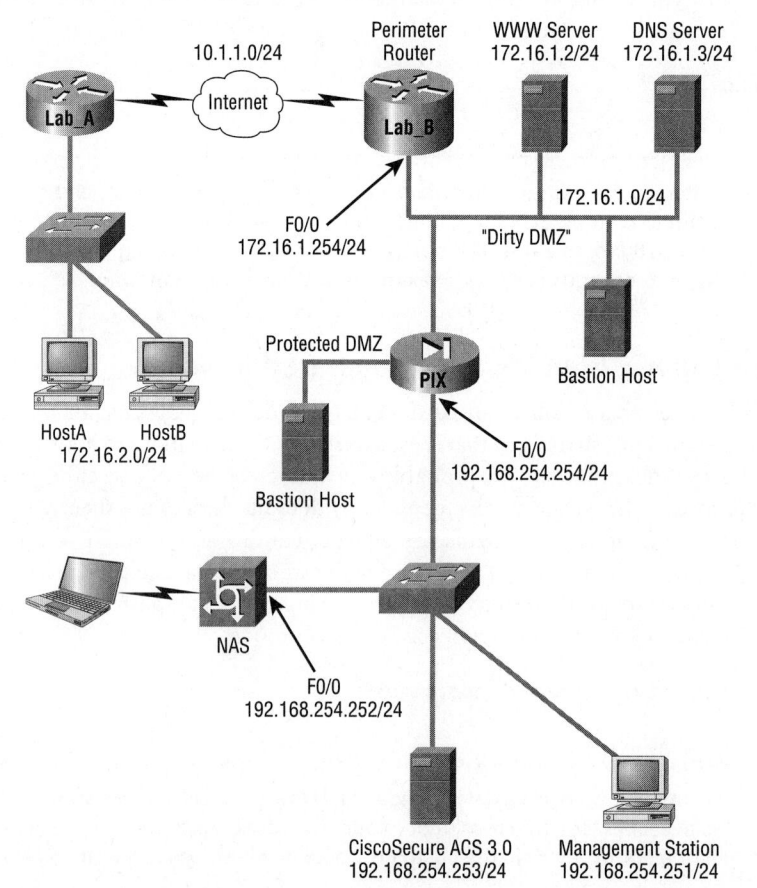

> **NOTE:** A word of advice: If you're taking the SECUR exam, which is probably a sure bet because you're reading this book, it would be wise to set up some routers and configure the next lab.

EXERCISE 8.1

Setting Up a VPN Using IKE

In this exercise, I'll guide you through configuring IKE using a VPN between the Lab_A device and the Lab_B device with the following parameters:

- Lab_A interface Serial 0/0 with IP address 10.1.1.1 /24
- Lab_B interface Serial 1/0 with IP address 10.1.1.2 /24
- Lab_A IKE policy priority equals 2
- Lab_B IKE policy priority equals 2
- 3DES message encryption
- MD5 message hash
- Authentication method is pre-share
- Default Diffie-Hellman group for both devices
- Default IKE SA lifetime for both devices
- IKE Identity is address for both devices
- Pre-shared key is cisco

Enter the following commands to create your IKE policies:

```
Lab_A#conf t
Enter configuration commands, one per line.  End with CNTL/Z.
Lab_A(config)#crypto isakmp enable
Lab_A(config)#crypto isakmp policy 2
Lab_A(config-isakmp)#encryption 3des
Lab_A(config-isakmp)#hash md5
Lab_A(config-isakmp)#authentication pre-share
Lab_A(config-isakmp)#exit
```

> **EXERCISE 8.1** *(continued)*

```
Lab_A(config)#crypto isakmp key cisco address 10.1.1.2

Lab_A(config)#^Z

Lab_A#


Lab_B#conf t

Enter configuration commands, one per line.  End with CNTL/Z.

Lab_B(config)#crypto isakmp enable

Lab_B(config)#crypto isakmp policy 2

Lab_B(config-isakmp)#encryption 3des

Lab_B(config-isakmp)#hash md5

Lab_B(config-isakmp)#authentication pre-share

Lab_B(config-isakmp)#exit

Lab_B(config)#crypto isakmp key cisco address 10.1.1.1

Lab_B(config)#^Z

Lab_B#
```

> Did you notice that the Diffie-Hellman group command and the `lifetime` command weren't entered? That's because the default settings were used, so you didn't need to use those commands.

Once the configuration is complete, you must always be able to verify what you have configured. The next section explains how to do this.

Verifying the IKE Policy

Now that the IKE policies have been configured, you need to verify that the device accepted them. You do this via the `show crypto isakmp policy` command, which displays the IKE policies currently configured on a device. With this in mind, let's verify the IKE policies on the Lab_A and Lab_B devices:

```
Lab_A#show crypto isakmp policy
Protection suite of priority 2
```

```
    encryption algorithm:      3DES--Triple Data Encryption Standard (168 bit
        keys)
    hash algorithm:            Message Digest 5
    authentication method:     Pre-Shared Key
    Diffie-Hellman group:      #1 (768 bit)
    lifetime:                  86400 seconds, no volume limit
Default protection suite
    encryption algorithm:      DES--Data Encryption Standard
    hash algorithm:            Secure Hash Standard
    authentication method:     Rivest-Shamir-Adleman Signature (56 bit keys)
    Diffie-Hellman group:      #1 (768 bit)
    lifetime:                  86400 seconds, no volume limit
Lab_A#

Lab_B#show crypto isakmp policy
Protection suite of priority 2
    encryption algorithm:      3DES--Triple Data Encryption Standard
    hash algorithm:            Message Digest 5
    authentication method:     Pre-Shared Key
    Diffie-Hellman group:      #1 (768 bit)
    lifetime:                  86400 seconds, no volume limit
Default protection suite
    encryption algorithm:      DES--Data Encryption Standard
    hash algorithm:            Secure Hash Standard
    authentication method:     Rivest-Shamir-Adleman Signature
    Diffie-Hellman group:      #1 (768 bit)
    lifetime:                  86400 seconds, no volume limit
Lab_B#
```

Everything looks great! Now that you've verified that your IKE policies are configured on each device, you're ready to move on and configure IPSec.

Configuring IPSec

Just like pre-shared keys, there are important steps that you should keep in mind when configuring IPSec on your routers. Configuring IPSec on each device is a five-step process:

1. Create the transform set.
2. Set the IPSec SA lifetime.
3. Create the access list that specifies the traffic to encrypt.
4. Create the crypto map.
5. Apply the crypto map to an interface.

Creating the Transform Set

A *transform set* is your tool for protecting the data flow. It's made up of payload authentication, payload encryption, and an IPSec mode. For devices to peer, the transform set must match on each device, except (obviously) for their names. Also, in order for a transform set to be valid, it must have a unique name on the device and at least one transform. To configure a transform set, enter the following command in global configuration mode:

```
crypto ipsec transform-set transform-set-name {[transform1] [transform2]
      [transform3]}
```

The variables for the preceding command are as follows:

- *transform-set-name* should be a unique name for the transform set.
- *transform1* can be ah-md5-hmac or ah-sha-hmac.
- *transform2* can be esp-des, esp-3des, or esp-null.
- *transform3* can be esp-md5-hmac or esp-sha-hmac.

After you've issued the preceding command, the device enters transform set configuration mode, in which the IPSec mode for the transform set can be configured. The default IPSec mode is tunnel. To change the IPSec mode, enter the following command:

```
mode {tunnel | transport}
```

When you're configuring transform sets, it's important to make sure that both the transforms and the IPSec mode are the same on the device you want to peer.

Setting the IPSec SA Lifetime

To make sure you're clear on this, an *IPSec SA lifetime* is what you use to determine how long IPSec SAs remain valid until they need to be renegotiated. You can configure the IPSec SA two ways: globally, or per crypto map sequence. When you go with the configured-globally option, the IPSec SA lifetime is applied to every crypto map that exists on the device. And it's important to know that a global IPSec SA lifetime can be overridden by configuring a crypto map–specific IPSec SA lifetime. For now, I'll stick with global IPSec SA lifetimes. You'll learn about the crypto map–specific IPSec SA lifetimes later in this chapter.

Two types of global IPSec SA lifetimes exist on a device: seconds and kilobytes. The seconds global IPSec SA lifetime specifies the number of seconds that an IPSec SA remains active before it expires. The kilobytes global IPSec SA lifetime specifies the amount of traffic that can be transmitted between peers for a given IPSec SA before the SA expires.

To change the seconds global IPSec SA from its default of 3600 seconds, enter the following command in global configuration mode, where *seconds* is a value between 120 and 86,400:

```
crypto ipsec security-association lifetime seconds seconds
```

To change the kilobytes global IPSec SA from its default of 4,608,000 kilobytes, enter the following command, where `kilobytes` represents a value between 2560 and 4,608,000:

`crypto ipsec security-association lifetime kilobytes kilobytes`

> **Note:** Remember that both the kilobytes and seconds global IPSec SA lifetimes exist on a device at the same time.

Creating the Access List

So far you've created the transform set and set the global IPSec lifetimes. But what good is IPSec if you haven't specified any traffic to protect? That's where access lists come into play.

IPSec uses extended access lists to perform the following tasks:

- Choose the outbound traffic to protect.
- Process inbound traffic for selecting IPSec traffic.
- Process inbound traffic for filtering out traffic that should have been protected.
- When processing IKE negotiations, they determine whether to accept requests for IPSec SAs.

I'm not going to explain how to create extended access lists here. If you need more information about extended access lists, they're covered in detail in the *CCNA Study Guide* (Sybex, 2002).

> **Note:** Cisco recommends using symmetrical access lists for IPSec because doing so causes both outbound and inbound traffic to be compared against the same access list.

Creating the Crypto Map

IPSec SAs are established through the use of a *crypto map*, which is basically a combination of one or more sequences where each sequence represents an IPSec SA.

Each crypto map sequence specifies the following:

- What traffic to protect
- The remote peer the protected traffic should be sent to
- The transforms to use to protect the traffic
- Whether the IPSec SA will be established via IKE or manually
- Other parameters such as a description and a crypto map IPSec SA lifetime

> ### Real World Scenario
>
> **When Would You Need More Than One Sequence?**
>
> Because an interface can have only one crypto map applied to it, you can run into trouble when you need more than one IPSec tunnel to form over an interface. The following graphic illustrates a network that would need two IPSec tunnels over the same interface:
>
> *[Diagram: HQ router connected via S0/0 to the Internet, with Site_1 and Site_2 routers each connected via S0 to the Internet. Each site has a LAN segment.]*
>
> Company XYZ is made up of three sites: HQ, Site_1, and Site_2. All the sites are connected to the Internet for WAN connectivity. The HQ site needs to have one IPSec tunnel connection to Site_1 and one IPSec tunnel connection to Site_2. How do you do this when you already know that an interface can have only one crypto map applied to it? All you need to do is create a crypto map with two sequences: one for the connection to Site_1 and the other for the connection to Site_2.

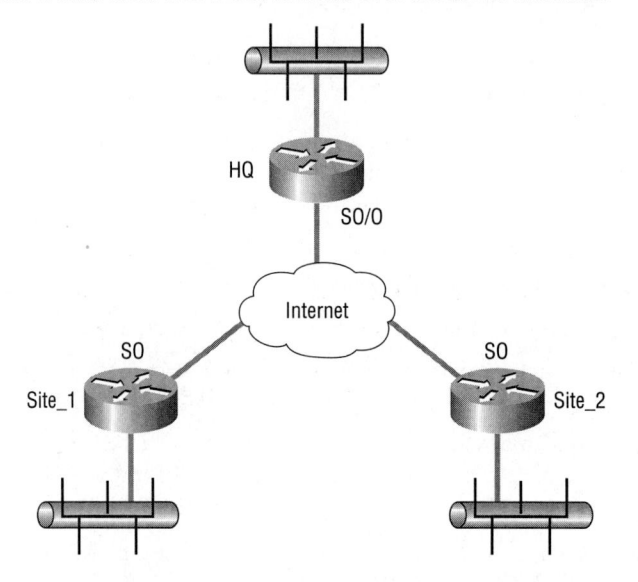

All sequences of a crypto map are tied together by the name of the respective crypto map. Each sequence can be one of the following types:

Cisco This sequence specifies that Cisco Encryption Technology will be used to protect traffic instead of IPSec.

IPSec-manual The IPSec-manual sequence specifies that IKE won't be used to establish IPSec SA. This type of sequence is discussed in more detail later in this chapter.

IPSec-isakmp This sequence specifies that IKE will be used to establish IPSec SAs.

Dynamic The dynamic sequence specifies that this sequence references a preexisting crypto map. This book doesn't cover dynamic crypto maps because they are beyond the scope of the SECUR exam.

To create a crypto map sequence that utilizes IKE, enter the following command in global configuration mode, where *map-name* is the name of the crypto map and *seq-num* is the sequence number of the crypto map sequence, which is a value between 1 and 65,535:

`crypto map map-name seq-num ipsec-isakmp`

Logically, the sequence number is what you use to specify the order in which traffic is compared to the crypto map; the lowest sequence number is compared first. So it's a very good idea to give the sequences that will be matched most often a lower sequence number—they'll process through more quickly that way.

Once you've created the sequence with the `crypto map` command, the device enters crypto map configuration mode. This is where you configure the specific parameters of the sequence. Table 8.1 lists the commands you can enter in crypto map configuration mode for a sequence using IKE.

TABLE 8.1 Crypto Map Configuration Mode Commands

Command	Purpose
`match address {access-list-number	name}`	A mandatory command that specifies the extended access list to use for defining the traffic to protect
`set peer {peer-address	peer-hostname}`	A mandatory command that specifies the IPSec peer
`set transform-set transform-set-name [transform-set-name2 transform-set-name6]`	A mandatory command that specifies a list of transform sets, in order of priority, to use for protecting traffic.
`description text`	An optional command that can be used to provide a description for a crypto map sequence
`set security-association lifetime seconds seconds`	An optional command that can be used to override the seconds global IPSec SA lifetime for the sequence
`set security-association lifetime kilobytes kilobytes`	An optional command that can be used to override the kilobytes global IPSec SA lifetime for the sequence
`set pfs {group1	group2}`	An optional command that can be used to specify the Diffie-Hellman group to use when requesting new security associations for this sequence
`set security-association level per-host`	An optional command that can be used to specify that separate IPSec SAs should be requested for each source/destination host pair

> **Note:** You can configure multiple peers for each sequence—very cool when you want to set a backup path for the IPSec tunnel in case the primary path goes down. When multiple peers are set for a sequence, the device begins with the first one entered and proceeds down the list until an IPSec SA is set up.

Once you've created your crypto map, you need to apply it to an interface.

Applying the Crypto Map

When you create IPSec tunnels without using Generic Routing Encapsulation (GRE) tunnels, the crypto map has to be applied to the outgoing interface. If you use GRE tunnels instead, you need to apply the crypto map to both the tunnel interface and the egress interfaces. The *egress interfaces* are any that may be used to form the GRE tunnel. You can have more than one GRE interface.

To apply a crypto map to an interface, enter the following command in interface configuration mode, where *map-name* is the name of the crypto map being applied to the interface:

`crypto map map-name`

For redundancy, you could apply the same *crypto map set* to more than one interface. The default behavior is as follows:

- Each interface has its own piece of the security association database.
- The IP address of the local interface is used as the local address for IPSec traffic originating from or destined to that interface.

If you decide to apply the same crypto map set to multiple interfaces, you need to specify an identifying interface. Doing this causes the following:

- The per-interface portion of the IPSec security association database (SAD) is established one time and shared for traffic through all the interfaces that share the same crypto map.
- The IP address of the identifying interface is used as the local address for IPSec traffic originating from or destined to those interfaces sharing the same crypto map set.

To designate the identifying interface, enter the following command in global configuration mode, where *map-name* is the name of the crypto map and *local-id* is the IP address of the identifying interface:

`crypto map map-name local-address local-id`

> **Warning:** You must use this `crypto map` command if you're applying a crypto map to a GRE tunnel, because the crypto map will be applied to both the tunnel interface and the egress interface.

Configuring Cisco IOS IPSec for Pre-shared Keys Site-to-Site 181

> **WARNING** When you specify an identifying interface, you must use the IP address of that interface whenever you configure the peer statements on the remote peers.

Before you move on to the final step in the process of configuring IPSec for pre-shared keys—testing and verifying IPSec—let's run through a sample IPSec configuration.

In Exercise 8.2, you'll build upon the configuration you began in the IKE section of this chapter. For a refresher, the following graphic illustrates the network you began configuring:

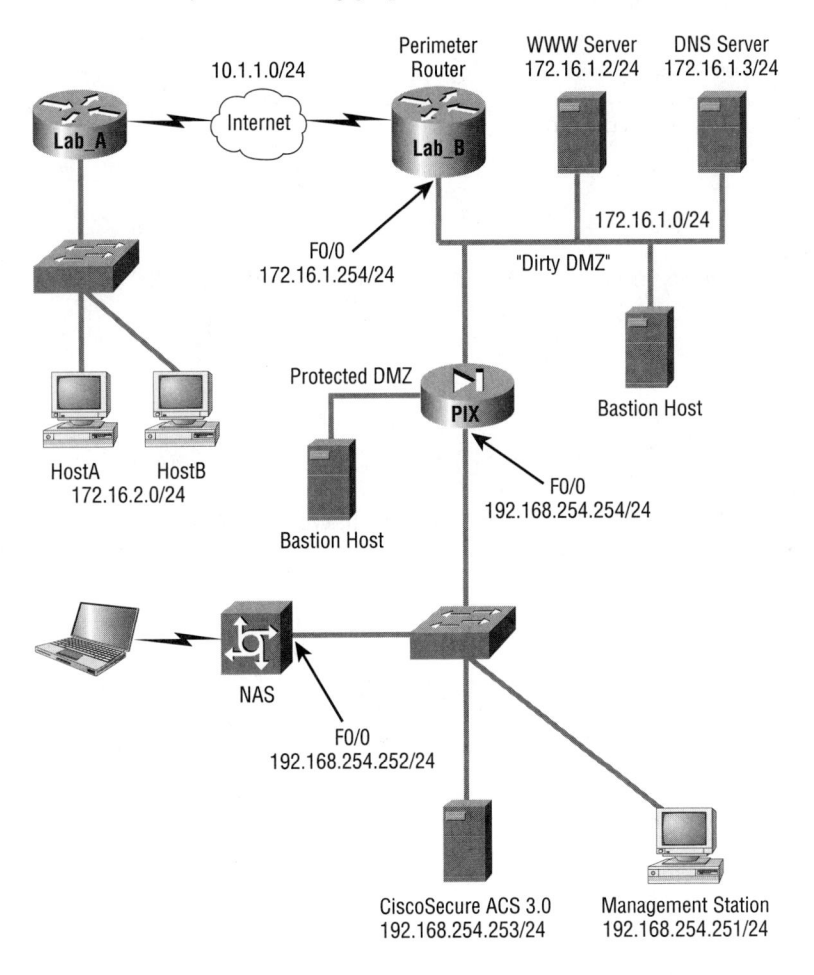

But before you jump into configuring IPSec, let's take another look at how the devices have been configured so far:

```
Lab_A#conf t
Enter configuration commands, one per line.  End with CNTL/Z.
Lab_A(config)#crypto isakmp enable
Lab_A(config)#crypto isakmp policy 2
Lab_A(config-isakmp)#encryption 3des
Lab_A(config-isakmp)#hash md5
Lab_A(config-isakmp)#authentication pre-share
Lab_A(config-isakmp)#exit
Lab_A(config)#crypto isakmp key cisco address 10.1.1.2
Lab_A(config)#^Z
Lab_A#

Lab_B#conf t
Enter configuration commands, one per line.  End with CNTL/Z.
Lab_B(config)#crypto isakmp enable
Lab_B(config)#crypto isakmp policy 2
Lab_B(config-isakmp)#encryption 3des
Lab_B(config-isakmp)#hash md5
Lab_B(config-isakmp)#authentication pre-share
Lab_B(config-isakmp)#exit
Lab_B(config)#crypto isakmp key cisco address 10.1.1.1
Lab_B(config)#^Z
Lab_B#
```

EXERCISE 8.2

Configuring IPSec on the Sample Corporate Network

Now you're ready to configure IPSec. You need to add IPSec to your currently configured network with IKE using the following steps:

1. Create a transform set on each device named `test` using esp-des and tunnel mode.

2. Leave the global IPSec SA lifetimes set to their defaults.

3. Create an extended access list on each device that will identify interesting traffic.

4. Create a crypto map on each device using the name `test1` and sequence number 100. Each sequence should use the transform set test and the extended access list just created, and set the peer to the IP address of the outgoing interface of the remote device.

EXERCISE 8.2 *(continued)*

5. Apply the crypto map to each device's outgoing interface.

6. Use the following commands to configure the Lab_A router:

   Lab_A#**conf t**

   Enter configuration commands, one per line. End with CNTL/Z.

   Lab_A(config)#**crypto ipsec tramsform-set test esp-des**

   Lab_A(cfg-crypto-trans)#**exit**

   Lab_A(config)#**access-list 100 permit ip 172.16.2.0 0.0.0.255 172.16.1.0 0.0.0.255**

   Lab_A(config)#**cryto map test1 100 ipsec-isakmp**

   Lab_A(config-crypto-map)#**match address 100**

   Lab_A(config-crypto-map)#**set transform-set test**

   Lab_A(config-crypto-map)#**set peer 10.1.1.2**

   Lab_A(config-crypto-map)#**exit**

   Lab_A(config)#**interface s0/0**

   Lab_A(config-if)#**crypto map test1**

   Lab_A(config-if)#**^Z**

   Lab_A#

   Lab_B#**conf t**

   Enter configuration commands, one per line. End with CNTL/Z.

   Lab_B(config)#**crypto ipsec tramsform-set test esp-des**

   Lab_B(cfg-crypto-trans)#**exit**

   Lab_B(config)#**access-list 100 permit ip 172.16.1.0 0.0.0.255 172.16.2.0 0.0.0.255**

   Lab_B(config)#**cryto map test1 100 ipsec-isakmp**

   Lab_B(config-crypto-map)#**match address 100**

   Lab_B(config-crypto-map)#**set transform-set test**

   Lab_B(config-crypto-map)#**set peer 10.1.1.1**

> **EXERCISE 8.2 *(continued)***
>
> Lab_B(config-crypto-map)#**exit**
>
> Lab_B(config)#**interface s1/0**
>
> Lab_B(config-if)#**crypto map test1**
>
> Lab_B(config-if)#^Z
>
> Lab_B#

As always, you have to be able to verify your configurations. The next section guides you through this process.

Testing and Verifying IPSec

It's test-and-verify time again. With network operations, you can't skip these steps. So, now you'll take some time to review the commands you need to use to verify IPSec operation.

The show crypto isakmp sa command is one of the most widely used commands for verifying IKE operation after IPSec has been configured. It gives you information about all the active IKE SAs on the device. Here's a sample of the output you'll get when you use this command:

```
Lab_A#show crypto isakmp sa
    dst        src        state       conn-id  slot
  10.1.1.2   10.1.1.1    QM_IDLE         82      0
```

Have a problem? For troubleshooting, it may be important to reset IKE SAs using the clear crypto isakmp *conn-id* command. With it, you can clear a single IKE SA. Alternatively, you can use the clear crypto isakmp * command to clear all active IKE SAs.

If you need more information, use the debug crypto isakmp command to display messages about IKE events. In addition, you can use the debug crypto ipsec command to learn even more.

If you want to get a look at the configuration of all IPSec transform sets on a certain device, use the show crypto ipsec transform-set command. Here's a sample of its output:

```
Lab_A#show crypto ipsec transform-set
Transform set test: { esp-des }
   will negotiate = { Tunnel, },
```

The aptly named show crypto map command displays the configuration of all crypto maps currently configured on a device—a great way to find out if someone blew their crypto map configuration.

To verify that an IPSec SA is working okay, use the show crypto ipsec sa command. Here's a sample of its output:

```
Lab_A#show crypto ipsec sa
interface: Serial0/0
    Crypto map tag: test1, local addr. 10.1.1.1
    local  ident (addr/mask/prot/port):
    (10.1.1.1/255.255.255.255/0/0)
    remote ident (addr/mask/prot/port):
    (10.1.1.2/255.255.255.255/0/0)
   current_peer: 10.1.1.2
     PERMIT, flags={origin_is_acl,}
    #pkts encaps: 10, #pkts encrypt: 10, #pkts digest 10
    #pkts decaps: 10, #pkts decrypt: 10, #pkts verify 10
    #send errors 10, #recv errors 0

    local crypto endpt.: 10.1.1.1, remote crypto endpt.: 10.1.1.2
    path mtu 1500, media mtu 1500
    current outbound spi: 20890A6F

    inbound esp sas:
     spi: 0x257A1039(628756537)
       transform: esp-des ,
       in use settings ={Tunnel, }
       slot: 0, conn id: 26, crypto map: test1
       sa timing: remaining key lifetime (k/sec): (4607999/90)
       IV size: 8 bytes
       replay detection support: Y

    inbound ah sas:

    outbound esp sas:
     spi: 0x20890A6F(545852015)
       transform: esp-des ,
       in use settings ={Tunnel, }
       slot: 0, conn id: 27, crypto map: test1
       sa timing: remaining key lifetime (k/sec): (4607999/90)
       IV size: 8 bytes
       replay detection support: Y

    outbound ah sas:
```

There are also several commands you can use to reset an IPSec SA. Table 8.2 lists these commands and describes what they do.

That's all there is to configuring IPSec utilizing pre-shared keys. You're not completely done yet though, because next I'll show you how to configure IPSec without using IKE. If you're on a roll, great—keep going. But get some coffee or get up and stretch, because you're only about halfway through this chapter.

TABLE 8.2   IPSec SA clear Commands

Command	Purpose
clear crypto sa	Resets all IPSec SAs on a device
clear crypto sa peer {ip-address | peer-name}	Resets the IPSec SA for the specified peer
clear crypto sa map map-name	Resets the IPSec SA for the specified crypto map
clear crypto sa entry destination-address protocol spi	Resets the IPSec SA for the specified address, protocol, and SPI
clear crypto sa counters	Resets the IPSec traffic counters for all IPSec SAs on the device

Configuring IPSec Manually

If you configure IPSec manually, you don't have to use IKE. But doing this means you'll have to specify the inbound and outbound keys to use on each device for establishing the IPSec SA manually. And no doubt you remember me telling you that wasn't such a great idea back in Chapter 7, "Understanding Cisco IOS IPSec Support," for two reasons: It's not as secure as using IKE, and it's harder to scale.

It follows, then, that you don't need to bother creating an IKE policy if you manually configure IPSec, right? Right, but you don't get to skip any of the other steps that were laid out for configuring IPSec utilizing pre-shared keys.

Other than having to give the inbound and outbound keys your personal attention, the main difference in configuring IPSec manually is how you create the crypto map. Let's look at that now. While in global configuration mode, you create a manual crypto map sequence by entering the following command, where *map-name* is the name of the crypto map and *seq-num* is the sequence number of the crypto map sequence, a value between 1 and 65,535:

crypto map *map-name seq-num* **ipsec-manual**

All the commands defined previously in Table 8.1 still apply to manual crypto map sequences, but four more mandatory commands must be entered in crypto map configuration mode (see Table 8.3).

TABLE 8.3 Additional Commands for Manual Crypto Map Sequences

Command	Purpose
set session-key inbound ah *spi hex-key-string*	A mandatory command that specifies the inbound key to use for Authentication Header (AH)
set session-key outbound ah *spi hex-key-string*	A mandatory command that specifies the outbound key to use for AH
set session-key inbound esp *spi cipher hex-key-string [authenticator hex-key-string]*	A mandatory command that specifies the inbound key to use for Encapsulating Security Payload (ESP)
set session-key outbound esp *spi cipher hex-key-string [authenticator hex-key-string]*	A mandatory command that specifies the outbound key to use for ESP

WARNING The outbound key of one device must be the same as the inbound key of the remote peer.

Configuring IPSec for RSA-Encrypted Nonces

RSA-encrypted nonces require you to perform two tasks: manually generate the public/private keys and then manually enter the public key of a device on the remote peer. Configuring IPSec for RSA-encrypted nonces is a five-step process:

1. Prepare for IPSec using RSA-encrypted nonces. This includes planning how to distribute the public keys.
2. Generate the RSA public/private keys manually.
3. Configure IKE using RSA-encrypted nonces.
4. Configure IPSec.
5. Test and verify IPSec.

You'll work through each of these steps in this section.

Preparing for IPSec Using RSA-Encrypted Nonces

You need to answer all those questions outlined in the "Preparing for IKE and IPSec" section at the beginning of this chapter, plus one more: What's your plan for distributing the public keys to potential peers? (This has to be accomplished out of band.)

Generating the RSA Public/Private Keys Manually for RSA-Encrypted Nonces

This step is the biggest change from configuring IPSec utilizing pre-shared keys. It's also the most involved step. When you're generating the RSA public/private keys manually, you've got five steps to follow:

1. Plan for configuring RSA.
2. Configure the device's hostname and domain name.
3. Generate the RSA public/private keys.
4. Manually enter the RSA public key on remote devices.
5. Manage the RSA keys.

Planning for Configuring RSA

There are a few more questions to answer before you jump in and configure RSA, so the number of errors that can occur during configuration are kept to a minimum:

- What peers will use RSA encryption? Make a list of these devices.
- What type of RSA keys will you use? You have two choices: general-usage or special-usage keys.
- What size of key modulus—a value between 360 and 2048 bits—do you want to use? The higher the bit value, the stronger the encryption.

Configuring the Device's Hostname and Domain Name for RSA-Encrypted Nonces

Armed with the answers to the preceding questions, you're ready to begin configuring these three items:

- Hostname
- Domain name
- Static hostname-to-address mapping for each peer

Because RSA encryption uses these three items for IKE identity, they must be properly configured in order for RSA to function. To configure the hostname of a device, enter the following command in global configuration mode, where *hostname* is the name of the device:

hostname *hostname*

The domain name is used in conjunction with the hostname to produce the fully qualified domain name for the device. You configure this by entering the following command in global configuration mode, where *domain-name* is the name of the domain:

`ip domain-name` *domain-name*

If a DNS server isn't available, you only need to configure a static hostname-to-address mapping for each peer by entering the following command in global configuration mode:

`ip host` *name* `[`*tcp-port-number*`]` *address1* `[`*address2 address8*`]`

The parameters for the preceding command are as follows:

- *name*: The name of the remote device.
- *tcp-port-number*: The CP port number to connect to when using the defined hostname in conjunction with an EXEC connect or Telnet command.
- *address1*: The IP address you want bound to the hostname.
- *address2 address8*: You can bind seven more addresses to the hostname.

Generating the RSA Public/Private Keys

Now you're ready to generate the RSA public/private keys on each device; but before issuing the command to generate the keys, you need to decide if you want to create *special-usage keys* or *general-usage keys*. Special-usage keys generate two public/private key pairs per device—a good choice when you're using RSA signatures and RSA-encrypted nonces on the same device and you don't want them using the same keys. General-usage keys create one public/private key pair that will be used by both RSA signatures and RSA-encrypted nonces.

With the key-type decision out of the way, it's time to start configuring. Enter the following command in global configuration mode:

`crypto key generate rsa [usage-keys]`

Be sure to use the `usage-keys` keyword when you want to generate special-usage keys.

Once you've entered the command to generate the keys, the device prompts you to enter the modulus length. This value tells the device the level of encryption strength to use—the higher the number, the stronger the encryption. Keep in mind that entering a higher value also means it will take longer to generate those keys.

Let's take a second and see what this process looks like on a device. Keep in mind that this device already has its hostname and domain name configured:

```
Lab_A#conf t
Enter configuration commands, one per line.  End with CNTL/Z.
Lab_A(config)#crypto key generate rsa
The name for the keys will be: Lab_A.mycorp.com
```

```
Choose the size of the key modulus in the range of 360 to 2048 for your
    Signature Keys.
Choosing a key modulus greater than 512 may take a few minutes.
How many bits in the modulus [512]: 512
Generating RSA keys
[OK]
% Key pair was generated at 10:22:30 UTC Dec 23 2002
Lab_A(config)#
```

After your RSA keys have been generated, you need a way to view them so you can take the public key from one device and input it into another one. To check out the RSA public key, enter the following command in privileged-exec mode:

show crypto key mypubkey rsa

Here's a sample of what Lab_A will then show you:

```
Lab_A#show crypto key mypubkey rsa
Key name: Lab_A.mycorp.com
 Usage: General Purpose Key
 Key Data:
  005C300D 06092A86 4886F70D 01010105 00034B00 30480241 00C5E23B 55D6AB22
      04AEF1BA A54028A6 9ACC01C5 129D99E4 64CAB820 847EDAD9 DF0B4E4C 73A05DD2
      BD62A8A9 FA603DD2 E2A8A6F8 98F76E28 D58AD221 B583D7A4 71020301 0001
```

The information below the words *Key Data* is the public key. Since you need to input this key into any device you want to peer with, it's a good idea to copy it down so you can transmit it out of band to remote devices.

Entering the RSA Public Key on Remote Devices Manually

Before you can enter the public key on any remote devices, you need to get into public key chain configuration mode. Do this by entering this command while in global configuration mode:

crypto key pubkey-chain rsa

You must specify whether the key is an addressed key or a named key. How the IKE identity has been configured on the device that generated the key decides this. If the IKE identity is address, you use the addressed key; if it's hostname, use the named key. You can also specify whether the key is an encryption key or a signature key with the following rules:

- **Encryption** specifies that the key will be an encryption special-usage key. Use this when you've generated special-usage keys and you're inputting the encryption key.

- **Signature** specifies that the key will be a signature special-usage key. Use this when you've generated special-usage keys and you're inputting the signature key.

- Not specifying the type of key makes it a general-purpose key. Use this when you generate general-usage keys.

While in public key chain configuration mode, enter one of the following commands:

addressed-key *key-address* {**encryption** | **signature**}

named-key *key-name* {**encryption** | **signature**}

In the addressed-key command, *key-address* is the IP address of the device that generated the key. In the named-key command, *key-name* is the fully qualified domain name of the device that generated the key.

Once you've specified the type of key and entered public key configuration mode, it's time to issue the key-string command. After that, you input the public key. Then, use the quit command to return to public key configuration mode. Here's the output caused by entering the key generated by Lab_A on Lab_B:

```
Lab_B#conf t
Enter configuration commands, one per line.  End with CNTL/Z.
Lab_B(config)#crypto key pubkey-chain rsa
Lab_B(config-pubkey-chain)#addressed-key 10.1.1.1
Lab_B(config-pubkey-key)#key-string
Lab_B(config-pubkey)#005C300D 06092A86 4886F70D 01010105 00034B00 30480241
      00C5E23B 55D6AB22 04AEF1BA A54028A6 9ACC01C5 129D99E4 64CAB820 847EDAD9
      DF0B4E4C 73A05DD2 BD62A8A9 FA603DD2 E2A8A6F8 98F76E28 D58AD221 B583D7A4
      71020301 0001
Lab_B(config-pubkey)#quit
Lab_B(config-pubkey-key)#^Z
Lab_B#
```

Verify that the key has been accepted by entering the command show crypto key pubkey-chain rsa in privileged-exec mode:

```
Lab_B#show crypto key pubkey-chain rsa
Codes: M -  Manually configured, C - Extracted from Certificate


Code   Usage       IP-Address      Name
M      General     10.1.1.1
```

To check out the actual key that you or someone else entered, use the show crypto key pubkey-chain rsa {address *address* | name *name*} command in privileged-exec mode:

```
Lab_B#show crypto key pubkey-chain rsa address 10.1.1.1
Key name:
Key address: 10.1.1.1
 Usage: General Purpose Key
 Source: Manual
```

Data:
  005C300D 06092A86 4886F70D 01010105 00034B00 30480241 00C5E23B 55D6AB22
    04AEF1BA A54028A6 9ACC01C5 129D99E4 64CAB820 847EDAD9 DF0B4E4C 73A05DD2
    BD62A8A9 FA603DD2 E2A8A6F8 98F76E28 D58AD221 B583D7A4 71020301 0001

Managing the RSA Keys

To keep your system clean, it's crucial to remove keys that are no longer valid. To spruce things up, get into public key chain configuration mode and issue the no form of either the addressed-key command or the named-key command.

It's nice that those last three steps in this process are pretty much identical to those for configuring pre-shared keys, isn't it?

Configuring IKE Using RSA-Encrypted Nonces

You'll configure IKE almost exactly the same way as you did for pre-shared keys. The one exception is the authentication method. Instead of entering the authentication pre-shared command, you enter the authentication rsa-encr command. Verify that the IKE policy works the same way using the same commands you used earlier.

Configuring IPSec for RSA-Encrypted Nonces

IPSec for RSA-encrypted nonces is configured in the same way as IPSec utilizing pre-shared keys—no exceptions. For a refresher on configuring IPSec, refer back to the section titled "Configure IPSec," earlier in this chapter.

Testing and Verifying IPSec for RSA-Encrypted Nonces

Finally, to verify IPSec for RSA-encrypted nonces, you use the same commands you used in the "Testing and Verifying IPSec" section earlier in this chapter, along with the show commands described in this section.

Configuring Cisco IOS IPSec Certificate Authority Support Site-to-Site

IPSec for CA is the most scalable of all IPSec implementations because it allows a device to receive a digital certificate from a certificate authority (CA) server that the device uses to identify itself for IPSec peering.

This section describes all the steps you'll need to learn how to configure IPSec for CA.

Configuring CA Support Tasks

To configuring IPSec for CA, you must complete these five tasks:

- Prepare for IKE and IPSec.
- Configure CA support.
- Configure IKE.
- Configure IPSec.
- Test and verify IPSec.

When you find yourself at the end of this section, you'll be able to implement site-to-site IPSec for CA. Did you notice that some of these tasks overlap with the ones described previously in IPSec for pre-shared keys? I'll only touch briefly on the overlapping ones.

Preparing for IKE and IPSec

Once again, you need to answer those questions back in the "Preparing for IKE and IPSec" section of this chapter. This time, you get two additional questions to ponder:

- Which CA server are you going to use? You need to determine that in order to assign your certificate.
- Do you need to use trusted root CA servers? You need to configure them if you intend to peer with devices that aren't using the same CA server as you are.

Configuring CA Support

This step is the greatest departure from the method used in configuring IPSec utilizing pre-shared keys; there's lots of new stuff to learn in this section. If you want to configure CA support, you have to successfully complete each of the following nine steps:

1. Manage NVRAM memory usage.
2. Configure the device's hostname and domain name.
3. Generate the RSA public/private keys.
4. Declare a CA.
5. Configure a root CA (trusted root).
6. Authenticate the CA.
7. Request the device's certificate.
8. Verify CA interoperability.
9. Save your configurations.

Managing NVRAM Memory Usage

Certificates are stored locally on a device—something that usually won't give you any memory-related grief. But it can; so if you think your situation warrants it, or if you just don't want to take any chances, enter the following command in global configuration mode:

`crypto ca certificate query`

Doing this ensures that the device retrieves certificates from the CA server only when needed.

> **WARNING** Some ugly issues can arise when retrieving certificates if the CA server is down, so be sure the certificate server is up and running before performing your query.

Configuring the Device's Hostname and Domain Name for CA

I won't go over this step again, because you do it the same way you did for RSA-encrypted nonces. If you need a review, refer to the section "Configuring the Device's Hostname and Domain Name for RSA-Encrypted Nonces," earlier in this chapter.

Generating the RSA Public/Private Keys Manually for CA

This step is also accomplished the same way as it was for RSA-encrypted nonces. Refer back to the "Generating the RSA Public/Private Keys Manually for RSA-Encrypted Nonces" section, earlier in this chapter, if you need a review.

Declaring a CA

In order for CA to operate, you must first designate a CA server from which you'll request your certificates. Let's define a few terms before diving into configuration:

Simple Certificate Enrollment Protocol (SCEP)   Simple Certificate Enrollment Protocol (SCEP) is a CA interoperability protocol that permits compliant IPSec peers and CAs to communicate so that the IPSec peer can obtain and use digital certificates from the CA.

Certificate revocation list (CRL)   Certificate revocation lists (CRL) are lists of certificates that have been revoked and are no longer valid. IPSec peers can obtain the CRL from the CA server and check the CRL every time an IPSec peer attempts to establish a new IKE SA.

Registration authority (RA)   A registration authority (RA) is a server that acts as a proxy for the CA so that CA functions can continue when the CA is offline.

This first step in declaring your CA is to enter the following command in global configuration mode, where *name* is the name you'll use to refer to the CA:

`crypto ca identity name`

Entering this command places the device in ca-identity configuration mode where you can spell out the CA-specific information such as the enrollment URL.

That's what you'll do next: enter the URL of your CA. This is the address to which the router will send certificate requests. To configure the enrollment URL, enter the following command in ca-identity configuration mode, where *url* is the URL to which the certificate requests will be sent:

enrollment url *url*

If the CA server you're communicating with provides an RA, you need to enable enrollment RA support by entering the following command in ca-identity configuration mode:

enrollment mode ra

Each of the next four commands should also be entered in this mode.

If your CA server provides an RA and supports Lightweight Directory Access Protocol (LDAP), and your CA server supports both RA and LDAP, you need to specify a URL to query. To do so, enter the following command, where *url* is the LDAP URL to query for retrieving certificates:

query url *url*

By default, the CRL option is disabled. You can enable this function; when it's enabled, a device requires that an IPSec peer's certificate be checked against the appropriate CRL for authentication. If your peer's certificate is found in the CRL database, then your device will respond by rejecting the IPSec peer, and authentication will fail. To avoid this snag, use the following command:

crl optional

By default, devices send the CA server certificate requests every minute until they receive a valid certificate in return. You can change this default behavior with the following command, where *minutes* is a value between 1 and 60:

enrollment retry period *minutes*

Devices also send CA server certificate requests until they receive a valid certificate back—something you'd probably love some control over. Good news: You can limit the number of times a device will request the certificate via this command, where *number* is a value between 1 and 100:

enrollment retry count *number*

You've now successfully declared your CA server. Before moving on, let's look at how this works.

In the following example, device Lab_A is configured to declare a CA that is creatively dubbed test_ca. The enrollment URL is http://ca_server. The CA doesn't support RA or LDAP, and the device is configured to ignore the CRL if one can't be found:

```
Lab_A#conf t
Enter configuration commands, one per line.  End with CNTL/Z.
Lab_A(config)#crypto ca identity test_ca
```

```
Lab_A(ca-identity)#enrollment url http://ca_server
Lab_A(ca-identity)#crl optional
Lab_A(ca-identity)#^Z
Lab_A#
```

Configuring a Root CA (Trusted Root)

A *trusted root CA* is the aptly named CA server that devices trust certificates from even if those devices aren't enrolled with that CA. This is important because you need to know that an IPSec peer may be enrolled with a different CA server than your device.

The first thing you need to do is come up with a name you'll use to refer to your trusted root CA. Do this by entering the following command in global configuration mode, where *name* is the name you'll use for the trusted root CA:

crypto ca trusted-root *name*

When you enter the preceding command, you put the device into trusted root configuration mode—the place from which you'll specify the trusted root–specific information such as the URL from which the trusted root certificates will be received.

Once your trusted root has its name squared away, you need to decide if the device will use SCEP or Trivial File Transfer Protocol (TFTP) to query the trusted root CA. If SCEP is your winner, enter this command in trusted root configuration mode, where *url* is the URL of the trusted root CA:

root CEP *url*

The next three commands are all issued from within the trusted root configuration mode.

If you want to use TFTP, use the following command instead, where *url* is the URL of the trusted root CA:

root TFTP *url*

If the trusted root CA is utilizing an HTTP proxy server, you need to define the URL of the proxy server with the following command, where *url* is the URL of the trusted root CA proxy server:

root PROXY *url*

You also get an option to indicate the URL to query using LDAP for CRLs from the trusted root server. To make this your reality, use the following command, where *ldap-url* is the LDAP URL to use for querying:

crl query *ldap-url*

With your CA server declared and everything including your trusted root servers configured, it's time to move on to authentication.

Authenticating the CA

You need only one command to authenticate a CA server. From within global configuration mode, enter the following command, where *name* is the name you used for the CA server:

crypto ca authenticate *name*

Once your CA server is authenticated, it receives the public key of the CA server. After you've entered the preceding command, the device asks if you accept the certificate, to which you reply either yes or no. Here's an example of authenticating the CA server declared on device Lab_A:

```
Lab_A#conf t
Enter configuration commands, one per line.  End with CNTL/Z.
Lab_A(config)#crypto ca authenticate test_ca
Certificate has the following attributes:
Fingerprint: 0123 4567 89AB CDEF 0123
Do you accept this certificate? [yes/no]#y
Lab_A(config)#
```

Requesting the Device's Certificate

After authenticating the CA, a device needs to request its own certificate from the CA server. To request a certificate, enter the following command in global configuration mode, where *name* is the name you used for the CA server:

crypto ca enroll *name*

Entering the preceding command starts the inquisition—you're then asked a number of questions, as you can see in the following output:

```
Lab_A#conf t
Enter configuration commands, one per line.  End with CNTL/Z.
Lab_A(config)#crypto ca enroll test_ca
%
% Start certificate enrollment ..
% Create a challenge password. You will need to verbally provide this password
        to the CA Administrator in order to revoke your certificate. For security
        reasons your password will not be saved in the configuration. Please make
        a note of it.
Password: cisco
Re-enter password: cisco
% The subject name in the certificate will be: Lab_A.mycorp.com
% Include the router serial number in the subject name? [yes/no]: no
% Include an IP address in the subject name [yes/no]? yes
Interface: serial0/0
```

```
Request certificate from CA [yes/no]? yes
% Certificate request sent to Certificate Authority
% The certificate request fingerprint will be displayed.
% The 'show crypto ca certificate' command will also show the fingerprint.
Lab_A(config)#
```

Verifying and Saving Your Configurations

Once again, it's verification time. Verifying CA interoperability introduces two new **show** commands to the group you met earlier in the "Entering the RSA Public Key on Remote Devices Manually" section of this chapter:

- The `show crypto ca certificates` command can be entered in privileged-exec mode to display information about a device's certificate, the CA server certificate, and any RA certificates.

- The `show crypto ca roots` command can also be entered in privileged-exec mode to display information about the CA roots configured on the device.

You should always save your configuration after you make changes. After all this work, it would be a shame to lose it now.

Use the `copy system:running-config nvram:startup-config` command to save your configuration. This saves the RSA keys as well. Saving to a TFTP server or using the Remote Copy Protocol (RCP) to save your configuration won't save the RSA keys.

Configuring IKE Using CA

IKE is configured the same way it was for pre-shared keys and RSA-encrypted nonces, with one exception: the authentication method used. You need to enter the command `authentication rsa-sig` in IKE policy configuration mode. You verify the IKE policy using the same commands I showed you earlier.

Configuring IPSec for CA

IPSec for CA is configured in the same way as IPSec utilizing pre-shared keys and IPSec for RSA-encrypted nonces with no exceptions. If you're less than clear on this, refer back to the section "Configuring IPSec," earlier in this chapter.

Before we move on to testing and verifying IPSec for CA, let's look at how all these steps come together. To help you see the whole picture, you'll configure IPSec for CA between devices Lab_A and Lab_B in Exercise 8.3. Recall once again the corporate network shown in the following graphic.

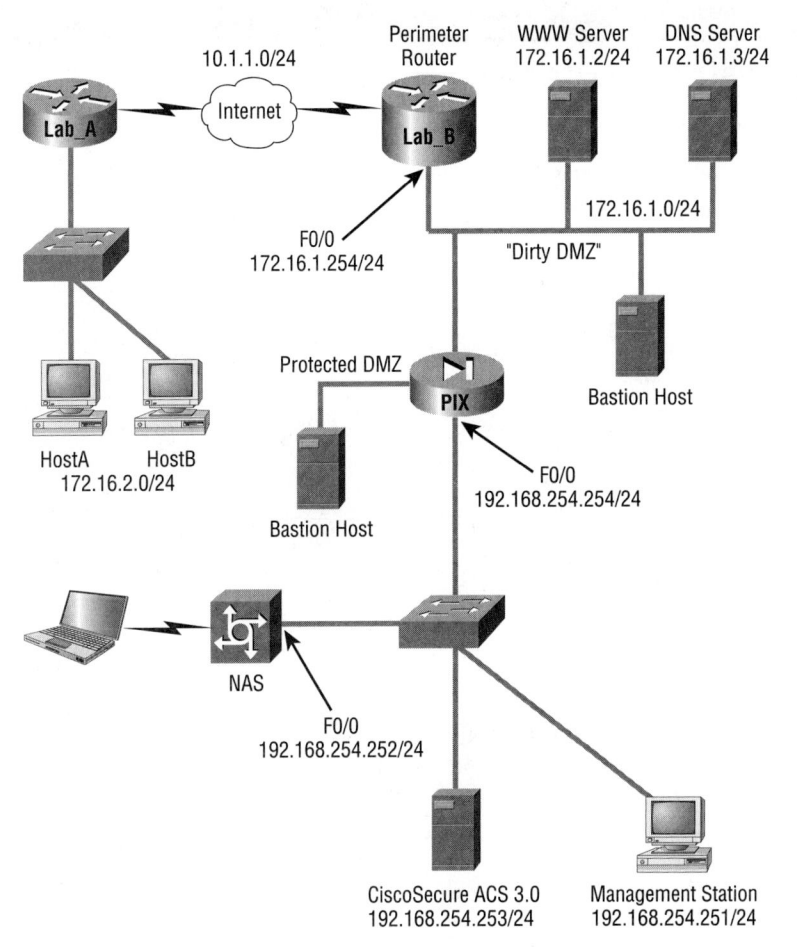

Configuring Cisco IOS IPSec Certificate Authority Support Site-to-Site

Let's get started by dividing the process of configuring IPSec for CA into four steps:

1. Generate RSA public/private keys.
2. Configure CA support.
3. Configure IKE.
4. Configure IPSec.

> **NOTE:** Both hostnames and domain names have already been configured on the devices.

EXERCISE 8.3

Configuring IPSec for the CA Network

This exercise has you configure IPSec using CA on the corporate network example.

1. Generate the public/private keys on each device using the following commands:

   Lab_A#**conf t**

   Enter configuration commands, one per line. End with CNTL/Z.

   Lab_A(config)#**crypto key generate rsa**

   The name for the keys will be: Lab_A.mycorp.com

   Choose the size of the key modulus in the range of 360 to 2048 for your
       Signature Keys.

   Choosing a key modulus greater than 512 may take a few minutes.

   How many bits in the modulus [512]: **512**

   Generating RSA keys

   [OK]

   % Key pair was generated at 10:22:30 UTC Dec 23 2002

   Lab_A(config)#

   Lab_B#**conf t**

   Enter configuration commands, one per line. End with CNTL/Z.

   Lab_B(config)#**crypto key generate rsa**

   The name for the keys will be: Lab_B.mycorp.com

   Choose the size of the key modulus in the range of 360 to 2048 for your
       Signature Keys.

   Choosing a key modulus greater than 512 may take a few minutes.

   How many bits in the modulus [512]: **512**

   Generating RSA keys

   [OK]

EXERCISE 8.3 *(continued)*

% Key pair was generated at 10:22:30 UTC Dec 23 2002

Lab_B(config)#

2. Configure CA support on each device using the following parameters:

    CA name: test_ca.

    Enrollment URL: http://ca_server.

    The devices need to ignore the CRL if one can't be found.

    The CA server doesn't support LDAP.

Use the following commands to configure CA support:

Lab_A(config)#**crypto ca identity test_ca**

Lab_A(ca-identity)#**enrollment url http://ca_server**

Lab_A(ca-identity)#**crl optional**

Lab_A(ca-identity)#**exit**

Lab_A(config)#**crypto ca authenticate test_ca**

Certificate has the following attributes: Fingerprint: 0123 4567 89AB CDEF 0123

Do you accept this certificate? [yes/no]#**y**

Lab_A(config)#**crypto ca enroll test_ca**

%

% Start certificate enrollment.

% Create a challenge password. You will need to verbally provide this password

    to the CA Administrator in order to revoke your certificate. For security

    reasons your password will not be saved in the configuration. Please make

    a note of it.

Password: **cisco**

Re-enter password: **cisco**

% The subject name in the certificate will be: Lab_A.mycorp.com

% Include the router serial number in the subject name? [yes/no]: **no**

> **EXERCISE 8.3** *(continued)*

% Include an IP address in the subject name [yes/no]? **yes**

Interface: **serial0/0**

Request certificate from CA [yes/no]? **yes**

% Certificate request sent to Certificate Authority

% The certificate request fingerprint will be displayed.

% The 'show crypto ca certificate' command will also show the fingerprint.

Lab_A(config)#

Lab_B(config)#**crypto ca identity test_ca**

Lab_B(ca-identity)#**enrollment url http://ca_server**

Lab_B(ca-identity)#**crl optional**

Lab_B(ca-identity)#**exit**

Lab_B(config)#**crypto ca authenticate test_ca**

Certificate has the following attributes: Fingerprint: 0123 4567 89AB CDEF 0123

Do you accept this certificate? [yes/no]#**y**

Lab_B(config)#**crypto ca enroll test_ca**

%

% Start certificate enrollment.

% Create a challenge password. You will need to verbally provide this password
 to the CA Administrator in order to revoke your certificate. For security
 reasons your password will not be saved in the configuration. Please make
 a note of it.

Password: **cisco**

Re-enter password: **cisco**

% The subject name in the certificate will be: Lab_A.mycorp.com

% Include the router serial number in the subject name? [yes/no]: **no**

EXERCISE 8.3 *(continued)*

```
% Include an IP address in the subject name [yes/no]? yes
Interface: serial1/0
Request certificate from CA [yes/no]? yes
% Certificate request sent to Certificate Authority
% The certificate request fingerprint will be displayed.
% The 'show crypto ca certificate' command will also show the fingerprint.
Lab_B(config)#
```

3. Configure IKE between the Lab_A device and the Lab_B device with the following parameters:

   Lab_A interface Serial 0/0 with IP address 10.1.1.1 /24

   Lab_B interface Serial 1/0 with IP address 10.1.1.2 /24

   Lab_A IKE policy priority equals 2

   Lab_B IKE policy priority equals 2

   3DES message encryption

   MD5 message hash

   Authentication method: rsa-sig

   Default Diffie-Hellman group for both devices

   Default IKE SA lifetime for both devices

   IKE identity as the address for both devices

   Use the following commands to configure IKE:

```
Lab_A(config)#crypto isakmp enable
Lab_A(config)#crypto isakmp policy 2
Lab_A(config-isakmp)#encryption 3des
Lab_A(config-isakmp)#hash md5
Lab_A(config-isakmp)#authentication rsa-sig
Lab_A(config-isakmp)#exit
```

> **EXERCISE 8.3** *(continued)*

Lab_A(config)#

Lab_B(config)#**crypto isakmp enable**

Lab_B(config)#**crypto isakmp policy 2**

Lab_B(config-isakmp)#**encryption 3des**

Lab_B(config-isakmp)#**hash md5**

Lab_B(config-isakmp)#**authentication rsa-sig**

Lab_B(config-isakmp)#**exit**

Lab_B(config)#

4. Configure IPSec, moving through the following list from beginning to end:

   a. Create a transform set on each device named `test` using esp-des and tunnel mode.

   b. Leave the global IPSec SA lifetimes set to their defaults.

   c. Create a symmetrical extended access list on each device that will permit traffic from networks 172.16.2.0 /24 and 172.16.1.0 /24.

   d. Create a crypto map on each device using the name `test1` and sequence number `100`.

   e. Each sequence should use the transform set test and the extended access list just created, and set the peer to the IP address of the outgoing interface of the remote device.

   f. Apply the crypto map to each device's outgoing interface.

   Use the following commands to configure IPSec:

   Lab_A(config)#**crypto ipsec tramsform-set test esp-des**

   Lab_A(cfg-crypto-trans)#**exit**

   Lab_A(config)#**access-list 100 permit ip 172.16.2.0 0.0.0.255 172.16.1.0 0.0.0.255**

   Lab_A(config)#**cryto map test1 100 ipsec-isakmp**

   Lab_A(config-crypto-map)#**match address 100**

   Lab_A(config-crypto-map)#**set transform-set test**

   Lab_A(config-crypto-map)#**set peer 10.1.1.2**

   Lab_A(config-crypto-map)#**exit**

EXERCISE 8.3 (continued)

Lab_A(config)#**interface s0/0**

Lab_A(config-if)#**crypto map test1**

Lab_A(config-if)#**^Z**

Lab_A#

Lab_B(config)#**crypto ipsec tramsform-set test esp-des**

Lab_B(cfg-crypto-trans)#**exit**

Lab_B(config)#**access-list 100 permit ip 172.16.1.0 0.0.0.255 172.16.2.0 0.0.0.255**

Lab_B(config)#**cryto map test1 100 ipsec-isakmp**

Lab_B(config-crypto-map)#**match address 100**

Lab_B(config-crypto-map)#**set transform-set test**

Lab_B(config-crypto-map)#**set peer 10.1.1.1**

Lab_B(config-crypto-map)#**exit**

Lab_B(config)#**interface s1/0**

Lab_B(config-if)#**crypto map test1**

Lab_B(config-if)#**^Z**

Lab_B#

You did it: You've configured IPSec for CA support all the way through! Oops, sorry—there's one more thing.

Testing and Verifying IPSec for CA

Verification. You have to verify stuff, and IPSec for CA is no exception. You complete this last gasp of a task using the same commands you learned earlier in the "Testing and Verifying IPSec" section of this chapter, along with the show commands introduced to in this section.

Summary

Do you feel as though you've run a marathon? This chapter was very long, packed with tons of things to remember.

It's imperative that you be able to configure IPSec, starting with how to configure IPSec utilizing pre-shared keys. In addition, you need to know how to create IKE policies and configure pre-shared keys. Configuring IPSec without IKE is done using the IPSec-manual crypto map. Manually configuring IPSec requires you to specify the inbound and outbound keys used for establishing IPSec peers.

In addition to IPSec with IKE, you can use RSA-encrypted nonces with IPSec. These require you to manually generate RSA keys and then manually input the public key into all the devices you intend to peer with. However, don't try this with large networks.

Configuring IPSec can also be accomplished using CA—the most scalable of all the implementation types. CAs allow a device to request a certificate from a CA server and use that certificate in all of its peering attempts.

You've covered a tremendous amount of material in this chapter, so don't feel bad if you didn't get it all on your first read through. Take as much time as you need to go back and review any areas you feel shaky about. Chapter 9, "Cisco IOS Remote Access Using Cisco Easy VPN," will be ready and waiting. The best news about Chapter 9 is that it's short and sweet, and it covers Easy VPN.

Exam Essentials

Understand the tasks required for IPSec utilizing pre-shared keys. Configuring IPSec with pre-shared keys requires the following four tasks, in this order:

1. Prepare for IKE and IPSec.
2. Configure IKE.
3. Configure IPSec.
4. Test and verify IPSec.

You must be able to perform each of these four tasks.

Be able to implement an IKE policy. Given the need for IKE, you must be able to create an IKE policy. Once the IKE policy is created, you must be able to implement it on the devices you wish to peer.

Be able to implement IPSec with IKE. You must be able to implement IPSec once you've configured IKE. This requires you to configure global IPSec SA lifetimes, transform sets, extended access lists, and crypto maps, and then apply the crypto map to an interface.

Be able to implement IPSec without IKE. You must be able to implement IPSec without the use of IKE. This requires you to manually configure the appropriate inbound and outbound session keys.

Be able to implement RSA-encrypted nonces. Given a scenario that requires the use of RSA-encrypted nonces, you must be able to implement it. This requires generating RSA public/private keys, manually entering the public key on devices you wish to peer with, configuring IKE using RSA-encrypted nonces, and configuring IPSec.

Understand the tasks required for IPSec with CA. Configuring IPSec with CA requires the following five tasks:

1. Prepare for IKE and IPSec.
2. Configure CA support.
3. Configure IKE.
4. Configure IPSec.
5. Test and verify IPSec.

You must be able to perform each of these five tasks.

Be able to implement IPSec with CA. Given a scenario that requires the use of CA servers, you must be able to implement it. This requires you to generate RSA public/private keys, declare a CA server, configure trusted root servers, authenticate the CA servers, request a certificate, configure IKE using RSA signatures, and configure IPSec.

Chapter 9

Cisco IOS Remote Access Using Cisco Easy VPN

THE FOLLOWING SECUR EXAM TOPICS ARE COVERED IN THIS CHAPTER:

- ✓ Understanding Cisco Easy VPN
- ✓ Understanding the Easy VPN Server
- ✓ Understanding the Cisco VPN software client
- ✓ Setting up the Easy VPN Server
- ✓ Setting up the Cisco VPN 4.6 Client

This short chapter introduces a cool development in VPN technology: Cisco Easy VPN. Although it can cut down considerably on labor, Cisco's Easy VPN won't work for you in every situation. I'll list which VPN features are supported and which aren't, and I'll include an overview of the Cisco VPN 4.6 Client Software.

I'll also present a configuration example that focuses on how you can make the Easy VPN Server into an IOS router (a relatively new feature) and make the Easy VPN Remote into the VPN 4.6 Client.

In addition, I'll explain some great tools you can use to eliminate unnecessary user interference when installing the VPN 4.6 Client software. This chapter wraps up with a hands-on lab where you'll get to install the Cisco VPN 4.6 Client on a Windows machine.

Configuring IOS Remote Access Using Cisco Easy VPN

Are you ready for something that's really as easy as its name implies? Look no further, because Cisco has become your genie—ready and waiting to grant your wish by bringing you the aptly named Cisco Easy VPN.

Virtual private networks (VPNs) have been around for some time, and you know there are many ways to configure them because we also covered some VPN configurations in Chapter 7, "Understanding Cisco IOS IPSec Support." VPNs can be as simple as two fixed IOS routers establishing a VPN between them, or they can be more complex, with multiple, mobile PC users and VPN Concentrators. Management in the first scenario is typically a snap, but in the second scenario, it's a lot more complicated.

This section focuses on a new feature in IOS that allows any capable IOS router to act as a VPN server, permitting your remote clients to establish VPN connections to the IOS router acting as a VPN server.

Introduction to Cisco Easy VPN

Cisco Easy VPN consists of two primary components: the Easy VPN Server and the Easy VPN Remote. The Easy VPN Server can be any of the following devices:

- IOS router
- PIX firewall
- VPN Concentrator device

The Easy VPN Server acts as a head-end device for either site-to-site or remote access VPN clients. It has the ability to push security policies to Easy VPN Remote clients before connections are actually established, ensuring that those clients always have current policies in place. Remember, anything that helps you to manage multiple remote devices is a good thing. Easy VPN Server goes a long way toward helping Cisco Easy VPN earn the moniker *easy*.

The Easy VPN Remote can be either a site-to-site device or the remote access VPN Client. In fact, it can be anything on the following list of devices:

- IOS router (800, 900, and 1700 series)
- PIX firewall
- VPN 3002 Hardware Client device
- VPN software client

As I said, the Easy VPN Remote can receive security policies from the Easy VPN Server, which minimizes the amount of configuration and maintenance required on remote devices and cuts your aggravation dramatically—especially if you have an ever-growing number of them.

You can see that there're quite a few possible combinations of Easy VPN Server and Easy VPN Remote options. The remainder of this chapter focuses specifically on how the Easy VPN Server becomes an IOS router, as well as how the Easy VPN Remote becomes the VPN software client.

The option of using the IOS router as the Easy VPN Server is a fairly recent development. The ability to use an IOS router instead of a PIX firewall or VPN Concentrator as the head-end to Easy VPN Clients offers a world of possibilities when you're establishing VPN connections throughout your existing, installed infrastructure. This flexibility is great, and adding VPN server capabilities to IOS can deliver the goods for you.

So, limiting our talk to this combination of server and remote, let's take a deeper look into the Easy VPN Server and Easy VPN Remote.

The Easy VPN Server

As of IOS release 12.2(8)T, the Cisco Easy VPN Server is available on an IOS router to support either the hardware Easy VPN Remote devices or the VPN software client.

End users have the capability to establish IPSec communications with these IOS routers, and the IOS routers acting as Easy VPN Servers have the ability to push security policies to these remote devices. The 12.2(8)T Easy VPN Server release of IOS adds support for the following VPN functions:

- Mode configuration version 6 support
- Xauth version 6 support
- IKE Dead Peer Detection (DPD)
- Split tunneling control
- Initial contact
- Group-based policy control

The IKE DPD is a form of keepalive for VPN connections. A number of problems could cause a VPN remote device to "disappear" or lose connectivity without being able to inform the VPN server. Ever had a dial-in line die? That's only one example. IKE DPD from the VPN server sends "R-U-THERE?" messages to idle VPN remote devices. If the idle devices fail to respond, the VPN server assumes the connection has been broken and responds by recovering the resources dedicated to maintaining that particular connection.

Split tunneling control gives the VPN remote the ability to maintain intranet and Internet access at the same time. Without split tunneling enabled, the remote will send all traffic—intranet and Internet—across the tunnel. If the VPN remote device is already Internet connected, it may not be necessary to have Internet traffic filled through the tunnel.

Initial contact solves this problem. Imagine that a VPN remote device is attached to a VPN server, and the connection is broken for some reason. The VPN remote device attempts to reestablish the VPN connection, only to find that its connection attempts are denied because it supposedly already has an established connection. "But," you sputter, "I'm not there anymore, I'm here!" In the formerly unforgiving world of VPN, those cries would have been ignored—or they would have flooded Help Desks—until now. Initial contact is supported by all Cisco VPN devices, meaning that whenever a new VPN connection is to be established, any previous connection information is reset.

But the Easy VPN Server doesn't support all possible IPSec options. Table 9.1 illustrates the options that are and aren't supported.

TABLE 9.1 Easy VPN Supported and Unsupported Options

Options	Supported	Unsupported
Authentication algorithm	HMAC-MD5 HMAC-SHA1	
Authentication types	Pre-shared keys RSA digital signatures	Digital Signature Standard (DSS)
Diffie-Hellman (DH) groups	2 5	1
IKE encryption algorithms	DES 3DES	
IPSec encryption algorithms	DES 3DES NULL	
IPSec protocol identifiers	ESP IPCOMP-LZS	Authentication Header (AH)
IPSEC protocol mode	Tunnel	Transport

In addition, a couple more options aren't supported: manual keys and perfect forward security (PFS).

Let's move on to the Cisco VPN software client and how it's installed and configured.

Introduction to the Cisco VPN Software Client

The Cisco VPN software client can be used to establish VPN connections to any of the Easy VPN Server devices listed earlier in this chapter, including an IOS router. The Cisco VPN software client is also available via Cisco Connection Online (CCO) to customers with SMARTnet support.

The Cisco VPN software client is available for the following operating systems:

- Windows 95, 98, Me, NT 4.0, 2000, and XP
- Linux (Intel)
- Solaris (UltraSPARC 32-bit)
- Mac OS X 10.1

Once installed, the VPN Client allows you to configure and select a number of possible VPN servers. When you launch the VPN Client, the window shown in Figure 9.1 appears.

Since no connections are configured, you need to add one by clicking the New button. When you do this, the Create New VPN Connection Entry Wizard appears. This window prompts you to name the connection and gives you the option of adding a description for the new connection entry. You must also enter the IP address of the VPN server you're connecting to in the window (see Figure 9.2).

FIGURE 9.1 Launching VPN Client

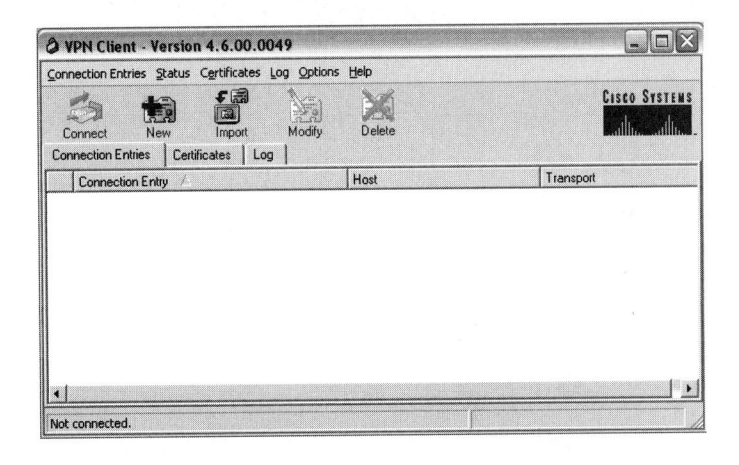

FIGURE 9.2 Creating a new connection entry

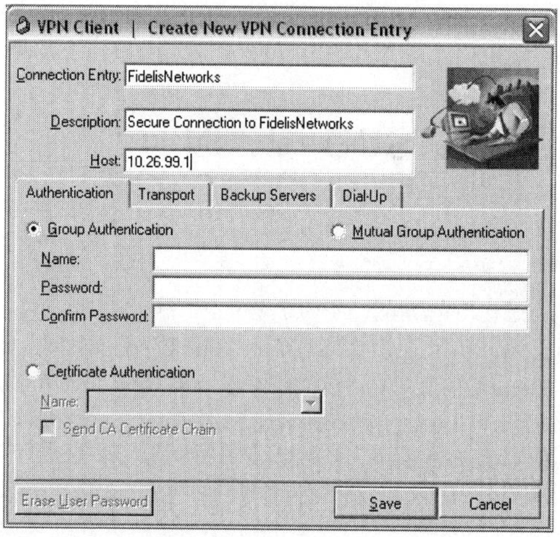

Next, fill out the group access or certificate information (Figure 9.3), and click the Save button. This is the only remotely challenging part of Easy VPN. If you're not doing this yourself, you must provide users with the correct information so they can fill out the screen.

Now, click Connect on the initial screen, as you can see in Figure 9.4.

You can add as many connections as you want and then select one to use from the connection entry window.

FIGURE 9.3 Entering group access information

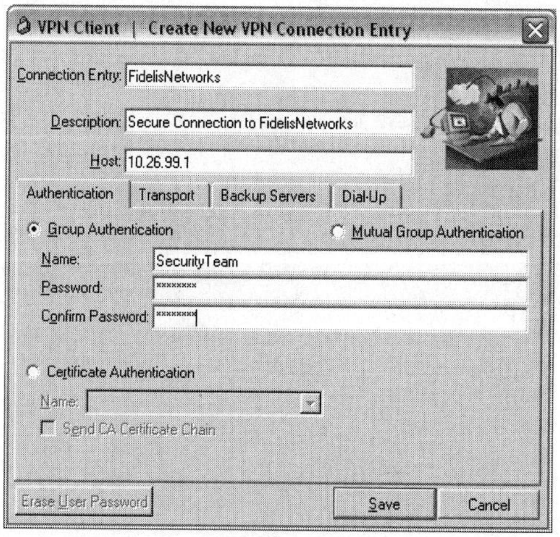

FIGURE 9.4 Connecting your VPN server

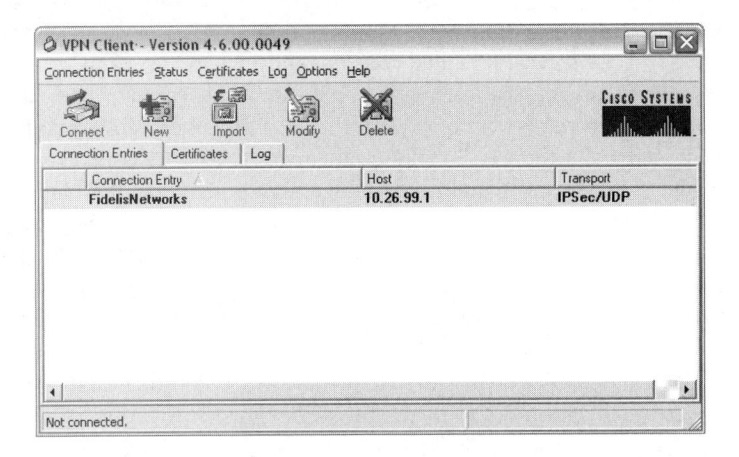

The VPN software client supports many VPN features. In fact, it's so supportive, it doesn't have some of the limitations that the IOS Easy VPN Server does. This requires a little thought when you're configuring connections, to avoid incompatibilities. Here's an example: VPN Client supports Diffie-Hellman groups 1, 2, and 5; but, as you know, the Easy VPN Server doesn't support DH1.

Easy VPN Server Configuration Tasks

Easy VPN Server configuration uses skills and commands I've already covered in previous chapters. Basically, you need to configure authentication, authorization, and accounting (AAA) and then configure IPSec. You can configure some optional features, such as DPD, but they're not required.

Cisco has defined the following seven steps to configure the Easy VPN Server:

1. Enable policy lookup via AAA.
2. Define group policy for mode configuration push.
3. Apply mode configuration and Xauth to crypto maps.
4. Enable Reverse Route Injection (RRI) for the VPN Client (optional).
5. Enable IKE Dead Peer Detection (optional).
6. Configure RADIUS server support (optional).
7. Verify the Easy VPN Server.

Each step itself consists of multiple steps. Step 1 involves enabling AAA. Steps 2 and 3 involve configuring IPSec. Steps 4 through 6 are specific to Easy VPN Server configuration, but as mentioned previously, they're optional. Finally, in step 7, you can use the `show crypto map interface` command to verify Easy VPN Server operation.

Preconfiguring the Cisco VPN Software Client

This book isn't a how-to on customer relations, but I've often observed a direct correlation between users who need to make software-related decisions and an increase in annoying telephone conversations between users and engineers. Therefore, it's usually in everyone's best interest to remove that ability from the keyboards of your expert users. Doing so is especially helpful because you're ultimately concerned about the security of the entire network—your control is essential to getting the job done right. Cisco seems to understand the ruinous potential of this conflict and has provided a way to streamline the installation of the VPN software client on Windows.

As the administrator of a Cisco VPN Software Client installation, you have the ability to preconfigure the connection configuration covered in the section "Introduction to the Cisco VPN Software Client" earlier in this chapter. You can also protect the user from making uninformed decisions during the installation of the VPN Client, such as, "Which directory should I install the software into?" You do this by creating three text files, which you then place in the same directory as the `setup.exe` file you used to install the VPN Client software:

The *oem.ini* file   The `oem.ini` file installs the VPN Client without user intervention. You get to perform tasks such as forcing the machine to reload after installation, selecting the directory to install the software into, and even turning off all user prompts during installation. In the end, the only thing the user has to do is double-click the `setup.exe` icon, and the file takes care of every standard query that follows during installation.

The *vpnclient.ini* file   The `vpnclient.ini` file is used to configure the global parameters of the VPN Client, which aren't normally queried as part of the installation wizard and are therefore not covered in the `oem.ini` file. You can customize these global parameters to whatever settings are appropriate for your environment.

The *.pcf* files   `.pcf` files add connection entries. You need to create one file for each connection you want to add, and you can use as many entries as you wish. Put them in the same directory as the `setup.exe` file, and they'll be added to the VPN Client.

> Refer to the documentation that came with your particular VPN Client software for the exact syntax of these files.

By using these three files, you can completely preconfigure the Cisco VPN software client and reclaim the network that is rightfully yours. The only thing left to do is send out a memo and get users to run the `setup.exe` program on the VPN Client machine.

Router and Security Device Manager Overview

Cisco Router and Security Device Manager (SDM) is a web-based tool that can greatly enhance productivity for both network and security administrators on the Cisco 830 through 7301 routers. The SDM software is stored in the router's flash. To verify that SDM is loaded, you can issue the IOS command: `show flash`. Cisco channel partners can utilize SDM for faster and easier deployment of Cisco routers for integrated services like dynamic routing, WAN access, firewalls, VPN, inline intrusion prevention (IPS), quality of service (QoS), and so on.

Cisco customers can utilize SDM for reducing the total cost of ownership (TCO) of their Cisco routers by relying on SDM-generated configurations. Configuration checks built into SDM reduce the possibilities of errors. SDM helps customers avoid potential network issues through monitoring of vital router performance statistics and system and firewall logs.

SDM offers smart wizards and advanced configuration support for LAN and WAN interfaces, NAT, stateful firewall policy, intrusion prevention, IPSec VPN, and QoS policy features. SDM also offers a one-click router lockdown and an innovative security auditing capability to check and recommend changes to router configurations based on ICSA Labs and Cisco TAC recommendations.

> **NOTE** There is a lot more to SDM than I can cover in this brief introduction. It's highly recommend that you read the SDM white paper at http://www.cisco.com/en/US/products/sw/secursw/ps5318/products_data_sheet0900aecd800fd118.html before you attempt the test.

Summary

The Cisco Easy VPN solution that Cisco provides can be deployed in various ways. The new Cisco features let you use the Easy VPN Server as an IOS router and employ the Easy VPN Remote as the VPN software client.

It's important to understand which features are supported and which features aren't supported in the VPN software client. For example, the Easy VPN Client supports Triple Data Encryption Standard (3DES), which is important, but it doesn't support DSS, Diffie-Hellman group 1 (DH1), and Authentication Header (AH).

You need to understand the process of adding a connection to the VPN software client, which we covered in detail in this chapter. If you have to, review the "Introduction to the Cisco VPN Software Client" section until you understand the process.

By truly understanding the process of adding a connection to the VPN software client, you can then streamline the installation of the VPN Client while ensuring that the ultimate control of your network remains where it should—in your hands.

Exam Essentials

Know the supported and unsupported IPSec features of the Easy VPN Server (see Table 9.1). DSS, DH group 1, and AH aren't supported features.

Know which files are used for which functions when preconfiguring the VPN software client. The oem.ini file is used to install without user prompts, the vpnclient.ini file is used to preconfigure global parameters, and the .pcf files are used to configure connections (one .pcf file per connection).

Know which devices can act as Easy VPN Servers and which devices can act as Easy VPN Remotes. The Easy VPN Server can be an IOS router, a PIX firewall, or a VPN Concentrator. The Easy VPN Remote can be an IOS router, a PIX firewall, a VPN 3002 Hardware Client, or VPN Client software.

Know the seven tasks for Easy VPN Server configuration. The seven Easy VPN Server configuration tasks are

1. Enable policy lookup via AAA.
2. Define group policy for mode configuration push.
3. Apply mode configuration and Xauth to crypto maps.
4. Enable Reverse Route Injection (RRI) for the VPN Client (optional).
5. Enable IKE Dead Peer Detection (optional).
6. Configure RADIUS server support (optional).
7. Verify the Easy VPN Server.

PART II

Cisco Secure PIX Firewall Advanced

Chapter 10

PIX Firewall Basics

THE FOLLOWING TOPICS ARE COVERED IN THIS CHAPTER:

- ✓ Firewall technology overview
- ✓ Overview of the PIX Firewall models
- ✓ Understanding PIX Firewall licensing
- ✓ Using the PIX Firewall user interface
- ✓ Defining the ASA security levels
- ✓ Overview of basic PIX Firewall configuration
- ✓ Using the Firewall Services Module (FWSM)

This chapter begins our detailed look at Cisco's firewall solutions, laying the groundwork for all the information you need to know for the Cisco Secure PIX Firewall Advanced (CSPFA) exam. We'll go into comprehensive coverage of installation and configuration in later chapters, but first, we'll take a broader view of firewalls in general.

We'll begin by discussing the role of firewalls in network security—what they can do and what they can't do. We'll cover the hardware and software components of the Cisco Secure PIX Firewall, including the different models and licensing available, and explain how they all fit together to help protect networks. Next will be an overview of the Catalyst 6500 series and Cisco 7600 series Firewall Services Module (FWSM) and how to do basic configuration. Finally, we'll cover the PIX Firewall command-line interface (CLI) and some of the basic commands used to manage the PIX Firewall.

Understanding a Firewall's Role in Network Security

Like many network devices, firewalls have evolved considerably since their inception, as networks themselves have evolved. In this section, we'll discuss what threats firewalls are designed to counter and some types of threats that firewalls are powerless against. We'll also look at the firewall in relation to the rest of the network and what the firewall actually is. We begin with a common definition.

What Is a Firewall?

A *firewall* is a system or group of systems that enforces an access-control policy between two or more networks: usually between the Internet and the internal networks of a company, but sometimes between internal networks. Although new classes of products, such as *personal firewalls* that reside on PCs, have now muddied that definition somewhat, it remains fundamentally accurate.

There are several important points regarding the effectiveness of a firewall, each of which is discussed in the following sections.

Policy Enforcement

A firewall is the mechanism that enforces a policy. It doesn't design or define the policy, nor is it the policy itself; it simply carries out the policy. In the discipline of policy management, which is rapidly becoming integrated with Cisco's security tools, a firewall is an example of a policy enforcement point (PEP). The decisions about the policy are made in a policy decision point (PDP), and the policy itself resides in a repository. In some implementations, one physical device might perform all three of these functions, but these distinctions are important nevertheless.

Firewall Location

To enforce a policy between two networks, the firewall must reside between those networks. Just like the firewalls in cars and buildings (typically made of large sheets of steel or fire-retardant material) that exist to slow the spread of real fires, network firewalls act as a border between the two systems to prevent something bad in one system from finding its way into the other system.

In a data network, the firewall must exist at the point through which the data passes on its route from one network to the other. If multiple paths exist, as they often do, there must be multiple firewalls to be effective. This is why a firewall can also be a group of systems.

Understanding the location of firewalls is crucial, because firewalls can help to secure only the perimeter of the network. They can't protect internal systems from internal users, nor can they prevent users from connecting modems to their desktops and accessing the internal network via dial-up analog lines. Again, if the physical path of the data as it travels through the network doesn't pass through the firewall, the firewall offers no protection.

Trusted Networks

A third, more subtle, point is that the presence of an access-control policy implies that one network is more trusted than another. In fact, this statement must be made from the perspective of a device on each network. You might consider your local network to be more secure than the network on the other side of the firewall. If not, why have a firewall at all? However, a device on the other side of the firewall might consider its local network more secure than your side of the firewall.

As you'll see later in the "The Adaptive Security Algorithm and Security Levels" section of this chapter, this relative level of trust is a key to the operation of the PIX Firewall.

Firewall Systems

As our definition points out, the firewall is a system. The firewall system itself can be implemented in many ways. In other words, it's not necessarily a black box with two Ethernet ports. It can be one physical box, several boxes, or none at all.

The most common firewall system is a software application that runs on top of a general-purpose operating system, such as Windows 2000 Server or Unix, with general-purpose hardware, such as the Intel-based PC or Sun Microsystems' Sparc Station. Another method of implementing firewall features uses custom hardware and software, designed with a single purpose in mind.

What Are the Potential Threats?

As described in the previous sections, the firewall is a point in the perimeter of the network that enforces an access-control policy between two networks that trust each other to varying degrees. To better understand the role of a firewall, we'll next look at the potential threats to network security. Three primary types of threats are addressed by network security:

Privacy violations Privacy violations occur when confidential data is exposed. This can occur on a host, such as the highly publicized web server break-ins that allowed hundreds of thousands of credit card numbers to be stolen. Privacy violations can also occur on the network itself. For example, an intruder with a packet sniffer might view confidential information, such as your password, as it's transmitted across the network.

Breach of integrity A breach of integrity occurs when data in a system is altered. Again, this can occur on a host or on the network itself. An example of a breach of integrity on a host is the defacement of a website. An example on the network could be a man-in-the-middle attack, where the data inside a packet is intercepted and modified as it traverses the network.

Denial of service (DoS) The two most common ways of denying service are on a host and in the network. Commonly, a flaw in the host is exploited to cause it to crash or waste CPU cycles or memory, starving the legitimate applications. In the network, an attack might try to use all available bandwidth or send invalid information to a routing protocol to cause it to redirect your traffic to the wrong location. A particularly nasty type of DoS attack is called the *distributed denial-of-service (DDoS)* attack. This term describes an attack where several (often thousands of) unsuspecting hosts are compromised and then used to attack a single target in unison.

The overall goal is to keep these threats from becoming a reality. The objective of network security is to create a policy that makes these attacks prohibitively difficult or expensive. The role of the firewall is to enforce this policy at the network perimeter.

Reviewing Firewall Technologies

Because there are many types of threats, there are many types of policies to deal with them. These policies operate at many different levels, so there are several different types of firewalls. Here, we'll concentrate on three common types:

- Application proxy (a type of dual-homed gateway)
- Packet-filtering firewall
- Stateful firewall

Of course, any given firewall product may implement one or more of these techniques.

Dual-Homed Gateways

There are several types of dual-homed gateways. *Application proxies* (often called *proxy servers*) and bastion hosts are common examples. All dual-homed gateways have one thing in common: Physically, and as far as the operating system is concerned, the dual-homed gateway is a host on two different networks at the same time. This device isn't a router or a switch; routers and switches forward packets at layer 2 or 3 (the Data-Link or Network layer of the OSI model). Rather, the dual-homed gateway acts as a host. Packets are sent to it, and it processes them in the same way as any other host, passing them all the way up to layer 7 (the Application layer), where they're inspected by a proxy application.

The proxy is application-aware. For example, a web proxy understands the HTTP protocol. It knows what the commands mean and can decide whether the users are allowed to access a certain URL or whether specific content returned to the client is allowed inside the network.

Generally speaking, dual-homed gateways are very useful for Application-layer filtering, and they excel at auditing. For instance, if you've used a web proxy server, you might have noticed that the log files are quite detailed and can grow very large.

Unfortunately, dual-homed gateways have several drawbacks:

- They're inherently slow. Their high latency often creates problems with real-time traffic, such as streaming media.
- Because they're application-aware, they must be programmed to understand the application. If the manufacturer doesn't support the particular service or protocol you need, you'll need to find another solution.
- Once they're compromised, the gateway can be used as a launch pad for attacks into the formerly protected network. This is typically possible on dual-homed gateways because they often run general-purpose operating systems, which makes it easy to develop attack software.

> **NOTE** Special-purpose operating systems and hardware rarely publish their application programming interfaces (APIs) and other specifications, so developing rogue programs to run on these systems would be an extremely difficult task.

Application gateways are very good at preventing unauthorized access to services or data, both inbound and outbound. They provide some protection against privacy violations on the hosts, but not for data in transit, and they actually become an additional point of failure for DoS attacks.

Packet-Filtering Firewalls

Packet-filtering firewalls operate at a much lower level of the OSI model than dual-homed gateways in the network. In fact, this functionality is often implemented on routers and switches, which process packets only at layers 2 through 4 (Data-Link, Network, and Transport).

Packet-filtering firewalls match values in the headers of frames and packets and permit or deny packets based on a set of rules. The most commonly used fields are as follows:

- The layer 2 source address and destination address, most often the MAC addresses
- The layer 3 source address and destination address, most often the IP or Internetwork Packet Exchange (IPX) addresses
- The options in the layer 3 header, such as the fragmentation bits
- The layer 4 source address and destination address, most often the TCP or UDP ports
- The options in the layer 4 header, such as the SYN bit

Packet-filtering technology has been around for some time and is often considered an old technology that is no longer useful, but it does have a few advantages:

- It's very cheap and widely available.
- The lower a function is on the OSI model, the faster it is, so packet-filtering firewalls generally have a tremendous speed advantage compared with application gateways.
- It's simple, fairly reliable, and easy to maintain. Its simplicity also makes it easy to implement in hardware.
- It's particularly useful in combination with other technologies. In modern security architecture, packet filtering is often used on screening routers.

On the other hand, packet filtering has its share of problems:

- The rules are commonly static in nature, so services such as FTP, which use random ports, are often blocked accidentally.
- Undesired packets can be fabricated to match the permit rules. For instance, a packet could be fabricated to appear as if it were already part of an established TCP connection, and it would be permitted to pass through the firewall.
- The order in which the rules are placed is critically important. If you have many rules, it's easy to make mistakes when manually maintaining them.
- Older packet-filtering platforms had difficulty with fragmented packets because only the first packet contains the header information. Sending specially formed, fragmented packets, or not sending the final fragment, would often crash older host systems.

Despite these shortcomings, packet-filtering technology is still useful because it provides a moderate amount of protection against all three of the primary threats described in the "What Are the Potential Threats?" section earlier in this chapter. Cisco has implemented this technology in the form of access control lists (ACLs) in all versions of the Cisco IOS software. Combining these ACLs with other firewalls, such as the PIX Firewall, can create a much more robust security system than either tool by itself.

Stateful Firewalls

Stateful firewalls operate in the same manner as packet-filtering firewalls, except they work on connections instead of packets. Put another way, a stateful firewall has the ability to permit or deny a packet based on other packets. For example, if a TCP packet arrives, claiming to be from an established connection (that is, it doesn't have the SYN bit set), the packet-filtering firewall would let it pass, but the stateful firewall will deny this packet if any of the following conditions are met:

- It hasn't seen the three-way handshake of SYN, SYN-ACK, and ACK for that connection.
- The TCP sequence and acknowledgment numbers aren't correct (these are based on the previous packet).
- The packet contains a response when there wasn't previously a command.

As you can see, when properly implemented, stateful filtering can make forging packets practically impossible.

Stateful firewalls also excel in preventing DoS attacks. For instance, conceivably, you could allow Ping traffic into your network. If someone attempted to send you 100,000 Internet Control Message Protocol (ICMP) requests at once, the packet-filtering firewall would let all of them through. However, the stateful firewall could be configured with a reasonable threshold, and after this threshold was crossed, the firewall would automatically deny all future requests until the flood subsided.

Generally, stateful firewalls provide the following benefits:

- Much higher performance than application gateways
- Stronger security than packet filtering
- Easy administration

However, because they don't necessarily operate at the Application layer, stateful firewalls don't offer as strong control over applications as do dual-homed gateways. This also means that their auditing isn't as detailed.

Firewall Technology Combinations

Each of the three firewall types mentioned in the previous sections has different strengths and weaknesses. While we compare them here academically, in the real world, they're often all used together.

For instance, the application gateway and proxy servers provide some protection for the application, but they themselves are vulnerable to other attacks, such as DoS attacks. To protect the proxy servers, you typically put them in what is called a *screened subnet* or a *demilitarized zone (DMZ)*. This is a protected network that sits between a trusted internal network and a totally untrusted external network. From the perspective of a typical company's internal network, the DMZ is trusted less than the internal network but more than the external network.

Two common screened-subnet designs are used today, as described in the following sections.

Packet-Filtering Router, Stateful Firewall, and Application Proxy Combination

One type of screened subnet employs a packet-filtering router to separate the outside network from the DMZ. Then a stateful firewall connects the DMZ to the inside network. An application proxy typically resides inside the DMZ, so traffic doesn't flow directly from the inside network to the outside network or from the outside network directly to the inside network.

Instead, all traffic from the inside network to the outside network flows to and from the proxy server. However, traffic from the outside network to the other servers, such as the web and FTP servers, doesn't pass through the proxy server, but goes directly to the appropriate server. The data flow of this design is shown in Figure 10.1.

> **NOTE** We use the terms *DMZ* and *screened subnet* interchangeably.

The combination of these three firewall technologies provides much more security than any one technology alone. The routers in this network provide high-performance packet filtering, and the application-aware proxy servers make attacks as difficult as possible. The stateful firewall protects the resources on the internal network without affecting the performance of web servers and other devices in the DMZ.

Another advantage of this design is that the access to the proxy server often requires authentication, based on the user's ID on the internal network (such as an account on a Windows domain). This makes access into the internal network more secure without requiring the management of an infinite number of accounts on the outside network, which are accessing your web and FTP services.

FIGURE 10.1 Traffic flow in a modern screened subnet

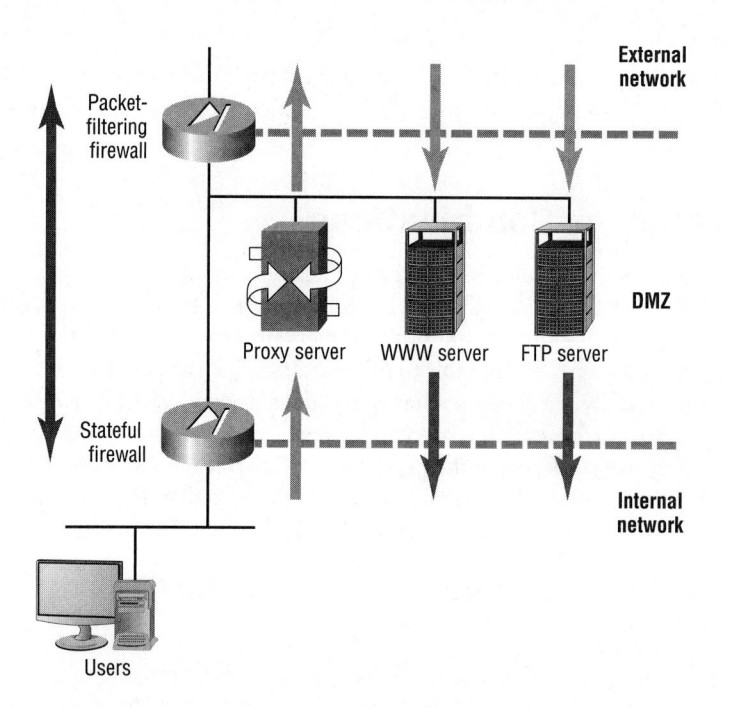

The combination of low-level support by the packet-filtering firewall, application-level support from the dual-homed gateway, and protection from DoS attacks is a classic case of synergy, where the whole is greater than the sum of the parts. This technique is sometimes called *defense in depth*.

A Stateful Firewall with Multiple Interfaces

The second type of screened-subnet design is similar to the one just described, but it's a little more efficient and cost-effective. It takes advantage of multiple interfaces on the newer, faster firewalls. However, the traffic flow is fundamentally unchanged. This design is shown in Figure 10.2.

This design has two inherent characteristics, which are both a result of all the data passing through a single firewall. The negative characteristic is that the additional traffic might affect performance. The positive characteristic is that seeing all the traffic might allow the firewall to make more intelligent filtering decisions than a firewall that sees only part of the traffic.

FIGURE 10.2 A cost-effective alternative DMZ design

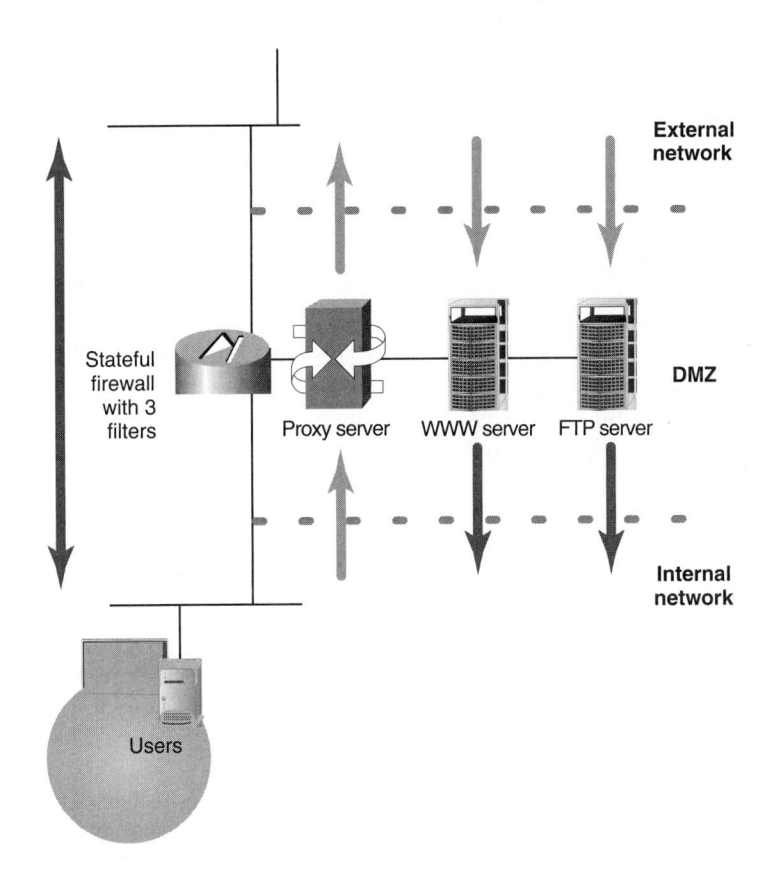

Hardware and Software Components of the Cisco Secure PIX Firewall

Now that you understand the basic firewall technologies and their usefulness, we can describe the basic characteristics of the PIX Firewall. The Private Internet Exchange (PIX) Firewall is one of the world's premier firewalls because its unique operation provides strong security and very high performance. It isn't based on a mainstream operating system, such as Windows or Unix, but on a hardened, secure, embedded operating system known as Finesse. In this section, we'll begin to discuss its operation and various features that contribute to its speed and protection.

> **NOTE**
> Admittedly, the information in this section is more marketing-related than technical; as such, isn't likely to be on the exam. However, it's important to understand the background and context in which Cisco places the PIX Firewall. This understanding will also benefit you immensely after the exam, when it comes time to select and install a firewall in your network.

The PIX Firewall has its roots in Network Address Translation (NAT), with the ability to maintain information about the state of each connection that passes through it, and then filter (permit or deny) traffic based on that state. For this reason, it's classified as a stateful firewall.

PIX Firewall Features

The PIX Firewall series uses specially designed hardware and a very small, proprietary, multi-threaded kernel. On the lower-end models, the hardware is fixed-configuration, but the higher-end models support modular interface cards for many different types of media, up to gigabit speeds. The advantage here is that the extraneous equipment and issues associated with hard drives, CD-ROMs, GUIs, monitors, keyboards, mice, and so on are eliminated, without losing the core functionality of the firewall.

The PIX Firewall features support for Internet Protocol Security (IPSec), virtual private networks (VPNs), cut-through proxy switching, inbound and outbound authentication, failover, and more. These features are covered in this section and in later chapters.

Another feature, which administrators will appreciate, is that compared with some firewalls (particularly those running on general-purpose operating systems), the PIX Firewall is easy to configure and hard to misconfigure. Unlike many firewalls, the PIX Firewall hardware and software are based on a *pessimistic*, or restrictive, security model. In other words, by default, everything is denied. To allow network traffic to pass through the PIX Firewall, it must be explicitly configured to accept that traffic.

The latest versions of the PIX Firewall operating system have even more new features. One of the most eagerly anticipated features is multicast support. The PIX Firewall now supports multicast routing (with the `mroute` command) and Internet Group Management Protocol (IGMP).

PIX Firewall Components

In this section, we'll explore the parts that make up the PIX Firewall. Before we get into the nuts and bolts, you should understand that simplicity is an important competitive advantage in the realm of security, because as components in a system become more complex, there are more opportunities to take advantage of the system. The PIX Firewall has succeeded in maintaining a simple, almost minimalist, list of components.

On the PIX Firewall, you can see some of these components by typing the show version command at the privileged exec prompt, as seen in Listing 10.1 (we've boldfaced the sections of interest here for clarity).

Listing 10.1: Using the show version command

```
PIX# show version

Cisco Secure PIX Firewall Version 6.0(1)

Compiled on Thu 17-May-01 20:05 by morlee

PIX up 58 secs

Hardware:   PIX-515, 64 MB RAM, CPU Pentium 200 MHz
Flash i28F640J5 @ 0x300, 16MB
BIOS Flash AT29C257 @ 0xfffd8000, 32KB

0: ethernet0: address is 0050.54ff.076d, irq 10
1: ethernet1: address is 0050.54ff.076e, irq 7
2: ethernet2: address is 00d0.b79d.8856, irq 9

Licensed Features:
Failover:          Enabled
VPN-DES:           Enabled
VPN-3DES:          Disabled
Maximum Interfaces:     6
Cut-through Proxy:      Enabled
Guards:            Enabled
Websense:          Enabled
Throughput:        Unlimited
ISAKMP peers:      Unlimited
```

```
Serial Number: 403420127 (0x180bb3df)
Activation Key: 0x9aa99a8d 0xc56166de 0x4ecd338a
  0x5b6d06eb
PIX#
```

As you can see, the components shown by the `show version` command are the central processing unit (CPU), random access memory (RAM), flash file system, system image, BIOS, interfaces, and licensed features. Let's take a closer look at each of these components.

CPU

The PIX Firewall uses the Intel Pentium line of processors as the CPU. This is where the software image is executed and most of the rules are processed. Also, tasks such as encryption using IPSec are performed here (unless an optional VPN accelerator card is installed, which offloads this processing to a dedicated processor).

The `show version` command shows the type and speed of the processor. The `show cpu usage` command gives the average processor utilization for the past five seconds, one minute, and five minutes, as in this example:

```
PIX# show cpu usage
CPU utilization for 5 seconds = 0%; 1 minute: 0%;5 minutes: 0%
PIX#
```

RAM

RAM is the primary memory used by the PIX Firewall. Instructions being executed by the CPU exist here. RAM is also used for packet buffers and the various tables, such as state information, dynamic NAT entries, the translation (xlate) tables (described in the "NAT Mechanisms" section later in this chapter), and more.

The sample `show version` output in Listing 10.1 shows that this PIX Firewall has 64MB of RAM. You can also use the `show memory` command to see the available or unused memory:

```
PIX# show memory
67108864 bytes total, 51089408 bytes free
PIX#
```

Flash File System

The physical flash memory used in PIX Firewalls is similar to that used in Cisco's router and switch platforms. However, the file system used by the PIX Firewall is considerably different.

The file system used in Cisco's IOS allows any number of files to be stored, including multiple images, copies of the configuration file, and so on. Each of these can be manipulated by a filename. However, the PIX Firewall flash file system version 1 divides the flash into four sectors. Each of these sectors contains one file. Version 2 of the flash file system adds one more sector, for a total of five, to support the GUI configuration software, PIX Device Manager (PDM).

The `show flashfs` command shows the length of each file but not the filenames:

```
PIX# show flashfs
flash file system:   version:2   magic:0x12345679
  file 0: origin:            0 length:2449464
  file 1: origin:      2490368 length:1463
  file 2: origin:            0 length:0
  file 3: origin:            0 length:0
  file 4: origin:      8257536 length:280
PIX#
```

The files are used as follows:

- File 0 is the PIX Firewall binary image. This is the BIN file. (See the next section for details on the PIX Firewall system image.)
- File 1 is the PIX Firewall configuration data, viewed with the `show config` command.
- File 2 contains the firewall's IPSec key and certificates.
- File 3 contains the PDM software.
- File 4 contains downgrade information for previous versions.

Access to these files is much more restricted than access to the Cisco IOS flash file system. To enhance security, the ability to copy files from flash to FTP, Trivial File Transfer Protocol (TFTP), another file on the flash, or other locations is no longer available. Also gone are flash partitions and detailed information, such as checksums. Although the lack of these features might not seem like an enhancement, their exclusion helps prevent your private keys from being stolen. The maintenance of the flash system—such as compacting, formatting, and squeezing—is handled automatically on the PIX Firewall.

System Image

The system image is a binary executable file that resides in file 0 in the flash. Older models store the image on 3.5-inch floppy disks. The image contains all the code for the PIX Firewall operating system and all the features—NAT, IPSec, filtering, and so on.

Unlike Cisco IOS images, where there are many images for each platform and each image contains only a certain set of features, there is only one image per software version for the PIX Firewall. This image contains all the features Cisco has developed for PIX Firewall, but certain features may be enabled and disabled by the licensing keys (see the "Licensed Features" section later in this chapter).

To install or upgrade an image, you must copy it across the network, typically with TFTP, or replace the flash memory with flash containing the new image. For PIX Firewall models that use floppy disks, simply swap the floppy with the one containing the new image, and reboot.

The PIX Firewall operating system itself is non-Unix, real-time, and embedded.

> ### 🌐 Real World Scenario
>
> **Flash Exploits**
>
> Years ago, it was a trivial (pun intended) exercise to gain unauthorized access to most Cisco routers. The primary reason was that most router administrators configured TFTP so that they could copy system images to and from the routers and make backup copies of their configuration files. Because TFTP has no authentication and doesn't even require a password, all intruders needed to know was the name of the configuration file, and they could send a TFTP Get request to the router. The router would promptly return the configuration file, which of course contained the login and enable passwords. Although the password was encrypted in the configuration file, it was just a matter of time before it was cracked. If the password could be found in a dictionary, this "matter of time" was probably a few seconds.
>
> Although it's still possible to configure routers like this, it's unusual. Newer versions of Cisco IOS have more secure default settings and support more secure protocols, such as FTP, which at least requires a username and password.
>
> With the PIX Firewall, security is much tighter. In fact, configuration file theft is exactly the type of attack the PIX Firewall's flash system is designed to thwart. It's immune to this type of attack because you can only send files to the PIX Firewall; you can't download from it.

BIOS

The BIOS of the PIX Firewall operates in the same way as the BIOS of other Intel processor–based computers. It's responsible for the initial boot sequence and loading the PIX Firewall software image located in file 0.

The BIOS is stored in a special chip, separate from flash. Although upgrades to the BIOS are seldom necessary (an example would be date fixes for the Y2K bug), upgrading it is possible.

Interfaces

Most PIX Firewalls have at least three fixed ports: RJ-45 (console connector), DB15 (failover connector), and USB (not currently used).

Depending on the model, PIX Firewalls also have one or two fixed Fast Ethernet interfaces for data traffic and a number of slots for optional interfaces. These interfaces are labeled much like router interfaces: 10/100 Ethernet 0, 10/100 Ethernet 1, and so on.

Internally, the interfaces are numbered and named. For instance, using the command `show interface ethernet1`, you can see that the interface numbered `ethernet1` is named `inside`:

```
PIX# show interface ethernet1
interface ethernet1 "inside" is up, line protocol is up
  Hardware is i82559 ethernet, address is 0050.54ff.076e
```

```
   IP address 10.1.1.20, subnet mask 255.255.255.0
   MTU 1500 bytes, BW 100000 Kbit full duplex
      395 packets input, 43128 bytes, 0 no buffer
      Received 395 broadcasts, 0 runts, 0 giants
      0 input errors, 0 CRC, 0 frame, 0 overrun,
        0 ignored, 0 abort
      1 packets output, 64 bytes, 0 underruns
      0 output errors, 0 collisions, 0 interface resets
      0 babbles, 0 late collisions, 0 deferred
      1 lost carrier, 0 no carrier
      input queue (curr/max blocks): hardware (128/128)
        software (0/2)
      output queue (curr/max blocks): hardware (0/2)
        software (0/1)
PIX#
```

All PIX Firewalls have at least two interfaces, but several models support six or more interfaces. By default, these two interfaces are named `inside` and `outside`. The name `inside` is reserved for a network that has a security level of 100 (the maximum). The name `outside` is reserved for a network that has a security level of 0 (the minimum). We'll discuss the security levels in more depth in the section "The Adaptive Security Algorithm and Security Levels," later in this chapter.

Secure PIX Firewall Product Line

The following is a brief description of the PIX Firewall product line, the chassis type, and the maximum number of interfaces supported. You can find a more detailed description at www.cisco.com/warp/public/cc/pd/fw/sqfw500/.

ModelInterfacesChassis

501 1 10BaseT and four-port 10/100 switch Desktop

506E 2 10BaseT Desktop

515E 6 FastE Modular

525 8 FastE or 3 GigE Modular

535 10 FastE or 9 GigE Modular

> **TIP**
> Some models of the PIX Firewall have more than one internal bus, which shuttles data from the interfaces to the CPU and RAM. For instance, the PIX 535 has three separate buses: two run at 66MHz or 33MHz, and the third runs at only 33MHz. Some interface cards, such as the Gigabit Ethernet interface card, come in 33MHz and 66MHz flavors, so the interface you use and the slot you choose can greatly affect your system's performance. Other interface cards, such as the VPN accelerator and four-port Fast Ethernet cards, can be placed only in 33Mhz slots, or the system will hang at boot time.

Licensed Features

Cisco has three basic licenses for the PIX Firewall:

- The Restricted license sets a limit on the number of connections and interfaces and disables failover.
- The Unrestricted license has no limit on connections, enables failover, and allows as many interfaces as the hardware supports.
- The Failover license, which is the least expensive, is intended for a backup firewall (when using the failover feature) and assumes the license characteristics of the primary firewall.

In addition to these licenses, each PIX Firewall comes with a license for IPSec encryption using 56-bit Data Encryption Standard (DES), Triple Data Encryption Standard (3DES) using 168 bits, or Advanced Encryption Standard (AES) with a variable-key length (128, 192, or 256 bits).

> **NOTE**
> The encryption and firewall licenses are independent from the version of the operating system. You can update the version of the operating system without affecting the licenses, and you can update the licenses without affecting the operating system version.

All features, including cut-through proxy, attack guards, N2H2, and Websense support, are included in the Unrestricted license. Older models of the PIX Firewall had multiple Restricted versions that were limited to 128 connections or 1024 concurrent connections.

Each PIX Firewall has a unique serial number. This serial number and the licenses purchased are used as the inputs to a mathematical formula that generates an activation key. You enter this key as the system image is being installed; it determines which features are available on the firewall. When you do a flash upgrade, you need the serial number of the flash card, too.

As of version 6.0, the `activation-key` command was added so that code and boot-time upgrades aren't needed to upgrade the activation key. For instance, if you purchase a license-activation key for 3DES encryption and wish to install it on your PIX Firewall, you must copy the system image to the flash (again). During this process, you'll be prompted for the activation code. The DES activation key provides 56-bit DES, and the 3DES activation key provides 168-bit 3DES.

PIX Firewall Operation

Now that you understand the components of the PIX Firewall, let's look at how they work together. As we mentioned earlier, the PIX Firewall has its roots in NAT. In fact, when the PIX Firewall was introduced in 1994, it was the first box capable of doing true RFC 1631 NAT.

Although it's possible to configure a PIX Firewall to not translate IP addresses, its switching process is based on NAT, and every packet must use this NAT mechanism. So, to understand how a PIX Firewall forwards packets, we must first define some NAT vocabulary. Then we'll discuss the sequence in which packets are processed, and finally, the Adaptive Security Algorithm.

> **WARNING** Even if the PIX Firewall filtering is configured so that its ACLs won't deny any packets, packets that aren't translated won't be forwarded. The PIX Firewall must have a translation slot to switch packets from one interface to another.

NAT Mechanisms

With NAT, a translation is a pair of IP addresses: local and global. The local address is on the network connected to the inside, or trusted, interface of the PIX Firewall. The global address is part of a network somewhere beyond the *outside interface* that is trusted less than the *inside interface*. The PIX Firewall translates the local address to the global address as the packet passes outbound through the firewall. It translates the global address to the local address as a packet passes inbound through the firewall.

Translations can be either static or dynamic. Static translations must be manually configured. Dynamic translations are created as packets that meet certain criteria arrive.

When the first packet in a series of packets arrives at the PIX Firewall from the inside interface, the PIX Firewall creates a *translation slot*. This "slot" is a software construct that keeps track of translations. Each translation uses one translation slot.

Connection slots are another software construct that the PIX Firewall uses to keep track of stateful information. A given pair of devices, such as a client and server, can multiplex several conversations between their two IP addresses. This is often accomplished via TCP and UDP ports. For instance, a client could connect to a server via telnet, FTP, and HTTP simultaneously, creating three separate TCP connections between the two devices. If this happened across a PIX Firewall, it would create a single translation slot and three connection slots. Each connection slot is bound to a translation slot.

> **NOTE** The Restricted licenses used in older PIX Firewall models limit the number of connection slots to either 128 or 1024. As of the time of this writing, "older" means the PIX Classic and those with model numbers that end in zero, such as PIX 520. The current models end in five, such as PIX 515, PIX 525, and PIX 535.

The translation table, which is usually abbreviated as *xlate table*, is the actual table in memory that holds all the translation slots and connection slots. It's important to distinguish this table from the configuration file of the PIX Firewall. Just because you've configured a static entry doesn't mean it will appear in the output of the show xlate command. The PIX Firewall places an entry in this table only when a packet arrives. After a certain amount of inactivity (that is, after the PIX Firewall doesn't see any more packets that are part of this conversation), the PIX Firewall removes the entry from the xlate table. Remember that the xlate table shows the current translations and connections.

Packet Processing

Now that you know how NAT works, let's look at how the PIX Firewall processes packets. We'll see how it handles outbound packets, inbound packets, and routing.

Outbound Packets

When a packet arrives on the inside interface, the PIX Firewall first checks the xlate table for a translation slot. Specifically, this means the PIX Firewall checks the source address of the IP header and searches the xlate table for a match. Its next actions depend on whether it finds a match.

Packets with Existing Translation Slots

If the PIX Firewall finds a match for the outbound packet's source address, it knows it has seen packets from this address before and has already created a dynamic translation slot, or it has a manually configured static translation slot. The PIX Firewall then processes the outbound packet as follows:

1. It takes the global address from the translation slot that corresponds to the local address it just looked up in the xlate table and overwrites the source address in the IP header of the packet with the value of the global address.
2. The other attributes, such as the checksums, are recalculated. (Otherwise, the packet would be discarded upon arrival, since the change in the IP header would change the value of the checksum.)
3. The packet is forwarded out the outside interface.

Packets without Existing Translation Slots

If the PIX Firewall receives a packet on the inside interface that doesn't have a current translation slot in the xlate table, it can dynamically create an entry if it's configured to do so. In this case, when the packet arrives, the PIX Firewall checks the source address and finds no match in the xlate table. It then follows these steps to process the outbound packet:

1. The PIX Firewall makes sure it has sufficient connections, which are determined by the license.
2. It creates the translation slot by reserving an unused IP address from the global NAT pool and entering this global address along with the source address from the IP header into the translation slot.

3. With the translation slot created, the source address is overwritten with the global address.
4. The checksum and other values are recalculated.
5. The packet is transmitted on the outside interface.

Inbound Packets

For packets that arrive on the outside interface, destined for the inside network, the PIX Firewall behaves quite differently than it does for packets that arrive on the inside interface. This is because the outside network is, by definition, less trusted. By default, packets from the outside don't create translation slots, so they can't be switched to the inside interface without a static NAT mapping. This makes the PIX Firewall very secure, from an architectural standpoint.

But even before the PIX Firewall checks for an existing entry in the xlate table, packets from an outside interface must match criteria specified in an ACL. Only after an incoming packet matches the ACL will it be processed further. The combination of the ACL and translation slot is the primary source of the PIX Firewall's security.

> **WARNING** Don't confuse the definition of stateful firewalls with this section's description of the operation of the PIX Firewall. There are many brands of stateful firewalls, but the PIX Firewall's operation is unique.

Routing

As you can see from the description of packet processing in the previous sections, the PIX Firewall isn't a router. This is an important distinction, because many other brands of firewalls are, in fact, routers, with packet-filtering or even stateful capabilities added on. For instance, the Cisco IOS Firewall is a full-featured, stateful firewall that runs on a Cisco router, but it processes packets just as it would if it were running a basic Cisco IOS image, except that it adds the stateful filtering feature. Although the mode of operation detailed in the previous sections makes the PIX Firewall much more secure, it also has some limitations related to its routing protocol support. We'll discuss the configuring of routing in the next chapter.

The Adaptive Security Algorithm and Security Levels

Cisco's Adaptive Security Algorithm (ASA) is the basis for the PIX Firewall's security, and it includes much of the information discussed in the previous sections. However, it can be summarized into a few rules that govern how packets are inspected and permitted or denied:

- All packets must have a connection slot to be transmitted.
- All packets are allowed to travel from a more secure interface to a less secure interface unless specifically denied (for example, by an ACL).
- All packets from a less secure interface to a more secure interface are denied, unless specifically allowed.

- All ICMP packets are denied unless you specifically configure the PIX Firewall to accept them.
- When the PIX Firewall denies a packet, the packet is *dropped* (received but not transmitted), and the action is noted in the logs.
- Monitor return packets to ensure that they're valid.

Security on the PIX Firewall is relative, and it's critical that you understand this. Specifically, what is allowed and disallowed by default depends on which interfaces a packet enters and leaves.

Each interface is assigned a value, called the *security level*, from 0 to 100, where 100 is completely trusted and 0 is completely untrusted. This allows a PIX Firewall with several interfaces to be configured securely.

For instance, you might have five interfaces on your PIX Firewall and assign them security levels as follows:

Connection	Security Level	Default Access
Internal network	100	All
Remote-access network	75	Business partner, DMZ, and Internet
Business partner	50	DMZ and Internet
DMZ	25	Internet
Internet	0	None

In this scenario, traffic from your internal network would, by default, be able to access any of the other four networks. Your remote users would be able to get to your business partner, the DMZ, and the Internet; however, you must explicitly configure the PIX Firewall to let them inside your internal network because it has a higher security level. Your business partners would be able to access your shared systems on the DMZ and the Internet by default, although you could restrict this with an ACL. Your partners wouldn't be able to get to your internal network or the modems on your remote-access network, unless you explicitly granted them permission in the configuration. The systems on the DMZ would be able to access only the Internet. Finally, the Internet wouldn't be able to access any of the other four networks, again, without explicit configuration.

In summary, the PIX Firewall controls access via the translation and connection slots we mentioned earlier. The PIX Firewall doesn't allow a packet from a less-trusted interface, destined for a more-trusted interface, to create a translation or connection slot, unless you explicitly configure the NAT translation and an ACL.

Working with the Firewall Services Module

If you want more firewall horsepower, you should consider using the Firewall Services Module (FWSM) for the Catalyst 6500 Series switch and the 7600 Series Internet router with either a Supervisor 1A with MSFC2 (Catalyst operating system only) or Supervisor 2 with MSFC2. The FWSM is based on Cisco PIX Firewall technology and uses the same time-tested Cisco PIX Firewall Operating System, a secure, real-time operating system.

This is a multigigabit firewall module with 1GB RAM and 128MB flash memory that provides up to 5Gbps of throughput. This module is switch fabric–aware and runs the entire PIX 6.0 software feature set and some PIX 6.2 features including command authorization, object grouping, and URL-filtering enhancements. It supports up to 100 virtual LANs (VLANs) with no physical interfaces.

There are some caveats to using the FWSM over a stand-alone PIX Firewall. It has no support for IDS signatures, Cisco Secure Policy Manager, conduit commands, Dynamic Host Configuration Protocol (DHCP) client, or VPN except IPSec for management purposes. If you need more than 5Gbps of throughput, then you can install up to four modules per chassis for a total of 20Gbps. However, there's no support for the Open Shortest Path First (OSPF) routing protocol, just as you'll find in version 6.3 of the PIX Firewall operating system.

This section presents a configuration overview and then discusses how to configure the switch for the FWSM using both IOS and Catalyst operating system (CatOS) based switches. Next we'll show you how to connect to the module and what tasks need to be completed for the FWSM to start protecting the secured VLANs.

Overview of Configuration

The FWSM can provide access control to the whole inside network, or it can segregate multiple security zones through VLAN interfaces of different security levels. These VLAN interfaces are known as secure VLANs because they're handled by the FWSM and not by the supervisor engine. There is one secure VLAN known as the secure VLAN interface (SVI), which provides a layer 3 secure VLAN interface between the module and the router on the supervisor engine so they can communicate with each other.

One SVI must be configured between each FWSM in the chassis and the supervisor engine module router. Only one SVI can exist between a given FWSM and the router on the supervisor engine. A device can have multiple SVIs, but only one can exist between each FWSM and the supervisor engine.

You can configure secure VLANs using both the Cisco IOS and CatOS operating systems. The secure VLAN information is passed from the switch operating system software to the firewall module when it comes on line. The module accepts traffic on the secure VLANs only after the firewall interfaces are configured on the module corresponding to the secure VLANs defined on the switch. The firewall software won't see traffic on VLANs that are unknown to the firewall module or on the secure VLANs without having corresponding firewall interfaces defined.

When the firewall module comes on line, the Network Management Processor (NMP) sends a message that specifies the secure VLANs that are defined for that particular firewall module. If a VLAN is active and is configured as a secure VLAN, the information about the new active VLAN is sent to the corresponding FWSM.

The FWSM configuration has the following characteristics:

- Each firewall interface is a layer 3 interface and has an IP address.
- Each firewall interface has a fixed VLAN, which is defined on the switch.
- The switch MSFC is used as a router for only the SVI so the devices can communicate.
- The module views all networks attached to an interface as having the same security level.
- Traffic from non-firewall VLANs is routed through the MSFC without being processed by the FWSM.

Configuring an IOS Switch

To set up the configuration for the FWSM on the switch using the Cisco IOS CLI, follow these steps:

1. Create the VLANs to be used by the module using the `vlan number` command.
2. Define an SVI on the MSFC using the `interface vlan number` command, or you'll be unable to configure VLANs on the module.
3. Create a firewall group of secure VLANs using the `firewall vlan-group firewall-group vlan-range` command.
4. Attach the VLAN and firewall group to the slot where the FWSM is located using the `firewall module module number vlan-group firewall-group` command.

You can also view the defined VLAN groups and the module(s) using the `show firewall vlan-group` and `show firewall module` commands. The following in an example of using these commands to create secure VLANs and the SVI, and tying the VLANs to the slot for the FWSM:

```
MSFC# conf t
Enter configuration commands, one per line. End with CNTL/Z.
MSFC(config)# vlan 15
MSFC(config-vlan)# vlan 16
MSFC(config-vlan)# vlan 17
MSFC(config-vlan)# exit
MSFC(config)# firewall vlan-group 10 15-17
MSFC(config)# firewall vlan-group 21 30-45
MSFC(config)# firewall module 8 vlan-group 10,21
```

Working with the Firewall Services Module

```
MSFC(config)# int vlan 55
MSFC(config-if)# ip address 192.168.1.1 255.255.255.0
MSFC(config-if)# no shut
MSFC(config-if)# end
MSFC# show firewall vlan-group
Group  vlans
-----  ------
10     15-17
21     30-45
MSFC# show firewall module
Module Vlan-groups
  8     10,21,
MSFC#
```

You can also see the SVI interface using the show interface vlan *number* command, as you can see from the following output:

```
MSFC# show int vlan 15
Vlan15 is up, line protocol is up
  Hardware is EtherSVI, address is 000A.2ed0.8c54 (bia 000A.2ed0.8c54)
  Internet address is 192.168.1.1/24
  MTU 1500 bytes, BW 1000000 Kbit, DLY 10 usec,
     reliability 255/255, txload 1/255, rxload 1/255
  Encapsulation ARPA, loopback not set
  ARP type:ARPA, ARP Timeout 04:00:00
  Last input never, output 00:00:08, output hang never
  Last clearing of "show interface" counters never
  Input queue:0/75/0/0 (size/max/drops/flushes); Total output drops:0
  Queueing strategy:fifo
  Output queue :0/40 (size/max)
  5 minute input rate 0 bits/sec, 0 packets/sec
  5 minute output rate 0 bits/sec, 0 packets/sec
  L2 Switched:ucast:196 pkt, 13328 bytes - mcast:4 pkt, 256 bytes
  L3 in Switched:ucast:0 pkt, 0 bytes - mcast:0 pkt, 0 bytes mcast
  L3 out Switched:ucast:0 pkt, 0 bytes
     0 packets input, 0 bytes, 0 no buffer
     Received 0 broadcasts, 0 runts, 0 giants, 0 throttles
     0 input errors, 0 CRC, 0 frame, 0 overrun, 0 ignored
     4 packets output, 256 bytes, 0 underruns
     0 output errors, 0 interface resets
     0 output buffer failures, 0 output buffers swapped out
Router#
```

> **NOTE:** To prevent trunks from carrying secure VLANs, you should remove those VLANs from any trunk connection using the `switchport trunk allowed vlan remov` *vlan-list* command.

Configuring a CatOS Switch

To set up the configuration on the switch for the FWSM using the Catalyst operating system CLI, you must be in the proper Virtual Terminal Protocol (VTP) mode to create VLANs (Server, Transparent, or Off modes all work), and then follow these steps:

1. Specify firewall VLANs and maps them to the module using the `set vlan` *vlan-list* `firewall-vlan` *module* command.
2. Set the VLAN SVI using the `set vlan` *vlan-number* command.

To display the range of VLANs specified for the FWSM, use the `show vlan firewall-vlan` *module-number* command. The following in an example of using these commands to create secure VLANs while tying those to the slot for the FWSM and setting the SVI:

```
Console>(enable) set vlan 17, 21-25, 29-30 firewall-vlan 8
Console>(enable) set vlan 19
Console>(enable) show vlan firewall-vlan 8
Secured vlans by firewall module 8:
17, 21-25, 29-30
Console>(enable)
```

Connecting to the Module

You might be asking yourself how you get to the module to configure it after you've set up the secure VLANs on the switch. For an IOS-based switch, the command is `session slot` *number* `processor 1`. The following is an example of connecting to the FWSM in slot 8:

```
MSFC# session slot 8 processor 1
The default escape character is Ctrl-^, then x. You can also type 'exit' at the
  remote prompt to end the session
Trying 127.0.0.81    Open

FWSM passwd:

Welcome to the FWSM firewall
```

Type help or '?' for a list of available commands.

FWSM>

If you're using the CatOS, you need to use the `session module` command to connect to the FWSM in the specified module. The following is an example of connecting to the FWSM in slot 8:

```
Console> session 8
The default escape character is Ctrl-^, then x. you can also type 'exit' at the
remote prompt to end the session
Trying 127.0.0.81    Open

FWSM passwd:

Welcome to the FWSM firewall

Type help or '?' for a list of available commands.

FWSM>
```

If the module doesn't boot into the application partition, you might need to reset the module with the `hw-module module slot-number reset cf:4` command for Cisco IOS and `reset module-number` for the CatOS-based switch.

Configuring the FWSM

The configuration of the module is the same if you're using the Cisco IOS or the CatOS-based switch. Plus, with a few exceptions, the configuration of the FWSM is basically the same as the stand-alone PIX Firewall. Each interface needs to be defined before it can be used for traffic using a command slightly modified for the FWSM. That command is `nameif vlan-number if-name security-level`, where `vlan-number` is in place of the `physical-interface` parameter.

> **NOTE** To allow traffic to flow from one interface to another, you must explicitly define an access list and map that access list to the appropriate interface. Unlike the PIX firewall, traffic from high-security-level interfaces isn't allowed to flow freely to an interface with a lower security level. By default, access lists are defined as deny any.

The following example shows how to configure the module:

```
FWSM(config)# nameif 15 inside 100
FWSM(config)# nameif 16 outside 0
```

```
FWSM(config)# ip address inside 10.1.1.1 255.255.255.0
FWSM(config)# ip address outside 192.168.1.2 255.255.255.0
FWSM(config)# access-list 1 permit ip any any
FWSM(config)# access-group 1 in interface inside
FWSM(config)# show nameif
nameif vlan15 inside security100
nameif vlan16 outside security0
FWSM(config)# show ip
System IP Addresses:
ip address inside 10.1.1.1 255.255.255.0
ip address outside 192.168.1.2 255.255.255.0
ip address eobc 127.0.0.61 255.255.255.0
Current IP Addresses:
ip address inside 10.1.1.1 255.255.255.0
ip address outside 192.168.1.2 255.255.255.0
ip address eobc 127.0.0.61 255.255.255.0
FWSM(config)# show access-list
access-list 1; 1 elements
access-list 1 permit ip any any (hitcnt=0)
FWSM(config)# show access-group
access-group 1 in interface inside
FWSM(config)#
```

Using the PIX Firewall CLI

Now that you know what the PIX Firewall is and how it works, it's time to get some hands-on experience with it. In this section, we'll discuss the various modes of the CLI as well as several basic commands. This chapter concentrates on the system and management commands and general navigation between the CLI modes. The bulk of the network and security configuration commands will be discussed in detail in later chapters.

CLI Access Methods

There are a number of ways to access the PIX Firewall's CLI. The most common method is via the console. This is a standard EIA/TIA-232 serial interface that uses a RJ-45 connector and a rolled cable. Typically, the console is connected to the COM port on a PC and accessed via a terminal emulator, such as HyperTerminal or TeraTerm.

Another way to access the CLI is via a Telnet session. However, this option comes with some major caveats. The Telnet protocol itself is almost totally insecure. Although a password is required, it's transmitted in plain text across the network. For this and other reasons, it's possible to telnet to a PIX Firewall from any interface, but sessions connecting to the PIX Firewall from the outside network must be inside an IPSec tunnel (Part III of this book, "Cisco Secure Virtual Private Networks," covers IPSec tunnels).

The preferred method of remotely accessing a PIX Firewall is using the Secure Shell Protocol (SSH). This method is similar to Telnet, but it provides data privacy via encryption.

We'll discuss the configuration of these access methods in the next chapter. Here, we'll continue by explaining what happens once you access and log on to the PIX Firewall.

CLI Modes

The PIX Firewall uses four basic modes of operation, similar to the Cisco IOS–based routers: Monitor mode, Unprivileged mode, Privileged mode, and Configuration mode.

Monitor Mode

This mode is sometimes overlooked in the Cisco documentation. You use Monitor mode when you need to upgrade the software on a PIX Firewall that doesn't have an internal floppy drive. None of the new PIX Firewalls have internal floppy drives.

You get into Monitor mode during the bootup sequence, when you're prompted to use either BREAK or Esc to interrupt the Flash boot. You have 10 seconds to interrupt the normal boot process. You then press the Esc key or send a BREAK character, which puts you in Monitor mode. The `monitor>` prompt is then displayed.

Unprivileged Mode

After the initial logon, you're in Unprivileged mode. This is a highly restricted mode that, by default, has only a few commands including `enable`, `pager`, and `quit`. The prompt in Unprivileged mode is marked by the greater-than symbol (>) after the system name.

Privileged Mode

To gain access to view and configure the PIX Firewall, you must type the command `enable` from the Unprivileged mode prompt. You're then prompted for the enable password. After successfully entering this password, you're in Privileged mode. This mode is marked by the pound symbol (#) after the system name.

The mode sequence looks like this:

```
PIX> ?
enable        Enter privileged mode or change privileged
                mode password
pager         Control page length for pagination
quit          Disable, end configuration or logout
PIX> enable
Password: *****
PIX#
```

From Privileged mode, you can manage the flash, view the configuration, use the `show` commands, view the logs, and enter any Unprivileged mode command. The command `disable` returns to Unprivileged mode from Privileged mode.

Configuration Mode

To enter Configuration mode on the PIX Firewall, type the `configure terminal` command. After you enter this command, the prompt changes to include the word `config`, indicating that you're in the Configuration mode.

While in this mode, you can modify the current running configuration in the PIX Firewall's memory. You can also enter any Unprivileged and Privileged command while in Configuration mode. So, if you want to view the configuration while in configuration mode, enter the `write terminal` command to view the current configuration in RAM. This is a different behavior from Cisco IOS, where you must exit the configuration mode to enter Unprivileged or Privileged commands. Any command you type will take effect immediately but still needs to be saved to flash memory, making the changes permanent. You can return to Privileged mode by typing the command `exit`.

Editing in the CLI

The PIX Firewall's CLI uses the same editing conventions as the Cisco IOS router software. These conventions are special Ctrl-key combinations or arrow keys that allow you to move the cursor to different places. Table 10.1 lists the key combinations commonly used when editing the PIX Firewall's configuration.

TABLE 10.1 PIX Firewall CLI Editing Keys

Key	Function
Ctrl+P or up arrow	Displays the previously accepted commands. This is handy when you need to enter several similar commands or the same command several times in a row.
Ctrl+N or down arrow	Displays the next accepted command. Note that if you make a syntax error and a command isn't accepted, it won't be displayed in the history.
Ctrl+W	Deletes the word to the left of the cursor.
Ctrl+U	Deletes the entire line.

Basic Commands

This section presents some of the basic Privileged mode commands. Other commands will be covered in other chapters when we discuss their respective technologies. These commands are used most often when configuring the PIX Firewall and are organized here alphabetically.

The *clear* Command

The clear command resets counters or caches held in the PIX Firewall's memory. This is useful during troubleshooting. You might want to clear the interface statistics, the ARP table, or the xlate table. You can also use this command to clear the PIX Firewall's configuration and clear the contents of the flash before installing a new image. The following is an example of the options available when you're running version 6.2 of the PIX Firewall operating system:

```
PIX# clear ?
arp         Change or view the arp table, and set the arp timeout value
blocks      Show system buffer utilization
capture     Capture inbound and outbound packets on one or more interfaces
flashfs     Show, destroy, or preserve filesystem information
local-host  Display or clear the local host network information
logging     Clear syslog entries from the internal buffer
pager       Control page length for pagination
passwd      Change Telnet console access password
shun        Manages the filtering of packets from undesired hosts
tcpstat     Display status of tcp stack and tcp connections
traffic     Counters for traffic statistics
uauth       Display or clear current user authorization information
xlate       Display current translation and connection slot information
PIX# clear
```

The *clock set* Command

PIX Firewalls use an internal clock, similar to that on PCs, for a number of purposes. The two primary uses are for generating timestamps on the Syslogs and as part of the Public Key Infrastructure (PKI) protocol, to make sure certificates and other security constructs are removed as they expire. Thus, it's important to set your clock correctly. To do this, use the clock set command.

The syntax is as follows:

clock set *hh:mm:ss month day year*

The *copy* Command

The copy command copies an image or PDM file from a TFTP server onto the flash. This command uses the URL syntax, as follows:

copy tftp[:[[//*location*][/*path*]]] flash[:[image | pdm]]

After you execute this command, the PIX Firewall will prompt you for the IP address of the TFTP server and the source filename that you want to copy.

> **WARNING** Unlike the copy TFTP operation on Cisco routers using IOS, when you're upgrading from 5.*x* to 6.*x* images, the PIX Firewall doesn't warn you about erasing all files on the flash or ask you over and over if you really, really want to copy the file. It just does it. Fortunately, once it has finished verifying that the copy was successful, you have the option of not installing the new image.

The *debug* Commands

The debug commands provide detailed, real-time information about events on the PIX Firewall. These include information about packets traversing the firewall, special services such as DHCP and failover, the crypto processes of IPSec and Internet Security Association and Key Management Protocol (ISAKMP), and more. Here's an example of the debug output for the RIP routing process:

```
PIX# debug rip
RIP trace on
PIX# 226: RIP: interface outside received v1 update
         from 10.2.0.6
227: RIP: interface outside received v2 update
         from 10.2.0.5
228: RIP: update contains 4 routes
229: RIP: interface inside sending v1 update
         to 255.255.255.255
230: RIP: interface outside received v2 update
         from 10.2.0.5
231: RIP: update contains 4 routes
```

Most debug operations use the command debug, followed by a keyword, such as rip, as in the previous example. However, the packet-debugging feature is much more powerful, and the syntax is correspondingly complex:

```
PIX# debug packet ?
usage: [no] debug packet ifname
       [src sip [netmask <smask>]]
```

```
          [dst dip [netmask <dmask>]]
          [proto
                  icmp |
                  tcp [sport <sport>] [dport <dport>] |
                  udp [sport <sport>] [dport <dport>] ]
          [rx|tx|both]
```

`PIX# debug packet`

As you can see, this feature allows you to explicitly define the types of packets you want to view. This is useful for verifying that your filters are operating as you intended.

The *enable* Command

The `enable` command controls access to Privileged mode. Usually, you'll use the command without any additional parameters, but there is an optional privilege-level parameter. The following is the `enable` command syntax:

`enable [priv-level]`

By default, the `enable` command asks for the level 15 enable password, but you can specify the privilege level from 0 to 15. We'll talk about how these privilege levels are used in Chapter 12, "ACLs, Filtering, Object Grouping, and AAA." Now let's see how to configure the enable password for each level.

The *enable password* Command

The `enable password` command sets the password that allows access to Privileged mode. The password is alphanumeric and can be at least 3 characters and up to 16 characters long. An optional a `level` parameter, followed by the privilege level, creates a password for that particular privilege level. The syntax is as follows:

`enable password password [level priv-level] [encrypted]`

If you're entering a password that is already encrypted, you must use the `encrypted` keyword after your password. Note that an encrypted string is always exactly 16 characters long (so you can't tell how long the unencrypted password is).

The *passwd* Command

The `passwd` command sets the password for Telnet and SSH access to the PIX Firewall. (Telnet and SSH are discussed in the next chapter.) The syntax is as follows:

`passwd password [encrypted]`

The `encrypted` keyword works just like it does for the `enable password` command.

The *perfmon* Command

The perfmon command provides a convenient interface for accessing a number of statistics all at once. This command has three parts:

```
PIX# perfmon ?
Usage:  perfmon interval seconds
        perfmon quiet | verbose
        perfmon settings
PIX# perfmon
```

The first command tells the PIX Firewall how often to report the statistics. The second command turns reporting on and off. The last command shows the current settings. Here is an example of these commands and the perfmon report:

```
PIX# perfmon interval 10
PIX# perfmon verbose
PIX# perfmon settings
interval: 10 (seconds)
verbose
PIX#
PERFMON STATS:      Current       Average
Xlates              0/s           0/s
Connections         0/s           0/s
TCP Conns           0/s           0/s
UDP Conns           0/s           0/s
URL Access          0/s           0/s
WebSns Req          0/s           0/s
TCP Fixup           0/s           0/s
TCPIntercept        0/s           0/s
HTTP Fixup          0/s           0/s
FTP Fixup           0/s           0/s
AAA Authen          0/s           0/s
AAA Author          0/s           0/s
AAA Account         0/s           0/s
PIX#
```

The *reload* Command

The reload command reboots the PIX Firewall after prompting you to confirm that you would like the PIX Firewall to reboot itself. Optionally, you can use the keyword **noconfirm** to bypass confirmation. The syntax is as follows:

```
reload [noconfirm]
```

The *show checksum* Command

To ensure the integrity of the configuration, the PIX Firewall calculates a cryptographic checksum of the configuration. The show checksum command has no optional parameters and displays the checksum as a series of four 4-byte numbers in hexadecimal format. As part of your security procedures, after the PIX Firewall is initially configured, you should use the show checksum command and record the checksum. You can then use this as part of your audits, to verify that no one has tampered with the configuration. Here's an example of the output of the show checksum command:

```
PIX# show checksum
Cryptochecksum: eb30f570 92b0f5e6 e29ee8dc 5f0aa42a
PIX#
```

The *show interface* Command

The show interface command is used often because it provides a great deal of information about the interfaces on the PIX Firewall. By default, all interfaces are set to the administratively down state. To verify that an interface has been initialized, you can use the following syntax:

show interface [*hardware_address*]

If the optional hardware address is given, the output is limited to information about the address specified; otherwise, information is displayed about all interfaces.

The show interface command is most often used to verify that the interface is *up/up*, which refers to the hardware and the line protocol—in this case, Ethernet. In other words, it checks layers 1 and 2 of the OSI model, respectively. The show interface command is also used to show the IP address and the activity on the interface, including packet and byte counts for inbound and outbound traffic, and error statistics. The following shows sample output of this command.

```
PIX# show interface ethernet0
interface ethernet0 "outside" is up, line protocol is up
  Hardware is i82559 ethernet, address is 0050.54ff.076d
  IP address 10.2.0.20, subnet mask 255.255.255.0
  MTU 1500 bytes, BW 100000 Kbit full duplex
      6063 packets input, 608203 bytes, 0 no buffer
      Received 1684 broadcasts, 0 runts, 0 giants
      0 input errors, 0 CRC, 0 frame, 0 overrun,
        0 ignored, 0 abort
      45 packets output, 3530 bytes, 0 underruns
      0 output errors, 0 collisions, 0 interface resets
      0 babbles, 0 late collisions, 0 deferred
      0 lost carrier, 0 no carrier
      input queue (curr/max blocks): hardware (128/128)
```

```
            software (0/1)
        output queue (curr/max blocks): hardware (0/1)
            software (0/1)
PIX#
```

The *show tech-support* Command

The show tech-support command has no optional parameters and is often used at the request of Cisco's Technical Assistance Center (TAC). It's a convenient way to dump the output of several show commands to the screen, so you can cut and paste the output into an e-mail message and forward it to the TAC to help them troubleshoot a problem.

The *shun* Command

The shun command allows an administrator to quickly respond to an incident by deleting the connection information of a given source address and rejecting any future packets from that source, without changing the configuration rules of the PIX Firewall. Because the configuration of ACLs and conduits can become complex, the shun command can save a great deal of time, which is often critical during an attack. We'll go into more detail about the shun command in Chapter 13, "Advanced Protocol Handling, Attack Guards, and Intrusion Detection."

The syntax of the shun command is as follows:

```
PIX# shun ?
Usage:  shun src_ip [dst_ip sport dport [prot]]
        no shun src_ip
        show shun [src_ip|statistics]
        clear shun [statistics]
PIX# shun
```

The *who* Command

The who command shows the TTY ID and IP address of each active Telnet session on the PIX Firewall. The TTY ID is important because this ID is used with the kill command to terminate active Telnet connections. You can provide an optional IP address parameter to display all sessions from that IP address. The following is an example of the command syntax:

```
PIX# who ?
Usage:  who ip
PIX# who
```

The *write* Command

You can use the `write` command to copy the current configuration to a number of different locations, as follows:

- To copy the current configuration to flash:

  `write memory`

- To display the current configuration on the terminal:

  `write terminal`

- To copy the current configuration to a TFTP server:

  `write network [[server_ip]:[filename]]`

- To copy the current configuration to a floppy disk, if one is available:

  `write floppy`

- To copy the current configuration to the failover standby server:

  `write standy`

You can also erase the configuration on the flash by using the following command:

`write erase`

The commands we covered in this section will get you started configuring your PIX Firewall. You'll refer back to this section often, because PIX Firewall administrators use these commands almost daily.

Summary

This chapter began by defining the term *firewall* and explaining that the role of a firewall is to protect the network at the perimeter from outside attacks. We then looked at the three common firewall technologies in use today:

- Packet-filtering firewalls use rules to deny packets based on the content of the headers.
- Application proxies are layer 7–aware programs that communicate with systems on untrusted networks on behalf of hosts in the trusted network.
- Stateful firewalls permit or deny packets based on other packets, typically on a session basis.

Next, we focused on the PIX Firewall. We examined the unique hardware and software components in a PIX Firewall and how they operate together to provide a formidable security solution. We then introduced the Firewall Service Module (FWSM), which runs the PIX Firewall operating system, and how to set up the module to work with both Cisco IOS– and CatOS-based switches.

Finally, we covered the PIX Firewall CLI and the common commands used in the day-to-day operation and management of the PIX Firewall.

Now that you have a basic understanding of firewalls, and the operation of the PIX Firewall specifically, this knowledge will provide a foundation for the advanced topics in later chapters.

Exam Essentials

Know what the PIX Firewall protects against and what it doesn't protect against. Understand the concept of a network's perimeter. Understand the types of attacks and which ones can be detected and defeated by firewalls.

Understand the difference between translation slots, connection slots, and the xlate table. Be able to describe the purpose of each of these components. Know when they're created and where they exist.

Know how to describe a modern screened subnet, or DMZ. Understand why DMZs exist and their advantages and disadvantages. Be able to describe the flow of information in and out of a DMZ.

Remember the differences between the various firewall technologies. Be able to describe the operation of application proxies, packet filters, and stateful firewalls, and identify the advantages and disadvantages of each type.

Understand the FWSM You need to be able to describe the features of the FWSM, the differences it has from a stand-alone PIX Firewall, and the commands to configure the module for both Cisco IOS– and CatOS-based switches.

Know the different modes of the CLI. Be able to distinguish between User mode, Privileged mode, and Configuration mode on the PIX Firewall operating system CLI. Know how to get to each mode and what passwords are required.

Know how to use the *show* commands. Be sure you can describe the output of common show commands. Know which command is the most appropriate for displaying various types of information.

Chapter 11

PIX Firewall Configuration

THE FOLLOWING TOPICS ARE COVERED IN THIS CHAPTER:

- ✓ Understanding the CLI and using some general commands
- ✓ How to configure the DHCP server
- ✓ An overview of Network Address Translation (NAT)
- ✓ An overview of Port Address Translation (PAT)
- ✓ How to configure remote access to the PIX Firewall
- ✓ Understand how to configure static, dynamic, and multicast routing

In this chapter, we'll discuss the configuration of the PIX Firewall. We'll begin by discussing the preparatory work you should complete before you configure a PIX Firewall, which includes configuring the hostname, remote access, and logging facilities. Then you'll learn how to set up a PIX Firewall to allow the traffic of your choice to pass between the inside, outside, and demilitarized zone (DMZ) interfaces. This includes the configuration of interfaces, Network Address Translation (NAT), and Port Address Translation (PAT). This chapter also covers how to configure a PIX Firewall to participate in Routing Information Protocol (RIP) domains and forward multicast traffic to downstream hosts that need it using Stub Multicast Routing (SMR).

Preparing for Firewall Configuration

To configure the PIX Firewall, you must answer the following questions at a minimum:
- What am I trying to protect?
- What am I trying to protect it from?
- How many networks will be connected, and what are their addresses?
- Which of these networks do I trust most?
- Which of these networks do I trust least?
- Are there any other paths to get from one network to another?
- What routing protocols are involved, and how are they configured?
- Will address translation be required?
- If so, how many addresses need to be translated, and how many addresses are available to translate them?
- What are my application requirements?
- Which applications will pass through the firewall, and on which interfaces will they arrive and depart?
- What protocol and/or port number will they use?
- Who are the users of each application?
- What are the source and destination IP addresses?
- What are my organization's security policies?

The answers to these questions will determine much of the configuration. As we go through the configuration procedures in the rest of this chapter, we'll point out where the answers to these questions are used.

> **NOTE**
> Cisco has provided a PDF file from Appendix A of the *PIX Firewall and VPN Configuration Guide* for PIX Firewall version 6.2 with tables so you can enter most of this information at URL http://www.cisco.com/univercd/cc/td/doc/product/iaabu/pix/pix_62/config/cfgforms.pdf.

Using Common Global Configuration Commands

Before we delve into the important aspects of configuring the PIX Firewall, let's take a brief look at several commands that are largely optional:

- `telnet`
- `ssh`
- `clock`
- `ntp`
- `domain-name`
- `hostnames`
- `name/names`
- `dhcpd`
- `logging`

Each of these commands plays a part in making the PIX Firewall more secure or more user friendly. They affect the PIX Firewall as a whole, rather than any one particular interface or rule.

The Remote Access Commands

By default, there is no remote access to the PIX Firewall, but the firewall can be configured to allow Telnet, SSH, and HTTP remote console access. We'll discuss the Telnet and SSH commands here; HTTP console access is discussed in Chapter 14, "Firewall Failover and PDM," when we talk about the Cisco PIX Device Manager (PDM).

The *telnet* Command

The `telnet` command is used to configure Telnet access to the PIX Firewall console. If you enter just an IP address, the firewall will add that IP address to each internal interface. Optionally, you can specify a network mask and interface name. If a mask is used, then the firewall will add the IP address and mask to each internal interface. If you specify an interface, then the firewall will add the IP address and mask to the specified interface only. If you want to allow Telnet access from any host, then use 0 0 as the IP address and mask.

Here is an example of using the `telnet` command, with the irrelevant portions omitted:

```
PIX(config)# telnet 0 0
PIX(config)# telnet 160.109.12.2 255.255.255.255 outside
PIX(config)# write term
Building configuration...
: Saved
:
PIX Version 6.2(2)
nameif ethernet0 outside security0
nameif ethernet1 inside security100
nameif ethernet2 dmz security99
hostname PIX
telnet 160.109.12.2 255.255.255.255 outside
telnet 0.0.0.0 0.0.0.0 inside
telnet 0.0.0.0 0.0.0.0 dmz
telnet timeout 5
PIX(config)#
```

As you can see from the output, the single `telnet 0 0` command produced two `telnet` commands in the configuration file. This is because it added the IP address and mask to all internal interfaces, which are `inside` and `dmz`. You can also see that there is a `telnet timeout` command with the value of 5 in the configuration. The default Telnet idle timeout is five minutes; you can change it to a value from 1 to 60 minutes with the `telnet timeout` command.

You might wonder why the PIX Firewall allows Telnet access to the outside interface, which doesn't sound very secure. The PIX Firewall allows direct Telnet console access to the outside interface only if the Telnet traffic is IPSec-protected. Therefore, to enable a Telnet session to the outside interface, you must configure IP Security (IPSec) on the outside interface, include IP traffic generated by the PIX Firewall in the access list, and then enable Telnet on the outside interface.

The *ssh* Command

Secure Shell (SSH) is a more secure access method than Telnet. You configure it just as you would Telnet, but with the `ssh` command. The PIX Firewall supports SSH version 1, which provides strong authentication and traffic encryption capabilities. It has the same parameter structure and default values as `telnet`, so we won't go over it again.

There are a couple of differences between Telnet and SSH. First, with SSH, you can directly access the PIX Firewall console on the outside interface without using IPSec. Since SSH is more secure than Telnet, the PIX Firewall allows direct access on the outside interface without the need to encapsulate the traffic in an IPSec tunnel.

The second difference is that, with SSH, you need to issue more commands to set up RSA encryption keys. To issue RSA keys, you need to set up a domain name (discussed later in this chapter) with the `domain-name` and `hostname` commands plus the `ca generate rsa key` and `ca save all` commands. For the `ca generate rsa key` command, the options are 512, 768, 1024, and 2048 (the modulus value). The `ca save all` command permanently saves the public keys to flash memory.

Here is an example of how to set up your RSA keys to enable SSH console access to the PIX Firewall:

```
pixfirewall(config)# hostname PIX
PIX(config)# domain-name sybex.com
PIX(config)# ca generate rsa key 1024
For key_module_size = 1024, key generation could
  take up to several minutes. Please wait.

PIX(config)# ca save all
PIX(config)#
```

If you haven't configured authentication, authorization, and accounting (AAA, discussed in the next chapter), then to gain access to the PIX Firewall console via SSH, at the SSH client, enter the username as `pix` and enter the Telnet password. You can set the Telnet password using the `passwd` command, discussed in Chapter 10, "PIX Firewall Basics," with the default Telnet password `cisco`.

The *clock* Command

You can use the `clock` command to set the system clock, time zone, and summer time information. Before version 6.2 of the PIX Firewall operating system, the syntax was too simple. The PIX Firewall's clock wasn't aware of daylight saving time (DST). Thus, it didn't automatically switch twice per year and didn't support time zones. We're thankful that this issue has been corrected, because both problems can cause headaches for those using the `logging timestamp` feature. All log entries are coded with the actual time, as opposed to the number of seconds elapsed since the last reboot, so you could be in for some head-scratching date math.

To set the time and clock on the PIX Firewall, use the `clock set` command followed by the time in the format *hh:mm:ss*, where *hh* is a 24-hour clock. You can optionally specify the *month day year* or *day month year*. The new `clock` command options allow you to set the time zone and when summer time starts and ends for DST. To configure the time zone, use the clock `timezone` command followed by the *zone-name* and *hour-offset* values. If you live in a time zone with half-hour offsets, you can optionally specify *minutes* after the *hour* value. Here is an example of setting the time zone for central daylight time (CDT):

```
PIX(config)# set timezone CDT -6
PIX(config)#
```

To ensure that the time will be adjusted for daylight saving, you must specify when the summer time occurs. This is done using the `clock summer-time` command. You need to specify the *zone-name* and then the keyword `recurring`. The following is an example of setting the summer time for the central time zone:

```
PIX(config)# set summer-time CDT recurring
PIX(config)#
```

To ensure that you've configured the clock settings correctly, you can use the `show clock` command with the optional `detail` parameter. Here is the output from these commands:

```
PIX(config)# sho clock
15:19:45.530 CDT Mon Apr 28 2003
PIX(config)# sho clock detail
15:19:48.760 CDT Mon Apr 28 2003
Time source is NTP
Summer time starts 02:00:00 CDT Sun Apr 6 2003
Summer time ends 02:00:00 CDT Sun Oct 26 2003
PIX(config)#
```

Now you're ready to make sure the time is always up to date using a Network Time Protocol (NTP) server.

The *ntp* Command

Setting the clock on the PIX Firewall is nice, but what happens if the clock loses a second every 24 hours? If you're like us, you want everything nice and synchronized so that when you're troubleshooting a problem, the time is the same on your firewalls and the routers or switches. That way, you know an event on your router happened two-tenths of a second after an event on your firewall.

The clock is pretty reliable on the PIX Firewall, but you would rather it be synchronized with other equipment on your network. You can use NTP to accomplish clock synchronization.

If you're familiar with NTP syntax in IOS, you'll be happy to find out it's very similar on the PIX Firewall. Here is the command used to set up the IP address of the server to get time:

```
ntp server ip_address [key key_number] source interace [prefer]
```

The *key_number* will be discussed later. The *interface* parameter specifies the interface used to communicate with the NTP server. Since you can have multiple NTP servers configured, you can set one to be preferred over the others with the *prefer* option.

You can use some commands to configure NTP authentication to make sure you're getting time from a trusted source. The `ntp authenticate` command globally enables NTP authentication for the PIX Firewall.

To configure a Message Digest 5 (MD5) authentication key, you use the `ntp authencication-key` *number* MD5 *value* command. The *number* is a number from 1 to 4,294,967,295, and the *value* is the key value, which is an arbitrary string of up to 32 characters. You can have multiple authentication keys configured, so you need to know which key to send to which server. This is where the *key_number* is used in the `ntp server` command discussed earlier.

The `ntp trusted-key` *key_number* command defines one or more key numbers that the NTP server needs to provide in its NTP packets for the PIX Firewall to accept synchronization with the NTP server.

To make sure your NTP communications are configured correctly, you can use the `show ntp status` command. You can also use the `show ntp associations` command to see the NTP peers and their stratum and reference clocks. The following is an example of using these commands to troubleshoot your NTP configuration:

```
PIX(config)# show ntp status

Clock is synchronized, stratum 5, reference is 135.166.127.25
nominal freq is 250.0000 Hz, actual freq is 249.9985 Hz, precision is
  2**18
reference time is C258009C.694453C1 (14:33:48.411 CDT Mon Apr 28 2003)
clock offset is 1.1066 msec, root delay is 33.49 msec
root dispersion is 8.10 msec, peer dispersion is 0.35 msec
PIX(config)# show ntp associations

  address          ref clock       st when  poll reach delay  offset  disp
*~135.166.127.25  175.172.8.85     4   43   128  377   3.5    -0.27   1.7
 * master (synced), # master (unsynced), - candidate, ~ configured
PIX(config)#
```

> **NOTE:** Remember that when you're configuring NTP support for the PIX Firewall, you need to allow inbound NTP traffic from the NTP server to reach the firewall. Otherwise your clock won't be able to synchronize.

The *domain-name* and *hostname* Commands

The `domain-name` command accepts a single parameter, the domain name, which is used to set the IPSec domain name. The `domain-name` and `hostname` commands combine to allow the administrator to specify the fully qualified domain name (FQDN). The primary purposes of these commands are to facilitate RSA keys, which use the FQDN as an input, and for IPSec.

The `hostname` command also accepts a single parameter: the name of the host. Although it's also part of the RSA key's input, this command is most often used to set the PIX CLI prompt. The following in an example of using these commands:

```
pixfirewall(config)# hostname PIX
PIX(config)# domain-name sybex.com
PIX(config)#
```

The *name/names* Commands

A few commands work together to provide aliases for IP addresses, much like the /etc/hosts file in a Unix host. The purpose of the name command is to make the configuration easier to read.

You can create an alias by using the name keyword followed by an IP address and the name (up to 16 characters) that you want to use. For instance, you might type the following:

```
PIX(config)# name 192.168.10.53 proxy1
PIX(config)# name 192.168.100.5 pix-outside
PIX(config)# name 192.168.10.1 pix-inside
PIX(config)#
```

Then you could use the word proxy1, pix-outside, or pix-inside in place of the IP address in all the access-list, ip address, nat, and conduit statements. Doing so enhances security by reducing the risk of incorrect configurations from typos. It also makes the output from show and other commands much easier to read, as you can see from the following example:

```
PIX(config)# ip address outside pix-outside 255.255.255.0
PIX(config)# ip address inside pix-inside 255.255.255.0
PIX(config)# show ip address
System IP Addresses:
        ip address outside pix-outside 255.255.255.0
        ip address inside pix-inside 255.255.255.0
Current IP Addresses:
        ip address outside pix-outside 255.255.255.0
        ip address inside pix-inside 255.255.255.0
PIX(config)#
```

The *dhcpd* Command

The PIX Firewall can act as both a DHCP client and a DHCP server. We'll be discussing the DHCP server in this section.

Support for the DHCP server within the PIX Firewall means that the firewall can use DHCP to configure clients directly connected to the inside interface. This DHCP feature is designed for the remote home or branch office that will establish a connection to an enterprise or corporate network.

> **NOTE:** The DHCP server feature doesn't support BOOTP requests and failover requests.

To configure a pool of addresses to use for client configuration, you need to use the dhcpd address command, followed by the start and end addresses in the range separated by a hyphen, and the interface where the client will reside. As stated earlier, the only interface that you can enable for DHCP for is the inside interface, so the address range must be in the same network as the IP address configured on the inside interface. Once the address range has been configured, you need to enable the DHCP server feature by using the `dhcpd enable inside` command.

Here is an example of the `dhcpd address` and `dhcpd enable` commands:

```
PIX(config)# dhcpd address 192.168.1.2-192.168.1.254 inside
PIX(config)# dhcpd enable inside
PIX(config)#
```

> **NOTE** If you're using the Cisco PIX 501 Firewall, there is a limit on the number of IP addresses that can be included in the DHCP address pool. If you have a 10-user license, you can have only 32 addresses in the pool; and if you have a 50-user license, you can have only 128 addresses in the pool.

You can use other DHCP commands to configure various DHCP options for the clients: `dns`, `wins`, and `domain`. The commands used to create these DHCP options are `dhcpd dns` followed by one or two IP addresses, `dhcpd wins` followed by one or two IP addresses, and `dhcpd domain` followed by a domain name.

The DHCP server feature can also support other option codes, which you might need to support for your DHCP clients. These options are configured using the `dhcpd option` command. You can specify either an ASCII string or IP address option types. For example, here are two options used by Cisco IP Phones to know where to contact a TFTP server to download their configurations:

```
PIX(config)# dhcpd option 66 ascii tftp.mynet.com
PIX(config)# dhcpd option 150 ip 10.109.23.3 10.109.23.4
PIX(config)#
```

Option 66 provides an IP address or hostname of a single TFTP server, and option 150 provides a list of TFTP server IP addresses where the IP phone can get its code and configuration.

What happens if you've configured the outside interface to get its IP address from an outside DHCP server, and you'd like to use the same DNS, WINS, and domain name options for your inside clients? You can do this with the `dhcpd auto_config client_interface` command, where the `client_interface` is the DHCP client interface. Currently, the only interface that can be enabled for DHCP client support is the outside interface, so the `client_interface` parameter should always be `outside`. This command automatically configures DNS, WINS, and domain name values from the DHCP client to the DHCP server. If you also configure the `dns`, `wins`, and `domain` options, then the CLI commands will overwrite the `auto_config` options.

You can adjust the DHCP lease time using the `dhcpd lease lease_length` command, which defaults to 3600 seconds but can be from 300 to 2,147,483,647 seconds. Other commands that need to be addressed are `show dhcpd`, which displays the `binding` and `statistics` information; and `clear dhcpd`, which clears all the `dhcpd` commands, bindings, and statistics information.

The *logging* Command

Simple Network Management Protocol (SNMP) and Syslog logging on the PIX Firewall are controlled by the `logging` command. This command directs the output of the logging process to several different places, including the console or a Syslog daemon on a Unix host (or software that mimics this on a Windows machine). The logs can also be displayed via Telnet. In all cases, logging must be explicitly enabled by using the following commands:

- To turn logging on and off, from the `config` prompt:

   [no] logging on

- To change the size of the of the queue for storing Syslog messages:

   logging queue *queue_size*

- To display the logs on the console:

   [no] logging console *level*

- To let the failover standby unit also send Syslog messages, which is disabled by default:

   [no] logging standby

- To store the logs in a buffer on the PIX that allows them to be displayed with the `show logging` command:

   [no] logging buffered *level*

- To include the device ID of the PIX Firewall in the Syslog message:

   [no] logging device-id {hostname | ipaddress *if_name* | string *text*}

- To send logs to a remote host using the Syslog facility:

   [no] logging host [*interface-name*]
        ip_address [*protocol/port*]

- To specify that Syslog messages sent to the server have a timestamp value on each message:

   [no] logging timestamp

- To display the logs on Telnet sessions:

   [no] logging monitor *level*

> **NOTE**
> It's possible to send these messages to multiple hosts. You might want to do this for redundancy or to let two different organizations keep tabs on the PIX Firewall, for example. However, sending messages to more than one host entails additional resource usage, so make sure that you don't overload the processor.

Configuring PIX Firewall Interfaces

The PIX Firewall must act as a gateway between two or more networks. As such, it must have, at a minimum, two physical network interfaces.

Configuring interfaces on the PIX Firewall is much different than configuring other Cisco devices, such as IOS routers and switches. For starters, you don't enter an Interface Configuration mode. Instead, you configure the interfaces from the `PIX(config)#` prompt. Also, you begin by assigning a name and security level to the hardware interface. After you've assigned these, most configuration commands use the name of the interface instead of its hardware address.

Since IP is the only layer 3 protocol supported by the PIX Firewall, you must gather some specific information before configuring its interfaces:

- IP address of each interface
- Subnet mask of each interface
- Relative security of each interface

Of course, each interface must be on a separate IP network, because the PIX Firewall doesn't currently support subinterfaces or secondary IP addresses (often called *multinetting*). However, if you're using the PIX Firewall's DHCP client, you don't need the IP address and subnet mask of the interface, but you'll need a DHCP server. The DHCP client feature is available only on the PIX Firewall outside interface.

Now let's talk about giving a meaningful name to your interfaces, so you can easily recognize what is being protected; assigning an appropriate security level for those interfaces; setting interface properties; assigning IP addresses; and changing the maximum transmission unit (MTU).

Naming an Interface and Assigning a Security Level

To name an interface, use the `nameif` command. The syntax for this command is as follows:

```
PIX(config)# nameif ?
usage: nameif hardware_id if_name security_lvl
       no nameif
PIX(config)#
```

Here, `hardware_id` represents the actual name, such as `ethernet0`, and `security_lvl` is any integer between 0 and 100. As for `if_name`, that's a little tricky: it's any string you make up, with the exception of `inside`, which is reserved for security level 100. The value 100, which indicates the most trusted interface, is always named `inside`. By convention, an interface with a security value of 0, which indicates the least trusted interface, is usually named `outside`; however, this isn't required—the interface with security level 0 can be named anything you want.

Here are some examples of using the `nameif` command:

```
PIX# show nameif
nameif ethernet0 outside security0
```

```
nameif ethernet1 inside security100
nameif ethernet2 DMZ security10
PIX# config term
PIX(config)# nameif ethernet1 inside 90
interface name "inside" is reserved for interface with security100
Type help or '?' for a list of available commands.
PIX(config)# nameif ethernet1 cheese 100
security 100 is reserved for the "inside" interface
Type help or '?' for a list of available commands.
PIX(config)#
```

Notice in the previous and later examples that when you try to give the same name to two different interfaces, the PIX Firewall's CLI swaps the name rather than give you an error or allow two interfaces to have the same name.

Also notice that the security value follows the displaced DMZ interface, but the interface named in your command (in this case, ethernet2) receives the security level specified in your command.

Next, let's look at some examples that show that it isn't necessary to have an inside interface or an outside interface.

```
PIX(config)# nameif ethernet0 cheese 0
PIX(config)# show nameif
nameif ethernet0 cheese security0
nameif ethernet1 inside security100
nameif ethernet2 DMZ security10
PIX(config)# nameif ethernet2 cheese 10
interface 0 name "cheese" swapped with interface 2 name "DMZ"
PIX(config)# show nameif
nameif ethernet0 DMZ security10
nameif ethernet1 inside security100
nameif ethernet2 cheese security10
PIX(config)# nameif ethernet2 cheese 0
PIX(config)# show nameif
nameif ethernet0 DMZ security10
nameif ethernet1 inside security100
nameif ethernet2 cheese security0
PIX(config)# nameif ethernet1 whiz security11
PIX(config)# exit
PIX# show nameif
nameif ethernet0 DMZ security10      same security as "cheese"
nameif ethernet1 whiz security11     no "inside" or "outside"
nameif ethernet2 cheese security10   same security as "DMZ"
PIX#
```

Notice in this example that when we chose the same security level for this interface, we created two interfaces with the same security level. This poses an interesting problem for the Adaptive Security Algorithm (ASA), because of the method in which NAT translation slots are created: Which interface will be permitted to access the other by default, and which interface will be denied by default? Cisco's answer is that both interfaces are denied by default. In fact, no direct communication is ever possible between two interfaces configured with the same security level.

> **TIP**
> Although accidentally configuring two interfaces with the same security level and having to troubleshoot the subsequent connectivity issue would be no fun, this feature can be not only valid, but also very useful. For example, if you wanted an extremely high level of security, you might want to force traffic between two networks through a proxy server or other bastion host. You could configure the two networks with the same security level and put the proxy on a third, higher-security network. This might also be useful in a B2B scenario, where you have two customer networks that need to communicate with you but definitely not with each other.

To summarize the use of the `nameif` command with one more example, if you wanted to give the first Ethernet interface of a PIX Firewall the name `YellowZone` and a security value of 20, you would type the following:

```
PIX(config)# nameif ethernet0 YellowZone 20
PIX(config)#
```

> **WARNING**
> For some reason, the PIX Firewall uses the term *Ethernet* somewhat liberally. Unlike with the IOS, where *Ethernet* refers only to the 10BaseT specification and *Fast Ethernet* refers to 100BaseTX and 100BaseFX, on the PIX Firewall, *Ethernet* refers to both 10Mbps and 100Mbps specifications. This is important because many administrators habitually define the auto-negotiation properties of Fast Ethernet, but not Ethernet. If you've hard-coded the speed and duplex values on your Catalyst switch, remember to define them in the PIX Firewall as well, even though the interface says *Ethernet*.

Setting Interface Properties and Shutting Down the Interface

After you enter a `nameif` statement for each interface on the firewall you wish to use, you'll continue the configuration by setting the layer 2 properties. To do this, use the `interface` command. The syntax of this command is as follows:

```
PIX(config)# interface ?
usage: interface hardware_id [hw_speed [shutdown]]
PIX(config)#
```

For Ethernet interfaces, the `interface` command controls the speed and duplex, and allows the interface to be administratively shut down.

The *hw_speed* parameter is one of the following keywords:

- `auto`, which sets the interface to use auto-negotiation
- `10BaseT`, which sets the interface to 10Mbps, half-duplex
- `100BaseTX`, which sets the interface to 100Mbps, half-duplex
- `100full`, which sets the interface to 100Mbps, full-duplex
- `aui`, which sets the interface to 10Mbps, half-duplex for an AUI cable
- `bnc`, which sets the interface to 10Mbps, half-duplex for a BNC cable

On older PIX Firewalls that support Token Ring, the available choices are 4, which sets the ring speed of the interface to 4Mbps, and 16, which sets the ring speed of the interface to 16Mbps.

Using the `shutdown` keyword is intuitively obvious. Just type the hardware address and the word `shutdown`, and the interface is disabled, like so:

PIX(config)# **interface ethernet0 shutdown**
PIX(config)#

However, once the interface is down, how to bring it back up isn't so obvious. Unlike with the IOS, you don't type `no interface ethernet0 shutdown` or `interface ethernet0 enable`. Instead, you enter the `interface` command again, but without the `shutdown` keyword. The tricky part is that when you disable the interface, you don't need to include the *hw_speed* value, but when you enable the interface, you must include this value.

> **WARNING** If you need to bounce an interface or disable it temporarily, be sure to make a note of the *hw_speed* setting. Otherwise, when you enable it, you could set the speed or duplex incorrectly, which would result in intermittent connectivity or no connectivity at all!

So, to bring this interface back up, issue the following command:

PIX(config)# **interface ethernet0 auto**
PIX(config)#

One last item of interest in this sequence is in the output of the `show interface` command. In the Cisco IOS, when an interface is *administratively down*, the line protocol is also down regardless of whether there is signal on that interface. Here, you can see that the interface is administratively down, but the line protocol is still up: This happens only if there is an Ethernet signal on that interface. Otherwise, the interface is administratively down and line protocol is down, like Cisco IOS:

PIX(config)# **interface ethernet0 shutdown**
PIX(config)# **exit**

```
PIX# show interface ethernet0
interface ethernet0 "YellowZone" is administratively down, line protocol is up

  Hardware is i82559 ethernet, address is 0050.54ff.076d
  IP address 10.2.0.20, subnet mask 255.255.255.0
  MTU 1500 bytes, BW 100000 Kbit full duplex
        15 packets input, 3153 bytes, 0 no buffer
        Received 15 broadcasts, 0 runts, 0 giants
        0 input errors, 0 CRC, 0 frame, 0 overrun, 0 ignored, 0 abort
        1 packets output, 64 bytes, 0 underruns
        0 output errors, 0 collisions, 0 interface resets
        0 babbles, 0 late collisions, 0 deferred
        1 lost carrier, 0 no carrier
        input queue (curr/max blocks): hardware (128/128) software (0/1)
        output queue (curr/max blocks): hardware (0/2) software (0/1)
PIX# conf t
PIX(config)# interface ethernet0 auto
PIX(config)#
```

From this point on, most of your configuration commands will refer to the interface by name instead of the hardware address. In this case, we'll use YellowZone instead of ethernet0.

Assigning an IP Address

Now, it's time to assign an IP address to the interface. For this, you use the ip address command. The syntax for this command is as follows:

```
PIX(config)# ip address ?
usage: ip address if_name ip_address [mask]
       ip address if_name dhcp [setroute] [retry retry_cnt]
       ip local pool poolname <ip1>[-<ip2>]
       ip verify reverse-path interface if_name
       ip audit [name|signature|interface|attack|info] ...
       show|clear ip audit count [global] [interface interface]
PIX(config)#
```

This command has two options of interest. For most users, all interfaces on the PIX Firewall will have static IP addresses. However, the PIX Firewall also supports dynamic address assignment via DHCP for use in the small office, home office (SOHO) environment, where cable modems and DSL-based Internet connections are common.

> **NOTE:** This dynamic address can also be used for PAT, which is explained later in this chapter.

In our example, we'll configure the `YellowZone` interface with an IP address of 10.1.1.1 /16:

```
PIX(config)# ip address yellowzone 10.1.1.1 255.255.0.0
PIX(config)#
```

Note that if the *mask* value isn't given, the default classful mask is used. As you would suspect, this is the mask of the interface. So, all hosts, routers, and other devices on this subnet should be configured with the same mask. Also note that although we entered the name `YellowZone` as proper case, and it displays in the `show` commands as proper case, when you're entering it in subsequent commands, it isn't case-sensitive.

If you were connecting the outside address to a cable modem of an ISP that doesn't use static addresses, you would enter the following command:

```
PIX(config)# ip address yellowzone dhcp setroute
PIX(config)#
```

Here, the `setroute` keyword tells PIX to enter a default route in its routing table. The route points to the *default gateway* address received from the cable modem's DHCP server.

> **WARNING:** The PIX Firewall failover feature isn't compatible with DHCP.

Setting the Maximum Transfer Unit

The last interface configuration command we'll cover is the `mtu` command. This command sets the maximum transfer unit (MTU), which is the maximum size of a layer 2 frame.

This command is used for both Ethernet and Token Ring. The default for Ethernet is 1500 bytes, and unless you have a good reason to change it, it should probably be left at the default setting. One of these good reasons is that when you're encrypting traffic using IPSec, if you leave it at the default, then when it's encrypted and encapsulated again it will be larger than 1500 bytes. Since Ethernet supports packets only up to 1500 bytes, the PIX Firewall will need to split the packet into two smaller packets, which is very inefficient. If you drop the MTU to 1400, then the resulting IPSec protected packet won't be larger than 1500 bytes and can be transmitted in a single packet.

The syntax for the `mtu` command is as follows:

```
PIX(config)# mtu ?
usage: mtu if_name bytes | (64-65535)
PIX(config)#
```

Configuring NAT and PAT

After you configure the interfaces on the PIX Firewall, the next step is to configure NAT and PAT. We'll begin this section with a brief introduction to NAT and PAT and then describe when and how to configure each.

> **Note:** In the previous chapter, we introduced the NAT mechanisms used by the PIX Firewall. Here, we'll provide a more generic explanation of address translation with NAT and PAT. Although we use Cisco's terminology, these concepts can be applied to any vendor, unless otherwise noted.

Understanding Address Translation

To be perfectly honest, address translation is a hack—a workaround, specified in RFC 1631 and RFC 3022, to provide IP address expansion and alleviate the problem of IP address depletion. As such, it breaks the rules of IP, which solves an immediate problem, but not without consequences.

To solve this problem of more hosts than addresses, RFC 1918 specifies three ranges of addresses (one from each class) that are reserved for private use:

- 10.0.0.0 to 10.255.25.255
- 172.16.0.0 to 172.31.255.255
- 192.168.0.0 to 192.168.255.255

The basic idea is that these addresses aren't globally unique. In other words, every organization in the world could use the 10.0.0.0/8 network at the same time; there is now a theoretically unlimited supply of addresses, because they can be reused. However, these addresses are blocked from the routing tables on the backbone of the Internet. Therefore, to get a packet from a private address across the Internet, it must be translated into a globally unique and registered address. There are two common techniques used to translate addresses: NAT and PAT.

NAT Global and Local Addresses

NAT is, in theory, a simple one-to-one mapping of addresses. When a packet with a source IP address such as 10.1.1.100 passes through the NAT process, the IP address in the packet is translated to a single public IP address, such as 202.199.17.23, and vice versa. These public, or global, IP addresses are unique and typically advertised on the Internet. If another host on the 10 network sent a packet through NAT at the same time, it would need to be translated into another public address; for example, 10.1.1.101 might be translated to 202.199.17.24.

In practice, NAT isn't so simple. Consider that each packet has two IP addresses: a source and a destination. Depending on the circumstances, you might want to translate either one or both of these IP addresses. Thus, it's necessary to distinguish between inside and outside IP addresses, as follows (these terms are consistent across both the PIX and IOS NAT implementations):

Inside local   The *inside local* address is the IP address that a host on the private network is using. In our example, this is 10.1.1.100.

Inside global   The *inside global* address is the IP address into which the inside IP address is translated. This is typically a globally unique and routable IP address, which hosts on the outside network use to communicate with the inside local address. In our example, this is 202.199.17.23.

> **NOTE** Obviously, all IP addresses are *routable* in the usual definition of the term, which is in the context of the OSI model. In this section, by *routable,* we specifically mean that the appropriate hosts on the network have a route to this IP address. For example, the Internet backbone routers don't know how to get to the 10 addresses because they don't have a route entry. So, we say that the IP address isn't *routable* on the Internet, although it might be routable inside your network.

Outside global   Typically, the *outside global* address is a globally unique and routable IP address of a host that resides on the outside network.

Outside local   The *outside local* address is the IP address used to translate the outside global IP address. This IP address may or may not be registered, but it must be routable on the inside network. Our simple example in the "PAT" section doesn't use an outside local IP address.

The terms *inside* and *outside* are used with respect to NAT, not the names of interfaces on the PIX Firewall. Remember that you might have several interfaces on a PIX Firewall, and you might need to translate IP addresses between each of them.

The outside global and outside local IP addresses typically come into play when you want to translate both the source and destination of a packet. We'll explore this in some of our examples in the "Configuring NAT on Multiple Interfaces" section later in this chapter.

Static and Dynamic NAT

To further complicate matters, NAT may be configured statically or dynamically. Static configuration is often used for inbound packets to web or other servers. For instance, you might have a web server on a DMZ, and the DMZ might be configured with private IP addresses. If a host on the global network wants to access the web server, it can't, because it has no idea which IP address is being used for translation. To resolve this problem, configure a static translation between the outside global and outside local IP addresses.

In a typical organization, there might be dozens of hosts, such as PCs, and only a couple registered IP addresses. When a host sends a packet to the global network, the PIX Firewall chooses the first available registered IP address from a pool of addresses that you configure. This is the inside global IP address. If another inside host sends a packet to the global network, the PIX Firewall again chooses the next available IP address. If there are no more available addresses, that host will be unable to communicate with the global network. This behavior is referred to as *dynamic,* because the host doesn't know (or care) what its inside global IP address will be, and it might be different every time it accesses the Internet. The host on the global network always knows what the inside global IP address is, because it's in the source address field of the IP header.

Although dynamic translation helps solve the address-depletion issue, it still constrains concurrent connections to the total number of registered IP addresses. For example, if you have 1000 computers on your network and only 32 registered IP addresses, only 32 of those 1000 computers can communicate with the Internet at a time. PAT, often called *overloading,* was created to solve this problem.

PAT

PAT is a method of multiplexing a potentially large number of private IP addresses through a single registered IP address. This is possible because the PIX Firewall keeps track of the source ports used and translates ports as well as IP addresses.

For instance, if a couple PCs on the local network request a web page from a server on the global network, the first PC sends a packet addressed as follows:

Source IP	Source Port	Destination IP	Destination Port
10.1.1.100	1026	199.206.253.29	80

For our example, suppose that the firewall's outside interface is addressed 199.206.12.143 and the server's IP address is 199.206.253.29. When this packet is received on the inside interface, the PIX Firewall modifies only the source IP address and port. It doesn't modify the destination information. The source IP address is changed to make the packet appear as if it originated from the outside interface of the PIX Firewall. In other words, the inside local IP address is replaced with the inside global IP address, just as with NAT. However, the source port is also translated to the first unused port above 1024. So, as the packet leaves the PIX Firewall, it looks like this:

Source IP	Source Port	Destination IP	Destination Port
199.206.12.143	1025	199.206.253.29	80

Now, when the next host sent a packet, if dynamic NAT were being used, with only one registered IP address, it would be denied. But with PAT, it's just given the next highest port. In this example, suppose the traffic is sent to the same server, although it could be any destination.

Source IP	Source Port	Destination IP	Destination Port
10.1.1.101	1032	199.206.253.29	80

When PIX receives this packet, it also translates it using the single registered IP address, but it uses a different source port, as shown below:

Source IP	Source Port	Destination IP	Destination Port
199.206.12.143	1026	199.206.253.29	80

To the web server, it appears as if the same host was making two requests, but it can distinguish between these via the source port. When the server responds, PIX knows where to send the response, because it knows which destination port maps to which local IP address and port.

Because there are 65,535 ports available to TCP and UDP, PAT is capable of supporting a very large number of privately addressed devices. Usually one outside IP address can support up to 64,000 inside hosts.

Address Translation Consequences

As we mentioned earlier, IP address translation comes with a few side effects. In addition to mild reactions such as headaches and dizziness as a result of trying to keep the "inside local, outside global" monikers straight, and the increased difficulty during troubleshooting, NAT actually breaks some things.

The most common problem is that many protocols include information about IP addresses in the payload of the packets, instead of taking it only from the headers. The security protocol IPSec is famous for being incompatible with NAT, because it tracks the sender's address for anti-spoofing and nonrepudiation purposes. When the receiver gets the packet, and the value in the IP source address field of the IP header is different from the value in the payload (because the header was translated), the packet isn't accepted or decrypted. This is now not such a problem since current versions of Cisco IOS can use IPSec over UDP that works with PAT, but DHCP, routing protocols, and other protocols are similarly affected.

Cisco's implementation of NAT makes special allowances to enable some protocols, such as DNS A and PTR records and queries, Microsoft's NetMeeting, and FTP. However, it doesn't support protocols with varying frame formats or frames that are encrypted, such as Simple Network Management Protocol (SNMP) and Point-to-Point Tunneling Protocol (PPTP). For this reason, it's possible to have traffic pass through the PIX Firewall without being translated, but the traffic is still handled as if it were being translated. This configuration is covered in the "Identity NAT" section later in this chapter.

NAT, PAT, and Security

In addition to the negative side effects discussed in the previous section, IP address translation produces a positive side effect as well: enhanced security. However, popular opinion regards this added security more highly than it deserves. Specifically, many people think that if a host is on the 10 network and connected to the Internet via NAT, hackers will be unable to reach this host because they don't have a route to it. The problem is that this is true only part of the time. The different types of address translation—static NAT, dynamic NAT, and PAT—offer different levels of security.

Static NAT offers no security whatsoever. Although it's true that there isn't a route to the 10.0.0.0 /8 network on the Internet backbone, that doesn't matter—the intruders can use the inside global address instead of the inside local address. In other words, any malicious traffic sent to the inside global address will be translated to the inside local address and passed on by NAT.

Dynamic NAT makes it practically impossible to directly communicate with a host on the inside network until that host attempts to communicate with the outside network. In other words, as long as there is no address translation in the firewall (called a *translation slot* in the PIX Firewall, as described in the previous chapter), you're fairly safe. However, the instant you open a browser window or any other application on a client that accesses the Internet, the firewall dynamically creates a translation. Until that translation times out, the host is just as vulnerable as it would be if it had a registered address. So, the only protection dynamic NAT really offers is that the internal hosts are moving targets. Attackers never know which host they will get when they attack an inside global address.

PAT offers a considerable amount of security because only the port you use is exposed to the Internet. For example, suppose you're running an anonymous FTP service on your host for internal use, and you also open a browser window and initiate a HTTP session to the Internet from the same host that uses a source port of 1026. When an intruder scans the firewall's address, it will find only your 1026 connection (which is fairly safe) and not the TCP port 21. The intruder will continue to be oblivious to the other listening ports on your host, including the anonymous FTP. With static and dynamic NAT, a ping sent to the inside global address is passed on to the host (inside local), but this is impossible with PAT.

The issue here is that many people assume all versions of NAT provide the same level of protection as PAT, which leaves them with a very false sense of security. Fortunately, if you're using a PIX Firewall, by default, it won't allow any of those outside connections—such as scans or pings—inbound, even with a static address translation entry. But even though the differences in the levels of security provided by address translation don't necessarily apply to PIX Firewall users, it's important to understand that it's the ASA of the PIX Firewall that is providing the protection, not the NAT process itself.

> **NOTE** Unfortunately, a lot of people have purchased cheap cable-modem routers that have been labeled "firewalls." Many of these "firewalls" perform only NAT. They have the ability to block ports, but ports aren't blocked by default. Without the ASA, the protection offered by NAT on these routers is nearly worthless.

Configuring NAT

Although NAT might appear confusing at first, it's simple if you understand one thing: NAT is always configured between a pair of interfaces. This makes it easy to focus on only two interfaces at a time, even if you have multiple interfaces to configure. And to make things even easier, there are only two commands to deal with—one per interface. If you're using NAT between multiple interfaces, you have a separate NAT command on the inside interfaces and one on the outside interfaces.

The address translation on the PIX is always performed between a local and global address, and all you need to do is pick the interfaces. You don't need to define which one is local and which one is global, because the local interface is always the higher security value. This will become very important later, when we look at examples of address translation between three and six interfaces in the "Configuring NAT on Multiple Interfaces" section.

Another important aspect of NAT configuration is the order of operation on the PIX Firewall. Knowing this order will help you understand why NAT is relevant only between pairs of interfaces, and it might help you troubleshoot problems later.

When the PIX Firewall receives an outbound packet (traveling from a higher-security interface to a lower-security interface), the first thing it does is to determine the outgoing interface based on routing information. At this point, it knows the incoming and outgoing interfaces, and which one is local and global, because it knows their relative security levels. Then it searches for a translation slot. Once it finds or creates one, it checks for security rules, such as access control lists (ACLs), and then translates the packet and sends it on its way.

For an inbound packet (traveling from a lower-security interface to a higher-security interface), the operation is a little different. First, the PIX Firewall checks the ACLs, and then it determines the outgoing interface, based again on routing information. Last, it checks for a translation slot.

> **NOTE** Of course, the PIX Firewall performs dozens more tasks. We've simplified the operation greatly to make it easier to understand. For more detailed information, visit the PIX Firewall documentation pages at www.cisco.com.

Now, let's look at the commands used to configure NAT. We'll begin with the simple examples and work progressively up to complex configurations, as we add interfaces and rules to deal with common, real-life situations.

The *nat* and *global* Commands

Two commands are used to configure NAT on the PIX Firewall: nat and global.

The nat command configures the local interface. It defines the networks to be translated. This command has the following syntax:

```
PIX(config)# nat ?
usage: [no] nat [(if_name)] nat_id local_ip [mask
               [max_conns [emb_limit [norandomseq]]]]
  [no] nat [(if_name)] 0 [access-list [acl-name]]
PIX(config)#
```

The global command configures the global interface. It defines what the translated network will be. The global command has the following syntax:

```
PIX(config)# global ?
usage: [no] global [(ext_if_name)] nat_id {global_ip
  [-global_ip] [netmask global_mask]} | interface
PIX(config)#
```

Notice that the nat command uses the *if_name* and *local_ip* parameters, whereas the global command uses the *ext_if_name* and *global_ip* parameters. The relationship of these is as follows: A host with address *local_ip* sending a packet to the PIX Firewall's *if_name* appears as *global_ip* to devices beyond the PIX Firewall's *ext_if_name*. The *emb_limit* is used to set the number of embryonic connections that will be supported to the protected systems. This is used to type and stop a SYN flood attack. We'll cover this more in Chapter 13, "Advanced Protocol Handling, Attack Guards, and Intrusion Detection."

For a simple example of using the nat and global commands to configure NAT, consider the two networks separated by a PIX Firewall, shown in Figure 11.1. One host is on the RFC 1918 private network 10.1.1.0 /24, and the other is on the public network 65.24.200.0 /24. Here, we want any packet that is sent from the inside network 65.24.200.0 to the outside network 10.1.1.0 to be translated.

> **WARNING** Don't be fooled by tricky questions: The local and global interfaces are determined only by the security values. It doesn't matter which address is private or public! Of course, in the real world, your most trusted inside network will almost always use private addresses, whereas your untrusted outside network will use public addresses. We've configured this example backward, just to demonstrate the point.

In this case, the *if_name* would be inside, and the *ext_if_name* would be outside. The *local_ip* would be 65.24.200.0 with a mask of 255.255.255.0.

FIGURE 11.1 Simple NAT example

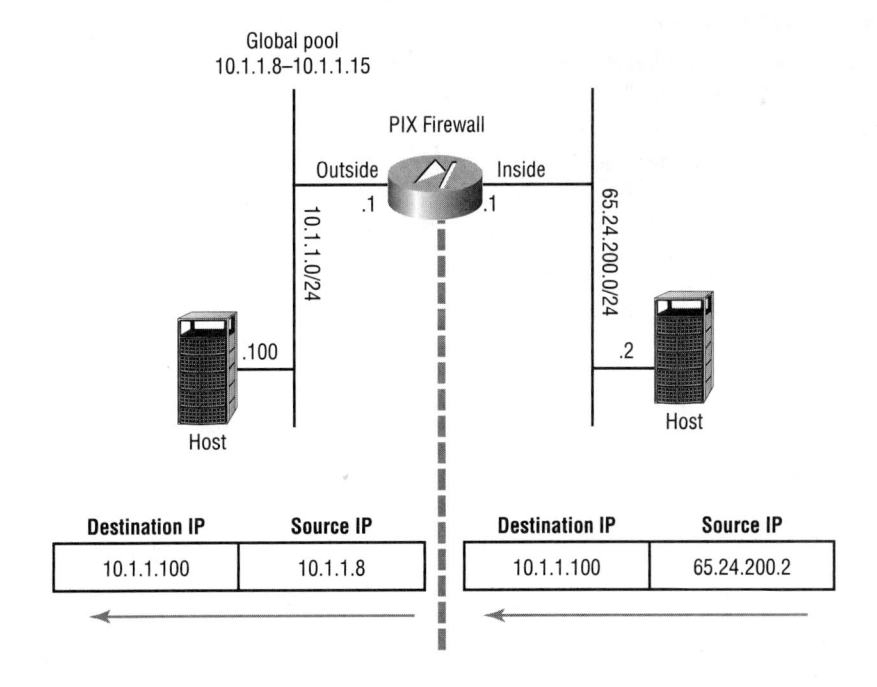

Destination IP	Source IP		Destination IP	Source IP
10.1.1.100	10.1.1.8		10.1.1.100	65.24.200.2

Global pool 10.1.1.8–10.1.1.15

The *global_ip* could be many different values, depending on your environment and how you want the PIX Firewall to behave. In this case, we'll assign the addresses 10.1.1.8 through 10.1.1.15 to the pool. This means up to eight hosts on the inside network could have translations at a time, and these eight hosts will appear to the outside world as .8 through .15.

The last required parameter for the nat and global commands is *nat_id*. The NAT ID is an arbitrary number between 0 and 2 billion, which allows you to tell the PIX Firewall which global addresses you want to use to translate internal addresses. This might make more sense when we start configuring multiple interfaces. For now, we can pick any number we want, as long as we use the same number in both the nat and global commands.

> **NOTE** Using a NAT ID of 0 tells the PIX not to do any translation. We'll discuss this in more detail later in the chapter, in the "Identity NAT" section.

We're ready to configure NAT on the PIX Firewall shown in Figure 11.1. We'll start by verifying that our interfaces are named and addressed correctly, using the show nameif and show ip commands:

```
PIX# show nameif
nameif ethernet0 outside security0
nameif ethernet1 inside security100
nameif ethernet2 intf2 security10
PIX# show ip
System IP Addresses:
        ip address outside 10.1.1.1 255.255.255.0
        ip address inside 65.24.200.1 255.255.255.0
        ip address intf2 127.0.0.1 255.255.255.255
Current IP Addresses:
        ip address outside 10.1.1.1 255.255.255.0
        ip address inside 65.25.200.1 255.255.255.0
        ip address intf2 0.0.0.0 0.0.0.0
PIX#
```

Now we tell the PIX Firewall which addresses we want translated, using the nat command:

```
PIX(config)# nat (inside) 1 65.24.200.0 255.255.255.0
PIX(config)#
```

> **WARNING** Don't forget the parentheses around the *if_name* and *ext_if_name* parameters.

Configuring NAT and PAT

The unusual thing about this command is the *mask* field. Unlike the `ip address` command, where you use the mask of the interface, here the mask is used to tell the PIX Firewall how many addresses to include in the range. For instance, even though the actual interface 65.24.200.1 has a 24-bit mask, we could use the following command:

```
PIX(config)# nat (inside) 1 65.24.200.0 255.255.255.128
PIX(config)#
```

This tells the PIX Firewall that we want only the first half of the address range (65.24.200.1 through 65.24.200.127) to be translated.

Similarly, we could use the following command:

```
PIX(config)# nat (inside) 1 65.24.200.14 255.255.255.255
PIX(config)#
```

By using the full 32-bit mask, we're telling PIX that we want only the host 64.24.200.14 to be translated. In this case, none of the other clients on that network would be translated.

Next, we tell the PIX Firewall which addresses we want these translated into, using the `global` command:

```
PIX(config)# global (outside) 1 10.1.1.8-10.1.1.15
PIX(config)#
```

> **Note:** Remember that the NAT ID (in this case, 1) can be anything you want, as long as it's the same in both the nat and global commands.

This is all that is required to allow hosts on the inside network to access the outside network. Once this command is in place, the default behavior of the PIX Firewall is to let all hosts included in the `nat` command (in this case, 65.24.200.1 through 65.24.200.254) make outbound connections, but hosts that want to initiate connections back in are still restricted. To allow a host on the outside network to initiate a connection, we use a third command: `static`.

> **Tip:** Optionally, you can allow all hosts on the inside to be translated by typing the command nat (inside) 1 0 0, where 0 0 is a shortcut for 0.0.0.0 0.0.0.0. As you can imagine, this can make configuration a lot less difficult, especially if you have a lot of subnets on your internal network that don't lend themselves to address summarization. However, it's a good idea to explicitly declare the IP addresses that are allowed out, because doing so makes spoofing almost impossible. Nobody wants the embarrassment or liability of having their network used as an attack launch pad because they haven't implemented anti-spoofing filters.

The *static* Command

The `static` command allows a host on the outside network to initiate a connection to a host on the inside network. The `static` command is different from the `nat` and `global` commands because it operates by itself. You enter all the information in one command rather than two. Here is the syntax of the `static` command:

```
PIX(config)# static ?
usage: [no] static [(internal_if_name, external_if_name)]
            {global_ip|interface} local_ip [netmask mask]
            [max_conns [emb_limit [norandomseq]]]
       [no] static [(internal_if_name, external_if_name)] {tcp|udp}
            {global_ip|interface} global_port
            local_ip local_port [netmask mask]
            [max_conns [emb_limit [norandomseq]]]
PIX(config)#
```

For example, let's say we have a web server on our inside network with an IP address of 65.24.200.22. We want all hosts on the outside network to be able to reach this service via the global address 10.1.1.16. To configure this, we enter the following command:

```
PIX(config)# static (inside, outside) 10.1.1.16 65.24.200.22
PIX(config)#
```

> **NOTE** The `static` command can be confusing because the interfaces are entered as inside then outside, but the IP addresses are entered as outside then inside. Just remember *inside outside, outside inside* for the `static` command, and you should be fine.

Identity NAT

Occasionally, you'll want the protection of a PIX Firewall but not need or desire address translation. This might be the case for several reasons:

- Your entire network is using registered addresses.
- The firewall's job is to protect some critical area of the internal network from the rest of the internal network, where both are using private addresses. An example is a large company's cluster of accounting or human resource systems that should be accessed only by people in certain departments.
- Using NAT breaks some protocols, such as SNMP, PPTP, and a lot of streaming media protocols.

The problem is that without a translation slot, nothing gets through the PIX Firewall, and translation slots are created only by the NAT process (as described in the previous chapter). The solution to this problem is to still send packets through the NAT process but not translate them. In other words, the source and destination fields in the IP headers aren't modified as they pass through the PIX Firewall. This is often called *identity NAT*.

You configure identity NAT by using the `nat 0` command. For example, if the inside interface of the PIX Firewall is 10.1.1.1 /24, and we don't want this network to be translated, we can accomplish this with the following command:

```
PIX(config)# nat (inside) 0 10.1.1.0 255.255.255.0
PIX(config)#
```

> **Note** that a corresponding `global` command isn't required for identity NAT.

When we enter this command, the PIX Firewall confirms our instruction:

```
PIX(config)# nat (inside) 0 10.1.1.0 255.255.255.0
nat 0 10.1.1.0 will be non-translated
PIX(config)#
```

> **Warning** The operation of the `nat 0` command, both syntactically and under the hood, has changed dramatically over the last several versions of the PIX operating system. This book deals with only the current implementation as of version 6.0(1). Even so, we're going into substantially more detail than you can expect to see on the exam. If you're using a different version, read the Command Reference documentation on Cisco's website before using the `nat 0` command.

Now, suppose we want the 10.1.1.0 subnet on the inside interface translated as usual. But one host, with IP address 10.1.1.15, frequently establishes IPSec-encrypted tunnels across the PIX Firewall, so we want every host on this network to be translated except 10.1.1.15. To configure this, we use two commands (not including the corresponding `global` commands on the outgoing interfaces):

```
PIX(config)# nat (inside) 1 10.1.1.0 255.255.255.0
PIX(config)# nat (inside) 0 10.1.1.15 255.255.255.255
PIX(config)#
```

Here is the output of the `show nat` command after these statements have been entered on the PIX Firewall:

```
PIX(config)# nat (inside) 1 10.1.1.0 255.255.255.0
PIX(config)# nat (inside) 0 10.1.1.15 255.255.255.255
nat 0 10.1.1.15 will be non-translated
```

```
PIX(config)# show nat
nat (inside) 0 10.1.1.15 255.255.255.255 0 0
nat (inside) 1 10.1.1.0 255.255.255.0 0 0
PIX(config)#
```

Notice that even though the commands were typed out of order, PIX sorted the longest subnet mask to the top of the list.

In these examples, using a zero in the *nat_id* field tells the PIX Firewall to allow packets from the specified hosts to pass through the firewall without being translated. However, there is another use for this command that can be quite confusing. We'll explain it in the next section, because it's important not to confuse it with identity NAT.

Access Blocking with ACLs

When there are many internal networks to be translated, it can be easy to make data-entry errors. To reduce this possibility, recent versions of the PIX operating system have made the **nat** command more powerful but somewhat confusing. In this section, we'll explain the proper way to tell the PIX Firewall which networks to translate.

As an example, let's say we have the 10.1.0.0 /20 subnet further broken into sixteen 24-bit subnets, from 10.1.0.0 /24 to 10.1.15.0/24. All of these access the Internet through the inside interface of our PIX Firewall. Further suppose that we want all of these networks to be translated except the hosts between 10.1.9.128 and 10.1.9.191. However, in this case, we're not talking about identity NAT, because we don't want these hosts to have any access at all. In other words, PIX should not create a translation slot for hosts in the range 10.1.9.128 /26.

We can accomplish this task two ways. The first is shown here, including the commands and the output of the **show nat** command:

```
PIX(config)# nat (inside) 1 10.1.0.0 255.255.255.0
PIX(config)# nat (inside) 1 10.1.1.0 255.255.255.0
PIX(config)# nat (inside) 1 10.1.2.0 255.255.255.0
PIX(config)# nat (inside) 1 10.1.3.0 255.255.255.0
PIX(config)# nat (inside) 1 10.1.4.0 255.255.255.0
PIX(config)# nat (inside) 1 10.1.5.0 255.255.255.0
PIX(config)# nat (inside) 1 10.1.6.0 255.255.255.0
PIX(config)# nat (inside) 1 10.1.7.0 255.255.255.0
PIX(config)# nat (inside) 1 10.1.8.0 255.255.255.0
PIX(config)# nat (inside) 1 10.1.9.0 255.255.255.128
PIX(config)# nat (inside) 1 10.1.9.192 255.255.255.192
PIX(config)# nat (inside) 1 10.1.10.0 255.255.255.0
PIX(config)# nat (inside) 1 10.1.11.0 255.255.255.0
PIX(config)# nat (inside) 1 10.1.12.0 255.255.255.0
PIX(config)# nat (inside) 1 10.1.13.0 255.255.255.0
PIX(config)# nat (inside) 1 10.1.14.0 255.255.255.0
PIX(config)# nat (inside) 1 10.1.15.0 255.255.255.0
```

```
PIX(config)# exit
PIX# show nat
nat (inside) 1 10.1.9.192 255.255.255.192 0 0
nat (inside) 1 10.1.9.0 255.255.255.128 0 0
nat (inside) 1 10.1.0.0 255.255.255.0 0 0
nat (inside) 1 10.1.1.0 255.255.255.0 0 0
nat (inside) 1 10.1.2.0 255.255.255.0 0 0
nat (inside) 1 10.1.3.0 255.255.255.0 0 0
nat (inside) 1 10.1.4.0 255.255.255.0 0 0
nat (inside) 1 10.1.5.0 255.255.255.0 0 0
nat (inside) 1 10.1.6.0 255.255.255.0 0 0
nat (inside) 1 10.1.7.0 255.255.255.0 0 0
nat (inside) 1 10.1.8.0 255.255.255.0 0 0
nat (inside) 1 10.1.10.0 255.255.255.0 0 0
nat (inside) 1 10.1.11.0 255.255.255.0 0 0
nat (inside) 1 10.1.12.0 255.255.255.0 0 0
nat (inside) 1 10.1.13.0 255.255.255.0 0 0
nat (inside) 1 10.1.14.0 255.255.255.0 0 0
nat (inside) 1 10.1.15.0 255.255.255.0 0 0
PIX#
```

Here, we type one `nat` statement for each 24-bit network except the 10.1.9.0 subnet, where we type two statements so as not to include the addresses that we don't want translated. In other words, we explicitly define all the networks that we want translated.

It's easy to see how you can make mistakes by issuing so many commands. To make matters worse, the PIX Firewall again sorts the longest subnet masks to the top of the list. This made it easier to read and understand things earlier but now makes it very difficult, because the subnets are no longer in numerical order. In large organizations, where there are often hundreds of networks, variable-length subnet masking (VLSM) is in use, and subnets often aren't contiguous, this situation could get out of hand very quickly.

Now compare that method with the `access-list` feature implemented as of version 5.3:

```
PIX(config)# access-list block permit ip 10.1.9.128 255.255.255.192 any
PIX(config)# nat (inside) 1 10.1.0.0 255.255.240.0
PIX(config)# nat (inside) 0 access-list block
PIX(config)# exit
PIX# show nat
nat (inside) 0 access-list block
nat (inside) 1 10.1.0.0 255.255.240.0 0 0
PIX# show access-list block
access-list block permit ip 10.1.9.128 255.255.255.192 any (hitcnt=0)
4PIX#
```

Again, although the corresponding `global` command has been omitted, we accomplished in 3 commands what previously took 17. Not only is the input far easier, and by extension less error-prone, but the output is much simpler and easier to comprehend. The difference is that the entire 10.1.0.0/20 network is covered in one easy-to-read statement, and the address ranges you don't want are defined in an ACL and then applied with the `nat 0` statement.

> **TIP** When you're troubleshooting a network problem or responding to an attack, time is critical. Any steps you can take to shorten the time required to understand your configuration will directly affect the time it takes to respond to the situation.

In this section and the previous section, you've seen not only the value of both identity NAT and the ability to block address translation using ACLs, but also that these commands are easily confused. Let's review their use:

- Use `nat (interface) 0 network subnet-mask` when you want certain hosts to be known outside the PIX Firewall by their actual address.
- Use `nat (interface) 0 access-list access-list` when you want to keep certain hosts from ever sending traffic through the PIX Firewall by preventing them from creating a translation slot.

> **NOTE** ACLs are covered in detail in the next chapter.

Configuring PAT

The configuration of PAT is even easier than NAT. You use the same `nat` command:

```
PIX(config)# nat (inside) 1 65.24.200.0 255.255.255.0
PIX(config)#
```

However, for the `global` command, you make one slight modification:

```
PIX(config)# global (outside) 1 10.1.1.8
PIX(config)#
```

By listing only a single address in the global pool (in this case, 10.1.1.8), all the hosts from 65.24.200.1 to 65.24.200.254 are seen on the outside network as 10.1.1.8. In other words, we've configured PAT. This IP address doesn't need to be the same address that is being used by the outside interface. Plus, you can have NAT and PAT configured concurrently, even to the same interface.

> **Note:** You might be asking yourself how you can use PAT when DHCP is used on the outside interface and you never know what the IP address will be. In this situation, you can substitute the outside IP address with the `interface` parameter, and the PIX Firewall will use the IP address from DHCP for PAT. The syntax is `global (outside) 1 interface`.

Here's an example of this command in action:

```
PIX(config)# global (outside) 1 10.1.1.8
Start and end addresses overlap with existing range
Type help or '?' for a list of available commands.
PIX(config)# no global (outside) 1 10.1.1.8-10.1.1.15
PIX(config)# global (outside) 1 10.1.1.8
Global 10.1.1.8 will be Port Address Translated
PIX(config)#
```

We start by attempting to configure a PAT address that is currently part of an existing global pool. As you can see, the PIX Firewall won't allow that. You can't have overlapping address ranges (although you can use NAT and PAT at the same time, as you'll see later in the "Configuring Six Interfaces" section). You must remove the first range before assigning the second. Another point of interest is that the PIX Firewall lets you know what you've done. This helps the PIX Firewall be more secure by preventing a lot of accidental misconfiguration.

Let's look at using static PAT for inbound traffic. A common situation for a small to medium business is to use PAT but want to have a few servers publicly available. Consider the example shown in Figure 11.2.

Here we have a web server, an FTP server, and a Unix-based server that is accessed via Telnet. Our fictitious business wants all three of these services to be available to the outside network, but it has only a single global address.

We'll readdress our networks so that the `inside` network is 192.168.1.0 /24 with the three servers using .2, .3, and .4 respectively. The PIX Firewall will be .1, of course. The ISP has assigned us a single registered address for our outside interface of 202.199.87.56.

This scenario presents a few challenges. First, we need to use the PIX Firewall's outside interface address as the global PAT address. Also, we need to direct inbound traffic as follows:

- Inbound HTTP traffic destined for TCP port 80 to 192.168.1.2
- Inbound FTP traffic destined for TCP port 21 to 192.168.1.3
- Inbound Telnet traffic destined for TCP port 23 to 192.168.1.4

No traffic to any other port will be allowed to pass inbound, but all the PCs on the 192.168.1.0 network must be able to access the Internet through the PAT translation. Our configuration will require three `static` commands: one for each service. And we'll need one `nat` command and one `global` command to allow our internal users outbound access.

FIGURE 11.2   Static PAT example

Destination IP: Port	Source IP: Port
192.168.1.2 : 80	x.x.x.x : y
192.168.1.3 : 21	x.x.x.x : y
192.168.1.4 : 23	x.x.x.x : y

After PAT translation

Destination IP: Port	Source IP: Port
202.199.87.56 : 80	x.x.x.x : y
202.199.87.56 : 21	x.x.x.x : y
202.199.87.56 : 23	x.x.x.x : y

Before PAT translation

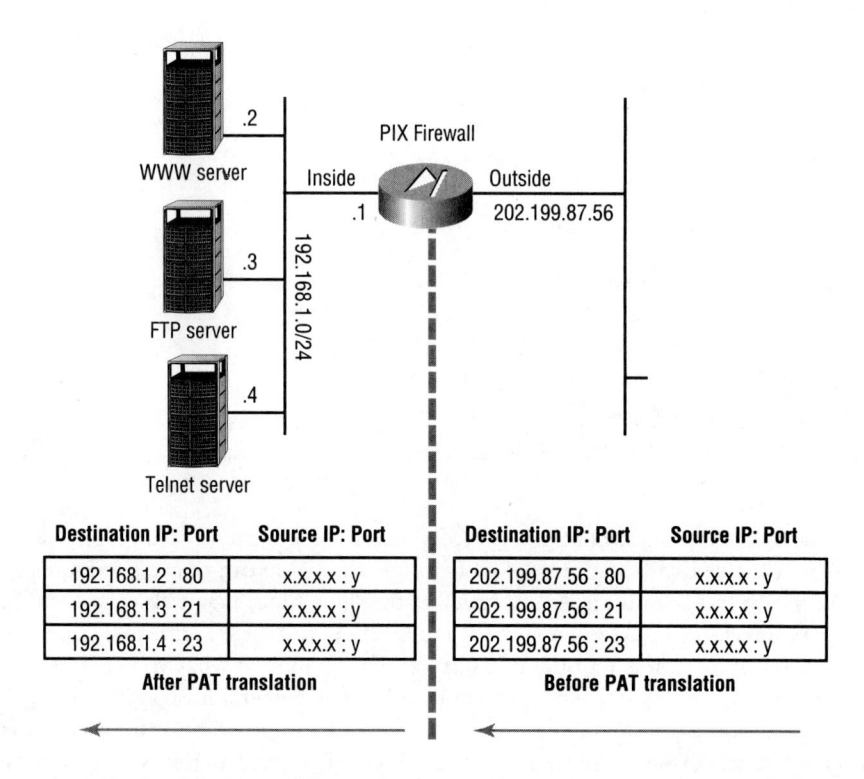

This scenario—where packets sent to a single global IP address are sent to different local IP addresses based on their TCP port—is often referred to as *port redirection*. Port redirection uses the same `static` command we used to map IP addresses on a one-to-one basis in the "Static and Dynamic NAT" section earlier in the chapter.

The major difference in static NAT and port redirection is that in port redirection, we add the optional port number and protocol. The protocol for all three of our requirements is TCP. The port number depends on the service, but it can be given in the decimal equivalent of the protocol's assigned number or as a keyword. We'll use both methods in the following configuration as an example.

The *static* Commands for Outside to Inside Requirements

Three `static` commands take care of our outside to inside requirements. (Although a few of these parameters, such as the two zeros on the end of each `static` command, are optional, we included them for completeness.)

For the inbound HTTP traffic, we use this command:

```
PIX(config)# static (inside, outside) tcp interface 80 192.168.1.2
➥80 netmask 255.255.255.255 0 0
PIX(config)#
```

This command tells the PIX Firewall that any traffic that arrives on the outside interface, destined for TCP port 80 of the outside interface, should be transmitted out the inside interface to 192.168.1.2, TCP port 80. It also tells the PIX Firewall to change the destination IP address field in the IP header to 192.168.1.2.

Notice the keyword `interface`. It's used to indicate the external or lower-security interface so that the actual IP address of the PIX Firewall's outside interface can be used, instead of dedicating a global pool of IP addresses as in the previous examples. Using this interface can occasionally be complicated, but it definitely saves IP addresses.

For the inbound FTP traffic, we use this command:

```
PIX(config)# static (inside, outside) tcp interface 21 192.168.1.3
➥21 netmask 255.255.255.255 0 0
PIX(config)#
```

This command tells the PIX Firewall that any traffic that arrives on the outside interface, destined for TCP port 21 of the outside interface, should be transmitted out the inside interface to 192.168.1.3, TCP port 21. It also tells the PIX Firewall to change the destination IP address field in the IP header to 192.168.1.3.

For the inbound Telnet traffic, we use this command:

```
PIX(config)# static (inside, outside) tcp interface telnet
➥192.168.1.4 telnet netmask 255.255.255.255 0 0
PIX(config)#
```

This command is just like the previous two, except that it sends the traffic destined for TCP port 23 to 192.168.1.4. Notice that we used the keyword `telnet` in this example, instead of the port number in decimal, to illustrate the flexibility. Note that in the `show` commands, and also in Configuration mode, PIX replaces these port numbers with its keywords automatically. One more thing to remember is that the port numbers don't need to be the same. You can change from port 53 (domain) on the outside to port 80 (www) on the inside. Doing so might be useful when you're trying to hide the outside port to an inside host by choosing a high port, such as 43234, to be translated to port 23 (telnet) to access an inside host.

The *nat* and *global* Commands for Inside to Outside Requirements

For internal hosts to also access the external network, we need `nat` and `global` statements. The `nat` statement is identical to the ones used previously; but in the `global` statement, we use the same `interface` keyword. This allows our internal hosts to use the same address as the outside interface as well, again saving IP addresses. Using the `interface` keyword allows us to change the IP address of the outside interface without having to change all the corresponding `nat`, `global`, and `static` commands:

```
PIX(config)# nat (inside) 1 192.168.1.0 255.255.255.0
PIX(config)# global (outside) 1 interface
PIX(config)#
```

These two commands tell the PIX Firewall to allow all traffic from the 192.168.1.0 network on the inside interface to access resources on the outside interface, after being translated with PAT using the IP address of the outside interface.

Checking the Configuration

After entering these commands, we exit the Configuration mode and type a few show commands to see how it looks:

```
PIX# show global
global (outside) 1 interface
PIX# show nat
nat (inside) 1 192.168.1.0 255.255.255.0 0 0
PIX# show static
static (inside,outside) tcp interface www 192.168.1.2 www netmask
 ⮕255.255.255.255 0 0
static (inside,outside) tcp interface ftp 192.168.1.3 ftp netmask
 ⮕255.255.255.255 0 0
static (inside,outside) tcp interface telnet 192.168.1.4 telnet
 ⮕netmask 255.255.255.255 0 0
PIX#
```

The show commands indicate that our commands were accepted as expected. Notice that the port numbers we typed have been converted to the recognized keywords for easy reading.

Now let's test it. We've set up hosts on either side of the firewall, attempted to telnet to 202.199.87.56, and then pointed our web browser to the same address. The show xlate command should prove our configuration is working. The output is shown here:

```
PIX# show xlate
2 in use, 2 most used
PAT Global 202.199.87.56(23) Local 192.168.1.4(23)
PAT Global 202.199.87.56(80) Local 192.168.1.2(80)
PIX#
```

As you can see, requests to port 23 were forwarded to 192.168.1.4 TCP port 23, and requests to port 80 were sent to 192.168.1.2 TCP port 80. FTP command sessions would work similarly, but without the fixup protocol command, our data sessions would be denied. We'll discuss this in more detail in Chapter 13.

Configuring NAT on Multiple Interfaces

In practice, networks often start out simply, much like the configurations we've shown in the previous sections; but they almost always grow both in size and complexity, as new segments and services are added and the amount of traffic increases. In this section, we'll explain the relationships between interfaces when there are more than just two.

> **TIP** The configuration of multiple interfaces might seem complicated because of the way packets are translated as they go from one network to another. But as long as you remember that translations always go between pairs of interfaces, and focus on just the pair in question, configuring multiple interfaces on the PIX Firewall will be much easier to comprehend and troubleshoot.

Configuring Three Interfaces

We'll start with a simple scenario with three interfaces, including the Internet on the outside interface, a DMZ network containing proxy and web servers, and two private networks on the inside interface. For the ASA, we'll assign 100 to the inside interface, 0 to the outside interface, and 10 to the DMZ interface. Here's a summary:

Interface	Security Level
Inside (two private networks)	100
DMZ (proxy and web servers)	10
Outside (Internet)	0

> **NOTE** Changing the DMZ interface to a security value of 50 won't change the PIX Firewall's behavior. That is, increasing or decreasing the value won't automatically make it more or less secure. What's important is the value relative to the other interfaces. In this case, as long as it's more than the outside interface and less than the inside interface (that is, between 1 and 99), any number will have the same effect.

This scenario, shown in Figure 11.3, is common. In this scenario, assume that our ISP is allowing us to use the 12 unused, registered addresses on the outside network for our NAT global pool. However, we have 100 user PCs on our 10.1.1.0 /24 subnet and another 100 user PCs on 10.1.2.0 /24 subnet. Since 200 is much larger than 12, we obviously need to make some allowances here.

Further, let's suppose the users on the 10.1.1.0 subnet are allowed unrestricted access directly to the Internet, but users on the 10.1.2.0 subnet must use a proxy server in the DMZ to access the Internet. These users will be translated from the inside to the DMZ using the global pool 192.168.1.101 to 192.168.1.199. If more than 99 simultaneous connections are needed, the .200 address should be used for PAT. If there are more than 99 simultaneous connections from the 10.1.1.0 subnet to the Internet, the 37.20.5.14 address should be used for PAT.

The proxy server (IP address 192.168.1.25) on the DMZ is allowed to initiate connections to the Internet using NAT, but it may not initiate connections to the inside network. The web server (IP address 192.168.1.75) is allowed to talk to a database (IP address 10.1.1.50) on the inside network.

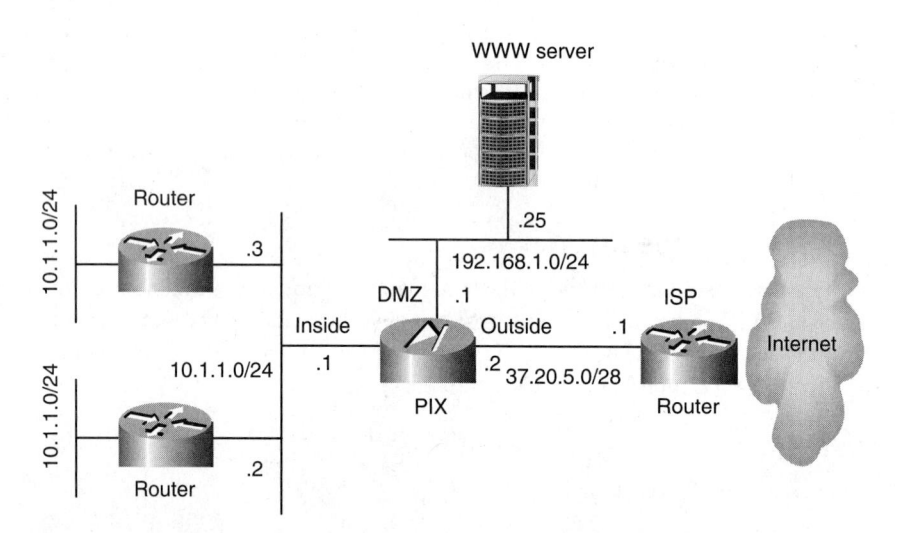

FIGURE 11.3 A simple multiple-interface scenario

Of course, hosts on the Internet aren't allowed to initiate any connections to the inside network, and they may initiate requests to the web server only on the DMZ network.

Configuring NAT between the Inside and Outside Interfaces

Now that you understand the requirements, let's begin by configuring NAT between the inside and outside networks. According to our requirements, the only connectivity allowed between the inside and outside interfaces is from the 10.1.1.0 network, and these addresses are supposed to be translated using the addresses 37.20.5.5 through 37.20.5.13. After those are used, any subsequent connections should be translated via PAT using the 37.20.5.14 address. No connections are required from the outside to the inside, so no `static` commands are necessary. The commands required for this configuration are as follows:

```
PIX(config)# nat (inside) 1 10.1.1.0 255.255.255.0
PIX(config)# global (outside) 1 37.20.5.5-37.20.5.13
PIX(config)# global (outside) 1 37.20.5.14
PIX(config)#
```

Configuring NAT between the Inside and DMZ Interfaces

Next, we configure NAT between the inside and DMZ interfaces. Our primary requirement here is to allow 10.1.2.0 devices access to the proxy server, so that they can access the Internet. However, any internal device is allowed to access the DMZ. These devices should be translated into 192.168.1.101 to 192.168.1.199. As we did with the outside interface, we'll use the 192.168.1.200 address for PAT, just in case more than 99 people are accessing it at once. So our commands are very similar, except that we also have a requirement for the web server to initiate connections into the inside network. This requires an additional `static` command:

```
PIX(config)# nat (inside) 2 0 0
PIX(config)# global (dmz) 2 192.168.1.101-192.168.1.199
PIX(config)# global (dmz) 2 192.168.1.200
PIX(config)# static (inside,dmz) 192.168.1.2 10.1.1.50 netmask 255.255.255.255
PIX(config)#
```

Now you can see the importance of having a NAT ID. This arbitrary number tells the PIX Firewall exactly which addresses we want to translate when there are multiple outbound interfaces. As you'll see in the next pair of interfaces, it also lets us tell the PIX Firewall which global addresses we want to use when there are multiple inbound interfaces.

Notice in the configuration above that the `nat` statement still uses the inside interface, but the corresponding `global` statements use the DMZ interface. In all these cases, the `nat` statement is used on the higher-security interface, whereas the `global` statements are used on lower-security interfaces.

Configuring NAT between the DMZ and Outside Interfaces

Next, we configure NAT between the DMZ and the outside interface. To fulfill the requirement that the proxy server be the only device allowed to initiate connections out, we choose yet another arbitrary NAT ID and use another pair of `nat` and `global` statements. To allow any external device to initiate connections to the web server, we need another `static` command. The commands are as follows:

```
PIX(config)# nat (dmz) 3 192.168.1.25 255.255.255.255
PIX(config)# global (outside) 3 37.20.5.4
PIX(config)# static (dmz, outside) 37.20.5.3 192.168.1.75 netmask
➥255.255.255.255
PIX(config)#
```

Here again, the interface with the highest security level is now the DMZ interface, so the `nat` statement is on the DMZ interface, whereas the `global` statement is on the outside interface. Also, by specifying just the proxy server and using a 32-bit mask (255.255.255.255), we've prevented any other host on that network from creating a translation slot in the PIX Firewall.

Reviewing the Configuration

We'll wrap up this example by showing the relevant part of the configuration (to save space, we've omitted the irrelevant information):

```
PIX# write term
Building configuration...
: Saved
```

```
:
PIX Version 6.0(1)
nameif ethernet0 outside security0
nameif ethernet1 inside security100
nameif ethernet2 dmz security10
hostname PIX
interface ethernet0 auto
interface ethernet1 auto
interface ethernet2 auto
ip address outside 37.20.5.2 255.255.255.240
ip address inside 10.1.0.1 255.255.255.0
ip address dmz 192.168.1.1 255.255.255.0
global (outside) 1 37.20.5.5-37.20.5.13
global (outside) 1 37.20.5.14
global (outside) 3 37.20.5.4
global (dmz) 2 192.168.1.101-192.168.1.199
global (dmz) 2 192.168.1.200
nat (inside) 1 10.1.1.0 255.255.255.0 0 0
nat (inside) 2 0.0.0.0 0.0.0.0 0 0
nat (dmz) 3 192.168.1.25 255.255.255.255 0 0
static (dmz,outside) 37.20.5.3 192.168.1.75 netmask 255.255.255.255 0 0
static (inside,dmz) 192.168.1.2 10.1.1.50 netmask 255.255.255.255 0 0
route inside 10.1.1.0 255.255.255.0 10.1.0.3 1
route inside 10.1.2.0 255.255.255.0 10.1.0.2 1
: end
[OK]
PIX#
```

Notice the routing statements required to make the connectivity work. Also notice that we've configured two different PAT addresses on the outside interface. This functionality was implemented in version 5.3. It works great, but it can be confusing. Be careful that you don't try to assign two PAT addresses to the same NAT ID.

Configuring Six Interfaces

Figure 11.4 shows the setup for our next example, which is much more complex than the one described in the previous section. Here, we have an organization with an internal network that is connected to the Internet and two partners. We also have a DMZ, which hosts servers that our business partners use, and a dedicated remote-access network, where users can dial in from home and access services such as their e-mail.

> ### Real World Scenario
>
> #### Outbound Connections from the DMZ
>
> It might seem safe to allow any device on your DMZ to initiate outbound connections to the Internet, but this isn't necessarily a good idea. Despite the fact that the network is more trusted than the Internet, it's not totally trusted. As an example of what can go wrong, consider the NIMDA virus and variants from September 2001. This outbreak was particularly annoying, because the virus had several delivery mechanisms. Aside from the often-used Outlook e-mail macros, it could also spread from IIS web server to IIS web server.
>
> The moral of the story is that a web server initiating a connection to the Internet is highly suspicious. Unless there is a well-documented need for this privilege, turn it off.

FIGURE 11.4   Complex six-interface NAT scenario

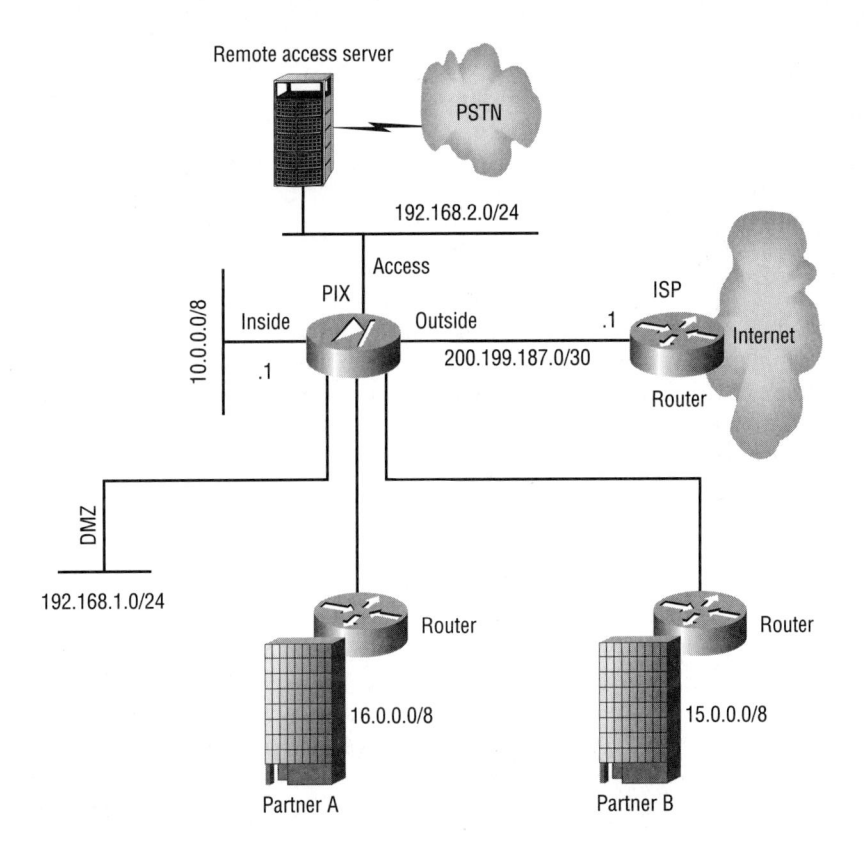

We want to implement the following basic rules:

- Hosts on the inside interface can access anything (we assume our partners have firewalls of their own, which prevent us from arbitrarily accessing their equipment).
- Only a small group of hosts on the 10.6.98.0 /24 inside interface need to access the remote-access segment, so they can use a shared bank of 32 modems to dial out.
- Hosts on the partner networks can access the DMZ.
- Hosts on the partner networks can't access each other or use our Internet connection. We assume they have their own ISP.
- Mobile users on the access segment can access anything except the inside interface. That is restricted to the e-mail server on 10.1.1.100.
- Hosts on the Internet can't initiate connections into any other network.

To implement this, we'll assign our interfaces the following security level values:

Interface	Security Level
Inside	100
Access	80
Partner A	40
Partner B	40
DMZ	20
Outside	0

Although we assigned all these values (except the inside network) arbitrarily, the relative numbers are important. They immediately accomplish several of the goals. Primarily, by assigning the same security value to both customer networks, we make it impossible for those two interfaces to communicate directly with one another. And the order of interfaces from highest to lowest allows us to configure the `nat` and `global` statements appropriately.

We'll start our configuration by addressing access to the interfaces in order of security value, from the lowest to the highest. It's critical that you remember that NAT is always between a pair of interfaces.

With six interfaces, we potentially have a lot of pairs of interfaces, but each pair doesn't require its own NAT ID. In fact, giving each its own NAT ID would create problems (although it's possible), because the `global` ranges can't overlap and the `nat` ranges can't be identical. Having several smaller ranges is much less efficient. So in the sections that follow, we'll combine the statements into groups based on the appropriate NAT IDs for efficiency and ease of understanding, but it doesn't change the fact that NAT operates only between a given pair of interfaces.

As an example, if a host on the inside network were translated to 192.168.2.50 for traffic to the DMZ interface, that same host could be translated to a completely different IP address when it conversed with devices through another PIX interface. In this case, that single host would have multiple translation slots.

Configuring the Outside Interface

The outside interface, of course, has the lowest security value. For this interface, we use one PAT address for all clients coming from the access and inside networks, as shown here:

```
PIX(config)# nat (inside) 1 10.0.0.0 255.0.0.0
PIX(config)# nat (access) 1 192.168.2.0 255.255.255.0
PIX(config)# global (outside) 1 interface
PIX(config)#
```

Here we demonstrate multiple nat statements paired with a single global statement, which is the opposite of the three-interface scenario described in the previous section. Note that neither of our partners or the DMZ hosts is allowed to use our Internet connection, but if access were allowed, we could easily add three more nat statements. (Note that it's impossible to combine these into one statement by aggregating addresses, because you still must specify the interface, and there are three different interfaces.)

Configuring the DMZ Interface

The next highest interface is the DMZ. Since everyone except the outside interface is allowed to access these hosts, we would normally have four nat commands that explicitly define their respective networks and one global command. However, the nat commands for the inside and access segments are already assigned explicitly with a NAT ID of 1. The problem is that you can't specify the same network in another nat command, because PIX will return a "duplicate NAT entry" error. Our solution is to shorten the subnet mask to include all networks for the inside and access segments, as shown here:

```
PIX(config)# nat (inside) 2 0 0
PIX(config)# nat (access) 2 0 0
PIX(config)# nat (partnera) 2 16.0.0.0 255.0.0.0
PIX(config)# nat (partnerb) 2 15.0.0.0 255.0.0.0
PIX(config)# global (dmz) 2 192.168.1.64-192.168.1.254
PIX(config)#
```

Normally this would be nominally less secure because it's theoretically possible to do spoofing. But because this is a DMZ segment, we accept that very small risk and leave our explicit (and correct) statement for use in the NAT ID 1 group that allows access to the Internet.

That takes care of our nat statements. For the global command, we reserve the first 62 addresses for servers on the DMZ segment, and we use the rest for our global NAT pool. It's also important to note that each of these four interfaces with a nat statement must have a higher security value than the interface with the global statement.

Configuring the Partner Interfaces

The next interfaces are our partner interfaces. Here, it's appropriate to reuse the nat statements from NAT ID 1, which permit only the inside and access segments, and use the interface addresses to do PAT. Thus, our statements are as follows:

```
PIX(config)# global (partnera) 1 interface
PIX(config)# global (partnerb) 1 interface
PIX(config)#
```

Configuring the Access Interface

Access to the access segment is next. We use another NAT ID to distinguish between the two we're already using on the inside interface. And since there are only 32 modems, there's no point to using more than 32 addresses in the global pool, because we can have only 32 simultaneous users:

```
PIX(config)# nat (inside) 3 10.6.98.0 255.255.255.0
PIX(config)# global (access) 3 192.168.2.64-192.168.2.95
PIX(config)#
```

Configuring the Inside Interface

Finally, we need to allow access to the inside network; but the only connectivity permitted here is from the access segment to an e-mail server, which requires only a single static statement. This statement allows hosts to access the server using a global address of 192.168.2.63. Therefore, it's important that this address be in the remote user's DNS or a static hosts file:

```
PIX(config)# static (inside,access) 192.168.2.63 10.1.1.100 netmask
➥255.255.255.255
PIX(config)#
```

> **NOTE** The static command doesn't actually allow access, of course. It allows the specified host only to create a translation slot from a lower-security interface to a higher one. To allow access, you must combine this statement with an access-list or conduit command. These commands are discussed in the next chapter.

Configuring Routing

In most cases, your network is made up of a number of subnetworks. There might be one or more at each branch office, or you might have the network configured so that each floor or each closet gets its own IP subnet. In any case, there are probably several internal routers. The hosts on most, if not all, of these subnets need access to external networks, such as business partners or the Internet.

These internal and external networks are, of course, separated by the PIX Firewall, so routing on the firewall becomes an issue. Typically, the internal routers use an internal routing protocol, such as Open Shortest Path First (OSPF) or Enhanced Internal Gateway Routing Protocol (EIGRP), to communicate Network layer reachability information (NLRI). Presumably, in such a case, each internal network knows about all the other internal networks. They also typically use a default route for destinations they don't know about. In most of your internal networks, this default route points to the PIX Firewall, which means all traffic leaving the network goes through the PIX Firewall. The PIX Firewall, in turn, generally needs a default route to which it can deliver the packets that pass inspection. Recall from the previous chapter that if the traffic doesn't pass through the firewall, the firewall can't possibly offer any protection.

In this section, we'll cover the commands used to configure IP routing on the PIX Firewall. Our goals are to configure the PIX Firewall

- To generate a default route so that internal routers know where to send packets destined for the external networks
- So that it knows where to send packets to internal destinations
- To route multicasting traffic without requiring you to configure Generic Routing Encapsulation (GRE) tunnels to pass multicast traffic

Configuring Dynamic Routing

Unfortunately, as of version 6.2 of the operating system, the only way for the PIX Firewall to communicate with other routers is via the RIP; even then, all it can do is generate a single default route and listen for other routes. So, in most circumstances, you may be better off configuring static default routes on your internal Cisco routers that point to the PIX Firewall's inside interface. One option is to allow the PIX Firewall to generate the default route via RIP, and then redistribute it into a more useful, stable, and secure routing protocol on the Cisco routers before the default route is passed to the rest of the network. Another option is to upgrade your PIX to version 6.3, which supports OSPF.

Generating a Default Route

To generate a default route using RIP, you use the `rip` command. The syntax of the `rip` command is as follows:

```
PIX(config)# rip ?
usage: [no] rip if_name default|passive [version <1|2>]
   [authentication text|md5 key key id]
PIX(config)#
```

Here's an example of a `rip` command:

```
PIX(config)# rip inside default version 2
PIX(config)#
```

This command sends the route 0.0.0.0 mask 0.0.0.0 to the multicast address 224.0.0.9 on the inside interface. This is received and processed by all RIPv2-speaking routers.

Specifying version 1 of RIP causes the same route to be sent to the broadcast address 255.255.255.255. This is illustrated here, using the output of the debug rip command:

```
PIX# debug rip
RIP trace on
PIX# configure terminal
PIX(config)# rip inside default version 1
PIX(config)# exit
PIX# 8: RIP: interface inside sending v1 update to 255.255.255.255
PIX# configure terminal
PIX(config)# rip inside default version 2
PIX(config)# exit
PIX# 9: RIP: interface inside sending v2 update to 224.0.0.9
PIX# no debug rip
RIP trace off
PIX#
```

> **NOTE** Although using RIP to broadcast the default route automates the route-learning process and is extremely easy to configure, it's less secure than using static routes. Distance-vector protocols such as RIP are also more susceptible to routing loops than their link-state cousins.

Configuring the PIX Firewall to Route Packets

The next issue to consider is configuring the PIX Firewall so that it knows where to send its packets.

If either the inside or outside networks are using the RIP protocol, you can configure the PIX Firewall to listen to those updates so that it learns its routes dynamically. This is accomplished with the rip command, using the passive keyword instead of the default keyword. For instance, to configure the PIX Firewall to listen for RIP updates on the inside interface, we use the following command:

```
PIX(config)# rip inside passive
PIX(config)#
```

You can also specify the version and enable authentication with this command.

Configuring Static Routing

The alternative to using dynamically learned routes is to manually configure static routes. These routes are configured using the route command, which has the following syntax:

PIX(config)# **route ?**
usage: [no] route *if_name foreign_ip mask gateway* [*metric*]
PIX(config)#

As an example, consider the network shown in Figure 11.5. This network includes three internal networks: the directly connected user segment, a remote-user segment, and the WAN link that connects them. The outside interface is connected to our ISP's router, which leads to the Internet, and the DMZ interface has a handful of servers.

FIGURE 11.5   *PIX Firewall routing example*

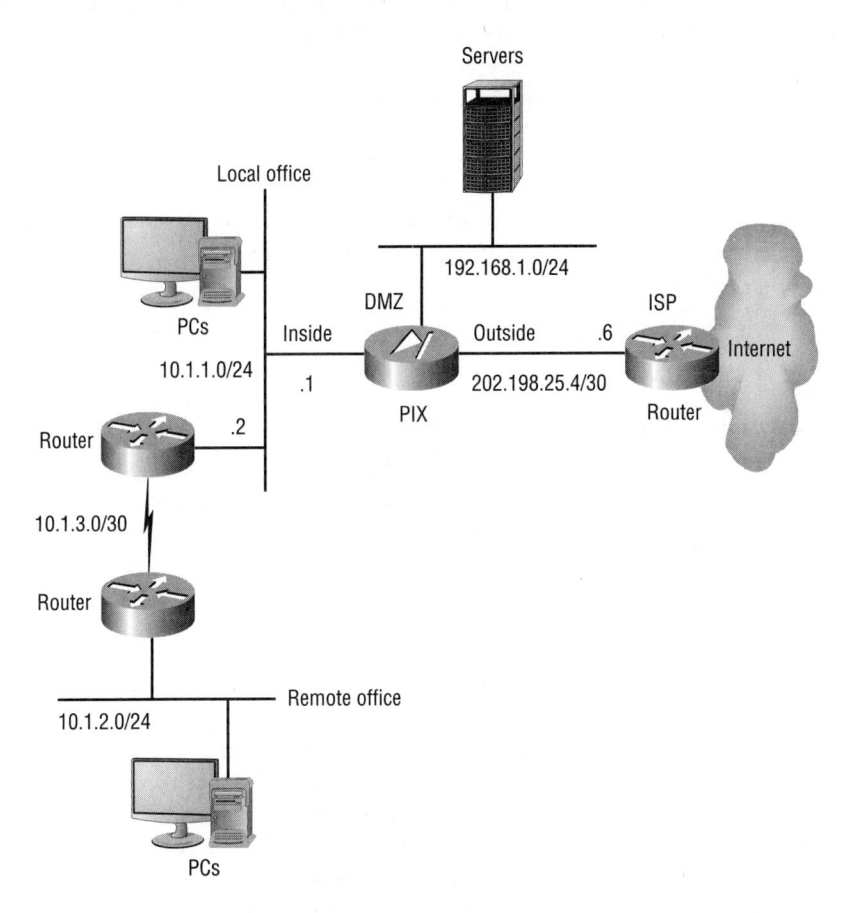

Before we begin entering commands, let's discuss what routes are needed. First, the PIX Firewall automatically enters directly connected networks in its routing table, so no manual entry is needed for the local-user segment, the DMZ, or the network attached to the outside interface. We can use the `show route` command to see the routing table, as follows:

PIX# **show route**
        inside 10.1.1.0 255.255.255.0 10.1.1.1 1 CONNECT static
        DMZ 192.168.1.0 255.255.255.0 192.168.1.1 1 CONNECT static
        outside 202.198.25.4 255.255.255.252 202.198.25.5 1 CONNECT static
PIX#

Notice that all three of the directly connected networks shown in Figure 11.5 are listed in this routing table.

Next, the PIX Firewall needs to know how to get to the remote-user segment. This requires a manual route. Since we assume there is no business need for external hosts to communicate with the routers that connect the local and remote offices, we don't need a route to the WAN subnet.

Last, we need a default route pointing to the ISP's router. This route also requires a manual entry.

Our commands to configure routing on the PIX Firewall in Figure 11.5 are as follows:

PIX(config)# **route inside 10.1.2.0 255.255.255.0 10.1.1.2**
PIX(config)# **route outside 0.0.0.0 0.0.0.0 202.198.25.6**
PIX(config)#

After entering these commands, we can check the routing table again to verify our changes.

PIX# **show route**
        outside 0.0.0.0 0.0.0.0 202.198.25.6 1 OTHER static
        inside 10.1.1.0 255.255.255.0 10.1.1.1 1 CONNECT static
        inside 10.1.2.0 255.255.255.0 10.1.1.2 1 OTHER static
        DMZ 192.168.1.0 255.255.255.0 192.168.1.1 1 CONNECT static
        outside 202.198.25.4 255.255.255.252 202.198.25.5 1 CONNECT static
PIX#

The two routes have been added as expected. In addition, although the routes are all static, the "static" routes are designated by the keyword OTHER, and the directly connected networks are designated by the keyword CONNECT.

One other point of interest in the output of the `show route` command is that the directly connected interfaces have the same metric (1) as the static routes. This might seem a little unusual if you're used to working with the IOS, where directly connected interfaces always have a metric of 0 and static routes with a next-hop IP address have a metric of 1. This curious situation might lead you to believe that it's possible to create all sorts of bizarre routing situations on the PIX Firewall, where traffic destined for directly connected interfaces could take a nonoptimal path.

To illustrate that this isn't the case, let's see what happens when we attempt to misconfigure the PIX Firewall shown in Figure 11.5:

```
PIX# configure terminal
PIX(config)# route dmz 10.1.1.0 255.255.255.0 192.168.1.2 1
➥Route already exists
PIX(config)# route dmz 10.1.1.0 255.255.255.0 192.168.1.2 2
➥Route already exists
PIX(config)# route inside 10.1.2.0 255.255.255.0 10.1.1.3 1
➥cannot add route entry
Type help or '?' for a list of available commands.
PIX(config)# route inside 10.1.2.0 255.255.255.0 10.1.1.3 2
PIX(config)# exit
PIX# show route
        outside 0.0.0.0 0.0.0.0 202.198.25.4 1 OTHER static
        inside 10.1.1.0 255.255.255.0 10.1.1.1 1 CONNECT static
        inside 10.1.2.0 255.255.255.0 10.1.1.2 1 OTHER static
        inside 10.1.2.0 255.255.255.0 10.1.1.3 2 OTHER static
        DMZ 192.168.1.0 255.255.255.0 192.168.1.1 1 CONNECT static
        outside 202.198.25.4 255.255.255.252 202.198.25.5 1 CONNECT static
PIX#
```

First, we attempt to reroute traffic destined for the local network on the inside interface out through the DMZ interface, with the same metric as the inside interface. PIX Firewall points out our mistake and rejects our command. Next, we try the same command, but with a higher metric. A higher metric on an IOS-based router would tell the router to use this route only if the first route fails. However, PIX Firewall doesn't like this either. These are unusual, but potentially useful, configurations, but keep in mind that the PIX Firewall consistently foregoes features in favor of security.

Next, we try to tell the PIX Firewall about an alternative route to the remote-user network, which isn't directly connected. By assigning an equal-cost route (both routes have a metric of 1), we might expect PIX Firewall to load-balance the traffic destined for 10.1.2.0 /24 between both the 10.1.1.2 and 10.1.1.3 (not pictured in Figure 11.5) routers. But alas, the PIX Firewall isn't too keen on load balancing either, although the error message it returns is somewhat less precise.

Finally, we try the same route again, but with a higher metric. The PIX Firewall adds this route to its table, as shown by the `show route` command.

The following are important points to remember about PIX Firewall routing:

- The PIX Firewall isn't a router.
- You can't achieve load balancing by manipulating route metrics.
- Static routes are more secure than those learned via RIP.

> **NOTE**
>
> Although the routing scenarios discussed here are common, you might need a far more complex routing environment. Thus, it isn't necessarily appropriate to replace a full-featured Cisco router with a PIX Firewall just because you need more security. This is particularly true if your network's routing is complex or if you wish to enable quality of service (QoS) or use features such as policy routing.

Configuring Multicast Routing

The PIX Firewall, in operating system version 6.2 or higher, supports *Stub Multicast Routing* (SMR), which enables it to pass multicast traffic between interfaces. The PIX Firewall acts as an Internet Group Management Protocol (IGMP) proxy agent, which forwards IGMP messages from hosts to the upstream multicast router. The PIX Firewall doesn't participate in a dynamic multicast routing protocol such as Distance Vector Multicast Routing Protocol (DVMRP) or Protocol Independent Multicast (PIM).

The SMR feature allows hosts to receive multicast traffic from a multicast router that's on another interface on the PIX Firewall, without having to create a GRE tunnel. The PIX Firewall forwards IGMP reports from downstream hosts to the upstream multicast router, and it forwards multicast traffic from the upstream multicast router to the downstream hosts.

By default, the PIX Firewall won't forward multicast traffic, so you need to enable the interface to forward multicast traffic by using the `multicast interface` command followed by the interface name. When you enter this command, you're placed in Multicast Configuration mode, and the prompt changes to (`config-multicast`)#. From this mode, you can only enter IGMP commands to configure multicast parameters. The following is an example of the Multicast mode:

```
PIX(config)# multicast interface outside
PIX(config-multicast)# ?
igmp              Configure IGMP on an interface
PIX(config-multicast)# igmp ?
Usage:  [no] igmp max-groups number
        [no] igmp forward interface interface_name
        [no] igmp access-group acl-id
        [no] igmp version [1|2]
        [no] igmp join-group group
        [no] igmp query-interval seconds
        [no] igmp query-max-response-time seconds
PIX(config-multicast)#
```

Now that the interface will forward multicast traffic on the interface, we need to enable the forwarding of all IGMP host Report and Leave messages received on the interface. The `igmp forward interface` command specifies the interface where the upstream multicast router is located so it can forward the IGMP messages out that interface. The IGMP commands are available only in the Multicast Configuration mode, with the exception of the `show igmp` and `clear igmp` commands.

Optionally, you can configure the PIX Firewall to join a multicast group and received multicast traffic for that group. You might do so for a client that can't respond via IGMP but still requires the multicast stream. The command to join a multicast group is `igmp join-group` followed by a Class D IP address to join. These Class D IP addresses are reserved for multicast traffic and are in the range from 224.0.0.0 to 239.255.255.255. Additionally, you can control which multicast traffic will be allowed by using the `igmp access-group` command followed by the name of an access list.

If the multicast traffic source is on a higher security level interface than the hosts receiving the stream, you must specifically configure the PIX Firewall to forward traffic from the source. The command to create a static route from the source to the multicast group address is `mroute`, followed by the source address and mask and inbound interface name, and then the destination address and mask and outbound interface name. The following is an example of using the `mroute` command:

```
PIX(config)# mroute 10.1.1.1 255.255.255.255 outside 225.1.1.1
➥255.255.255.255 inside
PIX(config)#
```

The other IGMP commands are used to customize the multicast on an interface. The `igmp version` command specifies the IGMP version to use; the default is 2. The `igmp query-interval` command configures the number of seconds between IGMP query messages. The maximum query response time can be used only with IGMP version 2 and can be configured by using the `igmp query-max-response-time` command. The `igmp max-groups` command configures the maximum number of groups allowed to be active on the interface.

The PIX Firewall has `show` and `debug` command that you can use to view and troubleshoot the multicast feature. The `show multicast` command displays the multicast routing configuration, and `show igmp` displays the IGMP parameters. Both of these commands can take an optional `interface` parameter followed by the name of the interface to view. The `show mroute` command lets you view the static and dynamic multicast routes active on the PIX Firewall. The only debug commands available are `debug igmp`, which enables debugging of IGMP events, and `debug mfwd`, which enables the debugging for multicast forwarding events.

Summary

In this chapter, we began by explaining what information you need to gather before configuring a PIX Firewall. Then we discussed the common global commands used to configure services such as DNS, DHCP, remote access, and logging, and how to set the system clock and NTP support.

Next, we discussed basic interface configuration, as well as advanced, multiple-interface configuration. Following that, we covered Network Address Translation (NAT) and Port Address Translation (PAT) in detail. Finally, we described how to configure the PIX Firewall to share a default route with other routers and how to receive information from other routers.

Exam Essentials

Know NAT and PAT inside and out.   You need to have a very solid grasp of the NAT and PAT operations, including the difference between static and dynamic NAT, what values you would expect to see in packets passing through the PIX Firewall, and how to configure both NAT and PAT.

Understand how to configure routing on the PIX Firewall.   PIX isn't a router, but it has limited IP and multicast routing capabilities. Know how to configure RIP to send and receive routes, how to set a static route, and how to get the PIX Firewall to forward multicast routing without GRE tunnels.

Understand the security level value.   Know what the security level value means in relation to other interfaces and how the ASA (Adaptive Security Algorithm) uses it. Also, know what the default values are for different names and interfaces and how to change them.

Know how to configure PIX Firewall interfaces.   Know how to set IP addresses, MTU, and layer 2 information, such as speed and duplex. Also know how to set the interface name.

Know the configuration basics.   Be able to configure logging, DHCP server, and remote access and to set the system clock, NTP support, and hostname. Know what other processes depend on this information.

Chapter 12

ACLs, Filtering, Object Grouping, and AAA

THE FOLLOWING TOPICS ARE COVERED IN THIS CHAPTER:

- ✓ Creating and using ACLs
- ✓ Converting conduit commands to ACLs
- ✓ Configuring URL filtering using Websense and N2H2
- ✓ Using the Point-to-Point Protocol over Ethernet (PPPoE) client
- ✓ Configuring and using group objects
- ✓ Configuring authentication, authorization, and accounting (AAA)
- ✓ Installing Cisco Secure Access Control Server for Windows 2000/NT (CSNT)
- ✓ Overview of using downloadable PIX ACLs
- ✓ Using TACACS+ for command authorization

In the previous chapters, we've mentioned access control several times in passing. This chapter is devoted to the various ways you can identify and block traffic from the Network layer through the Application layer.

We'll look at the specifics of access control lists (ACLs) on the PIX Firewall and how to convert conduit commands to access-list commands. Next we'll show you how the PIX Firewall can filter URLs using a Websense or N2H2 server, which are popular third-party products. We'll next discuss how to configure Point-to-Point Protocol over Ethernet (PPPoE) on the PIX Firewall.

We'll cover the configuration of object grouping and installation and configuration of an authentication, authorization, and accounting (AAA) server using Cisco Secure Access Control Server (ACS). Finally, we'll talk about downloadable PIX ACLs and how to configure and use them on a PIX Firewall.

Using PIX Firewall ACLs

The PIX Firewall operating system has a tiny fraction of the options and functionality for an ACL that a Cisco IOS router has. But then, those options and functionality aren't really necessary. If you think about it, all the functionality in Cisco IOS ACLs is basically an attempt to emulate a true stateful firewall. Almost all of these features are built into the PIX's Adaptive Security Algorithm (ASA).

ACLs on the PIX Firewall are fairly new. For the most part, they're meant to replace the `conduit` and `outbound` commands. ACLs also select which IP traffic IPSec protects and which it doesn't protect. In PIX Firewall 5.0 or higher, the `access-list` command replaces both of these statements. Unlike IOS ACLs, which can be bidirectional, PIX Firewall operating system ACLs affect only traffic inbound to the PIX Firewall on a given interface. Thus, an `access-list` statement must be bound to the inside and outside interfaces to control bidirectional traffic using the `access-group` command.

> **NOTE** Recall from Chapter 11, "PIX Firewall Configuration," that by default, all traffic from a lower security interface to a higher security interface is denied; however, a `static` statement can be created to allow certain traffic in. Conversely, all traffic from higher security interfaces to lower security interfaces is permitted by default, but the outbound command can be used to restrict certain traffic.

In fact, there are quite a few differences in the way ACLs are processed on the PIX Firewall versus how they're processed in the Cisco IOS, beyond the differences in features. The primary difference is that the order of a list isn't important on the PIX Firewall. In Cisco IOS ACLs, the rules are processed sequentially, and the first match is the rule that's used. In the PIX Firewall, when packets are evaluated against an ACL, they always take the longest match (the longest subnet mask).

In the following sections, we'll look at the syntax involved with creating ACLs on the PIX Firewall, applying a PIX ACL, and converting conduits to ACLs.

Creating a PIX ACL

The syntax for the PIX Firewall `access-list` command is as follows:

```
PIX(config)# access-list ?
Usage:  [no] access-list compiled
[no] access-list deny-flow-max n
[no] access-list alert-interval secs
[no] access-list id compiled
[no] access-list id [line line-num] remark text
[no] access-list id [line line-num] deny|permit
        protocol|object-group protocol_obj_grp_id
        sip smask | interface if_name | object-group network_obj_grp_id
        [operator port [port] | object-group service_obj_grp_id]
        dip dmask | interface if_name | object-group network_obj_grp_id
        [operator port [port] | object-group service_obj_grp_id]
        [log [disable|default] | [level] [interval seconds]]
[no] access-list id [line line-num] deny|permit icmp
        sip smask | interface if_name | object-group network_obj_grp_id
        dip dmask | interface if_name | object-group network_obj_grp_id
        [icmp_type | object-group icmp_type_obj_grp_id]
        [log [disable|default] | [level] [interval secs]]
Restricted ACLs for route-map use:
[no] access-list id deny|permit {any | prefix mask | host address}
PIX(config)# access-list
```

As you can see, the syntax of the `access-list` command closely resembles the syntax of the IP-extended ACL in the Cisco IOS. The *id* value can be either a number or a string. The *protocol* value is commonly IP, TCP, UDP, or ICMP. The source and destination IP address, mask, and port are much the same as well. One notable difference is that the source mask is a regular mask and not the wildcard bits used in Cisco IOS ACLs. The *operator* value is also similar; it's usually `eq` followed by a number from 1 to 254 (to represent other protocol numbers) or a keyword, such as `www`, `telnet`, or `ftp`.

Unlike in Cisco IOS, which has different types of access lists, there is only one type of access list on the PIX Firewall. In Cisco IOS, the number of the access list determines its type, but on the PIX Firewall, the number is meaningless: the access-list identifier can be any number or string value.

Another characteristic of the PIX ACL is the ability to add line numbers and remarks to the ACL statements:

```
access-list id [line line-num] remark text
```

This feature is cool, and it also comes in very handy. You know the deal with your IOS ACLs: if you mess something up, you have to remove it and start all over again. Well, that isn't so with the PIX ACL. When you're configuring a PIX ACL, you can include line numbers and remarks for each statement. These line numbers allow you to remove or reorder your statements instead of having to rebuild your ACL from scratch.

Let's talk about one feature that Cisco IOS ACLs and Cisco PIX Firewall ACLs have in common: compiled or turbo ACL. On the PIX Firewall, the turbo ACL feature is turned on globally with the `access-list compiled` command and turned off with the `no access-list compiled` command. By default, the turbo ACL feature is turned off, but the turbo ACL feature is used only for access lists with 19 or more entries. You can also turn on the turbo ACL feature for a certain access-list with the `access-list id compiled` command.

The turbo ACL feature on the PIX Firewall uses flash memory, so the minimum amount of flash memory required to run the feature is 2.1MB. If memory allocation fails, the turbo ACL lookup tables won't be generated. You can use the turbo ACL feature only on PIX Firewall platforms that have 16MB or more of flash memory.

> **NOTE** The Firewall Services Module (FWSM), which has 128MB of flash, has the turbo ACL feature enabled by default.

If the turbo ACL feature is configured, some ACL or ACL group modifications can trigger regeneration of the turbo ACL internal configuration. If you have a large number of ACLs, this could noticeably consume CPU resources. Consequently, we recommend modifying turbo-compiled access lists during nonpeak system-usage hours.

Applying a PIX ACL

The `access-group` command binds an ACL to an interface, just as it does in the Cisco IOS. The syntax for the PIX `access-group` command is as follows:

```
PIX(config)# access-group ?
usage: [no] access-group access-list in interface if_name
PIX(config)# access-group
```

The primary difference is that the keyword `in` is always used, because (as we mentioned previously) ACLs in the PIX Firewall operating system filter only inbound traffic. Thus, the `out` keyword doesn't exist. It's possible, however, to apply the same ACL to multiple interfaces. Also, this command is issued with the interface name as a parameter from the global-configuration prompt, rather than in the context of an interface, as is the case in the Cisco IOS, where your prompt is `Router(config-if)#`.

Converting Conduits to ACLs

Cisco has stated that the `conduit` command has been replaced with the `access-list` command and will no longer be supported in later releases of the PIX Firewall operating system. What are you supposed to do with older PIX Firewall configurations now that the `conduit` command soon won't be supported? We'll discuss how to convert those `conduit` commands to `access-list` commands in this section.

Since the `conduit` and `static` commands go hand in hand, we need to look briefly at the `static` command syntax. Remember from Chapter 11 that the `static` command syntax is

`static (high_interface,low_interface) global_ip local_ip netmask mask`

This translates a global IP address on the less trusted interface to a local IP address on the more trusted interface.

Before the `access-list` command was instituted, for a host to gain access to an inside IP address from the lower-trusted interface, you had to use a `conduit` command. Let's look at the format of the `conduit` command:

`conduit [deny | permit] protocol global_ip global_mask`
➥`global_operator global_port [global_port] foreign_ip foreign_mask`
➥`foreign_operatorforeign_port [foreign_port]`

Many of these can be collapsed by certain keywords, such as `host` or `any`. For example, here is a `static` and `conduit` command to allow web traffic from the outside interface to 109.135.102.5 to be translated and given access to the internal host at 192.168.1.5:

`PIX(config) # static (inside,outside) 109.135.102.5 192.168.1.5`
➥`netmask 255.255.255.255`
`PIX(config)# conduit permit tcp host 109.135.102.5 eq www any`
`PIX(config)#`

As you can see, the `conduit` command allows web access to the host at 109.135.102.5 from any IP address.

Now let's look at the syntax of the access-list command so you can get an idea how to do the conversion:

`access-list acl_name [deny | permit] protocol source_ip source_mask`
➥`operator port destination_ip destination_mask operator port`

To convert the previous `conduit` command to an `access-list` command, you must recognize that the *global_ip* is the same as the *destination_ip*, and the *foreign_ip* is the same as the *source_ip*. See Figure 12.1 for an illustration of this point. You must also remember that to implement the `access-list` command, you must use the `access-group` command on the inbound interface.

The following is the replacement access-list command with the corresponding access-group command on the inbound interface:

```
PIX(config)# access-list web_host permit tcp any host 109.135.102.5
➥ eq www
PIX(config)# access-group web_host in interface outside
PIX(config)#
```

FIGURE 12.1   Conduit to access-list conversion

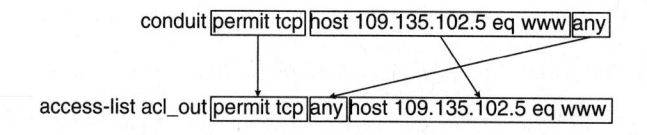

```
         conduit |permit tcp|host 109.135.102.5 eq www|any|

access-list acl_out|permit tcp|any|host 109.135.102.5 eq www|
```

URL Filtering

Websense and N2H2 are third-party products used by a Cisco Secure PIX Firewall. These products allow an administrator to filter URLs (typically HTTP web browsing) in a number of different ways. The most common is purchasing a subscription that periodically updates a database on a Windows server with a list of almost all the resources on the Internet. These URLs are put in categories such as news, sports, finance, and so on. This lets administrators set a policy on the Windows server, such as "our users aren't allowed access to sports websites." In theory, such policies provide some reduction of the legal liability for employers and other concerned organizations without inhibiting legitimate or work-related web-browsing activity.

In the following sections, we'll discuss how URL filtering works and how it's configured on the PIX Firewall.

How Does URL Filtering Work?

At a high level, the URL filtering architecture is consistent with the policy enforcement points (PEP) and policy decision points (PDP) we discussed at the beginning of Chapter 10, "PIX Firewall Basics." In this instance, the policy repository and PDP is the Windows server running URL-filtering software, and the PEP is the PIX Firewall.

The Websense and N2H2 products are implemented as plug-ins on a PIX Firewall. This plug-in communicates with a Websense or N2H2 server, which runs on a Windows server. Specifically, each time an HTTP request passes through the PIX Firewall, the PIX Firewall hands the requested URL to the plug-in and then transmits the URL request to the web server. The plug-in asks the URL server if the URL is approved and then returns the answer. By the time the requested web page is returned from the web server, the PIX Firewall usually has an answer from the Websense or N2H2 URL server and discards or forwards the web page as instructed.

Configuring the PIX Firewall for URL Filtering

Since the bulk of the intelligence is implemented on the Websense or N2H2 server, the configuration of the PIX Firewall is straightforward. There are only two base commands: `url-server` and `filter url`.

The first, `url-server`, tells the PIX Firewall the address of the Websense or N2H2 server. It has the following syntax:

```
PIX(config)# url-server ?
Usage:  [no] url-server [(if_name)] [vendor websense] host
➥ local_ip [timeout seconds] [protocol TCP|UDP [version 1|4]]
        [no] url-server [(if_name)] vendor n2h2 host local_ip
➥ [port number] [timeout seconds] [protocol TCP|UDP]
PIX(config)# url-server
```

If you're using Websense, you don't need to specify a vendor since it's the default server type. Typically, if you're using Websense, the `url-server` command is as simple as this:

```
PIX(config)# url-server (inside) host 10.1.1.5
PIX(config)#
```

The default timeout is five seconds for Websense, but you can change it by including the `timeout` keyword. You can also change the protocol type and version used to communicate with the Websense server.

> **NOTE** If you're using User Datagram Protocol (UDP) as the transport to the Websense server, which isn't the default, you must set the protocol version to 4.

As you can see from the earlier syntax, if you're using an N2H2 server, you must specify the `vendor n2h2` parameter. You also specify the same timeout and protocol options that are available under Websense, with the exception of the protocol version.

You can specify up to 16 URL servers, but only one type of URL filtering can be active at a time: either Websense or N2H2, but not both. In addition, if you change the configuration on the PIX Firewall, you must update the URL server; the firewall doesn't update the configuration on the URL server and vice versa.

The second base command, `filter url`, tells the PIX Firewall what traffic to pass to the Websense or N2H2 server for inspection. It has the following syntax:

```
PIX(config)# filter ?
Usage:  [no] filter url port [-port]|except lcl_ip mask
➥ frgn_ip mask [allow] [proxy-block] [longurl-truncate |
➥ longurl-deny] [cgi-truncate]
        [no] filter ActiveX|Java port [-port] lcl_ip mask
➥ frgn_ip mask
PIX(config)# filter
```

Here is an example:

```
PIX(config)# filter url http 10.0.0.0 255.0.0.0 0 0 allow
PIX(config)#
```

This command tells the PIX Firewall that all HTTP requests from 10.0.0.0/8 to any destination must be inspected by the URL server. If you don't specify the `allow` parameter, and the Websense or N2H2 server is unavailable, then the PIX Firewall will stop outbound HTTP traffic until the server is back online. You can specify a range of ports to filter with the *port [-port]* parameter, but you can also use the keyword `http` as we have in the previous example.

As you can see from the syntax of the `filter` command, you can also filter ActiveX and Java traffic from a local IP address range to a foreign IP address range on a specified port or ports. The `filter activex` command blocks outbound ActiveX, Java applets, and other HTML <object> tags from outbound packets. The `filter java` command filters out Java applets returning from a previously established outbound connection. Here is an example of Java applet and ActiveX blocking on all outbound connections:

```
PIX(config)# filter activex 80 0 0 0 0
PIX(config)# filter java 80 0 0 0 0
PIX(config)#
```

The `cgi-truncate` parameter sends a CGI script as a URL, and the `proxy-block` parameter prevents users from connecting to an HTTP proxy server. You can also specify a range of IP addresses to be excluded from the URL filtering using the `filter url except` command followed by the local IP address and foreign IP address ranges. This makes it easy to exclude some IP addresses from URL filtering.

If you're dealing with long URLs, then you can use the `longurl-deny` or `longurl-truncate` command to specify what the PIX Firewall should do with them. The `longurl-deny` parameter denies the URL request if it's over the URL buffer size limit or the URL buffer isn't available. The `longurl-truncate` parameter sends only the hostname or IP address to the Websense server if the URL is over the buffer limit. You can adjust the URL buffer size using the `url-block block` command followed by the block buffer size limit parameter. If you're using Websense, then you can optionally specify the long URL size with the `url-block url-size` command followed by a number from 2KB to 4KB specifying the size of the URL.

Let's touch on one more command briefly, for completeness: `url-cache`. This command caches web server responses that are pending a permit or denies a response from a Websense or N2H2 server. This is used if the web server responds faster than the Websense or N2H2 server, which prevents the web server's response from being loaded twice. You use this command to enable URL caching and set the size of the cache.

The command also increases throughput by caching the URL access privileges from the URL server. The PIX Firewall looks in the URL cache first for a matching permit or deny instead of forwarding the request to the URL server. The following is the syntax for the `url-cache` command:

```
PIX(config)# url-cache ?
Usage:   [no] url-cache dst|src_dst size Kbytes
PIX(config)# url-cache
```

The parameters of the `url-cache` command are `dst` or `src_dst`. You use the `dst` parameter if all users share the same filtering policy on the URL server and it will cache entries based upon the URL destination address. If all users don't share the same filtering policy on the URL server, then use the `src_dst` parameter, which caches entries based on both the source and destination of the URL request. These parameters must be followed by the `size` keyword and then a number that specifies the size of the cache in the range of 1–128KB.

Note that the `url-cache` command doesn't update the Websense accounting logs if you're using protocol version 1. They're updated for Websense protocol version 4 and if you're using the N2H2 URL server.

> **NOTE** If you change the filtering policy on the Websense or N2H2 server, you'll need to disable the cache with the no `url-cache` command and then re-enable the cache to make those policy changes apparent to the PIX Firewall URL cache.

PPPoE and the PIX Firewall

Support for the *Point-to-Point Protocol over Ethernet (PPPoE)* client was introduced in version 6.2 of the PIX Firewall operating system. It's mainly targeted to the small office, home office (SOHO) level PIX Firewalls (501 and 506E models), which might be hooked to a cable modem or DSL router. Currently, the PPPoE client is supported only on the outside interface, but it supports the Password Authentication Protocol (PAP), Challenge Handshake Authentication Protocol (CHAP), and MS-CHAP authentication protocols, with PAP being the default.

PPPoE provides an authenticated method of assigning IP addresses to client systems. PPPoE clients are typically personal computers connected to an ISP over a broadband connection. ISPs use PPPoE because it supports the higher-speed access speeds while using their existing remote access infrastructure and because it's relatively easy for customers to use.

The PPPoE client (in this case, the PIX Firewall) and the PPPoE server must be on the same layer 2 bridged networks. PPPoE uses two phases:

- In the Active Discovery Phase, the PPPoE client locates a PPPoE server, called an access concentrator (AC). A Session ID is assigned, and the PPPoE layer is established.
- In the PPP Session Phase, PPP options are negotiated, and authentication is performed. Once the link setup is completed, PPPoE functions as a layer 2 encapsulation method, allowing data to be transferred over the PPP link within PPPoE headers.

> **TIP**
> You must configure the PPPoE client username and password before enabling PPPoE on the interface.

In this section, we'll talk about how to enable, configure, and verify the operation of the PPPoE client on the PIX Firewall.

Configuring the PPPoE Client Username and Password

To configure the username and password used to authenticate the PIX Firewall to the AC, you use the vpdn command. The first step is to define the virtual private dial-up network (VPDN) group to be used for the PPPoE client, using the following command:

vpdn group *group_name* request dialout pppoe

You replace the *group_name* parameter with a descriptive name for the PPPoE client.

If your ISP requires authentication, you must select an authentication protocol using the following command:

vpdn group *group_name* ppp authentication *method*

The *group_name* is the group name you defined in the first step, and the method is one of the authentication methods: PAP, CHAP, or MS-CHAP.

> **NOTE**
> When you're using CHAP or MS-CHAP, the username may be referred to as the *remote system name*, and the password may be referred to as the *CHAP secret*.

Next, you need to create a username and password—which are usually assigned by the ISP—for the PPPoE connection, by using the following command:

vpdn username *username* password *pass*

Finally, you associate the username to the VPDN group by using the following command:

vpdn group *group_name* localname *username*

Enabling PPPoE on the PIX Firewall

The PPPoE client doesn't run by default; so, to enable PPPoE functionality on an interface, you use the `ip address` *interface* `pppoe` command. This command starts the PPPoE process and assigns the IP address received from the AC to the interface. You can optionally specify the `setroute` command, which allows the AC to set a default route for the client. You can reenter this command to clear and restart the PPPoE session. The current session will be shut down and a new one will be restarted.

> **NOTE** Remember, currently the PPPoE client can be enabled only on the outside interface.

PPPoE isn't supported in conjunction with DHCP because with PPPoE the IP address is assigned by the PPP server. The maximum transfer unit (MTU) size is automatically set to 1492 bytes, which is the correct value to allow PPPoE overhead within an Ethernet frame without having to fragment the outgoing Ethernet frame.

What happens if you're using a static IP address from your ISP? You can enable PPPoE in this situation by manually entering the IP address, using the following command:

`ip address` *interface ipaddress mask* `pppoe`

This command causes the PIX Firewall to use the specified IP address and mask instead of negotiating with the PPPoE server to assign an IP address dynamically.

The following is an example of the commands used to configure the PPPoE client on the PIX Firewall. Some of the irrelevant portions have been omitted:

```
PIX(config)#write terminal
PIX Version 6.2
nameif ethernet0 outside security0
nameif ethernet1 inside security100
hostname PIX
interface ethernet0 10baset
interface ethernet1 10full
ip address outside pppoe setroute
ip address inside 172.16.16.2 255.255.255.0
vpdn group pppoex request dialout pppoe
vpdn group pppoex localname sybex
vpdn group pppoex ppp authentication pap
vpdn username sybex password *********
: end
PIX(config)#
```

As you can see from this output, we're using the `setroute` option on the `ip address` command to create a default route back to the access concentrator. We have also defined the username of `sybex` and a password to be used for PAP authentication.

Verifying PPPoE Operation

To confirm that your configuration is working properly, Cisco has provided some diagnostic commands that show the configuration and operation of the PPPoE client.

The `show ip address outside pppoe` command displays the current PPPoE client configuration information. The following is the output from this command:

```
PIX(config)# show ip address outside pppoe
PPPoE Assigned IP addr: 192.168.121.1 255.255.255.255 on Interface:
➥ outside Remote IP addr: 192.168.148.36
PIX(config)#
```

The `show vpdn tunnel pppoe` command shows the information for the currently running PPPoE tunnels. Here is the output from this command:

```
PIX(config)# show vpdn tunnel pppoe

PPPoE Tunnel Information (Total tunnels=1 sessions=1)

Tunnel id 0, 1 active sessions
   time since change 20239 secs
   Remote MAC Address 00:08:E3:9C:4C:71
   3328 packets sent, 3325 received, 41492 bytes sent, 0 received
PIX(config)#
```

The `show vpdn session pppoe` command displays the status of currently active PPPoE sessions. The following is the output from this command:

```
PIX(config)# show vpdn session pppoe
PPPoE Session Information (Total tunnels=1 sessions=1)

Remote MAC is 00:08:E3:9C:4C:71
   Session state is SESSION_UP
     Time since event change 20294 secs, interface outside
     PPP interface id is 1
     3337 packets sent, 3334 received, 41606 bytes sent, 0 received
PIX(config)#
```

The `show vpdn pppinterface` command shows the interface identification value of the PPPoE tunnel. A PPP virtual interface is created for each PPPoE tunnel. Here is the command's output:

```
PIX(config)# show vpdn pppinterface
PPP virtual interface id = 1
PPP authentication protocol is PAP
Server ip address is 192.168.148.36
Our ip address is 192.168.121.1
Transmitted Pkts: 3348, Received Pkts: 3345, Error Pkts: 0
MPPE key strength is None
   MPPE_Encrypt_Pkts: 0,  MPPE_Encrypt_Bytes: 0
   MPPE_Decrypt_Pkts: 0,  MPPE_Decrypt_Bytes: 0
   Rcvd_Out_Of_Seq_MPPE_Pkts: 0
PIX(config)#
```

The `show vpdn group` command displays the group defined for the PPPoE tunnel, and the `show vpdn username` command displays the local username information. The following is the output from these commands:

```
PIX(config)# show vpdn group
vpdn group pppoex request dialout pppoe
vpdn group pppoex localname sybex
vpdn group pppoex ppp authentication pap
PIX(config)# show vpdn username
vpdn username sybex password *********
PIX(config)#
```

Object Groups

In an effort to improve the flexibility in the PIX Firewall configuration, as of version 6.2, Cisco has implemented the concept of the *object group*. You can use object groups with the standard `conduit` and `access-list` commands. They also reduce the number of entries required to implement a complex security policy. Four types of object groups can be used to make the configuration more readable, understandable, and easier to change:

- Protocol
- Network
- ICMP
- Service

In this section, we'll discuss how to create and use each type of object group to make it easier to configure and change access lists on the PIX Firewall.

Configuring Object Groups

To configure an object group, the command syntax is

object-group *group_type group_id*

where *group_type* is protocol, network, icmp-type, or service. The *group_id* is an identifier for the group and must be unique.

When you're configuring a service object group, you must also specify the protocol type being used:

- tcp
- udp
- tcp-udp

After you enter the object group command, you're placed in Object Group Configuration mode. In this mode, you specify the various objects within this group; you escape this mode with the exit command. You can also describe the object group with the description command used in Object Group Configuration mode.

Once you're in Protocol Object Group Configuration mode, the command syntax is

protocol-object *protocol*

where *protocol* is either a keyword, such as tcp, udp, or eigrp, or a decimal value of the protocol, such as 17 for UDP or 6 for TCP. This way, you can specify a group of protocols that are to be used together in an access list.

Following is an example of a protocol object group named branch-prot with the ESP, UDP, and AH protocol types:

```
PIX(config)# object-group protocol branch-prot
PIX(config-protocol)# protocol-object esp
PIX(config-protocol)# protocol-object ah
PIX(config-protocol)# protocol-object udp
PIX(config-protocol)#
```

If you want to specify a group of network objects to get the same treatment, then you need to get into Network Object Group Configuration mode. At this point, you have two options: either specify a host or specify a group of hosts.

The command syntax to specify a host is

network-object host *ip_address*

or

network-object host *hostname*

To use the *hostname* option, you must have already specified the host using the name command.

Object Groups

To specify a group of hosts or a network of hosts, the command syntax is

`network-object` `ip_address mask`

This allows you to configure a group of hosts. We've supplied an example of a network object group that specifies a host and a network to be grouped together:

```
PIX(config)# name 10.109.2.3 acs-server
PIX(config)# object-group network branch-net
PIX(config-network)# network-object host acs-server
PIX(config-network)# network-object 10.108.0.0 255.255.0.0
PIX(config-network)#
```

To specify a group of ICMP messages to use in an access-list statement, you need to get into ICMP Type Object Group mode. The syntax to add an ICMP type to the group is

`icmp-object` `icmp-type`

where `icmp-type` is either a keyword or one of the numbers found in Table 12.1.

The following is an example of an ICMP object group configuration:

```
PIX(config)# object-group icmp-type branch-icmp
PIX(config-icmp-type)# icmp-group echo
PIX(config-icmp-type)# icmp-group time-exceeded
PIX(config-icmp-type)#
```

As we mentioned earlier, a *service object group* is used to specify a range of TCP and/or UDP ports to be defined in a group; so, the object group command must specify TCP, UDP, or TCP-UDP. You can use two commands to add a port or range of ports to a service object group. The first command

`port-object eq` `service`

adds just one service to the service object group.

The second command

`port-object range` `begin end`

adds a range of ports to the service object. The `service`, `begin`, and `end` parameters can be either a keyword, such as `domain`, or a decimal value of the service. Here is an example of adding TCP and UDP ports to a service object group named `branch-svc`:

```
PIX(config)# object-group service branch-svc tcp-udp
PIX(config-service)# port-object eq domain
PIX(config-service)# port-object range 1024 65535
PIX(config-service)#
```

TABLE 12.1 ICMP Types

Number	Name of ICMP Type
0	Echo-reply
3	Unreachable
4	Source-quench
5	Redirect
6	Alternate-address
8	Echo
9	Router-advertisement
10	Router-solicitation
11	Time-exceeded
12	Parameter-problem
13	Timestamp-request
14	Timestamp-reply
15	Information-request
16	Information-reply
17	Address-mask-request
18	Address-mask-reply
31	Conversion-error
32	Mobile-redirect

You can also nest object groups within each other (also called *hierarchical* object grouping) to achieve greater flexibility and modularity when specifying access rules. For example, you can create two network object groups called Finance and Engineering. Then you can create another group called All_Nets, which contains both the Finance and Engineering group objects. The command to do this is group-object *object_id*, where *object_id* is the object to nest within the object being modified. You use the same command regardless of the object type being nested.

There are a couple of straightforward restrictions when you're nesting object groups. You can't nest an object group within itself, and you can't nest an object group of a different type. The following example shows the scenarios mentioned and what the PIX Firewall does when you attempt an illegal operation:

```
PIX(config)# object-group network Finance
PIX(config-network)# network-object 10.2.2.0 255.255.255.0
PIX(config-network)# exit
PIX(config)#object-group network Engineering
PIX(config-network)# network-object 10.2.3.0 255.255.255.0
PIX(config-network)# group-object Engineering
Adding obj (group-object Engineering) to grp (Engineering) failed;
➥ cause a loop in grp hierarchy
PIX(config-network)# exit
PIX(config)# object-group network All_Nets
PIX(config-network)# group-object Finance
PIX(config-network)# group-object Engineering
PIX(config-network)# exit
PIX(config)# object-group icmp-type branch-icmp
PIX(config-icmp-type)# object-group Finance
Adding obj to object-group (branch-icmp) failed; object and group
➥ type inconsistent
PIX(config-icmp-type)#
```

If there is another subnet added to the finance network, the only thing you need to do is to add that network to the Finance network object group. Doing so also adds the same network to the All_Nets object group, and your access lists are automatically updated.

Using Object Groups

To use a group object in an access list, you need to add the keyword **object-group** in front of the object identifier within the access list. The following is an example of using each type of object group in an access list and combining multiple object groups per access-list line:

```
PIX(config)# access-list 101 permit object-group protocol_object
➥ 10.12.3.0 255.255.255.0 any
PIX(config)# access-list 102 deny ip any object-group network_object
PIX(config)# access-list 103 permit icmp any any object-group
➥ icmp_object
PIX(config)# access-list 104 deny tcp any object-group
➥ service_object any
PIX(config)# access-list 100 permit object-group protocol_object
➥ object-group network_object1 object-group service_object1
➥ object-group network_object2 object-group service-object2
PIX(config)#
```

If you're familiar with other vendor firewalls, you'll realize the concept of object groups is one that has been missing from the Cisco PIX for a while. The reason for the inclusion of object groups from Cisco will become more apparent when we go over the PIX Device Manager (PDM) in Chapter 14, "Firewall Failover and PDM."

Authentication, Authorization, and Accounting (AAA) Services

AAA is a mechanism used to let a device, in this case a PIX Firewall, know who a user is, what the user can do, and what the user did. You can have authentication without authorization, but you can't have authorization without authentication. A user must be authenticated before the PIX Firewall knows what that user can do.

With traditional authentication, a user can gain access to the network by entering their assigned local username and password for that device. You can't allow Telnet access for one user and not another. If the user has entered the correct username and password combination, they have access to the entire network. Plus, local user administration becomes a nightmare as you get more users and more network access devices. People who leave the company must be removed from every device they had access to, and there is no way a user can change their password periodically.

With AAA services, you can allow certain users to have access to Telnet and FTP services without allowing them to browse the Web using the HTTP protocol. Once a user has been authenticated, the PIX Firewall can find out what services they're authorized to access. After this information is cached, the PIX Firewall uses a technique known as *cut-through proxy* to transparently verify the identity of users as they use any TCP- or UDP-based applications. This dramatically increases performance without affecting security.

In this section, we'll go through the installation and configuration of Cisco Secure Access Control Server for Windows NT (CSNT), how to implement AAA services on the PIX Firewall, and how to configure downloadable ACLs.

> **NOTE**
> The ACS server will run both on Windows NT/2000 and Sun Solaris, but we'll cover only the Windows product here.

Installing Cisco Secure ACS for Windows 2000/NT

For anyone who has installed and configured Windows software, CSNT installation is relatively straightforward. Let's go through the installation of the software for version 3.1.

We'll step through how to install the CSNT version 3.1 on a system without a previous version. Please complete the following steps:

1. Log in as the local system administrator to the computer on which you're installing the software.
2. Insert the Cisco Secure ACS CD into your CD-ROM drive, which will open the installation window.
3. Click Install, and the Software License Agreement window opens.
4. Read the Software License Agreement, and click Accept to agree to the terms and conditions. The Welcome screen opens.
5. Click Next to open the Before You Begin window.
6. You're presented with the following list of conditions that must be met before installation can take place:
    - End-user clients can successfully connect to the AAA clients.
    - This Windows 2000 Server can ping the AAA clients.
    - Any IOS clients are running Cisco IOS release 11.1 or later.
    - Microsoft Internet Explorer v5.5 or 6.0 or Netscape 6.2 is installed.

    Verify that each condition is met, select the check box for each item, and click Next.
7. The Choose Destination Location window opens. To install the software in the default directory, click Next. To use a different directory, click Browse, and enter the directory to use. If the directory doesn't exist, you're prompted to create it. Click Yes.
8. The Authentication Database Configuration window opens. Click the radio button for the authentication databases to be used by CSNT. Select either the CSACS Database Only or Windows NT User Database option. If you select the first option, the software will use only the Cisco Secure ACS database for authentication; if you select the second option, the software will check the Windows database if the user isn't found in the CSACS database. (If you select the Windows NT User Database option, you can use the "grant dial-in permission" attribute on the user to determine access permissions. This enables you to control a user's access permissions directly from Windows 2000/NT without using the Cisco Secure administration interface.) Click Next to continue to the Network Access Server Details window.
9. You have to set up one Network Access Server (NAS) to continue with the software installation. You need to supply the following information about the NAS:
    - How you'll authenticate users:
      TACACS+ (Cisco IOS)
      RADIUS (Cisco Aironet)
      RADIUS (Cisco BBSM)
      RADIUS (Cisco IOS/PIX)
      RADIUS (Cisco VPN 3000)

RADIUS (Cisco VPN 5000)

RADIUS (IETF)

RADIUS (Ascend)

RADIUS (Juniper)

RADIUS (Nortel)

RADIUS (IPass)

- The name of the access server
- The IP address of the access server
- The Windows Server IP Address
- The key value to be used for TACACS+ or RADIUS

Once this information has been entered, click Next to copy the files from the CD to the computer's hard drive.

10. The Advanced Options window appears. This is where you choose how to customize the Cisco Secure Administration Interface. You have the following options to either enable or disable in the interface:

    - User Level Network Access Restrictions
    - Group Level Network Access Restriction
    - Max Session
    - Default Time of Day/Day of Week Specification
    - Distributed System Settings
    - Database Replication

    Once you have enabled the desired options, click Next.

11. The Active Service Monitoring window opens. To enable the Cisco Secure ACS monitoring service, click the Enable Log-in Monitoring check box. You can then select the action to take when then login process fails:

    - No Remedial Action leaves the service operating as is.
    - Reboot restarts the computer where it's running.
    - Restart All restarts all Cisco Secure ACS services (the default).
    - Restart RADIUS/TACACS+ restarts only the RADIUS and TACACS+ services.

    From this window, you can also check the box to Enable Mail Notification. If this option is selected, you must supply the fully qualified domain name (FQDN) of the SMTP mail server and mail account to notify. Click Next.

12. The Network Access Server Configuration window opens. The installation software can help you configure an NAS. If this isn't desired, then deselect the Yes, I Want To Configure Cisco IOS Now check box, and click Next.

13. The Cisco Secure ACS Service Initiation window is the last window. Select any of the following tasks that you want performed:
    - Yes, I Want To Start The Cisco Secure ACS Service Now.
    - Yes, I Want Setup To Launch The Cisco Secure ACS Administrator From By Browser Following Installation.
    - Yes, I Want To View The Readme File.

    Click Finish to complete the installation.

Now, let's discuss the system requirements, how to administer the server, and how CSNT works, and then have an overview of additional features.

System Requirements

As of the publication of this book, the system requirements to install CSNT are the following:

- Pentium III processor running at 550MHz or faster
- CD-ROM drive
- English-language version of Microsoft Windows 2000 Server with at least Service Pack 3
- Microsoft Internet Explorer 5.5 or 6.0 or Netscape Communicator 6.2 or later
- 256MB of RAM required; 512MB recommended
- 250MB of free hard disk space (more might be required if your database will be on the same machine)
- A monitor with 256 colors, 800×600 resolution

Administration

Once the installation process is completed, you'll see a final installation window, which asks if you would like to do one of the following:

- View the readme file.
- Start the Cisco Secure ACS service now.
- Launch the Cisco Secure ACS Administrator from your browser.

Administration of CSNT is usually handled using a web browser pointing to TCP port 2002 on the machine running CSNT. This means that to administer CSNT, you need a common web browser; no special client is required, and you don't even need to be on the CSNT server to administer it. You do need to have one of the web browsers listed in the system requirements mentioned earlier.

Once the server is running, you can access, configure, and troubleshoot CSNT using an HTML/Java interface. Accessing the web-based administration tool is as simple as opening a web page. For example, if you were on the console of the NT server running CSNT, you might type **http://127.0.0.1:2002** into your web browser to bring up the web-based administration tool. CSNT must be running before you can access the web-based administration interface!

Alternatively, if you were trying to access the web-based administration tool from a remote machine, you would type **http://10.160.10.31:2002**, where 10.160.10.31 is the IP address of the server.

How CSNT Works

CSNT will work with any network-access device. You can use it with dial-up NASs and firewalls, or you can use it to manage access to switches and routers. The NAS can be literally any device capable of using the Terminal Access Controller Access Control System Plus (TACACS+) or Remote Authentication Dial-In User Service (RADIUS) protocol. In this section, we'll discuss CSNT when used with Cisco PIX Firewalls.

The PIX Firewall must be configured so that rather than checking local user databases for authentication, the user-access request is redirected to CSNT for authentication and authorization. (We'll discuss the specific syntax later in this chapter.) The firewall uses either the RADIUS or TACACS+ protocol to send the authentication request to CSNT. CSNT then verifies the username and password (we'll discuss that process shortly) and replies to the firewall. Once the user has been authenticated, CSNT sends a set of authorization attributes to the firewall. Finally, accounting can be done to keep track of user activity on the network. As we mentioned, this can become advantageous in situations where you have multiple firewalls.

Let's talk about how a user can be authenticated to an external user database, how the database can be maintained, and some additional features of CSNT.

CSNT Authentication through User Databases

CSNT maintains its own database, called the Cisco Secure User Database. When a user-access request arrives at CSNT, it first checks the Cisco Secure User Database for information regarding that user. If no matching information is found, CSNT can be configured to check a number of additional user databases, including the following:

- Windows NT
- Novell Directory Services (NDS)
- Directory Services (DS)
- Microsoft Commercial Internet System Lightweight Directory Access Protocol (MCIS LDAP)
- Open Database Connectivity (ODBC)

Additionally, CSNT can use any of the following token-card servers for authentication:

- Axent
- CRYPTOCard
- SafeWord
- Security Dynamics, Inc. (SDI)

Cisco Secure User Database Population

The Cisco Secure User Database can be populated in a number of ways:

- Manually
- With the Database Replication utility
- With the Database Import utility

Manual population means the users are added by hand; but to avoid all this work, you can use the replication and import utilities provided with CSNT.

The Database Replication utility provides fault tolerance and redundancy of your Cisco Secure User Database by allowing several independent CSNT servers to synchronize their data. In this manner, a new CSNT server can be introduced to the network, configured for database replication, and thus be populated with a replica of the existing Cisco Secure User Database.

A third option is to use the included Database Import utility, `CSUtil.exe`. If you have an existing ODBC-compliant database, you can use this utility to import user information from that database. (Refer to Cisco's documentation for formatting and import syntax.)

CSNT Features

CSNT has a rich set of features that allow you to customize and control the AAA process. The following list is by no means comprehensive, but it does include some of the highlights:

- Password aging
- User-changeable passwords
- Multilevel administration
- Group administration of users
- Maximum sessions for users and groups
- Ability to disable an account on a specific date
- Time-of-day and day-of-week access restrictions
- Ability to disable an account after an amount of failed attempts
- Ability to see logged-on users, and to view detailed information for each user
- Per-user TACACS+ or RADIUS attributes
- Downloadable ACLs
- Support for Voice over IP (VoIP)
- Windows NT Performance Monitor support for real-time statistics viewing
- Configurable accounting and auditing information stored in comma-separated values (CSV) format
- Authentication forwarding

- Relational database management system (RDBMS) synchronization
- Database replication
- Scheduled ACS system backup and ability to restore from the backup file

These and other features give you extremely granular control over the AAA process. You have the ability to control user access. Additionally, CSNT gives you the tools to monitor the CSNT server, as well as to manipulate the user database.

Implementing AAA on the PIX Firewall

Once ACS has been installed and configured on the server, you need to configure AAA services for the PIX Firewall. AAA can be configured to use the TACACS+ and/or RADIUS protocol in addition to LOCAL authentication. By default, the PIX Firewall comes preconfigured with the AAA groups tags of RADIUS, TACACS+, and LOCAL.

The RADIUS group tag is configured with the protocol type of radius, and TACACS+ group tag is configured with the protocol type of tacacs+. With the following command

aaa-server tag_name protocol protocol_type

you can configure another AAA group tag, where the protocol_type is either tacacs+ or radius.

Next you need to tie one or more servers to the AAA group tag. You do so with the following command:

aaa-server tag_name (interface) host ip_address key_value timeout timeout_value

The (interface), key_value, and timeout timeout_value are optional parameters. The first server configured will be used first, and if that server is unreachable, then the firewall will use the second server configured, and so on, until all configured servers have been attempted. The AAA server must be reachable from the specified (interface) or from the inside interface if the interface parameter isn't specified. The default timeout is set to 10 seconds if the timeout parameter and value aren't specified. If the key_value isn't specified, the communications between the AAA server and the PIX Firewall will be unencrypted. The PIX Firewall will inform you of this fact when you enter the command without the key_value.

The following is an example of the aaa-server commands:

```
PIX(config)# aaa-server fred protocol tacacs+
PIX(config)# aaa-server fred host 10.109.2.3
no encryption key found. Using unencrypted mode.
PIX(config)# aaa-server RADIUS (dmz) host 10.108.3.4 abc123 timeout 20
PIX(config)# aaa-server RADIUS (inside) host 10.109.5.4 a1b2c3 timeout 10
PIX(config)#
```

For RADIUS servers, the PIX Firewall uses the old default TCP/UDP port numbers described in RFC 2058. These port numbers are 1645 for authentication and 1646 for accounting. Some newer RADIUS servers may use the port numbers 1812 for authentication and 1813 for accounting, as defined in RFC 2138 and RFC 2139. If your RADIUS server uses ports other than 1645 and 1646, then you need to define ports using the following command prior to starting the RADIUS service with the aaa-server command:

aaa-server radius-authport *number* and aaa-server radius-acctport *number*

> **NOTE** RFC 2058 has been updated to reflect that early deployment of RADIUS was done using the erroneously chosen port number 1645.

When you view the configuration now, you'll see that the PIX Firewall has filled in the defaults for the interface and timeout values. Here is an example with the irrelevant portions of the configuration removed:

```
PIX(config)# write term
Building configuration...
: Saved
:
PIX Version 6.2(2)
hostname PIX
aaa-server TACACS+ protocol tacacs+
aaa-server RADIUS protocol radius
aaa-server RADIUS (dmz) host 10.108.3.4 acb123 timeout 20
aaa-server RADIUS (inside) host 10.109.5.4 a1b2c3 timeout 10
aaa-server LOCAL protocol local
aaa-server fred protocol tacacs+
aaa-server fred (inside) host 10.109.2.3 timeout 10
PIX(config)#
```

Now that the AAA server has been installed and configured and the PIX Firewall has been configured to communicate with the AAA server, you must tell the firewall what to authenticate, authorize, or account with the AAA server(s).

Authentication

The PIX Firewall can be configured to authenticate certain inbound or outbound traffic through the firewall and also certain traffic terminating on the firewall itself. For authentication of inbound and outbound traffic through the firewall, you use this command:

aaa authentication include | exclude *authen_service* inbound |
➥ outbound | interface *local_ip local_mask foreign_ip foreign_mask* group_tag

The **include** parameter specifies which traffic is authenticated, and the **exclude** parameter excludes traffic that was previously included with the **include** command.

The *authen_service* is the application with which a user is accessing the network. The value can be any, ftp, http, or telnet. The any parameter enables authentication for all TCP services. To have users prompted for authentication credentials, they must use ftp, http, or telnet.

The inbound, outbound, or *interface* parameter specifies which direction the traffic to be authenticated will be traveling, or the interface from which to authenticate users. The *local_ip local_mask foreign_ip foreign_mask* is the pattern of the traffic to be authenticated. The address for *local_ip* is always on the highest security level interface, and *foreign_ip* is always on the lowest.

The *group_tag is* the previously configured AAA server(s) using the specified tag to use for user authentication.

Here is an example of a configuration to authenticate users from 10.109.0.1 through 10.109.0.254 using the default RADIUS group, with the host 10.109.0.24 not needing authentication:

```
PIX(config)# nat (inside) 1 10.109.0.0 255.255.255.0
PIX(config)# aaa authentication include any outbound 0 0 RADIUS
PIX(config)# aaa authentication exclude outbound 10.109.0.24
➥ 255.255.255.255 RADIUS any
PIX(config)#
```

Let's look at a second example where the firewall permits inbound access IP addresses 160.109.200.1 through 160.109.200.30 using all services permitted by the access-list command. The aaa authentication command permits authentication using ftp, http, or telnet, depending on what the authentication server handles. The authentication server is at IP address 10.12.16.2 on the inside interface. Here is the example:

```
PIX(config)# aaa-server AuthIn protocol tacacs+
PIX(config)# aaa-server AuthIn (inside) host 10.12.16.2 thisisakey timeout 20
PIX(config)# static (inside,outside) 160.109.200.0 10.12.16.0
➥ netmask 255.255.255.224
PIX(config)# access-list acl_out permit tcp 10.12.16.0 255.255.255.0
➥ 160.109.200.0 255.255.255.224
PIX(config)# access-group acl_out in interface outside
PIX(config)# aaa authentication include any inbound 0 0 AuthIn
PIX(config)#
```

In addition to authenticating traffic using AAA, the PIX Firewall can authenticate users who attempt to gain access to the firewall itself. The firewall can authenticate Telnet, SSH, and HTTP, and enable access to the firewall in addition to the physical serial console connection.

To authenticate access to the PIX Firewall, use this command:

```
aaa authentication [serial | enable | telnet | ssh | http] console group_tag
```

You still need to allow access to the firewall with the respective access commands before the authentication can take place. For example, you must use the `telnet` or `ssh` command before the `aaa authentication telnet console` *group_tag* or `aaa authentication ssh console` *group_tag* commands will work.

We need to discuss some default behaviors using authentication to the PIX Firewall. If an `aaa authentication` *service* `console` *group_tag* command statement isn't defined, you can gain access to the PIX Firewall with no username and the PIX Firewall enable password (set with the `password` command). If the `aaa` commands are defined but the authentication requests time out, which implies the AAA server might be down or not available, you can gain access to the PIX Firewall using the username `pix` and the enable password. By default, the enable password isn't set.

Authorization

Authorization can be accomplished only by using the TACACS+ protocol, because RADIUS authorization isn't supported on the PIX Firewall. One thing to note about authentication versus authorization is that the `aaa authorization` command requires a previously configured `aaa authentication` command. However, use of the `aaa authentication` command doesn't require the use of the `aaa authorization` command.

Once a user has been authenticated to access a service or group of services the PIX Firewall can separately authorize that user to use a service or group of services. The command used to ask the AAA server to authorize certain traffic is

```
aaa authorization include | exclude author_service inbound |
➥ outbound | interface local_ip local_mask foreign_ip foreign_mask group_tag
```

The `include` and `exclude` parameters are used in the same way as for the `authentication` command.

The *author_service* is the application with which a user is accessing the network. This values can be `any`, `ftp`, `http`, `telnet`, or *protocol/port*. The *protocol/port* parameter specifies a protocol, which is either a name (such as TCP or UDP) or a decimal value (6 for TCP, 17 for UDP, 1 for ICMP, and so on) followed by an optional port number. For ICMP, the port number is the ICMP message type instead of a port number.

The `inbound`, `outbound`, and *interface* parameters are used in the same way as for the `authentication` command, as are the *local_ip*, *local_mask*, *foreign_ip*, *foreign_mask*, and *group_tag* parameters.

The following example enables authorization for DNS lookups from the outside interface:

```
PIX(config)# aaa authorization include udp/53 inbound 0.0.0.0 0.0.0.0 TACACS+
PIX(config)#
```

You can also specify a range of ports for authorization. In this next example, we want to exclude all higher UDP ports from authentication:

```
PIX(config)# aaa authorization exclude udp/1024-65535 outbound
➥ 0.0.0.0 0.0.0.0 TACACS+
PIX(config)#
```

Another authorization that can be accomplished with TACACS+ is the use of command authorization. Each command entered at the PIX Firewall console can be sent to the AAA server for authorization. When we say *AAA server* in the context of command authorization, we'll referring to a TACACS+ server because this is the only server type capable of command authorization.

Command authorization can also be done locally, but you need to use the `privilege` command and assign individuals a certain privilege level to a local user with the `username` command and change those commands they should have access to their privilege level or below. Doing command authorization on the AAA server allows it to scale because making changes to each PIX Firewall would be tedious and error prone.

The command to use AAA for command authorization is

```
aaa authorization command tacacs_server_tag
```

> **NOTE:** Certain configuration tasks need to be performed on the TACACS+ server to accomplish command authorization, but they're beyond the scope of this book. For further information, refer to http://www.cisco.com/en/US/products/hw/vpndevc/ps2030/products_tech_note09186a00800949d6.shtml.

Accounting

The accounting aspect of AAA is one of the most useful when you want to keep an eye on what users are doing with either your web servers or your outbound traffic. The command syntax to enable accounting is similar to that for the `authentication` and `authorization` commands. The accounting command syntax is

```
aaa accounting include | exclude acctg_service inbound | outbound |
➥ interface local_ip local_mask foreign_ip foreign_mask group_tag
```

As with the `authorization` command, the `include` and `exclude` parameters are used to include or exclude traffic.

The *acctg_service* is the application with which a user is accessing the network. This value can be `any`, `ftp`, `http`, `telnet` or *protocol/port*. The *protocol/port* parameter specifies a protocol, which is either a name (such as TCP or UDP) or a decimal value (6 for TCP, 17 for UDP, and so on) followed by an optional port number.

The `inbound`, `outbound`, and *interface* parameters are used in the same way as used for the `authentication` and `authorization` commands, as are *local_ip*, *local_mask*, *foreign_ip*, *foreign_mask*, and *group_tag*.

The following is an example of using the `aaa accounting` command and sending the accounting information to the configured server(s) defined under the default RADIUS group tag for all outbound TCP traffic:

```
PIX(config)# aaa accounting include tcp outbound 0 0 0 0 RADIUS
PIX(config)#
```

Virtual HTTP and Telnet

When you're using the PIX Firewall aaa commands to authenticate web traffic, the command assumes the AAA server database is shared with the web server. The PIX Firewall automatically provides the AAA server and web server with the same information. You can get around this limitation by using the @ symbol in the username and password. The username to the left of the @ symbol is sent to the AAA server, and the username to the right of the @ symbol is sent to the remote server.

This is also true with the password: The one on the left of the @ symbol is the password for the AAA user, and the other is the password for the remote user. This works with both FTP and HTTP services. For example, if you're authenticating to an FTP server called fred on the protected side of a PIX Firewall, you would use the following username and password combination to authenticate to both:

```
C:\>ftp fred
Username: aaa-user@ftp-user
Password: aaa-pass@ftp-pass
230 User logged in, proceed.
ftp>
```

This sends the aaa-user and aaa-pass for authentication to the AAA server; if that is successful, it then sends ftp-user and ftp-pass to FTP server fred.

The PIX Firewall supports usernames up to 127 characters and passwords up to 63 characters. In addition, the username and password must not contain the @ symbol.

On the PIX Firewall, you can also use special virtual server commands. For example, the syntax of the virtual http command is as follows:

```
virtual http ip_address
```

This command has an optional warn parameter that is applicable only for text-based browsers where the redirect can't happen automatically.

The virtual http command works with the aaa command to authenticate the user (separating the AAA server information from the web client's URL request) and redirect the web client to the web server specified.

The virtual http command redirects the web browser's initial connection to the specified IP address, which resides in the PIX Firewall, authenticates the user, and then redirects the browser back to the URL that the user originally requested. For outbound use, the *ip_address* parameter must be an address routed to the PIX Firewall; and for inbound use, the *ip_address* must be an unused global address.

The following is an example of the virtual http command:

```
PIX(config)# static (inside,outside) 160.109.2.3 160.109.2.3 netmask
↪ 255.255.255.255
PIX(config)# access-list acl_out permit tcp any host 160.109.2.3 eq 80
PIX(config)# access-group acl_out in interface outside
```

```
PIX(config)# aaa authentication include any inbound 160.109.2.3
➥ 255.255.255.255 0 0 TACACS+
PIX(config)# virtual http 160.109.2.3
PIX(config)#
```

> **Tip:** Keep in mind that browsers cache username and passwords. If an HTTP session isn't timing out, the web browser might be sending the cached username and password back to the PIX Firewall and reauthenticating the session.

The `virtual telnet` command allows the Virtual Telnet server to provide a way to pre-authenticate users who require connections through the PIX Firewall using services or protocols that don't support authentication, such as streaming media connections. The following is the command syntax for the `virtual` commands:

```
PIX(config)# virtual telnet ?
Usage:  [no] virtual http ip [warn]
        [no] virtual telnet ip
PIX(config)# virtual telnet
```

You can use the `virtual telnet` command to log in and out of the PIX Firewall, which creates a cached entry in the firewall `uauth` table. When an unauthenticated user telnets to the virtual IP address, they're challenged for their username and password and then authenticated with the TACACS+ or RADIUS server. The user sees the message "Authentication Successful" once they're authenticated.

If the user wishes to log out and clear their entry in the PIX Firewall `uauth` table, the user can telnet to the virtual address. The user is again prompted for their username and password, the PIX Firewall removes the associated credentials from the `uauth` table, and the user gets the message "Logout Successful."

If inbound users on either the perimeter or outside interfaces need access to the Virtual Telnet server, a `static` and `access-list` command pair must accompany use of the `virtual telnet` command. The global IP address in the `static` command must be a real IP address, and the local address is the IP address of the virtual server.

The following is an example of the `virtual telnet` command:

```
PIX(config)# virtual telnet 160.109.201.65
PIX(config)# static (inside,outside) 160.109.201.65 160.109.201.65
➥ netmask 255.255.255.255
PIX(config)# access-list acl_out permit tcp any host 160.109.201.65 eq telnet
PIX(config)# access-group acl_out in interface outside
PIX(config)#
```

Here is an example of what a Virtual Telnet session would look like:

```
/bsd/host%telnet 160.109.201.65
Trying 160.109.201.65
Connected to 160.109.201.65
Escape character is '^]'.
Username: username
TACACS+ Password: password
Authentication Successful
Connection closed by foreign host.
/bsd/host%
```

The username and password are those for the user on the TACACS+ server.

Downloadable PIX ACLs

The Downloadable PIX ACLs feature enables you to enter an ACL once in a Cisco Secure ACS and then have many PIX Firewalls download that ACL when authenticating using the RADIUS protocol. This is more efficient than entering the ACL into each PIX Firewall. Also, when you need to change the ACL, you'll have to change it in only one place. You need to configure the PIX Firewall to authenticate using only the RADIUS protocol, since it's the only protocol that supports this feature.

To configure an ACL on the Cisco Secure ACS, you must enter each PIX ACL command on a separate line. The downloadable PIX ACLs aren't limited in size, but because this feature uses the standard RADIUS Cisco AV-pairs, you can have a maximum of 4KB. When you're entering the ACL using the HTML ACS interface, don't use the access-list keyword or name, but enter the rest of the command as if you were typing at the PIX Firewall CLI. Here is an example of what your ACL should look like:

```
permit tcp any host 121.30.200.254
permit udp any host 121.30.200.254
permit icmp any host 121.30.200.254
permit tcp any host 121.30.200.253
```

The Cisco Secure ACS can back up all the ACLs entered, or it can replicate that data to another ACS box. You can attach the ACL to an ACS user or group profile once you've configured the ACL as a named shared profile component. When the Cisco Secure ACS returns an attribute with a named ACL as part of the RADIUS access accept packet, the PIX Firewall applies the ACL to the user's session. The Cisco Secure ACS includes a versioning stamp as part of the transaction to make sure the PIX Firewall has cached the latest version of the ACL. If a PIX Firewall responds and doesn't have the current version of the ACL, the Cisco Secure ACS automatically uploads the updated ACL to the PIX Firewall.

To enter a downloadable PIX ACL to the ACS, log in to the ACS server and follow these steps:

1. In the navigation bar, click Shared Profile Components.
2. Click Downloadable PIX ACLs.
3. Click Add, which makes the Downloadable PIX ACLs page appear.
4. In the Name box of the Downloadable PIX ACLs, enter the name of the PIX ACL. This must be unique.
5. In the Description box, you can optionally enter a description.
6. In the ACL Definitions box, enter each line of the PIX ACL in the format that we discussed earlier.
7. When you've completed specifying the PIX ACL, click Submit.

These changes take effect immediately, and the ACL is available to be sent to any PIX Firewall that is attempting to authenticate a user who has the ACL name attached to their user or group profile.

To assign a downloadable PIX ACL to a user account, navigate to the user account and click on the Assign PIX ACL box. Then, select one from the list of previously configured PIX ACLs, and click Submit.

To assign a downloadable PIX ACL to a group profile, you need to edit the setting of the group. At the top of the page, in the Jump To list, click Downloadable ACLs. Select the Assign PIX ACL check box, select one from the list of configured PIX ACLs, and click Submit.

Summary

In this chapter, we explained access-control techniques for the PIX Firewall and how to implement URL filtering using both Websense and N2H2 server types. We introduced you to the new PPPoE client and how to configure the PIX Firewall to work in conjunction with an ISP using a PPPoE server.

Then, we described how the PIX Firewall processes ACLs. You learned that PIX Firewall ACLs affect only traffic inbound to the PIX Firewall on a given interface. Therefore, `access-list` statements must be bound to the inside and outside interfaces to control bidirectional traffic. Next, we discussed object groups and how they can make your configuration easier to read and update.

We discussed the AAA concept and how to install and configure the CSNT server. Then we talked about how to implement AAA services on the PIX Firewall. Finally, we discussed downloadable PIX ACLs and how they can save you configuration time.

Exam Essentials

Remember the syntax PIX operating system ACLs. Know how to apply the ACLs to the desired interfaces and in the proper direction.

Understand what URL filtering does and how it works. Be able to describe the flow of information between the PIX Firewall plug-in and the URL server. Know how to configure the PIX Firewall to support URL filtering for both Websense and N2H2 servers.

Be able to configure the PPPoE client. Know the commands used to set up the PPPoE client authentication type, username, and groups. Also know how to enable the PPPoE client using both static and dynamic IP addressing.

Understand object groups. Be able to tell why you should use object groups and the different types of object groups. Know when you can nest object groups and when you're in Object Group Configuration mode.

Know how to install and configure CSNT. Be able to install and configure the Cisco Secure Access Control Server for Windows 2000/NT. This includes the options for external authentication including Windows NT, Novell NetWare NDS, LDAP, and any OBDC database.

Be able to configure AAA services for the PIX Firewall. Know which AAA services are available for the PIX firewall and how to configure both traffic-based AAA services in addition to AAA services that terminate on the firewall.

Know how to configure downloadable PIX ACLs. Know what a downloadable PIX ACL is and why you would want to use one. Also know how to configure the PIX Firewall and ACS for downloadable PIX ACLs.

Chapter 13

Advanced Protocol Handling, Attack Guards, and Intrusion Detection

THE FOLLOWING TOPICS ARE COVERED IN THIS CHAPTER:

- ✓ Configuring advanced protocol support on the PIX Firewall
- ✓ PIX Firewall support of multimedia applications
- ✓ Overview of attack guards and how to configure them
- ✓ Using intrusion detection on the PIX Firewall

When we defined firewalls back in Chapter 10, "PIX Firewall Basics," we said that three academic distinctions define a firewall as an application proxy, a packet-filtering firewall, or a stateful firewall. Although most firewalls are primarily one type or another, in actual implementation, they usually have some features from all three categories. This is certainly the case for the Cisco Secure PIX Firewall.

You saw in the previous two chapters that the PIX Firewall is primarily a stateful firewall. In this chapter, we look at some features of the PIX Firewall that are an interesting mix of application proxy and stateful filtering.

In the first part of this chapter, we'll discuss some hoops the PIX Firewall needs to jump through to make several popular, but poorly designed, protocols operate. In the second part, we'll discuss an opposite goal: how to keep undesired features of certain protocols from working. In the last part, we'll discuss how the PIX Firewall uses a scaled-down version of the Cisco Intrusion Detection System (IDS) and how you can quickly stop an attack in progress by using the shun command.

Advanced Protocol Handling

Unfortunately, not all protocols are as simple and straightforward as Telnet and HTTP. Many protocol designers feel the need to use multiple ports at the same time or, worse, to embed their protocol in other protocols in an attempt to escape the detection of corporate firewalls. These and other nonstandard behaviors make a stateful firewall's job much more difficult because the firewall must be programmed to understand how such problem protocols operate.

For instance, the firewall needs to know when to expect a new TCP connection to be opened and which source and destination ports the server and client will use, because these nonstandard or random high ports are blocked by default. The only alternative to programming the firewall to deal with each specific problem protocol is to change your entire security policy so that you permit everything by default and deny only specific traffic that you don't want. Obviously, this isn't an acceptable solution for most organizations.

The special programming required for each protocol isn't the only downside of advanced protocol handling. For each of these protocols, the PIX Firewall must look deep into the packet, all the way to the Application layer, to find the information it needs for the Adaptive Security

Algorithm (ASA) to process the special protocol. But even though an obligatory performance loss is associated with this processing, the PIX Firewall does a good job of minimizing it, particularly relative to firewalls that are primarily application proxies.

> **Note:** In this chapter, we explain several protocols in some detail. Although it's unlikely you'll see individual protocols covered on the test at this level, it's nevertheless critical that you understand these protocols if you intend to pursue a career in network security.

Special Protocol Support Basics

For the PIX Firewall to know which set of rules to apply to a given conversation, you need to tell it which protocol is being used. You accomplish this in the PIX Firewall operating system command line by associating a Transmission Control Protocol (TCP) or User Datagram Protocol (UDP) port number with the name of the protocol, using a keyword. This keyword is different for each type of protocol supported on the PIX Firewall. We'll now look at the rules regarding the advanced protocol support and how to configure it using the `fixup protocol` command.

Advanced Protocol Support Rules

It's important to remember these two rules when you're configuring advanced protocol support:

Advanced protocol support is enabled on a per-protocol basis. It's possible to enable support for one protocol, such as File Transfer Protocol (FTP), and disable it for another, such as RealTime Streaming Protocol (RTSP).

Advanced protocol support is configured globally. It isn't configured on a per-interface basis. For example, you can't define port 10000 as FTP only on `ethernet3` and port 20000 as FTP only on `ethernet2`. You can define both ports 10000 and 20000 as FTP, but this assignment will apply to all interfaces on the PIX Firewall. Or you can disable FTP support entirely, which will disable it for all interfaces on the PIX Firewall.

> **Note:** If you didn't know already, you might have gathered from this discussion that there is nothing magical about port numbers. In fact, they are assigned arbitrarily. The port numbers with which you're familiar, such as DNS on port 53 and HTTP on port 80, are assigned by the Internet Assigned Number Authority (www.iana.org); but technically, it's possible to use almost any port between 1 and 65535 for any service. For most Unix and Linux operating systems, these numbers are defined in the /etc/services file, but they can be easily changed.

The *fixup protocol* Command

You use the `fixup protocol` command to invoke the special protocol handling. The syntax for the `fixup protocol` command is as follows:

```
PIX(config)# fixup ?
usage: [no] fixup protocol prot [option]
  port [-port]
PIX(config)# fixup
```

To see the advanced protocol support enabled by default, you can use the `show fixup` command or the `write terminal` command (because the information is also listed in the configuration file). The following is the output of the `show fixup` command as of version 6.2 of the PIX Firewall:

```
PIX# show fixup
fixup protocol ftp 21
fixup protocol http 80
fixup protocol h323 h225 1720
fixup protocol h323 ras 1718-1719
fixup protocol ils 389
fixup protocol rsh 514
fixup protocol rstp 554
fixup protocol smtp 25
fixup protocol sqlnet 1521
fixup protocol sip 5060
fixup protocol skinny 2000
PIX#
```

One of the advantages of the `fixup protocol` syntax is its flexibility. For instance, you can assign multiple ports to a protocol, as shown here:

```
PIX# conf t
PIX(config)# fixup protocol ftp 10000
PIX(config)# exit
PIX# show fixup
fixup protocol ftp 21
fixup protocol http 80
fixup protocol h323 h225 1720
fixup protocol h232 ras 1718-1719
fixup protocol ils 389
fixup protocol rsh 514
fixup protocol rstp 554
fixup protocol smtp 25
fixup protocol sqlnet 1521
```

```
fixup protocol sip 5060
fixup protocol skinny 2000
fixup protocol ftp 10000
PIX#
```

It's common for host administrators to attempt to elude port scans by configuring services on nonstandard ports. For instance, if you administer a system with a web interface, you might set the web server on that device to use port 40080 instead of port 80. If this is the only inbound web connection you're expecting, you need to first delete the default connection by typing no `fixup protocol http 80`, and then configure the new port with the command `fixup protocol http 40080`.

It's also possible to configure a range of ports, as in `fixup protocol http 8000-8080`. This might be necessary to connect to some management applications. The Cisco Secure Access Control Server (ACS) product, for example, assigns a random port after connection.

Note that if you disable support for a protocol, it doesn't mean the protocol will be denied. For instance, if you created an access control list (ACL) that allowed all IP traffic from any source to any destination, and then typed no `fixup protocol ftp 21`, your client's FTP traffic would be allowed to flow freely through the PIX Firewall. But if you're going to have a policy like that, there's no real point in having a firewall. Conversely, enabling support doesn't mean that a protocol will be accepted. You still must create the appropriate translation and connection slots and `access-list` statements.

The benefit of the `fixup protocol` command is that you can have a restrictive policy and use a problem protocol at the same time. The `fixup protocol` command configuration provides instructions for the PIX Firewall on how to look inside each packet for information about ports that might be changing. Without this, the PIX Firewall doesn't know how to read the HTTP or FTP instructions saying that the connection should use a different port number. It also doesn't know how to allow the new traffic in.

Now that you have a basic grasp of the commands, in the next sections, we'll look at a few of these misbehaving protocols in some detail. We'll cover some of the more popular ones: FTP, RSH, SQL*Net, RTSP, and H.323. If you encounter a protocol that isn't on this list, check Cisco's website to see if it's supported. If it isn't, you might need to use an alternative solution. We'll discuss a few of these in the "Alternative Solutions to Problem Protocols" section, later in the chapter.

File Transfer Protocol

File Transfer Protocol (FTP) is certainly one of the most widely-used protocols. As its name indicates, its purpose is transporting files from one host to another.

FTP follows the client/server model, where one host (the server) runs a program that listens for connection requests from other hosts (clients) on port TCP 21, by default. When a client initiates a TCP connection to port TCP 21 on the server, with a high port as the source port (this typically starts with port 1025 and goes up as additional connections are made), and finishes the three-way handshake, the listener program (`inetd` in Unix) starts the FTP server service. In Unix-land, this is typically a daemon called `ftpd`. The `ftpd` daemon and the client can now talk to each other over the TCP connection. As you use the FTP client to navigate through directories, the traffic, such as lists of files and directories, is sent to and from TCP port 21 on the server, which is also known as *FTP command* or *FTP control*.

So far, FTP is behaving just like any other TCP-based application, and configuring a firewall rule via an ACL would be a walk in the park. However, once your client issues the GET command to download a file, FTP does something unusual. Your client begins listening on the next available high port (such as TCP 1026) and sends the PORT 1026 command to the server (this command is still sent over the existing connection to port 21). This command instructs the server to initiate a TCP connection for the actual file data to port TCP 1026 on the client, and from port TCP 20 on the server. TCP port 20 is also known as *FTP data*.

In theory, this architecture allows someone to continue issuing commands to TCP port 21 while simultaneously receiving the data from TCP port 20. However, this poses a huge problem for firewall administrators: Any inbound connections to clients are frowned upon. From a security point of view, you don't want any devices on an untrusted network initiating TCP connections to clients on your internal network. But it gets worse: Because the FTP protocol allows the destination port for the FTP-data connection to the client to be any random high port, the firewall administrator would need to open all high ports for FTP to work!

To solve this problem, you can use Active-mode FTP (the PIX Firewall default) or Passive-mode FTP. We'll look at these two modes, at using ACLs for packet-filtering FTP, and at setting some restrictions to provide a more secure FTP in the next sections.

> Another method for handing FTP would be to write an FTP client program that allowed the user to specify a port for the FTP-data connection. You could then configure your firewall to allow inbound connections on only this TCP port. Unfortunately, that feature isn't included in the common FTP clients in use today. Furthermore, it would leave computers unnecessarily vulnerable because that port would remain open 24 hours per day on the firewall even when you weren't currently using the connection.

Using Active-Mode FTP

The solution the PIX Firewall employs is to listen to the entire FTP transfer conversation on the FTP-control port. This is called *Active-mode FTP*, which occurs with the default `fixup protocol ftp` command:

```
PIX(config)# fixup protocol ftp 21
PIX(config)#
```

When the PIX Firewall sees the PORT *TCP port number* command sent across the network, it automatically allows the corresponding inbound connection. Of course, the source and destination IP addresses must be the same, and the destination TCP port must be the same port specified in the PORT command that the PIX Firewall intercepted.

Using Passive-Mode FTP

Since many organizations use firewalls that aren't as intelligent as the PIX Firewall, a workaround in the protocol was necessary. This is commonly known as *Passive-mode FTP*.

In Passive-mode FTP, the control session is set up just as it is in Active mode. The client initiates a connection to port 21 (typically) on the server. However, when it's time to open a data session, instead of sending the PORT command, the client sends a PASV command to the server. If the server supports Passive mode, it opens a random port of its own and responds with a PORT command to the client, which includes the number of the TCP port it just opened. Finally, the client initiates the FTP-data session to the random port on the server, as instructed by the PORT command.

Since this process is a little bizarre, we'll illustrate it with an example. Suppose a client, 10.1.1.100, decides to download a file via FTP from a server 10.1.2.200. Here is the sequence of messages and connections for this transfer:

1. The server begins listening on port 21.
2. The client opens port 10.1.1.100:1025 and establishes an FTP-control connection to TCP port 10.1.2.200:21.
3. The client sends a PASV command to the FTP server over the existing TCP session.
4. The server begins listening on port 1025.
5. The server sends a PORT 1025 message to the client across an existing TCP session.
6. The client opens port 10.1.1.100:1026 and establishes an FTP-data connection to TCP port 10.1.2.200:1025.

ACLs for Packet-Filtering FTP

Although the `fixup protocol` command on the PIX Firewall handles Passive-mode and Active-mode FTP nicely, when your firewall consists of packet-filtering ACLs and isn't stateful, you need to pay attention to the type of FTP your clients are using. This is because the ACLs must be built differently.

For Active-mode FTP, the safest (most restrictive) policy you can set without breaking the protocol is to allow outbound traffic to port 21, create another rule for inbound traffic that uses the `established` keyword to allow the return traffic back in, then allow inbound traffic to random high ports (TCP 1024 through 65535), and, again, use another rule with the `established` keyword for the return traffic.

For Passive-mode FTP, you allow connections to be initiated outbound to ports TCP 21 and anything in the range of 1025 through 65535. Again, create similar rules for inbound traffic using the `established` keyword.

> Fortunately, many common FTP servers allow you to specify the range of ports used for passive connections. If your server is configurable, set this range to something other than the default. The range should be as small as possible but still adequate for the number of anticipated simultaneous connections. This allows your corresponding firewall rules to be as restrictive as possible.

Setting FTP Restrictions

The `fixup protocol ftp` command does more than just allow the session to operate. It also inspects the FTP commands that are sent across the FTP-control session to ensure they're valid. As an administrator, you have the option of making this more restrictive by using the `strict` keyword at the end of the `fixup protocol ftp` command. The `strict` keyword adds two restrictions:

- It prevents web browsers from sending embedded commands in FTP requests.
- It limits the server so that it can generate only a 227 command. The client is also restricted so that it can generate only a `PORT` command.

Remote Shell

Remote Shell (RSH) is one of a group of Unix programs collectively referred to as the *r commands*, written long ago by folks at Berkeley. This group includes programs such as rlogin, rexec, rwho, rcp (remote copy), and more. The RSH protocol is used to open a shell on a remote computer. This shell can be used to execute commands and return the output to the local computer.

When the r commands were written, security wasn't an issue. Therefore, RSH doesn't even require you to log on to execute the commands on the remote host. These commands do include an authentication method, but it's so easily bypassed that the r commands have been almost totally replaced by *s commands*. RSH has been replaced by Secure Shell (SSH). Nevertheless, the PIX Firewall includes support for this aging command.

The specific support required is much like that of FTP. The RSH command uses what Berkeley refers to as *back-channel connections*. Just as your FTP commands travel over one TCP connection and your data travels over another, RSH's `stdin` and `stdout` traffic goes over the primary TCP connection, but the RSH server (which is typically a daemon named rshd) initiates a separate TCP session to return `stderr` traffic to the client.

> **NOTE** `stdin` (standard in), `stdout` (standard out), and `stderr` (standard error) are components of the Unix operating system that are related to libraries in the C programming language. I cover these here for completeness, but you don't need to know this for the test.

The primary connection for RSH uses TCP port 514 by default. This default can't be changed, but you can add other ports. Support for RSH on the PIX Firewall is enabled with the `fixup protocol rsh` command, as follows:

```
PIX(config)# fixup protocol rsh 514
PIX(config)#
```

SQL*Net

*SQL*Net* is a complex protocol used by Oracle to transfer data between database clients and servers. At a high level, this protocol is responsible for initiating and closing connections and allows both synchronous and asynchronous data transfer. The SQL*Net protocol is based on *Transparent Network Substrate* (TNS).

Oracle database servers handle incoming connections in an odd and complicated fashion, which is described in part as follows:

1. The server starts by pre-spawning a lot of server processes in anticipation of the connections. These server processes listen on different wildcard addresses.
2. The server starts a special listener, which listens on a well-known address.
3. When a client finally initiates a connection to the database, the special listener receives and authenticates the connection.
4. If the client is accepted, the special listener sends a redirect message to the client, containing the address of one of the pre-spawned server processes.
5. The client closes its connection to the special listener.
6. The client takes the address it received from the special listener in the redirect message and initiates another connection.
7. The database server pre-spawns another service to replace the one the client is using. The Oracle server keeps several services ready to receive connections in case a lot of connection requests come in at the same time. This prevents lag as a result of the time it takes to create a new process.

As you can see in this sequence, the client begins the conversation on a well-known port and is quickly redirected to use a different and, for practical purposes, random port. This makes it difficult to create simple packet-filtering rules—not even Cisco routers have psychic abilities to predict the ports you'll use.

The PIX Firewall, however, is capable of sifting through the Application layer of the redirect message and picking out the port that will be used. Based on this information, it can temporarily allow packets with the specific source and destination sockets seen in the initial request and the redirect message.

Support for SQL*Net on the PIX Firewall is enabled with the `fixup protocol sqlnet` command, as follows:

```
PIX(config)# fixup protocol sqlnet 1521
PIX(config)#
```

> **WARNING** In addition to being a badly-behaved protocol, SQL*Net doesn't even use the right port! According to IANA, Oracle's `orasrv` protocol belongs on port 1525. Since Oracle is using port 1521, which rightfully belongs to nCube, the PIX Firewall also uses port 1521 as a default. So if you happen to use nCube, you might need to disable the default command.

Multimedia Support

So far, you've seen how older and relatively simple protocols such as FTP, RSH, and SQL*Net cause problems for firewalls by opening multiple connections either inbound or outbound. When it comes to problem multimedia protocols, support becomes a little more challenging. As you work with many newer protocols, you might notice a disturbing trend in complexity. We hope that the recent focus on security in the technical world will result in new protocols that are full-featured, but not at the expense of security.

In the following sections, we'll look at two of these problem protocols. You'll see how the PIX Firewall supports the RTSP protocol and H.323 multimedia applications.

Real-Time Streaming Protocol

Real-Time Streaming Protocol (RTSP) is similar to the Real-Time Transport Protocol (RTP). RTP is primarily used for Voice over IP (VoIP). RTSP is designed especially for streaming media and is used by Cisco's IP/TV, Apple's QuickTime, RealPlayer, RealAudio, and RealNetworks. RTSP is designed for large-scale use, where a few high-speed servers stream a lot of traffic to a lot of clients at a lot of remote locations. The protocol allows clients to use special features, including pausing, rewinding, and fast-forwarding the stream. RTSP was defined in 1998 using RFC 2326.

RTSP is challenging because it has several different modes of operation. RTSP itself is a control protocol like RTP Control Protocol (RTCP). Both RTSP and RTCP are part of the RTP suite. This means the RTSP session was designed to pass commands, much like the FTP-control session. However, the data can be passed in several different channels. The following are some of the more common methods:

- Interleaving the data with the commands in the actual RTSP session (that is, using the same TCP connection)
- Creating a separate TCP session to carry the data
- Creating a separate UDP session to carry the data
- Tunneling the data through an HTTP session
- Using RTP to carry the data

RTSP can use almost any protocol to carry the data. For instance, RealServers use one of two methods: RTP or their own proprietary protocol, Real Data Transport (RDT).

Needless to say, it's impossible to maintain any semblance of security with a mere packet-filtering router when RTSP is a requirement. Not only would you need to open all the TCP ports, but you would need to open all the UDP ports as well!

Fortunately, the PIX Firewall's `fixup protocol` command allows you to mine the application data from the control session so that you can intelligently open only the necessary ports for the data-transport session. RTSP support is the first one that we've mentioned that isn't turned on by default for older versions of the PIX Firewall operating system. It's now enabled for newer versions. To enable this support, use the `fixup protocol rtsp` command:

```
PIX(config)# fixup protocol rtsp 554
PIX(config)#
```

When you're working with RTSP, the port used depends entirely on the application. Unfortunately, this command comes with a lot of caveats. The following is true of the PIX Firewall's support of RTSP (according to Cisco's *Command Reference*):

- The PIX Firewall won't fix any RTSP messages that pass through UDP ports.
- The PIX Firewall doesn't support the RealNetwork's Multicast mode (`x-real-rdt/mcast`).
- Port Address Translation (PAT) isn't supported with RTSP `fixup` support.
- The PIX Firewall can't recognize RTSP messages hidden in HTTP messages (HTTP *cloaking*).

In the following sections, we'll discuss how to support RTSP while using NAT, how to configure your RealPlayer to support RTSP, and how to support Cisco's IP/TV through the PIX Firewall.

> **Note:** The following information regarding how RTSP works with NAT and RealPlayer is based on material in Cisco's *Command Reference*.

RTSP and NAT

The PIX Firewall can't perform NAT on RTSP messages because the embedded IP addresses are contained in the Session Description Protocol (SDP) files as part of HTTP or RTSP messages. Packets could be fragmented, and PIX Firewall can't perform NAT on fragmented packets.

You can configure NAT for Apple QuickTime 4 or RealPlayer. Cisco IP/TV works with NAT only if the Viewer and Content Manager are on the outside network and the server is on the inside network. With Cisco IP/TV, the number of NATs the PIX Firewall performs on the SDP part of the message is proportional to the number of program listings in the Content Manager (each program listing can have at least six embedded IP addresses).

RTSP and RealPlayer

To configure PIX Firewall support for RealPlayer, use an `access-list` statement from the server to the client, or vice versa. You don't need to use a `fixup protocol rtsp` command if you're using TCP mode on RealPlayer. If you're using UDP mode, you need to use a `fixup protocol rtsp` *port* command.

In RealPlayer, you need to change the Transport mode (by selecting Options ≻ Preferences ≻ Transport ≻ RTSP Settings). For both TCP mode and UDP mode on RealPlayer, select the Use TCP To Connect To Server option. For TCP mode, select the Attempt To Use TCP For All Content check box. For UDP mode, and for live content not available via multicast, select the Attempt To Use UDP For Static Content check box.

RTSP and Cisco's IP/TV

Cisco's IP/TV uses the RTSP protocol on port 554 and port 8554. Therefore, you must enter two commands to support Cisco's IP/TV through a PIX Firewall:

```
PIX(config)# fixup protocol rtsp 554
PIX(config)# fixup protocol rtsp 8554
PIX(config)#
```

H.323

Unlike RTSP, H.323 is a conferencing protocol, designed for a moderate to small number of multimedia users in a peer-to-peer fashion. It's frequently referred to as an *umbrella protocol* because a large number of related protocols are included in H.323, and it's convenient to speak of them collectively as simply "H dot three twenty-three."

The `fixup protocol h323 h225 1720` and `fixup protocol h323 ras 1718-1719` commands, which are enabled by default, are used by applications such as CUseeMe and Microsoft's NetMeeting, as well as by Cisco's IP phones and telephony servers. However, these commands provide a different service than the previous examples of `fixup protocol` commands. According to the PIX Firewall *Command Reference,* the `fixup protocol h323` command allows the PIX Firewall to provide faster call setup (or more correctly, to not inhibit faster call setup) by supporting Fast Connect or Fast Start Procedure. It also allows H.245 tunneling.

Since version 6.2, the PIX Firewall supports PAT for the H.323 protocol. Prior to version 6.2, there was only one default `fixup` command for H.323. If you're viewing a PIX Firewall configuration and the only H.323 command is `fixup protocol h323 1720`, then you should know that this is the default command prior to version 6.2.

Alternative Solutions to Problem Protocols

Occasionally, you'll implement a bleeding-edge technology that has an unpredictable effect on your network. After doing your due diligence on Cisco's website and other support avenues, you might come to the conclusion that your PIX Firewall simply won't support this new application. In this case, there are a few alternatives or workarounds you can use, although none of them are particularly elegant.

One example of a workaround is to use a combination of policy routing and encapsulation. If you have Cisco IOS routers on either side of the PIX Firewall, you can use the following approach:

1. Identify the problem traffic as narrowly as possible with ACLs.
2. Create a VPN tunnel between the two routers, which passes through the PIX Firewall. IPinIP or Generic Routing Encapsulation (GRE) works well for this situation.
3. Use policy routing to direct the traffic matching your ACL through the VPN tunnel to the other router.

You'll need to design this setup carefully, to make sure you don't create routing loops, break your NAT or default routing, or introduce other problems. You also need to allow the IPinIP or GRE tunnels through the PIX Firewall with an ACL.

This solution is inherently less secure, because any traffic that goes through the tunnel will be allowed through the firewall. Therefore, if someone compromises the router and changes the ACL, your network is wide open. It's also worth noting that the logging utility on your PIX Firewall and any other devices, such as your intrusion detection system (IDS), are now blindfolded.

Other alternative solutions are limited only by your imagination, but keep in mind that you should make every attempt to use the ASA where possible and to keep your solutions scalable and manageable.

Attack Guards

Not only does the PIX Firewall solve several bona fide application issues with its `fixup protocol` command, but it also has a few features designed to keep attackers from exploiting applications, commonly called *attack guards*.

The PIX Firewall attack guards are diverse. Some operate at the Application layer, filtering undesirable commands and requests. Others operate at the lower layers of the OSI model to make sure packets are correctly formed. Some even work to protect the PIX Firewall's own subsystems. In any case, they all change the PIX Firewall's behavior. Sometimes you'll want these features enabled, and other times you'll want them disabled, so the PIX Firewall operating system allows you to toggle them on and off.

The following sections describe the AAA Flood Guard, SYN Flood Guard, Mail Guard, IP Fragmentation Guard, and DNS Guard features.

AAA Flood Guard

The *AAA Flood Guard* feature is one of the simpler guards. Its goal is to watch the PIX Firewall's uauth subsystem, which handles user authentication and helps optimize authentication, authorization, and accounting (AAA) system resource utilization. You should remember the uauth subsystem from the previous chapter, when we discussed AAA services on the PIX Firewall. Under normal circumstances, users establish a TCP connection from their node to the PIX Firewall to pass authentication information, such as usernames and passwords, to the PIX Firewall. Of course, this TCP connection starts with the famous three-way handshake.

The vulnerability here is that all hosts can support only a finite number of TCP connections and an even smaller number of connections that are in an *embryonic state*. A connection made in the embryonic state is made between the first and third part of the TCP handshake. This limitation is a function of the TCP/IP protocol stack, which is usually part of the operating system or a driver. It doesn't depend on hardware. In other words, a fast computer with loads of memory is just as vulnerable as a slow computer.

To exploit this weakness, attackers will often flood a service with requests. Attackers can generate thousands of bogus authentication requests per second, but the trick is not getting caught. After all, it's not hard to read a log and find the source IP address and trace it to the owner. As a result, most floods use bogus or spoofed source IP addresses, which can't be easily tracked. But that gives the target another problem: When the PIX Firewall receives the SYN packet, which is the first part of the TCP three-way handshake, it responds immediately with the second part, which is the SYN ACK. However, it sends the SYN ACK packet to the bogus IP address. For this reason, the attacker never receives a response and never finishes the third part of the handshake, the final ACK. This means the PIX Firewall never receives the ACK, and this connection never leaves the embryonic state.

The easily recognizable symptom of an AAA flood attack, commonly called a *SYN flood*, is a large number of TCP connections in an embryonic state. This is why the AAA Flood Guard process watches the uauth subsystem. When it detects this condition, the AAA Flood Guard immediately sets about freeing up the system resources. It closes TCP connections in the following order:

- Timewait
- Finwait
- Embryonic
- Idle

AAA Flood Guard is enabled by default. You can turn it off and on with the `floodguard` command, which has the following syntax:

```
floodguard enable | disable
```

For troubleshooting and management, the `show` and `clear` commands are also useful:

```
show floodguard
clear floodguard
```

It's important to note that the `floodguard` command protects only the PIX Firewall itself. The PIX Firewall can provide protection for other hosts against SYN floods. In the next section, we'll discuss the SYN Flood Guard that is used to protect other hosts from a SYN flood attack.

SYN Flood Guard

To protect hosts on the internal networks against a SYN DoS attack, the PIX Firewall can be configured to limit the number of embryonic connections allowed to the internal host using the *SYN Flood Guard*. Setting the maximum embryonic connections in the `nat` and `static` commands controls this type of protection, which is also called *TCP Intercept*. Let's review the syntax of these commands.

```
PIX(config)# static ?
Usage:  [no] static [(internal_if_name, external_if_name)] {global_ip|interface}
local_ip [dns] [netmask mask] [max_conns [emb_limit [norandomseq]]]
        [no] static [(internal_if_name, external_if_name)] {tcp|udp} {global_
ip|interface} global_port local_ip local_port [dns] [netmask mask] [max_conns
[emb_limit [norandomseq]]]
PIX(config)# static
```

and

```
PIX(config)# nat ?
Usage:  [no] nat [(if_name)] nat_id local_ip [mask [dns] [outside]
➥[max_conns [emb_limit [norandomseq]]]]
        [no] nat [(if_name)] 0 [access-list acl-name [outside]]
PIX(config)# nat
```

As you can see, each of these commands has an *emb_limit* parameter that can be set. Once this embryonic connection limit's reached, and until the number of connections falls below this threshold, every SYN packet bound for the internal host is intercepted. While it's intercepting these packets, the PIX Firewall responds on behalf of the internal host by sending an empty SYN/ACK packet back to the sender. The PIX Firewall then keeps some state information about the connection attempt, drops the packet, and waits for the sender's acknowledgment.

If the ACK is received from the sender, the PIX Firewall uses the retained state information to send a SYN packet to the internal host. The three-way handshake happens between the PIX Firewall and the internal host. Once the handshake completes, the PIX Firewall allows the normal connection to resume between the sender and internal host.

This feature was enhanced in version 5.2 of the PIX Firewall operating system. Before this version, the PIX Firewall just dropped any new connections once the embryonic connection limit was reached. This could allow even a modest attack to stop traffic to a company's web server and make it unavailable to the outside world.

Mail Guard

Mail Guard is an example of a guard that inspects Application layer traffic. Not only does it make decisions about whether to allow a packet through based on this application data, but it also has the ability to rewrite certain data.

Mail Guard is an excellent feature, but it does have its drawbacks. In 1982, Jon Postel wrote RFC 821: Simple Mail Transfer Protocol (SMTP). This protocol defined several four-letter commands that form the basis of today's e-mail. However, we've made a lot of progress since then. In the name of security, Mail Guard ignores two decades of enhancements and takes us all the way back to RFC 821; even then, it allows only a subset of the commands originally specified. The commands allowed by Mail Guard are listed in Table 13.1.

TABLE 13.1 Commands Allowed by Mail Guard

Command	Function
EHLO, HELO	Identifies the sender
MAIL	Initiates the mail transaction
RCPT	Identifies the recipient
DATA	Contains the text of the mail message
RSET	Aborts the current mail message
NOOP	Instructs the receiver to send an OK reply
QUIT	Instructs the receiver to send an OK reply and terminate the session

> ### 🌐 Real World Scenario
>
> #### Gathering Information from SMTP Servers
>
> Let's look at some examples of the way different mail servers behave and how the PIX Firewall's Mail Guard feature protects you. We'll telnet to a few real-world mail servers and show the output. We won't do anything illegal or immoral; we'll just use a manual way of doing what Outlook Express does every time you check your mail. The manual way allows us to view the program's output.
>
> First, let's look at the ever-popular and often-abused www.msn.com. We begin by using nslookup, setting TYPE=MX, and then finding www.msn.com. Once we have the IP address, we issue the command telnet *xxx.xxx.xxx.xxx 25*, which establishes a TCP session between our Telnet program and the SMTP service on one of MSN's mail servers:
>
> ```
> C:\> telnet xxx.xxx.xxx.xxx 25
> 220 cpimssmtpa29.msn.com Microsoft ESMTP MAIL Service,
>    Version: 5.0.2195.3972 r
> ady at  Mon, 5 Nov 2001 19:42:25 -0800
> NOOP
> 250 2.0.0 OK
> VRFY joe
> 252 2.1.5 Cannot VRFY user, but will accept message
>    for joe@msn.com
> HELP
> 214-This server supports the following commands:
> 214 HELO EHLO STARTTLS RCPT DATA RSET MAIL QUIT HELP BDAT
> QUIT
> 221 2.0.0 cpimssmtpa29.msn.com Service closing transmission
>    channel
> Connection to host lost.
> C:\>
> ```
>
> We're immediately greeted with a lot of information, including the hostname (which verifies we are where we think we are), the name of the service, the version (which makes it easy to look up its vulnerabilities), and the date and time. The -0800 time zone information also gives us a good idea where the server is physically, assuming we know where the company has data centers.
>
> Next, we issue the NOOP command and receive the 2.0.0 OK. Then we attempt to verify that user joe exists. Fortunately, MSN's server doesn't give this information away, but many mail servers still do. The HELP command tells us quite a bit about what we can and can't do here. Finally, we terminate the session with the QUIT command.

Next, let's look at another server from a popular ISP:

```
C:\> telnet xxx.xxx.xxx.xxx 25
220 xxxx.com ESMTP *** FOR AUTHORIZED USE ONLY! ***
NOOP
250 2.0.0 OK
VRFY joe
252 2.5.2 Cannot VRFY user; try RCPT to attempt delivery
   (or try finger)
HELP
214-2.0.0 This is sendmail version 8.11.6
214-2.0.0 Topics:
214-2.0.0        HELO    EHLO    MAIL    RCPT    DATA
214-2.0.0        RSET    NOOP    QUIT    HELP    VRFY
214-2.0.0        EXPN    VERB    ETRN    DSN     AUTH
214-2.0.0        STARTTLS
214-2.0.0 For more info use "HELP topic".
214-2.0.0 To report bugs in the implementation send email to
214-2.0.0        sendmail-bugs@sendmail.org.
214-2.0.0 For local information send email to Postmaster
   at your site.
214 2.0.0 End of HELP info
QUIT
221 2.0.0 xxxx.com closing connection
Connection to host lost.
C:\>
```

This server starts out much better. The only thing we know from the greeting is that it's enhanced (ESMTP) and that these administrators know how to replace the default greeting with one of their own. Next, our attempt to verify a user is met with a message similar to the MSN server. However, they blow it on HELP. Here, we get the server name and version again, along with all the commands they support. Because this particular mail server comes standard on Unix and Linux, we've also narrowed down the operating system. All of this information can help us choose specific exploits. From an administrator's point of view, you should be able to understand how limiting this mail-server information is critical to your security.

Finally, let's look at a mail server that is protected by the PIX Firewall's Mail Guard:

```
C:\> telnet xxx.xxx.xxx.xxx 25
220 **************************************************
***********************************
```

> **NOOP**
> 200 zzzz.com: Ok
> **VRFY joe**
> 500 zzzz.com: unknown command.
> **HELP**
> 500 zzzz.com: unknown command.
> **QUIT**
> 221 zzzz.com closing connection. Goodbye!
> Connection to host lost.
> C:\>
>
> Even a cursory glance tells you there is a huge difference here. It doesn't matter how much information their mail server returns in the banner, because it's all replaced with asterisks as it passes through the PIX Firewall. The NOOP command returns the name of the host (which we've have replaced with z's) and the Ok. The VERIFY and HELP commands both return unknown command. Given this information, attackers would need to try a lot of different attacks before they got lucky. Hopefully, your IDS will detect and notify you about these attempts before the attackers find a method that works.

Noticeably missing from the list in Table 13.1 are the VRFY, EXPN, and HELP commands. VRFY is used to identify a username. Although it's definitely useful, this command is often used by attackers to gather data. E-mail addresses and account names are often the same, so it's a trivial matter to do an nslookup for an organization's MX record in DNS to find the IP address of their mail server, and then telnet to port 25 (SMTP) and use VRFY to find usernames. Once a match is found, the attacker can start guessing passwords. Because administrative accounts on many old systems automatically were associated with e-mail addresses of the same name, it used to be fairly simple to determine a great deal of information about a system.

The EXPN command works like VRFY, except it returns distribution lists.

HELP sends brief information and instructions about use of the system. There's nothing quite like giving your attacker instructions for using your systems.

Even though the commands are limited by the PIX Firewall, it's still possible to get information about the mail server because the mail server has a number of banners and error messages. Mail Guard puts a stop to this, as well. It changes all the characters in SMTP banners, except 2.0.0, to asterisks. One of the nice features of Mail Guard is that if a command isn't allowed, the firewall still responds with OK, making someone think that the command has been accepted.

> **NOTE**
> Earlier versions of the PIX Firewall operating system have had problems with parts of Enhanced SMTP (ESMTP). It's always a good idea to test and make sure an implementation will work before you place it into production. Don't assume a PIX Firewall running 4.x code with Mail Guard will work with ESMTP.

Mail Guard on the PIX Firewall is enabled by default on TCP port 25, which is the standard SMTP port. However, you might want to use the full-featured mail servers, harden your host, and then use the `fixup protocol` command to turn Mail Guard on and off, as follows:

```
PIX(config)# fixup protocol smtp 25
PIX(config)# no fixup protocol smtp 25
PIX(config)#
```

It's also possible to change the port by entering the command with a different port number and to enable multiple ports by entering the command multiple times with different port numbers.

IP Fragmentation Guard

IP Fragmentation Guard is used to protect hosts against certain attacks that take advantage of the fragmentation feature in TCP/IP. The TCP/IP stacks on many older hosts were vulnerable to many different methods of abusing the *fragmentation* feature of IP. This feature is used most often for packets that traverse networks that have different maximum transmission unit (MTU) sizes. For instance, if a host on a Token Ring segment wants to send a large amount of data, it may choose to create the largest frame it can, which is 4096 bytes. When a router or translational bridge moves this packet from the Token Ring segment to an Ethernet segment, it needs to split it into several smaller fragments because the maximum size of a frame in Ethernet is 1518 bytes (including headers) or 1522 bytes with support for VLAN tags.

Fragments are a problem for firewalls because only the first fragment in a series of fragments contains the header information of the higher layers, such as TCP and UDP ports. Thus, a lot of simple packet-filtering firewalls might accidentally permit or deny fragments.

Two of the 20 bytes in the IP header are devoted to fragmenting packets. This is separated into two parts: a 3-bit flags section and a 13-bit Fragment Offset field, as shown in Figure 13.1.

The first bit of the flags section is reserved and not currently used. The second bit is called the Don't Fragment bit. If the value of this bit is zero, any device in the path from the source to destination, such as a router or firewall, is allowed to fragment this packet. However, if the value is set to 1, devices aren't allowed to fragment this packet. This typically means that the device will be unable to forward the packet, because it exceeds the MTU of the next segment in the path. Therefore, the device will discard the packet and usually return an Internet Control Message Protocol (ICMP) message to the source to let it know that it dropped the packet because it couldn't fragment it.

The last bit of the flags section tells the receiver whether this is the last packet in the chain or if the receiver should expect another fragment to follow. If the value of this field is 0, it means the packet is either not fragmented or it's the last fragment in the chain. If the value is 1, the receiver should expect more fragments to follow.

The Fragment Offset field tells the receiver how to put the fragments back together to form a packet. This is important because the fragments might arrive out of order if there were multiple transmission paths. It's also important to note that only the destination host reassembles fragmented packets. For instance, if a packet is generated on a Fiber Distributed Data Interface (FDDI) segment, then fragmented into three pieces on an Ethernet segment, and then passed through another FDDI segment to get to its final destination, the fragments won't be reassembled into a single packet when they traverse the final FDDI segment. When the destination host receives the first fragment of a packet, it sets up a little buffer to collect all the fragments and reassemble them before passing them up.

After this little fragmentation refresher, you should be able to see why fragments are such a security problem. In fact, there were probably all kinds of alarms going off in your mind: What if someone sent a fragment with the wrong offset? What if someone kept sending fragments without ever sending the last fragment? And the list goes on. Unfortunately, the answer to most of these questions is that the host crashes or stops communicating with the network. Because of that, these attacks are quite popular. The most common examples are the teardrop, bonk, and NT fragmentation attacks.

FIGURE 13.1 Fields in the IP header

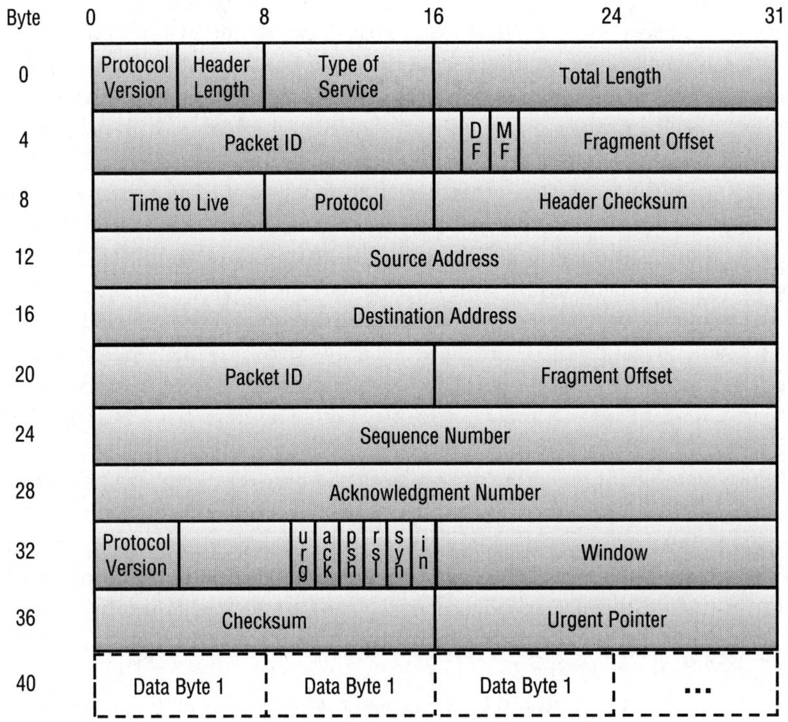

Byte	0	8	16	24	31
0	Protocol Version	Header Length	Type of Service	Total Length	
4	Packet ID			DF MF	Fragment Offset
8	Time to Live		Protocol	Header Checksum	
12	Source Address				
16	Destination Address				
20	Packet ID			Fragment Offset	
24	Sequence Number				
28	Acknowledgment Number				
32	Protocol Version		urg ack psh rst syn fin	Window	
36	Checksum			Urgent Pointer	
40	Data Byte 1	Data Byte 1	Data Byte 1	...	

To combat the attacks that take advantage of fragmentation, a number of recommendations are laid out in RFC 1858, and the ASA implements these suggestions. But often, even more protection is required. The PIX Firewall implements this in the IP Fragmentation Guard feature. This feature provides protection in two ways:

- It requires that each fragment in a chain after the first fragment be associated with a valid initial fragment. This takes advantage of stateful information to prevent attackers from manipulating the flags.

Attack Guards

- It limits the number of fragmented packets to less than 100 per second per host. This attempts to prevent hosts from being overwhelmed with the task of reassembling fragments.

Unfortunately, both of these controls can cause all kinds of problems for legitimate traffic, so the IP Fragmentation Guard feature is disabled by default. To enable the IP Fragmentation Guard feature, use the `sysopt security fragguard` command. The syntax for the `sysopt` command is as follows:

```
PIX(config)# sysopt ?
usage:
  [no] sysopt connection { permit-ipsec | permit-l2tp |
    permit-pptp | timewait | {tcpmss [minimum] bytes} }
  [no] sysopt ipsec pl-compatible
  [no] sysopt noproxyarp if-name
  [no] sysopt nodnsalias { inbound | outbound }
  [no] sysopt security fragguard
  [no] sysopt radius ignore-secret
  [no] sysopt uauth allow-http-cache
  [no] sysopt route dnat
PIX(config)# sysopt
```

> **NOTE** Once enabled, the IP Fragmentation Guard feature applies to all interfaces on the PIX Firewall. You can't selectively enable and disable per interface.

Separate from the IP Fragmentation Guard feature, the PIX Firewall also controls fragments with the `fragment` commands, which are described in Table 13.2.

TABLE 13.2 PIX Firewall *fragment* Commands

Command	Description
fragment size database-limit [interface]	Without the IP Fragmentation Guard feature, the PIX Firewall still keeps a table of fragments. This command allows you to allocate more or less memory as appropriate for your network.
fragment chain chain-limit [interface]	This command limits the number of fragments that can be created from a single packet.
fragment timeout seconds [interface]	This command limits the time that the PIX Firewall will wait for fragment stragglers.

TABLE 13.2 PIX Firewall *fragment* Commands *(continued)*

Command	Description
`clear fragment`	This command clears the table of fragments.
`show fragment [interface]`	This command shows fragment statistics.

DNS Guard

The *DNS Guard* feature is relatively simple, compared with the other attack guards. In the course of DNS operations, it's common for a request to be sent to many DNS servers. The DNS Guard feature monitors this request and allows only the first response inbound from any DNS server. All subsequent responses are dropped because the PIX Firewall tears down the UDP conduit created after the first response has passed through.

A host might need to query several different DNS servers, but each of these queries is handled separately. If a host sends four identical queries to four different DNS servers, the PIX Firewall creates four separate connections. As the queries are returned, the PIX Firewall tears down those connections individually.

What does this feature do to prevent an attack? By default, the PIX Firewall would normally need to wait for the outbound UDP connection to time out, but this could lead to the UDP session being hijacked. By closing this connection immediately following the first returning DNS reply packet and not waiting the timeout period, the PIX Firewall can prevent a DoS attack.

Because there isn't a reason to turn this feature off, there is no syntax to turn it on or off; it's always enabled.

Intrusion Detection

The PIX Firewall uses a scaled-down version of the Cisco *Intrusion Detection System* (Cisco IDS), which can identify a number of common IP-based attacks using *signatures* to detect patterns of misuse in network traffic. In the following sections, we'll talk about how to turn on intrusion detection using IP auditing and how to stop an attack using the shunning feature.

IP Audit

There are two signature classes: informational and attack. Both signature classes are tracked separately and have a default action. You can configure these default actions using the `ip audit attack action` and `ip audit info action` commands.

Intrusion Detection

Three actions can be taken for each of these signatures:

alarm   The `alarm` option indicates that when a signature match is detected in a packet, the PIX Firewall reports the event to all configured Syslog servers.

drop   The `drop` option drops the offending packet.

reset   The `reset` option drops the offending packet and closes the connection if it's part of an active connection.

The default is `alarm` for both informational and attack signatures. You can also specify multiple actions to occur. For example, you can specify the default action to take for attack signatures to be `alarm` and `reset` with the following command:

```
PIX(config)# ip audit attack action alarm reset
PIX(config)#
```

Before any traffic auditing can occur, you must create an *audit policy* with the `ip audit name` command. This audit policy can be either an attack or informational policy determined by the `attack` or `info` parameter after the policy name. You can also specify an action to take for this audit policy, with the `action` keyword followed by one or more of the three actions. If an action isn't specified, the default action is used.

For example, since we've changed the default attack signature action to `alarm reset`, when we create an attack audit policy without specifying an action, the action will be to alarm and reset. Here is the output to demonstrate this, with the irrelevant portions omitted:

```
PIX(config)# ip audit name attack-pol attack
PIX(config)# write term
Building configuration...
: Saved
:
PIX Version 6.2(2)
hostname PIX
ip audit name attack-pol attack action alarm reset
ip audit info action alarm
ip audit attack action alarm reset
PIX(config)#
```

IP auditing is performed by inspecting the IP packets as they arrive at an inbound interface. If a packet triggers a signature, and the configured action isn't to drop the packet, then the same packet could trigger other signatures.

You might wonder how the PIX Firewall knows which policy to apply to which interface. To apply an audit policy to an interface, you need to use the `ip audit interface` command followed by the interface name and the audit policy name. For example, if we wanted to apply the attack audit policy just created to the outside interface, we'd use the following commands:

```
PIX(config)# ip audit interface outside attack-pol
PIX(config)#
```

Cisco has provided a way to turn off or disable certain signatures from being checked globally on the PIX Firewall. The command to disable a signature is as follows:

```
ip audit signature signature_number disable
```

You can enable a previously disabled signature using the following command:

```
no ip audit signature signature_number
```

Why would you want to disable a signature in the first place? There might be times when you get false positives for legitimate traffic and you don't want to keep getting Syslog messages about this signature.

How do you find out the number for the signature you need to disable? You can look at the Syslog messages produced by the PIX Firewall to determine the number, which appears right after the IDS: keyword. You can also list the signatures on the system using the show ip audit count command, which is discussed in a moment.

The following is an example of some Syslog messages produced by the PIX Firewall IDS feature and syntax for how you can disable a signature globally:

```
%PIX-4-40013 IDS:2003 ICMP redirect from 10.4.1.2 to 10.2.1.1 on
   interface dmz
%PIX-4-40032 IDS:4051 UDP Snork attack from 10.1.1.1 to 192.168.1.1 on
   interface outside
PIX(config)# ip audit signature 6102 disable
PIX(config)#
```

To show how many attack and informational signatures have been triggered, you can enter the show ip audit count, which shows the IDS protected interface and the count for that particular signature. You can also use the interface parameter and then the specific interface name to show the count for only that signature, which must be configured for IDS protection. Finally, you can use the global keyword to show the counts for each signature regardless of the interface.

Following are some examples of using the show ip audit count command with the various parameters. You can see that this particular PIX is Internet-facing by the high number of signatures being triggered:

```
PIX# show ip audit count
Signature                          outside  DMZ   Global
1000 I Bad IP Options List         0        0     0
1001 I Record Packet Route         0        0     0
1002 I Timestamp                   0        0     0
```

1003	I	Provide s,c,h,tcc	0	0	0
1004	I	Loose Source Route	0	0	0
1005	I	SATNET ID	0	0	0
1006	I	Strict Source Route	0	0	0
1100	A	IP Fragment Attack	0	0	0
1102	A	Impossible IP Packet	0	0	0
1103	A	IP Teardrop	0	0	0
2000	I	ICMP Echo Reply	217610	96919	120691
2001	I	ICMP Unreachable	644046	0	644046
2002	I	ICMP Source Quench	7344	0	7344
2003	I	ICMP Redirect	17665	0	17665
2004	I	ICMP Echo Request	5830259	50330	5779929
2005	I	ICMP Time Exceed	153713	0	153713
2006	I	ICMP Parameter Problem	173	0	173
2007	I	ICMP Time Request	1506	0	1506
2008	I	ICMP Time Reply	231	0	231
2009	I	ICMP Info Request	1	0	1
2010	I	ICMP Info Reply	43	0	43
2011	I	ICMP Address Mask Request	501	0	501
2012	I	ICMP Address Mask Reply	0	0	0
2150	A	Fragmented ICMP	6880	0	6880
2151	A	Large ICMP	30415	0	30415
2154	A	Ping of Death	245	0	245
3040	A	TCP No Flags	278	0	278
3041	A	TCP SYN & FIN Flags Only	63866	0	63866
3042	A	TCP FIN Flag Only	762	0	762
3153	A	FTP Improper Address	5	0	5
3154	A	FTP Improper Port	2	0	2
4050	A	Bomb	43	0	43
4051	A	Snork	0	0	0
4052	A	Chargen	0	0	0
6050	A	DNS Host Info	0	0	0
6051	A	DNS Zone Xfer	0	0	0
6052	A	DNS Zone Xfer High Port	0	0	0
6053	A	DNS All Records	11	0	11
6100	I	RPC Port Registration	0	0	0
6101	I	RPC Port Unregistration	0	0	0
6102	I	RPC Dump	0	0	0
6103	A	Proxied RPC	0	0	0
6150	I	ypserv Portmap Request	0	0	0

```
6151 I ypbind Portmap Request             0      0      0
6152 I yppasswdd Portmap Request          0      0      0
6153 I ypupdated Portmap Request          0      0      0
6154 I ypxfrd Portmap Request             0      0      0
6155 I mountd Portmap Request             0      0      0
6175 I rexd Portmap Request               0      0      0
6180 I rexd Attempt                       0      0      0
6190 A statd Buffer Overflow              0      0      0
PIX# show ip audit count interface outside
Signature                               outside
1000 I Bad IP Options List               0
1001 I Record Packet Route               0
1002 I Timestamp                         0
1003 I Provide s,c,h,tcc                 0
1004 I Loose Source Route                0
1005 I SATNET ID                         0
1006 I Strict Source Route               0
1100 A IP Fragment Attack                0
1102 A Impossible IP Packet              0
1103 A IP Teardrop                       0
2000 I ICMP Echo Reply                   120691
2001 I ICMP Unreachable                  644047
2002 I ICMP Source Quench                7344
2003 I ICMP Redirect                     17665
2004 I ICMP Echo Request                 5779940
2005 I ICMP Time Exceed                  153713
2006 I ICMP Parameter Problem            173
2007 I ICMP Time Request                 1506
2008 I ICMP Time Reply                   231
2009 I ICMP Info Request                 1
2010 I ICMP Info Reply                   43
2011 I ICMP Address Mask Request         501
2012 I ICMP Address Mask Reply           0
2150 A Fragmented ICMP                   6880
2151 A Large ICMP                        30415
2154 A Ping of Death                     245
3040 A TCP No Flags                      278
3041 A TCP SYN & FIN Flags Only          63866
3042 A TCP FIN Flag Only                 762
3153 A FTP Improper Address              5
```

```
3154 A FTP Improper Port              2
4050 A Bomb                           43
4051 A Snork                          0
4052 A Chargen                        0
6050 A DNS Host Info                  0
6051 A DNS Zone Xfer                  0
6052 A DNS Zone Xfer High Port        0
6053 A DNS All Records                11
6100 I RPC Port Registration          0
6101 I RPC Port Unregistration        0
6102 I RPC Dump                       0
6103 A Proxied RPC                    0
6150 I ypserv Portmap Request         0
6151 I ypbind Portmap Request         0
6152 I yppasswdd Portmap Request      0
6153 I ypupdated Portmap Request      0
6154 I ypxfrd Portmap Request         0
6155 I mountd Portmap Request         0
6175 I rexd Portmap Request           0
6180 I rexd Attempt                   0
6190 A statd Buffer Overflow          0

PIX# show ip audit count global
Signature                             Global
1000 I Bad IP Options List             0
1001 I Record Packet Route             0
1002 I Timestamp                       0
1003 I Provide s,c,h,tcc               0
1004 I Loose Source Route              0
1005 I SATNET ID                       0
1006 I Strict Source Route             0
1100 A IP Fragment Attack              0
1102 A Impossible IP Packet            0
1103 A IP Teardrop                     0
2000 I ICMP Echo Reply                 217610
2001 I ICMP Unreachable                644047
2002 I ICMP Source Quench              7344
2003 I ICMP Redirect                   17665
2004 I ICMP Echo Request               5830278
2005 I ICMP Time Exceed                153713
```

```
2006 I  ICMP Parameter Problem        173
2007 I  ICMP Time Request             1506
2008 I  ICMP Time Reply               231
2009 I  ICMP Info Request             1
2010 I  ICMP Info Reply               43
2011 I  ICMP Address Mask Request     501
2012 I  ICMP Address Mask Reply       0
2150 A  Fragmented ICMP               6880
2151 A  Large ICMP                    30415
2154 A  Ping of Death                 245
3040 A  TCP No Flags                  278
3041 A  TCP SYN & FIN Flags Only      63866
3042 A  TCP FIN Flag Only             762
3153 A  FTP Improper Address          5
3154 A  FTP Improper Port             2
4050 A  Bomb                          43
4051 A  Snork                         0
4052 A  Chargen                       0
6050 A  DNS Host Info                 0
6051 A  DNS Zone Xfer                 0
6052 A  DNS Zone Xfer High Port       0
6053 A  DNS All Records               11
6100 I  RPC Port Registration         0
6101 I  RPC Port Unregistration       0
6102 I  RPC Dump                      0
6103 A  Proxied RPC                   0
6150 I  ypserv Portmap Request        0
6151 I  ypbind Portmap Request        0
6152 I  yppasswdd Portmap Request     0
6153 I  ypupdated Portmap Request     0
6154 I  ypxfrd Portmap Request        0
6155 I  mountd Portmap Request        0
6175 I  rexd Portmap Request          0
6180 I  rexd Attempt                  0
6190 A  statd Buffer Overflow         0

PIX#
```

Shunning

What happens when you start getting a lot of attack Syslog messages, or users are complaining about traffic coming from one or more IP addresses from the outside? If you determine that you're under attack, what do you do to stop the attack? You could always create an access list or modify the existing outside access list and stop all traffic from those IP addresses. But later, when the attack is no longer happening and the user has cleaned up the Trojan horse that started that attack, you'll need to go back in and delete those access-list lines you created. This is a hassle, and you might get the access list wrong and mess things up worse than before the attack started. Wouldn't it be nice if you could temporarily restrict access from an IP address? You can do so using the shun command.

The shun command applies a blocking or *shunning* function to the interface receiving the attack. Packets containing the IP source address of the attacking host are dropped and logged until the blocking function is removed manually. No traffic from the IP source address is allowed to traverse the PIX Firewall unit, and any remaining connections time out as part of the normal architecture. The blocking function of the shun command is applied whether or not a connection with the specified host address is currently active.

The shun command can take a single source IP address, or you can specify a destination IP address, which must also be accompanied by a source port and destination port with 0 (meaning all ports). One more option is to specify what protocol to block: TCP or UDP. If the protocol isn't specified, then the PIX Firewall blocks traffic on both TCP and UDP ports specified. If you use the shun command only with the source IP address of the host, then no further traffic from the offending host will be allowed.

Because the shun command is used to block attacks dynamically and temporarily, it isn't displayed in your PIX Firewall configuration. You can see the current shun commands by using the show shun command. To delete a shun entry, use the no shun command with the specific source IP address to delete. Optionally, you can use the clear shun command, which prevents all IP addresses from being shunned. Here is an example of using the shun command:

```
PIX(config)# shun 1.1.1.1
Shun 1.1.1.1 successful
PIX(config)# shun 2.2.2.2 3.3.3.3 23 0
Shun 2.2.2.2 successful
PIX(config)# show shun
Shun 1.1.1.1 0.0.0.0 0 0
Shun 2.2.2.2 3.3.3.3 23 0
PIX(config)# no shun 2.2.2.2
PIX(config)# show shun
Shun 1.1.1.1 0.0.0.0 0 0
PIX(config)# clear shun
PIX(config)# show shun
PIX(config)#
```

Summary

In this chapter, we discussed advanced protocol handling and the PIX Firewall attack guard features. First, we explained why some protocols pose challenges to packet-filtering and even stateful firewalls. Problematic protocols include FTP, RSH, SQL*Net, RTSP, and H.323. Then you learned how the PIX Firewall can be configured to make special allowances for these protocols.

Next, we looked at the PIX Firewall attack guards, which can protect against low-level attacks such as SYN floods, illegal fragmentation, and application-level attacks against SMTP and DNS. The attack guards include the AAA Flood Guard, SYN Flood Guard, Mail Guard, IP Fragmentation Guard, and DNS Guard features.

Finally, we looked at the intrusion detection services available on the PIX Firewall and how these are configured using the `ip audit` commands. We also discussed the `shun` command, a quick and easy way to temporarily stop traffic from a host that might be attempting to probe or attack your network.

Exam Essentials

Know how and when protocols create multiple TCP sessions. Understand when TCP sessions are created and why. Understand how the source and destination port numbers are selected. Given an ACL, be able to predict the outcome of attempts to connect protocols such as FTP across packet-filtering firewalls.

Remember how to configure advanced protocol support. Know how to enable and disable support for a given protocol. Know the default port numbers for the problem protocols, and be able to change the default port number to another number.

Know when to configure advanced protocol support. Understand when advanced protocol configuration is necessary and when it isn't. Be able to troubleshoot problems by predicting the outcome of enabling and disabling support.

Know what SMTP and DNS information is passed in and out of the PIX Firewall. Know how to enable and disable the Mail Guard feature, and understand the advantages and disadvantages of doing so.

Know how malformed packets can affect firewalls and the hosts they protect. Understand how session-based attacks at the TCP layer (such as the SYN flood) and lower-layer attacks (for example, fragmentation) can consume resources on hosts and allow some packets to sneak by a lesser firewall. Know what the Flood Guard and Fragmentation Guard features do and how they can be enabled and disabled.

Understand the PIX Firewalls intrusion detection and shunning capabilities Know how to turn on intrusion detection services and customize the PIX Firewall's response to traffic matching attack and informational signatures. Know the syntax of the `shun` command and that it doesn't show up in the configuration.

Chapter 14

Firewall Failover and PDM

THE FOLLOWING TOPICS ARE COVERED IN THIS CHAPTER:

- ✓ Understanding serial and LAN-based failover
- ✓ Configuring the PIX Firewall for failover
- ✓ Overview of the PIX Firewall PDM
- ✓ Preparing the PIX Firewall for the PDM
- ✓ Using the PDM to configure the PIX Firewall

In the previous chapters, you've seen how the Cisco Secure PIX Firewall deals with security issues, including stateful traffic filtering, special protocol handling, and more. In this chapter, we'll take a step away from security and focus on some advanced networking concepts. Specifically, we'll look at how the PIX Firewall compensates for system and network faults and how you can configure it for high-availability service. We'll talk about the PIX Device Manager (PDM) and what is required to install and operate the PDM from the PIX Firewall perspective. We'll also go over the PDM graphical user interface (GUI) and point out features and keys to using it. In addition, we'll identify the differences in using the PDM with the Firewall Services Module (FWSM).

We'll begin with an introduction to fault-tolerance concepts, defining the terms *point of failure* and *single point of failure* and looking at some typical fault-tolerant strategies. Then, for the rest of the chapter, we'll concentrate on the PIX Firewall failover feature—how it works and how to configure it.

Fault-Tolerance Concepts

Simply put, a *fault* is an event that occurs when a component of a system fails and causes a degradation or disruption of service. Faults are bad.

Fault tolerance refers to the ability of a system to experience a fault without a significant degradation or disruption of service. Fault tolerance is good, but it's often expensive and complicated. In this section, we'll look at what causes faults, how to evaluate them, and some common strategies to mitigate them.

> **NOTE** Recall that firewalls reside at the border of two or more networks, and for them to be effective from a security point of view, all network traffic must pass through them. Thus, users generally view the failure of a firewall as a failure of the entire network.

Points of Failure

Today's enterprise networks are incredibly complex. Even a simple peer-to-peer network requires hundreds of components to work together. Unfortunately, almost any one of these points could fail. We call each of them a potential *point of failure*.

Some points of failure are more important than others. When some components fail, they might cause the system to become slow or behave erratically, or the failure might be more subtle. For example, when a cooling fan wears out, it won't immediately cause a PC to fail. Instead, the rise in temperature in the CPU and motherboard may cause the system to "blue screen" intermittently. Often, it will cut in half the life expectancy of the rest of the parts, even though you may never notice that the fan failed.

When the failure of a single component causes a disruption in service for the entire system, we call this a *single point of failure*. For instance, if a backhoe cuts the fiber-optic cable that carries your WAN circuit into your building, all traffic across this circuit will immediately cease, even though the routers, switches, and PCs are all still functioning perfectly. This type of fault is particularly annoying.

Your goal is to identify possible or likely points of failure and eliminate single points of failure. When you eliminate all single points of failure in the entire system, that system is *highly reliable*.

Identifying Points of Failure

When you're identifying points of failure in a network, the phrase "throw a rock" comes to mind, because anything it hit would be a point of failure. Because there are so many points of failure, sometimes it's helpful to use a layered approach to identify them by following an application across the network as it interacts with another application. To demonstrate this approach, let's consider the case of a web server. We start at the application and go down (this list is by no means exhaustive, but it will help you understand how much is involved):

Web server application The web server application itself could fail, such as `httpd` on Unix or Microsoft's IIS. If this service crashes or stops for any reason, service will be totally disrupted. Some common culprits are application bugs, dependencies on other applications such as database backends, and misconfigurations.

Web server's operating system The server's operating system, such as Linux or Windows 2000, might crash. Bugs in the operating system (or even another application fighting for resources) could disrupt service completely. Again, misconfiguration is all too common a reason for this type of failure.

Device drivers Failures in the device drivers that control hardware—such as the network interface card, the video card, the controllers for hard drives or RAID arrays, and so on—are so common that the first words out of any hardware vendor's support department are invariably, "Have you downloaded the latest drivers from our website?"

Hardware Hardware components fail, too. It would take forever to list these, but a few of the most prone to failure are power supplies, memory modules (SIMMs, DRAMs, DIMMs, and so on), hard disks, cooling fans, motherboards, and wiring (particularly cables that are moved frequently or cables that are near users).

With a list like this, it's a wonder networks function at all. Even so, these applications and hardware components are all fairly obvious things you've probably considered before. However, many people don't realize that the protocols themselves can fail. Let's continue with our web server points of failure and look at the various protocols that can fail:

TCP/IP   TCP/IP can be a point of failure. In IP, each network is a broadcast domain. This means that a broadcast storm could disrupt service to every device in the subnet even if there are redundant routers and switches. This example illustrates another important point: Even if your application doesn't require a piece of hardware or software to function, if that other component misbehaves, it could affect your system. In this example, processing hardware interrupts caused by all the broadcasts on the network might use so much CPU time that your application is starved and an outage is perceived.

Routing protocols   Routing protocols often fail. Even a slight difference between two vendors' implementations of a standard protocol can cause disastrous results. Of course, simple misconfiguration is usually responsible for creating routing loops or *black holes* (places where traffic goes in but doesn't come out). In this way, an error in a remote part of the network can affect your system, even though your system doesn't ordinarily use those resources.

Support protocols   Peripheral and support protocols are vulnerable, too. Dynamic Host Configuration Protocol (DHCP), Domain Name Server (DNS), Windows Internet Naming Service (WINS), Address Resolution Protocol (ARP), and a host of other support protocols can fail. Higher layer protocols—such as FTP, HTTP, and others—can experience compatibility issues. Although these problems aren't common, they happen enough to justify an entire industry of companies that manufacture protocol analyzers, such as Wandel and Goltermann and Sniffer Technologies (formerly Data General).

The keys to detecting points of failure in a network are to keep an open mind and exhaustive documentation. After identifying the points of failure, you must understand what effect they will have on your network and then evaluate this impact. Evaluating the impact of each point of failure relative to other points of failure is important because eliminating every single point of failure in the network isn't practical. The complexity, effort, and cost would be prohibitive. After assessing the potential damage, you can address the points of failure in order of importance to the extent your resources allow.

PIX Firewall Points of Failure

Now that you have an idea about generic points of failure, let's look at some problems specific to the PIX Firewall. The PIX Firewall, of course, has most of the components listed in the previous section. It has software and hardware points of failure.

Although the PIX Firewall operating system is mature and highly stable, it's technically a potential point of failure. Cisco diligently addresses issues, particularly security vulnerabilities, and lists both bug fixes and outstanding issues in the release notes of each version.

When it comes to hardware, the PIX Firewall has all the usual suspects: power supplies, memory, flash, network ports, motherboard, and Pentium processor. In most models, each of these represents a single point of failure that would disable the entire system.

Real World Scenario

A Real-Life TCP/IP Subnet Failure

Although a TCP/IP type of failure is rare relative to physical failures such as power supplies and hard drives, I happened to experience just such an outage the same day I wrote this chapter.

The incident began in the early afternoon, with users from all over the campus reporting that the network was down. After a half hour or so, we had narrowed the problem to a single subnet. All affected users were on this subnet, which spanned multiple buildings via VLAN trunking, and none of the users on other subnets were affected. Furthermore, devices on the affected subnet could communicate with each other and could ping the default gateway, but they couldn't reach anything beyond that router. Many other subnets were also using this same router, but they weren't experiencing problems.

Because this router is actually a pair of large, non-Cisco routers in a complex Virtual Router Redundancy Protocol (VRRP) arrangement, with a detailed set of filtering rules that change often, we immediately suspected there was a problem with these filters or possibly a routing loop. After a few more hours of troubleshooting, we decided to shut off both the routers' interfaces on this network at the same time. Shortly afterward, we noticed that a continuous ping we had set up hadn't dropped a single packet, even though both of the interfaces we were pinging were down!

We checked the ARP cache on the desktop we had used for the ping test, and sure enough, the organizational unique identifier (OUI) in the MAC address didn't belong to the router's manufacturer. We looked it up, followed this address through the forwarding database tables in our switches, and eventually found that a server administrator had accidentally configured a new server with the IP address of our default gateway! This device was responding to ARPs and causing all traffic destined for other networks to be sent to it. Of course, it didn't have a route off the network, so it was discarding these packets. We unplugged the offending device, and connectivity was immediately restored. Elapsed time: more than four hours.

Although this incident was an accident, it could easily have been malicious. After all, any user with a laptop can give the machine a static IP and destroy an entire subnet. Even worse, how would you trace it if this laptop were hidden in a desk and connected to your network via an 802.11 wireless link?

It's common knowledge that the interface on the default gateway is a single point of failure, so we mitigate this issue by using protocols such as VRRP and Hot Standby Router Protocol (HSRP). The point of this story is that points of failure aren't restricted to hardware and software programs—even the IP address itself is a point of failure.

Fault-Tolerant Strategies

There are a number of different approaches to hardening a system, but the most common method by far is duplicating equipment. So, for one connection, you'd buy two routers, two switches, two firewalls, and so on. Although it's expensive, this approach gives you a number of options. In this section, we'll discuss two of those fault-tolerant options: redundancy and load balancing. We'll also cover how overengineering can make a network more complex.

Redundancy

The simplest method of connecting all this equipment is to make it redundant. In this arrangement, one component does all the work, and the other sits idly, waiting for the first to fail. In the event of a failure, the second component takes over the job of the failed component with as little ado as possible.

An example might be a pair of WAN circuits between two remote offices. In your routing protocol, you might assign a lower cost to the first circuit so that all the traffic uses this link. If it fails, the routers will begin using the circuit with the higher cost. You could also use HSRP to provide redundancy for routers.

Redundancy generally requires the backup component to be in a fully operational but idle state. The system must have some method of detecting a failure in the primary component and switching to the backup component.

Load Balancing

A more complex method of building a fault-tolerant system is by *load balancing*. If you configured the pair of WAN circuits with equal costs, a routing protocol such as Open Shortest Path First (OSPF) or Enhanced Internal Gateway Routing Protocol (EIGRP) would route some traffic across one link and other traffic across the other link.

The advantage of load balancing is that you use the capacity you have. Having a pair of WAN circuits is expensive, but you can essentially double the users' available bandwidth by using both circuits at the same time. During a failure of one of the links, the users may not notice the degradation of service.

Overengineering

It's important to realize that fault-tolerant strategies can go too far. The more complex systems become, the less reliable they are. Like exotic cars, they run well sometimes, but they spend more time in the shop than on the road. Also, more complex systems usually require higher-skilled engineers to maintain them, adding to their costs.

Failover systems often suffer from a bad case of overengineering. As more devices are added to the network for redundancy or load balancing, it becomes exponentially more difficult for administrators to create an exhaustive list of how the network will behave given a particular outage. When things go wrong, not only do you still have an outage, but it takes four times as long to solve because your environment is so complicated.

Many systems are also too sensitive and initiate a failover prematurely, causing an outage in an otherwise stable system. It's always a good idea to ensure failover will work in the way intended by testing it. (Of course, tests usually need to be done outside normal business hours.)

PIX Firewall Failover

The PIX Firewall failover feature is consistent with other features of the PIX Firewall in that it's as simple as possible. Failover is supported in the 515, 515E, 520, 525, and 535 models. Failover isn't supported in the PIX 501 and PIX 506E models. For the PIX Firewall to maintain simplicity, it imposes many restrictions on possible configurations, but when it's configured correctly, it's very reliable.

In the following sections, we'll discuss the features of failover, requirements for failover, how failover works, and configuring the PIX Firewall for failover operation.

PIX Firewall Failover Features

At a high level, the PIX failover feature consists of two identical PIX Firewalls in a redundant configuration. Only one firewall is operating at a time; the other monitors the first, waiting to take over in an emergency. The inside interfaces of both units are on the same IP subnet, and the outside interfaces of both units are on the same subnet. If you decide to use serial cable failover, then the units must also be physically close enough to be connected with the failover cable.

When serial cable failover occurs, the units swap both IP and MAC addresses. Although this redundant configuration doesn't offer the benefits of doubling your throughput, as does a load-balancing strategy, the simplicity of the PIX Firewall's failover has several advantages:

Transparency to users   Stateful failover is totally transparent to the users. Users continue sending their traffic to the same, single IP address. They don't even need to know that an IP address for the second PIX Firewall exists.

Unchanging addresses   Not only does the IP address not change, but the MAC address doesn't change either. This relates directly to user transparency, but it also means ARP tables are still valid and saves the downtime associated with waiting for entries in the hosts' ARP tables to expire and be repopulated.

Unchanging routes   Because both IP addresses are on the same subnet, no routing changes need to occur either. For instance, the next hop of a default route advertised by the Routing Information Protocol (RIP) would remain unchanged.

In fact, this strategy for failover is so simple that the only thing that must change is the forwarding database in the switches. However, for the PIX Firewall to implement this strategy, your failover configuration must meet specific requirements, as described in the next section.

PIX Firewall Failover Requirements

The requirements for using the PIX Firewall failover feature are as follows:

Two firewalls The failover feature requires two PIX Firewalls with identical model, number, and type of interfaces; software version; activation key type; flash memory; and amount of RAM. Failover shouldn't be confused with load balancing, because as far as the PIX Firewall is concerned, these two items aren't related. If you need additional firewall capacity, you'll need to buy a bigger PIX or the Firewall Service Module for the 6500 series switch and 7600 series router.

Licensing Cisco PIX software comes in two primary levels, restricted and unrestricted. Units with a restricted license can't be used for failover. Unrestricted licenses can be used in a firewall configuration as the primary or standby unit. Cisco offers a cheaper failover-only license; but the PIX Firewall can only be used for failover, and not as a stand-alone or long-term primary unit.

> **NOTE** If the PIX that's licensed only for failover doesn't hear from a PIX with a real license for 24 hours, it will begin rebooting at least once every 24 hours. If you can't get the fully licensed PIX up within the time limit, consider calling TAC to get a real license.

Failover cable For serial or cable-based failover, you need a failover cable that connects the two PIX Firewalls. This cable is fairly short, so in most circumstances, the PIX Firewalls should be within a few feet of each other. When you're using LAN-based failover, the PIX Firewalls can be geographically dispersed, or sitting in the same network rack, depending on your particular needs and configuration.

Now that we've covered what you need to use the PIX Firewall's failover feature, let's look at a typical PIX failover configuration.

How PIX Firewall Failover Works

As an example of how the PIX failover feature works, we'll use a typical small-business network. The network has one IP network (the 10.1.1.0/24 subnet) and one router connecting to the Internet. Figure 14.1 shows the physical connectivity.

> **NOTE** In these examples, we're providing failover only for the PIX. We don't attempt to address fault tolerance for the switches, routers, or WAN links, although you certainly wouldn't want to overlook these important components in your own network.

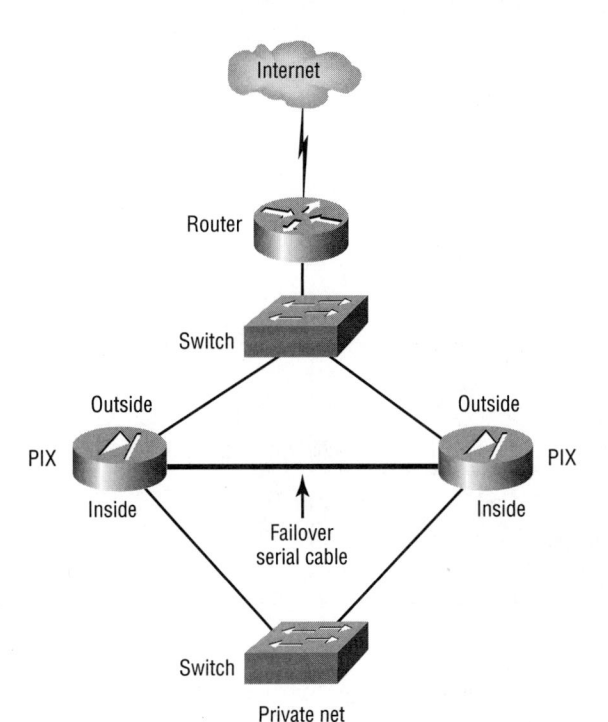

FIGURE 14.1 Physical diagram of a typical PIX failover configuration

In this diagram, you see the Ethernet interface of the router and both PIX Firewalls' outside Ethernet interfaces connected to a single switch, presumably with regular Category 5 cabling. It's possible to connect the firewalls to the router directly by means of a crossover cable, but doing so would require a router with two Ethernet interfaces. It would also require us to bridge those two interfaces together—for example, with Cisco's integrated routing and bridging (IRB), using a Bridge Virtual Interface (BVI)—since both firewalls' outside interfaces must be on the same subnet.

> **TIP** Adding a switch or hub between the router and firewalls has the extra benefit of providing a place to plug in an intrusion detection system (IDS) or protocol analyzers.

The inside interface of each PIX Firewall is connected to a second switch, to which the users' PCs and servers will also be connected.

So, logically, our network looks like the one shown in Figure 14.2. Here, you see that each PIX Firewall has an interface on both the 208.101.53.0 and 10.1.1.0 networks.

FIGURE 14.2 Logical diagram of a typical PIX failover configuration

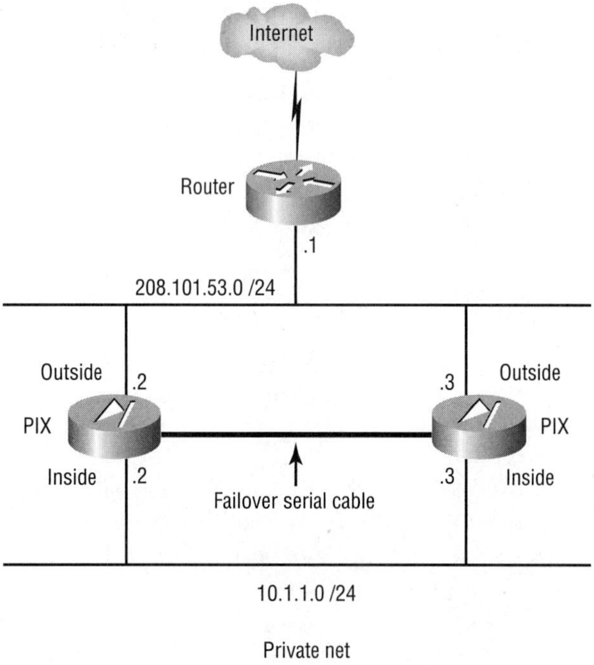

To make this example work, the clients need to point to one of the PIX Firewalls' inside interfaces as their default gateway. Both PIX Firewalls, in turn, need to point to the router's 208.101.53.1 interface as their default gateways. As we discussed in previous chapters, this can be accomplished via static routes or using passive RIP, assuming the router is advertising a default RIP route. Finally, the PIX Firewalls are responsible for Network Address Translation (NAT) from the 208.101.53.0 network to the 10.1.1.0 network and back.

When describing the PIX Firewall and its configuration, Cisco refers to the various units with several different labels:

Primary The *primary unit* is the one you've configured to be preferred. This unit attempts to assume the primary IP addresses and receives and forwards user traffic. It also handles routing updates and everything else.

Secondary The *secondary unit* is the one that isn't preferred. This unit brings all of its interfaces up, but it doesn't transmit or receive traffic (except for keepalive messages). It attempts to assume the backup IP addresses and monitors the other unit, waiting to take over if it fails.

Active Regardless of how it's configured, the *active unit* is the unit that is currently assuming the primary IP addresses and the responsibility for receiving and forwarding user traffic.

Standby Again, regardless of how it's configured, the *standby unit* is the unit that is currently not sending and receiving user traffic. Under normal circumstances, the standby PIX Firewall is responsible for monitoring the active PIX Firewall. However, if a failover has occurred, the standby unit is now the active unit. The formerly active unit is now the standby unit. The exception is when an administrator initiates a failover in the absence of an actual failure (as described later in this chapter, in the "Role Configuration" section).

So, at any given time, in a pair of PIX Firewalls configured for failover, one is primary (active) and the other is secondary (standby). When a failover occurs, the secondary unit becomes the active unit and the primary unit becomes the standby unit.

> **TIP** If it helps to distinguish between these roles, think about what would happen if you powered off both PIX Firewalls: One would still be the primary, and the other would still be the secondary, but neither would be the active or standby firewall.

Because the two PIX Firewalls are identical, aside from hostnames and licenses, there is rarely a reason to prefer one to another from a network design standpoint. Nevertheless, you must identify one of the units as the primary unit. When you're using serial cable-based failover, this is a function of hardware. The failover cable is labeled on each end as either Primary or Secondary. This cable controls which box is primary and secondary. To identify a box as the primary unit, connect the end of the failover cable labeled Primary to the desired unit. The device on the other end is the secondary unit. When you're using LAN-based failover, the primary unit is identified on the command line using the `failover lan unit primary` command.

At this point, you may have begun to wonder about the logistical details of the PIX Firewall's failover feature: How do the active and standby firewalls monitor each other for a failure? What do they monitor, and how often? How do you keep changes to the configuration synchronized? In the following sections, we'll answer all these questions and more.

Failover Monitoring

The standby unit monitors the active unit in three ways:

- By listening for hello packets via the LAN interfaces
- By listening for hello packets via the failover cable
- By testing the power status via the failover cable

All three of these activities happen on a periodic basis (every 15 seconds by default). Thus, a failure can be declared in several ways, including when an interface is down, when hello packets are missing, when a unit is powered off, or when the failover cable is unplugged.

A Down Interface

When a network interface is down, the PIX Firewall considers itself failed. This status is part of the operation of Ethernet. A report from the Data-Link layer tells you whether the interface is administratively down, down, or up. An administratively down interface won't cause a failover. This monitoring protects against low-level problems, such as an unplugged network cable, a damaged or out-of-spec cable, or a powered-off or otherwise inoperable hub or switch.

You can see the status of the interface in the output of the show interface command. For example, if we unplugged the cable connected to ethernet0 and shut down ethernet2, the show interface command might show the following output:

```
PIX(config)# interface ethernet2 shutdown
PIX(config)# exit
PIX# show interface
interface ethernet0 "outside" is up, line protocol is down
  Hardware is i82559 ethernet, address is 0050.54ff.076d
  IP address 37.20.5.2, subnet mask 255.255.255.240
  MTU 1500 bytes, BW 10000 Kbit half duplex
    0 packets input, 0 bytes, 0 no buffer
    Received 0 broadcasts, 0 runts, 0 giants
    0 input errors, 0 CRC, 0 frame, 0 overrun, 0 ignored,
      0 abort
    1 packets output, 64 bytes, 0 underruns
    0 output errors, 0 collisions, 0 interface resets
    0 babbles, 0 late collisions, 0 deferred
    1 lost carrier, 0 no carrier
    input queue (curr/max blocks): hardware (128/128)
      software(0/0)
    output queue (curr/max blocks): hardware (0/2)
      software (0/1)
interface ethernet1 "inside" is up, line protocol is up
  Hardware is i82559 ethernet, address is 0050.54ff.076e
  IP address 10.1.0.1, subnet mask 255.255.255.0
  MTU 1500 bytes, BW 100000 Kbit full duplex
    0 packets input, 0 bytes, 0 no buffer
    Received 0 broadcasts, 0 runts, 0 giants
    0 input errors, 0 CRC, 0 frame, 0 overrun, 0 ignored,
      0 abort
    1 packets output, 64 bytes, 0 underruns
    0 output errors, 0 collisions, 0 interface resets
    0 babbles, 0 late collisions, 0 deferred
    1 lost carrier, 0 no carrier
    input queue (curr/max blocks): hardware (128/128)
      software(0/0)
    output queue (curr/max blocks): hardware (0/2)
      software (0/1)
```

```
interface ethernet2 "dmz" is administratively down, line protocol is up
  Hardware is i82559 ethernet, address is 00d0.b79d.8856
  IP address 192.168.1.1, subnet mask 255.255.255.0
  MTU 1500 bytes, BW 100000 Kbit full duplex
    0 packets input, 0 bytes, 0 no buffer
    Received 0 broadcasts, 0 runts, 0 giants
    0 input errors, 0 CRC, 0 frame, 0 overrun, 0 ignored,
      0 abort
    1 packets output, 64 bytes, 0 underruns
    0 output errors, 0 collisions, 0 interface resets
    0 babbles, 0 late collisions, 0 deferred
    1 lost carrier, 0 no carrier
    input queue (curr/max blocks): hardware (128/128)
      software(0/0)
    output queue (curr/max blocks): hardware (0/2)
      software (0/1)
PIX#
```

Note that on Cisco IOS routers, when an interface is shut down, it's in an administratively down/down state; but on the PIX Firewall, the line protocol is up, even though `ethernet2` is administratively down. This condition occurs because the interface is getting link status but has been shut down by the administrator. If link status weren't present, the interface would be in an administratively down/down state. As far as failover is concerned, the line protocol status doesn't matter if the interface is administratively down.

Missing Hello Packets

Another way the PIX Firewall detects a failure is by missing hello packets. After three consecutive poll intervals (by default, 15 seconds each, for a total of 45 seconds) without receiving a hello packet on a network interface, the PIX Firewall puts that interface into a testing mode. If the interface fails this test, the PIX Firewall considers itself failed. This test is nonintrusive, which means the firewall continues forwarding traffic during the testing, if possible.

The interface test has four parts:

Test 1 The PIX Firewall begins by checking to see if the interface is up or down. This is the same as the previous check. If the interface passes this test, it continues to the next. If it's down, the unit is declared failed.

Test 2 If the interface is up, the PIX Firewall checks for activity on the interface. The PIX Firewall listens for a frame for 5 seconds. If a frame is received, the interface passes the test. If a frame isn't received for 5 consecutive seconds, it's still possible that the interface is okay but not very busy.

Test 3 The next test is more active. The PIX Firewall takes the last 10 IP addresses in its ARP cache and sends an ARP request for them, one at a time. If at any time the firewall receives a response to a request, the interface is declared okay and further testing is halted. In the unlikely event that the PIX Firewall goes through all 10 ARP requests without receiving a response (for instance, if the last 10 users had turned their PCs on, sent some traffic to the Internet, and then powered their PCs back off almost simultaneously), it continues to the next test.

Test 4 The last test is a desperation move to generate some traffic. The PIX Firewall sends a ping to the broadcast address of its subnet. If any device responds, the interface attempts the ARP test again. If no packets are received, the interface is declared down, and the PIX Firewall considers itself failed.

These last three tests are important because the active and standby units are often plugged into different physical switches for redundancy. After all, there isn't much point in paying for two firewall units if a single failure in a switch can render them both useless.

When the active and standby units are plugged into different switches, it's possible for some component upstream to fail, such as another port on the switch. Such a failure would prevent the PIX Firewall from communicating with the rest of the network without dropping the Ethernet circuit. If the PIX Firewall relied only on the interface status, many common upstream failures could occur, and the PIX Firewall would never switch over to the standby unit.

This higher-layer testing is particularly important because the last three tests aren't performed individually. One unit initiates the test, but after each test, that unit consults the other unit. If it sees traffic and the other unit hasn't, it fails the other unit. If it hasn't seen traffic and the other unit has, it fails itself.

Power Loss or Unplugged Failover Cable

In addition to determining which unit is primary and secondary, the failover cable's internal wiring is also wired in such a way that both units can tell if one or both ends of the cable are plugged in. This is accomplished by looping wires back inside the cable. Each unit can also tell if the other firewall is powered on.

When a unit detects that its partner is powered off, it assumes the active role. However, when the units detect that the failover cable is unplugged, they maintain their current status. This makes sense when you consider the alternatives: If both assumed the active role or both assumed the standby role, network connectivity would be disrupted.

Configuration Replication

Just as the physical configuration of the PIX Firewalls must be identical, the command-line configuration of the units also must be identical. Keeping these units identical could be a daunting, if not impossible, task in a volatile environment. Fortunately, the PIX Firewall makes this part easy by replicating the configuration from the active to the standby units in a few different ways:

Replication at startup When the primary unit finishes booting up and becomes the active unit, it copies its entire configuration to the standby unit over the failover cable. This ensures that both units begin service in sync.

Replication when commands are entered As you type configuration commands on the active unit (and you should type them only into the active unit), each instruction is also sent from the memory of the active unit across the failover cable to the memory of the standby unit. This ensures that the units stay in sync while they are in service. However, remember that you need to save the configuration changes to flash by using the `write memory` and `write standby` commands.

Replication on demand You also have the ability to force a complete configuration replication using the `write standby` command. This sends the entire configuration across the failover cable to memory in the standby unit.

Stateful Failover

After reading about how the PIX Firewall handles failover, you might still be wondering about what happens to the xlate table and how this affects existing sessions.

Stateful failover became available in version 5.0; however, prior to version 5.1 of the PIX operating system, very little information was passed over the failover cable. In fact, little more than the configuration information and hello packets were sent to the standby firewall. This was a problem because when a switchover occurred, the standby unit was correctly configured, but its xlate table was empty. Thus, the users of the network were forced to reestablish their sessions, even though they didn't need to reconfigure their machines. When a switchover occurred, the new active PIX Firewall had to reassign all the NATs and rebuild all its connection tables, because all knowledge of the translation slots and connection slots was lost.

Stateful failover provides the solution to this problem. It communicates information about current connections to the backup node. Some of the more notable information passed to the secondary node includes the global address pools and their status, the TCP connection table, and the xlate table. Other information helps perform miscellaneous failover tasks, such as keeping the clocks synchronized. This allows a switchover from the active to the passive node to be transparent to users of most applications.

Notably missing in this list of applications are HTTP and most UDP applications. Support for HTTP connections appeared in version 6.0. So, in version 6.0 and later, you have the option of including or not including stateful failover information for HTTP traffic. This is important because a significant amount, if not the majority, of traffic flowing through firewalls is web browsing. Turning on this feature could have a performance impact. And, to some extent, many users are conditioned by the typically unreliable Internet weather, and they are acquainted with the Refresh and Reload buttons.

In version 5.2, Cisco increased the speed of the failover serial cable from very, very slow (9600bps), to just very slow (115Kbps). However, this still isn't enough bandwidth to support the potentially massive state information, since practically every packet that passes through the PIX Firewall changes the state of some connection. Remember that the PIX not only keeps track of the source and destination addresses and ports, but also tracks the TCP sequence and acknowledgment numbers, which change in every packet.

Cisco's solution to the bandwidth problem is that stateful failover provides an optional dedicated 100Mbps Ethernet connection in addition to the serial failover cable. This means you need a spare Ethernet interface on both the primary and standby PIX Firewalls, configured with IP addresses and dedicated to failover. This is pictured physically in Figure 14.3 and logically in Figure 14.4.

FIGURE 14.3 Physical stateful failover

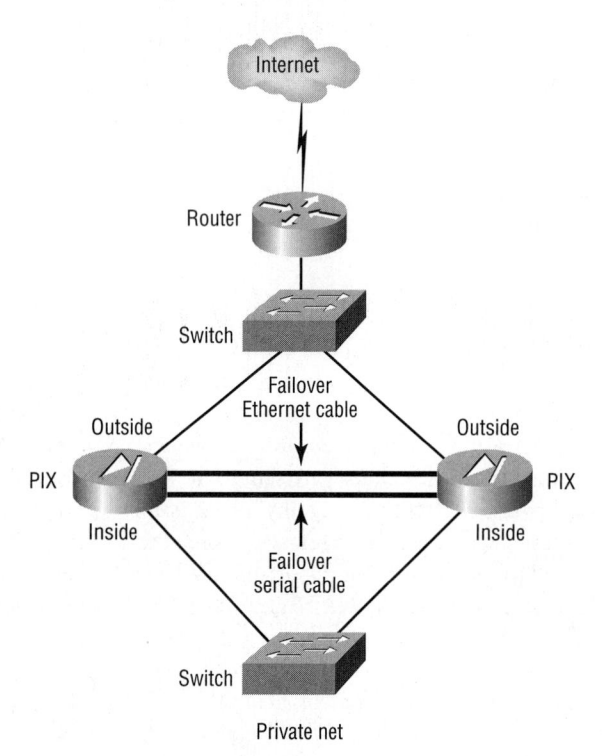

Basic Failover Configuration

Fortunately, configuring failover is simple. It takes only a few commands, and they're all a subset of the aptly named `failover` command. The syntax for this command is as follows:

```
pix(config)# failover ?
Usage:  [no] failover [active]
        [no] failover ip address if_name ip_address
        failover mac address ifc_name act_mac stn_mac
        failover reset
        failover link if_name
        failover poll seconds
        failover replication http
        failover lan unit primary|secondary |
                interface lan_if_name|
                key key_secret|
                enable
        show failover [lan [detail]]
```

FIGURE 14.4 Logical stateful failover

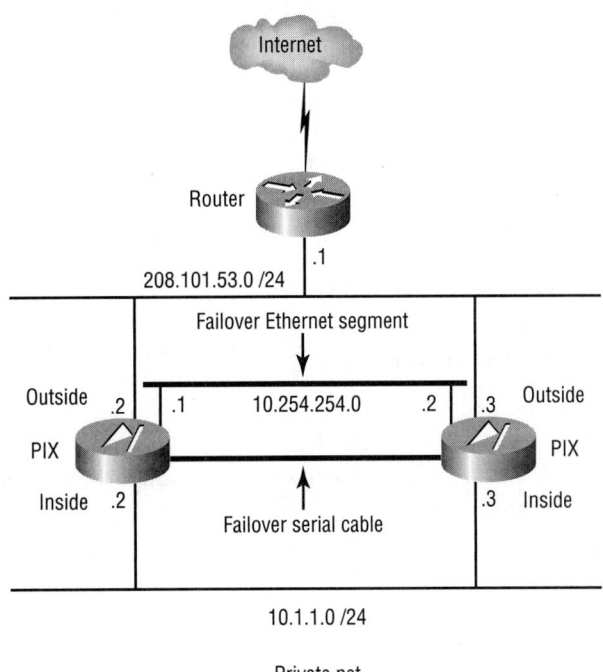

The defaults for these commands are as follows:

```
no failover
failover timeout 0:00:00
failover poll 15
failover ip address outside 0.0.0.0
failover ip address inside 0.0.0.0
failover ip address dmz 0.0.0.0
```

Note that it's possible to use stateful or nonstateful failover. Nonstateful failover might be appropriate in the following circumstances:

- You don't have a spare Ethernet interface because of cost or because you're using the maximum number of interfaces the PIX Firewall's chassis supports.
- You're primarily using UDP or other applications that don't require stateful information.
- In rare cases, performance might justify a decision to forego stateful failover.

Let's now discuss the difference between stateful and nonstateful failover configuration. We'll also discuss how and why to change both the polling interval and a PIX Firewall's role.

Nonstateful Failover Configuration

The `failover` and `failover ip address` commands are all that are required to configure nonstateful failover. Specifically, since the default is **no failover**, you need to issue the command `failover` to enable failover. And since you enter configuration commands only on the active node and not on the secondary node, you need a way to tell the secondary node what its IP addresses are. You do so with the `failover ip address` command.

For example, let's suppose you have inside, outside, and demilitarized zone (DMZ) interfaces, with the IP addresses 10.1.1.1, 10.1.2.1, and 10.1.3.1, respectively, on the active PIX Firewall. To configure the standby PIX Firewall, you issue the following:

```
PIX(config)# failover ip address inside 10.1.1.2
PIX(config)# failover ip address outside 10.1.2.2
PIX(config)# failover ip address dmz 10.1.3.2
PIX(config)#
```

Notice that the standby's interfaces can be any address on the same subnet. Because these interfaces will be used as part of the failover testing to determine whether an interface is up or down, each interface must have an IP address.

Stateful Failover Configuration

For stateful failover, you need to also specify the link you want to use for the failover link. For example, if you wanted to use `ethernet3` as the failover link, you could name it `faileth3` with the `nameif` command, and then use the `failover link` command, as follows:

```
PIX(config)# failover link faileth3
PIX(config)#
```

Once you enter the `failover link` command, stateful failover is enabled.

The state information is passed across this Ethernet (Fast Ethernet, actually) link via IP—specifically, IP protocol 105. Although it's recommended that you use a crossover cable and directly connect the two firewall units, you could run this connection through a hub or switch.

Finally, if you want to include web traffic in your stateful failover (available in version 6.0 and higher), you need to issue the following command:

```
PIX(config)# failover replication http
```

LAN-Based Failover Configuration

For LAN-based failover configuration, you need to specify the link that you want to use for the failover, just as in stateful failover configuration. The Ethernet interface for the failover link must also be identified. In addition, you must set one of the PIX Firewalls as the primary unit, as follows:

```
PIX(config)# failover link faillink
PIX(config)# failover lan interface faillink
PIX(config)# failover lan unit primary
```

As an option, you can encrypt the failover communications. As a default, all failover communications are sent in clear text. It's advisable to encrypt the failover communications with the following commands:

`PIX(config)# failover lan key `*`sharedkey`*

To enable the LAN-based failover, you need two final commands:

`PIX(config)# failover lan enable`
`PIX(config)# failover`

The secondary unit needs a basic configuration to allow the PIX Firewall to communicate with the primary unit and synch the configurations. The primary unit sends its configuration to the secondary unit, with the exception of the `failover lan unit` command. All the other `failover lan` commands are identical on both units, but they aren't replicated to the standby unit and must be saved in memory.

Poll Interval Configuration

Another common configuration is adjusting the polling interval. With most timers in IOS routers and switches, the default settings are typically the best, and it's recommended that you not change them unless you have a compelling reason to do so. The polling interval for the PIX Firewall failover feature is different. In most cases, you should change this number to better suit the characteristics of your network.

The polling interval is fairly simple. When two PIX Firewalls are configured for failover, the standby firewall sends messages to the active firewall on each interface every x number of seconds, where x is the polling interval. If the standby PIX Firewall doesn't hear a response from the active PIX Firewall for three polling intervals, it begins its failover sequence to become the active unit.

The default polling interval is 15 seconds. The minimum value is 3 seconds. So, by default, the standby PIX Firewall waits between 31 and 45 seconds (two polling intervals, plus part of a third, since we don't expect the active unit to fail precisely at the beginning of a polling interval) before initiating the failover sequence. If the polling interval were set to 3 seconds, the standby PIX Firewall would wait between 7 and 9 seconds before initiating the failover sequence.

As you can see, there is quite a difference between 9 and 45 seconds. Why not always set it to 3 seconds? The problem is that in a busy network, it's not unusual to see a link congested for 6 to 9 seconds. This could result in an accidental failover because the standby thinks the active is down, when in fact it's just busy. Of course, you might still have this problem with the default setting of 15 seconds, but it's much less likely to occur.

Finding the best setting for your network is a matter of trial and error. If your network isn't busy, go ahead and use the lower settings. If you experience unwarranted failovers, raise the poll interval until they stop.

For stateful failover, you need to consider the primary type of traffic you have. Some applications time out after 30 seconds and force you to reestablish them. If your PIX Firewall failovers always take 31 or more seconds, there isn't much point in exchanging all that stateful information, because the bulk of that information includes things such as TCP sequence numbers that are reset when your application session is reestablished. So, for stateful failover, you should use the lowest poll interval possible.

To set the polling interval, use the `failover poll` command. For instance, if you wanted to change the polling interval to 4 seconds, you would issue this command:

```
PIX(config)# failover poll 4
PIX(config)#
```

Also note that this timer is set for the entire system. Although it might be very useful, you can't set different interfaces to have different poll intervals.

Role Configuration

As we explained earlier in the chapter, by default, the active unit is the primary unit. However, for maintenance and other purposes, you can force a failover to occur so that the secondary unit is the active unit. The command to force a failover is simple:

```
[no] failover active
```

To force the secondary unit to become active, you enter the following command from the primary unit:

```
failover active
```

To switch service back to the primary unit, enter the following command from the secondary unit:

```
no failover active
```

Cisco PIX Device Manager (PDM)

PIX Device Manager (PDM) is used to create security rules on a single PIX Firewall or FWSM from a web browser. We'll give you an overview of the PDM and what it does, its operating requirements, how to prepare for PDM, and using the PDM to configure the PIX Firewall.

PDM Overview

The PDM is a powerful GUI that assists you in setting up and configuring a PIX Firewall without requiring an extensive knowledge of the PIX Firewall command-line interface (CLI). It also offers a wide range of informative, real-time, and historical reports that provide a view into usage trends, performance baselines, and security events. Many security vulnerabilities are caused by poor configuration. Consequently, implementing security policy must be as straightforward as possible. PDM includes wizards, point-and-click configuration, and online help to simplify administration.

PDM offers helpful wizards for setting up a new PIX deployment. With just a few steps, the PDM Setup Wizard enables you to efficiently create a basic configuration that allows packets to flow through the PIX Firewall from the inside network to the outside network securely. You can also perform optional tasks such as configuring rules to allow outside access to a web or mail server. After you complete initial setup, intuitive pull-down menus and icons let you easily add and delete services and rules as well as access other feature settings. The PDM sends the correct CLI commands to the PIX Firewall unit for the configuration you choose.

Using the PDM, you can easily configure, manage, and monitor security policies across your network. The PDM's GUI provides a familiar tabbed layout using task-oriented menu choices, drop-down menus, and browse options with one-click access to common tasks. The point-and-click design is simple for even novice users, reducing orientation time. The result is cost savings through significant reductions in management time and maximum efficiency in network security management.

PDM is implemented in Java to provide robust reporting and monitoring tools that provide you with real-time and historical insights. At a glance, administrators can view graphical reports summarizing network activity, resource utilization, and event logs, allowing performance and trend analysis. Data from each graph can be displayed in increments you select (10-second snapshot, last 10 minutes, last 60 minutes, last 12 hours, last 5 days) and refreshed at user-defined intervals. The ability to view multiple graphs simultaneously allows you to do side-by-side analysis.

The PDM applet uploads to your workstation when you access the PIX Firewall from your browser. PDM works with the Secure Sockets Layer (SSL) protocol to ensure that communication with the PIX Firewall unit is secure. Cisco PDM has an integrated Syslog viewer, which allows you to view specific Syslog message types by selecting the desired logging level.

Similar to Telnet and Secure Shell (SSH) usage, PDM lets you protect access with a valid username and password. This can be either on the PIX Firewall or through an authentication server.

The FWSM has some differences from the standalone PIX Firewall. These differences also affect how the PDM interacts with the FWSM. Specifically, any OSPF or VPN configuration commands are ignored but not changed by PDM. Everything else in the PDM is compatible with the FWSM.

In the following sections, we'll look at the operating requirements and how to prepare the firewall for the PDM. Finally, we'll go over how to configure the PIX Firewall via the PDM, and we'll highlight some of its key features.

Operating Requirements

The firewall requirements for running PDM are as follows: a Cisco PIX Firewall 501, 506E, 515E, 520, 525, 535, or FWSM with at least 32MB of RAM and 16MB of flash (PIX Firewall 501, 506, and 506E require 8MB). The firewall must be running version 6.0 or higher or the PIX operating system with either DES or 3DES enabled.

The requirement for running PDM on the user machine is a Pentium or Pentium-compatible processor running 300MHz, but 500MHz is recommended. It must have at least 128MB of RAM, with 192MB recommended; and a display resolution of 800 × 600 pixels using 256 colors, with 1024 × 768 pixels and 16-bit color recommended. The minimum network connection speed is 56Kbps, with 128Kbps recommended.

Table 14.1 lists the operating systems and browser combinations and their respective versions. PDM isn't supported on computers running Macintosh, Windows 3.1, or Window 95 operating systems, including Solaris on IBM PCs.

TABLE 14.1 Operating Systems and Browsers Supported by PDM

Operating Systems	Browsers
Windows 2000 (Service Pack 1)	MS Internet Explorer 5.01 (Service Pack 1) or higher (5.5 recommended)
Windows NT 4.0 (Service Pack 6a)	Netscape Communicator 4.51 or higher (4.76 recommended)
Windows 98 (original or 2nd edition)	
Sun Solaris 2.6 or 2.8 running CDE or Open Windows window manager	Netscape Communicator 4.76
Red Hat Linux 6.2 or 7.0 running GNOME or KDE 2.0 desktop environment	

Preparing for PDM

If the PIX Firewall doesn't have the PDM loaded, or if you need to upgrade to a later version, then you need to Trivial File Transfer Protocol (TFTP) the PDM image from the TFTP server to the PIX Firewall. If you're familiar with upgrading the PIX Firewall software image, this is very similar. The command to download a software image to the PIX Firewall is `copy tftp flash`, and the command to download the PDM software image to the PIX Firewall is `copy tftp flash:pdm`. Here is an example of using this command to install the PDM onto a PIX Firewall:

```
PIX# copy tftp flash:pdm
Address or name of remote host [127.0.0.1]? 172.17.141.20
Source file name [cdisk]? pdm-211.bin
copying tftp://172.17.141.20/pdm-211.bin to flash:pdm
[yes|no|again]? yes
Erasing current PDM file
Writing new PDM file
    !!!!!!!!!!!!!!!!!!!!!!!!!!!!!!!!!!!!!!!!!!!!!!!!!!!!!!!!!!!!!!!!!
    !!!!!!!!!!!!!!!!!!!!!!!!!!!!!!!!!!!!!!!!!!!!!!!!!!!!!!!!!!!!!!!!!
    !!!!!!!!!!!!!!!!!!!!!!!!!!!!!!!!!!!!!!!!!!!!!!!!!!!!!!!!!!!!!!!!!
    !!!!!!!!!!!!!!!!!!!!!!!!!!!!!!!!!!!!!!!!!!!!!!!!!!!!!!!!!!!!!!!!!
```

```
!!!!!!!!!!!!!!!!!!!!!!!!!!!!!!!!!!!!!!!!!!!!!!!!!!!!!!!!!!!!!!!
!!!!!!!!!!!!!!!!!!!!!!!!!!!!!!!!!!!!!!!!!!!!!!!!!!!!!!!!!!!!!!!
!!!!!!!!!!!!!!!!!!!!!!!!!!!!!!!!!!!!!!!!!!!!!!!!!!!!!!!!!!!!!!!
!!!!!!!!!!!!!!!!!!!!!!!!!!!!!!!!!!!!!!!!!!!!!!!!!!!!!!!!!!!!!!!
!!!!!!!!!!!!!!!!!!!!!!!!!!!!!!!!!!!!!!!!!!!!!!!!!!!!!!!!!!!!!!!
!!!!!!!!!!!!!!!!!!!!!!!!!!!!!!!!!!!!!!!!!!!!!!!!!!!!!!!!!!!!!!!
!!!!!!!!!!!!!!!!!!!!!!!!!!!!!!!!!!!!!!!!!!!!!!!!!!!!!!!!!!!!!!!
!!!!!!!!!!!!!!!!!!!!!!!!!!!!!!!!!!!!!!!!!!!!!!!!!!!!!!!!!!!!!!!
!!!!!!!!!!!!!!!!!!!!!!!!!!!!!!!!!!!!!!!!!!!!!!!!!!!!!!!!!!!!!!!
!!!!!!!!!!!!!!!!!
PDM file installed.
PIX#
```

Now that you have the PDM installed, to prepare to run it you need to either run the **setup** command to configure the PIX Firewall to be accessible from one IP address, or manually enter the commands via the CLI for PDM operation. Here you can see an example of using the **setup** command on a PIX Firewall, which has an existing configuration (the irrelevant portions have been omitted):

```
PIX(config)# setup
Pre-configure PIX Firewall now through interactive prompts [yes]?
Enable password [use current password]:
Clock (UTC):
  Year [2003]:
  Month [Mar]:
  Day [20]:
  Time [11:52:43]:
Inside IP address [192.168.21.1]:
Inside network mask [255.255.255.0]:
Host name [PIX]:
Domain name [sybex.com]:
IP address of host running PIX Device Manager: 172.17.141.200

The following configuration will be used:
Enable password: current passwordClock (UTC): 11:52:43 Mar 20 2003
Inside IP address: 192.168.21.1
Inside network mask: 255.255.255.0
Host name: PIX
Domain name: sybex.com
IP address of host running PIX Device Manager: 172.17.141.200

Use this configuration and write to flash? y
```

```
Building configuration...
Cryptochecksum: d8ab4e71 a1881144 b7db3938 0a3f8bfa
[OK]
PIX(config)# wr t
Building configuration...
: Saved
:
PIX Version 6.2(2)
hostname PIX
pdm history enable
http server enable
http 172.17.141.200 255.255.255.255 inside
: end
[OK]
PIX(config)#
```

As you can see from this example, the PIX Firewall has turned on the HTTP server with the `http server enable` command and made it so the workstation at 172.17.141.200 has to access the PDM with the `http 172.17.141.200 255.255.255.255 inside` command. The `pdm history enable` command is a default command.

You can also manually place these commands in the PIX Firewall configuration if you aren't keen on using the `setup` command. To reiterate, you need to turn on the HTTP server with the `http server enable` command and then make sure you allow HTTP connections to the PIX Firewall using the `http` command followed by the IP address and mask of the allowed hosts and the interface they will be using.

> **Note:** Because the PIX Firewall uses the SSL protocol to provide a secure transport for the PDM traffic, you can configure HTTP access to the outside interface.

Using PDM to Configure the PIX Firewall

Once you've set up the PIX Firewall to run PDM, you need to open a browser of your choice from the ones supported. If your PIX Firewall was set up with the inside IP address of 172.17.140.23, then you need to type in the following URL: https://172.17.140.23. You may see a couple of security alerts; choose Yes to open a login window like the one in Figure 14.5.

If you've set up AAA authentication, then this is where you enter the username and password. If there is no AAA, then leave the username blank and use the enable password. If there is no enable password, then also leave the Password field blank. This will spawn two more windows; an example of the first is shown in Figure 14.6.

FIGURE 14.5 Login Authentication

FIGURE 14.6 Cisco PIX Device Manager Information Window

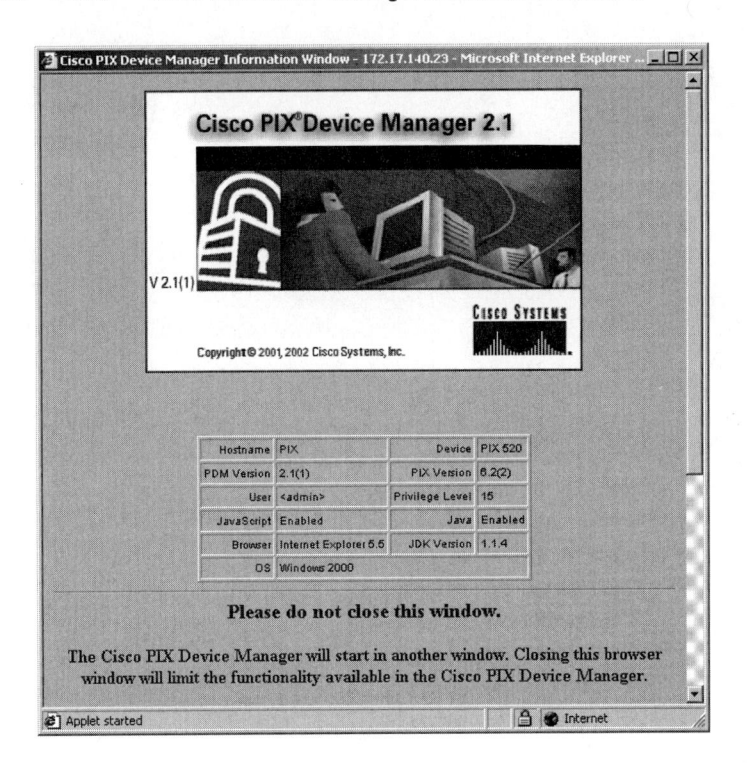

This window shows the PIX Firewall model, the software version, the PDM version, and information about your workstation. The second window is a Java window with the title Cisco PIX Device Manager followed by the version, as shown in Figure 14.7.

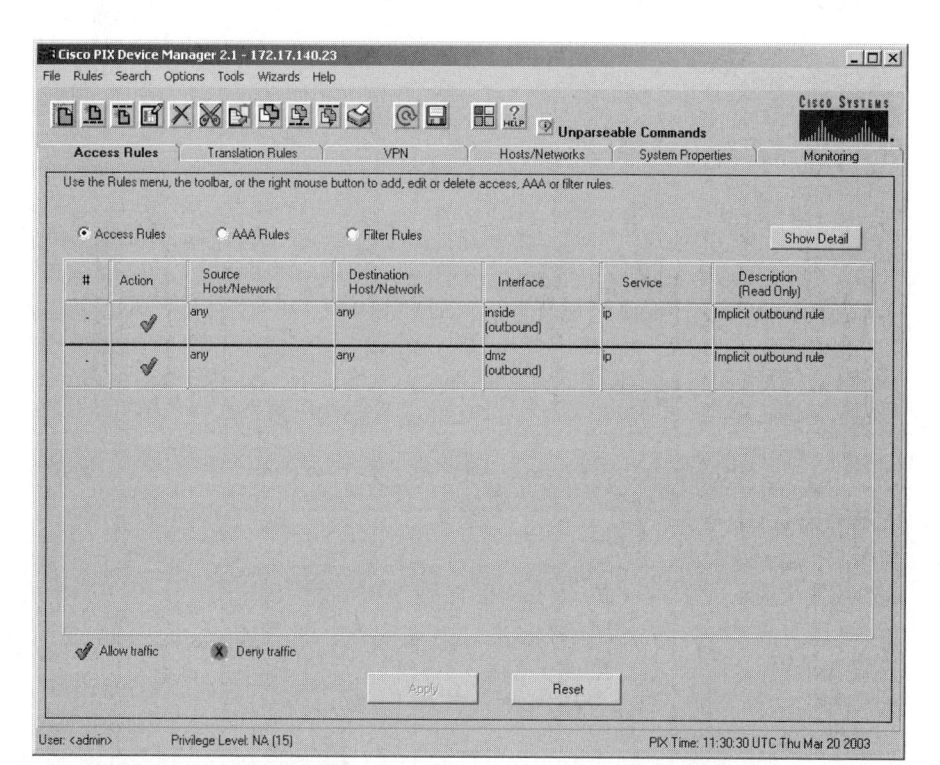

FIGURE 14.7 Cisco PIX Device Manager 2.1 window

You use this window to configure your PIX Firewall. If you look under the row of icons, you'll see tabs for Access Rules, Transition Rules, VPN, Hosts/Networks, System Properties, and Monitoring. We'll go over each of these so you're familiar with the user interface and what is configurable from each tab.

> **Note**
> We won't cover the VPN tab in this chapter; we'll discuss it in further detail in the next chapter when we talk about VPNs using the PIX Firewall.

Figure 14.7 shows the Access Rules tab, which lists the configured access rules, AAA rules, and filter rules. You can see the implicit outbound rule for each outside interface. The two rules represent the two outside interfaces (in this case, `inside` and `dmz`). Click the radio button next to the set of rules you'd like to see and configure. To add a rule, click the Rules drop-down menu on the top of the window and choose Add.

Figure 14.8 shows an example of adding a rule (in this case, an access rule) and the options available.

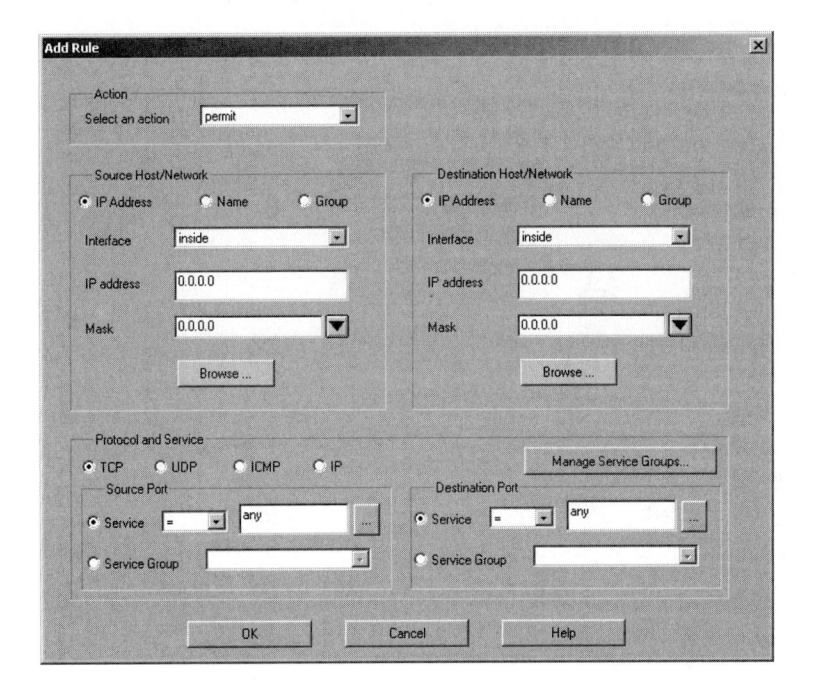

The Translation Rules tab shows the translation rules defined on the PIX Firewall. As you can see from Figure 14.9, there are currently no translation rules defined.

As on the Access Rules tab, by clicking the Rules drop-down menu on the top of the window and choosing Add, you can add a static or dynamic translation rule to the PIX Firewall configuration. Figure 14.10 is an example of the screen you'll see when adding a translation rule to the firewall.

Figure 14.11 shows the contents of the Hosts/Network tab. Remember that in Chapter 12, "ACLs, Filtering, Object Grouping, and AAA," when we talked about object groups, we said that they would be more apparent when talking about the PDM. The Hosts/Networks tab is where you set up network object groups; you can also nest one group inside another. You add a network or host by clicking on the Add button in the Hosts/Networks section; similarly, you can add a group of Hosts or networks by clicking on the Add button in the Hosts/Networks Groups section.

FIGURE 14.8 Adding an access rule

FIGURE 14.9 The Translation Rules tab

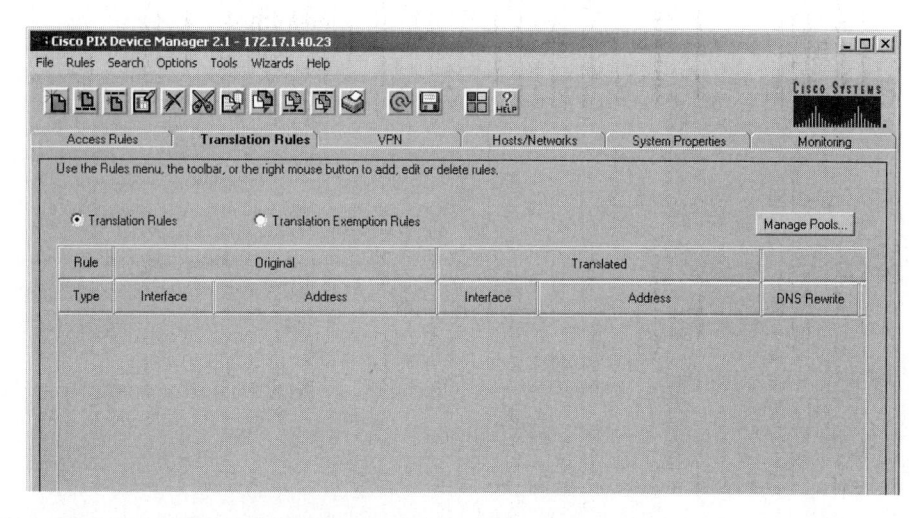

FIGURE 14.10 Adding a translation rule

FIGURE 14.11   The Hosts/Networks tab

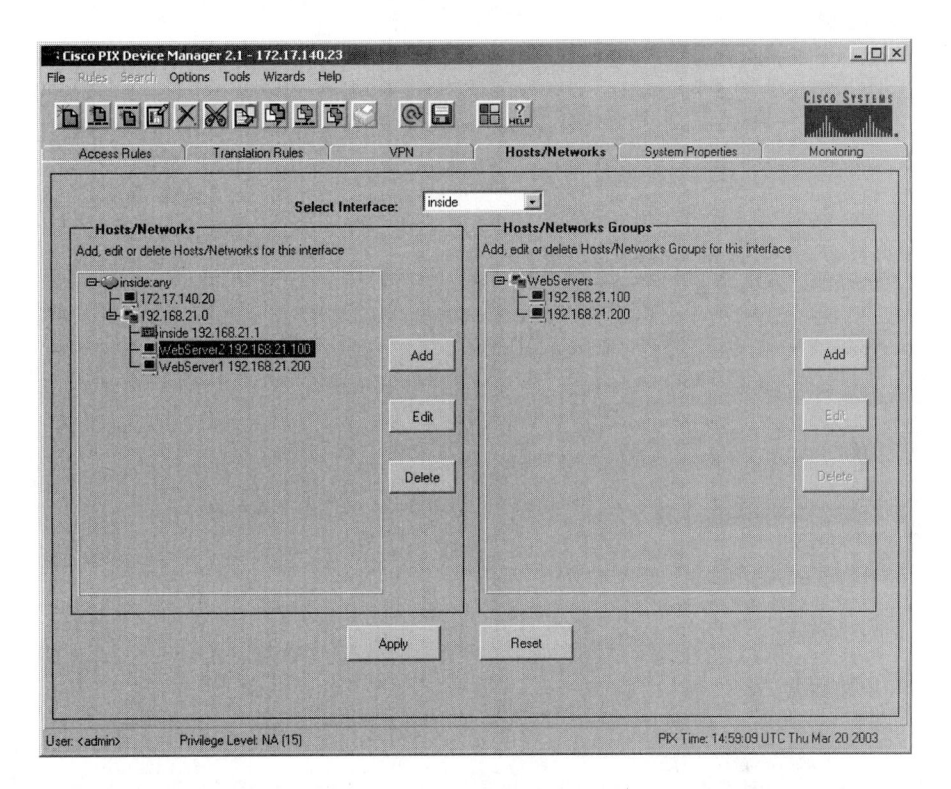

You can add individual hosts or whole networks to the PIX Firewall configuration and later use them in access rules to make your configuration more readable and scalable. You can also configure the NAT properties of the host or network at the time you create the object. As you can see in Figure 14.11, we've added two hosts called WebServer1 (IP address 192.168.21.200) and WebServer2 (IP address 192.168.21.100). We've also added a group called WebServers containing both WebServer1 and WebServer2. Now we can add an access rule to allow access to these web servers by using the WebServers group; we won't have to use their respective IP addresses.

The System Properties tab is used to view and configure the PIX Firewall system properties. Figure 14.12 shows the options available for configuration. We won't discuss each of them, but you should explore them when you have a chance.

The Monitoring tab is used to check on the health of the PIX Firewall. As you can see in Figure 14.13, many options are available to be monitored. If only the Monitoring tab is available in the PDM, a noncompatible configuration may exist.

FIGURE 14.12 The System Properties tab

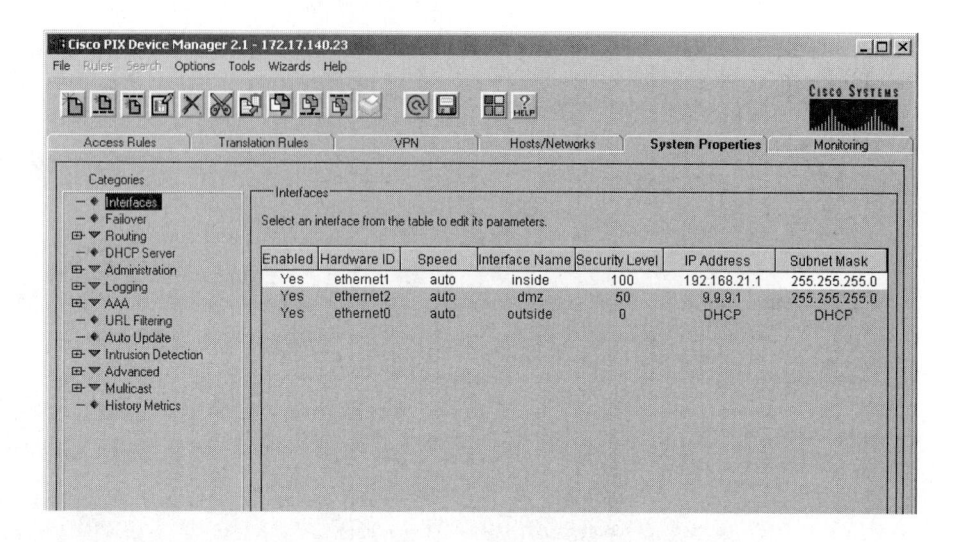

FIGURE 14.13 The Monitoring tab

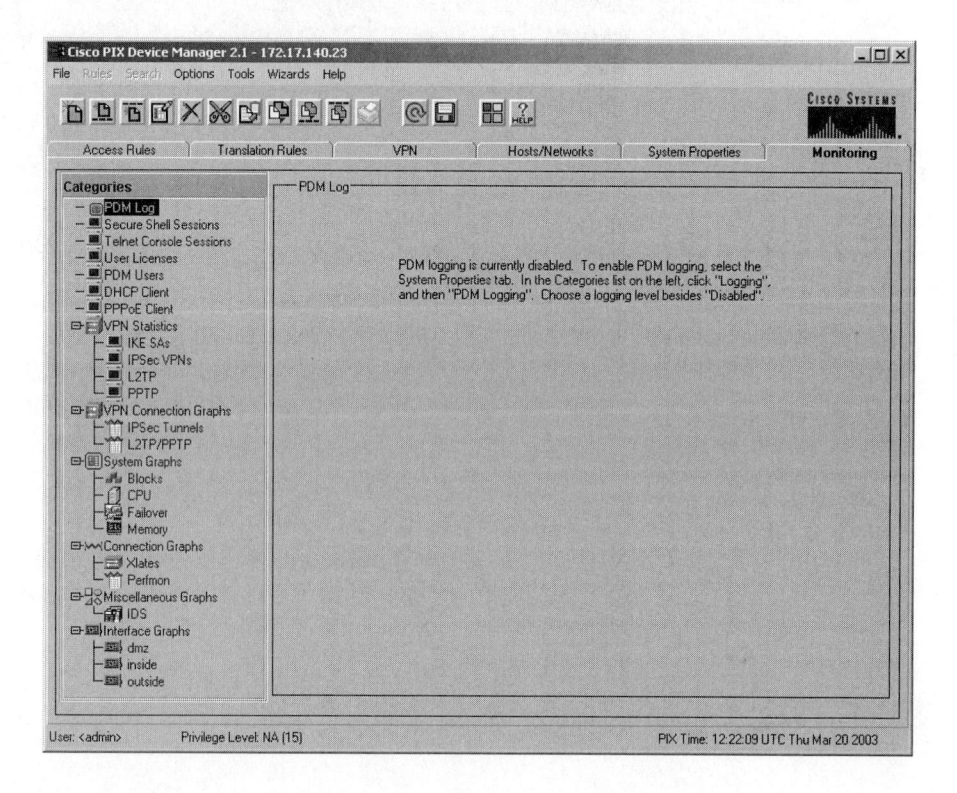

Cisco PIX Device Manager (PDM) 401

You can choose many different items to monitor in real time. Choose a category to view, and then select the available graphs within that category. You then add that graph to your selected graphs and click Graph It when you're done. In Figure 14.14, we've selected the CPU Utilization graph, and in Figure 14.15, we've selected the Memory Utilization graph.

You can select up to four graphs to view at a time, but multiple graph windows can be open at a time. Figure 14.16 shows an example of what you'll see when you click the Graph It button.

FIGURE 14.14   Selecting the CPU Utilization graph

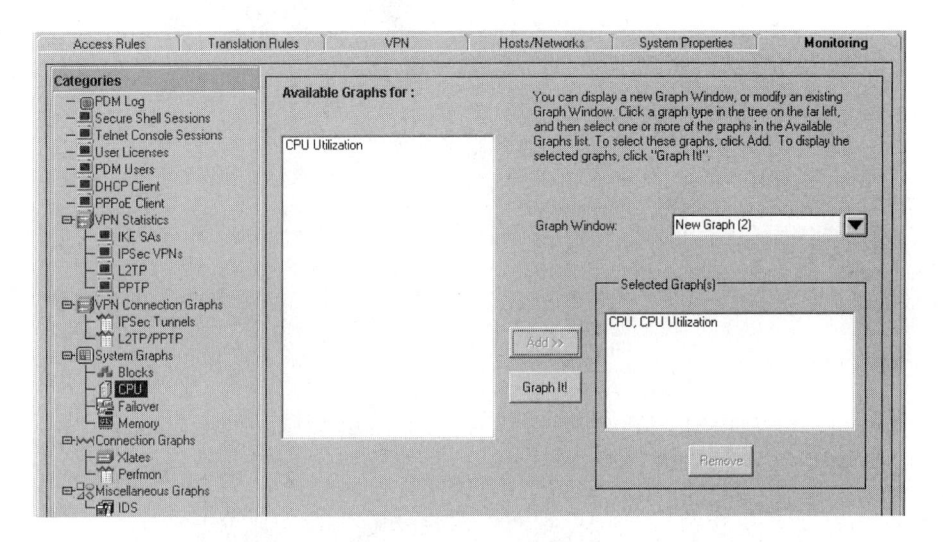

FIGURE 14.15   Selecting the Memory Utilization graph

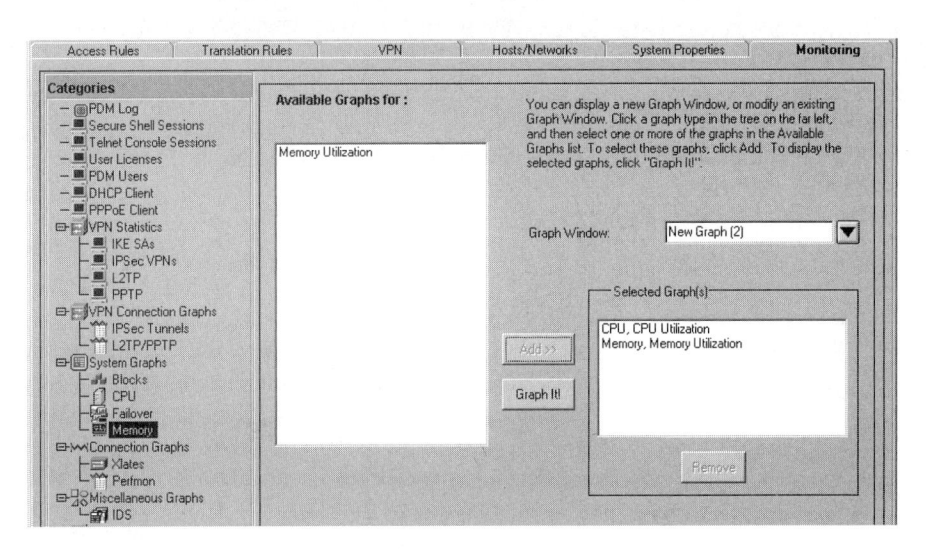

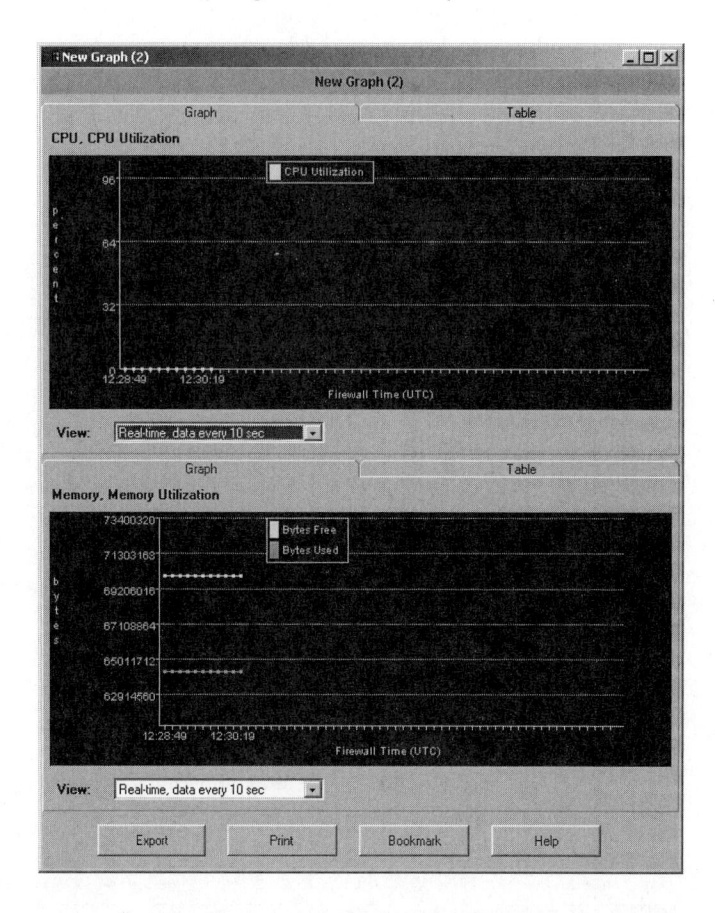

FIGURE 14.16 Graphing CPU and memory utilization

You need to be aware of two icon buttons that you may use often in the PDM. They're together in the middle of the icon button bar below the drop-down menus (you can see them in Figure 14.7).

The first icon button looks like a circular arrow; when you move the mouse over it, the text reads *Refresh PDM with the Running Configuration on the Firewall*. This button updates the PDM with the configuration of the firewall. It's used to make sure the PDM has the latest configuration from the firewall. There is no way for the PDM to know that someone has modified the configuration of the PIX Firewall from the console and not from the PDM.

The second icon button looks like a diskette; when you move the mouse over it, the text reads *Save Running Configuration to Flash*. This button is used to save the current running configuration in the PIX Firewall to flash. Changes are saved to the running configuration as you change from one tab to another, but this configuration isn't saved to flash until you explicitly save it.

Summary

In this chapter, we discussed the basic failover concepts of points of failure, single points of failure, and fault tolerance. We then explained how the PIX Firewall's hardware and software are points of failure, and how Cisco has mitigated the risk of failure using the failover feature.

We next discussed the PIX Firewall failover feature. You learned how PIX failover operates, what stateful failover is, and how to configure the PIX Firewall for failover.

The remainder of the chapter covered how to install and configure the PIX Firewall for configuration by the PIX Device Manager (PDM). We talked about the firewall and user requirements in addition to how the GUI operates, and some of its useful features.

Exam Essentials

Know what a point of failure is.   Understand the concept of *points of failure* and *single points of failure*. Be able to identify them and describe what to expect when they occur.

Understand the difference between redundancy and load balancing.   Be able to distinguish between these strategies. Understand the traffic patterns and special challenges associated with each one.

Understand the hardware requirements for configuring failover.   Remember what hardware you need. Know which cables must be connected where and what licenses you need to purchase. Be able to describe the special hardware requirements for stateful failover.

Know the configuration syntax used to configure failover.   Be able to identify the command lines required to configure failover and stateful failover. Know which unit to configure.

Understand the process used to fail over.   Know how the active and standby units communicate. Know what information is transmitted over the serial and Ethernet cables. Understand how polling works. Know what information is shared in stateful failover.

Understand what circumstances will trigger a failover.   Given a set of conditions, be able to determine whether the primary or secondary PIX Firewall will be active.

Know the PIX Firewall and user operating requirements to use PDM.   You should know which version of the PIX operating system must be installed to use the PDM. Know which user operating systems and browser versions will work with PDM.

Understand how to enable PDM on the PIX Firewall.   Know the methods used to enable PDM on the PIX Firewall using the `setup` command and manually configuring the `http` commands.

Chapter 15

VPNs and the PIX Firewall

THE FOLLOWING TOPICS ARE COVERED IN THIS CHAPTER:

- ✓ How a PIX Firewall enables a secure VPN
- ✓ Configuring the PIX Firewall for VPN support
- ✓ Configuring IKE and IPSec parameters on the PIX Firewall
- ✓ Testing and verifying the VPN configuration on the PIX Firewall
- ✓ How the Cisco VPN client operates
- ✓ How the PIX Firewall can scale for multiple VPNs
- ✓ Using the PDM to create site-to-site and remote access VPNs
- ✓ Using the PDM to configure access and translation rules
- ✓ Overview of PDM reporting, tools, and administration
- ✓ Overview of the auto-update server
- ✓ Setting the PIX Firewall and AUS communication settings
- ✓ Creating devices, images, and assignments in the PIX MC
- ✓ Using the PIX MC reports and administration

This chapter will describe how to configure the PIX Firewall to support IPSec tunnels using both pre-shared keys and digital certificates through certificate authorities. We'll discuss how to configure the IKE/ISAKMP parameters and explain the commands to test and verify your VPN configuration on the PIX Firewall. Next we'll talk about the Cisco VPN client and how to scale PIX Firewall VPNs. We'll show you how to use the PIX Device Manager to create both site-to-site and remote access VPNs.

Finally, we'll talk about how to do enterprise management and maintenance using the Cisco Secure Policy Manager and CiscoWorks2000. The PIX Firewall can be integrated into CiscoWorks2000 using two components of the VPN/Security Management Solution: the Management Console for PIX Firewalls and the Auto Update Server.

Preparing to Configure VPN support

The PIX Firewall enables a secure VPN by using IPSec tunnels, which can encrypt the tunnel using DES, 3DES, or AES encryption algorithms. When you're preparing for IPSec VPN configuration on a PIX Firewall, you need to decide what the tunnel will be used for, if this is the only tunnel, and what kind of security is required.

There isn't as much flexibility regarding tunnel termination when the tunnel ends at a PIX Firewall. Older versions of the PIX Firewall software required that a VPN terminate only on the outside interface. Newer versions (5.1 and later) allow tunnels to terminate on any interface.

To prepare for IPSec configuration, you'll need to perform the following tasks:

Gather information. Determine how the devices will refer to the peers—as either IP address or hostname—and what type of configuration will be used to build the IKE tunnel.

Decide which IKE policy (or policies) will be used for the tunnel. Are the Internet Key Exchange (IKE) policy parameter values using RSA signatures or a pre-shared secret for authentication? How will the information be encrypted between IKE peers? Which Diffie-Hellman group will be used? What is the tunnel's lifetime?

Decide how IPSec will be configured. Consider how IPSec security associations (SAs) will be formed, which transforms you'll use, and what type of traffic will be protected.

Make sure that network connectivity exists. The simplest way to do this is with a ping. Note that firewalls usually need to explicitly permit Internet Control Message Protocol (ICMP) traffic using the `icmp permit` command for this test to work properly.

Examine any existing ACLs to ensure that necessary traffic won't be blocked. Traffic from IKE/Internet Security Association and Key Management Protocol (ISAKMP; UDP port 500),

Authentication Header (AH; protocol 51), and Encapsulating Security Payload (ESP; protocol 50) should be permitted. The Adaptive Security Algorithm (ASA) on the PIX Firewall will allow traffic to return if it started on the local firewall, but if the client starts the session, the packets won't be allowed in unless the firewall is configured to allow the traffic through.

> **NOTE**: Cisco's ASA is the basis for the PIX Firewall's security. The ASA uses assigned security levels to allow interfaces to be configured securely. See Chapter 10, "PIX Firewall Basics," for more information about the ASA.

Configuring IKE on a Firewall

Configuring IKE is a simple task on the PIX Firewall primarily because each firewall comes with a default protection suite that can be used to build the IKE communication. ISAKMP is a framework that defines the procedures used for authenticating communication between two peers. IKE implements the Oakley and Secure Key Exchange MEchanism (SKEME) key exchange protocols within the ISAKMP framework, which automatically negotiates IPSec security associations and enables IPSec secure communications without manual preconfiguration.

In the following section, we'll show you how to enable IKE on a firewall interface, configure an IKE policy, and configure both pre-shared keys and digital certificates for IKE authentication.

Enabling IKE

IKE is enabled globally by default, and any changes that need to be made are configured on an interface-by-interface basis. This is different from the configuration on a Cisco IOS router, where ISAKMP is enabled or disabled globally.

Use the `isakmp enable` *interface-name* command to enable ISAKMP on the PIX Firewall for an interface. To disable IKE on an interface, place a `no` before the command; for instance, `no isakmp enable`. Leaving ISAKMP enabled on an interface that isn't acting as a VPN tunnel endpoint can be a security risk and should be avoided. The following is an example of the commands used to enable and disable IKE on an interface:

```
PIX(config)# isakmp enable outside
PIX(config)# no isakmp enable outside
PIX(config)#
```

Configuring the IKE Policy

When IKE is enabled on an interface, the next step is to configure the *IKE policy* or what the PIX Firewall calls a *protection suite*. To prepare for the configuration, examine the default policy template and decide how much of it may be used for the tunnel being created. For example, if you want to use pre-shared keys, you need to change the default authentication method from

RSA signatures to pre-shared keys. Figure 15.1 shows an example of an IKE policy using pre-shared keys.

Since the PIX Firewall has only one configuration mode, you issue all of the configuration commands from Global Configuration mode. Each command used to modify a policy property begins with isakmp policy *number*. Just as on the router, there aren't an overwhelming number of options, but each one is important. The following are the policy configuration commands:

- isakmp policy *number* encryption aes | aes-192 | aes-256 | des | 3des
- isakmp policy *number* hash md5 | sha
- isakmp policy *number* authentication pre-share | rsa-sig
- isakmp policy *number* group 1 | 2 | 5
- isakmp policy *number* lifetime seconds

> **NOTE**
> Remember that the *number* is the priority number, which links each of the separate lines together, and that the lower the priority number is, the higher the preference for that policy.

Once each device has a policy configured, and interesting traffic triggers the process, both devices can bring up an IKE tunnel. To allow the tunnel traffic to continue into the PIX Firewall, use the command sysopt connection permit-ipsec.

FIGURE 15.1 IKE tunnel details

IKE policy example		
Parameter	Site 1	Site 2
Encryption algorithm	DES	DES
Hash algorithm	MD5	MD5
Authentication method	Pre-shared keys	Pre-shared keys
Key exchange	768-bit D-H	768-bit D-H
IKE SA lifetime	86,400 seconds	86,400 seconds
Peer IP address	192.168.2.2	192.168.1.2

Configuring Pre-shared Keys

Using pre-shared keys is the simplest way of setting up authentication in preparation for building an IPSec tunnel. The disadvantages of using pre-shared keys are that they're inefficient for organizations that use many tunnels, and they're the least scalable method.

The preconfigured keys must match between two devices for them to form an IKE tunnel. A firewall may be configured with a key that is used to communicate with two other firewalls and a software client. The same key string may be used to communicate with many different end devices, or a firewall can be configured with a different key for each IKE tunnel that is to be created.

To configure a firewall to authenticate via a pre-shared key, specify the following:

ISAKMP peer   Use the `isakmp identity {address | hostname}` command to tell the PIX Firewall how it can expect peers to be defined. The identity of an ISAKMP peer is defined either by its IP address or by a hostname. This is a global command and applies to every peer that this PIX Firewall will be talking to. By default the PIX uses addresses not hostnames.

Hostname resolution   You can use the `name ip_address hostname` command to create a local name-to-address resolution table. If the first command was configured with the hostname option, the firewall needs a way to resolve hostnames to IP addresses. One way of doing this is with a DNS reference. Another is by creating a local translation table. This command isn't needed if the `identity` command specifies referencing with IP addresses.

ISAKMP key   Use the `isakmp key key_string {address | hostname} ip_address | hostname` command to establish what key will be used for what peer. This command establishes the key used, specifies if the peer will be referenced via IP address or via hostname, and then lists the address or hostname used. The key may be up to 128 characters in length.

> **NOTE**   Nothing prevents a PIX Firewall from using the same key to every one of the peer devices it talks to, although this wouldn't be a good security practice.

The following is an example of IKE configuration on a PIX Firewall:

```
PIX(config)# sysopt connection permit-ipsec
PIX(config)# isakmp enable outside
PIX(config)# isakmp key sybex address 192.168.244.33
PIX(config)# isakmp policy 80 authentication pre-share
PIX(config)# isakmp policy 80 encryption des
PIX(config)# isakmp policy 80 hash sha
PIX(config)# isakmp policy 80 group 1
PIX(config)# isakmp policy 80 lifetime 86400
PIX(config)#
```

Configuring the Use of Certificate Authorities (CAs) on a Firewall

Using a certificate authority (CA) for authentication on a PIX Firewall is the preferred method when you need to scale your VPN to a large number of devices. The information you must collect before enrolling a firewall with a CA and the procedure for enrolling are basically the same as for enrolling a Cisco IOS router, if you're familiar with that platform.

> **WARNING**
> Terminating several VPNs on a PIX Firewall is usually a bad idea. Doing so can create a resource overload on your firewall if adequate evaluation isn't performed. You can use a hardware accelerator card to allow the PIX Firewall to terminate many VPNs; but in general, if dozens or hundreds of tunnels are needed, it's best to consider using a VPN concentrator instead.

In the following section, we'll discuss how to configure the PIX Firewall to use digital certificates for authentication. We'll show how to prepare the PIX Firewall to communicate with a CA and how to enroll with the CA.

Preparing the Firewall for CAs

On a PIX Firewall, certificates are stored in flash memory. Several certificates may be generated when you enroll with a CA: an ID certificate for the device, the CA's ID certificate, and a registration authority (RA) ID certificate. Before enrolling with the CA, you should examine the flash to make sure space is available for storing the certificates and the keys.

Another preparatory step is to check the firewall clock setting to avoid problems with a certificate's validity time range. We strongly suggest using a timeserver in the network and configuring the firewall to talk to that server via Network Time Protocol (NTP). To set the PIX Firewall clock, use the `clock set` command (discussed in Chapter 11, "PIX Firewall Configuration").

In addition to setting the correct time, it's extremely important that you establish a proper hostname and domain name. It's possible to create the necessary keys without the domain being set up, but if a domain name isn't configured, the PIX Firewall uses a default domain of `ciscopix.com`. If the default name hasn't been changed, the administrator will be told to change it. To establish the domain name, use the command domain-name *domain*, which was also discussed in Chapter 11. You should use a unique hostname, because the host and domain names are used in the keys, and using identical names is a small security risk. To change the hostname, use the command `hostname` *name*.

Enrolling a Firewall with a CA

Before you enroll a firewall with a CA, you must generate the keys, identify the CA, and authenticate the CA. After these steps, you need to save the keys and configuration. The PIX Firewall has a separate command for configuring additional properties of the CA communication.

Generating the Keys

To generate the public and private keys that will be used with the certificates, use the `ca generate rsa key` *key_size* command. Recall from the last chapter that this command is also needed to run the PIX Device Manager (PDM) GUI. PDM uses the Secure Sockets Layer (SSL) protocol for secure communication, which uses the generated RSA key. The RSA key modulus default size is 768 bits, as opposed to the Cisco IOS router's default of 512 bits.

Here is an example of a general-purpose key configured on a PIX Firewall:

PIX(config)# **ca generate rsa key 512**
PIX(config)#

Identifying the CA

Use the following command to identify the name of a CA:

`ca identity` *name ip_address*

with an optional parameter for the script location. For example, the location might be :/certsrv/mscep/mscep.dll. Other commands reference the name that is specified here, and this command says that the named device is a CA.

In addition to specifying the IP address, you can add the Common Gateway Interface (CGI) script location and Lightweight Directory Access Protocol (LDAP) IP address at the end of the command. Once a CA is defined, you can't change the name without deleting the entire CA configuration. Here is an example:

PIX(config)# **ca identity MyCA 10.31.12.250 :/certsrv/mscep/mscep.dll**
PIX(config)#

Configuring Additional CA Communication Properties

You may use the `ca configure` *name type retry_period retry_count* command to configure additional properties of the CA communication. The PIX Firewall can optionally contact an RA instead of the usual CA. The *name* is the name of the CA identified with the `ca identity` command, and the type is either `ca` or `ra`. Optionally, you can use the `crloptional` parameter.

For example, you might decide that the PIX Firewall will get certificates only from a CA or that it can also get certificates from an RA. The retry period is used to determine how often the PIX Firewall will retry if the CA doesn't respond, and the retry count specifies how many times it retries before giving up. Here is an example of setting five retries, 10 seconds apart:

PIX(config)# **ca configure TestCA ca 10 5 crloptional**
PIX(config)#

The `crloptional` parameter makes the certificate revocation list (CRL) optional. Each time a new connection begins, the PIX Firewall attempts to download a new CRL. Ordinarily, if the CRL is unavailable, the tunnel setup is denied. Using `crloptional` says to allow the connection even if the CRL is unavailable. This is a security risk because it's possible for someone to use a hijacked certificate while a CA is experiencing a DoS attack, and the attempted connection would be allowed.

Authenticating the CA

The `ca authenticate` *name fingerprint* command authenticates the CA based on the method of authentication chosen by the CA administrator, either by an alphanumeric fingerprint or by a pre-shared password. The name used here is the same one used in the `identity` command. Including the expected fingerprint allows the PIX Firewall to compare what is received with what is expected. If the two don't match, the certificate is discarded. You obtain the fingerprint from the CA administrator. Here is an example:

```
PIX(config)# ca authenticate MyCA Sybex123
PIX(config)#
```

Enrolling the Firewall

Once you've authenticated to the CA, you have to request the certificate from the CA using the `ca enroll` *name password serial ipaddress* command. The optional parameters return the PIX Firewall serial number and IP address, respectively, in the certificate.

This sends a request with the Public Key Cryptography System (PKCS) 10. If everything is okay, the PIX Firewall gets a PKCS 7 back with the appropriate certificates.

The CA name is straightforward, and the password is used for the challenge from the CA, if it's required. A certificate on the PIX Firewall can include the serial number of the device and the IP address of the terminating interface; these are additional security measures to help prevent someone from hijacking a certificate. The following is an example of enrolling the PIX Firewall with a CA and using the additional parameters for higher security:

```
PIX(config)# ca enroll MyCA Sybex serial ipaddress
PIX(config)#
```

> **NOTE** The `ca enroll` command isn't entered into the configuration. If the PIX Firewall reboots after this command is issued but before certificates are received and saved, you'll need to reissue the request.

Downloading the CRL

The PIX Firewall automatically downloads a CRL whenever it receives a certificate. If the PIX Firewall is unable to download the latest CRL when it receives a certificate, it will reject the certificate, just as if the certificate were found on the CRL. To prevent this from happening, use the `crloptional` option with the `ca configure` command, as described earlier in this chapter in the "Configuring Additional CA Communication Properties" section.

Saving the Configuration

Saving your configuration provides a backup in case the firewall needs to be reconfigured. Use the `write mem` command to save everything that has been configured, with the exception of the CA enrollment command. Any RSA keys that have been generated are saved at the same time, but in a different area of the flash.

Another command you can use is ca save all, which saves configuration details regarding certificates. This command saves the RSA keys that were generated as well as the certificates received from the CA.

Showing Certificate Information

You can view the firewall's public key, certificates, and the CA's identity and configuration. To see the local PIX Firewall's public key, use the show ca mypubkey rsa command, as follows:

```
PIX(config)# show ca mypubkey rsa

% Key pair was generated at: 11:00:21 Nov 25 2001

Key name: PIX.sybex.com
 Usage: General Purpose Key
 Key Data:
   305c300d 06092a86 4886f70d 01010105 00034b00 30480241
   009956df 93f32f45 25d31b9d 1961754b 03d01f91 0b365a96
   162d77e2 b6eaba9e bad7684c 6d1533ac a7f13f7e 757dd91d
   5f0beb99 69ec35ef 8acc5136 8ce3d5ac af020301 0001
PIX(config)#
```

To view the local PIX Firewall's certificates, use the show ca certificate command:

```
PIX(config)# show ca certificate
CA Certificate
   Status: Available
   Certificate Serial Number:
     6246f2a3a959a6ab47df0ec86729079b
   Key Usage: Signature
     CN = CA Server
      OU = CASERVER
      C = US
   Validity Date:
     start date: 11:40:56 Nov 24 2001

     end   date: 11:49:17 Nov 24 2003


RA Signature Certificate
   Status: Available
   Certificate Serial Number: 6103a5c6000000000002
   Key Usage: Signature
```

```
    CN = Sybex
     O = Illustrated
     C = US
  Validity Date:
    start date: 11:51:13 Nov 24 2001

    end   date: 12:01:13 Nov 24 2002


RA KeyEncipher Certificate
  Status: Available
  Certificate Serial Number: 6103a6e0000000000003
  Key Usage: Encryption
    CN = Sybex
     O = Illustrated
     C = US
  Validity Date:
    start date: 11:51:13 Nov 24 2001

    end   date: 12:01:13 Nov 24 2002
PIX(config)#
```

To see the CA identity, use the command show ca identity. To see the CA configuration, use show ca configure. Here is an example of using both these commands:

```
PIX(config)# show ca identity
ca identity vpnca 172.31.1.50:/certsrv/mscep/mscep.dll
PIX(config)# show ca configure
ca configure vpnca ra 1 20 crloptional
PIX(config)#
```

Deleting CA-Related Items

You can use the following three commands to delete a firewall's keys and certificates:

The *no ca save all* command   This command erases the keys and certificates from flash.

The *ca zeroize rsa* command   This command eliminates the RSA keys that have been created, but it doesn't remove the certificates that are based on those keys.

The *no ca identity* command   This command, followed by the optional CA nickname, eliminates everything associated with the CA, including the firewall's ID certificate.

Configuring IPSec on a Firewall

After configuring IKE and your authentication method, you're ready to build your IPSec tunnel for the PIX Firewall. IPSec provides security for transmission of sensitive traffic over networks such as the Internet. IPSec provides the following network security services:

Data confidentiality The IPSec sender can encrypt packets before transmitting them across a network.

Data integrity The IPSec receiver can authenticate packets sent by the IPSec sender to ensure that the data hasn't been altered during transmission.

Data origin authentication The IPSec receiver can authenticate the source of the IPSec packets sent. This service depends on the data integrity service.

Anti-replay The IPSec receiver can detect and reject replayed packets.

IPSec tunnels are sets of SAs that are established between two IPSec peers. The SAs define which protocols and algorithms should be applied to sensitive packets and also specify the keying material to be used by the two peers. SAs are unidirectional and are established per security protocol (AH or ESP).

On the PIX Firewall, the components for configuring IPSec are

- Crypto ACLs
- Transform sets
- Tunnel lifetime
- Crypto maps

Creating Crypto ACLs

Crypto ACLs are regular ACLs, but they're tied to a crypto map on the PIX Firewall. They're attached to the tunnel to determine which traffic may cross the tunnel. Consider the example of two firewalls connecting a tunnel across the Internet, shown in Figure 15.2. Both firewalls have a symmetric ACL configuration. Source and destination information is flipped from one PIX Firewall to the other, because when PIX1 sends a packet across the tunnel, it expects the reply to come in via the tunnel. If the reply doesn't come through the tunnel, there is obviously something wrong, and the packet should be dropped.

Remember that Network Address Translation (NAT) takes place before the PIX Firewall compares the outgoing packet with the ACL. This means the NAT address is the one that needs to be used in the ACL. Also, remember that PIX Firewall ACLs are slightly different from IOS ACLs. To specify a single IP address on the PIX Firewall, use a net mask value of 255.255.255.255 instead of 0.0.0.0.

FIGURE 15.2 Symmetric ACLs

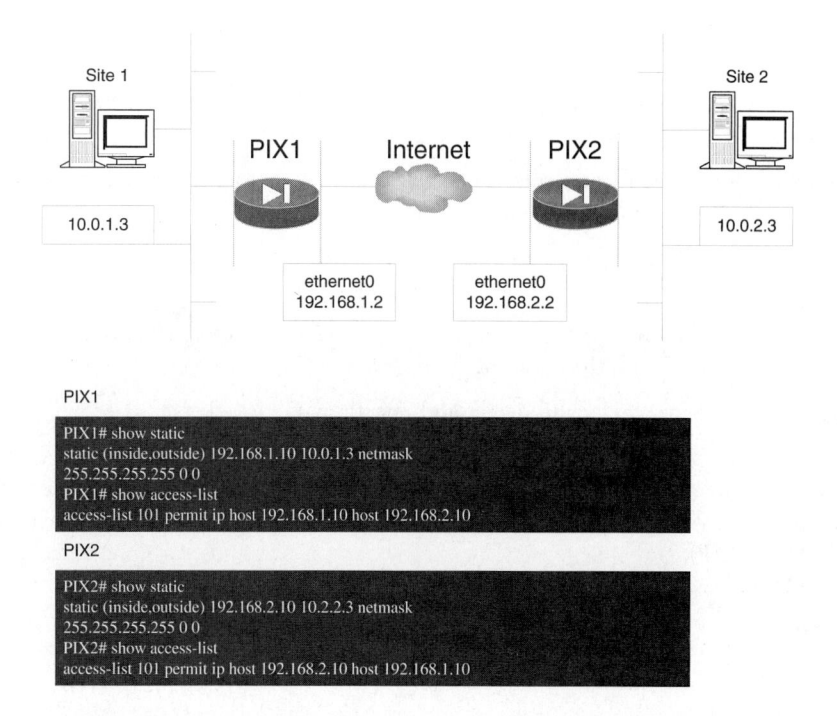

```
PIX1
PIX1# show static
static (inside,outside) 192.168.1.10 10.0.1.3 netmask
255.255.255.255 0 0
PIX1# show access-list
access-list 101 permit ip host 192.168.1.10 host 192.168.2.10

PIX2
PIX2# show static
static (inside,outside) 192.168.2.10 10.2.2.3 netmask
255.255.255.255 0 0
PIX2# show access-list
access-list 101 permit ip host 192.168.2.10 host 192.168.1.10
```

Creating and Configuring Transform Sets

To create the transform set for the PIX Firewall, use the `crypto ipsec transform-set` *name transform_1 transform_2 transform_3* command. Each transform set must have a name and at least one transform associated with it. Table 15.1 lists the transforms available. AES support is available only on PIX firewalls licensed for VPN-3DES, and version 6.3 or greater of the operating system.

An example of a configuring a transform set is as follows:

PIX(config)# **crypto ipsec transform-set testset esp-des esp-md5-hmac**
PIX(config)#

The transforms may be mentioned in any order when you enter the command, but you can have only one transform from each column. You should also know that `esp-3des` is available only if you have the Triple Data Encryption Standard (3DES) license installed. With version 6.3 of the PIX Firewall operating system, additional ESP encryption options include Advanced Encryption Standard (AES) with 128-, 192-, and 256-bit keys.

TABLE 15.1 Transforms for a PIX Firewall

AH Authentication	ESP Authentication	ESP Encryption
ah-md5-hmac	esp-md5-hmac	esp-3des
ah-sha-hmac	esp-sha-hmac	esp-des
		esp-null
		esp-aes-256

> **NOTE** Remember that transform sets between the peers must match for a tunnel to become established.

A Transport mode tunnel protects the data portion of the packet. A Tunnel mode tunnel protects the entire packet. You might wonder why you would want Transport mode over Tunnel mode. When you use Tunnel mode, the original IP address of the host is encapsulated, and the traffic looks as if it's coming from the PIX Firewall. When you use Transport mode, only the data portion of the packet is encrypted; the IP header is used from the original host, so the traffic looks as if it's coming from the original host and not the PIX Firewall. If you're using RFC 1918 address space, then the default of Tunnel mode is the best method to use. Figure 15.3 illustrates this concept.

FIGURE 15.3 Tunnel mode versus Transport mode

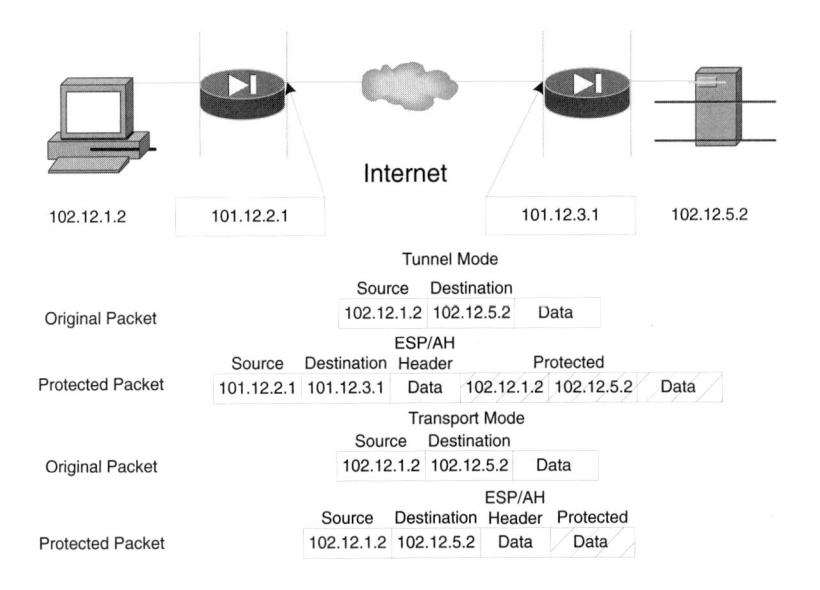

A Transport mode transform set can be used only with a dynamic crypto map; the PIX Firewall CLI will display an error if you attempt to tie a Transport mode transform set to a static crypto map. To create a Transport mode tunnel, use the `crypto ipsec transform-set` *name* `mode transport` command.

> **NOTE**
> The Windows 2000–native L2TP/IPSec client uses Transport mode, so Transport mode must be selected on the transform set. For PIX Firewall 6.0, Layer 2 Tunneling Protocol (L2TP) is the only protocol that can use the Transport mode. All other types of packets using Transport mode are discarded by the PIX Firewall.

Setting the Tunnel Lifetime

The *tunnel lifetime* is a value that can be expressed in seconds, blocks of data, or both. PIX Firewall software versions of at least 6.0 support using both of these methods to determine when the tunnel drops. When one of these values is reached, the tunnel is deactivated.

> **NOTE**
> Remember that tunnels are renegotiated 30 seconds before they're scheduled to expire. However, this renegotiation doesn't apply if perfect forward secrecy (PFS) is being used.

To configure the tunnel lifetime, use the `crypto ipsec security-association lifetime [seconds` *seconds* `| kilobytes` *kilobytes*`]` command. The following is an example of setting the tunnel lifetime:

```
PIX(config)# crypto ipsec security-association lifetime seconds 1600
PIX(config)# crypto ipsec security-association lifetime kilobytes 50000
PIX(config)#
```

You can specify both values, which will expire the SA with whatever value is reached first. You can also configure both values on the same command line, as shown by the following example:

```
PIX(config)# crypto ipsec security-association lifetime seconds 1600
➥kilobytes 50000
PIX(config)#
```

The default in time is 28,800 seconds; the default in data is 4,608,000KB. This method sets the timeouts on a global basis. You can configure individual tunnels differently by modifying the appropriate crypto map.

Creating Crypto Maps

A crypto map ties all the IPSec configuration information together. The command to create a crypto map is crypto map *name sequence_number sa_type*, where *sa_type* is ipsec-manual or ipsec-isakmp. However, a crypto map is configured on the PIX Firewall in a line-by-line format, as opposed to being placed into a Crypto Map Configuration mode as with a Cisco IOS router. Remember that only one crypto map statement per interface is allowed.

The following are the parameters that you can configure for each tunnel:

```
crypto map map-name seq-num ipsec-isakmp
crypto map map-name seq-num match address access-list-name

crypto map map-name seq-num set peer hostname | ip-address

crypto map map-name seq-num set transform-set transform-
    name1 [transform-name2] [transform-name3]

crypto map map-name seq-num set pfs [group1 | group2]
crypto map map-name seq-num set security-association
    lifetime seconds seconds | kilobytes kilobytes
```

To apply the crypto map to the appropriate interface, use the crypto map *map-name* interface | *interface_name* command.

> **NOTE** A PIX Firewall must be using at least software version 5.1 to be able to terminate a VPN on any interface. With version 5.0 and earlier, a VPN may be terminated only on the outside interface.

If a tunnel arrives from the outside and terminates at the PIX Firewall, it must terminate at the outside interface. Likewise, a tunnel coming from a DMZ network terminates at the DMZ interface. A VPN tunnel may pass through the PIX Firewall, but if it terminates at the PIX Firewall, it must do so at the first interface it hits. The following is an example of a crypto map configuration:

```
PIX(config)# crypto map TestVPN 10 ipsec-isakmp
PIX(config)# crypto map TestVPN 10 set peer 172.16.114.1
PIX(config)# crypto map TestVPN 10 set transform-set secureset
PIX(config)# crypto map TestVPN 10 match address 101
PIX(config)#
```

Real World Scenario

Using VPNs to Replace Expensive WAN Links

A company with an international Frame Relay network is looking to cut costs. The Frame Relay network costs $8,000 per month for the four-node network. We'll look at how the company can use its Internet connections at each location to implement a VPN so it can disconnect the expensive Frame Relay network. The company already has PIX Firewalls installed at each site, and we'll leverage them for the VPN network.

The following shows the internal IP addresses and outside PIX Firewall IP addresses at each location:

    Headquarters 216.10.200.0/22 205.13.25.67

    London 216.10.199.0/24 167.5.132.12

    Munich 216.10.198.0/24 43.159.13.56

    Tokyo 216.10.197.0/24 221.72.18.14

Management has dictated that the traffic must be encrypted using 3DES, but authentication headers don't need to be used. We'll use the 3DES encryption, Secure Hash Algorithm (SHA) for the hash, pre-shared key for authentication, and Diffie-Hellman Group 2 for the IKE tunnel negotiation.

We'll configure only the headquarters and London PIX Firewalls in this scenario. The others will look similar to the London router. The following are the steps used to set up the headquarters PIX Firewall:

```
HQ# config t
HQ(config)# access-list HQ_to_London permit 216.10.200.0 255.255.252.0
↪ 216.10.199.0 255.255.255.0
HQ(config)# access-list HQ_to_Munich permit 216.10.200.0 255.255.252.0
↪ 216.10.198.0 255.255.255.0
HQ(config)# access-list HQ_to_Tokyo permit 216.10.200.0 255.255.252.0
↪ 216.10.197.0 255.255.255.0
HQ(config)# isakmp enable outside
HQ(config)# isakmp policy 12 encryption 3des
HQ(config)# isakmp policy 12 hash sha
HQ(config)# isakmp policy 12 authentication pre-share
HQ(config)# isakmp policy 12 group 2
HQ(config)# sysopt connection permit-ipsec
HQ(config)# isakmp identity address
```

```
HQ(config)# isakmp key $yB3xcl$COc3RtlFlcAtlONS address 167.5.132.12
HQ(config)# isakmp key $yB3xcl$COc3RtlFlcAtlONS address 43.159.13.56
HQ(config)# isakmp key $yB3xcl$COc3RtlFlcAtlONS address 221.72.18.14
HQ(config)# crypto ipsec transform-set strong_enc esp-3des esp-sha-hmac
HQ(config)# crypto map Corp_VPN 10 ipsec-isakmp
HQ(config)# crypto map Corp_VPN 10 match address HQ_to_London
HQ(config)# crypto map Corp_VPN 10 set peer 167.5.132.12
HQ(config)# crypto map Corp_VPN 10 set transform-set strong_enc
HQ(config)# crypto map Corp_VPN 20 ipsec-isakmp
HQ(config)# crypto map Corp_VPN 20 match address HQ_to_Munich
HQ(config)# crypto map Corp_VPN 20 set peer 43.159.13.56
HQ(config)# crypto map Corp_VPN 20 set transform-set strong_enc
HQ(config)# crypto map Corp_VPN 30 ipsec-isakmp
HQ(config)# crypto map Corp_VPN 30 match address HQ_to_Tokyo
HQ(config)# crypto map Corp_VPN 30 set peer 221.72.18.14
HQ(config)# crypto map Corp_VPN 30 set transform-set strong_enc
HQ(config)# crypto map Corp_VPN interface outside
HQ(config)# exit
HQ#
London# config t
London(config)# access-list London_to_HQ permit 216.10.199.0 255.255.255.0
➥ 216.10.200.0 255.255.252.0
London(config)# access-list London_to_Munich permit 216.10.199.0 255.255.255.0
➥ 216.10.198.0 255.255.255.0
London(config)# access-list London_to_Tokyo permit 216.10.199.0 255.255.255.0
➥ 216.10.197.0 255.255.255.0
London(config)# isakmp enable outside
London(config)# isakmp policy 12 encryption 3des
London(config)# isakmp policy 12 hash sha
London(config)# isakmp policy 12 authentication pre-share
London(config)# isakmp policy 12 group 2
London(config)# sysopt connection permit-ipsec
London(config)# isakmp identity address
London(config)# isakmp key $yB3xcl$COc3RtlFlcAtlONS address 205.13.25.67
London(config)# isakmp key $yB3xcl$COc3RtlFlcAtlONS address 43.159.13.56
London(config)# isakmp key $yB3xcl$COc3RtlFlcAtlONS address 221.72.18.14
London(config)# crypto ipsec transform-set strong_enc esp-3des esp-sha-hmac
London(config)# crypto map Corp_VPN 10 ipsec-isakmp
```

```
London(config)# crypto map Corp_VPN 10 match address London_to_HQ
London(config)# crypto map Corp_VPN 10 set peer 205.13.25.67
London(config)# crypto map Corp_VPN 10 set transform-set strong_enc
London(config)# crypto map Corp_VPN 10 ipsec-isakmp
London(config)# crypto map Corp_VPN 10 match address London_to_Munich
London(config)# crypto map Corp_VPN 10 set peer 43.159.13.56
London(config)# crypto map Corp_VPN 10 set transform-set strong_enc
London(config)# crypto map Corp_VPN 10 ipsec-isakmp
London(config)# crypto map Corp_VPN 10 match address London_to_Tokyo
London(config)# crypto map Corp_VPN 10 set peer 221.72.18.14
London(config)# crypto map Corp_VPN 10 set transform-set strong_enc
London(config)# crypto map Corp_VPN interface outside
London(config)# exit
London#
```

Verifying and Troubleshooting IPSec Configuration on a Firewall

You can use a number of commands to verify that the PIX Firewall VPN tunnels are working properly, check the configuration, and troubleshoot it if necessary. In the following sections, we'll look at these in depth.

Viewing Configuration Information

You can view information about IKE policies, crypto ACLs, transform sets, crypto maps, tunnel lifetimes, and SAs. Being able to verify the configuration information is very important when you're troubleshooting problems: You'll be able to ensure the configuration is correct and all values are those that are expected. We'll look at how to do this for each in the following sections.

Viewing IKE Policies

The show isakmp policy command shows which IKE policies are configured on the PIX Firewall. The following shows the output from this command:

```
PIX# show isakmp policy
Protection suite of priority 10
    encryption algorithm:    DES - Data Encryption
       Standard (56 bit keys).
```

```
  hash algorithm:            Message Digest 5
  authentication method:     Pre-Shared Key
  Diffie-Hellman group:      #1 (768 bit)
  lifetime:                  86400 seconds, no volume limit
Default protection suite
  encryption algorithm:      DES - Data Encryption
     Standard (56 bit keys).
  hash algorithm:            Secure Hash Standard
  authentication method:     Rivest-Shamir-Adleman Signature
  Diffie-Hellman group:      #1 (768 bit)
  lifetime:                  86400 seconds, no volume limit
PIX#
```

Viewing ACLs, Transforms, and Tunnel Lifetimes

To view the contents of an ACL, use the command show access-list [*name*]. If you specify an ACL name, you'll see the requested list. If you enter just show access-list, you'll see all access lists.

The show crypto ipsec transform-set [*name*] command displays the configured transform sets. As with the show access-list command, you can specify a particular transform set to view by entering its name, or you can view all transform sets like this:

```
PIX(config)# show crypto ipsec transform-set

Transform set mine: { esp-des  }
   will negotiate = { Tunnel,  },

PIX(config)#
```

To view a summary of the tunnel configuration, issue the show crypto map [interface *interface_name* | tag *map_name*] command. If you reference an interface with this command, it displays only the tunnels that terminate at the specified interface. Using the name of the crypto map displays only the requested map. If you don't specify an interface or crypto name, the command displays all crypto maps. Here is an example:

```
PIX(config)# show crypto map

Crypto Map: "peer3" interfaces: { outside }

Crypto Map "peer3" 10 ipsec-isakmp
access-list 101 permit ip host 192.168.6.10 host
   192.168.3.10 (hitcnt=0)
```

```
        Current peer: 0.0.0.0
     Security association lifetime: 4608000
  kilobytes/28800 seconds
        PFS (Y/N): N
        Transform sets={ mine, }
PIX(config)#
```

If you'd like to see the current settings for the global tunnel lifetimes, use the `show crypto ipsec security-association lifetime` command. It's important to remember you can override these values for individual tunnels by setting the tunnel lifetime in the crypto map. The following is an example of using this command:

```
PIX(config)# show crypto ipsec security-association lifetime
Security-association lifetime: 4608000 kilobytes/28800 seconds
PIX(config)#
```

Viewing SAs

The `show crypto ipsec sa` command shows the status of the individual SAs that make up a VPN tunnel. This is a useful command if packets aren't making it across the tunnel but the tunnel is up. It easily detects when a packet should be encrypted but is being dropped because it isn't encrypted. Examining the `pkts` information tells you quite a bit. Here is an example of the output from this command:

```
PIX(config)# show crypto ipsec sa

interface: outside
   Crypto map tag: peer1, local addr. outside

  local  ident (addr/mask/prot/port):
    (192.168.2.10/255.255.255.255/0/0)
  remote ident (addr/mask/prot/port):
    (192.168.1.10/255.255.255.255/0/0)
  current_peer: 192.168.1.2
    PERMIT, flags={origin_is_acl,}
   #pkts encaps: 91, #pkts encrypt: 91, #pkts digest 0
   #pkts decaps: 77, #pkts decrypt: 77, #pkts verify 0
   #pkts compressed: 0, #pkts decompressed: 0
   #pkts not compressed: 0, #pkts compr. failed: 0, #pkts
     decompress failed: 0
   #send errors 55, #recv errors 0
```

```
    local crypto endpt.: outside, remote crypto endpt.:
      192.168.1.2
    path mtu 1514, ipsec overhead 44, media mtu 1514
    current outbound spi: 2efc960f

    inbound esp sas:
     spi: 0xe51b943c(3843789884)
       transform: esp-des ,
       in use settings ={Tunnel, }
       slot: 0, conn id: 4, crypto map: peer1
       sa timing: remaining key lifetime (k/sec):
         (4607998/4514)
       IV size: 8 bytes
       replay detection support: N

    inbound ah sas:

    inbound pcp sas:

    outbound esp sas:
     spi: 0x2efc960f(788305423)
       transform: esp-des ,
       in use settings ={Tunnel, }
       slot: 0, conn id: 3, crypto map: peer1
       sa timing: remaining key lifetime (k/sec):
         (4607995/4505)
       IV size: 8 bytes
       replay detection support: N

    outbound ah sas:

    outbound pcp sas:
PIX(config)#
```

This example shows the crypto map information applied to the SA and what device this PIX Firewall is peering with to create the tunnel. Further examination shows that the tunnel is made up of ESP and that AH isn't in use. It also shows the reason why this tunnel is up: It was activated by interesting traffic matching an ACL entry.

Understanding Error and Status Messages

IKE and IPSec can generate a number of status messages. Cisco doesn't provide a PIX Firewall–specific list of the messages, as it does for the IOS router, but the messages are usually self-explanatory.

One status message that it's always nice to see and that you might need to know for the test is `return status is IKMP_NO_ERROR`. This means ISAKMP managed to complete everything it needed to and the tunnel has come up.

Debugging

The commands used to troubleshoot a PIX Firewall tunnel are the `debug crypto` commands, beginning with `debug crypto isakmp` and then `debug crypto ipsec`.

> **NOTE**
> For information about all the debug commands available in PIX Firewall 6.2, refer to http://www.cisco.com/univercd/cc/td/doc/product/iaabu/pix/pix_62/cmdref/df.htm#1059143.

Understanding Remote Access VPN

For a remote computer to connect to the corporate network over the Internet, you must configure the PIX Firewall to accept these remote access VPN connections. This procedure involves more steps than setting up just a site-to-site VPN. You need to worry about authenticating the remote user and configuring the remote VPN client to appear as a client inside your network. We'll talk about how to configure the PIX Firewall for a remote access VPN. Then we'll use that information in the section "Installing and Configuring the Cisco VPN Client" to discuss how to configure the VPN clients to access the inside network.

There are additional steps for a remote access VPN, but the concept is the same as for a site-to-site VPN. We'll step through the procedure to set up the PIX Firewall, but let's first go over what makes the remote access VPN different.

Extended Authentication (Xauth)

The optional extended authentication *Xauth* feature allows the PIX Firewall to authenticate a VPN user using a TACACS+ or RADIUS server. Xauth is negotiated between IKE phases 1 and 2. IKE phase 1 is used for device authentication, and phase 2 is used for IPSec SA negotiation. If the Xauth fails, the IPSec SA isn't established, and the PIX Firewall deletes the IKE SA.

To enable the optional Xauth feature, use the command

`crypto map map-name client authentication aaa-group`

The *aaa-group* must be previously configured using the `aaa-server` command.

Remember, the PIX Firewall can support only one `crypto map` command per interface. What happens if you're also terminating a site-to-site VPN on that same interface? You don't want to add users to your TACACS+ or RADIUS server for the site-to-site VPNs. So, how do you configure the PIX Firewall not to authenticate those connections? If you're using a pre-shared key on your site-to-site VPN, then you need to add the `no-xauth` parameter to the `isakmp key` command. If you're using RSA signatures, then you need to add the `no-xauth` parameter to the `isakmp peer fqdn` *fully_qualified_domain_name* command. For example, the following is the command to not authenticate the site-to-site VPN peer at IP address 10.19.1.5 and one using the RSA signature at address `vpn1.Sybex.com`:

```
PIX(config)# isakmp key Sybex address 10.12.1.5 no-xauth
PIX(config)# isakmp peer fqdn vpn1.Sybex.com no-xauth
PIX(config)#
```

IKE Mode Config for Dynamic Addressing

You can use the *IKE Mode Config* feature to assign IP addresses dynamically to VPN clients. This feature allows the PIX Firewall to download an IP address and, optionally, other network-level configuration parameters to a VPN client as part of the IKE negotiation process. This IP address is used as an "inner" IP address encapsulated under IPSec, which provides a known IP address for a VPN client that can be matched against the IPSec security policy.

IKE Mode Config can be initiated two ways. First, the PIX Firewall can initiate the Configuration mode with the client. The client then responds, the IKE modifies the sender's identity, the message is processed, and the client receives a response. In the second method, the client initiates the Configuration mode with the PIX Firewall. The PIX Firewall responds with an IP address it has allocated to the client.

How does the PIX Firewall know which IP address to assign to which VPN client? You must first configure a pool of addresses using the `ip local pool` *name start_pool_ip-end_pool_ip* command. Next, you need to link the pool you created to the IKE configuration, using the `isakmp client configuration address-pool local` *name interface* command. The *name* is the name of the pool you created, and the *interface* is, optionally, the name of the interface on which to enable ISAKMP negotiation. Finally, you need to make sure that the `crypto map` you've assigned to the interface will give out these addresses to the VPN users. You do so using the `crypto map` *sequence-number client-configuration address* [initiate | respond] command. The `initiate` parameter indicates that the PIX Firewall will attempt to set IP addresses for each peer. The `respond` parameter indicates that the PIX Firewall will accept requests for IP addresses from any requesting peer.

The following is an example of using these commands to set up IKE Mode Config to assign dynamic addresses:

```
PIX(config)# ip local pool vpn-pool 10.192.12.100-10.192.12.199
PIX(config)# isakmp client configuration address-pool local vpn-pool outside
PIX(config)# crypto map vpnmap client configuration address initiate
PIX(config)#
```

Again, if you're using the same interface for site-to-site and remote access VPN connections, you need to let the PIX Firewall know that you don't want to assign an IP address to the site-to-site remote peer. As with the Xauth exception command, you can do this with the `no-config-mode` parameter added to either the `isakmp key` or `isakmp peer fqdn` *fully_qualified_domain_ name* command. This parameter can be combined with the `no-xauth` parameter to configure the PIX Firewall to not authenticate the site-to-site VPN peer or assign an IP address to the peer.

The following is an example of using both commands for a site-to-site VPN peer using a pre-shared key at IP address 10.19.1.5:

```
PIX(config)# isakmp key Sybex address 10.19.1.5 no-xauth no-config-mode
PIX(config)#
```

Pushing Additional Attributes to the VPN Client

The Cisco VPN 3000 Client version 2.5 and higher and the Cisco unified VPN Client have been extended so you can accept additional attributes for the client. The additional attributes are DNS, WINS, default domain, and Split Tunnel mode. To configure the PIX Firewall to support these extended attributes, you need to create a VPN group using the `vpngroup` command. This command has many parameters that are used to configure the Cisco VPN 3000 Client policy:

- `address-pool`
- `dns-server`
- `wins-server`
- `default-domain`
- `split-tunnel` settings
- `idle-time`

`address-pool` is the only required parameter; it ties a local address pool to the VPN group. The `dns-server` and `wins-server` parameters assign either one or two servers to their respective services. The `default-domain` command configures the default domain name used by the Cisco VPN 3000 Client. The `split-tunnel` parameter uses an access list to configure which IP addresses are IPSec-protected from the client and which are passed through unprotected. The `idle-time` parameter controls how long a client can be idle before disconnection.

The following is an example of using the `vpngroup` command with its parameters to set up a VPN group named Sybex:

```
PIX(config)# access-list 100 ip 10.192.12.0 255.255.255.0 10.192.13.0
➥255.255.255.0
PIX(config)# ip pool local pool1 10.192.12.100-10.192.12.199
PIX(config)# vpngroup Sybex address-pool pool1
PIX(config)# vpngroup Sybex dns-server 10.192.12.250
PIX(config)# vpngroup Sybex wins-server 10.192.12.251 10.192.12.252
PIX(config)# vpngroup Sybex default-domain sybex.com
```

```
PIX(config)# vpngroup Sybex split-tunnel 100
PIX(cofnig)# vpngroup Sybex idle-time 3600
PIX(config)#
```

Common Commands

Now, let's discuss what other commands are needed to get a remote access VPN up and running. As with a site-to-site VPN, you need to configure the IKE policy, peer IP address, and IPSec transform sets. You use the same commands to do this—with some changes. Let's talk about each of these steps.

To create an IKE policy for a remote access VPN, you use the `isakmp policy` command. Use the `encr`, `hash`, and `authentication` parameters to set the correct policy. If you're using the Cisco VPN 3000 Client 3.0 or above, make sure you include the command `isakmp policy number group 2`, because 3.0 and higher use Diffie-Hellman group 2.

The following is an example of an IKE policy that works with a Cisco VPN 3000 client 3.0 or higher:

```
PIX(config)# isakmp policy 13 encr des
PIX(config)# isakmp policy 13 hash md5
PIX(config)# isakmp policy 13 authentication pre-share
PIX(config)# isakmp policy 13 group 2
PIX(config)#
```

If you're using digital certificates and not a pre-shared key, you must use additional commands. Make sure you have a correct domain name and hostname defined before you create a digital certificate. You need to use the `ca generate rsa key key_size` command. The `key_size` is the size the key needs to be to generate the needed RSA key. Then you must identify the CA and the communication parameters. Authenticate and enroll to the CA before continuing. After you've verified your CA configuration, change the IKE authentication policy to use the RSA signature.

The following is an example of the IKE policy when using a CA for peer authentication:

```
PIX(config)# domain-name Sybex.com
PIX(config)# ca generate rsa key 512
PIX(config)# ca identity TestCA 10.192.12.254 10.192.12.254
PIX(config)# ca configure TestCA ca 1 20 crloptional
PIX(config)# ca authenticate TestCA
PIX(config)# ca enroll TestCA Sybex
PIX(config)# isakmp policy 14 encr des
PIX(config)# isakmp policy 14 hash sha
PIX(config)# isakmp policy 14 authentication rsa-sig
PIX(config)#
```

Now you need to specify the password and IP address of the VPN peer. The password is easy, but you don't always know what the IP address will be for each remote access VPN client. It seems that remote users are never in the same place twice, so they're always going to use a different IP address. You specify this information with a wildcard as the IP address in the peer command.

The following is an example of the command to use for remote access VPN clients using the pre-shared key Sybex:

PIX(config)# **isakmp key Sybex address 0.0.0.0 netmask 0.0.0.0**
PIX(config)#

You must configure the PIX Firewall to use an encryption and authentication scheme for these VPN clients. You do this as you did with the site-to-site VPN: by using the crypto ipsec transform-set command.

The following is an example of using this command to configure a good, strong encryption and authentication transform set:

PIX(config)# **ipsec transform-set strong-scheme esp-3des esp-sha-hmac**
PIX(config)#

Finally, you need to tie these elements together and add them to an interface. Because you don't know what the peer IP address will be beforehand, you must create a dynamic crypto map to associate the transform set. It will act as a template when a VPN client connects to the PIX Firewall. The crypto dynamic-map command sets up this dynamic template. Next you need to tie this dynamic map to a regular crypto map, which can be linked to the inbound VPN interface. You do so with the dynamic parameter of the crypto map command.

The following is an example of using these commands:

PIX(config)# **crypto dynamic-map RemClients 3 set transform-set strong-scheme**
PIX(config)# **crypto map VPN-Map 20 ipsec-isakmp dynamic RemClients**
PIX(config)# **crypto map VPN-Map interface outside**
PIX(config)#

Let's see what the PIX Firewall configuration might look like when it supports remote access VPN clients. The following is an example of a PIX Firewall configuration (the irrelevant portions have been removed):

PIX# **wr t**

Building configuration...
: Saved
:

```
PIX Version 6.2(2)
nameif ethernet0 outside security0
nameif ethernet1 inside security100
hostname PIX
access-list 100 permit ip 10.192.12.0 255.255.255.0 10.192.13.0 255.255.255.0
interface ethernet0 auto
interface ethernet1 auto
ip address outside 175.13.12.1 255.255.255.248
ip address inside 10.192.12.1 255.255.255.0
ip local pool pool1 10.192.12.100-10.192.12.199
nat (inside) 0 access-list 100
aaa-server RADIUS protocol radius
aaa-server RADIUS (inside) host 10.192.12.250 abcdef timeout 10
sysopt connection permit-ipsec
crypto ipsec transform-set good-scheme esp-des esp-sha-hmac
crypto dynamic-map RemClients 3 set transform-set good-scheme
crypto map VPN-Map 20 ipsec-isakmp dynamic RemClients
crypto map VPN-Map interface outside
isakmp enable outside
isakmp key ******** address 0.0.0.0 netmask 0.0.0.0
isakmp policy 13 authentication pre-share
isakmp policy 13 encryption des
isakmp policy 13 hash md5
isakmp policy 13 group 2
isakmp policy 13 lifetime 86400
vpngroup sybex address-pool pool1
vpngroup sybex dns-server 10.192.12.240 10.192.12.245
vpngroup sybex wins-server 10.192.12.241 10.192.12.246
vpngroup sybex default-domain sybex.com
vpngroup sybex split-tunnel 100
vpngroup sybex idle-time 3600
: end
[OK]
PIX#
```

In the next section, we'll talk about how to set up the VPN client to connect to the PIX Firewall we just configured.

Installing and Configuring the Cisco VPN Client

The VPN client is simple to install and operate and enables a user to establish secure end-to-end encrypted tunnels to a VPN server. The Cisco VPN client provides support for the following operating systems:

- Windows 95 (OSR2+)
- Windows 98
- Windows ME
- Windows NT 4.0
- Windows 2000
- Windows XP
- Linux (using Intel processors)
- Solaris (UltraSparc 32- and 64-bit processors)
- Mac OS X 10.1 and 10.2

The Cisco VPN client works with the following Cisco platforms:

- Cisco VPN 3000 Series Concentrator 3.0 and later
- Cisco IOS 12.2 T and later
- Cisco PIX Firewall 6.0 and later

After you've installed the VPN Client, you need to configure it to access the PIX Firewall.

If you need help installing the Cisco VPN 3000 Client software, refer to the documentation online at `http://www.cisco.com/univercd/cc/td/doc/product/vpn/index.htm`.

If you're using a pre-shared key for authentication, follow these steps to configure the client to interoperate with the PIX Firewall:

1. Click Start ➤ Programs ➤ Cisco Systems VPN 3000 Client ➤ VPN Dialer.
2. In the VPN Client main dialog box, click New.
3. Enter a name for this connection that isn't already being used. Click Next.
4. Enter the hostname or IP address of the remote PIX Firewall. Click Next.
5. Click Group Access Information.
6. Enter the name of the VPN group and the password. Click Next.
7. To complete the configuration, click Finish.

For the Cisco VPN 3000 Client to gain VPN access to the PIX Firewall using a digital certificate, you must first obtain the certificate from a CA server.

> **NOTE** We won't cover how you obtain a digital certificate for the client, but you can refer to the chapter "Obtaining a Certificate" in the Cisco VPN 3000 Client User Guide online at http://www.cisco.com/univercd/cc/td/doc/product/vpn/index.htm.

Only after this is done can you follow the steps below to create a VPN client connection using a digital certificate:

1. Click Start ➤ Programs ➤ Cisco Systems VPN 3000 Client ➤ VPN Dialer.
2. In the VPN Client main dialog, click New.
3. Enter a name for this connection that isn't already being used. Click Next.
4. Enter the hostname or IP address of the remote PIX Firewall. Click Next.
5. Click Certificate.
6. Click the name of the certificate you're using. Click Next.
7. To complete the configuration, click Finish.

You may wonder where is the VPN group name is configured in the client. The VPN group name is cleverly stored in the digital certificate as the Organization Unit (OU) field. So, if you change the name of the VPN group, you must obtain a new digital certificate with the correct VPN group stored in the OU field.

Deploying the VPN Client

The VPN client can be preconfigured for mass deployments, and the initial login requires very little user intervention. The VPN client access policies and configurations are downloaded from the central gateway and pushed to the client when a connection is established, which allows for simple deployment and management as well as a high degree of scalability.

The group of configuration parameters used for remote users to connect to a VPN server is called a *profile*. There are two varieties of profiles: global and individual. The *global profile* (vpnclient.ini) is a file that sets rules for all remote users; it contains parameters for the VPN client as a whole. The *individual profiles* are files that contain the parameter settings for each connection entry and are unique to that entry. They have a .pcf extension.

Profiles are created in two ways:

- When an administrator or a remote user, using the Windows or Macintosh client, creates connection entries using the VPN Client GUI
- When you create profiles using a text editor

When using the VPN client GUI, the user is also creating a file that can be viewed and edited through a text editor. You can start with a profile file generated through the GUI and edit it.

This approach lets you control some parameters that aren't available in the VPN Client GUI application—for example, auto-initiation or dial-up wait for third-party dialers.

The default location for all profile files for the various operating systems is

- Windows platforms: `C:\Program Files\Cisco Systems\VPN Client\Profiles`
- Linux, Solaris, and Mac OS X platforms: `/etc/CiscoSystemsVPNClient/Profiles/`

We'll explain how to create and edit the `vpnclient.ini` and individual profile files. Both files follow the normal Windows.ini file format convention. The following is a list of these conventions:

- Use a semicolon (;) to begin a comment.
- Section names are specified within brackets [*section name*], and they aren't case sensitive.
- Use key names to set values for parameters (keyword = value). For keywords without values, or unspecified keywords, the VPN client uses the defaults. Keywords can be in any order and aren't case sensitive, although using lowercase and uppercase makes them more readable.

To make an individual parameter read-only, so the client user can't change it within the VPN client applications, precede the parameter name with an exclamation mark (!). This controls what the user can or can't do within the VPN client applications only. You can't prevent someone from editing the global profile (`vpnclient.ini`) or individual profile (`.pcf`) files and remove the read-only designator.

Features Controlled by the Global Profile

The global profile file (`vpnclient.ini`) controls the following global features on all VPN client platforms:

- Start before logon
- Automatic disconnect upon logoff
- Control of logging services by class
- Certificate enrollment
- Identity of a proxy server for routing HTTP traffic
- Identity of an application to launch upon connect
- Missing-group warning message
- Logging levels for log classes
- RADIUS SDI extended authentication behavior
- GUI parameters—appearance and behavior of GUI applications

The `vpnclient.ini` file controls the following additional features when you're using a Windows platform:

- Location of the `Entrust.ini` file
- List of Graphical Identification and Authentication (GINAs) modules that aren't compatible with the VPN Client
- Auto-initiation

- Setting of the Stateful Firewall option
- Microsoft Outlook–to–Microsoft Exchange polling
- The method to use in adding suffixes to domain names on Windows 2000 and Windows XP platforms
- When working with a third-party dialer, the time to wait after receiving an IP address before initiating an IKE tunnel
- Network proxy server for routing HTTP traffic
- Application launching
- DNS suffixes
- Force Network Login, which forces a user on Windows NT, Windows 2000, or Windows XP to log out and log back in to the network without using cached credentials

> **NOTE** Profiles for the VPN Client are interchangeable between platforms, whereas keywords that are specific to the Windows platform are ignored by other platforms.

The following is a sample `vpnclient.ini` file, which shows what you might see if you open it with a text editor:

```
[main]
IncompatibleGinas=PALGina.dll,theirgina.dll
RunAtLogon=0
EnableLog=1
DialerDisconnect=1
AutoInitiationEnable=1
AutoInitiationRetryInterval=1
AutoInitiationList=techsupport,admin
[techsupport]
Network=172.17.0.0
Mask=255.255.0.0
ConnectionEntry=ITsupport
[admin]
Network=172.18.0.0
Mask=255.255.0.0
ConnectionEntry=Administration
[LOG.IKE]
LogLevel=1
[LOG.CM]
LogLevel=1
[LOG.PPP]
```

```
LogLevel=2
[LOG.DIALER]
LogLevel=2
[LOG.CVPND]
LogLevel=1
[LOG.CERT]
LogLevel=0
[LOG.IPSEC]
LogLevel=3
[LOG.FIREWALL]
LogLevel=1
[LOG.CLI]
LogLevel=1
[CertEnrollment]
SubjectName=Wade Edwards
Company=Sybex Corp
Department=Internal Relations
State=Utah
Country=US
Email=CCIE7009@hotmail.com
CADomainName=SybexCerts
CAHostAddress=10.11.12.13
CACertificate=CAU
[Application Launcher]
Enable=1
Command=c:\apps\apname.exe
[ForceNetLogin]
Force=1
Wait=10
DefaultMsg=You will be logged off in 10 seconds
Separator=****************************************
[GUI]
WindowWidth=578
WindowHeight=367
WindowX=324
WindowY=112
VisibleTab=0
ConnectionAttribute=0
AdvancedView=1
DefaultConnectionEntry=ACME
```

```
MinimizeOnConnect=1
UseWindowSettings=1
ShowToolTips=1
ShowConnectHistory=1
```

The VPN client uses parameters that must be uniquely configured for each remote user. These parameters together make up a user connection profile, which is contained in a *profile configuration file* (`.pcf` file) in the VPN client user's local file system.

Some of these parameters include:

- Remote server address
- IPSec group name and password
- Use of a log file
- Use of backup servers
- Automatic Internet connection via dial-up networking

Each connection entry has its own `.pcf` file. For example, if you have three connection entries named Sybex Server, Documentation, and Engineering, the Profiles directory shows the list of all these `.pcf` files.

Features Controlled by Connection Profiles

A connection profile (`.pcf` file) controls the following features on all platforms:

- Description of the connection profile
- Remote server address
- Authentication type
- Name of the IPSec group containing the remote user
- Group password
- Connecting to the Internet via dial-up networking
- Name of the remote user
- Remote user's password
- Backup servers
- Split DNS settings
- Type of dial-up networking connection
- Transparent tunneling
- TCP tunneling port
- Allowing local LAN access
- Enabling IKE and ESP keepalives
- Setting the peer response timeout
- Certificate parameters for a certificate connection

- Setting a certificate chain
- Diffie-Hellman group used
- Verifying the domain name (DN) of a peer certificate
- RADIUS SDI extended authentication setting
- Use of SDI hardware token setting
- Use of legacy IKE port setting

A .pcf file controls the following additional features when you're using a Windows platform:

- Dial-up networking phone-book entry for Microsoft
- Command string for connecting through an ISP
- NT domain
- Logging on to Microsoft Network and credentials
- Changing the default IKE port from 500/4500 (must be explicitly added)
- Enabling Force Network Login, which forces a user on Windows NT, Windows 2000, or Windows XP to log out and then log back in to the network without using cached credentials.

Here is a sample of a .pcf file:

```
[main]
Description=connection to Sybex server
Host=10.20.79.35
AuthType=1
GroupName=sybexusers
GroupPwd=
enc_GroupPwd=158E47893BDCD398BF863675204775622C494B39523E5CB65434D3C851
EnableISPConnect=0
ISPConnectType=0
ISPConnect=
ISPCommand=
Username=Wade
SaveUserPassword=0
UserPassword=
enc_UserPassword=
NTDomain=
EnableBackup=1
BackupServer=Doc1, Doc2, Doc3, Doc4
EnableMSLogon=0
MSLogonType=0
EnableNat=1
```

```
EnableLocalLAN=0
TunnelingMode=0
TCPTunnelingPort=10000
CertStore=0
CertName=
CertPath=
CertSubjectName
SendCertChain=0
VerifyCertDN=CN="ID Cert",OU*"Cisco",ISSUER-CN!="Entrust",ISSURE-OU!*"Sybex"
DHGroup=2
PeerTimeOut=90
ForceNetLogin=1
```

You can configure the VPN client for remote users by creating a profile configuration file for each connection entry and distribute the .pcf files with the VPN client software. These configuration files can include all or some of the parameters needed. Users must configure those settings that aren't already configured.

You can also distribute the VPN Client to users without a configuration file and let them configure it on their own. In this case, when they complete their configuration using the VPN client GUI, they're in effect creating a .pcf file for each connection entry, which can be edited and shared.

> **Note:** To protect system security, you shouldn't include key security parameters such as the IPSec group password, authentication username, or authentication password in .pcf files for remote users. You'll then supply users with the information they need to configure the VPN client for their individual installation.

Using PDM to Create VPNs

Recall that in Chapter 14, "Firewall Failover and PDM," we talked about the PDM but didn't show you how to create VPNs using the PDM. In this section, we'll show you how to use the PDM to create site-to-site and remote access VPNs.

Once you have the PDM up and running on your workstation, you need to navigate to the VPN tab, as shown in Figure 15.4.

> **Note:** Remember that if you're using the Firewall Services Module (FWSM), the VPN tab won't work because the FWSM doesn't support VPN services.

FIGURE 15.4   The PDM VPN tab

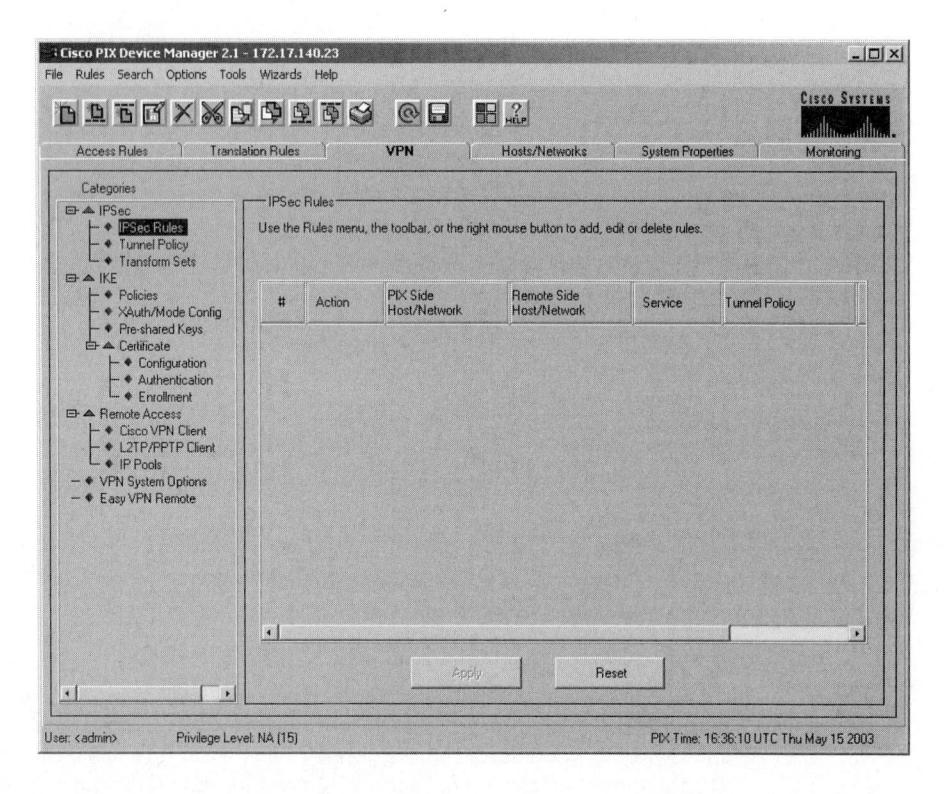

From the PDM VPN tab, you can choose to configure IPSec, IKE, remote access, and global VPN parameters on the PIX Firewall. Under the IPSec section, you can configure IPSec rules, tunnel policies, and transform sets. Under the IKE section, the options are policies, Xauth/Mode Config, pre-shared keys, and certificate parameters. When you're configuring a remote access VPN, this section of the GUI allows you to configure the Cisco VPN and L2TP/PPTP client plus the IP pools used for these clients. Finally, the global VPN parameters available are to enable the PIX Firewall to bypass the access check for IPSec, L2TP, and PPTP traffic plus configuring the PIX Firewall to act as an Easy VPN Remote.

You can set up all of these parameters through the GUI, but to make it easier, the PDM has a wizard to step you through the configuration of site-to-site and remote access VPNs. To access the VPN Wizard, select Wizards ➤ VPN Wizard from the drop-down menu, as shown in Figure 15.5.

Choosing the VPN Wizard opens another window. In the following sections, you'll see how to use the wizard to set up a site-to-site VPN and a remote access VPN.

FIGURE 15.5   Selecting the VPN Wizard

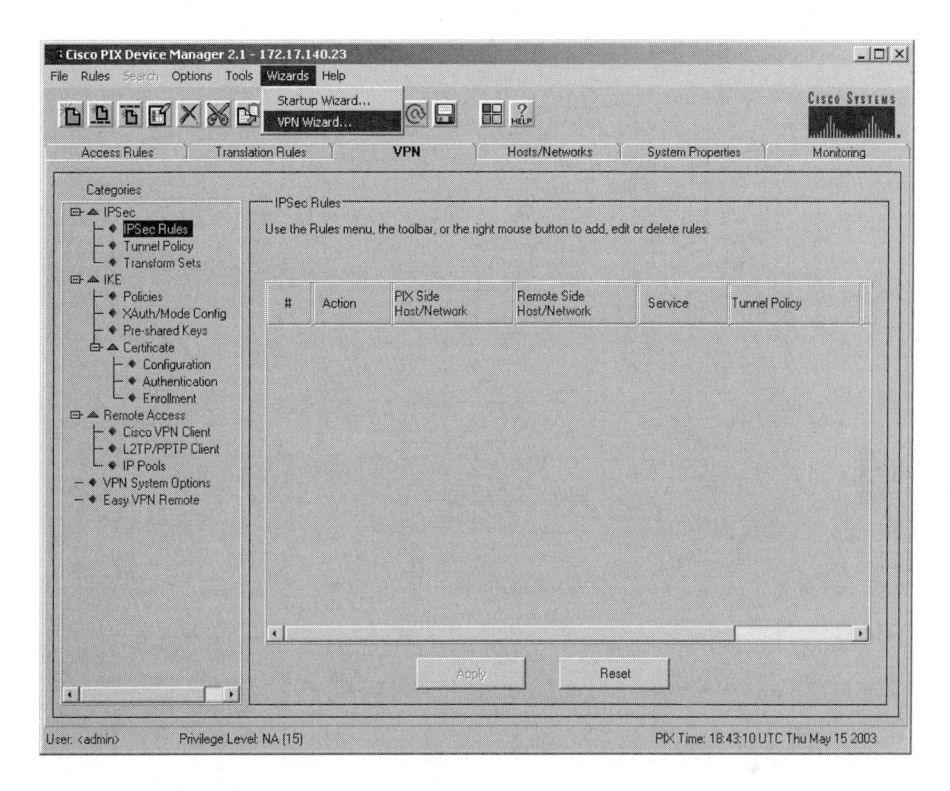

Setting Up a Site-to-Site VPN

Once you've activated the VPN Wizard, follow these steps to set up a site-to-site VPN:

1. On the VPN Wizard screen, shown in Figure 15.6, choose the Site To Site VPN option, and select the outside interface to terminate the VPN to. Then click the Next button.

2. Since this is a site-to-site VPN, you must specify a peer, or remote, IP address to terminate the other end of the VPN to. Select the method of authentication to use before negotiating IPSec. The choices on the Remote Site Peer screen are Pre-shared Key and Certificate. As you can see from Figure 15.7, when you choose the pre-shared key authentication method, you must enter the key to be used for authentication. If you choose to use a certificate, you must choose between using the IP address or a fully qualified domain name (FQDN) or DNS name for the peer. Click the Next button.

FIGURE 15.6 Selecting site-to-site VPN

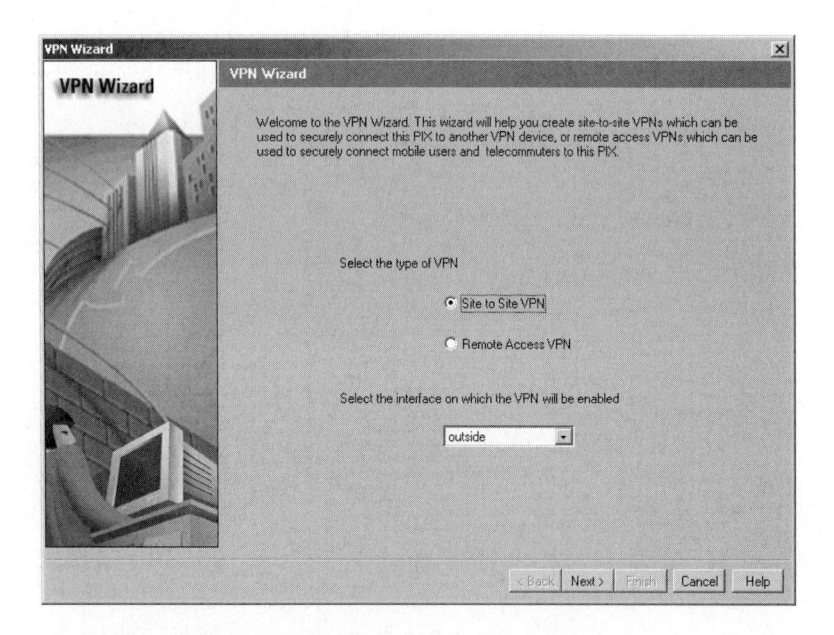

FIGURE 15.7 Choosing a remote site peer

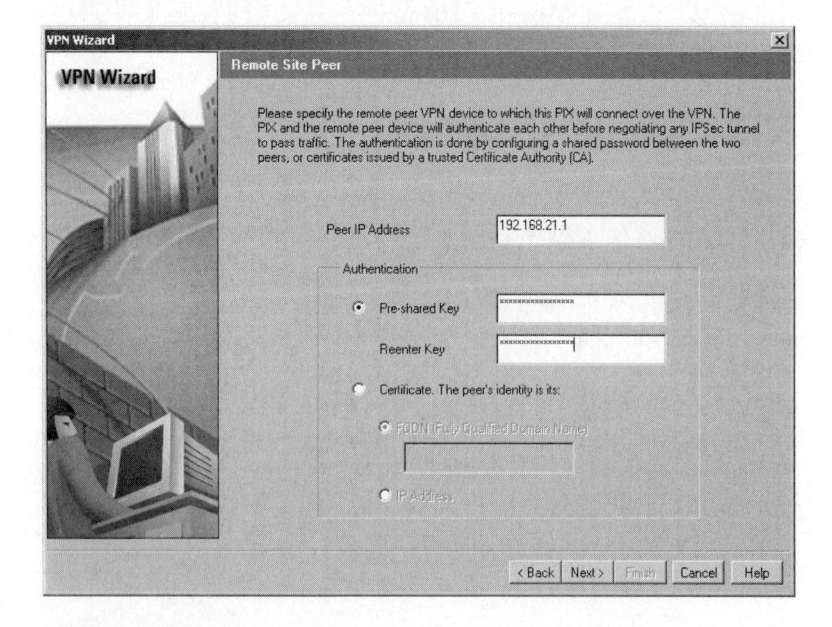

3. On the IKE Policy screen, create the IKE policy to use between the peers (see Figure 15.8). Here, you must choose the encryption and authentication methods in addition to which DH group to use. The authentication here is used to authenticate the IKE tunnel traffic and not the remote peer, like the previous screen setup. The options for encryption are DES and 3DES. The authentication scheme can be either SHA or MD5, and the DH group options are Group 1 or 2. Click the Next button.

4. On the Transform Set screen, create the transform set used by IPSec (see Figure 15.9). As on the previous screen, the IPSec transforms options are the same for encryption and authentication. The IKE policy (from Figure 15.8) and the IPSec transform set encryption and authentication options can be different. Click Next.

5. On the IPSec Traffic Selector screens, specify which source traffic on the local site will be protected by IPSec and which source traffic won't be protected (see Figure 15.10). In this example, you can see that we've chosen to use an IP address range to protect with IPSec, and this happens to be the range used by the inside interface of the PIX Firewall. We could also have chosen to use the name of a group of hosts or networks that have been previously configured on the PIX Firewall through the PDM. You must select the range you've entered by pressing the right arrow button to make it one of your selected networks. Click Next.

FIGURE 15.8 Specifying an IKE policy

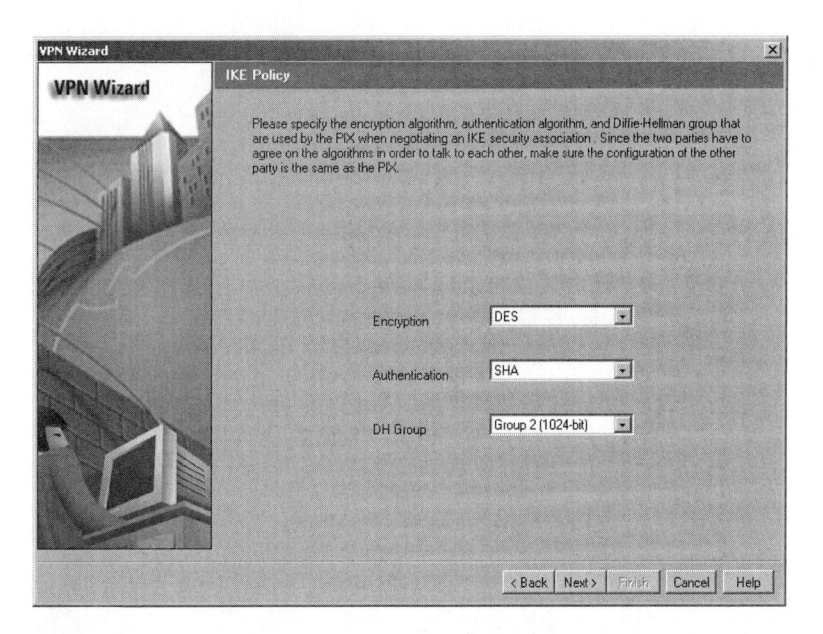

FIGURE 15.9 Creating the transform set

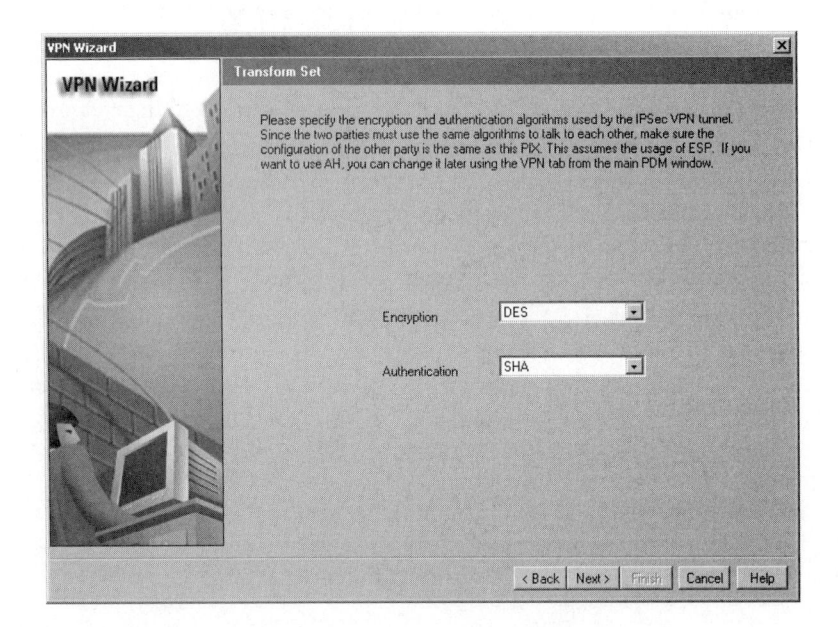

FIGURE 15.10 Selecting an IPSec traffic that is protected by IPSec

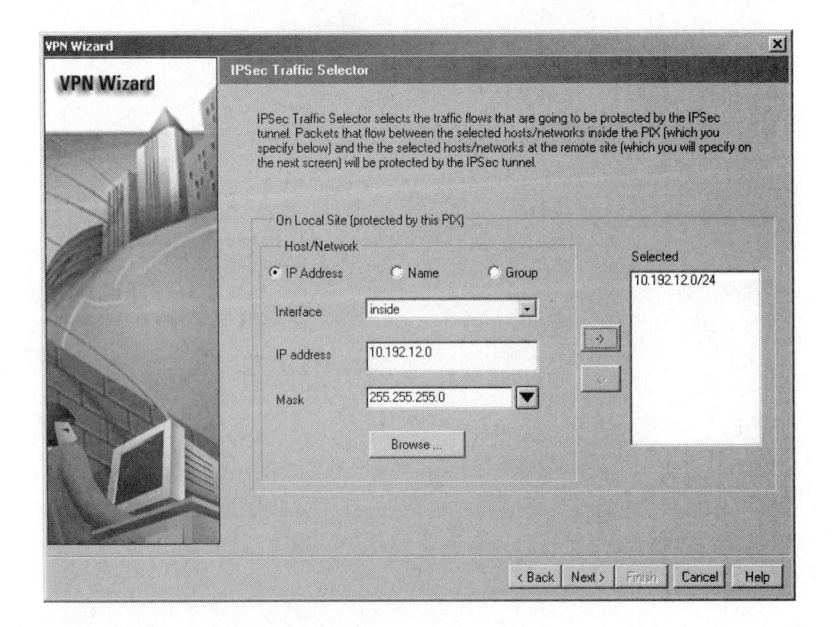

6. On the IPSec Traffic Selector (Continue) screen, select the remote traffic destination. This screen looks very similar to the previous screen, but in it you specify the remote site or destination traffic to protect with IPSec. Because the PIX Firewall doesn't know how to get to the remote network range, you get the message seen in Figure 15.11. You'll need to create and add the host or network to the PIX Firewall configuration. Use the Create Host/Network dialog box (shown in Figure 15.12) to create this remote network range, which is accessible from the outside interface, called the host/network Remote_Protected. Click Next.

7. Once you've created the host or network to protect on the remote site, select that network on the IPSec Traffic Selector (Continue) screen using the right arrow button, just as you did on the IP Traffic Selector screen. Figure 15.13 shows that we've selected the Remote_Protected network to protect with this IPSec tunnel.

FIGURE 15.11 The Add Host/Network? dialog box

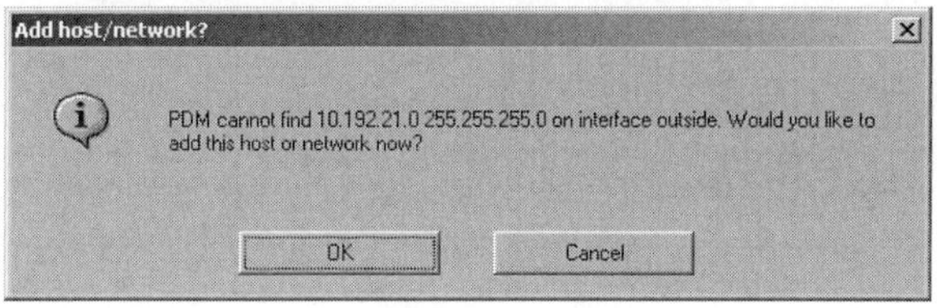

FIGURE 15.12 Creating a remote network range

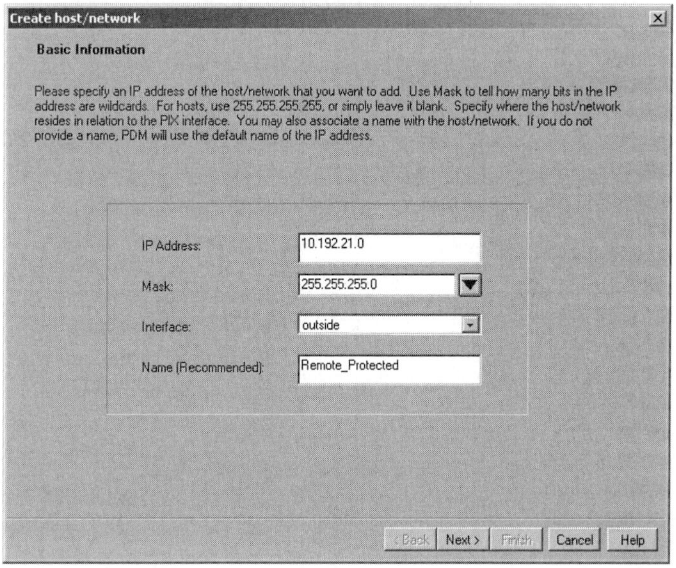

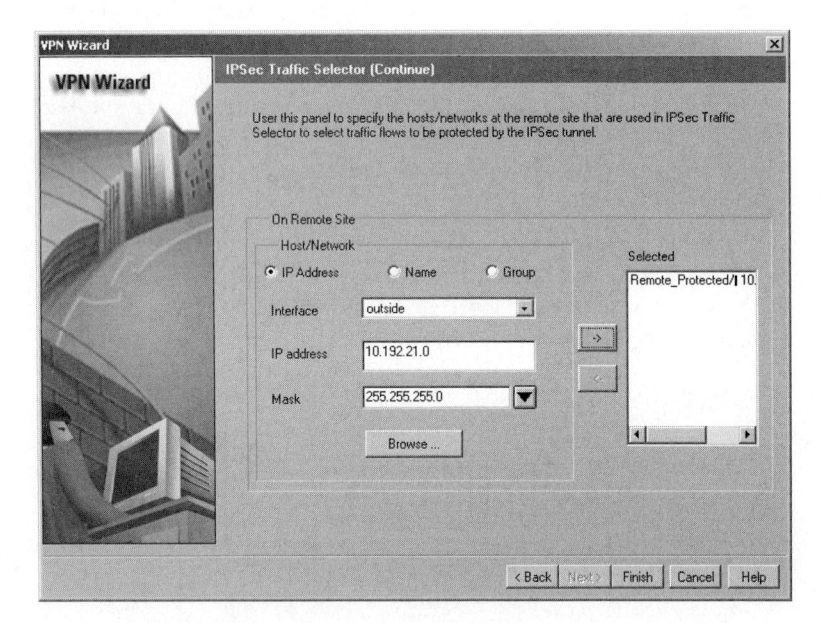

FIGURE 15.13 Selecting the network

8. To complete the wizard, click the Finish button on the IPSec Traffic Selector (Continue) screen.

You can now navigate through the options in the VPN tab to see the various parameters and objects created by the wizard. You can also change these to make changes to your site-to-site VPN.

Setting Up a Remote Access VPN

In the previous section, you saw how to set up a site-to-site VPN. Now we'll go through the VPN Wizard again, but this time we'll follow the remote access VPN track:

1. On the initial VPN Wizard screen (refer back to Figure 15.6), select Remote Access VPN and click Next.

2. On the Remote Access Client screen (see Figure 15.14), select the type of VPN client that will be accessing the PIX Firewall. In this example, our users will be using the Cisco VPN client 3.*x* or higher, so we need to select that option and click Next.

3. On the VPN Client Group screen (see Figure 15.15), create a VPN group and authentication method used by the clients. In this example, because we have a smaller group of people that will be accessing the VPN from remote, we use the Pre-shared Key option, which is also known as the *group password*. Call the group Sales_Force because the sales staff will be using this remote access VPN the most. (We could also select to use a certificate for authentication.) Click Next.

FIGURE 15.14 Selecting the remote access client

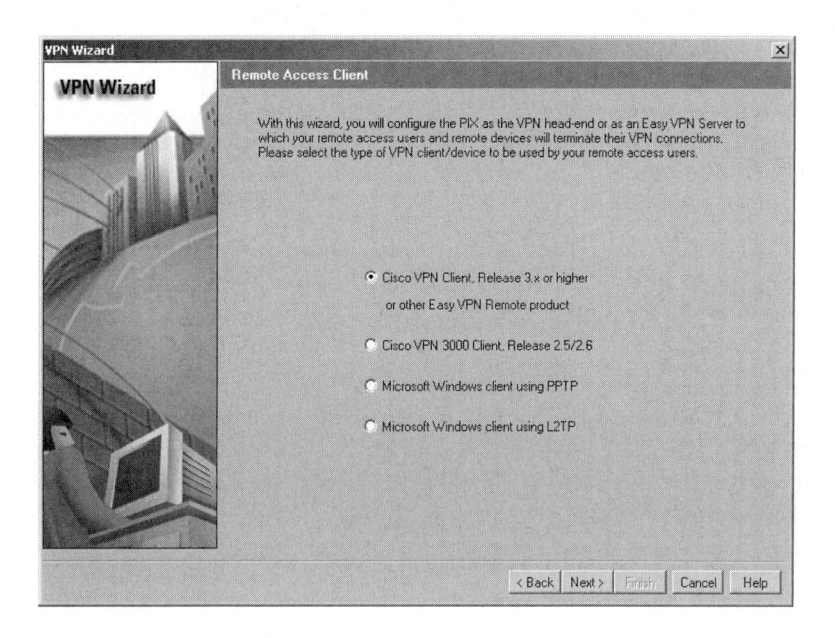

FIGURE 15.15 Creating a VPN group

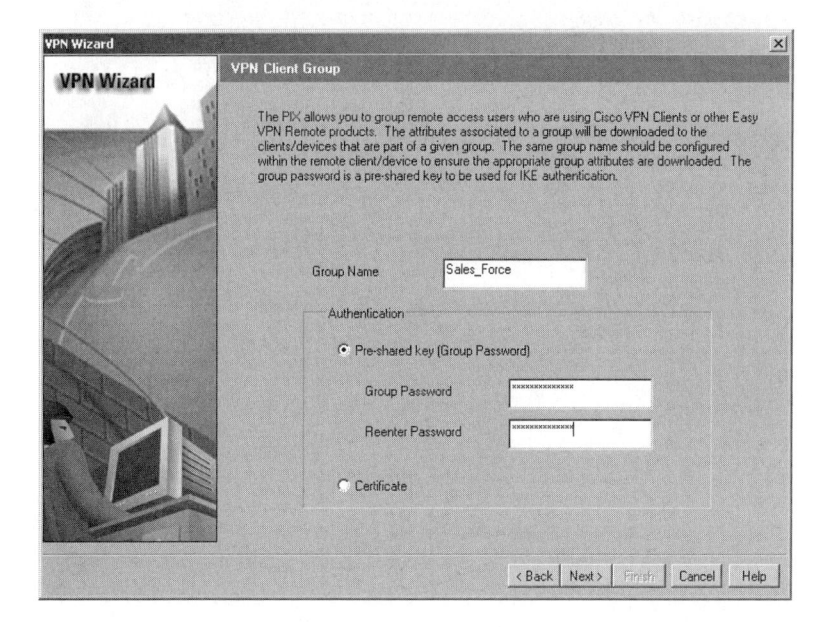

4. If you're using Xauth, you need to select the authentication, authorization, and accounting (AAA) server group that will be used to authenticate VPN users to this group. On the Extended Client Authentication screen (see Figure 15.16), select the Enable Extended Client Authentication check box to use AAA services for VPN client authentication. You can also create an AAA group if one isn't already created from this screen. You can also specify if this AAA server group is using the one-time password feature for greater security. If you aren't using Xauth, you can deselect the Enable Extended Client Authentication check box. Click Next.

5. On the Address Pool screen (see Figure 15.17), create or select the IP pool to use for clients in this VPN group. In this example, we've chosen to create a new pool called Sales_Pool and add 100 addresses to this pool. These IP addresses will be assigned to VPN clients authenticated to this group so they appear as nodes on the inside network. Click Next.

6. This next step is optional. On the Attributes Pushed To Client screen (see Figure 15.18), configure the VPN client with the DNS, WINS, and domain name of the inside network. In this example, we've chosen to push these attribute values to the VPN clients so they will be able to resolve internal DNS and WINS addresses as if they were on the inside of the network. Click Next.

FIGURE 15.16 Selecting an AAA server group

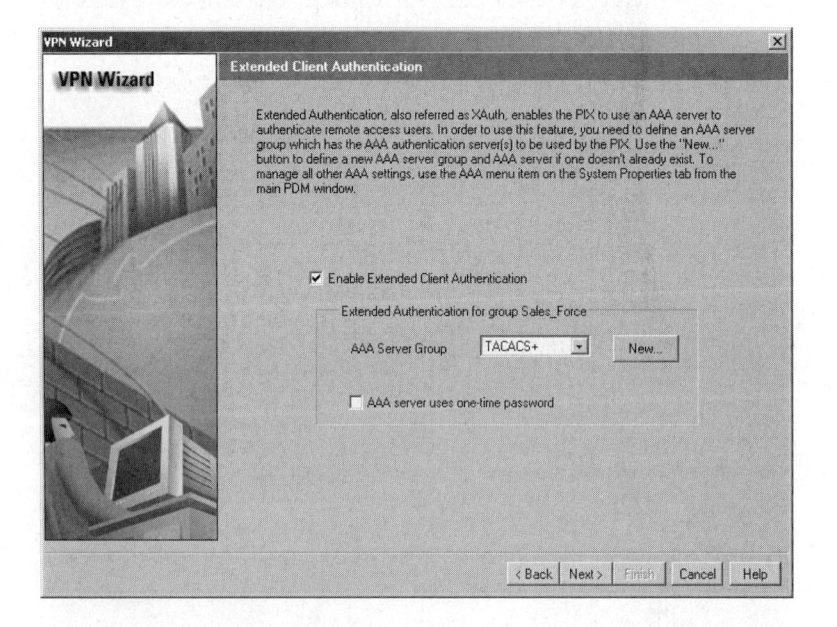

FIGURE 15.17 Creating an IP address pool

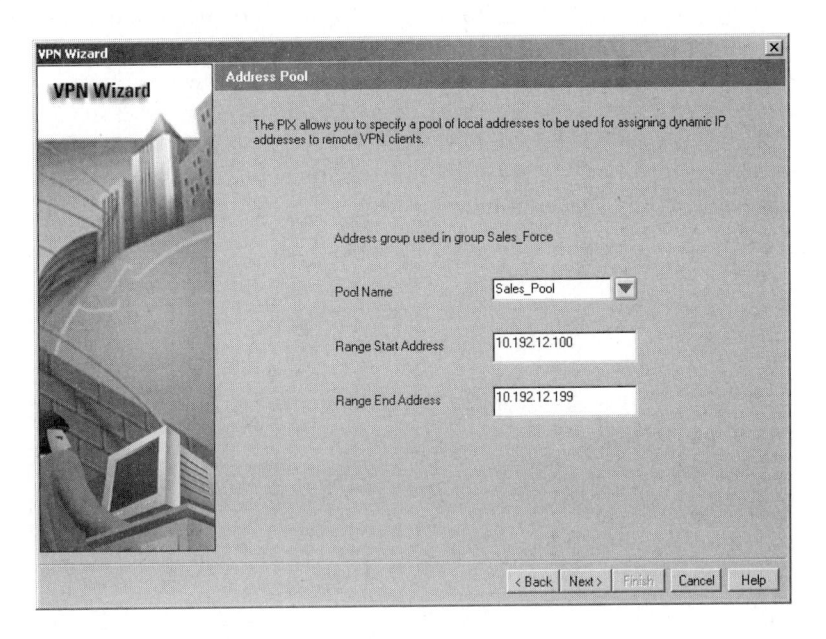

FIGURE 15.18 Pushing attributes to a VPN client

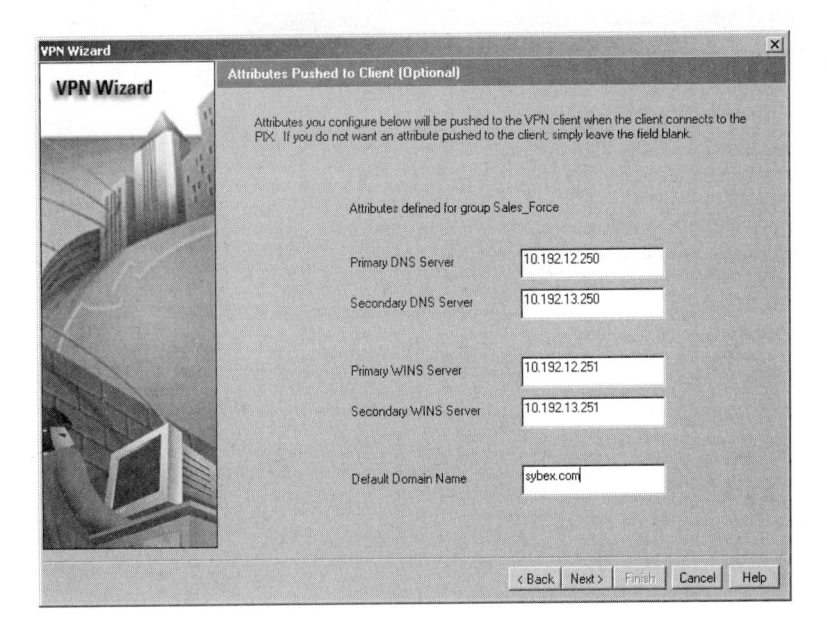

7. This next step is optional as well. On the Address Translation Exemption screen (see Figure 15.19), configure NAT for VPN users. Usually, you want to expose the real IP addresses on the internal network to the VPN users. If no selection is made, then no internal hosts will be NATed to the VPN users. One instance where this might be useful is if the remote VPN user is using a network address that is used inside the corporate network. You can create a rule here to NAT that address range from the corporate network to the VPN user so they will be able to see the resources on the corporate network. Click Finish to complete the VPN configuration.

Now that you've completed both the site-to-site and remote access VPN wizards, you can look through the VPN tab to see the changes that were made and the objects that were added. Figure 15.20 shows the VPN tab after the VPN configuration. There are two new IPSec rules: one for the site-to-site and one for the remote access VPN.

FIGURE 15.19 Choosing whether to make the internal network exposed to outside users

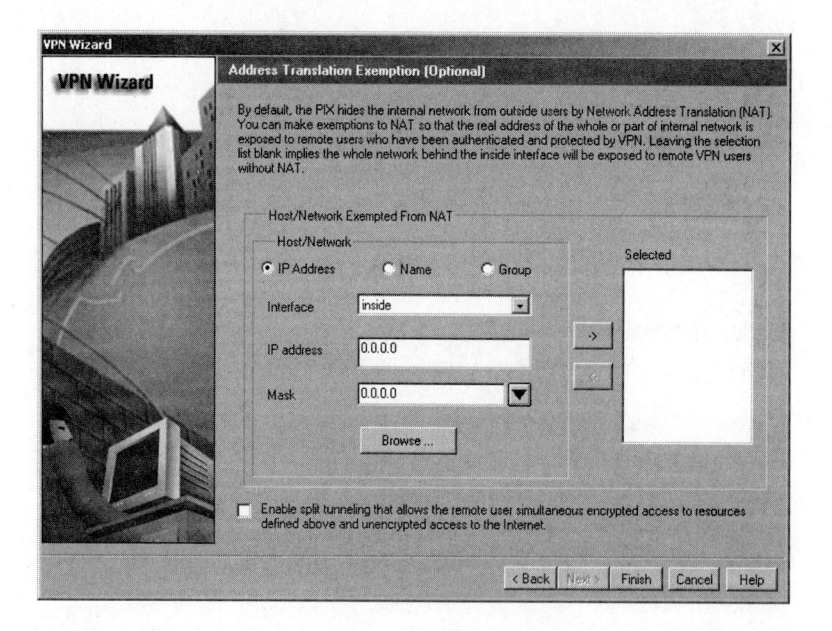

FIGURE 15.20 The VPN tab

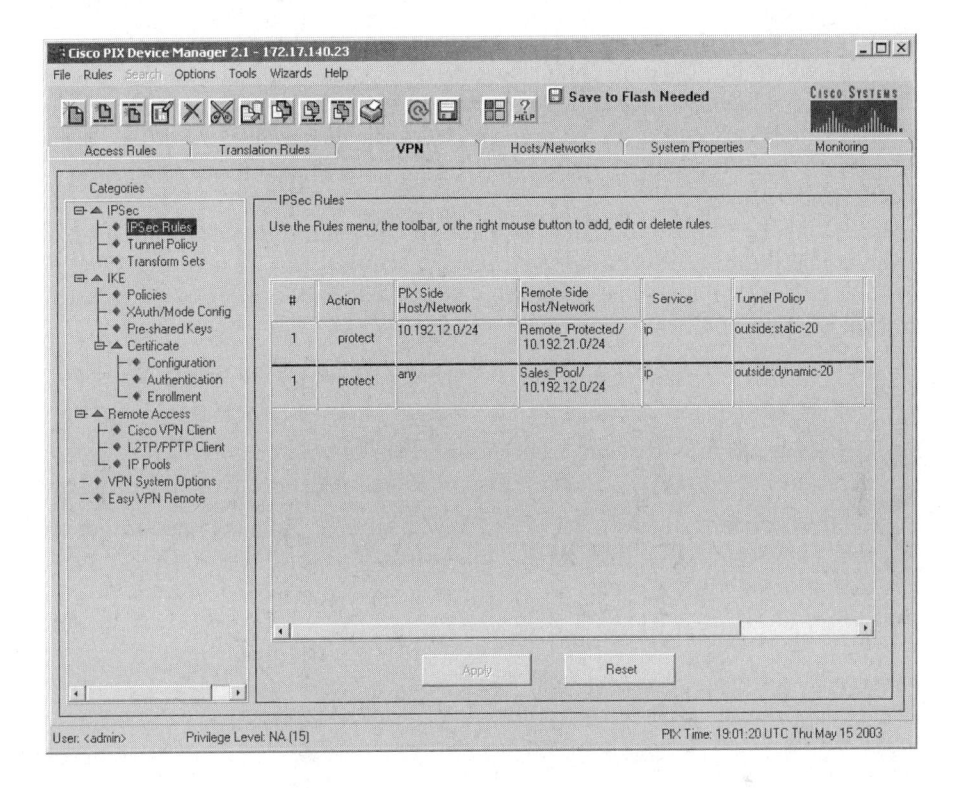

Enterprise PIX Firewall Management and Maintenance

When it comes to managing and maintaining the PIX Firewall, the PDM is good if you have one PIX Firewall. You can even manage several PIX Firewalls from a single workstation, but what if you have hundreds of PIX Firewalls? This is where the Cisco Secure Policy Manager and CiscoWorks VMS come into play.

In the following sections, we'll talk about the Cisco Secure Policy Manager, PIX Management Center, and the Auto Update Server and how you can use these tools to manage the PIX Firewall in the enterprise.

Cisco Secure Policy Manager (CSPM)

The CSPM is a scalable and powerful security-policy management system for Cisco PIX Firewalls, Cisco IOS firewalls, VPN routers, and intrusion detection system (IDS) sensors. Using CSPM, you can define, distribute, enforce, and audit network-wide security policies from a central location. CSPM streamlines the tasks for managing complex network security elements, such as perimeter access control, NAT, and IPSec-based VPNs. Figure 15.21 shows the CSPM screen and an example of a network topology.

CSPM is the cornerstone of the Cisco end-to-end security solution, and it simplifies the deployment of security devices and services within a Cisco-centric network. CSPM was produced to replace the PIX Firewall configuration completely, and it provides the following firewall management capabilities:

- Defines the interface settings such as the name, IP address, and security level.
- Defines device characteristics such as timeouts, flood guard, and logging.
- Defines access rules that can manage the traffic flow on Context-Based Access Control (CBAC) enabled routers, and can add commands generated from policy statements.
- Converts policy statements into PIX Firewall configuration commands that are inserted into an existing configuration for a router-based firewall. It completely replaces the configuration of a PIX Firewall.
- Manages remote and local devices over the network.

FIGURE 15.21 CSPM screen

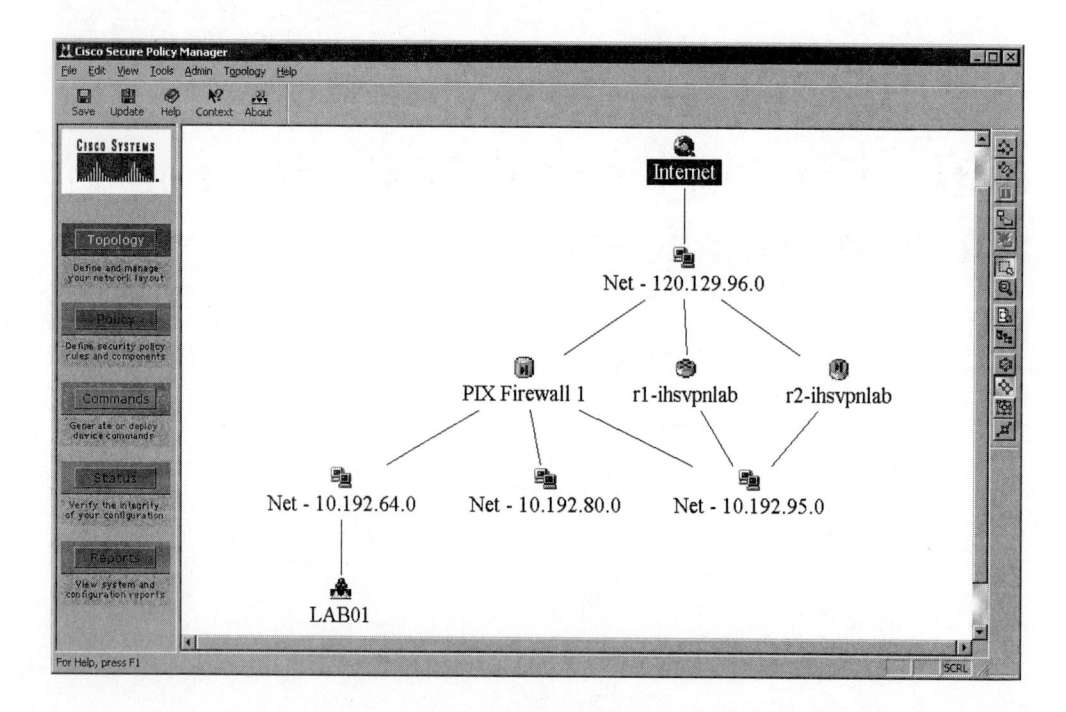

With CPSM, you can define high-level security policies visuals for multiple PIX Firewalls, routers, and IDS sensors. First, you need to define the network topology and how the controlled devices are situated in the network. Then you can define a global policy using the access and translation rules, which describe how different traffic flows should be treated. Since the CSPM has information about the relative position of controlled devices, the policy statements don't need to be defined per device. The software calculates which devices must enforce each policy statement and creates commands for those devices.

VPNs can be configured between multiple devices with CSPM. You can do this through the GUI or multiple IPSec templates for both full-mesh and hub-and-spoke networks. These templates add value in any security network environment by simplifying small security networks, multisite deployments, and large service-provider environments by centralizing and abstracting the management of security networks. After these policies have been created, you need to save and generate the device configurations. This goes through a consistency checker, which allows you to resolve any errors encountered.

Once they're checked and saved, the configurations can be distributed, or *pushed*, from a centralized location, eliminating the costly, time-consuming practice of implementing security commands on a device-by-device basis via the CLI. You do this under the Command tab of each device, where a certain level of version control can be accomplished. Carefully review the generated commands, and click the Approve Now button, which deploys the configuration to the target device.

For CSPM to manage a PIX Firewall, a special IPSec Bootstrap Configuration section is generated in the Command section of the PIX Firewall object. This section is located at the end of the Command box and is denoted by a hash mark (#) before each command. You must remove this character for these commands to be activated. Since CSPM accomplishes management through secure Telnet, you must also enable Telnet from the CSPM host.

PIX Management Center (MC)

Whereas the PDM addresses single-device management and CSPM addresses policy-based management, the *PIX* Management Center (MC) addresses the mid-level, multidevice management. The PIX MC is a component of CiscoWorks2000 under the VPN/Security Management Solution (VMS), uses terminology and concepts consistent with PDM, and has a look and feel consistent with PDM. It communicates with the PIX Firewall on TCP port 443 (HTTPS), so communications are secured.

The PIX MC is installed on the CiscoWorks2000 Server system. You must log in to the CiscoWorks2000 Server desktop and navigate to the VPN/Security Management Solution drawer. As you can see in Figure 15.22, you must expand the Management Center folder and click on the PIX Firewalls icon. Doing so launches the Management Center for PIX Firewalls in a separate window.

FIGURE 15.22   CiscoWorks2000

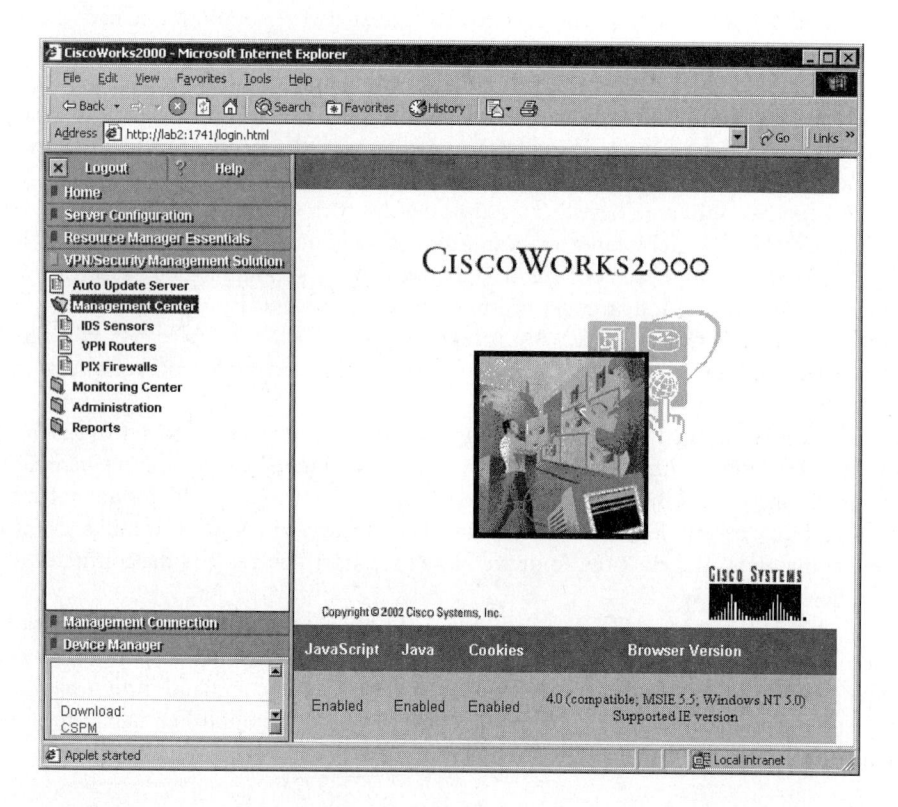

Figure 15.23 shows the PIX MC screen so you can see the options available.

The Devices tab is used to import PIX Firewalls to be handled in the Management Center, arrange them in groups, and administer those groups. The Configuration tab allows you to configure firewall settings, access rules, transition rules and building blocks, and view the configuration for each device. Using building blocks, you can create service groups. The Workflow tab is used to manage activities and jobs that can ensure the correct procedures are in place to approve device configuration changes. The Report tab lets you review audit records about actions that users have taken within an activity. Finally, the Admin tab is used to require approval for activities and jobs, perform database maintenance, and gather troubleshooting information through the MDCSupport utility when you're debugging problems.

Before you can import a PIX Firewall into the PIX MC, you must *bootstrap* the device by setting up the firewall with a minimum configuration. You need to name the PIX Firewall, assign an IP address, bring up the interfaces, create and enable a Telnet password, and enable the HTTP server to allow access from the PIX MC server, because the server uses TCP port 443 for secure communications.

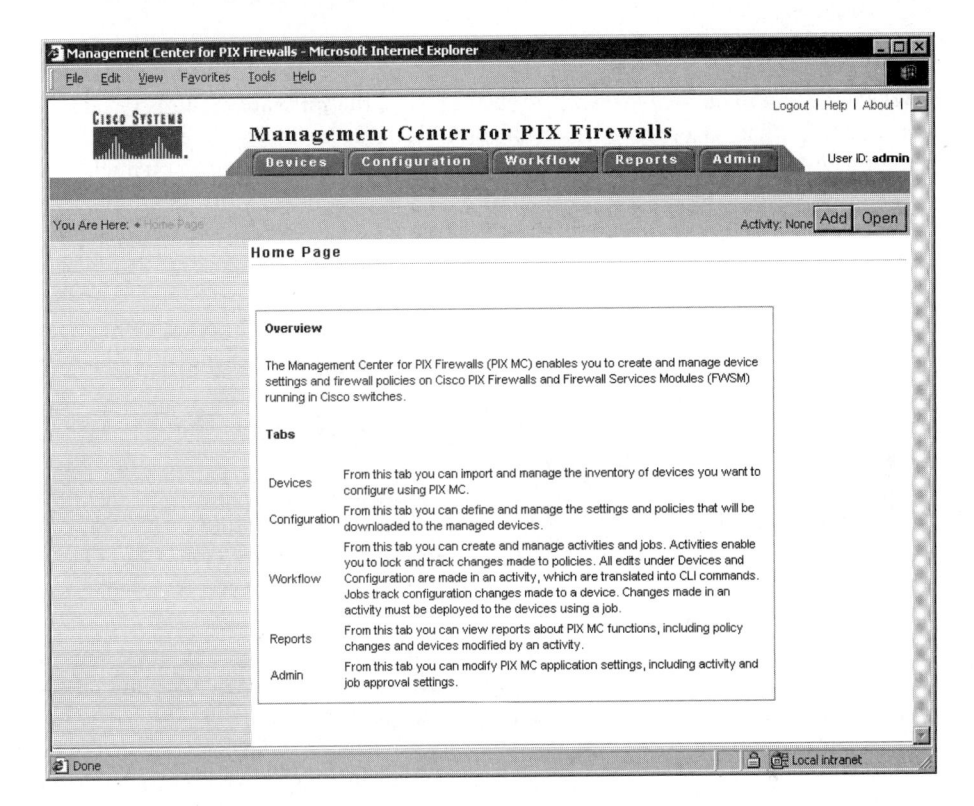

Enterprise PIX Firewall Management and Maintenance

FIGURE 15.23 Management Center for PIX Firewalls

Here is an example of a bootstrap configuration for the PIX Firewall, which allows the firewall to be imported into the PIX MC:

```
nameif ethernet0 outside security0
nameif ethernet1 inside security100
nameif ethernet2 dmz security60
enable password 2KFQnbNIdI.2KYOU encrypted
passwd 2KFQnbNIdI.2KYOU encrypted
hostname PIX
interface ethernet0 auto
interface ethernet1 auto
interface ethernet2 auto
ip address outside 120.110.1.1 255.255.255.0
ip address inside 192.168.10.1 255.255.255.0
```

```
ip address dmz-a 127.0.0.1 255.255.255.255
http server enable
http 192.168.10.11 255.255.255.255 inside
```

Whenever you're doing a task within the PIX MC, the software requires you to create an *activity*. This activity is a procedure for the PIX MC to accomplish. For example, importing or creating a device in addition to modifying the device requires an activity. You might think that's it: You approve the activity, and the changes are made. But the PIX MC has another workflow item called a *job*. A job is a collection of activities, and this is where the work is really done. You need to create a job, assign one or more activities to the job, and approve the job before the activities are executed.

Each job can be executed right away or sent to the Auto Update Server. When you choose to execute right way, you can choose to deploy to each affected device individually or all devices simultaneously.

Auto Update Server (AUS)

Like the PIX MC, the Auto Update Server (AUS) is accessible through the CiscoWorks2000 Server desktop and is under the VPN/Security Management Solution drawer. If you look at Figure 15.22, you'll see the Auto Update Server icon, which you click to launch the AUS in a separate window. Figure 15.24 shows the AUS screen and the options available.

From the Devices tab, you can see a summary of information about the devices known to the AUS. You can't add or delete devices from this tab; you can only view the summarized device information. You add and delete AUS-managed devices through the PIX MC. The Images tab displays information about the PIX Firewall software images, PDM images, and configuration files in the repository. It also allows you to add or delete PIX Firewall software images and PDM images. The Assignments tab lets the user change device-to-image and image-to-device assignments. The Reports tab displays the system information report and event report. The Admin tab allows the user to change the database password and configure the NAT address.

Sometimes the AUS is placed behind a firewall and isn't accessible from the outside network. The AUS needs to be able to update those devices outside the network, so there must be a mechanism to allow the outside devices to communicate with the AUS. The NAT address is used to control which IP address these outside devices use to communicate with the AUS. If you're managing all internal devices, then this should be the IP address of the AUS. If not, then it needs to be changed to the outside IP address, which is being NATed to the IP address of the AUS.

If you choose to manage a device using the Auto Update Server, you need to configure certain settings on the PIX Firewall to bootstrap it and others on the PIX MC. To bootstrap the PIX Firewall to communicate with the AUS for the first time, use the `auto-update` commands.

If you've enabled the unique identity feature, discussed in a moment, then use the `auto-update device-id` command together with the parameter for the type of unique identification. The identification parameter options include `hardware-serial`, `hostname`, `ipaddress`, `mac-address`, and `string`. If you use `ipaddress` or `mac-address`, then you must add an interface parameter. If you use `string`, then you must supply a unique string value.

FIGURE 15.24 Auto Update Server screen

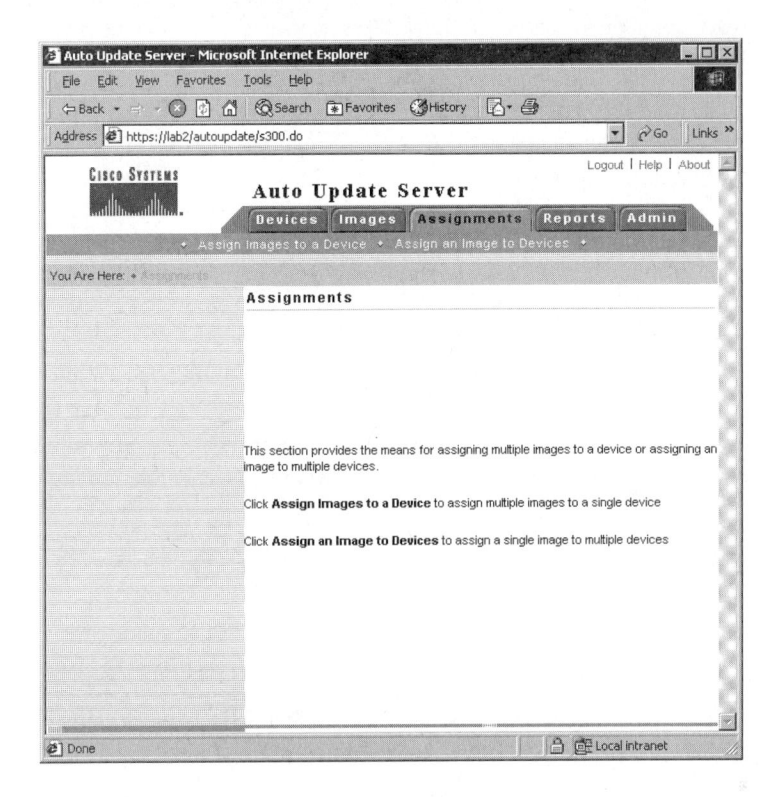

The `auto-update server` command takes one URL that is made up of several portions. The syntax is https://*username:password*@*ip-address*/*autoupdate*/*AutoUpdateServlet*. The *username* and *password* are the username and password to use on the PIX MC; this username must have the ability to add devices and add or delete configuration files. The *ip-address* is the IP address or hostname of the AUS.

You can also change the time between polling intervals with the `auto-update poll period interval` command. The polling interval is in minutes, and the default is 720 minutes. Now let's look at what it takes to add a PIX Firewall to the AUS.

The following is the list of settings on the PIX MC that you need to change. First, you need to configure the settings the PIX Firewall will use to connect to the AUS by following these steps:

1. Select Configure ➢ Settings ➢ Server and Services ➢ Auto Update Server. The Auto Update Server page appears.
2. Deselect the Inherit Settings check box.
3. Select the Enable Auto Update Server check box to activate the Auto Update Server feature on the PIX Firewall.
4. In the IP Address field, enter the IP address of the AUS.

5. In the Port field, enter the number of the port used for AUS. The default is 443 (HTTPS).
6. In the Path field, enter the directory path to the servlet that the device uses to access the Auto Update Server. The default path is /autoupdate/AutoUpdateServlet.
7. In the Username field, enter the username for the PIX Firewall.
8. In the Password field, enter the password for the PIX Firewall.
9. In the Confirm Password field, reenter the password for the PIX Firewall.
10. In the Poll Period (Minutes) field, enter the number of minutes for the PIX Firewall to wait between polls to AUS. The default is 720 minutes.
11. In the Poll Retry Count field, enter the number of times the PIX Firewall should try to connect to the AUS if the first try is unsuccessful. The default is 0.
12. In the Poll Retry Period (Minutes) field, enter the number of minutes between retries. The default is 5.
13. In the Deactivate PIX Firewall If No Update For field, enter the number of minutes the PIX Firewall should wait for updates from the AUS with no response before it deactivates itself.
14. Click Apply.

Then, you need to configure the method of identification that will be used between the PIX Firewall and the AUS by following these steps:

1. Select Configure ➤ Settings ➤ PIX Firewall Administration ➤ Unique Identity.
2. Deselect the Inherit Settings check box.
3. Select the Enable Device Unique Identity check box to activate the feature on the PIX Firewall.
4. Select the method to confirm the PIX Firewall identity. The options are as follows:
   - Host Name
   - Hardware Serial Number
   - IP Address
   - MAC Address
   - Unique Identity String
5. Click Apply.

Next, follow these steps to configure the information that PIX MC will use to contact the AUS:

1. Select Configure ➤ Settings ➤ PIX MC Control ➤ Auto Update Server Contact.
2. In the Auto Update Server Name field, enter the hostname or IP address of the AUS.
3. In the Auto Update Port field, enter the number of the port to access AUS. The default is 443 (HTTPS).
4. In the Unique ID field, enter the value that corresponds to the unique identity chosen in the Unique Identity page.

5. In the Username field, enter the username used to gain access to the AUS. The username should have permission to add devices and add or delete configuration files. You most likely should enter **admin**.
6. In the Password field, enter the password used to gain access to the AUS. You should use the password assigned to the username from step 5.
7. In the Confirm Password field, reenter the password.
8. Click Apply.

Finally, configure deployment of configuration files to AUS for the selected device by following these steps:

1. Select Configure ➢ Settings ➢ PIX MC Control ➢ Deployment.
2. Deselect the Inherit Settings check box.
3. In the Deployment Type field, select the destination to which configuration files are deployed. Choose the Auto Update Server option, which downloads the configuration files to the Auto Update Sever for later deployment to firewalls operating in Auto-Update mode.
4. Click Apply.

To bootstrap the PIX Firewall, which will allow the firewall to contact the AUS the first time, enter the following command:

```
PIX(config)# auto-update device-id hardware-serial
PIX(config)# auto-update server
➥https://admin:sybex@10.192.12.100/autoupdate/AutoUpdateServlet
PIX(config)#
```

You can verify the configuration is correct and how long before the next poll by using the `show auto-update` command. An example is shown here:

```
PIX(config)# show auto-update
Server: https://10.192.12.100/autoupdate/AutoUpdateServlet
Poll period: 720 minutes, retry count: 0, retry period: 5 minutes
Timeout: none
Device ID: host name [PIX]
Next poll in 0.83 minutes
PIX(config)#
```

Once you've configured the PIX MC and PIX Firewall to access the AUS, you can manage the firewall from the AUS. Whenever changes are made to the PIX Firewall from the PIX MC, those changes are sent to the AUS; then, on the next polling cycle, the PIX Firewall downloads those changes.

Summary

This chapter has described how to configure IPSec on the PIX Firewall, including the preliminary preparation, IKE configuration, pre-shared keys configuration, and CA configuration. Configuring IPSec on the PIX Firewall is easy; but the PIX Firewall doesn't like Transport mode tunnels, so it limits how those tunnels can be formed.

The PIX Firewall prevents traffic from coming into the firewall unless a device on the trusted side initiated the connection. Since this can be a problem with VPNs, the PIX Firewall needs to be configured to allow VPN traffic in from the outside.

We talked about how to manage and maintain the PIX Firewall in an Enterprise network using Cisco Secure Policy Manager and CiscoWorks2000. VPN/Security Management Solution is the CiscoWorks2000 software that consists of the PIX Management Center and the Auto Update Server. With these solutions, you can manage and maintain not only PIX Firewalls but also IOS routers and IDS Sensors.

Exam Essentials

Understand how the PIX Firewall implements IKE and IPSec. Know that the PIX Firewall uses IKE to authenticate and create a secure tunnel to communicate IPSec parameter to the VPN peer. Authentication can take place with a pre-shared key or by using digital certificates. IPSec provides secure tunnels between two peers and can protect and authenticate traffic inside the VPN tunnel using DES or 3DES encryption and SHA or MD5 hash for authentication using a transform set.

Know how to use IKE Mode Config for Xauth and dynamic IP addressing. IKE Mode Config can be used to authenticate remote access VPN users using Xauth to an AAA server group. This can also be used to configure the VPN Client with a dynamic IP address and other optional network parameters.

Remember how to configure and deploy the VPN Client. Understand the different options for the VPN Client and how to configure it for a VPN using pre-shared keys or digital certificate authentication. You should also know how to customize the deployment of the VPN Client to allow the user to install and run the software more easily.

Know how to use the PDM to create VPNs. You need to remember how to use the VPN Wizard to configure both site-to-site and remote access VPNs. You should also study the PDM interface to see how the different VPN settings can be modified and the impact this has on the PIX Firewall configuration.

Understand the role of the Cisco Secure Policy Manager. The CSPM is a stand-alone application that allows a user to remotely manage many Cisco security devices including the PIX Firewall. The CSPM uses policies for a high-level view of the security network. Each device implements its portion of the overall security policy and the CSPM pushes those portions to the respective device.

Know the components of VMS and how to access them. The PIX Management Center and Auto Update Server are both components of the VPN/Security Management Solution. The VMS has its own drawer, which is accessible from the CiscoWorks2000 Server desktop, where you can launch the AUS and management centers for PIX Firewall, routers, and IDS sensors.

Understand how to add a device to PIX MC and AUS. You should know what commands are needed to bootstrap the PIX Firewall to be managed by the PIX MC and AUS. You need to understand what configuration settings need to be implemented on the PIX MC to make a device manageable by AUS. You should also understand how to implement activities and jobs within the PIX MC and how to manage PIX Firewall configurations and images from the AUS.

PART III

Cisco Secure Virtual Private Networks

Chapter 16

Introduction to Virtual Private Networks

THE FOLLOWING TOPICS ARE COVERED IN THIS CHAPTER:

- ✓ The Cisco Secure virtual private network (VPN) product family developed by Cisco Systems
- ✓ IPSec and other open standards supported by Cisco Secure VPN products
- ✓ Component technologies of IPSec
- ✓ How IPSec works

This chapter introduces virtual private network (VPN) concepts and explains how VPN tunnels are created. The information presented here provides the foundation for the detailed, device-specific material in the following chapters.

We'll begin with some basics, including discussions of the types of VPNs and devices. The remainder of this chapter covers IPSec and Internet Key Exchange (IKE). IPSec is a standards-based method of negotiating a secure connection between peers. IKE is a protocol used to provide authentication between peers. We'll discuss the various authentication types, the different ways a VPN tunnel can be built, the steps involved in the process, and the order of events. Finally, we'll address potential problems associated with tunnels and how to troubleshoot them.

VPN Basics

A *virtual private network (VPN)* is an extension of a network. It's *virtual* because it doesn't use reserved circuits. A VPN may pass over a circuit that is used only for VPN traffic, but this isn't a requirement. It's *private* because it's a tunnel. This tunnel doesn't need to be encrypted or have any sort of protection for the data, although it can use encryption and other security measures. A device can be configured to allow only certain types of traffic to access the tunnel. It's a *network* because it extends an existing network past its natural boundaries.

In the following sections, we'll discuss the major types of VPN configurations used in most production environments today and the various Cisco devices on which they're configured.

Major Types of VPNs

There are many types of VPNs, but they're usually defined by how they're created and what purpose they serve. The following are three major types of VPNs:

Remote Access VPN   An Remote *Access VPN* connects to the network over a shared medium such as the Internet. People using the modem on their PC to connect to a modem at work are crossing the shared medium of the public telephone system. People connecting to their ISP to use the Internet to transport VPN traffic are connecting to two shared mediums. They first use DSL, cable, or dial-up connections to access their ISP, and then they use the Internet to go the rest of the way.

Intranet VPN   An *intranet VPN* connects two trusted locations to each other over a dedicated connection. An example would be a VPN between a corporate headquarters in Maine and a manufacturing facility in Thailand. The key elements are the trusted locations and connection dedicated to VPN traffic.

Extranet VPN An *extranet VPN* connects untrusted locations to each other over a dedicated connection. An example would be a headquarters office in Maine using a VPN to connect to the ordering system of a supplier in Ohio. There is a certain amount of trust, but not as much as there would be if both sides were part of the same corporate infrastructure.

VPN Devices

A VPN is a *tunnel,* and each tunnel must begin and end somewhere. Cisco has many devices that can act as one end of a VPN tunnel or manage it, including Cisco routers, the PIX Firewall, Cisco VPN Concentrators, and the Cisco Secure VPN client software.

> **NOTE** Cisco Secure is the name of the product line for Cisco's security products. *Cisco Secure Policy Manager* (CSPM), a component of Cisco Works, can be used to manage VPNs.

Cisco devices can talk to more than just other Cisco devices. A Cisco router can be set up for a direct VPN connection to a Windows 2000 server, a non-Cisco router, or another IPSec device.

IPSec is a standard, and as long as both vendors follow the instructions in the standard and both devices are set up with the correct configuration, they should be able to form a tunnel. (IPSec is discussed in detail later in this chapter, beginning with the "Introducing IPSec" section.)

Let's take a closer look at each type of Cisco VPN device and its capabilities.

Cisco Routers

Cisco routers come in various flavors and can do different tasks based on the available hardware and software. Different IOS feature sets give more or fewer options for creating a VPN tunnel. Cisco routers began supporting IPSec with IOS 11.3(T). Prior to this, they used Cisco Encryption Technology (CET), which shouldn't be used if IPSec is available.

Cisco IOS software can form many different types of tunnels. Along with IPSec tunnels, Cisco routers can build Layer 2 Forwarding (L2F), Layer 2 Tunneling Protocol (L2TP), Point-to-Point Tunneling Protocol (PPTP), IP in IP encapsulation (IPinIP), and Generic Routing Encapsulation (GRE) tunnels.

Even low-end routers can do encryption, but the type of encryption depends on the type of router, the version of IOS, and the amount of memory. Newer routers with enough flash and NVRAM can use an IOS image that allows for Triple Data Encryption Standard (3DES) encryption. A 1600-series router or a 2500-series router doesn't have the processing ability and is limited to basic Data Encryption Standard (DES) encryption. Some 800-series routers are capable of using 3DES. (DES and 3DES encryption are discussed in the "Encryption" section later in this chapter.)

It's normally not a good idea to terminate many VPN connections at even a robust router because of the amount of processing that goes on in the encryption and decryption process. The exception to this rule is when your router is outfitted with a VPN module. This module offloads the processing from the CPU, keeping valuable CPU cycles free for other tasks. (For more information about the VPN module, visit www.cisco.com/univercd/cc/td/doc/pcat/vpnnm.htm.)

> **Note:** Using Cisco routers for IPSec tunnels is discussed in detail in Chapter 18, "Configuring the VPN Concentrator."

The PIX Firewall

Cisco has a number of PIX Firewall models available, from the low-end 501 to the high-end 535. The PIX Firewall has supported IPSec since version 5.0. This firewall can form a tunnel with another device that is capable of a direct IPSec VPN connection, including Cisco routers, firewalls, and VPN Concentrators.

All PIX Firewalls can use AES, DES and 3DES encryption, but they must be licensed for it. A 3DES license can be purchased through a Cisco reseller. If you currently have a PIX Firewall that isn't licensed for encryption, you can get a free key for DES by registering at www.cisco.com/kobayashi/sw-center/ciscosecure/pix.shtml (access to this URL is available only with a valid CCO login ID and password).

> **Note:** Configuring PIX Firewalls for VPNs is discussed in detail in Chapter 18.

The Cisco VPN Concentrator

The Cisco VPN Concentrator is designed to terminate many client VPN connections. It can also form a tunnel with a router, firewall, or another concentrator.

You should use the VPN Concentrator if you have more than a few users who want to access a network via a VPN tunnel. The concentrator is a stand-alone network device that offloads the task of processing VPN tunnels from routers and firewalls. You can manage the VPN Concentrator via the command-line interface (CLI) or an HTML-based graphical user interface (GUI).

The 3000-series VPN Concentrators can terminate up to 10,000 user tunnels. The 5000-series VPN Concentrators can terminate up to 50,000 tunnels. Because the 5000 models are service-provider devices, neither this book nor the CSVPN exam covers them.

> **Note:** The features of the VPN Concentrator models are described in Chapter 17, "Introduction to Cisco VPN Devices." Details on configuring and managing VPN Concentrators are provided in Chapter 18, as well as Chapter 19, "Managing the VPN Concentrator."

VPN Client Software

VPN client software is used on PCs and servers as one end of a tunnel. When users create a VPN from their home PC, it terminates at a router, firewall, or concentrator.

The Cisco Secure VPN client comes in two flavors. The older one is the SafeNet client that Cisco uses to connect client PCs to routers and firewalls. There are two versions: 1.0 (which can't use a certificate from a Windows 2000 certificate authority) and 1.1 (which can use a certificate from a Windows 2000 or XP certificate authority).

The other type of client is the concentrator client, often referred to as the *Altiga* client. It's used to connect client PCs to the VPN Concentrator. There are two major versions of this client: 2.5 and 3.0. You should use whichever version of the client matches the software version on the concentrator; for example, use a 2.5 client if you have version 2.5 software on the concentrator.

Cisco realized that requiring two different clients when only one can be installed at a time was problematic. The company has merged the two into the Unified Client. The latest version of the Unified Client as of this writing is 4.0, which allows for VPNs to general Cisco devices. This version even comes with a transparent stateful firewall for the client. If you're using Windows XP, you must use version 3.1 or higher.

Real World Scenario

Why VPN Networking?

There are two main reasons why companies choose to install VPN technology: ease of administration and the all-important cost. Remote access and intranet WAN networking are the two most popular implementations for VPNs.

Remote Access

The use of Remote Access Services (RAS) has been a staple in remote IT connectivity for many years. This remote access method required administrators to keep up the extra devices needed such as modems, servers, operating systems, and so on. Then there were the phone-line access charges; and if remote users were beyond the local calling area, toll-free lines or calling cards need to be issued, adding another level of expense. With a remote-access VPN, a company can eliminate the need for RAS and the costly phone lines. There is still a cost for Internet access; however, companies can negotiate excellent access rates (some as low as $10 per month per user), and nationwide carriers boast local numbers from nearly everywhere, thus eliminating the need for long-distance charges. Administration and hardware upkeep cost are also reduced significantly. On average, a company that implements a VPN remote access solution realizes 60–70 percent in overall cost savings.

Intranet WAN Networking

Prior to VPN technology, any connections between offices had to be done with costly dedicated circuits. For most small/medium businesses (SMBs), the days of dedicated circuits between remote offices and headquarters are gone. A much more cost-effective solution has become connecting each office directly to the local Internet. Creating private VPN tunnels between those offices provides adequate protection for the data and the cost savings of having the dedicated lines. Offices have access to the Internet and the remote office with a single connection to the Internet. Multiple tunnels can even be configured to create remote-office-to-remote-office connectivity in a mesh configuration that once would have been cost prohibitive.

> Chapter 19 provides more details on using the VPN client software.

Introducing IPSec

IPSec is a standards-based way of creating a tunnel that data will travel along to get to its destination. An example of an IPSec tunnel is shown in Figure 16.1.

IPSec has the option of using several other standards to get the tunnel set up. One of these is Internet Key Exchange (IKE), which is a protocol that works with IPSec.

> IKE, RSA signatures, and certificate authorities are discussed in the "Internet Key Exchange" section later in this chapter.

We'll cover the IPSec components that provide authentication, encryption, and other services. These include the following:

- The Authentication Header (AH) and Encapsulating Security Payload (ESP) protocols
- Hashing
- Encryption
- Diffie-Hellman Key Exchange
- IKE
- Transform sets
- IPSec security associations (SAs)

However, before we discuss the individual components of IPSec, let's see what services it can provide.

FIGURE 16.1   An IPSec tunnel

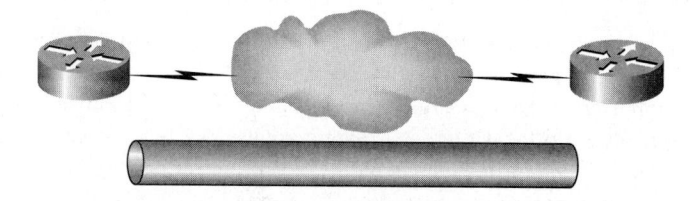

IPSec Services

IPSec can accomplish several tasks, if you wish to configure them. These include the following:

Data confidentiality   *Data confidentiality* can be ensured by encrypting traffic as the packets leave the router.

Data integrity   *Data integrity* can be ensured by verifying that packets haven't changed after they were sent. Hashing is used to verify that there haven't been any changes to transferred data.

Data-origin authentication   *Data-origin authentication* verifies the identity of the originator of the packet.

Anti-replay   *Anti-replay* is a process by which the receiver can detect that a packet has already been received and will reject any duplicate packets. (This doesn't interfere with the TCP retransmission function.)

> **NOTE** Configurations for all IP-related services are covered in depth in Chapter 18.

IPSec Building Blocks: AH and ESP

To establish an IPSec tunnel between two devices, those devices must negotiate how the tunnel will be built. IPSec operates at layer 3 (the Network layer) of the OSI model in such a way that it really inserts itself between layers 3 and 4 of the OSI model; but by ISO definition, encryption is a layer 7 function. There are two protocols to build tunnels and protect the data traveling across the tunnel:

- Authentication Header (AH) uses protocol 51.
- Encapsulating Security Payload (ESP) uses protocol 50.

Knowing what AH and ESP do is essential to creating a good tunnel blueprint. We'll look at each of these, as well as Tunnel and Transport mode, in the following sections.

The Authentication Header Protocol

AH, defined in RFCs 1826 and 2402, doesn't perform any sort of data encryption, so the information is passed in clear text. Its purpose is to provide data integrity and authentication as well as anti-reply service, which is optional. It ensures that a packet that crosses the tunnel is the same packet that left the peer device and that no changes have been made. It uses a keyed hash to accomplish this.

Figure 16.2 illustrates the hash creation. (Hashing is discussed in more detail a little later in this chapter, in the "Hashing" section.)

FIGURE 16.2 The Authentication Header (AH) process

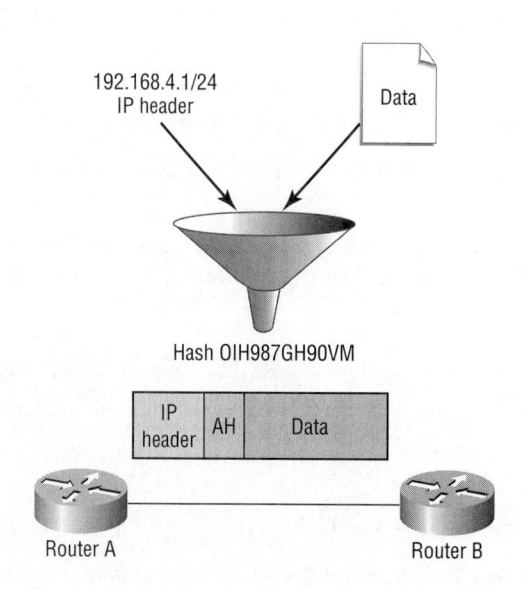

> **NOTE** Encryption is a very processor-intensive task, so there are situations where you might want to use just AH. For example, you might not want to bother to encrypt routing updates, but you'll want to make sure that the data inside the packets hasn't changed.

The AH information sits in the packet between the spots reserved for layers 3 and 4. The AH header consists of six fields:

Next Header   This 8-bit field identifies the protocol type after the AH. For example, for TCP or UDP, this field contains 4 or 17, respectively. When used as the IPSec protocol, the value in the Next Header field is 51.

Payload Length   This 8-bit field indicates the length of the IPSec header in 32-bit words, minus two. The fixed part of the length field is three words (96 bits) long. Although the Authentication Data portion is a variable length, it still has a standard length of three words for a grand total of six 32-bit words. When you accommodate for the deduction of two, the value entered in the Payload Length field is then four.

Reserved   These 16 bits are currently unused and consist of zeros.

Security Parameter Index (SPI)   This 32-bit field holds a pseudo, random, arbitrarily assigned number that is paired with the destination IP address and IPSec protocol to identify a particular tunnel. The SPI identifies AH information and links it to an appropriate peer IP address and SA.

Sequence Number This 32-bit field can be used to enable anti-replay, helping prevent old packets from being captured and reused. If anti-replay isn't used, this field still exists. The sequence number is an ever-increasing counter that isn't allowed to repeat for the duration of the SA. Often the number will be set to 0 when an SA is first established. The sequencing information isn't always used by the receiver; however, it's included from the sender just in case.

Authentication Data This field is where the data is stored to ensure that the packet hasn't been tampered with, and it contains the Integrity Check Value (ICV). The field size depends on the method used to do the hashing. The two methods used for Cisco devices, MD5 and SHA, truncate at 96 bits of information. Implementations in IPv4 require blocks of 32 bits, and IPv6 requires blocks of 64 bits. Padding is used to fill any spaces to reach the appropriate block size.

The AH process runs on the entire packet, with the exception of fields in layer 3 that are designed to change. For example, the Time to Live (TTL) field is designed to decrement as the packet goes from one network to the next.

AH takes the output from the process, encrypts it, and then truncates it so the result will fit in the Authentication Data field. When the packet arrives at the other end of the tunnel, the device performs the same calculation on the packet it received and compares the output it got with the one that was sent by the originator. If they match, the data is authenticated.

> **WARNING** The IP address is a field that isn't designed to be changed. However, many network implementations use Network Address Translation (NAT), which changes the IP address. Creating a tunnel that uses AH across a device using NAT will result in a broken tunnel.

Encapsulating Security Payload

ESP, defined in RFC 2406, can provide for data integrity and authentication, but its primary purpose is to encrypt the data crossing the tunnel. When using the hash to provide for authentication and integrity, ESP doesn't protect as much of the packet as AH does, but this can be a benefit in some situations.

There are two reasons why ESP is the preferred building block of IPSec tunnels:

- The authentication component of ESP doesn't include any layer 3 information. This means that it can work in conjunction with a network using NAT.
- On Cisco devices, ESP supports encryption using AES, DES or 3DES.

Figure 16.3 shows the ESP header and its placement in the packet, depending on whether IPSec is configured in Transport mode or Tunnel mode. These modes are discussed in detail in the next section.

Because ESP offers both authentication and encryption, it's possible to do both without needing to use AH. When you're using both ESP and AH, it's important to remember that encryption comes first. Everything from layer 4 through the end of the data is encrypted. Once the packet has been encrypted, the authentication process is applied.

FIGURE 16.3 The ESP header and packet

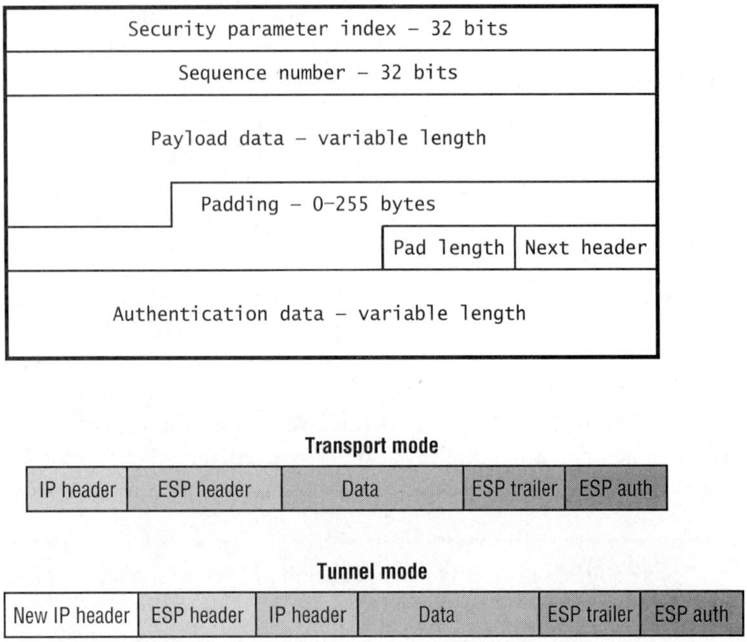

```
Security parameter index - 32 bits
Sequence number - 32 bits
Payload data - variable length
    Padding - 0-255 bytes
                         Pad length | Next header
Authentication data - variable length
```

Transport mode

| IP header | ESP header | Data | ESP trailer | ESP auth |

Tunnel mode

| New IP header | ESP header | IP header | Data | ESP trailer | ESP auth |

In addition to the ESP header, which sits right after the layer 3 information, ESP also has a trailer for encryption and a trailer for authentication. There are two 32-bit fields within the ESP header: the Security Parameter Index (SPI) and Sequence Number fields. These work in the same way they do in the AH header (described in the previous section). The ESP trailer contains three fields:

Pad Length This 8-bit field indicates how many bytes have been used for padding for encryption.

Next Header This 8-bit field identifies the type of data found in the Payload Data field.

Padding This field indicates how much padding has been used to get the encrypted packet to a fixed size. The size used depends on the encryption protocol, but it can be up to a block size of 2,040 bits.

The ESP authentication trailer contains a single field: the ESP Authentication field. This is where the authentication information is stored. Its size depends on the hashing algorithm.

Tunnel Mode and Transport Mode

An IPSec tunnel can be in either of two modes: *Tunnel mode* or *Transport mode*. Most of the IPSec sessions that Cisco devices deal with are using Tunnel mode. Figure 16.4 illustrates the difference between these modes.

FIGURE 16.4 Tunnel mode versus Transport mode

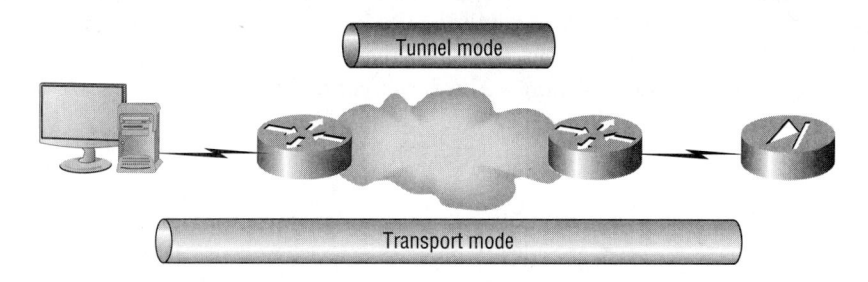

A Transport-mode tunnel encrypts from the device that originally created the packet all the way to the device that is receiving the packet. At no time does the packet leave the IPSec tunnel. If users wish to protect their e-mail as they send it to the server, they can encrypt it on their end, and the server will decrypt it. The message is protected from one end all the way to the other. Transport mode might be used if an administrator wanted to be able to administer the router from home via a VPN tunnel, for example.

If the IPSec tunnel doesn't protect the packet from end to end, then it's a Tunnel-mode tunnel. For example, if a company's headquarters has a router and the company's remote site has a router, there could be a Tunnel-mode tunnel between them. When users at the remote site check their e-mail, the traffic goes across the tunnel, but it isn't protected from end (user) to end (server).

The VPN concept deals with Tunnel-mode tunnels. A virtual network is created that spans some other network. A Tunnel-mode tunnel takes the packet and places it inside another packet. You end up with two IP addresses: one for the tunnel endpoint and one for the origination.

In the example shown in Figure 16.5, a packet with an IP header and payload is depicted at the top. If the packet needs to cross a Transport-mode tunnel, the AH process will run on the packet, and the AH header will be inserted. A Transport-mode tunnel does nothing to the IP header.

FIGURE 16.5 AH in Tunnel mode and in Transport mode

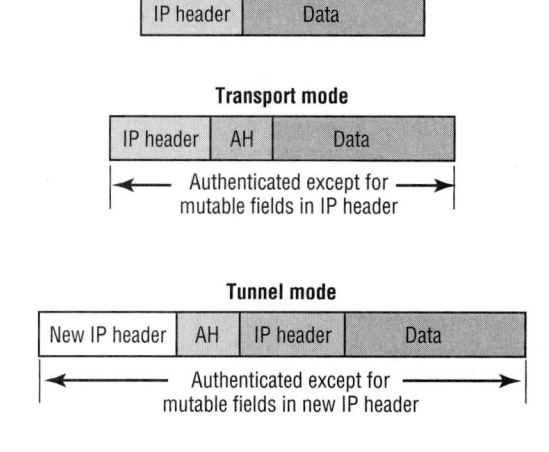

If the packet needs to cross a Tunnel-mode tunnel, the IPSec device takes the original packet and places it inside a new packet. The old IP address is now considered to be part of the data field. The new packet has a source IP address of the interface at one end of the tunnel and a destination IP address of the interface at the other end of the tunnel. ESP works the same way, except that if both encryption and authentication are used, encryption happens first.

Hashing

Hashing is used to verify that data hasn't changed or to hide data crossing the network. For example, Challenge Handshake Authentication Protocol (CHAP) uses hashing to disguise passwords. In the world of VPNs, hashing is used to verify that there haven't been any changes to data.

> **NOTE** The process of hashing an authentication is often referred to as a *Hashed Message Authentication Code* (HMAC).

A hash is a simple thing to create. For example, suppose that you want to send the number 12,345 across the network and use hashing to make sure there were no changes to this transmission. If the chosen algorithm said to multiply the data by 56,789, invert the result, and chop off all but the first four characters, here is what would happen:

Multiply $12,345 \times 56,789 = 701,060,205$

Invert $701,060,205 = 502,060,107$

Truncate $502,060,107 = 5,020$

When you send the number 12,345, the value 5020 is also included. To make sure that the data hasn't changed, the device on the other end of the tunnel performs the same computation on the value 12,345. Once it comes up with its own four-digit hash, it compares the hashes. If they match, the data hasn't changed.

A typical hash combines encryption and truncation or padding to get to a fixed-size authentication value. Cisco devices make good use of Message Digest 5 (MD5), which is 128-bit, as well as the Secure Hash Algorithm (SHA), at 160-bit, for hashing. These techniques perform the requisite encryption and then truncate or pad the message to 96 bits. Because of this, it's nearly impossible to regenerate the original value that was used to create the hash if it isn't already known. The value 5020 could have originally been 50,201, or it could have been 5,020,983,478.

Part of the negotiation of IPSec to set up the tunnel is the negotiation of various keys. The key used here is a shared secret, which will be explained in more detail in the "Diffie-Hellman Key Exchange" section, coming up shortly.

Encryption

Encryption is commonly associated with VPN tunnels, but encryption isn't a required component. Encryption involves a message, a key, and a way of combining the two.

One type of encryption takes a message and a key and lightly stirs the two together; whereas a stronger encryption is like putting the message and key in a blender and completely mixing the two. The result is a string of seemingly random characters that can be reversed at the other end into its clear-text form.

The tunnel endpoints must use the same type of encryption, which is verified before the tunnel comes up and data can be sent. If a message were encrypted in one form but the other side tried to decrypt it in another form, the output would be undecipherable.

Cisco devices currently support AES, DES and 3DES. DES uses 56-bit encryption, and so does 3DES, but 3DES uses it three times. Whereas DES negotiates a key, 3DES negotiates a key and then breaks it into three parts. The first part is 56-bit encryption, the second process is to decrypt the message with the second key, and then the third part is used to encrypt again. Because the first and second keys aren't identical, the second process is just another way of doing 56-bit encryption. 3DES yields encryption that is about twice as strong as regular DES. The Advanced Encryption Standard (AES) is based on an algorithm called Rijndael and is now supported in all PIX models. AES is designed to be more secure than DES and offers a larger key size and ensures that the only known approach to decrypt a message is for an intruder to try every possible key. AES also uses a variable key length, 128, 192 or 256-bit keys.

Diffie-Hellman Key Exchange

The *Diffie-Hellman* (DH) key exchange protocol, defined in RFC 2631, was created by Whitfield Diffie and Marten Hellman in 1976. The encryption protocol was designed to let two peers exchange a secret key without having any prior secrets and is an example of how two pairs can use different public keys to create a singe private key. This key exchange is used to create a *shared secret*. A shared secret is made when two networking devices create a key and then share part of it with the peer.

The first task is for each network device to create a key pair. One mathematical expression is generated, and from it, two keys are formed: a private key and a public key, as shown here:

The private key is never shared with any other device, but it's linked mathematically with the public key. Each network device sends its public key to its peer:

This results in each device having a copy of its private key, its public key, and the peer device's public key. Nothing more is done with its own public key, but the other two keys are very important. Each device mathematically combines its own private key with the peer device's public key. This process results in the shared secret:

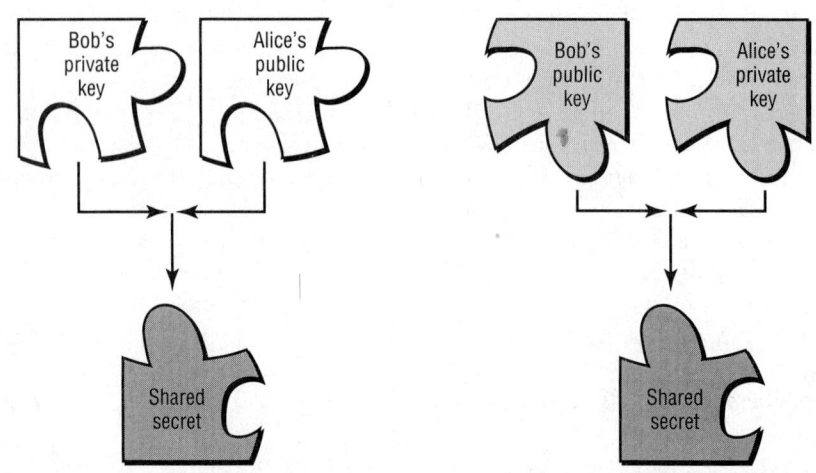

Because the keys are all linked together, each side ends up with the same key. Encrypting and decrypting data using the same key is called *symmetric key* encryption. (The other form is asymmetric key encryption, which encrypts using one key and decrypts using a different but mathematically related key.)

Diffie-Hellman is used to protect the IPSec tunnel setup process. The Diffie-Hellman tunnel is used to encrypt the IPSec negotiations that are required before the tunnel can come up. The Diffie-Hellman tunnel isn't used to encrypt conventional traffic—for that, you need the IPSec tunnel.

Several strengths of Diffie-Hellman are available, but most Cisco devices support only the two weakest types, called Group 1 and Group 2. Group 1 is 768-bit encryption; Group 2 is 1024-bit encryption.

> **Note:** With the approval of the new AES encryption standard, the IETF is working on increasing Diffie-Hellman up to 8192 bits.

Internet Key Exchange

The Internet Key Exchange (IKE) works hand in hand with IPSec and is defined in RFC 2409. IPSec sets up the tunnel for the traffic to cross in a protected fashion. IKE handles all of the administration and gets everything ready so that the IPSec tunnel can form. If there is no connection with IKE, IPSec has no chance of forming a tunnel.

IKE goes through two distinct processes when establishing an IPSec VPN tunnel. During phase 1, IKE is tasked with the authentication of the IPSec peers and negotiates an IKE security association between those peers on its way to initiating a secure tunnel using the Internet Security Association and Key Management Protocol (ISAKMP). In phase 2 of the IKE process, the peers use the tunnel established in phase 1 to negotiate the specified security parameters for the tunnel. Once negotiated, these parameters stay in place; the tunnel is either terminated by expiration of the SA lifetime or torn down manually.

> **NOTE** IKE is implemented on Cisco devices using transform sets. Configuration details and default settings are detailed in the section "Transform Sets."

Just as a foundation must be laid before a house can be built, an IKE tunnel must exist before IPSec information can be exchanged.

> **NOTE** The term *IKE* is used synonymously with *ISAKMP*. Throughout this book, the terms are used interchangeably.

IKE is configured manually on network devices and has several components that must match on both sides of the potential tunnel. Authentication is required to ensure that each device is talking to the correct peer. Cisco devices that support IPSec support two or three methods of authentication: pre-shared keys, RSA signatures, and RSA encrypted nonces. In larger networks, a *certificate authority* (CA) is the most efficient method for authentication due to the less cumbersome configuration and easier management.

In addition to determining how the devices will authenticate, the devices also need to be configured with a peer identifier. Acceptable methods of identifying a peer are via IP address and via a fully qualified domain name (FQDN). Whichever method is chosen applies to the router or firewall as a whole. You may not point to one peer via IP address and another via domain name.

Pre-shared Keys

A *pre-shared key* can be manually configured on each network device. When you're using pre-shared keys, it's vitally important that the two peers be given the same key. When the process starts, device A sends a packet to device B. This packet includes, among other things, a keyed hash and the data that made the hash. Device B creates a hash using its key and the data sent by device A. If the hashes match, then the two devices are using the same key and have authenticated.

Because pre-shared keys must be manually entered, this method of authentication isn't recommended for systems with many devices. However, it's a simple way of establishing authentication and works well when only a few devices are involved.

RSA Signatures

You can use an *RSA signature* if the devices have access to a CA. RSA signatures are keys that are generated on network devices and are used to authenticate the peer device. RSA signatures are the primary component when two network devices need to create a shared secret key (as explained in the "Diffie-Hellman Key Exchange" section earlier in this chapter). The peers use a public key and a private key to accomplish this, and they often use a CA to exchange keys.

Each device registers with the CA and gets a device-specific identity certificate. When attempting to authenticate, the devices exchange certificates.

> **NOTE** CAs are discussed in more detail in the "Certificate Authorities" section, after the discussion of RSA encrypted nonces.

The authentication is actually the process of being able to understand the certificate that was received. This method isn't efficient if only a few devices are involved, but it can save quite a bit of time if there are many devices using IPSec tunnels.

> **NOTE** *RSA* is a term that occurs frequently in encryption and security white papers and manuals. It stands for Rivest, Shamir, and Adleman, three doctors who invented the RSA Public Key Cryptosystem.

RSA-Encrypted Nonces

The *RSA-encrypted nonce* method employs everything that isn't desirable in the pre-shared key and RSA signature methods. It's manually configured on each device, so it increases the potential for making mistakes when entering data. Also, it depends on generated keys, so there is a risk that the keys will be compromised.

RSA-encrypted nonces start in the same way that RSA signatures do: Each network device must generate a large number, which gets split into public and private keys. The public key must be copied over to the peer device, where the nonce is encrypted in it. When the IPSec session needs to start and IKE needs to be authenticated, the devices exchange nonces. At this point, each side generates a shared secret in the same fashion that Diffie-Hellman key exchange operates.

RSA-encrypted nonces do have one advantage: They provide for a deniable transaction. A pre-shared key transaction can happen with only the peer that has the key. Since you have the IP address and the key, it's easy to prove. RSA signatures are difficult to deny because a trusted third party, the CA, maintains records of certificate serial numbers and can identify the device that registered. RSA-encrypted nonces have neither of these ways of proving the identity of the other device. After all, it isn't hard to spoof an address or hijack an IP address. If deniability is required, go with encrypted nonces.

Certificate Authorities

A CA is a trusted, third-party device that may or may not be under your administrative control. CAs are used to simplify administration of a large number of IPSec devices. Each device needs to register with the CA rather than have a separate configuration for every peer it might wish to create a tunnel with. A CA normally isn't recommended for small networks because of the initial cost in money and time to set one up.

It doesn't take long to set up four routers to do authentication via pre-shared keys for each of the other three routers in the group; it's a total of 12 keys. Expand the model from 4 routers to 400, and then add a new router. Not only will someone need to configure the new router for 400 pre-shared keys—one for each of the existing routers—but someone will need to log in to every one of the existing routers to add a single new key. Adding 800 keys will take quite a while, and troubleshooting the typos will take even longer. With a CA, you can avoid all this by registering the new router with the CA.

To enroll to a CA, a device needs to generate an RSA key. As explained earlier, part of the RSA key is a public key and part of it is a private key. During the certificate-enrollment procedure, the network device gets a copy of the CA's public key. The network device also sends its public key to the CA. The CA encrypts the client's public key in a certificate and sends it to the enrolling client.

When two devices wish to form a tunnel and are authenticating via certificates, they need to exchange the certificates. Because the certificates are nothing more than an encrypted packet, the peers must have the necessary information to decrypt them. Since they were encrypted using the CA's private key, a device needs the same CA's public key to decrypt the certificate. Once the certificate is decrypted, device A has a copy of device B's public key and vice versa.

It doesn't matter which CA you use; several are available to serve your needs. All CA applications that want to be compatible follow the format specified in the X.509 standards. The CA application gaining the most widespread usage is the one that Microsoft includes with Windows 2000 Server. There is no extra cost to use the CA supplied with Windows 2000, unlike other CA applications.

> **NOTE** Chapter 18, provides details on requesting and installing digital certificates for use with CAs.

Transform Sets

To build the IPSec tunnel, you need to tell the network device how to use AH and/or ESP. A *transform* is an option that describes how to build the tunnel. For example, a transform may tell a router to use ESP with DES encryption, tell a firewall to use AH with MD5 hashing, or say to use several items.

An IPSec blueprint, or *transform set*, can have up to three instructions in it: one AH transform and two ESP transforms (one for encryption and one for authentication). However, if more are needed, you can configure multiple transform sets within a given device's crypto policy to identify combinations. Figure 16.6 illustrates the options for transform sets.

Part of the configuration also involves telling the network device if the IPSec tunnel will use Tunnel mode or Transport mode. The default on the Cisco router is for Tunnel mode.

> **NOTE** Other types of transforms are available for odd purposes. For example, the ah-null transform is used to create a tunnel without authentication or encryption.

FIGURE 16.6 Transform set options

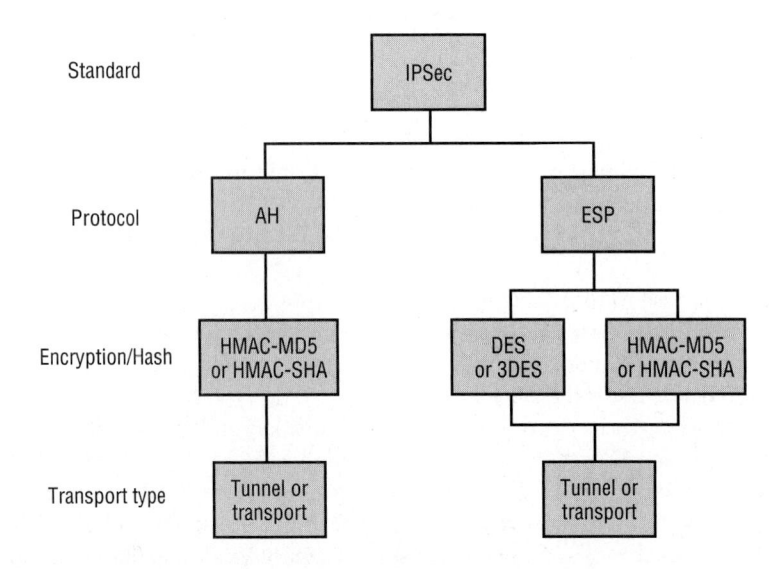

```
Standard                        IPSec
                                  |
                      ┌───────────┴───────────┐
Protocol             AH                      ESP
                      |                       |
                      |                ┌──────┴──────┐
Encryption/Hash   HMAC-MD5          DES         HMAC-MD5
                  or HMAC-SHA     or 3DES       or HMAC-SHA
                      |                └──────┬──────┘
Transport type    Tunnel or              Tunnel or
                  transport              transport
```

Building a transform set for an IKE tunnel on a Cisco device requires setting up five parameters for IKE phase 1 and three for IKE phase 2. The five parameters and their default settings for the VPN 3000 Concentrator Series are shown in Table 16.1.

> **WARNING** The parameters set for IKE phase 1 must match the opposite end of the tunnel exactly, or the tunnel won't establish the connection.

TABLE 16.1 IKE Phase 1 Parameters

Setting	Default	Option
Encryption algorithm	56-bit DES	168-bit 3DES
Hash algorithm	MD5	SHA-1
Authentication method	RSA digital signatures	Pre-shared keys, RSA encrypted nonces
Key exchange method	768-bit Diffie-Hellman Group 1	1024-bit Diffie-Hellman Group 2
IKE SA lifetime	86,400 seconds (1 day)	Variable*

*Shorter lifetime settings are an option and more secure but cause further use of processing cycles.

Once the IKE phase 1 configuration is complete, the only IKE phase 2 configuration requirements to establish the tunnel are shown in Table 16.2.

TABLE 16.2 IKE Phase 2 Parameters

Setting	Option
IPSec protocol	AH or ESP
Hash algorithm	MD5 or SHA-1
Encryption algorithm (ESP only)	DES or 3DES

IPSec Security Associations

An IPSec *security association* (SA) contains the instructions on how to build a tunnel to a given destination. When two peers decide that they will use ESP-DES and AH-MD5 for the IPSec tunnel, this information is stored somewhere along with items such as the SA lifetime and appropriate keys. All the properties of the blocks used to build an IPSec tunnel are placed in this database. The SA tells the router the recipe to use when sending traffic through the tunnel to a given destination.

An IPSec SA has several components:

- The peer IP address (the IP address of the other end of the IPSec tunnel)
- The Security Parameter Index (SPI), which is a pointer used to identify the characteristics of a tunnel
- The transform set used to build the IPSec tunnel
- Keys used to hash or encrypt the traffic that crosses the tunnel
- Optional attributes, such as the tunnel lifetime

Each tunnel has at least one SA associated with it. An IKE SA is bidirectional; the referenced properties apply in both directions. IPSec tunnels are unidirectional; they apply on a one-way basis only. Since the peers must negotiate and have identical ways of setting up the tunnel, the question, "Why are they unidirectional?" is often raised. The answer is that the router needs to be able to invert the access control list (ACL) for incoming traffic.

When the ACL is created, it applies to outgoing traffic, which is associated with the outgoing SA. To make sure that traffic coming in is protected in the way it should be, the router makes a mirror image of the ACL and associates it with incoming traffic for the incoming SA.

Each network device is responsible for setting up its outgoing SA. When router A receives traffic that wants to be encrypted, it sends the SA policy information to router B. This becomes router B's incoming SA. Router B compiles all the information it needs to determine appropriate characteristics for its outgoing SA and sends that to router A. The numbers identifying a particular SA (the SPI) are identical on both sides of the tunnel.

Figure 16.7 shows that there are two separate connections, based on the connection IDs in use (`conn id`). The SPIs are unique on a per-SA basis; each side uses the same SPI when referring to the same SA. Because there are two different SAs, there are two different SPIs. The other information must match across both SAs and on both sides.

> **NOTE** The `crypto map: mymap` shown in Figure 16.7 defines the crypto map used for IPSec configuration. The crypto map name (such as mymap in this example) doesn't need to match between the peers; it's a locally significant value. Chapter 18 provides more information about crypto maps for IPSec configuration.

IPSec SAs are traditionally negotiated through IKE (discussed in the next section). It's possible to create an SA manually, but doing so isn't advisable for most environments because it can require additional record keeping and increase the possibility of errors.

FIGURE 16.7 IPSec security associations (SAs)

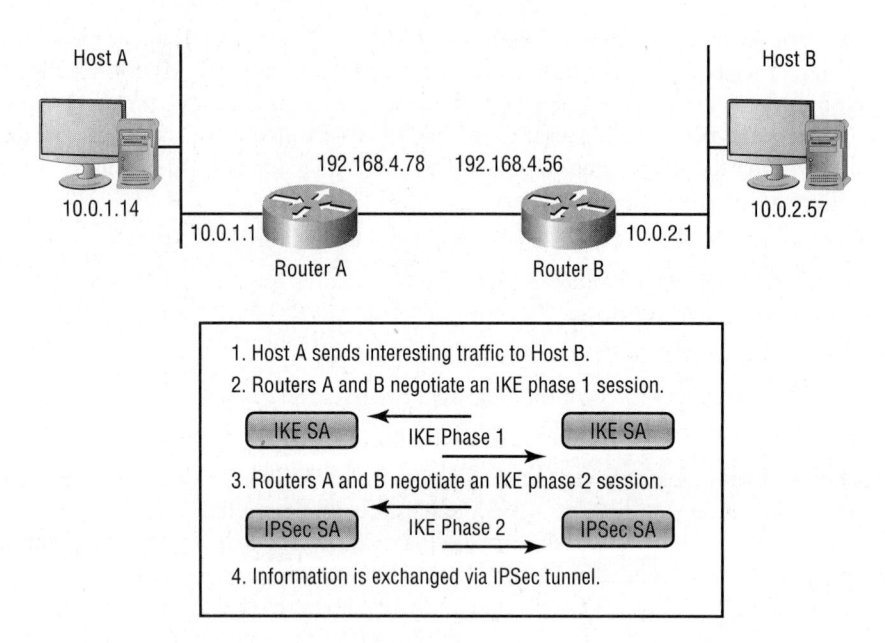

How IPSec Works

In the previous section, we introduced you to the IKE and explained that it must exist before IPSec can be set up. But before IKE or IPSec can perform their tasks, there must be some traffic that needs to cross the tunnel. This traffic is the entire purpose for setting up these tunnels in the first place and is defined as *interesting* traffic. Once that occurs, the router can communicate with the tunnel peer to set up the tunnel. IKE tasks are broken into two phases: The first is setting up the IKE tunnel, and the second does quite a bit of setup for IPSec.

In the coming sections, we'll look at the logical process of how a tunnel is set up, starting with how you define the interesting traffic that requires the tunnel to be set up. Next we'll examine the next steps as we look at both phase 1 and phase 2 of IKE. Finally, we'll look at the different decisions that need to be made as the tunnel is being used for various tasks.

Defining Interesting Traffic

Interesting traffic consists of packets that need to be transported to the opposite side of the tunnel. Without interesting traffic, there is nothing to trigger the tunnel creation. The tunnel must have a reason to exist, and traffic that wants to cross is that reason.

In the network pictured in Figure 16.8, routers A and B are configured to create a tunnel if traffic wants to go from the network that host A resides on to the network that host B resides on. To do this, an ACL needs to be configured.

The ACL won't be applied directly to an interface; instead, it's used to determine which traffic is able to use the tunnel. When you're building an ACL to determine which traffic will cross, use `permit` statements to permit traffic to use the tunnel and `deny` statements to prevent the traffic from using the tunnel. Traffic that is denied won't be protected by the tunnel. However, the traffic won't be blocked from leaving the router.

Consider the following `access-list` statement:

```
access-list 101 permit ip 10.0.1.0 0.0.0.255 10.0.2.0 0.0.0.255
```

This ACL will permit traffic originating from the 10.0.1.0 network to cross the tunnel if it's heading to a device on the 10.0.2.0 network. Since there are no other statements, all other traffic is denied by the implicit deny-all rule. The denied traffic can still access the network; it just won't cross in the tunnel.

FIGURE 16.8 Interesting traffic triggers tunnel creation.

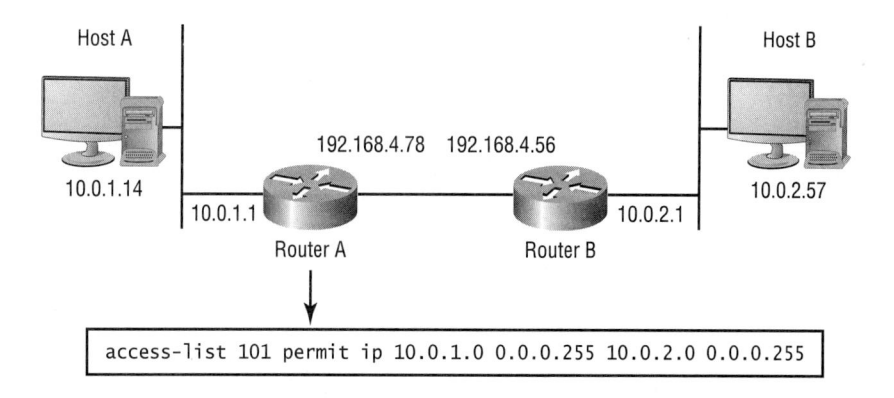

When an interesting packet arrives, the ACL determines if it should go across the tunnel. If so, the router determines what should be done and inserts the SPI (from the SA, as discussed in the "IPSec Security Associations" section earlier in the chapter) into the IPSec header. When the packet arrives at the destination peer, the device looks up the IPSec information based on the SPI in the packet.

IKE Phase 1

Once the router has received the interesting traffic and determined that the traffic needs to cross the tunnel, the router buffers the packet and starts the process to bring up the IPSec tunnel.

> **Note:** It isn't unusual to create an ACL that uses pings for interesting traffic. Ping the far side, and watch three to five pings fail. If this happens, test it by pinging again.

To bring up the tunnel, the two ends must negotiate what the IKE settings are supposed to be. The following items need to be negotiated:

- IKE SA
- Encryption
- Hash method
- Authentication method
- Diffie-Hellman group
- Tunnel lifetime

Each of these items must match on both sides of the tunnel, with the exception of the tunnel lifetime. A tunnel won't form if one side is using MD5 hashing and the other side is using SHA, or if one side is using Diffie-Hellman Group 1 and the other side is using Group 2. However, the tunnel lifetime values aren't required to match. This setting defaults to the shortest time value of the tunnel pair. For example, if one side leaves the lifetime at the default of one day and the other changes it to half a day, the tunnel will form, and it will expire in half a day.

Each Cisco network device has a default policy that is used for IKE phase 1 negotiations. This means that an administrator needs to make only the desired changes in the configuration. All other settings will use the defaults. For example, if you need to change only the default setting of using a CA for authentication, just change that to pre-shared keys in the profile. The rest of the profile settings will use the built-in defaults. Therefore, it's recommended that default settings be used for the initial configuration, leaving the custom requirements for the tunnels until after any necessary troubleshooting during initial setup.

IKE phase 1 has two different methods of communicating: *Main mode* and *Aggressive mode*.

Main Mode Communication

Main mode has three two-way exchanges between the peers:

1. In the first exchange, the devices agree on the algorithms and hashing that will be used.
2. The second exchange implements Diffie-Hellman to generate the shared secret key information and pass it back and forth.
3. The third exchange involves verifying the identity of the peer device. This process is protected by the Diffie-Hellman tunnel created in the second step.

Once everything is set up, an SA defines the tunnel. As explained in the "IPSec Security Associations" section earlier in the chapter, an SA is nothing more than a pointer to a database entry that defines how the IKE tunnel is formed. The appropriate information includes the hash method used, Diffie-Hellman information, how long the tunnel will stay up, and so on. It's important to remember that the IKE SA is bidirectional. The information the SA provides applies to both incoming and outgoing traffic.

Aggressive Mode Communication

Aggressive mode is great for reducing the latency involved with setting up the IKE tunnel, since only half of the communication is used. The downside is that there isn't enough communication to protect the identity information when it's being passed, because it's sent along with the Diffie-Hellman information.

The following Aggressive-mode steps are one-way communications:

1. Router A sends all the information it can to router B. This includes policy information such as the hash type and Diffie-Hellman group, the Diffie-Hellman public key information, and device identity information.
2. Router B sends back a similar packet, essentially saying what is being used so that router A knows that the tunnel is valid.
3. Router A acknowledges receipt of the packet that router B sent.

It's possible for someone to sniff the wire while an Aggressive-mode transaction occurs and find out the identity information, since it isn't protected the way that a Main-mode transaction is protected.

IKE Phase 2

The purpose of the second phase of IKE is to negotiate the IPSec tunnel parameters. The negotiations for this are protected by the IKE tunnel created in phase 1. Most of the items the two peers are negotiating are those configured in the transform sets. If the transform sets don't match, a tunnel won't be set up.

Phase 2 negotiation is also responsible for renegotiating the tunnel when the tunnel lifetime expires. There are two ways to do this: fully renegotiate the keys, or partially renegotiate the keys. When the keys are only partially regenerated, it saves computational power because not as much is being redone. It also isn't quite as secure. If you want the keys to be regenerated fully and have a new Diffie-Hellman tunnel to protect the negotiation, you need to ensure that you're using *Perfect Forward Secrecy* (PFS).

> **NOTE** PFS is a switch that tells the VPN device to go through the entire process of generating keys when the IPSec tunnel is about to expire. If PFS isn't used, part of the old key may be reused; and if the IKE tunnel is still up, it also may be reused. If PFS is enabled, the old IKE tunnel is torn down and rebuilt, and a totally new IPSec key is generated.

Once the IPSec tunnel has come up, packets move along it in both directions. ACLs are used to determine not only which packets need to exit through the tunnel, but also which packets should be arriving via the tunnel.

In the previous example, packets that originated on the 10.0.1.0 network and destined for the 10.0.2.0 network were to be encrypted. If the router received a packet from a 10.0.2.0 course heading for a 10.0.1.0 destination and the packet wasn't encrypted, the router would know there was something wrong and would discard the packet. ACLs determine which packets should be encrypted as they leave and which packets should be decrypted as they arrive.

The IPSec tunnel stays up for a certain duration. The choices for tunnel duration are a finite time limit in seconds or a number of kilobytes of traffic. The IPSec tunnel collapses once the timeout has been exceeded. More recent versions of code, such as IOS 12.1 and PIX software 6.0, allow for both ways to be used. For example, a router can be configured to have an IPSec tunnel that will expire in 12 hours or after 1GB of data has passed through it, whichever comes first.

The peers automatically renegotiate the tunnel 30 seconds or 256KB before the tunnel would expire. On a high-bandwidth link, the tunnel might expire in the middle of negotiations for a new tunnel, leaving a small gap in communications.

IPSec Task Flow

As traffic arrives and leaves, as traffic is encrypted and decrypted, decisions need to be made. Now that we've looked at the phases of IPSec tunnel creation, let's examine how the decisions are made in the process. Figure 16.9 shows a flowchart of the decision-making process.

Let's review each of the decisions in the process:

Does the traffic need to be encrypted? The IOS on the router needs to determine what it can do with traffic that arrives. The router compares the packet to the ACL and determines if the traffic should be encrypted. If the ACL denies the packet, the traffic is forwarded out the interface. If the ACL permits the packet, the traffic goes through the tunnel before leaving the interface.

FIGURE 16.9 IPSec decision-making flow

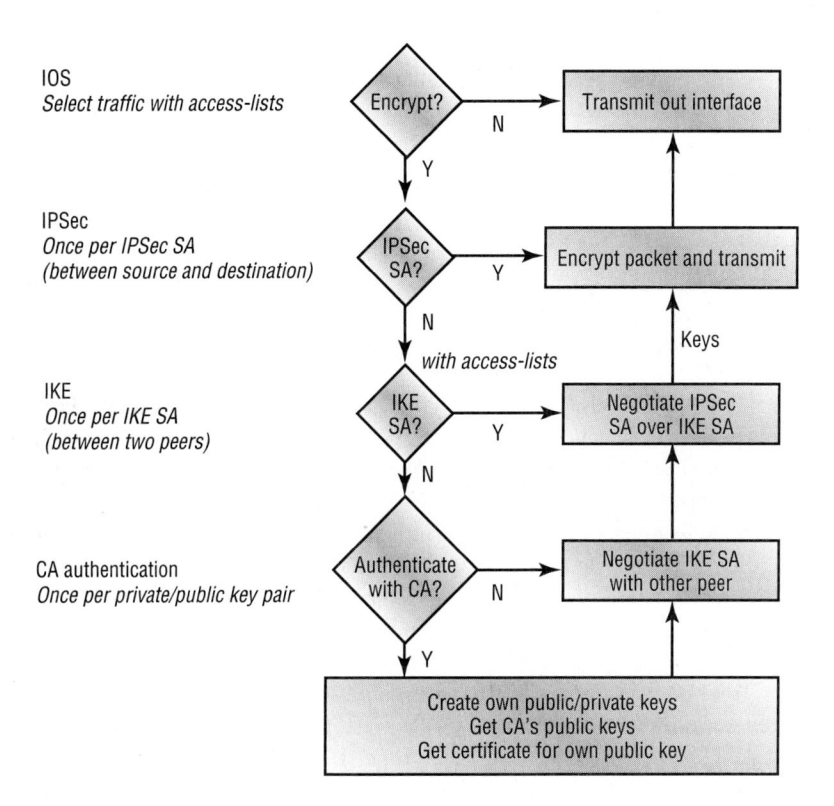

IOS
Select traffic with access-lists

IPSec
*Once per IPSec SA
(between source and destination)*

IKE
*Once per IKE SA
(between two peers)*

CA authentication
Once per private/public key pair

- Encrypt? → N → Transmit out interface
- Y → IPSec SA? → Y → Encrypt packet and transmit
- N (with access-lists) → IKE SA? → Y → Negotiate IPSec SA over IKE SA → Keys
- N → Authenticate with CA? → N → Negotiate IKE SA with other peer
- Y → Create own public/private keys; Get CA's public keys; Get certificate for own public key

Does the IPSec SA need to be negotiated? Before the traffic enters the tunnel, the router needs to make sure that the tunnel is up. If the IPSec tunnel already exists, the appropriate manipulations are performed on the packet before it goes on its way. If the tunnel isn't up, the router needs to do some more work.

Does the IKE SA need to be negotiated? The IPSec and IKE tunnels are two distinct entities. If the IPSec tunnel drops, it doesn't mean the IKE tunnel has dropped as well. If the IPSec tunnel is down, the characteristics need to be negotiated for it to come up. This can't happen if the IKE tunnel is down. If both the IPSec tunnel and the IKE tunnel are down, the IKE tunnel needs to be negotiated to protect the negotiations that go on to bring up the IPSec tunnel.

Does the traffic need to be authenticated with CA? A decision needs to be made to use either a CA or pre-shared keys. If a CA is used, the configuration, key creation, and certificate enrollment all take place before the IKE tunnel negotiation can begin.

IPSec Troubleshooting

IPSec is often a good choice for VPNs, but you must be aware of how changes will affect your network. Traffic that is crossing the network through an IPSec tunnel is still IP traffic. This means that you need to deal with standard IP issues when passing traffic through the tunnels. The issues you might need to troubleshoot include traffic delay, filtering, NAT, and ACLs.

In the following sections, we'll look at some of the more common problems associated with IPSec VPNs, including such issues as working with NAT and filtering, and we'll offer some suggestions for isolating trouble spots.

Traffic Delay Problems

There is a certain amount of delay associated with IP traffic. How much delay depends on several factors. There is propagation delay of about one microsecond per kilometer that the packet needs to travel. Packet travel isn't necessarily "as the crow flies," either. Do a `traceroute` to your destination to see the path being used.

Interfaces also have a delay associated with them. The slower the interface, the more time it takes to place the packet on the network. It also takes time to do the computations and processing to place a packet into the IPSec tunnel. Tests with three 2600-series routers connected via 10Mbps Ethernet showed about a 7-millisecond delay to place a ping packet into the IPSec tunnel using only DES encryption.

Encrypting Voice over IP (VoIP) traffic can be unnoticeable, or it can cause enough jitter (delay-triggered jerkiness) to make using VoIP connections undesirable. Test such applications as much as possible before implementing them on a wide-scale basis.

Filtering Problems

If the packets can leave the network device but never reach the far side, it's possible that some filtering is occurring somewhere in the network. If an intermediate router is filtering UDP port 500, then the IKE session won't complete. If the IPSec tunnel comes up but the intermediate router is filtering protocols 51 or 50, then packets with AH or ESP headers will be filtered.

The key to detecting filtering is to debug the setup of both IKE and IPSec and see how far the tasks complete. If the IPSec tunnel comes up, try to ping the far device without encryption. Then try to ping it with the ping configured as interesting traffic.

> **NOTE** With high-speed cable Internet connections growing, filtering is becoming more common. At least one cable provider is filtering IPSec packets generated by subscribers of their low-end residential service to force them to upgrade to the more expensive business package.

NAT Problems

Detecting a problem caused by NAT isn't surefire, but it's fairly easy. The main thing to look for is errors on encapsulated packets. If the packets are arriving and being discarded, and the device is configured to use AH, this is a good indication of NAT problems. An appropriate test would be to create a second tunnel from the same two devices using only ESP and then ping the far end across the tunnel.

ACL Problems

When an ACL is created on a router, the router uses that list to determine which traffic is privileged, or interesting, enough to cross the tunnel. The router also exchanges the source and destination information when examining incoming traffic to see what should have come in via the tunnel. If a packet should have come through the IPSec tunnel but didn't, the router will drop it.

It's very important that the ACLs on the peer devices are mirror images of each other. If router A permits traffic from 10.1.2.3 to destination 99.5.6.7, then router B should have a line permitting 99.5.6.7 to 10.1.2.3.

Summary

This chapter has served as an introduction to the rest of the chapters dealing with VPNs. First, you learned about the major types of VPNs and the Cisco VPN devices.

The rest of the chapter dealt with IPSec and Internet Key Exchange (IKE). You learned that IKE is the base; IPSec couldn't exist without an IKE foundation. Authentication is a critical component of IKE, and one of the options supported is the certificate authority (CA).

As you learned, IPSec is largely a self-negotiating process. Whereas IKE tunnels can be manipulated in many ways, IPSec configurations usually specify the broad building blocks that will be used and let the two network devices negotiate the details. IPSec's Authentication Header (AH) and Encapsulating Security Payload (EPS) protocols are used to build tunnels. IPSec can use encryption (AES, DES or 3DES) and hashing techniques (MD5 or SHA) to enhance security. Transform sets define a device's IPSec requirements. Actual tunnel creation is triggered by traffic that needs to use a tunnel, as defined by ACLs.

This is an excellent chapter to refer back to as you head further into this section of the book. The remaining chapters in this part will provide product-specific configuration information.

Exam Essentials

Understand the relationship between IKE and IPSec.   For VPN tunneling, two tunnels need to be set up. IKE is used to provide for authentication between the two devices, and it sets up the first tunnel. This tunnel then protects the information the devices exchange to bring up the IPSec tunnel. Also, remember that the IKE tunnel is bidirectional, and there are two unidirectional tunnels used in IPSec.

Know what AH and ESP can do.   AH and ESP are the two protocols that make up IPSec tunnels. Each can provide building blocks in the form of transforms, and the individual transforms are responsible for building the tunnel. AH provides only for authentication. ESP transforms can provide for authentication and/or encryption.

Remember the IPSec order of events.   When two devices are configured for IPSec, a tunnel isn't created spontaneously. Some sort of traffic needs to arrive at one of the routers to start the whole process. Interesting traffic arrives at a router, and that device starts an IKE session with its peer. If IKE resolves, IPSec negotiations can begin; and if they're successful, the interesting traffic can cross the tunnel.

Understand hashing.   Hashing is used in authentication to ensure the data being sent across the wire hasn't been changed. The data is sent in clear text, but sent along with it is an identifying code. When certain processes are run on the plain-text data, the result is a code. If the two codes match, the receiving device knows that the data hasn't been changed.

Chapter 17

Introduction to Cisco VPN Devices

THE FOLLOWING TOPICS ARE COVERED IN THIS CHAPTER:

- ✓ Overview of the Cisco VPN 3000 concentrator series
- ✓ Cisco VPN 3000 concentrator series models
- ✓ Cisco VPN 3000 concentrator series client support
- ✓ Configure the Cisco VPN 3002 Hardware Client for remote access using pre-shared keys
- ✓ Configuring the Cisco Windows VPN software client
- ✓ Overview of the Cisco VPN software client auto-initiation
- ✓ Configuring the Cisco VPN software client auto-initiation
- ✓ Overview of the VPN 3002 reverse route injection feature

Although a router or firewall can be used to terminate a virtual private network (VPN), that isn't the best use of either of those devices' CPU cycles. If you have VPNs that need to be terminated, it's better to use a device optimized for VPNs. Cisco has two types of dedicated physical devices that can terminate VPNs: the VPN Concentrator and the VPN Hardware Client. Cisco also offers a software client, which is loaded on a computer so that a PC can terminate a VPN tunnel.

This chapter begins with an overview of the Cisco VPN Concentrator devices, including their main features. Next, we'll discuss the VPN Hardware Client and how to configure it using the Quick Configuration utility. Finally, we'll cover the VPN software clients, including how to configure them.

> **NOTE** Details on configuring and managing VPN Concentrators are covered in Chapter 18, "Configuring the VPN Concentrator," and Chapter 19, "Managing the VPN Concentrator."

Introducing the VPN 3000 Concentrators

As VPNs gained popularity, Cisco realized that being able to terminate a VPN on a router was a good selling point. However, terminating more than a few VPNs on a 2500 series router resulted in unacceptable performance degradation. Using a router for VPN termination might be acceptable for an office where one or two people at a time would be using a VPN. However, if an office decided to allow 50 users to telecommute, it often experienced performance problems.

The solution was to develop a hardware device dedicated to terminating VPNs, called a *VPN Concentrator*. Until 2002, Cisco offered two classes of VPN Concentrators: the 3000 series and the 5000 series. The 3000 series is designed for corporate enterprise use, and the 5000 series is designed for use by service providers (and handles more connections than the 3000 models). The two series operate in a similar fashion, but they aren't configured the same way. This book covers only the 3000 series because the 5000 series was announced as an End of Sales (EoS) in February 2002. Thus, there will be no further feature development for the Cisco VPN 5000 product line. Enterprise customers using Cisco VPN 5000 series concentrators have been encouraged to move to Cisco 7200 series routers. The CSVPN exam covers only the 3000 series.

> **Note:** Cisco's 3000 VPN Concentrator is often still referred to as the *Altiga* concentrator because Altiga developed it.

In the following sections, we'll introduce the VPN 3000 Concentrator series models and summarize their features. Chapters 18 and 19 cover configuring and managing VPN Concentrators.

Overview of the VPN 3005 Concentrator

The 3005 model is an entry-level VPN Concentrator designed for small-to-medium offices. This model is a good choice if your organization isn't growing very quickly. For example, if a 500-user company has anywhere from 30 to 50 salespeople on the road at any one time and 15 to 20 other off-site employees, this concentrator will handle the job. If the company is expanding at a rapid pace, however, the 3005 model isn't an appropriate choice.

The 3005 can support up to 100 simultaneous tunnels via software-based encryption and isn't upgradable. Like the other 3000 series models, it offers the option of using 40-bit or 56-bit Data Encryption Standard (DES), 128-bit or 168-bit Triple DES (3DES), or 40-bit or 128-bit Microsoft Point-to-Point Encryption (MPPE), or 128-bit, 192-bit, or 256-bit Advanced Encryption Standard (AES). It can also use Message Digest 5 (MD5) and Secure Hash Algorithm (SHA) for hashing and Diffie-Hellman for key exchanges. (Encryption, hashing, and Diffie-Hellman are covered in Chapter 16, "Introduction to Virtual Private Networks.")

> **Note:** MPPE is an encrypted form of a Point-to-Point Protocol (PPP) packet. For more information about MPPE, refer to RFC 3078.

The VPN 3005 is a 1U device. A *U* is a measurement of height for placement in a rack and is equal to 1.75 inches (4.45 centimeters). For comparison, other 1U devices include the Cisco 2500 and 2600 series routers and the thin Catalyst 1900, 2900, and 3500 series switches.

Table 17.1 summarizes the characteristics of the VPN 3005 Concentrator.

Figure 17.1 shows the front and back of a 3005. Although the front of the 3005 is fairly nondescript, the 3005 comes with two LAN interfaces on the back. One interface is for the outside connection and is labeled *public*. The other interface is for the inside connection and is labeled *private*. A default configuration comes with each VPN Concentrator, so it's important that these interfaces are attached to the correct locations on your network. In addition to the LAN connections, there is also a DB9 interface for the console port. A standard RS-232 straight-through serial cable can be used for console access. As with most Cisco devices, a terminal emulation configured for 9600-N-8-1 is the default configuration.

TABLE 17.1 Characteristics of the VPN 3005 Concentrator

Feature	Description
Memory	64MB (fixed)
Simultaneous users	Up to 100
Power supply	Single
Height	1U
Encryption throughput	4MB
Encryption	Software based
Upgradability	None
Processor	Motorola PowerPC
Console port	DB9 Async (9600-N-8-1)
Client license	Unlimited

Each of the LAN interfaces supports 10/100 Ethernet. There is no provision for other types of LAN media (Token Ring, Fiber Distributed Data Interface [FDDI], or Copper Distributed Data Interface [CDDI]) at this time. The interfaces also have LEDs to indicate link, collision, transmit, and receive status.

Site-to-site tunnels are more complex than remote access tunnels because they create a tunnel between two concentrators and encrypt all the traffic that flows between. Because the amount of traffic is usually higher, the number of site-to-site tunnels that are supported is lower than the number of remote access (user) tunnels. The 3005 can support 100 site-to-site tunnels.

FIGURE 17.1 The VPN 3005 concentrator

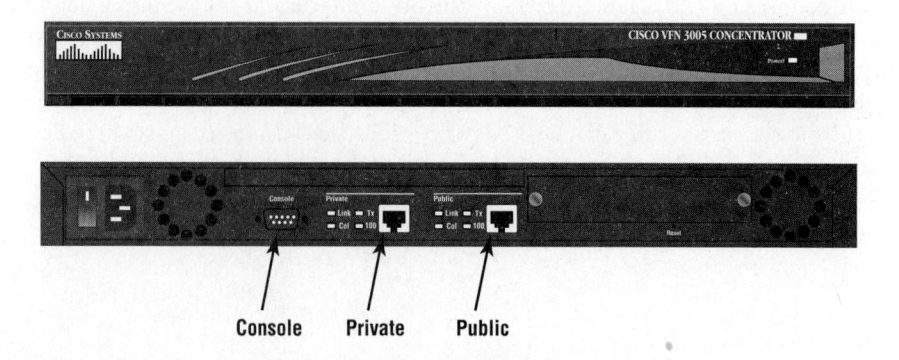

Overview of VPN 3015 through 3080 Concentrators

Models 3015 through 3080 are 2U VPN Concentrators that are more flexible than the 3005. If your organization is growing rapidly or already needs more than 100 tunnels terminated at a time, these are the models to consider.

The 3015 has the same tunnel capacity as the 3005, but it's upgradable to add support for more tunnels. The 3030, 3060, and 3080 models use hardware-based encryption and decryption. Since these tasks are offloaded from the CPU, more tunnels can be terminated by these devices than by the 3005. All of these models can use 40-bit, 56-bit, or 128-bit DES, 3DES, Advanced Encryption Standard (AES), or MPPE encryption; MD5 or SHA for hashing; and Diffie-Hellman for key exchanges.

> **WARNING** DES/SHA encryption transforms aren't supported in newer versions of the hardware and software clients. This might cause clients to stop working after an upgrade.

Table 17.2 summarizes the capabilities of the 3015, 3030, 3060, and 3080 models.

TABLE 17.2 Base Characteristics of the VPN 3015, 3030, 3060, and 3080 Concentrators

VPN Concentrator	3015	3030	3060	3080
Simultaneous users	100	1500	5000	10,000
Encryption throughput	4Mbps	50Mbps	100Mbps	100Mbps
Encryption method	Software	Hardware	Hardware	Hardware
Encryption (SEP) modules	0	1	2	4
Available expansion slots	4	3	2	2
Upgradability	Yes	Yes	N/A	N/A
System memory	128MB	128MB	256MB	256MB
Dual power supply (hot swap)	Optional	Optional	Optional	Default
Processor	Motorola PowerPC	Motorola PowerPC	Motorola PowerPC	Motorola PowerPC

Figure 17.2 shows the back of a 3015. Just as on the 3005, the console port is a DB9. The concentrator has both public and private Ethernet ports, as well as a third port, which can be used to connect to another LAN segment, such as a DMZ or extranet. The 3015 also has an option for a redundant power supply and up to four *Scalable Encryption Processing (SEP)* modules. The SEP is what does the hardware-based encryption. Overall, the more memory and more SEPs, the higher the number of tunnels the concentrator can handle. The digital signal processors in the SEP can be reprogrammed as standards change.

Like the 3005 concentrator, the 3015 can support 100 site-to-site tunnels. The 3030 can support 500, and the 3060 and 3080 can each support 1000.

> **NOTE** Cisco used to sell T1/E1 modules for VPN 3015 through 3080 Concentrator models, and Altiga sold a 3005 that had a T1/E1 port. These devices have been discontinued, and support for them in CiscoView is nonexistent after version 5.3. Customers using these products should see "Field Remediation Efforts" at http://www.cisco.com/warp/public/cc/pd/hb/vp3000/prodlit/eoswm_pb.htm.

In Figure 17.3, we take a glimpse at the 3015, 3030, 3060, and 3080 Concentrators. The 3015 is upgradable, whereas the 3005 isn't. All of these models share the same case, so only the 3015 is illustrated. Unlike the 3005, the front of the 3015 shows some information. There are quite a few LEDs on the front panel that show the status of the concentrator. See Chapter 19 for information about what each of the LEDs indicates.

> **NOTE** On the VPN Concentrator, a blinking green LED for link status doesn't mean that data is passing through the interface. Instead, it means that the link is connected but disabled.

FIGURE 17.2 The rear of the VPN 3015 concentrator

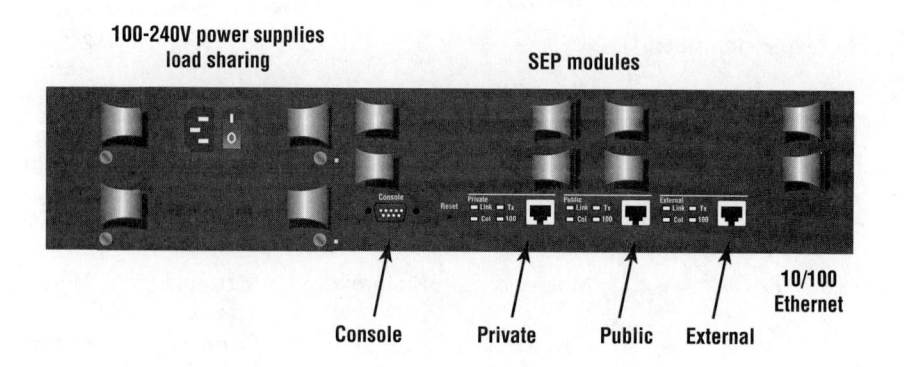

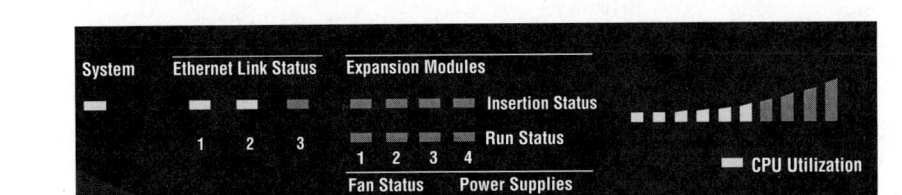

FIGURE 17.3 The front panel of the VPN 3015 Concentrator

On the right side of the LED panel is an LED meter. Below that are a button and three categories. Pressing the button migrates the lit LED through the three choices of CPU Utilization, Active Sessions, and Throughput. The meter displays whichever of these three is active.

VPN Concentrator Client Support

You should place the VPN Concentrator somewhere near the entrance to your network, generally in parallel or just behind the firewall. It isn't a good idea to have too many encrypted tunnels going too far into your network because they present a security risk. Figure 17.4 illustrates the concept of a VPN crossing a shared network.

Figure 17.4 shows the client connection coming across the Internet, passing through the router, and terminating at the concentrator. If the router were set to block a certain type of traffic, that router wouldn't be able to check the traffic inside the tunnel as it passed through. This becomes a more serious risk when a firewall allows encrypted traffic through. Of course, it might not be possible or desirable to eliminate all VPNs passing beyond a firewall or concentrator, but with good design planning, the number of VPNs that do this can be minimized.

FIGURE 17.4 Client support for a VPN Concentrator

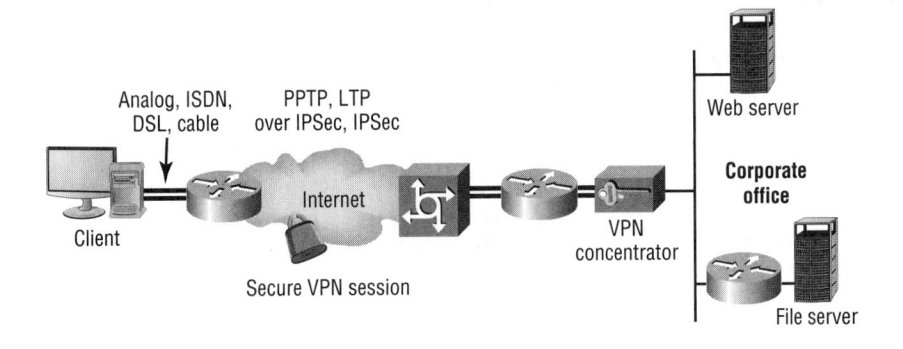

Introducing the 3002 VPN Hardware Client

The VPN Hardware Client is a great tool if your network has several users that need to communicate via a tunnel, but it's impractical to purchase a piece of hardware for every user. Unlike the VPN Concentrator, which was developed by Altiga and picked up by Cisco, the hardware client was developed by Cisco.

The hardware client is nothing more than a very basic router with the strong point of creating a tunnel to another location that is serviced by a VPN Concentrator. The purpose of using the VPN Hardware Client is to offload the client-processing requirements when there are several clients on the same network creating VPNs to the same destination. While this device supports up to 253 users, it's most appropriate for a small network with fewer than 50.

Figure 17.5 is an illustration of the VPN 3002 Hardware Client. There is an RJ-45 console connection, if one is required, but unlike the VPN Concentrator, the hardware client comes with an IP address preset on the active private interface. This makes it easy for someone to use a web browser to surf to the administration page to set up the device. An optional 8-port Ethernet switch is also available, which makes the 3002 the perfect solution for remote office locations that require little or no IT support.

> **NOTE** In addition to accessing the hardware client via a web browser, using HTTP or HTTPS, the VPN 3002 Hardware Client also supports administrative connections via Telnet and SSH.

The client is configured for the IP address of 192.168.10.1 on the private interface. The hardware client uses Port Address Translation (PAT) to provide address translation out to the Internet. You can disable the PAT feature, if necessary. The public interface can be configured to use Dynamic Host Configuration Protocol (DHCP) to request an IP address from the service provider.

FIGURE 17.5 The VPN 3002 Hardware Client

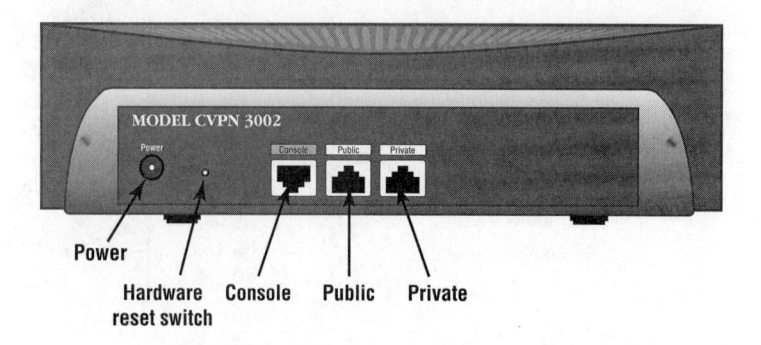

Once the client is up and running, anyone with the proper credentials can log in and make changes. The client needs to be configured, and then the tunnel needs to be brought up manually. Until this happens, secure communication between the sites doesn't exist. We'll look at how to configure the hardware client in the next section.

Configuring the 3002 CLI Quick Configuration Utility

When you first remove the 3002 from the box, you must start the configuration process from the command-line interface (CLI). Everything required to be configured on the 3002 can be done from the CLI. We'll look at how to configure the hardware client using the CLI in the following sections.

Interface Configuration

The following steps show you how to configure the interface:

1. The system prompts you for the configuration of the interfaces:

    ```
    1) Modify Ethernet 1 IP Address (Private)
    2) Modify Ethernet 2 IP Address (Public)
    3) Configure Expansion Cards
    4) Save changes to Config file
    5) Continue
    6) Exit
    Quick -> _
    ```

    Press 1 and Enter to select the option to modify the private-side Ethernet interface.

2. The CLI returns a table showing the existing configuration, including IP addresses and subnet masks:

    ```
    This table shows current IP addresses.
    Interface IP Address/Subnet Mask MAC Address
    -----------------------------------------------------------------
    Ethernet 1 - Private  | 10.10.4.6/255.255.0.0| 00.10.5A.1F.4F.07
    Ethernet 2 - Public   |      0.0.0.0/0.0.0.0 |
    Ethernet 3 - External |      0.0.0.0/0.0.0.0 |
    -----------------------------------------------------------------

    > Enter IP Address for Ethernet 1 (Private)
    Quick -> [ 0.0.0.0 ]
    ```

    When you enter the IP Address and press Enter, the system prompts you for the subnet mask. The default setting automatically takes the natural mask for the IP address entered.

3. The system prompts you to set up the speed of the interface. The default is to set to auto-detect.

4. The 3002 now requires the configuration of the transmission mode for the interface; the default is option 1 (Half/Full/Auto):

```
1) Enter Duplex - Half/Full/Auto
2) Enter Duplex - Full Duplex
3) Enter Duplex - Half Duplex
Quick -> [ 1 ] _
```

Configure System Information

To configure the system information, follow these steps:

1. The CLI prompts you to assign a system name to the 3002; the name must be unique to the system:

   ```
   -- : Assign a system name to this device.
   > System Name
   Quick -> _
   ```

2. The system prompts you for a DNS server IP address:

   ```
   -- : Specify a local DNS server, ...
   > DNS Server
   Quick -> [ 0.0.0.0 ]
   ```

3. You're prompted to enter the domain name for the system:

   ```
   -- : Enter your Internet domain name; ...
   > Domain
   Quick -> _
   ```

4. The next prompt is the default gateway:

   ```
   > Default Gateway
   Quick -> _
   ```

   This is the IP address that packets should be sent to where the system has no routing information. This IP address must be different from any of the other configured interfaces; you can also leave it blank to configure no forwarding gateway.

Configure a Tunneling Protocol

To configure the tunneling protocol, follow these steps:

1. The system first shows that PPTP and L2TP are both enabled with no encryption in the default configuration setting:

   ```
   -- : Configure protocols and encryption options.
   -- : This table shows current protocol settings
   PPTP | L2TP |
   ```

```
-----------------------------------------
|     Enabled       |     Enabled       |
| No Encryption Req | No Encryption Req |
-----------------------------------------
1) Enable PPTP
2) Disable PPTP
Quick -> [ 1 ]
```

2. You're asked to choose whether to require encryption:

   ```
   1) PPTP Encryption Required
   2) No Encryption Required
   Quick -> [ 2 ]
   ```

3. The system prompts you to enable or disable L2TP:

   ```
   1) Enable L2TP
   2) Disable L2TP
   Quick -> [ 1 ]
   ```

4. You're asked whether you wish to force encryption:

   ```
   1) L2TP Encryption Required
   2) No Encryption Required
   Quick -> [ 2 ] _
   ```

5. The next prompt is for IPSec:

   ```
   1) Enable IPSec
   2) Disable IPSec
   Quick -> [ 1 ] _
   ```

Configure IP Addresses

To configure the IP addresses, follow these steps:

1. To begin the setup of the DHCP addressing, the system prompts you to enable or disable a client-specified address assignment:

   ```
   -- : Configure address assignment for PPTP, L2TP and IPSec.
   1) Enable Client Specified Address Assignment
   2) Disable Client Specified Address Assignment
   Quick -> [ 2 ]
   ```

2. The system prompts you to enable or disable address assignment on a per-user basis:

   ```
   1) Enable Per User Address Assignment
   2) Disable Per User Address Assignment
   Quick -> [ 2 ] _
   ```

3. The system asks if you're going to use DHCP:

   ```
   1) Enable DHCP Address Assignment
   2) Disable DHCP Address Assignment
   Quick -> [ 2 ] _
   ```

4. You're prompted for the DHCP server address:

   ```
   > DHCP Server
   Quick -> _
   ```

5. The next prompt is for the pool assignment:

   ```
   1) Enable Configured Pool Address Assignment
   2) Disable Configured Pool Address Assignment
   Quick -> [ 2 ] _
   ```

6. The system asks you to configure the pool:

   ```
   > Configured Pool Range Start Address
   Quick -> _
   ```

7. You're prompted for the ending address:

   ```
   > Configured Pool Range End Address
   Quick -> [ 0.0.0.0 ]
   ```

Configure the IPSec Group

To configure the IPSec group, follow these steps:

1. The system prompts you for an IPSec group name:

   ```
   > IPSec Group Name
   Quick -> _
   ```

2. Once you enter the group name, the system prompts you for a password and asks for verification:

   ```
   > IPSec Group Password
   Quick ->
   Verify -> _
   ```

Change the Admin Password

To change the Admin password, follow these steps:

1. The system prompts you to change the Admin password:

   ```
   -- : We strongly recommend that you change the password ...
   > Reset Admin Password
   Quick -> [ ***** ] _
   ```

2. Enter your password, and then verify it:

`Verify -> _`

> **NOTE:** The system displays asterisks for your keystrokes.

Save and Exit the CLI

To save and exit the CLI, follow these steps:

1. You're prompted to either go to the main menu, save changes to the Config file, or exit:

   ```
   1) Goto Main Configuration Menu
   2) Save changes to Config file
   3) Exit
   Quick -> 2
   ```

2. Exit the system by selecting the default option, 3:

   ```
   1) Goto Main Configuration Menu
   2) Save changes to Config file
   3) Exit
   Quick -> 3
   Done
   ```

Configuring the Hardware Client with the Quick Configuration Utility

The hardware client is easy to set up through its Quick Configuration utility. You can walk a user through setup over the phone.

You can configure the client via the CLI through the console port, but most people choose to configure it via the web browser. However, the initial configuration (at least to get to configure the private-side IP address) must be done with the CLI as described in detail in the previous sections.

The first step is logging in to the device. Once the browser is pointed to the correct IP address, the login screen appears, as shown in Figure 17.6. No matter how the client is configured, the default username is `admin` and the default password is `admin`.

Anyone who is familiar with initial setup mode on a router will understand the concept of Quick Configuration. This utility's opening screen is shown in Figure 17.7. As you can see, it takes you through each configuration step:

1. Set the system time, date, and time zone.
2. Configure the Ethernet interface to your private interface.
3. Optionally, upload an existing configuration file.

4. Configure the public interface to a public network.
5. Specify a method for assigning IP addresses.
6. Configure the IPSec tunneling protocol.
7. Set the hardware client to use either PAT or LAN Extension mode.
8. Configure Domain Name System (DNS).
9. Configure static routes.
10. Change the Admin password.

Let's take a look at some of the Quick Configuration details.

FIGURE 17.6   Logging in to the hardware client

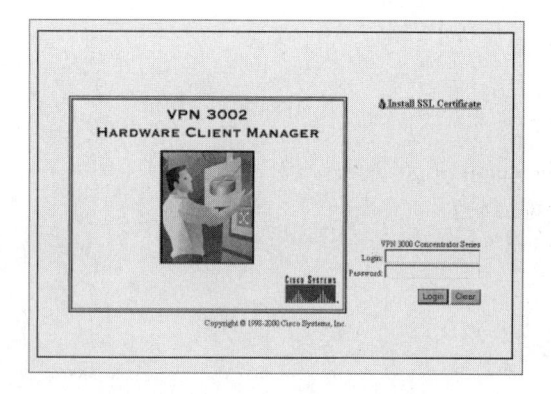

FIGURE 17.7   The opening Quick Configuration screen

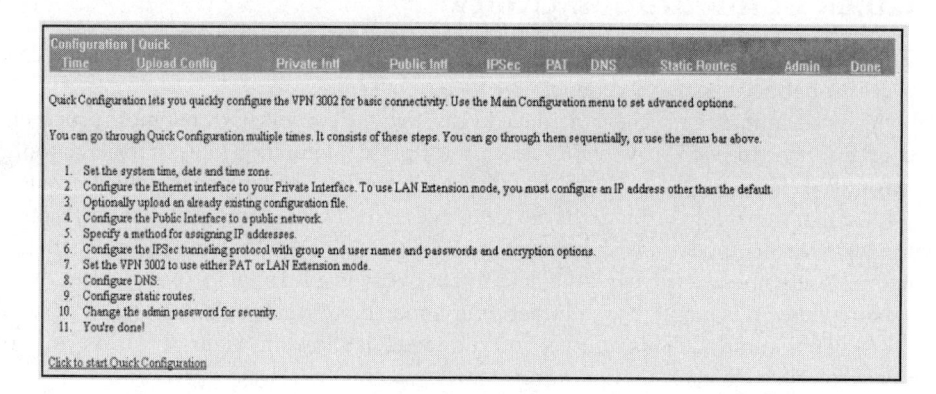

Setting the System Time

It's always advisable to ensure that the clock is set to the correct time. If the client will be using a digital certificate, it's also advisable to set the time and time zone to reflect Greenwich mean time (GMT). Setting the time on the client involves entering on the Time And Date screen (see Figure 17.8) the time, date, and time zone and specifying whether daylight savings time (DST) is used.

Using an Existing Configuration File

The next step allows the administrator to upload a configuration file. You do so using a web-based transfer tool. No Trivial FTP server is needed, but the file does need to reside on a drive that the administrator can access. If the file is on a mapped network drive, you can access it by clicking the Browse button.

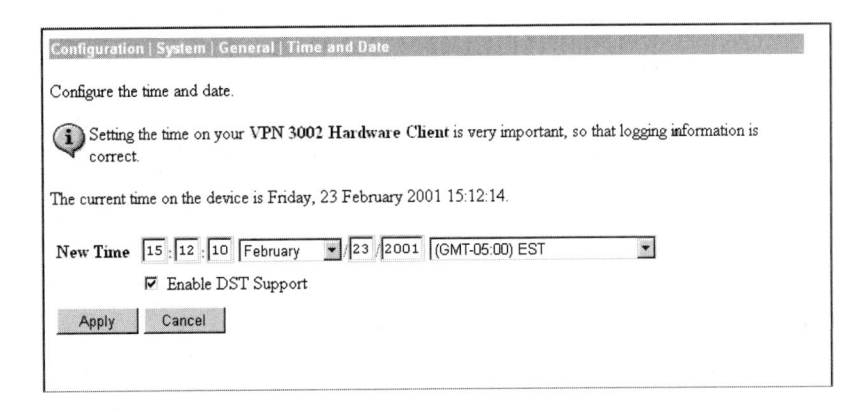

Configuring the Private Interface

The Private Interface screen, shown in Figure 17.9, displays the properties of the interface for inside the network. By default, it has an IP address of 192.168.10.1 with a 24-bit mask. If you want to change the IP address, select the Yes radio button. Also make sure that the interface has a DHCP server for client addressing if your site requires such support.

Configuring the Public Interface

The Public Interface screen, shown in Figure 17.10, contains properties for the interface going out to the Internet. The IP address may be statically configured or it may be set up via DHCP. Since many DHCP servers require the use of a valid hostname, this is an option on the Public Interface screen.

The public interface also has routing information associated with it. You can configure a default gateway. You can configure other routes later, but most networks that use the hardware client won't have a router further inside the network.

FIGURE 17.8 Configuring the time

FIGURE 17.9   Configuring the private interface

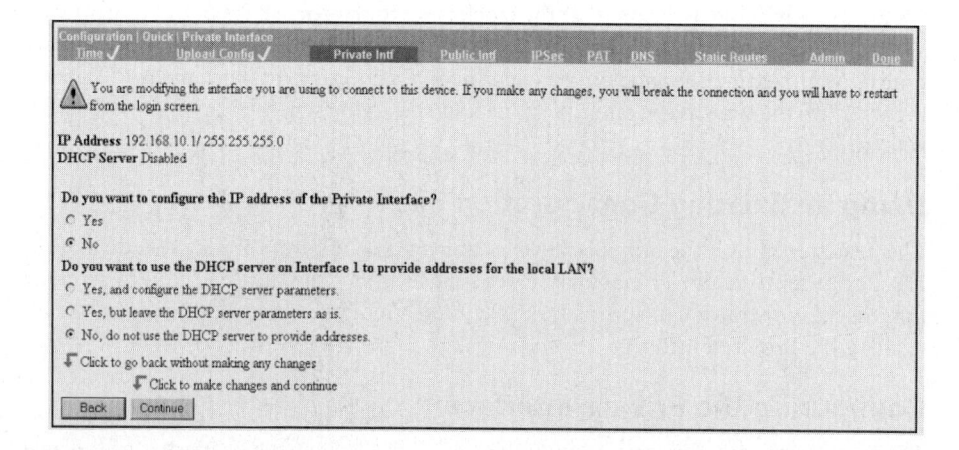

FIGURE 17.10   Configuring the public interface

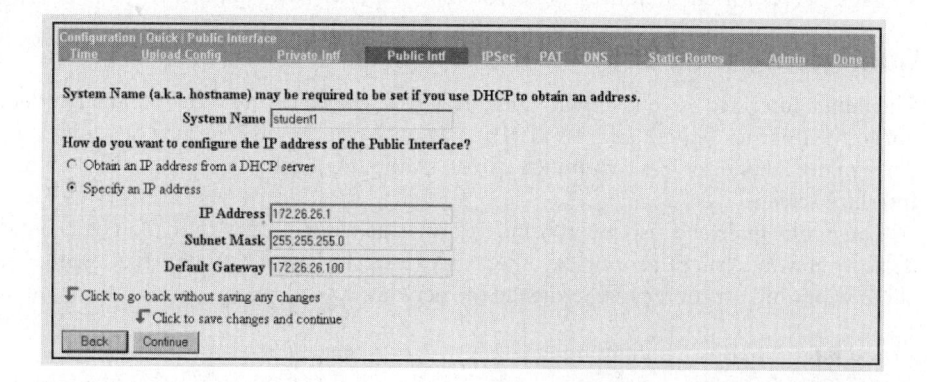

Configuring IPSec

All VPNs consist of a tunnel with two endpoints. Since the hardware client is one end of the tunnel, it needs to be told where the other end is. You configure this information on the IPSec screen, shown in Figure 17.11.

You can set up IPSec to use a group name and password, as well as a username and password for remote authentication via a database (such as a Windows domain or Active Directory database). Alternatively, IPSec can be set up to use digital certificates. These settings must match on both sides of the tunnel.

FIGURE 17.11 Configuring the IPSec peer

Configuring PAT or LAN Extension Mode

Port Address Translation (PAT) is used to translate from one IP address to another. If the default IP address of 192.168.10.1 remains on the private interface, PAT will remain enabled and can't be disabled. If you don't want to use PAT, you'll need to use some other IP address; if the packets will be seen by Internet devices, the IP address must be routable. Also, PAT must be disabled (and a different IP address used) if you want to use LAN Extension mode.

When you're configuring PAT, the first screen you come to is the Policy Management screen, as seen in Figure 17.12.

> **NOTE** PAT is a way that a network device can translate several IP addresses into a single IP address. Each IP address and port assignment will equal a like IP address and port assignment when a packet wishes to enter the Internet. This allows the potential for more than 64,000 IP addresses to use a single registered address, although the functional limit is about 4000.

Next you're sent to the Traffic Management screen, as seen in Figure 17.13. To configure the Port Address Translation, click PAT.

On the PAT screen (see Figure 17.14), click Enable.

FIGURE 17.12 The Policy Management screen

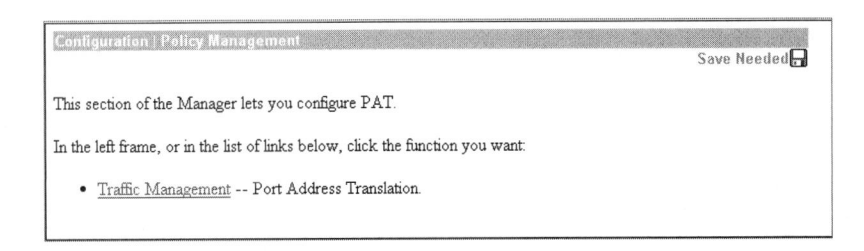

The Enable screen (see Figure 17.15) finally lets you enable PAT, which will effectively apply PAT to any traffic flowing from the private to the public interface.

LAN Extension mode allows the hardware client to present a routable network to the tunneled network. IPSec encapsulates all traffic from the private network behind the hardware client to networks behind the central-site concentrator. PAT doesn't apply; therefore, devices behind the concentrator have direct access to devices on the hardware client private network through the tunnel.

FIGURE 17.13   The Traffic Management screen

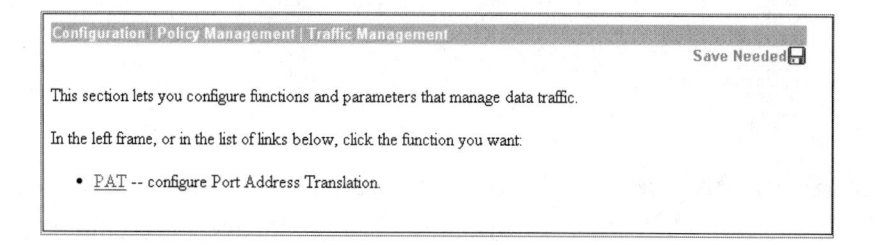

FIGURE 17.14   The PAT screen

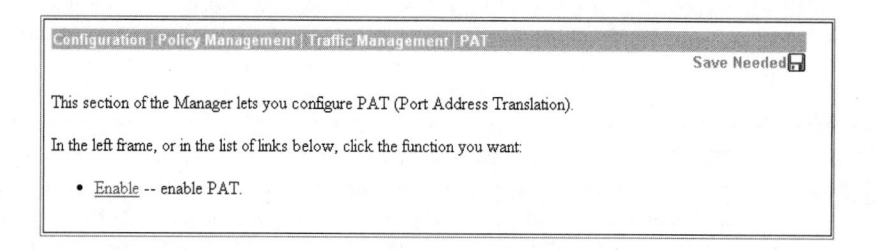

FIGURE 17.15   The Enable screen

Configuring DNS

The DNS screen of the Quick Configuration utility contains settings that allow the hardware client to communicate with a DNS server and for a local domain to be configured (see Figure 17.16). The domain name can be important when you're requesting an IP address via DHCP from some service providers.

FIGURE 17.16   The DNS screen

The DNS screen identifies and configures the servers that will be used for name resolution. The following options are available:

Enabled   To enable the DNS functions, select the Enabled check box. The default is for the DNS services to be enabled. If you don't wish to use the DNS services, then you can clear the box.

> **WARNING**   Disabling DNS affects more than just server IP address lookups. Many certificate services use DNS names for identification rather than IP addresses. Turning off DNS might prevent certificate usage.

Domain   This field allows you to assign a domain name field to be appended to hostnames before sending them to a DNS service for resolution. A 48-character limit is put on the field.

Primary DNS Server   Enter the IP address of the primary DNS server in this field.

Secondary DNS Server   Enter the IP address of the secondary DNS server in this field. The secondary DNS server is used as a backup if the primary server isn't available or doesn't respond before the specified timeout.

Tertiary DNS Server In this field, enter the IP address of the DNS server to be queried if the primary and secondary DNS servers don't respond within the specified timeout.

Timeout Period In this field, enter the time in seconds. A query will wait before going to the next level of backup server (Secondary, Tertiary). The default is 2 seconds, with a maximum value of 30 and minimum of 1.

Timeout Retries In this field, enter the attempts to cycle through each of the DNS servers before displaying an error. The default value is 2 times, with a maximum of 10 and minimum of 0.

Apply/Cancel Click Apply when you're satisfied with your input; click Cancel to return to the previous menu without keeping the input.

Configuring Static Routing

The Static Routes screen is used to configure static routes for the client. The public interface has a setting for a default route, but if other routing information is required, you'll need to configure static routes. If you need to remove a route, select it and choose Delete. Click the Add button to display the Add screen, shown in Figure 17.17.

FIGURE 17.17 The Add screen

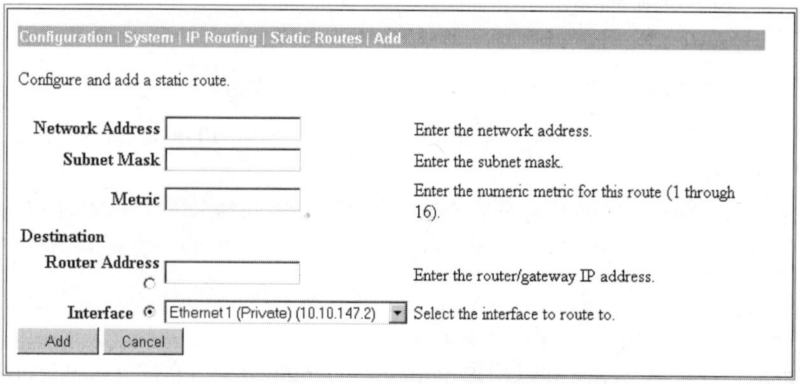

Changing the Admin Password and Enabling Users

The Admin screen allows you to change the Admin password. After you set a new Admin password (for security), the Quick Configuration utility displays a screen that lists four other users who are disabled by default:

- The *config* user is used for quick configuration and monitoring.
- The *monitor* user has read-only privileges.

You can enable one or both of these users by selecting the Enabled check box next to the appropriate user.

> These default users can be useful as templates for a multiclass administrative system that delegates certain authority to different persons or groups.

Managing the Hardware Client

After you've completed the Quick Configuration utility's steps, the Hardware Client Manager screen appears, as shown in Figure 17.18. This screen has links to three broad areas:

- The Configuration option is for configuring device properties such as IP addressing.
- The Administration option allows you to change user passwords.
- The Monitoring option shows system statistics and allows you to create the tunnel.

To see the status of a tunnel, click the Monitoring link, then System Status, which brings up the System Status screen. If a tunnel exists, it can be disabled. If a tunnel doesn't exist, you can activate one by clicking the Connect Now button, as shown in Figure 17.19. This screen also shows how long the client has been up and the type of software running.

If a tunnel currently exists, the Monitoring screen shows other information, including how long the tunnel has been up, the IKE and IPSec building blocks used to create the tunnel, and how much traffic has passed through the tunnel.

FIGURE 17.18 The Hardware Client Manager opening screen

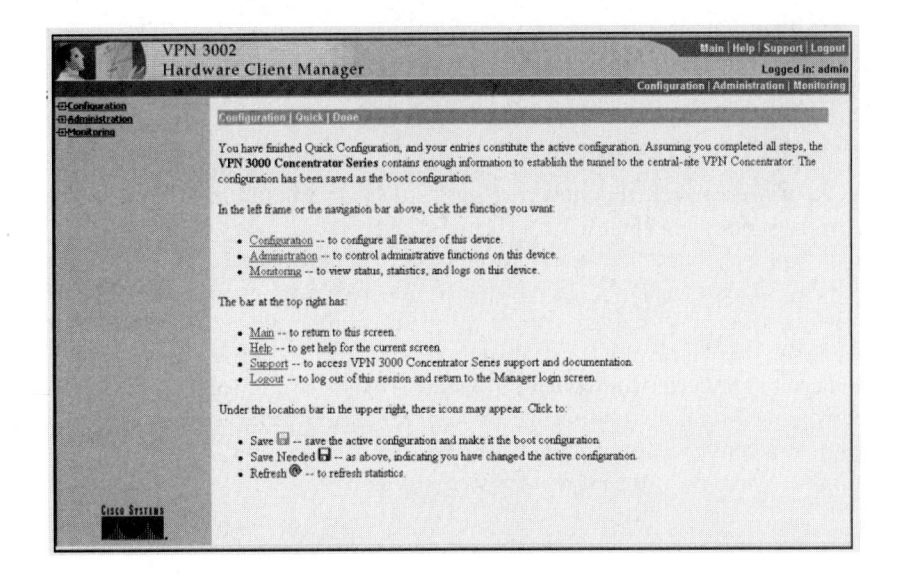

FIGURE 17.19   Bringing up the tunnel

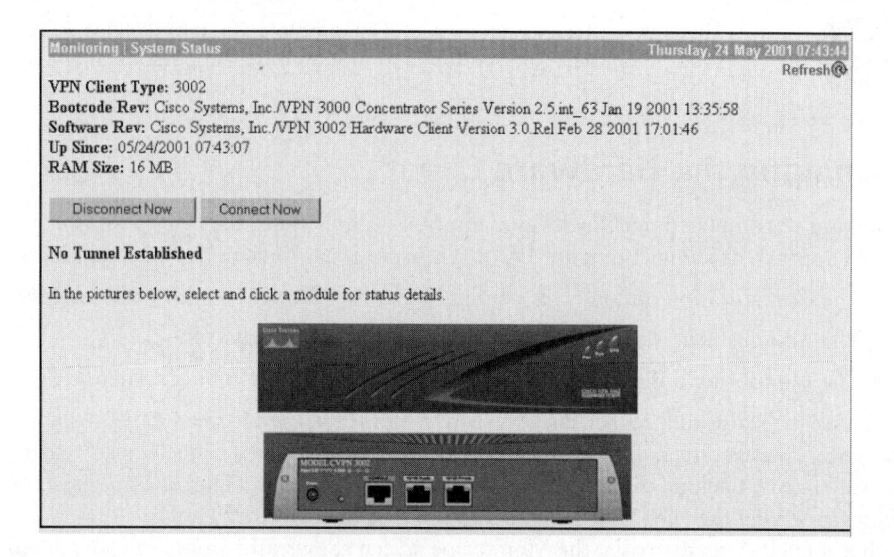

Additional VPN 3002 Client Features

In addition to the configuration options available during Quick Configuration, there are several ways of configuring the VPN 3002 so it's more secure or to alleviate problems found during setup. Some of these features are version dependent and may require up to version 3.6 software to exist on the client, concentrator, or both.

Reverse Route Injection

Reverse Route Injection (RRI) is how routes are added into a VPN Concentrator. These routes are then advertised out to the remote VPN clients or LAN-to-LAN connections. RRI is a feature supported on the concentrator that forwards routing information to the hardware client. Although this affects the client's routing table, it needs to be configured on the concentrator. The concentrator advertises the assigned IP address of the hardware client for other devices to be able to reach it.

The Cisco 3002 Hardware Client doesn't require any configuration to use RRI. The only requirement is to be in Network Extension Mode (NEM). The only routing protocols used by RRI are the Routing Information Protocol version 2 (RIPv2) and Open Shortest Path First (OSPF). Each of these is configured on the network interfaces. You access the interfaces to make those configurations through their respective Interfaces screen.

> **WARNING**   Use caution when you're using Virtual Router Redundancy Protocol (VRRP) with RRI. Routing loops may be created, because both the primary and backup servers will advertise the same routes.

At minimum, there must be at least an outbound RIPv2 configuration on the private interface. Outbound RIPv2 must also be configured to enable Autodiscovery. RRI setup details are covered in Chapter 18.

IPSec Over TCP and Backup Servers

You can configure IPSec over TCP as well as backup servers on the VPN 3002 by going to the IPSec screen (see Figure 17.20).

At the top of the screen is the address for the primary concentrator, and below it is a box where you can add IP addresses for tunnel termination. The easiest way to configure additional servers is to fill in the appropriate public IP addresses of concentrators in the Mode Config tab on the concentrator and then select Use The List Below. When a hardware client connects, the concentrator pushes the list of available backup servers to the client. The client can also have IP addresses hard configured, and if this is used, the Mode Config setting should be to use the client configured list.

FIGURE 17.20 The IPSec screen

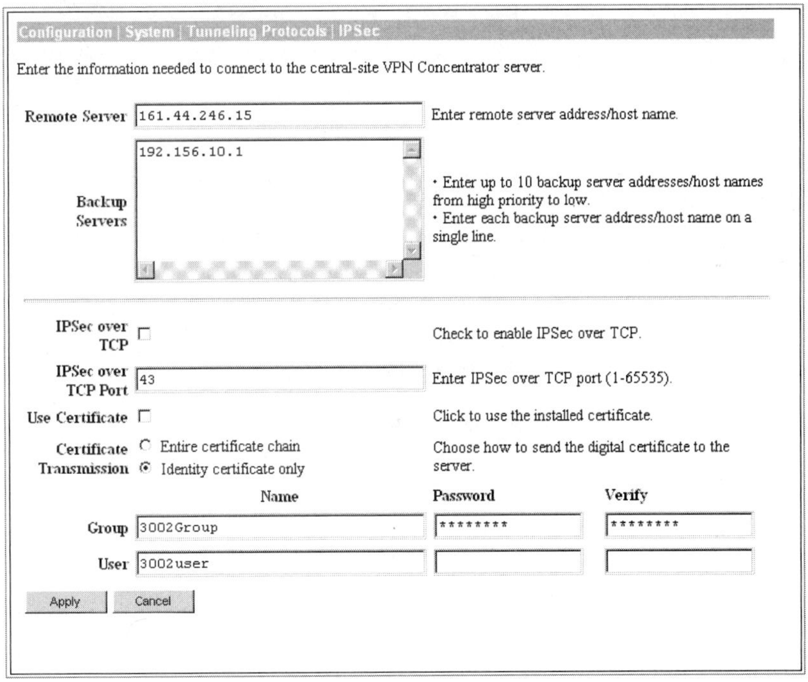

At the bottom of the page, you set up IPSec over TCP. Select the check box for IPSec over TCP, and ensure the proper port number is set up. The default on both the concentrator and the VPN 3002 is port 10000. Be sure to fill in the appropriate username, group name, and passwords for both, and ensure the port number is set correctly. This feature is useful when a device is performing PAT or filtering IPSec along the path the encrypted traffic will take. PAT doesn't support encrypted traffic well due to changing the port used during ISAKMP negotiations and also because ESP and AH don't have ports to translate.

Interactive Authentication

When a hardware client allows all traffic from the local network to cross to the VPN Concentrator on the far side, a potential security risk emerges. To combat this, Cisco has a feature on the VPN 3002 that requires a user to authenticate before the VPN 3002 will encrypt the traffic. This works well if you don't want some users, such as contractors, using the tunnel.

The username and password for the VPN 3002 itself can also be left off and provided when the tunnel needs to come up. This is more secure than the default storage method and is useful if the VPN 3002 is in a location that isn't secure. By default, the unit password is permanently stored in the hardware client's memory.

Configuration is accomplished on the concentrator, but authentication takes place on the client. Authentication is checked on the concentrator and pushed down to the client during tunnel negotiations.

The following instructions assume that both client and user authentication are required:

1. From the VPN 3002 Hardware Client Manager login screen, click the Connection/Login Status button (see Figure 17.21).

FIGURE 17.21 The VPN 3002 Hardware Client Manager login screen

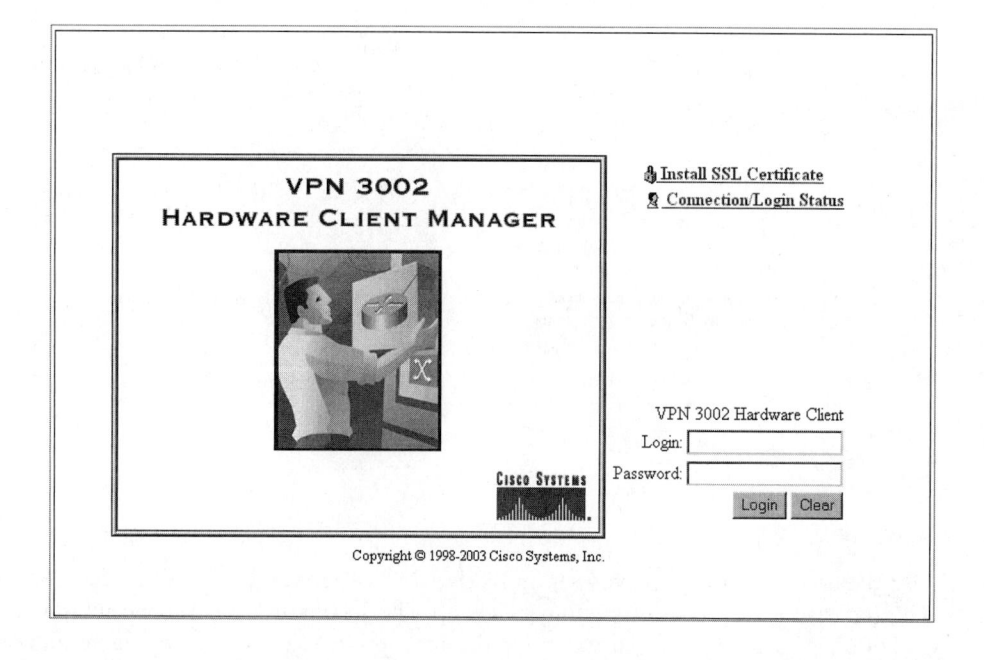

2. The Connection/Login Status screen appears (see Figure 17.22). Click Connect Now.
3. The VPN 3002 Interactive Authentication screen appears (Figure 17.23). Enter the username and password for the VPN 3002, and click Connect.
4. If everything was entered correctly, the client should indicate it's now connected. To authenticate a user, at the Connection/Login Status screen, click Log In Now (see Figure 17.24).
5. The Login screen appears. Enter the username and password, and click Login.
6. The IP address of the connection is now associated with the user who just logged in.

FIGURE 17.22 The Connection/Login Status screen

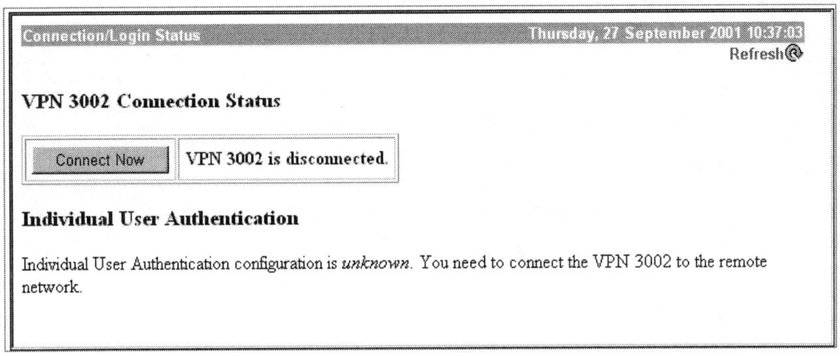

FIGURE 17.23 The VPN 3002 Interactive Authentication screen

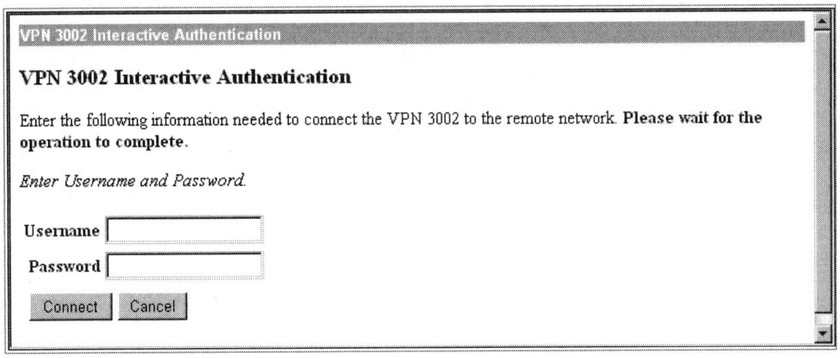

FIGURE 17.24 The Connection Login Status screen

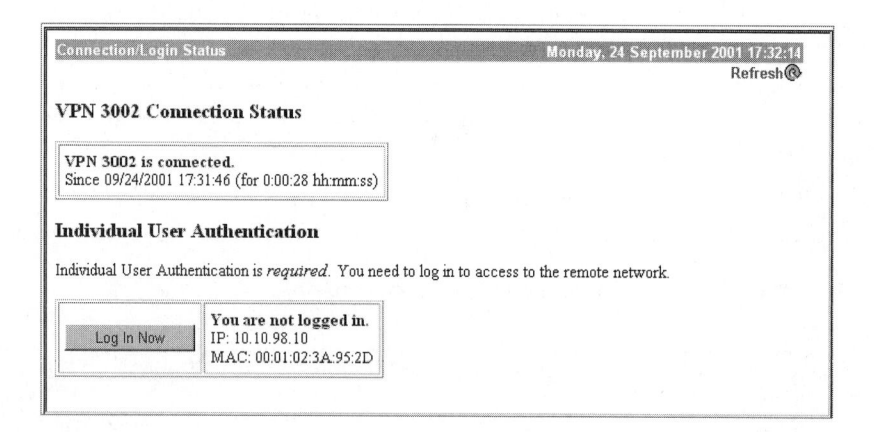

```
Connection/Login Status                        Monday, 24 September 2001 17:32:14
                                                                       Refresh

VPN 3002 Connection Status

  VPN 3002 is connected.
  Since 09/24/2001 17:31:46 (for 0:00:28 hh:mm:ss)

Individual User Authentication

Individual User Authentication is required. You need to log in to access to the remote network.

              You are not logged in.
  Log In Now  IP: 10.10.98.10
              MAC: 00:01:02:3A:95:2D
```

Load Balancing

Load balancing is a feature supported by configuring the concentrator; however, it works only with the hardware client version 3.5 or higher or Cisco VPN Clients running version 3.0 or higher. LAN-to-LAN and other connections may establish tunnels with concentrators that are set up for load balancing, but these devices won't participate in the load balancing by being directed away from the primary connection point. If the hardware client doesn't have the necessary software, then the client needs to point to the IP address of a real concentrator, not the IP address of the fake aggregating device that then shares the connections with real concentrators.

Due to the fact that the 3002 only receives the benefit of the load balancing, there is no configuration requirement at this end of the tunnel. Just remember to use the virtual IP address of the cluster at the opposite end of the tunnel.

> **WARNING** VRRP and load balancing shouldn't be used together with the same concentrator. VRRP uses a hot stand-by for redundancy if the primary device fails, meaning that only the primary passes traffic while the backup is in stand-by. Conversely, load balancing requires that all devices in the cluster be active at all times.

> **NOTE** No configuration is required to enable load balancing on the 3002. Load-balanced traffic is received when the proper virtual IP address for the remote end of the tunnel is used.

VPN Concentrators are configured together in a single virtual cluster. Within that cluster is a *virtual cluster master* (VCM). This cluster is assigned a single IP address that is the only address known to the opposite sides of the peer's tunnel.

The job of cluster master is determined by the election of the most eligible candidate. Each of the devices that are eligible to become the cluster master has an assigned priority value between 0 and 10. Table 17.3 lists the default priority settings. The highest priority number in the cluster wins the election and subsequently becomes the VCM. If two concentrators have the same priority values and there is a tie in the election process, then the device with the longest uptime value becomes the VCM. Default priority values are assigned in such a way that the faster, more capable concentrators have the higher priority values, making them more likely to become the master when clustered with a less-capable device.

You can override these default priority values on the Load Balancing screen if need be (see Figure 17.25). However, it's recommended that the most capable concentrator be allowed to become the VCM due to the processing overhead involved in being the master.

In the event the master of the cluster fails, an election will be forced and the next most capable concentrator will be elected. Additionally, any clients connected will be required to renegotiate their VPN tunnel.

When a client makes an attempt to connect to the cluster (cluster addresses should be configured on the remote end, not on any of the actual IP addresses of any of the devices in the cluster), the master handles the request by first determining which device in its cluster, including itself, has the most processing cycles. Second, the master hands the actual, hard-coded IP address of that device back to the requestor, who then reinitiates the IKE negotiations and sets up the tunnel with that concentrator; at that point, the load-balancing processing is complete, and the communication is only with the requestor and the assigned concentrator.

When a cluster receives a request for a connection, the IPSec group settings are negotiated to attempt to establish a tunnel. Every VPN Concentrator must have identical settings for the groups, and, of course, one of those groups must match the requesting peer for a tunnel to be successfully established.

> **Note:** Configuration for load balancing is covered in Chapter 18.

TABLE 17.3 Default Priority Settings by Model

Model	Priority
3080	9
3060	7
3030	5
3015	3
3005	1

FIGURE 17.25 The Load Balancing screen

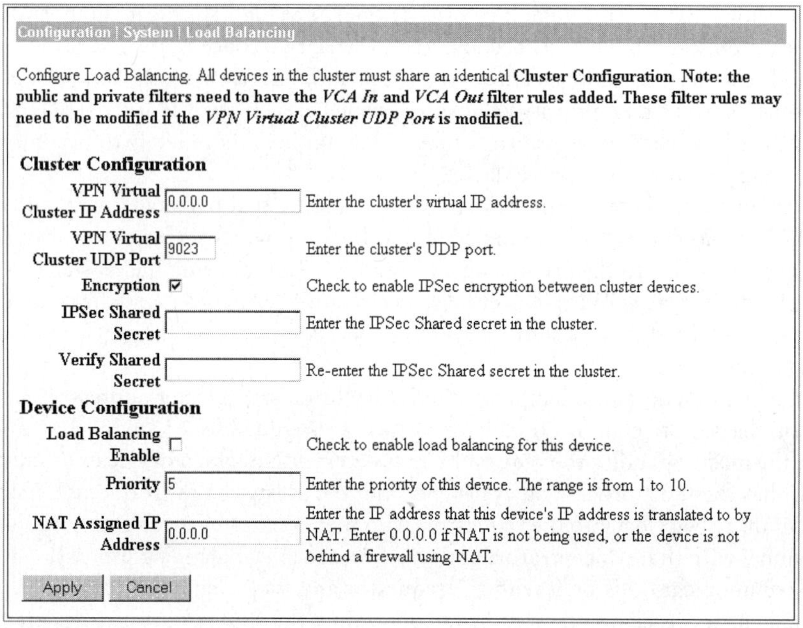

Introducing the VPN Software Clients

Another alternative Cisco offers for VPN termination is the VPN software client. This software allows a single PC or server to act as one end of an IPSec tunnel.

Cisco's VPN offerings were derived from four independent engineering groups. As a result, early versions of Cisco's VPN clients were specific to the type of VPN Concentrator device. The VPN 3000 series of VPN Concentrators were added to Cisco's offerings through the acquisition of Altiga Networks. The original Altiga-only client is still available, but Cisco has developed a common VPN Client that supports both the Altiga-derived devices as well as IOS router–based and PIX firewall VPNs. IOS-based VPNs were first supported in version 12.2T. Unity clients are supported on the PIX firewall after version 6.0. Prior to these versions, IOS- and PIX-based VPN connections were available only by using the older Cisco SafeNet client.

Cisco initially released version 3.0 of the VPN Client in the spring of 2002. This version, which was commonly referred to as the Unified Client, was the first to support multiple types of head-end devices. The version 4.0 software client has since replaced the version 3.x client. Our discussions will deal with this newer version of the Unified Client.

When the VPN Client starts, nothing is configured by default, as shown in Figure 17.26. To configure the client, you need to set up the connection and set properties.

FIGURE 17.26 The VPN Client at initial startup

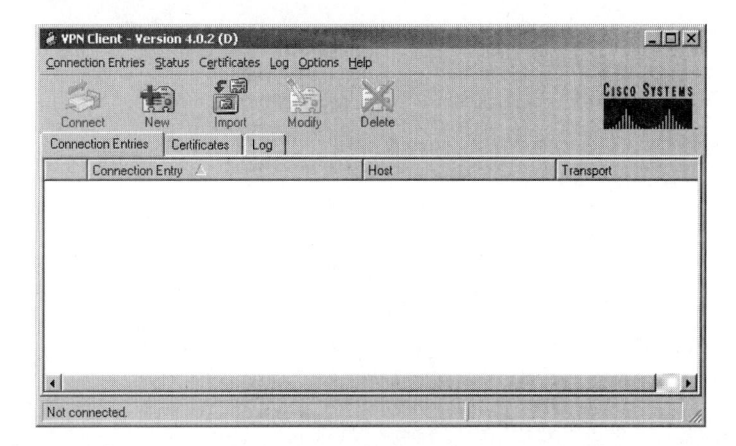

> **Note:** Unified Client versions 3.0 and lower don't support Windows XP. If you install version 3.1 and then upgrade your system to XP, XP might report that the client isn't supported, even though it is. The solution is to uninstall and reinstall the same client.

In the following sections, we'll look at the specifics in configuring the Unified Client.

Configuring the Connection

To configure the connection, click the New button to start the process. On the Connection Setting screen, set the name of the connection along with a description, and click Continue.

At the top of the Create New VPN Connection Entry screen (see Figure 17.27), specify a name for the connection, a description of the connection, and the IP address or hostname of the terminating device.

Setting Authentication Properties

Authentication can take place via either a digital certificate or a pre-shared key. The Authentication tab of the Properties dialog box, shown in Figure 17.28, allows you to set either group parameters or certificate information.

The group name and password used for the pre-shared–key method of authentication must match the ones set up on the destination device.

To use a certificate for authentication, select the Certificate Authentication radio button, and then select the certificate you wish to use from the drop-down list.

FIGURE 17.27 The Create New VPN Connection Entry screen

FIGURE 17.28 The Authentication tab

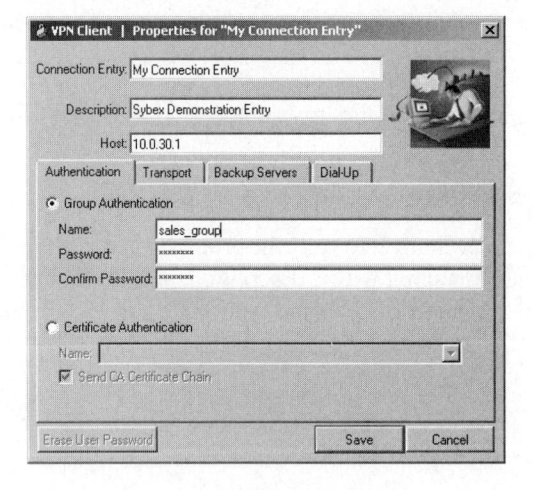

> **NOTE** A certificate must exist before options are available in the drop-down box. This is covered later in this chapter, in the section "Installing a Certificate."

The Send CA Certificate Chain check box is selected by default. This option instructs the client to send the full Certificate Authority (CA) certificate chain to the VPN Concentrator. This might be necessary when the VPN Concentrator and the VPN Client use certificates from different subordinate CAs that have the same root CA. If this option isn't selected, the VPN Concentrator must directly trust the subordinate CA that issued the client's certificate.

Setting Connection Properties

The Connections tab of the Properties dialog box, shown in Figure 17.29, allows you to define the other end of the tunnel for this particular configuration. Entries can be added with the Add button and deleted with the Remove button.

Multiple concentrator IP addresses are supported when the Enable Backup Servers check box is selected. If the concentrator with the first IP address is unavailable, the second IP address is tried. This allows an organization to use multiple concentrators for failover purposes.

FIGURE 17.29 The Connections tab of the Properties dialog box

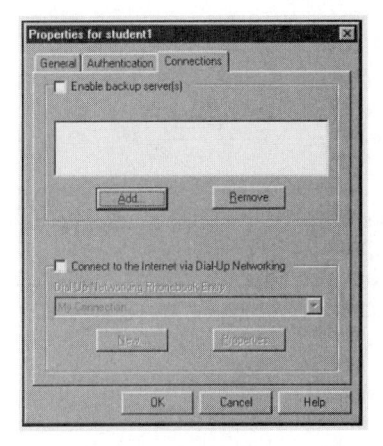

Installing a Certificate

You manage certificates from the Certificates tab on the main VPN Client screen, as shown in Figure 17.30. The Certificate Enrollment screen allows for two types of certificate enrollment: Online and File. The Cisco VPN Client can automatically request a certificate on line from a CA that supports Simple Certificate Enrollment Protocol (SCEP), or the certificate can be installed as part of an offline process. Additionally, a certificate that already exists as part of the internal Windows certificate store can be imported.

The following steps outline the process of requesting a certificate using the online method:

1. To request a certificate, click the Enroll icon at the top of the VPN Client screen, as shown in Figure 17.30.
2. The Certificate Enrollment screen opens, as shown in Figure 17.31. This screen has four fields: Certificate Authority, CA URL, CA Domain, and Challenge Password.
3. Select New to configure a new CA.

> **NOTE** Once a CA is successfully used for the first time, that CA's information is cached and automatically populates the CA URL and CA Domain fields when selected.

FIGURE 17.30 The Certificates tab

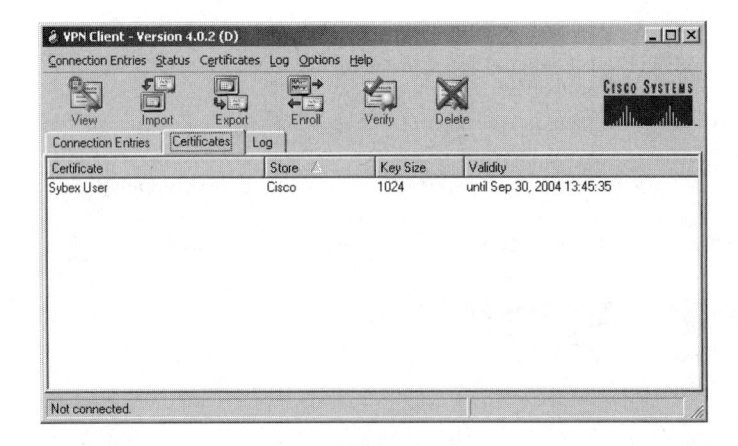

FIGURE 17.31 The Certificate Enrollment screen

4. Configure the CA URL to identify where to forward the certificate request. The listed URL is the standard SCEP URL for a Microsoft CA.

5. Configure the CA Domain. This field selects the domain of the authority that the CA services. This is often the IP domain name.

6. Configure the Challenge Password. The Challenge Password field is a simple authentication method that many CAs use to control certificate requests. If your CA doesn't require a challenge password, leave the field blank.

FIGURE 17.32 The second Certificate Enrollment screen

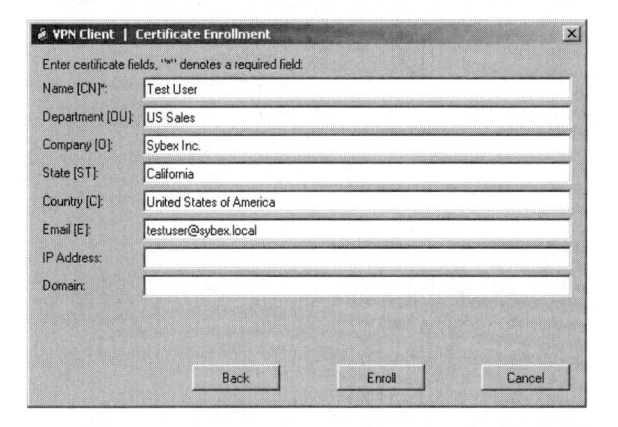

7. Click the Next button to display the second Certificate Enrollment screen, as shown in Figure 17.32.
8. This screen prompts you for certificate identification information. The only required field is the canonical name (CN). The field is usually the end user's full legal name.
9. Click the Enroll button to request the certificate. If the CA is configured to automatically issue the certificate, no further action is required.
10. If the CA authenticates requests manually, the certificate appears as Request in the Store column:

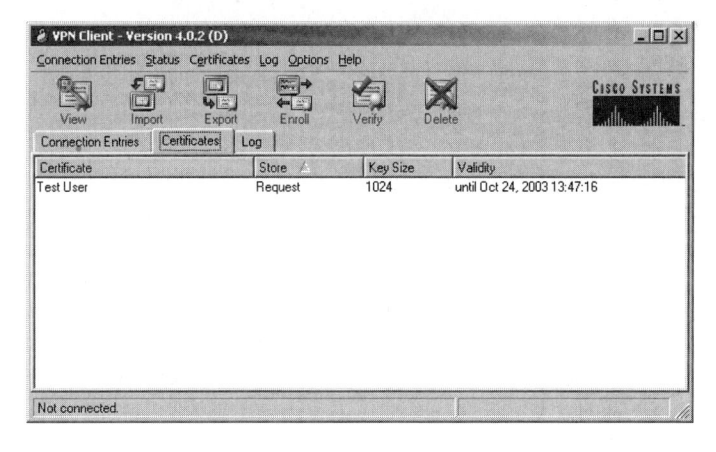

11. The client must periodically check with the CA to pick up the approved certificate. To manually check for the certificate, select the Certificates ➢ Retry Certificate Enrollment option:

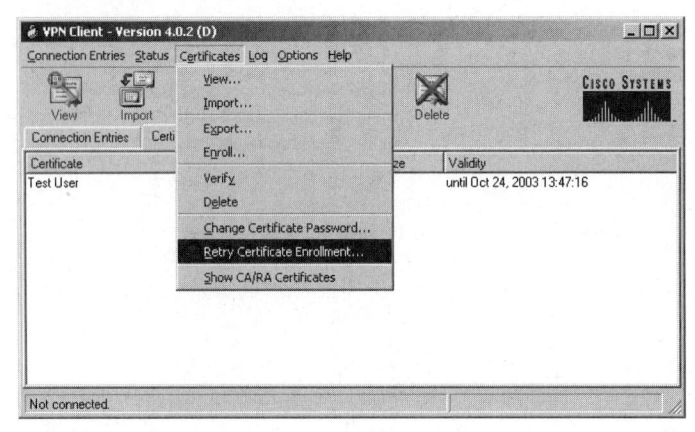

Preconfiguring the VPN Client

The software client needs to be loaded on each machine that is expected to form a tunnel end point. In many cases, it isn't practical for a member of the IT department to visit the home of a remote user just to install a single piece of software. Some people who work remotely can be talked through the setup via the phone, but others might find setup difficult. Cisco has attempted to make it easier to talk users through installations by "wizardizing" the process. Additionally, you can preconfigure the client for your users.

By preconfiguring the client, not only do you make it easier for the user to install the software, but you also can make sure that your users use particular settings. Recent versions of the VPN Client have a built-in stateful firewall. How effective is that firewall if users can easily turn it off? How secure is a wireless connection without a VPN? By requiring certain settings and making it difficult for users to stray from those settings, you can strengthen the security of your network.

When the VPN Client is being installed, the application can automatically configure itself based on custom parameters you create in the client's profile file. Global configuration parameters are stored in the `vpnclient.ini` file. Parameters relating to specific connections are saved in `.pcf` files. The `vpnclient.ini` configuration file is stored by default in the `c:\Program Files\Cisco Systems\VPN Client` directory. The `.pcf` connection configurations are stored in the `c:\Program Files\Cisco Systems\VPN Client\Profiles` subdirectory. Both types of files use the familiar Windows `.ini` format.

> **NOTE** Version 2.x of the Unified Client used a file called `IPSecdlr.ini` to hold configuration information.

Each profile file has many variables that you can configure. Here is an example of part of a vpnclient.ini file:

```
[MAIN]
!EnableLog=1
: This makes sure a log will always be kept.
DialerDisconnect=1
[LOG.DIALER]
LogLevel=1
: This enables dialer logging.
```

Table 17.4 lists the client configuration format for a profile file.

TABLE 17.4 Client Configuration Format

Symbol	Usage
!	Using the exclamation point as the first character makes this configuration item mandatory. Not all keys can be marked mandatory.
: or ;	The colon or semicolon is used to denote a comment.
=	The equal sign is a reserved symbol. It separates a keyword from a value.
[ ]	The square brackets are used for section headings. They usually denote a set of related keys and values.

> **NOTE** For full explanations of each VPN Client profile file variable, refer to http://www.cisco.com/univercd/cc/td/doc/product/vpn/client/3_6/admin_gd/vcach2.htm.

> **WARNING** It's possible to create custom .pcf and .ini files and forward them to the users. Although doing so is very convenient, it isn't a secure way of passing VPN passwords. Avoid the temptation to place authentication passwords and usernames in preconfigured files.

The user must place the client installation file, the vpnclient.ini file, and any .pcf files in the appropriate directories. When the client begins installation, it uses the properties found in the .ini file for customization. Cisco has made the VPN Client software available in both Microsoft Installer and InstallShield formats. Although the process is outside the scope of this text, savvy support personnel can easily script the installations to minimize user intervention and error.

> ### Real World Scenario
>
> #### Rolling Out a Number of VPN Concentrators
>
> It's common in a corporate or value added reseller (VAR) environment to install many VPN Concentrators with very similar configurations. Here are some suggestions for reducing the quantity of work and improving the quality of the installation.
>
> **Take Advantage of Client Preconfiguration Tools**
>
> It's not unusual to have to install the software client on hundreds of PCs during the initial rollout and during upgrades. You can use a combination of preconfiguration files, installer scripts, and CA tools to make the installation of the software client a one-click operation.
>
> Use the ! operator in the configuration files to restrict changes to the client configuration. Mark the configuration files read-only and/or set security on the files to prevent casual modification or loss of the files.
>
> **Clone VPN Concentrator Configurations**
>
> Most experienced router administrators have discovered that configuring a new router is about 95 percent repetitive and 5 percent unique information. Because of this, many have created a minimal template to paste into a router to set up things such as AAA and DNS and to disable unused features. Some administrators have even gone so far as to write a script that does things such as update the firmware and software and generate the encryption keys.
>
> You can upload and download the complete VPN Concentrator configuration as a text file. The basic format of the text file is very similar to the vpnclient.ini file. We've been unable to find a detailed Cisco-authorized manual for the text format, but the key names are very descriptive and can be easily figured out by an experienced administrator.
>
> For example, many companies have several locations. In a wireless LAN (WLAN) installation, you might need to configure many concentrators that have identical configurations except for IP addressing. In this case, it might be easiest to configure one of the concentrators using the CLI or web interface and then upload the configurations wholesale and make the address changes.
>
> **Standardize the Client Operating Systems**
>
> The software VPN Clients operate with subtle differences between versions of the client operating systems. For example, Windows NT/2000/XP versions of the client often handle capitalization differently than Windows 9x versions do. This can cause problems with keys, passwords, and the parsing of configuration files. Standardizing a client operating system makes sure that the features and installation process are consistent.

> **Note:** For more information about installation automation using MSI or InstallShield, refer to http://www.cisco.com/en/US/products/sw/secursw/ps2308/products_administration_guide_chapter09186a00802d3ab4.html.

Another file, oem.ini, controls the way the VPN Client looks. If you want to change the client software's text or graphics from the defaults, you can use the oem.ini file. In this file, you can provide the custom text or the location for custom text or graphic files.

> **Note:** For more information about using the oem.ini file, refer to http://www.cisco.com/univercd/cc/td/doc/product/vpn/client/rel_3_0/admn_gd/vcach4.htm.

Overview of the Cisco VPN Software Client Auto-Initiation

The Cisco VPN software client includes an *auto-initiation* feature. This feature allows the client software to automatically start the VPN connection process based on other network criteria. Typically, this feature is used in WLAN environments where an untrusted wireless network is used to access services on an otherwise secure wired LAN. Figure 17.33 shows an example network.

FIGURE 17.33 A wireless network with VPN

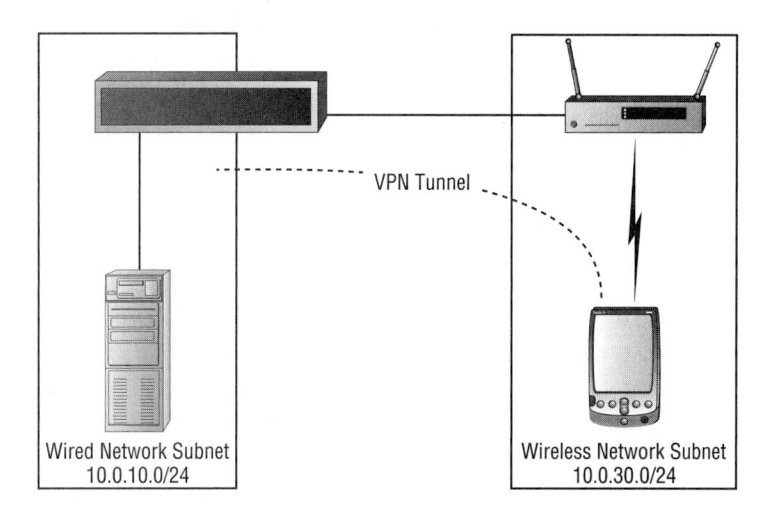

In this configuration, the VPN Concentrator provides two functions. First, it acts as a gateway between the wireless and wired networks. This allows the network administrator to authenticate wireless connections on a per-user basis. Second, the VPN Concentrator allows for a per-client encryption mechanism using standard VPN encryption methods. These features are unavailable using standard Wired Equivalent Privacy (WEP) protocols and are only partially provided with the new Lightweight and Efficient Application Protocol (LEAP)/Protected Extensible Authentication Protocol (PEAP) wireless security protocols.

The VPN Client isn't aware of the physical media being used for network connection. This means that an alternative indicator must be used to trigger a VPN connection. The Cisco VPN Software client uses a list of known IP subnets to determine when a WLAN network has been connected. Each of the known IP subnets is tied to a preferred VPN connection.

Configuring the auto-initiation feature is a three-step process:

Step 1: Create and configure the connection that will be used for the WLAN VPN. No special configuration is required for an auto-initiation connection. Configure it as you would any other VPN connection.

Step 2: Enable the auto-initiation feature in the *vpnclient.ini* file. The auto-initiation feature can't be enabled from the GUI and must be configured manually by editing the `vpnclient.ini` file. You must add two keys to the [MAIN] section to enable auto-initiation:

```
AutoInitiationEnable=1
AutoInitiationList=WLANList
```

The `AutoInitiationEnable=1` key enables the auto-initiation feature.

`AutoInitiationList=WLANList` ties the auto-initiation feature to a list of subnets named `WLANList`.

Step 3: Configure the selection criteria for the WLAN and tie it to the connection created in step 1. The selection criteria require a header and four keys to configure:

```
[WLANList]
Network=10.0.30.0
Mask=255.255.255.0
ConnectionEntry=WLANConnection
```

The `[WLANList]` header identifies the subnet listing. This header must match the key value of the `AutoInitiationList` key from step 2.

The `Network` and `Mask` keys identify the IP subnetwork that is assigned to the WLAN you wish to VPN through.

The `ConnectionEntry` key ties the subnetwork to the VPN connection that will be automatically initiated. This value must match the Connection Entry field in the GUI.

Although they aren't absolutely required for operation, several other keys are very useful when dealing with the auto-initiation feature. These are listed in Table 17.5.

TABLE 17.5 Other Important vpnclient.ini Keys

key/Value	Usage
AutoInitiationRetryInterval=3	Sets the retry timer to a number of minutes. The default setting is 1 minute.
DialerDisconnect=1	Instructs the VPN Client to disconnect the VPN connection when the user logs off their system.
RunAtLogon=1	Instructs the VPN Client to initiate the VPN connection prior to logon. By default, the VPN connection is initiated after the user logs on to the machine. Use this key to ensure that VPN clients are properly authenticated to the secured LAN.

Summary

Each VPN tunnel has two ends, and each end is a client of the tunnel. Three VPN components—the concentrator, hardware client, and software client—are able to offload the VPN process from other network equipment to some dedicated device or service.

The software client is portable but requires user intervention to run. At the very least, the user must start the application and log in. The hardware client and concentrator don't require user intervention, but they aren't portable.

The hardware client is totally GUI-driven and is simple enough to set up that someone could be talked through the configuration over the phone. Even better, you have the option of using a preconfiguration file that can be loaded into the client to provide the configuration.

The Unified software client is simple to configure and has a number of options for automating and standardizing the installation process for users.

Exam Essentials

Know the capabilities of the different VPN Concentrator models.   The VPN Concentrators come in two sizes. The 3005 is 1U; all the others are 2U. Normally, a higher number means increased capabilities for the unit. Going from the 3005 to the 3015 is an exception. The 3015 is upgradable, but otherwise has the same limitations that the 3005 does. Make sure you know the memory each model comes with and the maximum number of connections it can handle.

Understand how to configure the VPN Hardware Client.   Configuring the hardware client is similar to configuring the concentrator. However, there are differences, such as the fact that the hardware client comes with a preconfigured IP address.

Understand how to configure the VPN software client.   Know where to configure properties for the VPN Client. Know where to configure the tunnel end point and how to start a new configuration. Also know how to use a preconfiguration file.

Chapter 18

Configuring the VPN Concentrator

THE FOLLOWING TOPICS ARE COVERED IN THIS CHAPTER:

- ✓ Overview of remote access using pre-shared keys
- ✓ Initial configuration of the Cisco VPN 3000 Concentrator Series for remote access
- ✓ Browser configuration of the Cisco VPN 3000 Concentrator Series
- ✓ Configure users and groups
- ✓ CA support overview
- ✓ Certificate generation
- ✓ Validating certificates
- ✓ Configuring the Cisco VPN 3000 Concentrator Series for CA support
- ✓ IPSec Software Client
- ✓ Overview of the software client's firewall feature
- ✓ The software client's Are You There feature
- ✓ The software client's Central Policy Protection feature
- ✓ The software client's Stateful Firewall feature
- ✓ Client firewall statistics
- ✓ Customizing firewall policy
- ✓ Overview of the hardware client interactive unit and user authentication feature
- ✓ Configuring the hardware client integrated unit authentication feature
- ✓ Configuring hardware client user authentication

- ✓ Monitoring hardware client user statistics
- ✓ Configuring the VPN 3002 backup server feature
- ✓ Configuring the VPN 3002 load balancing feature
- ✓ Overview and configuration of the VPN 3002 software auto-update feature
- ✓ Monitoring the VPN 3002 software auto-update feature
- ✓ Overview of Port Address Translation
- ✓ Configuring IPSec over UDP
- ✓ Configuring NAT-Transversal
- ✓ Configuring IPSec over TCP
- ✓ Cisco VPN 3000 IPSec LAN-to-LAN
- ✓ LAN-to-LAN configuration
- ✓ LAN-to-LAN overview
- ✓ Configuring the concentrator LAN-to-LAN NAT feature
- ✓ Root certificate installation
- ✓ Identity certificate installation

When you pull a switch out of its box, you can place it into a rack, plug in the users, and the switch will work. But unlike a switch, a VPN Concentrator doesn't get its information from analyzing traffic that passes through it. A concentrator needs to be configured before it can be functional.

This chapter explains how to configure the Cisco VPN Concentrator from either the command-line interface (CLI) or from the browser-based GUI. The GUI is the preferred access method for most administrators and is more intuitive than the CLI. However, you'll need to perform the initial configuration from the CLI before you can use the browser-based GUI. Then you can use the GUI's Quick Configuration mode to perform the basic configuration.

To begin the opening setup, you need to gather the necessary information for your environment. At a minimum, you need the following:

- Private interface IP address, subnet mask, interface speed, and mode configuration
- Public interface IP address, subnet mask, interface speed, and mode configuration
- Device or system name
- System date and time
- Whether IP Security (IPSec), Point-to-Point Tunneling Protocol (PPTP), or Layer 2 Tunneling Protocol (L2TP) will be used
- DNS server IP address
- Domain name
- Default gateway IP address or hostname

You also might need the following information:

- IP addresses, subnet masks, interface speed, and mode for and additional interfaces.
- If you intend to hand out IP address information such as IP address range, subnet mask, and gateway to remote users, you'll need the Dynamic Host Configuration Protocol (DHCP) server information.
- IP address or hostname, port number, and server secret (or password) of any external RADIUS server.
- If you're using Windows NT Domain user authentication, you'll need the IP address, port number and Primary Domain Controller (PDC) information.
- If you're using any external SDI user authentication, you'll need the IP address and port number for the SDI server.

- Usernames and passwords for all internal VPN users. If you're using the per-user address assignment, you'll also need the IP address and subnet mask.
- If you're using the IPSec tunneling protocol, you'll need the name and password for the IPSec tunnel group.

Once the basic setup is completed, you're ready to configure the concentrator to allow users to build tunnels. We'll cover how to configure concentrator groups, users, authentication, access hour policies, and filters. The chapter will wrap up with information about configuring IPSec using digital certificates and installing them on the concentrator and the client.

Using the CLI for Initial Configuration

Because the VPN Concentrator doesn't have a default IP address, you can't use a web browser for initial concentrator configuration. You need to use the CLI to configure at least two things: an IP address on the private interface and a subnet mask if the default doesn't work for the network setup.

In the following sections, we'll review the CLI interface and all the nuances of making the initial configurations of the concentrator such as the initial interface configuration and routing configurations.

Starting the CLI

To get started with configuration, use the enclosed blue or black console cable to attach a laptop to the concentrator via a serial port. Next, set up a communications program, such as HyperTerminal, to communicate through the correct serial port on 8N1 (8 data bits, no parity, and 1 stop bit) with no flow control. These are the same settings used to talk to a router, switch, or firewall.

> **TIP** The VPN 3000 series is one of the few Cisco devices that doesn't come with an RJ45 console connector. In the absence of the bundled console cable, you can connect to the VPN Concentrator using two standard DB9 to RJ45 converters and a standard Ethernet cable.

> **WARNING** The concentrator has at least two sides and may have three, depending on the model purchased. The inside, or private, interface is the trusted part of the network. When you're attaching cables to the concentrator, make sure that the appropriate cables are plugged into the appropriate interface.

If the communications program has been configured correctly, when you press Enter, you'll be prompted to enter a login (default name `admin`) followed by a password (default is also `admin`):

```
Login: admin
Password:
```

If the VPN Concentrator has no configuration, it displays the CLI Quick Configuration Wizard. This wizard walks you through enough of the configuration to make your concentrator available for basic use. The Quick Configuration Wizard uses the same format as the CLI configuration tool on the VPN 3002 hardware client. The wizard prompts the administrator for information and provides a default suggested value in square brackets. Pressing the Enter key without entering a value sets the default value and moves to the next option.

The Quick Configuration Wizard can be aborted after the private interface has been configured. At that point, the VPN Concentrator is available to configure via the web configuration interface.

To provide the basic VPN concentrator configuration using the Quick Configuration Wizard, follow these steps:

1. Set the current system time:

    ```
                Welcome to
                Cisco Systems
        VPN 3000 Concentrator Series
            Command Line Interface
    Copyright (C) 1998-2003 Cisco Systems, Inc.




    -- : Set the time on your device. The correct time is very important,
    -- : so that logging and accounting entries are accurate.

    -- : Enter the system time in the following format:
    -- :        HH:MM:SS.  Example  21:30:00  for 9:30 PM

    > Time

    Quick -> [ 11:42:38 ]
    ```

2. Set the current system date:

    ```
    -- : Enter the date in the following format.
    -- : MM/DD/YYYY  Example 06/12/1999  for June 12th 1999.

    > Date

    Quick -> [ 09/28/2003 ]
    ```

3. Select the time zone:

    ```
    -- : Set the time zone on your device. The correct time zone is very
    -- : important so that logging and accounting entries are accurate.
    ```

```
-- : Enter the time zone using the hour offset from GMT:
-- :  -12 : Kwajalein    -11 : Samoa      -10 : Hawaii        -9 : Alaska
-- :   -8 : PST           -7 : MST         -6 : CST           -5 : EST
-- :   -4 : Atlantic      -3 : Brasilia   -3.5 : Newfoundland -1 : Mid-
Atlantic
-- :   -1 : Azores         0 : GMT         +1 : Paris         +2 : Cairo
-- :   +3 : Kuwait       +3.5 : Tehran     +4 : Abu Dhabi   +4.5 : Kabul
-- :   +5 : Karachi      +5.5 : Calcutta +5.75 : Kathmandu    +6 : Almaty
-- : +6.5 : Rangoon        +7 : Bangkok    +8 : Singapore    +9 : Tokyo
-- : +9.5 : Adelaide      +10 : Sydney    +11 : Solomon Is. +12 : Marshall
Is.

> Time Zone

Quick -> [ -6 ]
```

4. Enable or disable daylight savings time observation:

```
1) Enable Daylight Savings Time Support
2) Disable Daylight Savings Time Support

Quick -> [ 1 ]
```

5. Set the IP address of the private network interface:

```
This table shows current IP addresses.

    Intf         Status      IP Address/Subnet Mask      MAC Address
    -----------------------------------------------------------------
    Ether1-Pri|Not Configured|      0.0.0.0/0.0.0.0       |
    Ether2-Pub|Not Configured|      0.0.0.0/0.0.0.0       |
    -----------------------------------------------------------------
DNS Server(s): DNS Server Not Configured
DNS Domain Name:
Default Gateway: Default Gateway Not Configured

** An address is required for the private interface. **

> Enter IP Address

Quick Ethernet 1 -> [ 0.0.0.0 ] 10.0.10.190
```

At this point, the CLI will pause for a moment while the interface is brought up.

6. After the interface is initialized, enter the subnet mask for the private interface:

   ```
   Waiting for Network Initialization...

   > Enter Subnet Mask

   Quick Ethernet 1 -> [ 255.0.0.0 ]
   ```

7. Set the interface speed:

   ```
   1) Ethernet Speed 10 Mbps
   2) Ethernet Speed 100 Mbps
   3) Ethernet Speed 10/100 Mbps Auto Detect

   Quick Ethernet 1 -> [ 3 ]
   ```

8. Select the interface duplex:

   ```
   1) Enter Duplex - Half/Full/Auto
   2) Enter Duplex - Full Duplex
   3) Enter Duplex - Half Duplex

   Quick Ethernet 1 -> [ 1 ]
   ```

9. Set the interface maximum transmission unit:

   ```
   > MTU (68 - 1500)

   Quick Ethernet 1 -> [ 1500 ]
   ```

   Enough of the configuration has now been entered to allow a user to configure the VPN Concentrator from the local subnet using the web interface. The entire VPN Concentrator can be configured from the CLI. You could select option 4 in step 10 to configure the entire VPN Concentrator from the wizard. However, we'll concentrate on the web interface. Administrators shouldn't have great difficulty moving from the CLI to the Web and back, since Altiga and Cisco took great care to ensure that the main structures of the CLI and web interfaces are identical.

10. To save the configuration, select option 3, and then select 5 to exit and log off:

    ```
    1) Modify Ethernet 1 IP Address (Private)
    2) Modify Ethernet 2 IP Address (Public)
    3) Save changes to Config file
    4) Continue
    5) Exit

    Quick -> 3
    ```

```
1) Modify Ethernet 1 IP Address (Private)
2) Modify Ethernet 2 IP Address (Public)
3) Save changes to Config file
4) Continue
5) Exit

Quick -> 5
```

11. Sometimes it isn't possible to connect the VPN Concentrator and the configuration PC to the same IP subnet. In this case, you might need to configure a static route to permit web access. To do this, log back on to the CLI. You'll no longer be in the CLI Quick Configuration Wizard:

```
Login: admin
Password:
```

> **TIP** In the standard CLI, each menu has a title associated with it. The title of the opening menu is Main, as you can see at the command prompt at the very bottom of the menu screen. The cursor is sitting next to the text-based arrow (->), waiting for a number to be entered.

12. From the main menu, select option 1:

```
              Welcome to
            Cisco Systems
       VPN 3000 Concentrator Series
           Command Line Interface
Copyright (C) 1998-2003 Cisco Systems, Inc.



1) Configuration
2) Administration
3) Monitoring
4) Save changes to Config file
5) Help Information
6) Exit

Main ->
```

13. From the Configuration menu, select option 2:

```
1) Interface Configuration
```

2) System Management
   3) User Management
   4) Policy Management
   5) Back

Config ->

14. From the System Management menu, select option 4:
   1) Servers (Authentication, Authorization, Accounting, DNS, DHCP, etc.)
   2) Address Management
   3) Tunneling Protocols (PPTP, L2TP, etc.)
   4) IP Routing (static routes, OSPF, etc.)
   5) Management Protocols (Telnet, TFTP, FTP, etc.)
   6) Event Configuration
   7) General Config (system name, time, etc.)
   8) Client Update
   9) Load Balancing Configuration
   10) Back

System ->

15. From the Routing menu, select option 1:
   1) Static Routes
   2) Default Gateways
   3) OSPF
   4) OSPF Areas
   5) DHCP Parameters
   6) Redundancy
   7) Reverse Route Injection
   8) DHCP Relay
   9) Back

Routing ->

16. Select option 1 to add a static route:

```
Static Routes
-------------
Destination     Mask            Metric Destination
-----------------------------------------------------------
No Static Routes Configured
```

```
1) Add Static Route
2) Modify Static Route
3) Delete Static Route
4) Back
```

> **TIP** Don't overthink the routing at this point. You need only one route to the configuration PC's local subnet so you can log on to the web interface. Point the next hop to the nearest router in the PC's direction.

17. Enter the network address and subnet mask:

    ```
    > Net Address

    Routing -> 10.0.11.0

    > Subnet Mask

    Routing -> 255.255.255.0
    ```

18. Select option 1 to set the next hop as an address:

    ```
    1) Destination is Router
    2) Destination is Interface

    Routing ->
    ```

19. Set the next hop address and metric:

    ```
    > Router Address

    Routing -> 10.0.10.1

    > Route Metric (1 - 16)

    Routing -> [ 1 ]
    ```

20. The new static route is displayed. Select the Back option several times until you reach the Main menu (the options are numbered 4, 9, 10, and 5):

    ```
    Static Routes
    -------------
    Destination       Mask              Metric Destination
    -----------------------------------------------------------
    10.0.11.0         255.255.255.0         1 10.0.10.1
    ```

```
1) Add Static Route
2) Modify Static Route
3) Delete Static Route
4) Back

Routing ->
```

21. Select option 4 to save the configuration and then option 6 to log off:

```
1) Configuration
2) Administration
3) Monitoring
4) Save changes to Config file
5) Help Information
6) Exit

Main -> 4

1) Configuration
2) Administration
3) Monitoring
4) Save changes to Config file
5) Help Information
6) Exit

Main -> 6

Done
```

> **NOTE** The public interface filters HTTP (web browser) traffic by default. This prevents someone from administering the VPN Concentrator from the Internet. If administration from outside the network is necessary to initially configure the concentrator, you must modify the filter on the public interface to allow this access.

Using Web Quick Configuration Mode

Once the concentrator has been configured with an IP address and routing using the CLI Quick Configuration Wizard, as described in the previous section, you can log in to it via a web browser on a PC or laptop. The login is the same as it is for the CLI—the username and password are both admin. (The login screen is similar to the one used by the hardware client, discussed in Chapter 17.)

Chapter 18 · Configuring the VPN Concentrator

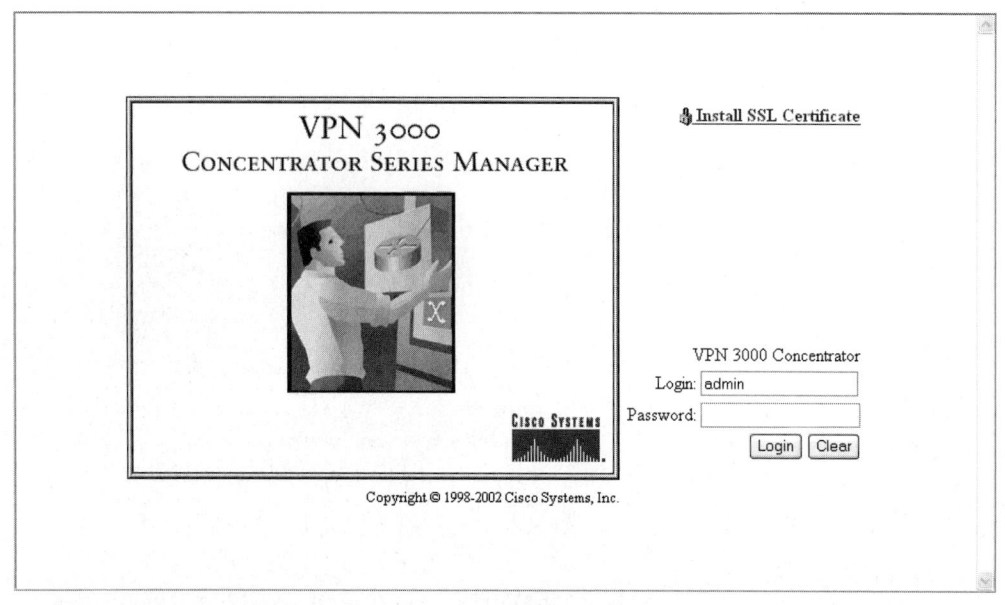

[VPN 3000 Concentrator Series Manager login screen]

When you access a VPN Concentrator with a basic configuration, it recognizes that more needs to be configured before it's fully functional. Just as an IOS router goes into Setup mode when you start it, the concentrator will offer to go into Quick Configuration mode:

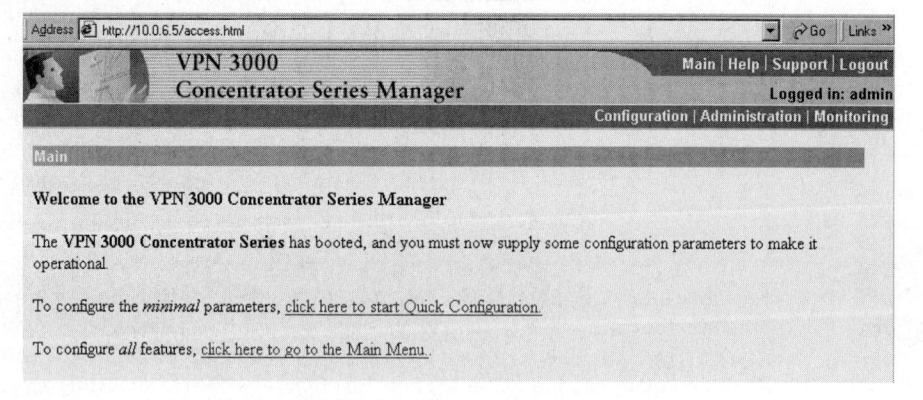

[VPN 3000 Concentrator Series Manager Main welcome screen]

NOTE: After you've made configuration changes and saved them, the only way to go back into Quick Configuration mode is to wipe the configuration and reboot.

Click the Quick Configuration mode link to configure the minimal parameters to make the concentrator functional. (Initial configuration via Quick Configuration mode is optional; it isn't required.) As described in the following sections, the utility will guide you through configuring physical interfaces, system information, tunnel-creation method, address assignments, authentication, and the `admin` password.

Configuring Physical Interfaces

The first Quick Configuration screen—the Quick Configuration Interfaces screen—allows you to configure concentrator interfaces, as shown in Figure 18.1. A VPN Concentrator can have three physical interfaces, although the example shown is from a model 3005, which has two interfaces. (WAN interfaces are referenced in the figure but are no longer sold by Cisco.)

Each interface is shown with its current status and any IP configuration. Click an interface to make changes to it.

> **WARNING** Be careful when making changes to the interface to which you're currently connected. You might inadvertently disconnect yourself from the concentrator and be forced back to the CLI interface for configuration.

FIGURE 18.1 The Quick Configuration Interfaces screen

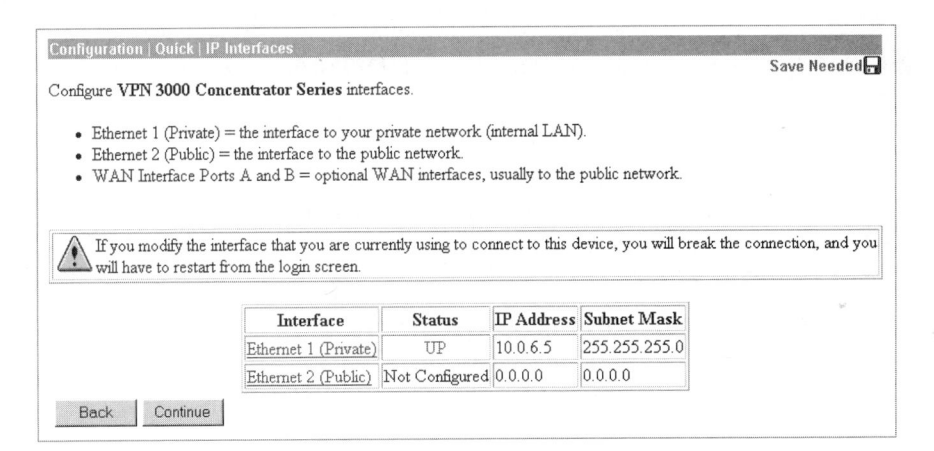

Configuration | Quick | IP Interfaces

Save Needed

Configure **VPN 3000 Concentrator Series** interfaces.

- Ethernet 1 (Private) = the interface to your private network (internal LAN).
- Ethernet 2 (Public) = the interface to the public network.
- WAN Interface Ports A and B = optional WAN interfaces, usually to the public network.

If you modify the interface that you are currently using to connect to this device, you will break the connection, and you will have to restart from the login screen.

Interface	Status	IP Address	Subnet Mask
Ethernet 1 (Private)	UP	10.0.6.5	255.255.255.0
Ethernet 2 (Public)	Not Configured	0.0.0.0	0.0.0.0

Back   Continue

Setting System Information

The System Info screen, shown in Figure 18.2, is extremely important if you'll be using digital certificates. Here, you set the time, a system name, domain information, and the address of the device serving as the default gateway.

If you're using certificates, it's very important that the correct time is set. Also, establishing system and domain information is required for the certificate process.

> **NOTE** The certificate process will be explained in the "Configuring the Use of IPSec Digital Certificates" section later in this chapter.

FIGURE 18.2   The Quick Configuration System Info screen

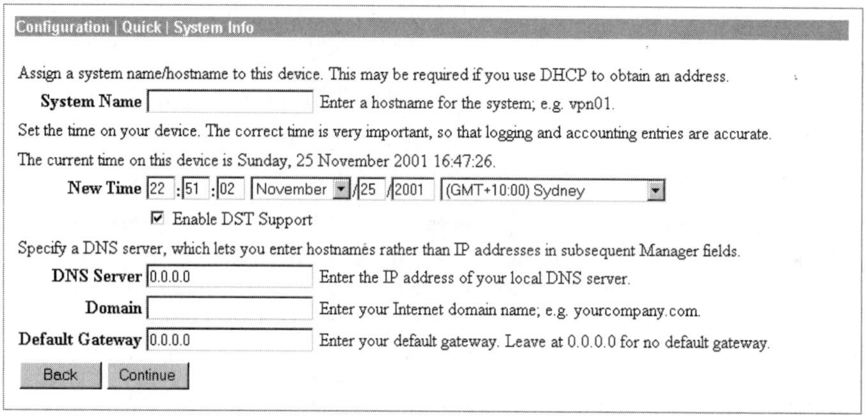

Setting the Tunnel-Creation Method

The Quick Configuration screen presents three methods of creating tunnels. The VPN Concentrator supports tunnels made with PPTP and L2TP. If one or both of these are enabled, you must decide if encryption is required or optional. Microsoft Challenge Handshake Authentication Protocol (MS-CHAP) is required to establish an encrypted tunnel with either of these methods. The third option is to use IPSec to build tunnels. Any or all of the protocols may be enabled at this time.

Setting the Address Assignment

When a client creates a tunnel to the VPN Concentrator, it needs an address for the tunnel. The Quick Configuration Address Assignment screen, shown in Figure 18.3, allows you to select the way in which the client gets the address.

FIGURE 18.3   The Quick Configuration Address Assignment screen

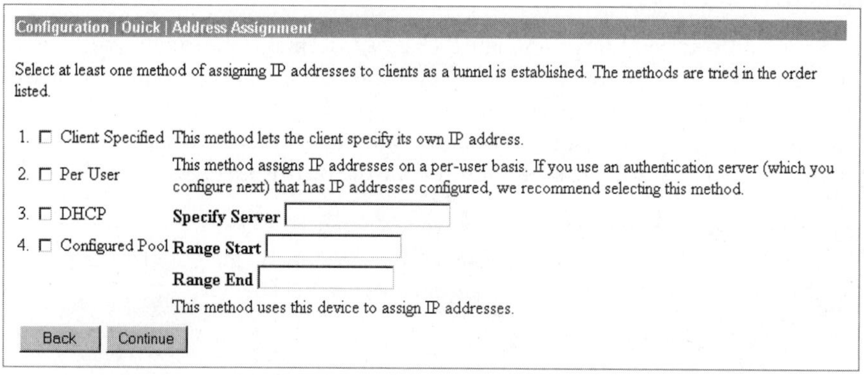

The first method listed, Client Specified, is usually the least desirable because it gives the administrator no control over the addressing on the local network. Also, client-specified addressing doesn't work with most implementations of IPSec and is usually reserved for tunnels using Microsoft technologies.

The remaining three methods are all valid for use with IPSec and are easy to configure. If you're using an authentication, authorization, and accounting (AAA) server, IP addresses to be used can be configured on a user-by-user basis.

> **NOTE** Cisco uses AAA to standardize the security service configuration, regardless of which type of security is implemented.

You can also use DHCP to provide addressing. If a DHCP server is used in the organization, select the pool option and specify the IP address of the DHCP server. If a pool server isn't in use, you can configure a local pool on the concentrator.

On this screen, you can choose multiple address-assignment methods. The concentrator will apply the rules from the top down. If the preferred method of providing addresses is to use the per-user or DHCP methods, it's advisable to also create a local DHCP pool, just in case the first method is unreachable or unavailable. Make sure that the IP addresses of the two or three methods don't overlap.

Configuring Authentication

If your organization has an AAA server, such as CiscoSecure Access Control Server (ACS), you can configure the concentrator to talk to the server to authenticate incoming tunnel requests. Figure 18.4 shows the Quick Configuration Authentication screen.

FIGURE 18.4 The Quick Configuration Authentication screen

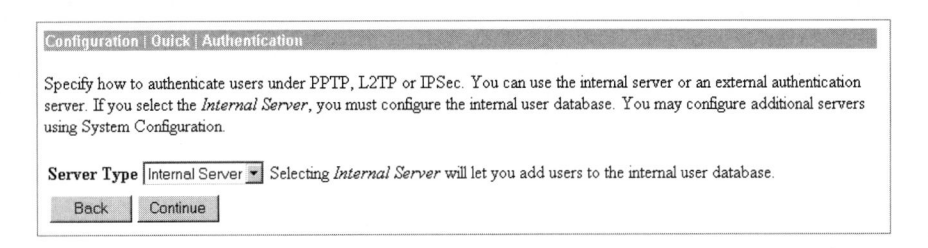

> **TIP** If there are many users, using an AAA server is highly recommended. It helps reduce the number of passwords users are required to remember and it doesn't require administrative intervention when a user changes a password.

If you specify an external server for authentication, more options will appear so that you can configure necessary attributes, such as the server IP address, hostname, timeout length, and number of retries. If a computer running Windows NT will be used for authentication, be sure to specify the computer name in the Domain Controller Name field.

> **Note:** The concentrator GUI offers RADIUS communication but only the more recent versions offer TACACS+. If you want to use TACACS+ but the concentrator doesn't list it as an option, you'll need to upgrade to the latest version of the software.

If you aren't using an AAA server, you can configure the concentrator with a local authentication database (just as a router can have a local database). You'll need to populate the database with appropriate user and group information so users can establish tunnels. When you're creating user and group information, Quick Configuration prompts you for a group name and password. Note that the internal database is limited to a maximum of 100 users and groups. If you need more than 100 users and/or groups, you'll have to establish an external authentication method. When you're configuring the group and password, a group name fulfills the same function as a username.

Setting a Group Name

For IPSec to work, a group and group password must be selected. This group ties a user to a particular set of parameters including encryption options, IP addressing, and access times. The Quick Configuration prompts you for this information, as shown in Figure 18.5. It isn't necessary to configure a group as part of the quick configuration, and it's therefore recommend that you leave the group blank until the Quick Configuration is complete.

FIGURE 18.5 IPSec Group Configuration screen

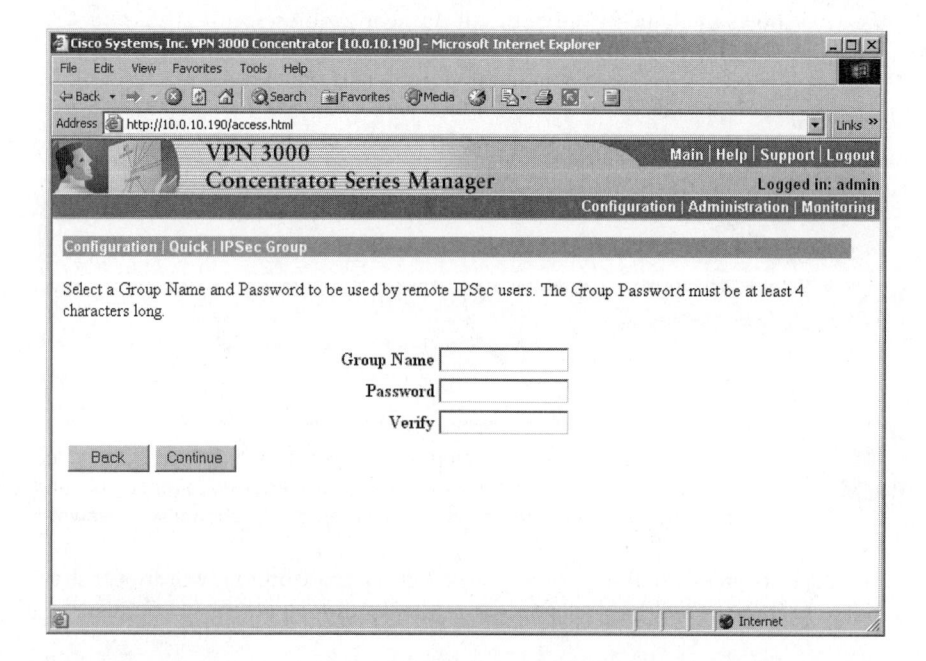

Changing the *admin* Password

The last screen in Quick Configuration—the Admin Password screen—deals with the `admin` password, as shown in Figure 18.6. Anyone who has set up a VPN Concentrator knows the default username and password. For security purposes, it's strongly recommended that a concentrator not be placed into production until this password has been changed.

Along with `admin`, other insecure passwords for a piece of Cisco equipment include `cisco`, `sanfran`, and `sanjose`. (Of course, any passwords that use all letters and form a word, as well as static passwords, are insecure.)

> **NOTE** Although versions 3.0 and later of the concentrator software allow for password recovery, older versions don't, requiring that the concentrator be shipped to the factory for the password to be reset.

FIGURE 18.6 The Quick Configuration Admin Password screen

Configuring User and Policy Management

Once you've set up the bare-bones configuration through Quick Configuration, the VPN Concentrator may be accessed but isn't fully utilized. To fully utilize the concentrator, you need to tell it who can create tunnels. The most efficient way of doing this is by configuring groups and users from the Main mode, rather than the Quick Configuration mode. In this mode, you can choose administration options by clicking hyperlinks in the GUI (web browser–based) window.

In the following sections, we'll discuss the basic configuration details of the VPN Concentrator. We'll look at the setup of users and groups, some of the rules for access and how they're set up and applied, and system load balancing for redundancy. Larger networks will benefit from our discussion of updating clients automatically; and no network can be considered complete unless you implement the proper security, so we'll cover the basics of the integrated stateful firewall feature set.

Navigating the GUI

The VPN Concentrator Manager window has three main frames:

Menu choices In the left frame, you'll see a menu with three main choices: Configuration, Administration, and Monitoring. Clicking Configuration expands the Configuration menu to show additional options. Clicking User Management shows the options in that category:

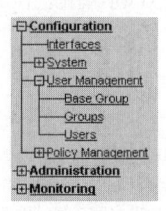

```
-Configuration
    -Interfaces
    -System
    -User Management
        -Base Group
        -Groups
        -Users
    -Policy Management
-Administration
-Monitoring
```

The structure here is identical to the structure found inside the CLI. The difference is that rather than typing numbers to change from one menu to another, you click the mouse.

Settings and information The bottom-right frame—the largest one—is where you set configuration options and view information. At the very top of the frame, you can see the path taken to get to this location, like this:

`Configuration | User Management | Base Group`

If there has been a material change to the configuration, the concentrator will remind you that a save is needed by displaying the following message and icon at the top of this frame (a *material change* is one that will severely affect how the concentrator operates if it reboots, such as changing an IP address):

`Save Needed`

Toolbar The toolbar is in the top frame in the browser window. It shows the name of the management application, VPN 3000 Concentrator Series Manager, and who you're currently logged in as. There are also quick selections for Help, Logout, and the three main menu choices.

> **NOTE** Although the GUI is where most people prefer to configure the concentrator, it's possible to configure it from the CLI. This book focuses on using the GUI (after initial configuration). If you're interested in the corresponding CLI techniques, when a task is done in the GUI in the Configuration section, then it will be done in the same section in the CLI.

Setting Up Groups

The VPN Concentrator comes with a default group called the *base group*. A *group* is used to gather users into a single entity for administration. It's a lot easier for an administrator to change the properties of a group and have the changes apply to all the users in the group than it is to change the properties of multiple users.

You can add groups to the concentrator to suit the needs of your organization. Each administrator-created group is placed as a member of the system-wide base group. If you create users and don't place them into an administrator-created group, those users are members of the base group directly. If you delete an administrator-created group, all of that group's users are placed in the base group (their member profiles aren't deleted).

In the following sections, you'll see how to create groups, set general group properties, and configure IPSec properties for a group.

Creating Groups

To add a group, from the main VPN Concentrator Manager window, select Configuration ➢ User Management ➢ Groups. You'll see the list of existing groups and actions you can take, as shown in Figure 18.7.

If you click the Add Group button under the Actions heading, the form shown in Figure 18.8 appears. On the Identity tab, supply a group name, specify a password (which is entered twice for verification), and choose the authentication type. The name of the group is important if you're using digital certificates because the group name on the concentrator must match the organizational unit (OU) name on the client's identity certificate. For the authentication type, internal authentication is always acceptable, assuming the database isn't full. Other options include Windows NT authentication and a RADIUS server. TACACS+ is supported on newer versions of concentrator software.

> **TIP** To modify an existing group, click the group you wish to modify on the Groups screen to highlight it, and then click the Modify Group button.

You can continue to configure the group by setting properties on the other tabs of the group configuration form, as described in the following sections.

FIGURE 18.7 The Groups screen

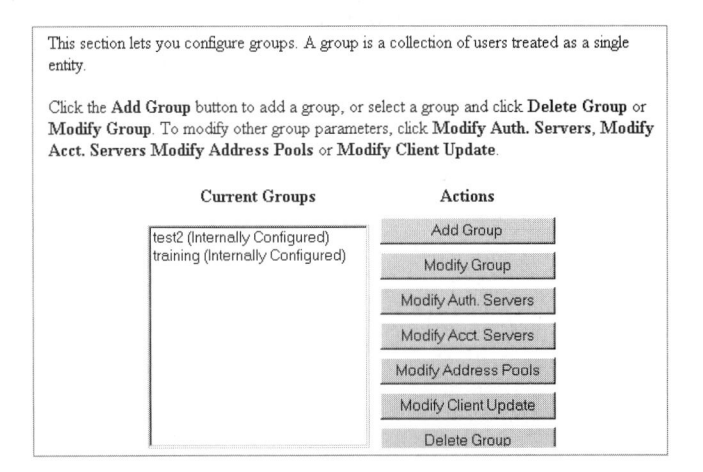

This section lets you configure groups. A group is a collection of users treated as a single entity.

Click the **Add Group** button to add a group, or select a group and click **Delete Group** or **Modify Group**. To modify other group parameters, click **Modify Auth. Servers, Modify Acct. Servers Modify Address Pools** or **Modify Client Update**.

Current Groups:
- test2 (Internally Configured)
- training (Internally Configured)

Actions:
- Add Group
- Modify Group
- Modify Auth. Servers
- Modify Acct. Servers
- Modify Address Pools
- Modify Client Update
- Delete Group

FIGURE 18.8 Adding a concentrator group

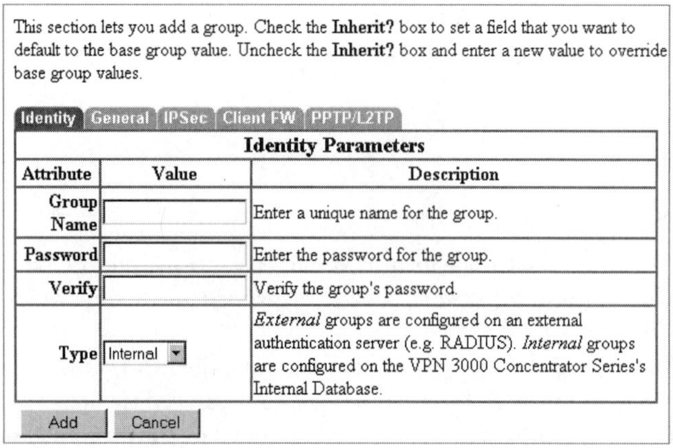

Setting General Group Properties

When you create a group, by default, it inherits the properties of the base group. Usually, you'll want to customize some of the properties to suit the members of the group. For example, telecommuters working normal business hours in customer service might have restrictions placed on their access hours, but traveling salespeople might need to be able to access their e-mail at all hours.

To customize group properties, click the General tab on the group form. You'll see the General Parameters options, as shown in Figure 18.9.

You can configure the following options:

- Access hour restrictions (choices are No Restriction, Never, Business Hours, and any custom policies you've defined)
- Number of simultaneous logins (three is the default)
- Minimum number of characters in the password
- Whether the password requires nonalphabetic characters (deselecting Alphabetic Only requires at least one nonalphabetic character in each password)
- An idle timeout, in minutes (30 is the default)
- Maximum connect time, also in minutes
- Traffic filter
- WINS information
- DNS information

- Strip authentication realm
- DHCP Network Scope for address assignment

You can configure the Access Hours and Filter parameters through the Configuration ➢ Policy Management section, as described in the "Configuring Access Hours and Filters" section later in this chapter.

Configuring IPSec and Remote Access Properties for a Group

The IPSec tab on the group form allows you to configure IPSec and Remote Access properties on a group-by-group basis.

To customize group properties, click the IPSec tab on the group form. You'll see the IPSec Parameters and Remote Access Parameters page, as shown in Figure 18.10.

FIGURE 18.9 General group properties

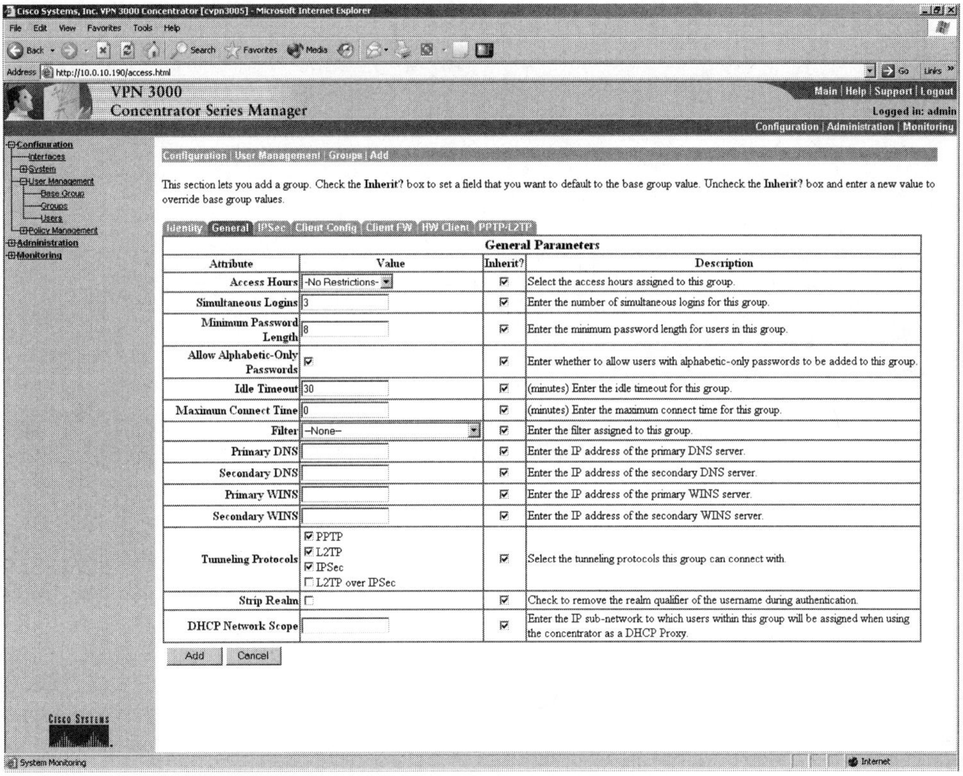

FIGURE 18.10 IPSec and Remote Access group properties

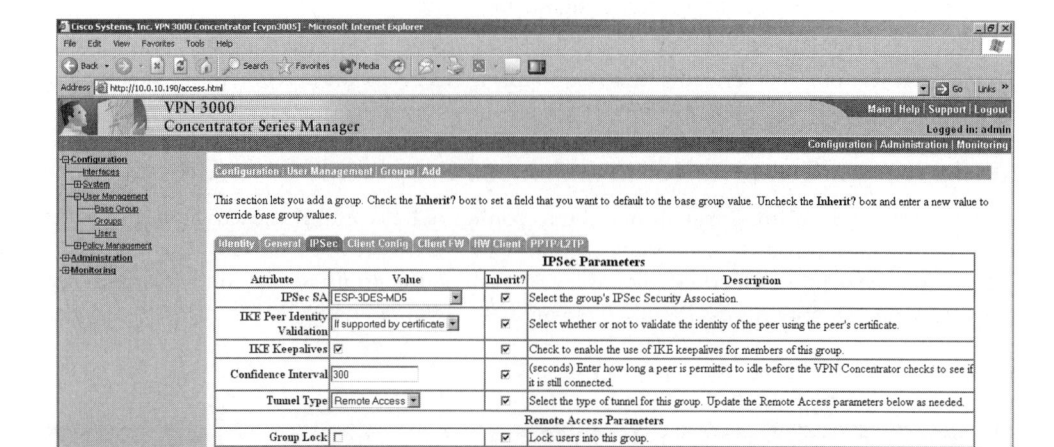

Seven options are available for configuration on this tab. All of them deal directly with the IPSec tunnel parameters or the authentication and authorization of the tunnel. Table 18.1 outlines the use of some of the attributes.

TABLE 18.1 Important IPSec Group Attributes

Attribute	Description
IPSec SA	Assigns a security association (SA) to the group.
IKE Peer Identity Validation	The VPN Concentrator can use an identity certificate to validate the user in addition to normal passwords. Three options are available: Required, in which the client must have a proper ID certificate; If Supported By Certificate, in which the client is authenticated if it presents appropriate certificate information; and Do Not Check, which means ignore all ID certificate information.

TABLE 18.1 Important IPSec Group Attributes *(continued)*

Attribute	Description
Tunnel Type	Allows you to choose the tunnel type. There are two options: Remote Access, which is the typical setting for hardware and software VPN clients; and LAN-to-LAN, which is reserved for whole network type connections and is typically used between two VPN 3000 Concentrators. If you select LAN-to-LAN, the IPSec SA attribute described previously is ignored. LAN-to-LAN tunnels are discussed in greater detail in the "Configuring LAN-to-LAN IPSec" section later in this chapter.
Group Lock	If this attribute is deselected, the concentrator won't enforce the association between an authenticated user and their membership in this group. Any authenticated user can use these IPSec group parameters even if they aren't specifically configured as a member of this group.
Authentication	Selects the destination server type for authentication of users who attach using this group.
Authorization Type	Selects the destination server type for authorization of users who attach using this group.
DN Field	Tells the concentrator which certificate field to use as the username when authenticating and authorizing clients.

Configuring Client Properties for a Group

The Client Config tab is an extension of the attributes of the IPSec tab. In fact, previous versions of the concentrator grouped the Client Config and IPSec attributes together under one tab.

To customize client properties, click the Client Config tab on the group form. You'll see the Client Configuration Parameters options page, as shown in Figure 18.11.

Six options are available on this tab. The tab is broken down based on the type of client. The top section deals with the Cisco Client, the middle section sets information for the Microsoft Client, and the bottom section has attributes that apply to both. Table 18.2 outlines the use of some of the attributes.

> **Note:** Newer versions of the concentrator software support a feature called *local LAN access*. It allows split tunneling to the point that the client can access local LAN objects so that a user can be connected remotely and print locally to a network printer.

FIGURE 18.11 Client Config group properties

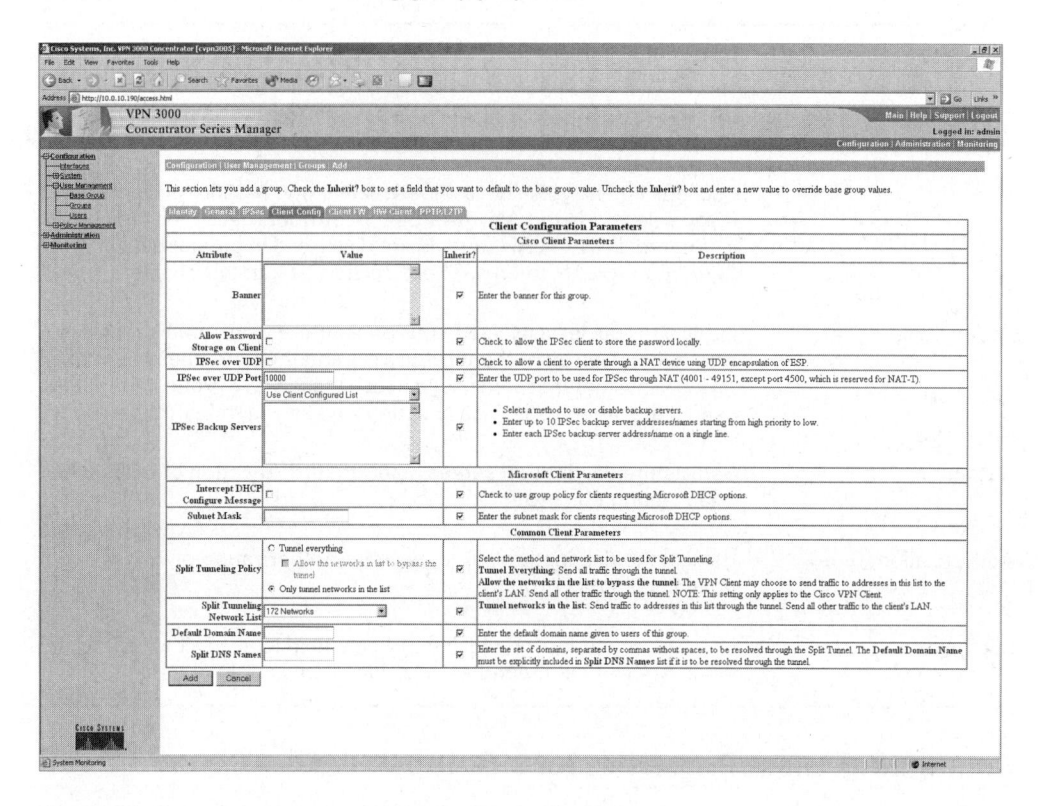

TABLE 18.2 Important Client Configuration Group Attributes

Attribute	Description
Allow Password Storage on Client	Forces the client to destroy any saved client passwords.
IPSec over UDP	Allows the client to connect by encapsulating the Encapsulating Security Payload (ESP) data into a User Datagram Protocol (UDP) packet. This method is often used when operating through Network Address Translation (NAT).
IPSec over UDP Port	Sets the IPSec over UDP port number.

Configuring User and Policy Management

TABLE 18.2 Important Client Configuration Group Attributes *(continued)*

Attribute	Description
Split Tunneling Policy	Has two basic settings: Tunnel Everything, which sends all data via the tunnel; and Only Tunnel Networks In List, which sends only specific networks via the tunnel. Allow The Networks In List To Bypass The Tunnel is a suboption of the Tunnel Everything attribute. It's the opposite of the Only Tunnel Networks In List option.
Split Tunneling Network List	Selects a preconfigured list of networks for evaluation by the Split Tunneling policy. These lists are configured from the Configuration ➢ Policy Management ➢ Traffic Management ➢ Network Lists menu.
Split DNS Names	When using split tunneling, you may wish to use the tunnel to resolve certain domain names while allowing others to be resolved normally. This attribute is a comma-separated list of domain names that will use the tunnel.

Real World Scenario

How and When Should I Configure Split Tunneling?

Like many features, the use and configuration of split tunneling varies widely. If you ask 10 system administrators if and how you should configure split tunneling, you're likely to get 10 different answers. Here are some things to consider:

Security

Split tunneling is always a security issue. By default, split tunneling is disabled, and all network traffic is delivered via the tunnel. Using split tunneling opens the door for bypassing security measures. Two primary issues arise. First, most corporate network infrastructures include security features such as firewalls and web filtering. Use of split tunneling may allow a user to circumvent the protections of the firewall and the restrictions of the web filters. Second, if the client is permitted to contact other network devices independently of the tunnel, it becomes a potential entry point for hackers or worms to piggyback their data on the client's tunnel to gain access to a network that is otherwise secure.

Cisco has addressed the second issue to some extent with the addition of support for third-party and built-in firewalls in the VPN client.

Performance

On the other side of the coin is the performance trade-off. Forcing traffic that isn't ultimately destined for the other end of the tunnel wastes both bandwidth and encryption capacity. Assume a telecommuting client takes a lunch break and starts surfing the Web at an average rate of 56Kbps. Further assume that the client's company is using the same service for both VPN traffic and general web access. That user will waste about 114Kbps (56Kbps in + 2.5 percent IPSec overhead + 56Kbps out) of Internet access bandwidth that could be avoided with split tunneling. Additionally, VPN Concentrators have a limited encryption capacity. This user's web surfing consumes about 1 percent of the capacity of a 3005 only to have the 3005 tear down the traffic and send it back out unencrypted anyway.

Politics and Support

A third factor that's rarely considered are the political and support issues of split tunneling. Often, VPN clients aren't just internal corporate employees. Many times, VPN access is opened to business partners and independent contractors. In this case, consider whether it's appropriate for the client to be sending personal or unrelated data via the tunnel. Where will the support responsibilities fall when the VPN configuration causes problems with other services? Does the administrator have the legal or political right to enforce firewall and security configurations on a PC system that their company doesn't own?

For example, I recently visited a customer that was doing independent transcription work for a local hospital. The hospital had installed a Cisco VPN 3030 and expected the client to use the tunnel to pick up and drop off materials. Most of the hospital's contractors were individuals who worked from home on single PCs. However, this customer was a small company with an internal network and server. The hospital had decided to disable split tunneling since the VPN tunnel was used only to pick up and drop off data. The hospital had the expectation that the contractors would connect and disconnect as needed. Since split tunneling was disabled, the customer lost access to their file server every time they tried to connect to the hospital. Should I send the bill to my customer or to the hospital?

Suggestions

Try to classify users into groups based on the concerns listed here. Balance your need for security with the costs of supporting the client and providing additional hardware and network capacity. Consult your company's computer usage and security policies. Often, third-party computer users are bound by a security policy as part of a contract. This might authorize the administrator to install and enforce rules on the contractor's system. Have a clear understanding of the political ramifications for support and security issues with each of these groups of users.

Setting Up Users

In addition to adding and configuring groups to the concentrator, you can also add and configure *users*. To add a user, from the main VPN Concentrator Manager window, choose Configuration ➤ User Management ➤ Users. On the Users screen, click the Add button to create a new user. You can also select an existing user and click the Modify button to change that user's properties or click the Delete button to remove that user.

After you click the Add or Modify button, you'll see the user form, as shown in Figure 18.12.

The username and password configured here are what the user will need to enter into the VPN client when the user wants to create a tunnel. This username and password function the same as a shared secret key for IPSec (discussed in Chapter 16, "Introduction to Virtual Private Networks").

FIGURE 18.12 Configuring a user

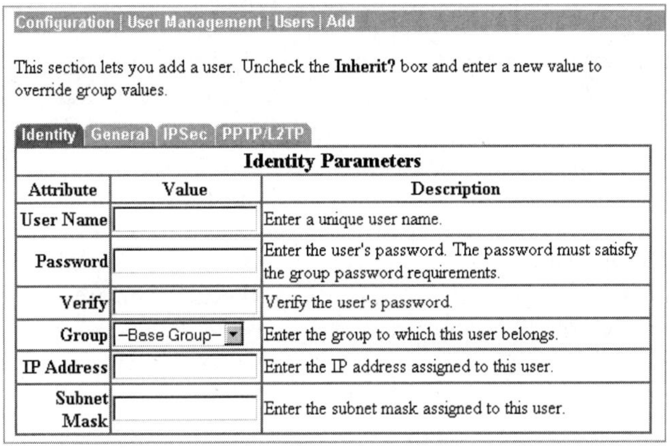
Configuration | User Management | Users | Add

This section lets you add a user. Uncheck the **Inherit?** box and enter a new value to override group values.

Identity | General | IPSec | PPTP/L2TP

Identity Parameters

Attribute	Value	Description
User Name		Enter a unique user name.
Password		Enter the user's password. The password must satisfy the group password requirements.
Verify		Verify the user's password.
Group	-Base Group-	Enter the group to which this user belongs.
IP Address		Enter the IP address assigned to this user.
Subnet Mask		Enter the subnet mask assigned to this user.

In addition to forcing the change of a password, you can change which group the user belongs to. (As noted earlier, users belong to the base group by default.) You can also assign a static IP address for this user whenever a tunnel is created.

Remember that a maximum of 100 total objects can be placed in the internal authentication database. If you set up more than 100 users and/or groups, you must establish an external authentication method, as described in the next section.

Configuring an Authentication Server

Rather than configure the internal user database, you can configure the VPN Concentrator to use an external authentication server. To set up an authentication server, from the main VPN

Concentrator Manager window, select Configuration ➤ System ➤ Servers ➤ Authentication. You'll see a list of currently configured authentication servers and the actions you can perform:

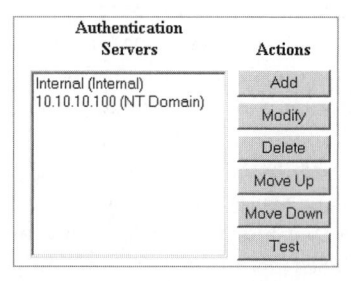

The order in which the servers are shown is the order in which they will be tried. It's a good idea to configure the internal database with administration logins. That way, if the authentication server is unavailable for some reason, an administrator will still be able to authenticate. Because the order is important, two buttons let you move a server up or down in the list.

To add an authentication server, click the Add button. You can modify the properties of an existing authentication server or delete one by clicking the appropriate button.

The Test button allows you to verify that communications exist between the VPN Concentrator and the authentication server, and that the authentication server is correctly configured. Use this testing method before putting the concentrator into production. When you click the Test button, you're prompted to enter a username and a password. Then click OK to perform the test. If communication between the concentrator and the authentication server is set up correctly and the authentication server can validate the authentication request, you'll see the response "Authentication Successful," as shown here:

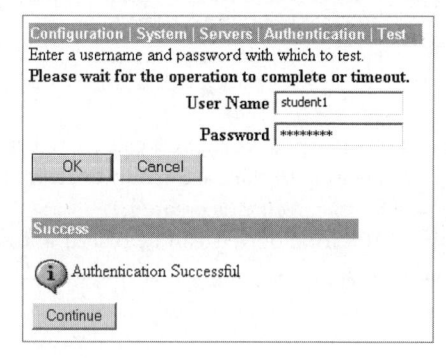

Configuring Access Hours and Filters

The IT department often needs to work with the Human Resources department to determine what users can and can't do with their computers. Telecommuting, traveling users, and users taking laptops home bring up new issues. How can you extend corporate policies to remote connections? Setting access hours policies and filtering traffic don't provide total solutions, but they do help.

Setting Access Hours

Configuring an *access hours policy* determines the hours during which a user can create a tunnel. A user may be authorized to create a tunnel between the hours of 6 A.M. and 7 P.M. Monday through Friday, but not during any other time.

To set access hours, from the main VPN Concentrator Manager window, select Configuration ≻ Policy Management ≻ Access Hours and then click the Add button. You'll see the Add screen, shown in Figure 18.13.

Specify a name for this policy profile. Then set whether the user can or can't access the network during the given time span, and specify the starting and stopping time for each day.

After you've configured the access hours policy, you can assign it to users and groups by choosing it on the General tab of the configuration form (as described in the "Setting Up Groups" and "Setting Up Users" sections earlier in this chapter). An access hour policy won't be put into effect automatically.

FIGURE 18.13 Setting access hours

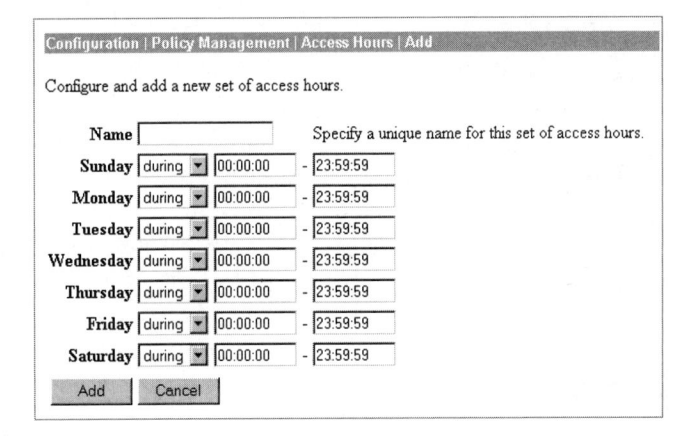

Filtering Traffic

A *rule* is a single statement that allows something to be done or prevents it from happening. A rule is responsible for traffic headed to UDP port 500 (ISAKMP) being permitted to enter the concentrator. A rule can be compared to a single line in an access control list (ACL).

The concentrator uses rules to build *filters*. A filter is just a big set of `permit` statements. If the traffic trying to come into the concentrator matches one of the types of traffic that is permitted, then the packet may continue on its way. You can configure filters and place them on physical interfaces to prevent undesirable traffic from entering the concentrator.

WARNING You can place filters on any of the concentrator's physical interfaces. Just be careful not to filter out administrative traffic on the appropriate interface!

> ### Real World Scenario
>
> **Access Hours Restriction Considerations**
>
> Determining the hours during which a user can connect is a task best left to management. It isn't unusual for one department to want very restrictive access, while another department wants wide-open access.
>
> To get an initial feeling for how things can pan out, look around your company. Salespeople tend to have a lot of flexibility, and their managers will probably request the same for access to network resources. Customer service agents generally don't have much flexibility, and their managers usually want to give them access hours that approach regular working hours plus expected overtime.
>
> Be careful when making recommendations regarding hours of access. It isn't unusual for administrator to get calls on weekends and evenings to extend access for users who need it.

To add a filter, from the main VPN Concentrator Manager window, select Configuration ➢ Policy Management ➢ Traffic Management ➢ Filters, and then click the Add button. You'll see the screen shown in Figure 18.14. Specify a name for your filter, and enter a description. You can change the settings for the Default Action, Source Routing, and Fragments options, but the defaults are acceptable in most cases.

Because the default for a filter is to drop packets, a filter with no rules in it won't allow any traffic through. Click the Add button to add rules to the filter. You'll see the Assign Rules to Filter screen, as shown in Figure 18.15.

FIGURE 18.14 Creating a filter

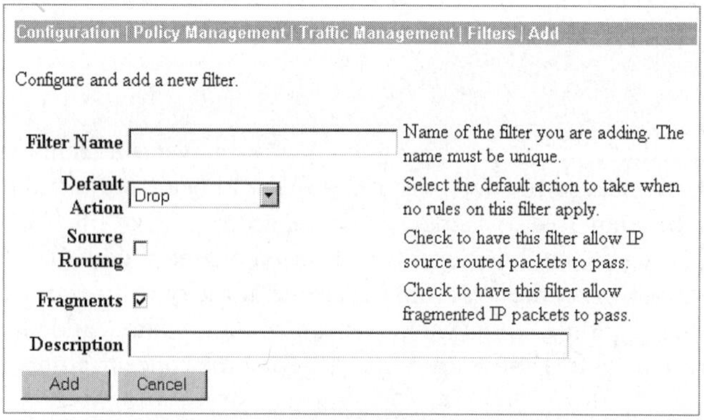

FIGURE 18.15 Adding rules to a filter

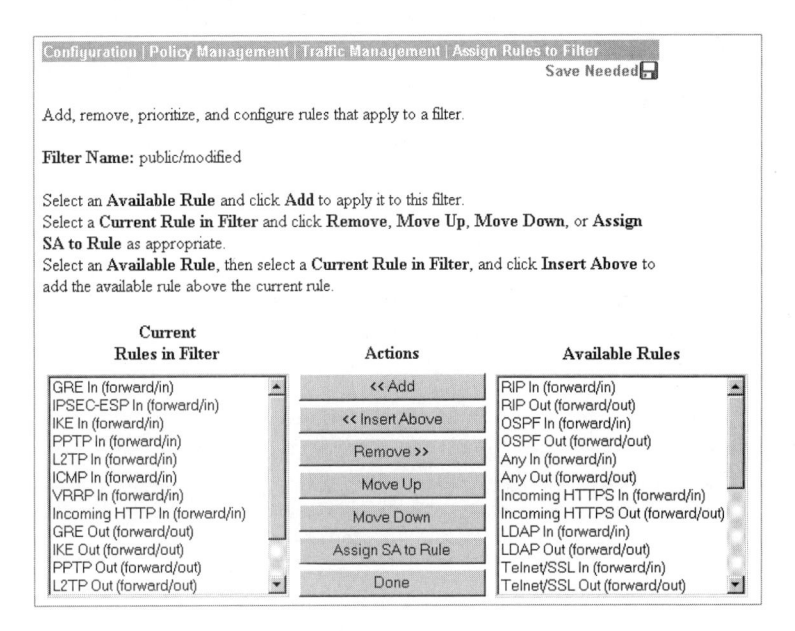

Select the available rules that you wish to include in the filter, and click on the Add button. The traffic represented here is the type that will be hitting the interface. For the public interface, this will consist of some management traffic but mainly tunnel protocols. The private interface can have tunnels, but it usually deals with basic traffic.

The default filter for the private interface allows HTTP traffic; the default filter for the public interface doesn't. If it's necessary to configure the concentrator from outside the trusted network, you must either allow HTTP (which isn't recommended) or create a tunnel to permit this access.

Configuring Backup on the Hardware Client

The purpose of the backup server is for the VPN 3002 Hardware Clients to have an alternative location in the event the site configured as the primary fails. Backups can be configured either by the group on the concentrator or, in the case of the 3002 Hardware Client, on an individual basis.

A company can have two locations that their remote users can attach to. In Figure 18.16, the primary connection point has been configured as 161.44.246.15. If, for whatever reason, the primary isn't available for default 8-second timeout period, the client will automatically switch over to the second site 192.156.10.1. Up to 10 backup servers can be listed, and the concentrator will try each one in succession (but only one time through, if no connections are made).

FIGURE 18.16 The Backup Configuration

As you'd expect, the backup list must be configured prior to the client connection as it's downloaded at connection; therefore a backup server list can't be downloaded from a backup on the primary upon connection. Any changes made to the server won't take effect until the next time the client connects to the primary.

Configuring Load Balancing

There's a difference between setting up a concentrator to back up another concentrator and setting up two concentrators to share the load. Configuring a backup, or *hot spare*, concentrator is accomplished with the Virtual Router Redundancy Protocol (VRRP). Configuring load balancing involves setting up concentrator clusters. Concentrators can do both backup and load balancing, but not at the same time.

> **NOTE** This section covers cluster configuration for load balancing. For information about configuring VRRP, refer to www.cisco.com/univercd/cc/td/doc/product/vpn/vpn3000/3_6/config/iprout.htm#xtocid42.

Understanding Clusters

Routers, firewalls, and other static devices that support a large number of clients through a single tunnel attach to a specific concentrator. This way, the administrator can distribute the processing load. This is helpful because the load varies: At a certain time, a LAN tunnel might be supporting just a few packets per second; then, a minute later, it might be supporting thousands of packets.

Software and hardware clients also connect to concentrators. Because of the dynamic nature of client tunneling and the relatively small number of packets crossing the tunnel, it's advantageous to make attaching to concentrators as flexible as possible.

To recap, remote access sessions and clients can be load balanced, but LAN-to-LAN connections, routers, firewalls, and other concentrators can't.

A cluster works as follows:

1. Clients attach to a virtual cluster master using a virtual cluster IP address. This address must be on the same IP network as the IP address on the cluster members' public interfaces.
2. The master device forwards the real IP address of a secondary cluster member, which is the concentrator that is currently carrying the least load.
3. The client requests a VPN session with that device.

Redundancy rules require that devices in the cluster be able to take over for the master if it fails. When you're setting up a cluster, the faster device will most likely become the cluster master. Each concentrator model has a default priority, ranging from 1 through 10, as shown in Table 18.3. The priority is used to determine which device will become the master when a master isn't present. For example, if a 3015 Concentrator (default priority 3) comes on line 5 minutes before a 3080 Concentrator (default priority 9), the 3015 will remain the master; there is no forced election. If they came up at the same time, the 3080 would become the master because it has the higher priority. You can change the priorities as part of cluster configuration, as described in the next section. If there is a tie, the device with the lowest IP address becomes the master.

TABLE 18.3 Load Balancing Default Priorities

Concentrator Model	Default Priority
3005	1
3015	3
3030	5
3060	7
3080	9

Concentrators use the *Virtual Cluster Agent (VCA)* protocol to communicate with other cluster members. Because VCA communications aren't designed to be routed, each member of the cluster must belong to the same IP network as every other cluster member, on both the public and private interface. For cluster communications to work, each member must allow the VCA packets in and out. Because each interface has a filter set, you need to ensure that VCA is allowed in and out of the concentrator on both the public and private interfaces. Figure 18.12 (shown earlier) gives an example of changing the rules for a filter.

Configuring the Cluster

Cluster configuration is fairly easy for each member. The main point to remember is that the configurations for the members need to support the same clients, because these devices will be doing load sharing.

To configure a cluster for load balancing, from the main VPN Concentrator Manager window, select Configuration ≻ System ≻ Load Balancing. Here, you configure several items:

Cluster IP Address This is the virtual IP address that clients initially talk to. Each cluster member needs to know this IP address in case it becomes the master.

Cluster UDP Port This is the port used for cluster communication. This port is used in the filter when VCA has been allowed. If the wrong port is specified, no communication occurs.

Encryption Should IPSec be used to encrypt the VCA communication among cluster members? All devices should have the same setting for this: enabled or disabled.

IPSec Shared Secret This is the shared secret that's used for IPSec encryption of the VCA. You'll need to enter the shared secret twice.

Enable Load Balancing This is a check box for enabling and disabling load balancing on the device.

Priority You can change the default priority (based on the hardware model) by changing the number in this field.

After you've configured the Load Balancing screen options, click the Apply button, and load balancing can begin. Don't forget to save the configuration.

Configuring LAN-to-LAN IPSec

A *LAN-to-LAN IPSec* tunnel exists when two concentrators are serving as the ends of a tunnel and there is a separate IP network on each side of the tunnel. Setting up LAN-to-LAN IPSec on routers and PIX Firewalls is part of the overall IOS IPSec configuration; however, the concentrator deals with this setup a bit differently.

To configure LAN-to-LAN IPSec on a concentrator, from the VPN Manager window, choose Configuration ≻ System ≻ Tunneling Protocols ≻ IPSec ≻ IPSec LAN-to-LAN. You'll see the IPSec LAN-To-LAN screen, as shown in Figure 18.17.

To add a LAN-to-LAN connection, click the Add button. You'll see the screen shown in Figure 18.18.

Configuring User and Policy Management 567

FIGURE 18.17 The VPN Manager IPSec LAN-To-LAN screen

FIGURE 18.18 LAN-to-LAN configuration

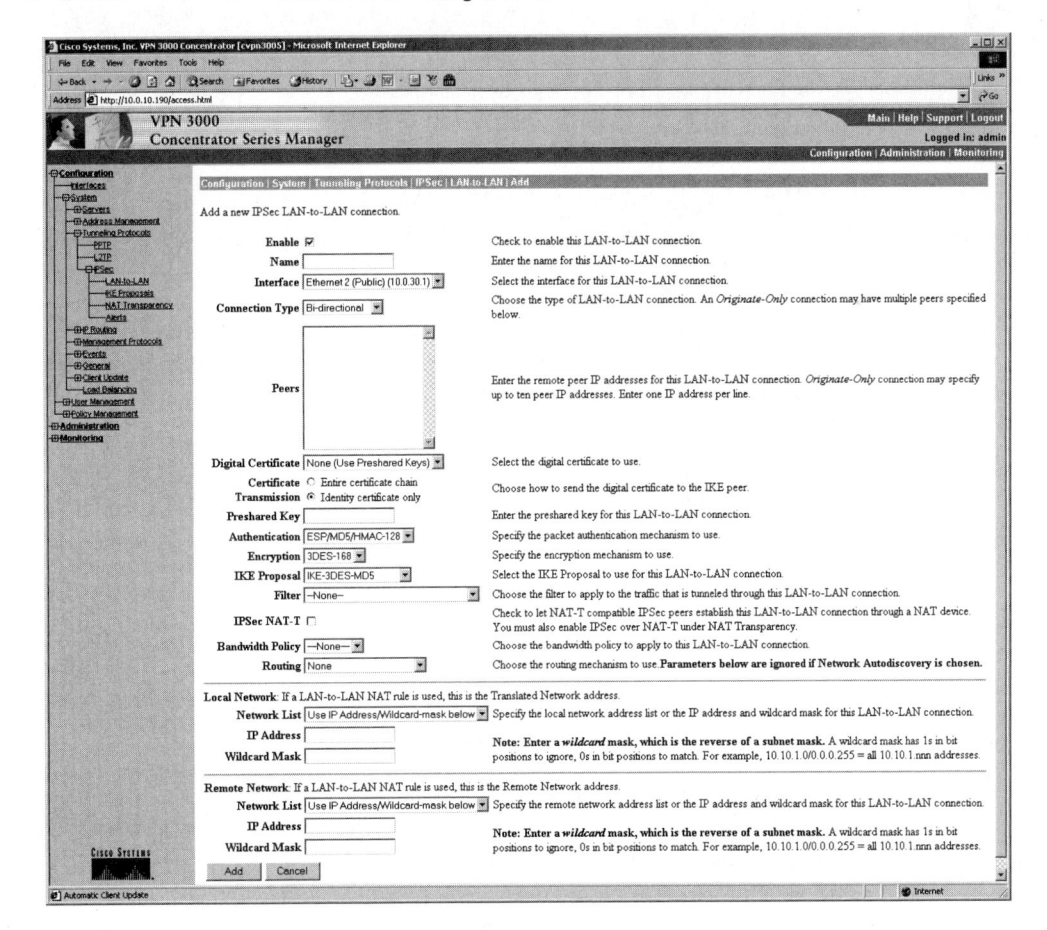

Specify the information for the new connection, as follows:

1. In the Name field, give the configuration a name.
2. From the Interface drop-down list, select the interface that the tunnel terminates on.
3. In the Peer field, enter the public IP address of the peer on the other end.
4. Choose the authentication method: digital certificate or pre-shared key.
5. Configure IKE by selecting an authentication method from the Authentication drop-down list.
6. Configure IPSec by selecting the encryption method from the Encryption drop-down list.
7. Select the IKE proposal from the drop-down list.
8. Select the Network Auto-Discovery check box if you're unsure of the networks available locally or remotely.
9. Configure what type of traffic needs to be protected for the local network. Choose a network list or select the Use IP Address/Wildcard Mask Below option, and then set a network in the fields below. Take care to use a wildcard mask instead of a normal network mask.
10. Configure what type of traffic needs to be protected on the remote network by specifying its network list or IP address and wildcard mask.
11. When each section has been configured, click Add to add the LAN-to-LAN IPSec connection.

In the next section, we'll look at basic troubleshooting for LAN-to-LAN connections.

Troubleshooting LAN-to-LAN Connections

Any LAN-to-LAN tunnel can have problems during setup, like any other tunnel. Check in Administration ➢ Sessions to see if the tunnel has come up. Remember that LAN-to-LAN sessions are listed separately from administrative and remote-access sessions.

If the tunnel hasn't come up, the issue may be related to configuration. One side might be set to use a pre-shared key while the other uses certificates; this would be an authentication issue. If pre-shared keys are used, one might have been entered incorrectly. There could also be a routing issue, or the policies or proposals might be different. Make sure that configuration items are identical where needed.

Updating Clients Automatically

If you're responsible for the VPN connections for many users, and you discover that their VPN software is flawed or outdated, what do you do? The correct answer is to update it. What if those people are scattered around the country, or even around the world? No, you don't e-mail them a file; instead, you automatically update the client.

Understanding Automatic Client Updates

You can automatically update both software and hardware clients. When an update is sent out, it's an Internet Key Exchange (IKE) packet with an encrypted message detailing the update information.

Configuring User and Policy Management

If the update is being sent to a hardware client, the update includes the location of a Trivial File Transfer Protocol (TFTP) server where the client can automatically update its software. The hardware client stores images in two locations: one is the active image, and one is the backup. The client runs a check to ensure that the file is a valid image before marking it active and rebooting. In the event there is a problem, an administrator can mark the backup file as active and reboot.

If you're sending the update to software clients, things get a bit tricky because users are involved. If the client needs updating, users are told where they need to get the file. The update location is a web server where you've placed the file. How does this differ from your e-mailing the file? The IKE packet checks to see whether the person is using an acceptable version (which you specify when you configure the client update process, as described in the next section) and informs the user of the update and its location *only* if the version in use isn't acceptable. This is easier for an administrator than keeping records of exactly which software version is running on every remote computer.

Configuring Automatic Client Updates

You need to take two steps to configure automatic client updates: enabling the process and configuring client update properties. These steps begin from the Client Update screen, accessed from the main VPN Concentrator Manager window by selecting Configuration ➢ System ➢ Client Update, as shown in Figure 18.19.

To enable the process, click the Enable link on the Client Update screen. The Enable Client Update screen contains an Enabled check box. Select it, and then click Apply (see Figure 18.20).

FIGURE 18.19 The Client Update screen

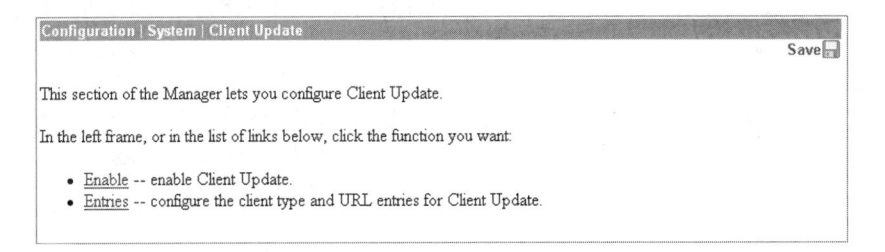

FIGURE 18.20 The Enable screen

To configure the client update process, click the Entries link on the Client Update screen. On the Entries screen, as seen in Figure 18.21, you can start configuring the process. If client update entries are already listed, you'll see the type of client and the acceptable version. Click the Add button to create a new entry. This brings up the Add screen, shown in Figure 18.22

FIGURE 18.21 The Entries screen

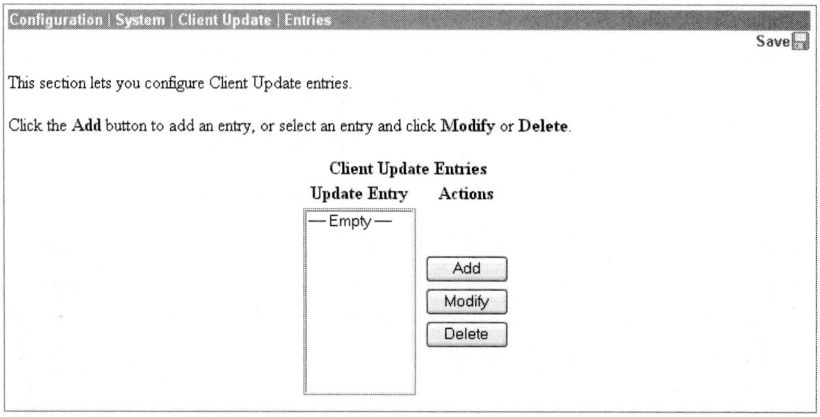

FIGURE 18.22 The Add Screen

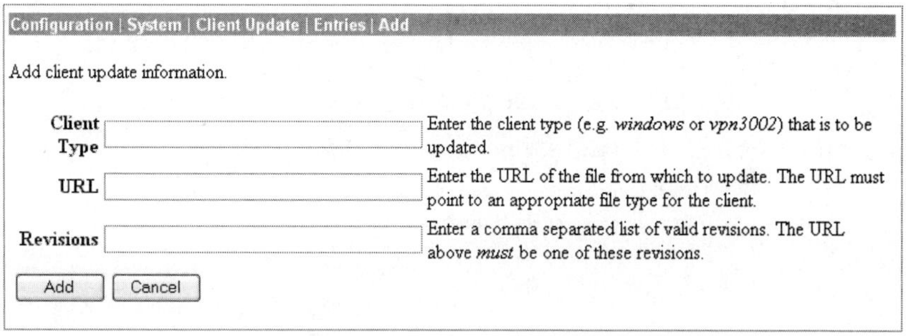

You need to configure three properties for client updates to work properly:

Client Type Configuring the client type is simple but exacting. You have a choice of four options or keywords: Windows, Win9*x*, WinNT, or vpn3002. You must use the correct case and spelling for the type of client you want. Using Windows as the client type means that the update will go to both types of Windows clients—those designed for Windows 95/98/Me and those designed for Windows NT/2000/XP. Use the Win9*x* client type if you want to send an update only to clients using Windows 95/98/Me. Use the WinNT client type if you want to send an update only to clients using Windows NT/2000/XP. Use the vpn3002 client type to send update messages to the hardware client.

URL The URL is the path to the update file. To activate the Launch button for the software client notification, the path must be an HTTP or HTTPS URL. For the hardware client to get its update, the file must be found on a TFTP server, so the URL must be a TFTP path.

Revisions When you configure the concentrator for updating, you state which software versions are available and which versions are acceptable for current use. You might decide that 3.6 is the only version available, but one of the versions listed must match the version of the file accessed by the path in the URL field.

Monitoring Auto-Updates

You can track client auto-update notifications using the event log. The event log keeps two types of entries that are useful for tracking updates and versions. Here is an example of two such entries:

```
20 09/30/2003 04:33:52.010 SEV=5 IKE/184 RPT=1 10.0.30.99
Group [sybex] User [testuser]
Client OS: WinNT
Client Application Version: 4.0.2 (D)

37 09/30/2003 04:33:53.030 SEV=4 AUTOUPDATE/19 RPT=1
Sending IKE Notify: Autoupdating clients in group [sybex]
Client delay: 0, instID: 000003EA
```

The top entry is from the IKE event class. It identifies the version of the client as 4.0.2 (D) with an OS of WinNT. The second entry is from the AUTOUPDATE event class. This log entry explains that a client has connected and has been notified that an update is available.

Since the update process involves downloading the software from another system, there isn't a good way to determine if the client actually updated without manually associating the client with another IKE message showing a newer client version. Many Syslog servers can relay statistical information to the administrator. It may be useful to forward the number of AUTOUPDATE notifications that are sent; this is a good indication of the number of unupdated clients still out there.

Setting Up the Stateful Firewall

The VPN client has an integrated Zone Labs firewall, which is part of the Cisco Integrated Client (CIC). CIC is a combination of the Unified Client and a firewall. You can use this firewall to filter Internet traffic when the VPN is active.

The stateful firewall feature is a setting on the VPN client that the user might or might not be able to turn off and on. If the firewall is on, it's on for all types of traffic. By default, it allows all types of traffic out but only DHCP and ESP traffic in. It's convenient but rather inflexible in its most basic form.

Another way to set up the stateful firewall is through the concentrator and its centralized protection policy (CPP). The CPP allows an administrator to define a set of rules for permitting and denying Internet traffic. A policy for the CPP is defined on the concentrator, and then the policy is pushed down to the CIC for use during the VPN connection. This allows for dynamic settings for each firewall. Not all firewalls that can be used support this particular feature.

The concentrator has the flexibility to require a firewall, require no firewall, or make it optional. When the VPN tunnel is first set up, the client notifies the concentrator which firewalls are available for use. If the optional setting is used and the client doesn't have the correct type of firewall, the tunnel remains up. If a specific type of firewall is required and the client doesn't have it, the tunnel is shut down.

> **TIP** Consider making firewalls optional during a major upgrade. Doing so will avoid problems if the newly installed client is unable to correctly negotiate parameters with the concentrator.

Next, let's take a closer look at the setup of the CIC and the CPP.

Using the CIC

The easiest way to provide firewall-based protection is to use the CIC included in the VPN client. It filters most inbound connections, excluding the VPN tunnel itself. It's easy to set up, since the user can turn it on. Also, as explained in Chapter 17, "Introduction to Cisco VPN Devices," you can preconfigure the client with this setting and force it on by placing this entry in the vpnclient.ini file:

```
!StatefulFirewall=1
```

The user won't be able to change the setting from inside the VPN client.

The client PC can use regular firewall software as a firewall, and each can be configured as necessary to keep out certain types of traffic. Many types of external firewalls are supported: Sygate Personal Firewall, Sygate Pro, Sygate Security Agent, ZoneAlarm, ZoneAlarm Pro, Zone Labs Integrity, and BlackICE Defender. Each of these may be configured to provide more flexibility to the filter than the CIC's "always on" feature offers.

Using the CIC isn't a popular option for security-conscious companies because the administrator doesn't have much control over it. One way you can retain control is to use the Zone Labs Integrity Agent and Integrity server. You can configure the server with the policies, and the agent on each PC will grab the policies and configure the local firewall. (For more information about using Zone Labs products, visit the company's website at http://www.zonelabs.com.)

Configuring CPP

To use the concentrator's CPP to set up the firewall, you must first configure the policy you want enabled on your clients. You configure this policy in the same way that you configure policies for interface traffic, as shown earlier in Figures 18.14 and 18.15. You need to define a rule, create a policy, link the rule to the policy, and assign the policy to the CPP.

Once you've configured a new policy for the clients, you need to configure the CPP. To do so, go to the appropriate group. Begin by selecting Configuration ➢ Settings. On the Settings screen, select Base Group to specify settings for the base group, or select a specific group to set up. Modify the group, and click the tab for Client FW. In the firewall configuration pane, select whether the firewall is to be required or optional, the type of firewall, and the policy.

Among your choices for the policy are Policy Pushed, which requires you to select the filter policy you just configured, and Policy from Server, which uses a *centralized protection server* (a Zone Labs Integrity server) to provide policies to the client. If you're using a centralized protection server, you must tell the concentrator where the server is located. Choose Configuration ≻ System ≻ Servers ≻ Firewall, and enter the IP address of the server and the port number for communication (see Figure 18.23).

As of concentrator version 3.6, all supported firewall types are listed in the drop-down list. For future expansion, there are also vendor and product codes that can be used. The codes for the currently supported CIC software are shown in Table 18.4.

FIGURE 18.23 The Firewall screen

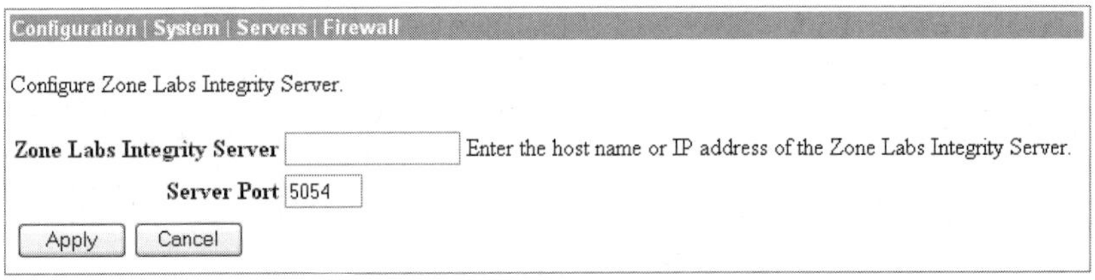

TABLE 18.4 Currently Supported Vendor and Firewall Codes

Vendor	Vendor Code	Product	Product Code
Cisco	1	Cisco Integrated Client	1
Zone Labs	2	ZoneAlarm	1
		ZoneAlarm Pro	2
		Zone Labs Integrity	3
NetworkICE	3	BlackICE Defender	1
Sygate	4	Sygate Personal Firewall	1
		Sygate Pro	2
		Sygate Security Agent	3
Cisco	5	Cisco Intrusion Prevention Security Agent	1

Configuring the Use of IPSec Digital Certificates

IPSec is one of the methods you can use to create tunnels between the VPN concentrator and the client, in addition to L2TP and PPTP. IPSec has two methods of authenticating the ends of the tunnel: pre-shared keys and digital certificates.

Setting up the VPN Concentrator to use a pre-shared key is simple because all that is required is the user's password. Setting up the concentrator to use a digital certificate is more complicated because the concentrator doesn't have a way to talk directly to the certificate authority (CA). All communications must be done via a third party—a PC that has access to the CA.

In the following sections, we'll take a closer look at Public Key Infrastructure (PKI). You must have a good understanding of how to request, install, and configure a certificate as well as the management of the user tunnels.

Introducing the Public Key Infrastructure

One of the most important concepts for certificates is the *Public Key Infrastructure (PKI)*. The word *public* here is a misnomer, because the infrastructure doesn't need to be public at all. The PKI refers to the directory of objects linked together via certificates.

At the core of the PKI is the CA. Although more than one server can be responsible for generating certificates, there is only one root CA, which is in charge of the entire system. The other servers that generate certificates are known as *subordinate CAs* or *registration authorities* (*RAs*). So, the PKI includes the root CA, any RAs, and any users that have received a certificate from any of the servers. An RA acts as a proxy for the CA. Figure 18.24 illustrates the PKI hierarchy.

FIGURE 18.24 The Public Key Infrastructure (PKI) hierarchy

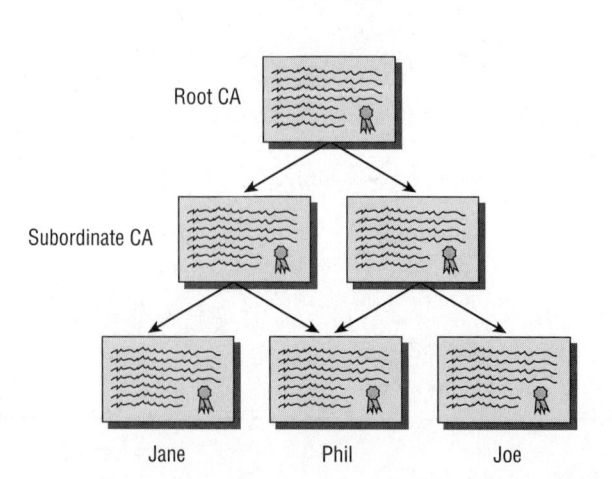

> **Note:** When you're configuring a concentrator to use certificates, the IKE authentication needs to specify RSA Keys instead of a pre-shared key.

If a device gets a certificate from an RA, then it gets an identity certificate for the RA, as well as one for the root CA. Every device in the PKI has a copy of the root CA's public key so it can decrypt certificates from other devices in the PKI.

When you're attempting to get a certificate from a PKI, the request can often be directed only to the CA. If there are any RAs, they will often forward the request to the CA, but this usually defeats the purpose of placing RAs in the PKI in the first place. If the CA is handling all the requests, there is a significant delay in large networks. Many certificate server implementations allow the server administrator to specify that if a request states it's to be handled only by the CA, that request is dropped.

Requesting and Installing Concentrator Certificates

You would choose to use digital certificates because you need to verify both ends of the tunnel, but there are too many devices to make using pre-shared keys a viable option. The CA fills the role of a trusted third party and can be hosted in-house, or the service can be bought on a certificate-by-certificate basis. The standard for certificates is X.509.

Several vendors have CA products that can provide certificates to Cisco networking devices as well as to PCs. The CA that comes with Windows 2000 Server instantly became one of the most popular products of this type when Windows 2000 was released. In addition, Entrust, Verisign, and Baltimore Technologies offer CA products.

Each device that wishes to communicate securely needs to have a certificate installed on it. Each device must transfer information to the CA to request the certificate. The standard for the method of communication to the CA is called *Public Key Cryptography Standard #10 (PKCS #10)*.

Once the PKCS #10 certificate request is sent to the CA, the CA needs to run through several steps before a certificate can be sent back to the requesting device. The first thing the CA must do is determine that the request came from a source that should be receiving a certificate. There are a couple of ways to do this:

- The administrator of the CA often sets up the CA so that requests are approved manually. CAs have an area where pending certificate requests reside until they're approved or discarded.
- The CA may require a password before generating the certificate. This method works well with routers and firewalls.

Once the request has been authenticated, the PKCS #10 is turned into an identity certificate. An *identity certificate* identifies a particular device. The PKCS #10 is combined with some information about the CA, and a hash is generated. The hash is then encrypted using the CA's private key, and the hash is added to the identity certificate. Finally, the certificate is sent to the requestor. This process is illustrated in Figure 18.25.

When the concentrator gets the certificate, it extracts the CA's public key from the CA ID certificate, assuming it has a copy of the certificate for the CA. It then decrypts the two certificate hashes and verifies their authenticity.

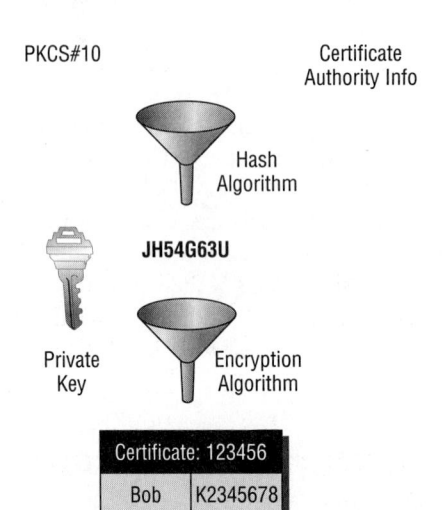

FIGURE 18.25 Generating the certificate

Now that we've looked at the overall process, let's see how to configure certificate requests and installations for the VPN Concentrator.

Configuring the Request for a Concentrator Certificate

To configure the request for a certificate for the concentrator, from the main VPN Concentrator Manager window, select Administration ➢ Certificate Management ➢ Enrollment. You'll see the form shown in Figure 18.26. This form can be used to generate certificates for both IPSec and SSL.

You must fill in the information needed by the CA before it can generate the certificate:

Common Name (CN) The CN of an object is what it's known as. A user might be known by the username, and a computer might be known by a serial number or asset tag number.

Organizational Unit (OU) An OU is normally a subdivision of the Organization. If the Organization is large, the OU might be a division. If the Organization is small, the OU might be a department.

Organization (O) An O refers to the entire organizational entity. Cisco would be an O, whereas Sales would be an OU under Cisco.

Locality (L) The L is normally the city the device resides in, but it could be a county, township, or some other method of identifying a geographic location.

FIGURE 18.26 Creating a certificate request

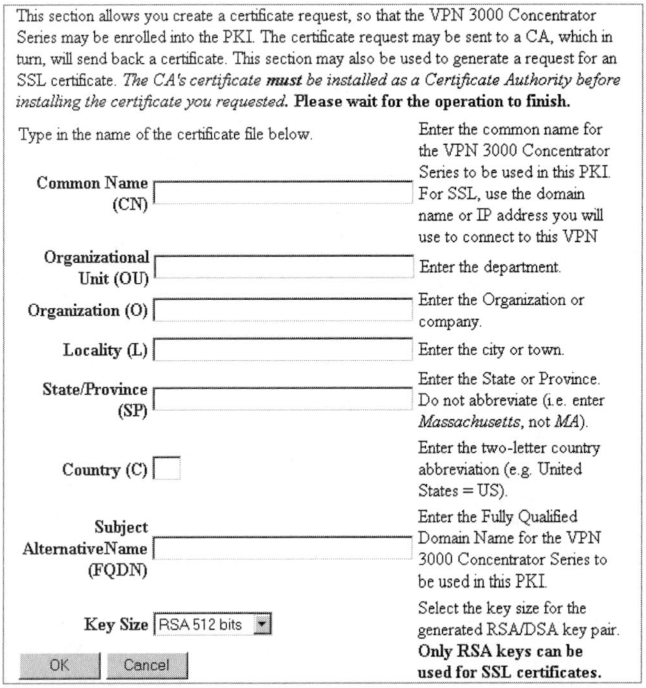

[Figure: Certificate request form with fields for Common Name (CN), Organizational Unit (OU), Organization (O), Locality (L), State/Province (SP), Country (C), Subject AlternativeName (FQDN), and Key Size (RSA 512 bits), with OK and Cancel buttons.]

State/Province (SP) The SP is usually used to define the state, province, county, or other political division.

Country (C) The C is the name of the country in which this device resides.

Subject Alternative Name (FQDN) The Fully Qualified Domain Name (FQDN) refers to the name of the device. An example of a server name would be `testbox.sales.cisco.com`.

Key Size This value sets the key size for the generated RSA/DSA key pair. Although most PKI implementations support RSA keys, many don't support another option offered here: Directory System Agent (DSA). Verify with the administrator of the CA what type of key should be used.

The key that is generated is actually a set of keys: a *public key* and a *private key*. The private key doesn't go anywhere; it resides on the concentrator. The public key is included with the information that was entered into the fields and sent to the CA. The keys are used to encrypt traffic to the other device, using that device's public key. If a public key is used to encrypt traffic, only the linked private key may decrypt it. This is called *asymmetric encryption*.

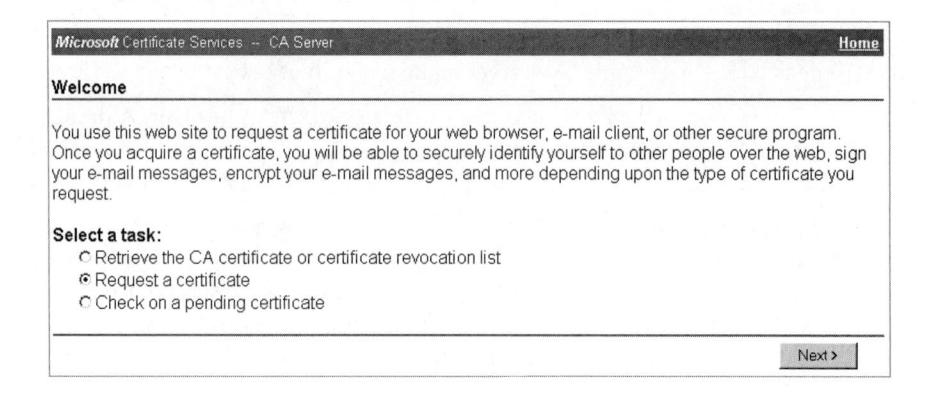

After you've filled in the certificate request form and clicked OK, the VPN Concentrator Manager opens another browser window that contains the information that the CA needs to create a new certificate, as in the example here:

```
-----BEGIN NEW CERTIFICATE REQUEST-----
MIIBGzCBxgIBADBmMRQwEgYDVQQDFAtzdHVkZW50IDEyMjERMA8GA1UECxQIdHJh
aW5pbmcxDzANBgNVBAoUBk15IENvLjEQMA4GA1UEBxMHUGhvZW5peDELMAkGA1UE
CBMCQVoxCzAJBgNVBAYTAlVTMFkwDQYJKoZIhvcNAQEBBQADSAAwRQJAYTUfYYPU
azIe6G2ND7XZ11NL0ycXPe5dzBtA49cO2fysrQsD2eIacpT4xqmtJP4zPKgnch1I
Pqyd8YgD16KVkQIBBzANBgkqhkiG9w0BAQQFAANBAD1vPGOz7g683KI/35r9ijmu
4SmpmDY1pAkIczRhQQkD3vi4a7oEyOHUVGZw2B8AKww6PLD4LCun1J0ZAIHlEvo=
-----END NEW CERTIFICATE REQUEST-----
```

Highlight all the information shown in this window, and copy it. You'll paste it into another browser window shortly. For safety's sake, you might want to paste it into a text file for temporary storage.

Generating the Concentrator Certificate

After you've copied the certificate request information generated by the Concentrator management utility, point the browser to the CA's URL. The CA used in this example is the one that comes with Windows 2000 Server. Figure 18.27 shows the Microsoft Certificate Services Welcome screen and choices. Select the Request A Certificate radio button, and click Next to continue.

The next page asks how the request should be input. You'll use this form to generate the certificate for the PC.

Since the data was copied from the concentrator, choose to use a Base64 Encoded PKCS #10 file. Then paste the PKCS #10 information that the VPN Concentrator Manager generated when you configured the request (as described in the previous section) into the Saved Request box, as shown in Figure 18.28. There is also the option to browse for a text file that contains the necessary information. Other options allow enrollment using a form and smart-card enrollment.

FIGURE 18.27 Choosing to request a certificate from the CA

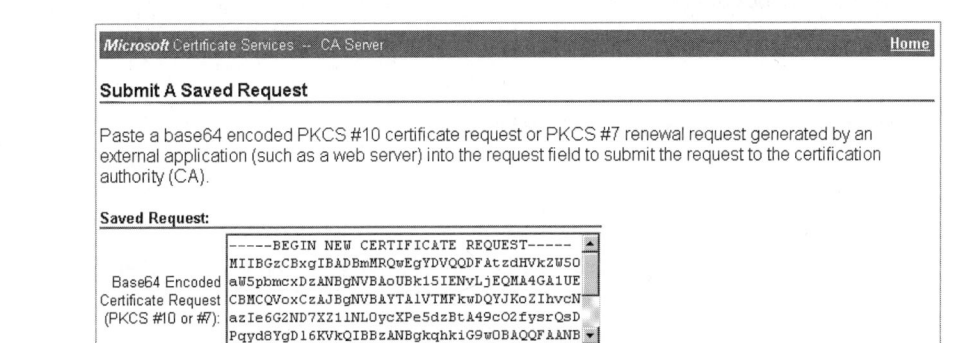

FIGURE 18.28 Pasting the PKCS #10 into the CA's certificate request form

In addition to starting the certificate request process, the CA's certificate request screen is also used to request a certificate revocation list (CRL). Occasionally, it's necessary to terminate a certificate before it would naturally expire. A CRL is a file generated by the CA that states which certificates are no longer valid, using the serial number of the certificate to uniquely identify the certificate in question. Updating the CRL isn't a required action, but it should be done. How often the CRL should be updated depends on your organization's security requirements.

When a connection is first made, the peers request a new copy of the CRL from the CA. Each peer then makes sure that the certificate it was just given isn't on the CRL. Some equipment is capable of ignoring an unavailable CRL, whereas others must have a new CRL for the connection to continue. This reduces the chance that a stolen certificate and denial of service attack on the CA can allow someone into your network. CRL requesting is on by default and requires HTTP access to the CA. The CRL distribution point is usually included in the certificate received from the CA, eliminating some configuration steps.

Downloading the Concentrator Certificate

Once the CA has generated the certificate, it must be downloaded. The next page has two options for certificate retrieval: DER encoded or Base64 encoded. Choose Base64 encoded for the concentrator.

At this point, the certificate for the concentrator must be downloaded to the PC. Make sure that it's placed in a secure location; there is no sense in placing it in a directory that everyone in the company can access.

Each certificate is a separate download, so be sure to collect the identity certificate, the root CA certificate, and the CRL. When you're using the Windows 2000 CA, collect the Concentrator ID certificate first and then click the Home hyperlink to continue downloading the remaining files.

Installing the Concentrator Certificate

After the certificate has been downloaded, it must be installed on the concentrator. From the main VPN Concentrator Manager window, choose Administration ➢ Certificate Management ➢ Install. You'll see the screen shown in Figure 18.29.

Choose the type of certificate downloaded, enter any required password, and tell the browser where the certificate can be found.

FIGURE 18.29 Installing the certificate on the concentrator

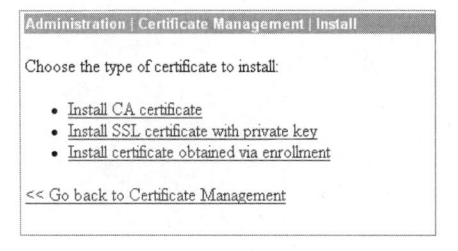

Viewing the Concentrator Certificate

Once the certificate has been installed, it's occasionally useful to be able to check something on it, such as the expiration date. You may also need to install a new CRL or even delete the certificate.

To view concentrator certificates, from the main VPN Concentrator Manager window, choose Administration ➢ Certificate Management ➢ Certificates. As shown in Figure 18.30, different certificate types are listed on this screen:

Certificate Authorities The Certificate Authorities section shows the CAs for which the concentrator has an ID certificate.

Identity Certificates The Identity Certificates section shows information regarding the ID certificates for the concentrator. These are certificates that are traded to authenticate.

SSL Certificates The SSL Certificate section shows the certificate that will be used in the event an SSL session is requested when administering the VPN Concentrator.

In each case, the screen shows issuer and expiration information. You can also delete the certificate or view details. To view a certificate, click the View link under Actions. Figure 18.31 shows an example of the details displayed. The View screen shows ownership and registration information. It includes subject and issuer information (Common Name, Country, and so on), the serial number that identifies the individual certificate, the hashing algorithm, the key size, and the type of key used. The Validity line at the bottom shows the period during which the certificate is valid.

Configuring the Use of IPSec Digital Certificates 581

FIGURE 18.30 Checking installed certificates

FIGURE 18.31 Viewing certificate details

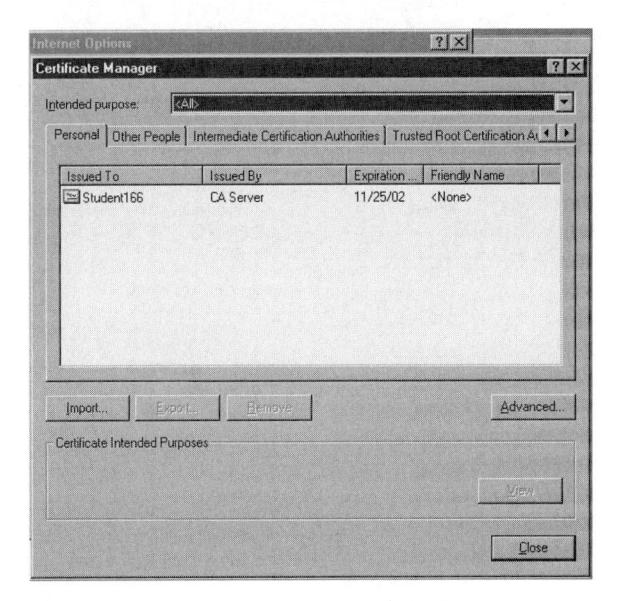

> If you've successfully requested and installed a certificate, but you receive an error message about the certificate not being valid yet, compare the validity time to the clock on the VPN Concentrator. Time zone offset is usually the cause of a certificate not being valid for a few more hours.

When certificates are exchanged, the peers make sure the certificates are good. The certificates must be valid, falling in the time range between issuance and expiration; the certificate must have been signed by a trusted CA; and the certificate serial number must not be listed in the CRL. The receiving device extracts the public key from the certificate for use in encryption.

Managing User Tunnels

The Unified Client (discussed in Chapter 17) doesn't provide a way for users to build their own tunnel attributes (the SafeNet client does allow this). Since the user connecting to the VPN Concentrator won't have a way to specify how the tunnel is to be built, the concentrator must provide this information. The administrator needs to make sure that the policies in effect recognize how the tunnel should be built and configure the group for digital certificate support.

The administrator must complete three tasks for user tunnel management:

1. From the main VPN Concentrator Manager window, select Configuration ➤ System ➤ Tunneling Protocols ➤ IPSec ➤ IKE Proposals. Make sure that the desired IKE proposal is the active one. Proposals are grouped together by encryption and hash method.

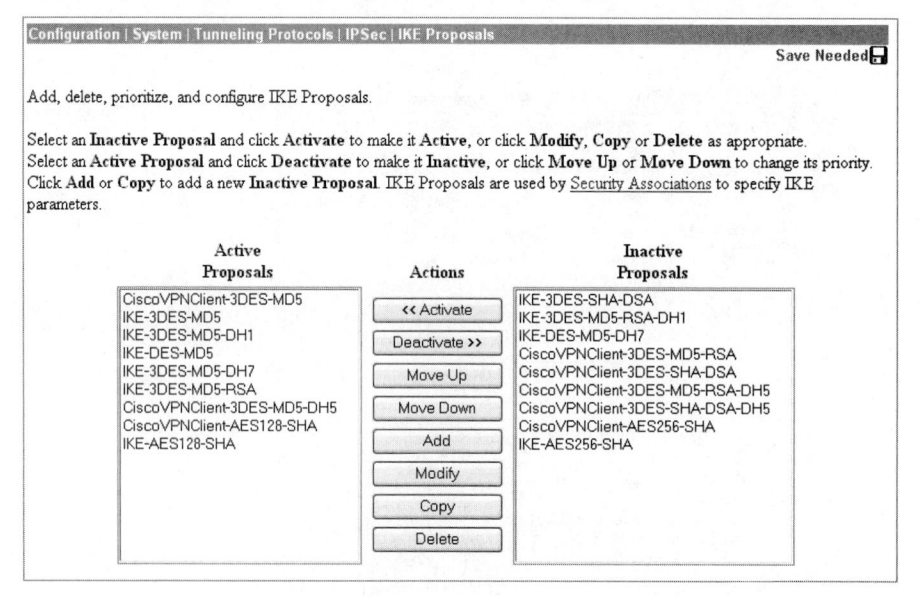

```
Configuration | System | Tunneling Protocols | IPSec | IKE Proposals
                                                                         Save Needed

Add, delete, prioritize, and configure IKE Proposals.

Select an Inactive Proposal and click Activate to make it Active, or click Modify, Copy or Delete as appropriate.
Select an Active Proposal and click Deactivate to make it Inactive, or click Move Up or Move Down to change its priority.
Click Add or Copy to add a new Inactive Proposal. IKE Proposals are used by Security Associations to specify IKE
parameters.

        Active                                              Inactive
       Proposals              Actions                      Proposals

  CiscoVPNClient-3DES-MD5                          IKE-3DES-SHA-DSA
  IKE-3DES-MD5             [ << Activate ]         IKE-3DES-MD5-RSA-DH1
  IKE-3DES-MD5-DH1                                 IKE-DES-MD5-DH7
  IKE-DES-MD5              [ Deactivate >> ]       CiscoVPNClient-3DES-MD5-RSA
  IKE-3DES-MD5-DH7         [   Move Up    ]        CiscoVPNClient-3DES-SHA-DSA
  IKE-3DES-MD5-RSA                                 CiscoVPNClient-3DES-MD5-RSA-DH5
  CiscoVPNClient-3DES-MD5-DH5  [ Move Down  ]      CiscoVPNClient-3DES-SHA-DSA-DH5
  CiscoVPNClient-AES128-SHA                        CiscoVPNClient-AES256-SHA
  IKE-AES128-SHA           [     Add      ]        IKE-AES256-SHA
                           [    Modify    ]
                           [     Copy     ]
                           [    Delete    ]
```

Configuring the Use of IPSec Digital Certificates

2. Choose Configuration ➤ Policy Management ➤ Traffic Management ➤ Security Associations. Select the IPSec SA that will be used, such as ESP-DES-MD5. Click Modify, and select the correct digital certificate for the VPN Concentrator.

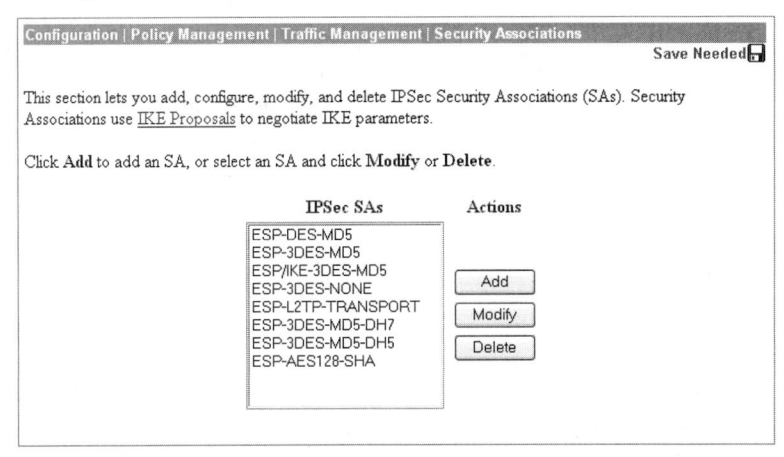

```
Configuration | Policy Management | Traffic Management | Security Associations
                                                                Save Needed

This section lets you add, configure, modify, and delete IPSec Security Associations (SAs). Security
Associations use IKE Proposals to negotiate IKE parameters.

Click Add to add an SA, or select an SA and click Modify or Delete.

                    IPSec SAs              Actions
                ESP-DES-MD5
                ESP-3DES-MD5
                ESP/IKE-3DES-MD5
                ESP-3DES-NONE              [  Add   ]
                ESP-L2TP-TRANSPORT
                ESP-3DES-MD5-DH7           [ Modify ]
                ESP-3DES-MD5-DH5
                ESP-AES128-SHA             [ Delete ]
```

3. Choose Configuration ➤ User Management ➤ Groups, and select the group that needs to be modified for digital certificate support. As mentioned previously, make sure that the group name on the Identity tab matches the OU field on the ID certificate for the concentrator. On the General tab, make sure IPSec is selected under Tunneling Protocols. On the IPSec tab, make sure that the IPSec SA is set to the SA type that is to be used.

> **NOTE** The tasks for creating a tunnel from one concentrator to another concentrator, router, or firewall in a LAN-to-LAN configuration are the same as those for creating a tunnel to a client PC. Make sure that the device on the far side supports the IKE proposal used on the concentrator.

Requesting and Installing Client Certificates

Requesting and installing a certificate for a PC are simple tasks. Each starts the same way it did to request a certificate for a concentrator. Begin by opening a web browser to the correct URL. From the browser, select Request A Certificate ➤ Advanced Request ➤ Submit A Certificate To This CA Using A Form. Figure 18.32 shows an example of the Microsoft Certificate Services Advanced Certificate Request form.

FIGURE 18.32 The client certificate request form

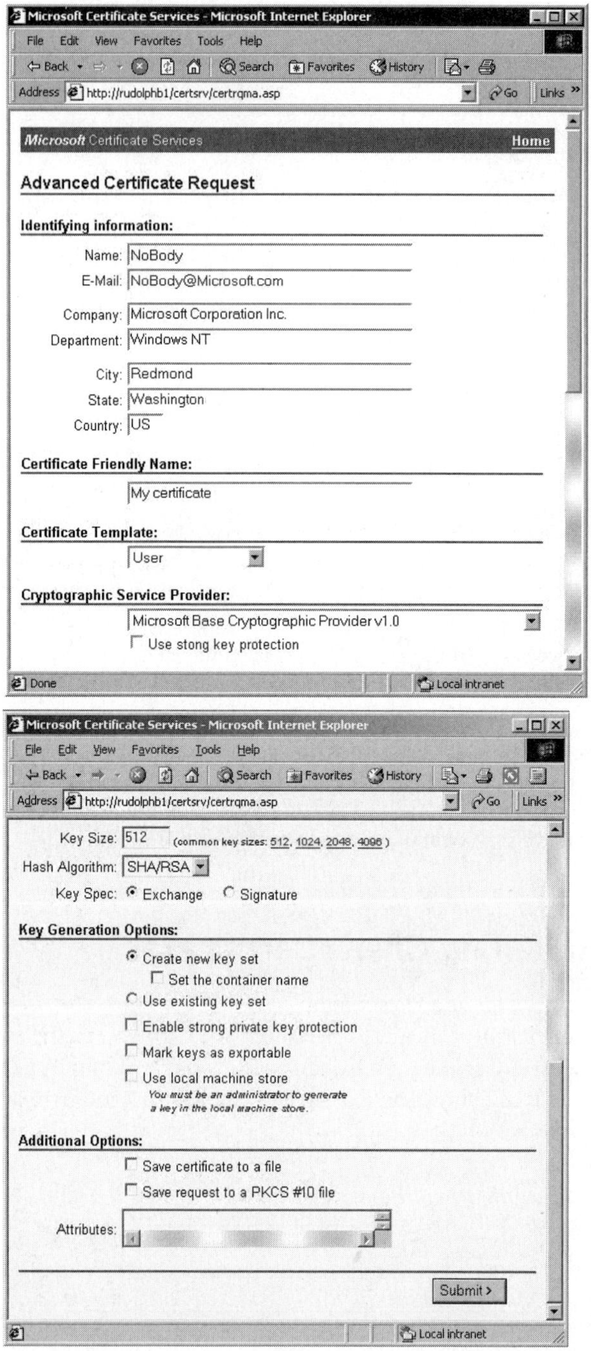

The name and department are very important. The Department field entry must match the name of the user's group on the concentrator. Also, make sure you supply the appropriate key size, as well as the appropriate policy information. These need to match the settings used for the concentrator certificate. For example, if MD5 is used on the concentrator, SHA shouldn't be used on the PC.

It's usually a good idea to set the Key Usage to Both and to choose the Mark Keys As Exportable option. This will allow the keys to be saved in a PKS #12 file, which means that the keys can be moved to a different PC, if necessary. Otherwise, you need to generate a new certificate for the PC.

After you've filled in the form, click Submit. The CA will generate the certificate and display a message indicating that the certificate was issued.

Click the Install This Certificate hyperlink to start the process of installing the certificate on the PC. Next, you'll see a verification message.

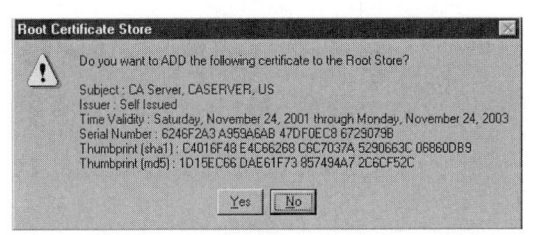

This message includes information about the certificate that you should examine before clicking Yes. Check the thumbprint against what the administrator of the CA says it should have generated. Make sure that the certificate is valid for a correct amount of time. If this information is correct, click Yes to install the certificate.

Each operating system has its own place to store certificates and its own method of viewing them. To view the certificates currently installed on a Windows-based PC, open Internet Explorer, and select Tools > Internet Options > Content > Certificates. Several types of certificates can be installed in the PC. If no custom certificates have been installed, the Personal tab of the Certificate Manager dialog box will be blank. If the certificate installation was successful, a certificate should be listed.

Double-click the certificate to see some information about it. The General tab of the Certificate dialog box shows to whom the certificate was issued (this is the same name as the one in the Name field on the certificate request form), the identity of the device that generated the certificate, the period that the certificate is valid, and that there is a private key associated with this certificate.

Selecting the Details tab of the Certificate dialog box provides more specific information about the certificate, as shown in Figure 18.33. You can select any of the fields on this tab; if there is additional information, as there would be for the key fields, it will be displayed in the text box at the bottom of the dialog box.

The final verification that the certificate is installed correctly is to activate the VPN client, open the Properties window, and select the Authentication tab. If the certificate is installed properly, the radio button next to Certificate should be selectable. If multiple certificates are installed, you'll be able to select the one to use from the drop-down menu. Each certificate is identified by the name used when filling out the form on the CA.

FIGURE 18.33 Viewing certificate details

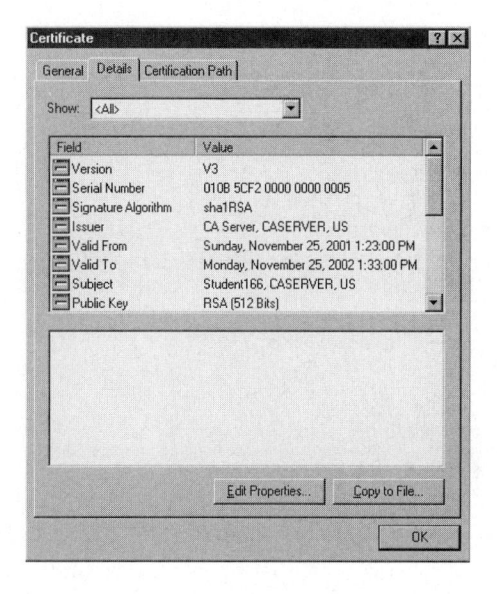

Firewall Feature Set for the IPSec Software Client

Every Cisco VPN Concentrator comes with the VPN Client software, or you may download Cisco VPN Client version 3.6 from the Cisco website. This software-based client is available for Windows versions 95, 98, Me, 4.0, 2000, and XP. Additionally, versions are available for Intel-based Linux, 32- and 64-bit Solaris UltraSparc, as well as Mac OS X 10.1. The client enables you to use secure tunnels from any of the previously mentioned workstations to any Cisco Easy VPN Server such as the PIX Firewall (6.0 or newer), any Cisco IOS–based system newer than 12.2(8)T, or any of the Cisco VPN 3000 Concentrators.

The VPN Concentrator may be configured to require a specific configuration. When a client attempts to connect, the internal rule base will be reviewed. The configuration is required, and if it doesn't match, then no tunnel is established. If the VPN Concentrator is configured to use the optional mode, it allows the client to connect and download the desired firewall with the correct configuration onto the client's PC. Additionally, the concentrator won't permit a VPN tunnel to be set up if a firewall is required by the concentrator and there is none. However, if a firewall isn't required and one exists, a tunnel may still be established. In this section, we'll discuss the following:

- The Are You There feature
- The Stateful Firewall feature
- The Central Policy Protection feature
- Client firewall statistics
- Customizing firewall policies

Software Client's Are You There Feature

Rather than define policies on the personal firewall, you may want to use a simple, albeit less secure, method of ensuring that the software client is running. With the client's Are You There (AYT) feature, the VPN client polls the firewall installed on the client PC once every 30 seconds. If there is no answer to the polls, the VPN client drops the tunnel. Only the polling traffic is passed between the concentrator and the firewall. AYT works with ZoneAlarm, ZoneAlarm Pro, Sygate, and BlackICE.

Software Client's Stateful Firewall Feature

You can configure the Stateful Firewall feature on the VPN client to prevent inbound connections from other networks without consideration of encryption type or tunneling configuration. All connection requests are denied with only a few exceptions:

- Traffic from the head-end network
- DHCP requests
- Encapsulating Security Payload (ESP) traffic

ESP rules are packet filters–based, not session-based filters. Using ESP allows split tunneling. This enables secured, encrypted traffic to the head-end network while still allowing communication via nonsecured connections to other outside networks such as the Internet. You enable this feature by deselecting the Always On option.

Software Client's Central Policy Protection Feature

If you require a more versatile and scalable solution for managing your firewall policies, you may want to consider the central policy protection (CPP) feature. The CPP can be set to deny or allow specific ports and protocols. The concentrator acts as the distribution point for the configured policies and pushes the rule base down to the client at connection during the negotiation process.

Once the predefined policies are received from the concentrator, they're passed to the CIC for enforcement. As with the Stateful Firewall, the Always On option gives more flexibility with restrictions on external or Internet-bound traffic.

Client Firewall Statistics

To view the firewall statistics from the VPN client, double-click the yellow padlock in the system tray to open the general information screen. Select Status ➢ Statistics, and click the Firewall tab (see Figure 18.34). The Firewall tab identifies the type of firewall and firewall policy as well as provides details about the firewall filter rules. These rules are configured from the CPP, as described in the previous section.

The Tunnel Details tab (Figure 18.35) shows you the IP addresses of the client and server as well as the encryption method and authentication for these connections.

On the Tunnel Details tab of the Statistics screen, you can see more details about your connection, including the following:

- **Bytes Received:** The count of total bytes of secure data received
- **Bytes Sent:** The count of total bytes of secure data transmitted
- **Packets Decrypted:** The count of total encrypted packets received and decrypted on the port
- **Packet Encrypted:** The count of total encrypted packets transmitted from the port

FIGURE 18.34 The Firewall tab of the VPN Client Statistics dialog box

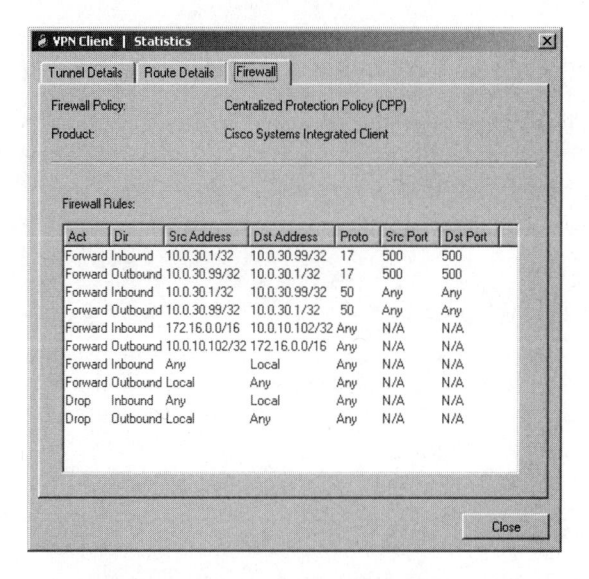

- Packets Bypassed: The count of total data packets not processed because no encryption was necessary
- Packets Discarded: The count of total data packets that the VPN client rejected because they didn't originate from the gateway

The Route Details tab, shown in Figure 18.36, shows the local LAN and secured routes. In the figure shown, the VPN client is configured to use the tunnel only for traffic destined for the 172.16.0.0/16 private network. All other traffic is unprotected.

FIGURE 18.35 The Tunnel Details tab of the VPN Client Statistics dialog box

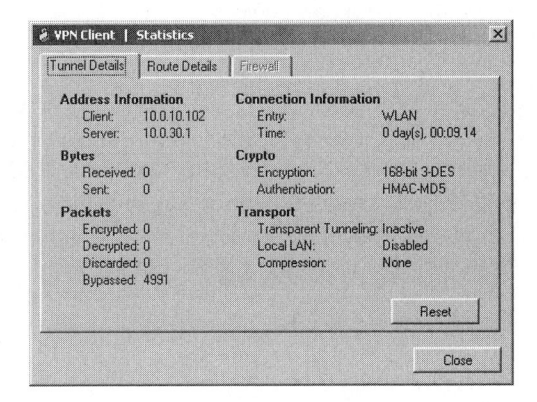

FIGURE 18.36 The Router Details tab of the VPN Client Statistics dialog box

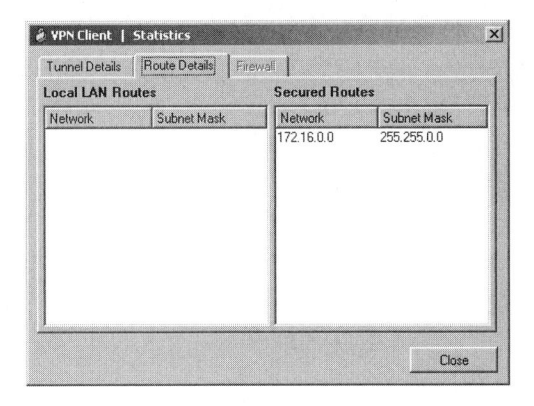

Customizing Firewall Policy

As with most default configurations, the overall security of your network would be inadequate if the defaults were left in place. Realistically, the default rules are there to supply some security and aid you in the process of setting up rules that are specific to your environment. These rules can be applied to a specific interface or to a VPN group.

The Filter Rules selection list on the Rules screen, shown in Figure 18.37, contains the default rules, which can be modified as you see fit. However, you'll probably want to create your own rules that are more specific to your environment. The text in parentheses after each option describes the action of the rule and the direction of the traffic that will be affected. The buttons on the side enable you to add, modify, copy, and delete your rules.

To modify the filter rules, highlight a rule and click the Modify button. Doing so brings you to the Modify window, as shown in Figure 18.38.

Notice that the norm for the default rules is to forward traffic to Use IP Address/Wildcard mask, which carries a default value of 0.0.0.0 255.255.255.255 (the equivalent to any address). One exception to the rule is the VRRP Out, which uses the multicast address 224.0.0.18/0.0.0.0, as assigned by the Internet Assigned Numbers Authority (IANA)

FIGURE 18.37 The Rules screen

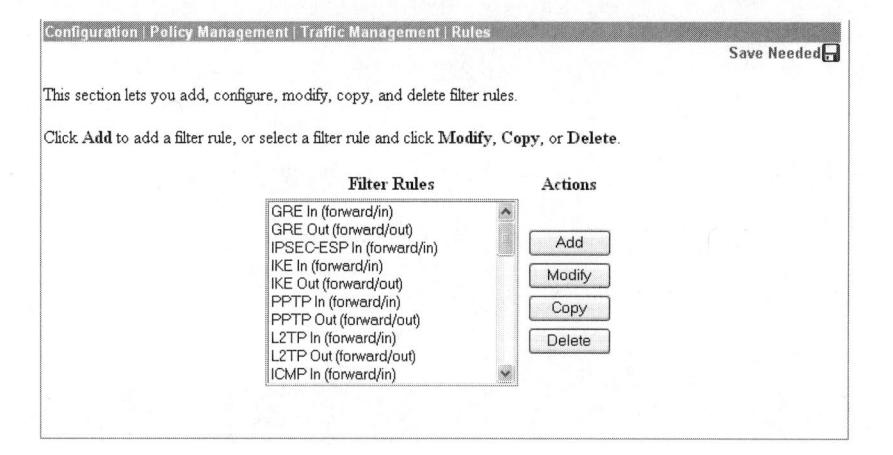

FIGURE 18.38 The Modify screen

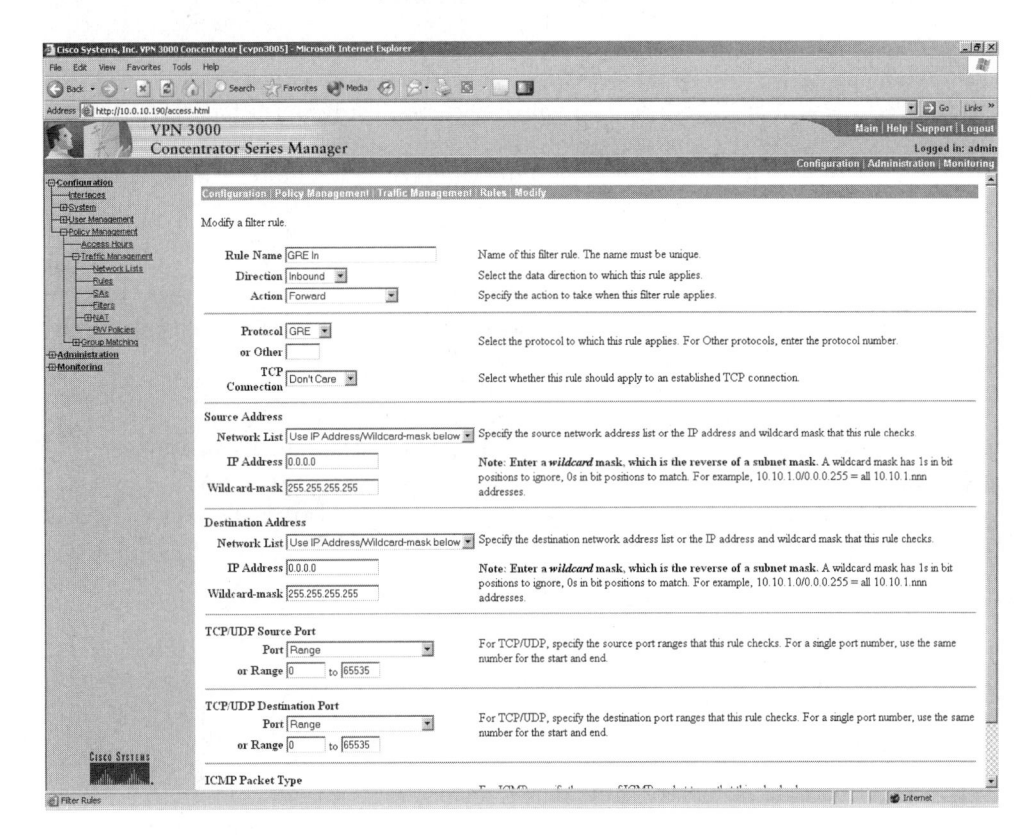

Configuring the VPN 3000 Concentrator for IPSec over UDP and IPSec over TCP

As we discussed in Chapter 16, Internet Protocol Security (IPSec) is the standard that enables a secure connection from the client to the VPN Concentrator. IPSec allows address data privacy, authentication, integrity, key management, and tunneling. There are two options for IPSec: IPSec over TCP and IPSec over UDP. Only one of these options can be used at a time, because when you pick one, the other is automatically disabled. The next sections describe each of the methods as well as some of their companion configurations in more detail.

Overview of Port Address Translation

Port Address Translation (PAT) is similar in nature to Network Address Translation (NAT). In PAT, the TCP or UDP port is translated in addition to the IP source or destination address. Using PAT lets you use one IP Address for multiple machines. The distinguishing feature between them becomes the unique port and not the unique IP address. NAT is a one-to-one translation, whereas PAT is a one-to-many translation. Additionally, PAT translates TCP and UDP ports as well as the source or destination address. Version 3.*x* of the software must be running to use PAT and Network Extension mode.

> **WARNING** Some applications expect to use specific ports. Because PAT changes the ports used, this can cause problems with this type of application.

You'll probably come across some old DOS applications that embed the workstation address with the data instead of depending on IP to carry the address. These applications predate even the OSI seven-layer model. Needless to say, they won't work with NAT or PAT, because data payload won't have been involved in the translation process and will retain the original addresses.

Configuring IPSec over UDP

The VPN 3002 Hardware Client fully supports User Datagram Protocol Network Address Translation Transparent IPSec (UDP NAT Transparent IPSec). There are three requirements for running UDP NAT Transparent IPSec:

- You must be running version 3.0.3 or later software.
- The client and concentrator must be configured for the same port.
- The VPN Concentrator must be configured with IPSec over UDP for the group.

With this configuration, the effects of NAT and PAT are completely bypassed due to the encapsulation of the data traffic within the new UDP packets. Rather, NAT mappings are kept intact through the use of keepalive packets being sent on a regular basis.

> **TIP** UDP Transparent IPSec bypasses the effects of NAT and PAT by encapsulating the data traffic within new UDP packets

Of course, this additional traffic does cause overhead, but it's necessary. UDP is connectionless by definition, which causes some limitations; one is that only a single VPN device may be behind the NAT device.

> **TIP** IPSec over UDP won't work if you're using PAT and you attempt to have more than one VPN 3002 Hardware Client behind the firewall.

Configuring the VPN 3000 Concentrator for IPSec over UDP and IPSec over TCP

The device and the client must both be configured for the same port for the connection to work; the default port is 10000, although the acceptable range is from 4001 to 49151. On the outbound side, the IPSec process encrypts, encapsulates, and then adds a new UDP header if required. From the inbound side, the UDP traffic goes directly to the IPSec processing for decryption and de-encapsulation before being routed. These rules may be removed from the filter under one of three conditions: when a group is deleted, when the last active IPSec over UDP security association (SA) for that group is deleted, or when IPSec over UDP is disabled for the group.

To configure IPSec over UDP, go to the Configuration ➤ System ➤ Tunneling Protocols ➤ IPSec screen, shown in Figure 18.39, and enter the remote server IP address and whether to use IPSec over TCP. If you wish to use something other than the default, you can take the default of using IPSec over UDP and change the port number. With this type of setup, you need to use pre-shared keys, so make certain the Use Certificate box is cleared. Next, enter the group, group password, user, and user password to complete the configuration.

FIGURE 18.39 The IPSec screen

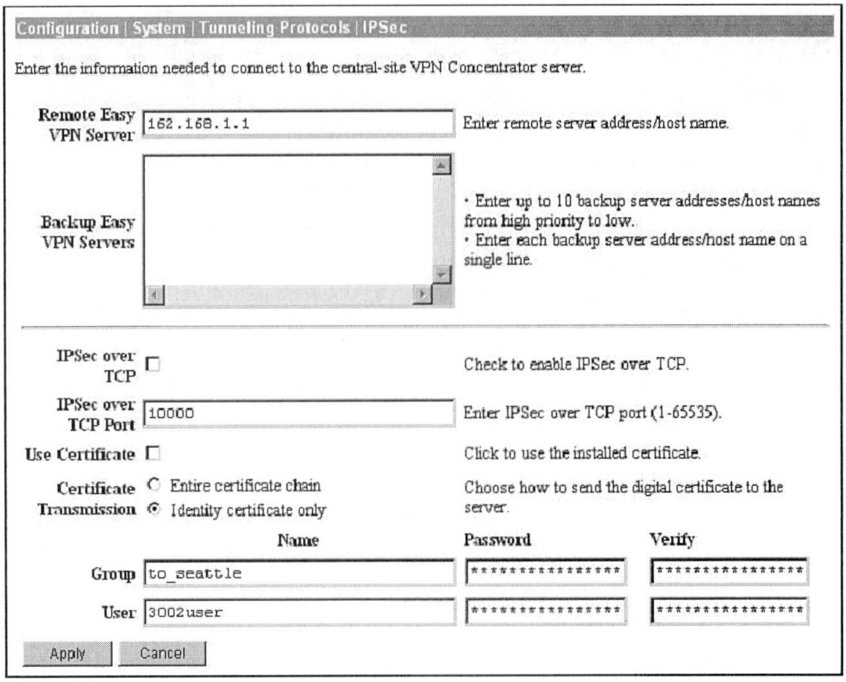

Configuring NAT-Transversal

As we previously mentioned, you'll inevitably run across an older DOS application that doesn't work over NAT or PAT because the IP address is embedded inside the payload. The solution for such a dilemma is to configure NAT-Transversal. In this configuration, the client encapsulates the data traffic with the new UDP packet, thus bypassing the effects of the NAT or PAT translation. Since this method is also UDP connectionless–based, it incurs the overhead of periodic keepalive packets to make sure that the tunnels stay up. It also has similar limitations to IPSec over UDP in that there can be only a single VPN device behind the NAT device.

> **TIP** UDP Transparent IPSec bypasses the effects of NAT and PAT by encapsulating the data traffic within new UDP packets.

NAT-Transversal is configured the same way as IPSec over UDP.

Configuring IPSec over TCP

IPSec over TCP is fully supported on the Cisco VPN Client and the Cisco VPN 3002 Hardware Client running version 3.5 or later software. With IPSec over TCP, the data is fully encrypted and encapsulated within the TCP packet and works through NAT and PAT devices, whereas ESP or IKE won't. Because of this encapsulation, the encryption won't work with a proxy server. As with the others, the same port numbers must be configured on both ends when IPSec over TCP is enabled.

You configure IPSec over TCP/IP by selecting the check box to enable IPSec over TCP and selecting the TCP port to use. The default port is 10000, but any port between 1 and 65635 may be used. Take caution not to select a well-known port number such as 25 (SMTP) or 80 (HTTP); expect a system warning message if you do, letting you know that the port you've chosen will no longer be available for that service. The VPN 3002 Hardware Client allows only one TCP port; however, on the VPN Client, you can separate up to 10 port numbers in the configuration with commas to use a different port for each hardware client.

To configure IPSec over TCP on the VPN 3002 Hardware Client, look on the Configuration ≻ System ≻ Tunneling Protocols ≻ IPSec screen. On the VPN Concentrator, configuration settings for IPSec over TCP are made on the Configuration ≻ System ≻ Tunneling Protocols ≻ IPSec ≻ NAT Transparency screen, shown in Figure 18.40.

FIGURE 18.40 The NAT Transparency screen

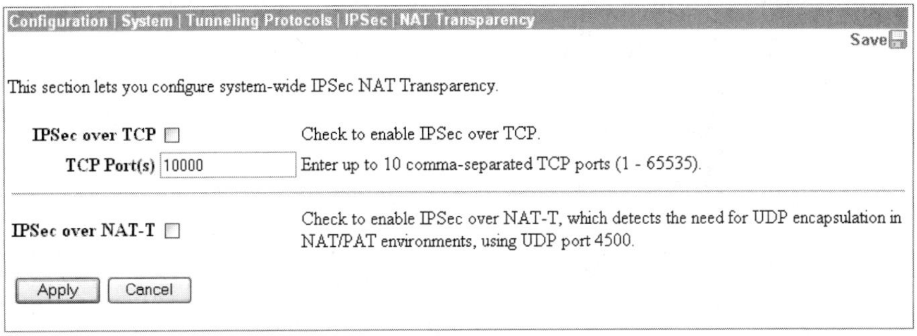

```
Configuration | System | Tunneling Protocols | IPSec | NAT Transparency
                                                                      Save

This section lets you configure system-wide IPSec NAT Transparency.

    IPSec over TCP  ☐          Check to enable IPSec over TCP.
       TCP Port(s) 10000       Enter up to 10 comma-separated TCP ports (1 - 65535).

    IPSec over NAT-T ☐         Check to enable IPSec over NAT-T, which detects the need for UDP encapsulation in
                               NAT/PAT environments, using UDP port 4500.

    [ Apply ]  [ Cancel ]
```

Summary

This chapter explained how to allow users to create tunnels and terminate them at the concentrator. First, we covered how to get the VPN Concentrator up and running. You use the CLI for initial configuration, and then you can use the management utility's Quick Configuration mode to configure minimal parameters.

Next, we described how to configure groups, users, and authentication (either locally or on a remote authentication server). We also showed how policies can be implemented to allow user access only during certain times and to prevent certain types of traffic from entering the concentrator.

We covered the use of digital certificates. Configuration for digital certificates requires that both the concentrator and the user PC request and install certificates.

Finally, configuring the VPN Concentrator might seem overwhelming when you look at all the tasks involved; but if you take one task at a time, it's fairly easy. Remember that there are distinct phases of configuration, just as there are on a router.

Exam Essentials

Understand the relationship between users and groups. The VPN Concentrator has a default base group, but you can add other groups. When a user is created, that user is a member of the base group unless the user is placed in a different group. You can configure a group with a policy, and that policy will then apply to all users who are members of the group. If a custom group is deleted, all the user members become members of the base group.

Understand the Public Key Infrastructure (PKI). The PKI is the relationship for all devices receiving certificates from a given CA. CAs can be stand-alone systems; there is no overall CA for the entire world. Setting up a server with certificate software in a home lab, then configuring a VPN Concentrator and a client to get certificates and form a VPN tunnel, is an example of a very small PKI.

Know the steps to request and install a digital certificate. Digital certificates are the most complex part of IPSec, but they're also the most in demand. Certain pieces of information, such as host and domain names, are required before a certificate request can be created.

Learn the details of the auto-update feature. The auto-update feature requires to the administrator to use several keywords to identify the client types. Memorize the keywords: `Windows`, `Win9x`, `WinNT`, and `vpn3002`.

Learn the steps to configure and use filters. The filtering capability is used on both the VPN Concentrator itself as well as on client firewalls. Get used to using the web tool to configure the rules and assign them to interfaces or client groups. Remember that all rules use a wildcard mask instead of a standard subnet mask.

Chapter 19

Managing the VPN Concentrator

THE FOLLOWING TOPICS ARE COVERED IN THIS CHAPTER:

- ✓ Monitoring and administering Cisco Secure VPN 3000 for remote-access networks
- ✓ Monitoring the VPN Concentrator
- ✓ Administering the VPN Concentrator
- ✓ Bandwidth management

In the last chapter, you saw how to configure the Cisco VPN Concentrator. Once the VPN Concentrator has been configured and tested, little needs to be done with it on a day-to-day basis beyond adding new users and groups when necessary. However, an administrator occasionally must monitor the concentrator to make sure that the network is running smoothly and troubleshoot any problems that occur. Of course, the administrator needs to perform administrative tasks, such as managing access and files.

The VPN Concentrator includes a management utility that makes it easy to access the concentrator reports and administration functions. This chapter covers the concentrator's monitoring and administration tools. This management tool includes statistical and logging information that can be used to troubleshoot security problems or bandwidth management configurations.

Monitoring the VPN Concentrator

To make sure the network is running properly, network administrators need to keep an eye on what the equipment is doing. Devices that use VPNs can gather many statistics about the network. There are two main ways to manage network equipment:

- *Simple Network Management Protocol (SNMP)* logs information to a management console in real time. This is the method that CiscoWorks and HP OpenView use to manage devices.

- A *Syslog server* is primarily used for historical logging. Syslog output is saved in tables for viewing at a later time.

> **NOTE** If you already have CiscoWorks, another management option is to use the Cisco VPN/Security Management Solution product. For more information about this product, visit www.cisco.com/warp/public/cc/pd/wr2k/vpmnso.

In the following sections, we'll take a deep look into the concentrator. You'll learn how to look at the system status, routing table information, and other general statistics that help keep the concentrator in good health.

Viewing Concentrator Monitoring Information

The VPN Concentrator tracks several types of statistics. To access the statistics, select Monitoring from the VPN Concentrator Manager window. You'll see the main Monitoring screen, as shown in Figure 19.1. The monitoring options include

- Routing Table
- Dynamic Filters
- Filterable Event Log
- System Status
- Sessions
- Statistics

When you select a hyperlink, the screen displayed contains the most recent data-capture available. Some screens have a Refresh button, which you can click to show the most up-to-date information. The following sections describe some of the more common options. We'll discuss the Event Log section in greater detail later in this chapter.

FIGURE 19.1 The VPN Concentrator's Monitoring screen

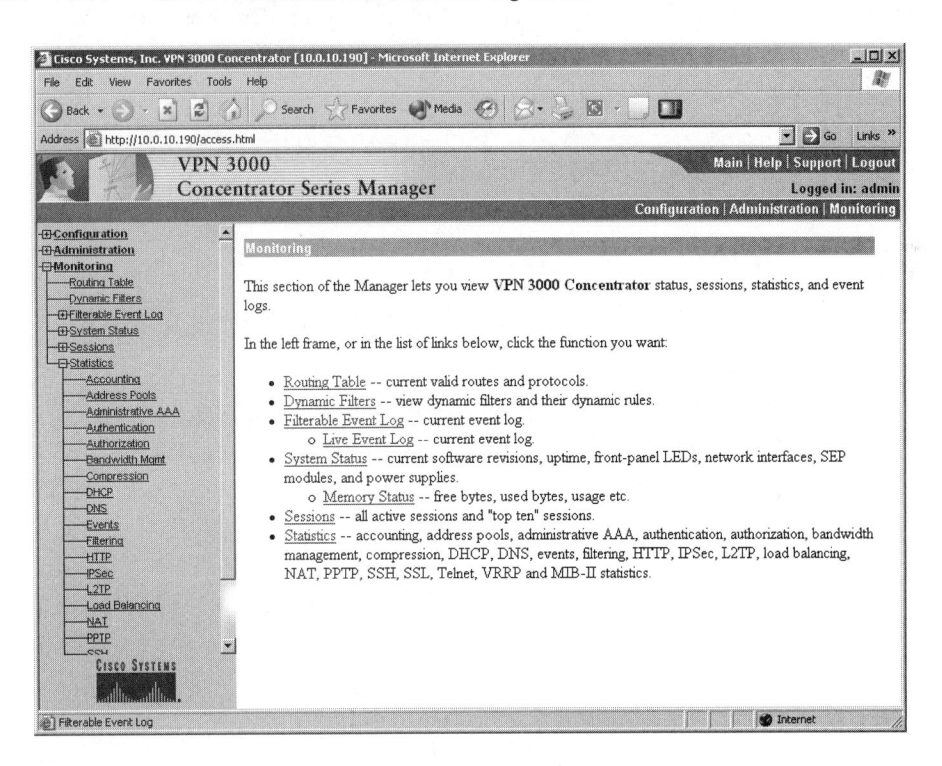

Viewing System Status Information

The System Status category provides a way to monitor the physical aspects of the concentrator, which is particularly helpful if the box is remote. Click the System Status link on the main Monitoring screen to see the System Status screen, shown in Figure 19.2.

This screen shows the type of device that is being examined and the general system status statistics. You can see the fan speed and temperature for the CPU, as well as throughput and processor utilization. This screen provides quick and easy checks of the basic systems operations.

Clicking an interface displays information about that interface, as shown in Figure 19.3. The interface in this example is using the IP address 10.0.6.5, is physical interface #1, and has a status of UP, so it's active. This interface has had around 1150 unicast packets flow in each direction, received almost 104,000 broadcasts, and sent out a few broadcasts as well.

Monitoring the power supplies is normally an easy thing to do. If you can access the screen at all, just click the interface's power supply on the System Status screen. There often isn't too much to worry about, because power supplies are generally quite dependable; but if the concentrator is in a locale where power isn't very stable and is subject to surges and sags, then the Power screen, shown in Figure 19.4, can be an invaluable addition to a UPS.

Monitoring LEDs is a time-honored tradition in the networking industry. The general rule to follow is that green LEDs are good, and other colors or no LED are bad. Figure 19.5 shows the LED Status screen, which appears when you click the front panel LEDs (on concentrator models 3015 through 3080) on the System Status screen. Table 19.1 explains what each of the LEDs indicates.

FIGURE 19.2 The System Status screen

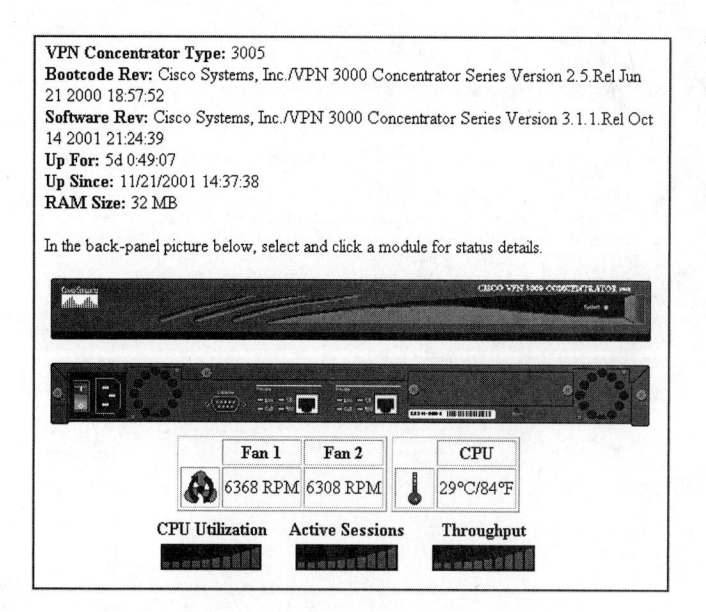

FIGURE 19.3 The Interface Statistics screen

Monitoring | System Status | Ethernet Interface 1   Monday, 26 November 2001 15:28:08
Refresh

Back

Interface	1
IP Address	10.0.6.5
Status	UP
Rx Unicast	1206
Tx Unicast	1077
Rx Multicast	220
Tx Multicast	0
Rx Broadcast	103737
Tx Broadcast	15

FIGURE 19.4 The Power screen

Monitoring | System Status | Power   Monday, 26 November 2001 15:42:09
Refresh

Back

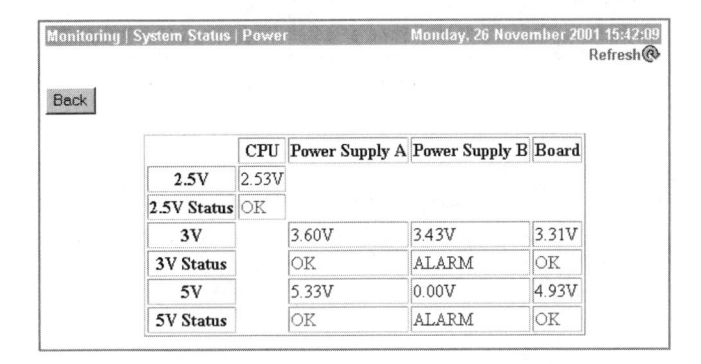

	CPU	Power Supply A	Power Supply B	Board
2.5V	2.53V			
2.5V Status	OK			
3V		3.60V	3.43V	3.31V
3V Status		OK	ALARM	OK
5V		5.33V	0.00V	4.93V
5V Status		OK	ALARM	OK

FIGURE 19.5 The LED Status screen

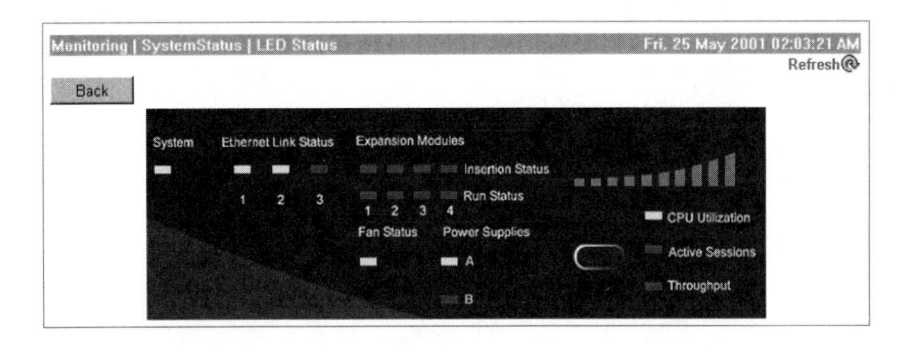

Monitoring | SystemStatus | LED Status   Fri, 25 May 2001 02:03:21 AM
Refresh

Back

System Ethernet Link Status Expansion Modules
                              Insertion Status
            1   2   3   Run Status
                              1 2 3 4
                              Fan Status Power Supplies
                                           A
                                           B

CPU Utilization
Active Sessions
Throughput

TABLE 19.1   LED Status on a VPN Concentrator

Indicator	Green	Amber	Off
System	Normal	System failed	Power off
Ethernet link status	Steady means connected to network; blinking means connected but disabled	N/A	Not connected
Expansion module insertion status	SEP installed	N/A	SEP not installed
Expansion module run status	SEP operational	N/A	If installed, encryption disabled or SEP failed (diagnostics)
Fan status	Normal	Below normal RPMs	N/A
Power supplies	Installed and running normally	Voltage outside acceptable range	Power supply not installed

> **NOTE** It isn't unusual for a properly working system to have one or more LEDs indicating an error state. For example, if a concentrator has two power supplies installed but only one is plugged in, the second will have voltage below the acceptable limit. Knowing your network is the key to knowing if a warning LED is an indication of a problem.

Viewing Routing Table Information

The concentrator can learn routes from several sources. In addition to Routing Information Protocol (RIP) and Open Shortest Path First (OSPF) derived routing information, the concentrator can understand static routes, default routes, and locally attached networks. To see routing information, select the Routing Table link from the main Monitoring screen. Figure 19.6 shows an example of the Routing Table screen.

FIGURE 19.6 The Routing Table screen

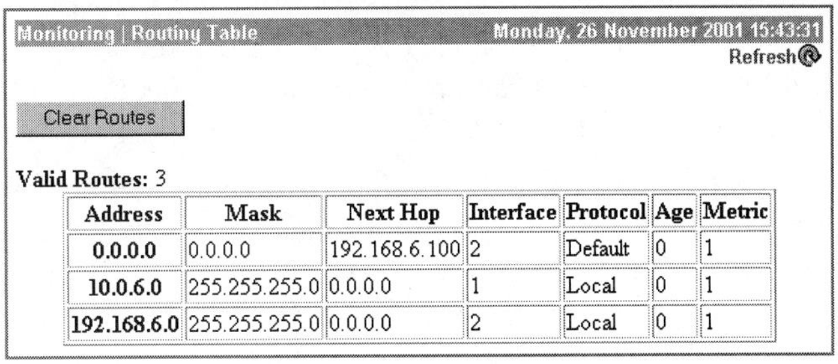
Monitoring | Routing Table
Monday, 26 November 2001 15:43:31
Refresh
Clear Routes
Valid Routes: 3
Address
Mask
Next Hop
Interface
Protocol
Age
Metric
0.0.0.0
0.0.0.0
192.168.6.100
2
Default
0
1
10.0.6.0
255.255.255.0
0.0.0.0
1
Local
0
1
192.168.6.0
255.255.255.0
0.0.0.0
2
Local
0
1

Viewing General Statistics

Click the General Statistics link on the main Monitoring screen to bring up the Statistics screen, shown in Figure 19.7. You can track a number of items via this screen:

- Point-to-Point Tunneling Protocol (PPTP), Layer 2 Tunneling Protocol (L2TP), and IPSec tunnels
- HTTP exchanges
- Event information
- Telnet sessions
- DNS information
- Authentication and accounting information
- Filtering information
- Virtual Router Redundancy Protocol (VRRP) information
- Secure Sockets Layer (SSL) sessions
- Dynamic Host Configuration Protocol (DHCP) leases and duration
- Address pool configurations and allocated addresses
- Secure Shell (SSH) sessions
- Load-balancing state
- Compression statistics
- Administrative authentication, authorization, and accounting (AAA) requests, authentications, and failures
- Network Address Translation (NAT) sessions and statistics

- Management Information Base (MIB) II interfaces and protocols
- Bandwidth management statistics

For example, if you click the PPTP link, you'll see the screen shown in Figure 19.8. All the statistics that appear on this screen have been captured since the concentrator was last booted. The screen shows three broad types of information:

Tunnels   The total number of tunnels is the aggregate number of tunnels created since the concentrator was last powered on. Active tunnels are the number currently active. You can update this number by clicking the Refresh icon. The maximum tunnels value is the highest number of tunnels active at one time since the concentrator was booted.

Sessions   The session information includes the total number of sessions, number of active sessions (which can be updated by clicking the Refresh icon), and maximum number of sessions active at one time, in the same format as the tunnel information. It's important to remember that several user sessions can be active through a tunnel.

Data and Control   The data and control information appears below the tunnel and session information. The information collected is divided into octets and packets transmitted and received.

FIGURE 19.7   The Statistics screen

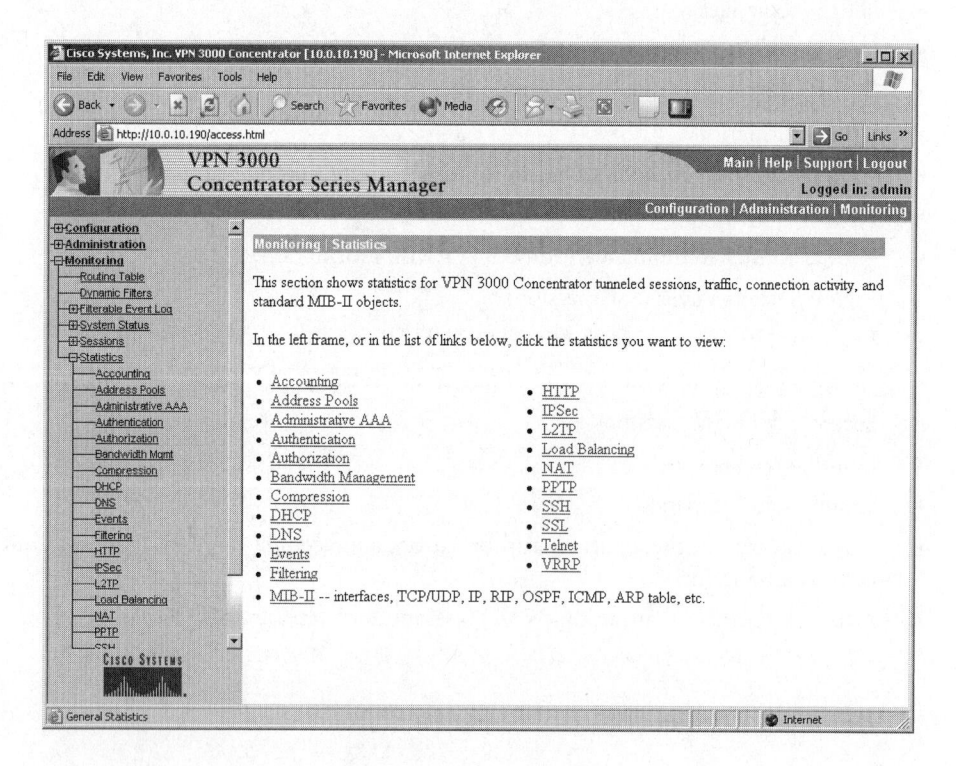

FIGURE 19.8 PPTP statistics

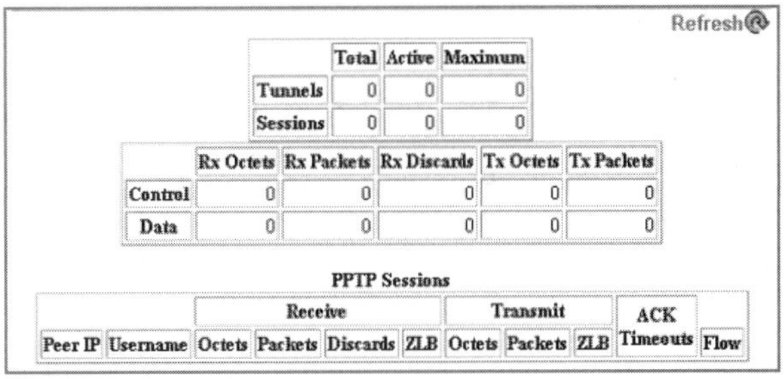

Table 19.2 describes the statistics collected for the PPTP tunnel type. The statistical information for each type of tunnel varies slightly; however, the PPTP statistics page is fairly representative of what you can expect to find on similar pages for L2TP or IPSec.

Another section of the Statistics menu, the Bandwidth Management screen, shown in Figure 19.9, provides important information on bandwidth controls.

TABLE 19.2 Tunnel Statistics

Data Field	Description
Tunnels	The number of tunnels that have been created since the VPN concentrator has been rebooted, the number of tunnels that are currently active, and the most that have been simultaneously connected.
Sessions	The number of sessions that have been created since the VPN concentrator has been rebooted, the number of sessions that are currently active, and the most that have been simultaneously connected.
Control/Data	The total number of PPTP-related bytes (octets) and packets that have been sent, received, or discarded since the VPN concentrator last rebooted.
Peer IP	The IP address of a currently connected peer. Fields to the right of the IP address identify specifics about the session related to this address.
Username	Username used to authenticate this session.
Octets/Packets	The number of bytes (octets) and packets sent or received since the session was started.
ZLB	Zero Length Body (ZLB) increments when the tunnel needs to acknowledge reception of a packet but no return packet is available on which to piggyback the acknowledgement.

TABLE 19.2 Tunnel Statistics *(continued)*

Data Field	Description
Discards	The total number of packets discarded.
ACK Timeouts	The number of times that the tunnel has exceeded its timer for sending an acknowledgement because no data was available for it to piggyback on. This should trigger a ZLB. Under normal circumstances, ZLB and ACK timeouts should be the same.
Flow	The flow-control status of this tunnel. The value can be one of four states: Local means the number of unacknowledged packets that have been received equals the window size for the tunnel, so the remote client is holding data; Peer means the number of unacknowledged packets that have been sent equals the window size for the tunnel, so the VPN concentrator is holding data; Both means the Windows in both directions are full, so both sides are holding data; and None means the tunnel has available window space in both directions and is able to send data (this is the normal condition).

FIGURE 19.9 The Bandwidth Management screen

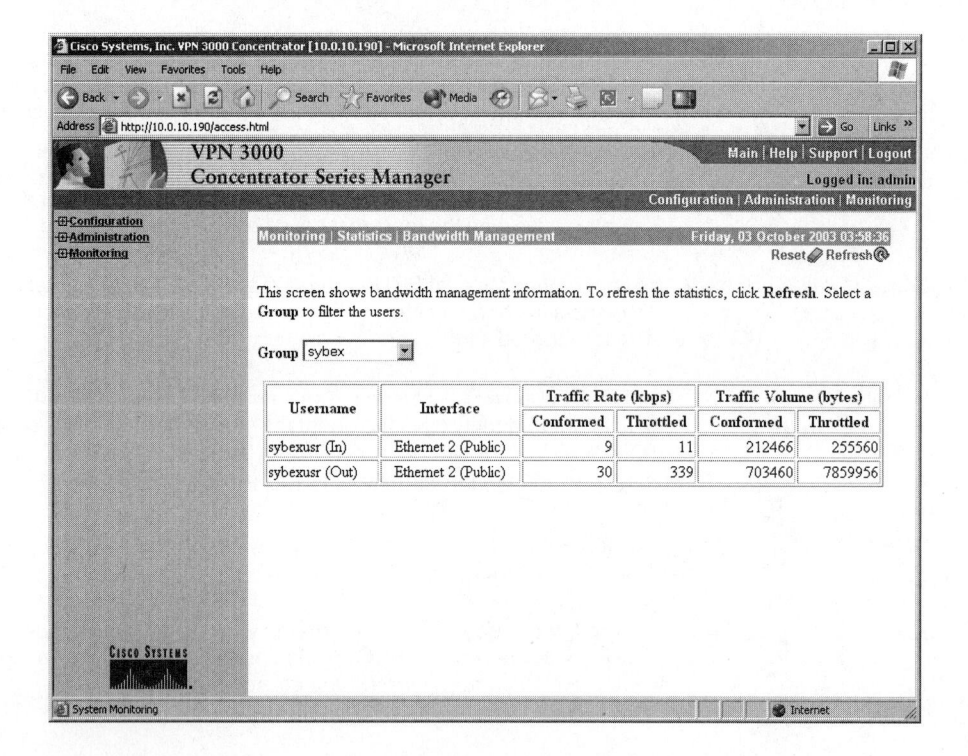

Table 19.3 describes the information available on the Bandwidth Management screen.

Other screens from the Management menu provide similar information in a similar table-based format. Each screen might or might not provide useful information depending on how your concentrator is configured and how you use it. At a minimum, you should be familiar with the PPTP, L2TP, IPSec, Authentication, Filtering, and Bandwidth Management sections.

TABLE 19.3 Bandwidth Management Statistics

Data Field	Description
Group	This option is contained in a drop-down menu and can be the Base Group, an administrator-defined user group, or the keyword All, which is used to select statistics for all groups.
Username	This column identifies the username associated with the tunnel statistics listed to the right. Each tunnel is displayed once for each direction in which the bandwidth policy is applied. In current versions, the bandwidth policy can't be applied unidirectionally.
Interface	The inbound or outbound interface on which the policy is being enforced.
Conformed Rate/Volume	The conforming speed or number of bytes sent or received for this tunnel.
Throttled Rate/Volume	The nonconforming speed or number of bytes for this tunnel.

Viewing Session Monitoring

The Sessions screen, shown in Figure 19.10, appears when you click the Sessions link on the main Monitoring screen. Several types of sessions are supported on the concentrator. At the top of the screen is a summary of the sessions, including totals of each type and all sessions. Further down the screen is detailed information on each type of session as well as information regarding each particular session. The different session types include

LAN-to-LAN Sessions   In a *LAN-to-LAN session,* two network devices form a tunnel between each other. The purpose of the tunnel is to protect information generated by the VPN clients. A concentrator-to-firewall VPN protecting data flowing from one LAN to another is an example of a LAN-to-LAN connection.

Remote-Access Sessions   A *remote-access session* is started by a client machine that has data it wants protected by a VPN. A user dialing up an ISP and then using a VPN client to talk to the concentrator is an example of a remote-access session.

Management Sessions   A *management session* is used to manage the concentrator. An example would be an administrator using a web browser to monitor or administer the concentrator.

FIGURE 19.10 The Sessions screen

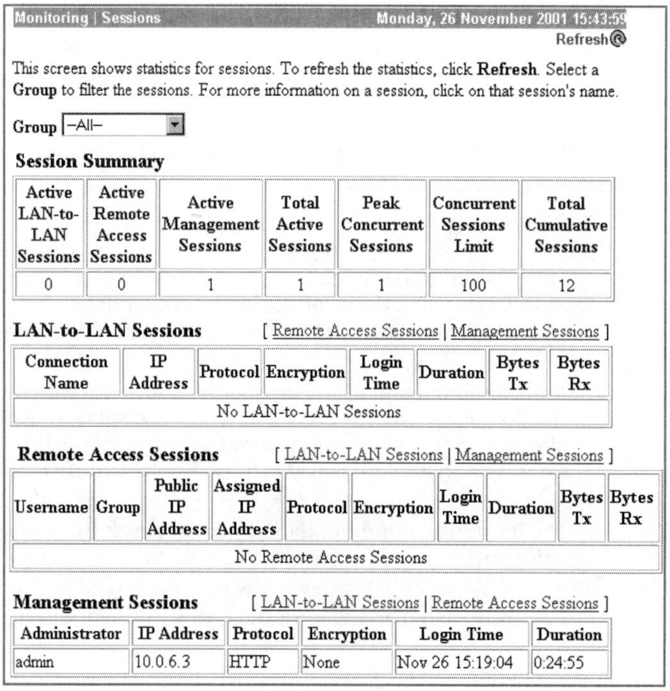

	Active LAN-to-LAN Sessions	Active Remote Access Sessions	Active Management Sessions	Total Active Sessions	Peak Concurrent Sessions	Concurrent Sessions Limit	Total Cumulative Sessions
	0	0	1	1	1	100	12

LAN-to-LAN Sessions [Remote Access Sessions | Management Sessions]

Connection Name	IP Address	Protocol	Encryption	Login Time	Duration	Bytes Tx	Bytes Rx
No LAN-to-LAN Sessions							

Remote Access Sessions [LAN-to-LAN Sessions | Management Sessions]

Username	Group	Public IP Address	Assigned IP Address	Protocol	Encryption	Login Time	Duration	Bytes Tx	Bytes Rx
No Remote Access Sessions									

Management Sessions [LAN-to-LAN Sessions | Remote Access Sessions]

Administrator	IP Address	Protocol	Encryption	Login Time	Duration
admin	10.0.6.3	HTTP	None	Nov 26 15:19:04	0:24:55

Each of the three is displayed with a number of statistics that are relevant to that type of session. For example, the Remote Access Sessions section is the only one that identifies the assigned tunnel IP address. All the information on this screen is available in different sections of the statistics screen found under the main Monitoring menu. However, this screen provides a concise, single-page source for current usage information.

In addition to the information shown on the Monitoring | Sessions screen, you can display the Monitoring | Sessions | Protocols screen to see a breakdown of a session on a protocol-by-protocol basis. The Protocols screen shows sessions for just IPSec or another tunnel type as well as encryption information. Clicking the connection itself provides details about the connection, including the username and IP address assigned to the connection.

Another option, not shown in Figure 19.10, is the ability to access top-10 session information. On the Monitoring | Sessions | Top Ten Lists screen, you can see which connections are the top 10 for connection time or bandwidth usage. To see the top-10 sessions in bytes per second, select Throughput.

Configuring Logging and SNMP Traps

Remote management takes two forms on the concentrator:

- The concentrator can use Management Information Bases (SNMP MIBs) and traps. This allows you to collect and parse information into a real-time format that you can use to make decisions when monitoring the network.

- You can use a Syslog server to collect data so someone can go through it at a later date.

Both methods are configured by choosing Configuration from the VPN Concentrator Manager window and then selecting System ➤ Events. You'll see the Events screen, shown in Figure 19.11.

In the following sections, we'll illustrate how to configure event logging by configuring the event classes on the concentrator as well as the configurations required by SNMP for management and by the Syslog server for additional logging. We'll also look at viewing the local log.

Configuring the Events to Log

To begin logging events, select the General link on the Events screen to set up default event handling. Figure 19.12 shows the General screen, which is used for configuring the types of events to be logged.

This screen is very flexible. You can have one type of event logged to a Syslog server, another type of event sent to SNMP, and a third e-mailed to a pager that is carried by whoever is on call.

FIGURE 19.11 Choosing a method of logging

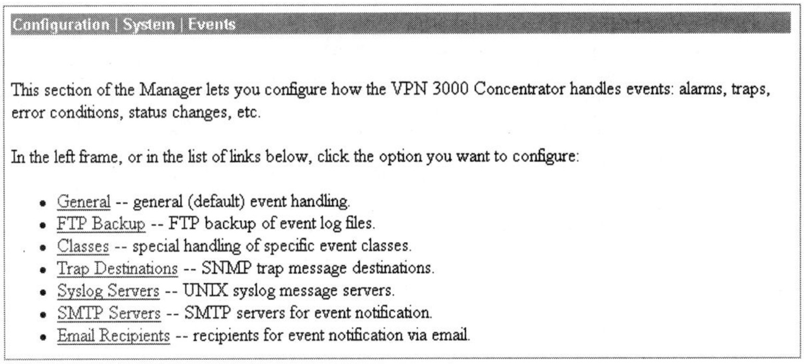

Configuration | System | Events

This section of the Manager lets you configure how the VPN 3000 Concentrator handles events: alarms, traps, error conditions, status changes, etc.

In the left frame, or in the list of links below, click the option you want to configure:

- General -- general (default) event handling.
- FTP Backup -- FTP backup of event log files.
- Classes -- special handling of specific event classes.
- Trap Destinations -- SNMP trap message destinations.
- Syslog Servers -- UNIX syslog message servers.
- SMTP Servers -- SMTP servers for event notification.
- Email Recipients -- recipients for event notification via email.

FIGURE 19.12   The General screen

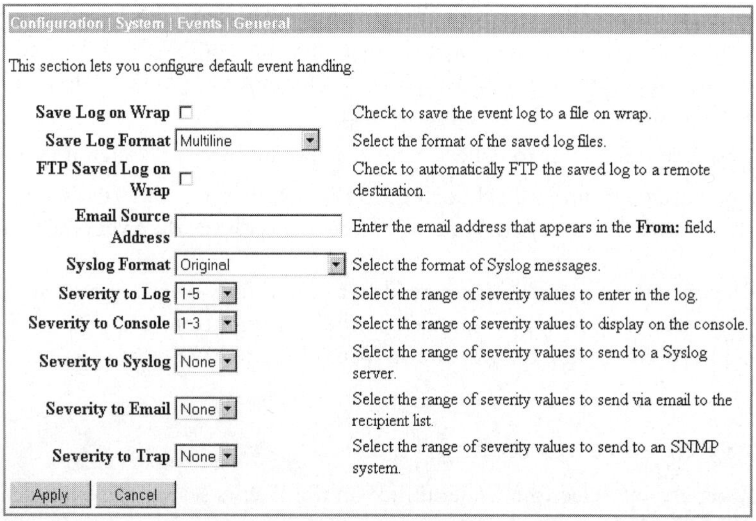

If you check the Save Log On Wrap check box, the log file will be saved when it's about to wrap after 2048 entries on the 3015–3080 models. The 3005, however, is limited to only 256 events. Each save consumes approximately 334KB. If the space available on the flash drops below 2.56MB, the concentrator will delete the oldest logs.

There are three choices for the log format:

- Multiline breaks the event entry into multiple lines of 80 characters each.
- Comma Delimited separates event-entry fields by commas.
- Tab Delimited separates event-entry fields by tabs.

If desired, you can enter an e-mail source address and select the format of Syslog messages. In the remaining fields, you can set severity levels for logging, displaying on the console, sending to a Syslog server, sending to an e-mail recipient list, and trapping.

You can view the log residing in memory any time from the administration console. To do so, access the log by choosing Event Log from the main Monitoring screen. You can filter the log by choosing specific classes and priorities to view (hold down the Ctrl key to make multiple selections).

Creating Custom Event Classes

If the preconfigured events aren't sufficient for your needs, the concentrator also gives you the opportunity to create custom event classes that can log information. Figure 19.13 shows the first screen of this process, the Classes screen. To open this screen, click the Classes link on the Events screen. If you want to change an existing custom event, select it and click Modify. To create a new custom event, click Add.

FIGURE 19.13   Selecting event classes

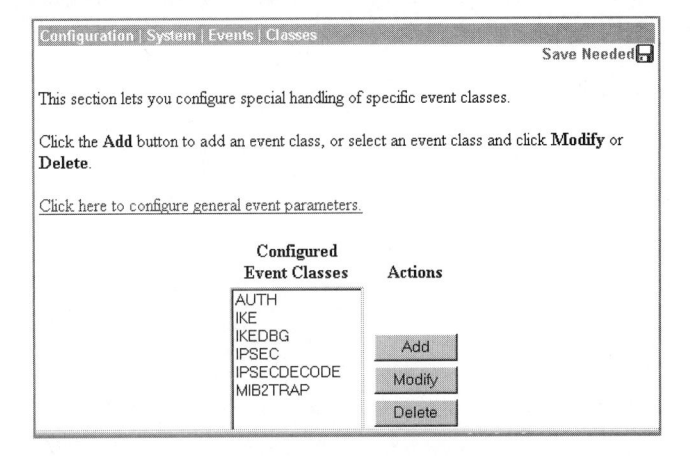

Each custom event can log events from severity values 1 (critical) to 13 (low-level hex dump). Levels 1 through 6 are normal alarms, levels 7 through 9 are debug alarms, and levels 10 through 13 are hex-dump events.

Configuring SNMP

The VPN Concentrator must be configured before trap information can be sent to an SNMP management station. To configure SNMP, select Trap Destinations from the Events screen. Through the Trap Destinations screen, shown in Figure 19.14, you can add or modify trap destinations.

FIGURE 19.14   Configuring SNMP traps

When you click the Add button on the Trap Destinations screen, you'll see the Add screen, shown in Figure 19.15. Entering the correct destination IP address is very important when you're configuring a trap. Choose the SNMP version of the trap, and enter the community string for this device.

FIGURE 19.15   Configuring a specific entry

> **WARNING**
> The default community string, `public`, is a popular SNMP community string. It's strongly recommended that default community strings *not* be used.

Logging On to a Syslog Server

A Syslog server is another type of network device that can capture and store logs generated by a concentrator. Before those logs can be sent out, you must set up a Syslog server and point the concentrator in the right direction. To configure a Syslog server, click the Syslog Servers link on the Events screen to open the Syslog Servers screen shown in Figure 19.16. You'll notice that setting up the Syslog server is similar to setting up SNMP. If there isn't an existing entry, click Add to create a new one.

FIGURE 19.16   Creating a Syslog entry

> ### Real World Scenario
>
> #### Using the Internal Logging Tools
>
> When working on this book, I tried to simulate every possible scenario that was discussed. One of the things that we covered in Chapter 17, "Introduction to Cisco VPN Devices," was the auto-initiation feature and its usage in a WLAN environment.
>
> When simulating the WLAN environment, I didn't have a DHCP server on the WLAN side of the concentrator, so I configured the DHCP forwarding feature. I spent about three hours trying to get my laptop to pick up a DHCP address and eventually tracked the problem to a configuration problem. Here is the process I used to find the issue.
>
> **Setting up logging**
>
> By default, detailed DHCP and IP packet information isn't logged to the Syslog server, the console, or to the internal log. The first step was to reconfigure the logging settings to track the information I wanted. Since I didn't have a computer handy to act as a Syslog server, I used the internal log.
>
> First I navigated to the Configuration | System | Events | General page. I selected the drop-down menu for the Events to Log. By default, you can log only event levels 5 or higher. I needed to see detailed debugging-level events, so I had to select the Use Event List option.
>
> To create the event list, you need to know the event class names. I don't have all these memorized, and Cisco makes us type them in by hand without a reference. Fortunately, you can click to the Filterable Event Log page and cheat by looking at the drop-down options under the filters.
>
> I created an event list that included the DHCP, DHCPDBG, and DHCPDECODE event classes.
>
> **Viewing the log**
>
> From the Live Event Log page, I was able to watch the DHCP-related events occur when I released/renewed my address on my laptop. The logs showed the DHCP request coming into the concentrator, the concentrator forwarding the request, and the DHCP server sending a reply. However, the laptop never received the reply because the VPN concentrator wasn't sending it back on the WLAN side.
>
> **Curing the problem**
>
> Once I knew that the problem was centered at the VPN concentrator and I had narrowed the locations where the packet could be lost, I was able to find the source of the issue. In my haste to reconfigure the concentrator, I had neglected to properly update the outbound filter on the public-side interface. I updated my filter, saved my configuration, and was able to successfully simulate the WLAN scenario.

Clicking Add brings up the Add screen, shown in Figure 19.17. Here, you need to specify the correct IP address. A Syslog server will install on UDP port 514 by default. If the Syslog application was installed with a different port or facility tag, you must enter the correct values.

Navigating to the Monitoring | Filterable Event Log | Live Event Log screen displays events as they are logged in almost real time. The screen is updated every five seconds and displays logs of events that occur on the concentrator. Leaving this screen open is one way to avoid having an administrative session terminated due to an idle timer. The refresh requests that occur every five seconds reset the idle timer.

FIGURE 19.17 Configuring a Syslog server

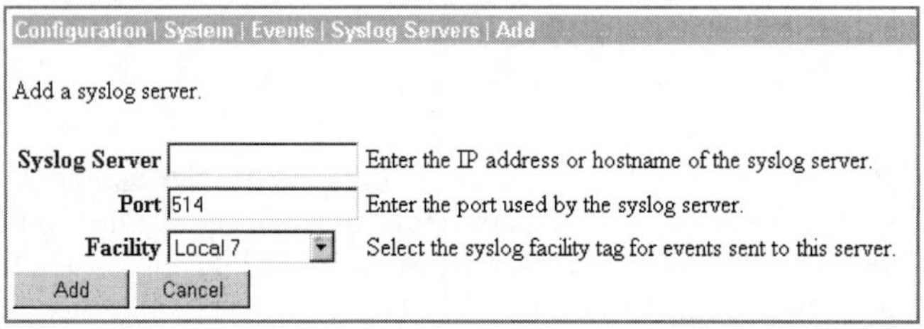

Viewing the Local Log

In addition to being able to send logging information to SNMP and Syslog servers, the VPN concentrator can store a small number of log entries locally. To view the local log, select the Monitoring screen from the main menu. From there, select the Event Log option. Note that older version of the concentrator had a single Event Log option.

The new version, shown earlier in Figure 19.1, has two options. The Live Event Log is an applet-based log that isn't filterable but automatically updates and includes a scrolling interface. The live event log has no configurable parameters. The Filterable Event Log, shown in Figure 19.18, has a number of options to allow the administrator to narrow the information displayed.

Table 19.4 describes the options available on the Filterable Event Log screen.

TABLE 19.4 Filterable Event Log Options

Option	Description
Event Class	Filter based on the class of the event.
Severities	Allows filtering based on specific severity levels.
Client IP Address	Allows filtering based on the address of the client. This applies only to events that are tagged with the information.

TABLE 19.4 Filterable Event Log Options *(continued)*

Option	Description
Events/Page	Number of events displayed per page. The Tape/VCR Type buttons allow movement between the pages.
Group	Allows filtering based on user group.
Direction	Changes the direction of listing from oldest to newest or newest to oldest.
Get/Save/Clear Log	Updates, saves, or erases the internal log.

FIGURE 19.18 The Filterable Event Log screen

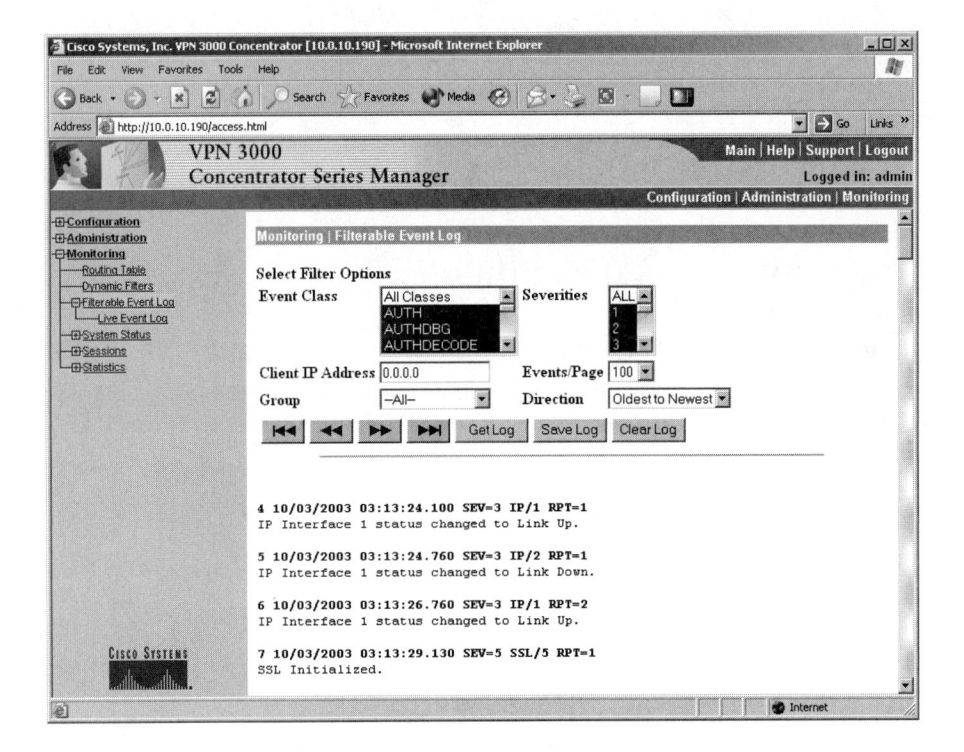

Administering the VPN Concentrator

In addition to monitoring the concentrator, administrators need to perform many miscellaneous administrative functions from time to time. All these functions are accessed through the Administration screen, shown in Figure 19.19. To access this screen, choose Administration from the VPN Concentrator Manager window. In Chapter 18, "Configuring the VPN Concentrator," we used the Certificate Management link on this screen to request and install digital certificates. Here, we'll look at the other options.

FIGURE 19.19 The main Administration screen

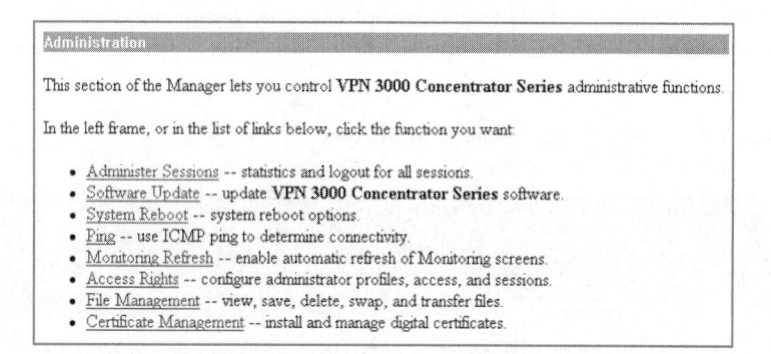

> **Administration**
>
> This section of the Manager lets you control **VPN 3000 Concentrator Series** administrative functions.
>
> In the left frame, or in the list of links below, click the function you want:
>
> - Administer Sessions -- statistics and logout for all sessions.
> - Software Update -- update **VPN 3000 Concentrator Series** software.
> - System Reboot -- system reboot options.
> - Ping -- use ICMP ping to determine connectivity.
> - Monitoring Refresh -- enable automatic refresh of Monitoring screens.
> - Access Rights -- configure administrator profiles, access, and sessions.
> - File Management -- view, save, delete, swap, and transfer files.
> - Certificate Management -- install and manage digital certificates.

Configuring Access Rights

Access control is an important part of any security policy. The concentrator allows the network administrator to have fairly detailed control over many access characteristics. You can configure Access Control Lists, set idle timeouts, and allow additional administrators access to the device. Overall, the purpose of an administrator is to determine access and rights in the concentrator software functional areas.

Adding Administrators

You can create multiple administrator accounts for the concentrator. In fact, the concentrator comes with five preinstalled administrator accounts, as shown in the Administrators screen in Figure 19.20. (To get to this screen, select Access Rights from the main Administration screen, and then select Administrators.) The default accounts and the default rights assigned to each account are listed in Table 19.5.

Fortunately, only one of these accounts is enabled by default (but it isn't impossible for an organization to accidentally get a configured concentrator that was used by another company and then returned). If two administrators are logged in at the same time, the first one gets read-and-write access and all subsequent logins get read-only access.

FIGURE 19.20 Configuring administrators

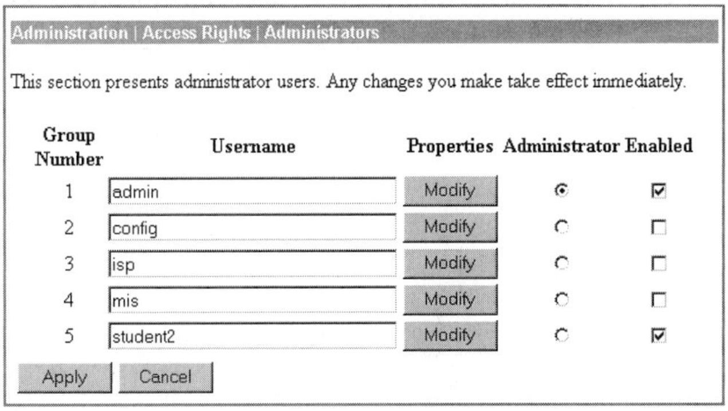

Notice that the administrator account names are in text boxes. This means that these account names can be changed. In the example shown in Figure 19.20, the account name for the group 5 user was changed from its default of `user` to `student2`. The default password for each of these accounts is its username (for example, `admin` for the `admin` account and `config` for the `config` account). There can be only one super administrator (Administrator) account, but you can enable each of the accounts by checking the box in the Enabled column.

TABLE 19.5 Default Concentrator Administrator Accounts

Group	Username	Description
1	admin	System administrator with access to and rights to change all areas. This is the only administrator enabled by default and the only one who can log in to and use the VPN Concentrator Manager as supplied by Cisco.
2	config	Configuration administrator with all rights except SNMP access.
3	isp	ISP administrator with limited general configuration rights.
4	mis	Management information systems administrator with the same rights as `config`.
5	user	User administrator with rights to view only system statistics.

Modifying Administrator Access Rights

If you have multiple administrators in a department and they shouldn't have the same level of ability on the concentrator, you can modify their *access rights*. Click the corresponding Modify button on the Administrators screen to modify the properties of the accounts, as illustrated on the screen shown in Figure 19.21.

FIGURE 19.21 Modifying access rights

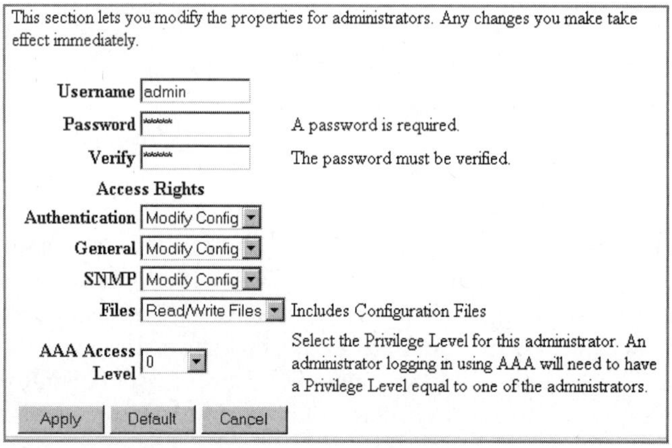

On this screen, you can change the properties of a particular administrator account as well as the username and password. For the Authentication, General, and SNMP access rights, the possible settings include the following:

Setting	Description
None	Administrator has no authority.
Stats Only	Administrator can access only the Monitoring section of the concentrator.
View Config	Administrator can view some items but not make changes (such as User mode on a router).
Modify Config	Administrator can view and change the configuration.

For files, rights can be assigned as follows:

Setting	Description
None	Administrator has no access.
List Files	Administrator can list files residing in flash.
Read Files	Administrator can read files residing in flash.
Read/Write Files	Administrator can read and write files to and from flash and save log files.

Adding an ACL

For security, you want to make sure that only those devices that are permitted to administer the concentrator are able to access it. When the ACL is empty, the concentrator doesn't block any device from sending HTTP packets to it in an attempt to do administration. To allow only certain machines to have this access, you need to filter out other devices.

To create a new ACL, select Access Rights from the main Administration screen, select Access Control List, and click Add. On the Add screen, shown in Figure 19.22, specify the IP address that can access the concentrator and the subnet mask. Then assign this device to a particular administrative group. Make sure the group is enabled (as described previously, in the "Adding Administrators" section) if you want the user to be able to perform any administrative tasks.

After you've created a new list, you can make changes to it by highlighting it on the Access Control List screen and clicking Modify.

FIGURE 19.22 Creating a new ACL

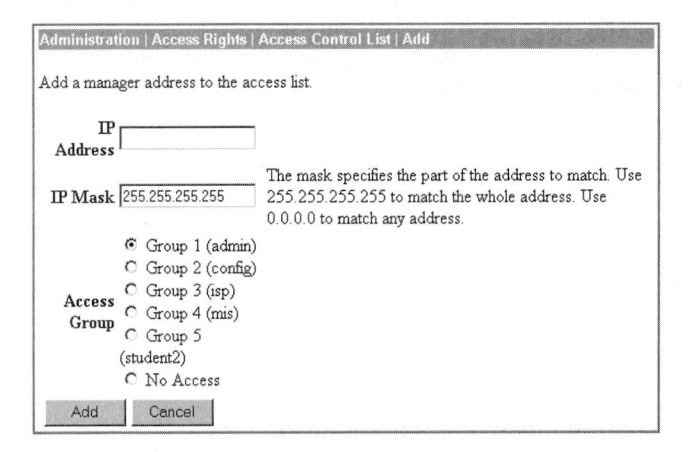

Managing Access Settings

Generally, you won't need to worry about the settings for administrative sessions. To see the session idle timeout and session limit settings, select Access Rights from the main Administration screen, and then choose Access Settings.

As shown in Figure 19.23, each administrative session has a default timeout of 10 minutes (600 seconds), and there can be no more than 10 administrative sessions at a time, by default. If necessary, you can change these values. This screen also has a check box for configuration file encryption. By default, sensitive items inside the configuration file are encrypted. If necessary, you can deselect this setting to disable encryption.

FIGURE 19.23 The Access Settings screen

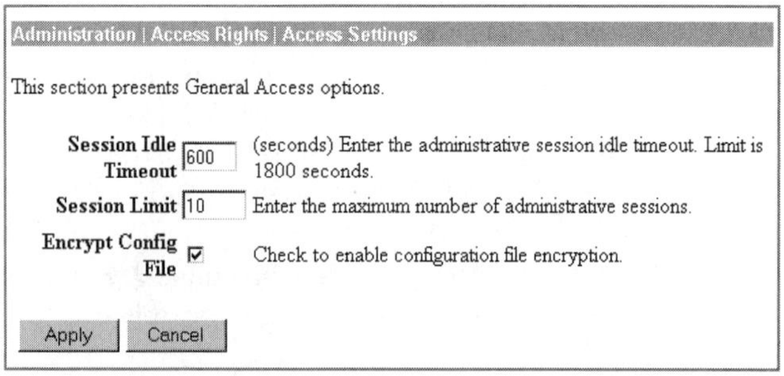

Administering Sessions

The Administer Sessions screen, displayed by choosing Administer Sessions from the main Administration screen, is very similar to the Sessions screen accessed from the main Monitoring screen (shown earlier in Figure 19.10). There is only one small difference: the Management Sessions section of the Administer Sessions screen allows you to ping the device accessing the management console as well as log out that user, as shown in Figure 19.24.

FIGURE 19.24 The Management Sessions screen

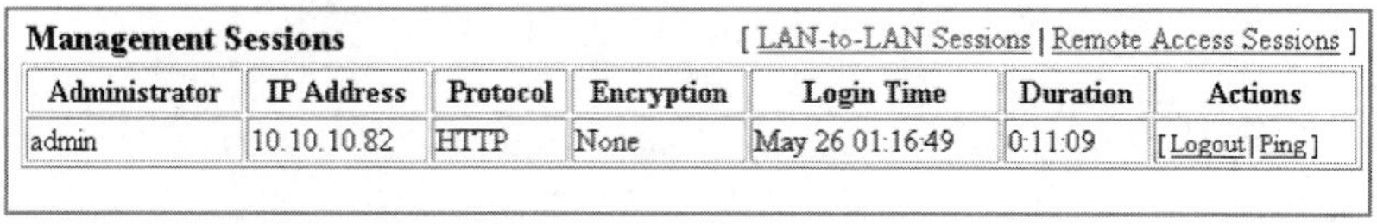

Administering File Management

The File Management screen provides options for managing files, swapping the configuration files, and transferring files via Trivial File Transport Protocol (TFTP). To open the File Management screen, click File Management on the main Administration screen. We'll look at this screen's options in detail in the following sections.

Managing Files

When you click the Files link on the File Management screen, you see the screen shown in Figure 19.25, with each file's name, size, and creation date and time. You can view, delete, or copy these files by selecting the appropriate action.

Two files that are commonly found here are CONFIG and CONFIG.BAK. CONFIG is the latest saved version of the configuration. CONFIG.BAK is the prior saved version of the configuration.

FIGURE 19.25 The Files screen

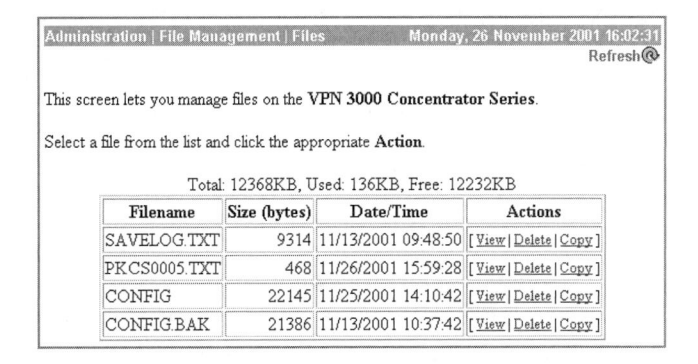

Swapping Configuration Files

If someone makes a configuration mistake and saves the changes, you can go back to the previous version of the configuration file (CONFIG.BAK). To do this, choose Swap Configuration Files from the File Management screen. You'll see the screen shown in Figure 19.26.

FIGURE 19.26 The Swap Configuration Files screen

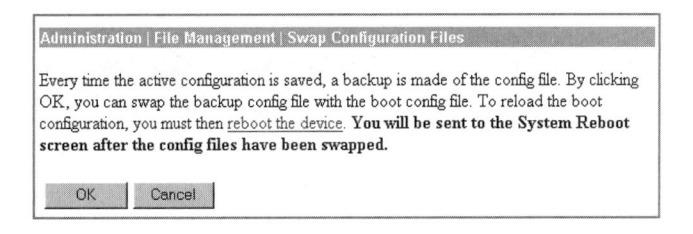

When you click OK, the System Reboot screen appears, as shown in Figure 19.27. (You can also access this screen directly by choosing System Reboot from the main Administration screen.) From here, you can make several choices about the reboot, including when it will happen, whether the configuration will be saved beforehand, and so on. All in all, a reboot normally takes a bit over a minute. If you don't save the current configuration, any changes you make will be lost.

Transferring Files using TFTP

Trivial File Transport Protocol (TFTP) is one way of getting files from another network device to the concentrator. Choosing TFTP Transfer from the File Management screen displays the screen shown in Figure 19.28.

FIGURE 19.27   The System Reboot screen

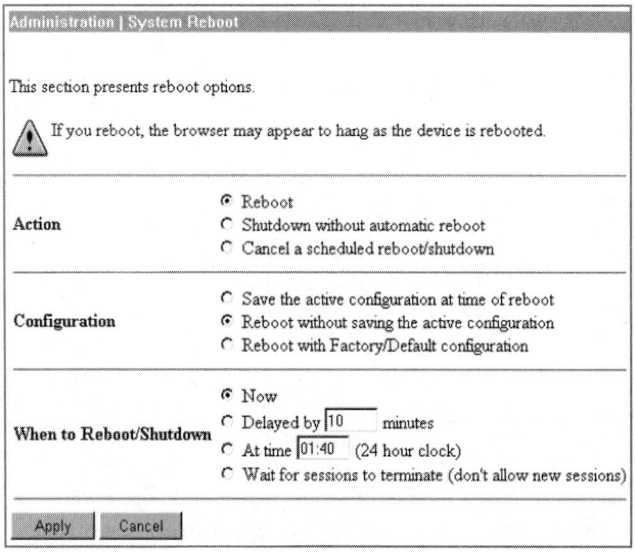

FIGURE 19.28   The TFTP Transfer screen

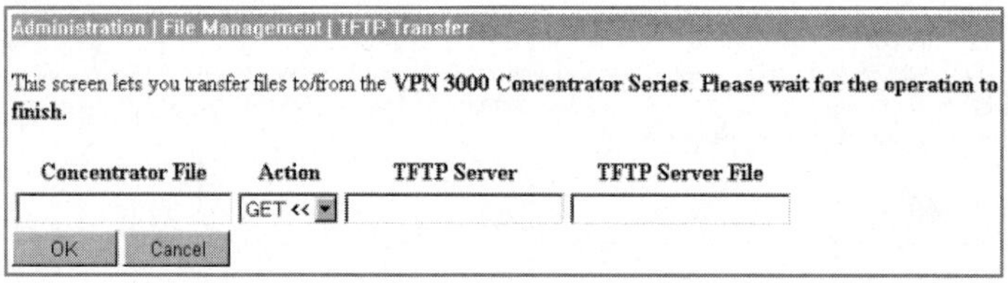

The TFTP Transfer screen accepts four options:

Concentrator File   This is the filename as shown on the concentrator.

Action   The action is the direction of the transfer as viewed from the perspective of the concentrator.

TFTP Server   This is the name or IP address of the server the file will be copied to or from.

TFTP Server File   This is the filename as shown on the TFTP server. It need not be the same as the name on the concentrator.

Note that the TFTP Transfer menu isn't used to upgrade the operating system on the concentrator. TFTP is appropriate for copying the configuration to a TFTP server and back.

Updating Software

Upgrading the software on the concentrator is easy. Select Administration ➢ Software Update ➢ Concentrator from the main menu. The Software Update | Concentrator screen, shown in Figure 19.29, shows what type of software is currently loaded and provides an option to upgrade.

FIGURE 19.29 The Concentrator screen

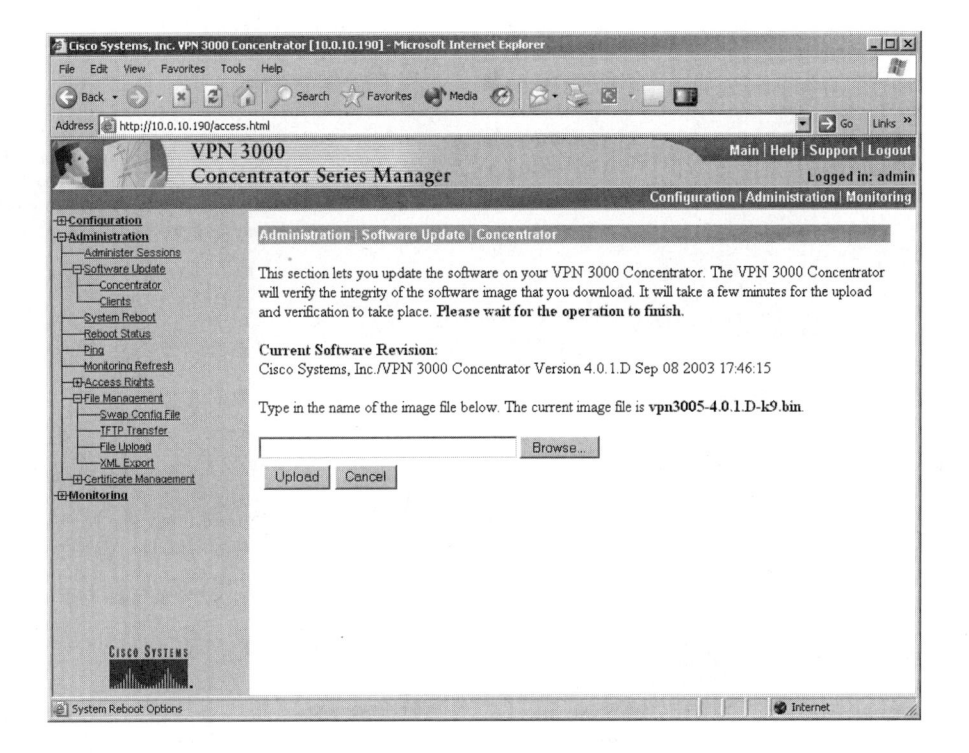

If you want to upgrade software, place the updated version of the software on the local PC or on a network drive the PC can access. Then click the Browse button to find the correct file, and place the path in the box next to the Browse button. With the correct path specified, click the Update button to upgrade the software. Once the software has been updated, the concentrator will need to reboot. Be sure to save the configuration, or any changes will be lost.

You can also use the software update feature to notify users of available updates to the client. This will tell them the location to go to download the update files. To do so, navigate to the Clients screen under the Software Update menu and select the group you wish to notify.

Pinging Devices

The concentrator can ping another device to ensure it exists on the network. One way to do this is by selecting Ping from the main Administration screen, which brings up the Ping screen, shown in Figure 19.30. Enter the IP address of the device to test, and click the Ping button to generate a response. The desired response is that the destination "is alive."

FIGURE 19.30 The Ping screen

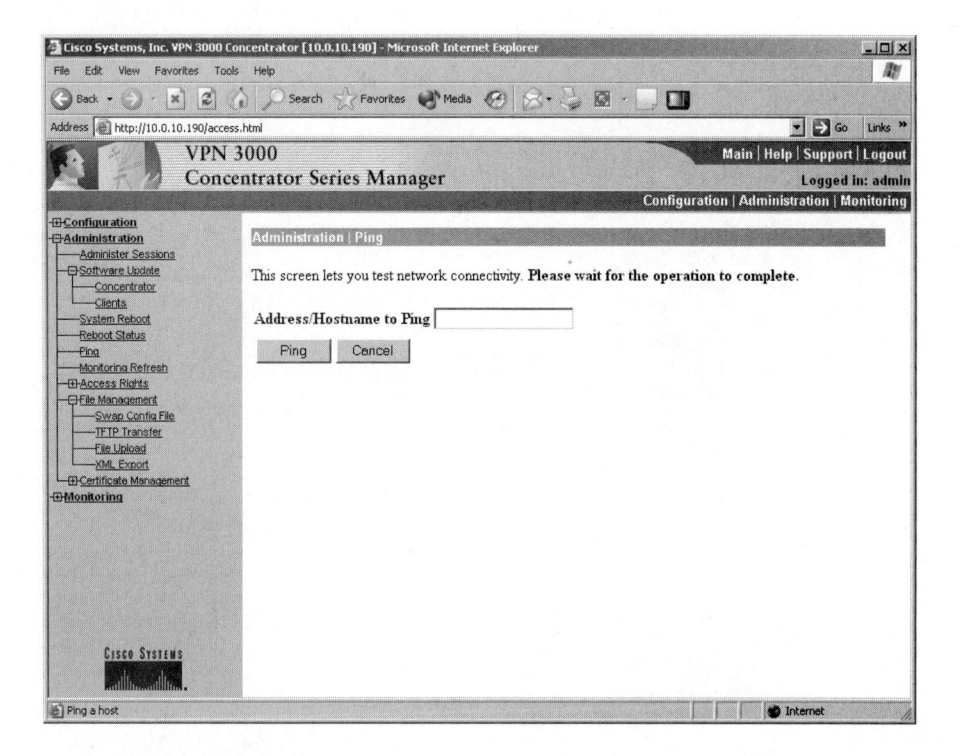

Summary

This chapter covered two areas of the VPN Concentrator's management utility: monitoring and administering.

Typically, you won't need to check the Monitoring section on a daily basis, but you should check it occasionally. Remember that both SNMP and system logging (through a Syslog server) allow the concentrator to inform other network devices of what is going on. Some form of semi-permanent storage of the logs is always a good idea, in case you need to refer to those logs.

The Administration section is a large catchall area for items that don't easily fit under Configuration and are often directly related to administration of the concentrator. The two broad items covered here are administrator configuration and file management.

Exam Essentials

Know that there are three primary sections for managing the VPN Concentrator. The three modes are Monitoring, Configuration, and Administration. Configuration is where the concentrator configuration occurs. Administration is where policy-related items are configured and tested. Monitoring is used to see what is going on with the concentrator and network.

Understand that while the VPN Concentrator Manager is a Cisco product, some Cisco features aren't enabled on it. The CVPN 3000 series product line provides many common features using methods that differ from a router or firewall. For example, a router typically uses Cisco's proprietary Hot Standby Router Protocol (HSRP) for redundancy. The VPN concentrator uses Virtual Router Redundancy Protocol (VRRP), which is an equivalent IETF draft-standard protocol. Terminology can also differ. An access control list (ACL) is used to control access to the web or virtual console on a VPN concentrator, and a filter rule is used to control traffic through the VPN concentrator. An ACL on a Cisco router is used to identify traffic for filtering, security, or traffic prioritization.

Know how to manage the concentrator. There are four different ways to manage the concentrator. Telnet and console access allow you to manage it via a command line. HTTP (or HTTPS) is required to use the GUI. SNMP management is available. A part of CiscoWorks also works well as a management tool.

Understand the meaning of each of the bandwidth management statistics. The bandwidth management statistics provide important information about both permitted and filtered bandwidth usage for users and groups. Make sure you can verify correct bandwidth management configurations by using these statistics.

Understand how configuration files are stored on the concentrator. The configuration instructions are stored in CONFIG and CONFIG.BAK. The CONFIG file is the most recent save. The CONFIG.BAK file is the second most recent save.

Know how to upgrade concentrator software. To upgrade the software, you store the software where your PC can access it and then give the path to the concentrator. The concentrator then downloads the files through your PC.

PART IV

Cisco Secure Intrusion Detection Systems

Chapter 20

Introduction to Intrusion Detection and Protection

CISCO SECURE INTRUSION DETECTION SYSTEMS EXAM TOPICS COVERED IN THIS CHAPTER:

- ✓ Defining intrusion detection
- ✓ The difference between true and false, and positive and negative alarms
- ✓ The relationship between vulnerabilities and exploits
- ✓ The difference between HIP and NIDS
- ✓ Various techniques used to evade intrusion detection
- ✓ Features of the various IDS Sensor appliance models

It should come as no surprise that there are many security threats that may attack a network, including attacks that are extremely complex in nature and that are over within seconds. To protect networks from security threats, you need intelligent defensive systems that can understand the characteristics of each attack, enabling them to positively distinguish intrusive activity from large, continuous streams of network traffic. *Intrusion detection* describes the detection of intrusive activity on the network, which indicates that a possible attack or unauthorized action is occurring on the network. *Intrusion protection* describes the ability to protect an organization's private network and information assets from attacks and unauthorized activity in real time.

An *intrusion detection system (IDS)* provides intrusion detection functionality—once an attack is detected, an IDS can respond to the threat and notify intrusion protection systems, allowing these systems to block further attacks. Intrusion protection systems are typically firewalls or routers with access control lists configured to filter traffic inbound and/or outbound on an external interface.

Cisco provides an excellent IDS solution that can detect a large number of documented attacks, with frequent updates that ensure that new attacks are detected as they appear on the Internet. The Cisco Secure IDS also provides the necessary tools to let you manage your network security on an ongoing basis.

In this chapter, we begin with a discussion of the security threats that result in the need for network security. Next, you'll see how to actually implement network security. Then we'll review intrusion-detection basics. Finally, we'll provide an overview of Cisco Secure IDS. The information covered in this chapter provides a foundation for the IDS installation and configuration details in the following chapters.

Understanding Security Threats

Before you can secure a network, it's important to understand the characteristics of *security threats*, so you know what you need to defend against. For intrusion-detection purposes, security threats are loosely classified as the parties responsible for initiating attacks on your network. There are various types of fundamental security threats, which relate to hacker expertise (structured or unstructured) and where an attack originates from (external or internal). There are also several types of attacks that are executed by security threats. First, we'll look at hacker characteristics that determine the nature of threats, and then we'll look at the various types of attacks.

Hacker Characteristics

The expertise of the hacker determines who is attacking your network and how likely they are to break into your network or cause disruption. The location of the hacker determines where the threat exists.

Hacker Expertise

In the past, hackers needed to have a deep understanding of networking, operating systems (especially Unix), programming, and Internet protocols such as DNS and FTP. These days, tools are readily available on the Internet that automate many of the hacking functions that used to require this expertise. Consequently, hacking can now be performed by many of the masses of people who have access to the Internet. Two distinct categories of hacker expertise have emerged: *unstructured threats* and *structured threats*.

Unstructured Threats

Unstructured-threat hackers typically have low to moderate skills and are trying to hack into your network just for the heck of it. These hackers are also known as *script kiddies* because they typically use scripts created by other highly skilled hackers as their tools.

Generally, an unstructured attack leaves a noticeable trail, and it's a fairly blatant attack on your network. This is because these hackers are more interested in accessing or bringing down your network as quickly as possible than they are in being undetected. As soon as these hackers have succeeded or failed, they generally move on to the next target, without trying to obtain private information contained on your network.

Even though the unstructured-threat hacker may not be after your company's top-secret business plan, the hacker can cause substantial disruption to the network, often without detection. A hacker may attempt to run scripts against your system that are supposed to grant unauthorized access to the system; but instead they may inadvertently crash the system, causing an outage that could cost your company dearly in both revenue and reputation. Many unstructured threats are also targeted at bringing down a network resource, to give the hacker a sense of power, control, and self-gratification.

Structured Threats

Structured-threat hackers are highly skilled individuals who intimately understand networking, operating systems, programming, and the mechanics of Internet protocols. These hackers can program tools that may exploit a new vulnerability or modify existing tools to suit their own requirements. Often, a structured-threat hacker attacks a system only if required. For example, a rival organization might hire a hacker to break into your network and obtain your five-year business plan. This hacker would try to break into your network as stealthily as possible, often over a period of weeks or months. The hacker could break into several systems, each providing access one step closer to the hacker's ultimate goal.

A structured threat represents a real danger not only to your network but also to the ongoing survival of your business. If your private and sensitive business information is compromised and ends up in the hands of your competition, you could be out of business within months.

Hacker Location

Any attack on your network starts from a specific location. An obvious location is a computer somewhere on the Internet (an external threat). A less obvious location is on a computer located on your internal network (an internal threat). You must understand where potential attacks can originate in order to position your security-defense systems appropriately.

External Threats

An attack that originates from a system that is outside your administrative control is considered an *external threat*. The most common external threat is one that originates from the Internet. Extranet connections to external vendors, business partners, and customers can also pose external threats.

The external threat is well known and is perceived as the most common threat to the network. Most organizations at the very least place a firewall between the Internet and their internal network to protect against external threats on the Internet. Firewalls and other security measures in place at the border of your network can detect and report on these external attacks.

Internal Threats

An attack that originates from a system that is within your administrative control is considered an *internal threat*. An interesting fact that is highlighted in numerous studies is that most attacks originate from an internal source. The internal threat is almost always somebody who has some form of access to your network. This includes current employees, contractors, disgruntled former employees, and employees of external service organizations who may frequently work on your network or systems.

Many organizations implement no network security measures whatsoever on the internal network, meaning an attack from an internal threat will generally succeed and won't be detected. If you're serious about securing your network, you must consider internal threats and implement adequate security mechanisms to protect against this form of attack.

Attack Types

The primary function of an IDS is to detect intrusive activity directed against your network and/or systems, which can be loosely classified as an attack. In order for an IDS to detect an attack, it must be programmed with the various criteria that combined together uniquely identify an attack. The collective criteria that characterize an attack are normally referred to as the *signature* of an attack. A signature allows an IDS to uniquely identify a specific attack. Many attacks are based upon hacker tools and scripts that exploit known vulnerabilities in network protocols, operating systems, and applications.

A *vulnerability* is a weakness that compromises the security and/or functionality of a system. For example, a network device such as a router or firewall may ship with default passwords that are public knowledge, which if left unchanged are vulnerable to compromise. Another example of a vulnerability might be the exchange of private and sensitive data in clear text, enabling an intermediate party to capture the data, compromising the privacy of that data.

An *exploit* takes advantage of vulnerabilities and is often implemented in the form of hacking tools and scripts. For example, a password cracker is designed to provide the fast cracking of weak passwords based on common words in the dictionary. This exploit takes advantage of the vulnerability associated with weak passwords.

> **Note:** Make sure you understand exactly what a vulnerability is and what an exploit is, and the difference between them.

Attacks can be characterized by many different criteria, and it's important to understand these criteria to determine how you can identify and react to an attack. Attacks can be classified into the following three types:

- Reconnaissance attacks
- Access attacks
- Denial of service (DoS) attacks

Each of these attack types is now discussed in more detail.

Reconnaissance Attacks

Reconnaissance attacks are the process of collecting various pieces of information about your network and organization. The goal of reconnaissance attacks is to obtain as much useful information as possible about your network, allowing any potential weaknesses or vulnerabilities in your network to be discovered. In modern warfare, reconnaissance is an important part of the overall attack process. Reconnaissance could include photography of enemy target locations, which allows the attacking side to find any potential weaknesses in the defense systems of the target.

Identifying these weaknesses helps increase the chance of the attack being successful. Just as in warfare, reconnaissance is an important part of the network hacking process and allows a hacker to discover a chink in the security systems of a target organization. The presence of reconnaissance attacks against your network normally indicates that an access or DoS attack (discussed later) is about to occur.

Two types of tools can be used for reconnaissance attacks:

- Administrative tools
- Scanning tools

Administrative Tools

Administrative tools aren't designed specifically for network security purposes. These tools have been developed for administrative and informational purposes, allowing network administrators to administer and obtain information about network resources. Unfortunately, these tools can also allow hackers to administer or obtain information about a target system. Some examples of common informational tools include:

Ping This tool uses Internet Control Message Protocol (ICMP) echo requests and echo responses to verify that an IP system is alive on the network.

Nslookup This is a command-line tool used to query DNS databases for information.

Telnet This utility provides virtual terminal access (terminal emulation) over TCP/IP to a remote system.

Finger This is a utility that allows you to query a host for information about user accounts on a remote system.

Scanning Tools

Scanning tools have been developed especially for testing the security of your network. These tools are a double-edged sword: Although they can be used by security administrators to find potential weaknesses in the network, they can also be used by hackers to find those same weaknesses. Scanning tools are designed to gather network resource information quickly and efficiently, presenting it in a format relevant to the administrator's or hacker's goals. Some scanning tools include *stealth* features, which minimize the chances of scans or probes (by the tool) being detected by security defense systems on the target network. Some examples of common scanning tools include:

Nmap This is an essential component of any hacker's toolkit. It provides a variety of port scanning functions and includes advanced features such operating system detection of target hosts.

Security Administrator Tool for Analyzing Networks (SATAN) This tool analyzes hosts for common vulnerabilities, such as those present in Network File System (NFS) and sendmail.

Nessus This is an extremely powerful security analysis tool that can be extended by a scripting language and features plug-ins for different attack types.

Access Attacks

Access attacks are designed to allow an attacker to gain unauthorized access to one or more target systems. An access attack generally takes advantage of a vulnerability in a target system by executing a known exploit (such as a hacking tool or script) against the target system. Access attacks can be categorized as providing access via the following mechanisms:

Unauthorized data manipulation This refers to the unauthorized reading, writing, copying, moving, or deleting of information that normally isn't accessible by an intruder. This is commonly provided due to weak authentication or via the exploitation of trust relationships between two systems.

System access This refers to the ability of an intruder to gain access to a system without prior knowledge of or possession of an account for the system. System access is normally gained by exploiting known application vulnerabilities that may provide partial or full access to a target system. System access may also be provided by poor configuration or via back doors installed by an intruder during a previous system compromise.

Privilege escalation This refers to the ability of an intruder who has limited access to a system to escalate their privileges on the system to provide partial or full access. Privilege escalation is often used to allow an intruder to install a back door allowing future system access, install other hacking tools to aid attempts to hack deeper into the network, and also erase any trace of the intruder on the compromised system by performing actions such as the deletion of log files or event logs.

Now that you understand the general categories of access attacks, it's time to examine some of the vulnerabilities that exist and discuss the exploits by which an attacker can gain unauthorized access to target systems. These vulnerabilities and exploits relate to the following:

- Physical access
- Authentication
- Trust relationships
- Protocol weaknesses
- Poor configuration
- Application vulnerabilities
- Back doors

Physical Access

When a hacker attacks a system from a remote location, there are typically security defense mechanisms in place, such as a firewall between the hacker and the target system. This makes the hacker's job of gaining access to the system much harder. If a hacker can obtain physical access to a target system, then many security mechanisms can be bypassed. For example, an attacker could boot the target system from a floppy disk and access the hard drive file system without the normal operating system's file system security controls. You should always consider the physical security of sensitive systems, and it's advisable to implement the following recommendations:

- Place your key computer systems (for example, servers, routers, switches, and firewalls) in a secured facility, such as a purpose-built computer room that has locked, restricted access to computer-related personnel only. If your computer systems are located in a shared computer facility (such as a large data center), ensure that your racks are locked at all times.
- Implement some form of auditing of access to key computer systems. This could be as simple as maintaining a handwritten log book or as complex as integrating your door security access system into a security auditing system on your network.
- Implement power-on passwords and BIOS passwords on all systems where possible. This prevents unauthorized access to the BIOS settings on servers.
- Disable booting from removable media (floppy disk, CD-ROM, network) in the BIOS. This prevents a hacker from booting a floppy and obtaining access to a system's data.

Authentication

Most modern operating systems include security features that require you to authenticate in some manner before granting remote access to the system. The most common authentication mechanism is to present a username and password to the system that matches what is stored in the system's user database. Usernames are fairly easy to guess, because they typically follow common naming conventions (for example, matching the user portion of the user's e-mail address). A hacker needs to find out the username of an account that has access to a target and then attempt to crack the password. Many passwords are easy to guess, because they may be a default password or have something to do with the legitimate user.

A password can be cracked manually (the hacker gains initial access to a system, is prompted for username and password, and then manually enters a password guess); however, this can take a long time. Automated password-cracking tools exist that automatically attempt different passwords until a match is found. These tools commonly perform what is known as a *dictionary attack*, where the password cracker attempts to use common English words that are defined in a dictionary file. Because humans set passwords and need to be able to remember them, a lot of passwords are English words that the user can remember; so the dictionary attack can crack these passwords fairly quickly. If all else fails, the hacker can resort to a *brute force attack*, which attempts every possible combination of password. The brute force attack can take a long time, depending on the processing power of the attacking system and the actual length of the password.

Some examples of common password-cracking tools include:

LC3 Formerly called L0phtcrack, this is an extremely powerful application that can crack Windows NT and Windows 2000 SAM (user account) databases. LC3 can crack passwords from a number of sources, including via a sniffer that intercepts a Windows authentication session.

Crack by Alec Muffet This is a password cracker for Unix.

Brutus This cracks common services such as HTTP, FTP, and POP3.

Trust Relationships

A *trust relationship* exists when a particular system trusts another system based upon IP address. The trusting system authenticates access based on the IP address of a remote system. This is a very weak form of authentication, because many users can use a single computer and it's easy to spoof the source IP address of a packet. Older versions of the Unix *r utilities* (`rcp`, `rsh`, and so on) use IP-based authentication to grant access. A file containing the names or IP addresses of trusted hosts determines whether access is granted. By masquerading as a trusted host, the hacker can obtain access to the system. Figure 20.1 illustrates trust relationships.

In Figure 20.1, JUPITER is defined as the trusting host because remote users are attempting to gain access to it. The `/etc/hosts.equiv` file on JUPITER controls which hosts are trusted, which in this example is MARS. A superuser account called `alice` exists on JUPITER. Alice has an account on MARS called **bob** and wishes to access JUPITER remotely from MARS from time to time. The `/home/alice/.rhosts` file on JUPITER basically states that the account called **bob** from the remote host MARS has the same access rights as the `alice` account on JUPITER. This means that Alice can log on to MARS as Bob and send remote commands (using the `rsh` utility) to JUPITER that run in the context of Alice's account, without any authentication (because JUPITER trusts MARS, JUPITER trusts that MARS has successfully authenticated the user Bob and therefore shouldn't need to authenticate the requested remote access). Notice that if Alice logs on to VENUS as any user and attempts to execute a remote command, the request is rejected because VENUS isn't in the list of trusted hosts (`/etc/hosts.equiv`).

A hacker can exploit the configuration in Figure 20.1 by *pretending* to be the user Bob on MARS and sending an `rsh` command to JUPITER. This command could add the attacker's host to the `/etc/hosts.equiv` file and then add the user's account to the `/home/alice/.rhosts` file. Now the attacker's host system is trusted, and the attacker can execute remote commands in the context of Alice on JUPITER.

Protocol Weaknesses

Many of the protocols in use today on the Internet were created at a time when security wasn't a major concern on the Internet. The Internet then was considered a research network, and it consisted of researchers and educational institutions. Because of this, many network protocols have few or no security features built in, making them susceptible to misuse by hackers. Common protocols that have security weaknesses include:

- Address Resolution Protocol (ARP)
- User Datagram Protocol (UDP)
- Transmission Control Protocol (TCP)
- Internet Control Message Protocol (ICMP)
- Internet Protocol (IP)

As you can see, all the fundamental IP protocols are vulnerable to weaknesses.

> **NOTE** An example of a tool that can be used to exploit ARP is Ettercap. See http://ettercap.sourceforge.net for more details.

FIGURE 20.1 Trust relationships

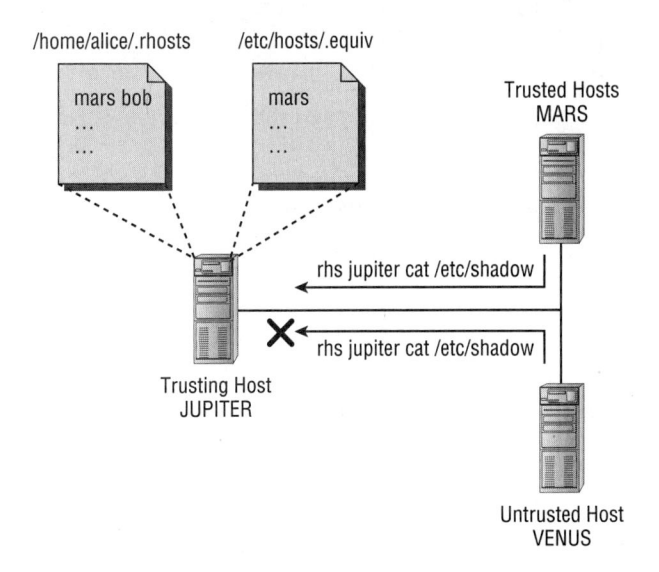

> ### Real World Scenario
>
> **An Example of a Protocol Weakness**
>
> Many network administrators understand that using a hub to connect hosts on a LAN segment represents a security vulnerability, because all hosts on the segment see all traffic on the segment and could sniff data off the wire to determine sensitive information. To circumvent this issue, you can use a switch that will only send *unicast* traffic out the ports attached to the source and destination of the unicast frame. This stops an eavesdropper attached to another switch port from eavesdropping; using a switch is generally accepted as the method to secure local unicast LAN communications from eavesdropping.
>
> However, the following illustrates an example of a protocol weakness in ARP that can be used to eavesdrop on unicast traffic, even if a switch is used to interconnect each host.
>
> This graphic illustrates the normal operation of ARP:
>
> **PLUTO**
> IP: 192.168.1.3
> MAC: 00-11-22-03-03-03
>
> **MARS**
> IP: 192.168.1.1
> MAC: 00-11-22-01-01-01
>
> **VENUS**
> IP: 192.168.1.2
> MAC: 00-11-22-02-02-02
>
> ① **ARP Request (Broadcast)**
> What is the MAC address for IP address 192.168.1.2?
>
> ② **ARP Reply (Unicast)**
> MAC address is 00-11-22-02-02-02
>
> ARP cache
> 192.168.1.2 00-11-22-02-02-02
>
> ③ Add IP ←→ MAC mapping to ARP cache
>
> The following describes the steps that take place during ARP operation:
>
> 1. MARS wishes to communicate with VENUS and determines that VENUS (192.168.1.2) is located on the same subnet. MARS checks the local ARP cache to see if a MAC address entry for 192.168.1.2 exists. An ARP entry doesn't exist, so MARS sends an ARP request broadcast, which requests the MAC address for 192.168.1.2 (VENUS). The broadcast is flooded to all hosts on the LAN segment.

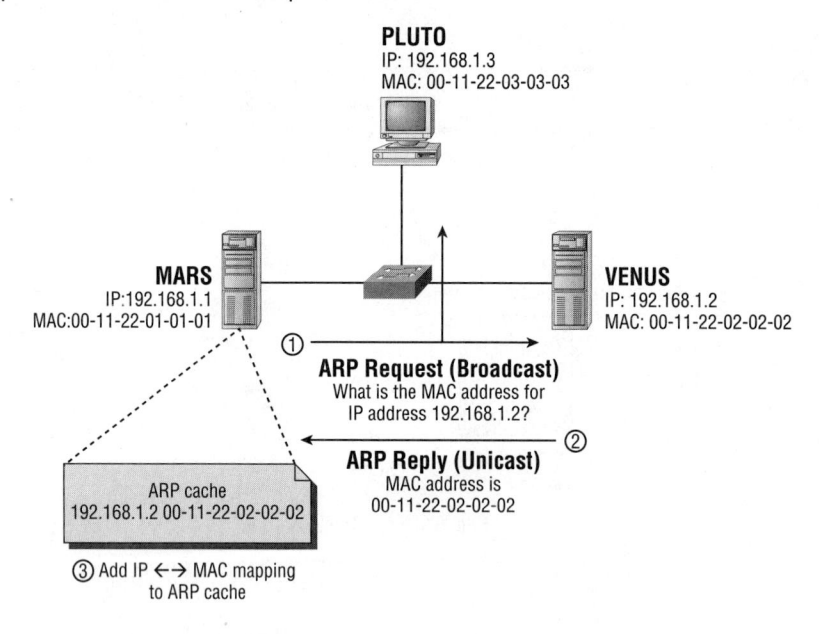

Understanding Security Threats

2. Because VENUS is the host with an IP address of 192.168.1.2, it responds with an ARP reply, which contains the MAC address of VENUS (00-11-22-02-02-02). This frame is sent directly to MARS.

3. MARS receives the ARP reply and adds an IP ← → MAC address mapping to its local ARP cache. MARS can now communicate with VENUS over the LAN.

Now consider the following graphic:

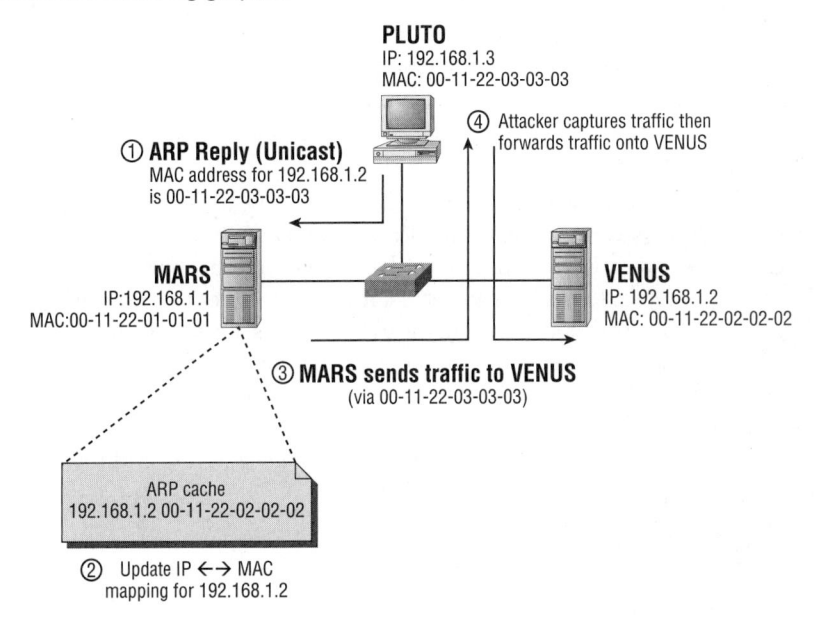

[Diagram: PLUTO (IP: 192.168.1.3, MAC: 00-11-22-03-03-03) — Attacker captures traffic then forwards traffic onto VENUS (4). ① ARP Reply (Unicast): MAC address for 192.168.1.2 is 00-11-22-03-03-03. MARS (IP: 192.168.1.1, MAC: 00-11-22-01-01-01) connected via switch to VENUS (IP: 192.168.1.2, MAC: 00-11-22-02-02-02). ③ MARS sends traffic to VENUS (via 00-11-22-03-03-03). ARP cache: 192.168.1.2 00-11-22-02-02-02. ② Update IP ← → MAC mapping for 192.168.1.2]

In the graphic, the following events take place:

1. An attacker on PLUTO continuously sends bogus ARP reply messages to MARS, which state that the MAC address of the host with an IP address of 192.168.1.2 (VENUS) is 00-11-22-03-03-03 (which is actually the MAC address of PLUTO).

2. MARS receives the ARP reply and updates the IP ← → MAC address mapping in its local ARP cache. MARS does this because it's feasible that a new host could have appeared on the network with an IP address of 192.168.1.2 (this could happen with Dynamic Host Configuration Protocol [DHCP]).

3. When MARS wishes to communicate with VENUS (192.168.1.2), it checks the local ARP cache and determines that the MAC address of the IP host 192.168.1.2 is 00-11-22-03-03-03 (which is really PLUTO). MARS transmits the packet to PLUTO (instead of directly to VENUS).

4. A sniffer running on PLUTO captures the traffic received from MARS that is really intended for VENUS. PLUTO then forwards the traffic on to VENUS to allow the communications to continue. The attacker on PLUTO can employ the same technique in step 1 for VENUS so that the return traffic is also redirected through PLUTO.

As you can see, a hacker can easily exploit protocol weaknesses to perform unauthorized, intrusive activity on your network. You can prevent the situation illustrated in this example from occurring by adding static ARP entries on each legitimate host for the remote host, which won't be overridden by bogus ARP replies. Of course, this is extra administration and could cause problems if a network interface card (NIC) in either host is replaced.

Application Vulnerabilities

Application vulnerabilities are bugs in an application that allow a hacker to gain unauthorized or privileged access to a system. A common application vulnerability is to cause a *buffer overflow* by sending an application malformed data. The data is placed into a buffer by the application; however, because the data is longer than expected, it causes a buffer overflow, which can allow the hacker to execute arbitrary code, often in the context of a system account with full administrative privileges. The application developer can remove these vulnerabilities by checking data before it's written into the buffer, ensuring that it's in the correct format. Keep in mind that tight timeframes and millions of lines of code mean even the most attentive programmer can leave these holes open. Some applications and services that contain well-known vulnerabilities include:

- Sendmail (SMTP mail server)
- BIND (DNS server)
- Microsoft IIS (Web server)

NOTE Many of the recent viruses that have wreaked havoc worldwide are due to buffer overflow.

Poor Configuration

When you install applications on systems that will provide services to external parties, it's important that you configure the applications with security in mind. Often, these applications aren't secured as much as they could be, which leaves them vulnerable to unauthorized access. Many times, the default installation includes features that aren't required and that represent security risks. If you plan your security well before installing and configuring an application, you should be able to identify any security concerns and remove them.

Back Doors

Back doors provide the hacker with a convenient method of unconventional access to a target system. A back door runs as a client/server application that provides access to the target system (the server side) on a TCP or UDP port. The hacker runs the back door client software to establish a connection to the target and gain unauthorized access. A back door must somehow be installed on the target host. Back doors are commonly inserted into other programs (called *transports*) and are silently installed on the target when the other program is executed. The transport program is normally a novelty application that may run a cute graphical animation or a game. A user on the target system could receive the transport program via e-mail and execute the transport program, unwittingly installing the back door onto the target system. Experienced hackers also commonly install back doors onto a system they've compromised, which allows easy access back to the system when required. Many back door programs are designed for stealth so that they can remain running undetected on a target system.

Another form of back door application (also known as a *Trojan horse*) modifies command utilities and applications on the target system. For example, a hacker may upload a modified version of the login utility, which provides login access to Unix systems. When a user logs on, the modified login utility performs the same functions as the normal login utility, except it also writes the username and password to a file.

Some common back door applications include the following:

- BackOrifice is a well-publicized back door that runs on Windows hosts.
- Whack-A-Mole installs a common back door application called *NetBus* on Windows hosts. The back door is delivered silently by a cute game (transport program).
- Loki is a back door application for Unix. It's unique in that it uses ICMP as the transport protocol between client and server. Loki tunnels an RSH/RCMD session in ICMP echo request packets. Many firewalls permit ICMP echo request traffic, so this allows the back door to run through a firewall.
- Rootkits are toolkits used by hackers once they've compromised a system. The rootkit installs Trojan horse command utilities and programs, a back door program, packet sniffers, and system-log cleaners (that wipe any indication the hacker has compromised the system). The rootkit is designed to allow a hacker to obtain unauthorized access further into the target network.

Denial of Service Attacks

Denial of service (DoS) attacks are designed to disrupt network services offered by the target organization. This could cost an organization millions of dollars in revenue due to system downtime. More important, consumer confidence can be severely damaged, often permanently, causing losses that are hard to quantify. The following types of DoS attacks exist:

- Network resource overload
- Host resource starvation
- Out-of-bounds attack
- Distributed attack

Network Resource Overload

Network resource overload refers to overloading a resource that is required for access to a target network's services. This almost always refers to network bandwidth: The DoS attack uses up all bandwidth, causing legitimate users to be unable to connect to a network service. The simplest network resource overload attack works by having a single host generate large amounts of data and send it continuously to the target network. This method requires the attacking network to have a greater amount of network bandwidth available than the target network. For example, an attacking host could send 5Mbps of data via a T3 (45Mbps) Internet connection to a target network that has a T1 (1.5Mbps) Internet connection, quickly eliminating any available network bandwidth at the target network and preventing service to legitimate users.

A network resource overload attack can also use the concept of *amplification* to increase the bandwidth consumed by the attack. For example, the attacking host may have a T1 (1.5Mbps) Internet connection, whereas the target network has a T3 (45Mbps) Internet connection. There is no way for the attacking host to singularly overload the target network Internet connection. However, if the attack occurred from 30 hosts with a T1 connection, the combined attack (30 1.5 = 45Mbps) would be sufficient to overload the target network's Internet connection. A common method of amplification is illustrated in Figure 20.2.

FIGURE 20.2 Common amplification methodology

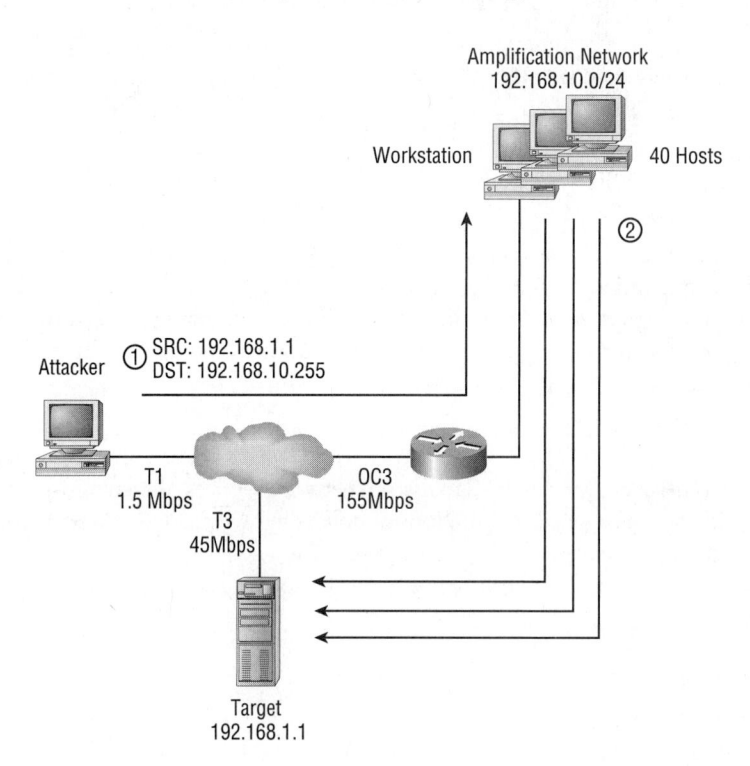

Figure 20.2 shows how an attacker can amplify a data stream at T1 speed into a data stream that exceeds the T3 connection to the target host, denying network bandwidth to the target host:

1. The attacker crafts large packets that contain the source IP address of the target host and a destination IP address of the amplification network's subnet broadcast. Because the packet is destined to the subnet broadcast address (192.168.1.255) of the amplification network (192.168.1.0/24), the router forwards the IP packet on to the amplification network as an Ethernet broadcast.

2. Each host on the amplification network responds to each packet by replying to the target host (192.168.1.1). The attacker is generating a packet stream of 1.5Mbps, so each host generates a reply packet stream to the target host of 1.5Mbps. Because there are 40 hosts on the network, an aggregate traffic stream of 60Mbps (40 1.5Mbps) is generated, saturating the T3 connection to the target host.

These are some common examples of network resource overload attacks:

- Smurf (amplification attack) uses ICMP ping packets.
- Fraggle (amplification attack) uses UDP packets.

Host Resource Starvation

Host resource starvation occurs when a DoS attack is directed against a host and uses up crucial resources that are required to allow the host to service network requests. The classic example of host resource starvation is the TCP SYN flood attack, which is illustrated in Figure 20.3.

The TCP SYN flood attack exploits the TCP three-way handshake that is used to set up a TCP connection. Normally, a SYN packet is sent from the local host to the remote host, the remote host replies with a SYN ACK packet, and the local host then responds with an ACK packet to complete the connection setup (SYN, SYN ACK, ACK). Figure 20.3 shows how this handshake process can be exploited:

1. The hacker sends a TCP SYN connection request to the target system, using a bogus source IP address that doesn't exist.

2. The target system receives the TCP SYN connection request and creates a new entry in the local TCP connection buffer that saves information such as the TCP sequence number in the SYN connection request. A SYN ACK reply is sent to the bogus IP address as part of the normal handshake process. The connection is in a *half open* state, because the handshake process is 50 percent complete.

3. Because the bogus IP address doesn't exist, no host can complete the TCP handshake by sending an ACK packet to the target system. If the bogus IP address did exist, it would send a RESET response because it never initiated the TCP SYN request. Thus, for the attack to succeed, the bogus IP address must not be alive.

FIGURE 20.3 TCP SYN flood attack

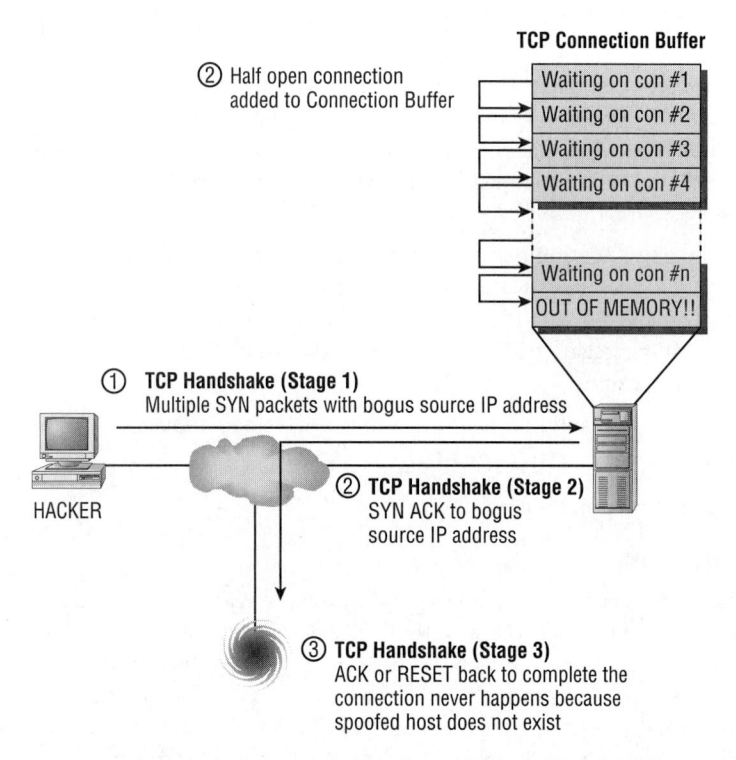

The attacker keeps on flooding TCP SYN connection requests to the target, with steps 1–3 cycling repeatedly. Eventually, the target system's TCP connection buffer maximum is reached, and the system can no longer accept TCP connections. The system is effectively down, because legitimate users can no longer access services provided by the system.

Out-of-Bounds Attack

An out-of-bounds attack refers to a DoS attack that uses illegal packet structure and data to crash a remote host's operating system. For example, a DoS attack may send IP packets that exceed the maximum IP packet length, or another may use an illegal combination of TCP flags in a TCP packet. Many TCP/IP stacks are written for normal TCP/IP operation, and developers never consider the possibility of some parameter of the TCP/IP packet being illegal. This means the stack doesn't know how to handle the illegal data, which can cause the operating system to crash (blue screen on Windows NT, Panic on Unix).

These are some common examples of out-of-bounds resource overload attacks:

- Ping of Death uses oversized ICMP ping packets (packets greater than 64Kb) to crash an (extremely confused) operating system.

- Teardrop uses overlapping fragments that exploit packet reassembly vulnerabilities in Linux and Windows.

- WinNuke sends out-of-band (data sent randomly) NetBIOS data to crash a Windows host.

Distributed Attack

Distributed DoS (DDoS) attacks have received much publicity in recent times. The concept of DDoS is similar to the amplification techniques examined earlier, except that DDoS uses a much more advanced client/server architecture. In DDoS attacks, the attacker uses a control system (server) that manages multiple zombie systems (clients) that actually perform the DoS attack. The control system issues a command to multiple zombie systems, instructing them to begin a DoS attack on a target system. Each zombie then performs the attack; the combined effect of each zombie system creates a massive DoS attack, leaving the target system little chance of survival. The client DDoS zombie is normally installed by using a transport application that secretly installs the Trojan horse. Figure 20.4 illustrates a DDoS attack:

FIGURE 20.4 Distributed denial of service attack

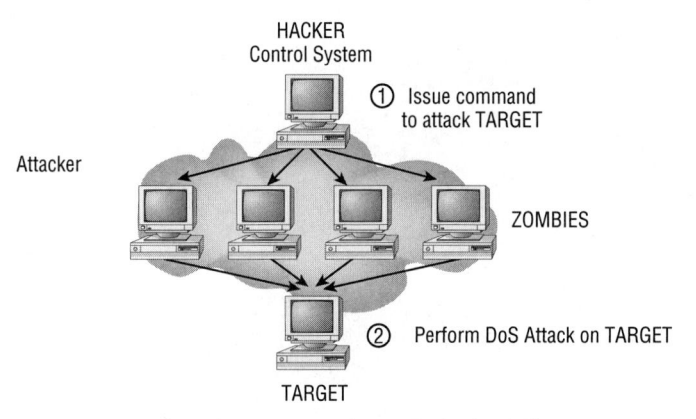

Some common examples of DDoS attacks include the following:

- Tribe Flood Network (TFN) uses ICMP, Smurf, UDP and SYN flood attacks. This attack was the first publicly available DDoS tool.
- Stacheldraht is similar to the TFN attack, but it allows for encryption of data between the control system and zombie systems.
- TFN2K is an updated version of the original TFN DDoS attack.

Real World Scenario

Preventing DDoS Attacks

Many organizations implement firewalls that restrict inbound access from untrusted networks, such as the Internet, to the internal network, but don't restrict outbound access from the internal network. It's good practice to restrict outbound access on your firewalls, because chances are that the outbound restrictions will block the DDoS services that a compromised machine may attempt to use. This may also be successful in limiting a back door connection from a compromised machine to an attacker.

Implementing Network Security

In order to secure your network, you need to define and implement a security policy that will achieve your organization's security goals. Once you've configured your network to adhere to your security policy, you need to continuously maintain and improve your security policy as the network changes and new threats arise. This process of implementing, maintaining, and improving network security is also known as the *Security Wheel*, which is an ongoing cycle that consists of four phases:

Phase 1—Securing the network

Phase 2—Monitoring network security

Phase 3—Testing network security

Phase 4—Improving network security

At the heart of the Security Wheel is the network security policy, which constantly evolves as demonstrated in the following diagram:

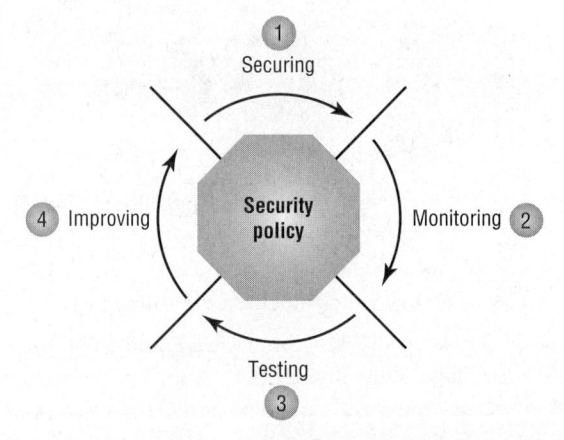

Each phase involves direct consultation and/or modification of the security policy. You need to complete each phase in the order shown, as described in the following sections, to properly manage your network security on an ongoing basis. Once the Security Wheel is complete, the cycle begins again with the implementation of network security enhancements, ongoing monitoring and testing, and back to the improvement of your network security. To ensure that your network security remains effective and up-to-date, you must continuously cycle through the Security Wheel.

Securing the Network

Securing the network refers to the process of configuring security to enforce your security policy. Your goal in securing the network is to protect network resources from unauthorized access and disruption in service. Your security policy needs to clearly define key areas that will easily translate to how you configure your network. Securing the network involves the following:

- Identifying your network
- Establishing security boundaries
- Implementing access control
- Eliminating vulnerabilities
- Protecting confidential data
- Preventing DoS attacks

Let's take a look at how you can accomplish each of these goals.

Identifying Your Network

Before you implement any security configuration, you should identify your network, which includes the following tasks:

Draw a network topology map To understand what you're securing, you must have a clear picture of your entire network topology, identifying computer systems, users, and network devices. Drawing a network topology map helps you understand the steps required to enable access between systems and/or users and also helps you identify any security weaknesses in your current topology.

Identify key assets and required access Key assets of your network might include file servers, databases, e-mail servers, web servers, and any system that contains information that is vital to the ongoing operation of the organization. You should clearly understand who requires access to these systems, when they require access, how they obtain access, and why they require that access.

Assess risks and the costs of mitigating those risks Assess the risk of information loss or theft on each key system—the impact such an event would have on your organization. For example, you might determine that your company accounting database is highly critical, and any loss or theft of information would have a major impact on the company. Determine the costs of protecting that information from loss or theft. The level of risk balanced against the cost of minimizing that risk ultimately determines the level of security you implement on your network.

With all this information in hand, you may identify improvements in your current network topology to enhance the security of key systems. You also have the necessary information to move on to the next phases of securing your network.

Establishing Security Boundaries

Before you implement any security configuration, you should clearly understand the security boundaries that exist in your network. A *security boundary* exists between *security zones*, which define an area under common security control. Establishing security boundaries and zones is important, because it can help identify where you need to implement access control and what type of access you should permit or deny. Your security policy document should clearly map the network, defining the various security zones in your network. The following are common security zones:

Intranet   This is the area of the network that your organization controls and that is trusted. Most network resources that belong to the organization reside in this area.

Extranet   This area defines connections to third-party vendors, partners, and customers. An extranet is outside the control of your organization and should be treated as a separate, untrusted security zone, even if you trust the third-party organization.

Internet   The Internet is a public area of the network that is outside the control of your organization. This is normally the most untrusted network.

Demilitarized zone (DMZ)   This is a staging area on your network for providing public access via the Internet or extranet to network resources. The network resources located in the DMZ are vulnerable, because they may be exposed to the Internet. By placing these public resources in a separate zone, you reduce the impact of a DMZ system being compromised (the compromised host must still cross a boundary to access your internal network).

Remote access   This zone defines an entry point for users to access the network from a remote location. Remote access can be via dial-up modem access, or it can be through some form of virtual private network (VPN) connection over the Internet or a service-provider network.

> ### Real World Scenario
>
> **Planning a Security Policy**
>
> Planning your security policy is important, and it's strongly recommended that you document your security requirements and policy. You must design your security policy with implementation in mind—it's no good to define a security policy that can't be achieved with current security technologies or practices. It's often useful to start the security policy process with a network security audit, ensuring you have a complete and up-to-date picture of the current network topology.
>
> A security policy document should, at the very least, contain the following:
>
> - High-level overview of security objectives
>
> - Detailed diagrams and inventory of the current network infrastructure
>
> - Risk assessment of key systems and areas of the network that are vulnerable to attack
>
> - Procedures outlining how services will be secured and provided
>
> - A methodology that ensures the security policy is enforced, is kept up to date, and is extensible
>
> - A well-defined incident response process, which is invoked when your network security is compromised

Some organizations may have multiple internal security zones (such as Marketing and Engineering), as well as multiple external security zones (such as dedicated links to third-party vendors and customers). Some form of security device (such as a firewall) usually exists at each boundary, interconnecting each zone and acting like a border post between two countries. All traffic between each zone must travel through the security device, so the security device becomes an obvious choice for controlling access between each zone.

After defining your security zones, you should determine the required interactions between each zone. These requirements dictate the necessary communications that must be enabled between two zones. For example, your organization may permit Web access from an internal proxy server to the Internet and allow both incoming and outgoing e-mail. Figure 20.5 illustrates security zones and the traffic patterns required between each zone.

Once you understand the required communications between each zone, you should determine how your security devices will restrict or allow traffic between each zone. There are two models when it comes to restricting or allowing traffic between security zones:

- Explicitly permit access. By default, all traffic is blocked by the firewall except for traffic that is explicitly allowed.

- Explicitly deny access. By default, all traffic is allowed by the firewall except for traffic that is explicitly denied.

FIGURE 20.5 Security zones and boundaries

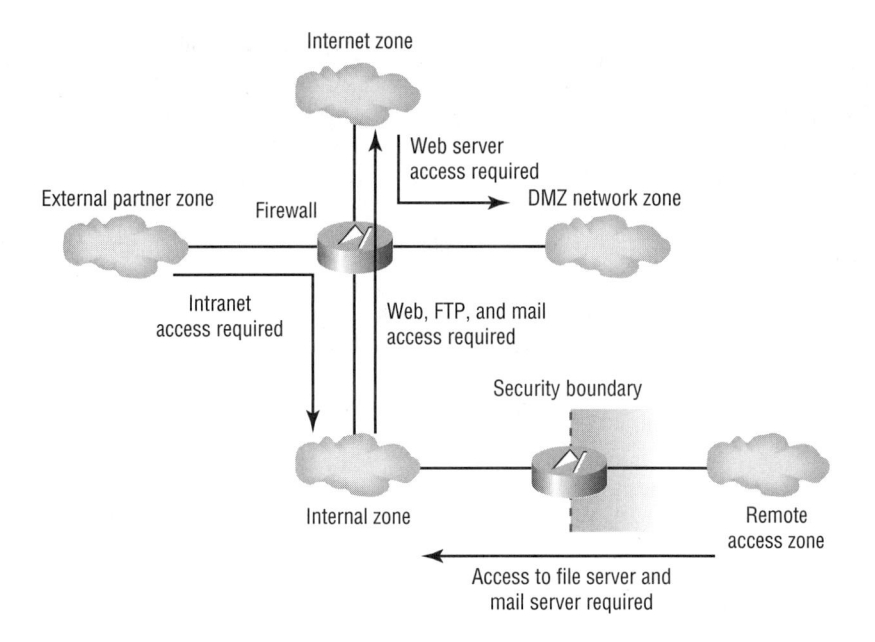

Which model you choose depends on how you measure risk against the transparency required. For example, a firewall that connects an organization's internal network to the Internet should only explicitly permit access, because the Internet poses a significant risk. However, a firewall that connects two internal IP networks may only explicitly deny access, because many forms of access are required between each network, and explicitly permitting access would become administratively difficult to manage.

Implementing Access Control

Implementing access control includes handling access between security zones and access to network resources. The previous section addressed access control between security zones via a firewall or other security device. Access to network resources can be defined as accessing a network service that is running on a particular computer system. When you're considering access to network resources, you need to consider the following:

- Using strong authentication
- Using authorization
- Eliminating anonymous access
- Eliminating trust relationships

These techniques for controlling network access are discussed in the following sections.

Using Strong Authentication

The most common form of authentication for access to network resources is to provide a username and password to the network resource you're accessing. Password-cracking tools can eventually crack a password by using a brute-force attack, so it's only a matter of time before someone can gain unauthorized access to a network resource. Strong-authentication methods are much harder to crack than a username/password combination. These methods include the following:

One-time passwords   This mechanism requires the user to present a different password to the target system each time. The target system may issue a random challenge string (a sequence of characters), and the user system then hashes the challenge and the user's password with a one-way function. A one-way function is irreversible, meaning that it's almost impossible to derive the original data from the hashed data. The user system then transmits the hash, which the authenticating system receives and compares to its own calculated hash value. If the hash values are identical, the user is authenticated.

Tokens   This mechanism is similar to a one-time password, except the user possesses a token card (which looks like a calculator). When the user wants to gain access to a system, the user enters a secret personal identification number (PIN) into the token card, and the token card hashes the PIN and some random form of data together. This method is considered highly secure because the user must physically possess a token card to gain access.

X.509 certificates X.509 certificates are part of a public key infrastructure (PKI) that allows users and systems to authenticate by using a certificate. A trusted certificate authority (CA) issues certificates to hosts/users, requiring each host/user to authenticate with the CA via some out-of-band manner (such as presenting a passport to the CA). Because all parties trust the CA, if the CA trusts a host, then all parties can trust the host.

> **NOTE** The security of an authentication procedure is determined by how many *factors* of authentication exist. In general, there are three factors of authentication: something you know, something you have, and something you are. A username and password are considered a one-factor authentication mechanism, because this is something you know. A token is considered a two-factor authentication mechanism, because you must know something (the PIN to unlock the token) and have something (the token itself). The more factors of authentication, the more secure the authentication mechanism.

Using Authorization

You can further enhance access control by defining authorization parameters when a user authenticates successfully. *Authorization* refers to which services users can access after they have authenticated. Each accessible service or action permitted is considered a privilege. A common flaw in many networks is to make use of an all-powerful administrative account (such as `root` or `administrator`) that's available to all network administrators. You should try to limit full administrative access to only those who are permitted it.

One of the most common uses of authorization is to provide group-level privilege access, where a profile or group is used as a template to set the appropriate level of privileges to a select group of users. For example, you may create a user group called Web Operators on a Windows NT system, with the group possessing sufficient rights (privileges) to successfully manage and maintain a website. Next, you grant the appropriate user accounts membership to the group, allowing each account to inherit the Web Operators group privileges. Rather than granting any Web Operator staff member full administrative privileges, which they could abuse, you have granted them only the required level of access specific to their jobs.

Eliminating Anonymous Access

Many techniques and vulnerabilities allow a hacker to convert a restricted anonymous connection into a full-fledged administrative connection. To prevent this privilege escalation, you should strive to disable anonymous access as much as possible.

Sometimes, disabling anonymous access is impossible, such as in the case of a web server serving the general public to provide organization information. When you do need to provide anonymous access, make sure you understand the implications and risks of enabling it. Thoroughly research any known vulnerabilities that might take advantage of the anonymous access, and apply patches for the known issues.

Eliminating Trust Relationships

Trust relationships have already been described as a method of authenticating access to a system based on an IP address only. Using IP addressing only to authenticate is open to misuse via address spoofing, and it doesn't allow for authentication based on the actual user accessing the system. Using trust relationships as the sole means of authentication is bad practice and should be eliminated in favor of user-based authentication. This approach also lets you grant the appropriate privileges based on the user who is attempting access. Using trust relationships in conjunction with user-based authentication enhances security by permitting access to only the appropriate users from specific systems.

> **TIP** On Unix systems, you can use a feature called *TCP wrappers* to control access to services (such as FTP) based on the source IP address of the system. If this security check is passed, the application/service then uses a user-based authentication scheme to permit or deny access. TCP wrappers also provide an audit log of successful and failed access attempts.

Preventing DoS

DoS attacks are the most conspicuous form of attack against a network. If a DoS attack is successfully applied against your network, you'll generally know about it fairly quickly, because you'll probably be called by irate employees and customers.

At all costs, you should try to prevent a DoS attack from being successful. If clients attempt to access a service that you actively promote, and they can't connect to it, they immediately have concerns about the reliability of your network. These concerns generally translate quickly to concerns about your products, services, and company as a whole. If clients discover that the outage was caused by a DoS attack, further questions about the security of your network are raised. Obviously, you want to avoid this sort of damage to your organization's reputation.

You can minimize the risk of DoS attacks using the techniques described in the following sections.

Rate-Limiting ICMP and TCP SYN Traffic

ICMP and TCP SYN traffic represent the most common types of traffic used in DoS attacks. Flooding TCP SYN connection requests can exhaust target host memory resources, and ICMP traffic can be used to exhaust network bandwidth. By rate-limiting this traffic to a low value (such as 16Kbps), DoS attacks in this format are thwarted.

You can also eliminate some common DoS attacks by disabling the ICMP directed-broadcast feature on router interfaces, which prevents the router from routing traffic sent to a subnet broadcast address. Another router-interface feature that you can disable is ICMP redirects, which are used to inform a system to reroute traffic through a specific device. A more direct approach to eliminating the ICMP flood threat is to block ICMP traffic altogether, but then you'll lose the useful features of ICMP—such as ping, traceroute, and maximum transmission unit (MTU) size monitoring.

> **NOTE** Rate-limiting or ICMP filtering works best when your ISP also implements it. This means the connection to your ISP isn't flooded, eliminating the DoS impact altogether (presuming the internal links of your ISP can handle the flood as well).

Employing Anti-Spoofing Countermeasures

Many DoS attacks rely on *address spoofing* (altering the source IP address). By filtering illegal source addresses on your Internet perimeter router, such as RFC 1918 private addresses and loopback addresses, you can eliminate many such attacks.

The following are some source IP addresses that you should block on the external interface of your perimeter router, applied to any traffic inbound on the interface:

- Old and new broadcast addresses (0.*x.x.x* and 255.255.255.255)
- RFC 1918 addresses (10.*x.x.x*, 172.16.*x.x*–172.31.*x.x*, 192.168.*x.x*)
- Loopback addresses (127.*x.x.x*)
- Link local networks (169.254.*x.x*)
- Test-NET (192.0.2.*x*)
- Class D (multicast 224.*x.x.x*–239.*x.x.x*), Class E (240.*x.x.x*–247.*x.x.x*), and unused address ranges (248.*x.x.x*–255.255.255.255)

Disabling IP Fragment Forwarding

Many DoS attacks are based on IP fragments. For example, a hacker can send overlapping fragments that can crash a target system. By disabling forwarding of IP fragments on a firewall device, you can eliminate these threats. If you require fragmentation support for legitimate fragmented traffic, configure your network security devices to reassemble each set of IP fragments received to ensure they're legitimate.

Eliminating Vulnerabilities

Many operating systems and applications have well-known vulnerabilities that allow an attacker to gain unauthorized access to your network. It's important to understand these vulnerabilities and implement the appropriate patches and service packs to remove the vulnerabilities. You should also disable any unnecessary services on your network, so that you're reducing the possible vulnerabilities on the network.

> **WARNING** Before implementing any new patches or service packs, install them on a test system in the lab to ensure that the stability of the operating system and applications isn't affected.

Protecting Confidential Data

Today, many sensitive communications are transmitted across untrusted links, such as the Internet. A hacker who has access to your internal network or to the service provider that manages your untrusted links could eavesdrop on your communications, obtaining sensitive information such as business secrets or login credentials.

> **NOTE** There is a common misconception that private service-provider networks and services (such as Frame Relay and ATM offerings) are secure. Like the Internet, these networks are also public and shared, although they're less at risk because they're typically under the full control of the service provider (although sometimes the service provider leases certain circuits from another provider). Realize that even a service-provider network is vulnerable (so you don't have a false sense of security).

To ensure that sensitive communications are protected from eavesdropping, you can use encryption to provide data confidentiality. A common method of encrypting data is to use a VPN, which encrypts data flows between two endpoints. Eavesdroppers located between each endpoint can still capture your communications, but they will find it extremely difficult to decrypt the encrypted information.

When you're planning a VPN connection, you need to consider untrusted links and VPN endpoints. Choosing your VPN endpoints is important. Many organizations define VPN endpoints between two VPN gateway devices, because each VPN gateway terminates an untrusted link and a VPN connection exists is transparent to the communicating hosts. However, this leaves the data between each host and the local VPN endpoint unencrypted. If an eavesdropper has access to the internal network, this will cause a security problem.

If your host operating system supports VPN communications, you may want to enable the VPN connection between each host, fully protecting the session while it's in transit. This method doesn't scale well and protects only the flow between the two hosts, requiring you to configure more VPN endpoints if you want other hosts to communicate securely. Figure 20.6 illustrates how choosing VPN endpoints dictates whether data is transmitted in clear text.

FIGURE 20.6   Choosing VPN endpoints

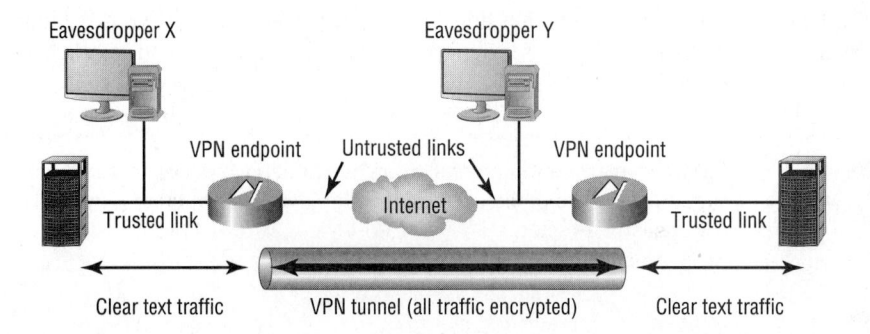

> **The Three Tenets of Network Security**
>
> There are three key tenets of network security:
>
> - *Confidentiality* refers to the ability to maintain the privacy of information.
>
> - *Integrity* refers to the ability to ensure that information isn't modified or falsely created by unauthorized parties.
>
> - *Availability* ensures that information is always accessible.
>
> Access attacks can affect all of these; however, an access attack is most commonly used to compromise confidentiality. DoS attacks most often affect availability but can also affect integrity via information corruption or defacement.

In Figure 20.6, the VPN endpoints between two networks are the firewall (gateways) for each network. This means that traffic is transmitted in clear text from each host to the local firewall over the trusted link; but it's then encrypted over the untrusted link until each packet reaches the remote firewall, where the packet is decrypted and forwarded in clear text to the remote host. Eavesdropper X can capture the transmission in clear text but must somehow gain access to your internal network. Eavesdropper Y can capture the transmission, but it's in an encrypted format that is nearly impossible to decrypt (assuming a strong encryption algorithm is used). If you need to ensure that the transmission can't be compromised, you must define each host as the VPN endpoints, protecting the transmission from both Eavesdroppers X and Y.

> **WARNING** Viewing your internal network as a trusted link is dangerous. A safer stance is to view your internal network as *more trusted* than other untrusted networks. Always be aware that threats can and do exist on your internal network.

Monitoring Network Security

Network security is much more than just configuring security. Many organizations purchase expensive network security equipment, configure it, install it, and then forget about it. Life proceeds normally, network services are accessible all the time, and there are no signs of security violations. The organization assumes that the security equipment is performing its job correctly, because there have been no obvious security breaches. The administrators here are in a dangerous state of mind—they have a false sense of security because no noticeable issues have arisen.

> **WARNING** New security threats are discovered daily, which underlines the importance of continuously updating your system. If your system is neglected and not properly updated, your network may be vulnerable to new security threats because your security systems were configured prior to the existence of the new threats.

An essential part of network security is the ongoing monitoring of your network security. If you proactively manage your network security, you'll detect violations to your security policy. By historically capturing attempted attacks, you'll be able to thwart future attacks more easily. You'll also be able to assess whether your network security policy is being implemented correctly.

> An IDS fits into the monitoring phase of the Security Wheel.

The following methods of monitoring exist:

Active monitoring   This involves turning on host system auditing. The host system is actively involved in collecting information. Administrators can review audit logs on each host system to check for security events, such as login success/failure and file system access.

Passive monitoring   This involves the automated monitoring of network traffic to detect unauthorized traffic on the network. An IDS provides this functionality and can automatically respond to suspicious activity by alerting security administrators and proactively blocking traffic from the suspicious party. The IDS is passive because it monitors traffic transparently to the rest of the network.

> Enabling security logging on each of your security systems is important, especially if you need legal evidence to prosecute an attacker.

Testing Network Security

Once you've implemented your network security configuration and have your monitoring mechanisms in place, you should test your configuration to ensure that it enforces your security policy and your network has no vulnerabilities. Two methods are available to test your network security configuration:

Security-scanner tools   These tools provide internal auditing. They vary in functionality, from performing simple reconnaissance such as port scanning to scanning specific network services for known vulnerabilities. Some tools—such as Nmap, SAINT (Security Administrator's Integrated Network Tool—previously SATAN), and Nessus—are freely available on the Internet. Most commercial tools include an extensible network security database that can be periodically updated to scan for new vulnerabilities as they become public knowledge. Examples of commercial scanning tools include Cisco Secure Scanner, ISS Internet Scanner, and ISS System Scanner.

Conducting an external audit   Conducting an external audit on a periodic basis involves having a professional, third-party security organization test your network security configuration. The external party hires experienced security personnel to attempt a break-in to your network, providing a real-world test of your network security. This is an excellent method of ensuring you haven't missed anything in your security configuration, and confirms that your network is secure from the eyes of a hacker.

It's advisable to use a combination of both methods to test your network security. Ideally, you should use scanning tools on a regular basis to verify that your security configuration is still working. You should then conduct an external audit on a less frequent basis to ensure that your configuration stands up to experienced hackers and sophisticated techniques.

Improving Network Security

The final phase of the Cisco Security Wheel is to collate the information gathered from the monitoring and testing phases and use that information to identify any improvements that may be necessary. Improving your network security also involves keeping up-to-date with security news, checking configuration files, and evaluating changes in your network topology.

Monitoring Security News

Every day, scores of security vulnerabilities are discovered and reported, so it's essential that you keep abreast of developments in network security. Two primary sources of security information are available on the Internet: mailing lists and websites. Mailing lists are useful for learning about new vulnerabilities as they become available. Websites are useful for quickly searching and finding information on vulnerabilities; many sites also have links to tools that exploit the vulnerabilities so you can test them against your network.

> Popular mailing lists include Bugtraq and other lists at www.securityfocus.com/archive/1, NTBugtraq at www.ntbugtraq.com, and SANS News Browser Service at www.sans.org/snb/. Popular websites include www.securityfocus.com, http://packetstormsecurity.nl, and http://www.cisco.com/pcgi-bin/front.x/ipsalerts/ipsalertsHome.pl.

Reviewing Configuration Files

In a perfect world, you, as the security administrator for your network, could configure a security device and sleep peacefully at night in the knowledge that the configuration would never change without your authorization. Unfortunately, this is seldom the case. Network emergencies often require administrators to quickly resolve problems, which may involve alteration of configuration to test theories and perform troubleshooting. Often, once the problem has been resolved, the changes to the network security device are left in place, creating a potential for new vulnerabilities on your network. Thus, it's important to periodically review your configuration files and ensure that the configuration is correct and hasn't been modified without prior permission.

The CiscoWorks 2000 network management suite includes functionality that allows you to store configuration files in the CiscoWorks database. Features such as configuration version tracking and change control management are also available.

Evaluating Changes in Your Network Topology

The modern network is a constantly evolving entity that needs to be able to grow as new services demand extra infrastructure. When your network topology changes, you need to evaluate any security implications and update your security configuration as appropriate.

Understanding Intrusion Detection Basics

Intrusion detection is the ability to detect intruder attacks against your network. These include reconnaissance, unauthorized access, and DoS attacks, as described in the "Attack Types" section earlier in this chapter.

IDS products are available with varying characteristics, based on the environment in which they're running. An IDS generates an alarm when it believes it has detected an attack, and it can optionally proactively respond to the attack. An attack is often related to a protocol or system vulnerability from which an exploit has been developed, often in the form of a hacking tool or script. An IDS relies on alarm criteria or triggers that let it identify possible attacks against the network. Of course, to be able to detect attacks, one or more IDS systems must be located appropriately in the network, either installed as network appliances monitoring traffic on the network or installed as agents on hosts monitoring suspicious operating system and application events. An IDS must also be able to detect more sophisticated attacks that use evasive techniques in an attempt to bypass the IDS and thus proceed undetected.

This section will discuss the following topics in details:

- Triggers
- IDS location
- IDS evasive techniques

Triggers

The primary goal of an IDS is to detect attacks directed against your network. *Triggers* define the criteria used to detect that an attack of some form has occurred. Triggers are a fundamental component of an IDS that control its effectiveness. There are two types of triggers: profile-based intrusion detection and signature-based intrusion detection.

Profile-Based Intrusion Detection

With *profile-based intrusion detection*, also known as *anomaly detection*, the IDS generates an alarm if the monitored network activity deviates sufficiently from what is considered "normal." To define what is considered normal, the IDS must baseline the network for a sufficient period of time, generating a profile of normal network activity. A profile must be generated for each user group in the network, so this process can take considerable time.

The major problem with profile-based intrusion detection is that each user group's traffic pattern must match the normal profile traffic pattern to avoid false alarms. Unfortunately, humans change their business and social habits frequently, so the network traffic generated by each user group in your network can often deviate from normal. This means that many false alarms may be generated, which you might circumvent by increasing the deviation at which an alarm is triggered. However, doing so can introduce false negatives: The IDS won't detect actual attacks because the deviation threshold is configured too high.

> **NOTE** A *false positive* occurs when an alarm is generated, but no attack is actually taking place. A *false negative* occurs when an attack does take place, but your IDS doesn't generate an alarm.

Profile-based intrusion detection has the following advantages:

- It makes it difficult for attackers to know which traffic will generate an alarm.
- It detects new, previously unpublished attacks.
- It detects insider attacks and data theft easily because the insiders' actions deviate from their normal profiles.

Profile-based intrusion detection has the following disadvantages:

- The IDS requires a suitable learning period to define normal network behavior.
- Many false positives can be generated.
- User profiles must be updated as a user's habits change.
- The alarms are difficult to understand.

Signature-Based Intrusion Detection

With *signature-based intrusion detection*, also known as *misuse detection* or *malicious activity detection*, the IDS generates an alarm if the monitored network traffic matches a predefined set of criteria that indicates the traffic is part of an attack.

All attacks have a certain set of criteria that can be examined to uniquely define various attacks. For example, a ping sweep has the following criteria:

- Each packet in the ping sweep is an ICMP Echo Request packet.
- The sweep consists of a number of ICMP Echo Request packets, each sent from the same source IP address to a range of destination IP addresses, often in sequential order.

The IDS constantly captures and analyzes traffic, so it could detect a ping sweep based on the above criteria. The criteria that make up an attack are known as the *signature* of the attack.

In the ping sweep example, the IDS must capture a number of packets to determine the second criteria. This is an issue with a signature-based IDS, because attacks can span multiple packets. To detect these types of attacks, the IDS must cache or maintain the state of monitored traffic for a specific amount of time that exceeds the period of an attack. This time period is known as the *event horizon*, and for some attacks, it can last for days or weeks. Obviously, the IDS has a finite amount of resources and can't indefinitely maintain state information.

A signature must be well designed; otherwise, the IDS may generate false positives or false negatives. A hacker can slightly modify an attack to attempt to bypass the normal attack signature. If your signatures are well designed and robust, a hacker will find it difficult to conceal an attack.

> **NOTE** False negatives are much more dangerous than false positives. A false negative means an attacker has managed to bypass your IDS. Your IDS needs to have well-defined signatures to ensure that it's providing the detection it claims to possess. False positives are an annoyance, because your management console can be flooded with events that never actually occurred. False positives represent a danger as well, because they may make it hard to pick up real attacks on the management console.

A signature-based IDS generally can detect attacks based on one or more of the following methodologies:

Pattern matching   Pattern matching is the simplest methodology. The IDS looks for a fixed sequence of information within each packet analyzed by the IDS. For example, a pattern-matching signature might search for the text *foobar* within a Telnet session. This requires the IDS to analyze all Telnet traffic and attempt to find the ASCII representation of *foobar* within the contents of each Telnet packet.

Stateful pattern matching   Pattern matching is very simple in that it only examines packets one by one, searching for a byte sequence in each packet separately. Many advanced attacks deliberately attempt to foil pattern matching by splitting attacks over several packets or by sending out-of-sequence packets. Stateful pattern matching extends the concept of pattern matching from being a purely packet-oriented methodology to being a methodology that understands that communications are based on connections and examines information received over a connection, rather than within a single packet. Taking this approach allows the IDS to reconstruct fragmented or out-of-sequence attacks, generating the actual data stream as it would be processed by the target system. Pattern matching takes place against the reconstructed data stream, allowing masked attacks to be detected.

Protocol analysis   Protocol analysis is essentially an extension to stateful pattern matching, where the IDS ensures that the data stream sent over a connection related to a specific protocol follows the rules of that protocol. This ensures that traffic is valid and isn't an attack designed to bypass security systems by using permitted application ports or an attack designed to cause denial of service by crashing a system due to illegal or invalid data passed to a target system. Such detection capabilities require an IDS to possess a knowledge of common protocols, such as TCP, UDP, HTTP, and FTP, and for the IDS to ensure that any traffic claiming to be using a specific protocol is in fact following the normal rules of operation for the protocol.

Heuristics   Heuristics provide attack detection based on algorithms that aren't associated with any normal methodology of misuse detection. Heuristic-based analysis often consists of complex algorithms and statistical relationships in order to detect certain types of attacks. For example, detecting a ping sweep requires an IDS to look for excessive ICMP packets sent to a large number of different destinations. This requires an algorithm that includes thresholds such as the maximum number of different destinations permissible from a specific source before generating an alarm.

Signature-based intrusion detection has the following advantages:

- It detects many known attacks.
- Alarms are easy to understand, because they match a specific attack.
- It's easier to set up, with no initial training period required.
- You can define custom signatures that detect new attacks.

Signature-based intrusion detection has the following disadvantages:

- It doesn't detect unpublished attacks.
- The signature database must be updated frequently.
- Traffic must be cached for a suitable period of time to detect attacks that span multiple packets.
- It's prone to false negatives if the attacker slightly modifies an attack.

> **NOTE** All Cisco Secure IDS sensors are signature-based intrusion detection systems that incorporate all the IDS methodologies discussed in this section.

IDS System Location

An important aspect of IDS design is understanding where to place your IDS components so that your network resources are protected. In general, there are two ways to locate the IDS: on the host or on the network.

Host-Based Intrusion Detection

With host-based intrusion detection, IDS software (known as an *agent*) runs on one or more host computer systems in your network. The agent examines many components of the operating system, including local event logs, error messages, and privileged access attempts. Figure 20.7 illustrates host-based intrusion detection.

Host-based intrusion detection has the following advantages:

- It detects attempts to bypass a network-based IDS, such as fragment reassembly and Time to Live (TTL) attacks.
- It detects attacks concealed from a network-based IDS by encryption, because host-based IDS analysis takes place before encryption and after decryption occurs.
- It lets you ascertain whether an attack succeeded. (A network-based IDS can detect attacks, but it has no way of determining whether the attack succeeded.)
- It doesn't require specialized IDS hardware.

FIGURE 20.7   Host-based intrusion detection

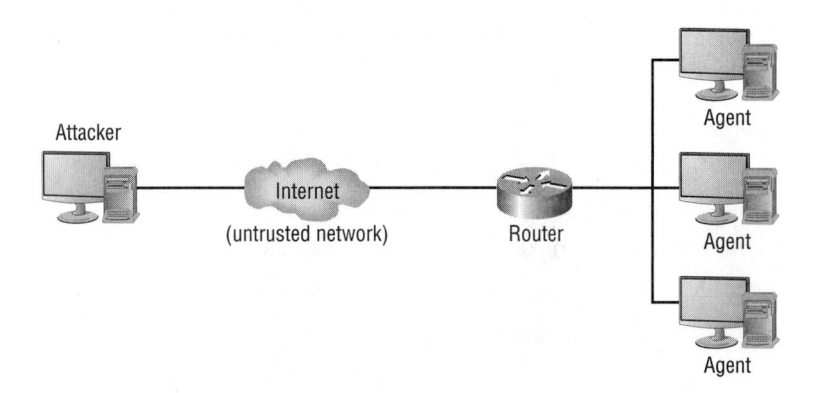

Host-based intrusion detection has the following disadvantages:

- It requires an agent per host that you wish to protect.
- It requires an agent that can support multiple operating systems.
- It can't detect reconnaissance scans, which often are a good indication that an attack is going to occur.
- It relies on the network stack of the host to communicate with a centralized IDS management platform. Some attacks may take out the network stack, preventing the agent from communicating with the IDS.

Network-Based Intrusion Detection

Network-based intrusion detection involves placing a dedicated IDS on a network segment that transparently monitors traffic through the segment. A network-based IDS can be placed on key segments throughout your network to provide protection for your entire network. Figure 20.8 illustrates network-based intrusion detection.

In Figure 20.8, all traffic from the Internet is passed to the router; the traffic is mirrored to a monitoring port on an IDS. A network-based IDS typically includes a promiscuous monitoring interface, which plugs into the network segment you wish to monitor. A network interface that operates in promiscuous mode captures all packets, regardless of their destination address. All traffic for the segment must be mirrored to the monitoring interface to ensure that all traffic that passes through the segment is analyzed. The network-based IDS doesn't interfere with normal network operation, and it operates transparently to the rest of the network.

> **NOTE**   The Cisco Secure IDS sensors covered in the CSIDS exam are network-based IDS. Cisco also offers the Cisco Security Agent, which is a host-based IDS.

An important consideration of network-based intrusion detection is bandwidth. For example, if you mirror the traffic of ten 100Mbps ports to a single 100Mbps monitoring port on the IDS, you can easily oversubscribe the monitoring port, missing traffic that could contain attacks against your network. Therefore, you need to carefully place your IDS, ensuring the monitoring interface won't be oversubscribed. A network-based IDS also requires significant CPU and memory resources to be able to analyze monitored traffic in real time.

Network-based intrusion detection has the following advantages:

- A single IDS can protect large portions of your network.
- It detects network-based attacks, such as a port scan or ping sweep.

Network-based intrusion detection has the following disadvantages:

- It requires installation on a segment that won't oversubscribe the monitoring interface.
- It requires monitoring of different parts of the networks using multiple IDS devices.
- It requires reassembly of fragmented traffic (IP traffic that is split into multiple IP fragments). This can be processor intensive.
- It can't detect attacks that are contained in encrypted communications.

> **NOTE** The most effective intrusion prevention strategy is to implement both host-based and network-based IDS. Typically, most organizations implement network-based IDS first, because it's effective against attacks originating externally. Adding host-based IDS further enhances protection from attack, especially from attacks that are generated from internal sources.

FIGURE 20.8 Network-based intrusion detection

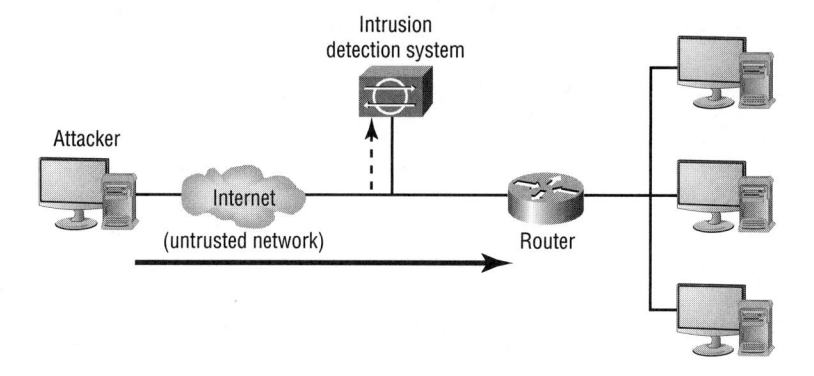

IDS Evasive Techniques

Intruders employ many techniques in an attempt to bypass IDS systems and escape detection. We'll discuss the following common evasive techniques in more detail:

- Flooding
- Fragmentation
- Encryption
- Obfuscation

Flooding

A very simple technique used to evade an IDS is to flood the IDS with *noise* or dummy traffic, which requires the IDS to utilize valuable CPU and memory resources to analyze the dummy traffic. If the performance of the IDS isn't sufficient to handle the traffic generated by flooding, then the intrusive activity performed by the intruder may be missed due to the excessive dummy traffic. Even if the real attack is detected, the IDS response may be significantly delayed due to the exhaustion of CPU and memory resources on the IDS.

Fragmentation

Fragmentation is a common evasive technique. An attack is fragmented into multiple packets in an attempt to bypass IDS systems that can't reassemble fragments for analysis. For an IDS to detect attacks concealed by fragmentation, it must be able to cache fragmented packets until all fragments have been received, reconstruct the fragmented packets, and then analyze the resulting data stream. This requires significant memory resources and is a processor-intensive operation; fragmentation can also be used as an advanced form of flooding to exhaust an IDS of system resources. To further complicate things, fragments can be accidentally or deliberately sent out of order, increasing the complexity of the code required to handle fragmented packets on the IDS. Fragmentation is normally associated with IP fragmentation; however, the same concepts apply to TCP, where an attack can be segmented across multiple TCP segments.

Encryption

Encryption technologies are becoming more prevalent, with VPNs and SSL-based encryption for web traffic and other traffic commonplace. A network IDS requires data to be sent in clear text so that the IDS can detect attacks. Encryption effectively renders the network IDS useless: All information is encrypted, and it can't be decrypted by the network IDS because the IDS has no knowledge of the keys used for encryption. Examples of encrypted traffic include the following:

- SSL communications to secure web servers
- VPN communications to VPN gateways and remote access VPN clients
- SSH communications to SSH servers

Obfuscation

Obfuscation hides attacks by altering the way data is encoded, allowing IDS systems that rely on simple pattern matching to be easily bypassed. Obfuscation attempts to confuse an IDS by inserting control characters (spaces, carriage returns, and so on) or by encoding data in a nonstandard format. For example, ASCII text can be encoded using Unicode, which requires an IDS to possess an understanding of Unicode.

Cisco Secure Intrusion Protection

It's important to understand that a complete intrusion protection system doesn't consist of just a single network-based IDS sensor or a collection of host-based IDS agents. A true intrusion protection solution includes many different components that protect different portions of the network and information systems. A complete intrusion protection solution must provide the following security services:

Detection *Detection* is the ability to identify intrusive activity directed against internal networks, systems, and applications.

Prevention *Prevention* is the ability to stop a detected attack, protecting target networks, systems, and applications.

Reaction *Reaction* is the ability to introduce countermeasures that protect the network and systems from future attacks.

To provide these services, Cisco has a number of products that include intrusion protection technologies based around the following security products and components:

Network sensors Network sensors include the Cisco Secure IDS 4200 series IDS sensors, which form the flagship of the Cisco intrusion protection product family.

Switch sensors Switch sensors are integrated into the switching backplane of Cisco Catalyst 6000/6500 switches, providing integrated intrusion protection for all portions of the network. The Catalyst 6000 Intrusion Detection System Module (IDSM) is the only switch sensor that Cisco has produced to date.

> **NOTE** Cisco has released an IDS network module for the 2600, 2800, 3600, 3700 and 3800 series family of routers, which capture packets from the internal data bus within the router. These IDS network modules provide the same IDS functionality as the 4200 series sensors and IDSM and shouldn't be confused with the Cisco IOS and Cisco PIX IDS software feature.

Router and firewall sensors   These are provided by an IDS software feature in the Cisco IOS Firewall feature set and Cisco PIX firewall. They provide basic inline intrusion detection services, ensuring that intrusive activity is blocked before being forwarded by a Cisco IOS router or Cisco PIX firewall.

> **NOTE**   You can use two fundamental methods to implement an IDS. A *passive IDS* (such as Cisco Secure IDS network and switch sensors) monitors traffic without actively being in the path of the traffic. An *inline IDS* (such as Cisco IOS Firewall sensors and Cisco PIX firewall sensors) sits directly in the path of traffic, analyzes traffic received, and only forwards traffic deemed nonintrusive. To provide intrusion protection, a passive IDS must instruct an external access control device (such as a border router or firewall) to apply temporary blocking for the source and/or destination of an attack. An inline IDS can drop any offending packets immediately without needing to consult external access control systems.

Host sensors   Host sensors provide host-based intrusion detection, protecting critical servers, hosts, and applications by detecting unusual operating system and application events that can be classified as intrusive activity.

Security management   Overlaying the Cisco intrusion protection offering is a comprehensive and robust security management and monitoring framework that allows complete intrusion protection management for the entire network. Cisco's security management products for intrusion protection enable an organization to manage and monitor all components of the intrusion protection solution centrally, allowing policy to be defined once from a central location and then pushed out to each intrusion protection component.

To provide a complete intrusion protection solution, you need to implement both host-based and network-based intrusion detection systems, which combined provide a *defense-in-depth* intrusion protection solution. Host-based intrusion protection protects critical servers and applications by providing the following features:

- Protecting applications
- Enforcing policy by controlling access to system resources
- Detecting buffer overflow attacks by monitoring the operating system kernel
- Protecting against attacks that bypass network-based IDS systems (such as encrypted attacks)

Network-based intrusion protection protects the network, attached systems, and applications by providing the following features:

- Detecting reconnaissance attacks
- Detecting buffer overflow and other access attacks
- Detecting DoS attacks
- Protecting the entire network from attacks by implementing intrusion protection at the appropriate enforcement points in the network

Combining host-based and network-based intrusion protection ensures that all intrusive activity can be detected. If you implement only one type of intrusion protection, it's impossible to ensure protection against all forms of intrusive activity.

Introduction to Cisco Secure IDS

Cisco Secure IDS is a network-based IDS that uses signature-based triggers to detect network-intrusion activity. The architecture of Cisco Secure IDS consists of several key components:

Sensor This performs real-time monitoring of network traffic, searching for patterns that could represent an attack.

Configuration manager The configuration manager provides configuration management for the sensor, pushing configuration and policy settings to the sensor. The configuration manager may be co-located with the sensor (typical for smaller sensor deployments) or may be separately located at a central location (typical for larger sensor deployments).

Event manager The event manager is used to collect events generated by sensors. An event is most often an alarm, which is generated if the sensor detects intrusive activity on the network it's currently monitoring. Cisco Secure IDS sensors have extremely limited event management capabilities; hence the event manager is always separate from the sensor.

> **NOTE** Prior to Cisco Secure IDS 4.0 software (the current release of Cisco Secure IDS software at the time of writing is 4.1), the Cisco Secure IDS architecture could be described based on two components: the sensor and the *Director*. The Director essentially performs the functions of the configuration manager and/or event manager; however, Cisco has removed this terminology from the Cisco Secure IDS architecture.

Cisco Secure IDS (CSIDS) isn't just a set of hardware components—it also includes software that has evolved over years. It's very important to understand that CSIDS is described in terms of the software version. For example, Cisco Secure IDS 4.1 represents the latest version of CSIDS. Historically, Cisco Secure IDS software started with version 2.2, was then updated to version 2.5, then to versions 3.0 and 3.1, and then to today's versions 4.0 and 4.1.

> **TIP** Cisco Secure IDS 5.0 is due for release in early 2005. The most notable new feature of this release will be the ability for a sensor to operate in an inline mode, providing the most effective intrusion protection capabilities.

Prior to Cisco Secure IDS 4.*x*, the sensor and sensor management components communicated via a proprietary protocol called the PostOffice protocol. This protocol provides reliable communications between the various IDS applications and services that run on each sensor and sensor management platform. The PostOffice protocol is UDP-based, operating on UDP port 45000 by default.

Starting from CSIDS 4.*x*, the sensor and management components communicate via a protocol called Remote Desktop Exchange Protocol (RDEP), which is an XML-based language that allows configuration and alarm events to be exchanged between CSIDS components.

> **TIP** The PostOffice protocol is a push-style protocol, which means that alarms are pushed from sensors to sensor management platforms as they occur. RDEP is a pull-style protocol, which means that alarms are received by the sensor management platform polling the sensor at regular intervals.

Figure 20.9 illustrates the Cisco Secure IDS architecture.

As an overview of the Cisco Secure IDS, we'll cover its primary features and the sensor and sensor management platforms.

FIGURE 20.9 The Cisco Secure IDS architecture

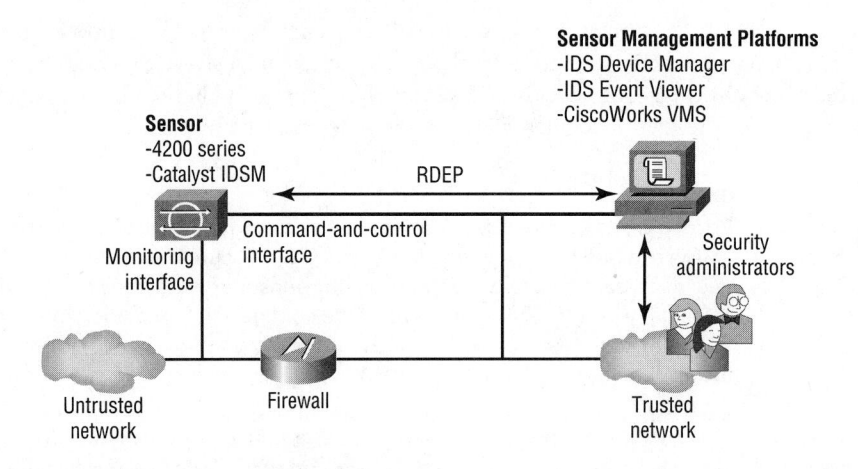

Cisco Secure IDS Features

Cisco offers a rich IDS product set that is part of Cisco's SAFE enterprise security blueprint. Cisco Secure IDS has many features that let you effectively detect and respond to security threats against your network. It provides the following fundamental capabilities:

- Alarm display and logging
- Intrusion response
- Remote sensor configuration and management

These features are discussed in the following sections.

Alarm Display and Logging

When a sensor detects an attack, it sends an alarm to the event management platform. On the event management platform, a graphical user interface (GUI) displays these alarms in real time, color-coding each alarm based on its severity. This display provides a quick indication that an attack has occurred and how dangerous the attack is. The sensor can also log more detailed alarm information in a local text-based log file, which allows for in-depth analysis of attack data and the use of custom scripts to present alarm data specific to your requirements. Figure 20.10 illustrates the alarm display and logging process.

Cisco Secure IDS event management platforms include a Network Security Database (NSDB), which includes detailed information about each attack that is detected by a sensor. This information provides analysis support for security administrators who must decipher and respond to detected attacks.

FIGURE 20.10 Alarm display and logging

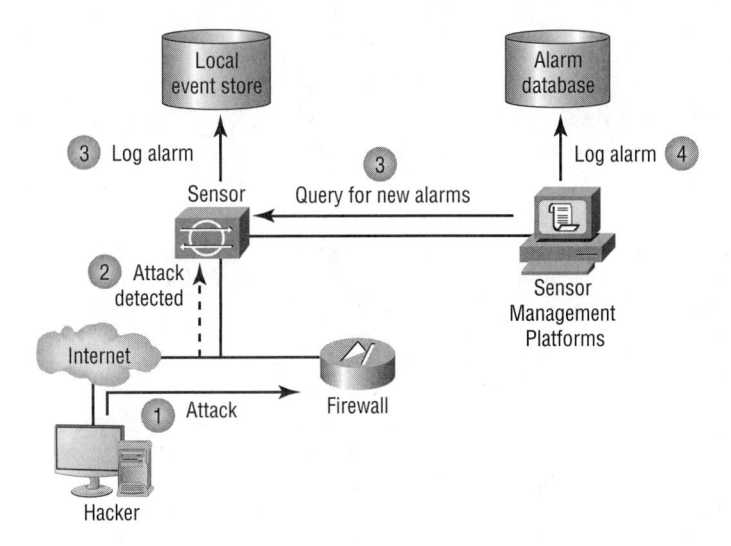

Intrusion Response

The Cisco Secure IDS sensor can directly respond to an attack using one or more of the following methods:

TCP reset The *TCP reset* response is available only for TCP-based attacks. It's implemented by the sensor sending a TCP reset packet to the host that is being attacked (the target). This causes the attacked system to close the connection, destroying any processes and memory associated with the connection. Figure 20.11 illustrates the TCP reset response.

FIGURE 20.11 TCP reset response

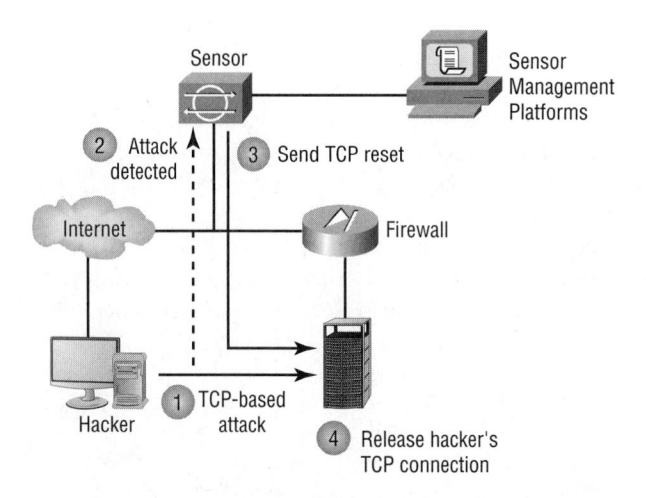

IP blocking The *IP blocking* response (also known as *shunning*) allows a sensor to apply an access control list (ACL) to a perimeter router interface, blocking IP connectivity from an attacking system. Figure 20.12 illustrates the IP blocking response. The blocking configuration is imposed for a configurable amount of time, after which it's removed. You can also manually block a host or network from the sensor management platform if you see any suspicious activity. (This manual blocking process is additive; in other words, a manual block is added to the current blocking ACL, updating the ACL to include the latest blocking configuration.)

IP logging When a sensor detects an attack, an alarm is generated and forwarded to the event management platform. The *IP logging* response allows a sensor to write alarm information to a local log file as well. The information written to the log file contains much more information than is sent to the event management platform, so you can use this option to provide detailed analysis of specific attacks. See Figure 20.10 (shown earlier) for an illustration of how IP logging works.

Each of these intrusion-response methods can be applied on a per-alarm basis, allowing for granular alarm response and management policy.

> **WARNING** You should use IP blocking only for signatures that have less chance of generating false positives; otherwise, legitimate traffic could be blocked if a false positive alarm is generated. A hacker who knows you're implementing IP blocking can also use your configuration as a DoS attack by crafting attack packets that have spoofed source IP addresses, with access from each spoofed address being blocked. Cisco Secure IDS allows you to configure IP addresses that will never be blocked, guarding critical hosts against such a DoS attack.

FIGURE 20.12 IP blocking response

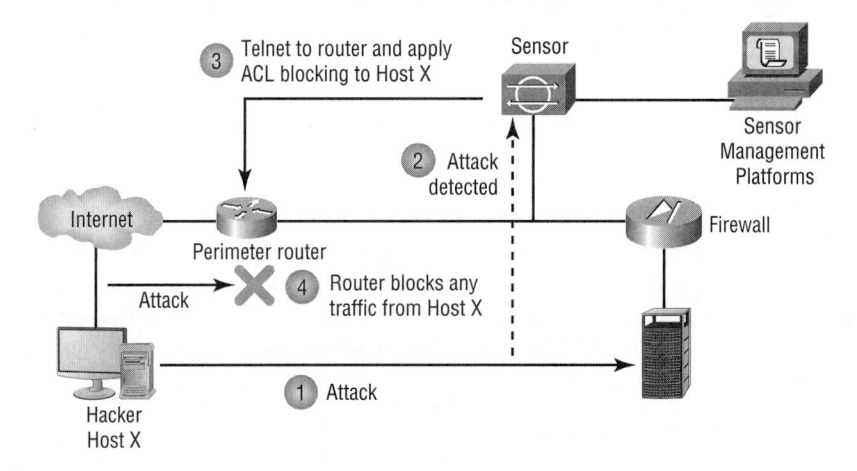

Remote Sensor Configuration and Management

Cisco Secure IDS sensor management platforms let you centrally manage and monitor multiple sensors located throughout your network. All sensor-related configurations are stored on a configuration management platform, with the configuration management platform responsible for pushing these configurations out to each sensor. Configuration attributes include the types of intrusive activity (signatures) that each sensor should monitor and how each sensor responds to a detected attack. Cisco Secure IDS also includes an Active Updates feature, which allows customers to subscribe to regular e-mail notifications generated by the Cisco Countermeasures Research Team (C-CRT), download new signature updates to a central location on the network, and then have multiple sensors automatically update their signature databases on a regular basis.

The Cisco Secure IDS configuration management platform lets you customize signatures, so that you create your own signatures that can detect some new attack. This functionality is provided by a complete signature language, which is similar to a scripting language, providing a powerful tool for customization.

> **NOTE** Customized signatures can only be applied to supported sensor platforms. See Table 20.1 for more details.

Cisco Secure IDS Feature Summary

A key feature of CSIDS 4.x is that all sensor platforms now run the same operating system and software, which means all features are common across all platforms.

Prior to CSIDS 4.x, it's important to understand that the features described in this section aren't supported on all sensor platforms. Table 20.1 summarizes each of the features discussed in this section and indicates the support for each feature of Cisco Secure IDS platforms.

> **NOTE** For CSIDS 4.x, all the features described in Table 20.1 are supported on all sensors except the router/firewall sensor.

TABLE 20.1 Cisco Secure IDS Feature Comparison for Sensors prior to CSIDS 4.x

Feature	Network Sensor (IDS 4200 Series)	Switch Sensor (Catalyst 6000 IDSM)	Router/Firewall Sensor (Cisco IOS and Cisco PIX)
TCP Reset	Yes	No	Yes
IP Blocking	Yes	Yes	Yes*
IP Logging	Yes	No	No
Customized Signatures	Yes	Yes	No
Active Updates	Yes	Yes	No
Analysis Support (NSDB)	Yes	Yes	Yes

*The router and firewall sensors don't provide IP blocking as such, but they provide a similar feature by possessing the ability to drop attack traffic due to the sensor sitting inline with network traffic sent and received.

Cisco Secure Sensor Platforms

The sensor platform is the most critical component of Cisco Secure IDS, because it detects, responds to, and reports intrusion activity to the sensor management platform. Each sensor is a hardware appliance that has been secured for the environment it works in, optimized for performance, and designed for ease of maintenance.

The sensor uses an extensive signature database that allows it to capture security attacks in real time from large amounts of IP traffic, and it possesses packet-reassembly features that prevent IDS bypass techniques. Once an attack is detected, the sensor sends an alarm to an event management platform and can optionally place that alarm information in a local log file. The sensor can also automatically reset a TCP-based connection that is associated with the attack and/or block the source IP address of the attacking system.

Cisco produces three main sensor platforms dedicated to IDS:

- 4200 series sensors
- Catalyst 6000/6500 IDS module (IDSM)
- Cisco 2600/3600/3700 IDS network modules

All of these sensor platforms are passive sensors, in that they passively monitor network traffic traversing one or more segments for intrusive activity. Each of these sensors contains two interfaces:

Command-and-control interface   This provides a management interface for the sensor. The command-and-control interface allows the sensor to be managed via TCP/IP and also lets the sensor send alarms to the event management platform. The command-and-control interface is the only interface that contains an IP address.

Monitoring interface   The monitoring interface operates in promiscuous mode, capturing all traffic on the attached segment and passing it to the IDS application for analysis. The monitoring interface doesn't have an IP address, ensuring that the sensor can be placed on an insecure segment and not be subjected to an attack itself.

Cisco also provides limited IDS capabilities using Cisco IOS Firewall and Cisco PIX sensors. These sensors are different from the 4200 series sensors and Catalyst IDSM and Cisco router IDS network modules in that they act as an inline IDS as opposed to a passive IDS and can only detect a reduced number of attacks.

4200 Series Sensors

The Cisco Secure 4200 series sensors are dedicated IDS appliances that can monitor up to 1Gbps of traffic from a single network segment. These sensors are available in three versions: IDS-4215, IDS-4235, and IDS-4250. All appliances are Intel-based servers that run a customized, security-hardened Linux operating system with a shell interface similar to Cisco IOS.

> **NOTE**   Prior to Cisco Secure IDS 4.0, 4200 series sensors ran a customized security-hardened version of the Solaris operating system for Intel.

The major difference between each platform is performance. The IDS-4215 can monitor traffic at a speed of up to 80Mbps, whereas the IDS-4235 can monitor traffic at a speed of up to 200Mbps. The IDS-4250 can monitor up to 500Mbps of traffic, with the ability to monitor 1Gbps of traffic with an optional accelerator card. Both the IDS-4235 and IDS-4250 can be attached to copper-based Gigabit Ethernet networks; the IDS-4250 also supports an optional dual 1000BaseSX card. Table 20.2 summarizes the differences between the sensors.

> **NOTE**   The IDS-4215 sensor replaces the IDS-4210 sensor, which is now end-of-sale (EOS; it can no longer be purchased as a new product) and provided 45Mbps of performance.

TABLE 20.2 4200 Series Sensor Comparison

Feature	IDS-4215	IDS-4235	IDS-4250
Performance	80Mbps	250Mbps	500Mbps1Gbps (with optional XL card)
Processor	n/a	Pentium III 1.3GHz	Dual Pentium III 1.3GHz
Memory	512MB	1GB	2GB
Monitoring NIC	10/100 Ethernet	10/100/1000 Ethernet	10/100/1000 Ethernet Optional 1000BaseSX
Chassis height	1U	1U	1U

> **Note:** Cisco also has released the IDS-4250-XL sensor, which can monitor up to 1Gbps of traffic. An existing IDS-4250 can be upgraded to an IDS-4250-XL sensor with the addition of a specialized dual 1000BaseSX card that includes onboard acceleration for IDS packet processing.

Catalyst 6000 IDS Module

The Cisco Catalyst 6000 IDS Module (IDSM) is a fully integrated line card that plugs into a Catalyst 6000/6500 switch. The IDSM exists in two versions:

- IDSM-1, which can monitor up to 100Mbps of traffic
- IDSM-2, which can monitor up to 600Mbps of traffic

> **Note:** The IDSM-1 is an EOS product and can only run Cisco Secure IDS 3.*x* software. The IDSM-2 replaces the IDSM-1 and can only run Cisco Secure IDS 4.*x* software.

The IDSM can take traffic directly off the switch backplane and analyze it with no impact on switch performance. It's capable of analyzing up to 600Mbps of traffic and can also analyze traffic from multiple VLANs (segments). The IDSM-2 possesses the same IDS functionality as the 4200 series sensors, and it can be managed through all sensor management platforms. The IDSM features are discussed in more detail in Chapter 21, "Installing Cisco Secure IDS Sensors and IDSMs."

IDS Network Module for Cisco 2600/2800/3600/3700/3800 Routers

Cisco has recently released an IDS network module for the modular Cisco 2600/2800/3600/3700/3800 family of routers (part code NM-CIDS-K9), which is effectively a server on a network module. The IDS network module has a completely separate operating system (the same Linux-based OS of the 4200 series sensors and IDSM) from the router (Cisco IOS); it uses the router to provide power and a connection to the data bus for an internal monitoring interface on the IDS network module. An external command and control interface is located on the network module, which allows for IDS network module management. Following are the specifications of the IDS network module:

- Processor: Intel Pentium III Mobile 500MHz
- Memory: 256MB (upgradeable to 512MB)
- Hard disk: 20GB IDE
- Monitoring interface: Internal port on router internal bus

The IDS network module can monitor up to 10Mbps of traffic in the 2600 and 3600 series routers, and 45Mbps of traffic in the 3700/3800 series routers. The IDS network module provides an excellent means of increasing security at the edge of the network, where many organizations deploy 2600, 2800, 3600, 3700, or 3800 series routers as border routers to the Internet.

Cisco IOS Firewall and Cisco PIX Sensors

The Cisco IOS Firewall and PIX sensors provide integrated intrusion detection in addition to the other integrated capabilities of each device (firewalling, VPN, routing, and so on). These sensors detect a limited number of devices, meaning they're useful only for smaller environments where the cost of implementing a dedicated IDS can't be justified.

> **WARNING** Don't confuse the IDS network module with the IDS features of the Cisco IOS Firewall feature set. The IDS network module is a fully functional Cisco Secure IDS sensor, supporting the same features as the 4200 series sensors and IDSM.

These sensors support the following features:

Signatures Cisco IOS FW includes 101 signatures, and Cisco PIX includes 55 signatures, which are based on a variety of common attacks. Signatures can be classified as *information signatures* (reconnaissance attacks) or *attack signatures* (access or DoS attacks).

> **TIP** In Cisco IOS 12.3(11)T, Cisco IOS includes over 700 signatures, making it comparable to Cisco Secure IDS sensors in terms of intrusion protection capabilities. Cisco has also announced that the new signatures developed by Trend Micro will be added to Cisco IOS in early 2005.

Alarm response Upon detection of an alarm, Cisco IOS FW and Cisco PIX sensors can respond with one (or more) of three different responses. These responses include generating an alarm that is sent via Syslog or PostOffice protocol to a sensor management platform, dropping intrusive activity, or resetting TCP sessions associated with an attack.

To support the IDS functionality on Cisco IOS or Cisco PIX, the following software versions and hardware platforms are required:

- Cisco IOS requires IOS version 12.0(5)T or higher and an IOS Firewall/IDS feature set installed on a 1700, 2600, 7100, 7200, 7500, or Catalyst 5000 RSM platform.
- Cisco PIX requires PIX OS version 5.2 or higher and is supported on the PIX 506E, 515E, 525, and 535 (it isn't supported on the PIX 501).

Cisco Secure IDS Management Platforms

Cisco Secure IDS management platforms are responsible for providing configuration management and event management for Cisco Secure IDS sensors. Cisco Secure IDS architecture offers several management platforms:

- IDS Device Manager and IDS Event Viewer
- IDS Management Center (IDS MC) and Security Monitoring Center (Security MC)

The IDS Device Manager and IDS Event Viewer are designed to be used in small installations with capability of managing up to five sensors. The IDS MC and Security MC are designed for large enterprise or service provider deployments where many sensors may be deployed throughout the network.

The functionality provided by the various management platforms includes configuration management (such as sensor configuration and sensor management) and event management (such as alarm response and alarm display) functions. With IDS Device Manager and IDS Event Viewer, event management is provided by IDS Event Viewer; configuration management functions are provided by IDS Device Manager. With the IDS MC and Security MC, event management is provided by the Security MC, and configuration management is provided by IDS MC.

> **NOTE** Cisco Security Agents require a separate management console called the Cisco Security Agent Management Center, which is included with CiscoWorks VMS as a separate application from the MC and the Security MC.

IDS Device Manager and IDS Event Viewer

IDS Device Manager and IDS Event Viewer are both web-based applications that enable stand-alone configuration management (IDS Device Manager) and event management (IDS Event Viewer) for up to five 4200 series sensors.

> **NOTE** Prior to Cisco Secure IDS 4.0, IDS Event Viewer could only monitor up to three sensors.

Because IDS Device Manager and IDS Event Viewer ship free with every Cisco Secure IDS 4.*x* sensor, they're ideal for use in small organizations looking to increase the security of their network by implementing an IDS without incurring high costs.

IDS Device Manager and IDS Event Viewer operate using a web-based, client/server architecture. The IDS Device Manager application runs from the sensor itself and manages the local sensor configuration. If multiple sensors are installed, you must use the local IDS Device Manager to manage each sensor independently, which obviously doesn't scale well if you're implementing more than a handful of sensors. The IDS Event Viewer application can collect alarms from up to five sensors and must be installed on a separate Windows NT or Windows 2000 server. IDS Device Manager provides a web-based interface for management, allowing management to be performed via any compatible web browser. IDS Event Viewer is a Java-based application that includes its own management console that you must run from the host on which the IDS Event Viewer is installed.

Figure 20.13 shows how IDS Device Manager and IDS Event Viewer manage Cisco Secure IDS sensors.

FIGURE 20.13   IDS Device Manager and IDS Event Viewer

IDS Device Manager
Runs from local web server on sensor
Can only configure local sensor

Alarms

IDS Event Viewer
Requires Windows 2000 Server
Collects alarms from up to 5 sensors

IDS Device Manager
Runs from local web server on sensor
Can only configure local sensor

Alarms

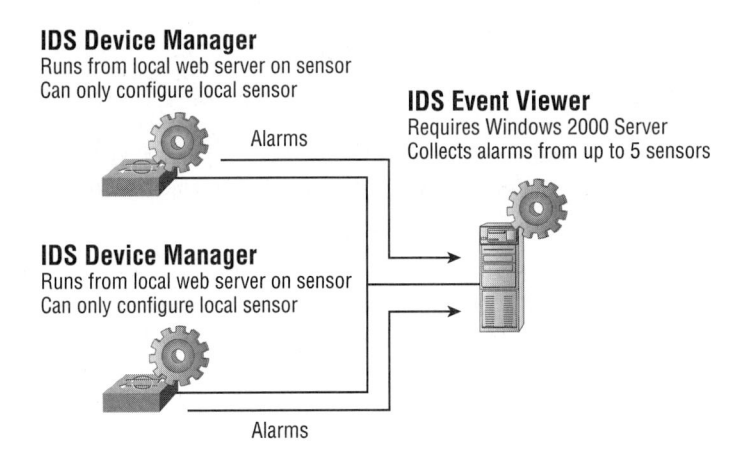

IDS Management Center and Security Monitoring Center

IDS Management Center and Security Monitoring Center form part of the CiscoWorks VPN and Security Management (VMS) bundle and provide the next generation of enterprise-class IDS sensor management and alarm management. Both products are designed to replace the older Cisco Secure Policy Manager and CSIDS Director for Unix management platforms, with the stated goals of providing the following enhancements over the older management platforms:

- Higher scalability, enabling support for hundreds of sensors and higher event volumes
- Group profiles to allow the same configuration to be applied concurrently to multiple sensors
- Event correlation to enable attacks to be identified that have been detected over multiple security systems
- Enhanced signature tuning to reduce false positives
- Richer reports and more flexible event notification schemes
- Web-based interface for easier management

> The IDS MC and Security MC can manage up to 300 sensors.

IDS MC and Security MC require CiscoWorks VMS to be installed on a Windows 2000 server. Both components can be installed on the same server; however, it's recommended that you separate each component, because the Security MC collects events not only from IDS sensors but also from Cisco routers and firewalls. Figure 20.14 shows how IDS MC and Security MC manage Cisco Secure IDS sensors.

Cisco Host IDS Platforms

The Cisco host-based IDS products provide a complete host-based IDS solution for the protection of critical systems and applications. Host sensor functionality is provided by Cisco Security Agent, which comes in a desktop and server version, whereas the Management Center for Cisco Security Agents is used to centrally manage desktop and server agents. We'll discuss each of these components next.

> The Cisco Security Agent product is fairly recent and resulted from the acquisition of the Okena StormWatch product. Prior to this acquisition, Cisco sold the Cisco Secure Host Sensor product, which was based on technology licensed from Entercept Security Technologies. The Cisco Secure Host Sensor product is now EOS.

Management Center for Cisco Security Agents

The Management Center for Cisco Security Agents is a component of the CiscoWorks VPN/ Security Management (VMS) 2.2 bundle. It's responsible for collecting and collating alarms from each agent as well as distributing agents to new hosts and updated agents with new software versions.

FIGURE 20.14 IDS MC and Security MC

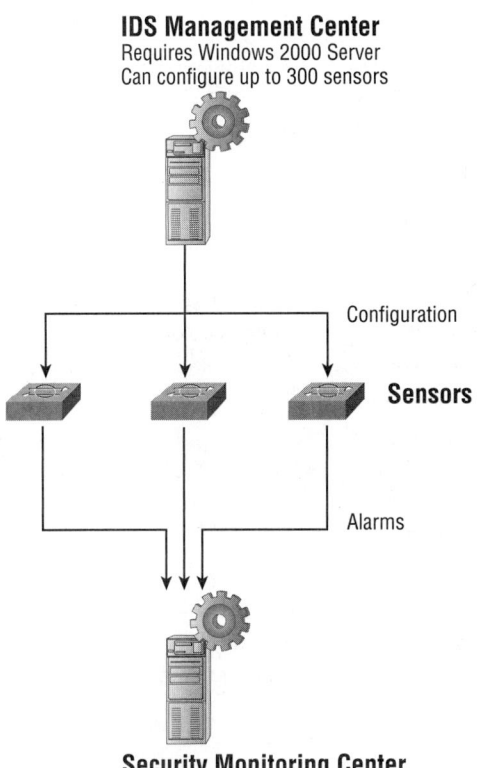

IDS Management Center
Requires Windows 2000 Server
Can configure up to 300 sensors

Configuration

Sensors

Alarms

Security Monitoring Center
Requires Windows 2000 Server
Can receive alarms from up to 300 sensors

Cisco Security Agent

The Cisco Security Agent consists of server and desktop agents. Server agents are available for Windows NT 4.0/Windows 2000 Server and Solaris 8 SPARC, and desktop agents are available for Windows NT 4.0 Workstation and Windows 2000/XP Professional.

The security agent resides between the operating system kernel and applications, enabling visibility of all system calls to memory, file, network, Registry, and COM object resources. The agent is configured with an appropriate level of behavior for specific applications; any deviation from the configured behavior causes the agent to detect unauthorized access or attack. The Cisco Security Agent is an example of an anomaly-based intrusion detection system, and as such is useful for detecting new attacks that are often impossible to detect with signature-based intrusion detection systems such as Cisco Secure IDS sensors.

The Cisco Security Agent provides a variety of features that ensure that critical systems and applications are protected from attacks. It's designed to detect known and unknown attacks based on the following intrusive activities:

Probing *Probing* relates to the activities associated with reconnaissance being performed against the host or an attempt to break into a host by guessing security information. The following are some of the probe attacks that the Cisco Security Agent detects:

- Ping
- Port scans
- Password and username guessing

Penetration *Penetration* refers to the process of gaining unauthorized access to processes running and/or data stored on the target system. The Cisco Security Agent can detect a possible attack based on events that indicate the host is in the process of being compromised or penetrated. The following are some of the events related to penetration attacks that the Cisco Security Agent detects:

- Mail attachments
- Buffer overflows
- ActiveX controls
- Back doors

Persistence *Persistence* refers to events that result from a successful attack and subsequent infection of a host system. The following are some of the events that indicate that a system has been compromised and that some form of unauthorized action, application, or service is present:

- File creation
- File modification
- Security settings modification
- Installation of new services
- Trap doors

Propagation *Propagation* refers to the automatic self-replication of an attack to other systems after an initial target system has been infected. The following are some of the events related to propagation that the Cisco Security Agent detects:

- E-mail copies of the attack
- Web and FTP connections
- Internet Relay Chat (IRC) connections
- Propagation via file shares

Paralyzing *Paralyzing* refers to the complete or partial removal of the availability and responsiveness of computing resources on a target system. The following are some of the events related to system paralysis that the Cisco Security Agent detects:

- File modification and deletion
- Computer crashes
- Denial of service
- Stealing of sensitive/confidential information

Summary

Because connectivity to networks such as the Internet is crucial for organizations to survive in today's increasingly competitive world, organizations must understand security threats and secure their networks against them. This chapter began with a discussion of security threats, including their identifying characteristics, attack types, and common exploits used to take advantage of vulnerabilities.

Next, we introduced how to implement network security and the Security Wheel, which is a continuous four-phase cycle of securing, monitoring, testing, and updating the network. You learned that an IDS is a device that helps you monitor the network, fitting into the monitoring phase of the Security Wheel.

Then we covered IDS basics, including the two major types of systems: profile-based and signature-based IDS, which can be either network-based or host-based. You learned that Cisco Secure IDS platforms covered on the CSIDS exam are signature-based and network-based.

Finally, we introduced the Cisco Secure IDS architecture, which provides features such as alarm display and logging, proactive intrusion response, and remote sensor management. The components of the Cisco Secure IDS are the sensor, which monitors network traffic, analyzing it for intrusive activity; the configuration manager, which provides configuration management for sensors; and the event manager, which manages alarms from the sensor when an attack is detected. Cisco Secure IDS sensors are available in a stand-alone appliance (the 4200 series sensors), as a blade in a Catalyst 6000/6500 switch (the Catalyst 6000 IDSM), or as a network module in a Cisco 2600/2800/3600/3700/3800 series router. Cisco IOS Firewalls and Cisco PIX firewalls also provide limited inline IDS capabilities. Two Cisco Secure IDS management platforms are available: IDS Device Manager and IDS Event Viewer provide management for small sensor deployments, whereas the IDS Management Center and Security Monitoring Center provide enterprise management for up to hundreds of sensor deployments.

Exam Essentials

Know the four primary security threats.   The four main security threats are unstructured, structured, external, and internal threats.

Remember each of the three types of attacks.   The types of attacks are reconnaissance, unauthorized access, and denial of service (DoS).

Understand each phase of the Security Wheel.   The Security Wheel defines securing, monitoring, testing, and improving your network security.

Understand the different types of IDS and where an IDS can run.   The two types of IDS are profile-based (anomaly detection) and signature-based (misuse detection). An IDS can run in a network-based location or on a host (host-based). Cisco Secure IDS sensors are signature-based and run in a network-based location.

Know the basic features of Cisco Secure IDS.   Alarm detection and management, intrusion response, and remote sensor management are the main features of Cisco Secure IDS.

Know which sensor platforms exist and the differences between them.   The IDS 4200 series sensors are stand-alone appliances. The 4210 supports up to 45Mbps 10/100 Ethernet traffic, the 4235 supports up to 200Mbps 10/100/1000 Ethernet, and the 4250 supports up to 500Mbps 10/100/1000 Ethernet. The Catalyst 6000 IDSM-2 is a blade module that supports up to 600Mbps traffic and can monitor traffic from multiple VLANs. The Cisco IOS Firewall feature set and Cisco PIX firewall software also provide limited IDS capabilities based on a small number of signatures.

Know which sensor management platforms exist.   Sensor management platforms include configuration-management and event management platforms. Configuration-management platforms include IDS Device Manager and the CiscoWorks VMS IDS Management Center. Event management platforms include IDS Event Viewer and the CiscoWorks VMS Security Monitoring Center.

Chapter 21

Installing Cisco Secure IDS Sensors and IDSMs

CISCO SECURE INTRUSION DETECTION SYSTEM EXAM TOPICS COVERED IN THIS CHAPTER:

- ✓ Features of the various IDS sensor appliance models
- ✓ The interfaces and ports on the various sensors
- ✓ Functions of the various Catalyst IDS module ports
- ✓ Initializing a Catalyst IDS module
- ✓ Verifying the Catalyst 6500 switch and Catalyst IDSM configurations
- ✓ Installing the sensor software image
- ✓ Installing the sensor appliance on the network
- ✓ Obtaining management access on the sensor
- ✓ Initializing the sensor
- ✓ Command-line modes
- ✓ Navigating the CLI
- ✓ Applying configuration changes made via the CLI
- ✓ Creating user accounts via the CLI
- ✓ Upgrading a sensor and an IDSM to an IDS major release
- ✓ The Cisco IDS directory structure
- ✓ The communication infrastructure of the Cisco IDS
- ✓ Locating and identifying the Cisco IDS log and error files
- ✓ The Cisco IDS configuration files and their function
- ✓ The Cisco IDS services and their associated configuration files
- ✓ Performing a configuration backup via the CLI

In the previous chapter, you learned about all about the reasons why intrusion protection is so important for organizations serious about network security, and you were introduced to the Cisco Secure IDS product family. In this chapter, you'll learn about the Cisco Secure IDS sensor platforms. The sensor is the actual device that monitors traffic, generating alarms if intrusive network activity is detected. The Cisco Secure IDS sensors include the Cisco Secure IDS 4200 series sensors, the Cisco Catalyst 6000 Intrusion Detection System Module (IDSM), and the Cisco 2600/3600/3700 IDS network module.

This chapter will initially look at the topic of sensor deployment, which is the process of planning where you should place your sensors on the network. You'll then learn how to install and initialize the sensor to a state where it's ready to be configured for intrusion detection.

Deploying Cisco Secure IDS

Before installing the Cisco Secure IDS sensor or Catalyst IDS module, you must understand the various deployment considerations that need to be taken into account. There are a number of locations in the network where you can place the sensor. Each location option has pros and cons, and your security, management, and cost requirements will ultimately dictate the optimal location for your sensor. You also must understand the interfaces that each sensor possesses, because they define the sensor's monitoring and management capabilities.

Once you understand the issues around sensor deployment, you can then decide exactly where you'll deploy your sensor(s). We'll cover the considerations and procedures for sensor deployment in this section.

These considerations include the following:

- Sensor selection considerations
- Sensor deployment considerations

Sensor Selection Considerations

When you're deploying network security for an organization, choosing the right device that is up to the job is important. If you're deploying an IDS solution that services a high-speed Internet connection and thousands of users, you're hardly going to buy an IDS designed for small to medium organizations. Instead, you're more likely to choose an enterprise IDS that can meet the current and future performance requirements of the organization, as well as other physical requirements such as support for specific types of network media (such as Gigabit Ethernet).

Performance Considerations

Choosing a sensor that can perform adequately in the environment it's deployed in is extremely important. An effective IDS shouldn't miss any intrusive activity targeted at systems and networks the IDS is protecting, even if the monitored link is under full load. Intrusion detection is a complex process that requires significant processing power and memory usage. Many attacks attempt to bypass an IDS by using techniques such as fragmentation, where an intrusive data stream is broken up into multiple IP fragments, or out-of-order TCP segment delivery, where TCP segments are delivered out of order but reconstructed at the target system into an intrusive data stream.

To detect such attacks, an IDS must be capable of keeping copies of packets received over a reasonable time frame, so that a data stream can be analyzed once all the fragments are available to reconstruct the data stream. This obviously consumes finite resources such as memory and CPU time, adding to the performance requirements of an IDS.

Other IDS bypass techniques also exist, where an attacker may flood the segment with harmless traffic an IDS is monitoring in an attempt to distract the IDS from a real attack hidden somewhere within the harmless traffic. The real test for an IDS is when it's being flooded with large amounts of traffic while an attack is being mounted that uses evasive techniques such as fragmentation—in this situation, an IDS must have enough system resources (CPU and memory) to still be able to accurately detect intrusive activity without missing a beat.

The Cisco Secure IDS sensor family includes a wide range of sensors that are designed to deliver complete intrusion protection performance from 10Mbps right up to speeds of 1Gbps. This means the Cisco Secure IDS sensor product family can effectively meet the intrusion protection requirements of all but a very few organizations. Although each sensor has a specified level of performance that generally provides an accurate representation of true system performance, it's important to understand that the quoted performance figures are based on fixed network conditions that aren't representative of real-world conditions.

Table 21.1 lists the various performance levels of each of the Cisco Secure IDS sensors and the conditions under which the quoted performance levels have been achieved.

TABLE 21.1 Cisco Secure IDS Performance

Product	Performance	Testing Conditions			
		New TCP Connections per Second	HTTP Transactions per Second	Average Packet Size (Bytes)	CSIDS Version Tested
NM-CIDS-K9	10Mbps (2600XM) 45Mbps (3700)	500	500	445	4.1
4210[1]	45Mbps	500	500	445	4.0

TABLE 21.1 Cisco Secure IDS Performance *(continued)*

Product	Performance	Testing Conditions			
		New TCP Connections per Second	HTTP Transactions per Second	Average Packet Size (Bytes)	CSIDS Version Tested
4215	80Mbps	800	800	445	4.0
IDSM-1[2]	100Mbps	1000	-	-[3]	-
4235	250Mbps	3000	3000	445	4.0
4250	500Mbps	2700	2700	595	4.0
IDSM-2	600Mbps	5000	-	450	4.0
4250-XL	1Gbps	5000	5000	595	4.0

[1]Cisco stopped selling the 4210 sensor after December 6, 2003.
[2]Cisco stopped selling the IDSM-1 after April 20, 2003.
[3]Cisco quotes the IDSM-1 as capable of processing up to 47,000 packets per second.

Network Media Considerations

All Cisco Secure IDS sensors are Ethernet-based, which means that if you want to monitor WAN connections for intrusive activity, you must place sensors on the Ethernet segment behind the appropriate WAN router.

> **NOTE** The exception to this is the IDS network module for the 2600/2800/3600/3700/3800 series routers, which includes an internal sensing interface that attaches to the data bus of the router. The router is independent of physical interface types on the router itself.

All Cisco Secure IDS sensors include two interfaces:

Command and control This interface is used for management and alarm notification communications with the sensor management platform(s).

Sensing Also referred to as the *monitoring interface*, this is used to capture and analyze traffic from one or more LAN segments.

In terms of network media considerations, the sensing interface is very important, because it limits the maximum theoretical throughput of the sensor. Cisco Secure IDS sensors are available that include 10/100Mbps Ethernet interfaces only, as well as sensors that include both fiber-based and copper-based Gigabit Ethernet connectivity.

> **Real World Scenario**
>
> **Cisco Secure IDS Sensors and Trunking**
>
> In a typical Cisco Secure IDS sensor deployment, the sensing interfaces of your sensor are connected to a switched LAN infrastructure (there are variations on this, which are discussed in the next chapter). Some LAN switches support *trunking*, where traffic from multiple VLANs can be sent to the sensor for analysis. With trunking, a VLAN ID is attached to each frame sent to the sensor, which identifies the VLAN to which the frame belongs. All Cisco Secure IDS 4.*x* 4200 and IDSM-2 sensors support the ability to monitor traffic from multiple VLANs sent on the same physical interface using 802.1q trunking. 802.1q is a standards-based protocol for trunking that is defined by the IEEE and is supported on most modern switches.
>
> So, if you want your sensor to monitor traffic from multiple VLANs over a single physical interface, you must ensure that the LAN infrastructure to which the sensor-sensing interface is connected supports 802.1q trunking.

Selecting a Sensor

The selection of a sensor is ultimately determined by the network environment that the sensor must protect. For example, a sensor monitoring an OC-3 Internet connection must be capable of monitoring traffic at speeds of up to 155Mbps, whereas a sensor monitoring an internal network typically requires the ability to monitor multiple VLANs. In summary, selecting a sensor comes down to two important criteria:

- Performance: How much traffic does the sensor need to be capable of supporting? What network environment is the sensor protecting?
- Network Media: What type of interfaces does the sensor require? Does the sensor need to monitor multiple segments (VLANs)?

Table 21.2 compares each of the various IDS sensor platforms, describing the performance capabilities, the network media (monitoring) supported, the typical network environment the sensor would be deployed for, and the cost (U.S. list price) of each sensor.

TABLE 21.2 Cisco Secure IDS Platforms

Product	Performance	Sensing Interface	Network Environment	Cost (U.S. List)
NM-CIDS-K9	10Mbps 45Mbps	Internal	T1/E1/T3/E3	$2,995
4210	45Mbps	10/100Mbps	T1/E1/T3/E3	End-of-sale (EOS)

TABLE 21.2 Cisco Secure IDS Platforms *(continued)*

Product	Performance	Sensing Interface	Network Environment	Cost (U.S. List)
4215	80Mbps	10/100Mbps	T1/E1/T3/E3	$7,295
IDSM-1	100Mbps	Internal 1000Mbps	Switched LAN (VLANs)	EOS
4235	200Mbps	10/100/1000Mbps	Multiple T3/E3 OC3	$12,500
4250	500Mbps	10/100/1000Mbps or 1000BaseSX	OC12 Switched LAN (VLANs)	$25,000 (10/100/1000Mbps) $27,000 (1000BaseSX)
IDSM-2	600Mbps	Internal 1000Mbps	Switched LAN (VLANs)	$29,995
4250-XL	1Gbps	1000BaseSX	Gigabit Ethernet	$40,000

Sensor Deployment Considerations

Once you've selected the appropriate sensor(s) for your environment, you must next assess any sensor deployment considerations before actually deploying your sensor. Sensor deployment considerations consist of the following:

- Sensor placement
- Sensor communications
- Sensor management

Sensor Placement Considerations

Network IDS systems are generally expensive pieces of equipment, so choosing the appropriate parts of the network to monitor is of critical importance. You must determine the exact number of IDS sensors that your network requires, as well as the optimal locations for each of these sensors. The following aspects of your network should be considered when evaluating IDS sensor deployment:

Connections to untrusted networks   You must understand all possible entry points into your network from untrusted networks (such as the Internet and extranets) and remote-access connections (such as dial-up and VPN client connections). Ideally, each entry point should be secured and monitored for traffic violations. You might also consider your internal trusted networks as monitoring points, especially on internal segments that host critical systems.

Critical resources Identifying the critical resources in your network often determines where you place your sensors. Critical resources may include servers, mainframes, routers, and firewalls. By placing a sensor in front of these resources, you can detect, send alerts in response to, and react to intrusive activity against the resource.

Performance requirements You must understand the bandwidth requirements of key connections in the network. For example, you may wish to monitor a link that uses 100Mbps bandwidth, so your IDS sensor must be able to handle this. You should also understand the different protocols in use (such as TCP, UDP, and HTTP) on the network, because each type of traffic has a different performance hit on an IDS system. If the network segment you wish to monitor will exceed a single sensor's capabilities, you can deploy multiple sensors.

Size and complexity Normally, the bigger your network, the more entry points there are to the network. This generally means you need to monitor more points in the network, which ultimately means you need to purchase more sensors.

Common Sensor Locations

Once you've determined and resolved the issues that you must consider before deploying sensors, you can determine where you want to place sensors. Sensors are commonly placed on entry points into the network. The most common sensor placement locations can be summarized as follows:

Internet connection The most common placement is on the Internet demilitarized zone (DMZ) network (the network between a perimeter router and firewall), where you can capture intrusive activity that originates from the Internet before it reaches the firewall. This way, you can understand exactly what threats are out there.

Intranet connection You can also place a sensor on your trusted network (also known as *intranet connections*), where you can detect internal intrusive activity. This is useful to detect any intrusive traffic that manages to pass through the firewall. You can also install host-based IDS agents to protect critical servers.

Remote-access and extranet connections Other common locations for placing IDS sensors are on remote-access networks and connections that terminate an extranet link.

Server farms Many organizations are centralizing servers into server farms, to increase performance, scalability, and availability. A common use of server farms is for public DMZ networks, where web servers, mail servers and other publicly accessible services are located. By installing host-based intrusion detection systems on each host, each public server is provided intrusion protection.

A truly complete intrusion protection solution implements a combination of network IDS sensors and host IDS agents, with sensors installed at entry points into the network and host agents installed on critical servers.

Figure 21.1 illustrates the various points in the network where you can place a sensor. Notice that each sensor is effectively monitoring an entry point into the network or a specific portion of the network.

FIGURE 21.1 Common sensor placement locations

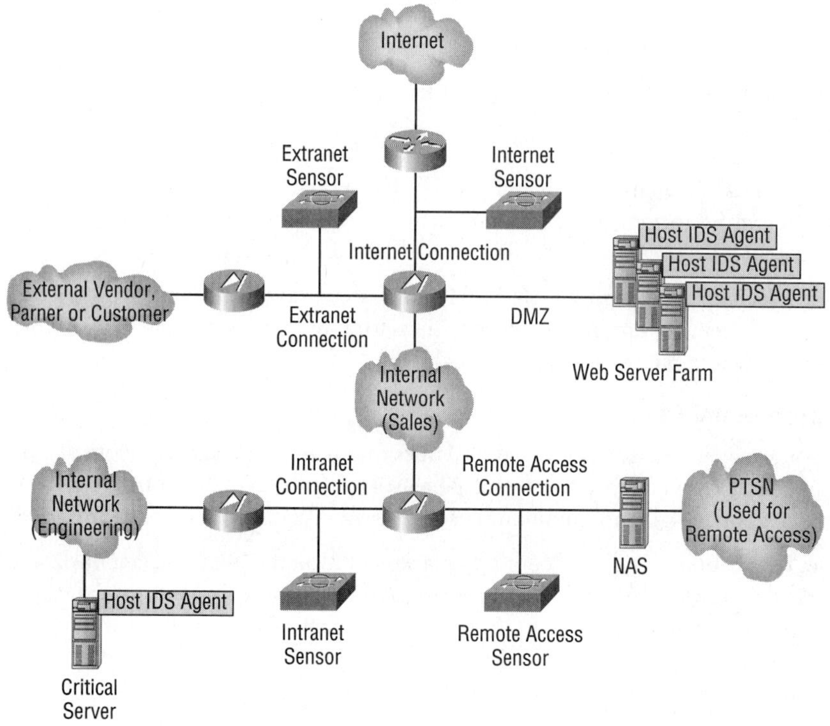

Traffic Capture

The locations where you attach your sensors must provide the capability for your sensor to capture all traffic sent and received on the segment the sensor attaches to. If the sensor is connected to a hub, this isn't a problem, because a hub is a shared network device that allows any connected device to capture all traffic passing through the hub. In a switched environment, however, a sensor will only see initial unicast traffic between devices, broadcast traffic, and multicast traffic if attached to a normal switch port. To ensure that sensors can monitor all traffic, even if attached to a switch, you must ensure that you can configure traffic-mirroring features on the switch, such as switch port analyzer (SPAN) and VLAN access control lists (VACLs). These traffic-capture mechanisms are discussed in Chapter 22, "Configuring the Network to Support Cisco Secure IDS Sensors."

Sensor Communications Considerations

When deploying Cisco Secure IDS sensors, it's common to deploy sensors such that the sensor management platform(s) that manage each sensor and receive alarm information from each

Deploying Cisco Secure IDS **691**

sensor are located at some other remote location in the network, possibly with a firewall in between the sensors and sensor management platform(s). Figure 21.2 demonstrates such a topology.

In Figure 21.2, the command and control interface on the sensor is attached directly to the firewall, with the sensor management platform attached to the internal network. This means that all sensor ← → sensor management platform communications must pass through the firewall. Hence, the appropriate rules must be configured on the firewall to permit these communications. Notice in Figure 21.2 that to support sensors running Cisco Secure IDS 4.*x*, SSH connections (TCP port 22) to the sensor from the sensor management platform must be permitted (for configuration management purposes), as well as HTTP (TCP port 80) or HTTPS (recommended – TCP port 443) connections to the sensor from the sensor management platform (for event management purposes using Remote Desktop Exchange Protocol [RDEP]).

> **NOTE**
> In Cisco Secure IDS 3.*x*, a proprietary protocol called the PostOffice protocol is used for sensor ← → sensor management platform communications. This protocol uses UDP port 45000.

FIGURE 21.2 Sensor communications through a firewall

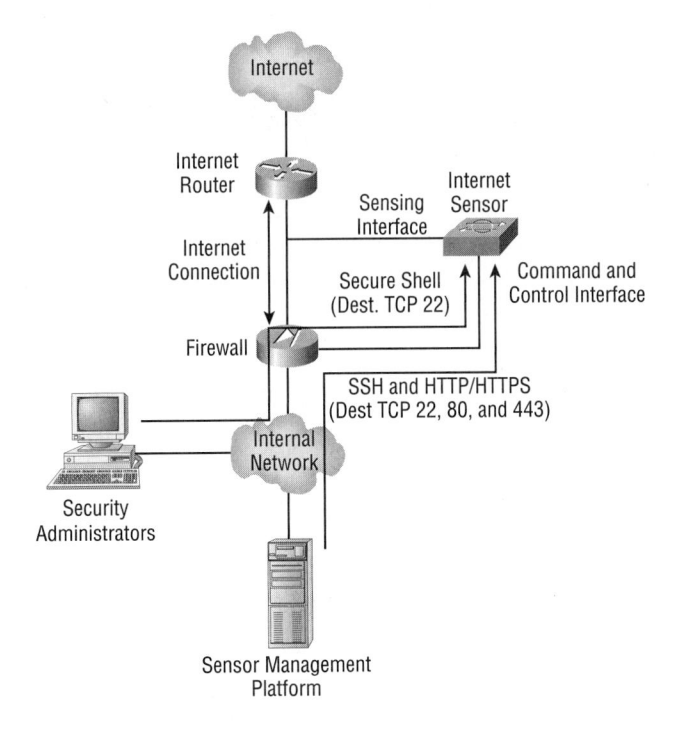

Sensor Management Considerations

A number of sensor management considerations exist when you're deploying Cisco Secure IDS. These considerations relate to the scalability and ongoing management of the Cisco Secure IDS architecture:

Sensor-to-management platform ratio For large networks where multiple sensors may be deployed, it's important to understand the practical limits as to how many sensors may be managed from a single sensor management platform. For example, IDS Event Viewer can receive alarms from only up to five sensors—anything above this number requires the Security Monitoring Center, which can in theory receive alarms from up to 300 sensors. The IDS Device Manager can only manage its local sensor, whereas the IDS Management Center can manage up to 300 sensors.

Software updates One of the most important ongoing management tasks for Cisco Secure IDS is to ensure that the most up-to-date signatures are installed on your sensors and sensor management platforms. It's critical that your sensors have the most up-to-date signatures installed so that new attacks can be detected. Your sensor management platform must also have the most up-to-date signatures installed so that it understands the alarms it must potentially enable/disable or tune, can interpret the alarms it receives, and can provide information as to the nature of the attacks that generate alarms and how to mitigate the attack.

Cisco Secure IDS 4.*x* supports a feature known as *automatic updates*, where sensors can be configured to obtain signature updates automatically from an FTP server. At this point in time, direct downloads from Cisco aren't supported; hence you still must manually populate the FTP server used to store the updates, which the sensors will then automatically download.

> **NOTE** Cisco posts signature updates every two weeks and occasionally posts signature updates outside of this schedule in response to new attacks. You can obtain signature updates from www.cisco.com/kobayashi/sw-center/ciscosecure/ids/crypto/ (requires a valid CCO login).

Alarm database management Alarm database management is an event management platform consideration. The event management platform collects alarms from each sensor and stores these alarms in a central database, enabling a single point of access to all alarms for all sensors. Because you never know how many alarms will be generated by your sensors, it's important to ensure that the event management platform has plenty of disk space. Of course, disk space is a finite resource; hence you must also consider how to limit the size of the alarm database by deciding how long to keep alarm information in the database before archiving it. Backing up the alarm database is also important, to ensure that you don't lose alarm information should the event management platform fail.

Installing and Configuring Cisco Secure IDS Sensors

In the previous sections, you learned about the design and planning issues you must consider before implementing Cisco Secure IDS sensors. In this section, you'll learn how to install and configure IDS sensors with a basic configuration.

When you're installing and configuring Cisco Secure IDS sensors for the first time, you must perform several tasks:

Plan the installation   Planning is an important component of any installation. In the case of Cisco Secure IDS, you need to be aware of some important issues, especially if you're upgrading a sensor from a previous software version.

Physically install and cable the sensor   This requires you to understand the physical layout of the various sensor platforms, so that you know where physical management and network interfaces are located.

Gain initial management access   When you're configuring a sensor for the first time, you must understand the methods available for initial management access.

Log in to the sensor   After you establish initial management access, you need to log in to the sensor for the first time. To do this, you must understand the default credentials required for management access and have an understanding of how to navigate the sensor command line interface.

Configure the sensor for the first time   After you log in and gain initial management access, you can then begin configuring the sensor. When you're configuring a Cisco Secure IDS sensor, you need to first configure basic configuration settings such as hostname, network addressing, and user accounts so that the command and control interface of the sensor can be attached to the network to allow communications with the appropriate sensor management platform(s) that will manage the sensor.

Administer the sensor   This includes basic day-to-day monitoring and administrative tasks that you may need to perform.

In the following sections, you'll learn how to perform the configuration tasks listed here for each of the Cisco Secure IDS sensor platforms. These platforms include the following:

- 4200 series sensors
- Catalyst 6000/6500 IDS module
- Cisco 2600/3600/3700 IDS network module

Planning the Installation

When you purchase a new Cisco Secure IDS sensor, the latest Cisco Secure IDS software should be already installed, meaning that you don't need to worry about installation of the base operating system and Cisco Secure IDS application files. A recovery/upgrade CD ships with each sensor, which is used for situations where you need to reinstall the base operating system and Cisco Secure IDS application files.

If you're upgrading an existing 4200 sensor to Cisco Secure IDS 4.x, it's important to understand that there are some upgrade considerations, due to the fact that Cisco Secure IDS 4.x uses a new base operating system (customized Red Hat Linux). Previous versions of Cisco Secure IDS on the 4200 series sensors used a customized build of Solaris 8 for Intel.

> **NOTE** The 4200 series are the only sensors that can be upgraded to Cisco Secure IDS 4.x from previous versions. The IDSM-1 can't be upgraded to Cisco Secure IDS 4.x (only the IDSM-2 supports Cisco Secure IDS 4.x), and the IDS network module only supports Cisco Secure IDS 4.x.

The following are important considerations you need to be aware of if you're upgrading to Cisco Secure IDS 4.x:

Upgrading from Cisco Secure IDS 3.x to 4.x   Customers with existing Cisco Secure IDS 3.x sensors who wish to upgrade to Cisco Secure IDS 4.x must purchase the Cisco Secure IDS 4.x recovery/upgrade CD (for customers with an active software support subscription, this CD is free but still must be ordered from Cisco).

The only way to upgrade from Cisco Secure IDS 3.x to 4.x is to perform a fresh installation of Cisco Secure IDS 4.x using the Cisco Secure IDS 4.x recovery/upgrade CD. All previous configuration settings are lost and should be recorded prior to installation of Cisco Secure IDS 4.x. Once Cisco Secure IDS 4.x is installed, the previous configuration settings must be manually configured on the new installation.

Upgrading from Cisco Secure IDS 4.0 to 4.1   You can upgrade from Cisco Secure IDS 4.0 to Cisco Secure IDS 4.1 and maintain your previous sensor configuration settings. The appropriate upgrade file is available from CCO for customers who have active software support subscriptions.

Memory requirements   If you're installing or upgrading to Cisco Secure IDS 4.1, it's important to note that this version requires all 4200 sensors to have a minimum of 512MB RAM.

BIOS revision requirements   If you're upgrading an IDS-4235 or IDS-4250 sensor to Cisco Secure IDS 4.x, a minimum BIOS revision level of A04 or higher is required. In the past, these sensors may have shipped with a revision level of A01, A02, or A03, which isn't suitable. You can create a BIOS upgrade diskette by running the file `BIOS_A04.EXE`, which is located in the BIOS directory on the recovery CD. Once the BIOS upgrade diskette has been created, boot the sensor from the diskette to upgrade the BIOS.

You can determine the BIOS revision level via keyboard/monitor or console when the sensor is first powered on, as demonstrated here:

```
Phoenix ROM BIOS PLUS Version 1.10 A03
Cisco Systems IDS-4235/4250
www.cisco.com
Testing memory. Please wait.
```

In this example, the last characters at the end of the first line indicate the current BIOS revision level is A03, which means the BIOS must be upgraded to revision level A4.

> **TIP** You can't upgrade the BIOS from a console connection; you must use a keyboard and monitor.

Upgrading the IDS-4220 and IDS-4230 sensors When you're upgrading an IDS-4220 or IDS-4230 sensor from Cisco Secure IDS 3.x to Cisco Secure IDS 4.x, it's important to note that the command and control and sensing interfaces are swapped. This means you must ensure that you swap the cables attached to each interface prior to upgrading to Cisco Secure IDS 4.x. In Cisco Secure IDS 4.x for the IDS-4220/IDS-4230, the onboard NIC (int0) is used as the sensing interface, and the NIC in a PCI slot (int1) is used as the command and control interface.

> **NOTE** The IDS-4220 and IDS-4230 sensors are legacy sensors that are no longer sold; however, many still exist in the field.

Physically Installing the Sensor

To correctly install an IDS sensor (for example, in a rack with appropriate space) and ensure that the appropriate physical connections are in place, you need to understand the physical characteristics of the sensor. This section describes the physical layout of the 4200 series, IDSM, and NM-CIDS sensors.

4200 Series Sensors' Physical Layout

The 4200 Series sensors are dedicated, stand-alone appliances that are basically Intel-based servers with the appropriate CPU, memory, storage, and network interfaces to perform IDS functions. Table 21.3 compares the physical hardware specifications of the current 4200 series models.

> **NOTE** Notice that the IDS-4215 sensor is more like a network appliance and less like an Intel-based server, with unique features such as an internal compact flash memory card for configuration storage and an RJ45 console port for direct management access (you can't attach a keyboard and monitor to the IDS-4215).

TABLE 21.3 4200 Series Sensor Physical Specifications

	4215	4235	4250/4250-XL
CPU	566Mhz	1.26Ghz	1.26Ghz (dual)
Memory	512MB	1GB	2GB
Storage	Compact flash (configuration) 20GB IDE (operating system)	20GB IDE (operating system)	20GB IDE (operating system)
Network Interfaces	2 x 10/100BaseT 4-port 10/100BaseT (optional)	2 x 10/100/1000BaseT	2 x 10/100/1000BaseT 1 x 1000BaseSX (optional) 4-port 10/100BaseT (optional) 2 x 1000BaseSX (upgrade to 4250-XL)
Physical Management Interfaces	Console (RJ45)	Keyboard/Monitor Console (DB9)	Keyboard/Monitor Console (DB9)
Performance Upgradeable	No	No	Yes (4250 to 4250-XL)

> Cisco will introduce two new sensors in early 2005: the IDS-4240 and the IDS-4255. Both of these sensors will be flash-based (no hard disks) and will provide 250Mbps and 600Mbps respectively when operating in inline mode. (Inline mode is a new feature of Cisco Secure IDS 5.0, which allows the sensor to act in a similar fashion to a firewall: It can actively block intrusive activity inline rather than having to instruct an external access control device to block.)

4215 Sensor Physical Layout

The Cisco Secure IDS 4215 sensor (Cisco product number IDS-4215) is Cisco's entry-level IDS sensor appliance. The IDS-4215 is a compact, slim-line network appliance that includes compact flash memory for storing configuration and a 20GB IDE hard disk for storing logging data. The IDS-4215 includes two 10/100BaseT interfaces for sensing and command and control functions, with an optional four-port 10/100BaseT card available to add more sensing interfaces.

Recall from our discussion earlier that the IDS-4215 is capable of monitoring up to 80Mbps of traffic (see Table 21.1). This means it's well suited for external connection segments, which typically use WAN connections to limit the amount of bandwidth to be processed. For example, the IDS-4215 is an ideal sensor to place on the Internet DMZ segment that connects an Internet connection of up to T3 (45Mbps) speed. The IDS-4215 isn't well suited to monitoring segments that have LAN speed (100Mbps) connections present (such as on an internal network segment).

If you're tasked with the installation of the IDS-4215, you need to understand its physical layout. Figure 21.3 shows the front panel layout for this sensor. If you're familiar with the Cisco 2600 series router, you can see that the front panel of the IDS-4215 is identical in layout, with a power LED, activity LED (indicates network activity), and network LED (indicates network connectivity).

FIGURE 21.3   Cisco Secure IDS 4215 sensor front panel

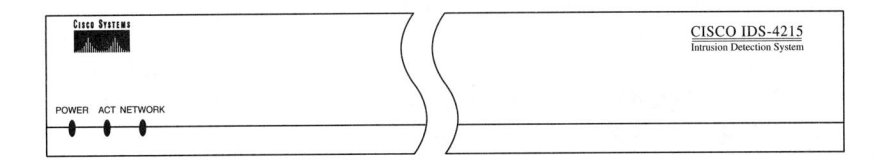

Figure 21.4 shows the rear panel layout for the IDS-4215. The rear panel features a power connector, power switch, RJ45 console port for management access, and several network ports. The server ships with two onboard NICs (int0 and int1), and you can order an optional four-port Ethernet network card (int2 thru int5) to increase the number of network interfaces. The following list describes the function of each network interface on the IDS-4215:

int0   This is the sensing interface (also known as the sniffing or monitoring interface). It needs to be attached to the LAN segment that you wish to monitor for intrusive activity.

int1   This is the command and control interface. It's configured with an IP address and provides the means to manage the sensor remotely via an IP network.

int2 to *int5*   These are additional sensing interfaces.

> Make sure you know the physical layout of *all* sensors for the exam.

FIGURE 21.4   Cisco Secure IDS 4215 sensor rear panel

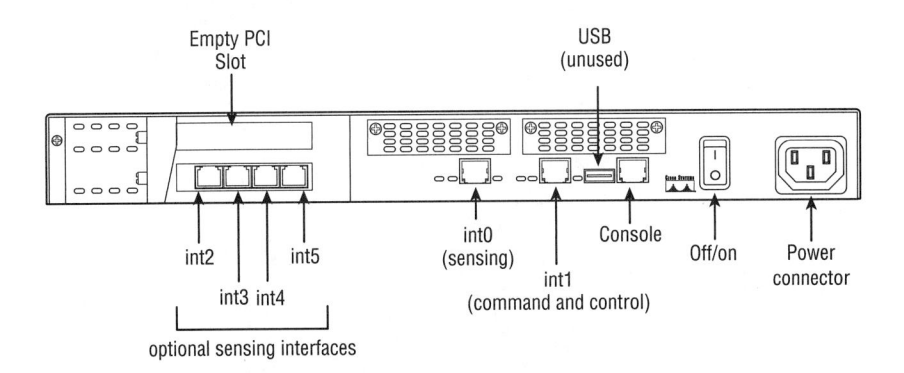

4235, 4250, and 4250-XL Sensor Physical Layout

The IDS-4235, IDS-4250, and IDS-4250-XL sensors all share the same base 1RU chassis; each sensor has different processor, memory, and network interface configurations. The IDS-4235 is well suited for monitoring multiple T3/E3 and OC3 Internet connections and possesses trunking capabilities that let it monitor internal network segments that run at a combined speed of up to 250Mbps. The IDS-4250 operates at up to 500Mbps, and the IDS-4250-XL operates at up to 1Gbps. The 4235 is a fixed-configuration sensor and can't be upgraded for higher performance or to add any optional interfaces. The 4250 can be performance upgraded to the 4250-XL sensor with the addition of a special acceleration card.

On the front of the 4235/4250/4250-XL sensor, a bezel hides the front panel of the sensor, which includes a number of interfaces, LEDs, and drive bays. Figure 21.5 shows the layout of the front panel behind the bezel for the IDS-4235.

> **TIP** Pressing the Identification button on the front panel causes the system status indicator LED on the front and back of the sensor to continuously blink until you press the Identification button again. This is useful if you need to locate the sensor in a rack full of servers.

Figure 21.6 shows the rear panel layout for the 4235/4250/4250-XL sensor. The rear panel features standard PC/server interfaces and includes onboard network interfaces that provide the command and control and sensing interfaces.

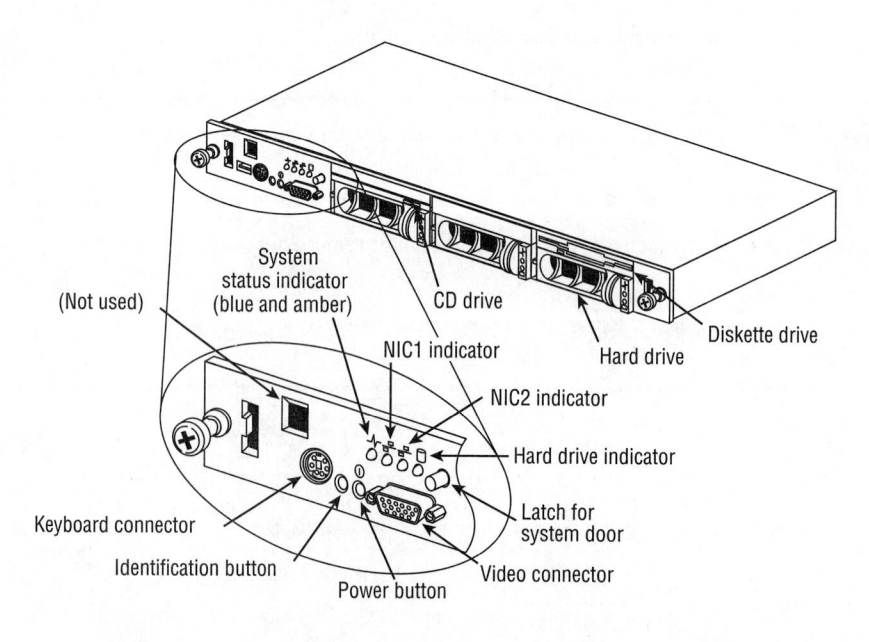

FIGURE 21.5 Cisco Secure IDS 4235/4250/4250-XL sensor front panel

FIGURE 21.6 Cisco Secure IDS 4235/4250/4250-XL sensor rear panel

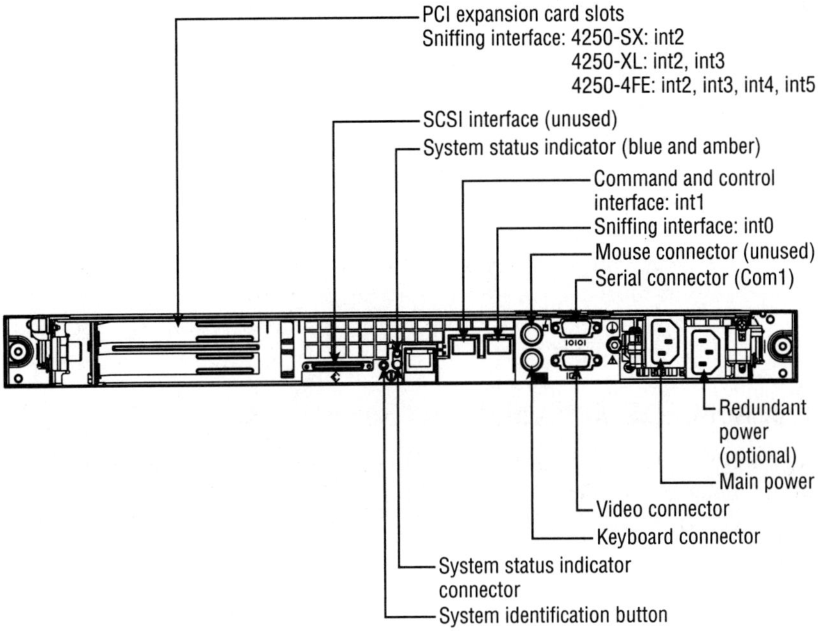
PCI expansion card slots
Sniffing interface: 4250-SX: int2
4250-XL: int2, int3
4250-4FE: int2, int3, int4, int5
SCSI interface (unused)
System status indicator (blue and amber)
Command and control interface: int1
Sniffing interface: int0
Mouse connector (unused)
Serial connector (Com1)
Redundant power (optional)
Main power
Video connector
Keyboard connector
System status indicator connector
System identification button

The function of each network interface varies depending on the sensor model. On the IDS-4235, only the onboard NICs (`int0` and `int1`) can be used; `int0` operates as the sensing interface, and `int1` acts as the command and control interface.

On the IDS-4250, the onboard NICs (`int0` and `int1`) ship standard with the sensor and perform the same functions as on the IDS-4235 sensor. In Figure 21.6, you can see that several optional interfaces exist, which serve to increase the number of sensing interfaces and performance of the sensor:

4250-SX This includes a single 1000BaseSX network interface that can be used for sensing. When installed, the 1000BaseSX sensing interface is identified as `int2` to the sensor operating system.

4250-4FE This includes four 10/100BaseT network interfaces that can be used for sensing. When installed, the sensing interfaces are identified as `int2` through `int6` to the sensor operating system.

IDS-XL-INT Installing this card upgrades the IDS-4250 sensor to a 4250-XL sensor. This card includes an onboard acceleration engine that boosts IDS performance, as well as two 1000BaseSX sensing interfaces. When installed, the 1000BaseSX sensing interfaces are identified as `int2` and `int3` to the sensor operating system.

> **TIP**
>
> Cisco Secure IDS sensors include a TCP reset feature, which allows a sensor to reset TCP connections associated with a detected attack. On most sensors, the TCP resets are generated from the sensing interface; however, on the IDS-4250-XL, only the onboard `int0` interface can be used to generate TCP resets. This means that if you wish to use the TCP reset feature, you must ensure that the `int0` interface is attached to the network. You must also ensure that the configuration of the `int0` interface matches the configuration of the `int2` and `int3` sensing interfaces. For example, if `int2` and `int3` are configured as access ports in a single VLAN, you must configure `int0` to belong to the same VLAN. If `int2` and `int3` are configured as trunk ports that can monitor multiple VLANs, you must configure `int0` as a trunk port and ensure that it's configured with the same native VLAN and is trunking the same VLANs as the sensing interfaces.

Catalyst 6000 IDSM Physical Layout

The Catalyst 6000 IDSM sensor is a line card that is designed for use with the Catalyst 6000 and 6500 family of switches. The IDSM adds value and functionality to an organization's investment in Catalyst 6000/6500 switches and lets the organization monitor traffic from one or more VLANs connected to the switch.

The IDSM is available in two models:

IDSM-1   This is the first-generation IDSM. It supports up to 120Mbps IDS performance. The IDSM-1 was no longer saleable as of April 2003, and no further signatures were released after April 2004. The IDSM-1 only supports CSIDS version 3.*x* software and runs a different code base than the 4200 series sensors, leading to some differences in features.

IDSM-2   This is the next-generation IDSM. It supports up to 600Mbps IDS performance. The IDSM-2 ships with Cisco Secure IDS version 4.*x* software and runs the same operating system and code base as the 4200 series sensors running Cisco Secure IDS version 4.*x*, ensuring feature parity across the two platforms.

IDSM-2 Physical Layout

The IDSM-2 is a fabric-enabled Catalyst 6000/6500 line card that can be placed in any spare slot on a Catalyst 6000/6500 switch, as long as the switch meets the minimum software and hardware requirements. Table 21.4 lists these requirements.

> **NOTE**
>
> *Fabric-enabled* refers to the ability to connect to an optional crossbar switching fabric, which boosts the aggregate throughput of the Catalyst 6500 from 32Gbps to 256Gbps (using Supervisor II) or 720Gbps (using Supervisor 720).

Installing and Configuring Cisco Secure IDS Sensors

TABLE 21.4 Minimum Hardware and Software Requirements for IDSM-2

Operating System	Supervisor Engine	Minimum Software Version
CatOS	Supervisor 1A Supervisor 2A	7.6(1)
Cisco IOS	Supervisor 1A with MSFC	12.1(19)E
	Supervisor 2 with MSFC	12.2(14)SY
	Supervisor 720	12.2(14)SX1

> **NOTE**
> A unique feature of the IDSM-2 is that it can use a feature known as *VLAN access control lists* (VACLs, discussed in Chapter 22). VACLs can capture only specific types of traffic for monitoring, without having to capture all the traffic received on a particular port, set of ports, or VLAN, as is the case with traditional capture technologies such as Switch Port Analyzer (SPAN). If you wish to use the VACL feature, the Catalyst 6000/6500 switch must have a policy feature card (PFC) installed. Any supervisor engine with an MSFC installed also has a PFC installed.

The IDSM-2 is a Catalyst 6000/6500 switch module with the appropriate backplane connectors to attach to the Catalyst 6000/6500 backplane and a front panel with a number of diagnostic buttons and other controls. Figure 21.7 shows the front panel of the IDSM.

The front panel of the line card includes a Status LED to indicate the state of the IDSM (see Table 21.5) and a Shutdown button, which can be used to shut down the sensor if you can't gain access to the sensor command-line interface (CLI).

FIGURE 21.7 IDSM front panel

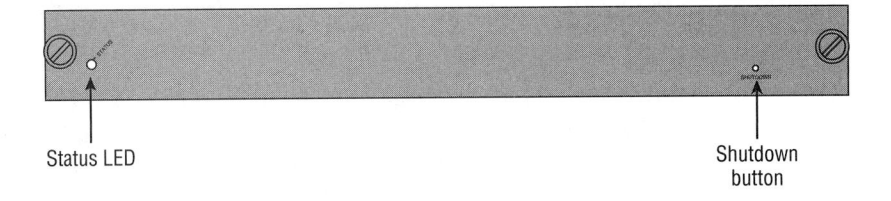

TABLE 21.5 IDSM-2 Status LEDs

Color	Description
Green	IDSM-2 is operational; all diagnostics tests passed okay.
Red	Diagnostic failed (other than an individual port test).
Amber	IDSM-2 is running self-tests or booting, or IDSM-2 is administratively disabled.
Off	IDSM-2 isn't powered on.

> **NOTE** The IDSM-2 must be shut down properly to prevent corruption of the IDSM-2 operating system. You'd normally shut down the IDSM-2 via a CLI session to the IDSM using the reset powerdown command. However, if you can't do this for some reason, you can push the Shutdown button to shut down the IDSM properly.

Internally, the IDSM-2 includes eight full-duplex 1 Gbps connections or traces to the Catalyst 6000/6500 backplane. Each trace is identified as an interface on the IDSM-2, with the first trace represented as int1 and the last trace represented as int8. For the Cisco Secure IDS exam, you need to ensure that you understand the function of each backplane interface (trace) on the IDSM-2:

- int1—Used for generating TCP resets if a signature is configured with this action
- int2—Command and control
- int3–int5—Unused
- int7—Sensing interface
- int8—Sensing interface

Cisco 2600/2800/3600/3700/3800 IDS Network Module Physical Layout

The IDS network module (NM-CIDS) is a network module for the Cisco 2600/2800/3600/3700/3800 series routers that enables traffic received by the router to be inspected for intrusive activity. The NM-CIDS provides a low-cost upgrade for routers at the edge of the network that connect to untrusted networks such as the Internet, without your needing to invest in a new IDS appliance.

When you install the NM-CIDS, it's important to understand the hardware and software requirements for the Cisco router in which the NM-CIDS is being installed. Not all of the models in the 2600/2800/3600/3700/3800 series family are compatible with the NM-CIDS, and to recognize and support the NM-CIDS, the router must be loaded with an appropriate version of Cisco IOS software. Table 21.6 lists the supported and unsupported routers for the NM-CIDS as well as the Cisco IOS software requirements.

TABLE 21.6 Supported Routers and Software Requirements for the NM-CIDS

Platform	NM-CIDS Supported?	Cisco IOS Requirements
2600 3620 3640/3640A	No	n/a
2600XM 2691 3660 3725/3745	Yes	12.2(15)ZJ or higher
2800	Yes	12.3(8)T
3800	Yes	12.3(11)T

Internally, the NM-CIDS includes an Intel Mobile Pentium III 500MHz processor, 512MB memory, and a 20GB IDE hard disk, all of which fit onto a standard Cisco network module form factor. Externally, the front panel includes a number of LEDs and a command and control network interface, as shown in Figure 21.8.

The front panel of the NM-CIDS includes LED indicators that describe the state of various components of the NM-CIDS (see Table 21.7) and a 10/100BaseT RJ45 Ethernet network interface, which is designated as the command and control interface for management purposes.

FIGURE 21.8 NM-CIDS front panel

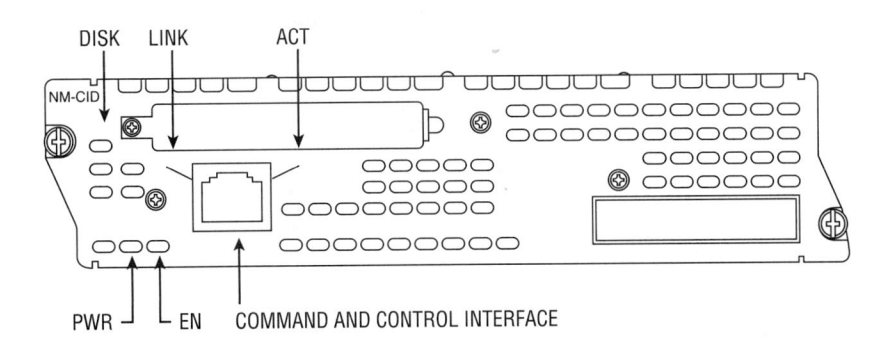

TABLE 21.7 NM-CIDS LED Indicators

Indicator	Description
ACT	Indicates network activity on the command and control interface
DISK	Indicates hard disk activity on the internal hard disk
EN	Indicates the NM-CIDS has passed the self-test and is operational
LINK	Indicates the command and control interface has a network connection
PWR	Indicates the NM-CIDS is powered on

Gaining Initial Management Access

Once you've physically installed and cabled a sensor appropriately, you need to obtain some form of management access to begin configuration of the box. There are five methods of management access, some of which aren't available for all sensors:

Keyboard and monitor   All 4200 series sensors except the 4215 include a keyboard and monitor port for CLI access. The IDSM-2 and NM-CIDS network module don't include a keyboard or monitor port.

Console port   All 4200 series sensors include a console port for CLI access, which requires a serial connection to a PC running terminal emulation software. The IDSM-2 and NM-CIDS network module don't have an external console port; instead, these sensors have an internal console port that can be accessed via the CLI of the operating system that runs the chassis in which the sensor is installed (for example, a Catalyst 6000/6500 switch or a Cisco 2600/3600/3700 router).

Telnet and Secure Shell   All sensors support CLI access via an IP network using Telnet and/or Secure Shell (SSH). Both methods of access require the sensor to be configured with an IP address and the management client to have a Telnet/SSH client installed.

> **NOTE**   By default, Telnet access is disabled and SSH access is enabled.

IDS Device Manager (IDM)   All sensors include the IDS Device Manager (IDM), which provides a web-based interface from which you can configure the sensor. This method of access requires the sensor to be configured with an IP address and requires the management client to have a supported web browser.

When you configure a sensor for the first time that has the default Cisco Secure IDS 4.*x* installation, you'll typically perform initial configuration of the sensor via the keyboard and monitor (4200 series) or internal/external console port (all sensors). By default, Cisco Secure IDS 4.*x* sensors ship with a command and control interface IP address of 10.1.9.201, subnet mask of 255.255.255.0, and default gateway of 10.1.9.1; if you connect the command and control interface to the network, you can use SSH or the IDS Device Manager as a means of initial management access.

> **WARNING** Avoid connecting your sensor to a production network for the purposes of initial configuration access. Doing so could expose the sensor to unauthorized access by individuals who are aware of the default IP configuration and credentials of the sensor.

The following section examines the tasks required to gain initial management access to each sensor platform.

Accessing the 4200 Series Sensor

Gaining initial management access to the 4200 series sensor is straightforward and can be achieved either by connecting a monitor and keyboard to the sensor or by attaching to console port on the sensor. The console port on a 4200 series is a male DB9 port except on the 4215 sensor, which uses an RJ45 console port. For sensors with a DB9 connector, an appropriate console cable is supplied with the sensor; a standard Cisco RJ45 console cable can be used to access the 4215 console port.

When establishing a console connection, use the following settings:

- 9600bps
- 8 data bits
- No parity
- 1 stop bit
- Hardware (or RTS/CTS) flow control

> **NOTE** The IDS-4215 sensor doesn't include monitor and keyboard interfaces; hence you must use the console port to gain initial management access.

Accessing the Catalyst 6000 IDSM

The IDSM doesn't include an external console port (only an internal console port). You can achieve initial console access to the IDSM only by first gaining management access to the Catalyst 6000/6500 operating system, which can be via any supported method of CLI access to the switch (console, Telnet, or SSH).

Before you attempt to establish access to the IDSM, you should first verify that the switch operating system can see the IDSM. You can do so using the `show module` command on both CatOS and Cisco IOS, as demonstrated here on a CatOS switch:

```
Console> (enable) show module
Mod Slot  Ports Module-Type                   Model            Sub Status
--- ---   ---   ---------------               ----------       --- ----
1   1     2     1000BaseX Supervisor          WS-X6K-SUP2-2GE  yes ok
15  1     1     Multilayer Switch Feature     WS-F6K-MSFC2     no  ok
2   2     48    10/100BaseTX Ethernet         WS-X6548-RJ-45   no  ok
4   4     8     Intrusion Detection System    WS-SVC-IDSM2     yes ok
Mod Module-Name       Serial-Num
--- -----------       ----------
1   SAD045618AB    15 SAD044509KZ
2   JAB02160499
3   SAD062212YX
4   SAD063999LS
```

In this example, notice that the switch can see the IDSM-2 and that the status is OK.

> **NOTE**
> While the IDSM is booting, the Status column of the `show module` output is set to other.

Once you've verified that the IDSM is operational, you can establish a console connection to it. If your Catalyst 6000/6500 switch is running CatOS software, then you can use the `session slot-number` command from privileged EXEC mode to establish an internal console connection to the IDSM. The following example demonstrates gaining console access to an IDSM installed in slot 4 of a Catalyst 6500 switch that runs CatOS:

```
Console> (enable) session 4
Trying IDS-4...

Connected to IDS-4.

Escape character is '^]'.

sensor login:
```

If your Catalyst 6000/6500 switch is running Cisco IOS software (also known as running in *native mode*), then you can use the `session slot slot-number processor 1` command from privileged EXEC mode to establish an internal console connection to the IDSM. The following example demonstrates gaining console access to an IDSM installed in slot 4 of a Catalyst 6500 switch that runs Cisco IOS:

`Switch# session slot 4 processor 1`

`sensor login:`

Accessing the Cisco 2600/3600/3700 IDS Network Module

The NM-CIDS sensor doesn't include an external console port; instead it includes an internal *ids-sensor interface*, which provides a means of allowing the router and NM-CIDS sensor to communicate with each other. Because the sensor doesn't include an external console port, you can achieve console access only by first gaining management access to the router in which the module is installed, via any supported method of CLI access to the router (console, Telnet, or SSH).

> **NOTE** The ids-sensor interface is configurable from the router and is referenced using the normal `slot-number/port-number` identification on Cisco 2600/3600/3700 routers (the port number is always 0). For example, if the NM-CIDS is installed in slot 1, the ids-sensor interface is represented to the router with an interface ID of 1/0.

Establishing an internal console connection to the NM-CIDS sensor is a little different than the IDSM, because the router uses a reverse Telnet connection using the ids-sensor interface. This means you must first configure the ids-sensor interface with an IP address, which you do by creating a loopback interface and configuring the ids-sensor as an IP unnumbered interface that uses the loopback interface IP address. The following example demonstrates configuring IP for the ids-sensor interface, assuming the NM-CIDS sensor is installed in slot 1 of the router:

`Router# configure terminal`
`Router(config)# interface loopback 0`
`Router(config-if)# ip address 1.1.1.1 255.255.255.255`
`Router(config-if)# exit`
`Router(config)# interface ids-sensor 1/0`
`Router(config-if)# ip unnumbered loopback 0`

> **NOTE** Indirectly addressing the ids-sensor interface ensures that it isn't vulnerable to attack. The loopback address needs to be unique but doesn't need to be a valid address on the network, because it's only used for establishing a reverse Telnet connection to the NM-CIDS sensor. The ids-sensor interface also shouldn't be confused with the command and control interface.

Once the ids-sensor interface is configured with IP, you can establish a reverse Telnet session to the sensor by executing the `service-module IDS-Sensor` *slot-number/port-number* `session` command from privileged EXEC mode. For example, the following command would access an NM-CIDS installed in slot 1 of a router:

`Router# service-module IDS-Sensor 1/0 session`

You can also establish a connection remotely to the sensor by telnetting directly to the router and specifying the appropriate port for the reverse Telnet connection. The port number is determined by the formula $2001 + 32 \times$ *slot-number*. For example, if the NM-CIDS sensor is installed in slot 1, the port number for accessing the sensor is $2001 + 32 \times 1 = 2033$. The following command would be used to gain access to the NM-CIDS sensor from a remote host using Telnet, assuming the router has the IP address 192.168.1.1 on the network:

`C:\> telnet 192.168.1.1 2033`

Logging In to the Sensor

Once you've connected via the appropriate management interface to the sensor, if you power up the sensor, the sensor will first boot and finally present you with a login prompt. Starting with Cisco Secure IDS 4.0, all sensors use a Linux-based operating system, which boots as follows:

- Machine BIOS detects and initializes hardware, such as the display, keyboard, hard disk, and CD-ROM.
- A boot loader program called GRUB starts, which allows multiple operating system images to be booted. With Cisco Secure IDS sensors, you can select two options, which are shown in Figure 21.9. The first option—Cisco IDS (2.4.18-5smpbigphys)—is the default selection; it boots the sensor normally. The second option—Cisco IDS Recovery—is used for recovery purposes, allowing you to re-image the sensor without needing to use the recovery/upgrade CD.
- Assuming the default selection is chosen at the GRUB boot loader, the sensor operating system (based on Red Hat Linux) loads.

If you select the Cisco IDS Recovery option, the sensor operating system is re-imaged. However, some configuration parameters are retained, as follows:

- The sensor's network settings remain the same.
- The `cisco` account password is set back to the default (`cisco`).
- All users except the `cisco` account are removed.
- All IDS settings are set to their default (such as signatures and filters).
- All iplogs, alerts, error messages, and status messages are cleared.

If you want to remove all configuration settings and reset the sensor to factory default settings, you must use the recovery/upgrade CD.

FIGURE 21.9 GRUB boot loader

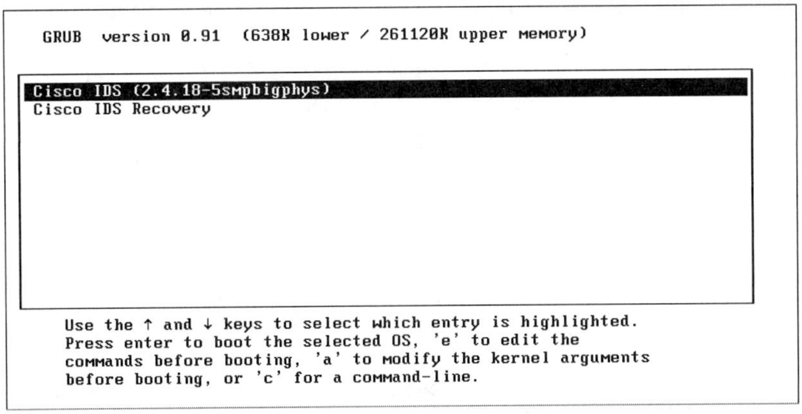

```
GRUB  version 0.91  (638K lower / 261120K upper memory)

 Cisco IDS (2.4.18-5smpbigphys)
 Cisco IDS Recovery




      Use the ↑ and ↓ keys to select which entry is highlighted.
      Press enter to boot the selected OS, 'e' to edit the
      commands before booting, 'a' to modify the kernel arguments
      before booting, or 'c' for a command-line.
```

After the sensor has completed booting up, you're prompted for a username and password. By default, a single administrative account exists that permits administrative access to the sensor that has a username of cisco and a default password of cisco. After authenticating with the default credentials, you're prompted to change the default password, as demonstrated in this example:

```
sensor login: cisco
Password: *****
You are required to change your password immediately (password aged)
Changing password for cisco
(current) UNIX password: *****
New password: ********
Retype password: ********
***NOTICE***
This product contains cryptographic features and is subject to United States and
local country laws governing import, export, transfer and use. Delivery of Cisco
cryptographic products does not imply third-party authority to import, export,
distribute or use encryption. Importers, exporters, distributors and users are
responsible for compliance with U.S. and local country laws. By using this
product you agree to comply with applicable laws and regulations. If you are
unable to comply with U.S. and local laws, return this product immediately.

A summary of U.S. laws governing Cisco cryptographic products may be found at:
http://www.cisco.com/wwl/export/crypto

If you require further assistance please contact us by sending email to
export@cisco.com
sensor#
```

> **Note:** The password you select must meet certain criteria to ensure that it isn't easily compromised. The password must be at least eight characters long, can't be based on a dictionary word, and must meet complexity requirements such as containing a mixture of alphanumeric characters.

In the previous example, notice that after the password has been successfully changed, a Cisco IOS-like `sensor#` prompt is displayed. All Cisco Secure IDS 4.x sensors include a custom shell that is designed to be consistent with the look and feel of Cisco IOS, with similar command syntax and execution.

Configuring the Sensor for the First Time

After you've logged in to the sensor, you're ready to begin sensor configuration. When you're configuring a sensor for the first time, the following configuration tasks are required:

1. Initialize the sensor.
2. Configure the sensor.

Initializing the Sensor

The first configuration task you'll normally perform is to initialize the sensor with the minimum parameters required to enable the sensor to successfully communicate on the network. All Cisco Secure IDS 4.x sensors include a `setup` utility, which presents an interactive dialog that allows you to configure the following initialization parameters:

Sensor name   By default, the sensor name is `sensor`. Change this to something meaningful that conforms to the naming conventions of your organization.

IP address, subnet mask, and default gateway   The command and control interface is configured with an IP address of 10.1.9.201/24 and default gateway of 10.1.9.1, which can be modified via the `setup` utility.

Telnet access   Telnet access is disabled by default; however, you can enable it via the `setup` utility.

Web server port   By default, port 443 is used for SSL connections to the local web server that runs the IDM. The `setup` utility allows you to configure a custom port.

Listing 21.1 demonstrates running the `setup` utility and configuring base configuration settings on a sensor:

Listing 21.1: Running the `setup` Utility

```
sensor# setup
```

Installing and Configuring Cisco Secure IDS Sensors

```
      --- System Configuration Dialog ---

At any point you may enter a question mark '?' for help.
User ctrl-c to abort configuration dialog at any prompt.
Default settings are in square brackets '[]'.


Current Configuration:


service host
networkParams
hostname sensor
ipAddress 10.1.9.201
netmask 255.255.255.0
defaultGateway 10.1.9.1
telnetOption disabled
exit
exit
!
service webServer
general
ports 443
exit
exit


Current time: Wed Sep 10 03:52:57 2003


Setup Configuration last modified: Wed Sep 10 03:39:57 2003


      Continue with configuration dialog?[yes]: yes
      Enter host name[sensor]: ids-4210
      Enter IP address[10.1.9.201]: 192.168.1.101
      Enter netmask[255.255.255.0]:
      Enter default gateway[10.1.9.1]: 192.168.1.1
      Enter telnet-server status[disabled]:
      Enter web-server port[443]:
```

The following configuration was entered.

```
service host
networkParams
hostname ids-4210
ipAddress 192.168.1.101
netmask 255.255.255.0
defaultGateway 192.168.1.1
telnetOption disabled
exit
exit
!
service webServer
general
ports 443
exit
exit
```

Use this configuration?[yes]: **yes**
Configuration Saved.
Warning: The node must be rebooted for the changes to go into effect.
Continue with reboot? [yes]: **yes**

Broadcast message from root (Wed Sep 10 04:20:58 2003):

A system reboot has been requested. The reboot may not start for 90 seconds.
ids-4210#
Broadcast message from root (Wed Sep 10 04:20:59 2003):

The system is going down for reboot NOW!

In the listing, notice that a summary of the current configuration is first displayed, after which you're asked to confirm whether you wish to continue. Assuming that you continue with configuration, you're then prompted to configure a number of parameters. In this example, you can see that the sensor has been configured as follows:

- Sensor name: `ids-4210`
- IP address: 192.168.1.101/24
- Default gateway: 192.168.1.1

After you complete the configuration, a summary of the new configuration is displayed, after which you must confirm that you wish to save the configuration changes.

Installing and Configuring Cisco Secure IDS Sensors

> **NOTE** If you modify the IP address, subnet mask, default gateway, or web port of the sensor, you must restart the sensor for the changes to take effect.

Configuring the Sensor

The `setup` utility provides a quick and easy way to get a sensor on the network and communicating. It's important, however, to understand how to configure the sensor without using the `setup` utility, because this will enable you to configure all the other network, system, and application parameters that aren't configurable via the `setup` utility. This section discusses the following:

- Understanding configuration modes
- Restricting network access
- Configuring known SSH hosts
- Configuring user and service accounts
- Configuring the sensor to capture traffic

Understanding Configuration Modes

Before you learn how to configure network and system parameters, it's important to understand the structure of the CLI used for Cisco Secure IDS 4.*x*. Just like Cisco IOS, the Cisco Secure IDS 4.*x* shell includes several different *command modes*, which enable you to configure, monitor, and manage different components of the system. The command mode structure is hierarchical and exists in several levels that operate in a parent/child type configuration. For example, the first-level CLI mode is the parent of the second-level CLI mode (in addition, the second-level CLI mode is the child of the first-level CLI mode). The following command modes are available:

Privileged EXEC mode This mode is the first level of command-line access, which you enter immediately after logging on to the sensor. Configuration isn't possible from this mode—you can only view configuration information and perform monitoring/diagnostic tasks. Privileged EXEC mode is represented in the command prompt by appending a single number sign (#) character to the sensor hostname. The following example demonstrates executing the `show version` privileged EXEC mode command, which displays software and hardware information about the system:

```
ids-4210# show version
Application Partition:

Cisco Systems Intrusion Detection Sensor, Version 4.0(1)S37


OS Version 2.4.18-5smpbigphys
Platform: IDS-4210
Sensor up-time is 56 min.
```

```
Using 240541696 out of 261312512 bytes of available memory (92% usage)
Using 528M out of 17G bytes of available disk space (4% usage)


MainApp           2003_Jan_23_02.00 (Release) 2003-01-23T02:00:25-0600 Running
AnalysisEngine    2003_Jan_23_02.00 (Release) 2003-01-23T02:00:25-0600 Running
Authentication    2003_Jan_23_02.00 (Release) 2003-01-23T02:00:25-0600 Running
Logger            2003_Jan_23_02.00 (Release) 2003-01-23T02:00:25-0600 Running
NetworkAccess     2003_Jan_23_02.00 (Release) 2003-01-23T02:00:25-0600 Running
TransactionSource 2003_Jan_23_02.00 (Release) 2003-01-23T02:00:25-0600 Running
WebServer         2003_Jan_23_02.00 (Release) 2003-01-23T02:00:25-0600 Running
CLI               2003_Jan_17_18.33 (Release) 2003-01-17T18:33:18-0600

Upgrade History:

  IDS-K9-maj-4.0-1-S36    17:23:41 UTC Tue Sep 09 2003

Recovery Partition Version 1.1 - 4.0(1)S37
```

Global Configuration Mode This mode is considered a second-level CLI mode and can be entered by executing the `configure terminal` command from privileged EXEC mode. From this mode, you can configure global system parameters as well as access other configuration modes specific to the various components that make up the sensor. Global configuration mode is represented in the command prompt by appending the text `(config)#` to the sensor hostname. The following example demonstrates accessing global configuration mode and executing the `hostname` global configuration command, which configures the sensor hostname:

```
ids-4210# configure terminal
ids-4210(config)# hostname sensor10
ids-4210(config)#
```

> **Note:** When modifying the hostname, you must reboot the sensor for the change to take effect.

Interface Configuration Mode This mode is considered a third-level CLI mode. It lets you configure parameters specific to the sensor network interfaces and is accessed by using the `interface` global configuration command. On Cisco Secure IDS, you can configure several types of interfaces: the command and control interface, sensing interface, and group interfaces.

The following example demonstrates accessing interface configuration mode for the command and control interface and configuring the command and control interface IP address:

```
ids-4210# configure terminal
ids-4210(config)# interface command-control
ids-4210(config-if)# ip address 192.168.1.101 255.255.255.0
```

Notice that interface configuration mode is indicated in the command prompt by the (config-if)# text.

Service Configuration Mode   This mode is considered a third-level CLI mode that allows configuration access to various services on the sensor, and it's accessed by using the service global configuration command. Several types of services exist. For example, the service host command provides access to the service host configuration mode and lets you configure host node settings such as the date/time and IP addressing. The following example demonstrates accessing the service host configuration mode:

```
ids-4210# configure terminal
ids-4210(config)# service host
ids-4210(config-host)# ?
exit                    Exit service configuration mode
networkParams           Network configuration parameters
no                      Remove an entry or selection setting
optionalAutoUpgrade     Optional AutoUpgrade configuration
show                    Display system settings and/or history information
timeParams              Time configuration parameters
ids-4210(config-host)# networkParams
ids-4210(config-host-net)# ipAddress 192.168.1.101
ids-4210(config-host-net)# exit
ids-4210(config-host)# exit
Apply Changes:?[yes]: yes
```

Notice in the example that several fourth-level CLI modes exist under the service host configuration mode; they're highlighted in response to the ? command. The networkParams command is then executed, which accesses a fourth-level CLI mode from which network parameters such as IP addressing for the sensor can be configured. Notice that you use the exit command to return to the parent CLI mode, and that once you exit a particular service configuration mode, you're prompted to apply the changes.

Restricting Network Access

Restricting network access refers to limiting the hosts that can establish network management connections (via Telnet, SSH, or IDM) to the sensor based on IP address. Hosts that are permitted to establish management connections are also known as *trusted hosts*.

Although the sensor requires management connections to be authenticated, limiting management connections to be established only from trusted hosts further enhances the operational security of the sensor. For example, if you have a number of network administrators whose PCs all reside on the 192.168.1.0/24 subnet, you can restrict management connections to be permitted only from hosts on this subnet, ensuring that hosts on other networks can't gain management access to the sensor.

> **Note:** By default, Cisco Secure IDS sensors are configured to only permit management connections from any address in the 10.0.0.0/8 network (10.*x.x.x*). However, it's recommended that you modify this default setting to suit your environment.

To restrict network access, you must first access the service host CLI mode using the **service host** global configuration command, and then access the networkParams fourth-level CLI mode by using the **networkParams** command. Once in this mode, you use the **accessList** command to define up to 512 trusted hosts or networks. The **accessList** command has the following syntax:

sensor(config-host-net)# **[no] accessList ipAddress** *ip-address* **[netmask** *subnet-mask*]

> **Note:** If you omit the optional netmask keyword, a 32-bit subnet mask of 255.255.255.255 (a host address) is assumed.

The following example demonstrates removing the default network access restrictions and then restricting management access to a particular host (192.168.2.100) and multiple hosts on a particular subnet (192.168.1.0/24).

```
sensor# configure terminal
sensor(config)# service host
sensor(config-host)# networkParams
sensor(config-host-net)# show settings
   networkParams
   -----------------------------------------------
      ipAddress: 192.168.1.101
      netmask: 255.255.255.0 default: 255.255.255.0
      defaultGateway: 192.168.1.1
      hostname: ids-4210
      telnetOption: enabled default: disabled
      accessList (min: 0, max: 512, current: 1)
   -----------------------------------------------
```

```
                ipAddress: 10.0.0.0
                netmask: 255.0.0.0 default: 255.255.255.255
        -----------------------------------------------
        -----------------------------------------------
        -----------------------------------------------
sensor(config-host-net)# no accessList ipAddress 10.0.0.0 255.0.0.0
sensor(config-host-net)# accessList ipAddress 192.168.2.100
sensor(config-host-net)# accessList ipAddress 192.168.1.0 netmask 255.255.255.0
sensor(config-host-net)# exit
sensor(config-host)# exit
Apply Changes:?[yes]: yes
```

In this example, notice the use of the show settings command, which displays the various configuration parameters related to the networkParams configuration mode. You can see that the default access list is in place, which permits access from any host in the 10.0.0.0/8 network.

> **NOTE** The show settings command can be executed from the various service third-level configuration modes as well as from any child fourth-level configuration modes for each different service.

Configuring Known SSH Hosts

Cisco Secure IDS sensors support the ability to automatically connect to other devices and perform automated tasks such as obtaining automatic upgrades and shunning. To ensure the security of these operations, SSH is used; it provides strong authentication, integrity, and confidentiality of the data transferred.

> **NOTE** *Shunning* (also referred to as *blocking*) refers to the ability of a sensor to establish a management connection to a perimeter router or firewall and apply a temporary access control list (ACL) to block the source and/or destination of a detected attack. Shunning is discussed further in Chapter 23, "Configuring Cisco Secure IDS Sensors Using the IDS Device Manager."

To enable sensors to communicate automatically with other hosts using SSH, you must add the *fingerprint* of each host. SSH is a client/server protocol, where SSH clients establish connections to SSH servers. In the scenario of automatic upgrades and shunning, the sensor is acting as an SSH client, establishing SSH connections to SSH servers. When an SSH client connects to an SSH server, the SSH server presents a public key, which has an associated fingerprint. The fingerprint is the MD5 hash of the public key and provides a means to uniquely identify the public key. By obtaining prior knowledge of the fingerprint of an SSH server, an SSH client can ensure that it's connecting to the correct SSH server and not an imposter by comparing the fingerprint presented for each connection with the stored fingerprint.

To add the fingerprint of an SSH server to which the sensor must communicate, you use the ssh host-key global configuration command, which has the following syntax:

sensor(config)# **ssh host-key** *ssh-server-address*

When you execute this command, the sensor attempts to establish an SSH connection to the IP address specified, after which the fingerprint of the SSH server is displayed. At this point, you're asked whether you wish to add the fingerprint to the *SSH known hosts table*, which is a table that stores the fingerprints considered authentic for each SSH server. If the fingerprint is accepted, the sensor will subsequently be able to connect to the SSH server and ensure that the SSH server is authentic by comparing the fingerprint received for each connection with the fingerprint stored in the SSH known hosts table. The following example demonstrates using the ssh host-key command to add the fingerprint of an SSH server (for example, this could be a perimeter router that the sensor needs to be able to apply shunning to) to the SSH known hosts table:

```
ids-4210# configure terminal
ids-4210(config)# ssh host-key 192.168.1.1
MD5 fingerprint is B2:F1:95:AB:28:BC:07:D5:E6:29:C9:1C:7C:2A:A5:C2
Bubble Babble is ximok-zefos-feceg-losyc-nyses-refac-virif-pivef-helal-rybor
Would you like to add this to the known hosts table for this host?[yes]: yes
```

To maintain the SSH known hosts table (manually add, view, or delete entries), you must access a service configuration mode for SSH known hosts, which is accessed by using the service SshKnownHosts global configuration command. Within this service configuration mode, you can execute two commands:

show settings   This command allows you to view the SSH known hosts table.

rsa1Keys   This command lets you manually add entries to the SSH known hosts table (you must manually enter the fingerprint and other parameters associated with the public key of the SSH server) and also delete entries from the SSH known hosts table. This command has the following syntax:

ids-4210(config-SshKnownHosts)# [**no**] **rsa1Keys id** *ssh-server-address*

If you're manually adding an SSH server to the SSH known hosts table, after executing the rsa1Keys command, you're placed into a fourth-level CLI mode that enables you to configure the fingerprint and other parameters specific to the SSH server.

The following example demonstrates viewing the SSH known hosts table and removing the host 192.168.1.1 from the table:

```
ids-4210# configure terminal
ids-4210(config)# service sshKnownHosts
ids-4210(config-SshKnownHosts)# show settings
   rsa1Keys (min: 0, max: 500, current: 1)
```

```
      ----------------------------------------------
         id: 192.168.1.1
         exponent: 65537
         length: 512
         modulus: 10572972567139699645614175438890717752502379884923858223386965804058815939971787381525338150234879043385392178150343443453125400634733752057797425625592877
      ----------------------------------------------
      ----------------------------------------------
ids-4210(config-SshKnownHosts)# no rsa1Keys id 192.168.1.1
ids-4210(config-SshKnownHosts)# show settings
   rsa1Keys (min: 0, max: 500, current: 0)
   ----------------------------------------------
   ----------------------------------------------
```

In this example, the `show settings` command is used to compare the SSH known hosts table before and after the `no rsa1Keys` command is executed.

Configuring User and Service Accounts

Cisco Secure IDS sensors use two types of accounts to identify, authenticate, and authorize users who wish to administer, monitor, and troubleshoot the sensor:

User accounts User accounts define administrators and operators that are permitted access to the sensor shell to perform a specific set of tasks. There are three different privilege levels to which a user account can be assigned:

Viewer Users with viewer privileges can view configuration information and events but can't modify any configuration parameters except their own passwords.

Operator Users with operator privileges can view configuration information and events and can configure the following parameters:

- Signature tuning
- Assignment of virtual sensor configuration to interface groups
- Managed routers
- Their own passwords

Administrator Users with administrator privileges have complete access to all configuration parameters configurable and all information viewable via the Cisco IOS-like sensor shell. This includes all the privileges of users with operator privileges, as well as the ability to do the following:

- Configure network addressing
- Configure trusted and known hosts

- Assign physical sensing interfaces to interface groups
- Enable or disable physical interfaces and interface groups
- Add users and passwords

> **NOTE** By default, all sensors ship with a single account with the username `cisco` and the default password `cisco`, which has administrator privileges.

To create a user account, you use the `username` global configuration command with the following syntax:

```
sensor(config)# username user [password password]
    [privilege {administrator | operator | viewer}]
```

The `password` keyword is optional; if it isn't specified, the sensor will prompt you to enter and confirm the password for the user. If the optional `privilege` keyword isn't specified, then a privilege level of Viewer is assumed.

Service account The service account is a special user account that is granted the service privilege. The service privilege allows BASH shell access to the Linux operating system without being restricted to the custom Cisco IOS-like shell that is normally used. Only a single service account (a user account granted the service privilege) can be created. To create the service account, you use the `username` global configuration command with the following syntax:

```
sensor(config)# username user password password privilege service
```

The `privilege service` portion of the command specifies that the account is a service account.

> **WARNING** The creation and use of the service account is recommended only for troubleshooting purposes and should take place only under the supervision of Cisco TAC.

The following example demonstrates creating a couple of user accounts and a service account, and then logging in to the sensor with the service account:

```
ids-4210# configure terminal
ids-4210(config)# username alice password ccie1024 privilege viewer
ids-4210(config)# username bob password ccie10000 privilege operator
ids-4210(config)# username justin password ccie6640 privilege service
ids-4210(config)# exit
```

```
ids-4210# exit

ids-4210 login: justin
Password: ********

***NOTICE***
This product contains cryptographic features and is subject to United
States and local country laws governing import, export, transfer and use.
Delivery of Cisco cryptographic products does not imply third-party authority
to import, export, distribute or use encryption. Importers, exporters,
distributors and users are responsible for compliance with U.S. and local
country laws. By using this product you agree to comply with applicable laws
and regulations. If you are unable to comply with U.S. and local laws, return
this product immediately.

A summary of U.S. laws governing Cisco cryptographic products may be found at:
http://www.cisco.com/wwl/export/crypto

If you require further assistance please contact us by sending email to
export@cisco.com.
Press Enter to continue

************************ WARNING ************************
UNAUTHORIZED ACCESS TO THIS NETWORK DEVICE IS PROHIBITED.
This account is intended to be used for support and
troubleshooting purposes only. Unauthorized modifications
are not supported and will require this device to be
re-imaged to guarantee proper operation.
**********************************************************
bash-2.05a$
bash-2.05a$ pwd
/home/justin
bash-2.05a$ ls /
bin  boot  dev  etc  home  initrd  lib  lost+found  mnt  opt  proc  root
   sbin  tmp  usr  var
```

In this example, notice that when the service account is used to log in, a BASH shell is presented; it accepts traditional Unix commands such as pwd and ls.

Configuring the Sensor to Capture Traffic

All Cisco Secure IDS sensors include sensing interfaces, which are intended to attach to the network and capture traffic from one or more LAN segments. All sensors have designated sensing interfaces, listed in Table 21.8.

TABLE 21.8 Sensing Interfaces for Cisco Secure IDS 4.x

Sensor Model	Sensing Interfaces
4210 4215 4220 4230 4235 4250	int0
4215-4FE 4235-4FE 4250-4FE	int0, int2, int3, int4, int5
4250-SX	int0, int2
4250-XL	int0, int2, int3
IDSM-2	int7, int8
NM-CIDS	int1

When you're setting up your sensor for the first time, an important configuration task is to configure your sensing interface(s) to ensure that the appropriate interfaces are configured to capture and monitor traffic. On Cisco Secure IDS 4.x, a *group interface* is used to define which interfaces are sensing. Using a group interface creates a *virtual sensor* that captures traffic from multiple sensing interfaces. Only a single group interface (interface group 0) exists, and any interface that belongs to the interface group 0 is configured as a sensing interface.

If you've installed a fresh installation of Cisco Secure IDS 4.x, each of the sensing interfaces listed in Table 21.8 is placed into interface group 0. If you're using Cisco Secure IDS version 4.0, by default all sensing interfaces are enabled; so, you don't need to perform any configuration to ensure that sensing interfaces will capture traffic. If, however, you're using version 4.1 software, all sensing interfaces are disabled by default and must be manually enabled via the IDS CLI or appropriate IDS management application.

> **NOTE** If you upgrade a version 4.0 sensor to version 4.1, the previous configuration for interface group 0 is maintained.

To manually add or remove sensing interfaces from interface group 0, you must first enter interface configuration mode by executing the `interface group 0` command from global configuration mode. Then, execute the `sensing-interface` command, which has the following syntax:

sensor(config-ifg)# [no] sensing-interface *interface-id*[,*interface-id*]

The following example demonstrates adding and removing sensing interfaces to interface group 0:

sensor# **configure terminal**
sensor(config)# **interface group 0**
sensor(config-ifg)# **no sensing-interface int4**
sensor(config-ifg)# **sensing-interface int0**
sensor(config-ifg)# **sensing-interface int2,int3**

In the example, notice that the `no sensing-interface int4` command is first used to remove `int4` as a sensing interface; then the `sensing-interface int0` command is used to add the `int0` interface into interface group 0. Finally, the `sensing-interface int2,int3` command demonstrates how you add multiple interfaces with a single command.

> **NOTE** Although you can assign any interface (including the command and control interface) to interface group 0, assigning an interface that isn't supported as a sensing interface (for example, the `int1` command and control interface on the 4200 series sensors) is an illegal configuration. In other words, you can't change which interfaces are command and control interfaces and sensing interfaces—you can only enable and disable sensing interfaces by adding or removing them from interface group 0.

Once you've assigned the appropriate interfaces to interface group 0, you next need to manually enable each sensing interface. On Cisco Secure IDS 4.0, all sensing interfaces are physically enabled; however, in Cisco Secure 4.1, all sensing interfaces are physically in a shutdown state by default and must be manually enabled. To enable a sensing interface, you must first enter interface configuration mode for the sensing interface you wish to enable by using the `interface sensing` *interface-id* command; then, execute the `no shutdown` command in interface configuration mode. The following example demonstrates enabling the sensing interface (`int0`) on a 4200 series sensor:

sensor# **configure terminal**
sensor(config)# **interface sensing int0**
sensor(config-ifs)# **no shutdown**

Remember that this configuration only needs to be performed on version 4.1 sensors—on version 4.0 sensors, sensing interfaces are enabled by default and require no explicit configuration.

Administering the Sensor

As a security administrator or engineer responsible for maintaining Cisco Secure IDS sensors, there are a number of common administrative tasks that you may need to perform frequently. These include the following:

Determining the current version   To determine the current version of Cisco Secure IDS software that is running, as well as other version information, execute the show version command from privileged EXEC mode. The following example demonstrates the output of the show version command on a 4200 series sensor:

```
sensor# show version
Application Partition:

Cisco Systems Intrusion Detection Sensor, Version 4.0(1)S37


OS Version 2.4.18-5smpbigphys
Platform: unknown
 Sensor up-time is 7 min.
Using 126742528 out of 129126400 bytes of available memory (98% usage)
Using 58M out of 4.3G bytes of available disk space (2% usage)


MainApp            2003_Jan_23_02.00 (Release) 2003-01-23T02:00:25-0600 Running
AnalysisEngine     2003_Jan_23_02.00 (Release) 2003-01-23T02:00:25-0600 Running
Authentication     2003_Jan_23_02.00 (Release) 2003-01-23T02:00:25-0600 Running
Logger             2003_Jan_23_02.00 (Release) 2003-01-23T02:00:25-0600 Running
NetworkAccess      2003_Jan_23_02.00 (Release) 2003-01-23T02:00:25-0600 Running
TransactionSource  2003_Jan_23_02.00 (Release) 2003-01-23T02:00:25-0600 Running
WebServer          2003_Jan_23_02.00 (Release) 2003-01-23T02:00:25-0600 Running
CLI                2003_Jan_17_18.33 (Release) 2003-01-17T18:33:18-0600

Upgrade History:

  IDS-K9-maj-4.0-1-S36    06:49:00 UTC Sun Sep 07 2003

  Recovery Partition Version 1.1 - 4.0(1)S37
```

Notice in this example that you can determine the Cisco Secure IDS version, as well as OS version, memory usage, and hard disk usage information.

Viewing the current configuration Cisco Secure IDS sensors possess a text-based configuration file, which includes all the various configuration parameters configured on the sensor. This configuration file is similar in concept to the configuration file on a Cisco router or switch, and you can use it to determine current configuration settings.

To view the current configuration of a sensor, execute the `more current-config` command from privileged EXEC mode. The following example shows the output of the `more current-config` command on a 4200 series sensor:

```
sensor# more current-config
! -----------------------------
service Authentication
general
attemptLimit 0
methods method Local
exit
exit
exit
! -----------------------------
service Host
networkParams
ipAddress 192.168.1.101
netmask 255.255.255.0
defaultGateway 192.168.1.1
hostname ids-4210
telnetOption enabled
accessList ipAddress 0.0.0.0 netmask 0.0.0.0
accessList ipAddress 192.168.2.100 netmask 255.255.255.255
exit
optionalAutoUpgrade
active-selection none
exit
timeParams
summerTimeParams
active-selection none
exit
exit
exit

    (Output truncated)
```

```
SERVICE.MSSQL
signatures SIGID 3702 SubSig 0
exit
exit
exit
exit
! -----------------------------
service alarm-channel-configuration virtualAlarm
tune-alarm-channel
systemVariables
exit
EventFilter
exit
exit
exit
```

> **NOTE** The output of the previous example has been truncated in the interest of conserving book pages.

The configuration file on a Cisco Secure IDS sensor is quite large when compared to a Cisco router or switch configuration file, because configuration exists for each signature that the IDS sensor is aware of.

Creating a backup configuration file Cisco Secure IDS includes the ability to create a *backup configuration file* that can be used for restoration or rollback purposes. To create a backup configuration file, you use the copy current-config backup-config command. This command literally copies the current configuration file to the backup configuration file. Here is an example:

```
sensor# copy current-config backup-config
Generating current config: /
sensor#
```

The copy current-config command can also be used to back up the current configuration to an FTP server, as demonstrated here:

```
sensor# copy current-config ftp://192.168.1.10/temp/current-config.cfg
User: administrator
Password: ********
Connected to 192.168.1.10 (192.168.1.10).
220 Microsoft FTP Service
ftp> user
(username) administrator
```

```
331 Password required for administrator.
Password:230 User administrator logged in.
ftp> 200 Type set to I.
ftp> put current.cfg current-config.cfg
local: current.cfg remote: current-config.cfg
227 Entering Passive Mode (192,168,1,10,4,95).
125 Data connection already open; Transfer starting.
226 Transfer complete.
36245 bytes sent in 0.0137 secs (2.6e+03 Kbytes/sec)
ftp>
```

In this example, notice that an FTP URL is specified as the destination to which the current configuration file should be copied. The sensor prompts for the appropriate credentials, after which you can see that the current configuration file (current.cfg) is transferred to the FTP server as the file current-config.cfg.

Restoring a backup configuration file   Using the copy command, you can restore a previous configuration file to the current configuration file by specifying the current configuration file as the destination. The following example demonstrates restoring the backup configuration file to the current configuration file:

```
sensor# copy backup-config current-config
Processing config: /
sensor#
```

In this example, you can specify an FTP URL as the source (instead of specifying backup-config).

When you're restoring configuration files, it's important to understand that using the copy command as demonstrated in the previous example *merges* the backup configuration with the current configuration. This means that although configuration settings in the backup configuration overwrite the current configuration, any configuration settings that are present in the current configuration and not explicitly defined in the backup configuration will remain. To totally replace the current configuration with only the settings defined in the backup configuration file, the /erase switch can be used with the copy command, as demonstrated here:

```
sensor# copy /erase backup-config current-config
Processing config: /
sensor#
```

Rebooting the sensor   To reboot the sensor, you use the reset command. The optional powerdown keyword, which shuts down the sensor instead of rebooting it, can also be specified. The following example demonstrates shutting down a sensor:

```
sensor# reset powerdown
Warning: Executing this command will stop all applications and power off the
node
```

```
            if possible. If the node can not be powered off it will be left in a state
            that
            is safe to manually power down.
            Continue with reset? : yes

            Broadcast message from root (Fri Oct  3 10:27:35 2003):

            A system shutdown has been requested.  This may take up to 90 seconds.
            Request Succeeded.

            Broadcast message from root (Fri Oct  3 10:27:46 2003):

            The system is going down for system halt NOW!

            Command terminated on signal 9.
```

If you're using the IDSM-2 or NM-CIDS, you can also reboot the sensor using the CLI of the switch or router in which the sensor is installed. On the IDSM-2, you can use the following commands to reboot the sensor:

- For CatOS, use `Console> (enable) reset` *IDSM-slot-number*
- For Cisco IOS, use `Router# hw-module module` *IDSM-slot-number* `reset`

On the NM-CIDS, the `service-module` command can be used to reboot, shut down, or reset the sensor:

```
Router# service-module ids-sensor ids-slot-number/0 {shutdown | reload |
reset}
```

The difference between the `reload` and `reset` options is that the `reload` option is used to gracefully reboot the sensor, whereas the `reset` option is used to forcefully reboot the sensor. The `reset` option is recommended for use only if the sensor is in a shutdown or hung state.

Cisco Secure IDS Architecture

For the Cisco Secure IDS exam, you need to possess a basic understanding of the underlying architecture of Cisco Secure IDS sensors. Cisco Secure IDS sensors are based on a Red Hat Linux operating system, which has been customized by Cisco and includes a Cisco IOS-like shell for everyday operation and maintenance.

Under the hood, Cisco Secure IDS comprises a number of applications and includes files and directories located on the underlying file system. The easiest way to learn about Cisco Secure IDS files and directories is to create a service account, log in with the service account, and take a look around the underlying operation system yourself. The main Cisco Secure IDS files are located in the /usr/cids/idsRoot directory, as shown here:

```
*********************** WARNING ***********************
UNAUTHORIZED ACCESS TO THIS NETWORK DEVICE IS PROHIBITED.
This account is intended to be used for support and
troubleshooting purposes only. Unauthorized modifications
are not supported and will require this device to be
re-imaged to guarantee proper operation.
********************************************************
bash-2.05a$ su
Password: ********
[root@sensor-a root]# cd /usr/cids/idsRoot
[root@sensor-a idsRoot]# ls -l
total 29
drwxrwxr-x   2 cids     cids         4096 Dec   6 03:45 bin
drwxrwxr-x   6 cids     cids         4096 Dec   6 03:38 etc
drwxrwxr-x   6 cids     cids         4096 Nov  21 08:04 htdocs
drwxrwxr-x   2 cids     cids         4096 Nov  21 08:04 lib
drwxrwxr-x   2 cids     cids         4096 Dec   6 03:45 log
drwxrwxr-x   3 cids     cids         1024 Jan  23  2003 shared
drwxrwxr-x   2 cids     cids         4096 Dec   6 03:44 tmp
drwxrwxr-x   7 cids     cids         4096 Dec   5 00:40 var
```

> **NOTE** The su command provides root-level access to the sensor operating system and uses the same password as the service account password.

In the previous example, notice that you use standard Linux commands to navigate the underlying operating system. Within the /usr/cids/idsRoot directory, you can see a number of directories:

bin The bin directory contains the various executable files for applications and utilities that compose Cisco Secure IDS. The following is a listing of the bin directory:

```
[root@sensor-a bin]# ls -l /usr/cids/idsRoot/bin
total 11136
-rwsrwx---   1 root     cids      1390050 Jan  23  2003 authentication
-rwxrwx---   1 cids     cids         5672 Jan  23  2003 cidDump
-rwxrwx---   1 cids     cids          534 Jan  23  2003 cidInstallArchive
```

```
-rwxrwx---   1 cids   cids        634699 Jan 23  2003 cidcli
-rwxrwx---   1 cids   cids       1405685 Jan 23  2003 cidwebserver
-rwsrwx---   1 root   cids         24045 Jan 23  2003 cleanUp
-rwxrwx---   1 cids   cids       1302086 Jan 23  2003 ctlTransSource
-rwxrwx---   1 cids   cids           166 Jan 23  2003 getEventStoreStats
lrwxrwxrwx   1 root   root            36 Nov 21 08:04 hotrod -> /usr/cids/
idsRoot/bin/hotrod_2_0.bin
-r--r--r--   1 cids   cids         56944 Jan 23  2003 hotrod_2_0.bin
-rwxrwx---   1 cids   cids         15818 Jan 23  2003 idsPackageMgr
-rwxrwx---   1 cids   cids        122699 Jan 23  2003 logApp
-rwsrwx---   1 root   cids       1527232 Jan 23  2003 mainApp
-rwxrwx---   1 cids   cids          6999 Jan 23  2003 merge.pl
-rwxrwx---   1 cids   cids       1052281 Jan 23  2003 nac
-rwxrwx---   1 cids   cids         67773 Jan 23  2003 sendCtlTrans
-rwxrwx---   1 cids   cids       3436747 Jan 23  2003 sensorApp
-rwxrwxr--   1 cids   cids        205504 Jan 23  2003 simulator
-r-xr-xr-x   1 cids   cids          7210 Jan 23  2003 superflash
-rwsr-x---   1 root   cids         57590 Jan 23  2003 terminal
```

For this example, the applications that make up Cisco Secure IDS are highlighted. They're described in more detail here:

- `authentication`: Runs the authentication subsystem, for authenticating communication requests to the sensor
- `cidcli`: Runs the custom Cisco IOS-like shell that is normally presented when you log on to the sensor CLI
- `cidwebserver`: Runs the IDS Device Manager, which provides web-based configuration to the sensor
- `logApp`: Responsible for logging sensor events and generating IP log files if required
- `mainApp`: Main application responsible for overseeing other applications
- `sensorApp`: Includes the various intrusion detection engines responsible for analyzing traffic and generating alarms as required.

etc This directory includes the configuration files that control how the various Cisco Secure IDS applications operate. Many files in this folder are defined in an XML format and provide default or current settings for different Cisco Secure IDS features.

htdocs This directory stores a number of HTML files used to provide the IDS Device Manager, online help, and network security database (NSDB) web pages.

lib The `lib` directory stores internal files used for Cisco Secure IDS operation.

log This directory stores the main event log file (`main.log`) and output files generated by the cidDump utility. The main event log file contains system events, warnings, and errors that are generated by the various Cisco Secure IDS applications.

Installing and Configuring Cisco Secure IDS Sensors

Real World Scenario

Cisco Secure IDS Internal Architecture

The Cisco Secure IDS sensor software is a series of applications that each provide a portion of the overall functionality of Cisco Secure IDS and interact with other applications in various ways. The following diagram shows the internal architecture of Cisco Secure IDS:

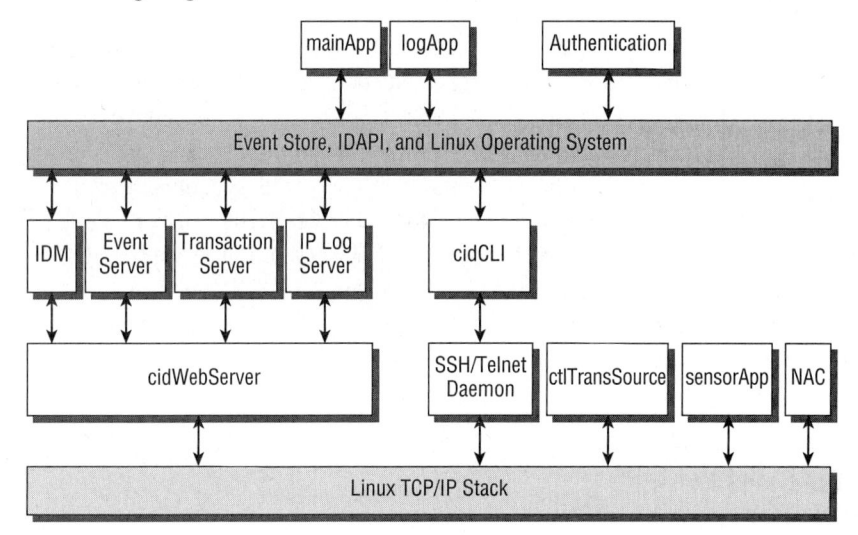

In terms of communications between Cisco Secure IDS components, there are two types of communication:

1. *Internal communication* is communication between components that reside on the same physical platform. Intrusion detection API (IDAPI) is used to facilitate internal communications.

2. *External communication* is communication between components that reside on separate physical platforms. Remote Desktop Exchange Protocol (RDEP) is used to facilitate external communications, which uses XML documents to exchange information. RDEP is transported in either HTTP or HTTPS over the network.

shared The shared directory stores the host.conf file, which contains basic sensor settings, such as network parameters (IP address, subnet mask, default gateway, and host name) and allowed hosts entries.

> **Note:** The cidDump utility generates a lot of information related to the Cisco Secure IDS application that is useful for Cisco technical support.

tmp   This directory stores temporary files that the sensor applications work with.

var   The var directory stores the current configuration file (current.cfg), the backup configuration file (backup.cfg), the event store where all alarms are stored, files that the various sensor applications work with, IP log files, and any updates that have been applied to the sensor. The contents of the var directory are as follows:

```
[root@sensor-a var]# ls -l /usr/cids/idsRoot/var
total 6516
-rw-rw----   1 cids     cids     4000002048 Nov 21 14:05 IdsEventStore
-rw-rw-r--   1 cids     cids             90 Dec  6 03:18 IdsEventStoreData
-rw-rw-r--   1 cisco    cids          36243 Nov 22 06:33 backup.cfg
-rw-rw-r--   1 cids     cids              4 Dec  6 03:19 cidwebserver.pid
-rw-rw-r--   1 cisco    cids          36243 Nov 22 06:33 current.cfg
drwxr-xr-x   2 cids     cids           4096 Nov 21 14:06 iplogs
drwx------   2 root     root          16384 Nov 21 07:59 lost+found
drwxrwxr-x   7 cids     cids           4096 Dec  3 07:22 updates
-rw-rw-r--   1 cids     cids            887 Dec  3 02:08 user.dat
drwxrwxr-x   2 cids     cids           4096 Dec  6 03:20 virtualSensor
```

Summary

In this chapter, you've learned about the hardware and system specifications of the Cisco Secure IDS sensor platforms: the Cisco Secure IDS 4200 series sensors, the Cisco Catalyst IDSM, and the Cisco 2600/2800/3600/3700/3800 NM-CIDS sensor. Understanding the hardware specifications of the various sensors is important, to ensure that you select sensors that meet the performance and media requirements of your network. Once you've selected a sensor, it's important to consider the issues associated with deployment of the sensor. These include exactly where you should place the sensor, so that the sensor can effectively monitor the appropriate network segments, as well as ensuring that the sensor can communicate with a sensor management platform and that the sensor management platforms you use are capable of supporting the combined load of the sensors you're deploying.

Once you're ready to begin installing and configuring your sensor, you need to gain initial management access to the sensor. Depending on the type of sensor, different methods of gaining initial management access are used, and it's important that you understand these methods. After you gain initial management access, the first step in configuring the sensor is to run the **setup** utility, which configures basic system parameters, such as hostname and network addressing. Other system parameters such as restricting management access, configuring known SSH hosts, and creating user accounts must be configured using other CLI commands. Once the appropriate system parameters are configured, you next need to ensure that the appropriate sensing interfaces of the sensor are in the group 0 interface, and you also need to explicitly physically enable each sensing interface.

Exam Essentials

Understand the common locations where IDS sensors are installed. IDS sensors are most commonly installed at entry points to your networks, including the Internet, extranets, intranets, and remote-access and server farm networks.

Remember the types of network interfaces that the Cisco Secure IDS sensor uses and the device names of the interfaces. The sensing or monitoring interface receives traffic and passes it to the IDS engine for analysis. The command and control interface has an IP address that lets the sensor communicate with the network for management and alarm notification purposes. With the 4200 series sensors, the sensing interface is always `int0` and the command and control interface is always `int1`. Additional sensing interfaces are identified as `int2`, `int3`, `int4`, and so on, depending on the number of additional sensing interfaces. On the IDSM, the sensing interfaces are `int7` and `int8`, with `int1` used for sending TCP resets. On the NM-CIDS, the sensing interface is `int0`.

Understand the performance specifications of the various Cisco Secure IDS sensors. See Table 21.1, which describes the throughput of each sensor in Mbps.

Remember the physical layout of each sensor. Be able to identify all physical ports and interfaces of the various sensor platforms.

Know the initial management access methods for each sensor and the login accounts available for access to each sensor. 4200 series sensors allow access via keyboard/monitor or console. The IDSM allows access via an internal console port, and the NM-CIDS allows access via reverse Telnet to an internal consoled port. All sensors by default have a single account called `cisco` with a default password of `cisco`.

Know how to perform initial configuration of each sensor. All sensors use the `setup` utility for initial sensor configuration.

Know the user account privileges. There are four privileges: administrator, viewer, operator, and service. Only a single service account can exist, which provides access to a BASH shell to allow access to the underlying Linux OS for troubleshooting purposes.

Know the various commands to configure the sensor. You need to understand the various CLI modes and how to configure all of the parameters discussed in this chapter.

Chapter 22

Configuring the Network to Support Cisco Secure IDS Sensors

CISCO SECURE INTRUSION DETECTION SYSTEM EXAM TOPICS COVERED IN THIS CHAPTER:

- ✓ Network devices involved in capturing traffic for intrusion detection analysis
- ✓ The traffic flows for each of the network devices
- ✓ Configuring Cisco Catalyst switches to capture network traffic for intrusion detection analysis

In order to detect intrusive activity, Cisco Secure IDS sensors require an accurate view of *all* traffic that is being sent and received on a particular network segment, to ensure that intrusive activity isn't missed by the sensor. This means that the network infrastructure devices that Cisco Secure IDS sensors connect to must be capable of passing or *mirroring* traffic sent and received on a particular network segment to the sensor.

In this chapter, you'll learn how to configure a Cisco switched infrastructure to support the capture of traffic for 4200 series sensors, the IDSM-2 sensor, and the NM-CIDS sensor. This includes using techniques such as switched port analyzer and VLAN access control lists.

Capturing Traffic

After you've installed and configured your sensor so that it's ready to begin receiving network traffic for intrusion detection analysis, it's important to ensure that the network infrastructure to which the sensor connects supports the ability to pass the appropriate network traffic from the protected network segments to the sensor.

> **NOTE** In the context of this chapter, you can think of a network segment as a broadcast domain, VLAN, or IP subnet.

Cisco Secure IDS sensors are network-based sensors that passively monitor network traffic, meaning that the LAN infrastructure to which the sensing interface of the sensor is attached must be capable of mirroring traffic from the monitored network segment. Depending on the type of sensor, several mechanisms are available to let the network mirror traffic to the sensing interface of the sensor. Table 22.1 describes each of the traffic-capture mechanisms supported for each type of sensor.

Notice in Table 22.1 that the 4200 series sensors are the only sensors that can monitor traffic received from an external device—the IDSM-2 and NM-CIDS both capture traffic from the backplane of the chassis in which they are installed. The following sections discuss the various traffic-capture mechanisms shown in Table 22.1 based on the following topics:

- Configuring traffic capture for the 4200 series sensors
- Configuring traffic capture for the IDSM
- Configuring traffic capture for the NM-CIDS

TABLE 22.1 Support for Traffic-Capture Mechanisms

Sensor	Traffic-Capture Mechanisms Supported
4200 series	External hub
	Network tap
	SPAN/RSPAN (via external switch)
	VACLs (via external switch)
IDSM	SPAN/RSPAN (via Catalyst 6000 backplane)
	VACLs (via Catalyst 6000 backplane)
NM-CIDS	Router backplane

> **TIP** Cisco IOS 12.3(4)T introduces a feature known as *IP Traffic Monitoring*, which allows Cisco routers to mirror traffic sent or received on one or more routed interfaces to Cisco Secure IDS sensors. See http://www.cisco.com/univercd/cc/td/doc/product/software/ios123/123newft/123t/123t_4/gt_rawip.htm for more details.

Configuring Traffic Capture for the 4200 Series Sensors

The 4200 series sensors feature physical sensing interfaces, which must be connected to an external traffic-capture device to capture traffic. Three generic types of LAN infrastructure devices can be used to capture traffic for the 4200 series sensors:

Hub   The traditional network capture device is the Ethernet hub, which allows for all traffic on a LAN segment to be captured without any additional features or hardware, based purely on the fundamental operation of a hub. A hub provides aggregation and interconnectivity for Ethernet devices by allowing interconnection to a *shared* internal communications media. Figure 22.1 demonstrates how an Ethernet hub operates.

In Figure 22.1, a hub is installed on an Internet DMZ segment with the Internet perimeter router and firewall attached; the sensing interface of the sensor is also attached to the hub. Any traffic sent or received by the hub is sent out all ports regardless of the type of traffic, due to the internal shared bus within the hub. This internal bus is essentially just a piece of wire, amplifying and propagating electrical signals received from attached devices to all other attached devices. This means the traffic flow between the firewall and perimeter router (all traffic sent between the internal network and Internet) can be captured by the sensing interface on the IDS or any other device attached to the hub. A hub is a physical layer device, because it propagates electrical signals and has no concept of layer 2 Ethernet frames.

Although a hub makes traffic capture easy for an IDS, the downside is the maximum network performance possible for devices communicating through the hub. Because a hub provides a shared Ethernet medium for attached devices to communicate on, each device must operate the Carrier Sense Multiple Access with Collision Detection (CSMA/CD) algorithm to detect the situation where two devices attempt to place data onto the medium at the same time, causing a collision. When a collision is detected, both sending devices back off for a small random amount of time in an effort to avoid a repeat collision; then they attempt to retransmit. The occurrence of collisions and the CSMA/CD algorithm used to avoid excessive collisions reduces the throughput of Ethernet media to 40–60 percent of the theoretical Ethernet throughput, depending on the number of devices attached to the shared media (for example, two devices communicating on a 100Mbps Ethernet hub can only hope to get approximately 60Mbps of throughput at best). If you have a low-performance Internet connection (such as T1 or 1.5Mbps full-duplex), then a 10Mbps or 100Mbps Ethernet hub is adequate; however, if you have a T3 Internet connection (45Mbps full-duplex), even a 100Mbps Ethernet hub isn't sufficient.

FIGURE 22.1 Ethernet hub operation

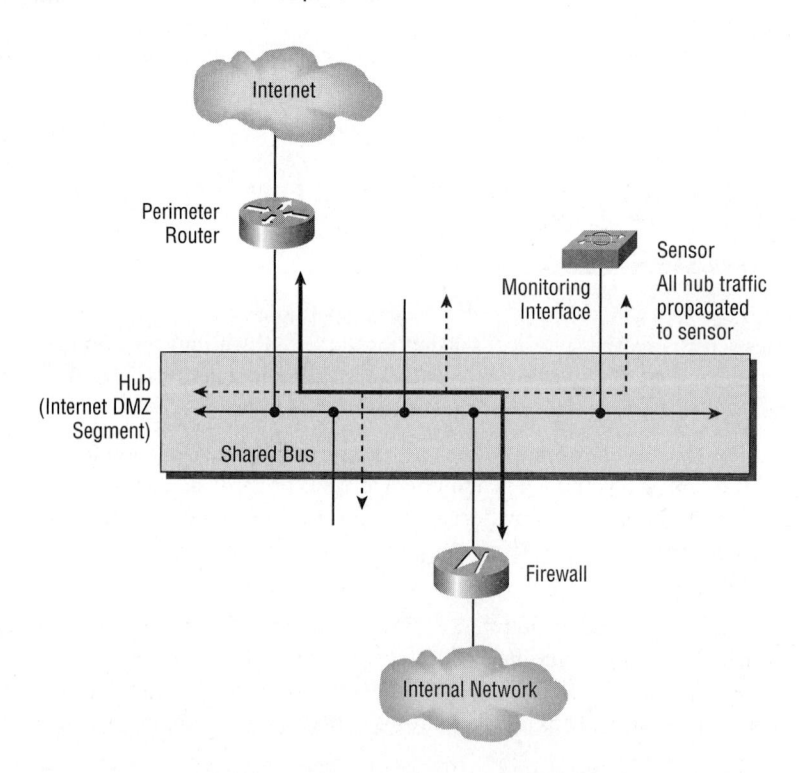

Capturing Network Traffic

All network-capture devices with network interfaces, whether IDSs or packet sniffers, require the network interface used for traffic capture to operate in *promiscuous mode*. When promiscuous mode is turned off, a network interface only forwards unicast frames received that are addressed to the MAC address of the network interface to the local host operating system (frames sent directly to the host—multicast and broadcast frames are also forwarded to the operating system). When promiscuous mode is turned on, the network interface forwards *all* frames received to the operating system for processing, regardless of their destination MAC address, ensuring that network capture applications are passing all frames captured from the network.

> **NOTE**
> A hub provides half-duplex operation, which means that a device can't send and receive at the same time. WAN technologies are full-duplex by nature (Ethernet can operate in full-duplex mode, although this requires a switch)—for example, a T3 connection can send and receive simultaneously at 45Mbps. This means that a T3 connection can generate a maximum of 90Mbps traffic of sent and received traffic, whereas a half-duplex 100Mbps Ethernet hub can only support a combined send and receive throughput of about 60Mbps at best—hence the reason a 100Mbps Ethernet hub isn't sufficient for T3 and higher Internet connections.

Switch LAN switches have steadily gained popularity over the past few years, such that switches are now considered a commodity networking device and can be easily obtained at low cost. Today the LAN switch has replaced hubs for the most part in corporate networks, because switches can eliminate collision domains and also can provide full-duplex Ethernet operation; thus devices can communicate with each other at rates closer to 90–95 percent of the theoretical maximum bandwidth possible with Ethernet. A switch is typically a layer 2 device, meaning that it intelligently forwards traffic based on the layer 2 properties of Ethernet frames received (the destination MAC address of a frame), rather than just propagating electrical signals as a hub does. The intelligence of a switch comes down to the fact that a switch dynamically learns where hosts are in the network, which allows it to switch frames addressed to hosts out only the port that the host is attached to, avoiding the unnecessary forwarding of those frames to other hosts in the network. This process is also known as *transparent bridging*, because the whole process is performed transparently to the end devices that attach to the switch. Figure 22.2 demonstrates how a switch operates.

In Figure 22.2, the hub used in Figure 22.1 has been replaced with a switch. Notice that the switch includes a *bridge table* (also known as the *CAM table*, or content-addressable memory table), which includes a list of destination MAC addresses (destination hosts) and the port that each destination MAC address is reachable from. The bridge table is dynamically learned by the switch examining the source MAC address of frames received from hosts, which allows the switch to determine where a host is located.

For example, if the firewall sends a frame to the Internet router, the source MAC address of the frame will be 0101.0101.0101 and the frame will be received on port 2/4 of the switch. By examining the source MAC address of the frame, the switch now knows that 0101.0101.0101 is reachable via port 2/4, and adds the entry into the bridge table. Any subsequent frames that are sent to the MAC address 0101.0101.0101 (the firewall) can then be intelligently forwarded out port 2/4. If a switch receives a frame with an unknown destination MAC address (the MAC address isn't present in the bridge table), then the switch will flood the frame out all ports (except the port upon which a frame was received)—once the destination host replies to the flooded frame, the switch learns exactly where the destination host is in the network (by reading the source MAC address of the reply frame), meaning that subsequent frames sent to the destination host can be forwarded out only the appropriate port.

> **NOTE** Unicast frames with unknown destinations, multicast frames, and broadcast frames are flooded out all ports (except the port the frame was received on). Some switches possess sufficient intelligence to also constrain the flooding of multicast frames out only those ports with devices attached that are members of a multicast group.

Given that a switch effectively constrains a unicast traffic flow between two hosts to only those ports to which each host attaches, to an external network capture device, which connects to a different port on the switch, the traffic sent between the hosts is invisible. This is obviously a problem for an IDS sensor, because a sensor can be effective only if it can analyze all traffic on a segment. To work around this issue, Cisco developed a feature called a switch port analyzer (SPAN) that lets you configure a set of ports or VLANs from which traffic should be captured and mirrored to a configured destination port on the switch. Today, all current Cisco Catalyst switches support SPAN (although some restrictions may apply depending on the switch platform). Some Cisco Catalyst switches also support a feature known as VLAN access control lists (VACLs), which can be used to classify specific types of traffic within a VLAN (such as HTTP traffic or FTP traffic sent to a specific host) and then mirror that traffic to a configured capture port. You'll learn about SPAN and VACLs later in this section.

Network tap   The least-used network capture device is called a *network tap*, which is inserted between two network devices on a LAN segment that are connected to each other using a back-to-back full-duplex connection via a crossover cable. This means that a network tap is only useful where only two devices, such as a router and firewall, are connected to the LAN segment you need to monitor. The network tap separates out the transmit circuit and receive circuits from both devices and attaches taps to each circuit; each mirrors traffic sent in a particular direction out an external capture port. Figure 22.3 demonstrates the operation of a network tap.

In Figure 22.3, the network tap sits between the firewall and router, with each device attached using an RJ-45 UTP cable. Notice that the network tap splits out the transmit and receive pairs on each port, effectively separating traffic sent from the firewall to the router (TXF ≻ RXR) and traffic sent from the router to the firewall (TXR ≻ RXF). An internal tap is then attached to each circuit that is wired to an external port on the network tap, which allows the traffic sent in each direction to be mirrored out each external tap port. Notice that a network tap still requires an Ethernet device such as a hub or switch to effectively allow the separated transmit and receive traffic captured from the tap to be mirrored to a single physical port of the hub/switch.

> **NOTE** A network tap is useful for monitoring devices that need to be mobile, where they're used for troubleshooting and analysis, requiring a temporary connection to the network. In this situation, attaching the network tap requires only a temporary disconnection and reattachment of cables to the network tap; no major changes to the existing network topology are necessary. For an IDS, a network tap offers no benefits over a switch or hub, because an IDS typically is located in a fixed location in the network and rarely needs to be moved.

The most common form of traffic-capture device used is the switch, and for the Cisco Secure IDS exam, you must understand how to configure Cisco Catalyst switches to mirror traffic to 4200 series sensors. The rest of this section focuses on configuring the switch port analyzer (SPAN) feature, which can be used on Cisco Catalyst switches to mirror traffic to a 4200 series sensor. SPAN lets you configure a switch to mirror traffic sent and/or received on a configurable set of source ports to a destination port, where you would attach the sensing interface of the sensor.

FIGURE 22.2 LAN switch operation

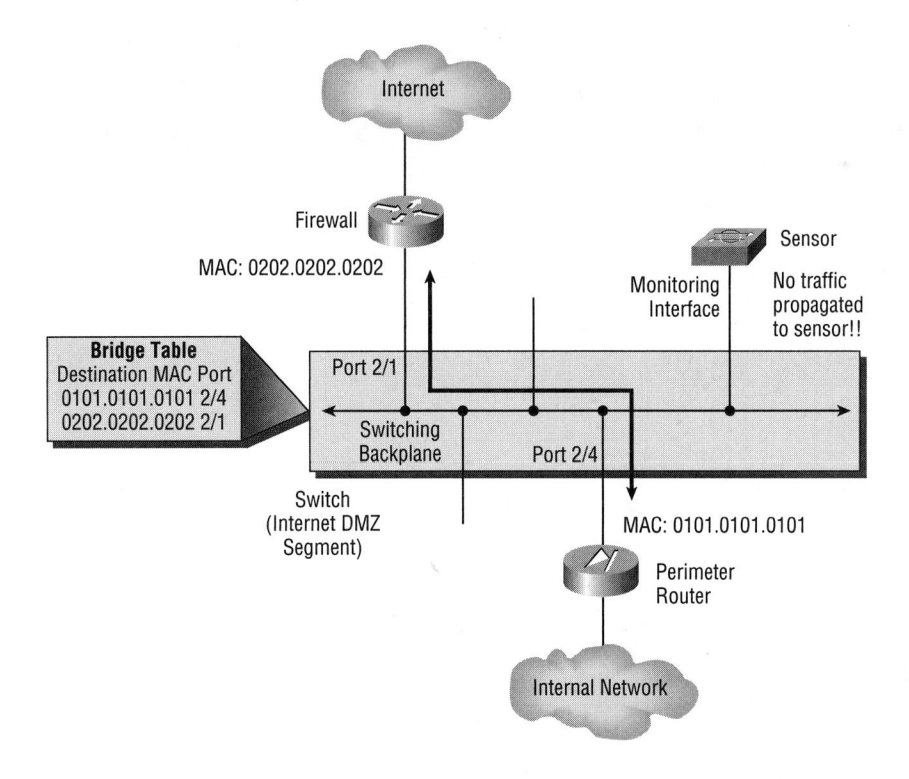

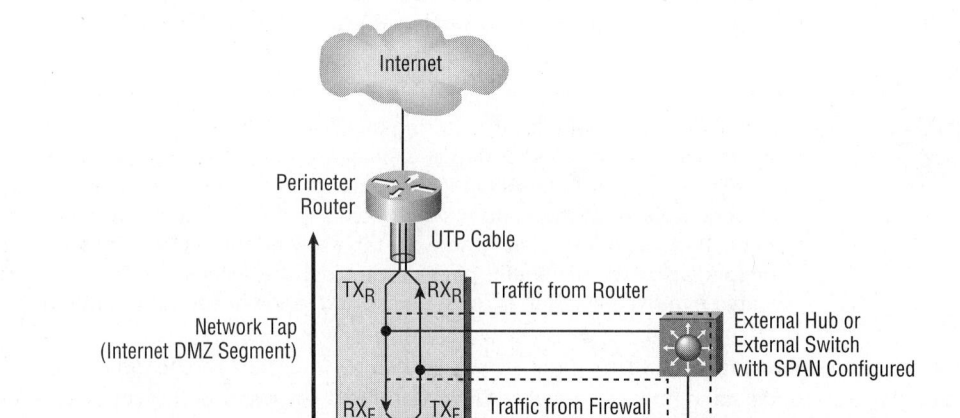

FIGURE 22.3 Network tap operation

One limitation of SPAN is that it only lets you monitor traffic generated on the same switch your sensor is attached to. An enhanced version of SPAN called remote SPAN (RSPAN) allows traffic from remote switch ports to be mirrored to a port on a separate Cisco Catalyst switch to which the sensing interface or a sensor is attached. In this section, you'll learn about the SPAN and RSPAN features and how to configure both on Cisco Catalyst switches. The following topics will be discussed:

- Configuring traffic capture using SPAN
- Configuring traffic capture using RSPAN

> **NOTE** VLAN ACLs can also be used to mirror traffic to the 4200 series sensors. VACLs are more commonly used in conjunction with the IDSM-2 and hence are covered in the later IDSM-2 section.

Configuring Traffic Capture Using SPAN

SPAN is the traditional method of mirroring traffic to an IDS sensor in a switched environment. When you configure SPAN for traffic capture, you must create a SPAN session, which has the following characteristics:

Set of source ports   This defines the source ports from which traffic will be mirrored. This set can include administratively defined physical ports or all the ports from one or more VLANs.

Capture direction on the source ports   This defines the type of traffic that you wish to capture from the set of source ports. For each source port you can capture traffic received (known as an *ingress SPAN* port), transmitted (known as an *egress SPAN* port), or both received and transmitted (referred to as ingress SPAN ports on Cisco switches). The direction is important, because it influences the maximum number of SPAN sessions you can run on the switch. On many Cisco Catalyst switches, more egress SPAN sessions (a SPAN session that captures traffic transmitted on source ports) are supported than ingress SPAN sessions (a SPAN session that captures traffic received on source ports). If a SPAN session has both egress and ingress SPAN ports, then the session is classified as an ingress SPAN session.

A single destination port   This defines the destination port that receives the mirrored traffic from the set of source ports. A SPAN session can have only a single destination port. When you're configuring SPAN for an IDS sensor, the destination port is attached to the sensing interface of the sensor. For example, on a 4215 sensor, the SPAN destination port must be attached to the `int0` interface on the sensor.

An important consideration when you're using SPAN for a sensor is whether the destination SPAN port accepts incoming packets from the network capture device (in this case, the sensor). Because sensors are capable of generating TCP resets on the sensing interface that are sent to the source of an attack and the destination target system to effectively tear down TCP-based intrusive activity, it's important if you wish to use this feature that the switch support incoming packets on the destination SPAN port (some Catalyst switches don't support this feature).

Figure 22.4 demonstrates a SPAN session.

SPAN and Oversubscription

A common problem with SPAN is the oversubscription of the destination port, which can easily happen if multiple source ports exist that are operating at the same speed as the destination port. If each source port is fully loaded, this causes congestion at the destination port; the switch may drop frames, possibly resulting in intrusive activity being missed by a sensor device attached to the destination port.

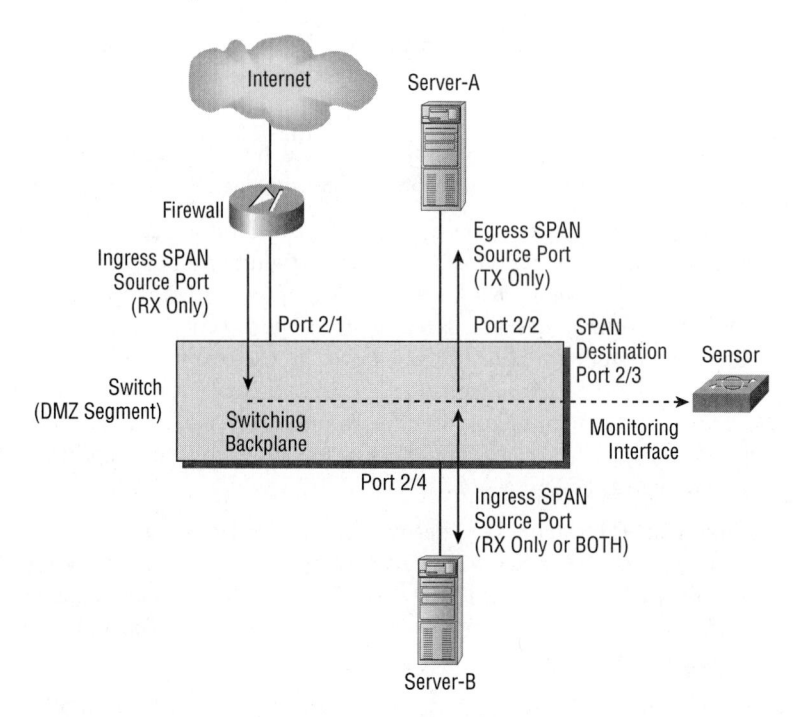

FIGURE 22.4 Components of a SPAN session

In Figure 22.4, a DMZ segment is shown, with two servers and a firewall attached. Notice that three source ports exist in total:

Port 2/1   This is an ingress SPAN port, because only traffic received inbound (RX) on the port is mirrored.

Port 2/2   This is an egress SPAN port, because only traffic sent outbound (TX) from the port is mirrored.

Port 2/4   This is an ingress SPAN port, because traffic either received inbound (RX) or sent and received in both directions (BOTH) is considered an ingress port.

All the traffic mirrored from the source ports is sent to the destination port, which is port 2/3 in Figure 22.4. The combination of the source ports, the direction for which traffic is mirrored (ingress or egress), and the destination port uniquely identifies a SPAN session. The SPAN session shown in Figure 22.4 is treated as an ingress SPAN session, because both egress and ingress source ports exist.

> **NOTE**
> It's important to understand that source ports in a SPAN can be determined dynamically by specifying a source VLAN instead of individual source ports. When this occurs, all ports that belong to a specific VLAN are automatically configured as source ports, with ports dynamically removed and added to the SPAN session as devices come and go. Specifying source VLANs for a SPAN session rather than source ports is referred to as *VSPAN*.

Before configuring SPAN, you must understand your IDS monitoring requirements and plan carefully for each of the parameters discussed previously. The following must be considered before implementing SPAN:

- SPAN session limits
- How the switch should handle incoming packets on the destination port (the port to which the sensing interface is attached), which is required for the TCP RESET alarm action
- 802.1q tagging of traffic on the destination port, which is required if monitoring traffic from multiple VLANs
- Destination port oversubscription

Table 22.2 describes each of the previous considerations on common Cisco Catalyst switch platforms. Destination port oversubscription is a problem on all platforms; hence it isn't included in Table 22.2.

TABLE 22.2 Cisco Secure IDS SPAN Features and Limitations

Platform	Maximum SPAN Sessions	Incoming Packets on Destination Port	802.1q Tagging on Destination Port
Catalyst 2900XL/3500XL	1	No	No
Catalyst 2950 (Standard Image)	1	No	No
Catalyst 2950 (Enhanced Image)	1	Yes	Yes
Catalyst 3550	2	Yes	Yes
Catalyst 4000/4500 (Supervisor I/II)	5	Yes	Yes
Catalyst 4000/4500 (Supervisor III/IV)	2 ingress; 4 egress	No	No
Catalyst 5000/5500	1 ingress; 4 egress	Yes	No
Catalyst 6000/6500 (CatOS)	2 ingress; 4 egress	Yes	Yes
Catalyst 6000/6500 (Native IOS)	2	Yes	Yes, IOS 12.2(SX)

As you can see in Table 22.2, the capabilities of each Cisco Catalyst switch vary depending on the switch platform and operating system. Notice that 802.1q tagging on the destination port is supported only on the Catalyst 2950 (Enhanced Image), the Catalyst 3550, and the Catalyst 6000/6500 running IOS 12.2(SX) or higher, meaning that these switches are suitable only for sensors that are monitoring multiple VLANs (such as the 4235, 4250, and IDSM) and where SPAN is configured.

> **NOTE** On the Catalyst 6000/6500 platform (CatOS or Native IOS), you can use VLAN access control lists (discussed later) to monitor traffic from multiple VLANs.

Cisco Catalyst switches ship with one of two operating systems, which means that the configuration tasks required depend on the operating system that ships with your switch:

Cisco IOS   Cisco IOS is the operating system that all Cisco Catalyst switches are being moved toward. Cisco IOS–based switches include the Catalyst 2900XL/3500XL, Catalyst 2950/3550/3750, Catalyst 4000/4500 with Supervisor III/IV, and Catalyst 6000/6500 operating in native IOS mode.

CatOS   Cisco Catalyst switches have traditionally supported CatOS, which has a different look and feel than Cisco IOS. CatOS provides all the features that Cisco IOS provides (in fact, CatOS to date is more feature-rich than Cisco IOS); however, in the long term, Cisco IOS will eventually replace CatOS. CatOS-based switches include the Catalyst 4000/4500 with Supervisor I/II, Catalyst 5000/5500, and Catalyst 6000/6500.

In the next sections, you'll learn how to configure SPAN on Cisco IOS and CatOS.

Configuring SPAN on Cisco IOS

In this section, you'll learn how to configure SPAN on a Cisco IOS–based Catalyst 3550 switch. Figure 22.5 shows a typical network topology where SPAN needs to be configured to mirror traffic to a sensor.

FIGURE 22.5   Example topology for SPAN on Catalyst 3550

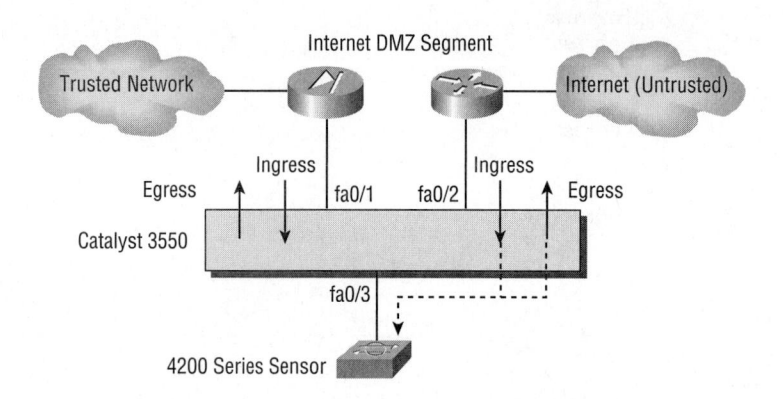

In Figure 22.5, a 4200 series sensor needs to monitor traffic sent from the Internet to the trusted network, as well as from the trusted network to the Internet. To achieve this, SPAN must be configured on the Catalyst 3550 switch in a manner that ensures that traffic sent in both directions between the firewall and router is mirrored to the sensor. This can be achieved in a number of ways:

- Capturing egress traffic on interface fastEthernet0/1 and fastEthernet0/2
- Capturing ingress traffic on interface fastEthernet0/1 and fastEthernet0/2
- Capturing egress and ingress traffic on either interface fastEthernet0/1 or fastEthernet0/2

The most efficient way to monitor traffic is to capture egress and ingress traffic on one of the interfaces, because only a single ingress SPAN session is used. Because only two devices are connected to the segment, this strategy captures all traffic—if more than two devices were attached to the segment, you would normally configure the segment VLAN as the source (configure VSPAN), capturing all ingress or egress traffic. In Figure 22.5, it's best to capture the traffic sent and received on the interface connected to the router (fastEthernet0/2), because this allows an attack that somehow affects the switch to be detected.

To configure SPAN on Cisco IOS–based Catalyst switches, you must perform the following tasks:

1. Configure one or more source ports or VLANs and specify the direction of traffic you wish to capture.
2. Configure a destination port.

On Cisco IOS, the monitor session global configuration command is used to configure a SPAN session. The following shows the syntax required to create a SPAN session and configure one or more source ports:

```
Switch(config)# monitor session session-id source interface
  interface-type interface-id [both | rx | tx]
```

The *session-id* parameter identifies the session, which is just a number that is used to reference the session for future commands. You can specify a source interface using the interface keyword and then define the direction for which traffic should be monitored using the rx (ingress traffic), tx (egress traffic), or both (ingress and egress traffic) keywords.

> **NOTE:** If you don't specify the direction, a direction of both is assumed.

To configure one or more source VLANs for a SPAN session, you use the following command syntax:

```
Switch(config)# monitor session session-id source vlan
  source-vlan(s) [rx]
```

Notice that when configuring a VLAN as a source, you can only mirror traffic received on the VLAN. This is to avoid duplicate packets being mirrored to the destination port, which would happen if both ingress and egress traffic were mirrored (a packet received entering the VLAN would be mirrored, and when the packet was transmitted exiting the VLAN, it would also be mirrored).

After defining the source ports or VLANs, you next define a destination port as follows:

```
Switch(config)# monitor session session-id destination interface
  interface-type interface-id [encapsulation
  {dot1q | isl | replicate}] [ingress vlan vlan-id]
```

The *session-id* parameter is used to map the destination interface configuration to the SPAN session created when the source ports and/or VLANs are defined. The optional `encapsulation` keyword is used to define how frames sent out the destination port should be tagged, which is important if you wish to configure your sensor to monitor multiple VLANs:

encapsulation dot1q   When configured, all frames are tagged with an 802.1q VLAN tag that identifies the VLAN on which the source port upon which the frame is being sent or received on belongs. Configure these keywords if you want your sensor to monitor traffic from multiple VLANs.

encapsulation isl   This works in the same manner as the `encapsulation dot1q` keywords, except that all frames are tagged with an ISL VLAN tag.

encapsulation replicate   When configured, the frame is mirrored in its original state (may or may not have VLAN tag information, depending on the type of port you're capturing traffic from).

Finally, the optional `ingress vlan` keywords enable incoming packets on the destination interface; the *vlan-id* defines the VLAN to which the frames received on the destination should be placed. This command is particularly important for Cisco Secure IDS sensors, because sensors can generate TCP resets as an alarm response mechanism; these are sent via the sensing interface of the sensor.

> **NOTE**   Cisco Secure IDS sensors only support 802.1q trunking; so, if you want to monitor traffic from multiple VLANs on a single interface, you must ensure either that the `encapsulation dot1q` keywords are configured or that the `encapsulation replicate` keywords are configured and a 802.1q trunk interface is specified as the source interface. Configuring a SPAN destination port with the `encapsulation isl` keywords isn't supported for Cisco Secure IDS sensors.

The following demonstrates configuring a SPAN session on the Catalyst 3550 switch in Figure 22.5, which mirrors traffic sent and received on the interface attached to the Internet router to the sensor (interface `fastEthernet0/2`). The destination port for the SPAN session (interface `fastEthernet0/3`) is also configured to accept TCP RESET packets that may be sent by the sensor.

```
Switch(config)# monitor session 1 source interface fastEthernet0/2 both
Switch(config)# monitor session 1 destination interface fastEthernet0/3
  ingress vlan 1
Switch(config)# exit
Switch# show monitor
Session 1
---------
Type                    : Local Session
Source Ports            :
    Both                : Fa0/2
Destination Ports       : Fa0/3
    Encapsulation       : Native
          Ingress       : Enabled, default VLAN = 1
```

Notice the use of the `show monitor` command, which can be used to troubleshoot your SPAN configuration.

Configuring SPAN on CatOS

In this section, you'll learn how to configure SPAN on a CatOS-based Catalyst switch. Figure 22.6 shows a topology similar to that from Figure 22.5, except the Cisco IOS–based Catalyst 3550 switch has been replaced with a CatOS-based Catalyst 4000 switch.

The SPAN configuration tasks required for CatOS are similar to Cisco IOS (configure source ports and a destination port), except that a single command (`set span`) is used to specify the source ports, traffic-capture direction, and destination port. The syntax of the `set span` command is listed here:

```
Console> (enable) set span {src_ports | src_vlans}
  dst_port [tx | rx | both] [inpkts enable] create
```

FIGURE 22.6 Example topology for SPAN on a CatOS-based switch

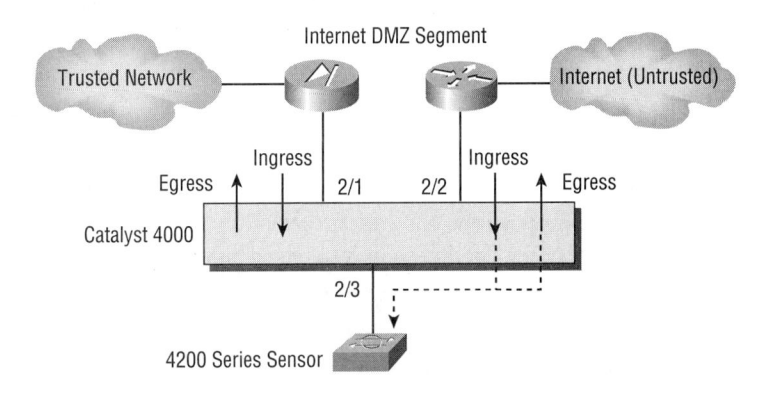

You can specify source ports or source VLANs for the span session and use the **tx**, **rx**, or **both** keyword to define the direction of traffic that is mirrored. The optional `inpkts enable` keywords allow packets received on the destination port to be forwarded by the switch, which is required if you wish to use the sensor's TCP RESET feature.

> **Note:** To remove a SPAN session, use the `set span disable` command.

The following demonstrates configuring a SPAN session on the Catalyst 4000 switch in Figure 22.6, which mirrors traffic sent and received on the interface attached to the Internet router to the sensor (port 2/2). The destination port for the SPAN session (port 2/3) is also configured to accept TCP RESET packets that may be sent by the sensor:

```
Console> (enable) set span 2/2 2/3 both inpkts enable create
SPAN destination port incoming packets enabled.
Enabled monitoring of Port 2/2 transmit/receive traffic by Port 2/3
Console> (enable) show span
---------------------------------------------------------
Destination       : Port 2/3
Admin Source      : Port 2/2
Oper Source       : Port 2/2
Direction         : transmit/receive
Incoming Packets: enabled
Learning          : -
Filter            : -
Status            : active
```

Notice the use of the `show span` command, which can be used to verify your SPAN configuration.

Configuring Traffic Capture Using RSPAN

One major limitation of SPAN is that all source and destination ports must be on the same switch. This means that any network capture devices must be co-located with the devices being monitored, which may cause inconvenience. Remote SPAN (RSPAN) lets you configure a set of source ports on a source switch, map the mirrored traffic to a special VLAN, and then transport all traffic within the VLAN (mirrored traffic) across the layer 2 network to a destination port on a remote destination switch. RSPAN obviously allows for greater flexibility; you can remotely locate network capture devices away from the production equipment being monitored. When you configure SPAN for traffic capture, you must create a SPAN session, which has the following characteristics:

Set of source ports and capture direction Just as for a SPAN session, this defines the source ports from which traffic will be mirrored as well as the direction of traffic that is mirrored; it's referred to as an *RSPAN source session*. One or more RSPAN source sessions can be configured to capture traffic and mirror captured traffic to the RSPAN VLAN. Just as Cisco switches have limitations as to SPAN sessions, so do switches in relation to RSPAN source sessions and RSPAN destination sessions.

A single destination port   The switch on which the destination port for an RSPAN session is located is referred to as having an *RSPAN destination session* configured. This defines the destination port that receives the mirrored traffic from the RSPAN VLAN, for which there can be only one destination port.

Transit switches   With RSPAN, a special type of VLAN is created, which can then be trunked to different parts of the network via existing LAN infrastructure. It's important to understand that all switches in the path between an RSPAN source session and RSPAN destination session *must* be capable of supporting RSPAN.

Figure 22.7 demonstrates how an RSPAN session works. Switch-A is configured with an RSPAN source session, because source ports are defined on Switch-A with traffic sent/received on these ports mirrored to VLAN 100. Traffic from VLAN 100 is then trunked over interswitch trunks, transiting Switch-B and Switch-C until it arrives at Switch-D.

FIGURE 22.7   RSPAN

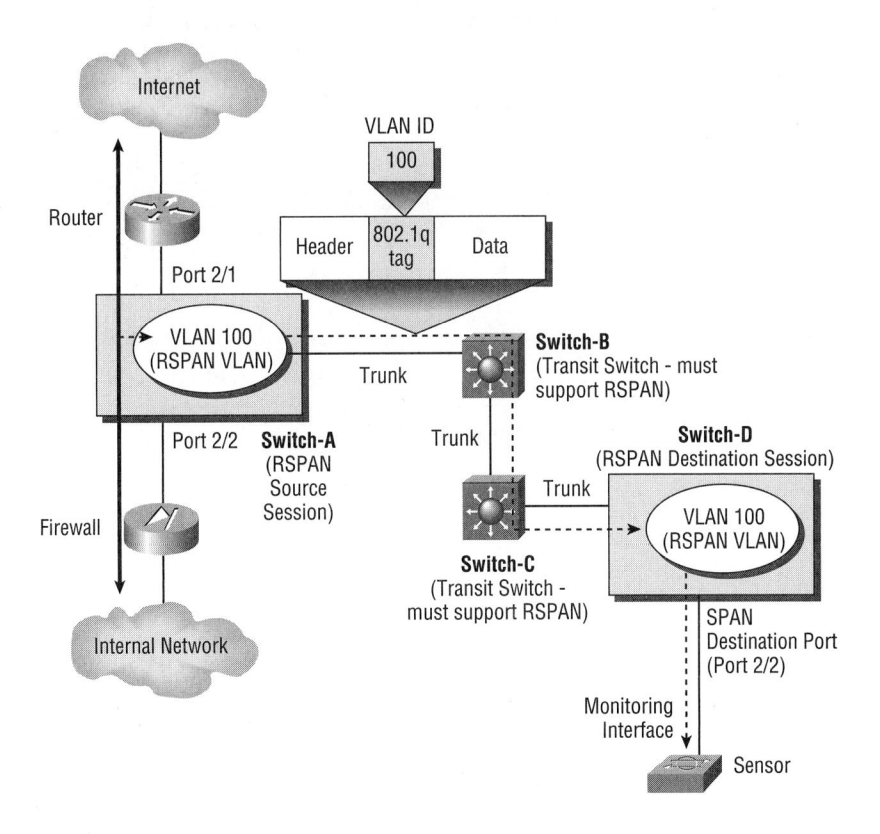

Notice that Figure 22.7 shows how each mirrored frame is transported across the network. An 802.1q tag is inserted into each frame (or an ISL tag is inserted if ISL trunks are used); the tag contains a VLAN ID of 100, identifying the frame as belonging to the RSPAN VLAN. At Switch-D, an RSPAN destination session is configured, where traffic received from VLAN 100 is mirrored out a single destination port.

> **NOTE**
> By default, traffic from all configured VLANs on a switch can be transported across a trunk interface. You can limit the VLANs that are trunked across a trunk—if you do this, you must ensure the RSPAN VLAN is on the list of allowed VLANs for each trunk.

Before configuring RSPAN, you must ensure that you understand the requirements, restrictions, and limitations of RSPAN. The following must be considered before implementing RSPAN:

- Support for RSPAN on Cisco Catalyst switches
- RSPAN session limits

> **NOTE**
> You must also consider other issues that are associated with traditional SPAN, such as whether incoming packets are supported on a destination port (required for TCP RESETS generated by the sensor), whether some form of VLAN tagging information is required, and the destination port subscription. See the earlier discussion of SPAN for more information.

Table 22.3 indicates support for RSPAN and lists the maximum RSPAN sessions that can be run on platforms that support RSPAN.

TABLE 22.3 Cisco Secure IDS Sensor Support for RSPAN

Platform	RSPAN Support	Maximum RSPAN Sessions
Catalyst 2900XL/3500XL	Not supported	—
Catalyst 2950 (Standard Image)	Not supported	—
Catalyst 2950 (Enhanced Image)	IOS 12.1(11)EA1 or higher	1 RSPAN source session and 1 RSPAN destination session[1] or 2 RSPAN destination sessions
Catalyst 3550	IOS 12.1(11)EA1 or higher	2 RSPAN sessions[1] (source or destination)

TABLE 22.3 Cisco Secure IDS Sensor Support for RSPAN *(continued)*

Platform	RSPAN Support	Maximum RSPAN Sessions
Catalyst 4000/4500 (Supervisor I/II)	CatOS 7.5 or higher	5 RSPAN sessions[1] (source or destination)
Catalyst 4000/4500 (Supervisor III/IV)	IDS 12.1(20)EW or higher	2 RSPAN sessions[1] (source or destination)
Catalyst 5000/5500	Not supported	—
Catalyst 6000/6500 (CatOS)	CatOS 5.3 or higher (requires PFC)	1 RSPAN source session[1]; 24 RSPAN destination sessions[2]
Catalyst 6000/6500 (Native IOS)	IOS 12.2(SX) or higher (requires PFC)	1 RSPAN source session[1]; 64 RSPAN destination sessions[2]

[1] A total of *n* x SPAN and RSPAN sessions collectively are supported. For example, if no SPAN sessions are configured on a Catalyst 3550, two RSPAN sessions are supported. If one SPAN session is configured, only one RSPAN session can be configured.
[2] RSPAN destination sessions aren't subject to the SPAN and RSPAN source session limitations.

As you can see in Table 22.3, support for RSPAN is limited and for those switches that support RSPAN, the RSPAN session limitations vary. It's important to understand that any transit switches in an RSPAN session (for example, Switch-B and Switch-C in Figure 22.7) don't use up RSPAN sessions, because RSPAN traffic is propagated via VLAN trunks rather than using RSPAN resources. The only limiting factor for transit switches is the maximum bandwidth available on each trunk that transports traffic from RSPAN sessions.

In the next sections, you'll learn how to configure RSPAN on Cisco IOS and CatOS.

Configuring RSPAN on Cisco IOS

In this section, you'll learn how to configure RSPAN on Cisco IOS–based Catalyst 3550 switches. Figure 22.8 shows a network topology where RSPAN needs to be configured to mirror traffic across a LAN infrastructure to a sensor.

In Figure 22.8, a 4200 series sensor needs to monitor traffic sent across the Internet DMZ segment that Switch-A provides. The sensor is connected to a remote switch (Switch-C), so RSPAN needs to be configured. Switch-A needs to be configured with an RSPAN source session that mirrors traffic sent and received on interface fastEthernet0/2 to a new RSPAN VLAN (VLAN 100). On Switch-C, an RSPAN destination session needs to be configured that mirrors RSPAN traffic received from VLAN 100 to the interface fastEthernet0/2 connected to the sensor. Trunking also needs to be configured on all switches, so that the RSPAN traffic in VLAN 100 is forwarded to Switch-C.

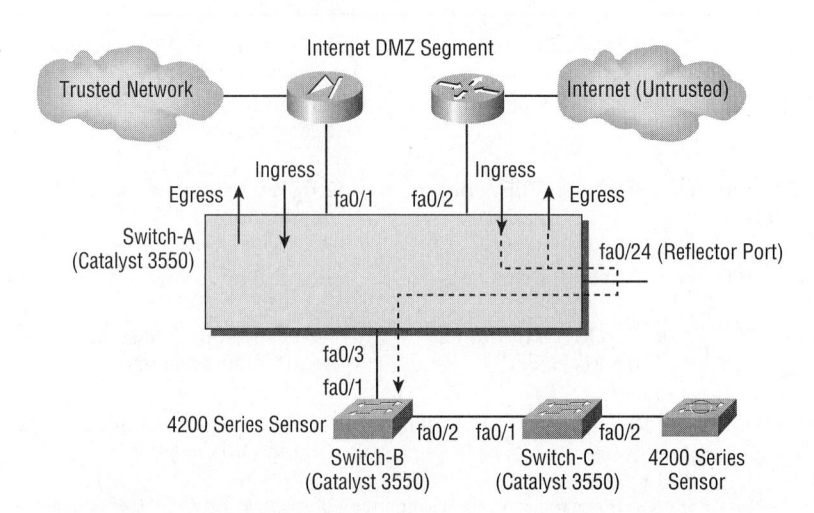

FIGURE 22.8 Example topology for SPAN on Catalyst 3550

To configure RSPAN on Cisco Catalyst switches, the following configuration tasks are required:

1. Create an RSPAN VLAN.
2. Configure trunking.
3. Configure an RSPAN source session.
4. Configure an RSPAN destination session.

Creating an RSPAN VLAN

A key requirement for RSPAN is that a separate VLAN is necessary for each RSPAN session that will transport traffic captured from an RSPAN source session. On Cisco Catalyst switches, an RSPAN VLAN is a special type of VLAN with properties specific to RSPAN operation; hence all switches that transport RSPAN VLAN traffic must support RSPAN. To create an RSPAN VLAN on Cisco IOS, you must use the `vlan` global configuration command as demonstrated here:

```
Switch-A(config)# vlan 100
Switch-A(config-vlan)# remote-span
Switch-A(config-vlan)# end
Switch-A# show vlan remote-span
Remote SPAN VLANs
------------------------------------------------------------------
100
```

> **Note:** To create VLANs on a switch, the switch must be configured in VTP server or transparent mode, which is achieved using the `vtp mode` global configuration command. Also, you can't create RSPAN VLANs using the older VLAN database configuration mode, which is accessed using the `vlan database` command from privileged mode access (Switch# `vlan database`).

In the previous configuration, the `vlan 100` command creates a new VLAN with an ID of 100; the subsequent `remote-span` command configures VLAN 100 as an RSPAN VLAN. Notice that the `show vlan remote-span` command can then be used to display all current RSPAN VLANs.

To support RSPAN across a distributed LAN infrastructure, the RSPAN VLANs used for RSPAN sessions must be configured on all RSPAN source and destination switches, as well as any transit switches. If you're using VLAN trunk protocol (VTP), you can create the RSPAN VLANs on your VTP server switches, which will then automatically propagate the new RSPAN VLANs to each of your VTP client switches. If you aren't using VTP, you must explicitly create the appropriate RSPAN VLANs on each switch. Therefore, in Figure 22.8, assuming VTP isn't being used, the RSPAN VLAN created on Switch-A must also be created on Switch-B and Switch-C:

```
Switch-B(config)# vlan 100
Switch-B(config-vlan)# remote-span

Switch-C(config)# vlan 100
Switch-C(config-vlan)# remote-span
```

Configuring Trunking

In a distributed LAN infrastructure, the interswitch connections that connect each switch are referred to as *trunks*. A trunk is different from a switch port that is connected to a host, in that it carries traffic from multiple VLANs rather than traffic from a single VLAN. Because RSPAN VLANs don't carry user traffic (only traffic mirrored from an RSPAN source session), a trunk is normally required between each switch to enable transportation of user and data VLANs as well as RSPAN VLANs.

By default, when you connect a Cisco IOS–based Catalyst switch to another Cisco IOS–based or CatOS-based Catalyst switch, a trunk forms with all VLANs being transported across the trunk. Dynamic Trunking Protocol (DTP) enables Cisco switches to detect connections to other Cisco switches and form a trunk if appropriate. DTP operates in several different modes; the default DTP mode of operation on Cisco IOS–based Catalyst switches is called *desirable mode*. In desirable mode, the switch actively tries to negotiate a trunk, so if another Cisco IOS–based Catalyst switch is connected, a trunk will form as they both try to actively negotiate a trunk.

> **TIP:** When configured in desirable or auto mode, a trunk forms only if the VTP domain names configured on each switch are identical.

If you need to force an interface to always become a trunk, you can use the `switchport` interface configuration command as demonstrated on Switch-A and Switch-B here:

```
Switch-A(config)# interface fastEthernet 0/3
Switch-A(config-if)# switchport trunk encapsulation dot1q
Switch-A(config-if)# switchport mode trunk

Switch-B(config)# interface fastEthernet 0/1
Switch-B(config-if)# switchport trunk encapsulation dot1q
Switch-B(config-if)# switchport mode trunk
```

In this example, the `switchport mode trunk` command configures the interface on each switch to always trunk. However, before you can configure this command, you must hardcode the trunk encapsulation to 802.1q or ISL using the `switchport trunk encapsulation dot1q` command or the `switchport trunk encapsulation dot1q` command.

Configuring an RSPAN Source Session

Once you've configured an RSPAN VLAN and ensured that trunks are in place so RSPAN traffic can be transported across the network, you can begin the configuration of an RSPAN session. An RSPAN session includes an RSPAN source session, which is configured on the switch from which traffic is being mirrored, as well as an RSPAN destination session, which is configured on the switch to which a network capture device is attached.

To configure an RSPAN source session, you must perform the following tasks:

1. Define one or more source ports or VLANs.
2. Define a destination of the RSPAN VLAN and specify a reflector port.

The syntax for defining one or more source ports or VLANs is identical to the syntax used to specify source ports or VLANs for a SPAN session. To define a destination of an RSPAN VLAN and to specify a reflector port, you use the `monitor session` command with the following syntax:

```
Switch(config)# monitor session session-id destination remote vlan
  rspan-vlan reflector-port interface-type interface-id
```

It's important to understand that the reflector port must be an unused physical interface on the switch; after being configured as a reflector port, it won't forward any traffic it may receive if a device connects to it. The following demonstrates configuring an RSPAN source session on Switch-A in Figure 22.8, defining traffic sent and receiving on interface `fastEthernet0/2` for the source port, and mirroring that traffic to the RSPAN VLAN 100 using a reflector port of interface fastEthernet0/24:

```
Switch-A(config)# monitor session 1 source interface fastEthernet 0/2 both
Switch-A(config)# monitor session 1 destination remote vlan 100
  reflector-port fastEthernet 0/24
Switch-A(config)# exit
Switch-A# show monitor
Session 1
---------
Type                 : Remote Source Session
Source Ports         :
    Both             : Fa0/2
Reflector Port       : Fa0/24
Dest RSPAN VLAN      : 100
```

In this example, after configuring the RSPAN source session, the `show monitor` command verifies the configuration of the new RSPAN session.

Configuring an RSPAN Destination Session

The final task required to configure an RSPAN session is to configure an RSPAN destination session on the switch to which a network capture device, such as an IDS sensor, is attached. To configure an RSPAN destination session, you must perform the following tasks:

1. Define the RSPAN VLAN as a source for the RSPAN destination session.
2. Define the destination port to which all traffic received from the RSPAN VLAN should be mirrored.

The syntax for defining the RSPAN VLAN as a source for an RSPAN destination session is as follows:

```
Switch(config)# monitor session session-id source remote vlan rspan-vlan
```

After defining the source RSPAN VLAN, you next define a destination port, which has the same syntax used to specify a destination port for a SPAN session. The following demonstrates configuring an RSPAN destination session on Switch-C in Figure 22.8, mirroring traffic received on VLAN 100 to the interface attached to the sensor, and ensuring the sensor can still send TCP RESET packets on VLAN 1.

```
Switch-C(config)# monitor session 1 source remote vlan 100
Switch-C(config)# monitor session 1 destination interface fastEthernet
  0/2 ingress vlan 1
Switch-C(config)# exit
```

```
Switch-C# show monitor
Session 1
---------
Type                   : Remote Destination Session
Source RSPAN VLAN      : 100
Destination Ports      : Fa0/2
    Encapsulation: Native
        Ingress: Enabled, default VLAN = 1
```

Configuring RSPAN on CatOS

In this section, you'll learn how to configure RSPAN on CatOS-based Catalyst 3550 switches. Figure 22.9 shows the same network topology as Figure 22.8, except this time each Cisco Catalyst 3550 switch has been replaced with a Catalyst 4000 switch running the CatOS operating system.

To configure RSPAN on CatOS-based Catalyst switches, the same configuration tasks required on Cisco IOS are also necessary:

1. Create an RSPAN VLAN.
2. Configure trunking.
3. Configure an RSPAN source session.
4. Configure an RSPAN destination session.

FIGURE 22.9 Example topology for configuring RSPAN on CatOS

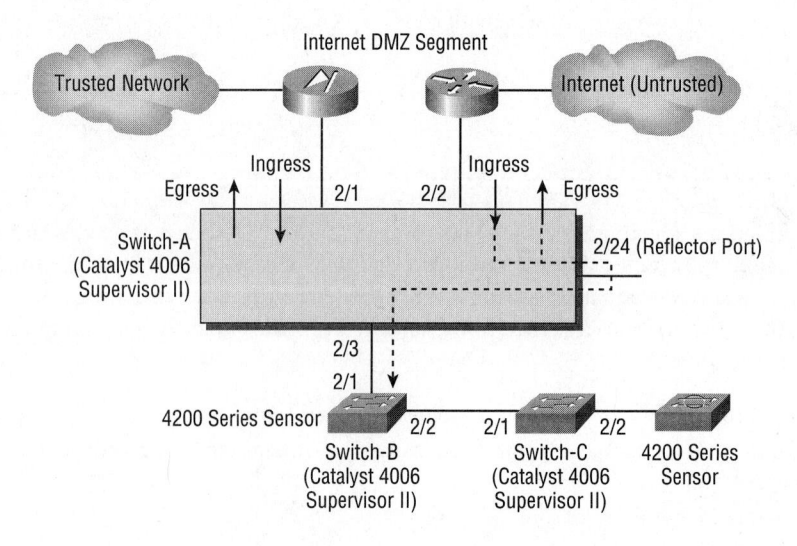

Creating an RSPAN VLAN

To create an RSPAN VLAN on CatOS, you must use the `set vlan` configuration command as demonstrated here:

```
Switch-A> (enable) set vlan 100 rspan
vlan 100 configuration successful
```

In this configuration, the `set vlan 100` command creates a new VLAN with an ID of 100; the `rspan` keyword indicates that VLAN 100 is an RSPAN VLAN.

To support RSPAN across a distributed LAN infrastructure, the RSPAN VLANs used for RSPAN sessions must be configured on all RSPAN source and destination switches as well as any transit switches. Assuming VTP isn't used, this means that the RSPAN VLAN created on Switch-A must also be created on Switch-B and Switch-C in the same fashion.

Configuring Trunking

As you've already learned, trunks are normally required for the interswitch connections between each switch that will transport RSPAN VLAN traffic. Unlike for Cisco IOS, when you connect a CatOS-based Catalyst switch to another CatOS-based Catalyst switch, a trunk will *not* form. This is because all switch ports on a CatOS-based switch operate in *auto mode* by default, which means the switch port forms a trunk only if the remote switch actively attempts to form the trunk. If both ends are configured in auto mode, a trunk can't form because neither switch port attempts to actively form the trunk.

> **NOTE** If you connect a Cisco IOS–based Catalyst switch to a CatOS-based Catalyst switch, by default a trunk will form, because the Cisco IOS–based Catalyst switch actively attempts to form a trunk (it's configured with a DTP mode of desirable).

The default trunking behavior of CatOS-based Catalyst switches means that each of the switches in Figure 22.9 needs to be configured so that each port connected to another switch forms a trunk. If you need to configure a port for trunking, you can use the `set trunk` command:

```
Console> (enable) set trunk module/port(s)
  {on | off | desirable | auto | nonegotiate}
```

The `on` keyword configures the specified port to always form a trunk, and the `off` keyword disables trunking. The `nonegotiate` keyword configures the specified port to always form a trunk and also to never send any DTP frames (useful for connecting to third-party switches). The following example demonstrates forcing a trunk to always form between Switch-A and Switch-B:

```
Switch-A> (enable) set trunk 2/3 on
Port(s)  2/3 trunk mode set to on.
```

```
Switch-B> (enable) set trunk 2/1 on
Port(s)  2/1 trunk mode set to on.
```

In Figure 22.9, Switch-B and Switch-C must also be configured to form a trunk between each other, as demonstrated here:

```
Switch-B> (enable) set trunk 2/2 on
Port(s)  2/2 trunk mode set to on.
```

```
Switch-C> (enable) set trunk 2/1 on
Port(s)  2/1 trunk mode set to on.
```

Configuring an RSPAN Source Session

To configure an RSPAN source session on CatOS, you must perform configuration tasks similar to those for Cisco IOS:

1. Define one or more source ports or VLANs.
2. Define a destination of the RSPAN VLAN, and specify a reflector port.

> **NOTE:** You don't need to configure a reflector port on Catalyst 6000/6500 switches, although you must on all other CatOS-based switches.

On CatOS, both of the previous configuration tasks can be completed using the set rspan source command, which is used to define RSPAN source sessions on CatOS:

```
Console> (enable) set rspan source {mod/port(s) | vlan-id(s)}
  rspan-vlan reflector mod/port [rx | tx | both] [create]
```

As for Cisco IOS–based switches, the reflector port must be an unused physical interface on the switch; after it's configured as a reflector port, it won't forward any traffic it may receive if a device connects to it. The following demonstrates configuring an RSPAN source session on Switch-A in Figure 22.9, defining traffic sent and receiving on port 2/2 for the source port, and mirroring that traffic to the RSPAN VLAN 100 using a reflector port of 2/24:

```
Switch-A> (enable) set rspan source 2/2 100 reflector 2/24 both create
Rspan Type   : Source
Destination  : -
Reflector    : Port 2/24
Rspan Vlan   : 100
Admin Source : Port 2/2
Oper Source  : Port 2/2
Direction    : both
```

```
Incoming Packets: -
Learning : -
Filter : -
Status : active
```

Configuring an RSPAN Destination Session

The final task required to configure an RSPAN session is to configure an RSPAN destination session on the switch to which a network capture device, such as an IDS sensor, is attached. To configure an RSPAN destination session on CatOS, you use the set rspan destination command to specify the destination port, the RSPAN VLAN from which traffic is received, and whether the switch should forward packets received on the destination port. The set rspan destination command has the following syntax:

```
Console> (enable) set rspan destination mod/port rspan-vlan
  [inpkts enable] [create]
```

The following demonstrates configuring an RSPAN destination session on Switch-C in Figure 22.9 and defining traffic received on VLAN 100 from Switch-B to be mirrored to port 2/2 attached to the sensor:

```
Switch-C> (enable) set rspan destination 2/2 100 inpkts enable create
Rspan Type : Destination
Destination : Port 2/2
Rspan Vlan : 100
Admin Source : -
Oper Source : -
Direction : -
Incoming Packets: enabled
Learning : enabled
Filter : -
Status : active
```

Configuring Traffic Capture for the IDSM

In order for the IDSM-2 to capture traffic for analysis, it must possess a network interface that allows capture of traffic. Figure 22.10 shows the internal architecture of the IDSM-2.

Figure 22.10 shows that the network interfaces of the IDSM-2 are internal and connect directly to the Catalyst 6000/6500 backplane. Each interface is a virtual interface that is part of the physical connection to the Catalyst 6000/6500 backplane.

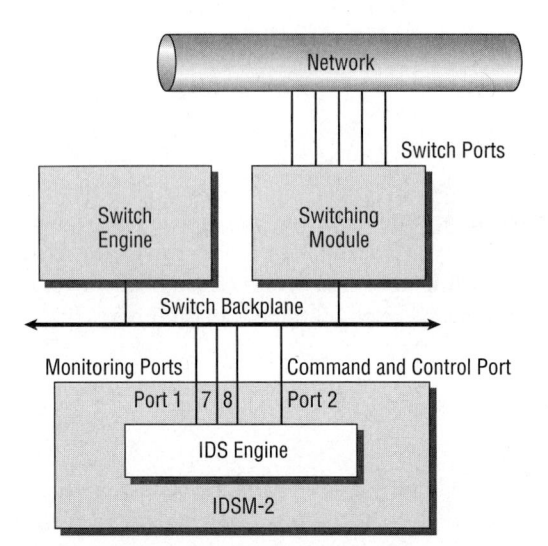

FIGURE 22.10   IDSM-2 internal architecture

The IDSM-2 includes the following interfaces:

Sensing interfaces   As shown in Figure 22.10, the IDSM-2 possesses three sensing interfaces (port 1, port 7, and port 8). Port 7 and port 8 are the main sensing interfaces and are used for capturing and analyzing traffic, whereas port 1 is only used for generating TCP RESETs in response to a detected attack. Each sensing interface is a trunking port, which allows it to receive traffic from multiple VLANs.

> **NOTE**   The numbering described in Figure 22.10 is specific to the CatOS operating system. If the switch is running Cisco IOS, the main sensing interfaces (port 7 and port 8 in Figure 22.10) are referred to as data-capture ports 1 and 2, respectively.

Command-and-control port   This is referred to as port 2 on the IDSM-2. This port provides the management interface (and is hence assigned an IP address) for the sensor application, allowing communications with sensor management platforms.

When you install the IDSM-2 module, you place it into a free slot that has a module number. For example, you might install the IDSM-2 into module 2. Each of the IDSM-2 ports is accessed by the switch using the same *module/port* designation used by the Catalyst 6000 switch. For example, if your IDSM-2 is installed in module 2, the sensing interfaces are identified as port 2/1, 2/7, and 2/8 to the switch, and the command-and-control port is identified as port 2/2 to the switch.

As you can see in Figure 22.10, the IDSM-2 has the same types of ports (interfaces) as the 4200 series sensors; however, the ports aren't visible and are internally connected to the

Catalyst 6000/6500 switch backplane. All traffic is captured off the switch backplane, and the IDSM-2 can monitor up to 600Mbps of traffic. Figure 22.11 illustrates how traffic is captured with the IDSM-2.

In Figure 22.11, a couple of hosts attached to a Catalyst 6000 switch are communicating. The data is switched over the switch backplane, and that data is mirrored to the IDSM-2 for analysis. If an alarm is detected, the alarm notification is sent out the command-and-control port and then forwarded out the appropriate port to the sensor event-management platform.

As you learned earlier in the chapter, when the 4200 series sensor is connected to a switched environment, you must use the SPAN feature on the switch connected to the sensing interface to mirror VLAN traffic to the sensor. Because the IDSM-2 is internally connected to a switch, you would expect that SPAN would also be used to mirror traffic to the IDSM-2 sensing interface. The IDSM-2 can use SPAN for traffic capture, but alternatively it can use VACL capture to monitor traffic.

VACLs allow layer 3 and 4 access controls to be applied to traffic on an entire VLAN basis. You can restrict IP traffic that flows within a VLAN based on the following:

- IP protocol type
- Source and destination IP addresses
- Source and destination TCP or UDP ports
- Combinations of the above

FIGURE 22.11 IDSM-2 traffic flow

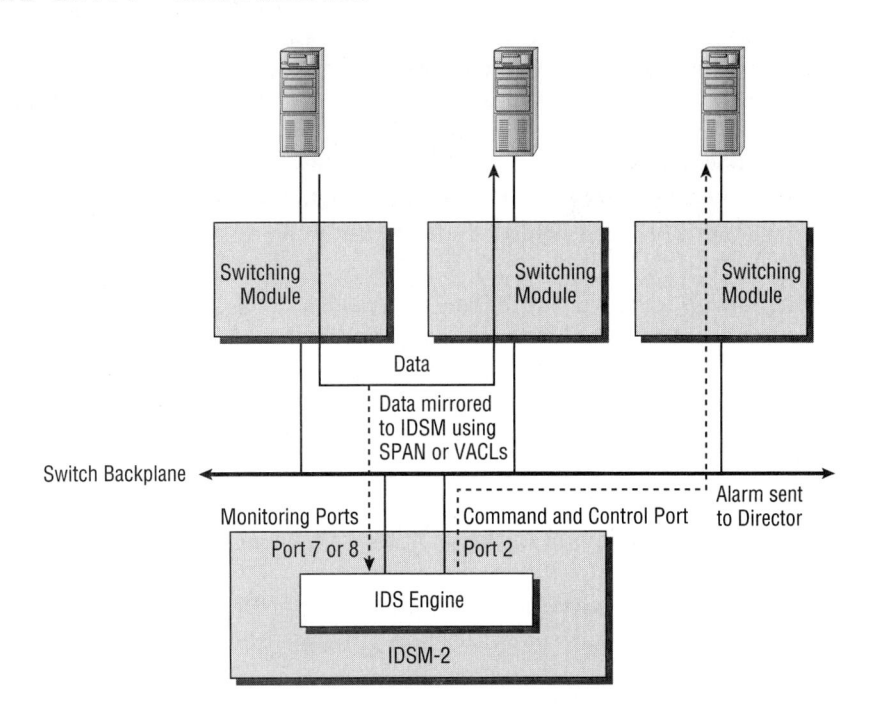

VACLs require the Catalyst 6000/6500 to have a *policy feature card* (PFC) installed. The PFC allows VACLs to be stored in ternary content-addressable memory (TCAM), which is a specialized memory structure that lets traffic be inspected against access control lists in hardware (at wire speed) rather than in software. This means that a Catalyst 6000/6500 with a PFC installed can apply access control via VACLs with no performance degradation.

VACLs also include a feature that lets you capture permitted traffic, where the permitted traffic is forwarded normally but is also mirrored to a capture list (a set of ports). If you add the IDSM-2 sensing interface to the capture list, you can analyze the traffic for intrusive activity. Only a single VACL per protocol (for example, IP or IPX) can be applied to a single VLAN. For the IDSM, this means that only a single IP VACL can be applied per VLAN. However, you can apply the same IP VACL to multiple VLANs. Figure 22.12 illustrates using VACLs to capture traffic for IDSM-2 analysis.

In Figure 22.12, incoming traffic into a particular VLAN is inspected using the shown VACL. If the packet matches the first statement (which permits web traffic), then the packet is forwarded *and* mirrored to the IDSM-2. This happens because the first statement specifies the `capture` keyword, which tells the switch to capture the traffic for the IDSM-2. Notice that traffic matching any `permit` statements that don't use the `capture` keyword is forwarded and isn't also passed to the IDSM-2 for analysis. Any traffic that is denied by the VACL is dropped and is also not passed to the IDSM-2.

Using VACLs to capture traffic for IDS analysis overcomes limitations of SPAN, which include the following:

Selective traffic monitoring With SPAN, *all* traffic sent, received, or sent and received is mirrored to the IDS sensor. SPAN provides no mechanism to selectively mirror certain types of traffic based on layer 3 or 4 parameters of the traffic. VACLs let you selectively capture traffic so that only permitted traffic is forwarded to the IDS sensor. This is important because the IDSM-2 can process a finite amount of traffic, and using SPAN with a set of source ports whose bandwidth sum exceeds the processing capability of the sensor means intrusive activity may be missed by the sensor. By using VACLs, you can selectively filter only certain types of traffic, allowing you to control the amount of traffic the IDS sensor must analyze.

SPAN session limitations Because the Catalyst 6000/6500 switch has SPAN session limits, you may be restricted in your IDS monitoring capabilities if you use SPAN. For example, you might install two IDSMs into a single Catalyst 6000/6500 switch, because you need to monitor more than 600Mbps of traffic. Assuming you're mirroring received traffic for both sessions, you've reached the SPAN session limits of the switch. You might also have a network probe that requires a SPAN session to capture traffic for network performance analysis. If you want to capture received traffic on the probe, this isn't possible because your SPAN session limits have been reached. You don't need to worry about SPAN session limitations when using VACLs.

Now that you've been introduced to the concepts of capturing traffic for the IDSM-2, it's time to learn how to configure Cisco Catalyst 6000/6500 switches to capture traffic using SPAN and VACLs.

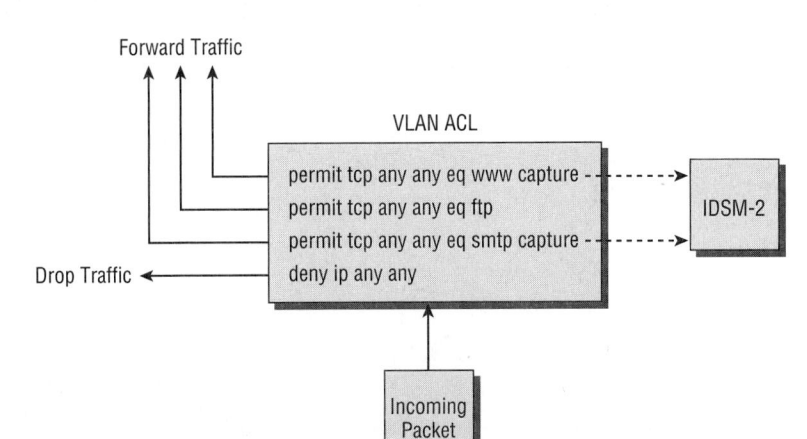

FIGURE 22.12 Using VACLs to capture traffic

Configuring SPAN for the IDSM-2

As listed in Table 22.1, traffic capture using either SPAN or VLAN access control lists (VACLs) is supported for the IDSM-2. Cisco Catalyst 6000/6500 switches run on either CatOS or Cisco IOS, and the configuration procedures vary for each operating system. In this section, you'll learn how to configure SPAN for the IDSM-2, for Catalyst 6000/6500 switches using CatOS and Cisco IOS.

> Depending on the Catalyst 6000 Supervisor module installed, if you use a SPAN session that monitors traffic in both the receive and transmit directions, you may get duplicates of the same packet forwarded to the IDSM-2. This will result in twice the number of alarms. This is a problem for the WS-X6K-SUP1A-PFC and WS-X6K-SUP1A-MSFC supervisor modules.

Configuring SPAN on CatOS

Configuring SPAN on CatOS-based Catalyst 6000/6500 switches for the IDSM-2 is identical to configuring SPAN for externally attached 4200 series sensors. The only configuration parameter that is different is the destination port, which must be one of the sensing interfaces on the IDSM-2. On CatOS, the two IDSM-2 sensing interfaces are represented to the switch operating system as *slot-number*/7 and *slot-number*/8, where *slot-number* represents the slot in which the IDSM-2 is installed. For example, if an IDSM-2 is installed in slot 4, the sensing interfaces are represented as 4/7 and 4/8 to the switch. To configure SPAN correctly, either of these ports must be used as a destination port for the SPAN session.

Figure 22.13 shows an example topology where an Internet DMZ needs to be monitored by an IDSM-2 installed in slot 3 of a Catalyst 6500 switch that provides LAN connectivity for the Internet DMZ.

In Figure 22.13, notice that the IDSM-2 sensing interfaces are attached to the switching backplane, which allows any traffic transported over the backplane to be mirrored to the IDSM-2. The following example demonstrates the configuration required to use SPAN to mirror traffic received on ports 2/1 and 2/2 to the first IDSM-2 sensing interface:

```
Console> (enable) set span 2/1-2 3/7 rx inpkts enable create
SPAN destination port incoming packets enabled.
Enabled monitoring of Ports 2/1-2 receive traffic by Port 3/7
```

FIGURE 22.13 Example topology for configuring SPAN on a CatOS-based Catalyst 6000/6500 switch with IDSM-2

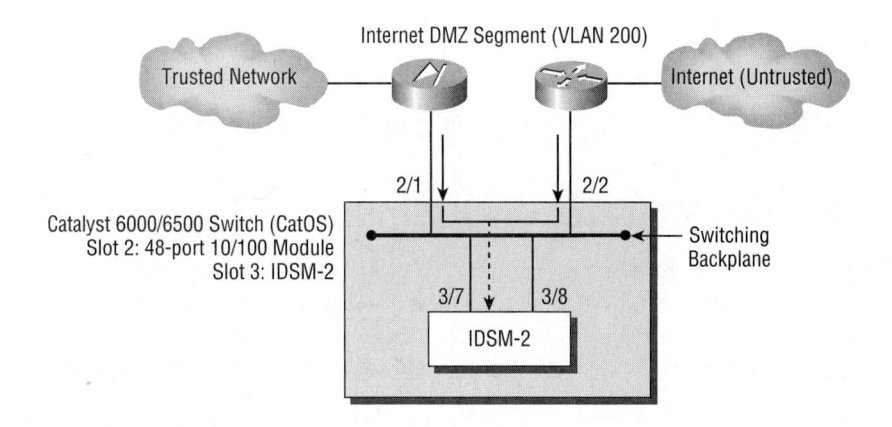

Configuring SPAN on Cisco IOS

Configuring SPAN on Cisco IOS–based Catalyst 6000/6500 switches for the IDSM-2 is slightly different than configuring SPAN on other Catalyst switches for externally attached 4200 series sensors. This is because the IOS operating system image for the Catalyst 6000/6500 switch has special support for the IDSM-2, since it's an integrated component of the switch.

To configure SPAN on Cisco IOS–based Catalyst 6000/6500 switches for the IDSM-2, you must configure the source interfaces/VLANs and destination interfaces for the session separately. To configure the source interfaces/VLANs, you use the same `monitor session source` command used on other Cisco IOS–based interfaces (discussed earlier in this chapter). To configure the destination interface, the syntax varies slightly from that which is used on other Cisco IOS–based Catalyst switches, as shown here:

```
Router(config)# monitor session session-id destination intrusion-
    detection-module slot-number data-port sensing-interface-number
```

Notice that the `intrusion-detection-module` keyword is used, and that you must specify which sensing interface is to be the destination interface using the `data-port` keyword.

> **WARNING** The sensing interfaces on the IDSM-2 are represented as data-port #1 and data-port #2, not as #7 and #8 as you might think based on the port numbering used on CatOS.

The following demonstrates configuring SPAN on the switch in Figure 22.13, assuming it's running Cisco IOS:

```
Router(config)# monitor session 1 source interface 2/1 rx
Router(config)# monitor session 1 source interface 2/2 rx
Router(config)# monitor session 1 destination intrusion-detection-
  module 3 data-port 1
```

In this example, the first two commands add interfaces 2/1 and 2/2 as source interfaces. The last command configures data-port #1 of the IDSM-2 installed in slot 3 as the destination interface.

Configuring Traffic Capture Using VACLs

The second traffic-capture mechanism available for the IDSM-2 is to use VACLs. Using VACLs to mirror traffic to your IDSM-2 lets you select which traffic you wish to mirror based on layer 2, layer 3, and/or layer 4 characteristics of the traffic. For example, you might want to capture only web traffic on a VLAN that has web servers attached, and VACLs allow the granularity to be able to do this. Compare this with SPAN, where you can only capture *all* traffic sent/received on a particular port or VLAN.

The use of VACLs requires the Catalyst 6000/6500 Supervisor engine (a line card that contains the main CPU of the switch) to have a policy feature card (PFC) installed. If you don't have a PFC installed, you can't use VACLs.

> **NOTE** The policy feature card adds layer 3/4 intelligence to Catalyst 6000/6500 switches, allowing the switch to filter layer 3/4 traffic for security purposes and also classify layer 3/4 traffic for quality of service purposes.

VACLs filter any traffic entering a specific VLAN to which the VACL is applied, with filtering based on *access control entries* (ACEs). Each ACE defines a specific type of traffic (such as web traffic or FTP traffic sent to a specific host) and lets you optionally specify a capture option that will mirror any traffic that matches the ACE to a capture port. You'll now learn how to configure VACLs on CatOS and Cisco IOS-based Catalyst 6000/6500 switches.

Configuring VACLs on CatOS

To configure VACLs on CatOS, you must perform the following steps:

1. Create a VACL that defines interesting traffic.
2. Commit the VACL to PFC memory.

3. Map the VACL to a VLAN.
4. Add the IDSM-2 sensing interface to the VACL capture list.

Because VACLs are more complex to configure than SPAN, a full VACL configuration example is included at the end of this section.

Creating a VACL

A VACL is identified by a name and can hold many entries that are known as ACEs. Each ACE defines a particular type of traffic that has certain layer 3 and layer 4 characteristics. To create a VACL, you use the `set security acl ip` command on the switch (not the IDSM). The syntax of the `set security acl ip` command depends on which layer 3 or layer 4 characteristics you specify. Here are some examples of VACLs:

```
set security acl ip TEST_VACL1 permit 192.168.1.0
  255.255.255.0 capture
set security acl ip TEST_VACL2 permit ip 10.0.0.0
  255.0.0.0 20.0.0.0 255.0.0.0 capture
set security acl ip TEST_VACL3 permit icmp 10.0.0.0
  255.0.0.0 20.0.0.0 255.0.0.0 echo capture
set security acl ip TEST_VACL3 permit tcp 10.0.0.0
  255.0.0.0 20.0.0.0 255.0.0.0 eq 80 capture
set security acl ip TEST_VACL4 permit udp host 10.1.1.1
  gt 1024 any eq 53 capture
```

Notice that each VACL ACE includes the **capture** keyword, which specifies that any traffic that matches the VACL ACE should be forwarded to the capture port list. It's crucial that you understand that the **capture** keyword is required to mirror traffic that matches the respective ACE. In the previous example, there are four VACLs:

- TEST_VACL1 allows any IP traffic from a source IP address that resides within the 192.168.1.0/24 subnet (such as 192.168.1.0–192.168.1.255).
- TEST_VACL2 allows any IP traffic from a source IP address that resides within the 10.0.0.0/8 subnet destined to the 20.0.0.0/8 subnet.
- TEST_VACL3 allows any ICMP traffic from a source IP address that resides within the 10.0.0.0/8 subnet destined to the 20.0.0.0/8 subnet. The VACL also has an ACE that allows any TCP web traffic from a client on the 10.0.0.0/8 subnet to a web server on the 20.0.0.0/8 subnet.
- TEST_VACL4 allows UDP DNS traffic from a DNS client at 10.1.1.1 destined to any DNS server. The DNS client must use a source port of greater than 1024. Notice the use of the **host** keyword to specify a single IP address and the **any** keyword to specify all IP addresses.

> **NOTE** You may notice that TEST_VACL1 doesn't include the `ip` keyword. This keyword isn't required for strictly IP traffic.

In each VACL, an implicit `deny any any` blocks any other traffic that isn't matched by the VACL.

Committing the VACL to PFC Memory

Once you've created your VACL, although the VACL is automatically stored in the switch NVRAM, you must manually commit the VACL to the PFC hardware. This loads the VACL into a special memory structure (the TCAM) on the PFC that allows the PFC to apply the VACL to traffic at wire speed, incurring no performance penalties.

To commit the VACL to hardware, use the `commit security acl` command from the switch (not the IDSM):

```
Console> (enable) commit security acl vacl_name | all
```

You can commit a specific VACL by specifying the VACL name, or you can commit all VACLs to hardware by specifying the `all` keyword.

Mapping the VACL to a VLAN

Now that your VACL has been created and committed to hardware, you can apply the VACL to one or more VLANs. By applying the VACL to a VLAN, you immediately start filtering traffic on the VLAN based on the VACL.

WARNING Be aware that the primary purpose of a VACL is to filter traffic. When using VACLs for IDS traffic capture, don't forget that a VACL is also filtering traffic. If you wish to only capture specific traffic, rather than filter it, add a `permit ip any any` ACE at the end of the VACL to override the implicit `deny any any` action. By using the capture keyword with specific ACEs above this `permit ip any any` ACE, you can control which traffic is monitored by the IDS, yet still permit all traffic through the VLAN.

As explained earlier, a single VLAN can have only a single VACL applied per protocol at any time. Because Cisco Secure IDS monitors only IP traffic, this means that each VLAN can have only a single IP VACL applied. However, you can map a VACL to multiple VLANs.

To map a VACL to a VLAN, use the `set security acl map` command from the switch:

```
Console> (enable) set security acl map vacl_name vlans
```

Adding the IDSM-2 Sensing Interface to the VACL Capture List

When you specify the `capture` keyword on a VACL ACE, any traffic that matches that ACE is mirrored to the VACL capture list. The VACL capture list is a list of switch ports to which any traffic captured by a VACL is mirrored. When an IDSM-2 is present in the system, the sensing interface on the IDSM-2 is automatically configured as the default destination capture port for all captured VACL traffic.

You can add other ports to the capture list by using the `set security acl capture-ports` command:

```
set security acl capture-ports module/ports
```

A VACL Capture Example for CatOS

Suppose that we have the sample network topology shown earlier in Figure 22.13. We wish to monitor only web and mail traffic (HTTP and SMTP) on the Internet DMZ segment but still permit other traffic without passing it to the IDSM-2 for analysis. First, we must create a VACL that specifies to capture only web and e-mail traffic and permits all other traffic without capturing it:

```
Console> (enable) set security acl ip TEST permit tcp
  any any eq 80 capture
TEST editbuffer modified.  Use 'commit' command to
  apply changes.
Console> (enable) set security acl ip TEST permit tcp
  any any eq 25 capture
TEST editbuffer modified.  Use 'commit' command to
  apply changes.
Console> (enable) set security acl ip TEST permit ip
  any any
TEST editbuffer modified.  Use 'commit' command to
  apply changes.
```

Notice that we use the `capture` keyword at the end of the ACEs that define web and mail traffic, but we omit the `capture` keyword on the `permit any any` ACE to capture only web and mail traffic.

The next step is to commit the VACL to hardware:

```
Console> (enable) commit security acl TEST
Hardware programming in progress...
ACL TEST is committed to hardware.
```

Now we must map the VACL to the Internet DMZ VLAN (200), using the `set security acl map` command:

```
Console> (enable) set security acl map TEST 200
ACL TEST mapped to vlan 200
```

Finally, we must assign the IDSM-2 sensing interface to the VACL capture list. We don't actually need to do this, because the IDSM-2 sensing interface is automatically assigned to the VACL capture list when the IDSM-2 is installed. However, for demonstration purposes, the following shows how to assign the IDSM-2 sensing interface (`port 3/7`) to the VACL capture list:

```
Console> (enable) set security acl capture-ports 3/7
Successfully set 3/7 to capture ACL traffic.
```

Configuring VACLs on Cisco IOS

Configuring VACLs on Cisco IOS is slightly different in concept than doing so on CatOS, due to differences in the command syntax and structure. To configure VACLs on Cisco IOS, you must perform the following steps:

1. Create an access control list that defines interesting traffic.
2. Create a VLAN access map that references the appropriate access control list(s).
3. Apply the VLAN access map to a VLAN.
4. Configure the IDSM-2 sensing interfaces as capture ports.

Creating an Access Control List

An access control list (ACL) is similar to a VACL on CatOS, in that it includes ACEs that define a particular type of traffic based on layer 3 and layer 4 characteristics. When used in conjunction with VACLs on Cisco IOS, ACLs are purely used for classification purposes, because another entity called a VLAN access map (discussed later) determines whether the traffic classified by an ACL should be permitted and/or captured.

To create an ACL, you can use either the `access-list` or `ip access-list` global configuration command. The following example demonstrates creating an ACL that classifies HTTP and FTP traffic:

```
Router# configure terminal
Router(config)# ip access-list extended WEB_FTP
Router(config-ext-nacl)# permit any any eq www
Router(config-ext-nacl)# permit any any eq ftp
Router(config-ext-nacl)# permit any any eq ftp-data
```

Creating a VLAN Access Map

After you've created the appropriate ACLs that define the traffic you wish to capture, you next need to create a VLAN access map that defines whether traffic classified within your ACLs should be forwarded, dropped, and/or captured.

A VLAN access map consists of multiple entries—when a packet is analyzed against a VLAN access map, each entry in the VLAN access map is read until the packet is matched to an entry, at which point the action defined in the VLAN access map entry is executed. To create a VLAN access map, you must create a VLAN access map entry, which is created using the `vlan access-map` global configuration command:

```
Router(config)# vlan access-map map-name seq-number
```

The *seq-number* parameter can be any value from 0 to 65535 and identifies a specific entry in the VLAN access map. The sequence number also defines an entry's relative position in the access map to other entries. Each VLAN access map is processed starting from the entry with the lowest sequence number to the entry with the highest sequence number until a match is made. Once you've created a VLAN access-map entry, you next need to reference an ACL that classifies the traffic you wish to match and define the action that should take place for packets that match the ACL:

```
Router(config-access-map)# match ip address acl-id
Router(config-access-map)# action {forward | deny} [capture]
```

Notice that you can specify an action of forward or deny and optionally specify an action of capture. Specifying an action of capture means matching traffic will be mirrored to the VACL capture ports.

The following example demonstrates creating a VLAN access map that ensures that all HTTP and FTP traffic is forwarded and captured and all other traffic is forwarded only.

```
Router# configure terminal
Router(config)# vlan access-map IDS 10
Router(config-access-map)# match ip address WEB_FTP
Router(config-access-map)# action forward capture
Router(config-access-map)# exit
Router(config)# vlan access-map IDS 20
Router(config-access-map)# action forward
```

In this example, an entry #10 identifies HTTP and FTP traffic (as classified by the ACL WEB_FTP created earlier) and specifies that this traffic should be forwarded and captured. The next entry (#20) implicitly matches all other traffic (no match ip address command is specified) and ensures that this traffic is forwarded but not captured. Entry #20 is required, because a VLAN access map has an implicit deny as the last entry in the access map—if entry #20 wasn't configured, then all non-HTTP and non-FTP traffic would be dropped. The sequence numbering in the previous example is also important, because entry #20 also matches HTTP and web traffic by virtue of the fact that any type of traffic matches this entry. Because entry #10 has a lower sequence number than entry #20, it's processed first; this ensures that HTTP and web traffic is forwarded and captured, not just forwarded, if it was matched to entry #20.

Applying the VLAN Access Map to a VLAN

After creating a VLAN access map, you next need to assign it to the appropriate VLAN from which you wish to capture traffic. This is achieved by using the vlan filter global configuration command:

```
Router(config)# vlan filter map-name vlan-list vlan-list
```

You can map a single VLAN access map to multiple VLANs, but you can't map multiple VLAN access maps to a single VLAN. The following example demonstrates mapping the VLAN access map created earlier to VLAN 100 and VLAN 200-205:

```
Router# configure terminal
Router(config)# vlan filter IDS vlan-list 100,200-205
```

Configuring the IDSM-2 Sensing Interfaces as VACL Capture Ports

The final VACL configuration task on Cisco IOS is to configure the IDSM-2 sensing interfaces as VACL capture ports for the appropriate VLANs. This is achieved by using the `intrusion-detection module` global configuration command to perform two tasks:

- Configure the IDSM-2 sensing interfaces as VACL capture ports. This is achieved by using the following command syntax:

Router(config)# `intrusion-detection module IDSM-slot-number data-port sensing-interface-number capture`

- Optionally, define the VLANs that are permitted to be captured. This is achieved by using the following command syntax:

Router(config)# `intrusion-detection module IDSM-slot-number data-port sensing-interface-number capture allowed-vlan vlan-list`

> **NOTE:** If you don't define the VLANs that are permitted to be captured, then all VLANs are permitted to be captured.

The following example demonstrates configuring the first sensing interface on an IDSM-2 installed in slot 4 of a Cisco IOS Catalyst 6000/6500 switch as a VACL capture port that is permitted to capture traffic from only VLAN 100 to 205:

Router# `configure terminal`
Router(config)# `intrusion-detection module 4 data-port 1 capture`
Router(config)# `intrusion-detection module 4 data-port 1 capture`
  `allowed-vlan 100-205`

A VACL Capture Example for Cisco IOS

Suppose we have the same sample network topology shown earlier in Figure 22.13. We wish to monitor only web and mail traffic (HTTP and SMTP) on the Internet DMZ segment but still permit other traffic without passing it to the IDSM-2 for analysis. First, we must create an access control list that classifies HTTP and SMTP traffic:

Router# `configure terminal`
Router(config)# `ip access-list extended WEB_MAIL`
Router(config-ext-nacl)# `permit any any eq www`
Router(config-ext-nacl)# `permit any any eq smtp`

Next we need to create a VLAN access map that specifies that HTTP and SMTP traffic classified by the `WEB_MAIL` ACL should be forwarded and captured, but all other traffic should simply be forwarded and not captured. The VLAN access map then needs to be mapped to the Internet DMZ VLAN (200):

```
Router# configure terminal
Router(config)# vlan access-map CAPTURE_WEB_MAIL 10
Router(config-access-map)# match ip address WEB_MAIL
Router(config-access-map)# action forward capture
Router(config-access-map)# exit
Router(config)# vlan access-map CAPTURE_WEB_MAIL 20
Router(config-access-map)# action forward
Router(config-access-map)# exit
Router(config)# vlan filter CAPTURE_WEB_MAIL vlan-list 200
```

Finally, we must configure an IDSM-2 sensing port as a VACL capture port:

```
Router(config)# intrusion-detection module 3 data-port 1 capture
```

Configuring Traffic Capture using the *mls ip ids* Command

It's important to note that in some configurations, traffic capture using SPAN or VACLs isn't supported. The following describes the specific situations when this is the case:

CatOS If you have a *multilayer switching feature card* (MSFC) installed and are running Cisco IOS Firewall Feature set software, you can't apply VACLs to a VLAN in which a Cisco IOS Firewall IP inspect rule has been applied.

Cisco IOS On Cisco IOS, it's possible to configure any switch interface as a *routed interface* (layer 3 interface), making the switch port operate in exactly the same fashion as an Ethernet interface on a traditional router. A routed interface doesn't attach to any VLANs, so VACLs can't be used to capture traffic.

> **NOTE** The MSFC is a daughter card for the Supervisor engine that turns the Catalyst 6000/6500 into a layer 3 switch, allowing it to perform both traditional LAN (layer 2) switching as well as route packets between VLANs in hardware. The MSFC runs a separate Cisco IOS operating system on CatOS-based Catalyst 6000/6500 switches (this mode of operating is referred to as *hybrid mode*). On Cisco IOS–based Catalyst 6000/6500 switches, the MSFC and switch processor run the same Cisco IOS operating system.

To capture traffic in the situations just described, you can use the mls ip ids interface configuration command.

Configuring the *mls ip ids* Command on CatOS

To capture packets carried on a VLAN for which an MSFC running Cisco IOS Firewall software has an IP inspect rule, the `mls ip ids` command can be applied to the appropriate VLAN interface on the MSFC:

```
Router(config-if)# mls ip ids acl-id
```

The `acl-id` parameter refers an ACL that lets you restrict the type of packets that are captured.

> **NOTE** When you're using the `mls ip ids` command, you must still configure the IDSM-2 sensing interface(s) as VACL capture ports.

The following example demonstrates enabling the capture of HTTP and SMTP packets on VLAN 100, in a switch that has an MSFC running Cisco IOS Firewall software with an IP inspect rule configured for packets received on VLAN 100:

```
Console> (enable) session 15
Trying Router-15...

Connected to Router-15.

Escape character is '^]'.

MSFC> enable
MSFC# configure terminal
MSFC(config)# ip access-list extended WEB_MAIL
MSFC(config-ext-nacl)# permit any any eq www
MSFC(config-ext-nacl)# permit any any eq smtp
MSFC(config-ext-nacl)# exit
MSFC(config)# interface vlan 100
MSFC(config-if)# mls ip ids WEB_MAIL
MSFC(config-if)# end
MSFC# exit

Console> (enable) set security acl capture 3/7
Successfully set 3/7 to capture ACL traffic.
```

In this example, notice that to gain access to the MSFC operating system on a CatOS switch, you use the `session 15` command. Slot 15 is a special slot number used to represent the internal MSFC connection to the switch backplane. After the MSFC has been configured, you still must ensure that the IDSM-2 data port(s) are configured as VACL capture ports.

Configuring the *mls ip ids* Command on Cisco IOS

To capture packets sent/received on a routed interface on a Cisco IOS–based (native IOS) Catalyst 6000/6500 switch, the same `mls ip ids` command discussed in the previous section (same syntax) can be applied. You must also ensure that the IDSM-2 sensing interface(s) are configured as VACL capture ports.

> **NOTE** By default, all interfaces on a Cisco IOS–based Catalyst 6000/6500 switch are routed interfaces.

The following example demonstrates enabling the capture of HTTP and SMTP packets on a routed interface of a Cisco IOS–based Catalyst 6000/6500 switch:

```
Router# configure terminal
Router(config)# ip access-list extended WEB_MAIL
Router(config-ext-nacl)# permit any any eq www
Router(config-ext-nacl)# permit any any eq smtp
Router(config-ext-nacl)# exit
Router(config)# interface fastEthernet 2/1
Router(config-if)# no switchport
Router(config-if)# ip address 10.1.1.1 255.255.255.0
Router(config-if)# mls ip ids WEB_MAIL
Router(config-if)# exit
Router(config)# intrusion-detection module 3 data-port 1 capture
```

In this example, the `no switchport` command configures the interface as a routed (layer 3) interface, allowing an IP address to be assigned to the interface. The `mls ip ids` command is then configured to enable capture of HTTP and SMTP traffic only. Finally, notice that a sensing interface on the IDSM-2 must be configured as a VACL capture port for this feature to work.

Configuring the Sensing Interface to Control Trunk Traffic

So far, you've learned all the necessary fundamentals to allow a Catalyst IDSM-2 to monitor traffic that passes through a Catalyst 6000/6500 switch. You can apply optional configuration on the sensing interface, which may be required in certain situations. Because the sensing interface of the sensor is a trunk interface, you may need to control which VLANs are trunked to ensure that the port isn't oversubscribed.

By default, the sensing interface on the IDSM-2 trunks traffic for *all* VLANs (VLANs 1 through 1024), meaning that the port is a member of all VLANs. In scenarios where you use multiple IDSMs in conjunction with VACL traffic capture, the same captured traffic is mirrored to each IDSM, because a single capture list is used. It's a good idea to limit the VLANs that are trunked on the sensing interface to only those that you wish the IDSM-2 to monitor.

In a multiple-IDSM-2 configuration, you typically use multiple IDSMs because you want to monitor more than 600Mbps of traffic. For example, if your VACL capture traffic may total

1000Mbps, you should clear VLANs from each trunk to limit the amount of traffic each IDSM-2 monitors to 600Mbps. Figure 22.14 illustrates this concept.

In Figure 22.14, each VLAN carries a constant stream of 250Mbps traffic. This means the total bandwidth aggregate on the backplane is 1000Mbps (4 250Mbps), which exceeds the capabilities of a single IDSM-2. To alleviate this, a second IDSM-2 is installed, and the aggregate backplane bandwidth is split into two 500Mbps streams by selectively trunking two VLANs on each IDSM-2 sensing interface trunk. Each IDSM-2 can handle 600Mbps, so all traffic can now be monitored.

You'll now learn how to control trunk traffic on both CatOS and Cisco IOS-based Catalyst 6000/6500 switches.

FIGURE 22.14   A multiple IDSM-2 configuration

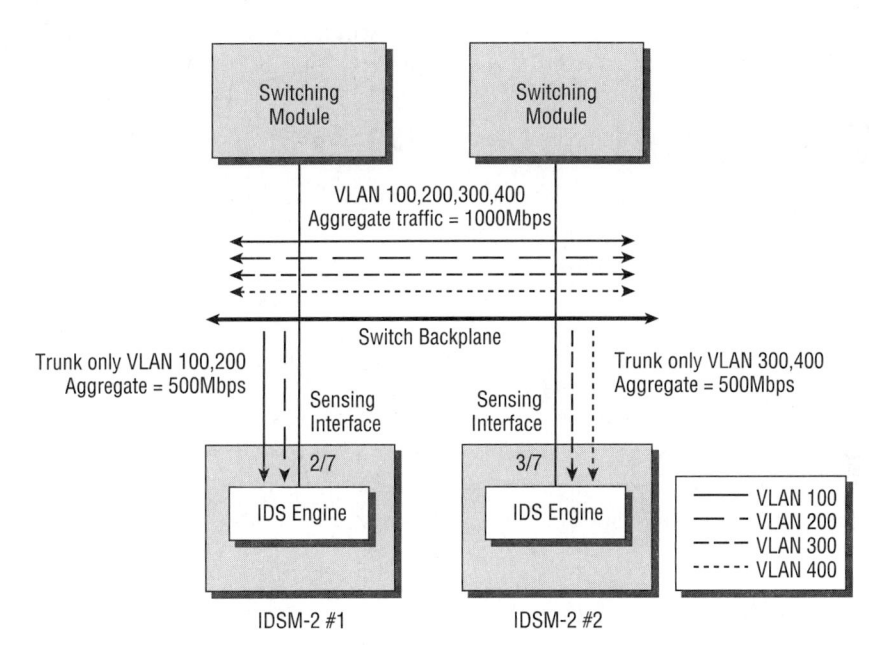

Restricting VLANs on CatOS

To control the VLANs that are trunked to the IDSM-2 sensing interface port, you must configure the Catalyst 6000/6500 operating system. On CatOS, you must first use the `clear trunk` command to remove all VLANs from the sensing interface and then use the `set trunk` command to selectively add VLANs to the sensing interface. The following example shows how you would map the appropriate VLANs in Figure 22.14 to each IDSM-2 sensing interface:

```
Console> (enable) clear trunk 2/7 1-1024
Removing Vlan(s) 1-1024 from allowed list.
Port 2/7 allowed vlans modified to none.
```

```
Console> (enable) clear trunk 3/7 1-1024
Removing Vlan(s) 1-1024 from allowed list.
Port 3/7 allowed vlans modified to none.
Console> (enable) set trunk 2/7 100,200
Adding vlans 100,200 to allowed list.
Port(s) 2/7 allowed vlans modified to 100,200.
Console> (enable) set trunk 3/7 300,400
Adding vlans 300-400 to allowed list.
Port(s) 3/7 allowed vlans modified to 300,400.
```

In this example, by trunking only VLANs 100 and 200 on port 2/7 (the sensing interface of IDSM-2 #1), only VACL capture traffic belonging to those VLANs is sent to the port. The same applies to the second IDSM-2 module (IDSM-2 2), where only VACL capture traffic belonging to VLANs 300 and 400 is sent to the sensing interface (port 3/7).

Restricting VLANs on Cisco IOS

To control the VLANs that are trunked to the IDSM-2 sensing interface on Cisco IOS, the `switchport trunk allowed vlans` interface configuration command must be configured on the appropriate sensing interfaces. The following example shows how you would map the appropriate VLANs in Figure 22.14 to each IDSM-2 sensing interface on Cisco IOS:

```
Router# configure terminal
Router(config)# interface GigabitEthernet 2/7
Router(config-if)# switchport trunk allowed vlan 100,200
Router(config-if)# exit
Router(config)# interface GigabitEthernet 3/7
Router(config-if)# switchport trunk allowed vlan 300,400
```

Assigning the Command-and-Control Port VLAN

To allow the IDSM-2 to communicate with external sensor management platforms, you must ensure that the command-and-control interface is attached to the appropriate VLAN so that the interface is in the correct logical IP subnet. For example, if your IDSM-2 has an IP address of 192.168.1.100 and a default gateway of 192.168.1.1, you should place your IDSM-2 into the same VLAN as the default gateway, ensuring that the IDSM-2 can communicate with the IP network correctly.

Assigning the command-and-control interface to a VLAN is performed via the switch operating system (not the IDSM-2), which means that you must understand how the command-and-control interface is identified to the switch. On CatOS, the command-and-control interface is always *IDSM-slot-number/2*—for example, if the IDSM-2 is installed in slot 4, the command-and-control interface is identified as port 4/2 to the switch operating system. On Cisco IOS, the command-and-control interface isn't identified by a numeric identifier—instead, it's identified as a *management-port*.

You'll now learn how to configure the command-and-control VLAN on CatOS and Cisco IOS.

Configuring the Command-and-Control VLAN on CatOS

To configure the VLAN to which the command-and-control interface belongs on CatOS, you use the `set vlan` command. The following example demonstrates configuring the command-and-control interface of an IDSM-2 installed in slot 3 of a Catalyst 6000/6500 switch to belong to VLAN 100:

```
Console> (enable) set vlan 100 3/2
```

Configuring the Command-and-Control VLAN on Cisco IOS

To configure the VLAN to which the command-and-control interface belongs on a Cisco IOS–based Catalyst 6000/6500 switch, the `intrusion-detection module` global configuration command is used. The following example demonstrates configuring the command-and-control interface of an IDSM-2 installed in slot 3 of a Catalyst 6000/6500 switch to belong to VLAN 100:

```
Router(config)# intrusion-detection module 3 management-port
  access-vlan 100
```

Notice that the `management-port` keyword is used to identify the command-and-control interface, rather than a numeric identifier.

Configuring Traffic Capture for the NM-CIDS

The NM-CIDS sensor sensing interface attaches to the data bus of the Cisco 2600/3600/3700 router in which the sensor is installed. Figure 22.15 shows the architecture of the NM-CIDS sensor.

In Figure 22.15, you can see that by connecting to the data bus of the router, the NM-CIDS can capture network traffic routed between the various interfaces that may be installed in the router. For example, in the figure, a serial interface and an Ethernet network interface are shown, and traffic routed between the two interfaces is mirrored to the internal sensing interface on the NM-CIDS sensor for analysis. The external command-and-control interface on the NM-CIDS sensor allows for IDS management and alarm notification.

Unlike the 4200 series sensor and IDSM-2, the NM-CIDS doesn't support traffic-capture technologies such as SPAN and VACLs, because the sensing interface on the NM-CIDS sensor isn't Ethernet-based. On the NM-CIDS, traffic capture is configured on a per-interface basis: You can selectively enable/disable the capture of traffic sent and received on each interface or subinterface. By default, no interfaces are configured for traffic capture; however, to configure traffic capture for a specific interface, you configure the `ids-service-module monitoring` interface configuration command, as demonstrated here:

```
Router# configure terminal
Router(config)# interface fastEthernet0/1
Router(config-if)# ids-service-module monitoring
```

In this example, any packets sent or received on interface `fastEthernet0/1` will be mirrored to the NM-CIDS sensor.

FIGURE 22.15 NM-CIDS sensor architecture

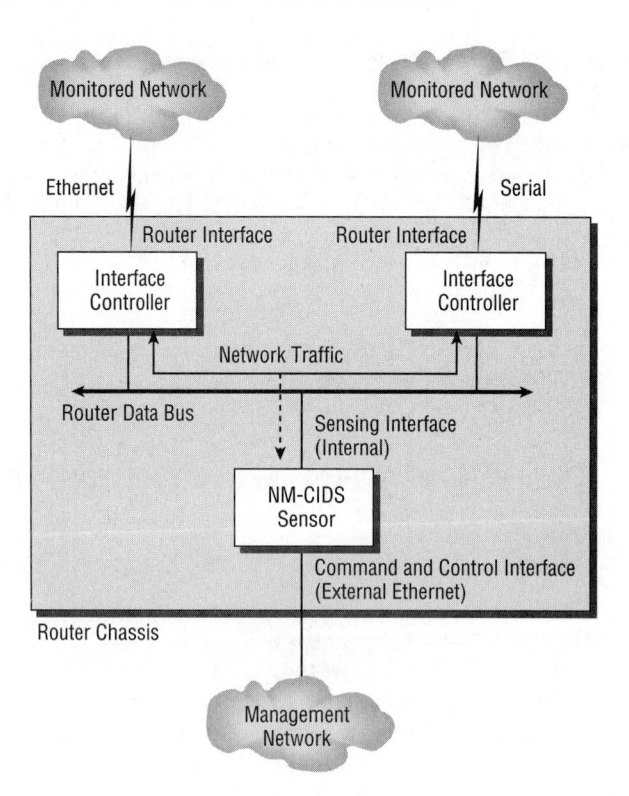

Summary

In this chapter, you learned how to configure the network infrastructure to capture traffic for Cisco Secure IDS sensors. For the IDS 4200 sensors, which contain external sensing interfaces, there are three generic traffic-capture devices: the hub, the network tap, and the switch. In modern LAN networks, most 4200 sensors must attach to a switched infrastructure; in this chapter, you learned that Cisco Catalyst switches support traffic-capture mechanisms such as switch port analyzer (SPAN), remote SPAN (RSPAN), and VLAN access control lists (VACLs).

For the IDSM-2 sensor, the sensing interfaces of the sensor are internal and connect to the backplane of the Catalyst 6000/6500 switch in which the IDSM-2 is installed. The Catalyst 6000/6500 supports SPAN/RSPAN and VACLs as traffic-capture mechanisms for the IDSM-2, since the sensing interfaces on the IDSM-2 can be identified as ports to the Catalyst switch operating system. Because each sensing interface is a trunk port, when you configure traffic capture for the IDSM-2, you can restrict captured traffic to specific VLANs by controlling the VLANs permitted on the trunk. You must also configure the appropriate VLAN for the command and control interface so that external sensor management platforms and sensor administrators can manage and monitor the IDSM-2.

Finally, the NM-CIDS sensor captures traffic directly from the router backplane and doesn't support mechanisms such as SPAN or VACLs. Traffic capture for the NM-CIDS requires the appropriate interfaces to be enabled for traffic capture, after which traffic sent and received on the interface is mirrored to the NM-CIDS sensor.

Exam Essentials

Understand the different types of network capture devices. There are three types of network capture devices: hubs, switches, and network taps.

Understand the issues with monitoring traffic in a switch LAN infrastructure. Unlike hubs, switches don't mirror traffic to all ports within a LAN segment, and hence they require a technology such as SPAN or VACLs to capture traffic.

Remember the different traffic-capture mechanisms available for each sensor. The 4200 series sensors support traffic capture from an external hub, switch (using SPAN/RSPAN or VACLs to an external capture port), or network tab. The IDSM-2 supports traffic capture using SPAN/RSPAN or VACLs. The NM-CIDS supports traffic capture from the router data bus only.

Know how to configure SPAN on Cisco IOS and CatOS. The `monitor session` command is used on Cisco IOS, and the `set span` command is used on CatOS. Make sure that you know the syntax for these commands on each platform.

Know how to configure RSPAN on Cisco IOS and CatOS. RSPAN requires all switches that transport RSPAN to support RSPAN. You must specify source ports/VLANs, configure a reflector port and specify the RSPAN VLAN as the destination on the source switch, ensure that the RSPAN VLAN is trunked through any transit switches, and ensure that the RSPAN VLAN is configured as the source on the destination switch. The `monitor session` command is used on Cisco IOS, and the `set rspan` command is used on CatOS.

Know how to configure VACLs to capture traffic for the IDSM-2 on Cisco IOS and CatOS. On Cisco IOS, you must create an access control list that classifies the traffic you wish to capture, create a VLAN access map that specifies that traffic matching the ACLs you've created should be captured, map the VLAN access map to one or more VLANs, and finally configure the IDSM-2 interfaces as VACL capture ports. On CatOS, you create a VACL that includes the `capture` keyword for the appropriate ACEs, commit the VACL to hardware, map the VACL to one or more VLANs, and finally configure the IDSM-2 interfaces as VACL capture ports.

Understand how to enable sensors to restrict the VLANs monitored from trunks. Both Cisco IOS and CatOS provide commands that let you restrict the VLANs captured on a sensing interface—make sure you know these commands.

Know how to assign the command-and-control VLAN on the IDSM-2. On CatOS, the `set vlan` command is used, with the command-and-control port as it appears to the switch referenced. On Cisco IOS, the `intrusion-detection module` *slot* `management-port access-vlan` *vlan-id* command is used to assign the command-and-control VLAN.

Understand the importance of the *mls ip ids* command. This command is required in two situations: when you wish to capture traffic from a VLAN on a hybrid mode switch that has an interface on the MSFC configured with an IP inspect rule, and when you wish to capture traffic sent and received on a routed interface of a native mode switch.

Chapter 23

Configuring Cisco Secure IDS Sensors Using the IDS Device Manager

CISCO SECURE INTRUSION DETECTION SYSTEM EXAM TOPICS COVERED IN THIS CHAPTER:

- ✓ Features and benefits of IDM
- ✓ The requirements for IDM
- ✓ Applying configuration changes made via the CLI
- ✓ Configuring sensor communication properties
- ✓ Configuring sensor logging properties
- ✓ Setting up sensors and sensor groups
- ✓ Sensor communications and sensor logging
- ✓ Creating signature filters to exclude or include a specific signature or list of signatures
- ✓ The device management capability of the sensor and how it's used to perform blocking with a Cisco device
- ✓ Designing a Cisco IDS solution using the blocking feature, including the ACL placement considerations, when deciding where to apply Sensor-generated ACLs
- ✓ Configuring a sensor to perform blocking with a Cisco IDS device
- ✓ Configuring a sensor to perform blocking through a master blocking sensor
- ✓ IDS software update files for a sensor and an IDSM
- ✓ Installing IDS signature updates and service packs

So far in this book, you've learned how to configure Cisco Secure IDS sensors using the command-line interface (CLI). Cisco Secure IDS sensors include a web-based management application called the IDS Device Manager (IDM), which eases management by providing a graphical interface that you can use to configure sensor settings. The IDM provides a secure management interface and gives you the flexibility to manage the IDS sensors securely from any device that has a web browser.

In this chapter, you'll learn how to use the IDM to configure Cisco Secure IDS sensors. You'll learn how to perform the same basic system configuration tasks discussed in Chapter 21, "Installing Cisco Secure IDS Sensors and IDSMs," configure intrusion detection, administer Cisco Secure IDS sensors, and monitor Cisco Secure IDS sensors, all using the IDM. For the exam, it's important that for each configuration task described, you understand how to perform the task using both the IDM and CLI. For all configuration tasks in this chapter, if the equivalent CLI configuration hasn't been discussed previously in this book, then you'll also learn how to perform the equivalent task using the sensor command line interface.

IDS Device Manager Introduction

The IDS Device Manager (IDM) is a web-based configuration management tool that lets you manage a Cisco Secure IDS sensor. The IDM is designed to make Cisco Secure IDS configuration simple, without your needing to rely on knowledge of the Cisco Secure IDS command-line interface (CLI). Before using the IDM, you must understand the components of the IDM and the requirements for using the IDM. Assuming that you've met the appropriate system requirements of the IDM, you can then connect to the IDM for the first time.

IDM Components and System Requirements

The IDM is a web-based application and therefore consists of a web server component and a web client (browser) component. Following is a discussion of each of these components, including any requirements for each component:

Web server   The web server component of the IDM resides on the sensor itself, which means that no additional hardware or software is required apart from the sensor. The IDM web server component is ready to run once an appropriate network configuration on the command-and-control interface (for example, IP address, subnet mask, and default gateway) has been configured on the sensor. By default, the IDM is configured to use Secure Sockets Layer (SSL), which operates over TCP port 443 and ensures the confidentiality and integrity of IDM communications.

> **Note:** It's recommended that you do not disable SSL, because doing so may potentially expose sensitive configuration information to unauthorized parties.

Web browser   The second component of the IDM is the client component, which can be any supported web browser. The following web browsers are supported:

- Netscape Navigator/Communicator 4.79 or higher
- Microsoft Internet Explorer 5.5 Service Pack 2 or higher

The IDM requires the use of *cookies*, which are used to temporarily store session information during an IDM configuration session. The cookies aren't used to store information permanently and are only used to store random numbers that enable the web server to bind HTTP transaction requests to a particular configuration session. If your browser has cookies disabled, the IDM won't work; hence you need to ensure that cookies are enabled before using the IDM.

Accessing the IDM for the First Time

You can access the IDM via any supported web browser by specifying the IP address of the sensor command-and-control interface as the URL (for instance, `https://sensor-ip-address`). Entering this URL into your web browser initiates an SSL connection to TCP port 443 on the sensor, after which HTTP transactions are exchanged over the secure communications channel setup via SSL.

To support SSL, the sensor web server includes a *self-signed certificate*, which ensures that the sensor can identify itself and provide the necessary parameters to begin cryptographic operations. The certificate is provided in an X.509 format, which ensures compatibility with web browsers that support digital certificates.

Because the sensor certificate is self-signed and not signed by a trusted certificate authority (CA), when you connect to the IDM for the first time you'll be presented with a warning indicating that the certificate presented by the sensor hasn't been issued by a trusted certificate authority. Figure 23.1 demonstrates the warning that is presented on Internet Explorer.

To continue after the warning, click the Yes button; however, the next time you connect to the sensor, you'll be warned again. To avoid being continually warned each time you establish a new session to the sensor IDM, you can choose to trust the certificate. First click the View Certificate button; Figure 23.2 shows the certificate that is displayed after you click the button.

In Figure 23.2, you can see further evidence that the sensor certificate isn't trusted. If you wish to trust the certificate, you can click on the Install Certificate button, which starts the Certificate Import Wizard. Using this wizard lets you place the sensor certificate in the Trusted Root Certification Authorities store, after which your browser will automatically trust the sensor certificate and no longer issue warnings at future connections.

FIGURE 23.1 Internet Explorer warning

FIGURE 23.2 Viewing the sensor certificate

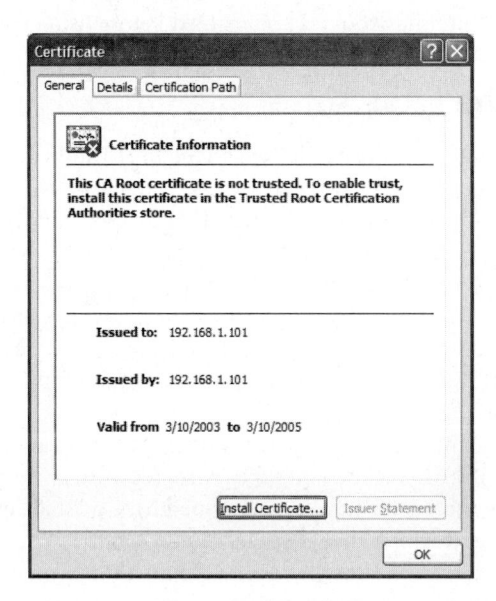

Assuming that you acknowledge the certificate warning, an SSL connection will be established to the IDM server running on the sensor. The first thing the sensor will do is attempt to authenticate the connection, challenging the connecting user for his/her credentials, as demonstrated in Figure 23.3.

> **NOTE** The credentials used for authentication to the IDM are the same credentials you would normally use for shell-based access to the sensor.

After successful authentication, the IDM will start, displaying a somewhat bare IDM start page, as shown in Figure 23.4. At this stage, you've successfully connected and authenticated to the IDM.

FIGURE 23.3   IDM authentication

FIGURE 23.4   IDM start page

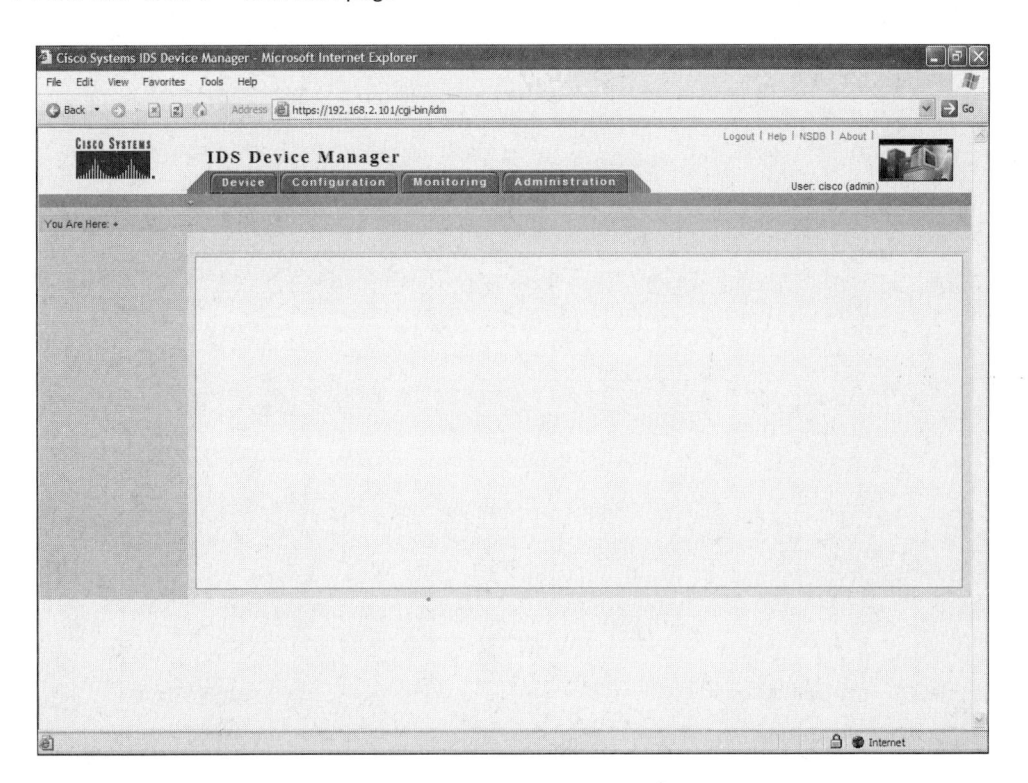

> Access to the IDM is restricted by the same access lists that restrict shell-based access. If you can't establish a connection to the IDM, ensure that the IP address of the web client you're using is permitted in the access list used to permit remote management. Remember that by default, connections from the 10.0.0.0/8 address range are permitted.

Only a single IDM session is supported at any time, which causes problems if another administrator attempts to establish a new IDM session while one is in progress or if an IDM session isn't terminated correctly and the sensor still thinks the existing session is still active. If such a situation occurs, the administrator attempting the new IDM session will be presented with the error message "User limit has been reached." This error includes an option to *force login*, which means that the other conflicting IDM session will be terminated, allowing the new IDS session to begin.

Navigating the IDM

Before you learn how to use the IDM to configure a sensor, it's important to understand the layout of the IDM. Figure 23.5 indicates key components of the IDM screen that let you navigate and access help for the various IDM configuration screens.

FIGURE 23.5 IDM layout

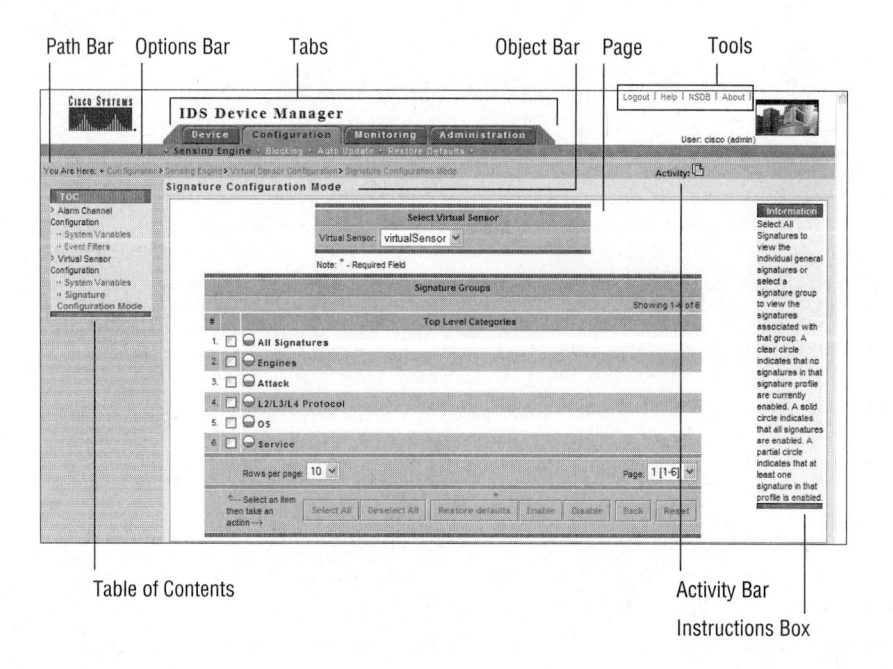

Each of the IDM GUI components shown in Figure 23.5 are described here:

Tabs   These provide access to the four main configuration areas of the IDM:

- Device provides options for setting up the sensor.
- Configure provides options for configuring intrusion detection on the sensor.
- Monitoring provides options for setting up monitoring on the sensor.
- Administration provides options for administering the sensor.

Each tab possesses a number of configuration options, which are displayed in the Options bar when you click a tab.

Options bar   This bar displays the options that are available for the selected tab. Each option may have suboptions, which are displayed in the TOC.

Path bar   The Path bar indicates the context or path of the configuration page currently being displayed. The path consists of the tab, option, and page you're working on.

Table of Contents (TOC)   The TOC displays the available configuration pages for the current option you're working on. For example, in Figure 23.5, the TOC shows the configuration pages available for the Configuration ➤ Sensing Engine option.

Object bar   The Object bar indicates the current configuration page that is selected from the TOC or Options bar.

Page   This is the area on which you provide and obtain information relative to the configuration option/suboption you're working with.

Tools   This section contains the following four buttons:

- Logout logs out the current user from the IDM.
- Help opens a new window that displays context-sensitive help for the currently displayed page.
- NSDB opens the network security database in a separate window that provides further information about vulnerabilities and exploits related to a detected attack.
- About shows the IDM version and copyright information.

Instructions box   The Instructions box provides instructions on how to use the currently selected configuration option/suboption.

Activity bar   The Activity bar shows a set of changes or additions to devices that must be submitted for approval.

In Figure 23.5, notice that the Configuration tab is selected, with the Sensing Engine option selected in the Options bar (as indicated by the blackened text). In the TOC, you can see the various configuration pages or suboptions available for the Sensing Engine option, and the Object bar indicates that the Signature Configuration Mode page is currently selected. Within the Signature Configuration Mode page, you can see that for the six signature profiles listed, at least one signature in the profile is enabled, based on the information contained within the Instructions box.

Configuring Cisco Secure IDS Sensors Using the IDM

The IDM is primarily used as a configuration tool, allowing you to configure system-level sensor parameters along with parameters related to intrusion detection operation on the sensor. In the following sections, we'll discuss performing sensor setup, as well configuring intrusion detection, blocking, and auto updates using the IDM.

Performing Sensor Setup Using the IDM

In Chapter 21, you learned how to set up Cisco Secure IDS sensors using the Cisco IOS–like shell that can be accessed via console, keyboard/monitor, or Telnet/SSH. You learned how to use the `setup` utility, which performs the initial configuration of the sensor and prepares it for operation on the network. After initial configuration using the `setup` utility, the IDM can be used to perform all subsequent configuration of the sensor, making it easy to configure and maintain the sensor using a graphical user interface (GUI) rather than a CLI.

When you're connecting to the IDM for the first time after running the `setup` utility, you'll normally complete the initial configuration of your sensor by accessing the Sensor Setup page, which lets you configure system parameters crucial to the ongoing operation of the sensor. To access the IDM Sensor Setup screen, select the Device tab and then select Sensor Setup from the Options bar. Figure 23.6 shows the resulting IDM view after selecting Device ➢ Sensor Setup.

FIGURE 23.6 The IDM Sensor Setup page

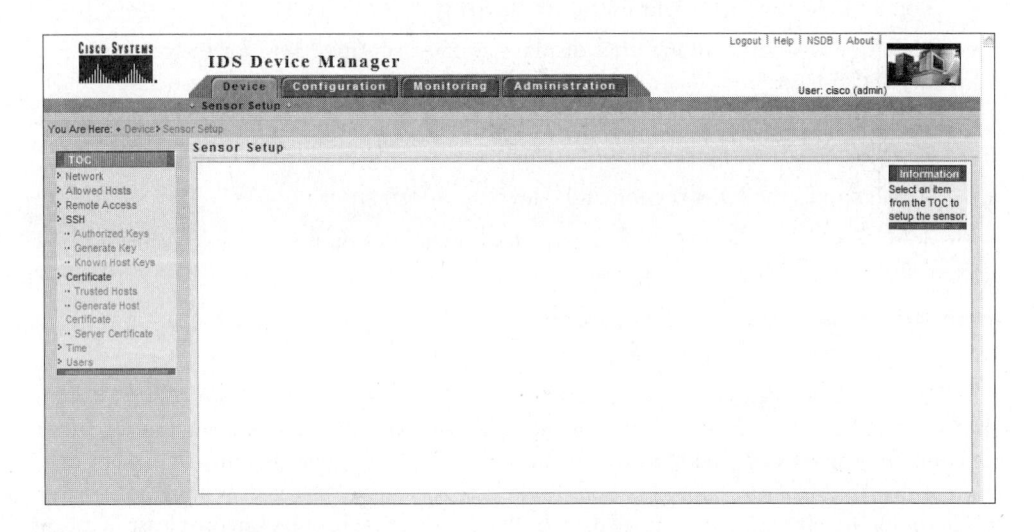

In Figure 23.6, notice that the Sensor Setup page itself is blank; however, the TOC shows the following different configuration suboptions:

Network The Network configuration page lets you configure the following network parameters:

- Host name
- IP address
- Subnet mask
- Default gateway
- Enabling/disabling the use of TLS/SSL to secure the IDM
- Web server port

Note that many of these parameters are configured using the setup CLI utility. Figure 23.7 shows the Device ➤ Sensor Setup ➤ Network configuration page.

In Figure 23.7, notice the Apply To Sensor and Reset buttons. The Apply To Sensor button applies any modifications made to the various network parameters to the sensor, whereas the Reset button returns any modified parameter back to its original value.

Allowed Hosts The Allowed Hosts configuration page lets you define the IP addresses of hosts that are permitted network management access to the sensor; this page is equivalent to the functionality provided by the `accessList` command within the `networkParams` subconfiguration mode of the service host configuration mode when using the CLI. Figure 23.8 shows the Device ➤ Sensor Setup ➤ Allowed Hosts configuration page.

Notice the Add, Edit, and Delete buttons, which let you define individual access list entries for explicitly permitting network management access to the sensor. In Figure 23.8, a single entry 0.0.0.0/0.0.0.0 has been added, which permits network management access from any IP address.

Remote Access The Remote Access configuration page lets you enable/disable Telnet access to the sensor. By default, Telnet access is disabled (only SSH access is permitted for remote shell-based management access), and it should be left disabled for maximum security.

SSH The SSH suboption isn't a configuration page as such but is essentially a container object for a number of configuration pages related to the configuration and operation of SSH on the sensor. Notice that there are three configuration pages within the SSH suboption:

Authorized Keys This page lets you define the public keys of authorized SSH clients that are permitted to connect to the SSH server of the sensor for remote shell access. By default, no authorized keys are defined, which means that any SSH client can connect. If you wish to restrict SSH access to specific SSH clients, you must enter the following parameters for each SSH client:

- Key modulus length
- Public exponent
- Public modulus

Generate Key This page lets you view the current public key used by the sensor SSH server and also regenerate the public key of the sensor if required (for example, if the private key of the sensor has somehow been compromised). If a new public key is generated, this key must be updated on all SSH clients that connect to the sensor SSH server.

Known Host Keys This page lets you define the public keys of any SSH hosts that the sensor needs to connect to (the sensor acts as an SSH client, and the host acts as an SSH server). This happens when the sensor needs to perform blocking in response to a detected attack, with the sensor establishing an SSH session to a perimeter device (for example, border router or firewall) and implementing the appropriate blocking configuration.

FIGURE 23.7 The Network configuration page

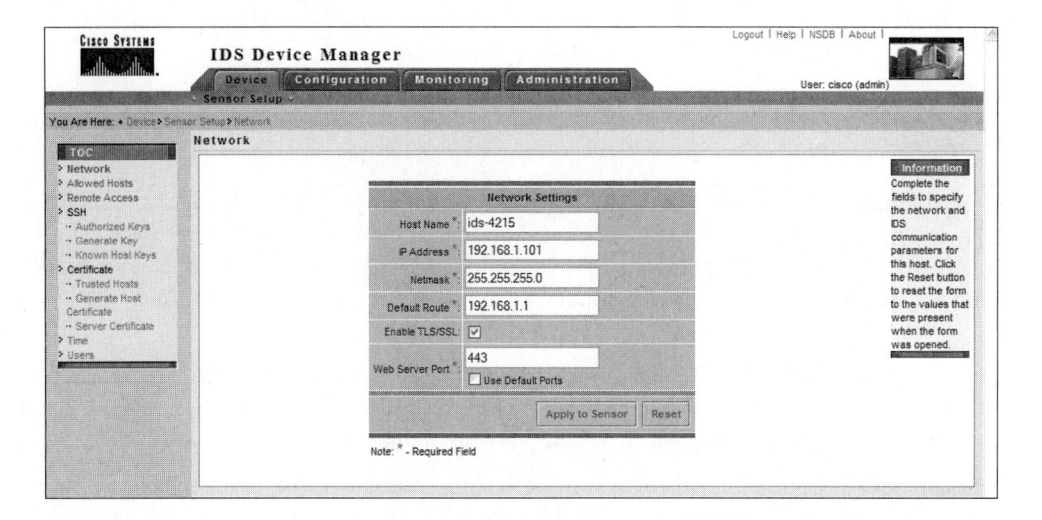

Certificate Similar to the SSH suboption, the Certificate suboption is a container object for a number of configuration pages related to the configuration and operation of digital X.509 certificates on the sensor. Notice that there are three configuration pages within the Certificate suboption:

Trusted Hosts This page lets you define the certificate fingerprint of hosts that the sensor needs to connect to. When you add a host, the sensor will automatically attempt to establish an HTTPS connection to the specified host and retrieve the fingerprint of the certificate presented by the host. In a master blocking sensor configuration (discussed later in this chapter), Cisco Secure IDS sensors may need to send a blocking request to a master blocking sensor. This is achieved by establishing an Remote Desktop Exchange Protocol (RDEP) connection over HTTPS, which involves the master blocking sensor presenting a digital certificate to identify and authenticate itself. For the connection to be accepted by the sensor that is connecting to the master blocking sensor, the master blocking sensor certificate fingerprint must be preconfigured.

Generate Host Certificate This page lets you view the Message Digest 5 (MD5) and Secure Hash Algorithm (SHA) fingerprint of the current certificate used by the sensor web server that is presented to HTTP clients connecting to the IDM and also used to initiate cryptographic operations related to the SSL connection. You can also regenerate the certificate of the sensor if required, by clicking the Apply To Sensor button. Figure 23.9 shows the Device ➢ Sensor Setup ➢ Certificate ➢ Generate Host Certificate configuration page.

Server Certificate   This page lets you view the MD5 and SHA fingerprint of the current certificate used by the sensor web server.

FIGURE 23.8   The Allowed Hosts configuration page

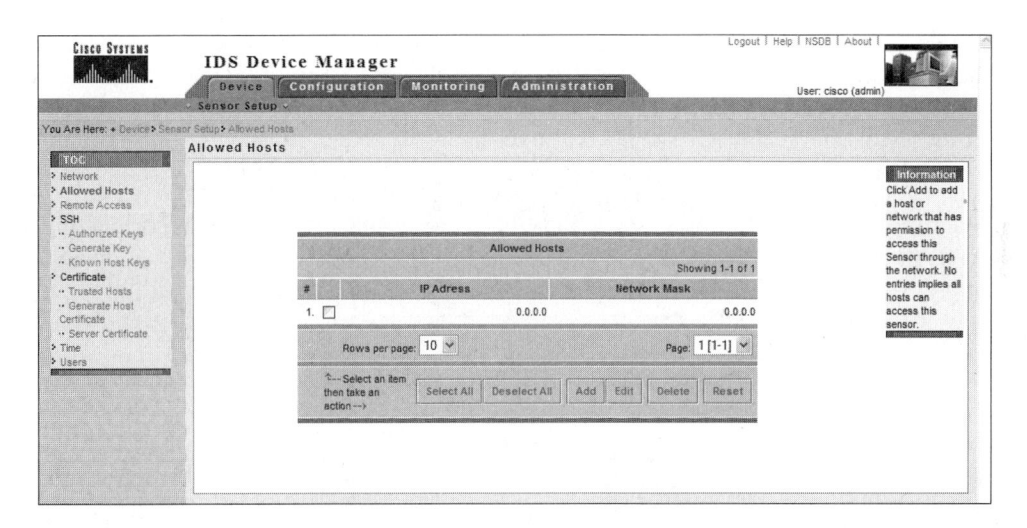

FIGURE 23.9   The Generate Host Certificate configuration page

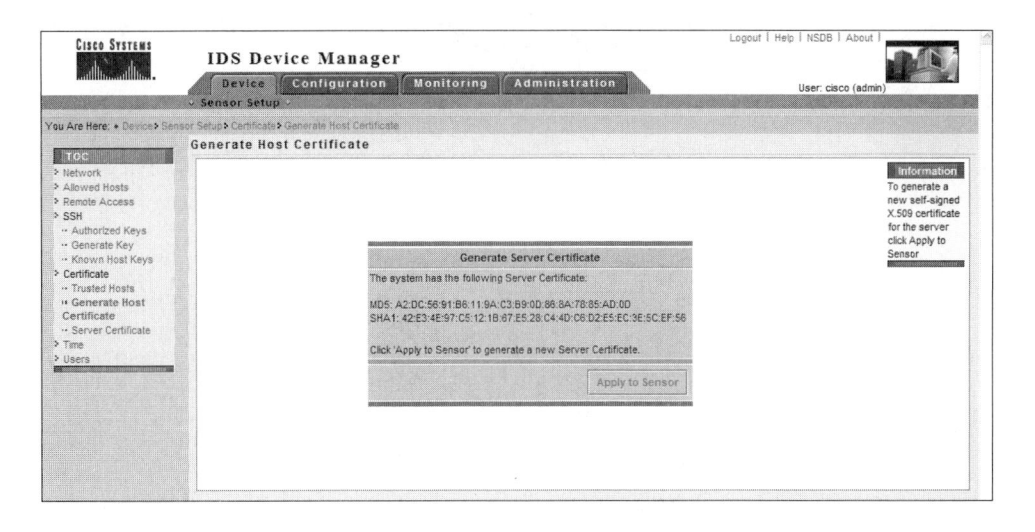

> You can view the sensor certificate from the CLI using the show tls fingerprint command.

Time This page lets you define the sensor system date and time settings. You can also configure the Network Time Protocol (NTP) client that is included with the sensor, which allows the sensor to obtain time from an external NTP server. Figure 23.10 shows the Device ➢ Sensor Setup ➢ Time configuration page.

In Figure 23.10, the current date and time are configured as well as NTP server settings and daylight saving settings. An NTP server of 192.168.2.1 is configured; *NTP authentication* is also configured, which ensures that the time received from the NTP server is authentic and hasn't been altered in transit. Daylight savings is also configured for New Zealand (my home country), where an hour of time is added at 2:00 A.M. on the first Sunday of October and an hour of time is deducted at 2:00 A.M. on the third Sunday of March.

FIGURE 23.10 The Time configuration page

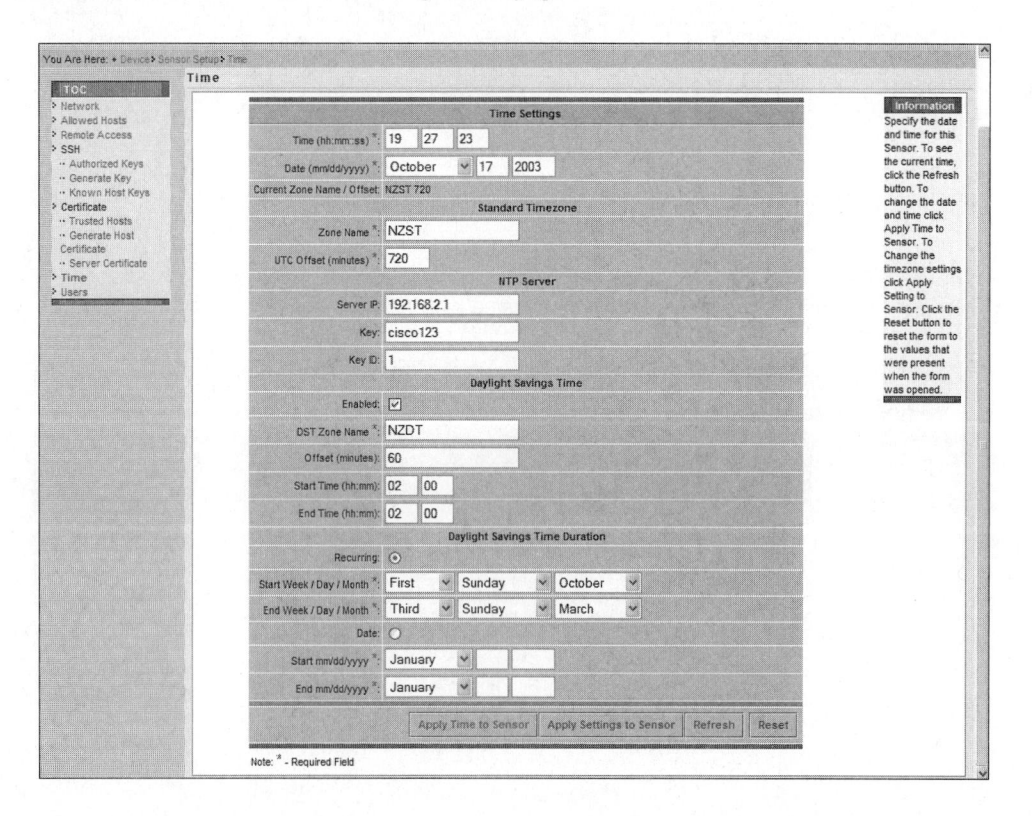

> **Note:** If possible, always use NTP and NTP authentication to ensure accurate time on your sensors. When you're configuring NTP authentication, you must specify a numeric key identifier (ID) as well as a key string (similar to a password). For NTP authentication to succeed, the NTP server must be configured with the same key ID and key string.

Users This page lets you add, edit, and delete user accounts that have some form of management access to the sensor. Figure 23.11 shows the Device ➢ Sensor Setup ➢ Users configuration page.

In Figure 23.11, notice that each user account is displayed (by default, only the `cisco` account exists), with the user account name and role listed. Recall from Chapter 21 that three different roles exist for user accounts (administrator, operator, and viewer), as well as a special service role that can only be applied to a single account. To add, modify, or delete user accounts, you can use the Add, Edit, or Delete button, respectively. Figure 23.12 demonstrates adding a new user by clicking the Add button on the Users page.

In Figure 23.12, a new user account called **bob** is being added, which has operator privileges. By clicking the Apply To Sensor button, the new user account will be added, and the Users page should be updated to include the new user account.

> **Note:** On Cisco Secure IDS 23.1, you must also explicitly enable sensing interfaces and assign sensing interfaces to the group 0 interface.

FIGURE 23.11   The Users configuration page

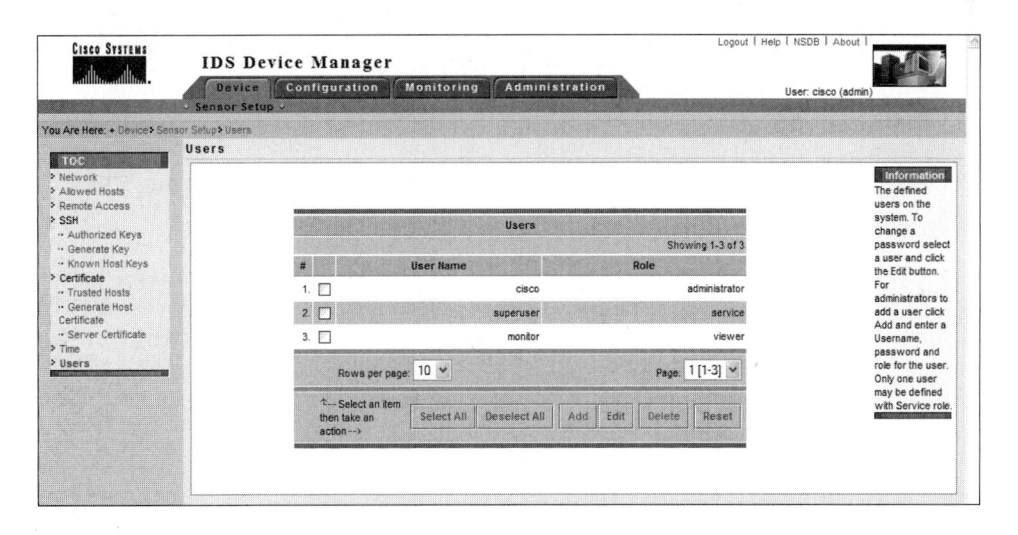

FIGURE 23.12   Adding a new user

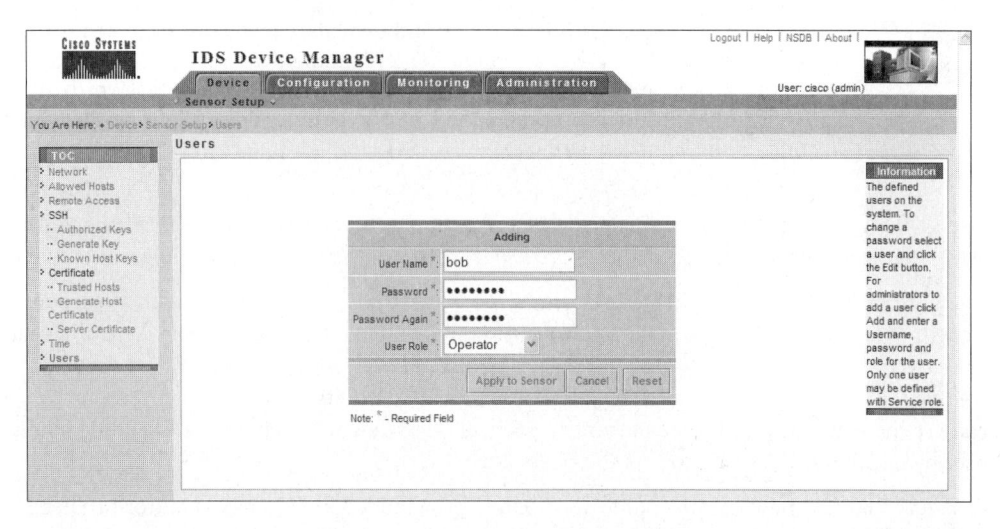

Configuring Intrusion Detection Using the IDM

Once you've configured system parameters using the IDM, the sensor should be ready to begin its primary purpose, which is to perform intrusion detection. Configuring intrusion detection consists of three main configuration tasks:

- Configuring signatures
- Configuring system variables
- Configuring event filters

Configuring Signatures

Signatures are a fundamental component of Cisco Secure IDS because they define the characteristics of intrusive activity, allowing sensors to positively identify such activity. A signature is essentially a set of rules and properties that uniquely identifies a specific form of intrusive activity. Cisco Secure IDS sensors process packets against each signature to determine whether the packets exhibit the characteristics or traits defined by a signature. If a packet or sequence of packets is deemed to exhibit the same characteristics defined in a signature—assuming the signature is enabled—a positive match is made against the signature, an alarm is generated, and additional actions may be invoked if they are configured for the signature.

Signatures aren't covered in this chapter; they're discussed in depth in Chapter 24, "Configuring Signatures and Using the IDS Event Viewer." It's important for this chapter, however, that you understand the basics of signatures—what they are and what they detect. If you aren't too sure about signatures, it might pay to read Chapter 20 again ("Introduction to Intrusion Detection and Protection").

Configuring Sensor System Variables

When you're configuring intrusion detection on Cisco Secure IDS, it's important to understand that a number of *system variables* exist, which let you define parameters and values that relate to how attacks are detected and how alarms are processed and filtered. System variables either control some specific parameter related to intrusion detection or allow you to define global constants (fixed values) that can be referenced within the configuration parameters for the various settings you can configure for intrusion detection.

There are two types of system variables:

- Alarm channel system variables
- Virtual sensor system variables

Configuring Alarm Channel System Variables

In Cisco Secure IDS 4.*x*, all alarms that are generated are sent to an *alarm channel*, which is essentially a processing engine where each alarm is filtered and aggregated. Once filtered and aggregated, alarms are stored in the event store, which is a local storage area on the sensor for alarms. Figure 23.13 illustrates how alarms are sent to the alarm channel, where they are filtered, aggregated, and then placed into the event store.

In Figure 23.13, raw alarms are generated by the IDS engine and are sent to the alarm channel. The alarm channel filters and aggregates raw alarms as per the filtering policy configured on the sensor, sending these alarms to the event store for storage.

To control the alarm-filtering policy, a number of *alarm channel system variables* control how alarms are filtered by the alarm channel. Each variable has a value, which can be modified to alter the alarm-processing characteristics of the sensor. System variables can be referenced by event filters, which are described later in this chapter.

> **NOTE** You can only change the value of an alarm channel system variable. You can't add, delete, rename, or modify the constraints or type of alarm channel system variables.

FIGURE 23.13 Alarm generation on Cisco Secure IDS

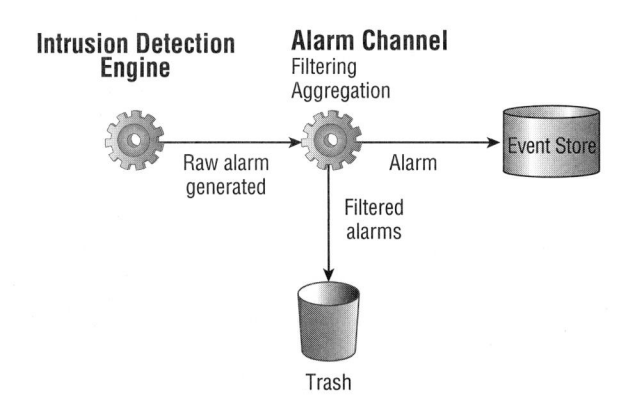

Cisco Secure IDS 4.*x* includes the following alarm channel system variables:

OUT The OUT system variable defines all networks that are considered external and has a fixed value of 0–255.255.255.255 (in other words, any IP address) that can't be modified.

IN The IN system variable defines all networks that are considered internal to the sensor; it's blank by default. Defining the networks that are internal is important, because it allows the sensor to identify the source and destination of intrusive activity as being either internal or external.

When you're defining the IN system variable, you need to enter the most significant portion of the address that uniquely identifies your internal networks. For example, if the 10.0.0.0/8 network is considered internal, you can specify the number 10 to define this network. If only the 10.20.0.0/16 network is considered internal, you would specify 10.20. You can specify multiple internal networks by separating each network with a comma, and you can also specify a range of networks by using the hyphen character. For example, if the IN system variable has a value of 10,192.168.1-192.168.10, then the networks 10.0.0.0/8 and 192.168.1.0/24–192.168.10.0/24 are considered internal.

DMZ1, DMZ2, and DMZ3 The DMZ1, DMZ2, and DMZ3 system variables can be used to define demilitarized zone (DMZ) networks in your network topology, which can then be used to filter alarms originating from or directed toward the DMZ networks. A DMZ network is a network that has a trust level in between external and internal networks and is often used to provide access for users and devices on external networks rather than providing direct access to the internal network. Figure 23.14 shows an example firewall topology that includes several DMZ networks.

In Figure 23.14, a public DMZ provides public web and mail access to external users and devices on the Internet, and a third-party DMZ provides access to third parties. A Cisco Secure IDS sensor monitors traffic sent from the Internet to the public DMZ as well as traffic sent from third parties to the internal network. The Cisco Secure IDS sensor can be configured with the following system variables to separately identify the DMZ networks:

- DMZ1 = 200.1.1
- DMZ2 = 172.16.1

You can then use these system variables within event filters (discussed in the next section) to define each DMZ rather than type in the IP address of the DMZ.

USER-ADDRS1, USER-ADDRS2, USER-ADDRS3, USER-ADDRS4, and USER-ADDRS5
The USER-ADDRS1 through USER-ADDRS5 system variables allow administrators to define one or more IP addresses that they may wish to filter alarms for. For example, an organization may set up a *honey pot*, which provides a lure for potential attackers by operating phantom services. Because the honey pot keeps a record of any intrusive activity performed against it, there is no point in capturing IDS alarms related to attacks on the honey pot. One of the USER-ADDRS variables can be configured with the IP addresses of the honey pot, so that a filter can be defined that excludes alarms for intrusive activity against the honey pot by referencing the variable in the event filter.

SIG1, SIG2, SIG3, SIG4, and SIG5 The SIG1 through SIG5 system variables can be used to define specific signatures, which can then be used to exclude alarms related to the signature.

FIGURE 23.14 Example topology with DMZ networks

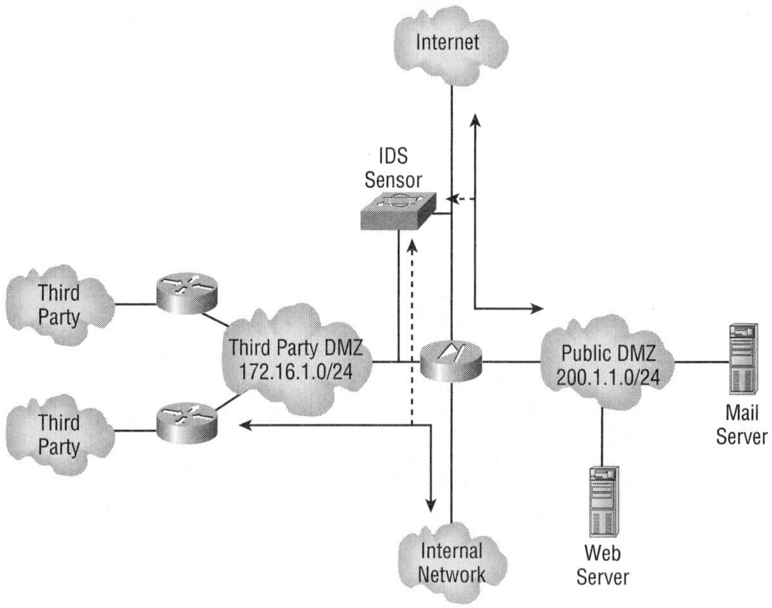

Real World Scenario

Internal and External Networks

When you're designing, implementing, and supporting network security systems, one of the key concepts relating to the system is the definition of external networks and internal networks.

An *external network* is normally an untrusted network. It's a network that is administratively not under your jurisdiction, meaning that you have no means of verifying the network security of the external network.

An *internal network* is normally a trusted network, because you have administrative control over either the entire network or some portion of the network, with other trusted administrators (that is, other staff within your organization) controlling the rest of the network. You can presume the internal network is trusted (or at least is more trusted than an external network), assuming the necessary steps to secure your network have been taken.

You configure alarm system variables using the IDM via the Configuration ➢ Sensing Engine ➢ Alarm Channel Configuration ➢ System Variables configuration page, as shown in Figure 23.15.

In Figure 23.15, notice that the only system variable that is configured by default is `OUT`, which is always `0-255.255.255.255` and can't be modified. The various `SIG` system variables aren't shown in Figure 23.15 but can be viewed by clicking the Page drop-down box and selecting Page 2.

To modify a system variable, select the appropriate check box next to the variable and then click the Edit button. Figure 23.16 demonstrates configuring the `IN` system variable.

> **NOTE** Although you can select multiple system variables, you can edit only one at a time. You can select multiple system variables and reset their values to their respective defaults by clicking the Reset button.

In Figure 23.16, a value of `192.168.1` is configured for the `IN` system variable, which defines the 192.168.1.0/24 network as internal. To apply the system variable value, click the OK button. At this point, a dialog is displayed, as shown in Figure 23.17, warning you that although the system variable value has been modified, you must still commit the configuration change.

After clicking OK, you're returned to a modified System Variables page, as shown in Figure 23.18. Notice that the `IN` system variable filter has been applied and that a new icon has appeared in the Activity bar. You must click this Save Changes icon in order for the system variable modifications to be permanently saved.

FIGURE 23.15 The System Variables configuration page

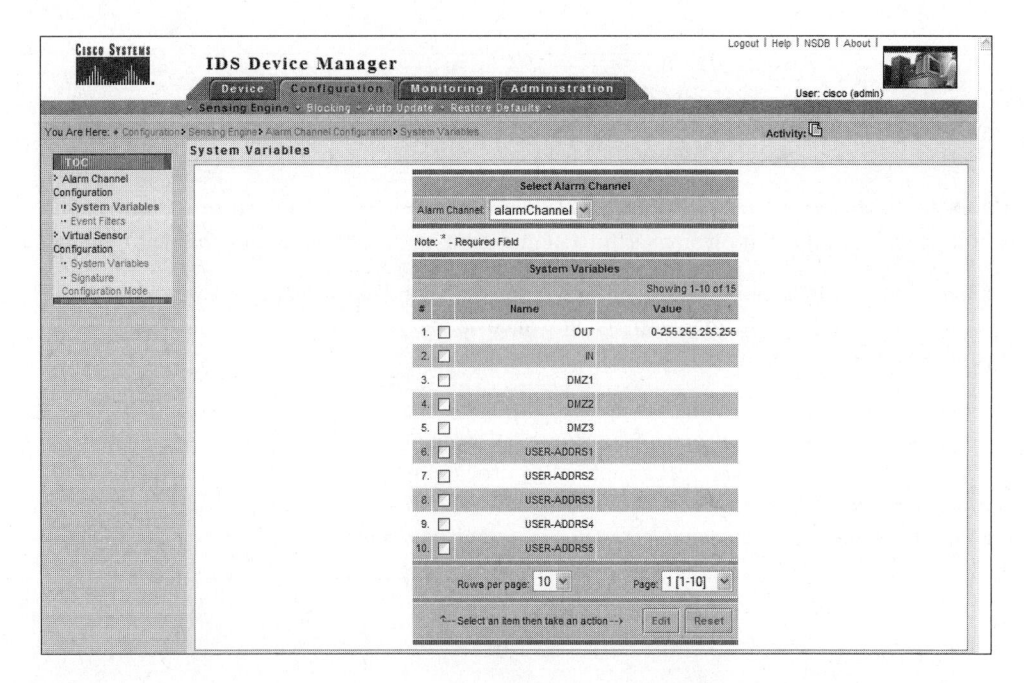

Configuring Cisco Secure IDS Sensors Using the IDM   801

FIGURE 23.16   Configuring the IN system variable

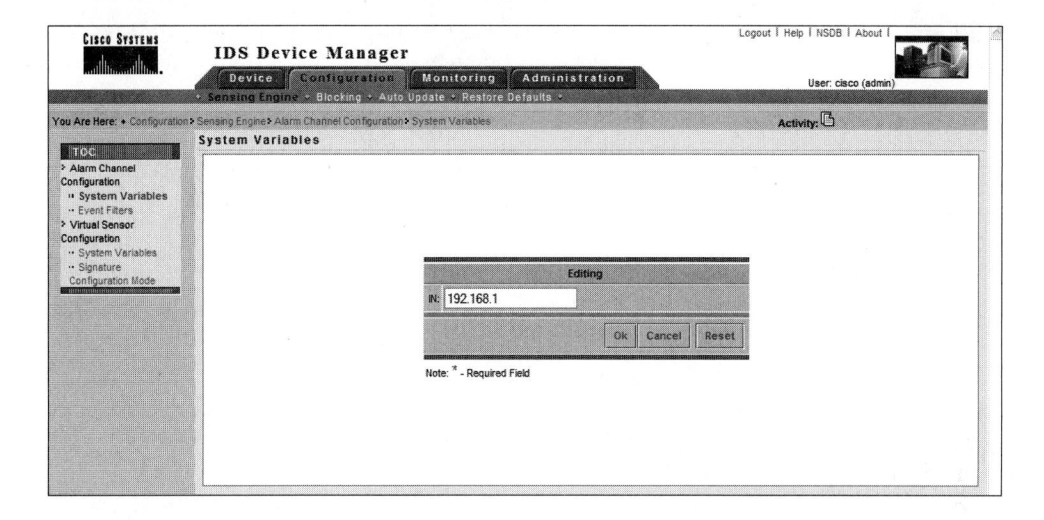

FIGURE 23.17   System variable configuration warning

FIGURE 23.18   System variable page after modification

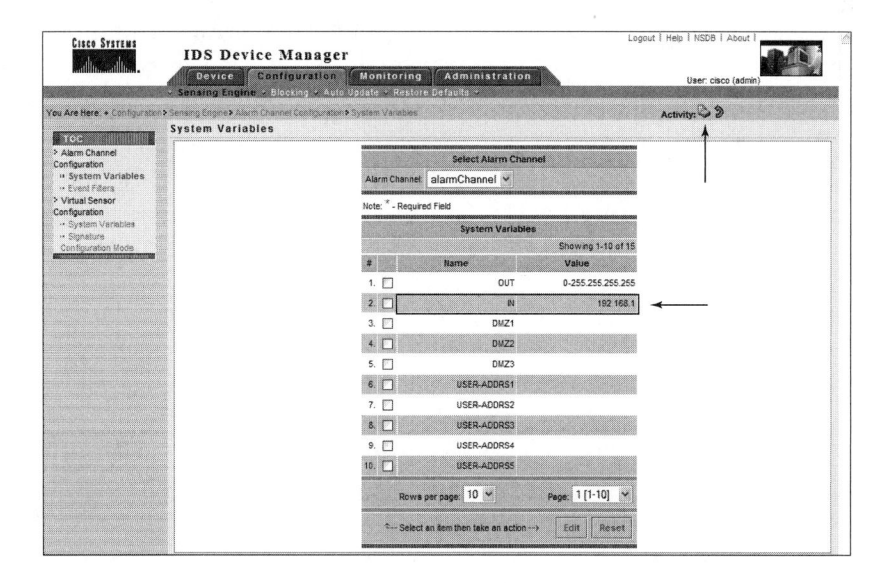

> **NOTE** After committing changes using the Activity bar, you may find that you're unable to configure the sensor for some time. This may continue for several minutes while any changes are committed.

CONFIGURING ALARM CHANNEL SYSTEM VARIABLES USING THE SENSOR CLI

To enable configuration of alarm channel system variables, the sensor CLI includes a fourth-level alarm channel configuration CLI mode. To configure alarm channel system variables, you must first access this CLI mode using the `service` global configuration command as follows:

sensor(config)# **service alarm-channel-configuration** *alarm-channel-name*

Notice that an *alarm-channel-name* parameter must be specified; it indicates the name of the *virtual alarm channel* you're configuring. In the current version 4.*x* release, only a single virtual alarm channel exists: `virtualAlarm`.

> **NOTE** Virtual alarm channels are used to enable support of multiple virtual sensors running on the same physical sensor platform in future software versions.

The following demonstrates accessing the alarm channel configuration CLI mode:

```
ids-4210# configure terminal
ids-4210(config)# service alarm-channel-configuration virtualAlarm
ids-4210(config-acc)# ?
```

Notice that the prompt changes to include `config-acc`, which indicates that alarm channel configuration mode has been accessed. Once you're in this mode, you use the `tune-alarm-channel` command to enter configuration mode for the alarm channel. Within this mode, you can configure system variables using the `systemVariables` command, or you can configure event filters (discussed later in this chapter) using the `EventFilter` command. The following demonstrates configuring alarm channel system variables using the `systemVariables` command, once you're in configuration mode for the alarm:

```
ids-4210# configure terminal
ids-4210(config)# service alarm-channel-configuration virtualAlarm
ids-4210(config-acc)# tune-alarm-channel
ids-4210(config-acc-virtualAlarm)# systemVariables
ids-4210(config-acc-virtualAlarm-sys)# ?
default         Set the value back to the system default setting
DMZ1            Defines the DMZ1 network space
DMZ2            Defines the DMZ2 network space
DMZ3            Defines the DMZ3 network space
```

```
exit              Exit systemVariables configuration submode
IN                Defines the protected network space (Should include ALL
                  protected addresses). 'OUT' equates to all addresses
                  NOT included in 'IN'.
show              Display system settings and/or history information
SIG1              User defined Signature set
SIG2              User defined Signature set
SIG3              User defined Signature set
SIG4              User defined Signature set
SIG5              User defined Signature set
USER-ADDRS1       User defined network space
USER-ADDRS2       User defined network space
USER-ADDRS3       User defined network space
USER-ADDRS4       User defined network space
USER-ADDRS5       User defined network space
ids-4210(config-acc-virtualAlarm-sys)# IN 192.168.1.0
ids-4210(config-acc-virtualAlarm-sys)# show settings
systemVariables
    -----------------------------------------------
       OUT: 0-255.255.255.255 <protected>
       IN: 192.168.1.0
       DMZ1:
       DMZ2:
       DMZ3:
       USER-ADDRS1:
       USER-ADDRS2:
       USER-ADDRS3:
       USER-ADDRS4:
       USER-ADDRS5:
       SIG1:
       SIG2:
       SIG3:
       SIG4:
       SIG5:
    -----------------------------------------------
ids-4210(config-acc-virtualAlarm-sys)# exit
ids-4210(config-acc-virtualAlarm)# exit
Apply Changes:?[yes]: yes
ids-4210(config-acc)# exit
```

In this example, notice that once you specify the `systemVariables` command, you're taken into another configuration mode that lets you set the same system variables that are configurable using the IDM. The 192.168.1.0/24 network is defined as an internal network in this example, after which the alarm channel system variable settings are verified using the `show settings` command. After the system variable configuration is complete, you must exit back to the alarm channel configuration mode to apply the changes.

Configuring Virtual Sensor System Variables

Cisco Secure IDS 4.*x* includes the concept of a *virtual sensor*, which is a logical sensor that has a specific policy applied and is similar in concept to the virtual alarm channel discussed earlier. The concept of a virtual sensor lets you create multiple sensors running on the same physical sensor, each with a separate policy. In Cisco Secure IDS 4.*x*, only a single virtual sensor exists, which means that the policy applied to the virtual sensor effectively is the policy enforced by the physical sensor.

> **NOTE** Multiple virtual sensors are expected to be supported in future software releases.

A number of system variables are available for the virtual sensor that can be used to modify the parameters used for signatures on the IDS sensor as well as modify the types of traffic that are analyzed against different IDS engines.

Virtual sensor system variables can be modified but can't be added, deleted, or renamed. You can modify each variable from the Configuration ➤ Sensing ➤ Virtual Sensor Configuration ➤ System Variables configuration page, which is shown in Figure 23.19.

The virtual sensor system variables are as follows:

WEBPORTS This defines the TCP ports that are considered to represent web traffic. Cisco Secure IDS includes a number of signatures that relate to web traffic; instead of processing every packet send by the IDS against each web signature, only packets matching the services defined by the WEBPORTS variable are inspected.

By default, the WEBPORTS variable has a value of 80, 3128, 8000, 8010, 8080, 8888, 24326—if you have a web application or service that uses a custom web port other than those listed, you can modify the WEBPORTS variable to ensure that packets associated with the custom service will be analyzed against web-based signatures.

Ports1–Ports9 The Ports variables let you define custom ports that you can apply to specific signatures that may only be analyzed against traffic received on well-known application port(s). For example, if a signature relates to a vulnerability in the Simple Mail Transfer Protocol (SMTP), the signature will only be processed against traffic with a source or destination port of 25, which is the well-known port for SMTP. If you're using SMTP on a custom port, you can define that custom port using one of the Ports variables to enable the sensor to also process traffic using the custom port against the SMTP-related signature.

By default, no Ports variables are defined.

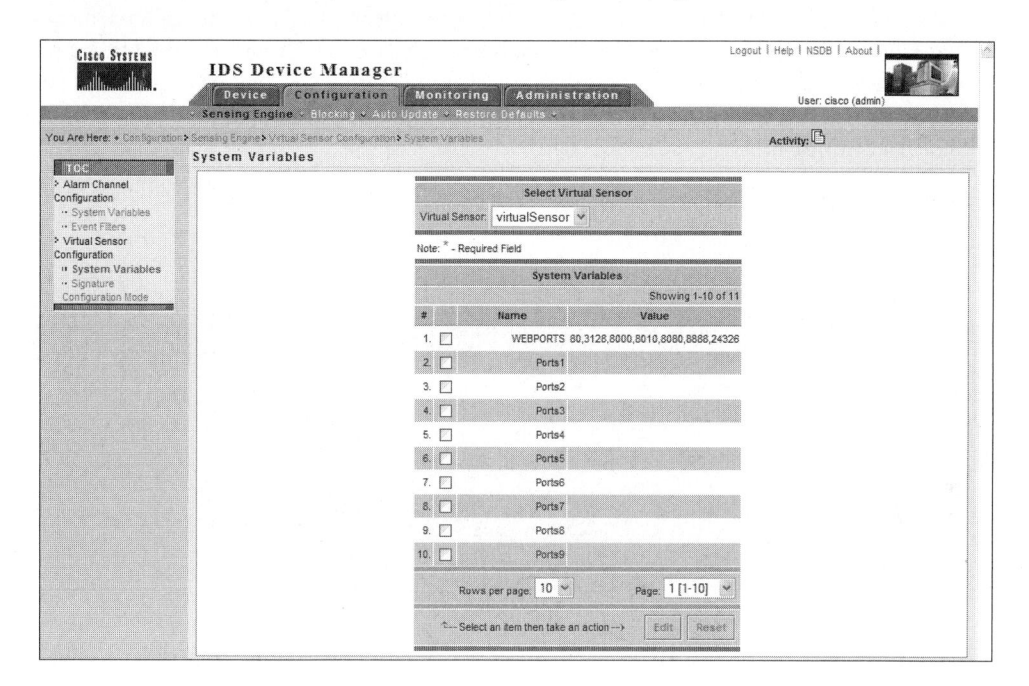

FIGURE 23.19 The System Variables configuration page

IPReassembleMaxFrags The `IPReassembleMaxFrags` variable lets you define the maximum number of fragments that the sensor will cache for fragment-reassembly purposes. Fragmentation is a common method used by attackers to avoid detection: Attack packets are split into multiple fragments. One issue with fragments is that the first packet of a fragment is the only packet that includes the various layer 4 protocol fields that identify the type of traffic (for example, a destination TCP port of 80 identifies web traffic). Subsequent fragments don't include a layer 4 header, which makes it impossible to associate the packet with a particular application-layer service or protocol if the fragment is analyzed by itself.

For an IDS sensor to detect attacks that are hidden within fragmented IP packets, the sensor must cache and reassemble all fragments associated with a fragmented IP packet, so that any potential attack packets that have been fragmented can be reconstructed into the original attack packet and subsequently detected.

By default, the `IPReassembleMaxFrags` variable has a value of 10000, which means that the sensor will cache 10,000 fragments. You can modify the number of fragments cached to any value between 1000 and 50,000 by setting the appropriate value for the `IPReassembleMaxFrags` variable.

To modify a system variable, check the box at the left of the variable that you wish to modify, and then click the Edit button. A new page will load, which lets you modify the variable.

Figure 23.20 demonstrates modifying the WEBPORTS system variable. Port 8081 is added to the WEBPORTS variable, which means that any TCP traffic with port 8081 will be analyzed against web signatures. After the modification has been made in Figure 23.20, clicking the OK button will apply the change. At this point, a warning similar to Figure 23.17 will be presented, indicating that a system variable has been changed and that the Save Changes icon in the Activity bar must be clicked to permanently save the changes.

FIGURE 23.20   Modifying a virtual sensor system variable

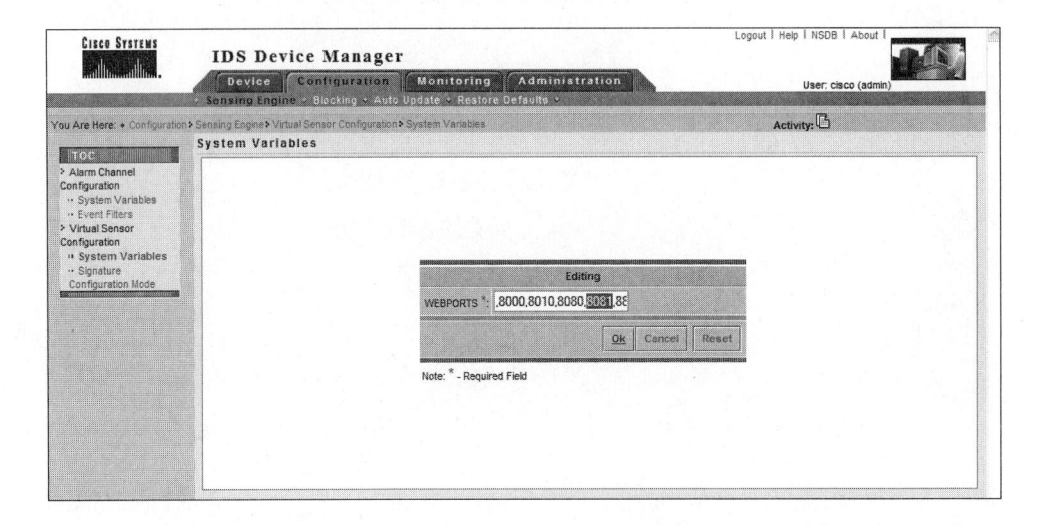

CONFIGURING VIRTUAL SENSOR SYSTEM VARIABLES USING THE SENSOR CLI

To enable configuration of virtual sensor system variables, the sensor CLI includes a fourth-level virtual sensor configuration CLI mode. To configure virtual sensor system variables, you must first access this CLI mode using the service global configuration command as follows:

sensor(config)# **service virtual-sensor-configuration** *virtual-sensor-name*

Notice that a *virtual-sensor-name* parameter must be specified; it indicates the name of the virtual sensor that you're configuring. As you learned in the previous section, in the current version 4.*x* release only a single virtual sensor exists. This is referred to as virtualSensor within the sensor CLI.

The following demonstrates accessing the virtual sensor configuration CLI mode:

ids-4210# **configure terminal**
ids-4210(config)# **service virtual-sensor-configuration virtualSensor**
ids-4210(config-vsc)# **?**

Understanding IP Fragmentation

IP fragmentation can be used to mask an attack by fragmenting the attack into IP fragments. IP fragments pose a problem not only for IDS sensors, but also for access-control devices such as firewalls and perimeter routers. An IP fragment is normally used to transport an IP datagram that is larger than the maximum transmission unit (MTU) for a network over which the datagram is being sent.

The MTU defines the maximum size of a frame or unit of data that can be sent across the network. For example, the MTU of an Ethernet network is 1518 bytes. This MTU defines the Ethernet header and data contents of a frame. Often, the data MTU is referred to. For example, any layer 3 protocol packets carried in Ethernet frames are transported in the data section of the frame. Because the Ethernet header is 18 bytes in size, the data MTU (or layer 3 MTU) for Ethernet is 1500 bytes (18 + 1500 = 1518 bytes).

When the IP datagram is larger than the MTU, the datagram must be split into fragments that are less than or equal in size to the MTU of the transit network. The following graphic demonstrates the process of fragmenting an IP datagram:

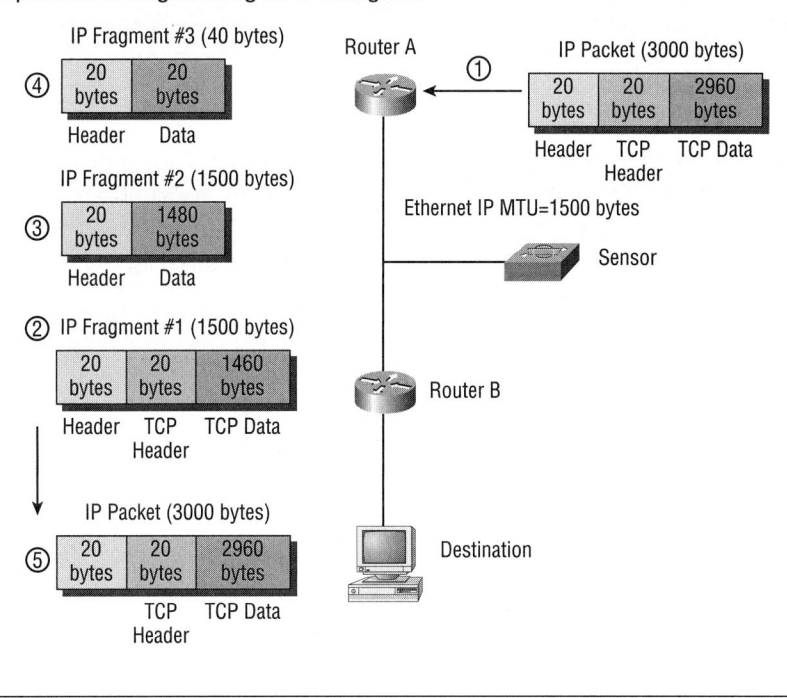

In the graphic, the IP MTU of the Ethernet link between each router is 1500 bytes, and the IP datagram size is 3000 bytes. The following events take place:

1. An IP packet of 3000 bytes is received by Router A. The packet includes an IP header of 20 bytes, a TCP header of 20 bytes, and TCP data of 2960 bytes (the IP data portion is defined as 2980 bytes). Because the next hop router (Router B) is connected by an Ethernet link with an IP MTU of 1500 bytes, Router A must fragment the packet.

2. Router A fragments the original packet and sends the first fragment, which contains an IP header of 20 bytes, the original TCP header of 20 bytes, and 1460 bytes of the original packet data.

3. Router A sends the second fragment, which contains an IP header of 20 bytes and 1480 bytes of the original packet data. Notice that the original TCP header isn't included in this fragment, so other devices on the network (such as firewalls or IDS sensors) can't determine the upper-layer protocol of the data contained in the packet.

4. Router A sends the third and final fragment, which contains an IP header of 20 bytes and 20 bytes of the original packet data. Notice that the original TCP header is also not included in this fragment, so other devices on the network (such as firewalls or IDS sensors) can't determine the upper-layer protocol of the data contained in the packet.

5. The destination host receives each fragment and reconstructs the original packet.

If you consider the fragments shown in the graphic, you'll notice that the first fragment contains the layer 4 (for example, TCP or UDP) header of the datagram, which indicates the Application-layer protocol data being transported in the packet. An IDS sensor receiving this first packet can identify the Application-layer protocol of the packet and apply the appropriate signature analysis to the packet.

The problems associated with IP fragments start with the subsequent fragments after the first one. No subsequent fragment includes the layer 4 header of the original packet; it has only an IP header that includes fragment-offset numbering that helps the destination system reassemble the fragment. This poses a problem for the IDS sensor, because the sensor has no idea to which Application-layer protocol the IP fragment belongs. If the fragment is legitimate, the sensor can assume the fragment belongs to the Application-layer protocol indicated in the first fragment. However, the fragments could be malicious, and they could be used to bypass access-control devices and mask intrusive activity contained within the fragments.

To determine the exact content of an IP fragment stream that is received, the IDS sensor must reassemble a fragmented IP datagram (just as a destination system must), which then allows the sensor to analyze the datagram in full. This process is known as *IP fragment reassembly*, and this feature is supported on the 4200 series sensors and the Catalyst IDSM.

Notice that when you access virtual sensor configuration mode, the prompt changes to include `config-vsc`. Once you're in this mode, you use the `tune-micro-engine` command to enter configuration mode for the virtual sensor. Within this configuration mode, you can configure system variables using the `systemVariables` command. The following demonstrates configuring alarm channel system variables using the `systemVariables` command once in configuration mode for the alarm:

```
ids-4210# configure terminal
ids-4210(config)# service virtual-sensor-configuration virtualSensor
ids-4210(config-vsc)# tune-micro-engines
ids-4210(config-vsc-virtualSensor)# systemVariables
ids-4210(config-vsc-virtualSensor-sys)# ?
default             Set the value back to the system default
                    setting
exit                Exit systemVariables configuration submode
IPReassembleMaxFrags Defines the maximum number of fragments to
                    allow the system to queue.
Ports1              User defined
Ports2              User defined
Ports3              User defined
Ports4              User defined
Ports5              User defined
Ports6              User defined
Ports7              User defined
Ports8              User defined
Ports9              User defined
show                Display system settings and/or history information
WEBPORTS            Defines the ports associated with the web service
ids-4210(config-vsc-virtualSensor-sys)# IPReassembleMaxFrags 20000
ids-4210(config-vsc-virtualSensor-sys)# WEBPORTS 80,81
ids-4210(config-vsc-virtualSensor-sys)# show settings
   systemVariables
   -----------------------------------------------
      WEBPORTS: 80,81 default: 80,3128,8000,8010,8080,8888,24326
      Ports1:
      Ports2:
      Ports3:
      Ports4:
      Ports5:
```

```
        Ports6:
        Ports7:
        Ports8:
        Ports9:
        IPReassembleMaxFrags: 20000 default: 10000
    ---------------------------------------------
ids-4210(config-vsc-virtualSensor-sys)# exit
ids-4210(config-vsc-virtualSensor)# exit
Apply Changes:?[yes]: yes
ids-4210(config-vsc)# exit
```

In this example, notice that once you specify the `systemVariables` command, you're taken into another configuration mode that lets you set the same system variables that are configurable using the IDM. The example sets the `IPReassembleMaxFrags` variable to 20000 and the `WEBPORTS` variable to 80 and 81, after which the new settings are verified using the `show settings` command. After completing the configuration, you must exit back to virtual sensor configuration mode to apply the changes.

Configuring Alarm Channel Event Filters

Event filters (also referred to as *signature filters*) let you configure the alarm channel to filter alarms for specific signatures, based on source and/or destination IP address or on any of the alarm channel system variables described earlier in the previous section.

To configure an alarm channel event filter, open the Configuration ➢ Sensing Engine ➢ Alarm Channel Configuration ➢ Event Filters configuration page, shown in Figure 23.21.

FIGURE 23.21   The Event Filters configuration page

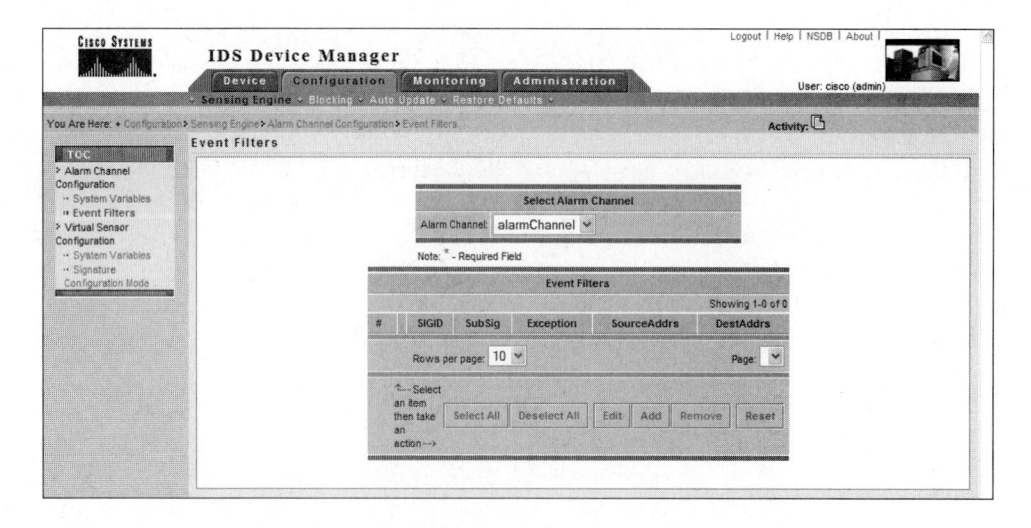

In Figure 23.21, notice that no event filters are configured by default. To add a new filter, click the Add button. Doing so displays the page shown in Figure 23.22.

In Figure 23.22, you can see that the composition of an event filter consists of the following components:

SIGID This value specifies the numeric signature ID of the signature that the filter excludes. You can also specify any SIG system variable if these have been defined. Notice in Figure 23.22 that a range of signatures has been specified (2001–2004). The asterisk character (*) can be used to specify all signatures.

SubSig Some signatures include *subsignatures*, which although unique inherit all the properties of the parent signature. The SubSig field identifies the subsignature ID that the filter excludes. The asterisk character (*) can be used to specify all subsignatures.

Exception If this option is enabled, it negates the filter, meaning that all alarms except for those matching the criteria of the event filter will be excluded.

SrcAddrs This field defines the source IP address of intrusive activity that is to be filtered. You can type in the desired addresses, or you can specify the DMZ or USER-ADDRS system variable. When you're specifying a numeric address, you can use *ip-address/mask-length* syntax. Notice in Figure 23.22 that the value 10.0.0.0 is specified, which references any IP address in the 10.0.0.0 Class A network. The asterisk character (*) can be used to specify all addresses.

DestAddrs This property defines the destination IP address of intrusive activity that is to be filtered. You can type in the desired addresses, or you can specify the DMZ or USER-ADDRS system variables. Notice in Figure 23.22 that the value 192.168.0.0 is specified, which references any IP address in the 192.168.0.0 network. The asterisk character (*) can be used to specify all addresses.

FIGURE 23.22 Creating an event filter

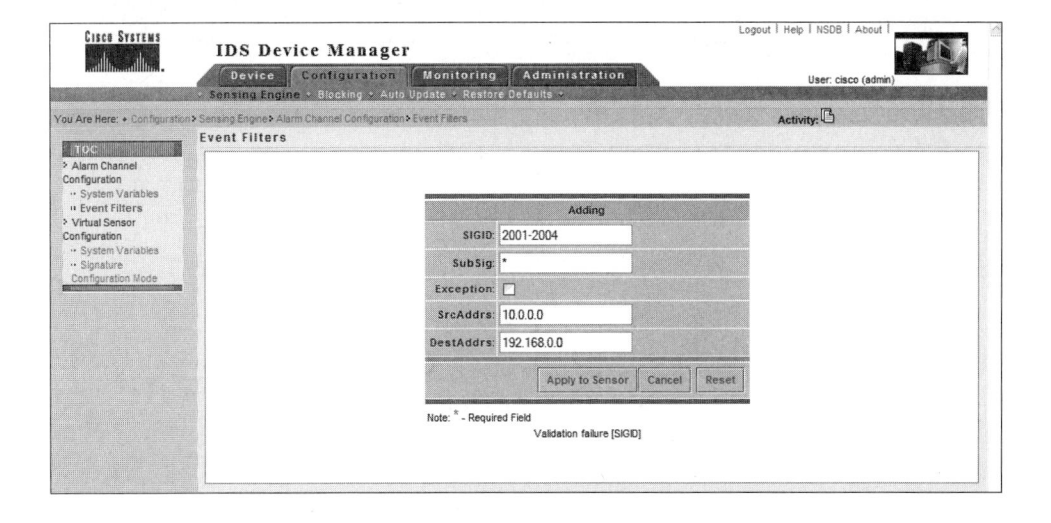

To complete the configuration of the event filter, click the Apply To Sensor button. At this stage, if you've mistyped or misconfigured any fields, a validation error will appear, identifying the field that has a problem. Assuming your configuration is correct, a warning will appear; it indicates that, although the event filter has been created, you still must commit the changes using the Activity bar (similar to Figure 23.17). After acknowledging this warning, the Event Filters page will be displayed again, this time with the new event filter as shown in Figure 23.23.

Notice in the Activity bar that the Save Changes icon has appeared; you must click it for the configuration changes to be permanently saved. The configuration of Figure 23.23 creates an event filter that won't exclude alarms from being generated for traffic with a source IP address of 10.*x.x.x* and a destination IP address of 192.168.x.x that triggers signatures with a signature ID of 2001–2004.

FIGURE 23.23 The Event Filters page after creating an event filter

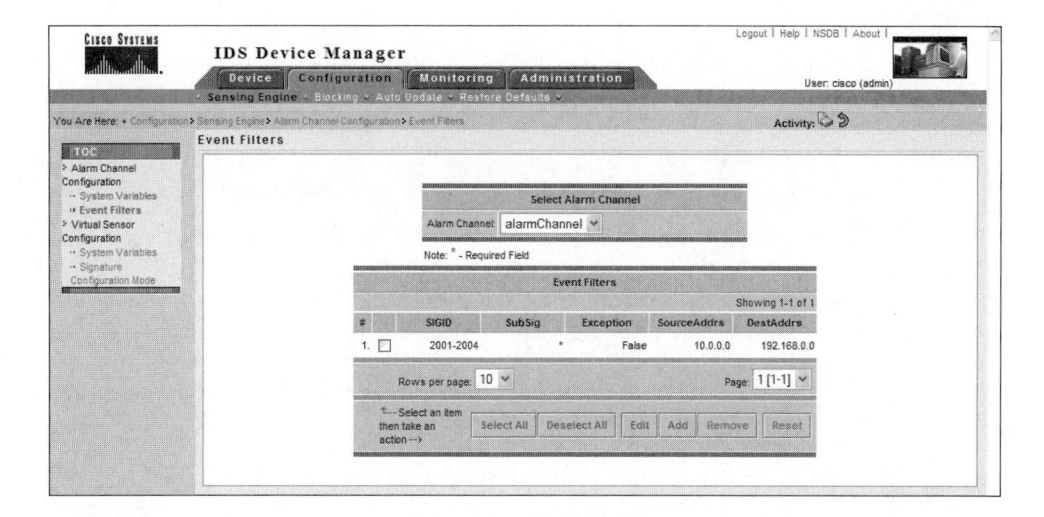

Configuring Alarm Channel Event Filters Using the Sensor CLI

To configure event filters using the sensor CLI, you must first access the fourth-level alarm channel configuration CLI mode by executing the `service alarm-channel-configuration virtualAlarm` command and then enter the `tune-alarm-channel` command. From here, you can specify the `EventFilter` command, which takes you to a new configuration mode where you can create event filters. To create a filter, you use the `Filters` command, which is demonstrated in the following example:

```
ids-4210# configure terminal
ids-4210(config)# service alarm-channel-configuration virtualAlarm
ids-4210(config-acc)# tune-alarm-channel
ids-4210(config-acc-virtualAlarm)# EventFilter
ids-4210(config-acc-virtualAlarm-Eve)# Filters ?
```

DestAddrs	Source Addresses of Events to which this filter should be applied.
Exception	Does this filter describe an exception to an event filter? This allows creating 'General Case' exclusions then adding more specific inclusions.
SIGID	Signature ID's of Events to which this filter should be applied.
SourceAddrs	Source Addresses of Events to which this filter should be applied.
SubSig	SubSigID's of Events to which this filter should be applied.

```
ids-4210(config-acc-virtualAlarm-Eve)# Filters SIGID 2001-2004 SourceAddrs
10.0.0.0 DestAddrs 192.168.0.0
ids-4210(config-acc-virtualAlarm-Eve)# show settings
   EventFilter
   -----------------------------------------------
      version: 4.0 <protected>
      Filters (min: 0, max: 5000, current: 1)
      -----------------------------------------------
         DestAddrs: 192.168.0.0 default: *
         Exception: False <defaulted>
         SIGID: 2001-2004 default: *
         SourceAddrs: 10.0.0.0 default: *
         SubSig: * <defaulted>
         -----------------------------------------------
      -----------------------------------------------
   -----------------------------------------------
ids-4210(config-acc-virtualAlarm-Eve)# exit
ids-4210(config-acc-virtualAlarm)# exit
Apply Changes:?[yes]: yes
ids-4210(config-acc)#
```

In this example, the same event filter created earlier using the IDM is created using the CLI. Notice that the Filters command lets you specify each of the parameters that compose an event filter. After the event filter configuration is complete, you must exit back to the alarm channel configuration mode to apply the changes.

Configuring Blocking Using the IDM

Cisco Secure IDS sensors can manage Cisco perimeter device access-control security by dynamically applying *access control lists (ACLs)* or *shun rules* to a perimeter router or firewall. ACLs are sets of ordered statements (each statement is referred to as an *access control entry*) that either permit or deny a specific type of traffic to be sent or received on a perimeter router or firewall interface. Cisco Secure IDS sensors can connect to Cisco IOS routers and Catalyst 6500 switches as required and apply an ACL to the appropriate interface(s) that include ACEs that block access from attacking hosts, protecting the network from attackers. Cisco Secure IDS sensors can also generate shun rules on Cisco PIX firewalls. A shun rule is a temporary block that is applied to traffic received by the PIX firewall and is applied in addition to the current ACLs defined on the PIX.

The ability to perform these actions is referred to as *device management*, with each perimeter and firewall device referred to as a *managed device*.

IP blocking (also referred to as *shunning*) is the process of using the device-management capabilities of a sensor to block an attacker from having further access to networks protected by a perimeter router or firewall. IP blocking is invoked by Cisco Secure IDS sensors in response to intrusive activity detected on the monitoring interface. Cisco Secure IDS lets you customize signatures so that if a signature match triggers an alarm, an action such as IP blocking can take place.

> **NOTE** In the next software release, titled Cisco Intrusion Prevention System (CIPS) version 5.0 (due early 2005), IP blocking is likely to become a thing of the past, because sensors will support inline operation in which they can drop malicious packets directly without requiring an external perimeter device. Inline intrusion prevention is more effective than blocking, because blocking allows initial attack traffic and isn't effective against single-packet attacks.

In the following sections, you'll learn about the various IP blocking architectures that you can configure, IP blocking considerations, and how to implement IP blocking.

Blocking Architectures

When you're considering blocking architectures, it's important to understand the number of sensors you have and the number of entry points into your network from external networks.

At each entry point to your network, you'll have at least one perimeter device. At the most basic level, perimeter devices control traffic flows between an external network and an internal network. In a well-designed network security topology, the perimeter device provides the first line of defense for the protected network and associated systems. Often, these devices are Cisco routers or Cisco PIX firewalls that use ACLs to control access in and out of the network. Blocking uses these perimeter devices to block systems that are trying to attack your network. This is the ideal blocking point, because it represents the outermost gateway between your network and untrusted networks, ensuring that attack traffic can't infiltrate any part of your network.

Many organizations also implement multiple entry points to external networks for high availability and performance benefits. Obviously, all perimeter devices at each entry point must be configured with the same IP blocking configuration to prevent an attacker from using other entry points to attack your network. A single IDS sensor can manage multiple perimeter devices at each entry point to your network; however, for some environments, it's recommended that you deploy multiple IDS sensors throughout your network.

To summarize, blocking is often implemented in one of the following scenarios:

- Single sensor with a single perimeter device
- Single sensor with multiple perimeter devices
- Multiple sensors with multiple perimeter devices

In the following sections, you'll learn about each of these architectures.

Single Sensor and Single Perimeter Device

The simplest blocking architecture is for a sensor to manage a single perimeter device, instructing the device to block attack traffic when the sensor detects it. Figure 23.24 shows the typical topology used for this architecture.

In Figure 23.24, the perimeter device is a Cisco IOS router. The following events occur that cause blocking to be invoked:

1. The sensor detects an attack from an external hacker. The signature that matches the attack has an action of blocking defined, which tells the sensor to block the source IP address of the attack traffic.
2. The sensor establishes a Telnet or SSH session to the perimeter router and implements the blocking configuration by applying an ACL for external traffic inbound to the router that blocks the attacking host.

FIGURE 23.24   Blocking with a single perimeter router

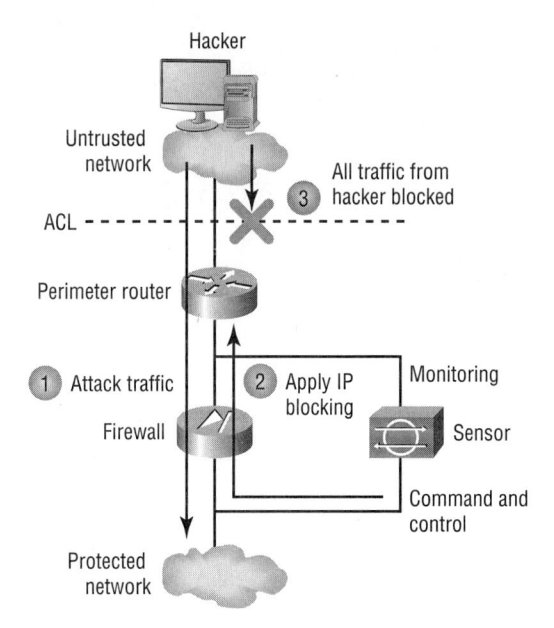

3. All subsequent traffic from the attacking host (the IP address that the hacker is attacking from) only is blocked. However, all other traffic is permitted. After a configurable amount of time, the sensor establishes another Telnet or SSH session to the perimeter router and removes the blocking.

> **Note:** Cisco Secure IDS lets you block all traffic from an attacking host, or block only the connection associated with the intrusive activity that fires the alarm.

Single Sensor and Multiple Perimeter Devices

Many organizations implement multiple connections to external networks to enhance the performance and availability of connectivity to the external network. There are many different ways that you can implement multiple external connections, each providing varying levels of redundancy with varying levels of cost and complexity. Figure 23.25 shows a simple network topology that provides multiple connections to an external network and demonstrates how a single sensor can manage multiple perimeter devices.

FIGURE 23.25 IP blocking with multiple perimeter devices

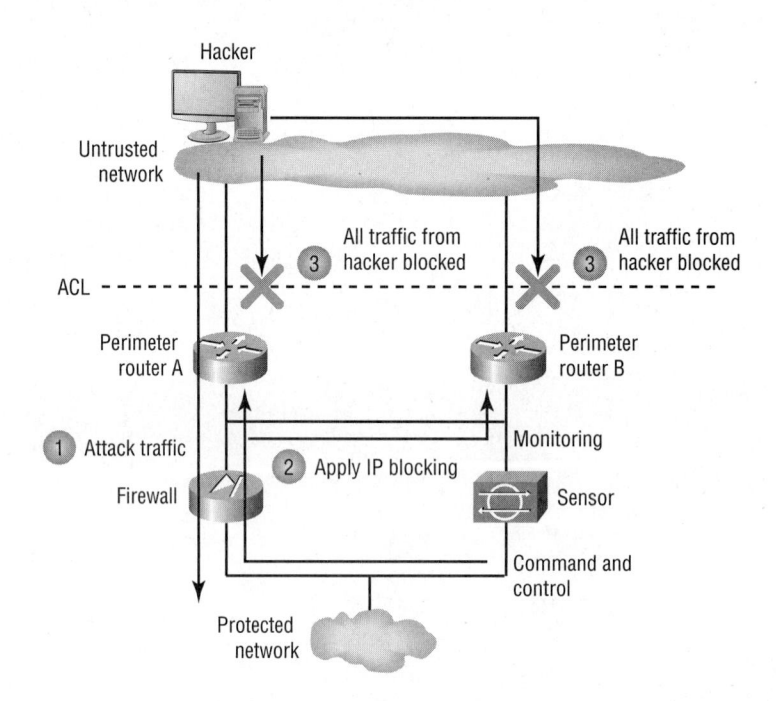

In Figure 23.25, the following events occur that cause IP blocking to be invoked:

1. The sensor detects an attack from an external hacker. The attack signature has an action of blocking defined, which tells the sensor to implement blocking of the source IP address of the attack traffic.
2. The sensor establishes a Telnet or SSH session to each perimeter router and implements the blocking configuration by applying an ACL for external traffic inbound to each router that blocks the attacking host.
3. Any subsequent traffic from the attacker (whether for attack or legitimate purposes) is blocked for the duration of the blocking timeout at both perimeter routers A and B. This ensures that the protected network is protected at all entry points into the network.

Using a single sensor to manage multiple perimeter routers for blocking works in the topology illustrated in Figure 23.25 because, although there are two external entry points to the network, they both provide access to a shared segment (Internet DMZ), which is monitored by a single sensor. A single sensor can detect attacks that traverse either entry point into the network, meaning that the blocking will always be invoked. In more complex environments, multiple sensors may be required because the entry points may be geographically dispersed, making it impossible for a single sensor to monitor traffic from all entry points.

Multiple Sensors and Multiple Perimeter Devices

Each sensor keeps track of the current ACLs configured on the devices it manages. If multiple sensors manage the same perimeter device, the ACL state information held on each sensor becomes obsolete as soon as another sensor applies a new ACL to the perimeter device. This confuses the sensor and leads to incorrect IP blocking configuration. To work around this restriction, Cisco Secure IDS allows a single sensor known as a *master blocking sensor* to be responsible for implementing blocking on all perimeter devices; all other sensors (known as *blocking forwarding sensors*) forward *blocking requests* to the master blocking sensor rather than applying blocking to perimeter devices themselves. This means that all perimeter devices are managed by only a single sensor, ensuring that conflicting blocking configurations don't result from multiple sensors attempting to manage a single device.

Each sensor can be configured with an optional master blocking sensor, which is a remote sensor that the local sensor instructs to implement blocking on behalf of the local sensor. Figure 23.26 illustrates the use of a master blocking sensor.

In Figure 23.26, the following occurs, causing blocking to be invoked at both the first perimeter router and at the second perimeter router:

1. Sensor A detects an attack from an external hacker. The attack signature has an action of blocking defined, which tells the sensor to implement blocking of the source IP address of the attack traffic.
2. Sensor A is configured as a blocking forwarding sensor and is configured with a master blocking sensor of Sensor B. Sensor A sends a blocking request via an HTTPS connection to Sensor B, requesting the blocking of the source of the detected attack on all perimeter devices.

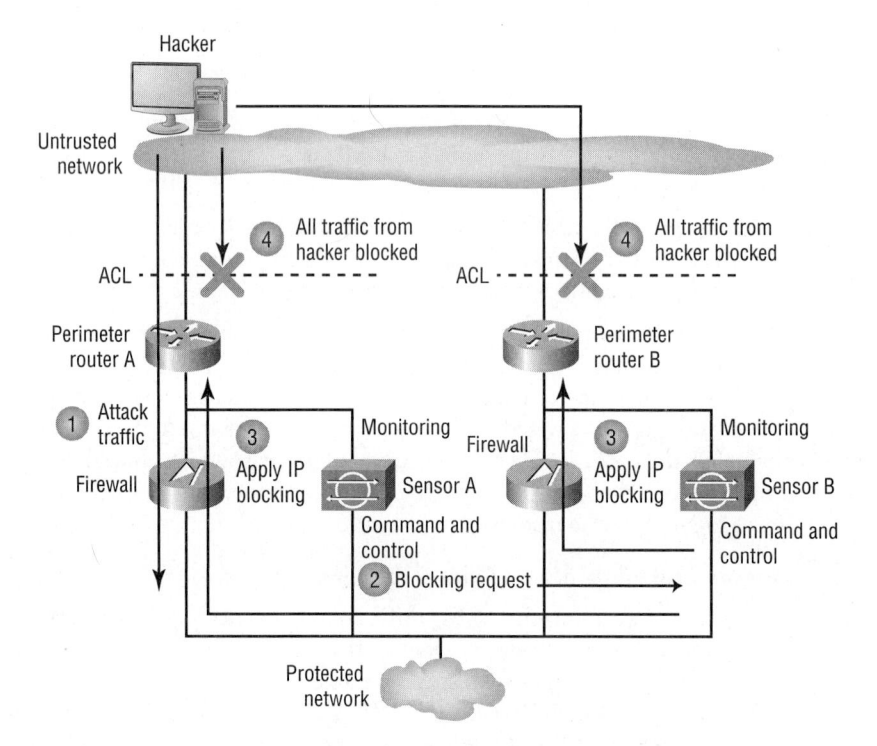

FIGURE 23.26 Blocking with a master blocking sensor

3. Sensor B accepts the blocking request, establishes a Telnet/SSH session to each managed device (in Figure 23.26, these are Router A and Router B), and applies the blocking configuration.
4. Any subsequent traffic from the attacker (whether for attack or legitimate purposes) is blocked for the duration of the blocking timeout at both perimeter routers A and B. This ensures that the protected network is protected at all entry points into the network.

Blocking Considerations

Blocking certainly sounds like a very useful feature. After all, if you're under attack from an external threat, it's desirable to be able to detect the attack and automatically block further IP traffic from the attacking system at the perimeter of your network. You must, however, be extremely careful when implementing blocking, because the feature itself can be used as a denial of service (DoS) tool.

For example, you might have an extranet link to a critical business partner via the Internet. An attacker could send traffic that is considered intrusive with spoofed source IP addresses of systems that belong to your partner. If you've configured your sensors to use blocking as a response to the intrusive activity, connections to your partner systems will be blocked by your perimeter device(s).

You can tune the security of your network to ensure that DoS via IP blocking is thwarted. Another key consideration for IP blocking is ensuring that an IP blocking configuration is applied at all entry points to your network.

Before implementing IP blocking, consider the following techniques that ensure its effectiveness:

Identify critical systems   By identifying all of the critical systems, you can configure your sensor to never block traffic from these systems. Critical systems include not only business systems, but also network systems that are critical for maintaining network connectivity. These systems can include authentication systems (for example, RADIUS or TACACS servers), DNS servers, network management systems, and so on.

> **TIP** When you configure TACACS authentication to gain management access to Cisco routers, you often configure a backup authentication mechanism to ensure that you can still gain management access in the event of the TACACS server being down. An attacker could masquerade (spoof) as the TACACS server performing an attack that triggered an IP blocking action, effectively blocking access to your TACACS server on the perimeter router. This would then allow attackers to bypass the TACACS authentication on your perimeter router, instead using another mechanism that might not be as secure.

Implement anti-spoofing filtering on your perimeter devices   For any perimeter device, it's good practice to examine and filter bogus source IP addresses from the external network (also known as *network ingress filtering*). If packets arrive at your perimeter device from the external network with source IP addresses that belong to internal systems or use RFC 1918 addressing (private addressing such as 10.*x*.*x*.*x*), these packets should be dropped because the source IP address has been forged. This will prevent attack traffic with spoofed internal addresses from triggering IP blocking for the spoofed internal systems, because the spoofed traffic is discarded at the perimeter of the network before the sensor sees it.

> **TIP** RFC 2827 (see www.faqs.org/rfcs/rfc2827.html) defines how you should implement network ingress filtering.

Configure blocking by exception only   Rather than implementing IP blocking for all signatures and then selectively disabling it for certain signatures, implement IP blocking for only the signatures that you feel require the feature. You should also consider the length of time an IP blocking configuration is applied. By default, this is 30 minutes. You may require a longer or shorter blocking time, depending on how slowly or quickly your security staff can respond to an incident.

Understand all entry points into your network   To ensure the effectiveness of your blocking configuration, make sure that you understand any alternative entry points to your network. The blocked system could use these other entry points to continue the attack, bypassing the effectiveness of the IP blocking feature. Cisco Secure IDS allows sensors to instruct other sensors at alternative entry points to implement blocking on the perimeter device at each entry point.

> **TIP** Dial-in access points are common entry points that are often overlooked.

ACL Placement for IP Blocking

Depending on the device on which you're implementing blocking, it's important to understand how ACL placement can affect blocking.

On the Cisco PIX firewall, blocking isn't implemented with ACLs; instead, it's implemented with shuns, which are implemented in addition to preexisting ACLs that may be in place. This means that you don't need to consider ACL placement on the PIX firewall.

On Cisco IOS routers and Catalyst 6500 switches, Cisco Secure IDS sensors use extended IP ACLs to configure blocking. Any ACL with a number in the range of 100 to 199, or 2600 to 2699, is considered an extended IP ACL. ACLs can be applied either inbound or outbound on an interface, which leads to the question of exactly where you should apply an ACL and in which direction. If you apply an IP ACL inbound on an interface, all IP traffic that is received by that interface is passed through the ACL. If you apply an IP ACL outbound on an interface, all IP traffic that is sent out that interface is passed through the ACL. Normally, you'll be applying blocking on a perimeter router, which regulates access between an external (untrusted) network and internal (trusted or protected) network.

In Cisco Secure IDS 4.x, you can define ACL entries that should be applied before the specific entries used for blocking (referred to as a *pre-block ACL*) as well as ACL entries that should be applied after the specific blocking entries (referred to as a *post-block ACL*). This ensures that any existing security policy configured on the router can be maintained if required and also ensures that specific rules are never overridden by blocking. For example, if a perimeter router is currently permitting web traffic to a critical host that should never be blocked, you can define a pre-block ACL that includes this web access. You can then define other security rules that are enforced after any blocking is implemented using a post-block ACL.

To ensure that all traffic either inbound to or outbound from the protected network is passed through the perimeter router, you must have a dedicated interface for both the external network and internal network. The interface that connects to the external network is designated an external interface. The interface that connects to the internal network is designated an internal interface. Understanding that a perimeter router possesses these interfaces (internal and external) and that ACLs can be applied either inbound or outbound on each interface is paramount to understanding how IP blocking can be configured.

The function of IP blocking is to protect the internal network from hosts on the external network that are sending attack traffic. This means that traffic from the external network going to the internal network must be analyzed and filtered appropriately. To achieve this, you can either apply an ACL inbound on the external interface or apply an ACL outbound on the internal interface. Figure 23.27 illustrates both ACL placement methods for IP blocking.

FIGURE 23.27 ACL placement for IP blocking

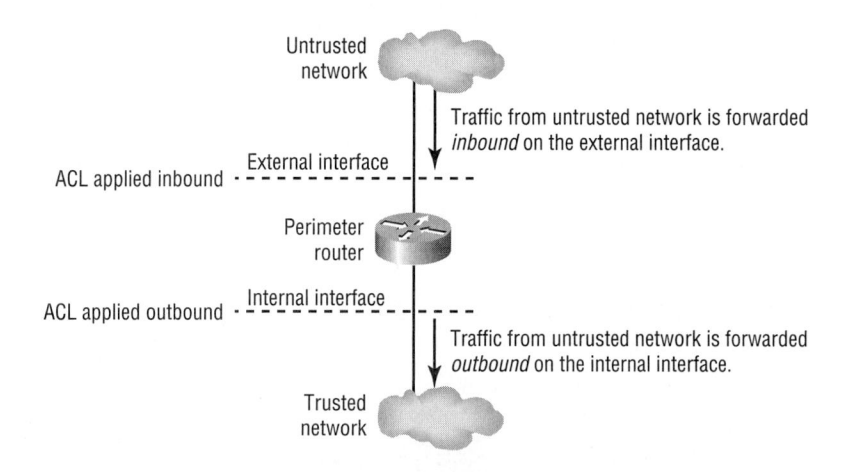

[Diagram: Untrusted network connects to External interface of Perimeter router (ACL applied inbound); traffic from untrusted network is forwarded inbound on the external interface. Internal interface connects to Trusted network (ACL applied outbound); traffic from untrusted network is forwarded outbound on the internal interface.]

> **TIP** Cisco Secure IDS sensors let you apply blocking to more than one interface. This is useful if you have a perimeter router that has multiple interfaces, which provide multiple connections to external networks.

If you choose to apply blocking inbound on the external interface of your perimeter router, consider that if blocking is invoked, attack traffic is dropped before it enters the router for subsequent routing. Also, you can't apply your own custom ACL inbound on the external interface, because the sensor will overwrite any custom configuration. Many organizations like to configure basic filtering at this point (before traffic enters the router) to provide a first level of security. If you require this functionality, you must either configure the ACL outbound on the internal interface or define the custom ACL entries in pre-block and post-block ACLs.

The second method (applying blocking outbound on the internal interface) is less secure, since the router now must receive and process all traffic, which makes the router itself vulnerable to attack. This is the case because attack traffic is dropped after it enters the router, which means the router isn't protected from the attacking system by blocking; hence it's preferable to implement the blocking ACL inbound on the external interface with any constant security rules defined in pre-block and post-block ACLs.

The Blocking Process

Now that you understand how ACLs are used on Cisco routers and the considerations for determining where you should apply them, it's useful to understand the IP blocking process in detail. Figure 23.28 shows the process that occurs when IP blocking is invoked.

FIGURE 23.28 The IP blocking process

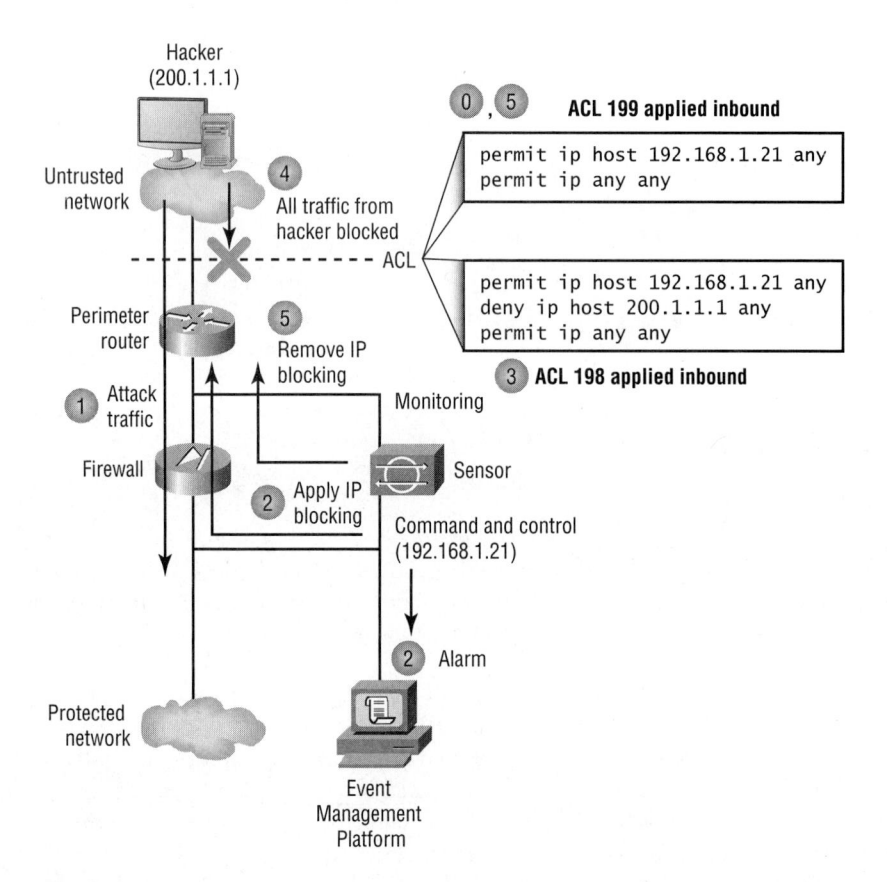

Figure 23.28 illustrates applying an ACL inbound on the external interface. Prior to the events in Figure 23.28, when device management support is initially configured on the sensor, it will apply a default ACL (numbered 199) to the perimeter router that permits all traffic. The default ACL contains the following entries:

```
access-list 199 permit ip host 192.168.1.21 any
access-list 199 permit ip any any
```

Notice that the sensor explicitly places a `permit` statement at the top of the ACL to ensure that the sensor itself (192.168.1.21) can access the perimeter router at all times. A `permit ip any any` access control entry (ACE) is added after the blocking ACE (at the end) to permit other traffic.

The following events occur in the IP blocking process illustrated in Figure 23.28:

1. An attacker sends traffic that is considered intrusive to a system hosted on the protected network. The traffic passes through a segment that the sensor is monitoring.

2. The sensor inspects this traffic, which triggers a signature that has an IP blocking action defined. An alarm is generated and sent to the event management platform. The sensor ensures that the source IP address of the attack traffic isn't on a list of IP addresses that IP blocking shouldn't be applied to (this is to protect critical systems from a DoS attack based on IP blocking).
3. The sensor establishes a Telnet/SSH session to the perimeter router (in the same manner a network administrator establishes a session), passes the appropriate Telnet and enable passwords to the router, and creates a blocking extended IP ACL. In Figure 23.28, this is one less (198) than the current ACL (199) in place, and this ACL denies all traffic from the attacking system (all traffic with a source IP address of the traffic that triggered the signature). The ACL is then applied to either the internal or external interface of the perimeter router.

> **Note**
>
> Management access to perimeter routers is often restricted to specific hosts by using the `access-class` command on the vty (Telnet or SSH) lines of the router. You must ensure that any ACLs referenced by this command permit access from the sensor; otherwise the perimeter router will block Telnet access from the sensor, and IP blocking will fail.

4. All IP traffic from the attacker is now blocked by the perimeter router. This includes traffic generated by the attacking system that might even be legitimate. In other words, the attacking system has been blocked, rather than the intrusive traffic.
5. After a configurable time period (the default is 30 minutes), the sensor removes the IP blocking configuration by applying a nonblocking ACL with a `permit ip host 192.168.1.21 any` ACE and a `permit ip any any` ACE. This ACL reverts back to number 199. This process of swapping ACL numbers is required to ensure that an ACL is applied to the interface at all times.

It's important to note in Figure 23.28 that if a pre-block ACL and post-block ACL are configured, the pre-block ACL entries will be included before the blocking ACE, and the post-block ACL entries will be included after the blocking ACE.

Configuring Blocking

Before you can configure blocking, your perimeter devices must be installed and configured correctly for routing on the network. The perimeter device must be reachable via IP from the sensor, and Telnet/SSH access to the device must be enabled. If your perimeter devices meet these requirements, you can configure blocking (no specific router configuration is required to implement blocking).

The following configuration tasks are required to implement blocking using the IDM:

1. Define blocking properties.
2. Exclude critical systems from blocking.
3. Configure logical devices.

4. Configure blocking devices.
5. Configure master blocking sensors.
6. Configure manual blocking.

Defining Blocking Properties

On the IDM, the Blocking Properties page lets you define two global settings that apply to blocking:

- Whether the sensor command-and-control IP address can be blocked
- The maximum combined number of block entries that exist at any time

To configure blocking properties using the IDM, select Configuration ➤ Blocking and then select Blocking Properties from the TOC displayed. Figure 23.29 shows the Blocking Properties configuration page.

In Figure 23.29, the default settings for the Blocking Properties configuration page are shown. Notice that the sensor IP address isn't permitted to be blocked by default, which means that an extra ACE permitting access to the sensor will be applied before any blocking ACEs (see Figure 23.28). The maximum number of block entries is 100 by default; you can modify it to any value between 0 and 250.

FIGURE 23.29 The Blocking Properties configuration page

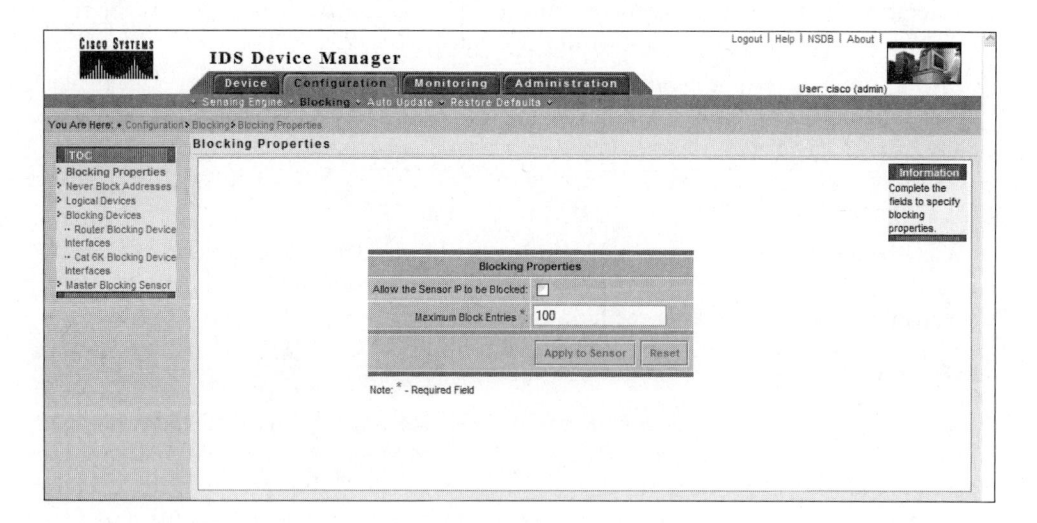

Excluding Critical Systems from Blocking

As we discussed earlier, blocking can be dangerous if it isn't implemented with some initial thought. Before configuring blocking, you should identify any critical systems in your network that should never be blocked, so that you can avoid attackers using blocking as a DoS attack.

To exclude critical systems from being blocked, you need to access the Never Block Addresses option within the TOC on the main Configuration ≻ Blocking page. Figure 23.30 shows the Never Block Addresses configuration page.

In Figure 23.30, notice that a single entry exists for host 200.1.1.10, which defines it as a critical system that should never be blocked. By default, no entries are defined on the Never Block Addresses configuration page; they can be added by clicking the Add button. This opens a page that lets you specify an IP address and subnet mask of the host(s) that you wish to exclude from blocking.

FIGURE 23.30 The Never Block Addresses configuration page

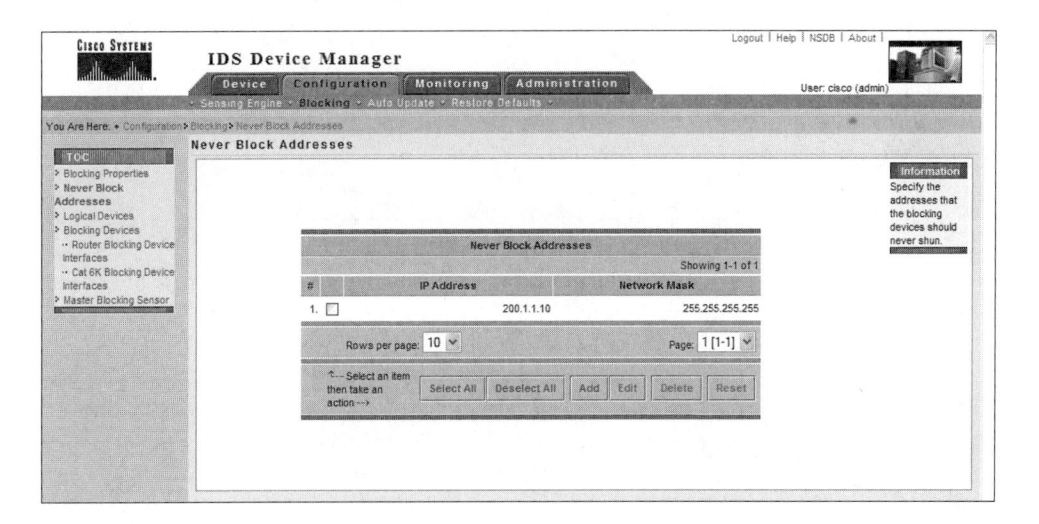

Configuring Logical Devices

Cisco Secure IDS uses the concept of *logical devices* with respect to blocking. A logical device essentially lets you configure a set of credentials that can later be applied to one or more blocking devices that you create. For example, you may have multiple perimeter routers that you wish to apply blocking to, which may all have the same authentication credentials for network management access. You can create a logical device that defines the credentials and then reference the logical device for each blocking device you define that represents each perimeter router, instead of having to specify the authentication credentials individually for each blocking device.

To configure logical devices, select the Logical Devices item from the TOC on the main Configuration ≻ Blocking page. Figure 23.31 shows the Logical Devices configuration page.

In Figure 23.31, notice that several parameters exist for each logical device:

Name This parameter defines a unique name that identifies the logical device.

Enable Password This parameter specifies the password required to gain enable mode (privileged mode) access to the logical device.

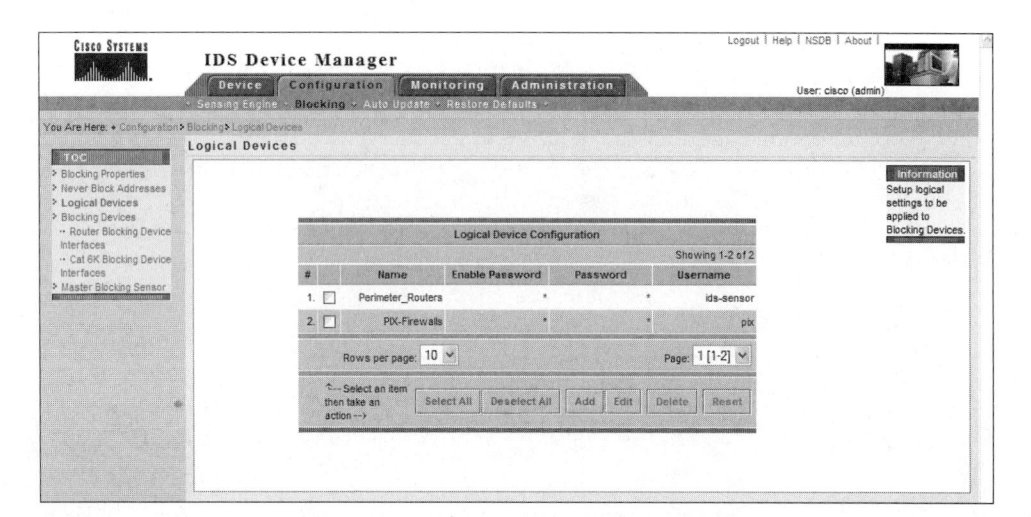

FIGURE 23.31   The Logical Devices configuration page

Password   This parameter specifies the password required to gain initial Telnet/SSH (user mode) access to the logical device.

> I have found that you must specify a username even if you don't use usernames to authenticate access to your routers. If your router doesn't prompt for a username, the sensor will only supply the appropriate password and ignore the username you've configured. If you don't configure a username, blocking never works: An error is generated in the sensor event log, indicating that no username could be found.

Username   This parameter specifies the username required to gain initial Telnet/SSH access if a username is required.

In Figure 23.31, notice that two logical devices are defined. As its name suggests, the first logical device is used to configure credentials for accessing perimeter routers, whereas the second logical device is used to configure credentials for accessing perimeter PIX firewalls. By default, no logical devices are defined; however, you can click the Add button to create a new logical device.

Configuring Blocking Devices

A *blocking device* defines a specific perimeter device and its associated parameters. When you're configuring a blocking device, two configuration tasks are required:

1. Create a blocking device.
2. Configure blocking interfaces.

CREATING A BLOCKING DEVICE

A blocking device in the IDM defines a number of parameters that uniquely identify a specific perimeter device to which blocking should be applied. The following parameters can be configured for a blocking device:

IP Address   This parameter defines the IP address of the perimeter device to which the sensor will attempt to establish a Telnet/SSH session.

NAT Address   This parameter specifies the network address translated (NATed) address of the sensor as it may be defined on the perimeter device. This setting is important when NAT is used to enable connectivity to the command-and-control interface of the sensor and you want to ensure that communications to the sensor aren't blocked. The sensor will create an ACE that permits access to the NAT address (rather than the real IP address of the sensor), ensuring that communications to the NAT address of the sensor aren't blocked.

Device Type   This parameter defines the type of perimeter device. Valid options in Cisco Secure IDS 4.*x* include Cisco router, Catalyst 6000 VACL, and PIX.

Logical Device   This parameter references the logical device that defines the credentials required to gain privileged access to the perimeter device.

Communication   This parameter defines the type of communications that should be used to gain access to the perimeter device. Valid options in Cisco Secure IDS 4.*x* include Telnet, SSH DES, and SSH 3DES.

> If you specify either SSH option, you must ensure that the public key of the blocking device has been defined as a known host key on the sensor. You can do so using the Device ➤ Sensor Setup ➤ SSH ➤ Known Host Keys page within the IDM.

To configure blocking devices, select the Blocking Devices option from the TOC on the Configuration ➤ Blocking page. Figure 23.32 shows the Blocking Devices configuration page.

In Figure 32.32, notice that a single blocking device has been defined, with an IP address of 192.168.1.1 (by default, no blocking devices are defined). The NAT address of the sensor is defined as 200.1.1.100, which will be used in any ACEs that are used to ensure that the sensor IP address isn't blocked. Notice that the device type is set to router-devices, which means that the blocking device is a Cisco router. The logical device for the blocking device has been defined as `Perimeter_Routers`, which was defined earlier as a logical device. This means that the sensor will use the authentication credentials defined for the `Perimeter_Routers` logical device when attempting to access the blocking device.

Finally, the communication protocol used to manage the blocking device has been configured as SSH with 3DES. Assuming the blocking device public key has been defined as a known host key, the sensor should successfully attempt and establish an SSH session for the purposes of applying blocking.

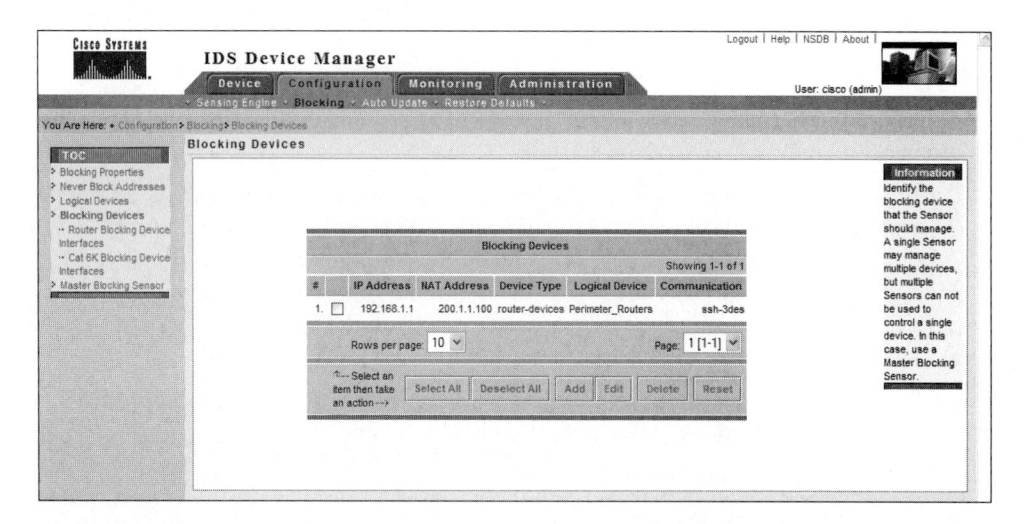

FIGURE 23.32 The Blocking Devices configuration page

CONFIGURING BLOCKING INTERFACES

After you create a blocking device, you must next define the interface and direction on the blocking device that you wish to apply the blocking ACL to. With Cisco Secure IDS 4.x, you can configure two types of blocking interfaces:

Router Blocking Interface This defines a blocking interface on a router, which can be any physical or virtual interface. As described earlier, ACLs can be applied either inbound or outbound to a router interface. The following parameters are configurable for router blocking interfaces:

IP Address This parameter defines the IP address of the blocking device.

Blocking Interface This parameter defines the interface ID of the interface to which the blocking ACL will be applied.

Blocking Direction This parameter defines the direction in which the blocking ACL should be applied.

Pre-block ACL Name Optionally, this parameter defines the name of a predefined ACL on the perimeter device that should be applied before any blocking ACL entries.

Post-block ACL Name Optionally, this parameter defines the name of a predefined ACL on the perimeter device that should be applied after any blocking ACL entries.

Cat6K Blocking Interface If you're using a Catalyst 6000/6500 switch as your blocking device, it's important to understand that if you need to filter traffic, these switches apply VLAN access control lists (VACLs) to VLANs rather than to interfaces, as is the case with routers. Unlike router ACLs, VACLs don't provide the option to specify a direction that you can apply the VACL. This is the case because a VACL is always applied whenever packets enter a VLAN to which the VACL is applied, as well as when packets leave the VLAN—this behavior is fixed and can't be modified.

The following parameters are configurable for Cat6K blocking interfaces:

IP Address   This parameter defines the IP address of the blocking Cat6K switch.

VLAN Number   This parameter defines the VLAN ID of the VLAN to which the blocking VACL will be applied.

Pre-block VACL Name   Optionally, this parameter defines the name of a predefined VACL on the perimeter device that should be applied before any blocking VACL entries.

Post-block VACL Name   Optionally, this parameter defines the name of a predefined VACL on the perimeter device that should be applied after any blocking VACL entries.

To configure blocking interfaces for a router or Catalyst 6000/6500 blocking device, open either the Configuration ➢ Blocking ➢ Blocking Devices ➢ Router Blocking Device Interfaces page or the Configuration ➢ Blocking ➢ Blocking Devices ➢ Cat 6K Blocking Device Interfaces page. Figure 23.33 shows the Router Blocking Device Interfaces configuration page.

By default, no blocking interfaces are defined; however, a blocking interface has been defined in Figure 23.33. Notice that the IP address of the blocking device configured in Figure 23.32 is selected, meaning the blocking configuration in Figure 23.33 will be applied to this blocking device. A blocking interface of fastEthernet0/0 is specified, with a blocking direction of inbound on the interface. Notice that a pre-block ACL and a post-block ACL are also defined; both must exist on the blocking device to be successfully applied.

> **NOTE**   You may wonder why you can't define blocking interfaces for the Cisco PIX firewall. Blocking is applied as a shun on the Cisco PIX, which is different from an ACL and is applied in addition to any existing ACLs that are applied. A shun applies for packets received on *any* interface rather than a specific interface or VLAN, as is the case for the other types of blocking interfaces.

FIGURE 23.33   The Router Blocking Device Interfaces configuration page

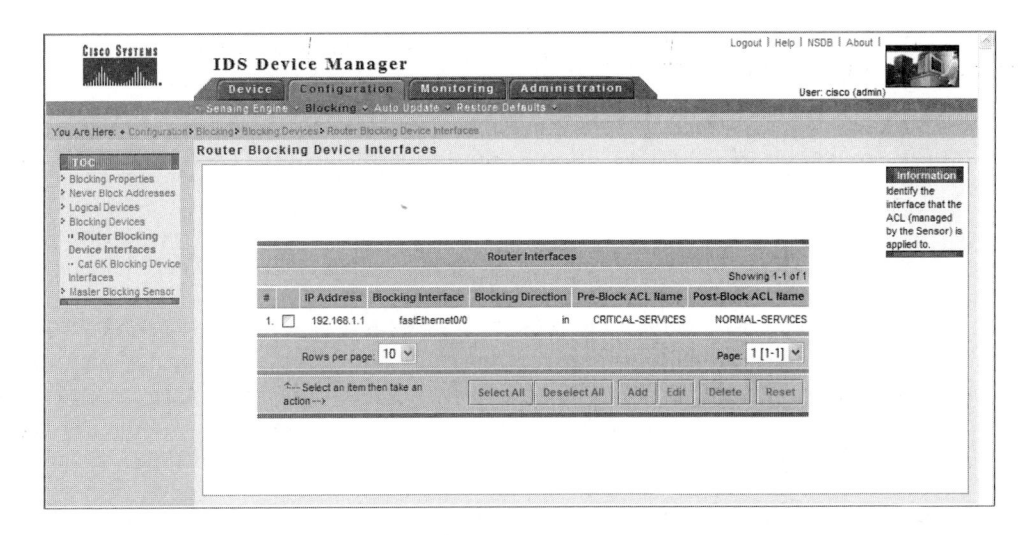

Configuring Master Blocking Sensors

As we explained earlier in the "Blocking Architectures" section, network topologies that have multiple connections to external networks can use multiple IDS sensors. To ensure that blocking is applied correctly in such an environment, you must designate a single master blocking sensor that is used to manage each perimeter device, and you must configure all other sensors as blocking forwarding sensors that forward blocking requests to the master blocking sensor. The configuration required for each type of sensor is different; we'll discuss them separately next.

CONFIGURING THE MASTER BLOCKING SENSOR

Once you've chosen the appropriate sensor to become the master blocking sensor, you next need to configure the sensor as a master blocking sensor. To configure a sensor as a master blocking sensor, you only need to define all blocking forwarding sensors that send block requests to the local sensor as being trusted hosts. As long as a remote sensor is configured as a trusted host, the master blocking sensor will accept blocking requests.

To configure blocking forwarding sensors as trusted hosts on the master blocking sensor, open the Device ➤ Sensor Setup ➤ Allowed Hosts page, and ensure that the IP addresses of each blocking forwarding sensor are defined as allowed hosts (see Figure 23.8 for an example of configuring allowed hosts).

CONFIGURING BLOCKING FORWARDING SENSORS

After you configure the master blocking sensor, you next need to define the master blocking sensor on each blocking forwarding sensor. When you're defining a master blocking sensor, you need to define a number of parameters:

IP Address This parameter defines the IP address of the command-and-control interface of the master blocking sensor.

Port This parameter defines the port used for establishing a connection to the master blocking sensor. The sensor uses the same XML-based method of communications that the IDM uses, so you should specify the same port that you use when configuring the master blocking sensor with the IDM.

User Name This parameter defines the username that should be used to authenticate the connection established to the master blocking sensor. Specify a user account that has administrative privileges on the master blocking sensor.

Password This parameter defines the password for the username specified to authenticate access to the master blocking sensor.

Use SSH When this parameter is enabled (recommended), all blocking requests sent to the master blocking sensor are secured using HTTP over SSL (not SSH, as the configuration option incorrectly suggests). If you enable this option, you must also define the master blocking sensor as a trusted TLS host. When you're configuring the master blocking sensor as a trusted TLS host, the blocking forwarding sensor will retrieve the server certificate of the master blocking sensor and add the certificate as a trusted certificate. This ensures that when a blocking forwarding sensor initiates an SSL connection to the master blocking sensor, the blocking forwarding sensor will automatically accept the master blocking sensor certificate and continue with the blocking request connection.

Configuring Cisco Secure IDS Sensors Using the IDM

> **NOTE** To add a trusted TLS host, you can use the Device ➢ Sensor Setup ➢ Certificate ➢ Trusted Hosts page in the IDM, or you can use the `tls trusted-host ip-address` CLI command.

To define the master blocking sensor on a blocking forward sensor, select Master Blocking Sensor from the TOC on the Configuration ➢ Blocking page. Figure 23.34 shows the Master Blocking Sensor configuration page.

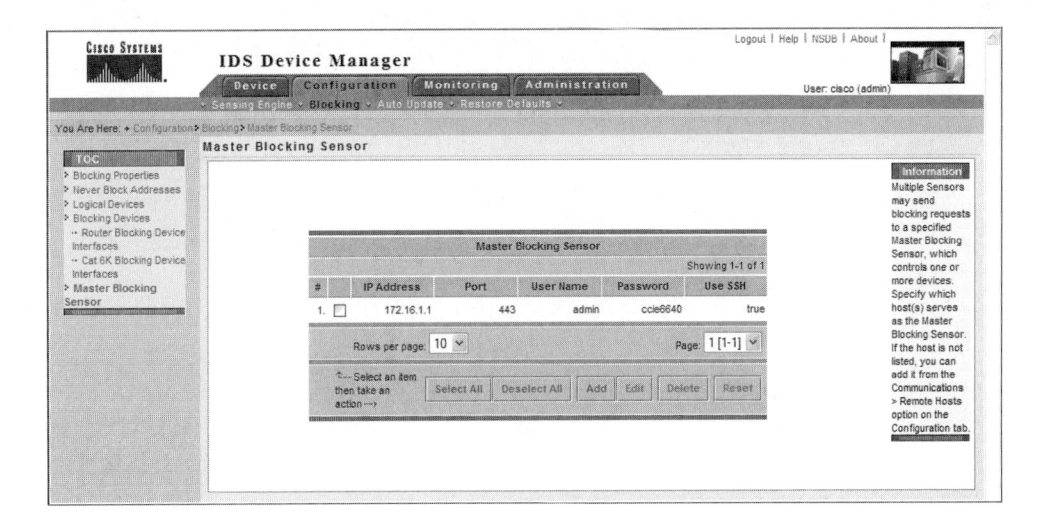

In Figure 23.34, notice that a single master blocking sensor has been defined, with an IP address of 172.16.1.1. The blocking forward sensor is configured to connect to port 443 on the master blocking sensor, and it sends a username of `admin` and password of `ccie6640` to authenticate the blocking request. Because the use SSH option is enabled in Figure 23.34, the master blocking sensor must also be defined as a trusted TLS host.

FIGURE 23.34 The Master Blocking Sensor configuration page

Configuring Manual Blocking

The ability of a sensor to manage perimeter devices and automatically apply blocking when an attack is detected is sometimes referred to as *automatic blocking*. Cisco Secure IDS sensors also allow administrators to configure *manual blocking*, where an administrator can define an arbitrary source host or network that should be blocking for a configurable amount of time. Manual blocking is useful if you don't wish to implement automatic blocking due to the risks associated with it (for example, it may be used as a DoS attack and may block legitimate hosts) and want to only apply blocking as required to ensure that genuine attackers are blocked.

To configure manual blocking, select Administration ➢ Manual Blocking, which opens the Manual Blocking TOC. This TOC contains two suboptions: Selecting Host Manual Blocks lets you block a single source system, whereas selecting Network Manual Blocks lets you block entire networks that may be sourcing attacks. The following shows the Host Manual Blocks configuration page, which you open by selecting Administration ≻ Manual Blocking ≻ Host Manual Blocks:

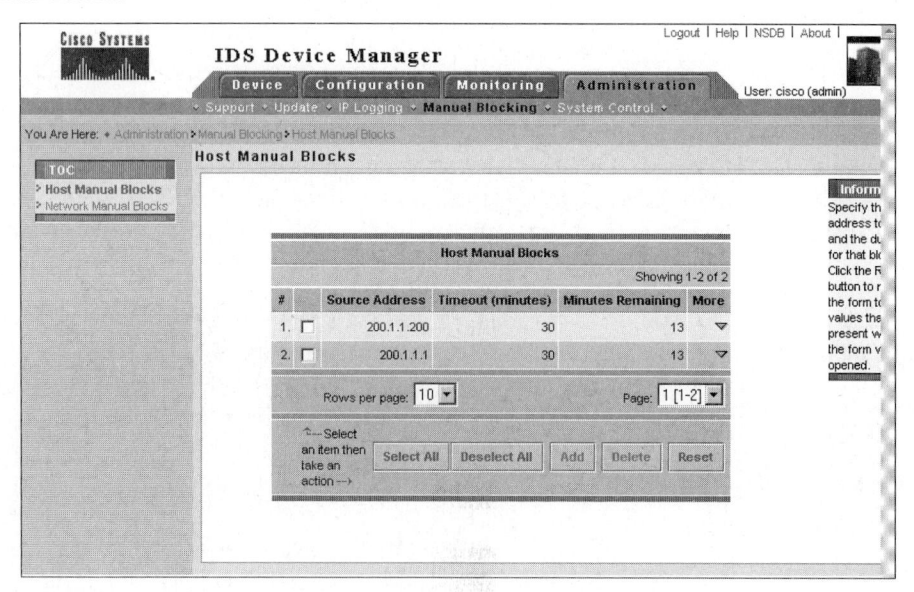

Notice that you can see two blocks that are currently active (for the source addresses 200.1.1.1 and 200.1.1.200). You can determine how long the block is to be applied and how much longer the block will be required. You can also remove current blocks by selecting the appropriate block(s) and clicking the Delete button.

> Any blocks that have been applied due to automatic blocking are also displayed within the Host Manual Blocks page.

Configuring Blocking Using the Sensor CLI

All blocking parameters described in the previous section can be configured using the sensor CLI. To configure blocking using the CLI, you must first access network access configuration CLI mode using the `service networkAccess` global configuration command. This mode provides the ability to configure all parameters associated with blocking and device management. We'll now discuss the following command-line configuration tasks:

- Defining general blocking properties using the CLI
- Configuring logical devices
- Configuring blocking devices

Defining General Blocking Properties Using the CLI

When you're using the CLI to configure blocking, you can configure a number of general blocking properties using the following commands from the network access configuration mode:

- `shun-enable` defines whether blocking is enabled.
- `master-blocking-sensors` defines master blocking sensors.
- `never-shun-hosts` and `never-shun-networks` define hosts and networks that should never be blocked.
- `shun-hosts` and `shun-networks` define hosts and networks that should always be blocked.
- `allow-sensor-shun` defines whether the sensor IP address can be blocked.
- `enable-acl-logging` defines whether ACL logging is enabled.
- `shun-max-entries` defines the maximum number of blocking entries that can be present at any one time.

Notice that you can configure many more blocking properties using the CLI as compared with using the IDM. For example, you can define hosts and networks that should *always* be blocked, and you can also enable or disable ACL logging.

> **NOTE** ACL logging is a feature that allows a sensor to accept Syslog traps from perimeter routers that relate to packets violating the ACLs configured on the router (for example, a packet matches a `deny ip any any log` statement on an ACL, causing a Syslog trap to be generated). Cisco Secure IDS sensors can generate alarms in response to Syslog traps generated from ACL violations, which is referred to as *ACL logging*.

The following demonstrates configuring general blocking properties using the sensor CLI:

```
ids-4210# configure terminal
ids-4210(config)# service networkAccess
ids-4210(config-NetworkAccess)# general
ids-4210(config-NetworkAccess-gen)# shun-enable true
ids-4210(config-NetworkAccess-gen)# allow-sensor-shun false
ids-4210(config-NetworkAccess-gen)# never-shun-network ip-address
  192.168.1.0 netmask 255.255.255.0
ids-4210(config-NetworkAccess-gen)# master-blocking-sensors
  mbs-ipaddress 192.168.2.101
ids-4210(config-NetworkAccess-gen-mas)# mbs-username cisco
ids-4210(config-NetworkAccess-gen-mas)# mbs-password cisco123
ids-4210(config-NetworkAccess-gen-mas)# mbs-tls true
ids-4210(config-NetworkAccess-gen-mas)# mbs-port 443
```

```
ids-4210(config-NetworkAccess-gen-mas)# exit
ids-4210(config-NetworkAccess-gen)# show settings
general
   -----------------------------------------------
      enable-acl-logging: false default: false
      allow-sensor-shun: false default: false
      shun-enable: true default: true
      shun-max-entries: 100 default: 100
      master-blocking-sensors (min: 0, max: 100, current: 1)
      -----------------------------------------------
         mbs-ipaddress: 192.168.2.101
         mbs-password: cisco123
         mbs-port: 443 default: 443
         mbs-tls: true <defaulted>
         mbs-username: cisco
         -----------------------------------------------
      -----------------------------------------------
      never-shun-hosts (min: 0, max: 100, current: 0)
      -----------------------------------------------
      -----------------------------------------------
      never-shun-networks (min: 0, max: 100, current: 1)
      -----------------------------------------------
         ip-address: 192.168.1.0
         netmask: 255.255.255.0
         -----------------------------------------------
      -----------------------------------------------
      shun-hosts (min: 0, max: 100, current: 0)
      -----------------------------------------------
      -----------------------------------------------
      shun-networks (min: 0, max: 100, current: 0)
      -----------------------------------------------
      -----------------------------------------------
ids-4210(config-NetworkAccess-gen)# exit
ids-4210(config-NetworkAccess)# exit
Apply Changes:?[yes]: yes
ids-4210(config)#
```

In this example, blocking is enabled, the sensor IP address is configured to never be blocked, and the 192.168.1.0/24 network is configured to never be blocked. A master blocking sensor is also configured; it has an IP address of 192.168.2.101. Notice that when you're configuring a master blocking sensor, you configure a number of parameters that enable the local sensor to communicate with the master blocking sensor, such as master blocking sensor username, password, whether TLS (SSL) is to be used, and the web server port to connect to. After the configuration of general blocking properties is complete, you must exit network access configuration mode to apply the changes.

Configuring Logical Devices

A logical device defines profiles that contain the credentials required to gain administrative access to the blocking devices the sensor is configured to manage. To configure a logical device using the CLI, you use the shun-device-cfg command from network access configuration mode, as follows:

```
sensor(config-NetworkAccess)# shun-device-cfg name logical-device-name
```

After creating the logical device, you're placed into a new configuration mode that lets you use the following configuration parameters specific to the logical device:

- Username used for Telnet access
- Password used for Telnet access
- Enable password used to gain privileged mode access

The following demonstrates creating a logical device and configuring the appropriate access settings for the device:

```
ids-4210# configure terminal
ids-4210(config)# service networkAccess
ids-4210(config-NetworkAccess)# shun-device-cfg name Router-Access
ids-4210(config-NetworkAccess-shu)# ?
default            Set the value back to the system default setting
enable-password    Enable password for device.
exit               Exit shun-device-cfg configuration submode
password           Password for the intial login.
show               Display system settings and/or history information
username           Username for account on device.
ids-4210(config-NetworkAccess-shu)# username cisco
ids-4210(config-NetworkAccess-shu)# password telnet123
ids-4210(config-NetworkAccess-shu)# enable-password enable123
ids-4210(config-NetworkAccess-shu)# exit
ids-4210(config-NetworkAccess)# exit
Apply Changes:?[yes]: yes
ids-4210(config)#
```

Configuring Blocking Devices

A blocking device defines a physical perimeter device, specifying parameters such as the IP addressing of the device, protocols used to communicate with the device, the logical device associated with the blocking device, and the interfaces to which blocking ACLs should be applied. To create blocking devices, you must be in network access configuration mode. As you've already learned, Cisco

Chapter 23 · Configuring Cisco Secure IDS Sensors Using the IDS Device Manager

Secure IDS sensors can apply blocking to three types of devices: Cisco IOS routers, Cisco Catalyst 6000 switches, and Cisco PIX firewalls. When you're creating or configuring a blocking device using the sensor CLI, different commands are available for each type of device, as shown here:

```
sensor(config-NetworkAccess)# router-devices ip-address device-ip
sensor(config-NetworkAccess)# cat6k-devices ip-address device-ip
sensor(config-NetworkAccess)# pix-devices ip-address device-ip
```

Notice that for each type of device you create, you must specify the device IP address. This IP address must be an actual IP address on the device, even if the device is reachable via a NAT address (you can add the NAT address later). Once you specify the IP address of the device and press Enter, you're placed into a configuration mode that lets you configure other parameters specific to the blocking device. The following demonstrates configuring a Cisco perimeter router as a blocking device:

```
ids-4210# configure terminal
ids-4210(config)# service networkAccess
ids-4210(config-NetworkAccess)# router-devices ip-address 192.168.1.100
ids-4210(config-NetworkAccess-rou)# ?
  communication      Indicates the method used to access the box. If
                     unspecified, SSH 3DES will be used.
  default            Set the value back to the system default setting
  exit               Exit router-devices configuration submode
  nat-address        CIDS NAT address.
  no                 Remove an entry or selection setting
  show               Display system settings and/or history information
  shun-device-cfg    Logical name of general device configuration to use
                     for this device.
  shun-interfaces    List containing interface names and directions.
ids-4210(config-NetworkAccess-rou)# nat-address 200.1.1.100
ids-4210(config-NetworkAccess-rou)# shun-device-cfg Router-Access
ids-4210(config-NetworkAccess-rou)# communication telnet
ids-4210(config-NetworkAccess-rou)# shun-interfaces direction in
                                    interface-name fastEthernet0/1
ids-4210(config-NetworkAccess-rou-shu)# pre-acl-name PREBLOCK_ACL
ids-4210(config-NetworkAccess-rou-shu)# post-acl-name POSTBLOCK_ACL
ids-4210(config-NetworkAccess-rou-shu)# exit
ids-4210(config-NetworkAccess-rou)# show settings
ip-address: 192.168.1.100
   communication: telnet
   nat-address: 200.1.1.100
```

```
    shun-device-cfg: Router-Access
    shun-interfaces (min: 0, max: 100, current: 1)
    -----------------------------------------------
       direction: in
       interface-name: fastEthernet0/1
       post-acl-name: POSTBLOCK_ACL
       pre-acl-name: PREBLOCK_ACL
       -----------------------------------------------
    -----------------------------------------------
ids-4210(config-NetworkAccess-rou)# exit
ids-4210(config-NetworkAccess)# exit
Apply Changes:?[yes]: yes
ids-4210(config)#
```

In this example, a Cisco perimeter router with an IP address of 192.168.1.100 is configured. A NAT address of 200.1.1.100 is configured for the device (`nat-address` command), and a logical device profile called Router-Access is referenced to specify the credentials that should be used for authentication (`shun-device-cfg` command). The sensor is configured to use Telnet for communications with the device (`communication` command), and blocking ACLs are configured to be applied inbound on interface `fastEthernet0/1` of the router using the `shun-interfaces` command. Notice that when you configure the blocking interface, you're placed into a subconfiguration mode, where you can optionally specify pre-block and post-block ACLs using the `pre-acl-name` and `post-acl-name` commands, respectively.

> **NOTE** When you configure other types of blocking devices (such as Cat6K or PIX), the options available for configuring blocking device parameters vary depending on the type of the device.

Configuring Auto Update Using the IDM

Auto Update is a feature that enables Cisco Secure IDS sensors to automatically retrieve signature updates from a central location, removing the burden of having to manually update each sensor in the network when a new signature update becomes available. Keeping your sensor up to date with the latest signatures is very important, because it ensures that your sensor can detect new attacks.

The Auto Update feature requires a central FTP or SCP (secure copy) server that acts as a central repository for signature updates. Signature updates must be manually downloaded and copied to this server—you can't configure your sensors to auto update directly from Cisco. Once the appropriate updates are in place on your FTP or SCP server, each of your sensors can then automatically obtain the updates on a periodic basis.

> **NOTE** Secure copy (SCP) is the most secure and recommended method for auto updates.

To configure auto updates on a sensor, select Configuration ➢ Auto Update within the IDM. Doing so opens the Auto Update page, where you can define the appropriate FTP or SCP server where updates are located and also define a schedule that controls how often the sensor should check for new updates. Figure 23.35 shows the Auto Update configuration page.

In Figure 23.35, an FTP server of 192.168.2.10 is specified as the update server. The appropriate credentials are specified, as well as a directory in which the IDS signature updates are installed. A schedule is also defined, with an hourly schedule selected. The configuration in Figure 23.35 means that updates will start at 12 midnight and will then occur every six hours as defined in the Frequency field.

Note that the following FTP servers are certified for use if you're updating the sensor via FTP:

- Sambar FTP Server Version 5.0 (win32)
- Web-mail Microsoft FTP Service Version 5.0 (win32)
- Serv-U FTP-Server v2.5h for WinSock (win32)
- Solaris 2.8

FIGURE 23.35 The Auto Update configuration page

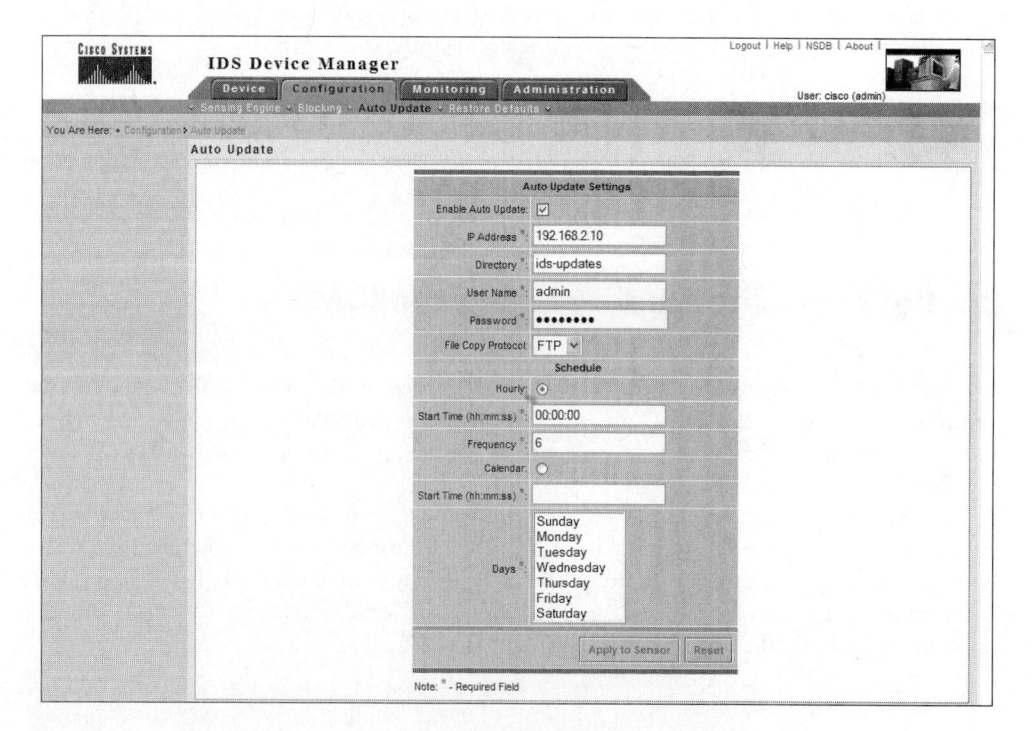

- HP-UX (HP-UX qdir-5 B.10.20 A 9000/715)
- Windows 2000 (Microsoft FTP server version 5.0)
- Windows NT 4 (Microsoft FTP server version 3.0)

Configuring Auto Update Using the Sensor CLI

To configure Auto Update settings using the sensor CLI, you must first access the service host configuration mode and then specify the optionalAutoUpgrade command. This takes you to a new mode where you must next specify the autoUpgradeParams command, which takes you into another mode where you can configure auto upgrade parameters such as update URL and schedule. The following demonstrates configuring Auto Update settings using the sensor CLI:

```
ids-4210# configure terminal
ids-4210(config)# service host
ids-4210(config-Host)# optionalAutoUpgrade
ids-4210(config-Host-opt)# autoUpgradeParams
ids-4210(config-Host-opt-aut)# ?
directory          upgrade host directory that contains the upgrade files
exit               Exit autoUpgradeParams configuration submode
fileCopyProtocol   file copy protocol
ipAddress          ip address of upgrade host
password           user password
schedule           auto upgrade schedule params
show               Display system settings and/or history information
username           user name
ids-4210(config-Host-opt-aut)# ipAddress 192.168.2.10
ids-4210(config-Host-opt-aut)# directory updates/sensors
ids-4210(config-Host-opt-aut)# FileCopyProtocol ftp
ids-4210(config-Host-opt-aut)# username cisco
ids-4210(config-Host-opt-aut)# password
Enter password[]: ********
Re-enter password: ********
ids-4210(config-Host-opt-aut)# schedule
ids-4210(config-Host-opt-aut-sch)# active-selection hourFreqUpgrade
ids-4210(config-Host-opt-aut-sch)# hourFreqUpgrade
ids-4210(config-Host-opt-aut-sch-hou)# startTime 00:00
ids-4210(config-Host-opt-aut-sch-hou)# frequency 1
ids-4210(config-Host-opt-aut-sch-hou)# exit
ids-4210(config-Host-opt-aut-sch)# exit
ids-4210(config-Host-opt-aut)# exit
ids-4210(config-Host-opt)# show settings
   -> optionalAutoUpgrade
```

```
            -----------------------------------------
*---> autoUpgradeParams
            -----------------------------------------
            schedule
                -----------------------------------------
                hourFreqUpgrade
                    -----------------------------------------
                    startTime: 00:00:00
                    frequency: 1 hours
                    -----------------------------------------
                -----------------------------------------
            ipAddress: 192.168.2.10
            directory: updates/sensors
            username: cisco
            password: <hidden>
            fileCopyProtocol: ftp
            -----------------------------------------
      -----------------------------------------
ids-4210(config-Host-opt)# exit
ids-4210(config-Host)# exit
Apply Changes:?[yes]: yes
ids-4210(config)#
```

In this example, the Auto Update server is configured with an IP address of 192.168.2.10, with FTP used as the protocol to obtain update files. Notice that the `schedule` command is used to configure the Auto Update schedule, which takes you into a new configuration mode. The `active-selection` command is used to specify that the update schedule will be performed using hour frequency settings (you can choose to use calendar frequency settings, where updates are scheduled based on calendar settings rather than hour settings). The hour frequency settings are then specified by entering the `hourFreqUpgrade` command and then specifying the start time (00:00) and the frequency in hours (every hour in this example) when checks for new updates should take place.

Administering and Monitoring Cisco Secure IDS Sensors Using the IDM

The IDM not only provides configuration access to sensors, it also provides access for monitoring and administrative purposes. In the following sections, you'll learn how to administer and monitor Cisco Secure IDS sensors using the IDM.

IDM Administration

The IDM provides a number of administration features that enable you to maintain the sensor and perform system-level administration tasks. Within the Administration tab on the IDM, you can select five different options:

- Support
- Update
- IP Logging
- Manual Blocking
- System Control

We'll discuss the features associated with each of these tabs in the following sections.

Obtaining Support Information

The Administration ➤ Support page on the IDM provides access to support information for the sensor, which is useful if you need to provide this information to a third-party support organization such as a Cisco reseller or Cisco TAC. Two sources of support information are available:

Diagnostics   This provides diagnostics information about the sensor. It requires execution of a diagnostics program on the sensor, which takes several minutes to execute before displaying any results.

System Information   This provides system information such as Cisco Secure IDS software version, Cisco Secure IDS components that are running, general statistics, network statistics, NTP statistics, memory usage, and SWAP file usage.

Generating and Viewing Diagnostics

To view diagnostic information about the sensor, you must first generate a diagnostics report, which is an HTML-based report that contains the results of various diagnostics tests conducted by the sensor. To begin generating a diagnostics report, select Administration ➤ Support ➤ Diagnostics in the IDM. Figure 23.36 shows the Diagnostics page on a sensor.

In Figure 23.36, notice that you must click the Run Diagnostics button to begin generating diagnostic information. If you click this button, a new page appears that indicates diagnostic information is currently being generated. This page also lets you cancel the diagnostics generation if required.

> **NOTE**   If you've previously generated a diagnostics report, a button labeled View Last Report is also present on the Diagnostics page.

Once the diagnostics generation is complete, a new page appears, indicating that diagnostics are complete. This page also provides a View Results button, which you can click to open a diagnostics report in a separate window, as shown in Figure 23.37.

FIGURE 23.36 The Diagnostics page

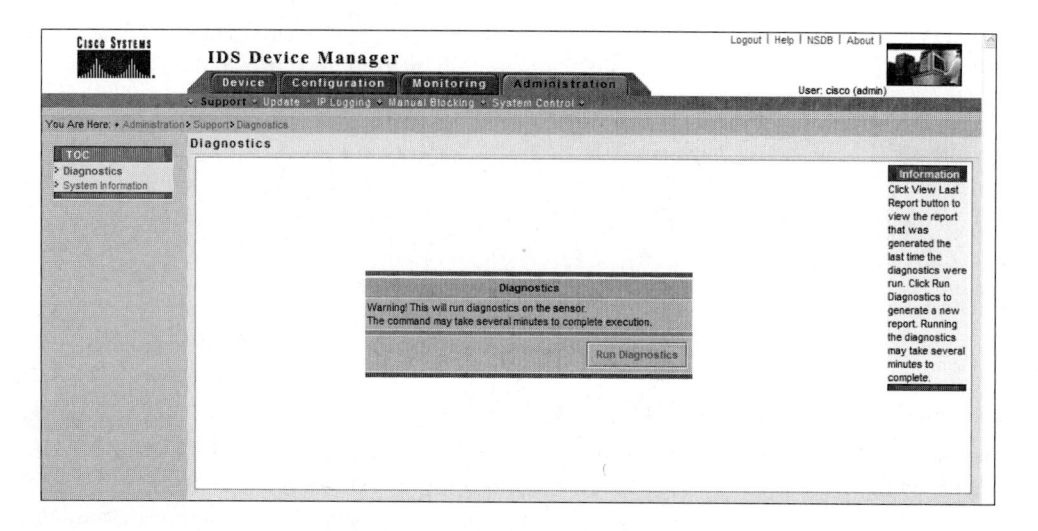

FIGURE 23.37 Viewing a diagnostics report

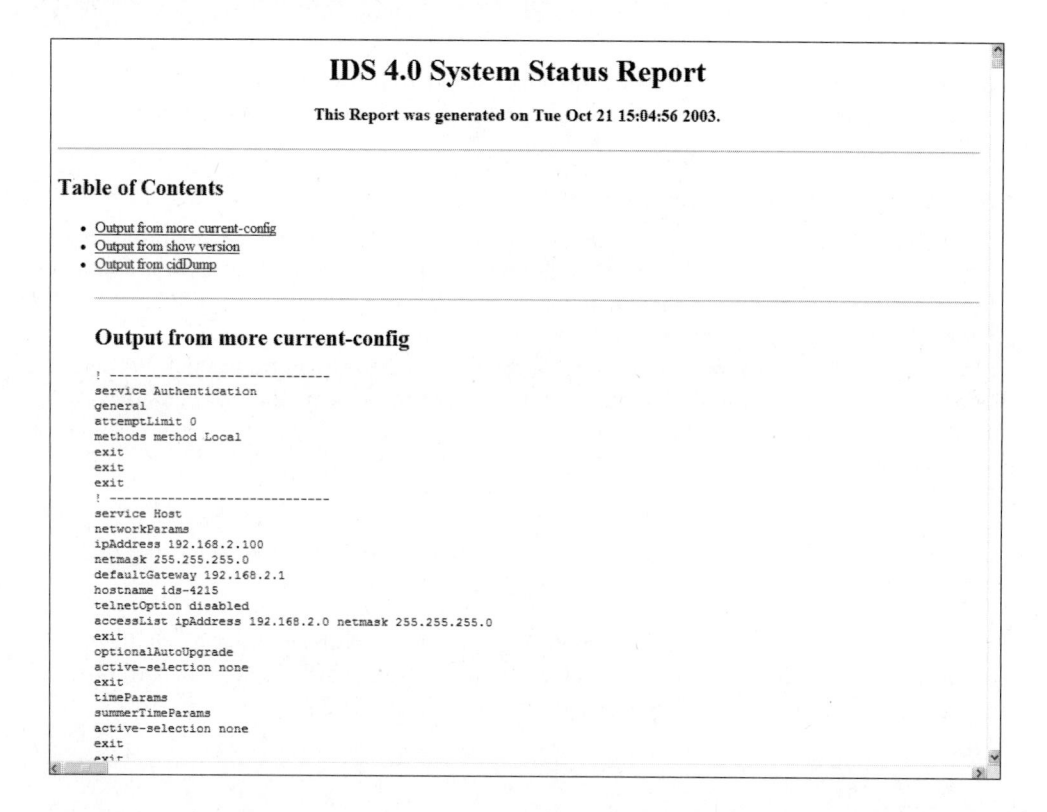

In Figure 23.37, notice that there are three top-level links:

Output from *more current-config* This provides a link to the current configuration of the sensor, which is obtained during diagnostics by using the `more current-config` command.

Output from *show version* This provides a link to the current version information for the sensor, which is obtained during diagnostics by using the `show version` command.

Output from *cidDump* This provides a link to various snippets of information that are collected by running a number of diagnostics commands using a script called `cidDump`. For example, you can see the output of the `uname` command, which displays information about the current kernel version that is running. Figure 23.38 shows some of the different types of information obtained by the `cidDump` script.

In Figure 23.38, you can see that `cidDump` collects the output of a number of different system-level commands (for example, `uname`, `netstat`, and `rpm`) and also displays the contents of various Cisco Secure IDS files that control sensor operation.

FIGURE 23.38   cidDump diagnostics

```
Output from cidDump

uname -a
uptime
ps -ef
/sbin/lsmod
ipcs
df -k
mount
/sbin/ifconfig -a
netstat -a
netstat -r
/sbin/arp -a
crontab -l
cat /etc/group
cat /etc/hosts
cat /etc/hosts.allow
cat /etc/hosts.deny
cat /var/log/.tac
rpm -qa
dmesg
ls -alR /usr/cids
cat /usr/cids/idsRoot/etc/IDMSetup.xml
cat /usr/cids/idsRoot/etc/NIGHTLY_VERSION
cat /usr/cids/idsRoot/etc/VERSION
cat /usr/cids/idsRoot/etc/VERSION_RP
cat /usr/cids/idsRoot/etc/auth.conf
cat /usr/cids/idsRoot/etc/boot.info
cat /usr/cids/idsRoot/etc/boot.info.diff
cat /usr/cids/idsRoot/etc/boot.info.old
cat /usr/cids/idsRoot/etc/cidsZoneInfo.txt
cat /usr/cids/idsRoot/etc/cidwebserver.conf
cat /usr/cids/idsRoot/etc/cliAdmin.conf
cat /usr/cids/idsRoot/etc/cliAdmin.conf.mp
cat /usr/cids/idsRoot/etc/cliOperator.conf
cat /usr/cids/idsRoot/etc/cliOperator.conf.mp
cat /usr/cids/idsRoot/etc/cliViewer.conf
cat /usr/cids/idsRoot/etc/cliViewer.conf.mp
cat /usr/cids/idsRoot/etc/credentials.conf
cat /usr/cids/idsRoot/etc/curHostConfig.xml
cat /usr/cids/idsRoot/etc/curNetworkAccessConfig.xml
cat /usr/cids/idsRoot/etc/curUserAccountConfig.xml
cat /usr/cids/idsRoot/etc/curWebServerConfig.xml
cat /usr/cids/idsRoot/etc/defAnalysisEngineConfig.xml
cat /usr/cids/idsRoot/etc/defAuthenticationConfig.xml
cat /usr/cids/idsRoot/etc/defHostConfig.xml
```

Viewing System Information

To view system information about a Cisco Secure IDS sensor, you can select Administration ➢ Support ➢ System Information in the IDM to display the System Information page, as shown in Figure 23.39.

In Figure 23.39, notice that the current Cisco Secure IDS software version is shown as (4.0(1)S37), as well as version information for each of the individual Cisco Secure IDS software components and whether the components are running. A number of statistics (such as network statistics) are also supplied.

> **NOTE** If you're having problems with your sensor and need to log a support incident with your reseller or Cisco TAC, you can use the show tech-support command from the CLI to obtain all the appropriate information required by Cisco TAC.

FIGURE 23.39 The System Information page

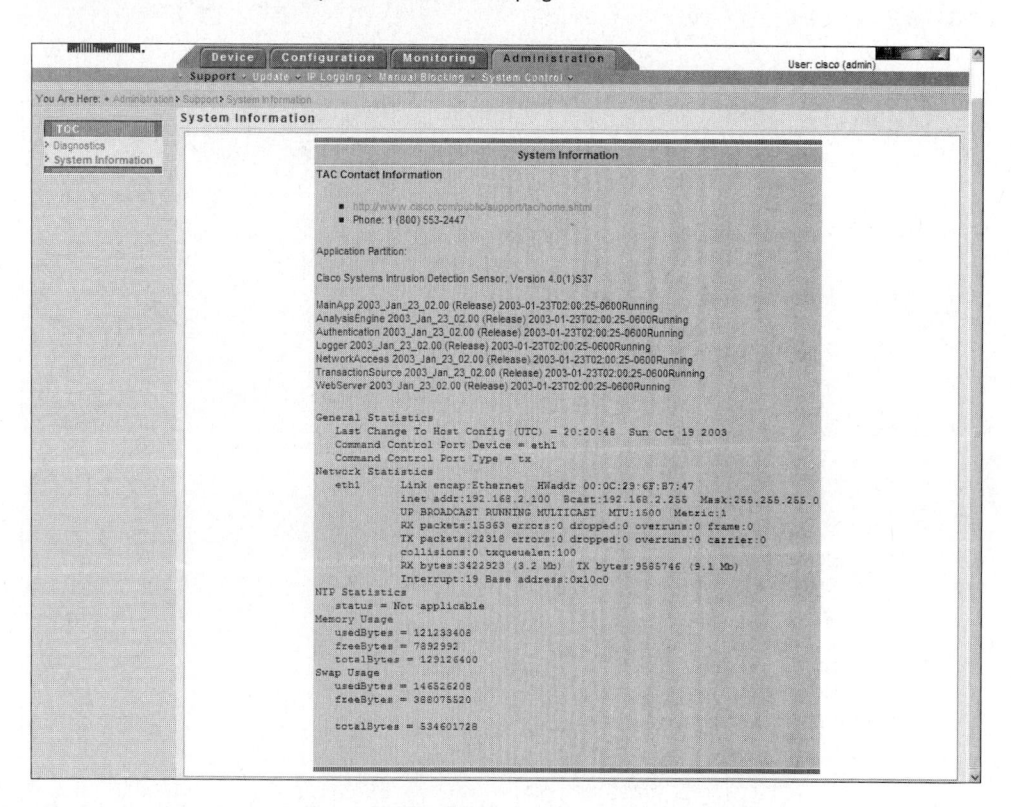

Updating the Sensor

The Internet is an evolving entity, and new attacks are released every day that could be used immediately by hackers against your network in an attempt to gain unauthorized access or perform some form of denial of service. IDS sensors must be able to keep pace with the continuously changing landscape of vulnerabilities and exploits that your network may be exposed to. Cisco releases signature updates every two weeks for sensors; however, it's up to you to ensure that your sensor(s) remain up to date. In this section, you'll learn about Cisco Secure IDS updates and how to update sensors using both the IDM and CLI.

Before discussing how you update Cisco Secure IDS sensors, it's important to first discuss update files and make sure that you understand how Cisco Secure IDS updates are named. This will ensure that you correctly identify update files and don't accidentally apply the wrong type of update. Several types of Cisco Secure IDS updates are released:

- Signature updates provide updates to the Cisco Secure IDS signature engines.
- Service packs provide application and operating system updates.
- Minor version updates provide minor updates to Cisco Secure IDS software. For example, a minor update file updates version 4.0 software to version 4.1.
- Major version updates provide major updates to Cisco Secure IDS software (for example, updating from version 3.x to 4.0). Major version updates typically require a fresh installation on the sensor.

> **NOTE** Signature updates, service packs, minor version updates, and major version updates are all platform independent. Cisco also makes other files available, such as recovery partition images and other application files, which are platform specific.

All update files have a common naming structure, which is shown here:

```
                Cryptographic Image  Software   Signature
                   (Optional)        Version    Version
                      ┌─┐              ┌─┐        ┌─┐
                IDS-K9-aaa-x.x-x-Sx.rpm.pkg
                      └─┘              └─┘
                      File           Service Pack
                      Type              Level
```

Notice the following components of each update file:

Cryptographic image (option) If an update file contains cryptographic software features, then the update file includes K9- after the initial IDS- portion of the update.

File type This component indicates the type of update file. Valid keywords include

- `sig`: Signature update
- `sp`: Service pack update
- `min`: Minor update file

Software version The software version indicates the software version that the update applies to or will upgrade to. It includes a major version number and minor version number. For example, a version of 4.1 indicates a major version of 4 and minor version of 1.

Service pack level This specifies the service pack level that the update applies to or will upgrade to. A number of service packs may be released for a specific minor version—for example, 4.1-1 refers to version 4.1 software with service pack 1 installed.

Signature version level This component indicates the signature version contained in the update. As new signature updates are released, the signature version level is incremented.

The following examples of update filenames describe each update file:

- `IDS-K9-min-4.1-1-S47.rpm.pkg`: This is a minor update file that will update version 4.0 sensors to version 4.1 service pack 1 with a signature version level of 47. The K9 in the filename indicates that the update file contains cryptographic software features.
- `IDS-K9-sp-4.1-3-S61.rpm.pkg`: This is a service pack file that will update sensors to version 4.1 service pack 3 with a signature version level of 61. The K9 in the filename indicates the update file contains cryptographic software features.
- `IDS-sig-4.1-3-S63.rpm.pkg`: This is a signature update file that will update sensors currently running version 4.1 service pack 3 software to a signature version of 63. Notice that because the file is a signature update only, the filename doesn't include cryptographic software features and the K9 keyword is missing.

> **NOTE** When you're updating files, make sure you read the README file that Cisco publishes for the update. Most updates require a minimum level of sensor software before you can apply the update. For example, to apply the signature update `IDS-sig-4.1-3-S63.rpm.pkg`, you need to ensure that the sensor is running version 4.1 service pack 3 (you can't apply this update to version 4.1 service pack 2 sensors).

Updating the Sensor Using the IDM

The Administration ➤ Update page on the IDM lets you manually install updates to the sensor if required. Before attempting to install an update, you must ensure that you've downloaded the appropriate updates and placed them on an appropriate network server that the sensor can access. Figure 23.40 shows the Update page.

In Figure 23.40, notice that you can specify the URL where the update is available as well as a password that authenticates access to the update if required. You specify the username used to connect to the server within the URL by prefixing the destination server with the username in the format *url-type://username@server/path*.

FIGURE 23.40 The Update page

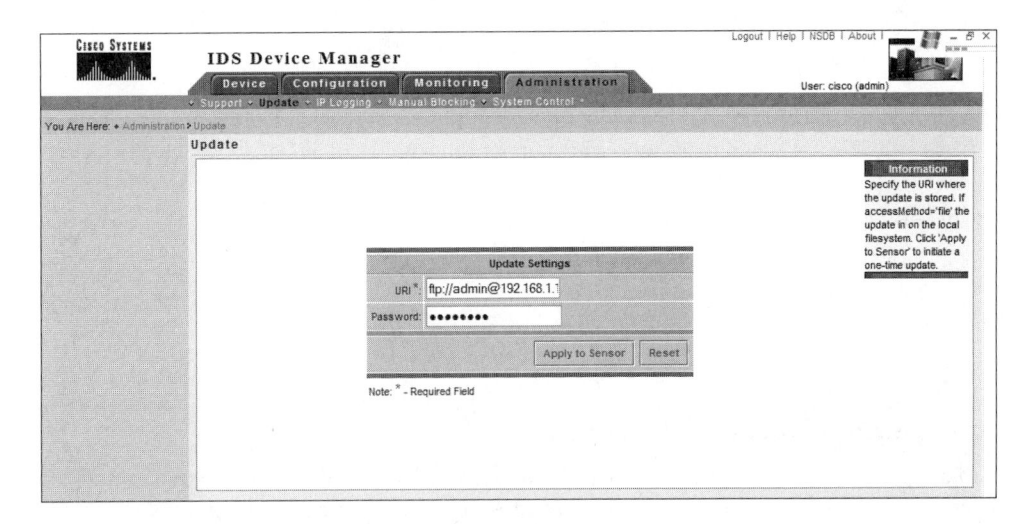

The URL can specify any one of these types of network servers:

FTP This is specified by placing `ftp://` in front of the update server URL. In Figure 23.40, you can see that the URL specified is an FTP URL.

SCP (secure copy) This is specified by placing `scp://` in front of the update server URL.

HTTP This is specified by placing `http://` in front of the update server URL.

HTTPS This is specified by placing `https://` in front of the update server URL.

Local File System This is specified by placing `file://` in front of the URL and then specifying the path to the update on the local file system.

Updating the Sensor Using the CLI

You can apply updates and upgrades to the sensor from the CLI using the `upgrade` global configuration command, which has the following syntax:

```
sensor(config)# upgrade source-url
```

After entering this command, you're prompted interactively by the sensor for additional information required to successfully connect to the specified URL. The following demonstrates applying an update using the CLI.

```
sensor# configure terminal
sensor(config)# upgrade ftp://192.168.2.1/IDS-sig-4.0-2-S43.rpm.pkg
User: anonymous
Password: ********
Warning: Executing this command will apply a signature update to the
application partition.
```

```
Continue with upgrade? : yes

Broadcast message from root (Wed Dec  3 07:15:04 2003):

Applying update IDS-sig-4.0-2-S43. This may take several minutes.
         Please do not reboot the sensor during this update.

Broadcast message from root (Wed Dec  3 07:21:53 2003):

Update complete.
         sensorApp is restarting
         This may take several minutes.
```

Configuring Manual IP Logging

IP logging is one of the actions that can be invoked when an alarm is detected, along with generating TCP resets and blocking a connection or device. When IP logging is specified as an action for a signature, the sensor captures all IP packets associated with any alarms generated by the signature. This enables administrators to obtain attack packets and analyze them for further information or understanding. Cisco Secure IDS sensors also support *manual IP logging*, where administrators can manually capture packets for a configurable time period or number of bytes, regardless of whether alarms have been generated. Manual IP logging is useful if you want to capture packets from a suspicious host or an attacker, so that you determine exactly what the attacker is trying to do.

The Administration ➤ IP Logging page on the IDM lets you configure the sensor to capture all IP packets associated with a specific host for a configurable period of time or for a configurable number of bytes. Figure 23.41 shows the IP Logging page.

By default, no IP logging entries are present. To add a logging entry, click the Add button, which brings up the IP Logging configuration pages shown in Figure 23.42.

In Figure 23.42, notice that you can define the follow parameters for an IP logging entry:

IP Address This parameter specifies the IP address that must be included in all packets that are captured.

Duration (minutes) Optionally, this parameter specifies how long the packet capture should last.

Number of Packets Optionally, this parameter specifies the number of packets that should be captured. If this number is reached, IP logging for the specified IP address is stopped.

Number of Bytes Optionally, this parameter specifies the number of bytes that should be captured. If this number is reached, IP logging for the specified IP address is stopped. In Figure 23.42, the manual IP logging entry is configured to log up to 8192 bytes of traffic.

FIGURE 23.41 The IP Logging page

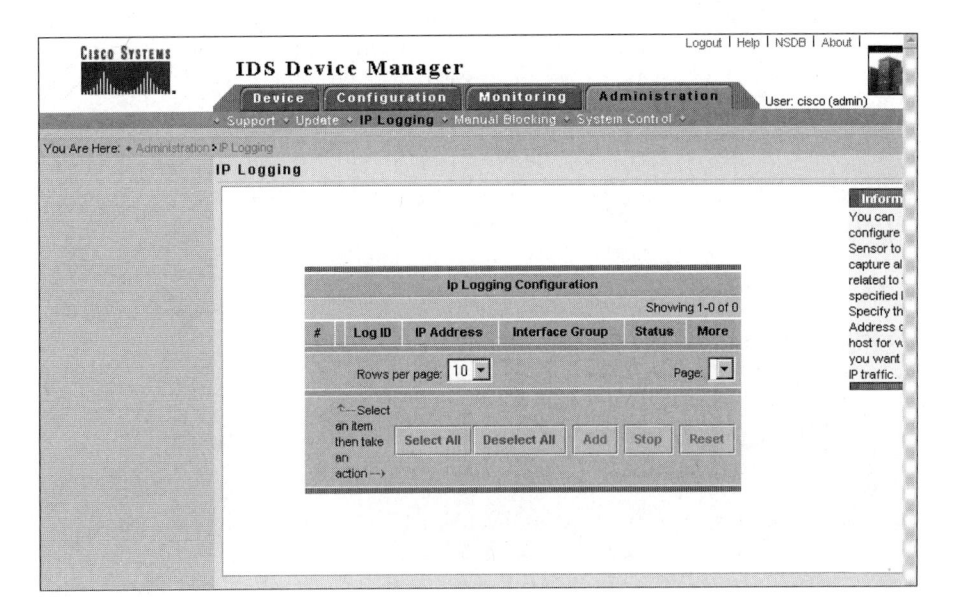

FIGURE 23.42 The IP Logging configuration page

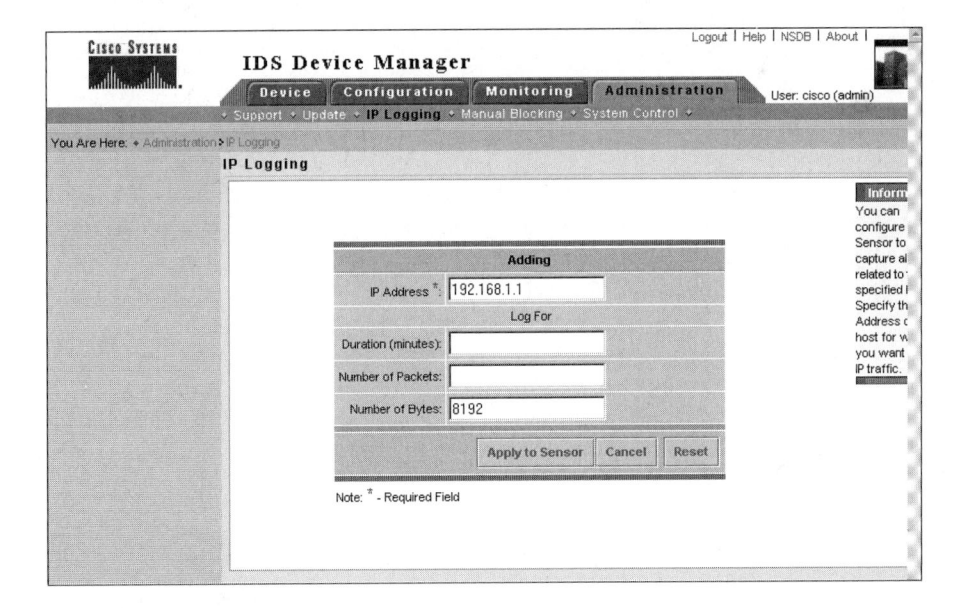

After you specify the appropriate parameters for IP logging, click the Apply To Sensor button to return to the main IP Logging configuration page. You should now see a new entry with a status of Started. You can view the information collected by manual IP logging by selecting Monitoring ➢ IP Logs, which lets you access IP log files on the sensor. Viewing IP log files is discussed later in this chapter.

> For manual IP logging to work, you must ensure that the event-logging level of the sensor is set to informational. This is configured via the Monitoring ➢ Events Display page, discussed later in this chapter.

Configuring Manual IP Logging Using the CLI

You can also configure manual IP logging using the sensor CLI by using the `iplog` command:

```
sensor# iplog group-interface-id ip-address [bytes num-of-bytes]
    [duration minutes] [packets max-packets]
```

On Cisco Secure IDS version 4.0 and version 4.1, there is only a single group interface (interface group 0); hence you always specify a value of 0 for the *group-interface-id* parameter. The following demonstrates configuring manual IP logging using the CLI:

```
sensor# iplog 0 200.1.1.1 duration 10 packets 1000
```

This configuration creates an IP log file that will contain packets with the IP address 200.1.1.1. Packets will only be captured for 10 minutes or up to a maximum of 1000 packets, whichever is reached first.

Configuring Manual Blocking

From time to time, you may wish to manually block a specific host or network that is initiating an attack against your network. Although you can use normal blocking to do this, many administrators often prefer the ability to manually exercise control over blocking. This ensures that any blocking implemented doesn't affect critical hosts (unless, of course, human error is involved), which can easily be the case if an attacker deliberately spoofs source IP addresses of your critical hosts in an attempt to get IDS sensors to block access to your critical hosts.

To configure manual blocking, open the Administration ➢ Manual Blocking page on the IDM. From here, you can create and manage manual blocks for specific hosts as well as specific networks by selecting either Host Manual Blocks or Network Manual Blocks. Figure 23.43 shows the Administration ➢ Manual Blocking ➢ Host Manual Blocks page.

To add a host manual block, click Add. Doing so displays the Adding page, which is shown in Figure 23.44.

In Figure 23.44, notice that the following parameters are available for a host manual block:

Source Address This parameter specifies the IP address of the attacking source you wish to block.

Source Port Optionally, this parameter specifies the source port of packets generated by the attacking source you wish to block. This value is specified only if you want to block a specific connection from an attacker rather than all packets from the attacking host.

Destination Address Optionally, this parameter specifies the destination IP address of packets generated by the attacking source you wish to block. This lets you limit the block to a specific source and destination if required.

FIGURE 23.43 The Host Manual Blocks page

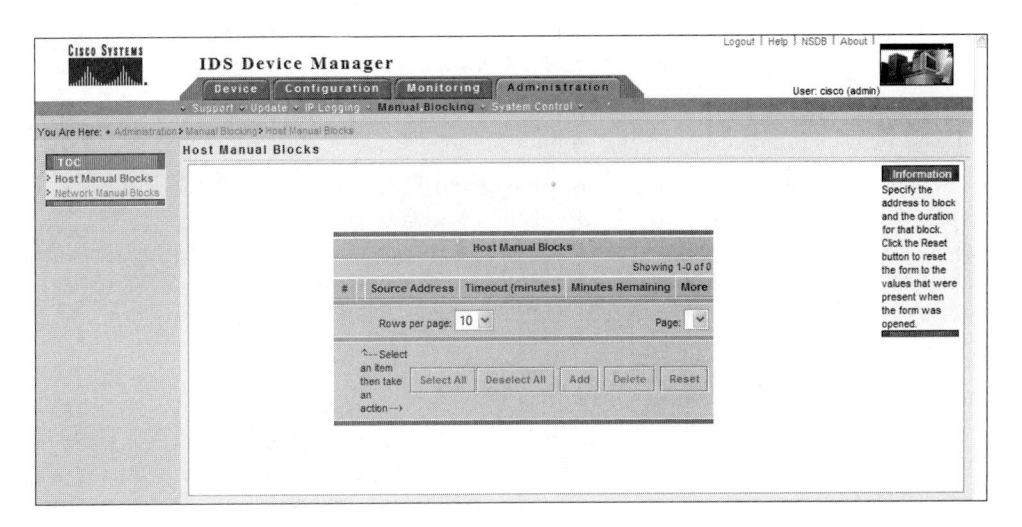

FIGURE 23.44 Adding a host manual block

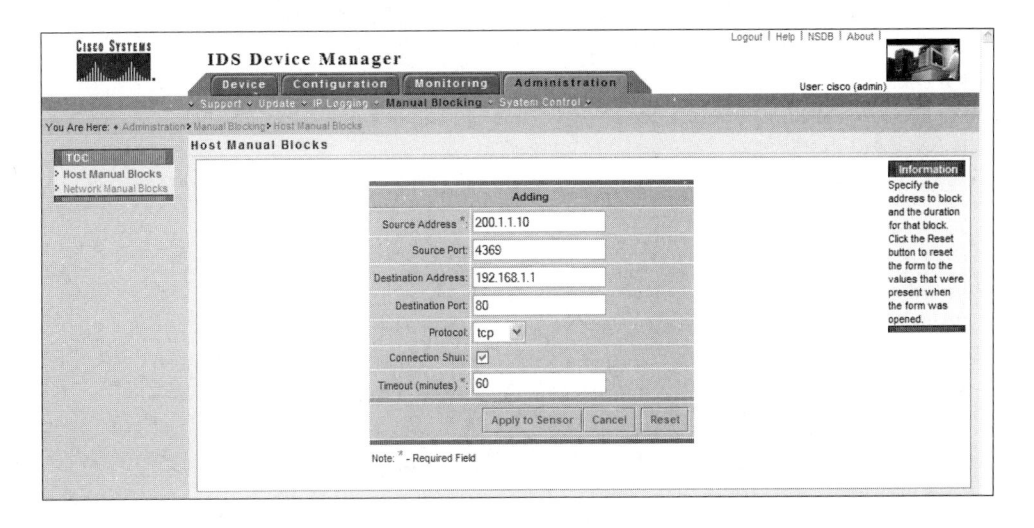

Destination Port Optionally, this parameter specifies the destination port of packets generated by the attacking source you wish to block. Configuring a destination port lets you restrict block connections associated with a particular application or server from an attacker rather than all packets from the attacking host.

Protocol Optionally, this parameter specifies the IP protocol that you wish to block. Valid options are none (all IP protocols are blocked), TCP (only TCP packets are blocked), and UDP (only UDP packets are blocked).

Connection Shun If enabled, this parameter indicates that only a single connection is being blocked, with the connection parameters defined using the source/destination port and address fields. If it's disabled, all IP packets that meet the criteria specified in the source/destination port and address fields will be blocked.

Timeout This parameter defines the amount of time the block will be applied.

In Figure 23.44, a single connection is being blocked between 200.1.1.10 and 192.168.1.1. Because the destination port is 80, the connection is a web-based attack.

After configuring the manual blocking entry, you next need to click the Apply To Sensor button. At this point, the sensor will attempt to add the manual block to all of its managed devices. If your sensor can't communicate with a managed device, the addition of the manual block will fail.

Configuring Manual Blocking Using the CLI

Earlier in this chapter, you learned that blocking is configured via the network access configuration mode within the sensor CLI. Recall that this configuration mode has a general mode, which lets you configure general blocking properties and also allows you to configure manual blocking using the **shun-hosts** and **shun-networks** commands. The following demonstrates manually blocking a host:

```
sensor# configure terminal
sensor(config)# service networkAccess
sensor(config-NetworkAccess)# general
sensor(config-NetworkAccess-gen)# shun-hosts ip-address 200.1.1.200
sensor(config-NetworkAccess-gen-shu)# ?
connectionShun     Set to True for conditional blocking, or False for
                   unconditional blocking.
default            Set the value back to the system default setting
dest-ip-address    Destination IP address to block.
dest-port          Destination port of device to block.
exit               Exit shun-hosts configuration submode
protocol-name      Specify IP protocol by name. If used, do not set
                   numeric type.
protocol-number    Specify IP protocol by number. If used, do not set
                   protocol name.
show               Display system settings and/or history information
```

```
source-port          Source port of device to block.
sensor(config-NetworkAccess-gen-shu)# exit
sensor(config-NetworkAccess-gen)# exit
sensor(config-NetworkAccess)# exit
Apply Changes:?[yes]: yes
sensor(config)#
```

This example blocks packets from the address 200.1.1.200. Notice the various options that are available if you wish to specify other criteria such as destination IP address and destination port that must be matched for blocking.

Configuring System Control

The final administration area in the IDM is the System Control area, which is accessed by selecting Administration ➢ System Control within the IDM. Figure 23.45 shows this page.

In Figure 23.45, notice the single drop-down box, which has an action of Reset selected by default. You can also select Shutdown from this box to shut down the sensor instead of rebooting it. Once you've selected the appropriate action, click the Apply To Sensor button to invoke the action. Figure 23.46 shows what happens if the sensor is configured to be shut down.

Configuring System Control Using the Sensor CLI

You can reset or shut down a sensor from the sensor CLI using the `reset` command, which has the following syntax:

```
sensor# reset [powerdown]
```

If you specify the optional `powerdown` keyword, then the sensor will shut down rather than reboot.

FIGURE 23.45   The System Control page

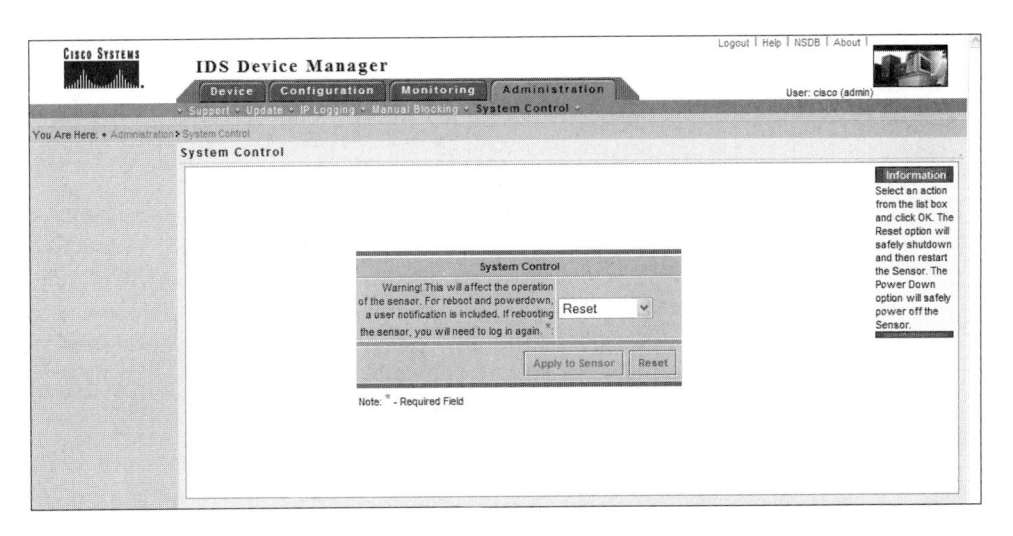

FIGURE 23.46 Shutting down a Cisco Secure IDS sensor

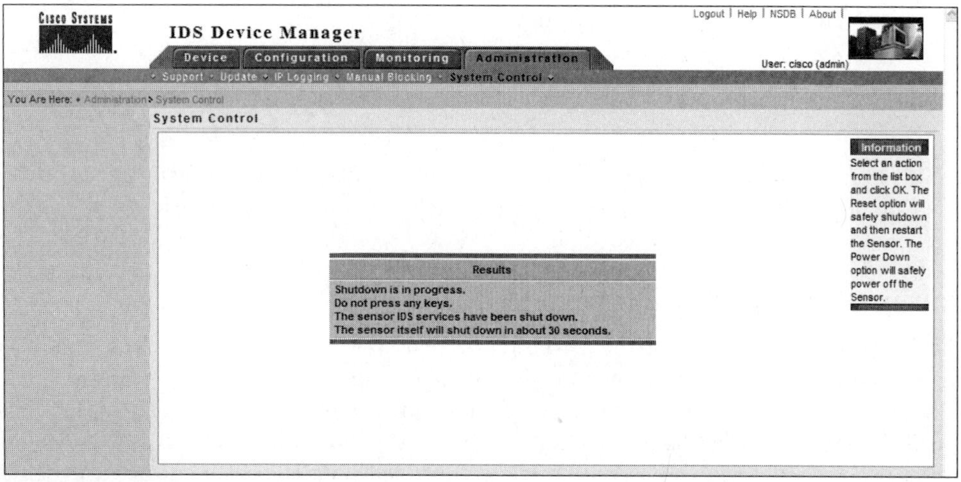

IDM Monitoring

The IDM provides a number of monitoring features that enable you to monitor sensor performance and also view additional intrusion detection information. Within the Monitoring tab on the IDM, you can select three different options:

- IP Logs
- Events
- Statistics

The features associated with each of these tabs are discussed in the following sections.

Viewing IP Logs

The Monitoring ➤ IP Logs page on the IDM provides access to all IP logging files stored on the sensor, which may have been generated in response to the event action of a signature, or because IP logging for a specific host has been defined (via Administration ➤ IP Logging page). Figure 23.47 shows the IP Logs page.

In Figure 23.47, notice that a single log file exists, which relates to an IP logging file that was created earlier (see Figure 23.42) for a specific host (192.168.1.1) via the Administration ➤ IP Logging page. All IP log files are stored in *tcpdump* format, which is a special format used by the Unix `tcpdump` network sniffer/analysis tool. To view the IP log files, you need a utility that can read tcpdump files, such as Ethereal. Figure 23.48 demonstrates using Ethereal to view the IP logging file shown in Figure 23.47, which can be downloaded by clicking the Log ID for the log file from the IP Logs page.

FIGURE 23.47 The IP Logs page

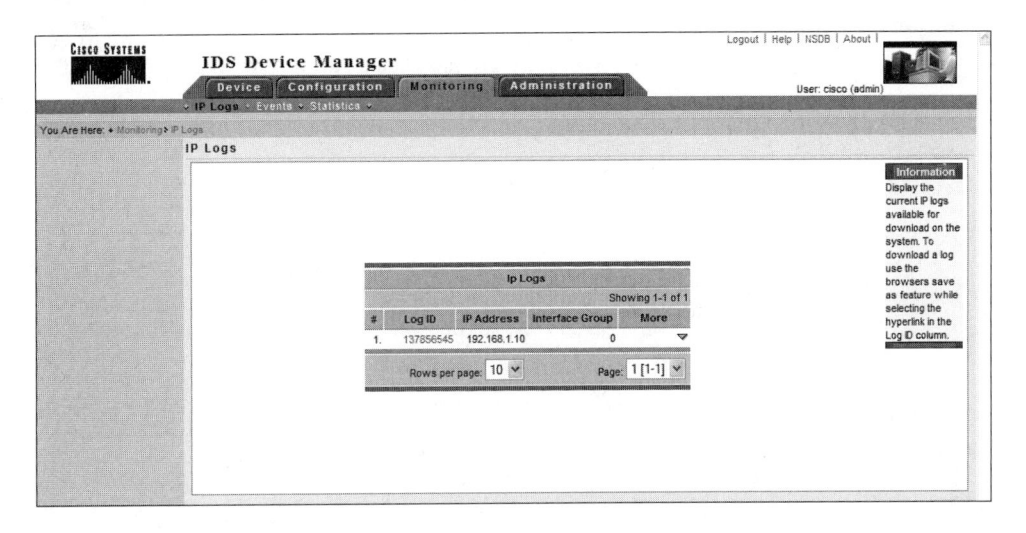

FIGURE 23.48 Example of an IP Logging file in Ethereal

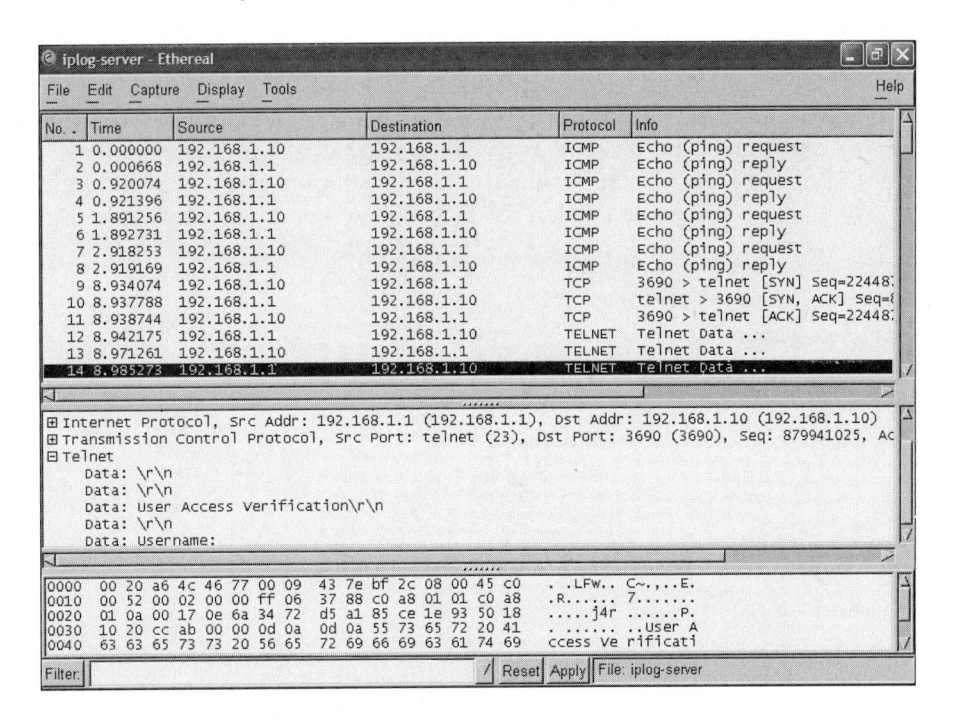

> Ethereal is a freeware network capture utility that you can download from http://www.ethereal.com. Ethereal is discussed further in Chapter 24, "Configuring Signatures and Using the IDS Event Viewer."

Viewing IP Logs Using the Sensor CLI

Using the standard sensor CLI, no commands are available for viewing the contents of IP log files. You can, however, view the status of IP log files using the CLI, and also copy IP log files to external servers.

To view the status of IP log files, you use the `iplog-status` command. The following demonstrates using this command:

```
sensor# iplog-status
Log ID:            137854304
IP Address:        192.168.1.10
Group:             0
Start Time:        1070584742402359000
End Time:          1070584744435327000
Bytes Captured:    1066
Packets Captured:  10
```

In this example, you can see that a single IP log file exists; it has a log ID of 137854304 (the log ID is important if you wish to copy an IP log file from the sensor to an external server). To copy an IP log file, you use the `copy iplog` command, specifying the log ID of the IP log file you wish to copy and the destination URL. The following demonstrates copying an IP log file using the sensor CLI:

```
sensor# copy iplog 137854304 ftp://192.168.2.1
User: anonymous
File name: iplog-example
Password: *******
Connected to 192.168.2.1 (192.168.2.1).
220 3Com 3CDaemon FTP Server Version 2.0
ftp> user
(username) anonymous
331 User name ok, need password
Password:230 User logged in
ftp> 200 Type set to I.
ftp> put iplog.1014.tmp iplog-example
local: iplog.1014.tmp remote: example
227 Entering passive mode (192,168,2,1,12,96)
```

```
125 Using existing data connection
226 Closing data connection; File transfer successful.
1066 bytes sent in 0.001 secs (1e+03 Kbytes/sec)
ftp>
```

In this example, an IP log file is copied to an FTP server with an IP address of 192.168.2.1.

Viewing Events

The Monitoring ➤ Events page on the IDM provides access to alarms and events stored in the event store, which is a local storage area on the sensor for alarms. Figure 23.49 shows the Events page.

In Figure 23.49, notice that you can specify a number of filter criteria for viewing events stored in the event store. Some of the filter criteria include the following:

Alerts You can specify whether alerts (alarms) should be displayed. You can also specify the severity level of alerts that should be displayed.

Other events You can indicate whether to view debug, error, log, network controller, and status events, if you wish.

Time You can specify a start date/time, an end date/time, and a time range for the events that you wish to view.

> **NOTE** If you leave all filter criteria blank, all events are displayed.

FIGURE 23.49 The Events page

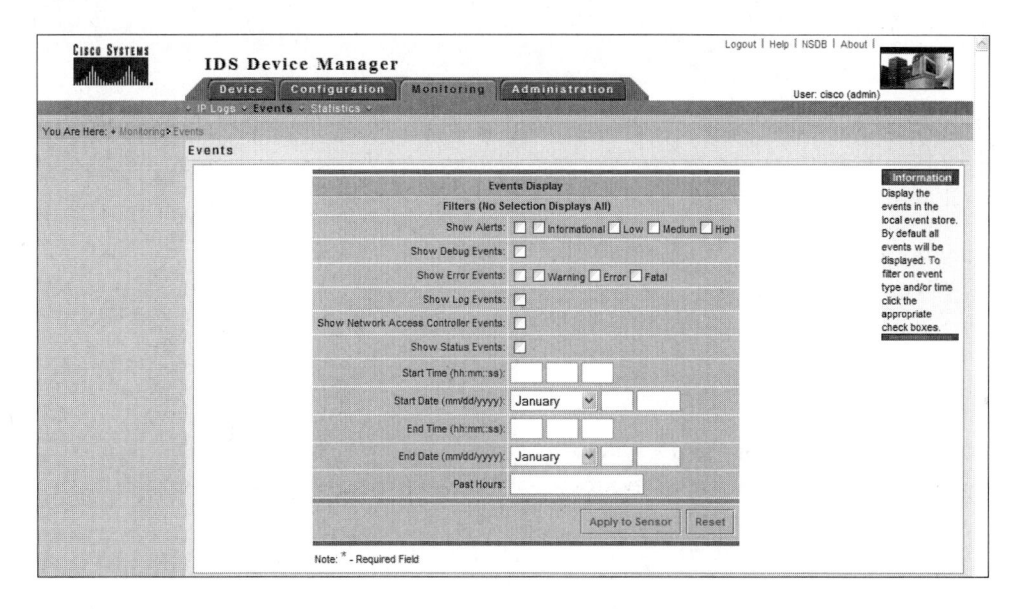

Once you've specified the appropriate filter criteria, then if you click the Apply To Sensor button, all events that match the filter criteria will be displayed, as demonstrated in Figure 23.50.

In Figure 23.50, you can see information for two events. Notice that each event includes a number of fields that provide specific information about the event. For example, event 1 is an alarm, because you can tell from signature details in the event, such as signature ID and a signature name.

FIGURE 23.50 Viewing events

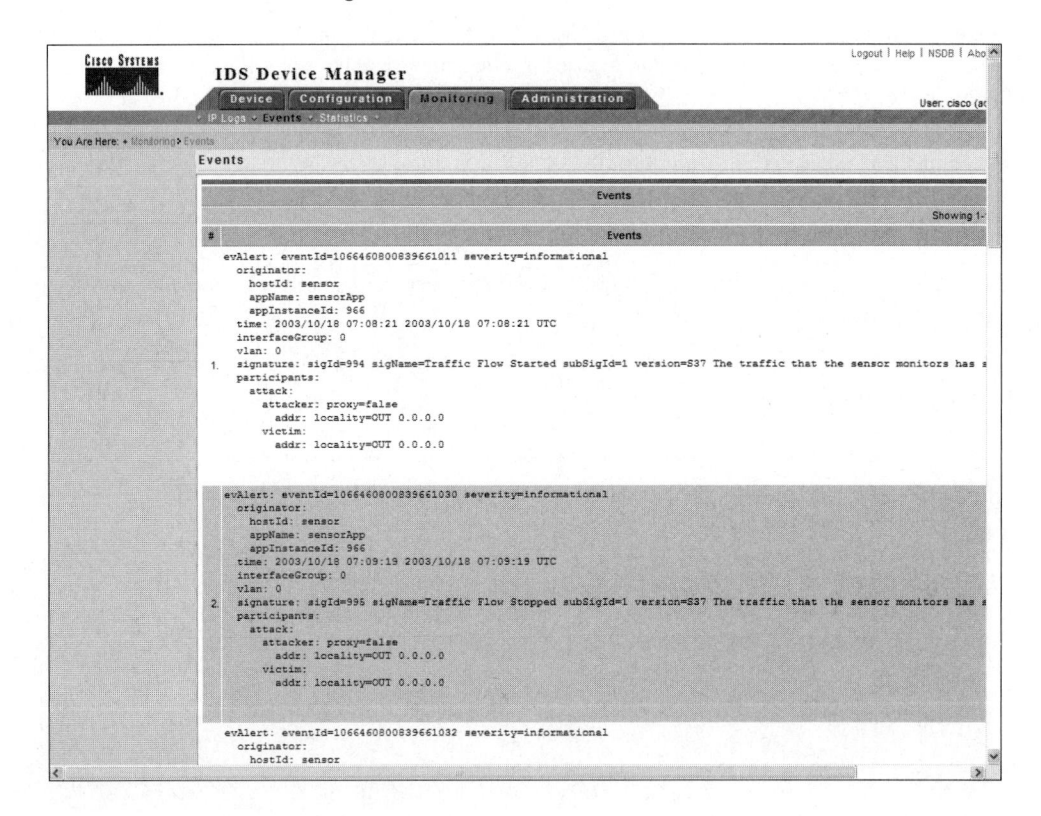

Viewing Events Using the Sensor CLI

You can view the sensor event store from the sensor CLI using the show events command. The following demonstrates using this command to view the sensor event store:

```
sensor# show events ?
<cr>
alert          Display local system alerts
error          Display error events
hh:mm[:ss]     Display start time
```

```
log             Display log events
nac             Display NAC shun events
status          Display status events
sensor# show events error

evError: eventId=1069519036718323014 severity=error
  originator:
    hostId: sensor
    appName: nac
    appInstanceId:
  time: 2003/12/05 00:28:14 2003/12/05 00:28:14 UTC
  errorMessage: name=errUnclassified sendDuplicateMessage() failed:
  error name = errTransport, error description = Connection failed
```

You can view all events by specifying the show events command with no options, or you can view specific types of events by specifying an appropriate option.

Viewing Statistics

The Monitoring ➤ Statistics page on the IDM provides access to statistics related to the Cisco Secure IDS intrusion detection engine. Statistics provided include the following:

WebServer Statistics This section provides information about the web server that handles IDM connections and connections from other IDS management platforms.

TransactionSource Statistics This section provides transaction source statistics.

TransactionServer Statistics This section provides transaction server statistics.

NetworkAccess Statistics This section provides information relating to the blocking configuration and state of the sensor.

Logger Statistics This section provides information relating to log events written to the event store.

Host Statistics This section provides system-level information about the sensor.

EventStore Statistics This section provides information about log events stored in the event store.

EventServer Statistics This section provides information about connections from an external monitoring platform such as the IDS event viewer.

AnalysisEngine Statistics This section provides information about packets processed and analyzed by the sensor.

Authentication Statistics This section provides information about failed authentication attempts for management access to the sensor.

Figure 23.51 shows the top portion of the Statistics page.

FIGURE 23.51 The Statistics page

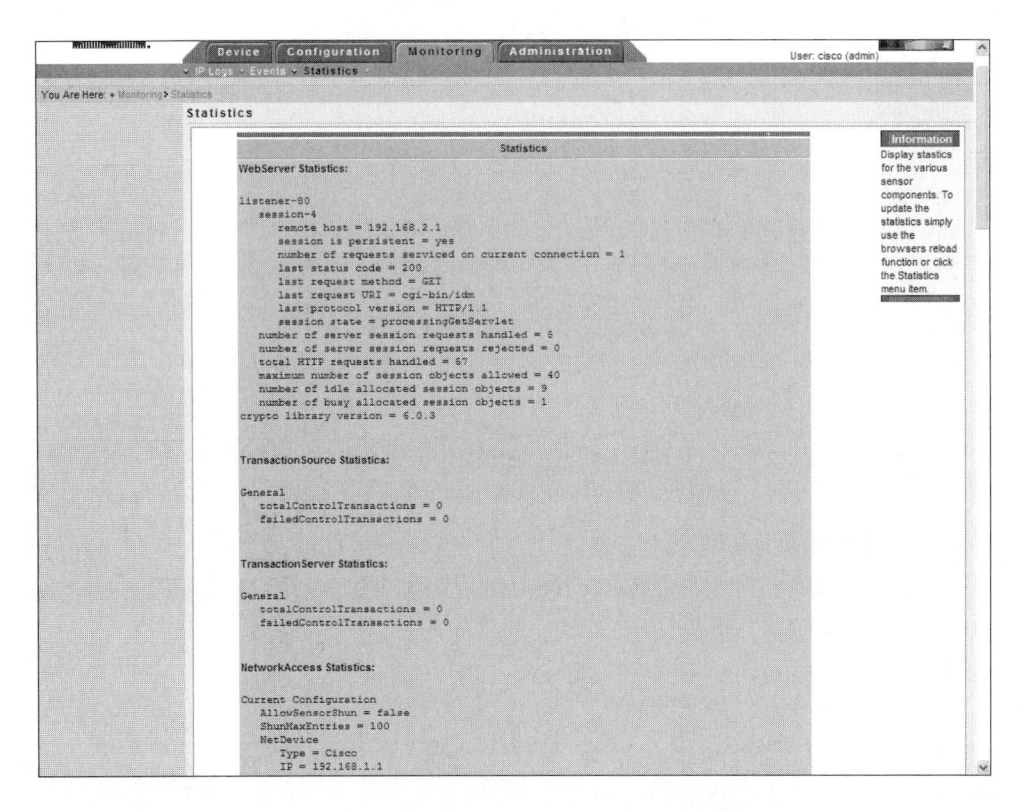

Viewing Statistics from the Sensor CLI

You can view statistics from the sensor CLI using the show statistics command. The following demonstrates using this command to view sensor statistics:

```
sensor# show statistics ?
Authentication      Display authentication statistics
EventServer         Display event server statistics
EventStore          Display event store statistics
Host                Display host statistics
Logger              Display logger statistics
NetworkAccess       Display network access controller statistics
TransactionServer   Display transaction server statistics
TransactionSource   Display transaction source statistics
WebServer           Display web server statistics
sensor# show statistics EventStore
Event store statistics
```

```
General information about the event store
   The current number of open subscriptions = 2
   The number of events lost by subscriptions and queries = 0
   The number of queries issued = 0
   The number of times the event store circular buffer has wrapped = 0
Number of events of each type currently stored
   Debug events = 0
   Status events = 59
   Log transaction events = 535
   Shun request events = 0
   Error events, warning = 37
   Error events, error = 101
   Error events, fatal = 3
   Alert events, informational = 267
   Alert events, low = 5648
   Alert events, medium = 0
   Alert events, high = 4
```

Summary

In this chapter, you learned how to configure, monitor, and administer Cisco Secure IDS sensors using the IDS Device Manager. The IDS Device Manager is a web-based application; the server component resides on the sensor, and the client component is any supported web browser. The IDS Device Manager is the recommended method of sensor management (unless you're using an enterprise IDS management platform such as IDS Management Center) and makes it easier to manage than using the at times cryptic command-line interface.

To get started with the IDS Device Manager, all you need to do is initialize the sensor with an IP configuration using the **setup** CLI utility and ensure that the IP address of the web browser you're using is a permitted host. Once these basic tasks are complete, you can then connect using the IDM. The IDM uses HTTP over SSL on TCP port 443 by default; however, you can modify the web server port and also disable SSL if required. You also need the credentials of a user account configured on the IDM that possesses the appropriate rights for the tasks that you'll perform using the IDM.

Once you've connected and authenticated successfully to the IDM, you can begin configuration tasks. If you're working with a new sensor, you can run through sensor setup screens, which configure system-level parameters necessary for the underlying operation of the sensor. You can then configure intrusion detection on the sensor, modifying signatures, system variables, and event filters. You can also configure blocking, which enables the sensor to manage perimeter devices such as routers, PIX firewalls, and Catalyst 6000/6500 layer 3 switches, applying access control lists to block the source of detected attacks. In a network topology with multiple sensors, you should configure a master blocking sensor, which is the only sensor that applies blocking ACLs to perimeter devices. All other sensors are configured as blocking forwarding sensors, because they forward blocking requests to the master blocking sensor rather than attempt to apply blocking to perimeter devices directly.

The IDM also lets you administer and monitor the sensor. In terms of administration, you can obtain support information, update sensor software, configure IP logging that captures all traffic from a specific host or set of hosts, manually apply blocks, and reboot/shut down the sensor. With monitoring, you can view IP logs (which are generated for any signature that has an event action of logging defined), view events in the event store (which are alarms generated by the intrusion detection engine as well as system and error events), and view statistics relating to various components of the sensor.

Exam Essentials

Know the requirements of the IDM.   The IDM requires a Cisco Secure IDS sensor and a client with a supported web browser. Supported browsers include Netscape Navigator/Communicator 4.79 or higher, and Microsoft Internet Explorer 5.5 SP2 or higher.

Know how to connect to the IDM.   By default, the IDM uses HTTP over SSL using TCP port 443, meaning that you normally use a URL of `https://sensor-ip-address`. When you're establishing the connection, you must authenticate to the IDM using an account configured locally on the sensor. Be sure that the IP address of the web browser is configured as an allowed host on the sensor.

Understand the layout of the IDM.   Ensure that you understand each of the following components of the IDM: tabs, Options bar, Path bar, TOC, Object bar, page, tools, Instructions box, and Activity bar.

Understand how to perform various sensor setup configuration tasks using the IDM.   The Device ➤ Sensor Setup option lets you configure network settings, define allowed hosts, enable/disable the use of Telnet, configure SSH authorized hosts, configure SSH known hosts, configure certificates (trusted hosts and local server certificate), configure time settings, and configure user accounts.

Know how to configure intrusion detection using the IDM.   The Configuration ➤ Sensing Engine page lets you configure signatures, alarm channel system variables, virtual sensor system variables, and event filters. The Configuration ➤ Blocking option allows you to configure blocking and master blocking sensors.

Understand the concepts of the alarm channel and virtual sensor.   The Alarm Channel filters and aggregates alarms generated by the intrusion detection engine before they are placed in the event store on the sensor. Cisco Secure IDS supports the concept of a virtual sensor, which is abstracted from the physical sensor itself. At present only a single virtual sensor exists; however, in the future, multiple virtual sensors are expected to be supported, allowing for separate IDS policies to be defined (one per virtual sensor).

Know how to configure blocking. To configure blocking, first configure general blocking properties (whether the sensor IP address can be blocked, maximum blocking entries that can exist). Next, define any critical hosts that you don't wish to apply blocking for. You next configure logical devices, which define credentials for authenticating to devices managed by the sensor, and then configure blocking devices, which define each perimeter device and the interface/VLAN and direction that you wish the block to apply to.

Know how to configure master blocking sensors. There should be only a single master blocking sensor, which has all perimeter devices configured as blocking devices. The master blocking sensor must also have each blocking forwarding sensor configured as an allowed host so that these sensors can connect to the master blocking sensor. If the master blocking sensor uses SSH to manage devices, you must ensure that the SSH host keys of each managed device are configured as known host keys.

Understand how Auto Update works. Auto Update allows sensors to automatically obtain updates from a central FTP or SCP server. It's important to understand that you must manually download the appropriate updates from Cisco and then place them on the FTP/SCP server.

Understand how to perform administration tasks using the IDM. Administration tasks include obtaining support information, manually updating the sensor, configuring IP logging, configuring manual blocking, and rebooting the sensor.

Understand how to perform monitoring tasks using the IDM. Monitoring tasks include viewing IP logs, viewing events, and viewing statistics.

Understand system variables. Alarm channel system variables define IP addresses or networks that can be referenced in event filters. Virtual sensor system variables define ports that are considered web ports, define a custom list of ports that can be referenced when configuring a signature, and define the maximum number of fragments that the sensor can cache.

Know how to configure sensors using the CLI. Make sure that for all tasks configurable using the IDM, you also understand how to use the CLI to perform the same tasks.

Chapter 24

Configuring Signatures and Using the IDS Event Viewer

CISCO SECURE INTRUSION DETECTION SYSTEM EXAM TOPICS COVERED IN THIS CHAPTER:

- ✓ Configuring the sensor's sensing parameters
- ✓ Configuring a signature's enable status, severity level, and action
- ✓ Tuning a signature to perform optimally based on a network's characteristics
- ✓ Creating a custom signature given an attack scenario
- ✓ Cisco IDS signature features
- ✓ Selecting the Cisco IDS signature engine to create a custom signature
- ✓ Global Cisco IDS signature parameters
- ✓ Engine-specific signature parameters
- ✓ Features and benefits of IEV
- ✓ Identifying the requirements for IEV
- ✓ Installing the IEV software and configuring it to monitor IDS devices
- ✓ Creating custom IEV views and filters
- ✓ Navigating IEV to view alarm details
- ✓ Performing IEV database administration functions
- ✓ Configuring IEV application settings and preferences

Signatures are the fundamental component of a signature-based IDS solution, because they provide the rules that define intrusive activity. Understanding how to tune signatures that ship with Cisco Secure IDS software and also how to create custom signatures for new attacks is crucial to the overall success or failure of your IDS sensor. Before you can tune or create signatures, you must have an in-depth understanding of how signatures are implemented within Cisco Secure IDS, the signature engines that categorize the various attacks detected by signatures, and the parameters that make up each signature.

Another key ingredient of any successful IDS solution is its capability to generate, gather, and display alarms to security operators in a concise, yet accurate and detailed, manner. An IDS sensor isn't much use if it can't somehow impart the fact that alarms have been detected to security administrators and operators responsible for responding to intrusion attempts. Hence, when you're choosing an IDS solution, it's important to look past the seemingly more important features such as performance and number of attacks detected, and ensure that the alarm-monitoring interface provided by the IDS is accurate, easy to use, and reliable. All Cisco Secure IDS sensors include an application called the IDS Event Viewer, which is the alarm-monitoring software installable on a separate Windows-based host machine that ships for free with every Cisco Secure IDS sensor purchased and is installable on a separate Windows-based host machine. The IDS Event Viewer is suitable for smaller Cisco Secure IDS deployments and can monitor alarms generated by up to five sensors.

In this chapter, you'll learn about signatures, how Cisco Secure IDS implements signature engines, and how to configure signatures using the IDM and sensor command-line interface. You'll also learn about the requirements for the IEV application, how to install the IEV, and how to use the IEV to view and manage alarms according to your requirements.

Cisco Secure IDS Signatures

Signatures are a fundamental component of Cisco Secure IDS, because they provide the set of rules and logic that allow sensors to successfully detect intrusive activity. For example, many denial of service (DoS) attacks place illegal data in packet fields that don't make sense to target systems, which may cause target systems to crash, creating a DoS condition. Assume that such an attack modifies a particular field in the TCP header of TCP packets to a value of 0x1010, which is illegal according to the TCP specification for the field. A signature for this attack might be defined as follows:

- Check IP protocol field has a value of 6 (the packet is a TCP packet).
- Check TCP field value. If value = 0x1010, then signature is matched.

If a packet or set of packets being analyzed matches the rules defined in a signature, then the sensor will generate an alarm, listing the signature ID matched and other information such as source IP address, destination IP address, and so on.

Cisco Secure IDS includes three types of signatures:

Built-in signatures   Cisco Secure IDS sensors ship with a number of signatures that are referred to as *built-in signatures* in their default configuration. Built-in signatures are organized based on *signature engines*, which are components of the sensor intrusion detection engine that detect specific types of attacks.

Tuned signatures   Cisco Secure IDS software lets you tune built-in signatures, which refers to the process of modifying configurable parameters that affect how traffic is analyzed against a signature. Any built-in signature that has been modified in any fashion is referred to as a *tuned signature*.

Custom signatures   Some signature engines allow for the creation of *custom signatures*, where security administrators specify the conditions that packets being analyzed must meet for the signature to be matched. Custom signatures are useful for detecting new attacks for which Cisco has not released a built-in signature, or to create signatures specific to the characteristics of the environment being monitored by your sensors.

Cisco Secure IDS signatures include a number of features that ensure Cisco Secure IDS sensors can provide effective intrusion detection whatever the environment the sensor is installed in. Following are descriptions of the features of Cisco Secure IDS signatures:

Alarm summarization   Some attacks (especially DoS attacks) are repetitive and can generate excessive alarms that cause IDS management platforms and applications to become overloaded. In this situation, important alarms may be difficult to detect or missed due to the large number of alarms being generated, causing a delayed or zero response to intrusive activity. Cisco Secure IDS signatures include an alarm summarization feature, which allows repetitive alarms to be summarized, reducing the overall number of alarms generated.

Configurable thresholds   Some signatures allow you to adjust thresholds that determine whether an alarm is triggered. For example, a signature that detects port scans might be configured to generate an alarm only if more than 10 ports are attempted to be connected to on the same target system from the same source within a one-second interval. The number of ports connected to and the interval over which to measure the number of ports connected to could be thresholds that are configurable.

Anti-evasive techniques   Some attacks attempt to bypass signature-based intrusion detection systems by using evasive techniques such as obfuscation and fragmentation. Cisco Secure IDS signatures include de-obfuscation and reassembly features that ensure anti-evasive techniques employed by attackers aren't successful.

Response actions   All Cisco Secure IDS signatures that are successfully triggered generate an alarm; however, you can also optionally define one or more response actions:

Log   The sensor captures subsequent IP packets from the source of the attack that triggered a signature (also referred to as *IP logging*).

Reset   The sensor sends TCP resets over the sensing interface to the source and destination hosts associated with an attack.

Block   The sensor configures a managed perimeter device to block IP traffic from the source of an attack.

Now that you've been introduced to signatures on Cisco Secure IDS, the following sections will focus on each of the Cisco Secure IDS signature engines and describe the various parameters for each signature engine.

Cisco Secure IDS Signature Engines

Cisco Secure IDS signature engines are components of the sensor intrusion detection engine that detect different types of attacks. The different signature engines are as follows:

ATOMIC engine   This engine detects attacks that are contained within a single packet. In other words, atomic signatures don't need to worry about the complexities of having to analyze multiple packets. A number of subengines exist within the ATOMIC engine:

>**ATOMIC.L3.IP**   This is a general-purpose layer 3 inspector that can inspect payload length and IP protocol number values, with the ability to handle fragments and perform partial Internet Control Message Protocol (ICMP) comparisons.

>**ATOMIC.ICMP**   This subengine detects single-packet ICMP attacks.

>**ATOMIC.UDP**   This subengine detects single-packet User Datagram Protocol (UDP) attacks.

>**ATOMIC.TCP**   This subengine detects single-packet Transmission Control Protocol (TCP) attacks.

>**ATOMIC.IPOPTIONS**   This subengine detects single-packet attacks that exploit the use of IP options.

>**ATOMIC.ARP**   This subengine detects single-packet Address Resolution Protocol (ARP) attacks.

FLOOD engine   This engine detects DoS attacks that attempt to cause a DoS condition by using flooding techniques such as saturating network links. FLOOD signatures monitor the packet-per-second rate associated with one or more source and destination hosts. A number of subengines exist within the FLOOD engine:

>**FLOOD.HOST.ICMP**   This subengine detects n to 1 attacks, where multiple ICMP packets are directed at a single destination host.

>**FLOOD.HOST.UDP**   This subengine detects n to 1 attacks, where multiple UDP packets are directed at a single destination host.

>**FLOOD.NET**   This subengine detects n to n attacks, where the packet-per-second rate for specific types of packets is measured.

SERVICE engine This engine is used for signatures that require inspection of layer 5 through layer 7 protocols, such as DNS, SQL, Simple Mail Transfer Protocol (SMTP), and HTTP. The following SERVICE subengines exist:

SERVICE.DNS This subengine detects attacks related to the DNS service.

SERVICE.FTP This subengine detects attacks related to FTP service.

SERVICE.GENERIC This subengine detects attacks related to custom services and payloads.

SERVICE.HTTP This subengine detects attacks related to HTTP service.

SERVICE.IDENT This subengine detects attacks related to TCP Client Identity Protocol (IDENT) service.

SERVICE.MSSQL This subengine detects attacks related to MSSQL service.

SERVICE.NTP This subengine detects attacks related to Network Time Protocol (NTP) service.

SERVICE.RPC This subengine detects attacks related to Remote Procedure Call (RPC) service.

SERVICE.SMB This subengine detects attacks related to Server Message Block (SMB) service.

SERVICE.SNMP This subengine detects inspects Simple Network Management Protocol (SNMP) version 1 packets only.

SERVICE.SSH This subengine detects attacks related to Secure Shell (SSH) service.

STRING engine This engine is used for regular expression-based pattern inspection of data from multiple transport protocols, including TCP, UDP, and ICMP. A regular expression lets you specify one or more strings, using a syntax that includes *metacharacters* and string values. Metacharacters are operators that allow you to compare a specified string value against the current string data being analyzed. Table 24.1 lists the various metacharacters.

STATE.STRING engine This engine is used for state-based regular expression-based pattern inspection of TCP streams by creating a string-based state machine. A *state machine* describes a specific event based on previous transactions that may have occurred. This allows for powerful signatures to be created that are useful for protocol decoding.

SWEEP engine This engine detects reconnaissance attacks where multiple connections are attempted from a single source to multiple ports on a single destination system or multiple destination systems. This engine includes the following subengines:

SWEEP.HOST.ICMP This subengine detects ICMP sweeps from a single source to multiple destination hosts.

SWEEP.HOST.TCP This subengine detects TCP sweeps from a single source to multiple destination hosts.

SWEEP.MULTI This subengine detects cross-protocol sweeps where both UDP and TCP ports are used. The SATAN utility can trigger signatures using this engine.

SWEEP.OTHER.TCP   This subengine detects nonstandard TCP sweeps, which use illegal TCP flag combinations and are often used to fingerprint the operating system of a target system (NMAP is an example of a utility that generates such sweeps).

SWEEP.PORT.TCP   This subengine detects TCP port sweeps from a single source to a single destination.

SWEEP.PORT.UDP   This subengine detects UDP port sweeps from a single source to a single destination.

SYSLOG engine   This engine is used to interpret incoming Syslog events from perimeter devices generated in response to access control list violations and to generate alarms based on each ACL violation.

TRAFFIC engine   This engine detects traffic irregularities, where a protocol is being used to provide a covert communications channel. For example, LOKI is a Trojan horse that can transmit data within ICMP packets, which are often permitted through firewalls. Only a single subengine called TRAFFIC.ICMP exists.

TROJAN engine   This engine detects Trojan horse attacks such as BackOrifice and Tribe Flood Net (TFN). This engine includes three subengines:

TROJAN.BO2K   This subengine detects the presence of BackOrifice Trojan horses used for backdoor access to compromised hosts.

TROJAN.TFN2K   This subengine detects the presence of TFN Trojan horses used for distributed denial of service (DDoS) attacks.

TROJAN.UDP   This subengine detects the presence of BackOrifice Trojan horses that are operating in UDP mode (communicating with a remote attacker using UDP rather than TCP).

TABLE 24.1   Regular Expression Metacharacters

Metacharacter	Description	Examples
[]	A range of characters is enclosed by square brackets. You can use a hyphen to indicate a range of characters.	[Rr]ed matches the strings *Red* and *red*. [a-c]12 matches the strings *a12*, *b12*, and *c12*.
.	Matches any single character, including white space.	r.d matches the strings *rad*, *rbd*, *r1d*, *r2d*, *r d*, and so on.
*	Matches zero, one, or more of the previous character in the expression.	AA* matches the strings *AA*, *AAA*, *AAAA*, and so on.

TABLE 24.1 Regular Expression Metacharacters *(continued)*

Metacharacter	Description	Examples
+	Matches one or more of the previous characters in the expression.	AA+ matches the strings *AAA*, *AAAA*, and so on, but doesn't match *AA*.
?	Matches zero or one occurrences of the previous character in the expression.	AA? matches the string *AA* or *AAA* but doesn't match *AAAA*.
^	Matches the start of a line.	^blah matches the string *blah* but doesn't match the string *I said blah*, because *blah* isn't at the start of the line.
[^]	Matches any characters not in the list specified within the brackets. The brackets can also be used to indicate special characters.	[^abc]123 matches the strings *d123*, *e123*, and so on, but doesn't match *a123*, *b123*, or *c123*. 1[+]2 matches the string *1+2*.
$	Matches the end of a line. $ can be used in conjunction with ^ to match an explicit string.	blah$ matches the string *blah* or *I said blah* but doesn't match the string *blah blah black sheep*, because the pattern *blah* isn't following by an end-of-line character. ^blah$ matches the string *blah* only and doesn't match *blah blah* or any other string with *blah* included.
\	When used in conjunction with particular characters, specifies the hidden tab (), newline.	3\+2 matches the string *3 + 2* where a tab character exists between the 3 and + characters and between the + and 2 characters.
()	Limits the scope of the expression to which you're applying a regular expression.	ba(na)+ matches one or more occurrences of the text *na* within the string: for example, *bana*, *banana*, *bananana*, *banananana*, and so on.
|	Matches either expression that is separated by the | metacharacter.	golf(ed|ing) matches either *golfed* or *golfing*.

An Analysis of Code Red

In mid-2001, the Code Red worm was released onto the Internet and compromised thousands of systems, causing millions of dollars in downtime and lost productivity. The Code Red worm uses a particular buffer overflow exploit, which involves the passing of a specific HTTP GET request to a remote Microsoft IIS server. Although Cisco Secure IDS includes a signature that specifically detects Code Red (signature ID #5126), it's interesting to understand exactly how Code Red works.

The Code Red worm sends a large amount of data to the default.ida ISAPI filter in Microsoft IIS. Because the buffer input is unchecked, a buffer overflow occurs that allows arbitrary execution of code with full system access rights. The following shows an example of the data that is passed to IIS that causes the buffer overflow:

```
GET /
default.ida?NNNNNNNNNNNNNNNNNNNNNNNNNNNNNNNNNNNNNNNNNNNNNNNNNNNNNNNNNNNNN
NNNNNNNNNNNNNNNNNNNNNNNNNNNNNNNNNNNNNNNNNNNNNNNNNNNNNNNNNNNNNNNNNNNNNNNNN
NNNNNNNNNNNNNNNNNNNNNNNNNNNNNNNNNNNNNNNNNNNNNNNNNNNNNNNNNNNNNNNN%u9090%u
6858%
ucbd3%u7801%u9090%u6858%ucbd3%u7801%u9090%u6858%ucbd3%u7801%u9090%u9090%u8190%u00c
3%u00
03%u8b00%u531b%u53ff%u0078%u0000%u00=a
```

After this data is sent, subsequent code is sent that replicates the Code Red attack onto the target system. The target system then attacks other systems automatically, causing a snowball effect, enabling the Code Red worm to spread extremely quickly.

To detect the previous GET request, you can use the following regular expression to match the attack string:

```
[/][Dd][Ee][Ff][Aa][Uu][Ll][Tt][.][Ii][Dd][Aa][?][a-zA-Z0-9]+%u
```

Let's examine the previous expression in more detail. If you consider the first three characters, [/], this represents the actual character /. This character must be enclosed in square brackets, because it's a special character for regular expressions. If you now consider the portion [Dd][Ee][Ff][Aa][Uu][Ll][Tt][.][Ii][Dd][Aa][?], it represents the default.ida? portion of the string. Because Microsoft IIS doesn't enforce case sensitivity, you need to use the previous expression to detect variants of the main Code Red exploit. For example, the expression matches the following strings:

```
/default.ida?
/DeFault.iDa?
```

> The next part of the regular expression reads [a-zA-Z0-9]+. The [a-zA-Z0-9] portion matches any alphanumeric character. The + symbol at the end means to match one or more instances of the previous pattern [a-zA-Z0-9], which means to match one or more alphanumeric characters. The last part of the regular expression reads %u, which means to match the string %u. The following show examples of strings that will match the expression:
>
> ```
> /default.ida?NNN%u
> /default.ida?NNNNNNNNN%u
> /default.ida?nnna123%u
> ```
>
> From this example, you can see that regular expressions can be very powerful and can be used to detect complex patterns within ASCII data streams.

Signature Engine Parameters

All signatures contain parameters that control how signatures are analyzed and how alarms are generated. The parameters that apply to each signature are dependent on the signature engine that the signature belongs to. In other words, each engine defines the parameters available for signatures that belong to the engine. All engine parameters are defined by a name that identifies the parameter and a value that is configurable for each signature.

When you're working with parameters, it's important to understand that there are two generic types of parameters:

Master engine parameters   *Master engine parameters* exist for all signature engines and provide the ability to configure features common to all signatures. Master engine parameter values can be different for different engines; however, the existence and meaning of the parameter is consistent for all signature engines.

Local engine parameters   Each signature engine also contains *local engine parameters*, which are parameters specific to the signature engine. Local engine parameters provide the ability to configure features unique to each signature engine.

For both master engine and local engine parameters, each parameter can have the following attributes:

Protected   A *protected parameter* can't be modified and always has the same value. For example, the SigName parameter is a parameter common to all signatures and defines the name of the signature. For all built-in signatures, this parameter is protected. In other words, you can't modify the signature name of a built-in signature.

Required   A *required parameter* is a parameter that must be configured with a nonzero value. Required parameters are essential for signatures to work and have meaning.

Optional   *Optional parameters* are all parameters that are configurable but don't require configuration.

In the following sections, we'll look at both the master engine and local engine parameters more closely.

Master Engine Parameters

Master engine parameters are available for all Cisco Secure IDS signatures; they control common signature features. The following are the different types of master engine parameters:

- Fundamental parameters
- Alarm count parameters
- Alarm summarization parameters

Fundamental Parameters

The basic parameters include the following:

SigName   This parameter defines the name of the signature.

SIGID   This parameter defines the signature ID of the signature.

AlarmSeverity   This parameter defines the severity of alarms generated by the matches against the signature.

Enabled   This parameter defines whether the signature is enabled or disabled.

EventAction   This parameter defines the action that should be taken by a sensor, should the signature be fired. Valid options include IP logging, TCP resets, and blocking.

MaxTTL   This parameter defines the amount of time that a logical stream of information should be inspected. During this time of analysis, an *inspector* is generated, which is essentially an instance of the signature that is used to analyze specific packets that have been captured. Once the MaxTTL timer expires, the inspector is destroyed.

Alarm Count Parameters

The alarm count parameters define how alarms are counted, generated, and summarized. There are two alarm count parameters, and we'll look at them in the following sections.

STORAGEKEY

The StorageKey parameter defines how signature hits should be counted and controls the number of alarms that are generated. The StorageKey value is defined in terms of an *address view*, which is an expression that indicates the combination of addressing information that should be used to uniquely identify and count each signature hit. Address views are defined using the following syntax:

```
src-address-indicator src-port-indicator dst-address-indicator
    dst-port-indicator
```

Each indicator value indicates whether signature hits should be recorded for each unique instance of the relevant indicator value. The following indicators are used:

- A = source address
- a = source port
- B = destination address
- b = destination port
- x = doesn't matter

For example, an address view might be defined as AaBb. This means that a hit should be generated for each unique combination of source address, source port, destination address, and destination port that fires the signature. If the address view is defined as Axxx, this means that a hit should be generated for each unique source address that fires the signature.

SUMMARYKEY

The SummaryKey parameter specifies the address view used for alarm summarization. For example, if the SummaryKey value is set to Axxx, then signature hits are counted (and summarized) separately for each unique source address. If the SummaryKey value is set to AxBx, then signature matches are counted (and summarized) separately for each unique combination of source address and destination address. Assume that the following signature matches take place:

- 60 signature matches with a source IP address of 200.1.1.1 and destination IP address of 200.2.1.1
- 60 signature matches with a source IP address of 200.1.1.1 and destination IP address of 200.3.1.1

If the SummaryKey is set to Axxx, then the count of signature matches will be 120, because the same source IP address has generated all signature matches. If the SummaryKey is set to AxBx, then the count will be 60 for A=200.1.1.1, B=200.2.1.1 and 60 for A=200.1.1.1, B=200.3.1.1.

Alarm Summarization Parameters

Cisco Secure IDS signatures include alarm summarization features, which limit the alarms generated by excessive matches against a signature. There are two types of alarm summarization:

- Simple mode
- Advanced mode

SIMPLE MODE

In simple mode, a signature must be fired a configurable number of times before an actual alarm is generated. Two parameters control simple alarm summarization:

MinHits This parameter defines the number of times a signature must be matched (also referred to as *signature hits*) before an actual alarm is generated.

AlarmInterval This parameter allows a timed interval to be used in conjunction with the hit count provided by MinHits.

If the AlarmInterval parameter isn't defined, then alarm count is purely used for summarization based on the value of the MinHits parameter for the lifetime of the alarm inspector

(MaxTTL value). If the `AlarmInterval` is used, then a summary alarm is generated for every *X* signature hits during interval *Y*, where *X* is the value of the `MinHits` parameter and *Y* is the value of the `AlarmInterval` parameter.

ADVANCED MODE

In advanced mode, a more advanced method of summarization is used. The following defines the parameters used in advanced mode:

ThrottleInterval The `ThrottleInterval` parameter is used as a timer for specifying the interval over which signature hits should be counted for alarm summarization features.

AlarmThrottle The `AlarmThrottle` parameter controls the number of alarms generated by a specific signature. The `AlarmThrottle` parameter can be configured with one of the following values:

FireOnce Only a single alarm is generated once for each address set for the lifetime of the inspector. The inspector lifetime is defined by the `MaxTTL` parameter and is a value between 0 and 1000 seconds.

FireAll An alarm is generated for each match against a signature, with no limit as to the alarms that are generated (no summarization).

Summarize An alarm is generated for the first signature match within the `ThrottleInterval` interval and then counts the number of signature hits that are detected within the interval. At the end of the interval, if more than one alarm was generated, a summary alarm is sent for the interval that includes the number of alarms generated during the interval. For example, if the interval is 10 seconds and 40 alarms are generated during an interval, two alarms are generated: one for the first alarm detected during the interval and a second summary alarm that specifies 40 alarms have occurred during the interval. Summary alarms are generated for each address set specified by the `SummaryKey` value.

GlobalSummarize This is identical in function to the `Summarize` value; however, the address view used for counting alarms is the global key (xxxx), meaning that all alarms are counted for the signature regardless of address. For example, if 20 alarms are generated by a source 200.1.1.1 and 40 alarms are generate by a source 201.1.1.1 during the interval, with the `AlarmThrottle` parameter set to `GlobalSummarize`, a single summary alarm will be generated indicating 60 alarms were generated during the interval. With the `AlarmThrottle` parameter set to `Summarize` and the `SummaryKey` set to anything other than xxxx, two summary alarms would be generated, one for each source.

ChokeThreshold The `ChokeThreshold` parameter can be used to change the alarm summarization technique used by a signature (change the `AlarmThrottle` parameter value) if the number of alarms exceeds the value configured as the `ChokeThreshold` parameter for each interval defined by the `ThrottleInterval` parameter. Configuring the `ChokeThreshold` parameter is referred to as configuring automatic alarm summarization, because the alarm summarization characteristics automatically change depending on whether the `ChokeThreshold` parameter is exceed. Table 24.2 defines how automatic alarm summarization works when the `ChokeThreshold` parameter is configured.

TABLE 24.2 Alarm Summarization

Original AlarmThrottle Parameter Value	AlarmThrottle **Parameter Value if** ChokeThreshold **Value exceeded within** ThrottleInterval	AlarmThrottle **Parameter Value if** 2 * ChokeThreshold **Value Exceeded within** ThrottleInterval
FireAll	Summarize	GlobalSummarize
Summarize	GlobalSummarize	—

To describe automatic alarm summarization, it's best to use an example. Let's say that the AlarmThrottle parameter for a signature is FireAll, that the ChokeThreshold parameter has a value of 100, and the ThrottleInterval is 10 seconds. If there are fewer than 100 signature hits within 10 seconds, then the alarm summarization technique remains as FireAll and 100 alarms are generated. If 150 signature hits occur within 10 seconds, 100 alarms are initially generated; however, after the hundredth signature match, the alarm summarization parameter will change to Summarize. This means that a single summary alarm will be generated at the end of the interval with a summary count of 150.

It's also important to understand that you can't use certain combinations of alarm summarization parameters, as described here:

- You can't use a value of FireOnce for the AlarmThrottle parameter with a value configured for the ChokeThreshold parameter.
- You can't use a value of FireOnce for the AlarmThrottle parameter with signatures that use a StorageKey value of xxxx.
- If an AlarmInterval value is specified, the value of the MinHits must be greater than 1, the value of the AlarmThrottle parameter must be FireAll, and the value of the ChokeThreshold must be ANY.

Local Engine Parameters

Local engine parameters are specific to each signature engine. Tables 24.3 to 24.8 describe the important local engine parameters for each different signature engine.

TABLE 24.3 ATOMIC Engine Parameters

Signature Engine	Parameter	Description
ATOMIC.ARP	ArpOperation	Operation code of ARP packets that the signature examines.
	RequestInBalance	Number of ARP requests for a specific IP address that can exceed the number of ARP replies before the signature fires.

TABLE 24.3 ATOMIC Engine Parameters *(continued)*

Signature Engine	Parameter	Description
ATOMIC.ICMP	IcmpCode	ICMP code to match in the ICMP header code field.
	IcmpID	ICMP ID value within the ICMP header identification field to match.
	IcmpSeq	Sequence value within the ICMP header sequence field to match.
	IcmpType	ICMP type to match in the ICMP header type field.
ATOMIC.IPOPTIONS	HasBadOption	Whether the IP options of packets being examined must be malformed for the packets to be analyzed against the signature.
	IPOption	IP option code of packets to be analyzed against the signature.
ATOMIC.L3.IP	MaxProto	Maximum IP protocol number of packets that are analyzed against the signature.
	MinProto	Minimum IP protocol number of packets that are analyzed against the signature.
	isRFC1918	When enabled, packets must have a source IP address within the private RFC1918 address ranges (10.x.x.x, 172.16.x.x—172.31.x.x, and 192.168.x.x) to be analyzed against the signature.
ATOMIC.TCP	DstPort	Destination port to match in the TCP header.
	SrcPort	Source port to match in the TCP header.
	SinglePacketRegex	String patterns to search for within a single TCP packet.
	TCPFlags	TCP flags to match in the TCP header when masked by the Mask value. For example, to match only TCP packets with a SYN flag (connection setup packets), set a value of SYN for TCPFlags.

TABLE 24.3 ATOMIC Engine Parameters *(continued)*

Signature Engine	Parameter	Description
	Mask	Mask used for comparison with the TCPFlags parameter. For example, if you have a value of SYN ACK for the TCPFlags parameter and a value of SYN for the Mask parameter, only packets with a SYN flag will be matched.
ATOMIC.UDP	DstPort	Destination port to match in the UDP header.
	MinUDPLength	Minimum length of the packet before it can be analyzed.

TABLE 24.4 FLOOD Engine Parameters

Signature Engine	Parameter	Description
FLOOD.HOST.ICMP	IcmpType	ICMP type to match in the ICMP header type field
	Rate	Maximum number of ICMP packets with the specified type allowed per second before the signature will fire
FLOOD.HOST.UDP	ExcludeDst1	Destination port to be excluded from flood counting
	ExcludeDst2	Another destination port to be excluded from flood counting
	Rate	Maximum number of UDP packets with the specified type allowed per second before the signature will fire
FLOOD.NET	Gap	Interval at which the peak count is set to 0 if matched traffic remains below the defined rate
	Peaks	Period of time above the specified rate necessary to fire the signature
	Rate	Maximum number of packets per second that shouldn't be exceeded

TABLE 24.5 SERVICE Engine Parameters

Signature Engine	Parameter	Description
SERVICE.DNS	QuerySrcPort53	Source port of packets must be port 53
	QueryValue	Whether DNS packets are queries or responses
SERVICE.FTP	ServicePorts	List of destination ports for which packets will be analyzed
	isPASV	Whether a PASV port spoof was detected
SERVICE.GENERIC	DstPort	Destination port to match
	SrcPort	Source port to match
SERVICE.HTTP	UriRegex	Pattern to match within the URI section of HTTP requests
	RequestRegex	Pattern to match within an HTTP request
	Deobfuscate	Whether to apply de-obfuscation features before examination
SERVICE.IDENT	MaxBytes	Maximum payload data size
	hasBadPort	Whether the signature fires due to a bad port number
SERVICE.MSSQL	sqlUsername	SQL username to match in SQL packet
	passwordPresent	Whether a password was used for SQL login
SERVICE.NTP	Mode	Mode of operation for NTP packets
	isInvalidDataPacket	Whether the signature fires dues to incorrect NTP packet size
SERVICE.RPC	RpcProgram	RPC program number to match in RPC messages

TABLE 24.5 SERVICE Engine Parameters *(continued)*

Signature Engine	Parameter	Description
	Unique	Maximum number of unique ports that can be used by an RPC mapper before the signature is fired
	isSweep	Whether to listen for RPC sweeps
SERVICE.SMB	AccountName	User account name that must be matched
	FileName	Name of a file that should fire a signature
SERVICE.SNMP	BruteForceCount	Maximum number of unique community strings that must be seen before the signature is fired
	IsBruteForce	Whether the signature should use the BruteForceCount gate
	IsValidPacket	Whether SNMP packets are valid
SERVICE.SSH	KeyLength	RSA key length to match
	UserLength	Maximum length of a new user name
SERVICE.SYSLOG	AclDataSource	List of IP addresses that are valid Syslog trap generators
	AclFilterName	Name of the ACL filter

TABLE 24.6 STRING Engine Parameters

Signature Engine	Parameter	Description
STRING.ICMP STRING.TCP STRING.UDP	Direction	Whether traffic is traveling to or from the destination
	RegexSpring	String pattern to match

TABLE 24.7 SWEEP Engine Parameters

Signature Engine	Parameter	Description
SWEEP.HOST.ICMP	IcmpType	ICMP type to match in the ICMP header type field.
	Unique	Minimum number of destinations to which ICMP packets must be addressed to fire a signature.
SWEEP.HOST.TCP	TCPFlags	TCP flags to match in the TCP header when masked by the Mask value. For example, to match only TCP packets with a SYN flag (connection setup packets), set a value of SYN for TCPFlags.
	Mask	Mask used for comparison with the TCPFlags parameter. For example, if you have a value of SYN ACK for the TCPFlags parameter and a value of SYN for the Mask parameter, only packets with a SYN flag will be matched.
	Unique	Maximum number of unique connections permitted.
SWEEP.PORT.TCP	TCPFlags	TCP flags to match in the TCP header when masked by the Mask value. For example, to match only TCP packets with a SYN flag (connection setup packets), set a value of SYN for TCPFlags.
	Mask	Mask used for comparison with the TCPFlags parameter. For example, if you have a value of SYN ACK for the TCPFlags parameter and a value of SYN for the Mask parameter, only packets with a SYN flag will be matched.
	Unique	Maximum number of unique connections permitted.
	PortRange	Port range to examine.
SWEEP.PORT.UDP	PortsInclude	List of ports to inspect.

TABLE 24.7 SWEEP Engine Parameters *(continued)*

Signature Engine	Parameter	Description
	Unique	Maximum number of unique port connections allowed.
SWEEP.OTHER.TCP	PortRange	Port range to examine.
	TCPFlags1	TCP flags for an equality comparison.
	TCPFlags2	TCP flags for an equality comparison.
SWEEP.MULTI	TcpInterest	Predefined TCP ports of interest.
	UdpInterest	Predefined UDP ports of interest.
	UniqueTcpPorts	Number of unique TCP connections allowed.
	UniqueUdpPorts	Number of unique UDP connections allowed.

TABLE 24.8 Other Engine Parameters

Signature Engine	Parameter	Description
TRAFFIC.ICMP	isLoki	Whether the signature is looking for the original Loki attack
	isModLoki	Whether the signature is looking for a modified Loki attack
OTHER	HijackMaxOldAck	Maximum number of dateless client-to-server ACKs before a Hijack is triggered
	SynFloodMaxEmbryonic	Maximum number of simultaneous embryonic (half-open) connections to any service
	TrafficFlowTimeout	Number of seconds that must pass with no traffic during a hijack for an alarm to be triggered

Configuring Cisco Secure IDS Signatures

Now that you understand about Cisco Secure IDS signatures, signature engines, and signature parameters, you're ready to begin configuring signatures. In the following sections, you'll learn how to configure signatures using the IDS Device Manager and using the CLI.

Configuring Signatures Using the IDM

To configure signatures using the IDS Device Manager (IDM), first log in to the IDM and then navigate to Configuration ≻ Sensing Engine ≻ Virtual Sensor Configuration ≻ Signature Configuration Mode. This opens the Signature Configuration Mode page, shown in Figure 24.1.

Notice that signatures are arranged based on *signature groups*. Signature groups are used to sort and display signatures based on different criteria. The following defines how each signature group displays signatures:

All Signatures   This group lists all signatures one by one from lowest signature ID to highest signature ID.

Engines   This group lists all signatures based on the signature engine that each signature belongs to. For example, you can view signatures that use the ATOMIC.TCP engine.

FIGURE 24.1   The Signature Configuration Mode page

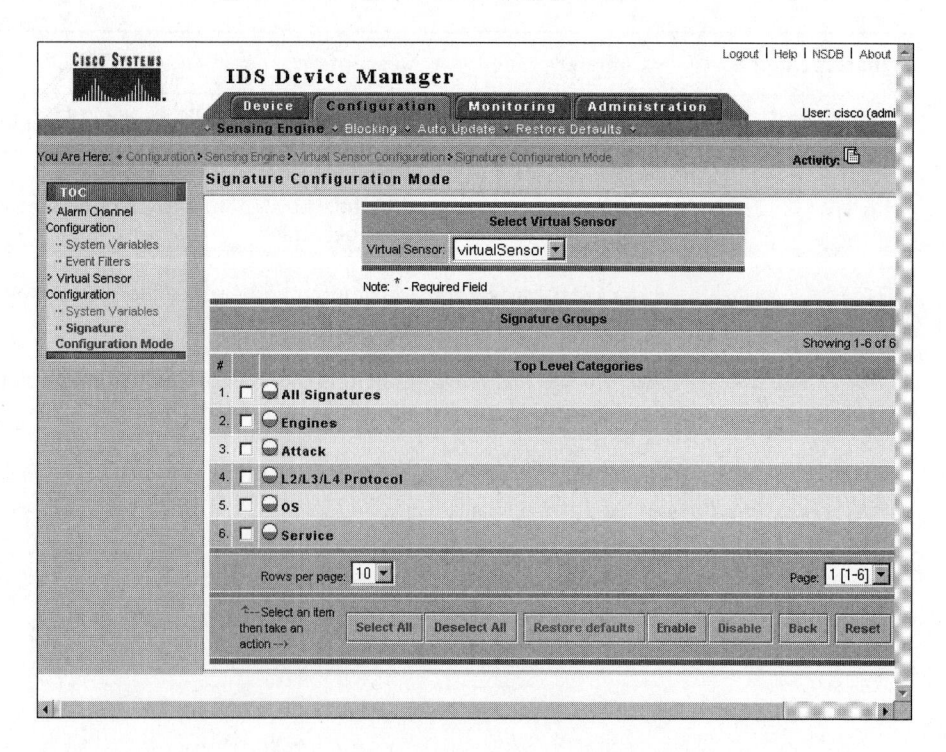

Attack This group lists all signatures based on the type of attack that each signature detects. For example, you can view signatures based on code execution, IDS evasion, or reconnaissance attacks.

L2/L3/L4 Protocol This group lists all signatures based on the layer 2, layer 3, or layer 4 protocol that the attack defined by each signature affects. For example, you can view signatures based on the ARP protocol or TCP/UDP combo sweeps (sweeps that use both TCP and UDP ports).

OS This group lists all signatures based on the operating system that the attack defined by each signature affects. For example, you can view signatures for attacks against Windows or Unix operating systems.

Service This group lists all signatures based on the layer 5, layer 6, or layer 7 service that the attack defined by each signature affects. For example, you can view signatures for attacks based on DHCP, HTTP, SMTP, and IMAP services.

Each top-level group may contain one or more child groups. To view the child groups within a top-level group, click the signature group name to open a new page focused on the appropriate group that you selected. For example, Figure 24.2 shows the Signature Configuration Mode page after clicking the Engines group in Figure 24.1.

FIGURE 24.2 The Signature Configuration Mode page for the Engines group

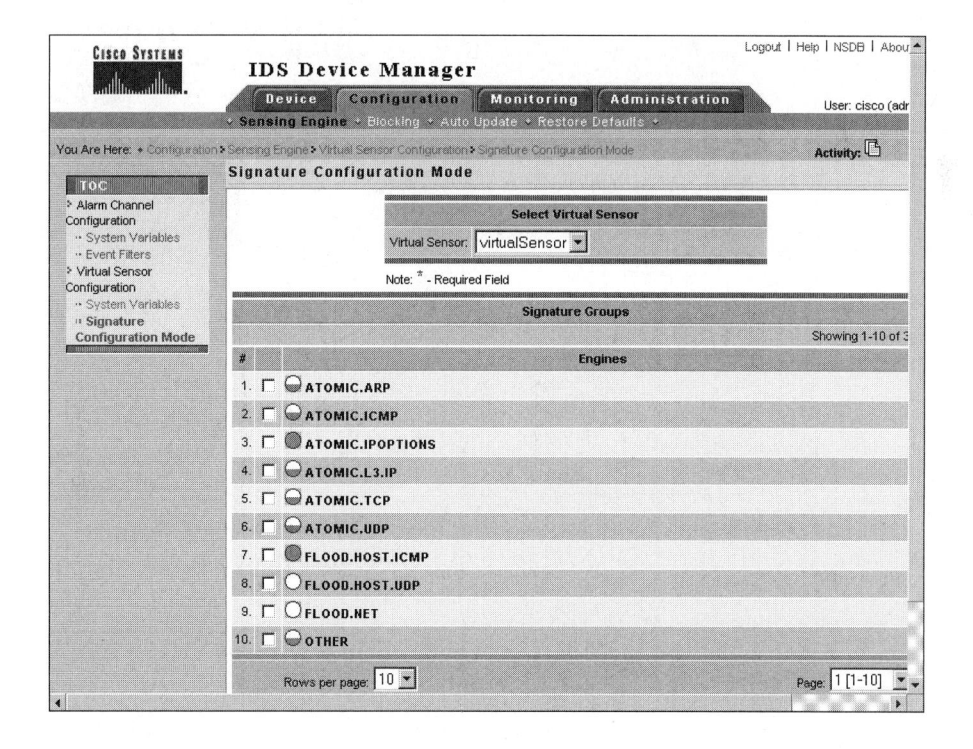

In Figure 24.2, you can see that several groups exist within the Engines group, each of which represents one of the various signature engines (ATOMIC.ARP, ATOMIC.ICMP, and so on). Each child group either contains specific signatures or may contain other groups depending on the levels of hierarchy within the top-level signature group you're working with. Figure 24.3 shows the Signature Configuration Mode page after clicking on the ATOMIC.ARP engine in Figure 24.2.

In Figure 24.3, you can see four specific signatures (IDs 7101, 7102, 7104, and 7105), which you can enable/disable and/or tune individually. Also notice the various columns in this figure, which provide information about key alarm parameters for each signature. A useful column is the More column, which is only present when viewing individual signatures. If you move the mouse over the small downward-pointing caret for a specific signature, a small comments box appears that shows the configuration of the various alarm parameters for the signature. Figure 24.4 shows the comments box that is displayed when you position the mouse over the More caret for a particular signature.

Notice that you can view the values of the various alarm parameters for the signature. For example, the `AlarmSeverity` parameter has a value of `Informational`, and the `AlarmThrottle` parameter has a value of `FireAll` (generate an alarm for each signature match).

FIGURE 24.3 The Signature Configuration Mode page for the ATOMIC.ARP group

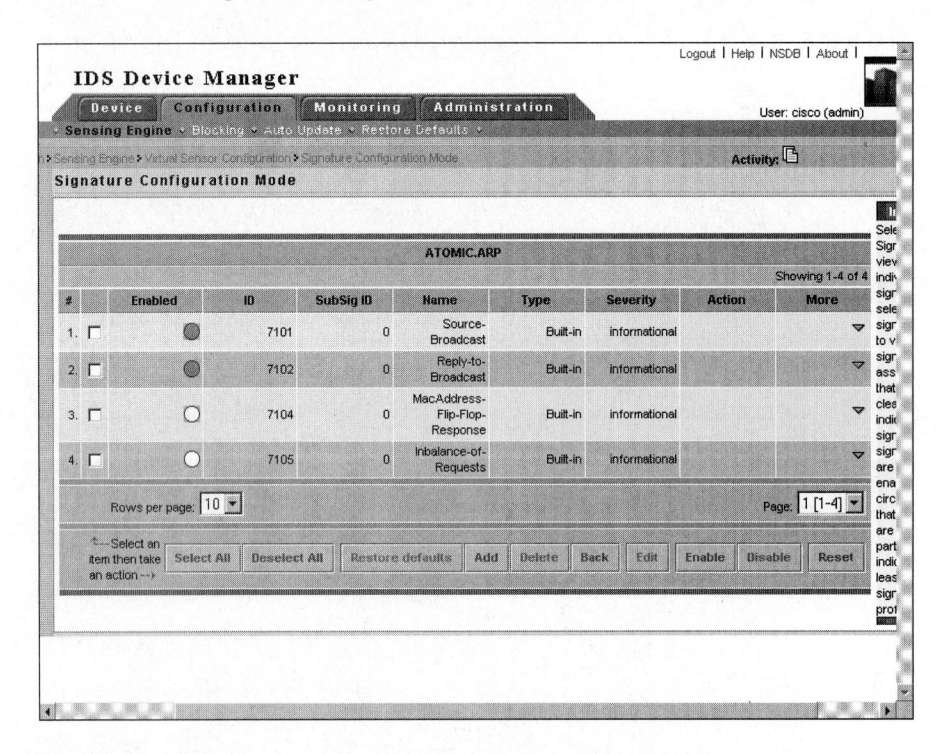

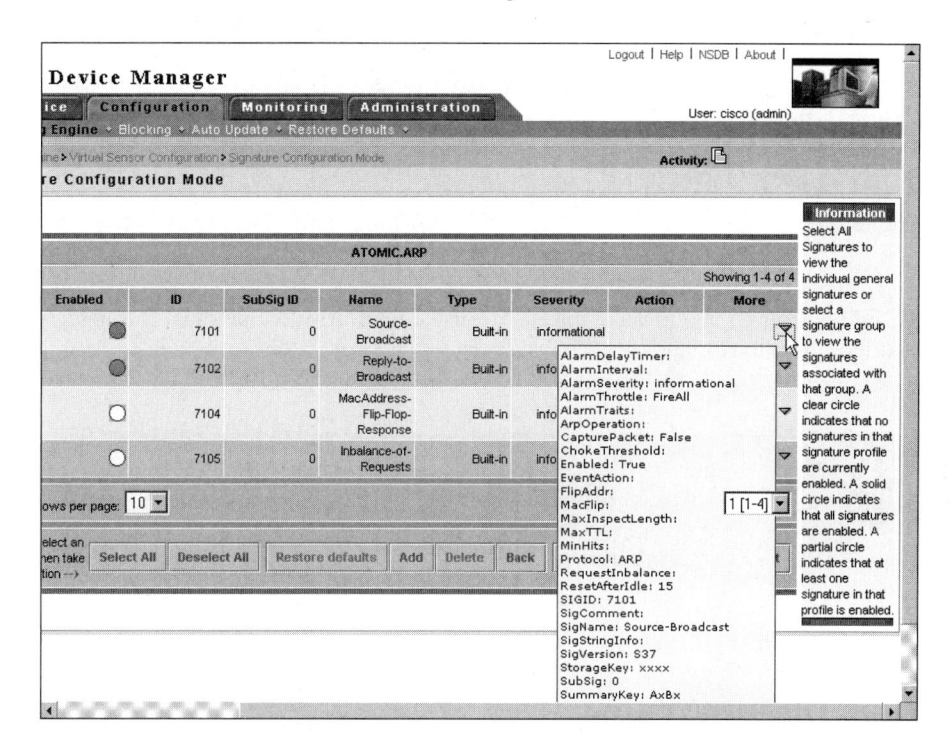

FIGURE 24.4 The More comments box for a signature

Enabling or Disabling Signatures

Within signature configuration mode, you'll notice that each specific signature or signature group has a circle icon to the left that indicates enabled/disabled status. The various circle icons are as follows:

Empty circle The signature is disabled, or the signatures within the signature group are all disabled.

Half-full circle Some (but not all) of the signatures within the signature group are enabled.

Full circle The signature is enabled, or all of the signatures within the signature group are enabled.

For example, referring back to Figure 24.2, you can see that the circle next to the ATOMIC.ARP group is half-full, indicating that some (but not all) signatures within the group are enabled (as confirmed in Figure 24.3, where only signatures 7101 and 7102 are enabled). The circle next to the ATOMIC.IPOPTIONS group is full, indicating that all signatures within the group are enabled, whereas the circle next to the FLOOD.NET group is empty, indicating that all signatures within the group are disabled.

To enable or disable a signature or signature group, select the check box next to the signature/signature group item and then click the Enable or Disable button at the bottom of the Signature Configuration Mode page. If you wish to restore the default enabled/disabled state and configuration of a signature or signature group, you can select the appropriate item and then click the Restore Defaults button.

Tuning Signatures

For all built-in signatures, you can modify alarm parameters associated with each signature. Any built-in signature that has been modified from the default configuration is referred to as a *tuned signature*. To tune a signature, select the check box next to the signature and then click the Edit button at the bottom of the Signature Configuration Mode page. Doing so opens a page that lets you edit the various alarm parameters that are configurable for the signature you're working with. Figure 24.5 demonstrates tuning a signature.

> **NOTE**
> Figure 24.5 shows only the top half of the page, because there are so many alarm parameters that they can't all fit within a single page. At the bottom of the page are three buttons: OK, Cancel, and Reset (which resets parameters to default values).

FIGURE 24.5   Tuning signatures using the IDM

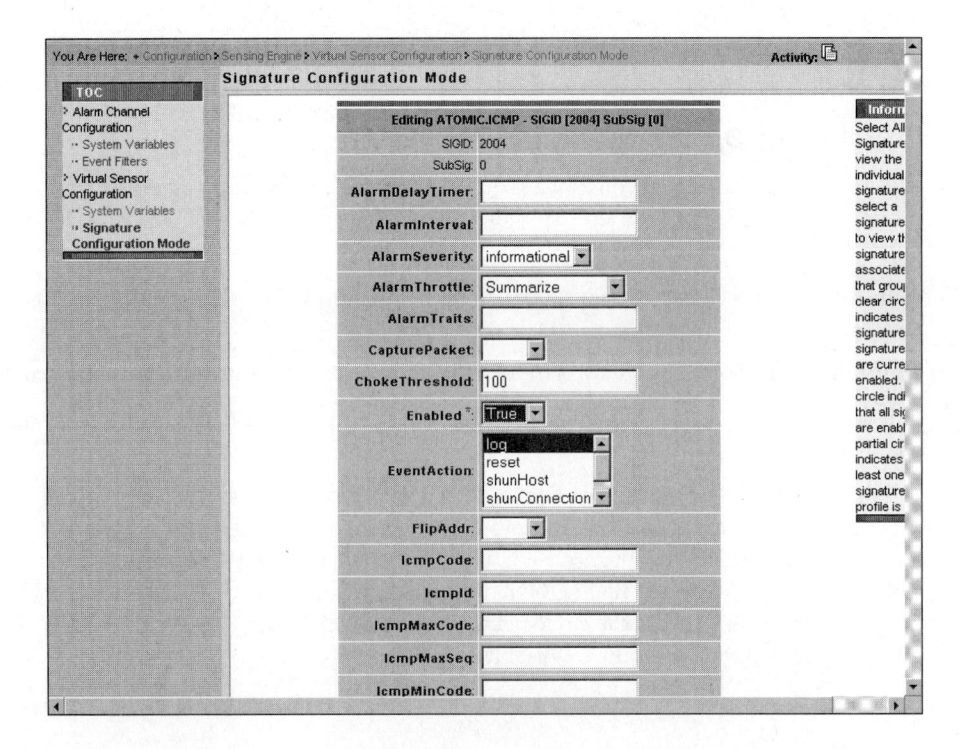

In Figure 24.5, the signature with ID 2004 (ICMP Echo Request) is being configured. The `Enabled` and `EventAction` parameters have been modified so that the signature is enabled (by default, this signature is disabled); and an event action of Log has been defined, which means that subsequent packets from sources that generate ICMP echo request packets will be captured and logged. Once you've completed your configuration, scroll to the bottom of the page and click the OK button to return to the previous Signature Configuration Mode page. After you've modified any signature settings, a Save Changes icon should appear in the Activity bar; you must click it for the signature configuration changes to be permanently saved.

Creating Custom Signatures

You can create custom signatures, which are often used to detect new attacks or more specific instances of a well-known attack. Before you create a custom signature, you must determine the appropriate signature engine that will analyze traffic for the new signature. Selecting the correct signature engine requires consideration of the following information related to the attack you're attempting to detect:

> You can't create custom signatures based on the Trojan signature engine.

Network protocol   Is the attack based on TCP, UDP, ICMP, or IP protocol traffic?

Target address   Is the attack directed against a target host or network?

Target port   What destination ports are used to manifest the attack?

Attack type   What type of attack is it (for example, DoS or reconnaissance)?

Payload inspection   What type of payload inspection is required (for instance, does a string pattern need to be searched for)?

For example, let's say an attack has just been published, and you need to create a signature for the attack. The attack is a DoS attack, and it manifests itself in TCP packets that have a destination port of 2002 with an illegal TCP flag combination of `SYN FIN`. For this signature, the ATOMIC.TCP signature engine can be used, because it permits the following:

- The signature will trigger based on the contents of a single packet.
- You can specify a destination port and specify the TCP flags in an ATOMIC.TCP signature (see Table 24.3).

As another example, let's say that you wish to detect excessive UDP connections to hosts on your network (in excess of 50 connections per second). For this signature, the SWEEP.PORT.UDP signature engine (see Table 24.6) can be used, because it permits the following:

- You can specify specific UDP source and destination ports.
- You can specify a maximum permissible rate of new connections that will trigger the signature if exceeded.

Once you've determined the signature engine that you're going to use to create your signature, you can begin the actual process of creating the signature. To create custom signatures using the IDM, you must select the Engines top-level group from the top-level Signature Configuration Mode page and then select the appropriate engine that you wish to create a custom signature for. For example, to create a custom signature that looks for the string *format flash* within Telnet connections (this signature will detect attempts to format the flash file system on a Cisco network device), you create the custom signature based on the STRING.TCP engine. Figure 24.6 shows the Signature Configuration Mode page after selecting the Engines signature group and then the STRING.TCP signature group.

Notice the Add button at the bottom of the page. Clicking this button lets you create a custom signature based on the STRING.TCP engine. Figures 24.7 and 24.8 show the top and bottom halves respectively of the Signature Configuration Mode page after clicking the Add button in Figure 24.6.

FIGURE 24.6 Signature Configuration Mode page for a signature engine

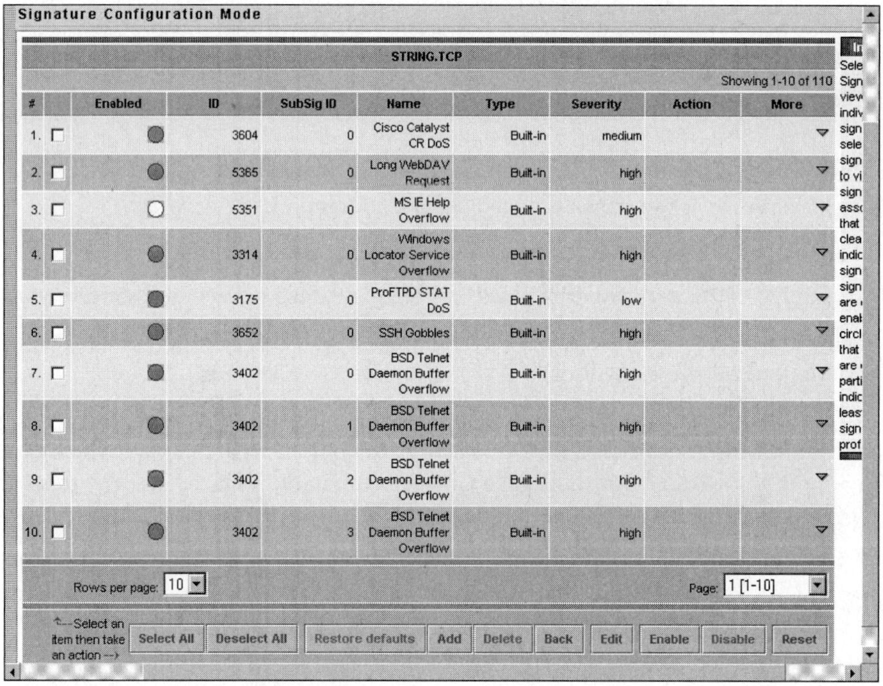

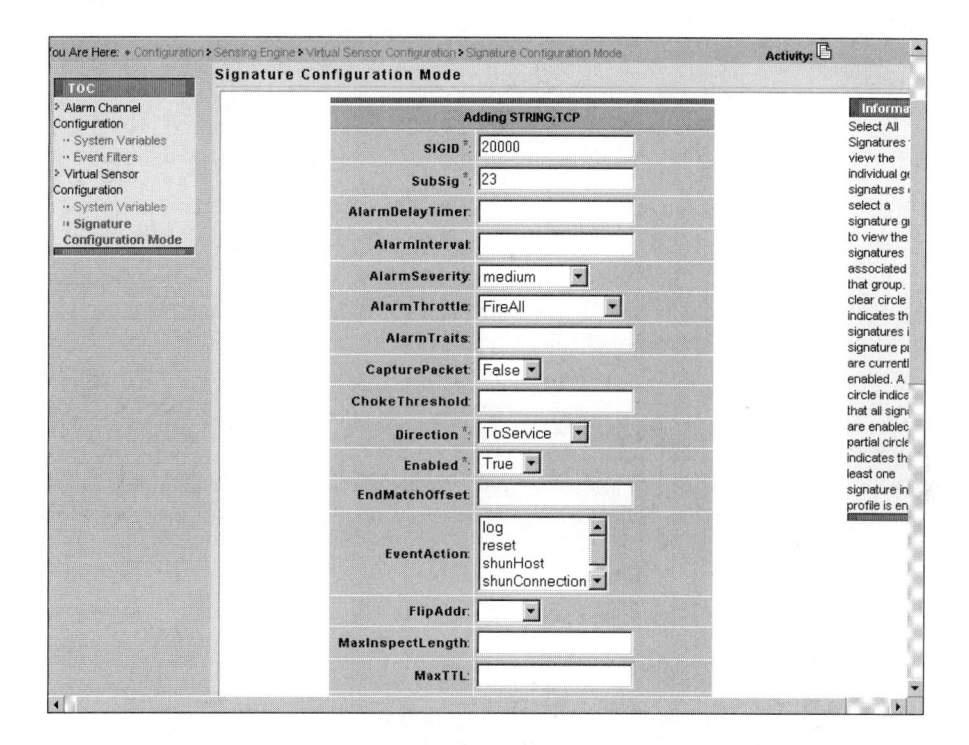

FIGURE 24.7 Creating a custom signature, part 1

All required parameters (parameters that must be configured with a value) are indicated with an asterisk. You can see that the following alarm parameters have been configured:

SIGID This is the signature ID, which by default is 20000.

SubSig This is the subsignature ID, which by default is 0 but has been modified to 23 in Figure 24.7.

Direction This indicates whether packets sent to the ports defined by the `ServicePorts` parameter should be analyzed (`ToService`) or if packets sent from the ports defined by the `ServicePorts` parameter should be analyzed (`FromService`).

Enabled This indicates whether the signature is enabled or disabled.

Protocol This value defines the IP transport protocol of packets that should be analyzed against the signature.

RegexString This defines the regular expression that should be searched for. In Figure 24.8, it's defined as `format flash`, which detects attempts to format the flash on Cisco devices.

> **NOTE**
>
> A better regular expression would be [Ff][Oo][Rr][Mm][Aa][Tt] [Ff][Ll][Aa][Ss][Hh], because it matches any variation of the format flash command regardless of case. Note that SERVICE.HTTP signatures include a `DeObfuscate` parameter that normalizes ASCII data so that obfuscation techniques (using capitalization is a very simple form of obfuscation) are detected.

ServicePorts   This field defines the ports of the services that must be included within packets that are being analyzed.

StorageKey   This defines the address view used for prealarm counters. In Figure 24.8, the `StorageKey` value is defined as `AaBb`, which means that counters will be maintained separately for each unique combination of source IP address, source TCP port, destination IP address, and destination TCP port.

SummaryKey   This defines the address view used for post-alarm counters. In Figure 24.8, the `SummaryKey` value is defined as `AaBb`, which means that counters will be maintained separately for each unique combination of source IP address, source TCP port, destination IP address, and destination TCP port.

FIGURE 24.8   Creating a custom signature, part 2

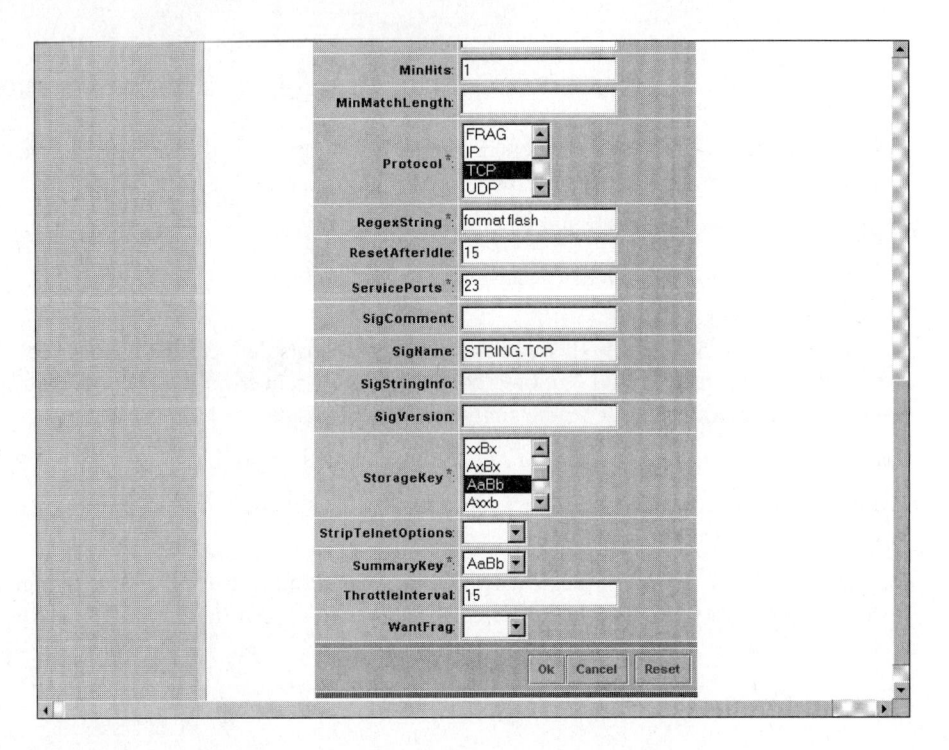

After you complete the configuration of alarm parameters, click the OK button to complete the creation of the new custom signature. The new custom signature should now be included within the signature engine group representing the engine that you based the custom signature on.

> **TIP** The Cisco Secure IDS 4.1 IDM includes a signature wizard, which allows for step-by-step assisted configuration guidance when creating new signatures.

Configuring Signatures Using the CLI

To configure signatures using the CLI, you must first access virtual sensor configuration mode by using the `service virtual-sensor-configuration virtualSensor` global configuration command. Next, enter the `tune-micro-engines` command to access configuration mode for the virtual sensor. At this point, if you type in the **?** character for online help, you'll notice that you can access the various signature engines from this configuration mode, as shown here:

```
sensor# configure terminal
sensor(config)# service virtual-sensor-configuration virtualSensor
sensor(config-vsc)# tune-micro-engines
sensor(config-vsc-virtualSensor)# ?
ATOMIC.ARP                  Layer 2 ARP signatures.
ATOMIC.ICMP                 Simple ICMP alarms based on Type,
                            Code, Seq, Id, etc.
ATOMIC.IPOPTIONS            Simple L3 Alarms based on Ip Options
ATOMIC.L3.IP                Simple L3 IP Alarms.
ATOMIC.TCP                  Simple TCP packet alarms based on TCP
                            Flags, ports (both sides), and single
                            packet regex. Use SummaryKey to
                            define the address view for MinHits
                            and Summarize counting. For best
                            performance, use a StorageKey of xxxx.
ATOMIC.UDP                  Simple UDP packet alarms based on
                            Port, Direction and DataLength.
exit                        Exit service configuration mode
FLOOD.HOST.ICMP             Icmp Floods directed at a single host
FLOOD.HOST.UDP              UDP Floods directed at a single host
FLOOD.NET                   Multi-protocol floods directed at a
                            network segment.  Ip Addresses are
                            wildcarded for this inspection.
FragmentReassembly          Fragment Reassembly configuration tokens
```

IPLog	Virtual Sensor IP log configuration tokens
OTHER	This engine is used to group generic signatures so common parameters may be changed. It defines an interface into common signature parameters..
SERVICE.DNS	DNS SERVICE Analysis Engine
SERVICE.FTP	FTP service special decode alarms
SERVICE.GENERIC	Custom service/payload decode and analysis based on our quartet tuple programming language. EXPERT use only.
SERVICE.HTTP	HTTP protocol decode based string search Engine. Includes anti-evasive URL deobfuscation
SERVICE.IDENT	Ident service (client and server) alarms.
SERVICE.MSSQL	Microsoft (R) SQL service inspection engine
SERVICE.NTP	Network Time Protocol based signature engine
SERVICE.RPC	RPC SERVICE analysis engine
SERVICE.SMB	SMB Service decode inspection.
SERVICE.SMTP	SMTP Protocol Inspection Engine
SERVICE.SNMP	Inspects SNMP traffic
SERVICE.SSH	SSH header decode signatures.
SERVICE.SYSLOG	Engine to process syslogs.
show	Display system settings and/or history information
ShunEvent	Shun Event configuration tokens
STATE.STRING.CISCOLOGIN	Telnet based Cisco Login Inspection Engine
STATE.STRING.LPRFORMATSTRING	LPR Protocol Inspection Engine
StreamReassembly	Stream Reassembly configuration tokens
STRING.ICMP	Generic ICMP based string search Engine
STRING.TCP	Generic TCP based string search Engine.
STRING.UDP	Generic UDP based string search Engine
SWEEP.HOST.ICMP	ICMP host sweeps from a single attacker to many victims.
SWEEP.HOST.TCP	TCP-based Host Sweeps from a single attacker to multiple victims.
SWEEP.MULTI	UDP and TCP combined port sweeps.
SWEEP.OTHER.TCP	Odd sweeps/scans such as nmap fingerprint scans.
SWEEP.PORT.TCP	Detects port sweeps between two nodes.

SWEEP.PORT.UDP	Detects UDP connections to multiple destination ports between two nodes.
systemVariables	User modifiable system variables
TRAFFIC.ICMP	Identifies ICMP traffic irregularities.
TROJAN.BO2K	BackOrifice BO2K trojan traffic
TROJAN.TFN2K	TFN2K trojan/ddos traffic
TROJAN.UDP	Detects BO/BO2K UDP trojan traffic.

To configure a signature using the CLI, you must know the signature engine that the signature belongs to. For example, the ICMP Echo Request signature (Signature ID #2004) belongs to the ATOMIC.ICMP engine. So, if you wish to configure this signature, you must specify the command ATOMIC.ICMP, which takes you to a new configuration mode that lets you configure signatures for the engine. Once you're in the appropriate signature engine configuration mode, you use the **signatures** command to create and modify signatures. The following shows the syntax for this command:

sensor(config-vsc-virtualSensor-ATO)# **signatures SIGID** *signature-id* **[SubSig** *subsignature-id*]

Once you specify the appropriate **signatures** command, you're placed into a new configuration mode that lets you define parameters for the specific signature you're working with. Each parameter is configured by specifying the name of the parameter, followed by the value of the parameter. The following example demonstrates enabling a signature and modifying other signature parameters:

```
sensor# configure terminal
sensor(config)# service virtual-sensor-configuration virtualSensor
sensor(config-vsc)# tune-micro-engines
sensor(config-vsc-virtualSensor)# ATOMIC.ICMP
sensor(config-vsc-virtualSensor-ATO)# signatures SIGID 2004
sensor(config-vsc-virtualSensor-ATO-sig)# Enabled true
sensor(config-vsc-virtualSensor-ATO-sig)# EventAction log
sensor(config-vsc-virtualSensor-ATO-sig)# ChokeThreshold 200
sensor(config-vsc-virtualSensor-ATO-sig)# show settings
SIGID: 2004 <protected>
   SubSig: 0 <protected>
   AlarmDelayTimer:
   AlarmInterval:
   AlarmSeverity: informational <defaulted>
   AlarmThrottle: Summarize <defaulted>
   AlarmTraits:
   CapturePacket: False <defaulted>
   ChokeThreshold: 200 default: 100
```

```
    Enabled: True default: False
    EventAction: log
     FlipAddr:
     IcmpCode:
     IcmpId:
     IcmpMaxCode:
     IcmpMaxSeq:
     IcmpMinCode:
     IcmpMinSeq:
     IcmpSeq:
     IcmpType: 8 <protected>
     IpTOS:
     MaxInspectLength:
     MaxTTL:
     MinHits:
     Protocol: ICMP <defaulted>
     ResetAfterIdle: 15 <defaulted>
     SigComment:
     SigName: ICMP Echo Req <protected>
     SigStringInfo:
     SigVersion: S37 <defaulted>
     StorageKey: xxxx <defaulted>
     SummaryKey: AxBx <defaulted>
     ThrottleInterval: 30 <defaulted>
     WantFrag:
sensor(config-vsc-virtualSensor-ATO-sig)# exit
sensor(config-vsc-virtualSensor-ATO)# exit
sensor(config-vsc-virtualSensor)# exit
Apply Changes:?[yes]: yes
sensor(config-vsc)#
```

In the previous example, notice that the show settings command lists the various parameters that are configurable for the signature. After configuring the signature, you must exit back to virtual sensor configuration mode to apply the changes.

> **TIP** Any parameter that is specified as <protected> can't be modified.

If you wish to create a signature, you use the same signatures command within the appropriate signature engine for the signature that you wish to create. When you're creating a signature, you must specify a signature ID between 20000 and 50000 that isn't used by other custom signatures. Once you've entered the signature configuration mode for the new signature, you can use the show settings command to determine which parameters must be configured:

```
sensor# configure terminal
sensor(config)# service virtual-sensor-configuration virtualSensor
sensor(config-vsc)# tune-micro-engines
sensor(config-vsc-virtualSensor)# STRING.TCP
sensor(config-vsc-virtualSensor-ATO)# signatures SIGID 20001
sensor(config-vsc-virtualSensor-ATO-sig)# show settings
   SIGID: 20001
   SubSig: 0 <defaulted>
   AlarmDelayTimer:
   AlarmInterval:
   AlarmSeverity: medium <defaulted>
   AlarmThrottle: Summarize <defaulted>
   AlarmTraits:
   CapturePacket: False <defaulted>
   ChokeThreshold:
   Direction: ToService <defaulted>
   Enabled: True <defaulted>
   EndMatchOffset:
   EventAction:
   FlipAddr:
   MaxInspectLength:
   MaxTTL:
   MinHits: 1 <defaulted>
   MinMatchLength:
   Protocol: TCP <defaulted>
-> RegexString: --> REQUIRED FIELD NOT SET <--
   ResetAfterIdle: 15 <defaulted>
   ServicePorts: 80,3128,8000,8010,8080,8888 <defaulted>
   SigComment:
   SigName: STRING.TCP <defaulted>
   SigStringInfo:
   SigVersion:
   StorageKey: STREAM <defaulted>
   StripTelnetOptions:
   SummaryKey: AaBb <defaulted>
   ThrottleInterval: 15 <defaulted>
   WantFrag:
```

In this example, notice that the `RegexString` parameter is a required parameter that has no value currently configured. The following shows the configuration required to create a custom signature that detects the string *format flash* within Telnet traffic and has a severity of high:

```
sensor# configure terminal
sensor(config)# service virtual-sensor-configuration virtualSensor
sensor(config-vsc)# tune-micro-engines
sensor(config-vsc-virtualSensor)# STRING.TCP
sensor(config-vsc-virtualSensor-ATO)# signatures SIGID 20001
sensor(config-vsc-virtualSensor-ATO-sig)# SigName
Enter SigName[]: CUSTOM_TELNET_SIGNATURE
sensor(config-vsc-virtualSensor-ATO-sig)# ServicePorts 23
sensor(config-vsc-virtualSensor-ATO-sig)# RegexString
Enter RegexString[]: [Ff][Oo][Rr][Mm][Aa][Tt] [Ff][Ll][Aa][Ss][Hh]
sensor(config-vsc-virtualSensor-ATO-sig)# AlarmSeverity high
sensor(config-vsc-virtualSensor-ATO-sig)# exit
sensor(config-vsc-virtualSensor-ATO)# exit
sensor(config-vsc-virtualSensor)# exit
Apply Changes:?[yes]: yes
sensor(config-vsc)#
```

> **TIP** To reset signature parameters to defaults, use the `reset-signatures` command under `virtualSensor` subconfiguration mode. You can reset settings for all signatures or settings for specific signatures.

Introduction to the IDS Event Viewer

The IDS Event Viewer (IEV) provides alarm monitoring, collecting alarms from up to five sensors and presenting them via a graphical interface to security administrators tasked with managing and responding to intrusion attempts. The IEV is an integral component of smaller Cisco Secure IDS deployments (up to five sensors)—after all, an IDS sensor isn't much use if you don't know when it detects intrusive activity.

Before we discuss the IEV, it's important that you understand how the IEV interacts with Cisco Secure IDS sensors. Figure 24.9 shows this interaction.

You can see that alarms generated by the sensor are filtered and aggregated by the alarm channel and then placed in the event store. The IEV accesses alarms stored in the event store by establishing an HTTP or HTTPS connection to the sensor web server and then pulling alarms stored in the event store using remote desktop exchange protocol (RDEP) requests. Notice that alarms filtered by the alarm channel on the sensor can't be viewed in the IEV, because they have already been discarded.

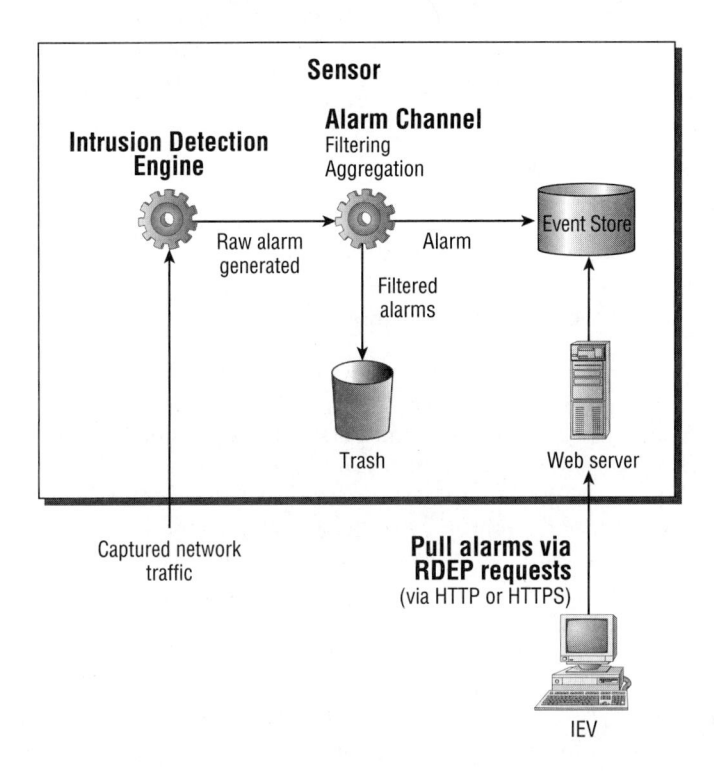

FIGURE 24.9   IEV interaction with Cisco Secure IDS sensors

Unlike the IDM, which runs locally on the sensor, the IEV is an external Java-based application that runs from an external Windows host. Running the IEV on a separate machine allows multiple sensors to be monitored, and in Cisco Secure IDS 4.*x*, up to five sensors can be monitored.

To install the IEV, a separate PC or server is required that has the following hardware specifications:

- Pentium III 800 MHz or higher
- 256MB memory
- 500MB free disk space

In addition to the above hardware specifications, note that the IEV can only be installed on one of the following operating systems:

- Microsoft Windows NT 4 Service Pack 6 (IEV 4.0 and 4.1)
- Microsoft Windows 2000 Service Pack 2 or higher (IEV 4.0 and 4.1)
- Microsoft Windows XP Service Pack 1 or higher (IEV 4.1 only)

During installation, the IEV installs the Java 2 Runtime Environment version 1.3.1 and MySQL Server version 3.2 as supporting applications for the IEV. In the following sections, we'll look at installing the IEV as well as accessing it for the first time.

Installing the IEV

To install the IEV, you must first obtain the IEV installation program, which is available on the Cisco website at `http://www.cisco.com/cgi-bin/tablebuild.pl/ids-ev`.

> **NOTE**: Access to the IEV URL requires a valid Cisco Connection Online (CCO) login.

The IEV installation file as of October 2003 is called `IEV-min-4.1-1-S48.exe` and is 36MB in size. Obviously this file installs version 4.1 of the IEV, however this version can be used to monitor earlier Cisco Secure IDS 3.*x* and 4.0 sensors.

> **NOTE**: If you've previously installed IEV 3.1, note that you can't upgrade from version 3.1 to version 4.x. Instead, you must first uninstall version 3.1 and then perform a new installation of version 4.*x*. You can upgrade from IEV 4.0 to IEV 4.1.

Assuming that you've obtained the appropriate installation file, after executing the file, a setup program will start that takes you through the IEV installation process. The first screen is a standard Welcome screen; clicking the Next button takes you to the Select Destination Location screen, where you can select the installation folder for the IEV. By default, the IEV is installed into the `SystemDrive\Program Files\Cisco Systems\Cisco IDS Event Viewer` folder, as shown in Figure 24.10.

After you specify the appropriate installation folder and click Next to continue, the Select Program Manager Group screen is displayed; here, you can select the appropriate program group where shortcuts to start the IEV application will be created. By default, the `Cisco Systems\Cisco IDS Event Viewer` program group is selected, as shown in Figure 24.11.

FIGURE 24.10 The Select Destination Location screen

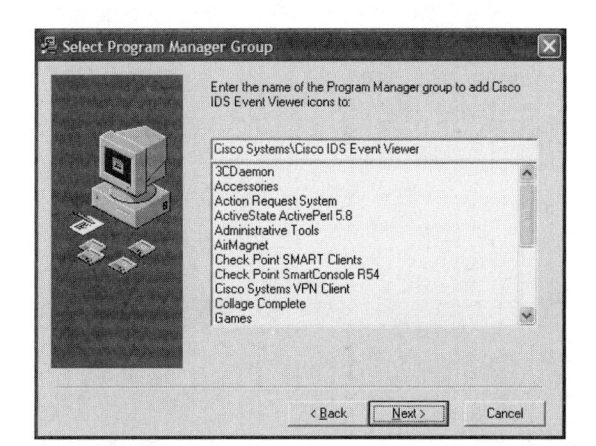

FIGURE 24.11 The Select Program Manager Group screen

Specify the appropriate program group and click Next, and the Start Installation screen will be displayed. This indicates that you're ready to install the IEV. Clicking the Next button will begin the IEV installation.

Once the file-copying process has completed, the Installation Complete screen will be displayed; click Finish to complete the IEV installation. At this point, you'll be prompted to restart the IEV host.

Accessing the IEV for the First Time

After you restart the IEV host, the IEV is ready to use. During the installation, a Cisco Systems ➢ Cisco IDS Event Viewer program group folder is created (as specified in Figure 24.11), which contains three shortcuts:

Cisco IDS Event Viewer This shortcut points to the `IEVClientStart.bat` batch file, which resides in the `IEV Install Folder\IEV\bin` folder and starts the IEV application. An identical shortcut also resides on the Windows Desktop, which can also be used to start the IEV application.

Help On IDS Event Viewer This shortcut points to the IEV help file, which provides online help for the IEV application.

Uninstall Cisco IDS Event Viewer Selecting this shortcut lets you uninstall the IEV application if required.

To start the IEV application, select Start ➢ Programs ➢ Cisco Systems ➢ Cisco IDS Event Viewer ➢ Cisco IDS Event Viewer, or open the shortcut to the Cisco IDS Event Viewer located on the Windows Desktop. The IEV application will start, which opens a window titled Cisco IDS Event Viewer: Thread Analysis Console, as shown in Figure 24.12.

FIGURE 24.12   The IEV application

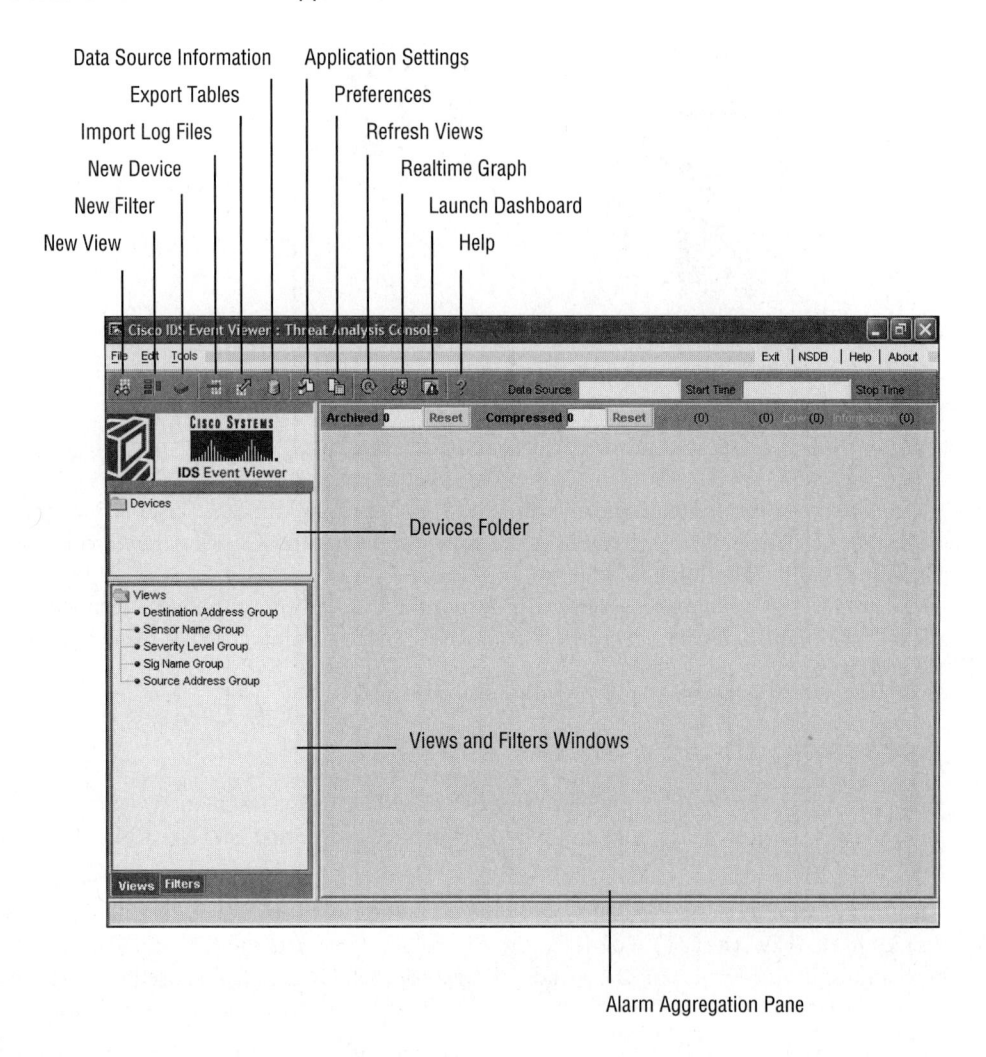

Labels pointing to the interface:
- Data Source Information
- Export Tables
- Import Log Files
- New Device
- New Filter
- New View
- Application Settings
- Preferences
- Refresh Views
- Realtime Graph
- Launch Dashboard
- Help
- Devices Folder
- Views and Filters Windows
- Alarm Aggregation Pane

> **NOTE** Each of the items pointed out in Figure 24.12 will be discussed in the following sections.

Configuring the IEV

Now that you're familiar with the IEV application and its layout, it's time to learn how to configure the IEV to monitor the Cisco Secure IDS sensor(s) that you've deployed in your network. Configuring the IEV consists of the following configuration tasks:

- Add sensors to the IEV.
- Configure filters and views.
- Configuring application settings and preferences.
- Administering the IEV Database.

Adding Sensors to the IEV

By default, the IEV isn't configured to monitor any sensors and must be explicitly configured to monitor the appropriate sensors in your network. To add a new sensor to the IEV that you wish to monitor, select File ➤ New ➤ Device from the main menu, or right-click the Devices folder and select New Device. Doing so opens the Device Properties dialog box, shown in Figure 24.13, which lets you specify the various parameters related to the sensor that you wish to add.

FIGURE 24.13 The Device Properties dialog box

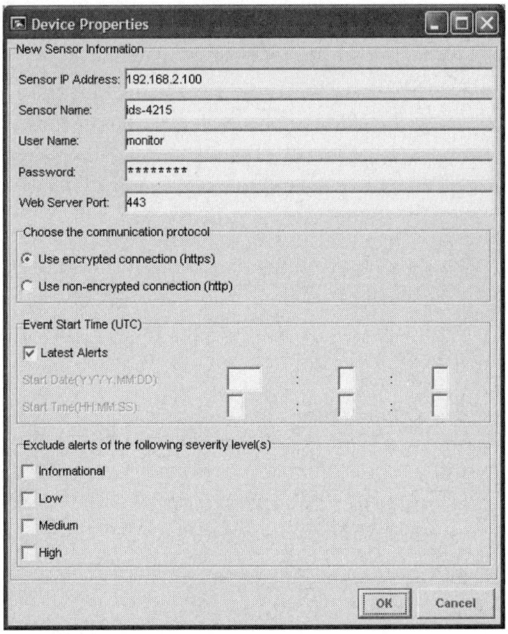

The following describes the various properties configurable in the Device Properties dialog box:

Sensor IP Address This is the IP address of the command-and-control interface of the sensor that you're adding. By default, this field is blank; however, in Figure 24.13 an IP address of 192.168.2.100 has been specified.

Sensor Name This is the hostname of the sensor that you're adding. By default, this field is blank; in Figure 24.13, a hostname of ids-4215 has been specified.

User Name and Password To enable the IEV to connect and authenticate successfully to the IEV, you must specify the credentials of a valid user account configured on the sensor. The user account specified must possess at least Viewer privileges. In Figure 24.13, the credentials of an account called `monitor` are provided. Assuming that this account has Viewer privileges, successfully authenticating with these credentials will enable the IEV to connect to the sensor for monitoring purposes.

Web Server Port This specifies the web server port on which the sensor is listening. By default, the sensor listens on port 443; however, if you've modified the web server port on the sensor using either the `setup` utility (see Chapter 21, "Installing Cisco Secure IDS Sensors and IDSMs") or the IDM (see Chapter 23, "Configuring Cisco Secure IDS Sensors Using the IDS Device Manager"), you must ensure that the custom port is specified for the sensor in the IEV.

Communication Protocol This defines whether encrypted communications should be used. The default setting is to use encrypted communications (HTTPS); however, you can use nonencrypted communications (HTTP) if desired. It's highly recommended that you always use encrypted communications between the IEV and sensors.

Event Start Time This defines the start time of the events that the IEV should obtain from the sensor. By default, the Latest Alerts check box is selected, which means that the IEV receives new alerts generated by the sensor only after the IEV has connected to the sensor. Alternatively, you can specify a start date and start time, which allows the IEV to receive historical alerts from the specified start date and start time, as well as any new alerts generated by the sensor after the IEV has connected to the sensor.

Alert Exclusions By default, the IEV pulls all alarms from the sensor, no matter what severity level. You can filter the alarms pulled by the IEV based on the severity of the alarm by selecting the appropriate severity levels on the Device Properties dialog box. For example, if you selected Medium in Figure 24.13, the IEV would not pull any alarms with a medium severity from the sensor.

Once you've configured the appropriate device parameters, click the OK button, and the IEV will attempt to establish a connection to the sensor IP address you've specified. If the IEV can't establish a connection to the sensor, check that the settings you entered in the Device Properties dialog box are correct and match the configuration of the sensor.

> **TIP** For the IEV to establish connectivity to a sensor, the IEV IP address must be in the Allowed Hosts access list on the sensor. It's configured using the `accessList` CLI command from the networkParams subconfiguration mode within the service host configuration mode, or via the Device ➢ Sensor Setup ➢ Allowed Hosts page in the IDM.

Assuming connectivity is established, if you're using encrypted communications (recommended), the IEV first obtains and displays the sensor certificate in the Certificate Information dialog box, shown in Figure 24.14.

Notice that the MD5 and SHA fingerprints of the certificate are displayed, which should match the actual fingerprint of the sensor certificate if the certificate being presented is authentic.

> **TIP** To view the actual fingerprint of the sensor certificate, you can issue the `show tls fingerprint` command from a sensor CLI session.

To accept the certificate presented by the sensor, click the Yes button. At this point, the sensor will be added as a device and should be displayed within the Devices folder, as shown in Figure 24.15.

> **TIP** You can automatically access the IDM for a particular sensor from the IEV by double-clicking the appropriate sensor in the Devices folder.

FIGURE 24.14   The Certificate Information dialog box

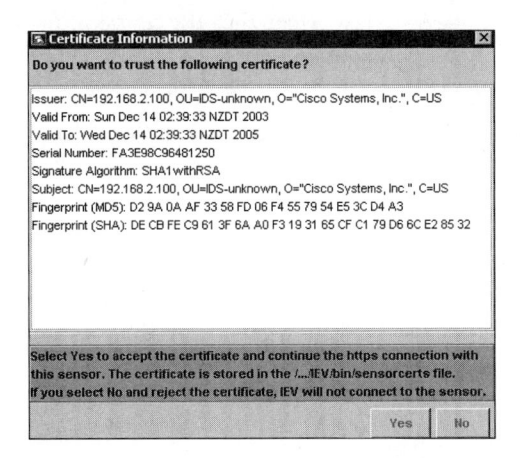

FIGURE 24.15 The IEV after a device is added

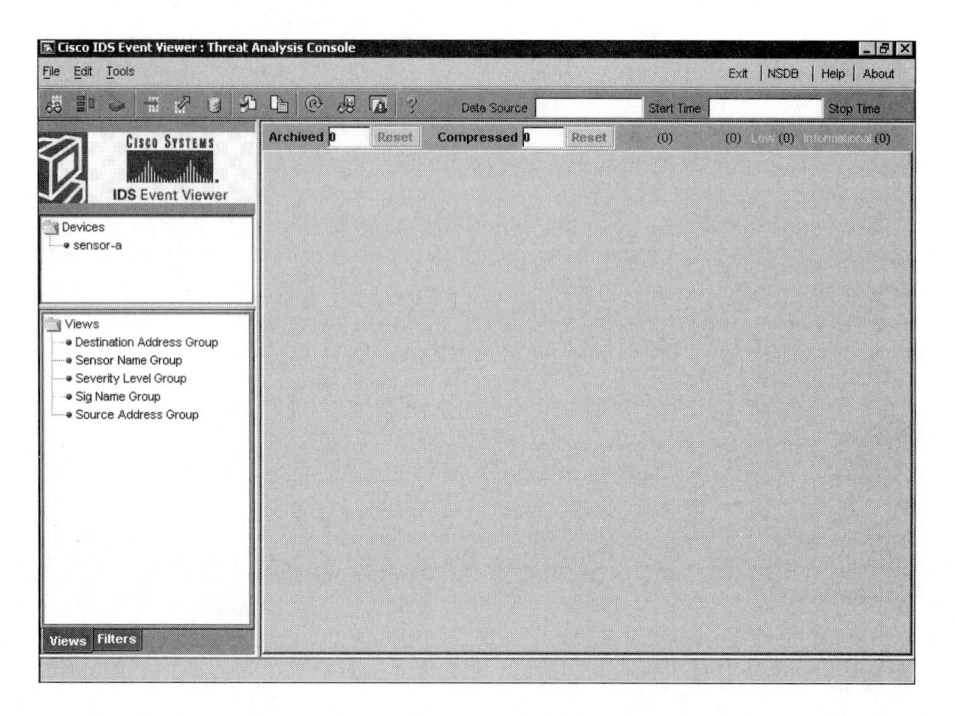

Viewing Device Status

After you've successfully added a sensor as a device, you can check the status of the device representing the sensor at any time. To check device status, right-click the device you wish to check and then select Device Status from the menu that appears. A Device Status dialog box will appear, as shown in Figure 24.16, which provides the following information:

Connection Status This indicates the current status of the connection between the IEV and sensor. The following messages may appear:

- Subscription not open yet.
- Subscription successfully opened.
- Failed to open subscription. Check communication parameters.
- Network connection error. Is the web server running?
- Status unknown. IEV server program may not be running.

In Figure 24.16, the text *Subscription successfully opened* indicates that the IEV is successfully connected to the sensor.

Sensor Version This indicates the software version of the sensor. In Figure 24.16, you can see that the sensor is running version 4.0(1)S37.

FIGURE 24.16 The Device Status dialog box

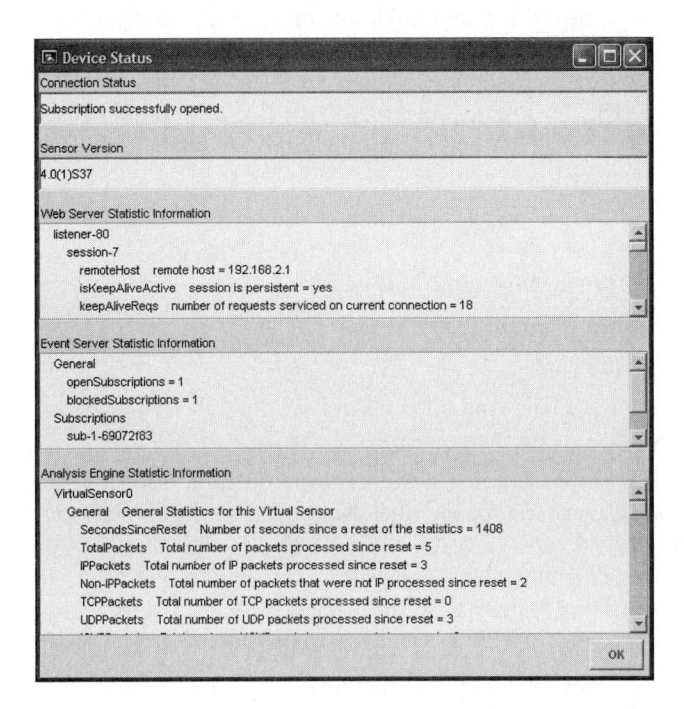

Web Server Statistic Information This provides statistics related to the web server, which accepts IDM and IEV connections. In Figure 24.16, notice that the first line indicates `listener-80`, which means that the web server on the sensor is currently running on port 80. The remaining lines show information about a current IDM or IEV session that is presently established to the sensor.

Event Server Statistic Information This provides statistics related to the event server on the sensor, which accepts IEV connections.

Analysis Engine Statistic Information This provides statistics related to the intrusion detection engine of the sensor. These statistics include the number of packets processed, TCP sessions analyzed, and alarms generated by the engine.

Configuring Filters and Views

One of the most difficult tasks in any IDS system relates to the process of managing alarms. On a busy network, a sensor can generate hundreds or even thousands of alarms within minutes, especially when the network is under attack. If your security administrators have to analyze large volumes of alarms that are continuously being generated, it's easy for critical alarms to be missed, reducing the overall effectiveness of the IDS. For this reason, possessing the ability to filter alarms is important, because it ensures that security administrators can apply filters that display only critical alarms and prevent less important alarms from being displayed that may obscure the critical alarms.

The IEV includes the ability to filter alarms, allowing administrators to drill down on specific alarms based on a number of different criteria. For example, an administrator might only be interested in high-severity alarms that are being generated for attacks to a specific target IP address, or an administrator might need to view all occurrences of a specific alarm during the time an attack took place. The IEV also includes views, which allow administrators to control how alarms are grouped and displayed, and can also incorporate filters. In the following sections, you'll learn how to create filters and views.

Creating a Filter

Three methods are available to create a filter:

- Select File ➢ New ➢ Filter from the main menu.
- Click the New Filter button.
- Click the Filters tab in the Views And Filters Window, right-click the Filters folder, and select New Filter from the menu that appears.

After you perform any of these methods, the Filter Properties dialog box is displayed, which lets you configure the various criteria for the filter. Figure 24.17 shows the Filter Properties dialog box.

You can define a name that identifies the filter, which by default is `UserFilter`. On the left side of the dialog box, notice the Filter Functions tree, which lets you specify the various criteria that make up the filter. As you see, you can filter on a number of criteria, each of which is described here:

Severity In Figure 24.17, the By Severity filter function is selected by default. On the right side of the dialog box are four severity levels you can filter on:

- Informational
- Low
- Medium
- High

The Informational severity level describes alarms generated by activity that may be used for legitimate administrative purposes but also could be related to intrusive activity. For example, the Ping utility is commonly used for troubleshooting purposes, but it can also be used for reconnaissance purposes by an attacker. The Low, Medium, and High severity levels describe alarms generated by intrusive activity; the severity level reflects the relative danger of the activity.

In Figure 24.17, notice that you can exclude one or more severity levels from the filter. Because the Informational and Low severity levels are selected in Figure 24.17, only alarms with a Medium or High severity level will be displayed by the filter.

NOTE Notice in Figure 24.17 that the small box to the left of the By Severity label is filled with a cross, which means that the By Severity criteria will be applied. If this box isn't filled, then the filter function won't be applied, even if the criteria on the right are configured.

FIGURE 24.17 The Filter Properties dialog box

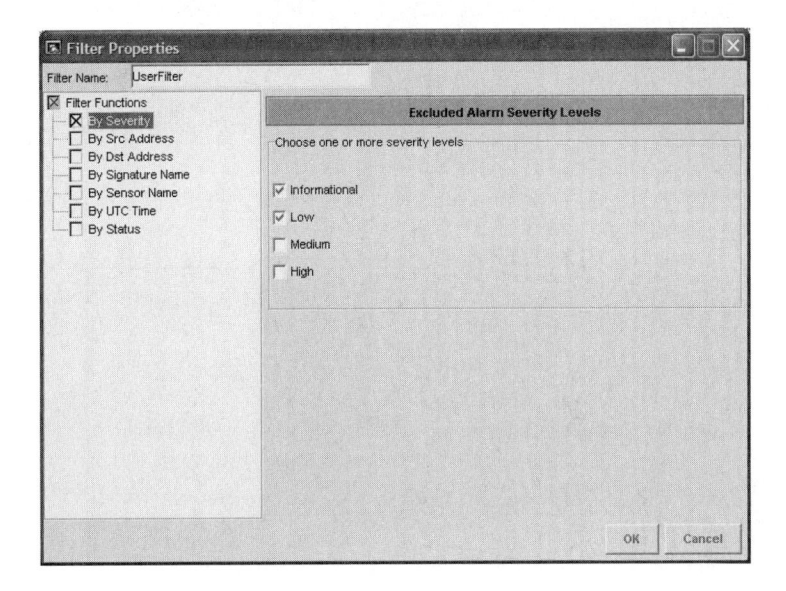

Source address The By Src Address filter function lets you filter based on the source IP address of the intrusive activity that generates an alarm. Figure 24.18 shows how you can configure the By Src Address filter function.

In Figure 24.18, notice that you can include or exclude a single IP address or range of IP addresses, and add them to a list along with other IP address inclusions/exclusions. The configuration of Figure 24.18 includes any alarms generated by traffic with a source IP address in the 192.168.2.0/24 subnet, except for alarms generated by traffic with a source IP address of 192.168.2.100.

> **NOTE** The source IP address typically identifies the attacker; however, be aware that it's very easy for an attacker to spoof an IP address. The IEV lets you define a list of addresses that should be either included or excluded from the filter.

Destination address The By Dst Address filter function lets you filter based on the destination IP address of the intrusive activity that generates an alarm. The criteria by which you can configure the By Dst Address filter function are identical to the By Src Address filter, with the ability to include or exclude a single IP address or range of IP addresses and add them to a list along with other IP address inclusions/exclusions.

> **NOTE** The destination IP address typically identifies the target of an attack.

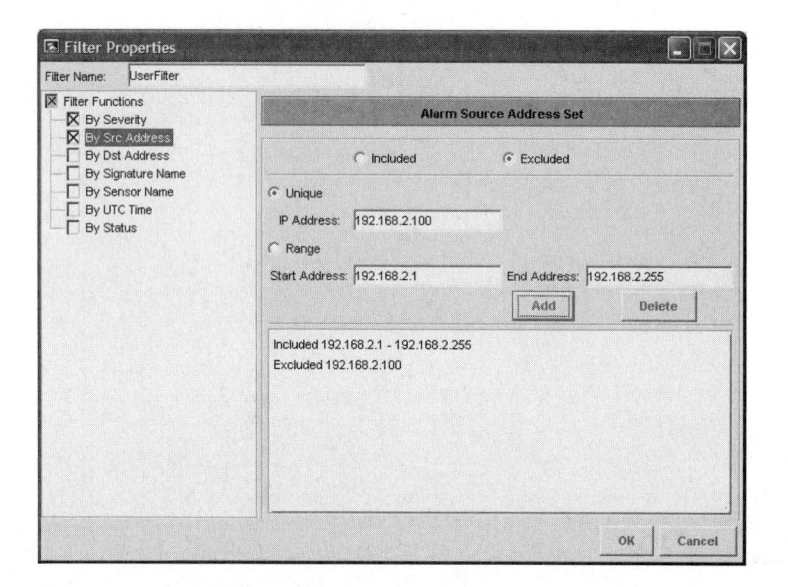

FIGURE 24.18   The By Src Address filter function

Signature name   The By Signature Name filter function lets you filter specific signatures based on a number of different criteria. Figure 24.19 shows the By Signature Name filter function.

In Figure 24.19, notice by the title of the right pane that you can only exclude signatures; you can't explicitly include signatures (only implicitly by virtue that a signature isn't excluded). The signatures are arranged by four different views:

L2/L3/L4 Protocol   This lets you exclude signatures based on the layer 2, layer 3, or layer 4 protocol each signature relates to. In Figure 24.19, all ICMP signatures (layer 3 protocol) are excluded and a specific TCP signature (3030) is excluded.

Attack   This lets you exclude signatures based on the type of vulnerability an attack is designed to exploit. You can exclude signatures related to a number of vulnerabilities, such as DoS, DDoS, code execution, viruses/worms/Trojan horses, and IDS evasion.

OS   This lets you exclude signatures based on the operating system that an attack is designed to exploit. You can exclude signatures related to attacks against Cisco IOS, Macintosh, Novell Netware, Unix (general Unix, AIX, HP-UX, IRIX, Linux, and Solaris), and Windows (general Windows, NT, 2000, and XP).

Service   This lets you exclude signatures based on the application-layer service that an attack is designed to exploit. You can exclude signatures related to attacks against a number of popular services, such as DHCP, DNS, HTTP, RPC, and SQL.

> **NOTE** It's important to understand that the L2/L3/L4 Protocol, Attack, OS, and Service tabs in the By Signature Name filter function are views that arrange the Cisco Secure IDS signatures into various categories. For example, the TCP SYN Host Sweep (3030) signature selected in Figure 24.19 is automatically selected in the Reconnaissance category within the Attack view, because this signature is considered a reconnaissance signature as well as a TCP signature.

Sensor name All Cisco Secure IDS alarms include a field that identifies the sensor that generated an alarm. The By Sensor Name function lets you explicitly exclude (you can't explicitly include) alarms from one or more sensors that the IEV is monitoring. Figure 24.20 shows the By Sensor Name function.

In Figure 24.20, each sensor defined in the Devices folder within the IEV is listed. You can select one or more sensors that you wish to exclude alarms from in the filter.

Time The By UTC Time function lets you exclude alarms from one or more time periods, as shown in Figure 24.21.

In Figure 24.21, notice that all alarms generated on October 22, 2003 are excluded.

FIGURE 24.19 The By Signature Name filter function

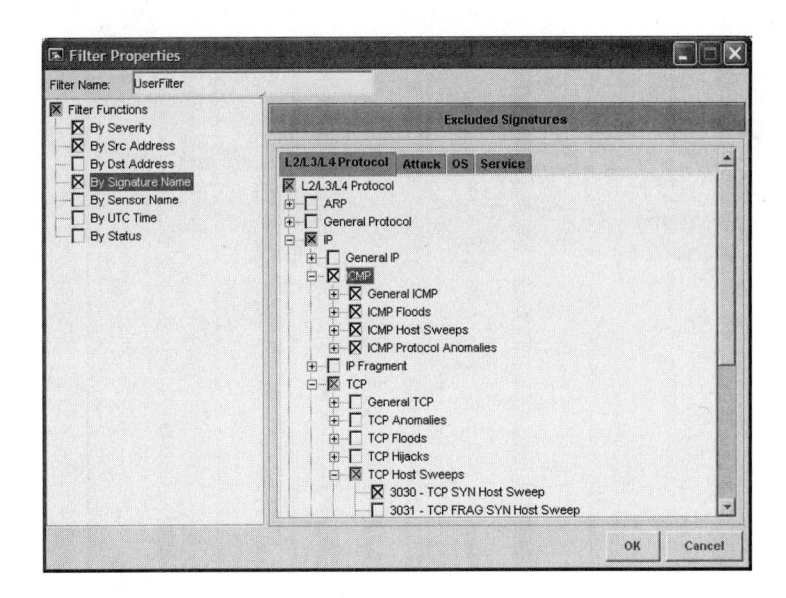

FIGURE 24.20 The By Sensor Name filter function

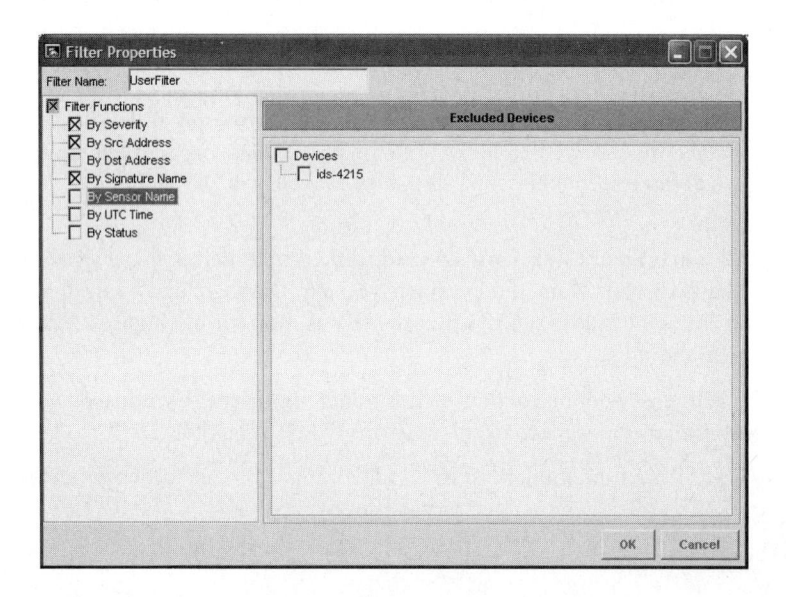

FIGURE 24.21 The By UTC Time filter function

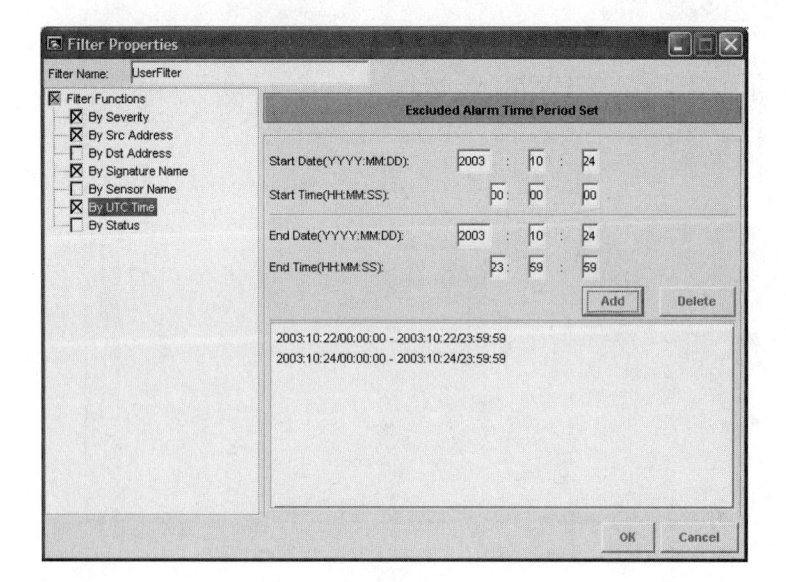

Status All alarms received by the IEV are assigned a status, which indicates whether an administrator is aware of an alarm, whether the alarm has been responded to, and whether the alarm has been resolved. Figure 24.22 shows the By Status function, which lets you exclude alarms from the filter based on the alarm status.

Notice the various statuses an alarm can possess:

New   The alarm is new.

Acknowledged   The existence of an alarm has been acknowledged by an administrator.

Assigned   The alarm has been assigned to an administrator for further investigation and action.

Closed   The alarm is resolved and has been closed.

Deleted   The alarm is deleted.

In Figure 24.22, all alarms that have been closed or deleted will be excluded from the filter.

Once you've assigned an appropriate name to the filter you've created and have defined its various filter functions, click the OK button in the Filter Properties dialog box to complete the creation of the filter. The filter will now appear in the Filters folder on the Filters tab of the IEV, as shown in Figure 24.23.

FIGURE 24.22   The By Status function

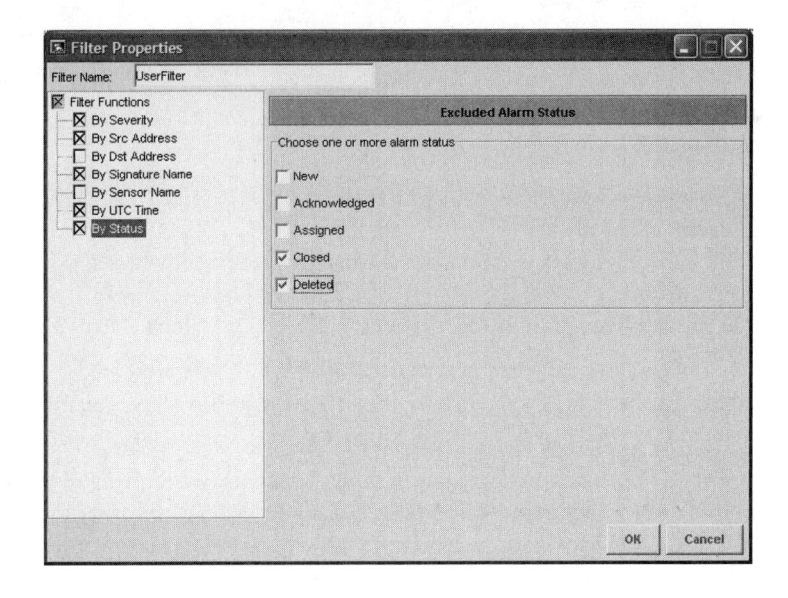

FIGURE 24.23 A filter after being created

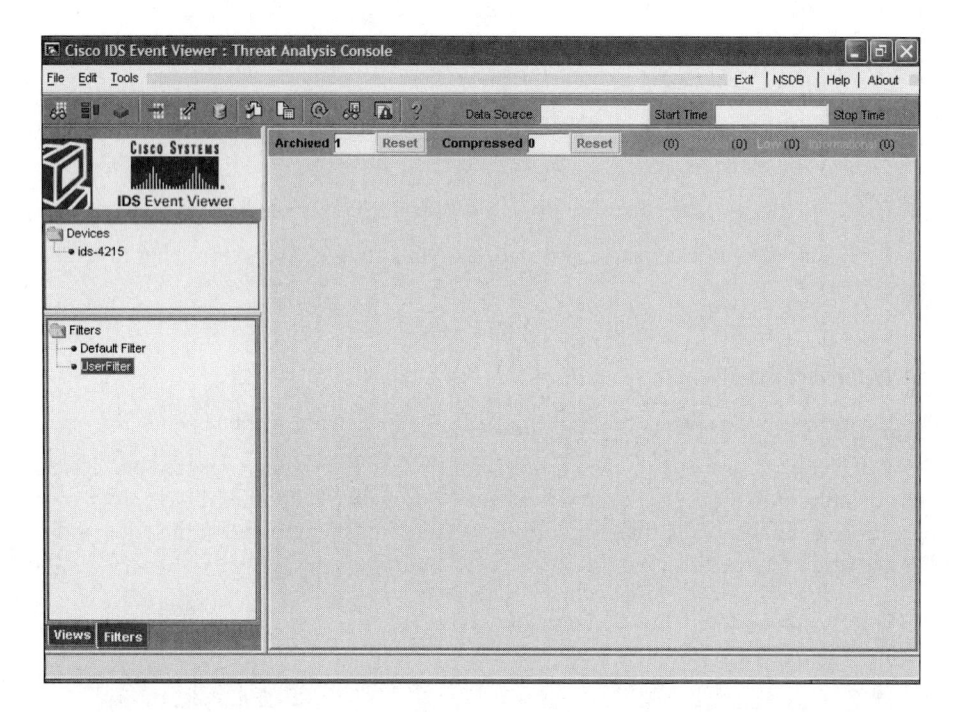

Creating a View

A *view* defines the parameters for the way in which alarms are presented and can also include a filter to define exactly which alarms are presented. It's important to understand the difference between a view and a filter. A view defines *how* alarms are presented, whereas a filter defines *which* alarms are presented.

A view includes the following parameters that define the way in which alarms are presented:

Filter A view can optionally specify a filter, which will filter alarms presented in the view according to the filter parameters. If you wish to filter alarms within a view, you must create an appropriate filter before you can reference it in your view.

Grouping style The IEV includes an aggregation table, which provides an aggregated display of all alarms within the view. The aggregation table consolidates alarm information, making it easier to manage. Within the aggregation table, you can group or sort alarms based on any of the following parameters:

- Signature name
- Source address

- Destination address
- Sensor name
- Severity level

For example, if you choose to group by sensor name, the aggregation table will group all alarms based on the sensor that generated the alarm. The grouping style lets you customize the view of the Alarm Aggregation table to suit your requirements.

Columns initially shown on Alarm Aggregation table Once alarms are grouped based on a specific parameter in the Alarm Aggregation table, other columns exist that provide summary or aggregated information about the grouped alarms. These columns include the following:

- Signature Name
- Source Address
- Destination Address
- Sensor Name
- Severity
- Total Alarm Count

The column that corresponds to the grouping style displays specific information, and the remaining columns display aggregated information and change names accordingly. For example, if you group alarms based on signature name, the Signature Name column will include a row for each different signature detected within all the alarms.

This means that if all alarms are related to just ICMP Echo Reply and ICMP Echo Request signatures, then two rows will exist: one for the ICMP Echo Reply signature and one for the ICMP Echo Request signature. All other columns will provide aggregated information—for example, if 63 different source addresses have been seen in ICMP Echo Request signatures, then the Source Address column (named Source Address Count, because it has been aggregated) will have a value of 63.

Within a view, you can define the columns that will initially be shown in the aggregation table. Some columns must always be shown; these include the column that relates to the grouping style selected and the total alarm count column. For example, if you choose to group by source address, the Source Address column and Total Alarm Count column will always be displayed. Other columns, however, can be configured to be initially displayed or not displayed.

Secondary sort order column This defines the column used to sort alarms on the Alarm Aggregation table after they have grouped based on the grouping style configured for the view. For example, if alarms have been grouped by sensor name, you can then configure the aggregation table to sort each row in the table based on the source address count column (from highest to lowest). By default, the column that corresponds to the grouping style is selected as the secondary sort order column, but any of the columns listed earlier can be defined as the secondary sort order column.

Data source This lets you select the default data source from which the IEV obtains alarms. The IEV can access alarms from several data sources:

event_realtime_table This data source contains all current alarms and receives new alarms.

Archived files By default, the IEV archives alarms every 24 hours into separate files. You can specify an archived file as the data source, which lets you view historical alarm information.

Imported log files This lets you import log files collected from sensors.

By default, the `event_realtime_table` data source is selected.

Columns initially shown on alarm information dialog table The Alarm Information Dialog table lists each of the alarms associated with a row in the Alarm Aggregation table and provides more columns that give further detail about each alarm. For each view, you can select the columns that are initially shown within this table. Table 24.9 describes the columns you can select, each of which typically relates to a field within each alarm.

Three methods are available to create a view:

- Select File ➢ New ➢ View from the main menu.
- Click the New View button.
- Click the Views tab in the Views and Filters Window, right-click the Views folder and select New View from the menu that appears.

TABLE 24.9 Alarm Information Dialog Table Columns

Column	Description
Signature Name	Name that describes the signature that generated the alarm (displayed by default)
Sig ID	Signature ID of the signature that generated the alarm (displayed by default)
Severity Level	Severity level of the signature (displayed by default)
Device Name	Name of the sensor that generated the alarm (displayed by default)
Event UTC Time	Time (expressed in UTC time) the alarm was generated (displayed by default)
Event Local Time	Local time the alarm was generated (displayed by default)
Src Address	Source IP address of the activity that generated the alarm (displayed by default)

TABLE 24.9 Alarm Information Dialog Table Columns *(continued)*

Column	Description
Dst Address	Destination IP address of the activity that generated the alarm (displayed by default)
Src Port	Source UDP or TCP port of the activity that generated the alarm (displayed by default)
Dst Port	Destination UDP or TCP port of the activity that generated the alarm (displayed by default)
Event ID	Sensor event ID assigned to the alarm
Trigger String	Used for summary alarms; describes the number of alarms detected over the summary interval
Alarm Status	Status of the alarm: new, acknowledge, assigned, or closed
App Name	Name of the signature engine that generated the alarm
Receive Date	Date the alarm was received by the IEV
Receive Time	Time the alarm was received by the IEV
Subsig ID	Subsignature ID of the subsignature that generated the alarm
Sig Details	Any custom details related to the signature that generated to the alarm
Sig Version	Signature version level of the sensor that generated the alarm
Total Attacks	If the alarm is a summary alarm, indicates the total number of attacks summarized by the alarm
Src Locality	Whether the source IP address of the activity that generated the alarm is an internal or external device
Dst Locality	Whether the destination IP address of the activity that generated the alarm is an internal or external device
Attack Details	Details about the attack that generated an alarm, collected by some signatures

TABLE 24.9 Alarm Information Dialog Table Columns *(continued)*

Column	Description
Summary Count	If the alarm is a summary alarm, indicates the number of individual events that generated the summary alarm
Summary Type	If the alarm is a summary alarm, indicates the criteria used to summarize the alarm
Interface Group	Interface group on the sensor that received the activity that generated the alarm
VLAN	VLAN on which the activity that generated the alarm was received
Context	Context buffer, which captures 256 bytes of incoming and outgoing data after a signature that supports this feature is triggered
IPLog Activated	Whether the alarm activated the IP Log event action and captured the packets associated with the intrusive activity
TCP Reset sent	Whether the alarm activated the TCP Reset event action and generated a TCP Reset that was sent to the source and destination of the intrusive activity
Shun Requested	Whether the alarm activated the Blocking event action and generated a blocking/shun request that was applied to perimeter device(s) or a master blocking sensor
Notes	Any notes that have been configured for the signature

After you perform any of the previous methods, the View Wizard dialog box is displayed. This wizard lets you configure the various criteria for the view.

In Figure 24.24, you can see the first screen of the View Wizard dialog box, where you can define the following parameters related to the view:

View Name A view name of UserView is configured.

Filter The UserFilter created earlier has been configured to be applied to the view.

Grouping style The grouping style is set to group based on signature name.

Initial columns for Alarm Aggregation table You can see that all columns are selected to be initially displayed.

Column Secondary Sort Order The Alarm Aggregation table is sorted by Signature Name column after the grouping style is applied.

Once you've defined the appropriate parameters on the first screen of the View Wizard dialog box, click the Next button to proceed to the next screen. Figure 24.25 shows the second screen of the View Wizard dialog box.

FIGURE 24.24 The View Wizard dialog box: step 1 of 2

FIGURE 24.25 The View Wizard dialog box: step 2 of 2

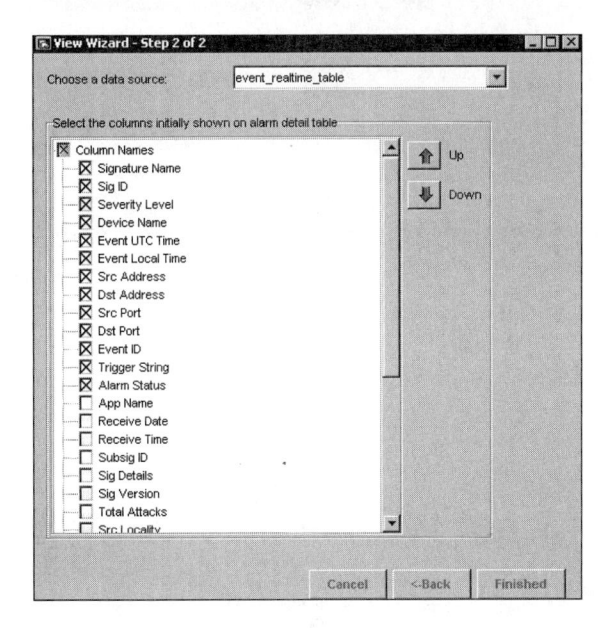

In Figure 24.25, you can see that the second screen of the View Wizard dialog box lets you configure the data source for the view (`event_realtime_table`) and the columns that should be initially displayed in the alarm information dialog table.

Once you've completed configuring the appropriate parameters, click the Finished button to complete the configuration of the view. Figure 24.26 shows the Views folder within the main IEV window after a custom view has been created.

In Figure 24.26, notice that the `UserView` view created in Figures 24.24 and 24.25 is displayed below five other views. These other views are default views that ship with the IEV and display alarms based on the grouping style that each view's name describes. For example, the Destination Address Group view groups alarms based on destination address, and the Sig Name Group view groups alarms based on signature name. The following describes the configuration of the other parameters associated with each default view:

Filter   No filter is applied.

Initial columns for Alarm Aggregation table   All columns are selected.

Secondary sort order   The column that corresponds to the grouping style is selected.

Data source   The `event_realtime_table` is selected as the data source.

Initial columns on alarm information dialog table   The columns as indicated in the alarm information dialog table (see Table 24.8) are displayed.

FIGURE 24.26   The Views folder in the IEV

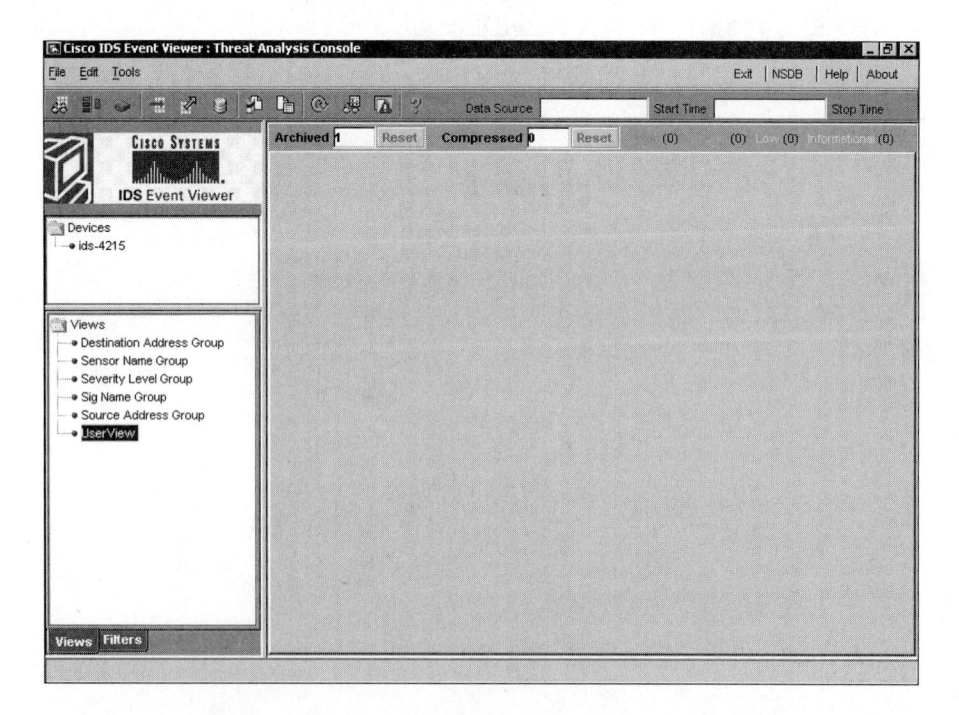

Configuring Application Settings and Preferences

The IEV includes a number of preferences and application settings that control how the IEV application refreshes event information, archives event information, and interacts with other helper applications and databases. The following sections describe how to configure these preferences and application settings.

Configuring Preferences

The IEV includes two main sets of preferences that allow you to control whether the alarm information presented in tables is refreshed on a periodic basis as well as control how and when historical alarm information is archived. We'll discuss the following preferences:

- Refresh Cycle settings
- Data Archival settings

Configuring Refresh Cycle Settings

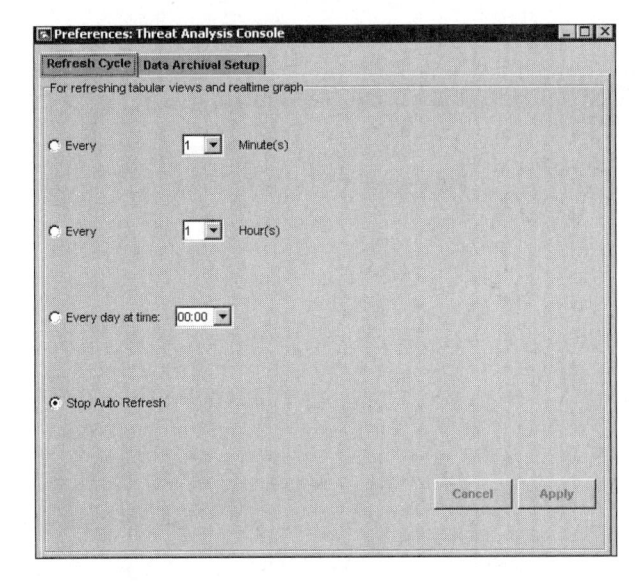

Refresh Cycle settings define how often information displayed in tables and the realtime graph is refreshed. By default, all information displayed in tables and the realtime graph is static and must be manually refreshed. However, you can configure the IEV to automatically refresh table and realtime graph information periodically.

To configure Refresh Cycle settings, select Edit ➢ Preferences from the IEV main menu and click the Refresh Cycle tab in the Preferences dialog box that appears. Figure 24.27 shows the Refresh Cycle tab.

FIGURE 24.27 Configuring Refresh Cycle settings

Notice that you can select one of four options for refreshing table and realtime graph data:

- Every *n* minutes
- Every *n* hours
- Every day at *nn:nn*
- Never (Stop Auto Refresh)

By default, the Stop Auto Refresh setting is selected, meaning data is never refreshed automatically.

Configuring Data Archival Settings

Data Archival settings define when realtime alarms (events) are archived from the `event_realtime_table` to an archive file. Two thresholds are used to trigger data archival:

Time   Events are primarily archived on a scheduled basis. The schedule can be every *n* minutes, every *n* hours, or daily at a specified time.

Maximum number of records   Events can also be archived if the number of events in the `event_realtime_table` exceeds a configurable threshold.

When data archiving occurs, events in the `event_realtime_table` that are eligible for archiving are written to an archive file with the filename `archive_table.timestamp`. Any events that have a status set to Deleted are removed from `event_realtime_table` but aren't archived.

To configure Data Archival settings, select Edit ➤ Preferences from the IEV main menu and click the Data Archival tab in the Preferences dialog box that appears. Figure 24.28 shows the Data Archival Setup tab.

FIGURE 24.28   Configuring Data Archival settings

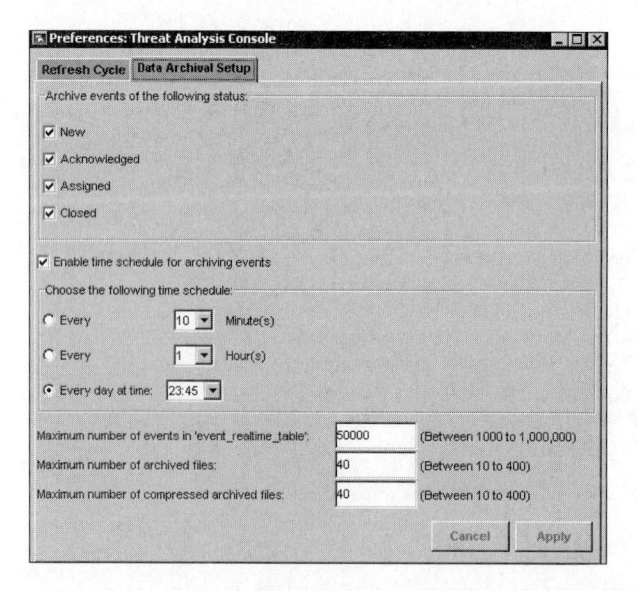

You can configure a number of settings:

Archive Events Of The Following Status This lets you define the status of events that can be archived. By default, events with a status of New, Acknowledged, Assigned, or Closed are eligible for archiving. Some administrators might wish to configure the IEV to never archive events with a status of New, which ensures that any events that are archived have been identified and acknowledged in some fashion.

Enable Time Schedule For Archiving Events This setting lets you define a scheduled time for archiving events in the `event_realtime_table`. You can see that by default this occurs every night at 23:45. However, you can modify the schedule to every *n* minutes, every *n* hours, or a custom time every day. You can also disable scheduled archiving if desired.

Maximum Number Of Events In *event_realtime_table* This defines the maximum number of events that can exist in the `event_realtime_table`. By default, up to 50,000 events are permitted in the `event_realtime_table`. However, you can define a maximum value between 1000 and 1,000,000.

Maximum Number Of Archived Files This setting defines the maximum number of archived files that can exist on the IEV host. By default, there can be up to 40 archived files, after which half of the oldest archived files will be compressed. You can adjust the maximum number of archived files to a value between 10 and 400.

Maximum Number Of Compressed Archived Files This defines the maximum number of compressed archived files that can exist on the IEV host. By default, there can be up to 40 compressed archived files, after which half of the oldest compressed archived files will be deleted. You can adjust the maximum number of archived files to a value between 10 and 400.

Configuring Application Settings

The IEV includes a number of application settings, which allow you to define external helper applications and files that will assist you when using the IEV, as well as control how the Alarm Aggregation table is updated after an alarm is deleted from the Drill Down Dialog table or Expanded Details Dialog table. To configure application settings, select Edit ➤ Application Settings from the IEV main menu to open the Application Settings dialog box, shown in Figure 24.29.

You can configure a number of settings:

Web browser location This setting specifies the path on the IEV to a web browser application. This enables administrators to invoke a web browser to connect to the IDM on sensors and to view information in the NSDB.

Ethereal application location Cisco Secure IDS sensors support the ability to capture packets that generate alarms, which can be achieved by configuring signatures with an event action of IP logging. The packets captured within IP log files are stored in a binary format known as tcpdump, which is difficult to interpret in its raw state without considerable knowledge of the protocols that compose each packet. The IEV lets you decode packets captured within IP log files using Ethereal, which is a free network protocol analyzer available for a wide range of operating systems, including Microsoft Windows 2000 and Windows XP (on which the IEV runs). When you use Ethereal with the IEV, the IEV will launch Ethereal and load the IP log file you're working with into Ethereal.

The Ethereal application location setting specifies the path on the IEV to the Ethereal application. If Ethereal has been installed before the IEV, the location is automatically configured during IEV installation. If you install Ethereal after the IEV, you must manually configure the path to Ethereal.

NSDB folder location This setting specifies the location of the NSDB folder, which houses the Network Security Database. The NSDB is used to provide information about alarms that are generated, giving security administrators a description of the possible attacks that generated the alarm and how to mitigate the vulnerability associated with the alarm.

Auto Refresh Parent View On Database Modifications This setting controls what happens to the parent Alarm Aggregation table when a row is deleted from the Drill Down Dialog table or Expanded Details Dialog table. By default, this setting is enabled, which means that any modifications made to the child tables are automatically updated in the parent Alarm Aggregation table. Disabling this setting means that you must manually refresh the Alarm Aggregation table after modifications are made to the child tables.

FIGURE 24.29 Configuring Application settings

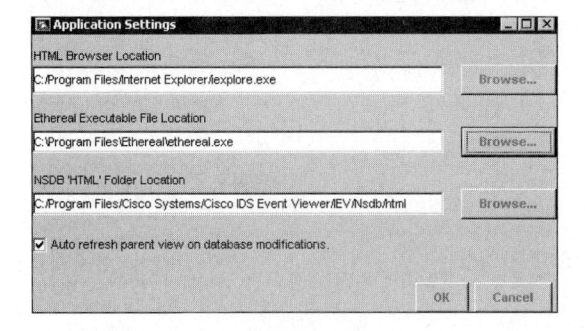

Administering the IEV Database

The IEV includes a database of alarm information, which contains several tables of alarms. Each data source is represented by a physical table in the IEV database; all alarms associated with the data source are stored in the table that represents the data source. For example, the `event_realtime_table` data source is stored as a table called `event_realtime_table` in the IEV database. When the information in the `event_realtime_table` data source is archived, a new table and corresponding data source are created in the IEV database for the archived alarms.

> **NOTE:** The various tables that you learned about earlier in this chapter (such as the Alarm Aggregation table) are logical tables that are built based on a view configured in the IEV from the alarms stored in the physical table that represents a data source.

The IEV lets you administer the physical IEV database, with the ability to view information about each physical table (data source) within the database as well as the ability to import and export alarm information. The following sections describe how to perform each of these administration tasks.

Viewing Data Source Information

As we described earlier, each data source in the IEV is actually a physical table stored within the IEV database. You can view information about each data source in the IEV by selecting File ➤ Database Administration ➤ Data Source Information, which opens the Data Source Information dialog box, shown in Figure 24.30.

In Figure 24.30, notice that there are seven tables, each of which represents an individual data source. Information about each table is provided by the various columns, which include the following:

- Table Name
- Total Events
- Table Size (In Bytes)
- Create Time
- Update Time

FIGURE 24.30 The Data Source Information dialog box

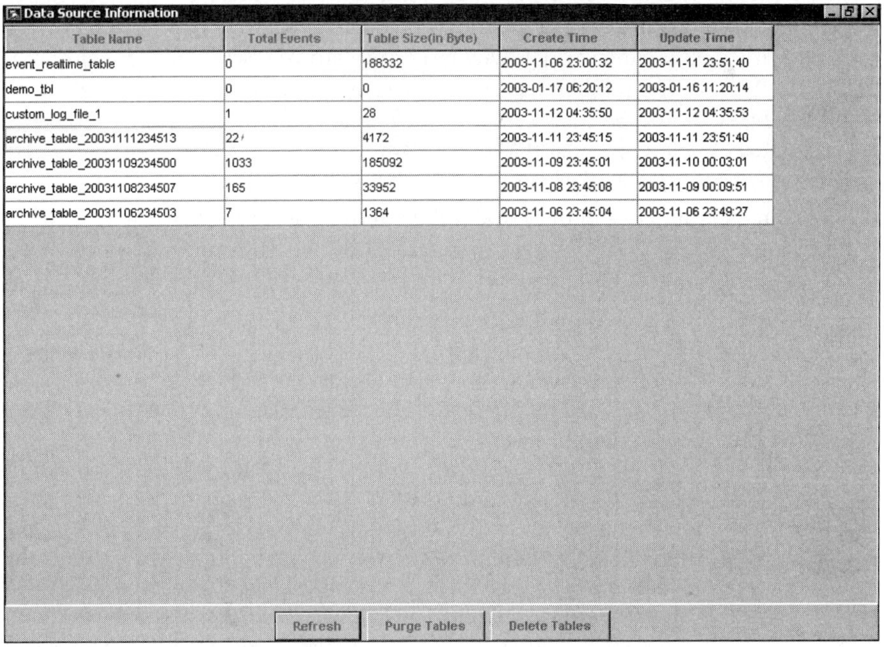

Table Name	Total Events	Table Size(in Byte)	Create Time	Update Time
event_realtime_table	0	188332	2003-11-06 23:00:32	2003-11-11 23:51:40
demo_tbl	0	0	2003-01-17 06:20:12	2003-01-16 11:20:14
custom_log_file_1	1	28	2003-11-12 04:35:50	2003-11-12 04:35:53
archive_table_20031111234513	22	4172	2003-11-11 23:45:15	2003-11-11 23:51:40
archive_table_20031109234500	1033	185092	2003-11-09 23:45:01	2003-11-10 00:03:01
archive_table_20031108234507	165	33952	2003-11-08 23:45:08	2003-11-09 00:09:51
archive_table_20031106234503	7	1364	2003-11-06 23:45:04	2003-11-06 23:49:27

In Figure 24.30, the first table is `event_realtime_table`, which includes all recent alarms. You can see that this table currently has 0 events (alarms), is approximately 188KB in size, and was created on November 6 around 11:00 p.m. The last four tables represent archived data sources; the number of alarms in each archived data source varies.

Viewing Alarm Information

The IEV provides an interface to alarm information collected from Cisco Secure IDS sensors, so it's important that you understand how to find and display the alarm information that you wish to view. The IEV organizes alarm information into tables, each of which provides varying degrees of detail about alarms that have been received from sensors. All tables are accessed based on a view, which defines how alarm information is displayed and sorted (you'll learn about views later in this chapter). The IEV also generates graphs based on the alarm information in the various IEV tables.

Working with Tables

All information in the IEV is presented in either a table or graph. A table provides a list of individual or aggregated alarms. This section describes each table, showing you how to access, view, and work with them.

THE ALARM AGGREGATION TABLE

The Alarm Aggregation table provides a summary of alarm information collected for a particular view and can be considered the master or parent table for all of the alarms matched by a view. When you open a view, the Alarm Aggregation table is the first table that is displayed; it's shown in the Alarm Aggregation pane (see Figure 24.12). Opening the Alarm Aggregation table first allows administrators to see a summary view of the alarms presented by the view they are working with. You can then drill down on specific alarms or sets of alarms within the view from the Alarm Aggregation table.

Figure 24.31 shows the Alarm Aggregation table for the Sig Name Group view, which is a default view that ships with the IEV that groups alarms based on the signature name of each alarm. The Alarm Aggregation table shown in Figure 24.31 can be viewed by double-clicking the Sig Name Group view in the Views folder within the Views and Filters Window.

In Figure 24.31, the Alarm Aggregation table shows six entries. Each entry (row) corresponds to the signature name of alarms collected by the IEV (as indicated in the Signature Name column), with the remaining columns providing aggregated information about the alarms collected for the specific signature. The first entry is colored red (you can't see this color in the figure, but you may notice that the first entry is a darker shade of gray), which indicates that the highest severity of alarms summarized by the row is High; the remaining entries are colored light blue, which indicates that the highest severity of alarms summarized by these rows is Informational.

> **NOTE**
> In the Sig Name Group view or any view that groups based on signature name, the Highest Severity column provides no aggregation features, because all alarms summarized will have the same severity (because they were generated by the same signature). The Highest Severity column is useful for views grouped by other parameters, because it allows entries that have generated high severity alarms to be quickly identified.

FIGURE 24.31 The Alarm Aggregation table

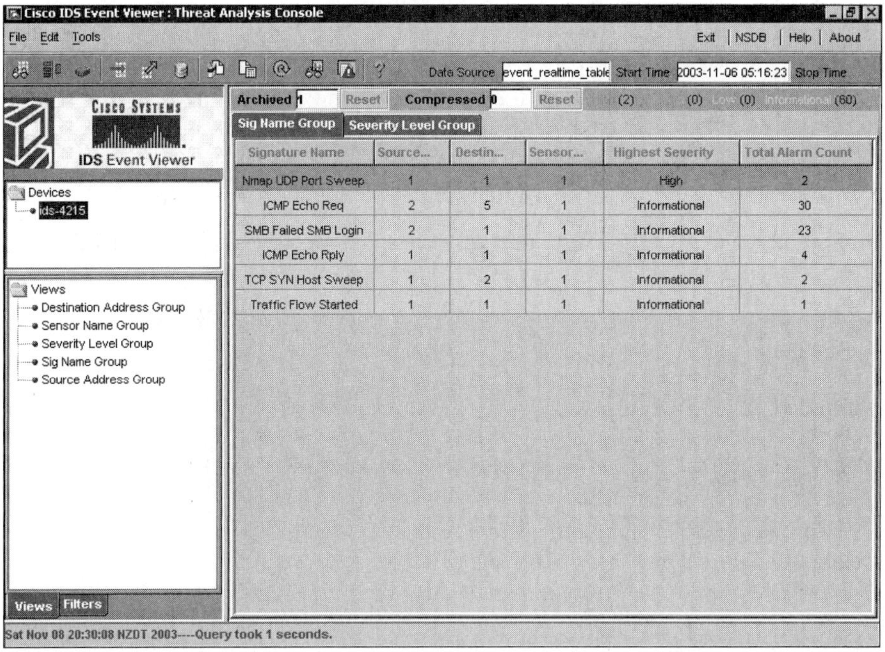

Looking in more detail at the entries in Figure 24.31, notice the second entry with a signature name of SMB Failed SMB Login; it relates to failed login attempts to a Windows file share. The Total Alarm Count column has a value of 30, which means that 30 alarms related to this signature have been collected. The Source Address Count column (in Figure 24.31, this column has been truncated due to size restrictions) has a value of 2, which means that two different sources have generated these alarms. The Destination Address Count column has a value of 1, which means that all alarms have the same destination IP address. The Sensor Name Count column has a value of 1, which means that all alarms were generated by a single sensor.

For each entry in the Alarm Aggregation table, you can perform a number of actions by right-clicking within the first column. Doing so displays a menu that includes the following items:

Expand Whole Details Selecting this item opens the Expanded Details Dialog table for the entry (discussed in detail in the next section).

NSDB Link The *network security database (NSDB)* is an HTML-based database that provides security information for each signature, giving a description of each signature and indicating any related benign triggers (legitimate traffic that could trigger the signature), vulnerabilities, and recommended actions to take. To view information about an alarm, you can right-click any field within an alarm and select the NSDB Link item from the menu that appears. Doing so opens the appropriate HTML page for the alarm in the system web browser on the IEV host. Figure 24.32 shows the NSDB page for the SMB Failed SMB Login alarm shown in Figure 24.31.

NOTE The NSDB Link option is available only for views that are grouped by signature name.

In Figure 24.32, notice the amount of information provided to describe the attack that generated the alarm. You can see that the alarm is related to failed Windows user authentication logins three or more times within a single SMB session. The NSDB is particularly useful if you come across an alarm that you aren't familiar with and require further information.

Set Status To This item is a submenu that lets you set the status of alarms associated with the entry selected in the Alarm Aggregation table. By default, any new alarms generated have a status of New. However, you can change the status to any of the following:

- New
- Acknowledged
- Assigned
- Closed
- Deleted

Delete Row From Database Selecting this item deletes all of the alarms associated with the entry selected in the Alarm Aggregation table from the current data source.

FIGURE 24.32 The NSDB

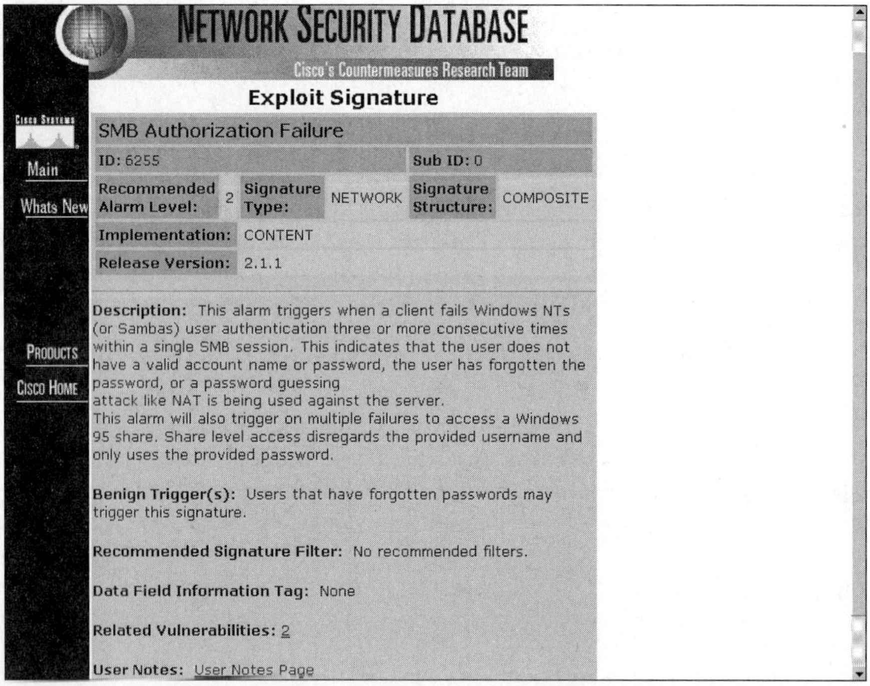
NETWORK SECURITY DATABASE
Cisco's Countermeasures Research Team
Exploit Signature
Main
Whats New
Products
Cisco Home
SMB Authorization Failure
ID: 6255
Sub ID: 0
Recommended Alarm Level: 2
Signature Type: NETWORK
Signature Structure: COMPOSITE
Implementation: CONTENT
Release Version: 2.1.1
Description: This alarm triggers when a client fails Windows NTs (or Sambas) user authentication three or more consecutive times within a single SMB session. This indicates that the user does not have a valid account name or password, the user has forgotten the password, or a password guessing attack like NAT is being used against the server.
This alarm will also trigger on multiple failures to access a Windows 95 share. Share level access disregards the provided username and only uses the provided password.
Benign Trigger(s): Users that have forgotten passwords may trigger this signature.
Recommended Signature Filter: No recommended filters.
Data Field Information Tag: None
Related Vulnerabilities: 2
User Notes: User Notes Page

THE EXPANDED DETAILS DIALOG TABLE

The Expanded Details Dialog table provides further details about specific entries in the Alarm Aggregation table and hence is considered a child table of the Alarm Aggregation table. For example, an entry in the Alarm Aggregation table might aggregate information about 20 alarms into a single entry; the Expanded Details Dialog table expands on the alarms associated with the single entry in the Alarm Aggregation table.

To open the Expanded Details Dialog table, right-click the first column of the entry that you wish to expand, and then select the Expand Whole Details item from the menu that appears. Figure 24.33 shows the Expanded Details Dialog table for the third entry (SMB Failed SMB Login) in the Alarm Aggregation table shown in Figure 24.31.

In Figure 24.33, you can see that the SMB Failed SMB Login entry from Figure 24.31 has been expanded into two entries in the Expanded Details Dialog table. Each entry contains specific information for each column—in other words, all the summarization provided by the Alarm Aggregation table has been removed (except the Total Alarm Count). The alarms associated with the SMB Failed SMB Login signature have been generated by two sources, 192.168.1.10 and 192.168.1.11. The destination for all alarms is the same (192.168.1.100), and you can see that the sensor that generated both sets of alarms is called `ids-4215`.

You can perform actions for entries in the Expanded Details Dialog table similar to those you can perform for entries in the Alarm Aggregation table, by right-clicking any field within an entry in the Expanded Details Dialog table. These include opening the NSBD for an alarm, setting the status of alarms, and deleting alarms from the current data source. You can also select the View Alarms option, which opens the Alarm Information Dialog table discussed next.

FIGURE 24.33 The Expanded Details Dialog table

Source Address	Destination Address	Sensor Name	Severity Level	Total Alarm Count
192.168.1.10	192.168.1.100	ids-4215	Informational	15
192.168.1.11	192.168.1.100	ids-4215	Informational	8

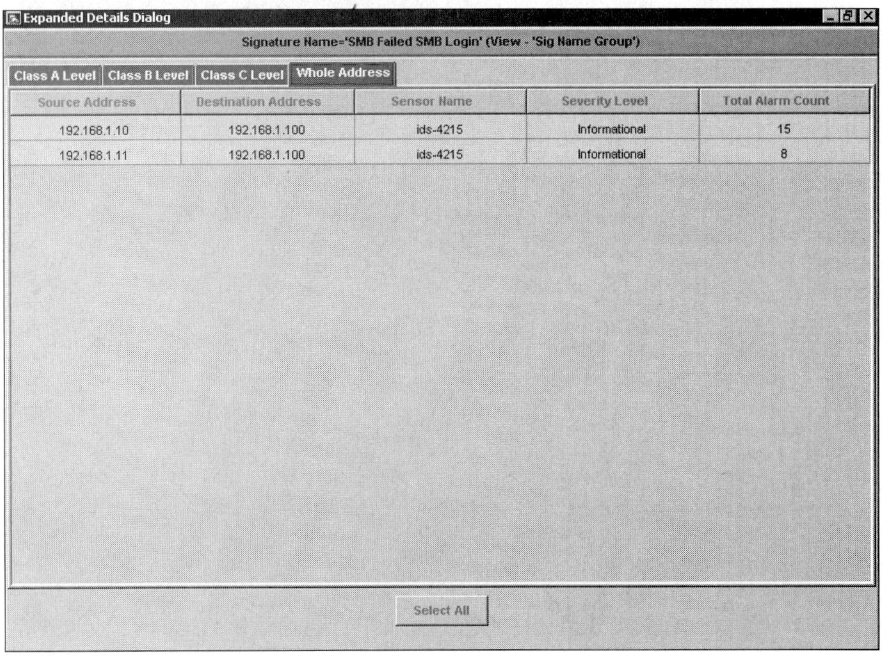

THE ALARM INFORMATION DIALOG TABLE

The Alarm Information Dialog table displays each specific alarm for an entry in the Alarm Aggregation table or the Expanded Details Dialog table. There are a couple of ways to open the Alarm Information Dialog table, depending on which table you're attempting to access it from:

- In the Alarm Aggregation table, double-click the Total Alarm Count column.
- In the Expanded Details Dialog table, right-click any column, and select View Alarms from the menu that appears.

Continuing from Figure 24.33, Figure 24.34 shows the Alarm Information Dialog table after right-clicking on any column within the first entry and selecting View Alarms.

In Figure 24.34, you can see each individual alarm associated with the first entry in Figure 24.33. Notice that you can see a lot more information in the Alarm Information Dialog table; in fact, there are many other fields not shown in Figure 24.34 that can be viewed by scrolling to the right.

THE DRILL DOWN DIALOG TABLE

The Drill Down Dialog table lets you drill down on a specific column within the Alarm Aggregation table, displaying each of the individual entries for the column. To open the Drill Down Dialog table, double-click any of the columns for a specific entry in the Alarm Aggregation table except for the first column and the Total Alarm Count column.

Figure 24.35 shows the Drill Down Dialog table that is opened when the Sensor Name Count column for the third entry (the SMB Failed SMB Login row) in the Alarm Aggregation table of Figure 24.31 is double-clicked.

FIGURE 24.34 The Alarm Information Dialog table

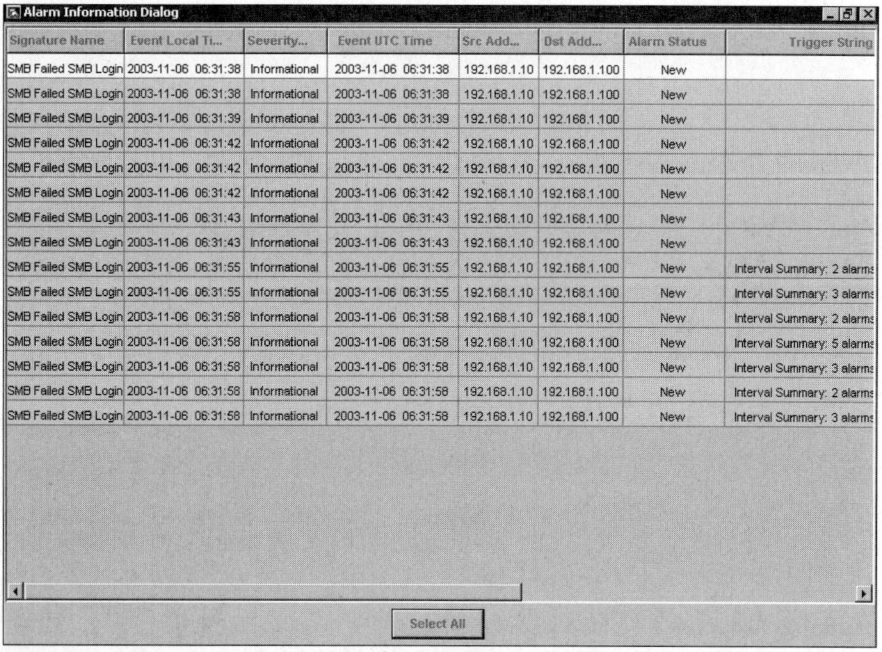

Signature Name	Event Local Ti...	Severity...	Event UTC Time	Src Add...	Dst Add...	Alarm Status	Trigger String
SMB Failed SMB Login	2003-11-06 06:31:38	Informational	2003-11-06 06:31:38	192.168.1.10	192.168.1.100	New	
SMB Failed SMB Login	2003-11-06 06:31:38	Informational	2003-11-06 06:31:38	192.168.1.10	192.168.1.100	New	
SMB Failed SMB Login	2003-11-06 06:31:39	Informational	2003-11-06 06:31:39	192.168.1.10	192.168.1.100	New	
SMB Failed SMB Login	2003-11-06 06:31:42	Informational	2003-11-06 06:31:42	192.168.1.10	192.168.1.100	New	
SMB Failed SMB Login	2003-11-06 06:31:42	Informational	2003-11-06 06:31:42	192.168.1.10	192.168.1.100	New	
SMB Failed SMB Login	2003-11-06 06:31:42	Informational	2003-11-06 06:31:42	192.168.1.10	192.168.1.100	New	
SMB Failed SMB Login	2003-11-06 06:31:43	Informational	2003-11-06 06:31:43	192.168.1.10	192.168.1.100	New	
SMB Failed SMB Login	2003-11-06 06:31:43	Informational	2003-11-06 06:31:43	192.168.1.10	192.168.1.100	New	
SMB Failed SMB Login	2003-11-06 06:31:55	Informational	2003-11-06 06:31:55	192.168.1.10	192.168.1.100	New	Interval Summary: 2 alarm
SMB Failed SMB Login	2003-11-06 06:31:55	Informational	2003-11-06 06:31:55	192.168.1.10	192.168.1.100	New	Interval Summary: 3 alarm
SMB Failed SMB Login	2003-11-06 06:31:58	Informational	2003-11-06 06:31:58	192.168.1.10	192.168.1.100	New	Interval Summary: 2 alarm
SMB Failed SMB Login	2003-11-06 06:31:58	Informational	2003-11-06 06:31:58	192.168.1.10	192.168.1.100	New	Interval Summary: 5 alarm
SMB Failed SMB Login	2003-11-06 06:31:58	Informational	2003-11-06 06:31:58	192.168.1.10	192.168.1.100	New	Interval Summary: 3 alarm
SMB Failed SMB Login	2003-11-06 06:31:58	Informational	2003-11-06 06:31:58	192.168.1.10	192.168.1.100	New	Interval Summary: 2 alarm
SMB Failed SMB Login	2003-11-06 06:31:58	Informational	2003-11-06 06:31:58	192.168.1.10	192.168.1.100	New	Interval Summary: 3 alarm

FIGURE 24.35   The Drill Down Dialog table

Sensor Name	Source Address	Destination Address	Severity Level	Total Alarm Count
ids-4215	2-->	192.168.1.100	Informational	23

Signature Name='SMB Failed SMB Login' (View - 'Sig Name Group')

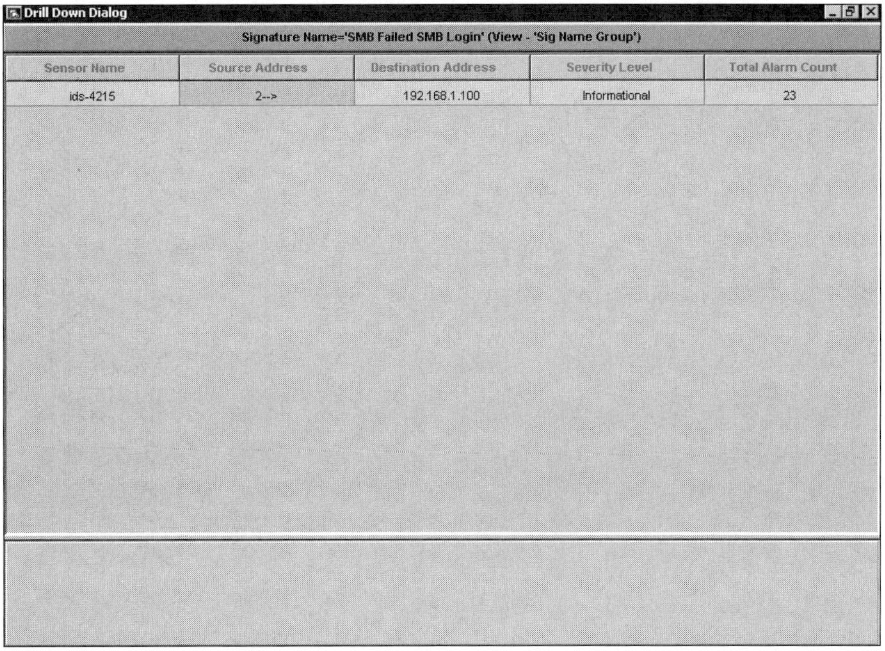

In Figure 24.35, notice that the specific entries related to the column (Sensor Name Count) double-clicked in the Alarm Aggregation table are displayed. The first column is Sensor Name, which groups the alarms related to the entry double-clicked in the Alarm Aggregation table based on Sensor Name. You can see that only a single entry exists, because only a single sensor has generated each of the alarms. Notice that the Source Address column in Figure 24.35 is a different shade (green, rather than light blue for the other columns) and that the value of the Source Address column is 2-->. This indicates that two different source addresses have generated the alarms associated with the entry. The Drill Down Dialog table lets you drill down even further on columns that are multivalued; Figure 24.36 shows what happens when the Source Address field for the entry is double-clicked.

In Figure 24.36, notice that two entries are displayed at the bottom of the window. These entries are grouped first on sensor name and then based on source address (since the Source Address field was double-clicked). You can see that 15 alarms have been generated for SMB Failed SMB Login signatures from 192.168.1.10 to 192.168.1.100, and 8 alarms for 192.168.1.11 to 192.168.1.100.

THE REALTIME DASHBOARD

The Realtime Dashboard displays alarms as they are generated in real time, unlike the other tables and graphs previously discussed, which by default must be manually refreshed to include information about new alarms. The Realtime Dashboard is useful for realtime monitoring, ensuring that security operators are notified of alarms as they occur.

FIGURE 24.36   The Drill Down Dialog table

Sensor Name	Source Address	Destination Address	Severity Level	Total Alarm Count
ids-4215	2-->	192.168.1.100	Informational	23

Sensor Name	Source Address	Destination Address	Severity Level	Total Alarm Count
ids-4215	192.168.1.10	192.168.1.100	Informational	15
ids-4215	192.168.1.11	192.168.1.100	Informational	8

> **NOTE**   Tables and graphs other than the Realtime Dashboard can be configured to auto-update on a scheduled basis. (For more information, see the section "Configuring Preferences.")

To open the Realtime Dashboard, you can either select Tools ➢ Realtime Dashboard ➢ Launch Dashboard from the main menu or click the Launch Dashboard button on the toolbar in the main IEV window. Figure 24.37 shows the Realtime Dashboard.

In Figure 24.37, notice that a number of alarms are shown—the Realtime Dashboard displays individual alarms and doesn't aggregate any alarms. When you start the Realtime Dashboard, no alarms are displayed; only alarms generated after the Realtime Dashboard is started are shown. Notice the buttons at the bottom of the Realtime Dashboard, which perform the following functions:

Pause   Clicking this button pauses the realtime display of the dashboard until you click the Resume button.

Resume   Clicking this button resumes the realtime display of the dashboard. This button is enabled only if the Pause button has been previously clicked to pause the realtime display.

Reconnect   Clicking this button clears all alarms from the realtime display and forces the sensor to reestablish connections to each sensor.

FIGURE 24.37   The Realtime Dashboard

Signature Name	Sig ID	Severit...	Device...	Event UTC Time	Event Local Time	Src Address	Dst Address
ICMP Echo Rply	2000	Informational	ids-4215	2003-11-06 13:02:09	2003-11-06 13:02:09	192.168.1.100	192.168.1.10
ICMP Echo Req	2004	Informational	ids-4215	2003-11-06 13:02:09	2003-11-06 13:02:09	192.168.1.10	192.168.1.100
Large ICMP	2151	Informational	ids-4215	2003-11-06 13:01:44	2003-11-06 13:01:44	192.168.1.100	192.168.1.10
ICMP Echo Req	2004	Informational	ids-4215	2003-11-06 13:01:42	2003-11-06 13:01:42	192.168.1.10	192.168.1.100
Large ICMP	2151	Informational	ids-4215	2003-11-06 13:01:42	2003-11-06 13:01:42	192.168.1.10	192.168.1.100
Large ICMP	2151	Informational	ids-4215	2003-11-06 13:01:41	2003-11-06 13:01:41	192.168.1.100	192.168.1.10
ICMP Echo Req	2004	Informational	ids-4215	2003-11-06 13:01:41	2003-11-06 13:01:41	192.168.1.10	192.168.1.100
Large ICMP	2151	Informational	ids-4215	2003-11-06 13:01:41	2003-11-06 13:01:41	192.168.1.10	192.168.1.100
Large ICMP	2151	Informational	ids-4215	2003-11-06 13:01:40	2003-11-06 13:01:40	192.168.1.100	192.168.1.10
ICMP Echo Req	2004	Informational	ids-4215	2003-11-06 13:01:40	2003-11-06 13:01:40	192.168.1.10	192.168.1.100
Large ICMP	2151	Informational	ids-4215	2003-11-06 13:01:40	2003-11-06 13:01:40	192.168.1.10	192.168.1.100
ICMP Echo Rply	2000	Informational	ids-4215	2003-11-06 13:01:39	2003-11-06 13:01:39	192.168.1.100	192.168.1.10
Large ICMP	2151	Informational	ids-4215	2003-11-06 13:01:39	2003-11-06 13:01:39	192.168.1.100	192.168.1.10
ICMP Echo Req	2004	Informational	ids-4215	2003-11-06 13:01:39	2003-11-06 13:01:39	192.168.1.10	192.168.1.100
Large ICMP	2151	Informational	ids-4215	2003-11-06 13:01:39	2003-11-06 13:01:39	192.168.1.10	192.168.1.100
TCP SYN Host Sweep	3030	Informational	ids-4215	2003-11-06 12:52:40	2003-11-06 12:52:40	192.168.1.100	202.239.129.204

Once alarms appear in the Realtime Dashboard, you can view further information about them by right-clicking any field within an alarm. The following describes the menu items that appear if you right-click an alarm:

Show Context   This option is available for some TCP and UDP-based signatures and lets you view up to 256 bytes of incoming and outgoing binary data that preceded the triggering of an alarm. This effectively lets you view the packet headers of any context-based intrusive activity.

> **NOTE**   *Signature implementation* defines where the information that triggers the signature is located within packets. *Context-based signature implementation* refers to signatures where trigger data is located within the packet header, and *content-based signature implementation* refers to signatures where trigger data is located within the packet payload.

Show Attack Details   Some signatures collect details about the attack that generated an alarm. For example, a TCP SYN Host Sweep alarm is generated when a single source attempts to establish a number of TCP connections to multiple destinations in quick succession. You can view details of each destination that a connection is attempted to by viewing attack details associated with the alarm. Figure 24.38 demonstrates viewing attack details for the TCP SYN Host Sweep alarm shown in Figure 24.37.

In Figure 24.38, you can see that the source host that generated the alarm has an IP address of 192.168.1.100 (as indicated by the Source1 row). You can also see each destination that the source host attempted to connect to, with destination IP address and destination port details provided.

NSDB Link   This provides a link to the NSDB for the selected alarm.

You can customize the operation of the Realtime Dashboard by selecting Tools ≻ Realtime Dashboard ≻ Properties from the main menu. Doing so opens the Realtime Dashboard Properties window, shown in Figure 24.39.

> **TIP**   You can also add notes to an alarm if you have the Notes column displayed in the dashboard. To add the Notes column to the dashboard, right-click any column header in the dashboard and select the Show All Columns option from the menu that appears. Locate the Notes column, and then double-click the cell for the alarm entry that you wish to add notes for. This activates a cursor in the cell, in which you can type any notes that you wish.

FIGURE 24.38   The Attack Details window

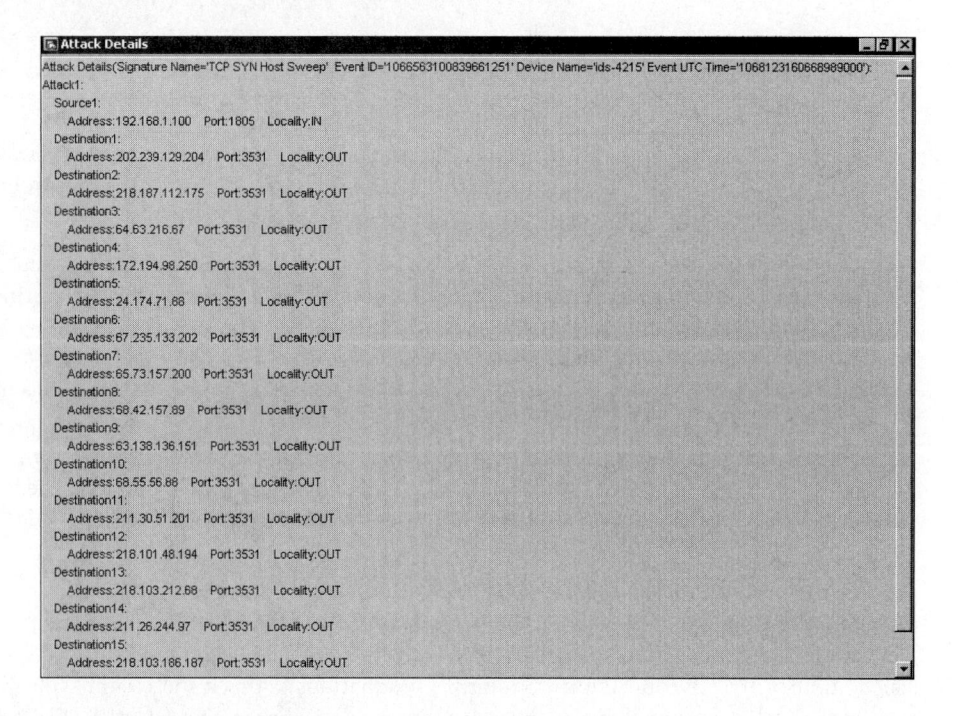

```
Attack Details(Signature Name='TCP SYN Host Sweep' Event ID='1066563100839661251' Device Name='ids-4215' Event UTC Time='1068123160668989000'):
Attack1:
    Source1:
        Address:192.168.1.100   Port:1805   Locality:IN
    Destination1:
        Address:202.239.129.204   Port:3531   Locality:OUT
    Destination2:
        Address:218.187.112.175   Port:3531   Locality:OUT
    Destination3:
        Address:64.63.216.67   Port:3531   Locality:OUT
    Destination4:
        Address:172.194.98.250   Port:3531   Locality:OUT
    Destination5:
        Address:24.174.71.88   Port:3531   Locality:OUT
    Destination6:
        Address:67.235.133.202   Port:3531   Locality:OUT
    Destination7:
        Address:65.73.157.200   Port:3531   Locality:OUT
    Destination8:
        Address:68.42.157.89   Port:3531   Locality:OUT
    Destination9:
        Address:63.138.136.151   Port:3531   Locality:OUT
    Destination10:
        Address:68.55.56.88   Port:3531   Locality:OUT
    Destination11:
        Address:211.30.51.201   Port:3531   Locality:OUT
    Destination12:
        Address:218.101.48.194   Port:3531   Locality:OUT
    Destination13:
        Address:218.103.212.68   Port:3531   Locality:OUT
    Destination14:
        Address:211.26.244.97   Port:3531   Locality:OUT
    Destination15:
        Address:218.103.186.187   Port:3531   Locality:OUT
```

In Figure 24.39, notice the following parameters:

Exclude alerts based on severity   You can exclude alerts (alarms) from being displayed in the Realtime Dashboard based on the alarm severity. By default, informational alarms are excluded; however, any combination of alarm severities can be excluded.

Exclude alarms based on sensor   You can exclude alarms from being displayed in the Realtime Dashboard based on the sensor that generated them. By default, no alarms are excluded; however, you can exclude alarms from any sensor defined as a device in the IEV.

Event retrieval   You can control the number of events that are retrieved from sensors and how often events are retrieved. By default, up to 100 events are retrieved every second.

Maximum events   You can control the maximum number of events that can be displayed in the Realtime Dashboard. By default, a maximum of 2000 events can be displayed; however, this can be modified to any value between 25 and 5000 events.

Working with Graphs

The IEV includes graphing features, which allow you to view graphs of the average number of alarms generated per minute based on each alarm severity level (informational, low, medium, and high). Graphs can either be *statistical graphs*, which are graphs generated from any historical data source, or *realtime graphs*, which are graphs generated from the `event_realtime_table` data source. We'll discuss each type of graph next.

FIGURE 24.39   The Realtime Dashboard Properties window

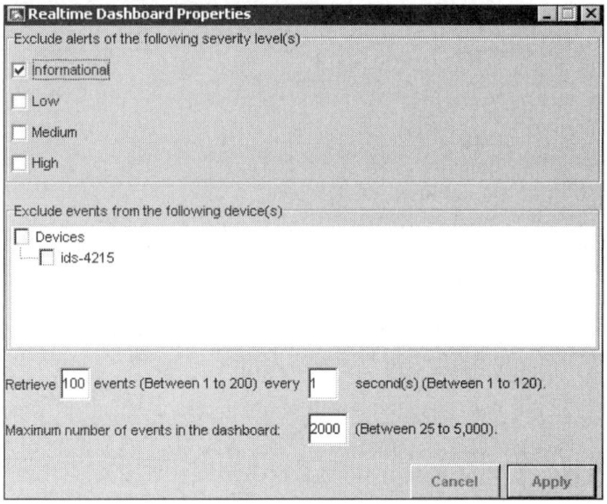

STATISTICAL GRAPHS

The IEV includes a statistical graphing feature, which lets you view graphs of the average number of alarms generated per minute for each alarm severity level from any data source. To open a statistical graph, right-click any view in the Views folder and select Statistical Graph from the menu that appears. The data source currently applied for the view will be used for the graph, which will graph the average number of alarms generated per minute for each alarm severity.

Figure 24.40 shows the Statistic Graph window, which opens when you right-click a view and select Statistical Graph.

In Figure 24.40, the graph that is displayed spans a 10-minute time period by default (13:47:00 to 13:57:00 in Figure 24.40), which can be altered by clicking the appropriate span button at the top of the window (10 Min, Hour, Day, or Week). Notice that the title bar of the Statistic Graph window indicates the data source, which is the `event_realtime_table` source in Figure 24.40.

Between 13:55:00 and 13:56:00, 24 alarms/minute were generated, and you can see that they were informational alarms since the bar is colored light blue. You can toggle the graph between a bar graph (default) and an area graph by clicking the Area or Bar button and refresh the graph by clicking the Refresh Graph button. You can also modify the start time of the graph by clicking the left and right arrow buttons, which respectively decrement or increment the start time by the current span of the graph.

FIGURE 24.40 The Statistic Graph window

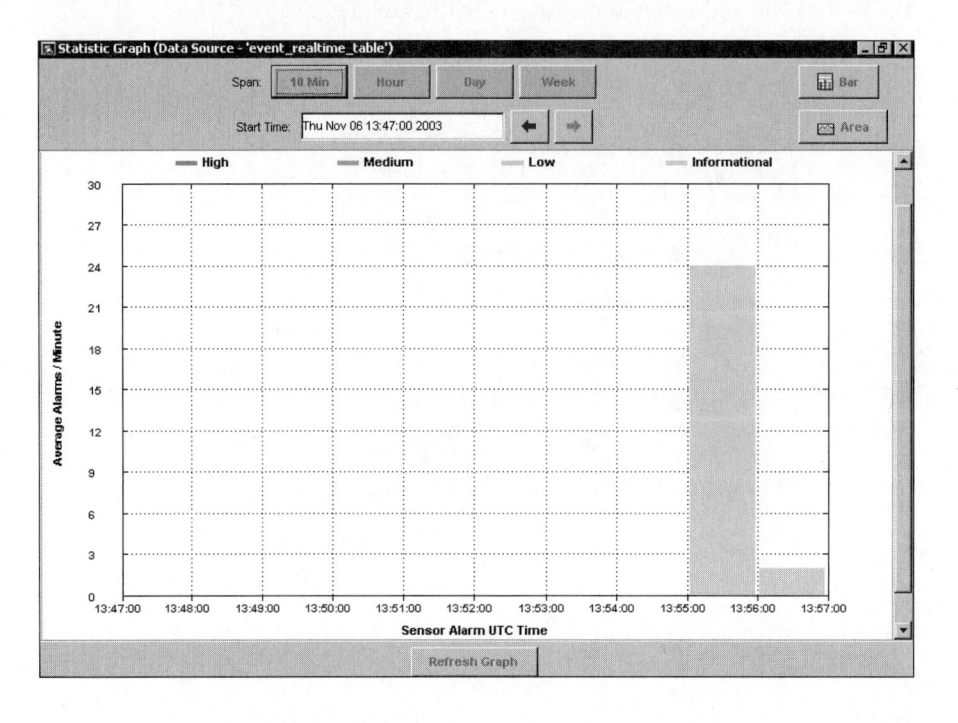

REALTIME GRAPH

As you learned in the last section, the IEV includes a statistical graphing feature, which lets you graph alarm information based on historical data. The IEV also includes a realtime graphing feature, which displays a realtime graph of the average number of alarms generated per minute for each alarm severity level.

To open the realtime graph, you can either select Tools ➢ Realtime Graph or click the Realtime Graph button on the toolbar in the main IEV window. Figure 24.41 shows the Realtime Graph window.

You can see in Figure 24.41 that the realtime graph is identical to the statistical graph—the only difference is that the realtime graph uses a data source of current alarms from when the graph is started, while the statistical graph uses any data source you specify. All features in the Realtime Graph window are identical to the Statistical Graph window (see Figure 24.40).

FIGURE 24.41 The Realtime Graph window

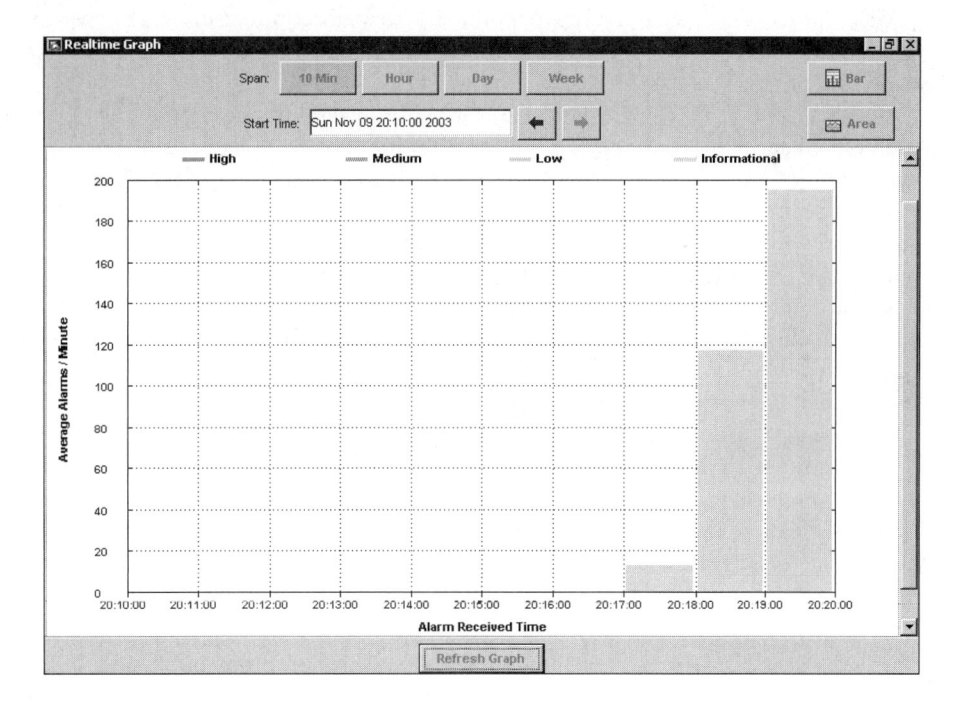

Summary

This chapter has been all about signatures, which detect intrusive activity, and alarms, which are the notifications generated about intrusive activity. Cisco Secure IDS includes a large database of powerful signatures, which are capable of detecting many sophisticated and complex attacks. Signature engines provide the intelligence and understanding of the various different types of attacks, and allow you to tune and create signatures for a wide variety of attacks. Each signature defines a number of local parameters, which control signature criteria specific to the signature engine the signature belongs to, as well as master parameters that are common to all signatures. You can configure and create signatures using either the IDM or sensor CLI.

In terms of alarm management, the Cisco IDS Event Viewer application provides an alarm management solution for small deployments of up to five sensors. When deployed, the IEV is installed on a Windows-based host and opens subscriptions to each sensor (referred to on the IEV as a device) that it's configured to monitor. These subscriptions involve the periodic polling of each sensor for alarm information that has been placed into each sensor's event store, using the RDEP protocol over HTTP or SSL-based HTTP.

The IEV consists of a single database that houses several physical tables referred to as data sources. A data source is a single table of alarm information that relates either to current and new alarm information (the `event_realtime_table` data source) or to historical alarm information that has been archived. You can also create data sources by importing alarm information contained within IP log files captured from sensors. From each data source, the IEV displays the alarm information contained within using views, which are a set of criteria that determine how alarm information is presented and optionally specify a filter that excludes a number of alarms. Each view creates a number of logical or virtual tables from a data source—a parent table called the Alarm Aggregation table is created, which aggregates alarm information and presents it in a summarized format. From the Alarm Aggregation table, you can drill down to more specific alarm information using the Expanded Details Dialog, Drilldown Dialog, and Alarm Information Dialog tables. The IEV also includes a Realtime Dashboard, which lets you view alarms as they are generated in real time. The Realtime Dashboard opens a continuously updated hook into the `event_realtime_table` data source, ensuring that any new alarms can be immediately detected without having to manually update a specific view.

You can also generate graphs based on the alarms associated with a specific view and data source. All graphs on the IEV represent the alarms generated per minute for each severity level of alarm. Statistical graphs are generated from archived data sources, whereas realtime graphs are generated from the `event_realtime_table` data source.

Exam Essentials

Know what signatures are.   A signature is a set of rules that define some specific form of attack or intrusive activity.

Understand signature engines.   Cisco Secure IDS includes a number of signature engines, each of which detects specific types of attacks. For example, the ATOMIC family of signature engines detects attacks implemented in single packets.

Understand signature parameters.   Each signature includes parameters, which can be defined by a name and value. Parameters can be either master parameters, which specify common signature parameters, or local parameters, which specify signature parameters specific to the signature engine the signature belongs to.

Know how to configure signatures.   Signatures can be configured using the IDM or via the CLI by accessing the virtual sensor service configuration mode. You can also use the IDS Management Center to create signatures, which is discussed in Chapter 25, "Enterprise Cisco Secure IDS Management."

Be able to determine and select the appropriate signature engine for custom signatures.   When you're creating custom signatures, you must be able to determine the signature engine that you'll base the signature on. This is determined by a number of criteria, including the protocol (such as TCP or UDP), the target system (such as host or network), the destination ports, and the type of attack.

Understand the system requirements for running the IEV.   The IEV must be installed on a separate host from the sensor, and it requires a minimum hardware specification of Pentium III 800MHz CPU, 256MB memory, and 500MB free disk space. The IEV can only be installed on Windows NT 4 SP6, Windows 2000 SP2 or higher, and Windows XP SP1 or higher.

Understand how to obtain the IEV application.   The IEV is available for download from the Cisco website at `http://www.cisco.com/cgi-bin/tablebuild.pl/ids-ev`.

Know how to add sensors to the IEV.   The IEV represents sensors as devices. To add a device to the IEV, you must know the IP address, sensor name, web port, and appropriate user credentials. You can also specify a start date and time if you wish to obtain historical alarms from a sensor, and you can exclude alarms from the sensor based on severity level.

Understand filters.   A filter filters alarm information based on a number of criteria, including by severity, by source address, by destination address, by signature name, by sensor name, by date/time, and by status. You can apply one or more of these criteria, allowing you to create powerful and fully customized filters.

Understand views.   A view defines how alarm information is organized and presented in the IEV. Every view builds an Alarm Aggregation table, which provides a summary of alarm information within the view grouped on a number of different criteria such as signature name, sensor name, source address, and destination address. You can specify parameters such as the grouping style for the Alarm Aggregation table, initial columns to include on the Alarm Aggregation tables and alarm information dialog tables, the secondary sort order column on the Alarm Aggregation table, and the default data source that the view applies to. A view can optionally include a filter, which restricts the alarms that the view applies to.

Understand how you can view alarm information in IEV. The IEV lets you view historical alarm information via the Alarm Information Dialog table. You can also view alarm information in real time using the Realtime Dashboard. You can view historical and realtime alarm statistics using graphs, and you can view IP log files using the network analyzer Ethereal.

Understand data sources. A data source is basically a table of alarms. There are two types of data sources: a single realtime data source called the `event_realtime_table`, which contains recent alarms and receives new alarms; and archived data sources, which are tables of historical alarms that are typically generated on a periodic basis (by default, every 24 hours). Each data source is used to generate logical tables of alarm information, which are built from the views that you configure.

Know how to configure IEV application settings and preferences. Application settings and preferences allow you to configure data refresh settings, data archival settings, the location of helper applications (such as web browser, Ethereal, and NSDB), and how information in the Alarm Aggregation table is refreshed if modifications are made to other child tables.

Know how to administer the IEV database. The IEV database consists of multiple data sources, each of which is a table of alarm information. You can import alarm information from IP log files generated by sensors creating a new custom data source, as well as export existing data sources to an external file. You can also delete data sources as required.

Chapter 25

Enterprise Cisco Secure IDS Management

CISCO SECURE INTRUSION DETECTION SYSTEM EXAM TOPICS COVERED IN THIS CHAPTER:

- ✓ Features and key concepts of the IDS MC
- ✓ Installing the IDS MC
- ✓ Generating, approving, and deploying sensor configuration files
- ✓ Administering the IDS MC Server
- ✓ Using the IDS MC to set up sensors
- ✓ Using the IDS MC to configure sensor communication properties
- ✓ Using the IDS MC to configure sensor logging properties

CiscoWorks VMS is an enterprise-securing management solution that provides management and monitoring of Cisco Secure IDS sensors. In previous chapters, you learned how the IDM and IEV provide management and monitoring for small Cisco Secure IDS sensor deployments. In this chapter, you'll learn about CiscoWorks VMS, which provides the ability to manage and monitor up to 300 Cisco Secure IDS sensors. CiscoWorks VMS can also manage other Cisco security devices, such as Cisco PIX firewalls and Cisco VPN routers, providing a complete security management solution.

In this chapter, you'll learn about the features of CiscoWorks VMS 2.2, learn how to install the various components of CiscoWorks VMS 2.2, and learn how to perform enterprise IDS management using the IDS management center.

Introduction to CiscoWorks VMS

CiscoWorks VMS provides the ability to manage many different Cisco security devices and as such is a reasonably complex product that includes many different components. Understanding the various components of CiscoWorks VMS, their requirements, and how they interoperate is important if you're planning to deploy CiscoWorks VMS. Once you have an understanding of the CiscoWorks VMS components that you need to deploy, you next need to determine whether your current server equipment meets the hardware and software requirements of those components. In this section, you'll learn about the various CiscoWorks VMS components, the system requirements for CiscoWorks VMS, and the architecture of the IDS management center that provides enterprise IDS sensor management.

CiscoWorks VMS Components

CiscoWorks VMS isn't just a single application; it's a package of applications that combine to provide enterprise security management and monitoring. The various CiscoWorks VMS applications can be installed onto a single physical server or can be distributed across multiple physical servers for higher scalability. The following components make up the CiscoWorks VMS package:

Common Services Common Services provides common software and services for the various VMS components and is a base component required to support all other components. In a distributed installation, the Common Services component must be installed on all CiscoWorks VMS servers before any other components. CiscoWorks Common Services also includes the following optional subcomponents:

CiscoView CiscoView provides a graphical device management tool for Cisco network and security devices. CiscoView version 5.5 is included with CiscoWorks VMS 2.2.

Integration Utility The Integration Utility provides support for third-party network management systems (NMS), such as HP OpenView. Version 1.5 of the Integration Utility is included with CiscoWorks VMS 2.2.

Resource Manager Essentials (RME) This provides a repository of network inventory information, enabling centralized storage and distribution of device configurations, software images, and software updates. RME also provides asset tracking and change management features. RME Version 3.5 is included with CiscoWorks VMS 2.2.

Auto Update Server (AUS) Auto Update Server version 1.1 is included with CiscoWorks VMS 2.2. It lets you automatically update and manage configurations for Cisco IOS and Cisco PIX devices.

Management Center for Firewalls This enables you to centrally manage and configure Cisco PIX firewalls and Cisco Catalyst 6000/6500 Firewall Services Modules (FWSMs). Version 1.3 is included with CiscoWorks VMS 2.2.

Management Center for VPN Routers This enables you to centrally manage and configure Cisco VPN routers, Cisco Catalyst 6000/6500 VPN Services Modules, and Cisco IOS firewalls. Version 1.2 is included with CiscoWorks VMS 2.2.

Management Center for IDS Sensors (IDS MC) The Management Center for IDS Sensors enables you to centrally manage and configure Cisco Secure IDS sensors, including the 4200 series sensors and Catalyst 6000/6500 IDS modules. Version 1.2 is included with CiscoWorks VMS 2.2. The IDS MC uses the PostOffice protocol to manage version 3.*x* sensors and Secure Shell (SSH) to manage version 4.*x* sensors.

Management Center for Cisco Security Agents This enables you to centrally manage and configure Cisco Security Agents that provide host-based intrusion protection for servers and desktops. Version 4.0 is included with CiscoWorks VMS 2.2.

Monitoring Center for Security (Security Monitor) The Monitoring Center for Security provides centralized monitoring, collection, and correlation of Cisco PIX firewall logs, network-based IDS events, and host-based IDS events. Version 1.2 is included with CiscoWorks VMS 2.2. The Security Monitor uses the PostOffice protocol to monitor version 3.*x* sensors and Remote Desktop Exchange Protocol (RDEP, over HTTP or HTTPS) to monitor version 4.*x* sensors.

VPN Monitor This provides centralized monitoring of LAN-to-LAN and remote access IPSec-based VPNs. Version 1.2.1 is included with CiscoWorks VMS 2.2.

To scale CiscoWorks VMS for larger deployments, it's recommended that you distribute the various components across multiple physical servers.

For more information on scaling CiscoWorks VMS deployments, refer to the *CiscoWorks VMS Solution Deployment Guide*, **which is located at** www.cisco.com/en/US/products/sw/cscowork/ps2330/prod_white_papers_list.html.

CiscoWorks VMS System Requirements

CiscoWorks VMS is a client/server application and hence has different server system requirements and client system requirements. Next, we'll discuss the system requirements for the client and server components of CiscoWorks VMS.

CiscoWorks VMS Server System Requirements

The system requirements for a CiscoWorks VMS Server depend on the components installed and the operating system used (Windows 2000 or Solaris 2.8). Table 25.1 lists the system requirements for a CiscoWorks VMS 2.2 server that only has Common Services installed:

> **NOTE** The requirements listed in Table 25.1 are suitable for small CiscoWorks VMS installations. For larger CiscoWorks VMS installations, you may require higher specification hardware components.

TABLE 25.1 CiscoWorks VMS 2.2 Server System Requirements

Component	Minimum Requirements
Hardware	Pentium III 1GHz CPU (Windows)
	Sun UltraSPARC 60MP with 440MHz CPU or higher (Solaris)
	Sun UltraSPARC III (Solaris)
	CD-ROM
	100Mbps network interface
Operating system	One of the following:
	Windows 2000 Professional, Server or Advanced Server SP3
	Sun Solaris 2.8 with the following patches:
	108528-13
	108827-15
	108528-13
	108827-15

TABLE 25.1 CiscoWorks VMS 2.2 Server System Requirements *(continued)*

Component	Minimum Requirements
Memory	1GB physical memory
	2GB virtual memory
Hard disk	9GB free disk space
Helper applications	Sun Java Plug-in 1.3.1-b24
	Microsoft ODBC Driver Manager 3.510 or later (Windows)

All VMS components can be installed on a Windows-based server; however, it's important to note that only the following components can be installed on a Solaris-based server:

- CiscoWorks Common Services
- Management Center for IDS Sensors
- Monitoring Center for Security
- Auto Update Server

When you're using Windows-based servers, note also that the following configurations aren't supported by CiscoWorks VMS:

- Installation on a primary or backup domain controller
- Installation on a server running Terminal Services
- Installation on a FAT file system (you must use NTFS)

This chapter focuses on the IDS MC and Security Monitor, which have their own system requirements if you choose to install these components on a CiscoWorks VMS server. Table 25.2 lists the system requirements for the IDS MC and Security Monitor.

TABLE 25.2 CiscoWorks VMS 2.2 IDS MC and Security Monitor System Requirements

Component	Minimum Requirements
Hardware	Pentium 1GHz CPU (Windows)
	Sun UltraSPARC 60MP with 440MHz CPU or higher (Solaris)
	Sun UltraSPARC III (Solaris)
	CD-ROM

TABLE 25.2 CiscoWorks VMS 2.2 IDS MC and Security Monitor System Requirements *(continued)*

Component	Minimum Requirements
	100Mbps network interface
Operating system	One of the following:
	Windows 2000 Professional, Server or Advanced Server SP3
	Sun Solaris 2.8 with the following patches:
	108528-13
	108827-15
	108528-13
	108827-15
Memory	1GB physical memory
	2GB virtual memory
Hard disk	12GB free disk space
Helper applications	Sun Java Plug-in 1.3.1-b24
	Microsoft ODBC Driver Manager 3.510 or later (Windows)

[1]When you're installing Windows 2000, only the US English version of Windows 2000 is supported. The US English regional setting is also the only regional setting supported.

If you compare Table 25.1 and Table 25.2, you can see that the only real difference is that the IDS MC and Security Monitor components require higher free disk space (12GB) compared to the Common Services components (9GB). All other system requirements are identical to the base CiscoWorks Common Services requirements.

> If you're installing a demo copy of CiscoWorks VMS on Windows 2000, make sure that you're using a retail copy. I have found that using a Microsoft Select copy of Windows 2000 caused licensing problems.

CiscoWorks VMS Client System Requirements

All CiscoWorks VMS server applications provide a web-based interface, which means that the only client requirement is a supported web browser with appropriate hardware and operating system specifications. Table 25.3 lists the client system requirements.

TABLE 25.3 CiscoWorks VMS 2.2 Client System Requirements

Component	Minimum Requirements
Hardware	Pentium 300MHz CPU or higher (Windows)
	Solaris SPARCstation or Ultra 10 with 333MHz CPU (Solaris)
Operating system	One of the following:
	Windows 2000 Professional or Server SP3
	Windows XP SP1
	Sun Solaris 2.8
Memory	256MB
Hard disk	400MB virtual memory (Windows)
	512MB swap space (Solaris)
Web browser	One of the following:
	Internet Explorer 6.0 SP1 with Microsoft Virtual Machine
	Netscape Navigator 4.79 (Windows)[1]
	Netscape Navigator 4.76 (Solaris)[1]
	The web browser must also have the following enabled:
	JavaScript
	Java
	Cookies

[1] The Firewall MC and Router MC are supported only on Internet Explorer 6.0; they aren't supported on Netscape Navigator.

Installing CiscoWorks VMS

Once you've verified that all system requirements are met, you can begin installation of CiscoWorks VMS. In this chapter, you'll learn how to install CiscoWorks VMS on a Windows 2000 platform to perform enterprise IDS management and monitoring tasks. This requires the following installation steps:

1. Install CiscoWorks Common Services.
2. Install the IDS Management Center (IDS MC) and Security Monitoring Center (Security Monitor).
3. Start the CiscoWorks Desktop.
4. Add users.
5. License CiscoWorks VMS components.

Before you can begin CiscoWorks installation, you must ensure that you have the appropriate CiscoWorks VMS installation CD-ROM. If you have a valid CCO login, you can download a 90-day evaluation copy from www.cisco.com/cgi-bin/Software/FormManager/formgenerator.pl?pid=10180&fid=10280. Note that you must supply valid CCO credentials to access this URL.

Installing CiscoWorks Common Services

The CiscoWorks Common Services provide low-level CiscoWorks component functionality and must be installed before any other component on any servers that are to have CiscoWorks VMS components installed.

To begin installation, insert the CiscoWorks VMS CD-ROM that is provided when you purchase CiscoWorks VMS. A splash screen should automatically start, which provides the option to initiate installation of CiscoWorks VMS. If the splash screen doesn't automatically start (for example, because the autorun feature of your CD-ROM is disabled), browse to the root directory of the CD-ROM, where an executable file called AUTORUN.EXE is located.

To begin the CiscoWorks setup program, click the Install button. This will start CiscoWorks setup; you can also start it by executing the SETUP.EXE application located in the root directory of the CiscoWorks CD-ROM.

The first screen that is displayed is the VMS Management and Monitoring Centers 2.2 screen, which lets you select which CiscoWorks VMS components you wish to install. Figure 25.1 shows this screen.

By default, all components are selected. If you're installing the first CiscoWorks components on the local server, you must first install the Common Services component by itself with no other components selected, as shown in Figure 25.1. Once the Common Services component is installed, you can then install management centers as required.

FIGURE 25.1 Selecting components to install

After you select the Common Services component and click the Next button, the Ready To Install The Program screen appears. Here, you're prompted to confirm that you wish to begin installation of the selected components. Clicking the Install button begins the installation process.

Now the setup program for Common Services starts. The first screen displayed is a Welcome screen, which provides initial information about the installation. Click the Next button, and a Software License Agreement screen will be displayed; you must accept the license by clicking the Yes button. At this point, the setup program checks to ensure that DNS is properly configured. The setup program attempts to resolve the local host name using DNS; if this fails, then the DNS requirements for installation have not been met and a warning is displayed, advising you of this.

Once the DNS check is complete, the Setup Type screen is displayed. It lets you choose the installation type, as shown in Figure 25.2.

You'll notice that there are three setup types:

Express Installation This installs all CiscoWorks Common Services components in the default location with default settings.

Typical Installation This lets you select CiscoWorks Common Services components and specify the installation path. This is the default selection and is recommended for most installations.

Custom Installation This allows you to select CiscoWorks Common Services components, customize component settings, and specify the installation path.

Assuming that you select Typical Installation, when you click the Next button the Choose Destination Folder screen is displayed, as shown in Figure 25.3. Here, you can specify the folder in which CiscoWorks VMS should be installed. By default, `C:\Program Files\CSCOpx` is selected as the destination folder.

Select the appropriate destination folder and click the Next button, and the Select Components screen is displayed. Here, you select the Common Services components that you wish to install. Figure 25.4 shows the Select Components screen.

FIGURE 25.2 The Setup Type screen

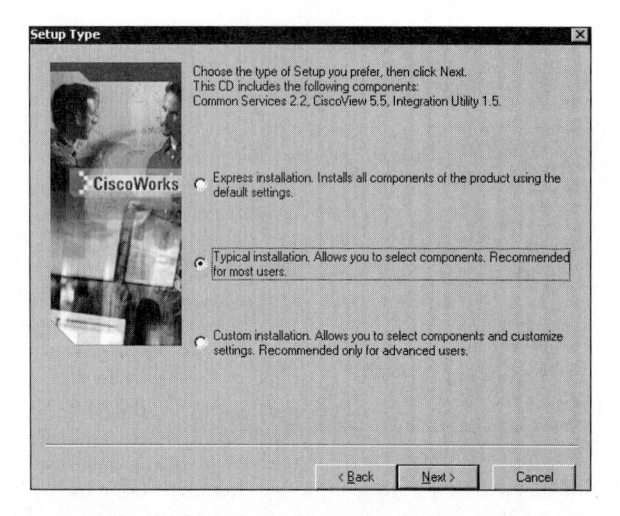

FIGURE 25.3 The Choose Destination Folder screen

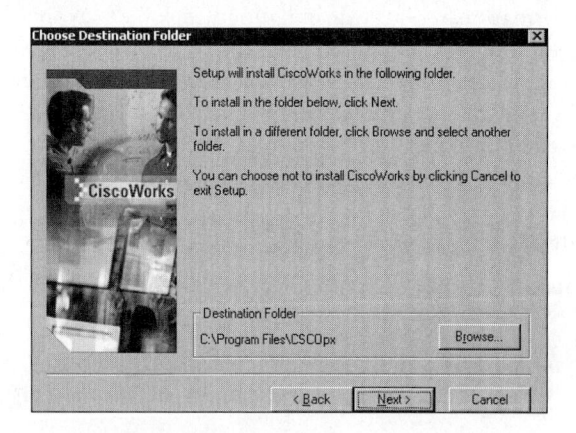

In Figure 25.4, all components have been selected:

- CiscoWorks Common Services 2.2 (CWCS)
- CiscoView 5.5
- Integration Utility 1.5

> **NOTE** Notice that you must install the CiscoWorks Common Services component if you wish to install CiscoView 5.5.

FIGURE 25.4 The Select Components screen

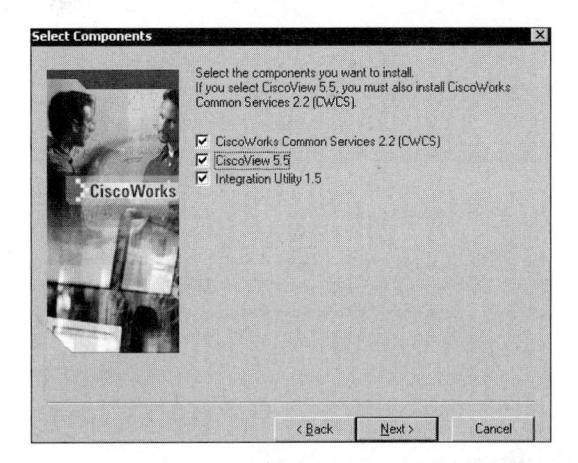

After you select the appropriate components and click the Next button, the setup program verifies that the current local system specifications meet the system requirements (such as memory and disk space) and displays a warning if any requirements aren't met. Assuming the local system specifications are sufficient, the Change Admin Password screen is displayed next. This screen lets you configure the administrative password used by CiscoWorks VMS.

The password specified must be at least five characters long and must begin with an alphabetic character. Configure and verify an appropriate password and click Next, and the Change Casuser Password screen is displayed, as shown in Figure 25.5. The `casuser` account is a special account that is created in the local Windows 2000 operating system user database; it's used to start the various services that CiscoWorks VMS installs.

FIGURE 25.5 The Change Casuser Password screen

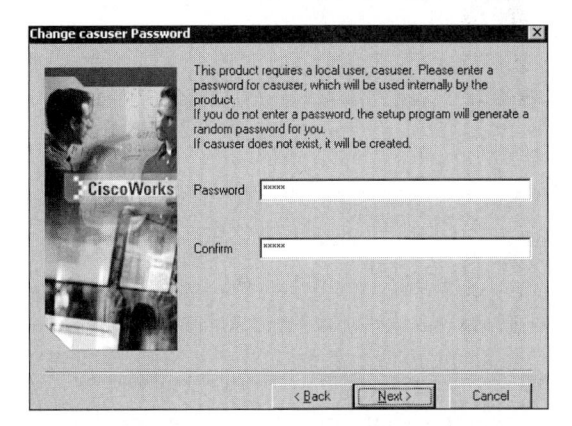

> **NOTE:** A group called casusers is also created in the local user database that contains the casuser account.

Configure and confirm an appropriate password, and click the Next button, and a final Summary screen is displayed that lists the various setup options you've configured. Figure 25.6 shows the Summary screen.

You can click the Show Details button to display all setup options, such as passwords and the various settings for each component. Clicking the Next button starts the installation process; the appropriate components are copied and installed to the local system.

After installation is complete, you'll be prompted to reboot the system. After reboot, the CiscoWorks Common Services components will be ready to use.

FIGURE 25.6 The Summary screen

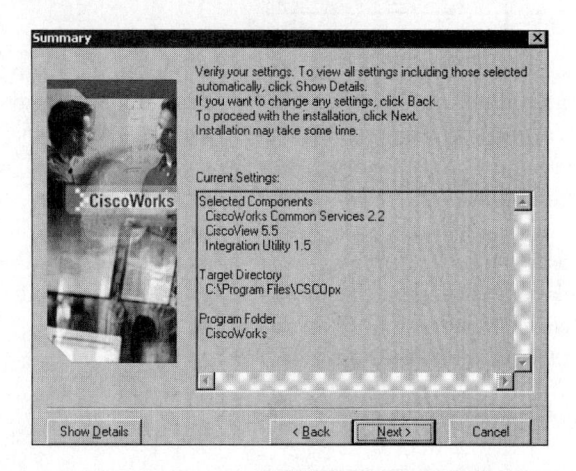

Installing the IDS Management Center and Security Monitoring Center

After the CiscoWorks Common Services are installed, you can next install the IDS Management Center and Security Monitoring Center. To begin the installation process, insert the CiscoWorks VMS CD-ROM and wait for the AUTORUN.EXE program to run, or execute the AUTORUN.EXE or SETUP.EXE program from the root directory of the CD-ROM. If you run the AUTORUN.EXE application, click the Install button to begin the main CiscoWorks VMS setup application.

When the main CiscoWorks VMS setup application starts, the VMS Management and Monitoring Centers 2.2 screen is displayed. To install the IDS Management Center and Security Monitoring Center, ensure that the appropriate option is selected, and then click the Next button to proceed. Figure 25.7 demonstrates selecting the correct option for installing the IDS MC and Security Monitor.

FIGURE 25.7 Selecting the IDS MC and Security Monitor components for installation

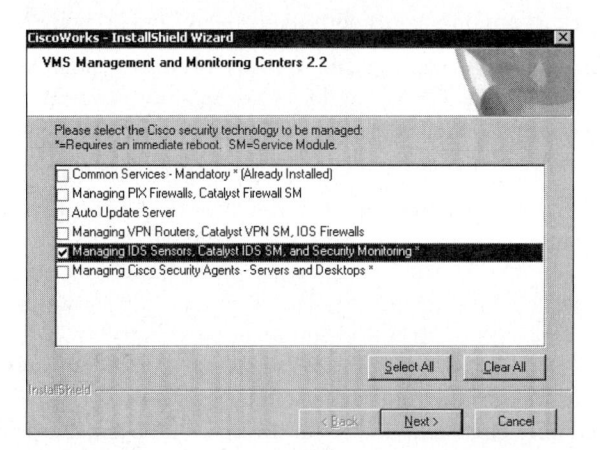

In Figure 25.7, you can see that the option Managing IDS Sensors, Catalyst IDS SM, And Security Monitoring is selected. Notice that the screen indicates that the mandatory Common Services are installed, meaning you can proceed with the installation of other components. Click the Next button, and the Ready To Install The Program screen will appear; it prompts you to confirm that you wish to proceed with the installation options you've selected. Click the Install button on this screen to start the setup program(s) for the component(s) you selected.

Assuming you've selected to install only the IDS MC and Security Monitor, the setup program for these components starts up, with a Welcome screen initially displayed. Click the Next button to proceed to the Software License Agreement screen, which you must accept by clicking the Yes button to continue. After accepting the Software License Agreement, you're next presented with the Setup Type screen, which is shown in Figure 25.8.

FIGURE 25.8 The Setup Type screen

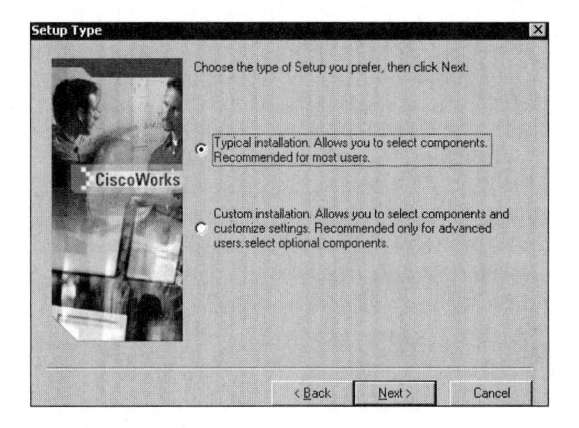

Notice that you can select one of two setup types:

Typical Installation   Selecting this option installs both the IDS MC and Security Monitor.

Custom Installation   Selecting this option lets you choose to install either the IDS MC by itself, the Security Monitor by itself, or both the IDS MC and Security Monitor. You can also modify settings such as the IDS MC/Security Monitor database location and password, PostOffice settings (required to support Cisco Secure 3.*x* sensors), and the UDP port used by CiscoWorks.

Assuming that you select the typical installation, after you click the Next button the setup program verifies that your system meets the requirements for the IDS MC and Security Monitor (see Table 25.2). Assuming that your system meets the requirements, the Summary screen is displayed; it shows the settings that will be used for installation. Figure 25.9 shows this screen.

In Figure 25.9, you can see that both the IDS MC and Security Monitor are to be installed to `C:\Program Files\CSCOpx`. If you wish to install only the IDS MC or the Security Monitor by itself, you must select the custom installation on the Setup Type screen.

Click the Next button, and the Select Database Location screen is displayed; it lets you choose where the IDS database will be installed. By default, this is `C:\Program Files\CSCOpx\MDC\Sybase\DB\IDS`.

Once you've selected an appropriate database location and clicked the Next button, the Select Database Password screen is displayed, where you configure the password for accessing the IDS database. Configure an appropriate database password, and the Select CiscoWorks Syslog Port screen is displayed; it prompts you to specify the UDP port on which the standard CiscoWorks Syslog server (installed with Common Services) should run. This is because the Security Monitor includes its own Syslog server, which runs on UDP port 514 and therefore clashes with the standard CiscoWorks Syslog server. By default, the standard CiscoWorks Syslog server is configured to operate on UDP port 52514, as shown in Figure 25.10.

FIGURE 25.9   The Summary screen

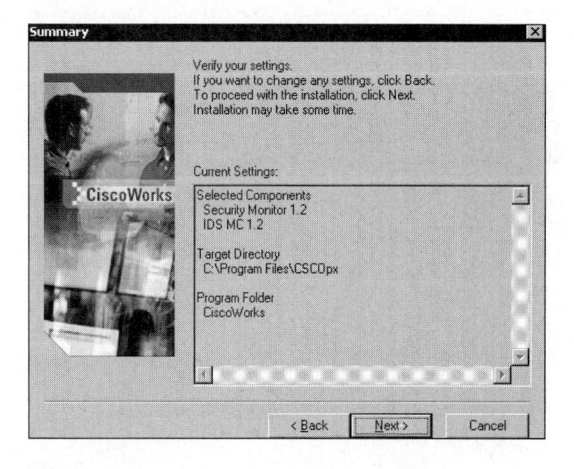

FIGURE 25.10 The Select CiscoWorks Syslog Port screen

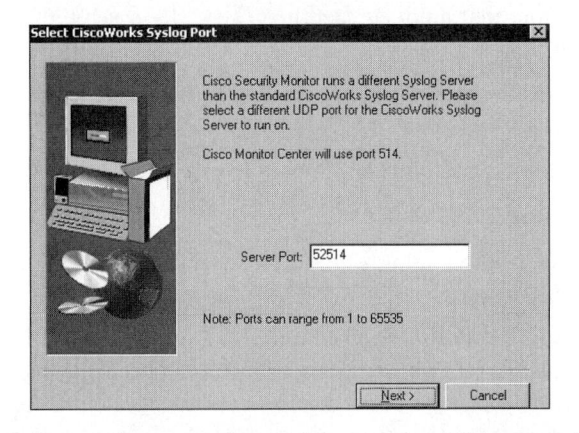

After you've configured the port to be used for the standard CiscoWorks Syslog server, the Configure Communication Properties screen is displayed, which is used to configure PostOffice communication parameters. The PostOffice protocol is a proprietary protocol used by Cisco Secure IDS 3.*x* sensors to communicate configuration information and alarm information to Director platforms (*Director* is the termed used for sensor management platforms prior to Cisco Secure IDS 4.x). If you specify PostOffice communication parameters, the CiscoWorks VMS server can manage and monitor older Cisco Secure IDS 3.*x* sensors. Figure 25.11 shows the Configure Communication Properties screen.

FIGURE 25.11 The Configure Communication Properties screen

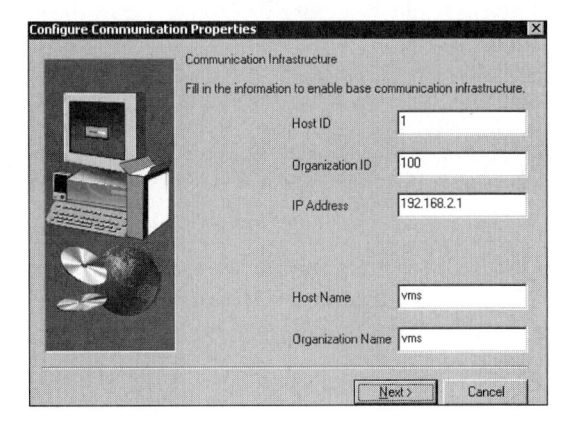

Notice the following parameters:

Host ID This is a numeric identifier that uniquely identifies the VMS server within a specific organization.

Organization ID This is a numeric identifier that uniquely identifies the organization to which the VMS server belongs.

IP Address This is the local IP address used for PostOffice communications to other devices.

Host Name This is the local host name.

Organization Name This is the descriptive name for the organization to which the VMS server belongs.

After you've specified the appropriate PostOffice communication parameters and clicked the Next button, the information-collecting phase of setup is complete and file copying begins. Once installation is complete, the Setup Complete screen is displayed. Click Finish to close the setup program. At this point, you must restart the server to complete the IDS MC and Security Monitor installation.

Starting the CiscoWorks Desktop

When CiscoWorks VMS installation is complete, you're ready to begin using CiscoWorks VMS. All CiscoWorks VMS interaction is web-based, meaning that you only need a supported browser to use all CiscoWorks VMS components. The CiscoWorks Desktop provides a common interface that is used for CiscoWorks VMS and gives you the ability to start any CiscoWorks VMS component that you wish to use.

To start the CiscoWorks Desktop, you must connect to the CiscoWorks web server, which by default listens on TCP port 1741 rather than TCP port 80. You can start the CiscoWorks Desktop using either of the following methods:

> **TIP** You can modify the web server port on Windows by executing the `changeport.exe` command-line utility, which is located in the `C:\Program Files\CSCOpx\lib\web` directory.

On the CiscoWorks VMS server On the CiscoWorks VMS server itself, you can start the CiscoWorks Desktop by selecting Start ➤ Programs ➤ CiscoWorks ➤ CiscoWorks. Doing so opens the local browser and opens the URL `http://vms-hostname:`1741.

On a remote browser You can connect via a remote browser to the CiscoWorks Desktop by opening the URL `http://vms-ip-address:`1741. If you've enabled SSL (recommended), you can connect using the URL `https://vms-ip-address:`1742 (notice that the TCP port used for SSL is 1742 instead of 1741 for normal web-based access).

> **NOTE** SSL is disabled by default, but it's recommended to ensure that remote management communications are secured. To enable the use of SSL, select Server Configuration ➢ Administration ➢ Security Management ➢ Enable/Disable SSL from the navigation tree on the CiscoWorks Desktop. This opens a page that lets you enable/disable SSL.

Figure 25.12 demonstrates connecting to the CiscoWorks Desktop via a remote web browser. Notice the Login Manager frame on the left, which prompts you for the appropriate credentials to gain access to the CiscoWorks Desktop. To gain access, specify the administration credentials that you configured during CiscoWorks Common Services installation and then click the Connect button. Figure 25.13 shows the CiscoWorks Desktop after successful authentication.

Notice that the CiscoWorks Desktop comprises several different components:

Logout and Help buttons The Logout button logs out the current logged-in administrator, and the Help button opens online help in a separate browser window. The online help provides procedural and conceptual information about CiscoWorks VMS, as well as an index, search engine, and glossary of CiscoWorks terms. Figure 25.14 demonstrates the online help feature included with CiscoWorks VMS.

FIGURE 25.12 Accessing the CiscoWorks Desktop

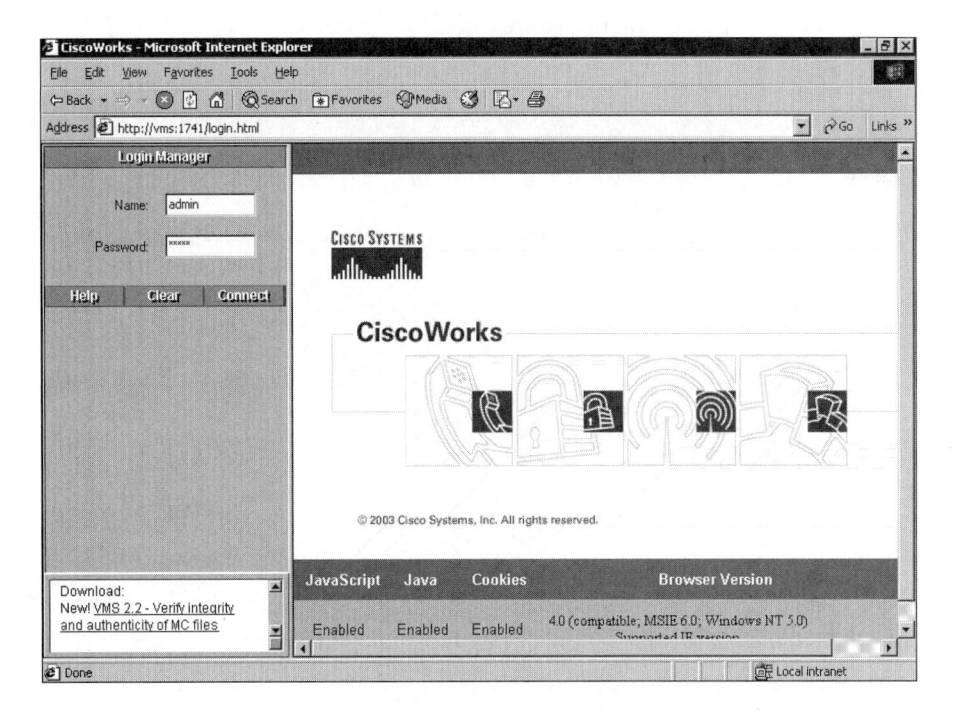

Navigation tree This is located on the left-hand frame, and provides a means to navigate between the various CiscoWorks VMS components. The navigation tree consists of five drawers (the Home drawer is open in Figure 25.13):

Home This is the default drawer, providing links to additional resources on CCO and a folder called My Shortcuts for storing frequently performed tasks. You can create a shortcut by dragging any item within the Navigation Tree to the Home drawer.

Server Configuration This drawer provides tools for configuring, administering, and diagnosing CiscoWorks VMS.

Management Connection This drawer provides applications for adding external links to CiscoWorks and also provides a collection of links to commonly used tools on CCO.

Device Manager This drawer lets you start applications used for device management, such as CiscoView.

VPN/Security Management Solution This drawer provides applications and tools for configuring and managing the management centers included in CiscoWorks VMS. This drawer is available only if one or more management centers (such as IDS MC) is installed on the local server.

FIGURE 25.13 CiscoWorks VMS online help

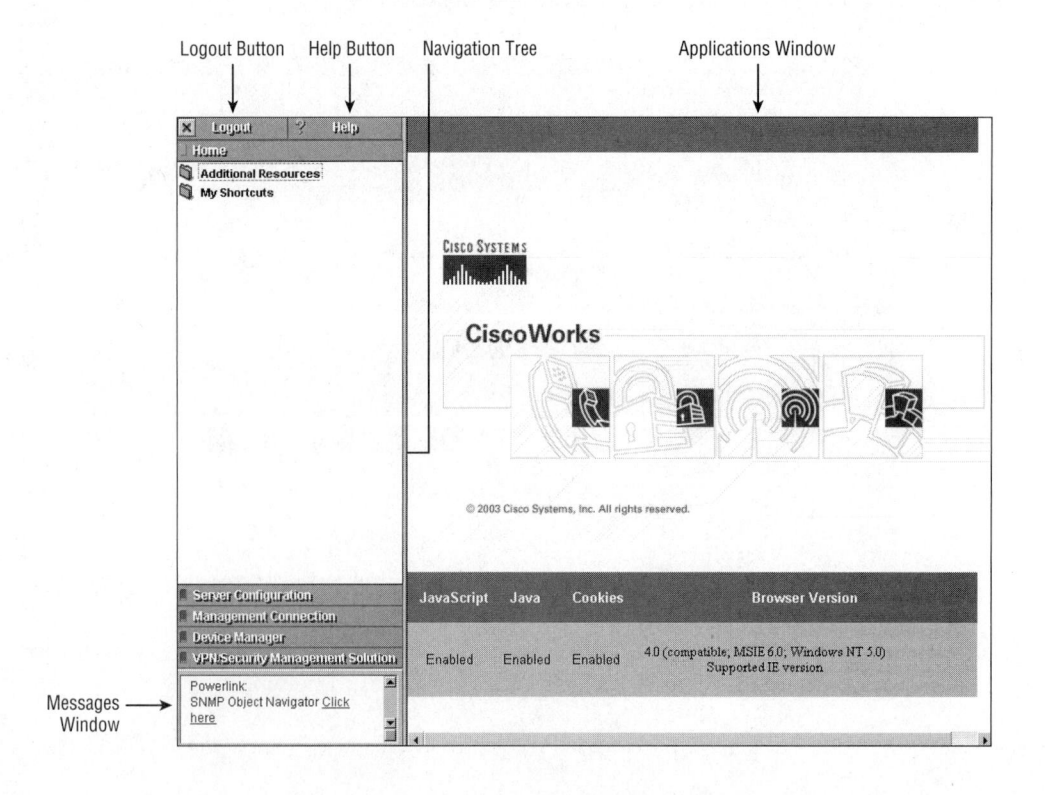

Applications window This is the right-hand frame, which displays the pages and information associated with the current feature you're working with in the navigation tree.

Messages window This is located at the bottom of the left-hand frame below the navigation tree. It provides a rolling Tips of the Day ticker-style window. Messages displayed are automatically updated every 24 hours from the `Cisco.com` website.

> **TIP** You can customize the content of the messages window by modifying the file `UserMessageFile`, which is located in `C:\Program Files\CSCOpx\lib\classpath\com\cisco`.

FIGURE 25.14 The CiscoWorks Desktop after successful authentication

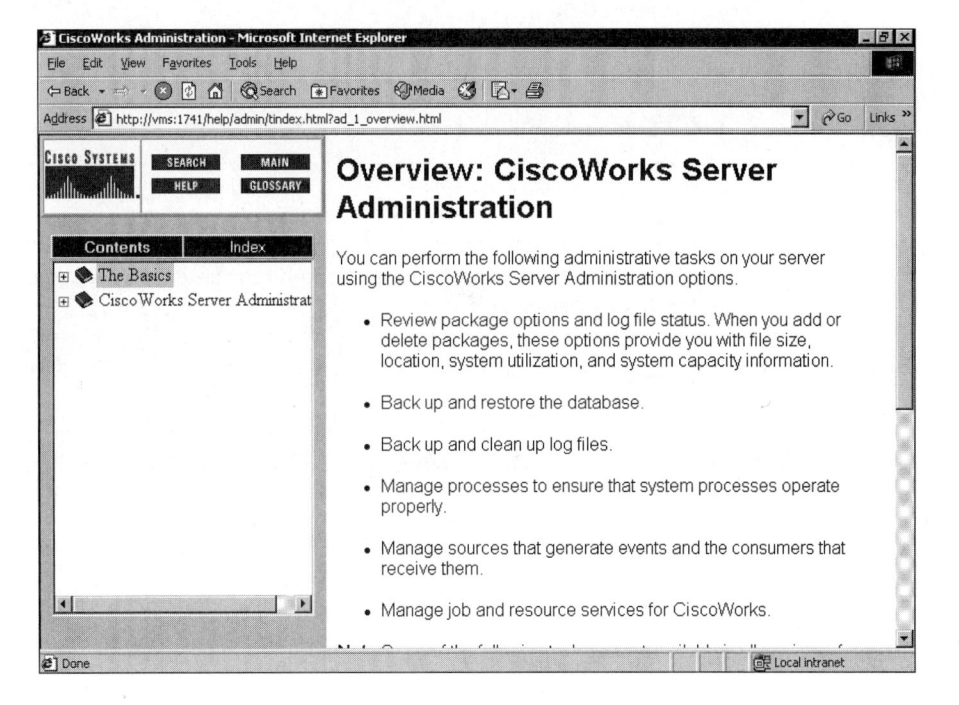

Adding Users

CiscoWorks VMS provides several different *security levels*, which are essentially roles or sets of privileges that can be assigned to user accounts used to administer and manage CiscoWorks VMS. Table 25.4 lists each of the security levels on CiscoWorks VMS.

TABLE 25.4 CiscoWorks VMS Security Levels

Security Level	Role
0	Help Desk
1	Approver
2	Network Operator
4	Network Administrator
8	System Administrator
16	Export Data
32	Developer
64	Partition Administrator

> **NOTE** The Export Data, Developer, and Partition Administrator roles are available only for third-party developers.

In this chapter and the next, you'll learn what tasks each of the roles in Table 25.4 can perform for the various components of CiscoWorks VMS.

To add a new user to CiscoWorks, select Server Configuration ➢ Setup ➢ Security ➢ Add Users from the CiscoWorks Desktop. Doing so opens the Add User page, shown in Figure 25.15, where you can add a new user.

> **NOTE** You can configure fallback authentication options in CiscoWorks VMS, where local operating system credentials can be used in the event that you forget the appropriate logon credentials to access CiscoWorks.

Licensing CiscoWorks VMS Components

When you install CiscoWorks VMS, all components are installed with a 90-day evaluation license by default. To ensure that you can still use CiscoWorks VMS after the 90-day evaluation period expires, you must obtain a *production license* from Cisco, which fully licenses your CiscoWorks VMS product for ongoing use. To obtain a production license, you must have the *Product Authorization Key (PAK)*, which is printed on a label attached to the box that CiscoWorks VMS ships in.

Once you have the PAK, navigate to the URL `http://www.cisco.com/pcgi-bin/Software/FormManager/formgenerator.pl`, which provides an online registration form. After you've completed the registration form (you'll need to submit the PAK on this form), a production license file will be sent to you via e-mail from Cisco. Copy this file to the CiscoWorks VMS server, which you can then load into CiscoWorks via the CiscoWorks Desktop.

To add a production license using the CiscoWorks Desktop, select VPN/Security Management Solution ➢ Administration ➢ Common Services ➢ Licensing Information from the navigation tree. This will open the License Information page in the Applications window, as shown in Figure 25.16.

To add a production license to CiscoWorks VMS, enter the path to the license file in the Filename field and then click the Update button. This will load the license file and update the licensing information.

FIGURE 25.15 The Add User page

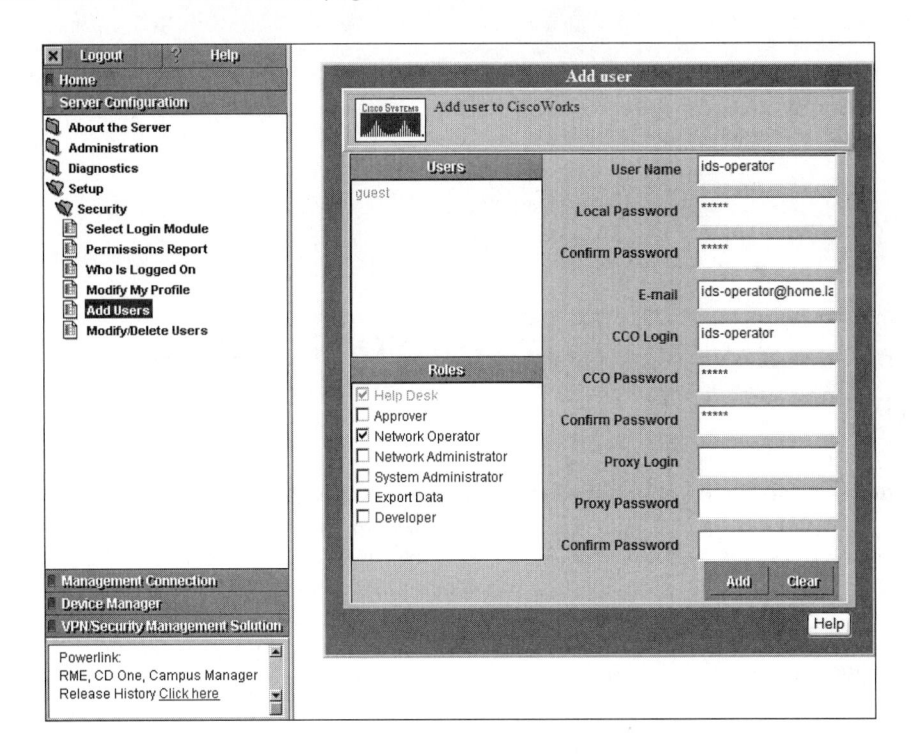

FIGURE 25.16 License Information page

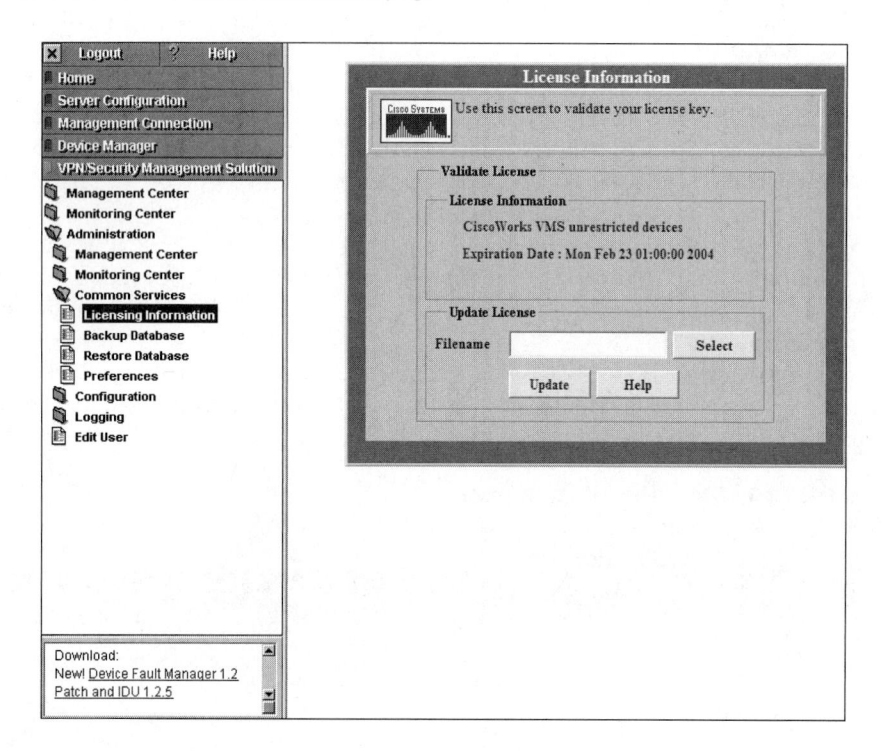

Configuring IDS Sensors Using the IDS MC

After you install and license the CiscoWorks Common Services, IDS Management Center, and Security Monitoring Center, you're ready to begin working with CiscoWorks VMS. This section describes how to use the IDS Management Center to provide enterprise IDS management of Cisco Secure IDS sensors. We'll discuss the following configuration tasks:

- IDS MC architecture
- Starting the IDS MC
- Creating sensor groups
- Adding sensors to the IDS MC
- Configuring intrusion detection using the IDS MC

IDS Management Center Architecture

The IDS Management Center (IDS MC) provides enterprise management of up to 300 Cisco Secure IDS sensors, allowing for a single, centralized point of administration for large Cisco Secure IDS sensor deployments. The IDS MC is an application that is part of the CiscoWorks VMS product suite, providing the necessary interface and logic to manage Cisco Secure IDS sensors. The IDS MC interacts with several different entities:

IDS sensor The IDS MC manages sensors by establishing secure shell sessions and automatically configuring sensors.

Administrators The IDS MC provides an HTTP/HTTPS interface that allows for graphical, web-based management and deployment of sensor configurations.

CiscoWorks Common Services The IDS MC uses CiscoWorks Common Services to provide a data store for IDS sensor configuration information and other information.

The following illustrates the architecture of the IDS MC and how it interacts with the entities just listed:

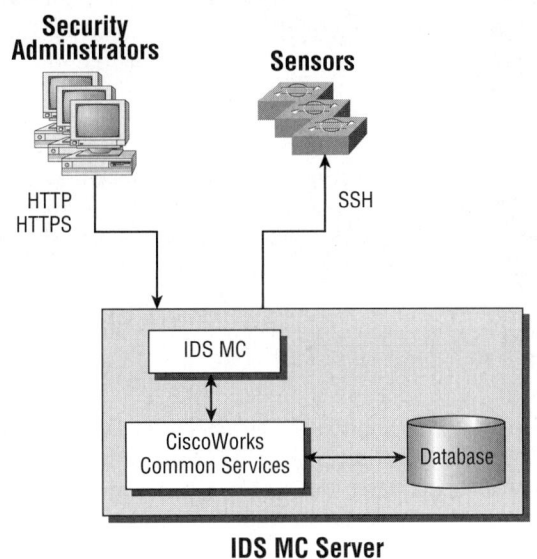

On the IDS MC server, the IDS MC application is installed within the `C:\Program Files\CSCOpx\MDC` folder. The installation includes a number of different folders, as listed here:

- `Apache` provides the web server that is used for generating the IDS MC web interface.
- `Sybase` provides the backend database used for storing IDS MC configurations.
- `Tomcat` provides Java servlets and Java server pages for the IDS MC web interface.
- `etc\ids\updates` stores updates for sensors managed by the IDS MC.

A number of processes make up the IDS MC application; each provides different functions and features of the IDS MC. The following are the important processes that make up the IDS MC:

- `IDS_Analyzer` processes event rules and requests user-specified notifications if required.
- `IDS_Backup` backs up and restores the IDS MC and Security Monitor database.
- `IDS_DbAdminAnalyzer` periodically applies active database rules.
- `IDS_DeployDaemon` manages all configuration deployments.
- `IDS_Notifier` receives notification requests (script, e-mail, and/or console) from other subsystems and performs the requested notification.
- `IDS_Receiver` receives IDS and Syslog events and stores them in the database.
- `IDS_ReportScheduler` generates all scheduled reports.

Starting the IDS Management Center

Now that you understand a little about the architecture of the IDS MC, it's time to learn how to start the IDS MC and begin using it. To start the IDS MC, you must first open the CiscoWorks Desktop as described earlier in this chapter. Once you've accessed the CiscoWorks Desktop, you can start the IDS MC by selecting VPN/Security Management Solution ➢ Management Center ➢ IDS Sensors from the navigation tree.

> **NOTE** When you start the IDS MC, an HTTPS connection on port 443 is made to the IDS MC web server. It's important to understand that the CiscoWorks Desktop (which uses port 1741 or 1742 by default) and IDS MC applications (which uses port 443) run from different web servers.

Once the IDS Sensors item is selected, the IDS MC opens in a separate browser window, as shown in Figure 25.17.

You can see that the IDS MC looks very similar to the IDS Device Manager (IDM) discussed in Chapter 23, "Configuring Cisco Secure IDS Sensors Using the IDS Device Manager." The IDS MC has been designed with the same look and feel as the IDM, which ensures that administrators familiar with using the IDM can easily transition to the IDS MC. The following describes each component of the IDS MC interface:

Path bar This provides the context for the current page, which is described in terms of the tab, option, and page selected.

TOC This component lists the available suboptions (pages) within the current option selected in the Options bar.

Options bar This lists the available options for the tab that is currently selected.

Configuring IDS Sensors Using the IDS MC

Tabs Tabs provide access to major product functionality areas of the IDS MC. The following tabs are available in the IDS MC:

Devices This tab provides options for adding, editing, and deleting sensors and groups of sensors.

Configuration This tab lets you configure settings for sensors or sensor groups managed by the IDS MC.

Deployment This tab lets you generate, approve, and deploy configurations to sensors.

Reports This tab provides the ability to generate reports.

Admin This tab provides the ability to administer the IDS MC.

Tools This area provides access to the Close, Help, and About buttons.

Instructions box This provides context-specific instructions related to the current page being viewed in the Security Monitor.

Action buttons These are located within each page and initiate commands or actions for a page.

FIGURE 25.17 The IDS Management Center

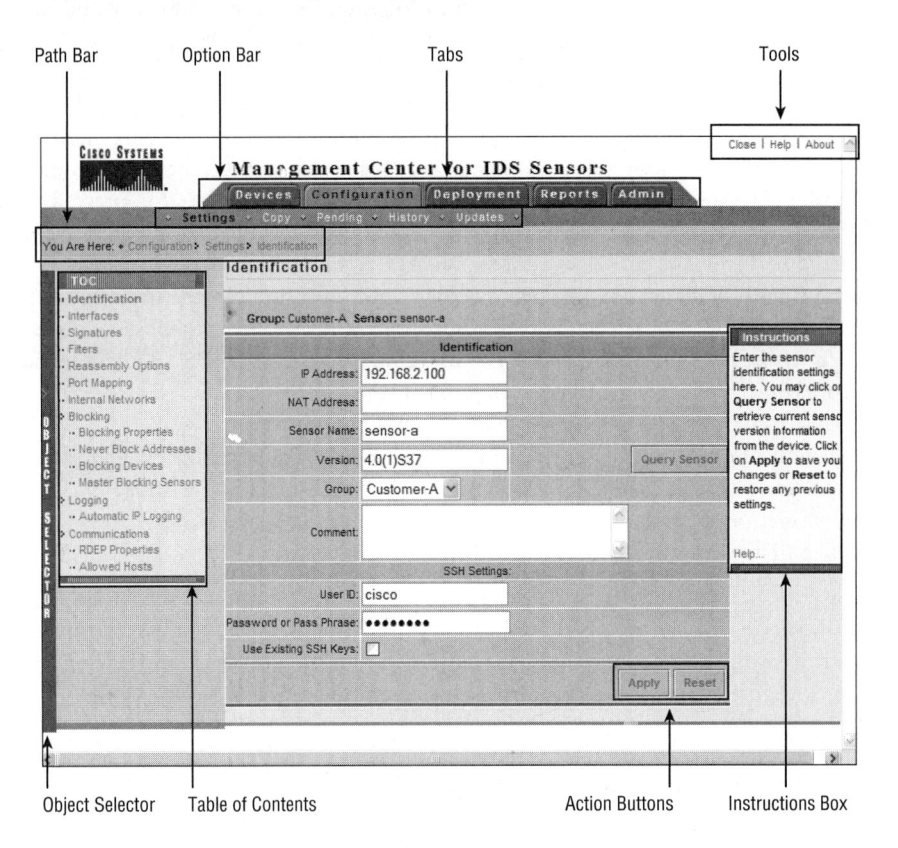

Configuring Sensor Groups

A key concept of the IDS MC is *sensor groups*, which enable you to group sensors. You can also nest sensor groups, where a group can contain not only sensors, but also other groups. For example, a group might consist of several sensors, whereas another group might consist of several sensor groups. A group can also consist of sensors and other groups if required.

Sensor groups provide a hierarchy of groups and sensors that enables you to apply a single policy to multiple sensors by configuring a policy for the group that sensors belong to. The IDS MC hierarchy consists of a single top-level group, by default called Global, which is the parent of all other sensors and sensor groups. Under the Global group, you can create multiple levels of sensor groups, each of which inherits configuration settings from parent sensor groups. The IDS MC hierarchy allows for extremely flexible and scalable enterprise management of multiple Cisco Secure IDS sensors.

When you're configuring the IDS MC, it's best to first determine the appropriate sensor groups that you need to use to enable the various sensor policies to be applied to each sensor that is managed by the IDS MC. For example, imagine that the IDS MC is being used by a managed services provider (MSP) that manages Cisco Secure IDS sensors for multiple customers. In this scenario, it would be typical for sensor groups representing each customer to be created under the top-level global group, which ensures that the Cisco Secure IDS sensors belonging to each customer are separated. Within each customer group, one or more subgroups may exist, depending on the sensors deployed for the customer. For example, Customer X might have a couple of sensors monitoring Internet traffic and another couple of sensors monitoring internal traffic. It's likely that the policies configured on each sensor will be quite different for each location; hence a group could be created for Internet sensors and another group created for internal sensors, both of which belong to the Customer X group. This configuration allows for common configuration settings to be applied to all sensors belonging to Customer X by configuring the Customer X group settings. Configuration settings specific to each location can then be applied by configuring each configuring the settings for the appropriate Internet or Internal sensor group.

Once you've determined the sensor groups required within the IDS MC, you next need to create them within the IDS MC. To create a sensor group, select Devices ➤ Sensor Group in the IDS MC. This displays the Sensor Group page, shown in Figure 25.18.

To create a new group, select the appropriate parent group of the new group that you wish to create, and then click the Create Subgroup button. Doing so opens the Add Group page, shown in Figure 25.19.

Notice that you can configure the following parameters:

Settings This parameter lets you define where the initial settings for the group will be applied from. Two options are available: the Default (Use Parent Values) option configures the group to inherit settings from the parent group of the new group, and the Copy Settings From Group option configures the group to inherit settings from the selected group.

Group Name This is the name of the new group.

Description This is a description of the group.

FIGURE 25.18 The Sensor Group page

FIGURE 25.19 The Add Group page

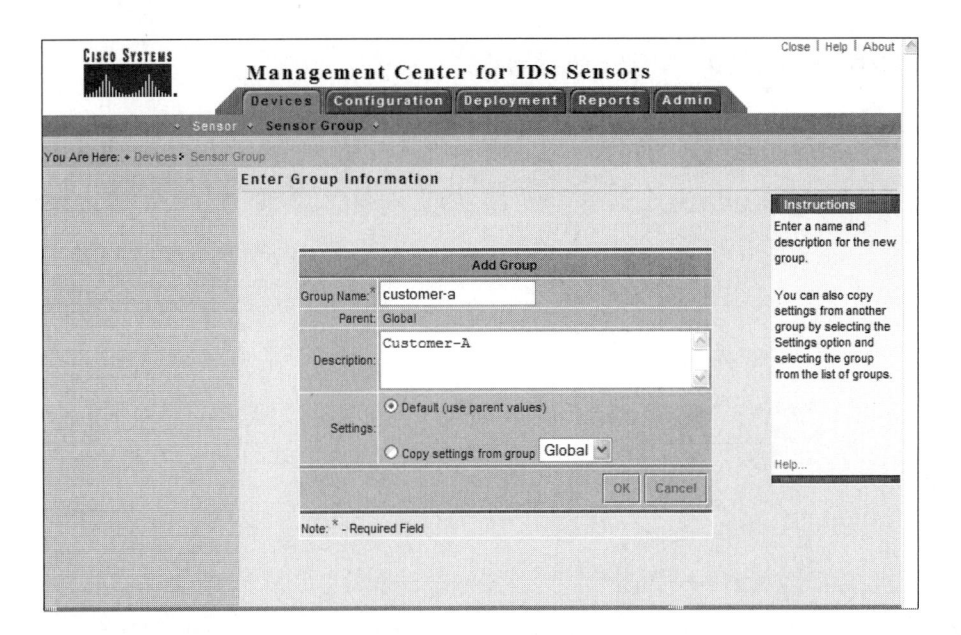

Once you've configured the Add Group page, click the OK button to complete the addition of the new group. This will display the Sensor Group page, which should now show the new group that you've created.

Adding Sensors to the IDS MC

When you're adding sensors to the IDS MC, you must add each sensor to a sensor group and define sensor identification information. To begin the process of adding a sensor to the IDS MC, select Devices ➢ Sensor to open the Sensor page, as shown in Figure 25.20.

To add a sensor, click the Add button. This will open the Select Group page, where you must select the group that you wish the sensor to belong to. Figure 25.21 shows the Select Sensor Group page.

In Figure 25.21, notice that the customer-a group, created earlier, is selected. Once you've selected the appropriate group, click the Next button to continue. The Enter Sensor Information page is displayed, where you can define a number of parameters that identify the sensor, as shown in Figure 25.22.

The following settings can be configured that identify the sensor you're adding to the IDS MC:

IP Address   This is the IP address of the command-and-control interface of the sensor.

NAT Address   This is the NAT address used to represent the command-and-control interface of the sensor. For example, if a sensor has a private IP address of 192.168.1.100 but is reachable via the NAT address 200.1.1.100, you must configure 200.1.1.100 as the NAT address for the sensor.

FIGURE 25.20   The Sensor page

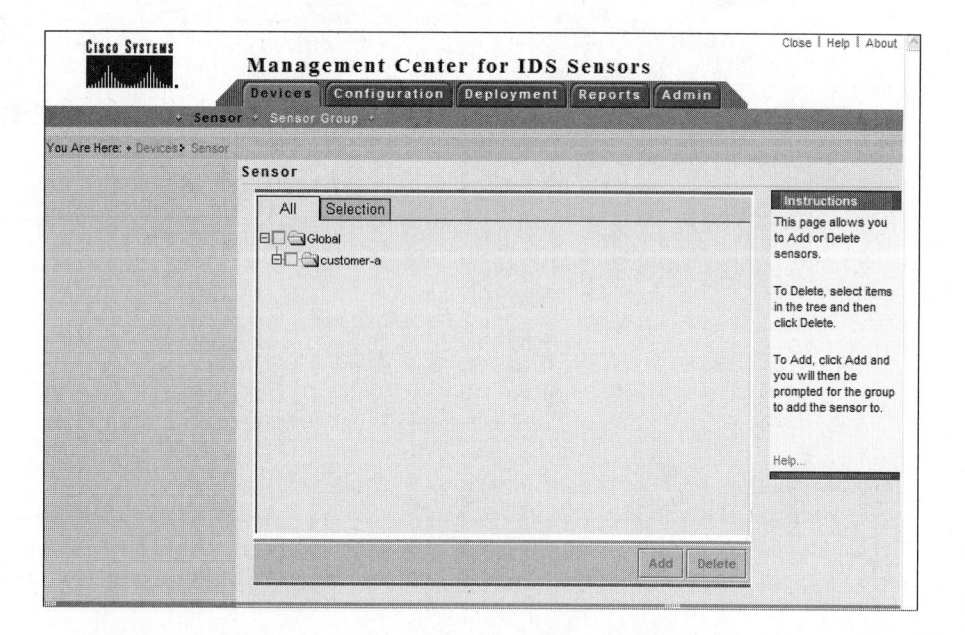

FIGURE 25.21 The Select Sensor Group page

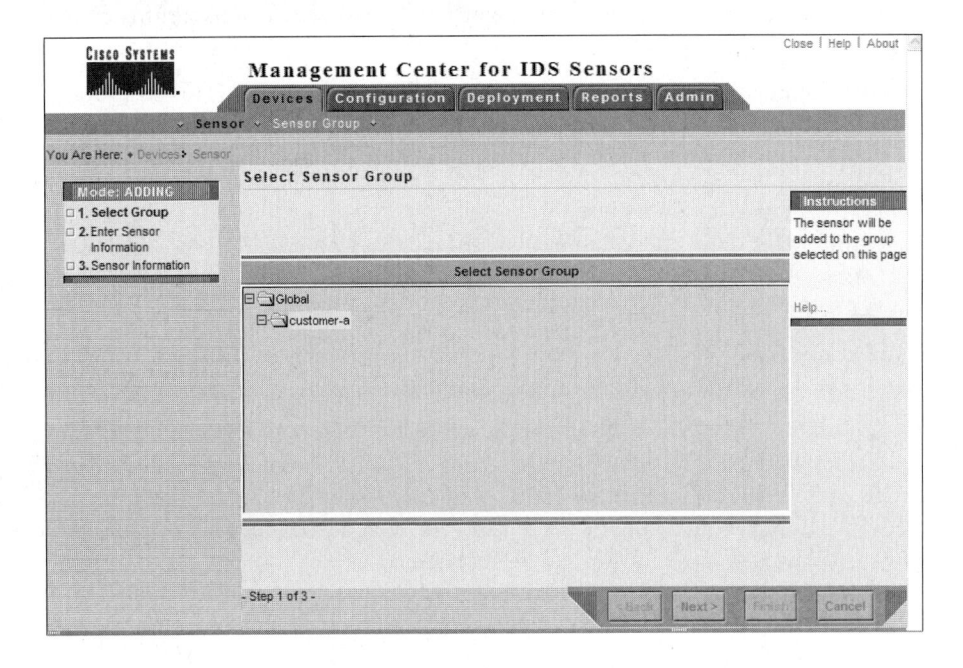

FIGURE 25.22 The Enter Sensor Information page

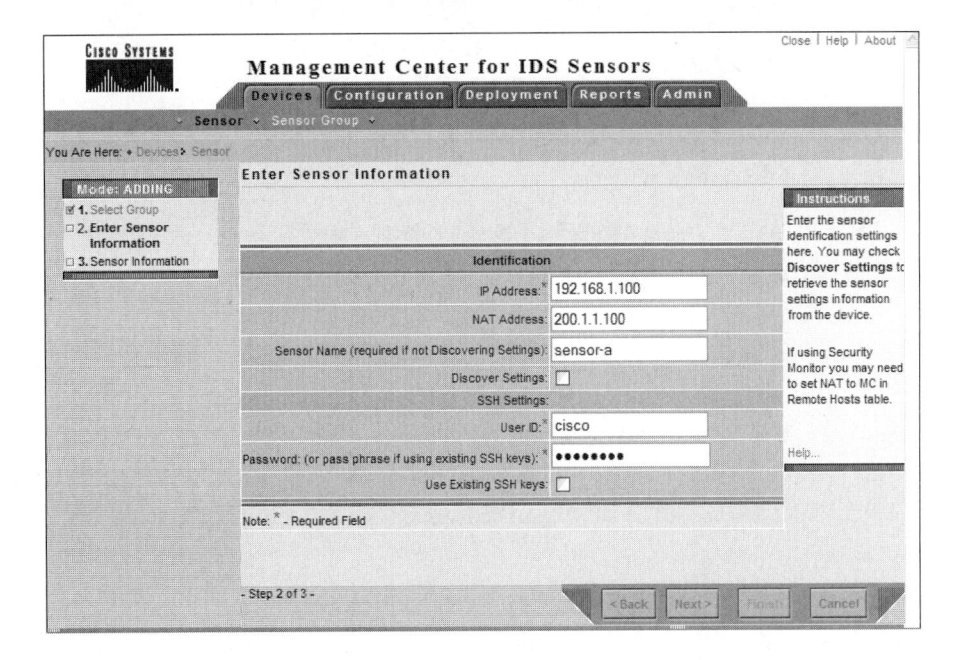

Sensor Name This is the hostname of the sensor. You don't need to configure this if you enable the Discover Settings parameter, which retrieves the sensor name after connecting to the sensor IP address.

Discover Settings Enabling this parameter configures the IDS MC to retrieve sensor settings from the sensor.

User ID This defines the account name on the sensor that can be used for SSH access to the sensor.

Password This setting defines the password of the account on the sensor that can be used for SSH access to the sensor. If the Use Existing SSH Keys option is selected, you must specify the correct passphrase used to unlock the public key of the sensor.

Use Existing SSH Keys SSH can use either passwords or public keys for authentication. If you've configured the public key of the sensor in the IDS MC already, you can choose to use the public key by selecting this option.

After you configure the appropriate sensor identification settings, click the Next button to proceed to the Sensor Information page, shown in Figure 25.23.

Notice that you can configure the sensor version and a comment associated with the sensor. In Figure 25.23, the version selected is 4.0(1)S37.

FIGURE 25.23 The Sensor Information page

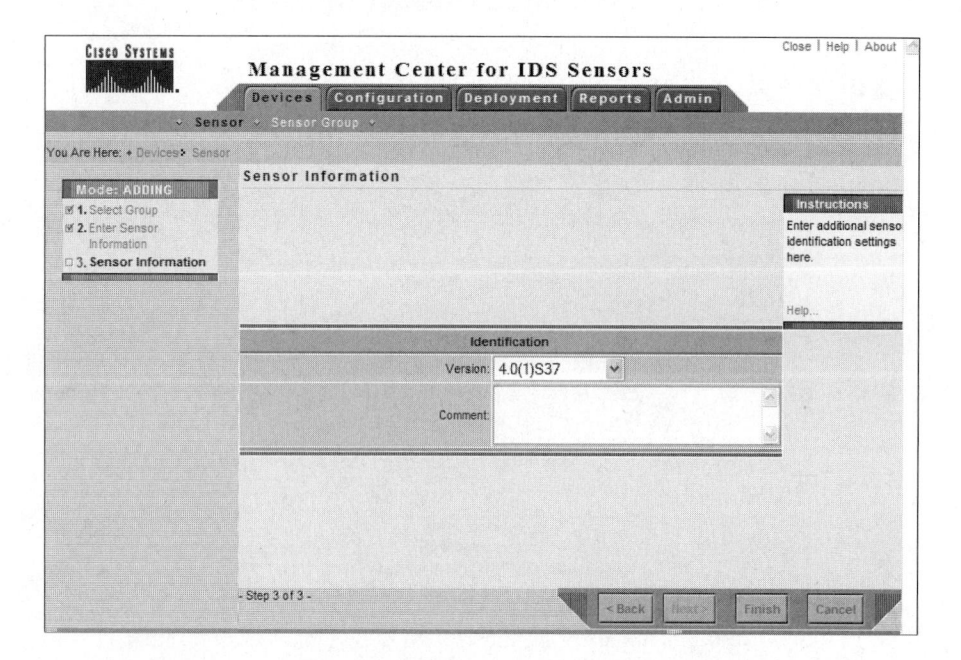

Configuring IDS Sensors Using the IDS MC   971

> **NOTE** If you configure a version 3.x sensor, you must also specify PostOffice settings for the sensor, which are displayed below the Identification settings in Figure 25.23 when version 3.x is selected from the Version field. PostOffice settings that must be configured are the host ID, organization name, and organization ID of the sensor.

To complete adding the sensor to the IDS MC, click the Finish button to return to the Sensor page. At this point, you should see the new sensor that you've added to the IDS MC.

Configuring Sensors Using the IDS MC

Once you've installed CiscoWorks VMS, created sensor groups, and added sensors to each group, you're ready to begin configuring your sensors. On the IDS MC, sensors are configured by clicking the Configuration tab, which opens the Configuration page shown in Figure 25.24.

Notice that the Object Selector bar is expanded, which lets you select the appropriate object that you wish to configure. An object could be a single sensor, or it could be a group of sensors. To select an object, click the appropriate object within the hierarchy. Once you've selected the object that you wish to work with, you can click the Settings option in the Options bar to open the Settings page. The Settings page includes the Settings TOC. The Settings TOC lets you configure various sensor parameters, and is shown in Figure 25.25.

FIGURE 25.24   The Configuration page

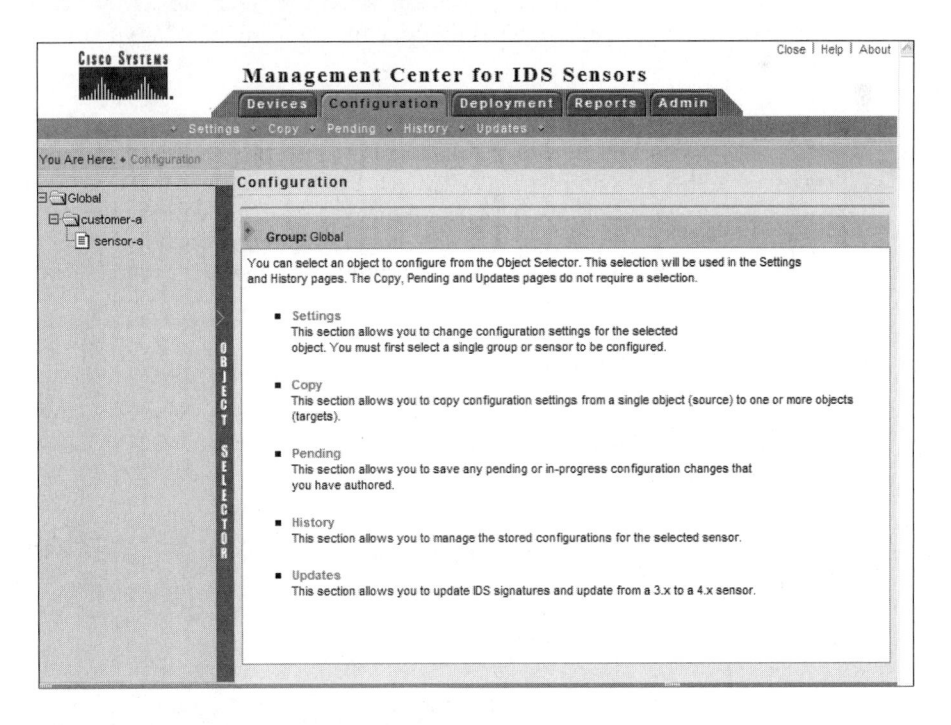

FIGURE 25.25 The Settings page

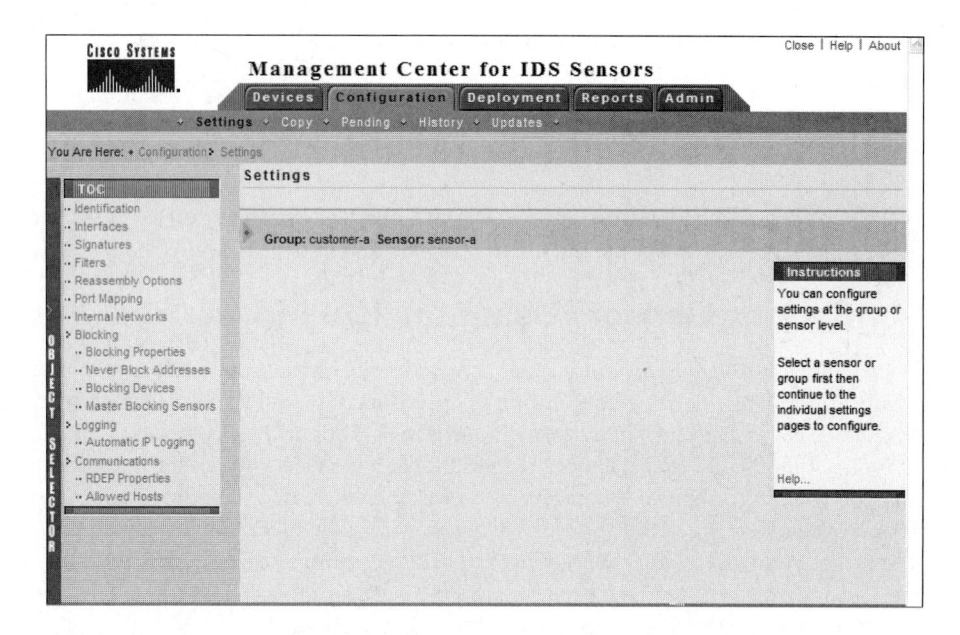

Notice the TOC on the left and the various sensor configuration parameters available. The Object Selector is collapsed, but you can click it to select a different object. The current object that you're working with is listed beneath the page title. In Figure 25.25, you can see that the current object is sensor-a.

> **NOTE**
> For the configuration tasks discussed in this chapter, it's assumed that you've added a version 4.x sensor to the IDS MC and selected that sensor object using the Object Selector. This means that each configuration page will be specific to a version 4.x sensor. Be aware that configuration options and pages vary for version 3.x sensors or if you're configuring a sensor group that contains a number of sensors.

Next, we'll discuss the following configuration tasks:

- Configuring communications settings
- Configuring intrusion detection settings
- Configuring blocking
- Configuring logging
- Configuring signatures

Configuring Communications Settings

The IDS MC lets you configure a number of communication settings, which control how Cisco Secure IDS sensors communicate with the IDS MC and other devices. The following communications settings are configurable using the IDS MC:

- Configuring identification settings
- Configuring allowed hosts
- Configuring RDEP settings

Configuring Identification Settings

Identification settings in the IDS MC are the settings that you specify when you add a sensor to the IDS MC (see Figures 25.21–25.23). These settings include the following parameters that relate to a specific sensor:

- IP address
- NAT address
- Sensor name
- Sensor version
- The group the sensor belongs to
- SSH username and password

To configure identification settings, select the Identification option from the Settings TOC to open the Identification page, shown in Figure 25.26.

Configuring Allowed Hosts

Cisco Secure IDS sensors include an *allowed hosts* list, which defines the IP addresses of hosts that are permitted management access to a sensor. For example, if a security administrator is using a PC with an IP address of 192.168.1.50, the Cisco Secure IDS sensor that the security administrator manages must have this IP address (or a subnet address that includes his IP address) configured as an allowed host.

To configure allowed hosts using the IDS MC, select the Communications ➤ Allowed Hosts option from the Settings TOC. This will open the Allowed Hosts page, shown in Figure 25.27.

In Figure 25.27, you can see that hosts in the 192.168.1.0/24 subnet are configured as allowed hosts. If you wish to add allowed hosts, click the Add button.

> **TIP** You must define at least one entry in the Allowed Hosts list before the IDS MC will allow you to generate and deploy a sensor configuration.

FIGURE 25.26 The Identification page

FIGURE 25.27 The Allowed Hosts page

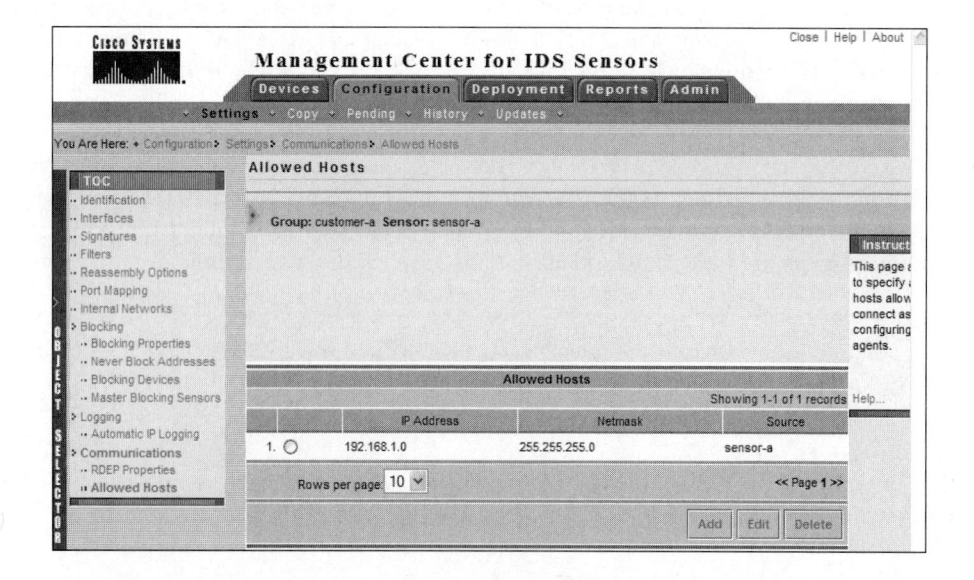

Configuring RDEP Properties

Cisco Secure IDS 4.*x* sensors use the RDEP protocol for communicating alarm information to remote monitoring platforms such as the Security Monitor. RDEP is a subset of the HTTP/1.1 protocol, enabling alarm information to be communicated using HTTP transactions. The IDS MC lets you modify properties that relate to RDEP operation, such as the web server port used for RDEP communications and whether SSL should be used to secure RDEP communications. To configure RDEP properties, select the Communications ≻ RDEP Properties option from the Settings TOC, which opens the RDEP Properties page, shown in Figure 25.28.

FIGURE 25.28 The RDEP Properties page

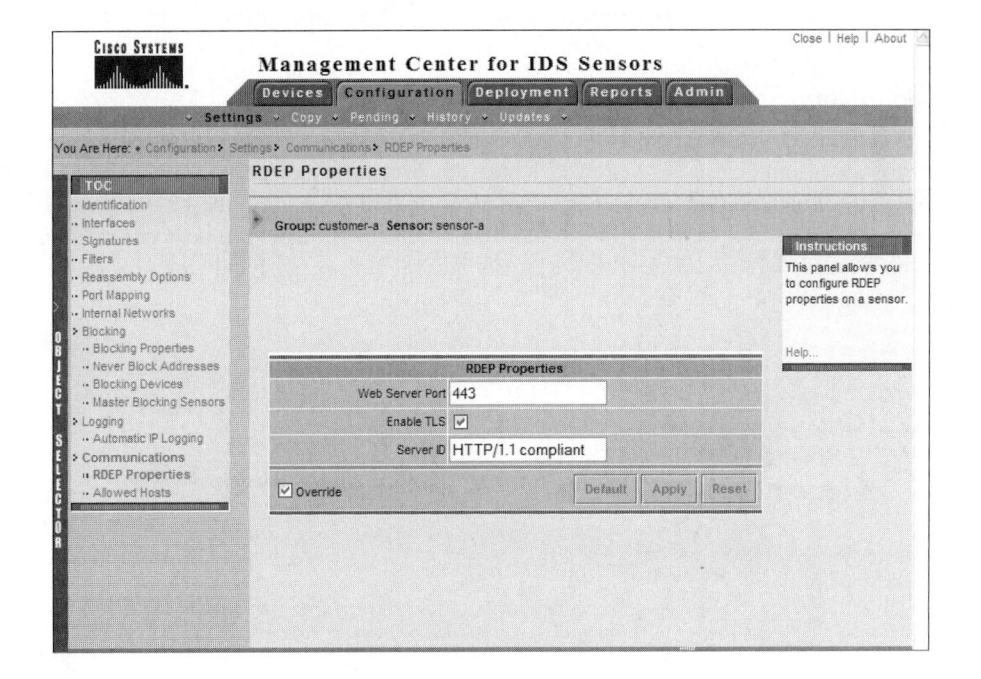

Configuring Intrusion Detection Settings

The IDS MC lets you configure a number of settings related to the intrusion detection behavior of a sensor. These include the following:

- Configuring sensing interfaces
- Identifying internal networks
- Identifying additional ports used by specific signatures
- Configuring reassembly options
- Configuring filters

Configuring Sensing Interfaces

If you're configuring a Cisco Secure version 4.1 sensor or higher, you can configure multiple sensing interfaces by adding each sensing interface to interface group 0 on the sensor. To configure sensing interfaces on the IDS MC for version 4.1 sensors, select the Interfaces option from the Settings TOC. This will open the Interfaces page, shown in Figure 25.29.

If you click the Query Interfaces button, the IDS MC connects to the sensor you're currently configuring, queries the sensor for a list of its sensing interfaces, and then displays the sensing interfaces in the Interfaces page (this is the case in Figure 25.29). Once the IDS MC has determined the sensing interfaces available for a sensor, you can then selectively enable/disable each interface. Enabling an interface adds it to the group 0 interface on the sensor, which is the group interface that captures traffic and passes captured traffic to the intrusion detection engine of the sensor for analysis.

Identifying Internal Networks

In Chapter 23, you learned that a sensor includes an alarm channel system variable called IN, which defines IP addresses that are considered part of the internal network, as well as the variable OUT, which defines IP addresses that are considered external. These system variables allow the Source Location and Destination Location fields of an alarm to be accurately populated with a value of IN or OUT, enabling security administrators to quickly identify where an attack is originating from and where an attack is directed.

FIGURE 25.29 The Interfaces page

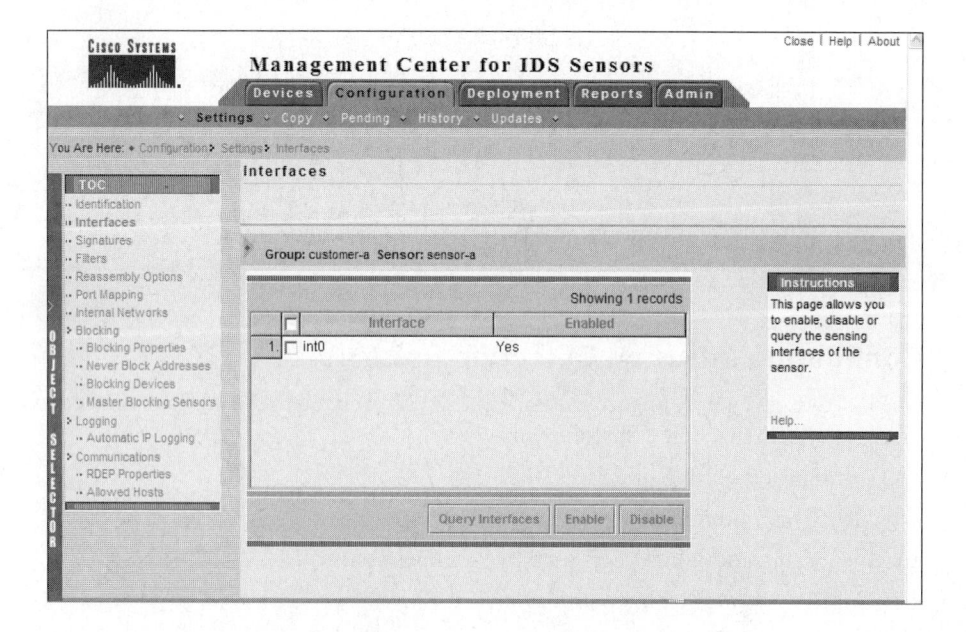

To identify internal networks using the IDS MC, select the Internal Networks option in the Object Selector to open the Internal Networks page. This page lets you add the network's address ranges that are considered internal, as demonstrated in Figure 25.30.

Identifying Additional Ports Used by Sensors

Certain signatures relate to traffic based on a specific Application-layer protocol such as HTTP or Telnet. By default, sensors typically inspect traffic only on the well-known ports associated with these protocols. If you're using custom ports for these protocols, the sensor won't inspect the protocol traffic against the protocol-specific signatures, meaning that intrusive activity could be missed.

Using the IDS MC, you can configure sensors to inspect traffic for a specific protocol that is using a custom port by selecting the Port Mapping option from the Settings TOC. This opens the Port Mapping page, as shown in Figure 25.31 for a version 4.*x* sensor.

In Figure 25.31, notice that for version 4.*x* sensors, you can define only web ports, which define the TCP ports of traffic that will be inspected against signatures that relate to web-based attacks. By default, ports 80, 88, 90, and 8000–9900 are configured as web ports; however, in Figure 25.31 port 5555 has also been added so that traffic with a destination port of 5555 will be inspected against web-based signatures.

FIGURE 25.30 The Internal Networks page

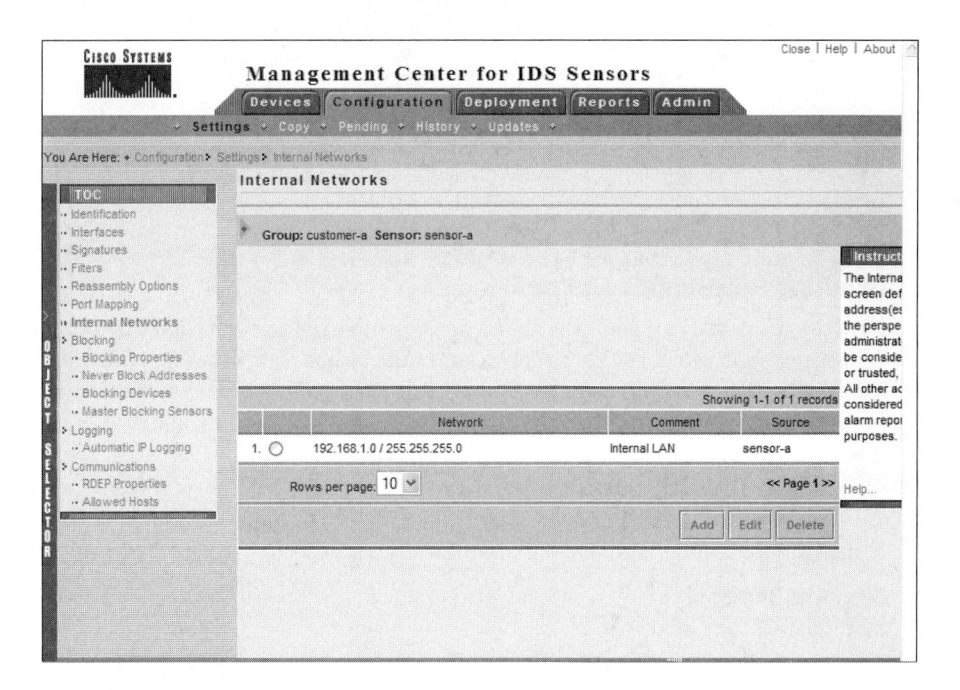

FIGURE 25.31 The Port Mapping page

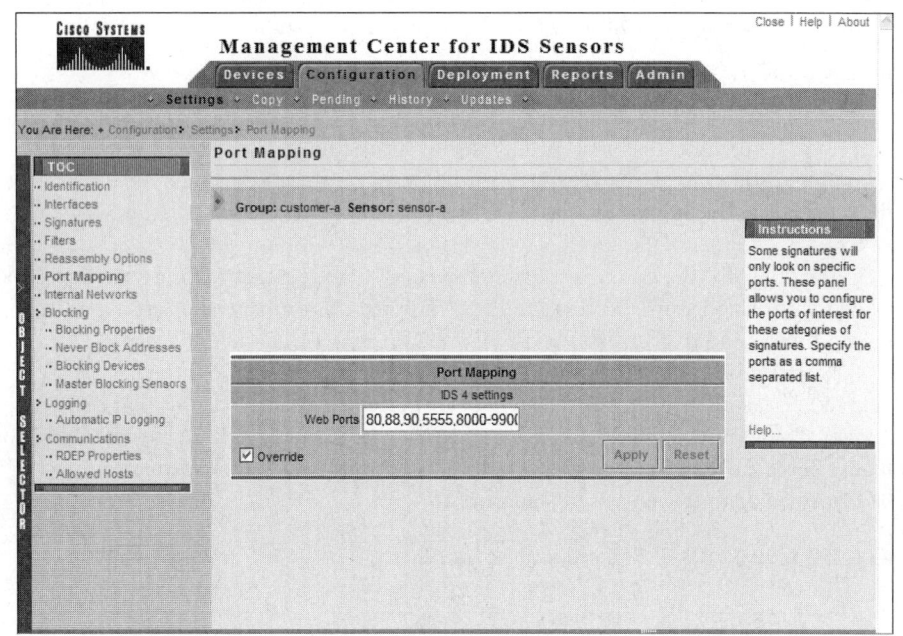

> **NOTE** For version 3.*x* sensors, you can modify port mappings for TCP HIJACK, TCP SYNFLOOD, Telnet, and web signatures.

Configuring Reassembly Options

Cisco Secure IDS sensors include the ability to reassemble IP fragments and TCP segments, which ensures that attackers can't mask attacks by splitting attack traffic into multiple IP fragments or TCP segments. The IDS MC includes a number of reassembly options; you can ensure that not too many sensor resources are allocated to traffic reassembly by controlling a number of parameters associated with IP fragment and TCP segment reassembly.

To configure reassembly options, select the Reassembly Options item from the Settings TOC, which opens the Reassembly Options page shown in Figure 25.32.

Notice the following parameters that are configurable:

IP Fragment Reassembly   This section lets you configure the following parameters associated with IP fragment reassembly:

> **IP Reassemble Mode**   The IP Reassemble Mode defines the mode that should be used to reassemble fragments, based on common operating systems including NT (Windows NT), Linux, Solaris, and BSD. By default, NT is selected as the reassemble mode.

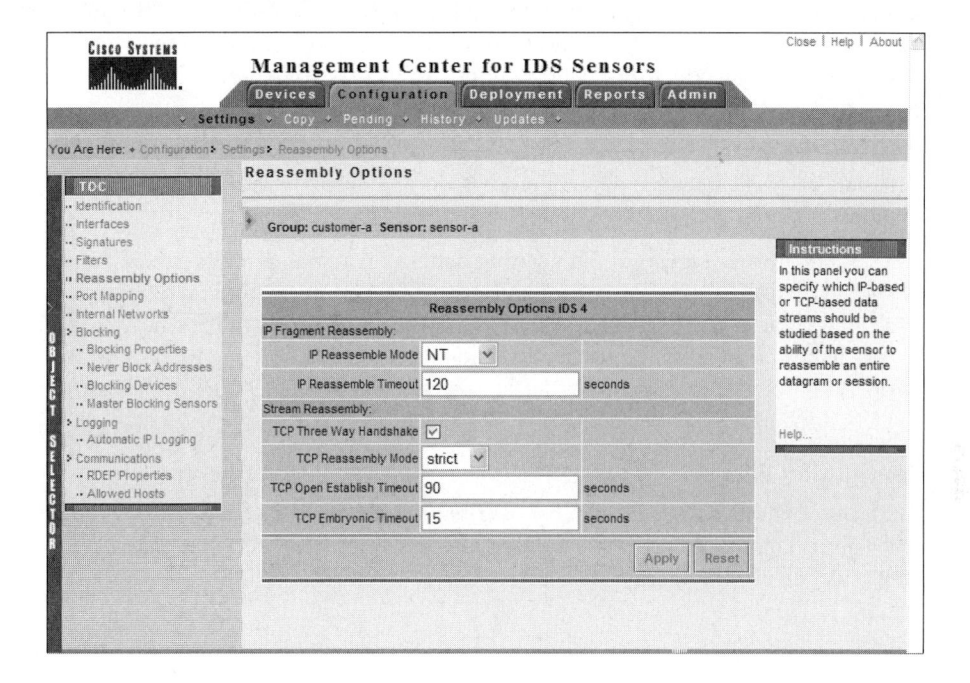

FIGURE 25.32 The Reassembly Options page

IP Reassemble Timeout This defines the maximum amount of time an incomplete packet should be cached. By default, this timeout is 120 seconds. This setting is the equivalent of the virtual sensor tune micro engines.

Stream Reassembly Some attackers attempt to mask TCP-based attacks from sensors by splitting an attack into multiple TCP segments, meaning that sensors that can only inspect single packets won't detect the attack. The Stream Reassembly section lets you configure the following parameters associated with reassembling a TCP stream or session:

TCP Three-Way Handshake When enabled, sensors will ensure that a TCP three-way handshake (SYN, SYN ACK, ACK) has taken place before attempting to cache and reassemble TCP segments associated with each TCP session. By default, this setting is enabled, ensuring that the sensor resources required for TCP session reassembly are used only for valid TCP connections.

TCP Reassembly Mode The TCP Reassembly Mode defines what the sensor should do if it's unable to completely reconstruct a TCP session due to some TCP segments not being received. Two options are available:

- Loose: The sensor will attempt to reassemble a TCP session, even if some TCP segments have not been received.
- Strict: The sensor will ignore any incomplete TCP sessions that can't be completely reconstructed and discard all TCP segments associated with the incomplete session. This means that the incomplete TCP session won't be analyzed by the intrusion detection engine.

Choosing the Strict option (default) ensures that sensors don't waste resources reassembling and analyzing incomplete TCP sessions; however, there is a chance that the sensor may miss intrusive activity. Choosing the Loose option ensures that intrusive activity masked by an incomplete TCP session won't be missed; however, this may result in more sensor resources being utilized.

TCP Open Establish Timeout   This option defines the maximum amount of time the sensor should cache TCP session data for established TCP sessions without receiving any subsequent data associated with the session. The default value is 90 seconds.

TCP Embryonic Timeout   This setting defines the maximum amount of time the sensor should cache TCP session data for half-open TCP sessions without receiving any subsequent session data. A half-open TCP session is a session that hasn't fully completed the TCP three-way handshake (in other words, the session has been initiated but not fully established). This option protects the IDS sensor from caching too many TCP sessions during a prolonged TCP SYN flood attack. The default value is 15 seconds.

Configuring Filters

Filters allow you to reduce the number of false positives generated by a sensor by filtering alarms at the alarm channel before they're placed into the event store. As you learned in Chapter 23, a filter is defined by the following criteria:

- Signature
- Source address
- Destination address

Recall that every filter has an action, which is to either include (permit alarms that match the filter criteria) or exclude (discard alarms that match the filter criteria).

To create a filter, click the Filters item in the Settings TOC to open the Filters page, shown in Figure 25.33.

To create a filter, click the Add button in the Filters page to open the Enter Filter page, shown in Figure 25.34.

In Figure 25.34, a filter called Custom-Filter is created, which specifies an action of exclude. Notice that the Signatures, Source Addresses, and Destination Addresses options each include a link to another page, which lets you configure the appropriate values for each of these fields. Figure 25.35 shows the Enter Signatures page, which opens when you click the Signatures link in Figure 25.34.

In Figure 25.35, you can see that the 1000 BAD IP OPTION and 1005 SATNET ID signatures have been selected. Click the OK button, and you'll be returned to the Enter Filter page, which should reflect the selection made in Figure 25.35. To add addresses to the filter, you must first click either the Source Addresses or Destination Addresses link in the Enter Filter page (see Figure 25.34), which opens either the Filter Source Addresses or Filter Destination Addresses page. Figure 25.36 shows the Filter Source Addresses page, which opens when you click the Source Addresses link in Figure 25.34.

FIGURE 25.33 The Filters page

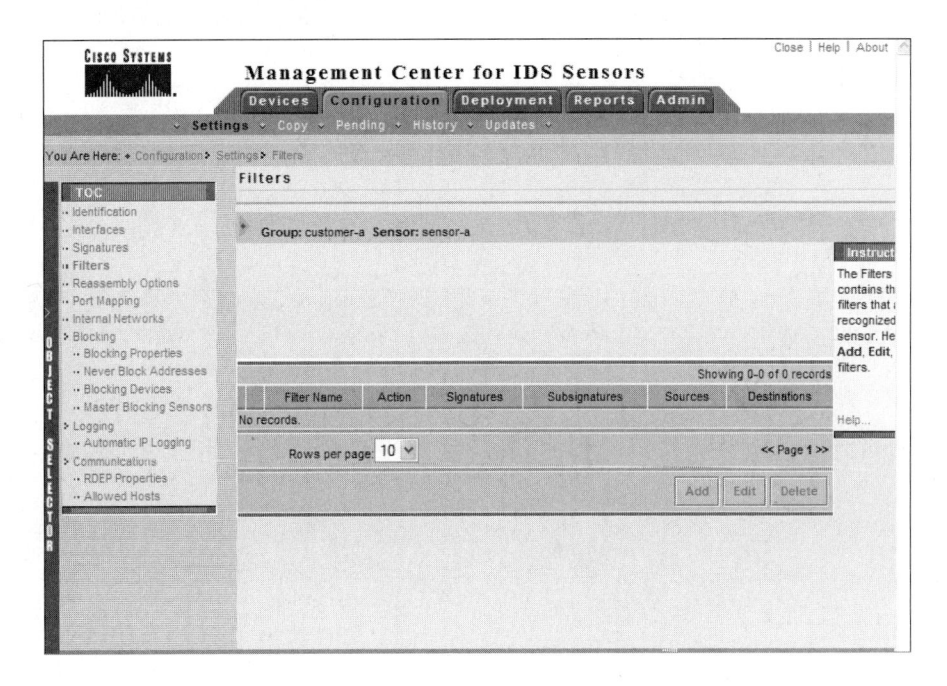

FIGURE 25.34 The Enter Filter page

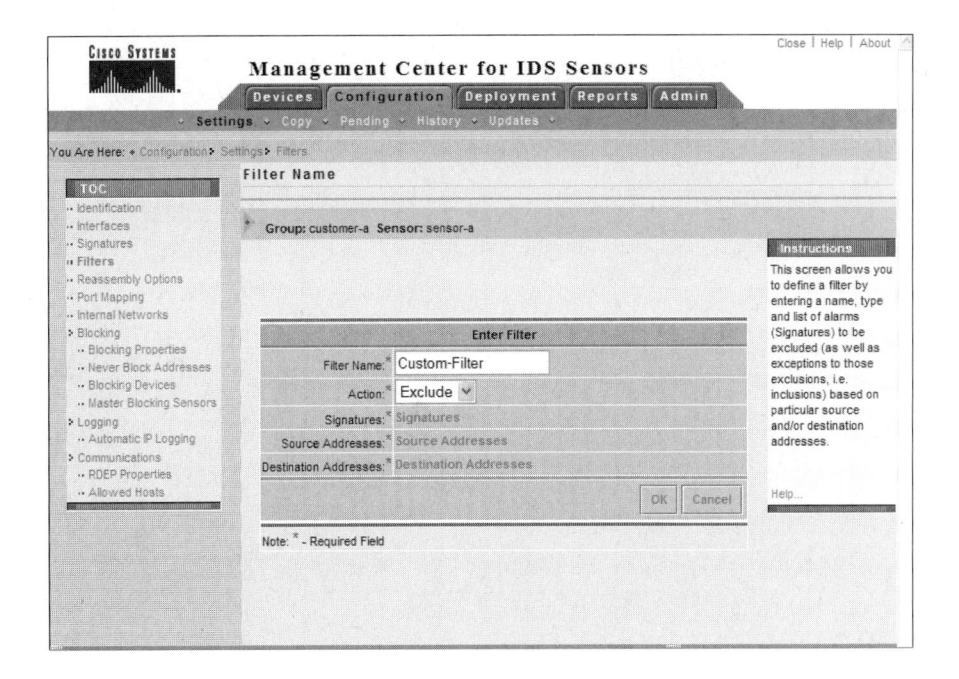

FIGURE 25.35 The Enter Signatures page

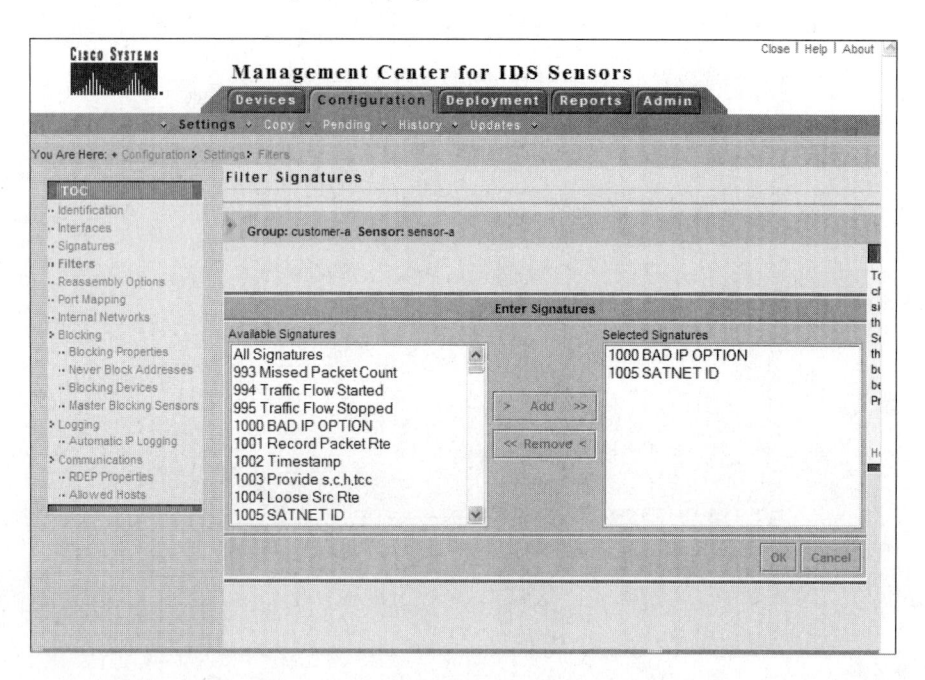

FIGURE 25.36 The Filter Source Addresses page

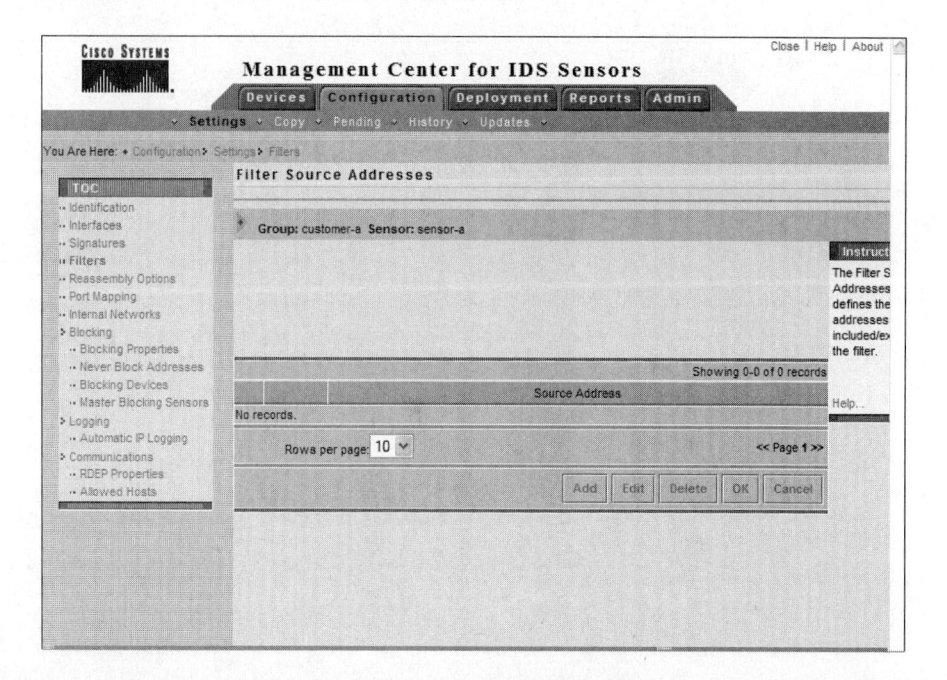

Notice that you can add one or more entries to the Filter Source Addresses page by clicking the Add button. When you click the Add button, the Enter Filter Address page is displayed, as shown in Figure 25.37.

Notice that you can select from a number of different options to define a source (or destination) address. The Internal and External options reference the IN and OUT system variables, respectively, whereas the Single, Range, and Network options allow you to manually define a numeric address or set of addresses.

Once you've specified the appropriate addressing information, click the OK button to return to the Filter Source Addresses page; you should see a new entry with the addresses you configured. Click OK again to return to the Enter Filter page, which will now include the signature configuration you applied earlier in Figure 25.35, as well as the source address configuration you applied in Figures 25.36 and 25.37. At this point, you must also specify a destination address by clicking the Destination Addresses link shown in Figure 25.34 (if you don't specify a destination address, you won't be able to finalize the creation of the filter). Assuming you've configured the appropriate signatures, source address, and destination address to filter, Figure 25.38 shows the Enter Filter page after the configuration of Figures 25.35–25.37.

FIGURE 25.37 The Enter Filter Address page

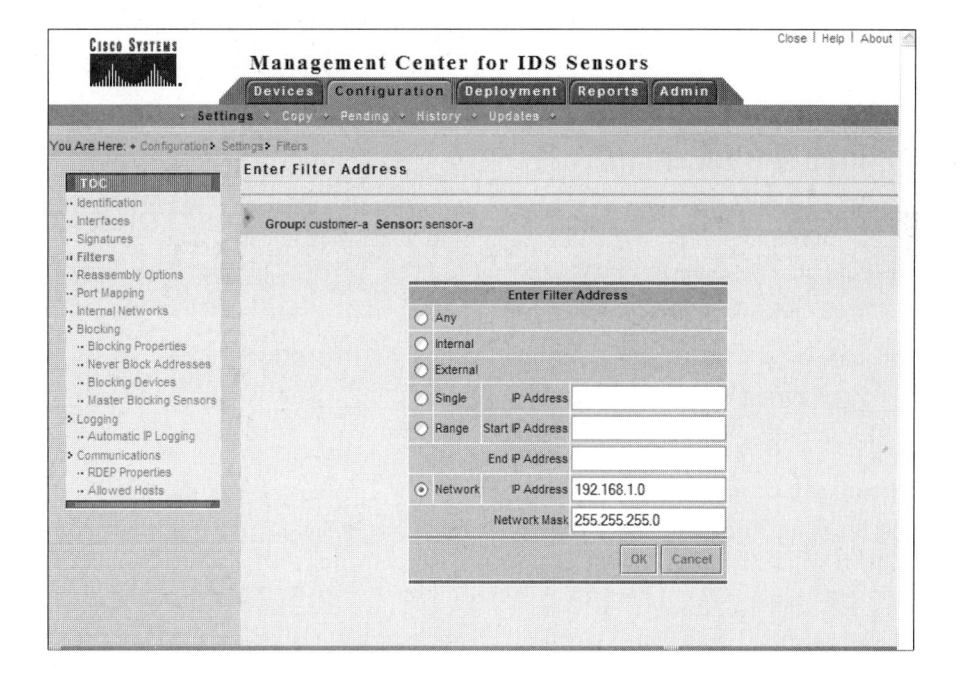

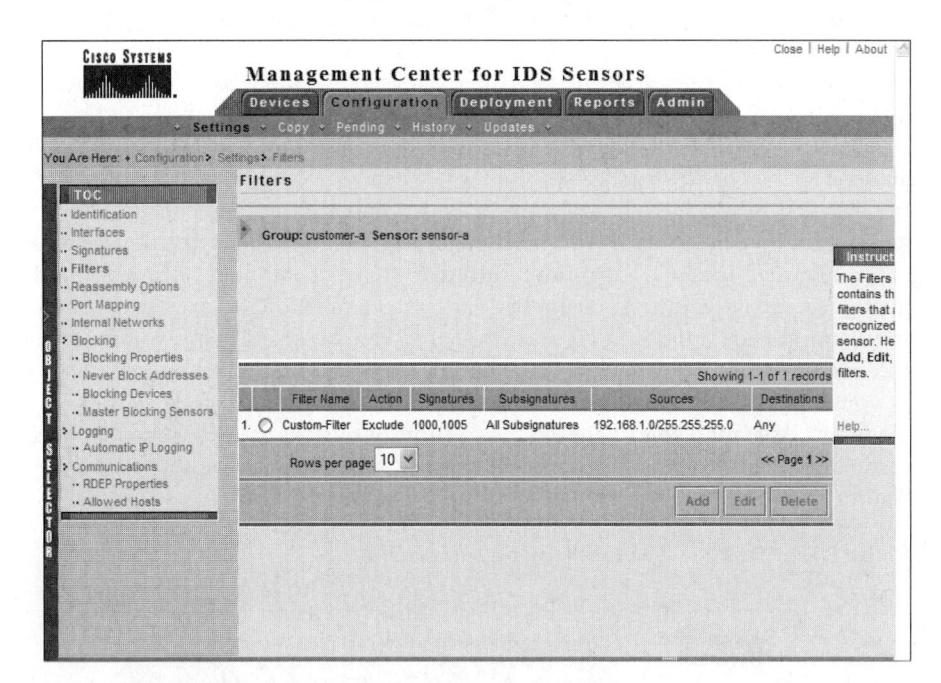

FIGURE 25.38   The Enter Filter page after configuration

Configuring Blocking

Blocking refers to the ability of sensors to automatically log on to perimeter devices and apply access control lists that block access from hosts generating intrusive activity. The IDS MC lets you configure blocking as follows:

- Specifying blocking properties
- Specifying networks and hosts that should never be blocked
- Configuring blocking devices
- Configuring master blocking sensors

Specifying Blocking Properties

The Blocking Properties page within the Settings TOC is similar to the Blocking Properties page in the IDM (see Chapter 23) and enables you to configured the following parameters related to blocking:

Blocking Length   This option specifies the amount of time a block is applied before being removed.

Maximum ACL Entries   This parameter specifies the maximum number of ACL entries that can be maintained by a sensor.

Enable ACL Logging   Enabling this option configures ACL policy violations to generate Syslog messages.

Allow Blocking Devices To Block The Sensor's IP Address By default this option is disabled, which means that sensors will include an access control entry that permits access to the sensor's IP address to ensure that blocking access control entries don't block access to the sensor. Enabling this option means that access to the sensor may be blocked.

Figure 25.39 shows the Blocking Properties page in the IDS MC.

> **NOTE** By default, the Override check box isn't clicked, which means settings from the Global group are used and can't be modified. Checking the Override option lets you configure custom blocking properties.

Specifying Networks and Hosts that Should Never Be Blocked

A key concern when configuring blocking is the possibility that blocking could be used as a DoS attack, where attackers generate intrusive activity with spoofed IP addresses of critical hosts and thus cause access from critical hosts to be blocked. To prevent this from happening, you should always identify critical hosts and networks that should never be blocked and then configure sensors to never block for those addresses.

To specify networks and hosts that should never be blocked by sensors managed by the IDS MC, select the Blocking ≻ Never Block Addresses option in the Settings TOC. Figure 25.40 shows the Never Block Addresses page that is displayed.

FIGURE 25.39 The Blocking Properties page

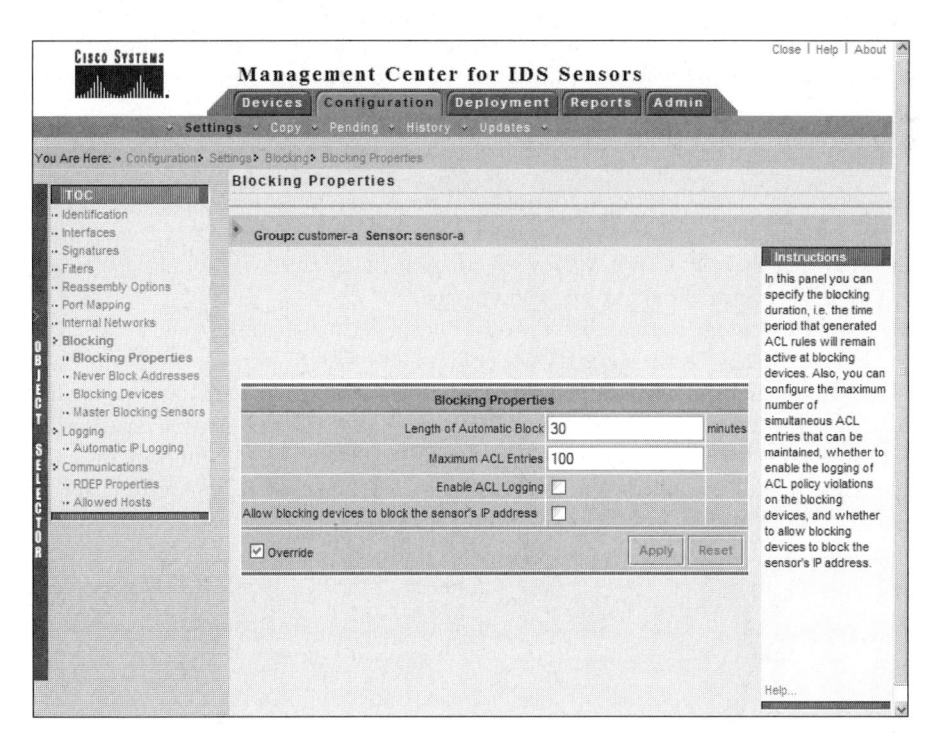

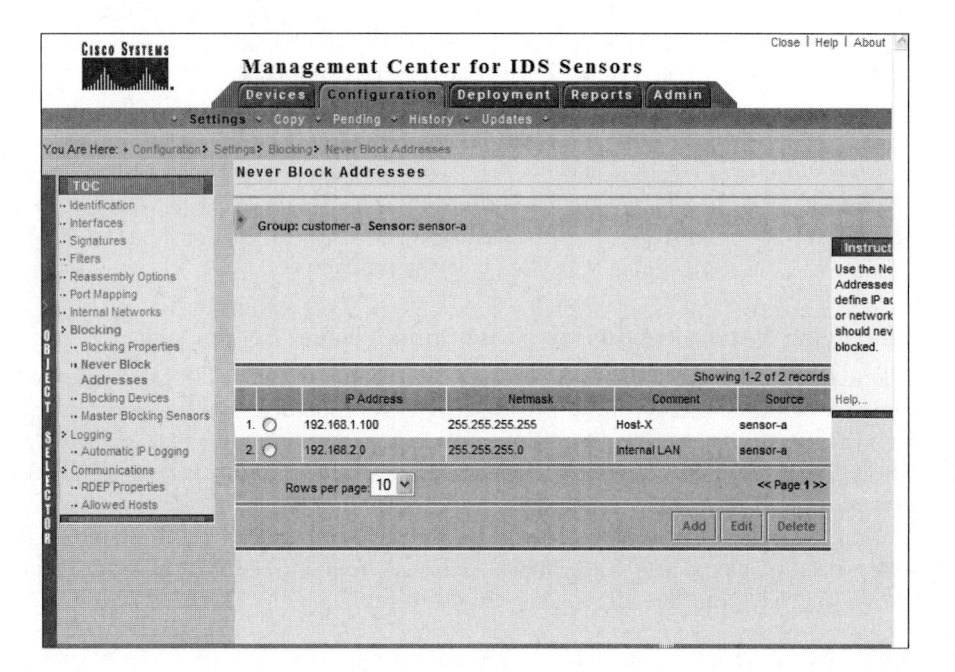

FIGURE 25.40 The Never Block Addresses page

In Figure 25.40, two entries have been added that define a protected host (192.168.1.100) and a protected network (192.168.2.0/24). You can add these protected hosts and networks by clicking the Add button.

Configuring Blocking Devices

For sensors to apply blocking to perimeter devices, you must define each perimeter device that is to have blocking applied to it. Such perimeter devices are referred to as *blocking devices*; you can configure them in the IDS MC by selecting the Blocking Devices option in the Settings TOC. Figure 25.41 shows the Blocking Devices page.

To add a blocking device, click the Add button in the Blocking Devices page. This will open the Enter Blocking Device page shown in Figure 25.42.

Here, you can specify parameters that enable the sensor to manage the specified device, including IP Address, NAT Address, Username, Password, and Enable Password. Notice the Edit Interfaces hyperlink, which lets you specify the interface and interface direction to which blocking should be applied. When configuring a blocking device, you must ensure that at least one blocking interface is defined. Figure 25.43 shows the Enter Blocking Device Interfaces page, which opens when you click the Edit Interfaces hyperlink.

FIGURE 25.41 The Blocking Devices page

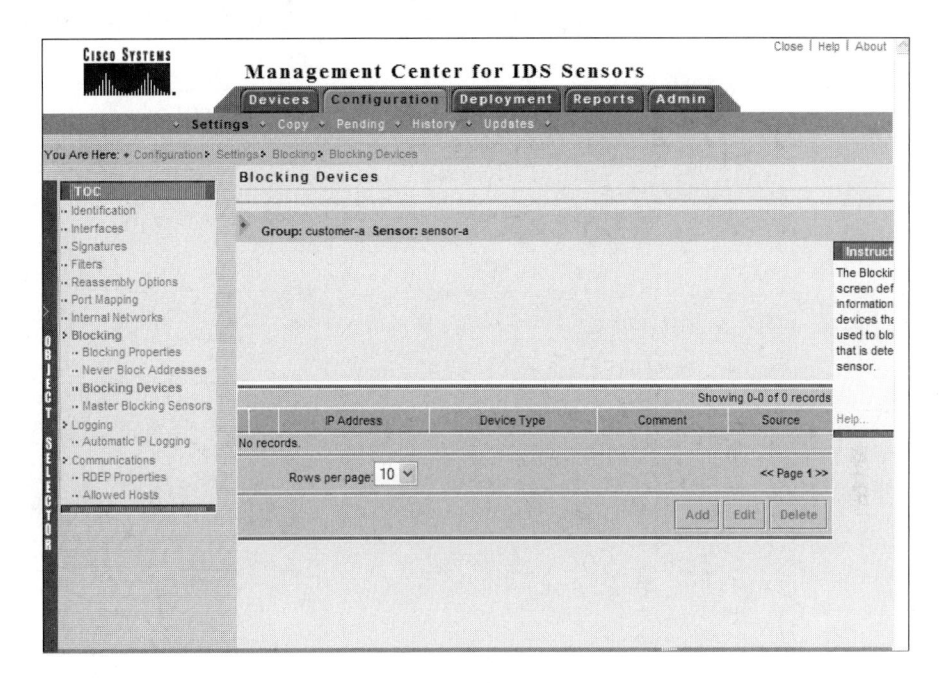

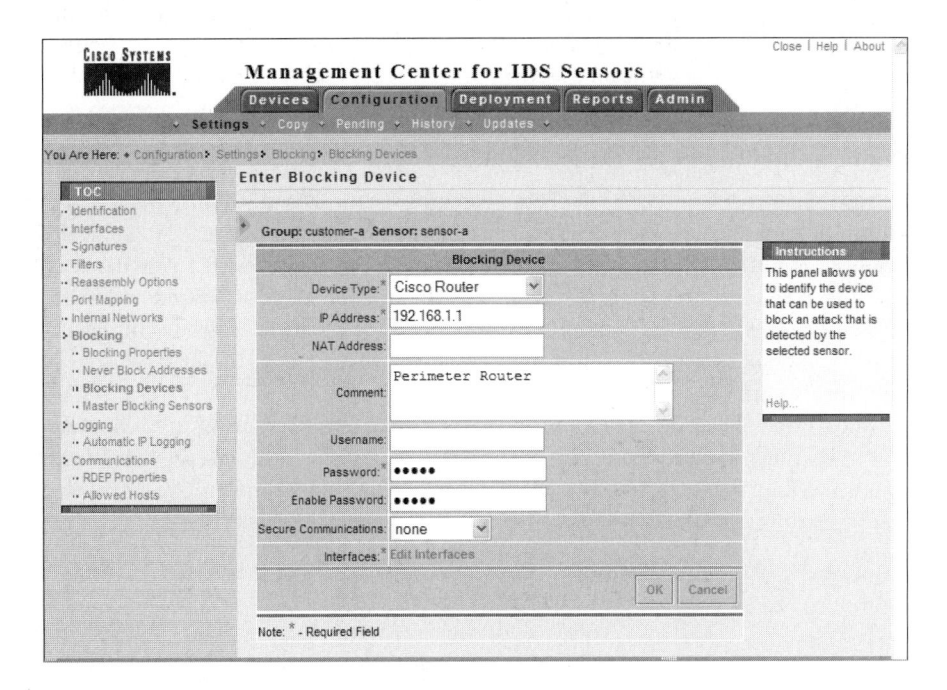

FIGURE 25.42 The Enter Blocking Device page

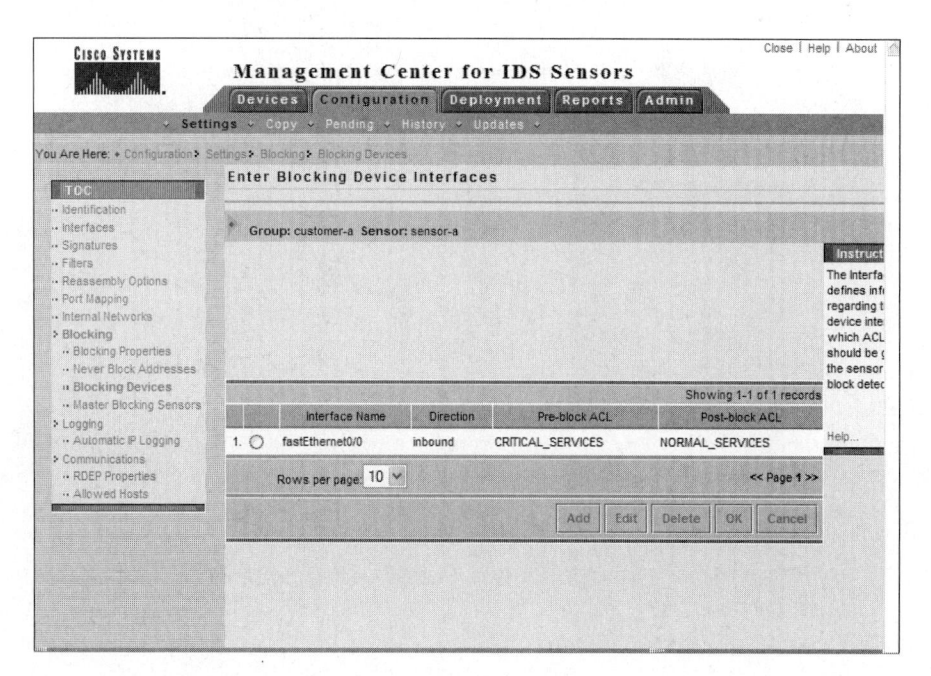

FIGURE 25.43 The Enter Blocking Device Interfaces page

You can add a new blocking interface by clicking the Add button. A blocking interface has already been defined in Figure 25.43, and you can see that you must specify the interface name, blocking direction, and optional pre-block/post-block ACL names. After specifying blocking interfaces, click the OK button to return to the Enter Blocking Devices page, and then click OK again to add the blocking device and return to the Blocking Devices page.

Configuring Master Blocking Sensors

As we discussed in Chapter 23, a master blocking sensor is used in multisensor deployments with multiple perimeter devices, where a single master blocking sensor is used to apply all blocking on behalf of other sensors. Each sensor that forwards blocking requests to the master blocking sensor is referred to as a *blocking forwarding sensor* and must be configured with the master blocking sensor. To specify the master blocking sensor for a sensor or group of sensors, select the Master Blocking Sensors option from the Settings TOC. Figure 25.44 shows the Master Blocking Sensors page.

The Master Blocking Sensors page shows the current sensor that is configured as a master blocking sensor for the sensor you're configuring. You can add or remove master blocking sensors by clicking the Add or Delete button. Figure 25.45 shows the Enter Master Blocking Sensor page, which is displayed after you click the Add button.

FIGURE 25.44 The Master Blocking Sensors page

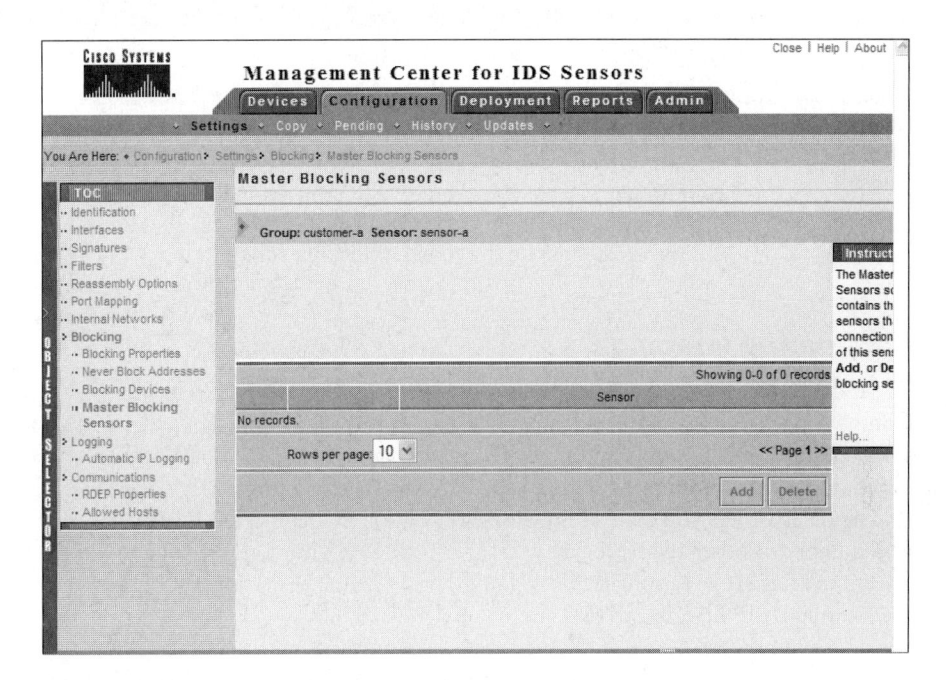

FIGURE 25.45 The Enter Master Blocking Sensor page

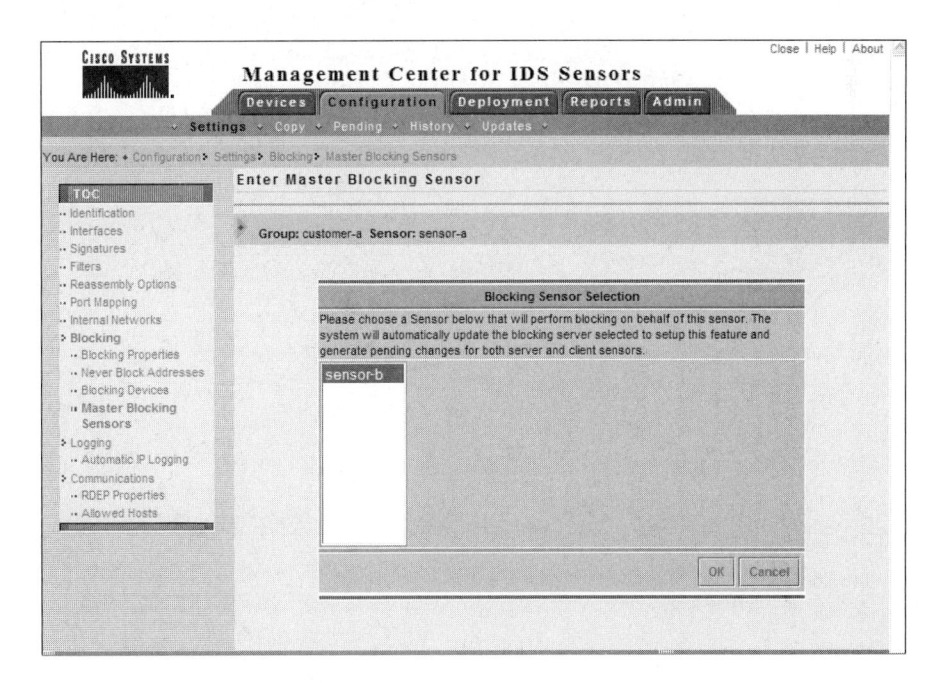

In Figure 25.45, notice that a sensor called sensor-b is shown in the list of blocking sensors. Selecting this sensor and then clicking the OK button specifies sensor-b as a master blocking sensor for the current sensor that is being configured.

> **NOTE** To be eligible to be configured as a master blocking sensor, a sensor object that is configured with at least one blocking device must be present in the IDS MC. Also, remember that you must define the master blocking sensor as a trusted TLC host and that the blocking forwarding sensors must be included in the Allowed Hosts list on the master blocking sensor.

Configuring Logging

The IDS MC lets you control how sensors perform IP logging, which refers to the alarm response where the packets associated with an attack are captured and logged to a file. For version 4.x sensors, you can configure only automatic IP logging options; automatic IP logging is invoked when a signature that is configured with an event action of IP logging is triggered.

The IDS MC lets you control how long automatic IP logging should capture packets, as well as a number of other related parameters. To configure automatic IP logging on the IDS MC, select the Logging ➢ Automatic IP Logging option from the Settings TOC. Figure 25.46 shows the Automatic IP Logging page.

FIGURE 25.46 The Automatic IP Logging page

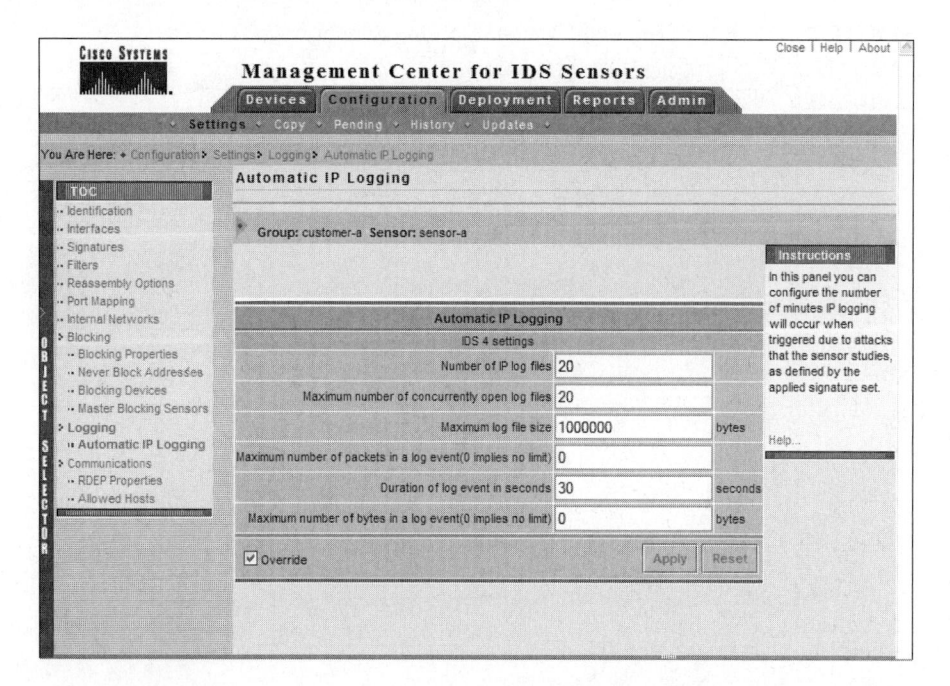

Notice the various parameters that you can configure for a version 4.x sensor. You can configure the maximum number of IP log files, maximum number of concurrently open log files, log file size limits, and the duration that logging should occur.

Configuring Signatures

Signatures are a fundamental component of any signature-based IDS, because they're the entities that allow sensors to identify various types of intrusive activity. The IDS MC lets you configure built-in Cisco Secure IDS signatures and also allows you to create custom signatures.

To configure signatures, select the Signatures option from the Settings TOC. Figure 25.47 shows the Signatures page.

FIGURE 25.47   The Signatures page

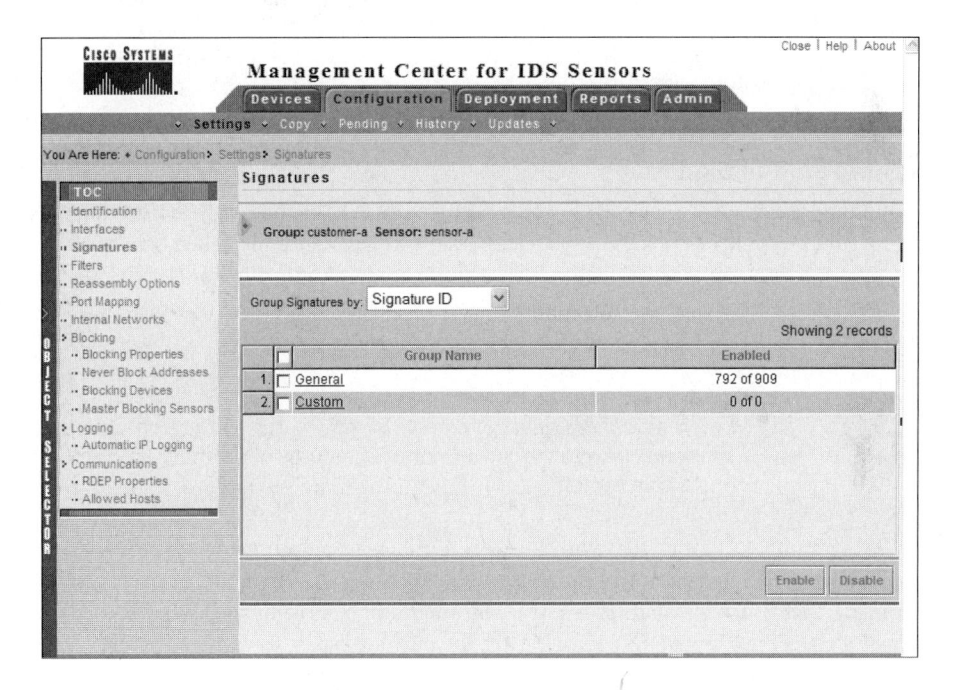

Notice the Group Signatures By drop-down box, which lets you select the *grouping style* that is to be applied to Cisco Secure IDS sensors. There are several grouping styles, which group signatures based on different criteria:

Signature ID   This is the default grouping style, as shown in Figure 25.47, which includes two top-level groups:

General   This group lists each signature that ships with Cisco Secure IDS software, from the lowest signature ID up to the highest signature ID.

Custom   This group lists custom signatures that have been created by administrators. You can also create custom signatures using this group.

L2/L3/L4 Protocol This groups signatures based on the layer 2, 3, and 4 protocols associated with the attacks detected by each signature. Examples of these groups include ARP, General IP, General TCP, General UDP, and TCP floods.

Service This groups signatures based on the Application layer protocols associated with the attacks detected by each signature. Examples of these groups include SQL, DNS, HTTP, FTP, and NetBIOS.

Attack This groups signatures based on the type of attack that triggers each signature. Examples of these groups include DoS, DDoS, Reconnaissance, and Viruses/Worms/Trojans.

OS This groups signatures based on the operating system that is targeted by the attack that fires each signature. Examples of these groups include General Windows, Solaris, and Red Hat Linux.

When you're configuring signatures, you can perform two major configuration tasks:

- Tuning built-in signatures
- Creating custom signatures

Each of these configuration tasks will now be discussed separately.

Tuning Built-in Signatures

To configure signatures, select the appropriate grouping style that lets you find the signatures that you wish to work with. Once you've selected a grouping style and clicked on a specific group, the Signature(s) In Group page is displayed; it's built based on the group you've selected. Figure 25.48 shows the Signature(s) In Group page after you select the L2/L3/L4 protocol grouping style on the Signatures page and then click the General ICMP group.

> **TIP** You can quickly enable or disable all signatures within a group by selecting the check box next to the group in the Signatures page and then clicking the Enable or Disable button.

In Figure 25.48, notice that you can see a number of signatures, which are all General ICMP signatures. The Signature Group drop-down list shows the current signature group you're working with (such as General ICMP), and the Filter Source drop-down list lets you filter the list of signatures displayed. You can filter the current list of signatures by selecting one of the criteria in the Filter Source drop-down list and then specifying a string or text to filter on in the text field next to the Filter Source drop-down list. The following are the criteria you can choose in the Filter Source drop-down list:

ID This option lets you filter signatures within the current signature listing by specifying all or part of the signature ID of the signatures you wish to view.

Subsig ID This option lets you filter signatures within the current signature listing by specifying the subsignature ID of the signatures you wish to view.

> **NOTE** If a signature doesn't have subsignatures, the subsignature ID of the signature is always zero (0).

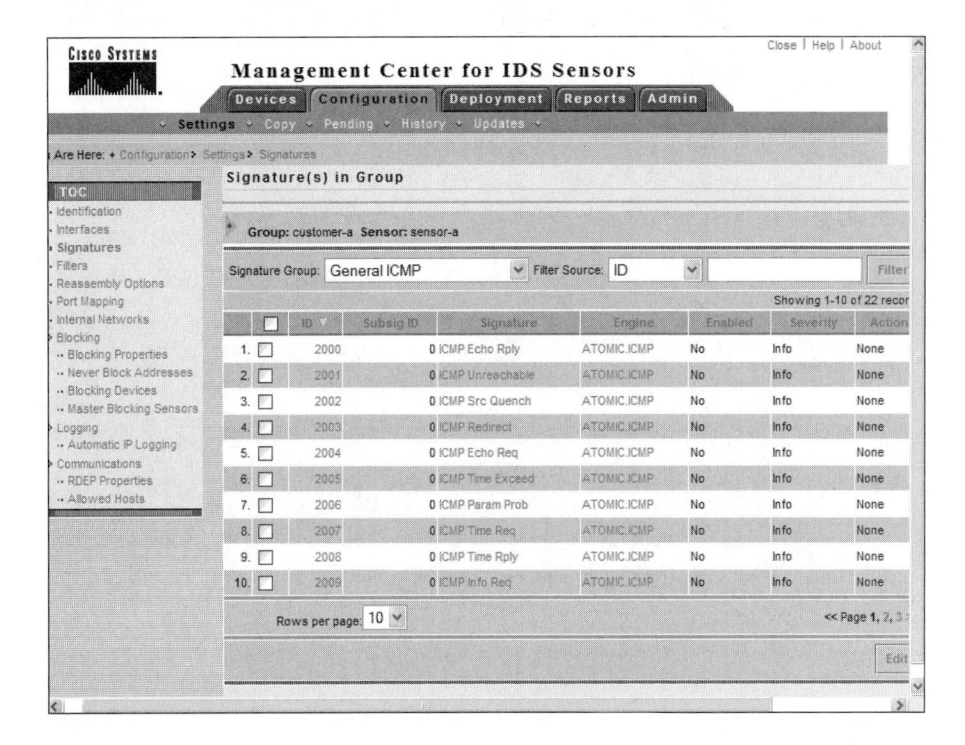

FIGURE 25.48 The Signature(s) In Group page

Signature   This option lets you filter signatures within the current signature listing by specifying all or part of the signature name of the signatures that you wish to view.

Engine   This option lets you filter signatures within the current signature listing by specifying all or part of the engine name (such as ATOMIC.ICMP) of the signatures you wish to view belong to.

Enabled   This option lets you filter signatures based on whether they're enabled or disabled. To view all enabled signatures, filter on the text Yes. To view all disabled signatures, filter on the text No.

Severity   This option lets you filter signatures based on signature severity. You must specify the text that describes the severity of signatures that you wish to view (for example, Info, Low, Medium, or High).

Action   This option lets you filter signatures based on the action taken by signatures should they be triggered. You must specify the text that describes the action taken by signatures that you wish to view (such as Log, Reset, BlockHost, or BlockConnection).

Once you've found the signatures that you wish to configure, select the check box next to the appropriate signatures and then click the Edit button. The Edit Signature(s) page will open, which lets you tune parameters associated with the signatures. Figure 25.49 shows the Edit Signature(s) page for the ICMP Echo Reply signature.

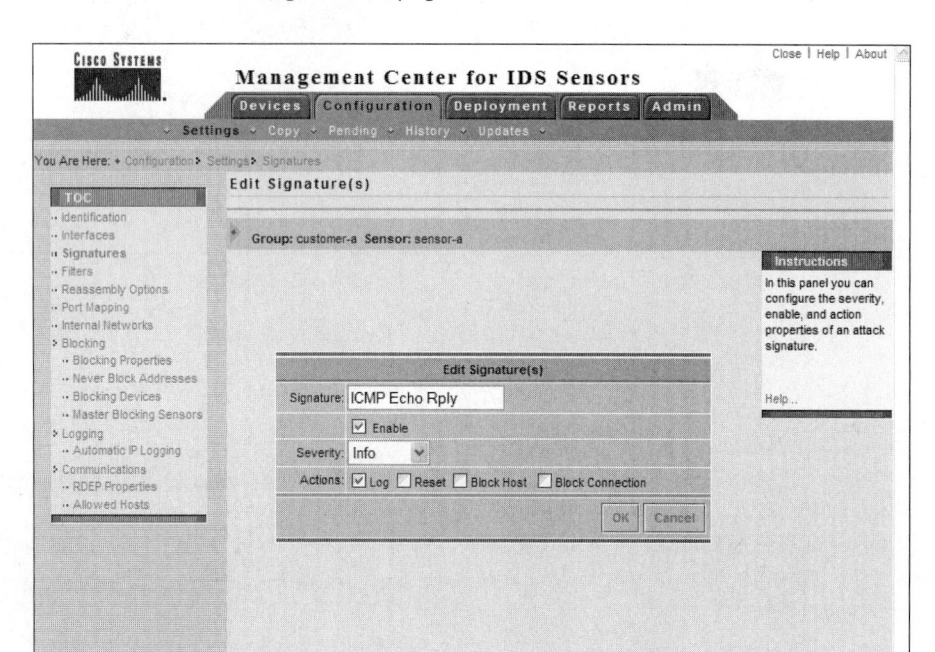

FIGURE 25.49   The Edit Signature(s) page

Notice that you can view the signature name (you can't modify built-in signature names), enable or disable the signature, define the severity of the signature, and define the action that sensors should take if the signature is triggered. In Figure 25.49, the ICMP Echo Reply signature has been enabled and has an action of Log configured. By default, this signature is disabled and has no action associated with it.

Creating Custom Signatures

The IDS MC lets you create custom signatures, which enable you to extend the functionality of sensors to detect new attacks for which built-in signatures have not yet been released. To configure and create custom signatures, open the Signatures page and ensure that the Signature ID grouping style is selected. Within the Signatures page, a group called Custom is listed, which allows you to configure and create custom signatures. Figure 25.50 shows the Signature(s) In Group page after you click the Custom group hyperlink.

Notice that by default no custom signatures exist. To add a new custom signature, click the Add button to open the Tune Signature page, as shown in Figure 25.51.

You can specify various parameters that define a custom signature. These include the signature name, the engine used for the custom signature, and an alarm parameter table for the signature. The alarm parameter table lists the configurable alarm parameters and indicates whether each parameter must be configured (as indicated by the Required column).

In Figure 25.51, a signature called Custom_Worm is being created, which is based on the STRING.TCP engine. The STRING.TCP engine lets you create signatures that search for a specific string using regular expressions within TCP sessions for the services (ports) listed in the `ServicePorts` parameter for the signature (for example, 80, 3128, 8000, 8010, 8080, and 8888 in Figure 25.51). Notice that the `RegexString` parameter in Figure 25.51 is listed as a required parameter but isn't configured. This parameter defines the regular expression that specifies the string you want to look for. Figure 25.52 shows the Edit Parameter page, which is opened by selecting the radio button next to the `RegexString` parameter and then clicking the Edit button.

FIGURE 25.50 The Signature(s) In Group page for custom signatures

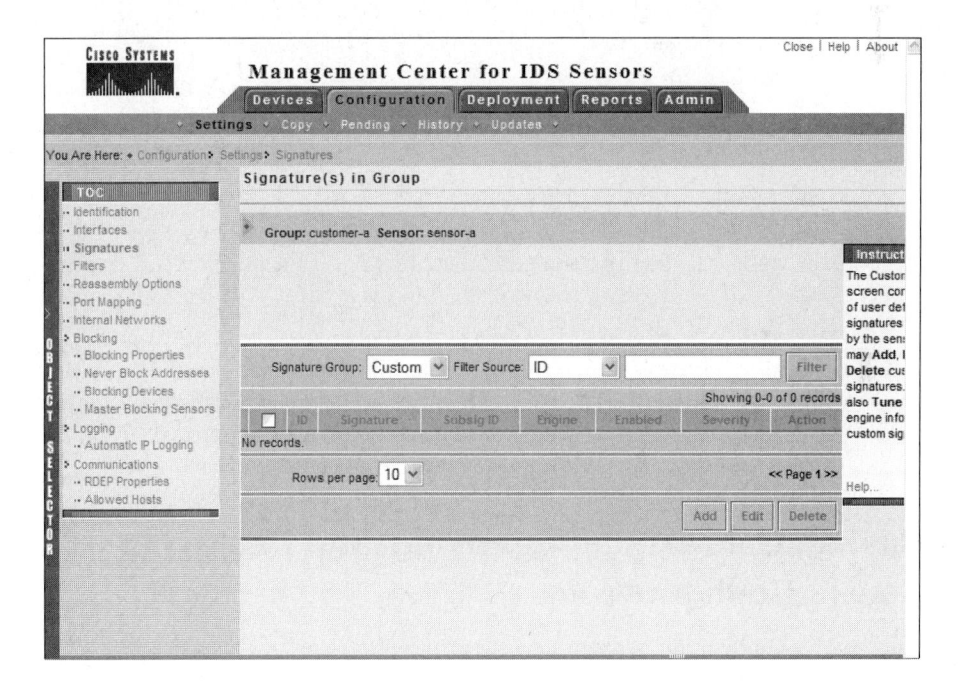

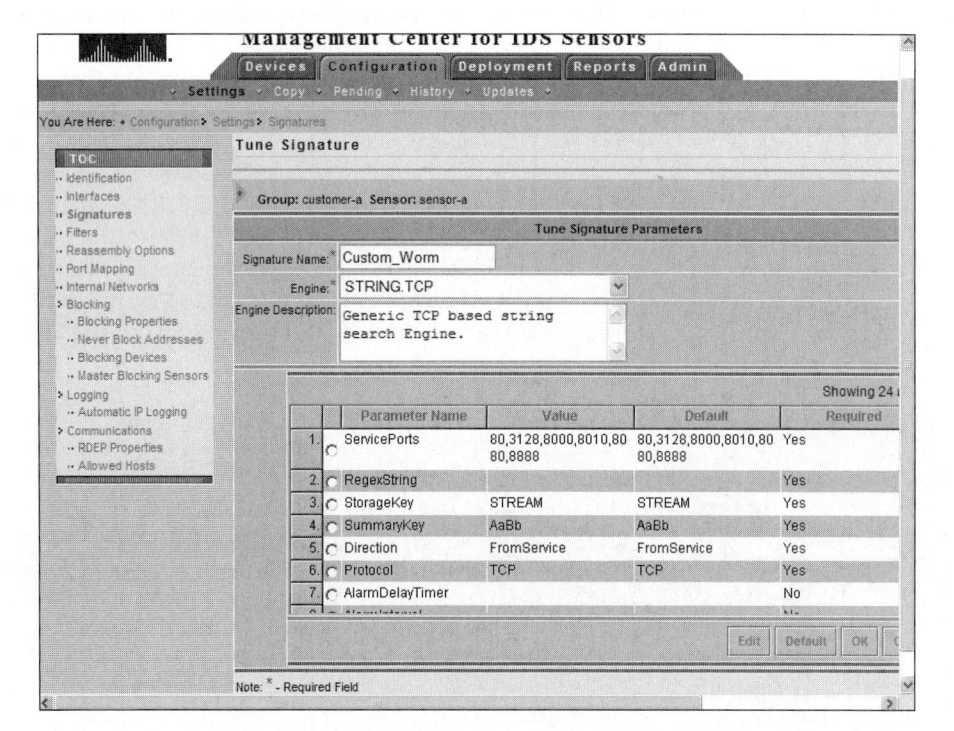

FIGURE 25.51   The Tune Signature page

In Figure 25.52, the text *format flash* is defined as the regular expression, meaning the signature will match TCP traffic that includes the text *format flash*. Click the OK button to return to the Tune Signature Page. You should be able to click OK to complete the creation of the custom signature, now that all required parameters have been configured.

Saving, Generating, Approving, and Deploying Sensor Configurations

Once you've configured a sensor or sensor group using the Settings TOC, you must save the configuration changes to the IDS MC database, generate the appropriate configuration file for each sensor that you wish to modify, approve the configuration, and then push or deploy the configuration to the appropriate sensors. This section describes performing each of these tasks using the IDS MC.

FIGURE 25.52 The Edit Parameter page

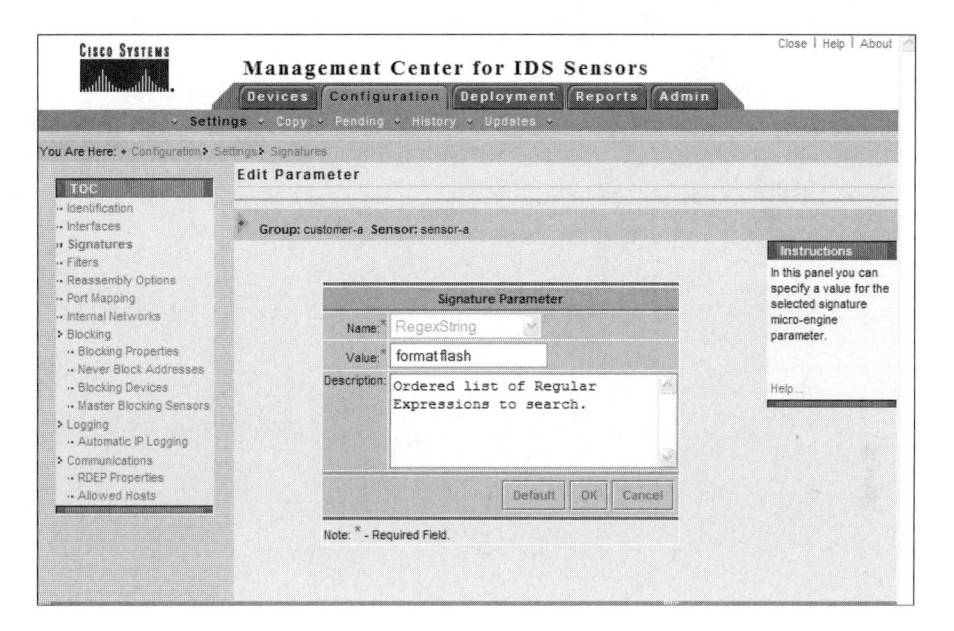

Saving Sensor Configurations

When a change is made to the IDS MC database, a new configuration is generated that is designated a pending status. Any configuration that is in a pending status must be explicitly saved to be written to the IDS MC database permanently, after which configuration files specific to the sensors managed by the IDS MC can be generated, approved, and deployed to each sensor.

To view any pending configurations, select Configuration ➤ Pending to open the Pending page shown in Figure 25.53.

In Figure 25.53, notice that a configuration called Global.customer-a.sensor-a is present in the Pending table. To save the pending configuration, enable the check box next to the configuration and click the Save button. Once a pending configuration is saved, it disappears from the Pending page, and you can continue the process of generating, approving, and deploying sensor configurations.

> **TIP** You can use the Configuration ➤ Copy page to start the Copy Wizard, which lets you copy the partial or complete settings from a specific sensor or group into another sensor or group within the IDS MC. After the Copy Wizard is complete, a new configuration is generated in the Pending page.

FIGURE 25.53 The Pending page

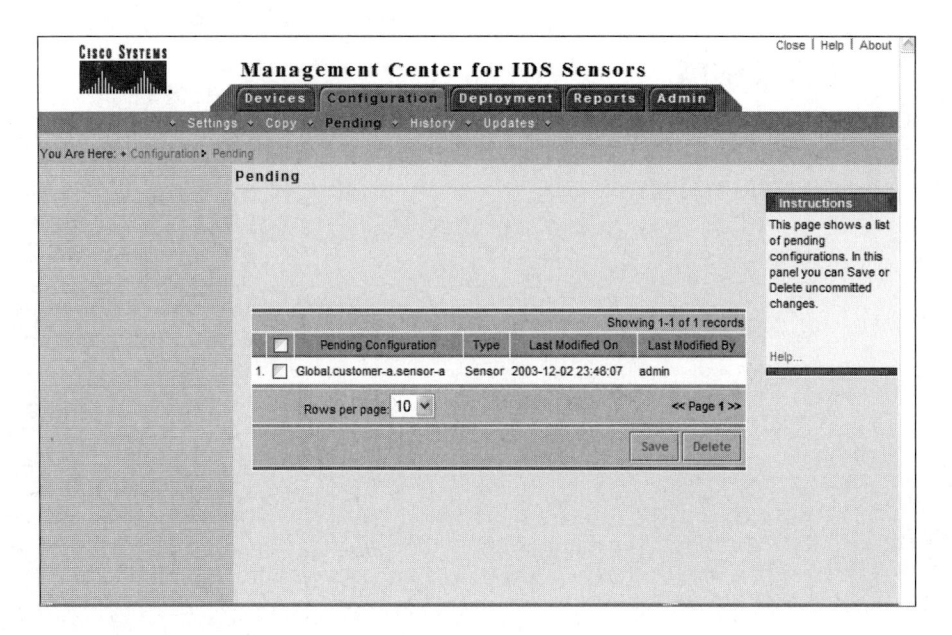

Generating Sensor Configurations

Before you can approve and deploy a sensor configuration, you must generate the appropriate sensor configuration file on the IDS MC, which is based on the configuration you've applied to sensors and sensor groups and saved to the IDS MC database. Only accounts with system administrator privileges can generate sensor configurations.

> **NOTE** To generate sensor configurations based on new configuration information you've applied, you must ensure that the configuration changes have been saved to the IDS MC database.

To generate a sensor configuration, open the Deployment tab within the IDS MC and then select the Generate option. This will open the Generate page, which lets you choose a sensor or sensor group for which you wish to generate a new configuration file. Figure 25.54 shows the Generate page.

In Figure 25.54, sensor-a has been selected. Clicking the Generate button generates a new configuration file for the sensor, with all current configuration settings that have been saved in the IDS MC database. After generating a configuration file, you can view the configuration file you've generated by selecting Configuration ➢ History, which opens the History page, shown in Figure 25.55.

FIGURE 25.54 The Generate page

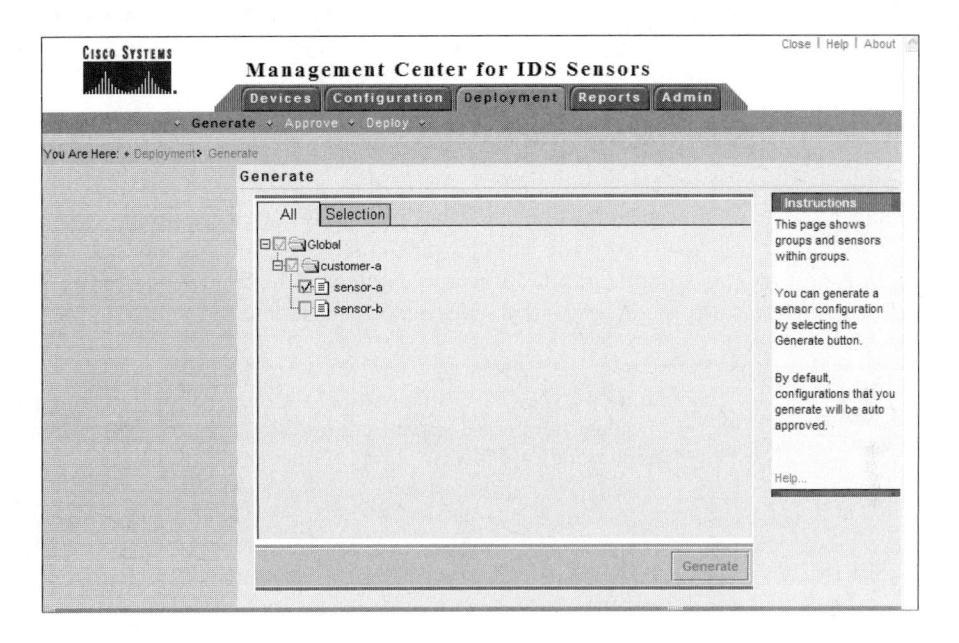

FIGURE 25.55 The History page

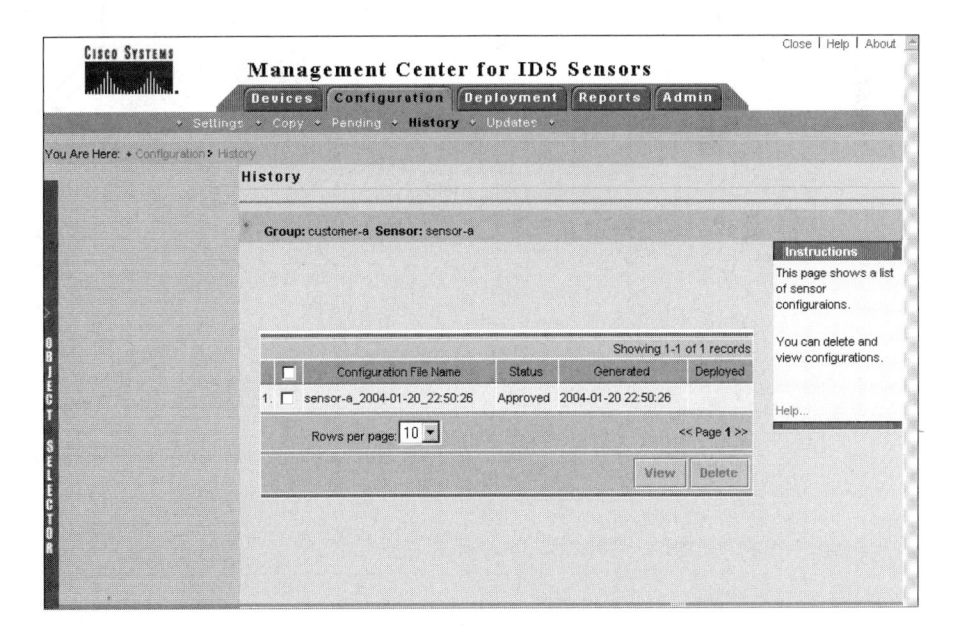

You can see in Figure 25.55 the configuration file that was generated, which includes a date/time stamp of when the file was generated. Notice that the status of the file is Approved. The status isn't Generated, because any generated files are automatically approved by default. The Deployed column indicates whether the configuration file has been deployed.

Approving Sensor Configurations

After you've generated a sensor configuration, the configuration must be approved before you can deploy the configuration to a sensor. By default, the IDS MC automatically approves any configurations that are generated; so if you leave the default settings in place, you don't need to worry about approving sensor configurations. If you've configured the IDS MC so that you must manually approve sensor configurations, then you need to understand the manual approval process.

> **NOTE**
> To configure the IDS MC so that manual approval of sensor configurations is required, select Admin ➤ System Configuration and then select Configuration File Management from the TOC that is presented.

> **NOTE**
> Only user accounts with either Approver or System Administrator privileges are permitted to manually approve sensor configurations.

To manually approve sensor configurations, select Deployment ➤ Approve, which opens the Approve page shown in Figure 25.56.

FIGURE 25.56 The Approve page

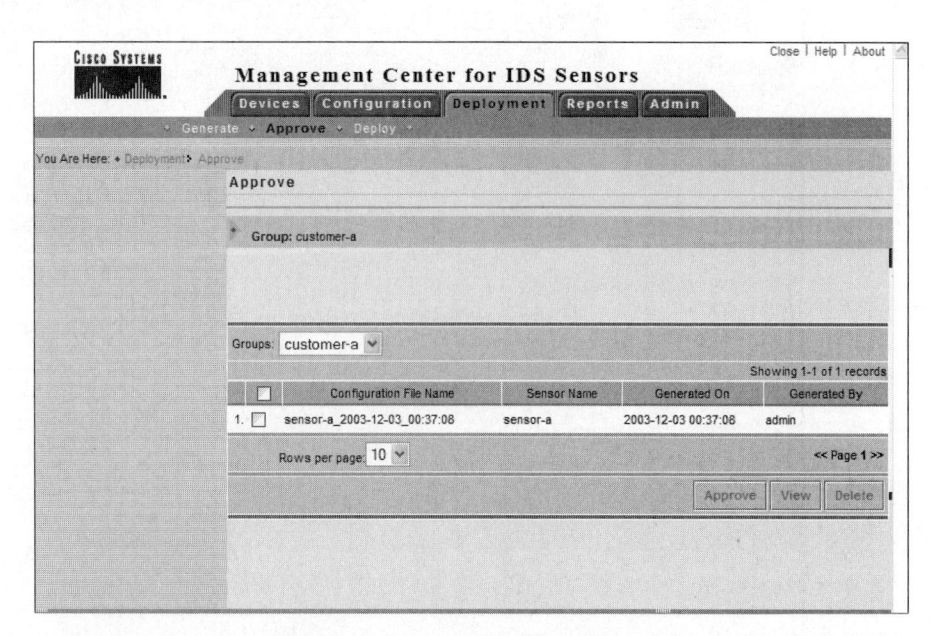

In Figure 25.56, you can see a list of all configuration files that have been generated but not yet approved for a specific group. To approve a configuration file, select the appropriate check box next to the configuration file and then click the Approve button. Notice that you can view or delete configuration files pending approval by clicking the View or Delete button, respectively.

Deploying Sensor Configurations

Once a sensor configuration has been generated and approved, the configuration is ready for deployment to the sensor.

> **NOTE** Only users with system administrator privileges can deploy sensor configurations.

To deploy sensor configurations, select Deployment ➢ Deploy and then open the Submit option from the TOC that appears. This will open the Submit page, shown in Figure 25.57.

Notice that you can select a sensor or group of sensors to which you wish to deploy a configuration. As soon as you select a sensor and click the Deploy button, the Select Configurations page is displayed automatically, as shown in Figure 25.58; here you can select the configuration that you wish to apply.

After you select the configuration you wish to apply, click the Next button to open the Enter Job Properties page, shown in Figure 25.59. This page lets you configure scheduling and other options for the sensor deployment.

FIGURE 25.57 The Submit page

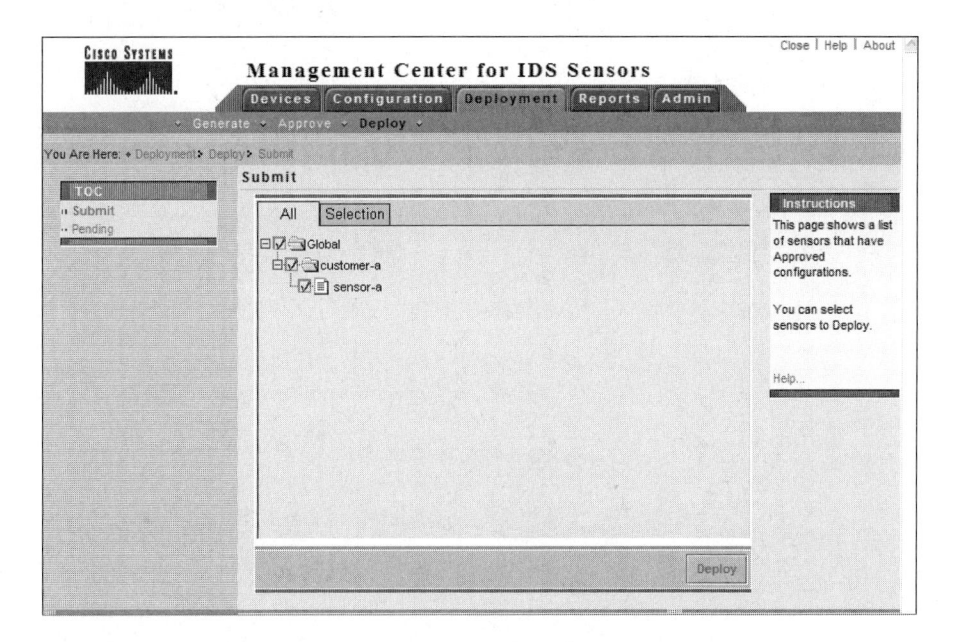

FIGURE 25.58   The Select Configurations page

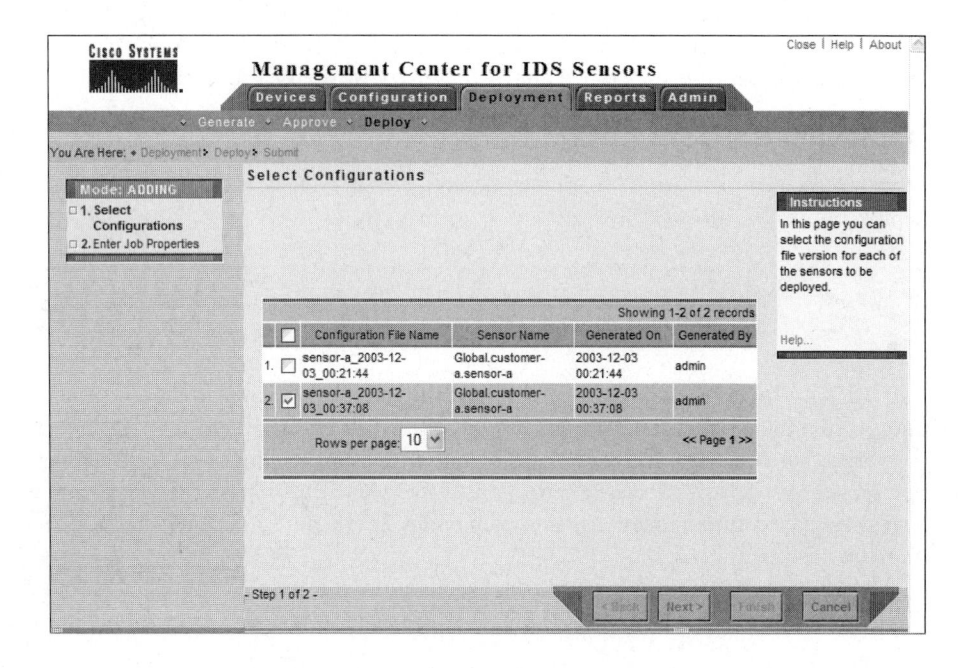

FIGURE 25.59   The Enter Job Properties page

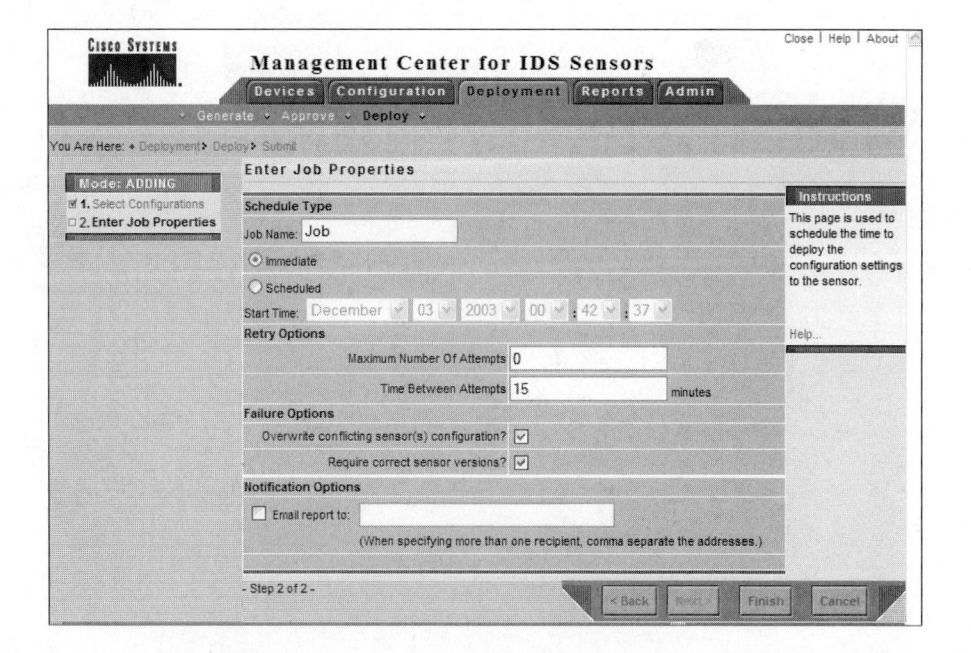

You can configure the following parameters related to configuration deployment:

Scheduling   You can schedule deployment to occur immediately or at a specific date and time.

Retries   You can specify the maximum number of retries. should a deployment operation fail, as well as the time the IDS MC should wait between retries.

Other settings   You can configure deployment so that any conflicting configuration is overwritten, configure the IDS MC to verify that the sensor software version is correct before deployment, and also configure e-mail notification options for the success or failure of the deployment.

After you configure properties for the deployment, click the Finish button in the Enter Job Properties page. If the deployment is scheduled for immediate deployment, the configurations will be deployed immediately at this point. If you've scheduled the deployment for a future date and time, the job will move into a pending status until it's deployed at the scheduled date and time.

> **NOTE**   You can view, edit, and delete any pending jobs by selecting the Pending option from the Deployment ➢ Deploy TOC.

Updating Cisco Secure IDS Sensors

The IDS MC lets you update Cisco Secure IDS sensor software, which includes service packs and signature updates. To apply updates, the following configuration tasks are required:

- Downloading updates
- Updating sensors

Downloading Updates

Before you can update sensor software, you must download the update files from the Cisco website. Cisco Secure IDS software updates can be downloaded from the URL `www.cisco.com/cgi-bin/tablebuild.pl/mgmt-ctr-ids`, which requires a valid CCO login. When you're downloading updates for the IDS MC to deploy to sensors it manages, you must save all updates in the `C:\Program Files\CSCOpx\MDC\etc\ids\updates\` folder. Once you've placed update files in this folder, they're available in the IDS MC interface for deployment.

Updating Sensors

After you've downloaded the updates that you wish to apply to a sensor, you can use the IDS MC to apply updates to the appropriate sensors. To update sensor software, select the Configuration ➢ Updates option from the IDS MC, which opens the Updates page shown in Figure 25.60.

FIGURE 25.60 The Updates page

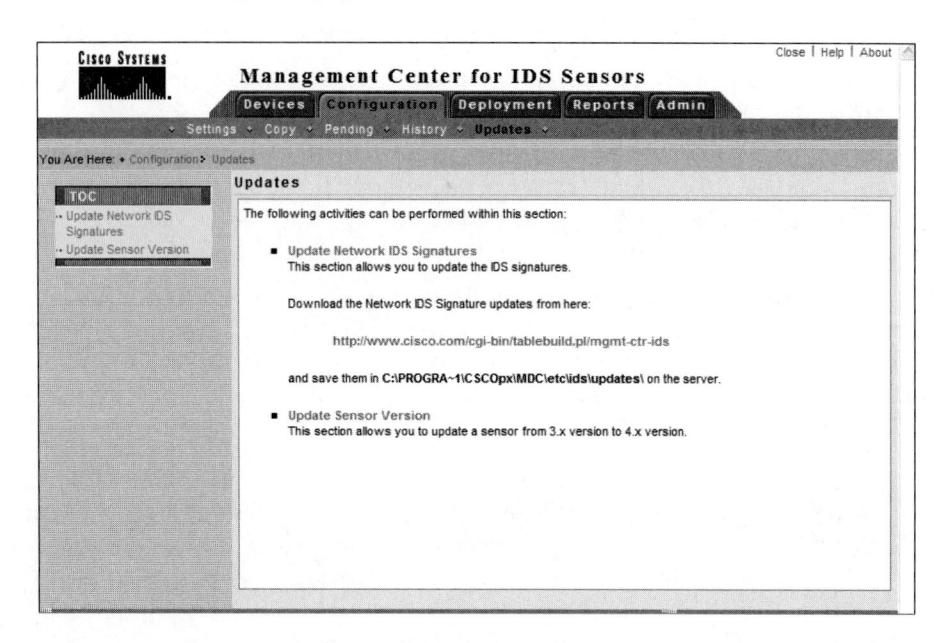

Notice that the TOC lists two options:

Update Network IDS Signatures   This option lets you update Cisco Secure IDS signatures and apply service packs.

Update Sensor Version   This option allows you to update Cisco Secure IDS 3.x sensors managed by the IDS MC to version 4.x.

To update signatures or apply service packs to sensors, select the Update Network IDS Signatures option from the TOC. This will open the Update Network IDS Signatures page, as shown in Figure 25.61.

Notice the Update File drop-down list, which lists all files that are currently located in the C:\Program Files\CSCOpx\MDC\etc\ids\updates\ folder. In Figure 25.61, you can see that the file IDS-sig-4.0-1-S42.zip is listed, which includes version 4.0-1 S42 signatures. Select the appropriate update file, and click the Apply button to open the Select Sensors To Update page shown in Figure 25.62.

After you select the sensors that you wish to update, click the Next button, which will open the Update Summary page. Click the Finish button, and the IDS MC server will attempt to apply the update to the specified sensors.

FIGURE 25.61 The Update Network IDS Signatures page

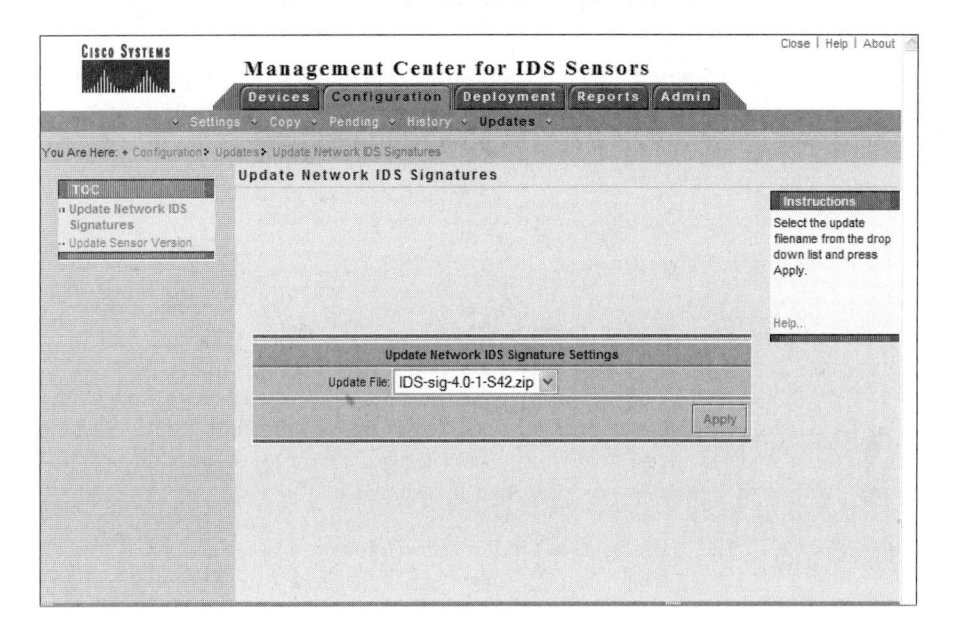

FIGURE 25.62 The Select Sensors To Update page

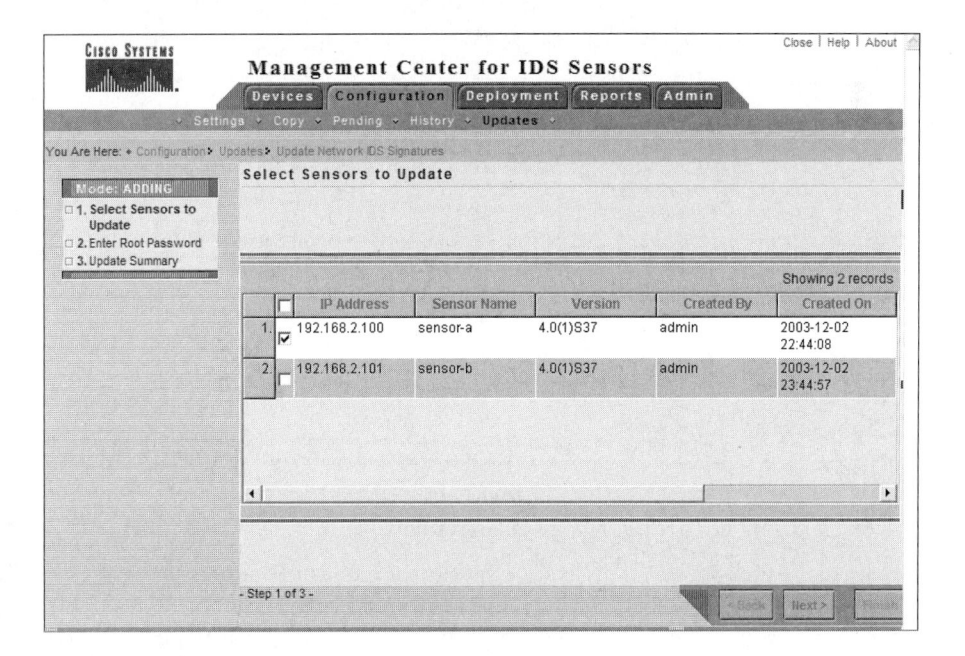

Administering the IDS MC

The IDS MC includes a number of system configuration and report settings, which allow you to control how events are pruned from the IDS MC database, configure a number of system-level settings, and also generate reports. Administering the IDS MC consists of the following tasks:

- Configuring system configuration settings
- Configuring database rules
- Configuring report settings

Configuring System Configuration Settings

The IDS MC includes a number of system configuration settings, each of which defines the behavior of various aspects of the IDS MC. To configure system configuration settings, click the Admin tab and select the System Configuration option from the Options bar. Figure 25.63 shows the System Configuration page that is displayed.

FIGURE 25.63 The System Configuration page

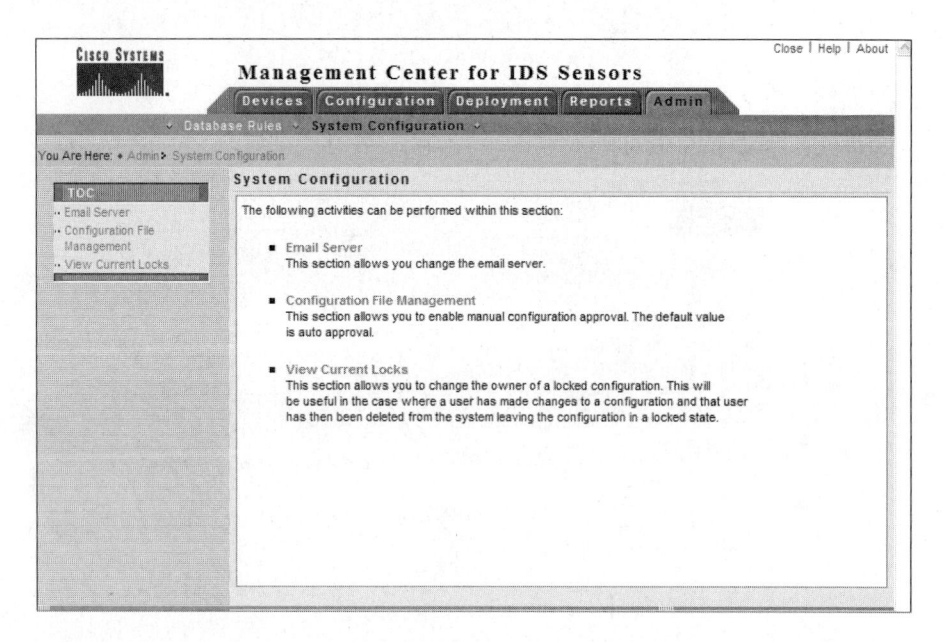

You can configure the following system settings:

Defining an e-mail server This lets you specify the name or IP address of an SMTP server that should be used for any e-mail notifications generated by the IDS MC. For example, database rules (discussed in "Configuring Database Rules" later in this chapter) include an option for generating an e-mail notification. To define an e-mail server, select the Email Server item from the System Configuration TOC.

Configuring manual approval of configuration files   By default, the IDS MC automatically approves configuration files that are generated by administrators. If you wish to require that configuration files be manually approved after generation, the Configuration File Management option in the System Configuration TOC lets you enable/disable automatic approval. Disabling automatic approval requires that any configuration files generated must be manually approved by an IDS MC user with appropriate rights.

View current locks   This lets you change the owner of configuration changes that are currently locked. This option is useful when a user account has been deleted from CiscoWorks, locking a particular configuration element in the IDS MC database.

Configuring Database Rules

The IDS MC includes a number of *database rules* that allow some action to take place on a scheduled basis or based on a database threshold being exceeded. If a database rule is triggered, an action takes place, which can include a notification being generated (via e-mail or console notification) and/or a custom script being executed. Database rules are primarily used to ensure that the IDS MC database doesn't become too large.

To configure database rules, click the Admin tab in the IDS MC and then select the Database Rules option from the Options bar. This will open the Database Rules page, shown in Figure 25.64.

FIGURE 25.64   The Database Rules page

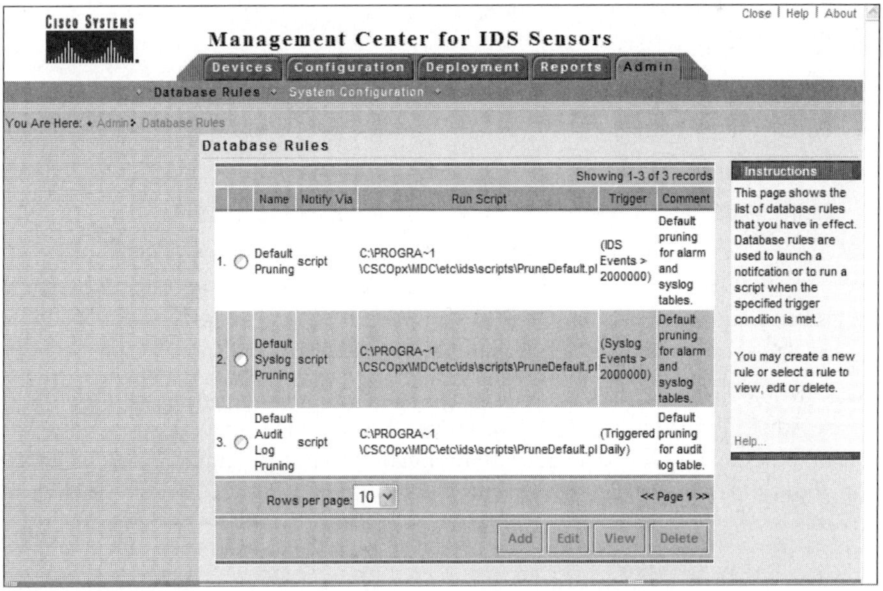

Notice that three rules exist by default:

Default Pruning   This rule is triggered when the total number of IDS events in the IDS MC database exceeds 2,000,000. The rule includes an action of running a script called `PruneDefault.pl`, with options that prune the oldest 1,800,000 events from the `alert` and `syslog` tables within the IDS MC database.

Default Syslog Pruning   This rule is triggered when the total number of Syslog events in the IDS MC database exceeds 2,000,000. The rule includes an action of running the `PruneDefault.pl` script, with options that prune the oldest 1,800,000 events from the `alert` and `syslog` tables within the IDS MC database.

Default Audit Log Pruning   This rule is triggered on a daily basis, and includes an action of running the `PruneDefault.pl` script with options that prune the oldest 25,000 events from the `auditlog` table in the IDS MC database.

> **TIP**   All pruned events are archived to the `C:\Program Files\CSCOpx\MDC\Sybase\DB\IDS\AlertPruneData` directory by default.

Notice on the Database Rules pages that you can add, edit, or delete database rules. When you add or edit a database rule, you must first specify the trigger conditions for the rule and then the actions that should be taken if the rule is triggered. Figure 25.65 demonstrates editing the Default Pruning rule, with the Specify The Trigger Conditions displayed first.

Notice the various trigger conditions that you can define. You can trigger a rule based on any one of the following criteria:

- IDS MC database size
- Free disk space
- Total IDS events
- Total Syslog events
- Total events
- Daily schedule

After you specify the trigger conditions, clicking the Next button takes you to the Choose The Actions page, where you specify the actions that take place should a rule be triggered. Figure 25.66 shows this page.

You can specify one or more of the following actions:

Generate a mail notification   This option is available only if you've defined an e-mail server via the Admin ➢ System Configuration ➢ Email Server page. You can specify the recipients, subject, and message content for the mail notification that is generated. You can include information about the rule that triggered the mail notification using the keyword substitutions shown in Table 25.5.

FIGURE 25.65 The Specify The Trigger Conditions page

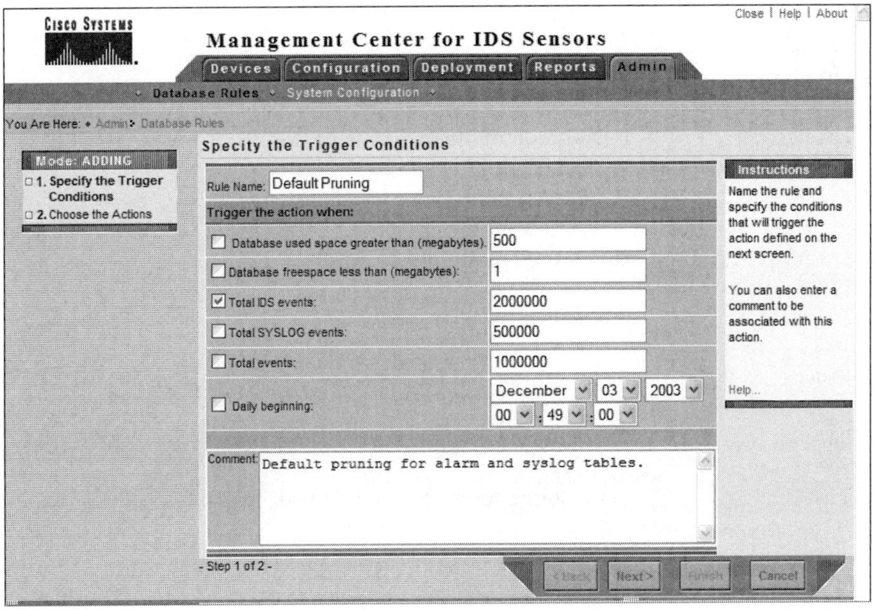

FIGURE 25.66 The Choose The Actions page

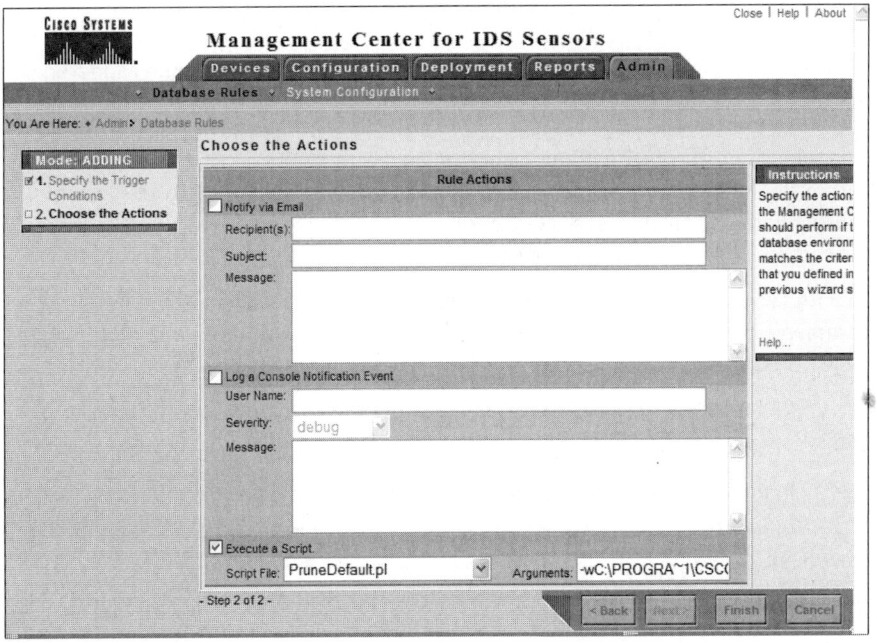

TABLE 25.5 Database Rule Mail Notification Keyword Substitutions

Keyword	Description
${RuleName}	Name of the database rule
${RuleDescr}	Description of the database rule
${Filter}	Query filter for the rule, which includes the trigger conditions for the rule
${Interval}	Query interval for the rule
${Initial}	Initial threshold for the rule
${Repeat}	Repeat threshold for the rule
${DateStr}	Date stamp for when the rule was triggered, in YYYY/MM/DD format
${TimeStr}	Time stamp for when the rule was triggered, in HH:MM:SS TZ format
${GmtDateStr}	GMT date stamp for when the rule was triggered, in YYYY/MM/DD format
${GmtTimeStr}	GMT time stamp for when the rule was triggered, in HH:MM:SS TZ format (TZ is always UTC)
${MsgCount}	Number of matches that occurred in the current interval that caused the rule to be triggered
${Threshold}	Threshold that was met to cause the rule to be triggered

Generate a console notification event Selecting this option writes an event to the audit log within the IDS MC, with a configurable severity and configurable message content. To view console notification events, select Reports ➢ Generate to open the Select Report page and then select the Console Notification Report option.

Execute a script Selecting this option enables you to execute a script and also specify the parameters to pass to the script. The IDS MC includes a number of PERL scripts (located in the C:\Program Files\CSCOpx\MDC\etc\ids\scripts folder) that you can select:

- PruneByAge.pl prunes events older than the specified number of days.
- PruneByDate.pl prunes events generated on or before a specific date.
- PruneBySeverity.pl prunes events based on alarm severity.
- PruneDefault.pl by default prunes 1,800,000 alarms from the IDS MC, but can be customized by specifying different command-line parameters.

- `PruneMarkedForDeletion.pl` prunes events already marked for deletion.
- `PruneSpecifyCmdLine.pl` prunes specific alarms from the database based on a combination of age, date, severity, and whether events are marked for deletion.

Once you've selected the appropriate script that you wish to execute, you can also specify command-line parameters to pass to the script. Each script has a number of mandatory and optional parameters, as demonstrated by the syntax for the `PruneSpecifyCmdLine.pl` script:

```
PruneSpecifyCmdLine.pl -r"tablelist" [-p] [-t"date"] [-a#] [-s"severities"] [-w"dirname"]
```

The following are the various options for the script:

- `-r"tablelist"`: Specifies the table to be pruned. You can list more than one table in a comma-delimited list. Tables include `syslog`, `alert`, `auditlog`, `deploy`, and `sysconfig`. This option is required.
- `-p`: Prunes all events marked for deletion.
- `-t"date"`: Runs all events older than the specified date.
- `-a#`: Prunes all events older than the specified number of days.
- `-s"severities"`: Prunes all events with the severity level(s) specified. You can specify multiple severity levels in a comma-delimited list.
- `-w"dirname"`: Outputs comma-delimited files of pruned events to the specified directory.

Once you've completed specifying the actions, click the Finish button in the Choose the Actions page. This will complete the creation or modification of the database rule you're working with.

Configuring Report Settings

The IDS MC includes a number of reports that allow you to summarize and present information related to IDS MC activities in an easy-to-read format. To configure reports, click the Reports tab, where you can generate and view reports.

Generating Reports

To generate a report, select Reports ➢ Generate to open the Select Report page, shown in Figure 25.67.

You can generate one of the following predefined reports:

Subsystem Report   This report includes audit records ordered by the IDS subsystem and is filterable by event severity, date/time, and subsystem.

Sensor Version Import Report   This report includes audit records that are generated when the software version of sensors is queried and imported into IDS MC. These records indicate success or failure of the operation and are filterable by device, event severity, and date/time.

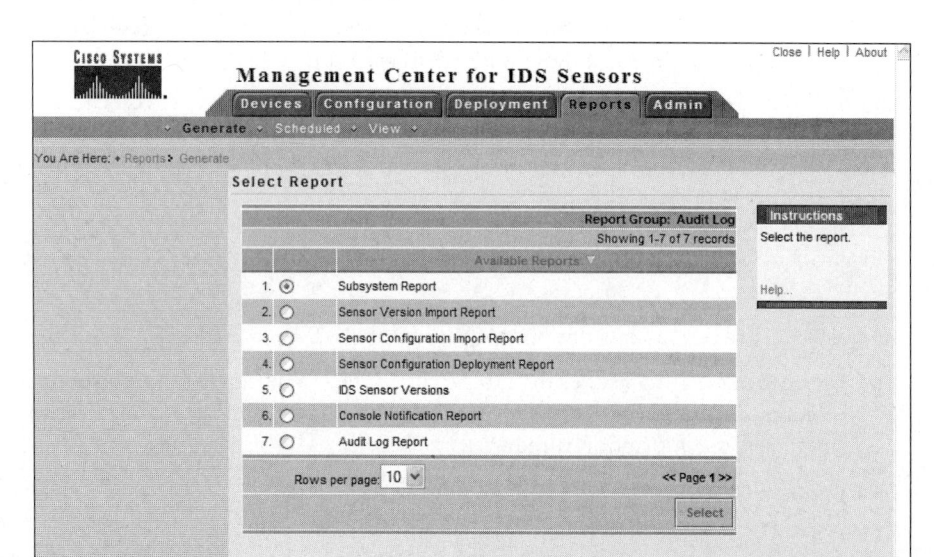

FIGURE 25.67 The Select Report page

Sensor Configuration Import Report This report includes the audit records that are generated when you import sensor configurations into IDS MC. These records indicate success or failure of the operation and are filterable by device, event severity, and date/time.

Sensor Configuration Deployment Report This report includes records related to sensor configurations deployed to devices using the IDS MC. These records indicate success or failure of the operation and are filterable by device, event severity, and date/time. Each record also includes any error messages for failure events.

IDS Sensor Versions This report lists each sensor and specifies the current Cisco Secure IDS software version loaded on each sensor.

Console Notification Report This report includes console notification records generated by the notification subsystem, which can be used by database rules. Events are filterable by event severity and date/time.

Audit Log Report This report includes audit records by the server and application. Unlike the other report templates, this report template provides a broad, non–task-specific view of audit records in the database and is filterable by task type, event severity, date/time, subsystem, and applications.

When you generate a report, you're asked to specify filtering and scheduling options for it. With respect to filtering, you can define the time period over which the report should be generated, the severities of events to include in the report, and other parameters specific to the report you're generating. With respect to scheduling, you can choose to generate the report immediately, or you can specify a schedule for generating the report. You can also export the report to an HTML file and generate an e-mail notification when the report runs.

> **Note**: If you wish to modify the scheduling parameters of a scheduled report, select Reports ➢ Scheduled, which opens the Edit Scheduled Reports page.

Viewing Reports

To view reports that you've generated, select Reports ➢ View to open the Choose Completed Report page, shown in Figure 25.68:

You can select the appropriate report that you wish to view and then click either the View button (report will open in the same window) or the Open In Window button (report will open in a new browser window). You can also delete generated reports from this page.

FIGURE 25.68 The Choose Completed Report page

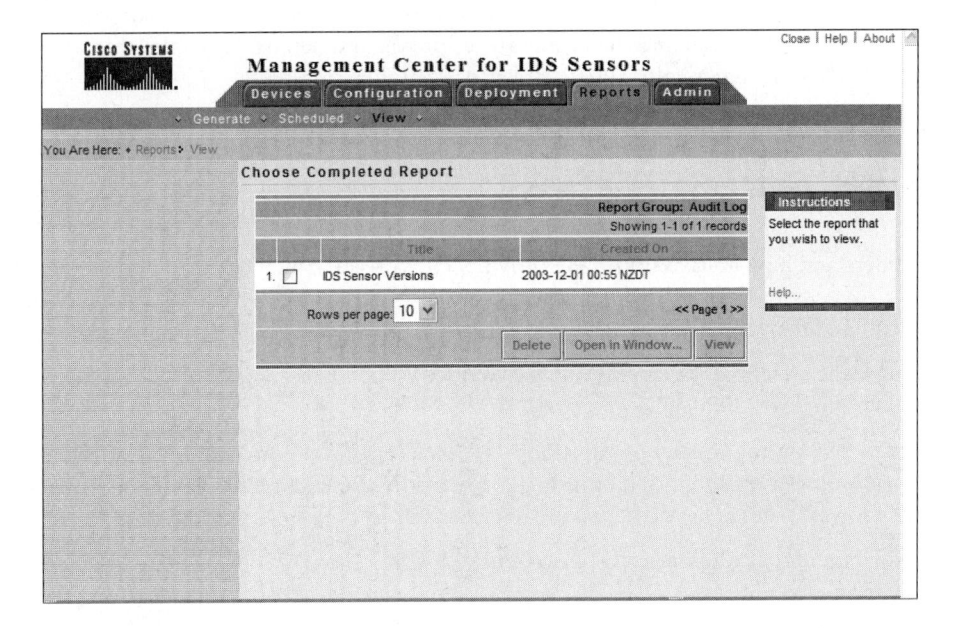

Summary

CiscoWorks VMS 2.2 provides an enterprise management platform not only for Cisco Secure IDS sensors, but also for other Cisco security devices and products. CiscoWorks VMS can manage up to 300 Cisco Secure IDS sensors, ensuring that it can meet the management and scalability demands of even the largest networks. CiscoWorks VMS 2.2 is actually a set of components, each of which provides some form of security management or monitoring functionality.

To install CiscoWorks VMS 2.2, you must first ensure that the CiscoWorks VMS server meets the minimum system requirements. Assuming this is the case, you must then install the CiscoWorks Common Services component, which is a mandatory component for all CiscoWorks VMS servers. After Common Services are in place, you can then install the IDS MC and Security Monitor. CiscoWorks permits you to separate the IDS MC and Security Monitor onto separate physical services if required.

Once you've installed CiscoWorks VMS 2.2, you can begin managing Cisco Secure IDS sensors. Managing sensors starts with adding sensors and sensor groups to the IDS MC—a sensor group lets you group sensors for the purposes of deploying a common configuration or common base settings (from a parent group) to each sensor within the group. After adding sensors to the IDS MC, you can then configure the various sensor configuration parameters, including communication settings, intrusion detection settings, signatures and logging. When you've configured the IDS MC with the appropriate settings for your sensor(s), you must next save the configuration and then generate, approve, and deploy the configuration. By default, the IDS MC automatically approves sensor configuration files.

Exam Essentials

Understand how CiscoWorks VMS provides enterprise IDS management and monitoring. CiscoWorks VMS includes the IDS Management Center, which provides enterprise IDS management, and the Security Monitoring Center, which provides enterprise IDS monitoring.

Know the system requirements of CiscoWorks VMS. CiscoWorks VMS can be installed on either Windows 2000 SP3 or Solaris 2.8.

Know the unsupported configurations of CiscoWorks VMS on Windows. CiscoWorks VMS on Windows isn't supported on primary or backup domain controllers or any server running Windows Terminal Services, and it can't be installed on a FAT partition.

Understand the components of CiscoWorks VMS. CiscoWorks VMS includes several components:

- CiscoWorks Common Services, including the optional CiscoView 5.5 and Integration Utility 1.5 components
- Resource Manager Essentials 3.5
- Auto Update Server 1.1

- Firewall MC 1.2
- VPN Router MC 1.2
- IDS MC 1.2
- Security Agent MC 4.0
- Security Monitor 1.2
- VPN Monitor 1.2.1

Know how to install CiscoWorks VMS. All CiscoWorks VMS components can be installed on a single stand-alone server or distributed across multiple servers. On any CiscoWorks VMS server, you must install CiscoWorks Common Services first. You can then install the components that you require (such as IDS MC and Security Monitor).

Know how to start the IDS MC. To start the IDS MC, you must first start the CiscoWorks Desktop via the URL `http://server-ip-address:1741` or `https://server-ip-address:1742` if SSL is enabled, and you must authenticate as a valid user. You can then start the IDS MC by opening the VPN/Security Management Solution drawer in the navigation tree and clicking the Management Centers ➤ IDS Sensors option. This starts the IDS MC in a separate browser window.

Know how to add IDS sensors and sensor groups to the IDS MC. You can add sensor groups via the Devices ➤ Sensor Groups page in the IDS MC, and you can add sensors via the Devices ➤ Sensors page.

Know how to configure IDS sensors using the IDS MC. All sensor configuration is performed in the IDS MC by opening the Configuration ➤ Settings TOC and selecting the appropriate sensor or sensor group object using the Object Selector.

Understand how to generate, approve, and deploy sensor configurations. After you've configured sensor or sensor group objects in the IDS MC, you must next generate sensor configurations for each sensor, approve the configurations (by default, all configurations are automatically approved), and then deploy sensor configurations. All of these tasks are performed using the Deployment tab within the IDS MC.

Understand how to administer the IDS MC. The IDS MC lets you configure database rules for database management, configure miscellaneous system parameters, and generate reports.

Chapter 26

Enterprise Cisco Secure IDS Monitoring

CISCO SECURE INTRUSION DETECTION SYSTEM EXAM TOPICS COVERED IN THIS CHAPTER:

- ✓ Features and key concepts of the Security Monitor
- ✓ Installing and verifying the Security Monitor functionality
- ✓ Monitoring IDS devices with the Security Monitor
- ✓ Administering Security Monitor event rules
- ✓ Creating alarm exceptions to reduce alarms and possible false positives
- ✓ Using the reporting features of the Security Monitor
- ✓ Administering the Security Monitor server

In the last chapter, you learned about the IDS Management Center component of CiscoWorks VMS and how it provides enterprise management of up to 300 Cisco Secure IDS sensors from a single server. CiscoWorks VMS also includes the security monitoring center (Security Monitor), which provides enterprise monitoring of the alarms generated by Cisco Secure IDS sensors and other Cisco security devices. The Security Monitor can monitor alarms from up to 300 sensors and, in conjunction with the IDS MC, provides a fully featured, scalable enterprise IDS management and monitoring solution.

In this chapter, you'll learn how to use the Security Monitor. In the last chapter you learned how to install CiscoWorks VMS and its components (including the Security Monitor), so it's assumed you understand how to install the Security Monitor. You'll learn how to start the Security Monitor, define sensors that you wish to monitor, view alarms generated by those sensors, configure other notification methods, and administer the Security Monitor database.

Introduction to the Security Monitor

The Security Monitor is a component of the CiscoWorks VMS solution, and it provides security monitoring for networks that include Cisco Secure IDS sensors and other Cisco Security devices. In the following sections, you'll learn about the features of the Security Monitor, devices supported by the Security Monitor, and how to access the Security Monitor for the first time.

Security Monitor Features

The Security Monitor includes a number of features that enable you to easily and effectively manage security events in your network. The Security Monitor provides the following key features:

Realtime Event Viewer The Security Monitor includes an Event Viewer application, which provides a realtime view of events (alarms) as they're generated. Alarm information is arranged in a tabular view and can be easily manipulated so that alarm information is aggregated and summarized to provide an overview of the current status of security events in the network. You can also drill down on specific alarms if required and re-sort alarm information into custom views. The Event Viewer also provides graphing features, provides the ability to view the context data associated with a signature, and can access the Network Security Database (NSDB) for further information on an alarm.

Event Notification   *Event notification* lets you generate e-mail notifications and/or custom scripts in response to an alarm being generated. Event notification is enabled by creating event notification rules, which specify the criteria for when an event notification should take place and the actions associated with the event notification.

> **NOTE**   Event notification is a key differentiator between the IDS Event Viewer (IEV) product that ships free with Cisco Secure IDS sensors (see Chapter 24, "Configuring Signatures and Using the IDS Event Viewer") and the Security Monitor. The IEV doesn't support event notification.

Event Reporting   *Event reporting* provides a snapshot view of security events on your network and can be generated from historical or realtime event data. All reports are generated in an HTML format for easy viewing from any supported web browser and can also be e-mailed or exported to another format. The Security Monitor includes a series of filters that you can apply to refine reports; you can also configure scheduled reports that are automatically generated on a scheduled basis.

Event Correlation   You can perform *event correlation* using the Event Viewer, reporting, and event rule subsystems of the Security Monitor. By default, the Event Viewer displays all alarms; however, you can reorder events to correlate to specific events based on specific attributes such as signature name, source address, destination address, and so on. You can also filter the event information used to generate reports, allowing you to create a correlated snapshot view of specific events. Finally, event rules provide the ability to create logical relationships between events produced by different monitored devices and generate e-mail notifications or execute custom scripts based on those logical relationships.

Version 1.2 of the Security Monitor is included with CiscoWorks VMS 2.2; it provides some new features over and above older versions of the Security Monitor. The following features are new to version 1.2 of the Security Monitor:

- Support for receiving alarms from Cisco Security Agent MC servers
- The ability to generate firewall reports based on firewall events
- Enhanced data import and export mechanisms
- A database-compact utility that can reclaim disk space

Supported Devices for the Security Monitor

The Security Monitor supports receiving alarms not only from Cisco Secure IDS sensors but also from other Cisco security devices, which allows for centralized collection of security events from all security devices in your network. Table 26.1 lists the security devices, software versions, and types of events supported by version 1.2 of the Security Monitor.

TABLE 26.1 Supported Devices, Software Versions, and Events on the Security Monitor 1.2

Device	Software Version	Type of Events Supported
Cisco Secure IDS Sensors	3.x, 4.x	IDS alarms (via PostOffice or RDEP)
Cisco PIX Firewall	6.x	All firewall and IDS events (via Syslog)
Firewall Services Module	1.1.1, 1.1.2	All firewall events (via Syslog)
Cisco IOS Router	12.2 Mainline	IDS subsystem alarms only (via Syslog or PostOffice protocol)
Cisco IDS Host Console	2.5	IDS alarms
Cisco Security Agent MC Server	4.0	IDS alarms

With respect to Cisco Secure IDS 4.x sensors, the Security Monitor supports collection of alarms from these devices using the Remote Desktop Exchange Protocol (RDEP) over HTTP/HTTPS, in the same fashion as the IEV. Recall from Chapter 24 that the IEV pulls alarms from the local event store on each sensor using RDEP. The Security Monitor uses exactly the same mechanism to collect alarms from version 4.x sensors.

Accessing the Security Monitor for the First Time

Assuming you've installed the CiscoWorks VMS common services and the Security Monitor (see Chapter 25, "Enterprise Cisco Secure IDS Management"), you're ready to start the Security Monitor. Before accessing the Security Monitor, you need to ensure that you're logged into the CiscoWorks Desktop with an account that possesses the appropriate rights for the tasks you need to perform with the Security Monitor. Table 26.2 lists the various user roles that exist within CiscoWorks VMS and describes the tasks that each can perform within the Security Monitor.

Assuming you have the appropriate privileges to access the Security Monitor, you can start the Security Monitor by opening the VPN/Security Management Solution drawer within the CiscoWorks Desktop navigation tree and then selecting Monitoring Center ➤ Security Monitor. Figure 26.1 shows the navigation tree view used to open the Security Monitor.

After you select Monitoring Center ➤ Security Monitor in Figure 26.1, a separate browser window opens that displays the Security Monitor interface. Figure 26.2 shows the Security Monitor interface.

TABLE 26.2 Security Monitor Privileges

Role	Security Monitor Tasks
Help Desk	Can view any alarm or report. Can't delete alarms or reports. Can't generate reports.
Approver	Can view any alarm or report. Can't delete alarms or reports. Can't generate reports.
Network Operator	Can view any alarm or report. Can delete any alarm or report. Can generate reports.
Network Administrator	Can view any alarm or report. Can delete any alarm or report. Can generate reports. Can edit device configurations.
System Administrator	Can perform all tasks.

FIGURE 26.1 CiscoWorks Desktop navigation tree view used to Open Security Monitor

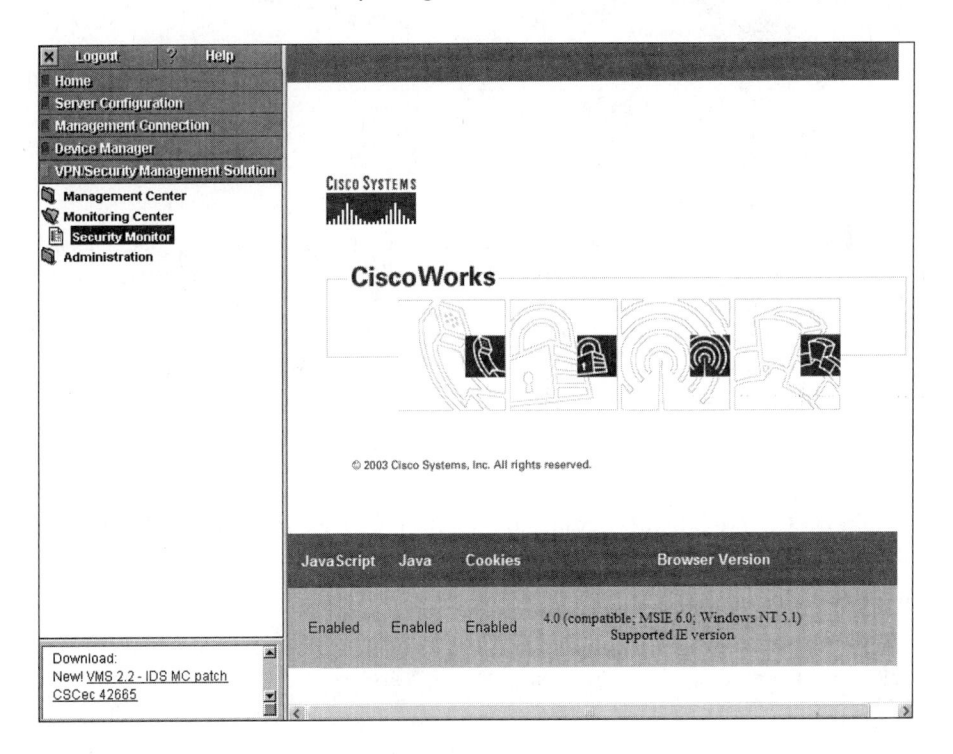

FIGURE 26.2 The Security Monitor interface

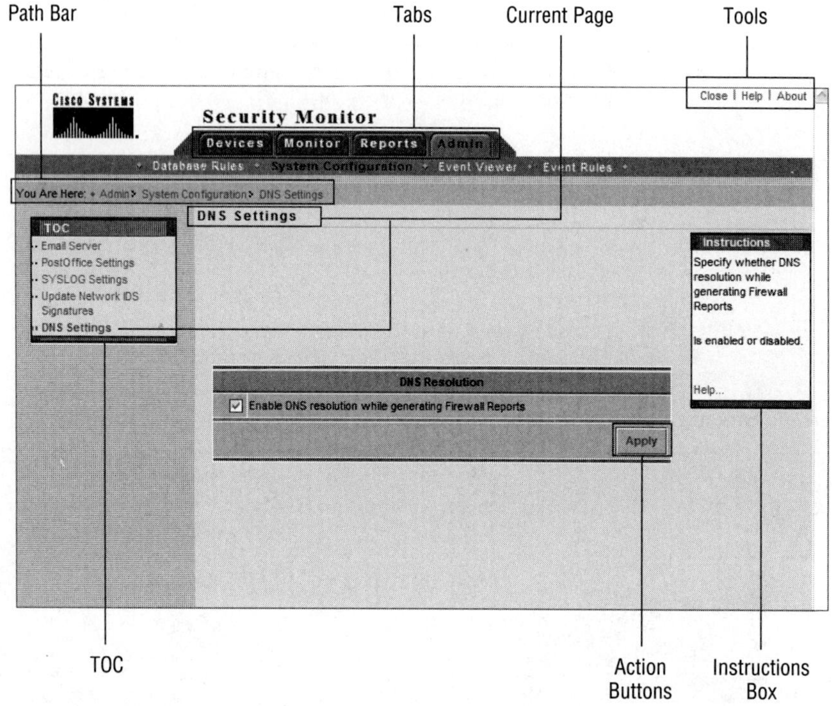

In Figure 26.2, the Admin > System Configuration > DNS Settings page has been opened, which includes all the various components of the Security Monitor interface. You can see that the look and feel of the Security Monitor is similar to the IDS MC and includes the same basic elements, such as a Path bar, TOC, Options bar, tabs, tools, Instructions box, and action buttons. The Security Monitor includes four tabs that access the major functionality areas of the Security Monitor interface:

Devices This tab provides options for adding, editing, deleting, and importing monitored devices.

Monitor This tab provides options for monitoring device status and viewing alarms using the Event Viewer application.

Reports This tab provides options for generating, viewing, and scheduling reports.

Admin This tab provides options for configuring database rules, system configuration, event rules, and Event Viewer preferences.

Configuring the Security Monitor

Now that you understand how to start the Security Monitor and are familiar with the look and feel of the Security Monitor interface, it's time to learn how to configure the Security Monitor to provide monitoring of Cisco Secure IDS sensors. The Security Monitor can manage a number of Cisco security devices, including Cisco Secure IDS sensors, Cisco IOS routers, Cisco IDS host sensors, Cisco PIX firewalls, and Cisco Security Agents. This book only covers Cisco Secure IDS 4.x sensors; hence in this chapter you'll learn how to define 4.x sensors so that the Security Monitor can monitor them for alarm information. Configuring the Security Monitor for IDS sensor monitoring requires the following tasks:

- Configure sensors to support the Security Monitor.
- Define devices to monitor.
- Verify sensor connection status.

Configuring Sensors to Support the Security Monitor

Before you add sensors to the Security Monitor, you must ensure that each sensor is configured to permit alarms to be monitored by the Security Monitor. On Cisco Secure IDS 4.x sensors (RDEP-based sensors), the Security Monitor server must be configured as an allowed host. You can add the Security Monitor as an allowed host by using any one of the following methods:

- Sensor CLI (see Chapter 23, "Configuring Cisco Secure IDS Sensors Using the IDS Device Manager," for more details)
- Sensor IDM (see Chapter 23 for more details)
- IDS MC (see Chapter 25 for more details)

> **NOTE** The Security Monitor connects to Cisco Secure IDS 4.x sensors in the same fashion as the IEV (see Chapter 24). The Security Monitor opens a subscription to each sensor and periodically pulls events from the sensor event store, using RDEP messages within HTTP/HTTPS transactions.

Defining Devices to Monitor

Once you've ensured that the sensors you wish to monitor will accept connections from the Security Monitor, you can begin configuring the Security Monitor by adding the devices (sensors) that you wish to monitor. The Security Monitor must be configured with the appropriate communication settings for a sensor (for example, IP address, web server port, username/password) so that it can communicate with the sensor and receive alarms. Cisco Secure IDS sensors can be added to the Security Monitor in one of three ways:

- Manually adding sensors
- Importing sensor information from the IDS MC
- Importing PostOffice settings from sensors running PostOffice communications (Cisco Secure IDS 3.x only)

> **NOTE** Importing PostOffice settings from sensors isn't discussed in this chapter, because version 3.x sensors aren't covered on the exam.

Manually Adding Sensors

You can add sensors manually to the Security Monitor by manually specifying the appropriate communication settings for the sensor. The communication settings you must define depend on the version of sensor you're adding—this section only discusses adding version 4.x sensors.

To begin adding sensors as devices to the Security Monitor, select the Devices tab in the Security Monitor, which opens the Devices page, as shown in Figure 26.3.

To add a sensor, click the Add button at the bottom of the Devices page, which opens the Select Device Type page, as shown in Figure 26.4. This page lets you select the type of security device you're adding.

You can add several types of IDS devices, as well as Cisco PIX/FWSM and Cisco Security Agent management console devices. To add a version 4.x sensor, you must select the RDEP IDS option on the Select Device Type page. Assuming that you select an RDEP IDS, clicking the Next button opens the Enter Device Information page. This page lets you specify the various communication settings that are required for the Security Monitor to communicate with the sensor you're adding. Figure 26.5 shows the Enter Device Information page.

In Figure 26.5, notice that you can specify settings similar to those used when you add a device to the IDS MC (see Chapter 25). In Figure 26.5, a sensor called sensor-a has been added, which has an IP address of 192.168.1.100 and a NAT address of 200.1.1.100 (the sensor is reachable from the Security Monitor via the address 200.1.1.100) and uses encryption (SSL over HTTP) for secure communications. The Security Monitor is also configured to receive only alarms with a medium severity (default) or higher from the sensor. Once you've completed the Enter Device Information page, click Finish to complete the device-creation process; the Devices page should now show the new sensor.

FIGURE 26.3 The Devices page

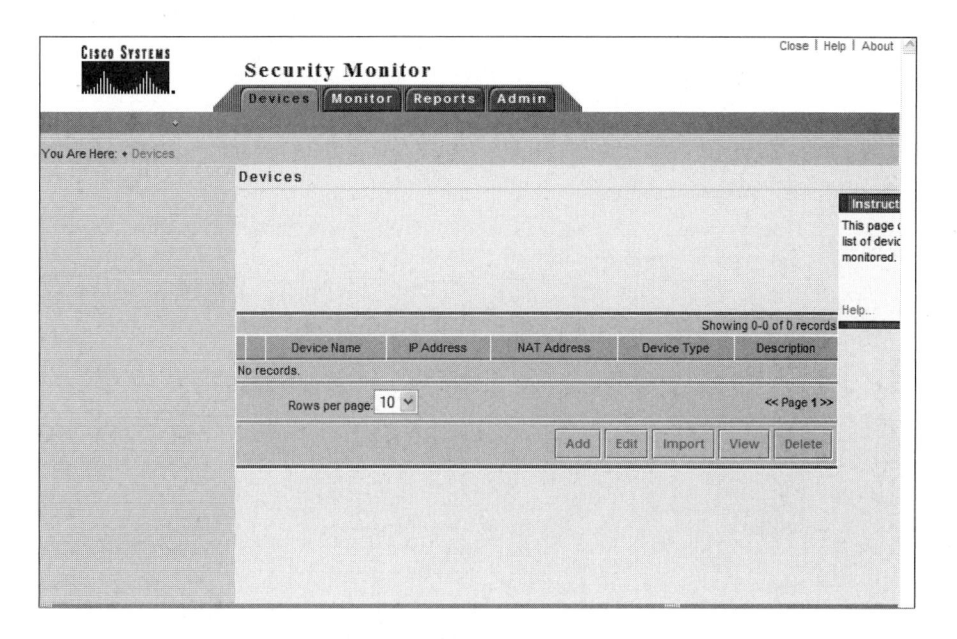

FIGURE 26.4 The Select Device Type page

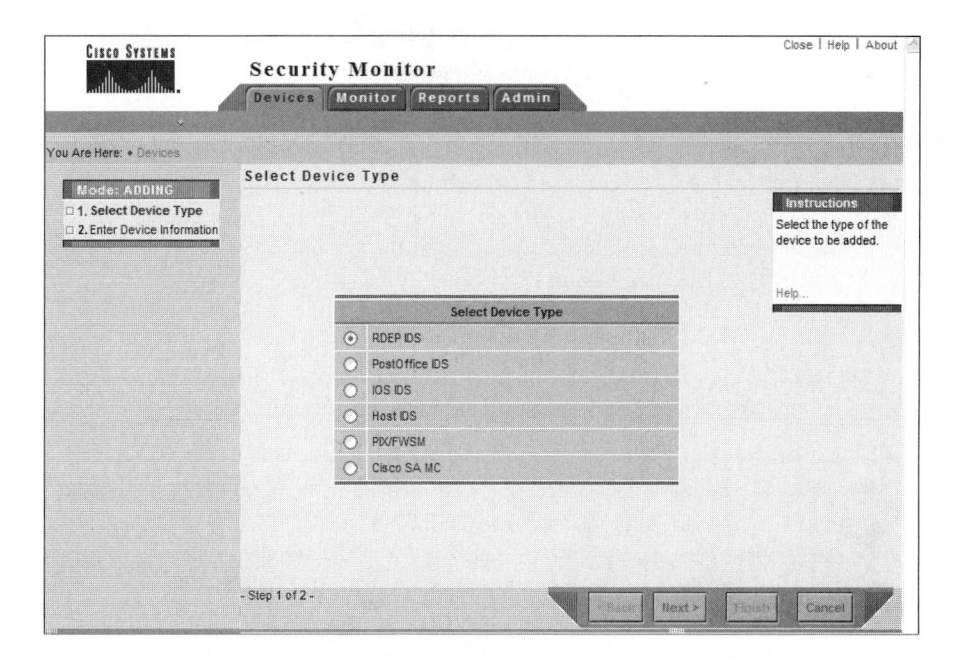

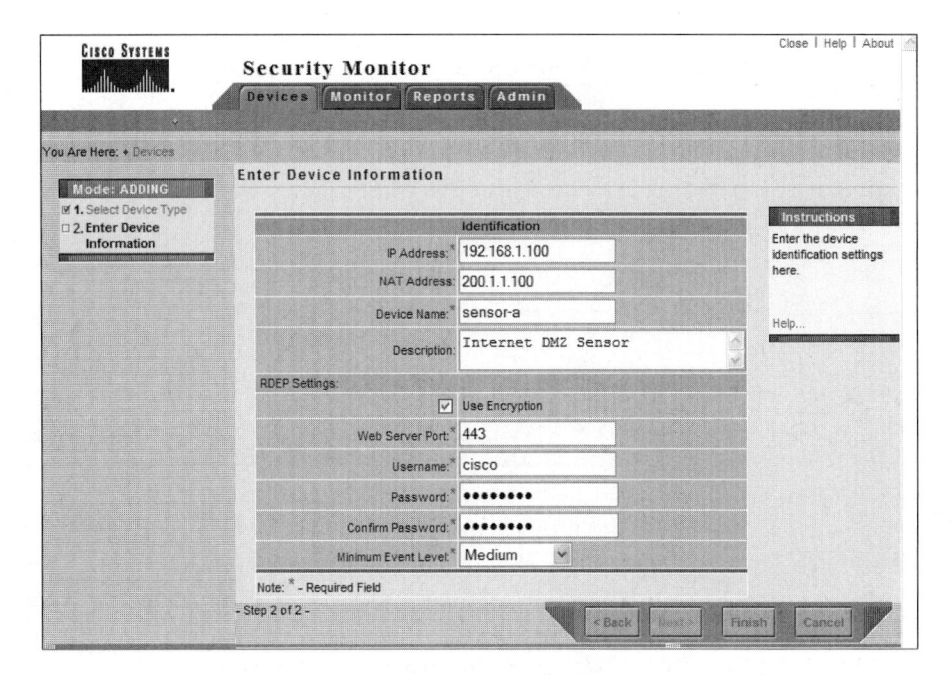

FIGURE 26.5 The Enter Device Information page

Importing Sensor Information from the IDS MC

If you use the IDS MC to manage sensors that you wish to monitor with the Security Monitor, you'll have already configured many of the settings required to communicate with the sensor within the IDS MC. These settings can be imported into the Security Monitor, which saves you from having to manually re-enter sensor settings.

To import sensor information from the IDS MC, open the Devices page by clicking the Devices tab (see Figure 26.3), and then click the Import button. This will open the Enter IDS MC Server Information page, shown in Figure 26.6.

Notice that you must configure the IP address of the IDS MC server (this can be the same server as the Security Monitor or a different server), the web server port on which the IDS MC operates (HTTPS is used to communicate with the IDS MC server and uses a default port of 443), and an appropriate username and password for accessing the IDS MC server.

> **NOTE** An account with system administrator privileges must be specified to import sensor settings from the IDS MC.

After you specify the appropriate parameters in the Enter IDS MC Server Information page, click the Next button. At this point, the Security Monitor server connects to the IDS MC server via HTTPS, authenticates, and obtains a list of sensors currently configured within the IDS MC. This list of sensors is displayed in the Select Devices page, as shown in Figure 26.7.

Configuring the Security Monitor   1027

FIGURE 26.6   The Enter IDS MC Server Information page

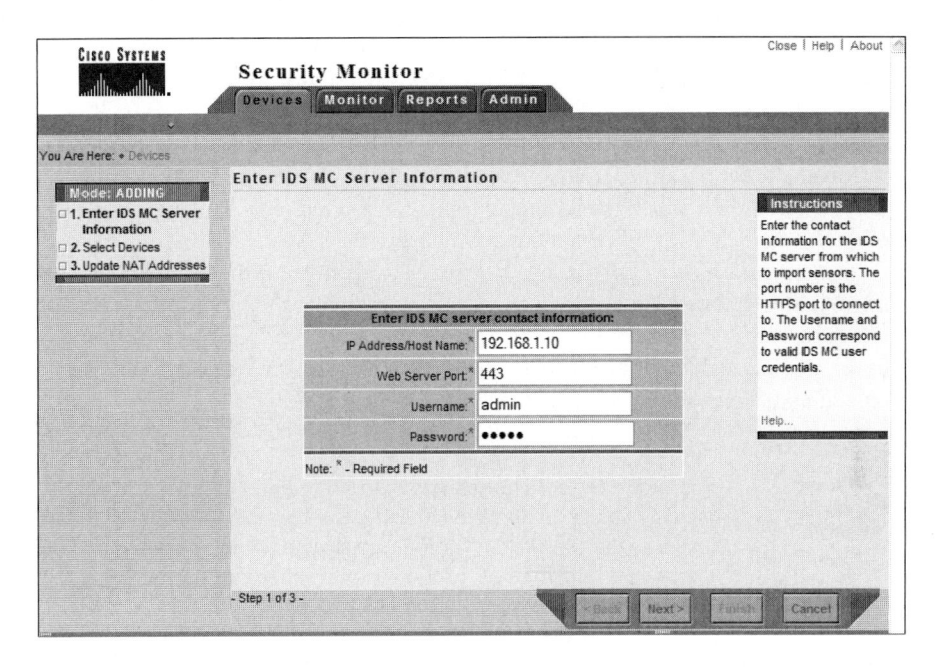

FIGURE 26.7   The Select Devices page

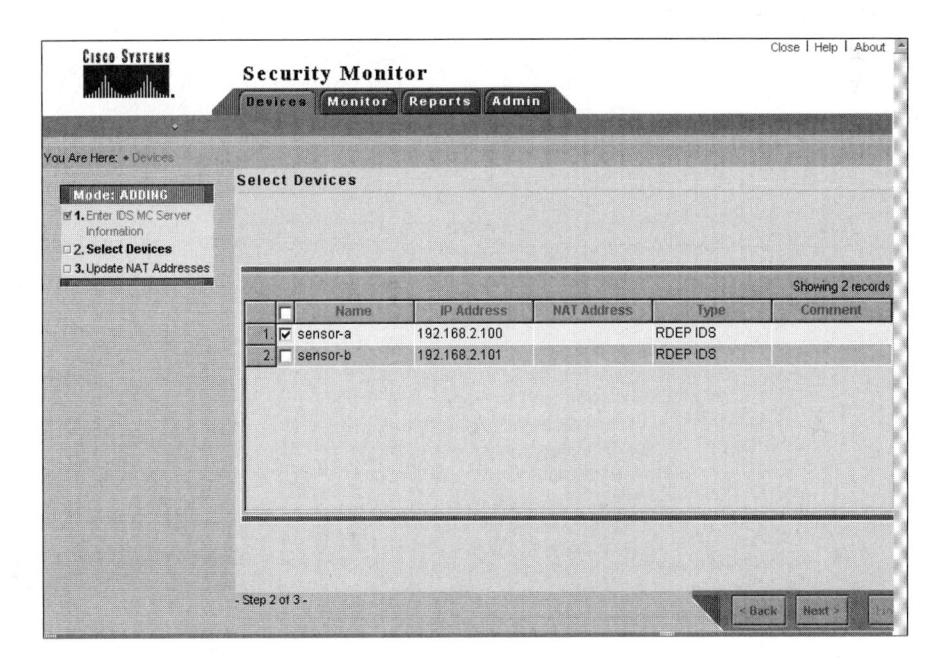

In Figure 26.7, two sensors are displayed: sensor-a and sensor-b. You can select one or more sensors that you wish to import by checking the box next to the appropriate sensor(s) and clicking the Next button. Doing so opens the Update NAT Addresses page shown in Figure 26.8, which lets you configure the NAT addresses for each sensor that you're importing if it's reachable via a NAT address.

If you need to configure a NAT address, click the appropriate cell within the NAT Address column and enter the appropriate NAT address. In Figure 26.8, a NAT address of 200.1.1.100 is being configured, which the Security Monitor will attempt to connect to rather than the real IP address of the sensor when pulling alarms from the sensor.

To complete the import of the sensors you selected on the Select Devices page, click the Finish button in the Update NAT Addresses page after specifying the NAT address for each sensor (if required). This will open the Import Summary page, which indicates whether the configuration import was successful. Click OK on this page to return to the Devices page, where the sensors you've imported should now be displayed.

> **NOTE** You can view, edit, or delete devices by selecting the appropriate device from the Devices page and then clicking the View, Edit, or Delete button. You can also use the Monitor ➤ Connections page, which shows device connection status and information on the various sensor subsystems.

FIGURE 26.8 The Update NAT Addresses page

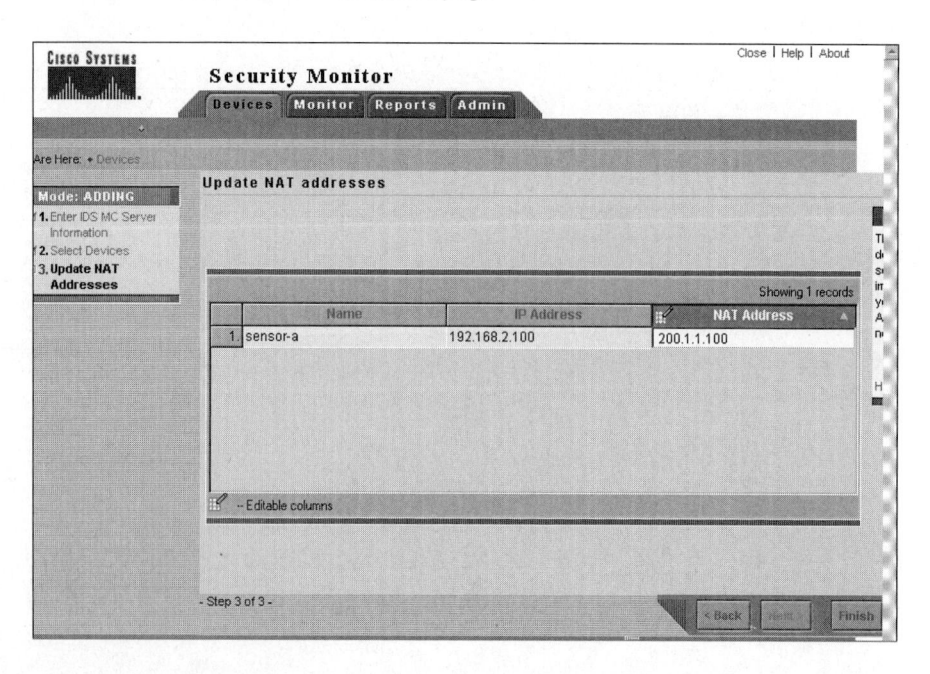

Verifying Sensor Connection Status

After you add a sensor to the Security Monitor, the Security Monitor attempts to open a connection to the sensor and establish a *subscription*, where the Security Monitor periodically pulls events from the event store on the sensor. To verify that a subscription has been successfully established with sensors, select Monitor ➢ Connections from the IDS MC, which will open the Connections page shown in Figure 26.9. This page indicates the current status of all devices monitored by the Security Monitor.

In Figure 26.9, notice that sensor-a currently has a status of Connected, which means that the Security Monitor has successfully established a working subscription with the sensor. If a sensor has a status of Not Connected, then the Security Monitor hasn't been able to successfully connect.

> The Security Monitor and IDS Event Viewer poll sensors for new events every five seconds.

FIGURE 26.9 The Connections page

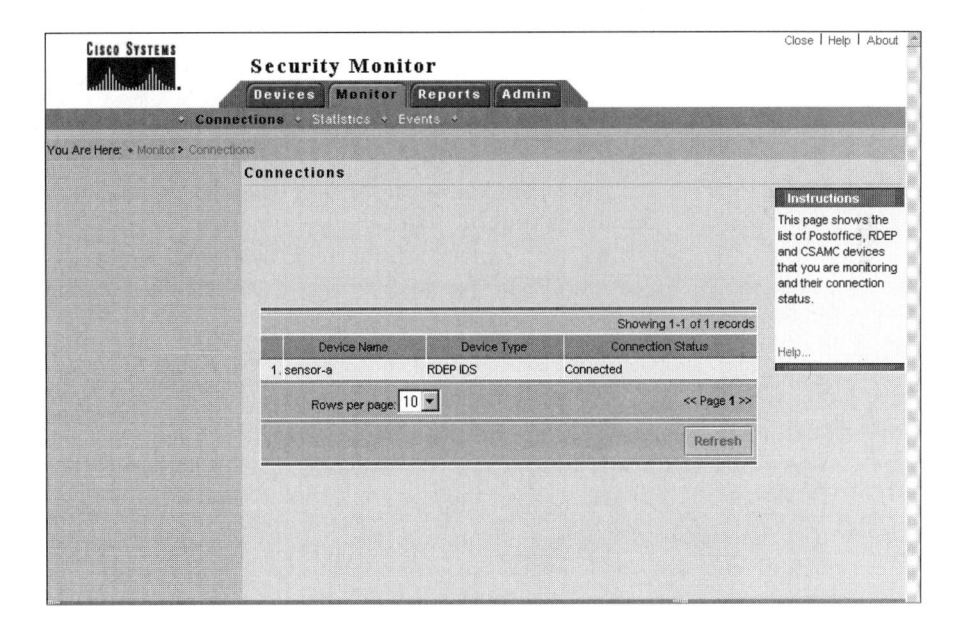

Working with Events

After you've successfully configured the Security Monitor with the devices it monitors and verified that the Security Monitor is connected to those devices, the Security Monitor should start receiving security events, such as IDS alarms from sensors. In this section, you'll learn how to work with events, which consists of the following tasks:

- Viewing events
- Defining notifications using event rules

Viewing Events

Once the Security Monitor establishes a working subscription to one or more sensors, it will receive alarms from the sensors. All alarms and other security events are placed into the Security Monitor database, which you can then view using the Event Viewer application that is included with the Security Monitor. In the next sections, you'll learn about the following tasks associated with viewing alarm information in the Security Monitor:

- Starting Event Viewer
- Working with Event Viewer
- Configuring Event Viewer preferences

Starting Event Viewer

Before starting Event Viewer, you must define the set of alarms that you wish to work with. This set of alarms could be historical, or it could be alarms as they're collected in real time. You launch Event Viewer from the Security Monitor interface by opening the Monitor tab and then selecting the Events option. This opens the Launch Event Viewer page, as shown in Figure 26.10.

The following parameters need to be defined:

Event Type This setting lets you select the type of event that you wish to view. By default, All IDS Alarms is selected, which will display network IDS and host IDS alarms collected from sensors, Cisco IOS routers, Cisco PIX firewalls, Cisco Host IDS consoles, and Cisco Security Agent MC servers. Other options include network IDS alarms, host IDS alarms, and many different PIX alarm types.

Column Set This setting defines the columns that you wish to display in Event Viewer. Each column typically represents a field within each alarm that is collected. You can choose to open the custom column set you used the last time you used Event Viewer (the Last Saved option), the default column set, or all columns.

Event Start Time This setting specifies when the oldest events in the Event Viewer should start. Selecting the At Earliest option views events starting with the oldest stored in the Security Monitor database, whereas configuring the At Time option lets you view events from a certain time onward.

FIGURE 26.10 The Launch Event Viewer page

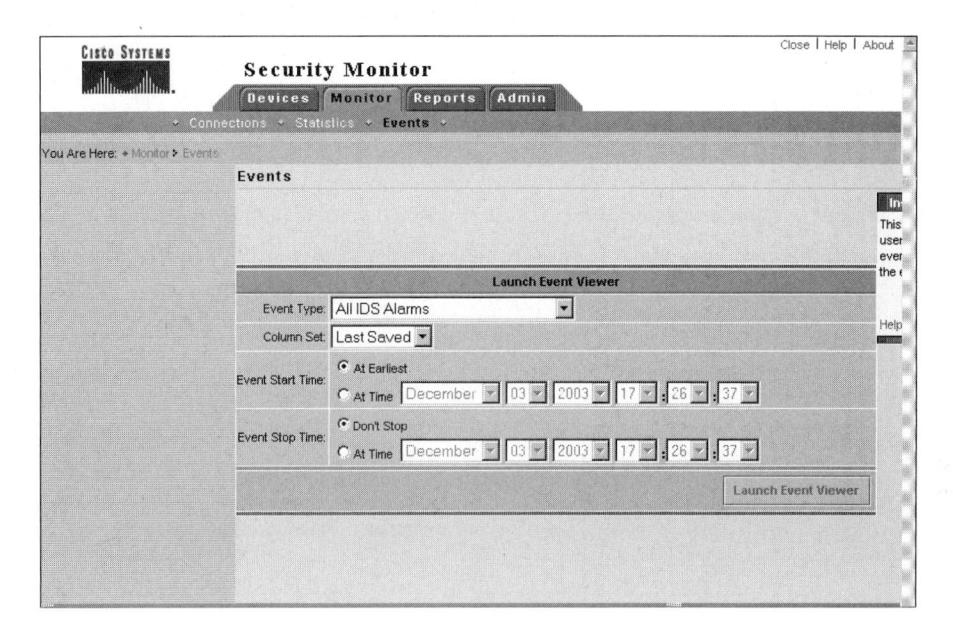

> **WARNING** The timestamp on alarms in the Security Monitor is the time that the Security Monitor server received the alarms, not the time that the sensor generated the alarm. Always ensure that the Security Monitor and each of your sensors are synchronized to the same time source (for example, using an NTP server) to ensure that alarm date and time information in the Security Monitor is accurate.

Event Stop Time This setting specifies the most recent events that should appear in the Event Viewer. If you select the Don't Stop option, the Event Viewer will provide realtime events; however, if you select the At Time option, the Event Viewer will display historical alarm information.

After you configure the appropriate information in the Launch Event Viewer page, click the Launch Event Viewer button to start the Event Viewer, displaying alarms based on your configuration specified in the Launch Event Viewer page. Figure 26.11 shows the Event Viewer window.

> **NOTE** The different buttons on the Event Viewer toolbar will be discussed throughout the rest of this section.

Event Viewer provides a lot of information with respect to each alarm, allowing you to quickly determine the type of alarm, the severity of the alarm, where the alarm was generated, who was responsible for generating the alarm, and what date and time the alarm occurred. The Event Viewer interface consists of several components:

Menu bar This provides the Edit, View, Graph, and Actions menus, which give you quick access to a number of Event Viewer features and functions.

Toolbar This contains buttons that provide fast access to common tasks performed in the Event Viewer.

Grid pane This contains the various rows of individual and aggregated alarm information. Each row contains cells that correspond to a specific alarm field.

FIGURE 26.11 The Event Viewer window

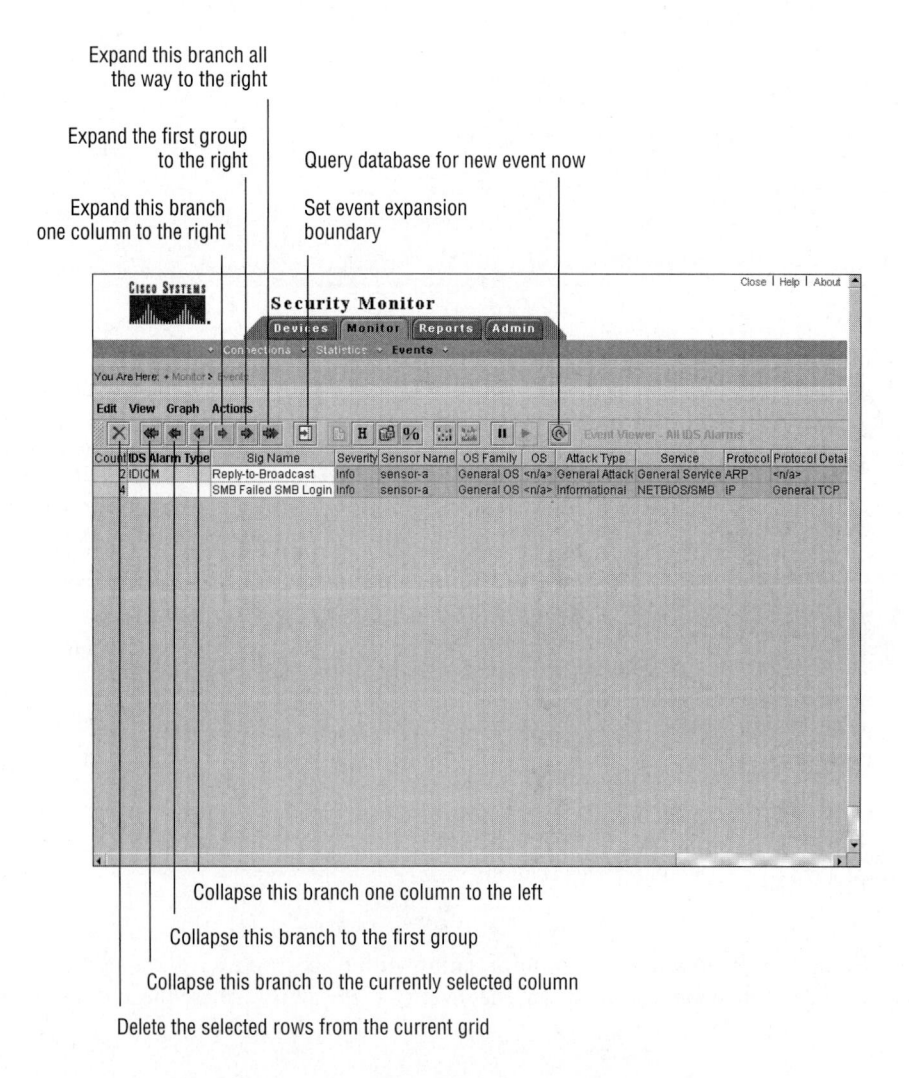

It's important to understand that Event Viewer can display cells in a number of ways, depending on how event information is currently arranged. Table 26.3 describes the various ways in which cells can appear in Event Viewer.

TABLE 26.3 Cell Appearance in IDS Event Viewer

Color	Content	Description
White	Not empty	Cell is expanded and contains unique information.
White	Empty	Cell is expanded but has the same value as the previous alarm entry.
Grey	Not empty	Cell is collapsed (aggregated) but only a single value exists for the cell; hence the cell information is displayed.
Grey	Empty	Cell contains aggregated information (more than one unique value for the cell).
Grey	+	Cell is the first aggregated node for subsequent nodes.

Working with Event Viewer

A key feature of any alarm monitoring system is that it must be easy to read and use yet still display adequate and appropriate information. This means it's important that you're very familiar with how Event Viewer displays alarms and how you can work with Event Viewer to display alarm information according to your own custom requirements. In the next sections, we'll look at the following tasks that relate to working with Event Viewer:

- Expanding events
- Collapsing events
- Setting the event expansion boundary
- Working with columns
- Suspending and resuming event display
- Refreshing event data
- Viewing event information
- Graphing event data
- Deleting events

Expanding Events

When you first open Event Viewer, you might notice that alarm information is aggregated past the second column (IDS Alarm Type) by default. This means that alarm information in the first and second columns is unique (if multiple values exist in the first or second column, then separate entries or rows per unique value are present), whereas alarm information in the third column onward is aggregated. For example, if you have the same type of alarm generated by multiple sensors, only a single entry will exist by default, because the sensor name column isn't one of the first two columns.

> **NOTE** The point at which alarms are aggregated is referred to as the *event expansion boundary*. Alarm information in columns to the right of the event expansion boundary is aggregated (collapsed), and alarm information in columns to the left of the event expansion boundary is expanded.

If you wish to expand aggregated alarm information so that you can view more specific alarm information or individual alarm entries, you can use the expansion buttons located on the Event Viewer toolbar.

> **NOTE** You can also expand events using the Edit menu in Event Viewer.

There are three expansion buttons:

Expand This Branch One Column To The Right This expands the current row one column to the right of the current event expansion boundary. The following examples demonstrate clicking the Expand This Branch One Column To The Right button for an alarm entry in the Event Viewer:

| 7 | SMB Failed SMB Login | Info | sensor-a | General OS | <n/a> | Informational | NETBIOS/SMB | IP | General TCP |

| 7 | SMB Failed SMB Login | Info | sensor-a | General OS | <n/a> | Informational | NETBIOS/SMB | IP | General TCP |

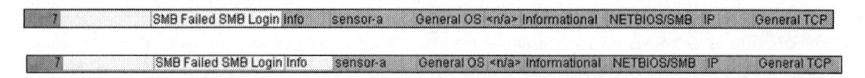

In these examples, notice that the cell with the text Info is colored gray before the button is clicked but is colored white after the button is clicked. This indicates that alarms have been expanded one column to the right. In the example, no expansion is evident, however, because the column that has been expanded was already fully expanded beforehand. If the next column to the right has aggregated information (as indicated by gray shading and a value of +), then clicking Expand This Branch One Column To The Right will expand the aggregated information.

Expand The First Group To The Right This expands the current row at the next aggregated field past the current event expansion boundary in the row. The following examples demonstrate clicking the Expand The First Group To The Right button for an alarm entry in the Event Viewer:

| 7 | SMB Failed SMB Login | Info | Informational | NETBIOS/SMB | + |

| 8 | SMB Failed SMB Login | Info | Informational | NETBIOS/SMB | <n/a> | | OUT | OUT |
| 1 | | | | | Interval Summary: 2 alarms this interval | OUT | OUT |

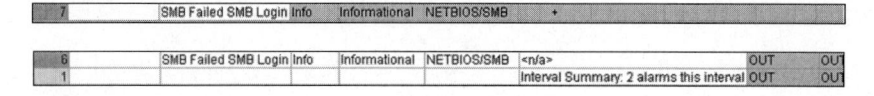

In these examples, notice that a single entry exists before the button is clicked, with the events expanded up to the cell with the value SMB Failed SMB Login, as indicated by the white shading of these cells. To the right of these cells, event information isn't expanded, as indicated by the gray shading. Notice that the cell to the right of the cell with the value *NETBIOS/SMB* is a collapsed cell (this is the Alert Details field), indicating that there are multiple entries with different values in the cell. By clicking the Expand The First Group To The Right button, the collapsed cell is expanded, expanding the single alarm entry into two alarm entries. The first alarm entry includes six alarms, all with the same Alert Details field value of *<n/a>*; the second alarm entry includes a single alarm with an Alert Details value of *Interval Summary: 2 alarms this interval*.

Expand This Branch All The Way To The Right   This expands all entries that may be aggregated within the current row at the next aggregated field past the current event expansion boundary in the row. In the previous example, you saw how a single alarm entry was expanded into two entries by clicking the Expand The First Group To The Right button. The following shows what happens when you click the Expand This Branch All The Way To The Right button:

1	SMB Failed SMB Login	Info	Informational	NETBIOS/SMB	<n/a>	OUT	OUT
1							
1							
1							
1							
1							
1					Interval Summary: 2 alarms this interval	OUT	OUT

You can now see each of the seven individual alarm entries.

Collapsing Events

Collapsing events is the opposite of expanding events—aggregating alarm information rather than drilling down on more specific alarm information. To collapse events, you can use either the Edit menu in the Event Viewer or the collapse buttons located on the Event Viewer toolbar.

The following describes each of the collapse buttons:

Collapse This Branch One Column To The Left   This collapses alarm entries one column to the left of the current leftmost aggregated (collapsed) column.

Collapse This Branch To The First Group   This collapses alarm entries to the first column that can be aggregated due to multiple occurrences of the same value in the column.

Collapse This Branch To The Currently Selected Column   This collapses alarm entries to the currently selected column in an alarm entry.

> **NOTE**   You can also collapse alarm entries to the first group by right-clicking an expanded alarm entry and selecting Collapse First Group from the menu that appears.

Setting the Event Expansion Boundary

The event expansion boundary defines the number of columns to which a new alarm entry will be expanded by default. For example, if the event expansion boundary is the third column in

Event Viewer, any new alarm entries will be expanded to the third column (and shaded white), with any subsequent columns aggregated if possible and shaded gray. The current event expansion boundary is indicated in the column headers, with the event expansion boundary column header text shown in bold text. For example, if you refer back to Figure 26.11, you can see that the column header IDS Alarm Type is highlighted bold, indicating that this column is the current event expansion boundary.

> **TIP**
> For Cisco Secure IDS 4.*x* sensors (RDEP sensors), the value for the IDS Alarm Type field for alarms generated is always *IDIOM*.

To modify the event expansion boundary, click in the cell of any alarm entry that is within the column that you wish to become the event expansion boundary, and then either select Edit > Set Event Expansion Boundary from the Event Viewer menu or click the Set Event Expansion Boundary button on the Event Viewer toolbar.

After you set the event expansion boundary, the column header that you've selected as the event expansion boundary should be highlighted bold. Any new alarm entries will be expanded to the new event expansion boundary by default.

Working with Columns

Each time you work with Event Viewer, you can customize the set of columns that are displayed in the Event Viewer window, and you can create views of alarms that contain only specific information.

> **NOTE**
> The set of columns currently displayed in Event Viewer is referred to as a *column set*.

One surprising limitation of Event Viewer is that you can delete columns from the current Event Viewer view, but you can't add columns. This means that if you need to create a custom view, you typically need to start Event Viewer with all columns displayed by selecting All from the Column Set drop-down list in the Launch Event Viewer page (see Figure 26.10), and then delete columns that you don't wish to appear. Once you have the final column set that you wish to work with, you can then save the currently displayed columns as a custom column set.

To delete columns from Event Viewer, click in a cell within the column that you wish to delete, and then select Edit > Delete > Column from the Event Viewer menu. A dialog box will appear, asking you to confirm that you wish to delete the column indicated. Click Yes, and the column will be removed from the Event Viewer display.

> **NOTE**
> You can't delete the Count column.

To save the current column set in the Event Viewer display, select Edit ➢ Save Column Set from the Event Viewer menu. A dialog box will appear, asking you to confirm that you wish to save the column set.

Notice that when you save a column set, it's saved as the last saved column set, which is an option in the Column Set drop-down list of the Launch Event Viewer page (see Figure 26.10). This means that you can have only a single custom column set stored at any one time.

Suspending and Resuming Event Display

If you're viewing events in real time using the Event Viewer, you may wish to suspend new events from being displayed from time to time. This is most likely if a flurry of new events is generated, which you wish to view and analyze without being interrupted by new alarms being generated.

To suspend event display in the Event Viewer, you can either select Actions ➢ Suspend New Events from the Event Viewer menu or click the Pause New Event Database Queries button on the Event Viewer toolbar. To resume event display, you can either select Actions ➢ Resume New Events from the Event Viewer menu or click the Resume New Event Database Queries button on the Event Viewer toolbar.

Refreshing Event Data

By default, the Event Viewer application automatically queries the Security Monitor database for new events every five minutes, refreshing the current Event Viewer display with the most up-to-date alarm information. Sometimes you may wish to manually refresh the Event Viewer display, which initiates an immediate query of the Security Monitor database for new events.

> **NOTE** You can modify the default automatic query interval used by Event Viewer by modifying Event Viewer preferences, discussed later in this chapter.

To manually refresh the Event Viewer display, you can either click the Query Database For New Events Now button on the Event Viewer toolbar or select Actions ➢ Refresh Events from the Event Viewer menu.

Viewing Event Information

The Event Viewer application can provide further information about events, such as providing a link to the network security database (NSDB) or displaying the context information associated with a signature. You can also resolve all IP addresses in the Event Viewer to hostnames and view statistics about a particular alarm entry in Event Viewer.

The following describes each source of event information:

Viewing context information Some alarms include a context buffer, which captures up to 256 bytes of incoming traffic and 256 bytes of outgoing traffic when the signature associated with the alarm is triggered. If you've selected an alarm that contains context information, you can either click the Context Buffer button on the Event Viewer toolbar or select View ➢ Context Buffer from the Event Viewer menu to view context information. The Context Data Buffer dialog box is shown in Figure 26.12.

In Figure 26.12, the context data being viewed relates to the Sendmail Reconnaissance signature (ID #3103), which is triggered if the EXPN or VRFY command is issued in an Simple Mail Transfer Protocol (SMTP) connection. Notice that context data for the attacker (the commands issued by the attacker) and victim (the responses issued by the target system) are displayed separately.

Resolving hostnames When you're working with Event Viewer, you'll often work with the Attacker Address and Victim Address columns, which identify, respectively, the source and destination of attack traffic that generated the alarm. You may wish to resolve these IP addresses to hostnames in an attempt to further identify the source or destination of an attack. Event Viewer includes a utility for resolving all IP addresses currently listed in Event Viewer to hostnames, which you can execute by either clicking the Hostnames button on the Event Viewer toolbar or selecting View ➢ Hostnames from the Event Viewer menu. Figure 26.13 shows the resulting Hostname Resolution dialog box.

Using the Network Security Database The NSDB provides an online database of information about the attacks and vulnerabilities associated with each signature, allowing security operators to quickly determine the intent, impact, and possible benign triggers of attacks. You can launch the NSDB from Event Viewer by either clicking the Network Security Database button on the Event Viewer toolbar or selecting View ➢ Network Security Database from the Event Viewer menu. You can also reach the NSDB on CiscoWorks VMS servers with the Security Monitor installed via the URL `https://idsmc-server/vms/nsdb/html/all_sigs_index.html`.

FIGURE 26.12 The Context Data Buffer dialog box

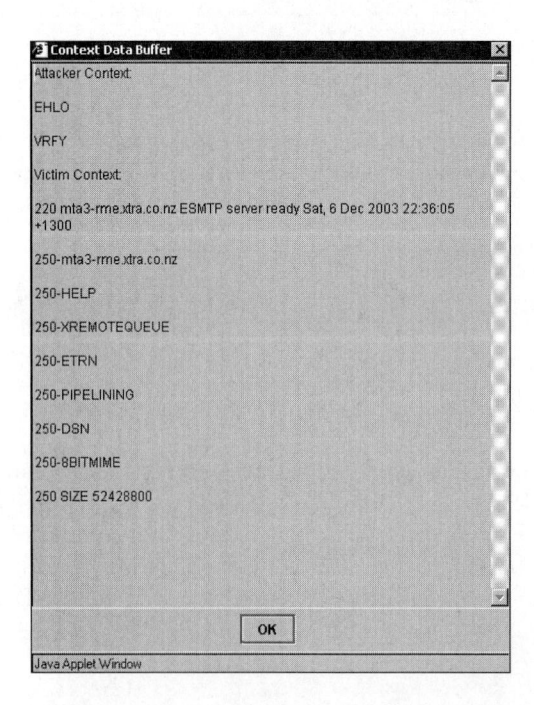

FIGURE 26.13 The Hostname Resolution dialog box

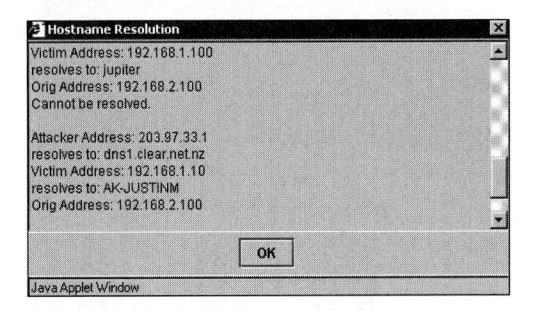

Viewing event statistics Event Viewer lets you view a number of statistics associated with an alarm entry that you've selected. Statistics that you can view include the number of events associated with the currently selected entry, a severity breakdown of events, the number of child nodes in the entry, and an indication as to the percentage of total alarms currently displayed in Event Viewer that the current alarm entry comprises. To view Event Statistics for a particular alarm entry in the Event Viewer, first select the appropriate alarm entry, and then either click the Statistics button on the Event Viewer toolbar or select View ➢ Statistics from the Event Viewer menu. Figure 26.14 shows the Event Statistics dialog box that is displayed as a result.

FIGURE 26.14 The Event Statistics dialog box

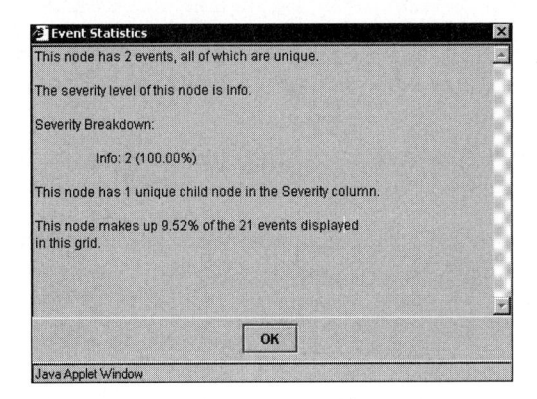

Graphing Event Data

Event Viewer includes a graphing function, where you can graph events by the child node of a particular alarm entry, or graph events over time for an alarm entry. You can create graphs by using the various graphing buttons on the Event Viewer toolbar.

You can also create graphs by using the Graph menu in Event Viewer, which includes the By Child and By Time menu items. Figures 26.15 and 26.16 demonstrate graphs generated by the Graph By Child and Graph By Time functions, respectively.

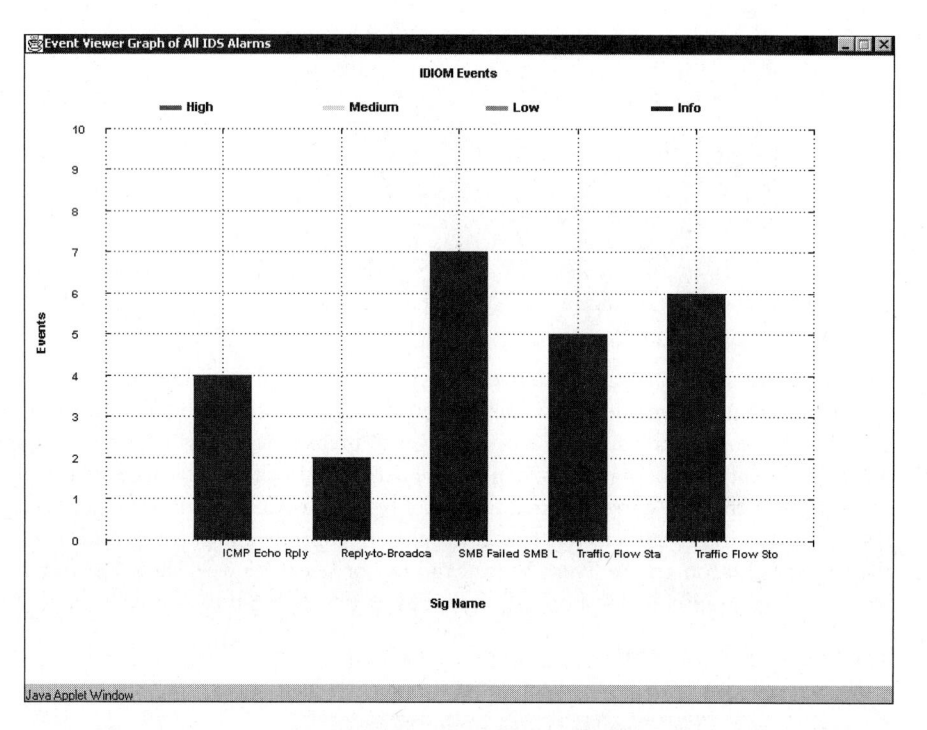

FIGURE 26.15   Graphing By Child

In Figure 26.15, the child node for the alarm entry that was selected in Event Viewer is the Signature Name field, so Signature Name serves as the x-axis for the graph. For both graphs, the y-axis provides the event count. Each bar is further classified into informational, low, medium, and high alarms, as indicated by the different colors in the legend shown.

Deleting Events

The Event Viewer application lets you delete events, either temporarily from the Event Viewer display or permanently from the Security Monitor database. Deleting an event temporarily means that you can view the event at a later time by resetting the current Event Viewer display. If you delete an event permanently from the Security Monitor database, you'll never be able to view the event again, regardless of whether you reset the Event Viewer display.

To delete events temporarily, first select the row that you wish to delete and then either click the Delete The Selected Rows From The Current Grid Only button on the Event Viewer toolbar or select Edit ➢ Delete ➢ From This Grid from the Event Viewer menu.

After you initiate the action to delete events from the current grid, a dialog box will be displayed asking for confirmation of the action. Click the Yes button to complete the action, or click the No button to cancel the action.

If you wish to delete events permanently from the Security Monitor database, first select the row that you wish to delete, and then select Edit ➢ Delete ➢ From Database from the Event Viewer menu. A dialog box will be displayed, asking for confirmation of the action. Clicking the Yes button will permanently delete the events, and clicking the No button will cancel the action.

FIGURE 26.16 Graphing By Time

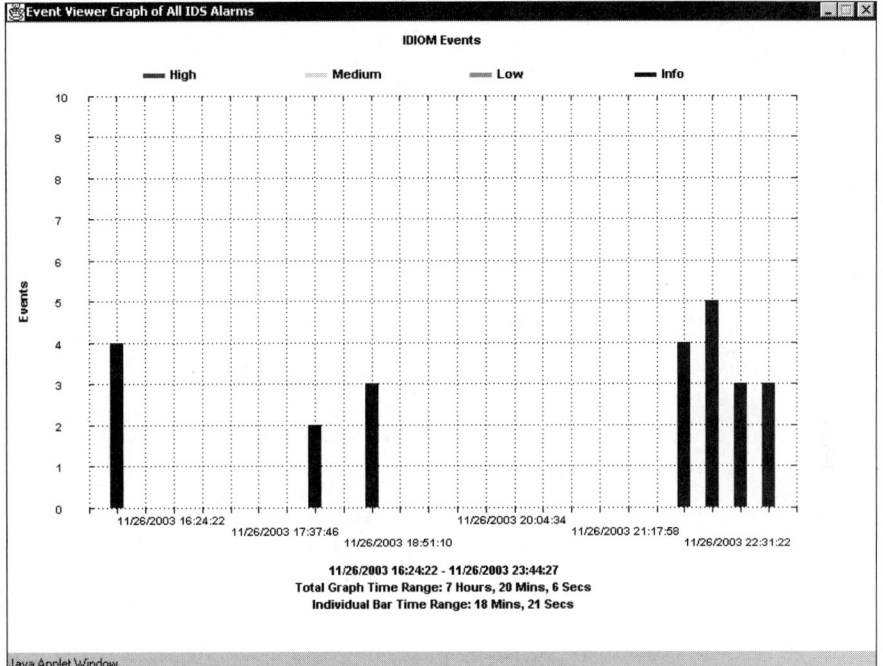

Configuring Event Viewer Preferences

Event Viewer includes a number of preferences that control the default behavior of the application. To configure Event Viewer preferences for the current Event Viewer session, select Edit ➢ Preferences from the Event Viewer menu to open the Preferences dialog box, shown in Figure 26.17.

The sections of the Preferences dialog box are as follows:

Actions This defines settings that relate to the manual blocking feature supported for version 3.*x* sensors. Manual blocking isn't discussed in this chapter, because it isn't included as a feature for version 4.*x* sensors.

Cells This includes the Blank Left and Blank Right options, with Blank Left enabled by default. When Blank Left is selected, if multiple child alarms have the same value in expanded cells to the left of the event expansion boundary, only the first child alarm will display actual values in the expanded cells with the same value; remaining child alarms will have blank cells. When Blank Right is selected, collapsed cells are always collapsed (as indicated by the + value at the cell where aggregation occurs); subsequent cells are blanked, even if only a single event exists for the collapsed cell. By default, Blank Right isn't enabled, meaning the values for collapsed cells that only include a single entry are displayed.

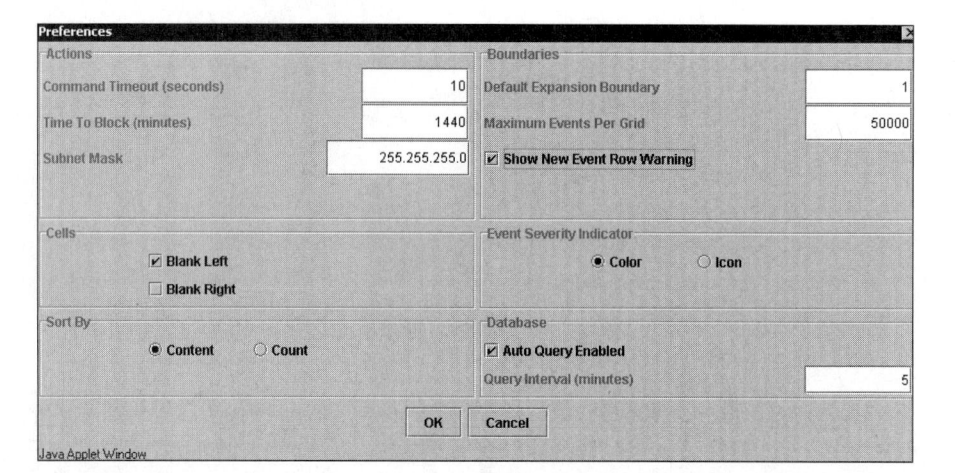

FIGURE 26.17 The Preferences dialog box

Sort By   This determines how events are ordered in the Event Viewer display. By default, Content is selected, which sorts events alphabetically based on the value of the column to the right of the count column (the IDS Alarm Type column by default). If Count is selected, events are sorted from the highest to lowest values in the Count column.

Boundaries   This determines the default event expansion boundary and defines the maximum number of events that can be displayed in a single Event Viewer grid. By default, the event expansion boundary is 1, which means one column to the right of the count column (the IDS Alarm Type column by default). The default maximum number of events is 50,000; you can adjust this to any value between 0 and 250,000.

Event Severity Indicator   By default, event severity is indicated by the color of the count column. You can modify this so that event severity is indicated by an icon rather the color. Figure 26.18 shows the Event Viewer with the event severity indicator set to icon.

In Figure 26.18, notice that icons now appear in the Count column that indicate the severity of each alarm.

Database   This section defines whether Event Viewer automatically refreshes events by allowing you to enable or disable automatic querying of the Security Monitor database. If enabled, you can also define how often events from the Security Monitor database should be updated. By default, automatic querying is enabled to run every five minutes.

If you use Edit ➢ Preferences from the Event Viewer menu to modify preferences, it's important to understand that this only configures preferences for the current Event Viewer session. If you start a new Event Viewer session, any preference modifications will be lost, and the default Event Viewer preferences will be loaded. You can modify Event Viewer preferences permanently via the Admin ➢ Event Viewer page within the Security Monitor, as shown in Figure 26.19.

FIGURE 26.18 Event Viewer with icon set as the event severity indicator

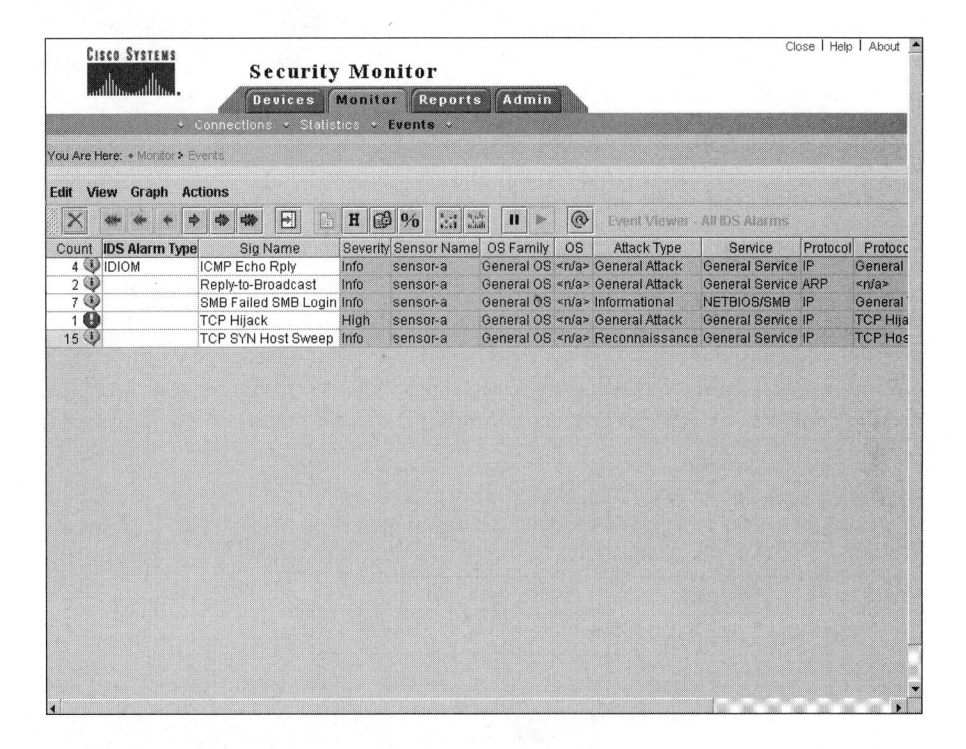

FIGURE 26.19 The Admin ➢ Event Viewer page

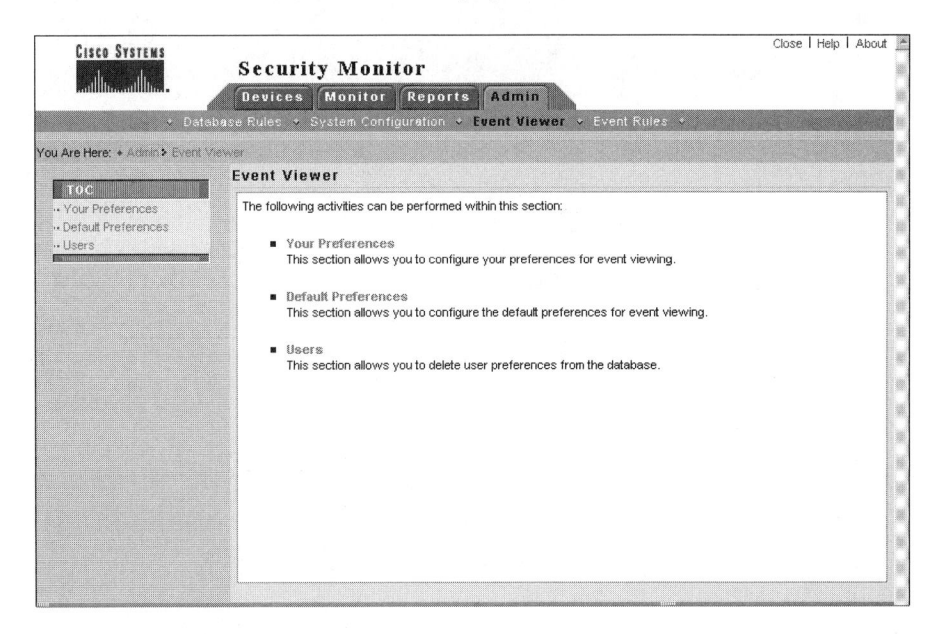

Notice that there are three options within the Event Viewer page:

Your Preferences   Selecting this option opens the Your Preferences page, which lets you configure custom Event Viewer preferences for your user account that are loaded when you start the Event Viewer application. Figure 26.20 shows the Your Preferences page.

All the preferences you learned about earlier in the Preferences dialog box (see Figure 26.17) can be configured. Modifying these preferences affects the Event Viewer preferences used when Event Viewer is started for the currently logged-in user account.

Default Preferences   Selecting this option opens the Default Preferences page, which lets you configure the default Event Viewer preferences that should apply for any user who doesn't have any custom preferences defined.

Users   Selecting this option opens the Users page, which lists each of the event preference configurations that have been configured by users. From this page, you can delete a specific user's Event Viewer preferences, ensuring that they will receive the default Event Viewer preferences.

FIGURE 26.20   The Your Preferences page

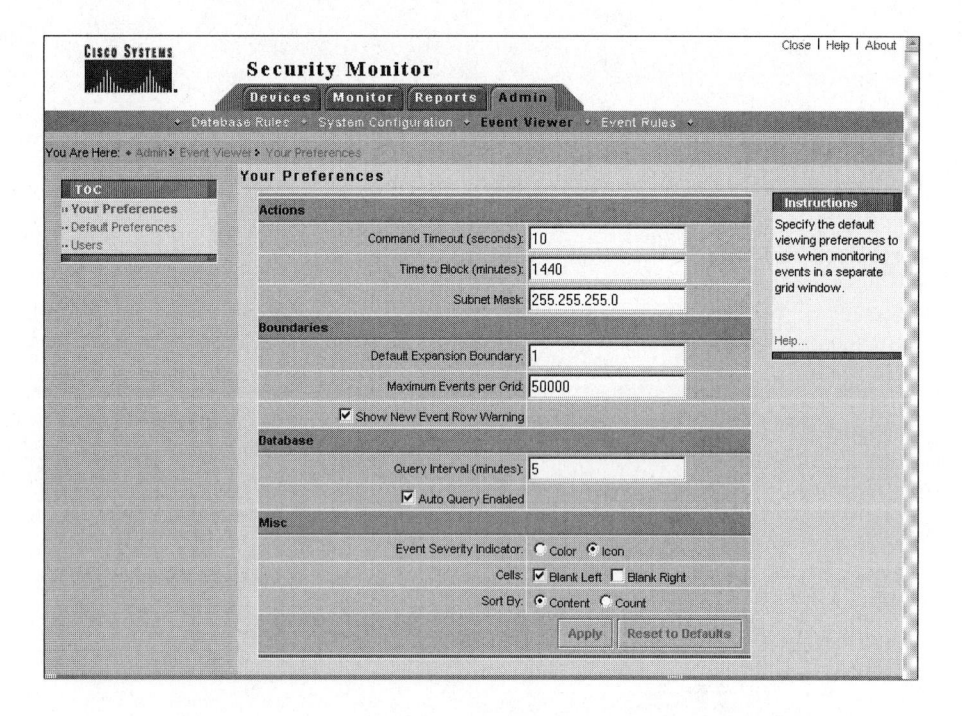

Defining Notifications Using Event Rules

In large deployments of IDS sensors, it's common for a great deal of event data to be generated, which can make it difficult to isolate real attacks and respond to them quickly when you're a dashboard-style product such as Event Viewer. *Event rules* extend the functionality of the Security Monitor so that you can define a set of criteria related to the occurrence of one or more events that meet certain conditions and thresholds and then generate a custom action, such as generating an e-mail notification or running a custom script. Event rules are most commonly used to notify security operators of specific events or a pattern of events.

An event rule consists of three components:

Event filter The *event filter* specifies the criteria that must be met for the event rule to be triggered.

Action If the event rule is triggered, an *action* is initiated. Three actions are available:

- Send an e-mail notification.
- Log a console notification to the audit log.
- Execute a script.

Thresholds and intervals To avoid excessive event actions being initiated, you can configure *thresholds*, which define the number of occurrences of a particular event that must occur before the event rule is triggered, as well as *intervals*, which define the time period used to implement the timers measured by each clock.

You can enable, disable, create, modify, and delete event rules by selecting Admin ➤ Event Rules within the Security Monitor. Doing so opens the Event Rules page, shown in Figure 26.21.

Notice that by default, no event rules exist. To create a new event rule, click the Add button on the Event Rules page to initiate a wizard that steps you through four configuration pages:

- Identify The rule
- Specify The Event Filter
- Choose The Actions
- Specify The Thresholds And Intervals

Identifying the Rule

The first page displayed when adding a new event rule is the Identify The Rule page, which is shown in Figure 26.22. On this page, you configure a name and description for the rule.

FIGURE 26.21 The Event Rules page

FIGURE 26.22 The Identify The Rule page

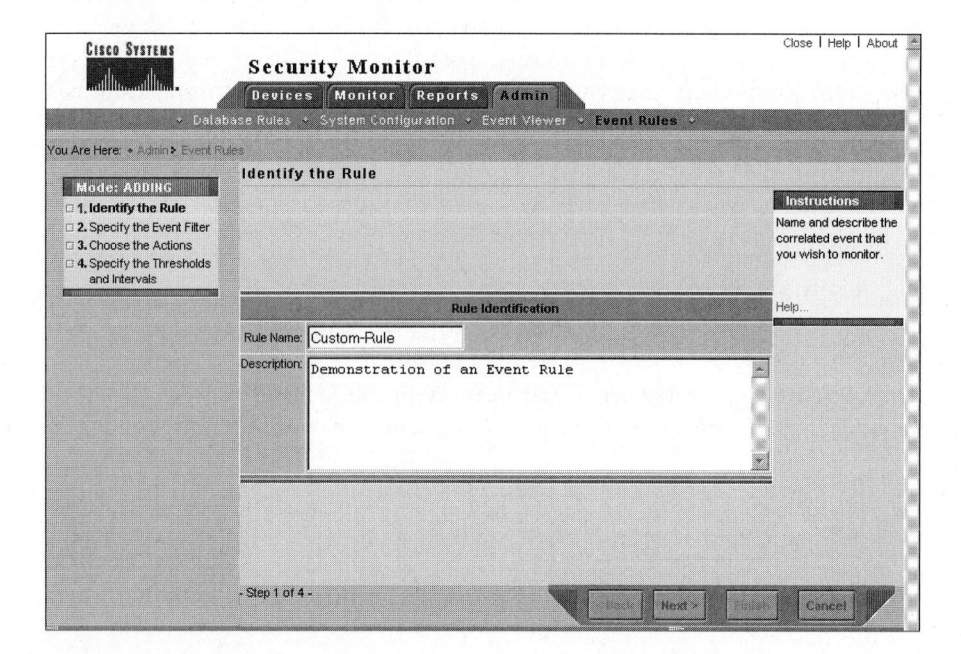

Specifying the Event Filter

After you configure the Identify The Rule page and click the Next button, the Specify The Event Filter page is displayed, as shown in Figure 26.23. This page defines the criteria that should be applied to events to determine whether events match the rule. You can specify up to five statements, each of which lets you compare the value within event fields against a value that you specify. If you specify multiple statements, you also specify the logical operations that should be used to combine the outcome of each statement, allowing for powerful and flexible filters to be built.

For each statement, you can examine the values of the following event fields:

- Originating Device
- Originating Device Address
- Attacker Address
- Victim Address
- Signature Name
- Signature ID
- Severity

When you select one of these event fields to examine, the Specify The Event Filter page updates appropriately. For example, if you select Signature Name, the page updates so that the value field includes a drop-down list of all signatures.

FIGURE 26.23 The Specify The Event Filter page

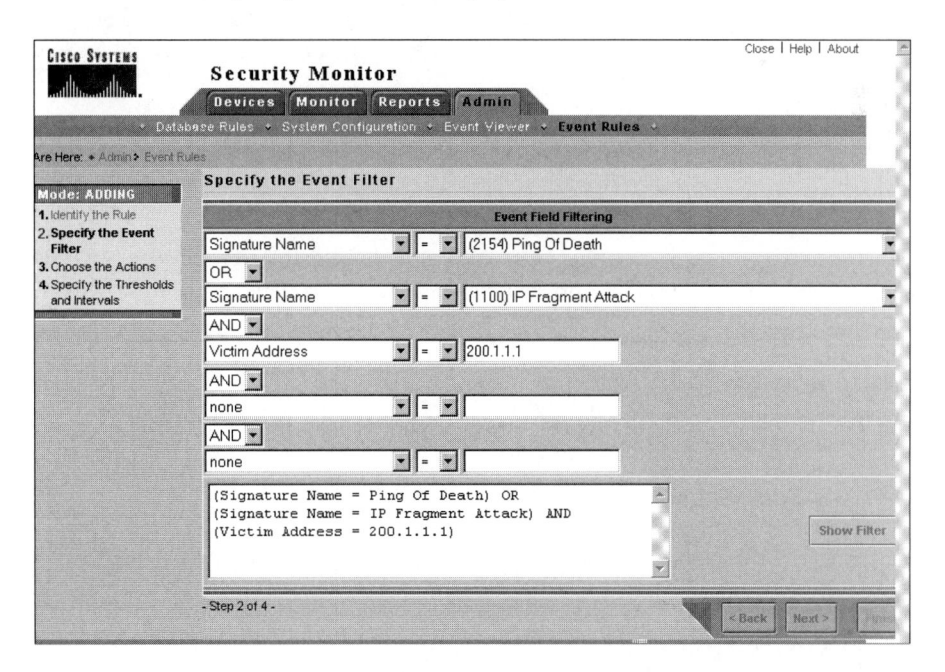

Now you need to define the comparison operator that you wish to use. The following comparison operators can be used:

- Less than (<)
- Less than or equal to (<=)
- Equals (=)
- Doesn't equal (!=)
- Greater than or equal to (>=)
- Greater than (>)

Next, you need to specify a value that you wish to compare against the value of the event field you're examining. Once you've specified a value, the statement is complete.

When the Security Monitor is executing an event rule, each statement you've defined generates a Boolean value of either TRUE or FALSE. For example, if you defined the statement Signature Name = ICMP Echo Rply, then any events that have a value of ICMP Echo Rply in the signature name field will cause the statement to be evaluated as TRUE. Once each statement has been evaluated as either TRUE or FALSE, these outcomes are compared using the Boolean operations specified in the drop-down lists between each statement. The following Boolean operations are supported:

- AND
- OR
- NOT

After you define your filter statements, it's useful to click the Show Filter button, which displays the complete Boolean statement in the text field at the bottom of the page. For example, in Figure 26.23, the Show Filter button has been clicked; you can see the complete Boolean statement, as follows:

```
(Signature Name = Ping Of Death) OR
  (Signature Name = IP Fragment Attack)
  AND (Victim Address = 200.1.1.1)
```

This statement means that the event rule will only be matched for events generated from the Ping of Death or IP Fragment Attack signatures that are targeted as the host with an IP address of 200.1.1.1.

Choosing the Actions

After you configure the Specify The Filter page and click the Next button, the Choose The Actions page is displayed, as shown in Figure 26.24. This page defines the actions that should take place if the event rule is matched for a particular event. You can choose to execute one or more of the following actions:

- Send an e-mail notification.
- Log a console notification event to the audit log.
- Execute a custom script.

Notice in Figure 26.24 that the e-mail notification and console notification actions are enabled. If you look closely at the message of the e-mail notification, you can see the use of keyword substitutions (${DateStr} and ${TimeStr}), which you learned about in Chapter 25 for database rules in the IDS MC. You can use the same keyword substitutions used in IDS MC database rules.

> **NOTE** See Table 25.5 in Chapter 25 for a complete list of the keyword substitutions available.

FIGURE 26.24 The Choose The Actions page

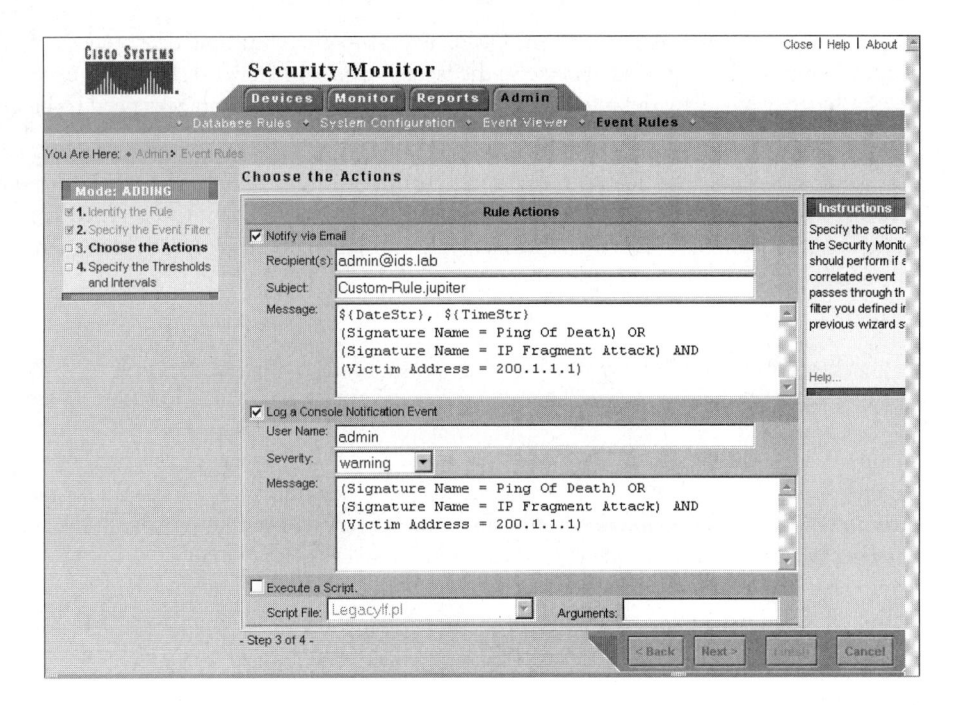

> **NOTE** If you choose to execute a script, you must select it from the Script File drop-down list, which contains a list of PERL scripts located in c:\Program Files\CSCOpx\MDC\etc\ids\scripts. By default, all of these scripts relate to database maintenance for database rules (see Chapter 25). You can create your own custom scripts and copy them to this folder, after which they can be selected from the Script File drop-down list.

Specifying the Thresholds and Intervals

After you configure the Choose The Actions page and click the Next button, the Specify The Thresholds And Intervals page is displayed, as shown in Figure 26.25. This page lets you define thresholds for executing actions when the rule is matched, as well as also intervals relating to when actions should be executed once again for repeat triggering of the rule.

The following thresholds and intervals can be configured:

Issue Action(s) After (# Event Occurrences) This defines the number of events that must match the event rule before the actions defined for the rule are executed. For example, if this threshold is set to three events (the default value), and if the event filter is configured to match signatures with a name of ICMP Echo Reply, three ICMP Echo Reply signature alarms must be generated for the actions in the event rule to be executed.

Repeat Action(s) Again After (# Event Occurrences) When multiple occurrences of an event occur after an action was issued because the Issue Action(s) After threshold was exceeded, this threshold (five events by default) is used to define how many occurrences need to be detected before the event rule actions are repeated.

For example, assume that 20 events that meet the criteria event filter of the event rule take place. If you're using the default values for the Issue Action(s) After (# Event Occurrences) and Repeat Action(s) Again After (# Event Occurrences) thresholds (3 and 5, respectively), then the event rule actions will be executed as follows:

- Event #3 (first occurrence)
- Event #8 (repeat occurrence)
- Event #13 (repeat occurrence)
- Event #18 (repeat occurrence)

Reset Count Every (Minutes) This interval defines when the event count used for the previous thresholds is reset; by default, the event count is reset every 30 minutes. For example, assume that one event that meets the criteria event filter of the event rule is generated per minute. If you're using the default values for the Issue Action(s) After (# Event Occurrences) threshold, Repeat Action(s) Again After (# Event Occurrences) threshold, and Reset Count Every (Minutes) interval (3, 5, and 30 minutes, respectively), then the event rule actions will be executed as follows:

- Event #3 (first occurrence)
- Event #8 (repeat occurrence)
- Event #13 (repeat occurrence)
- Event #18 (repeat occurrence)
- Event #23 (repeat occurrence)
- Event #28 (repeat occurrence)
- Event #33 (first occurrence after event count reset)
- Event #38 (repeat occurrence)

Real World Scenario

The Importance of Thresholds and Intervals

When you're designing event rules, it's very important to understand the nature of the attacks that you're configuring event rules to notify you about. Configure your thresholds and intervals too low, and you risk excessive notifications being generated; on the other hand, configure your thresholds and intervals too high, and you risk not being notified at all about an attack.

For example, if you're configuring an event rule to notify you of an attack that is currently spreading rapidly throughout the Internet (such as an Internet worm), you might expect the signature that detects the attack to fire thousands of times within a few minutes. Using the default thresholds and intervals in this scenario, your event rule will also be fired thousands of times, which typically isn't desirable (for example, getting 2000 e-mails due to 10,000 occurrences of the same attack in a few minutes isn't productive and is annoying). For this type of attack, you might set a low Issue Action(s) threshold (so that the fact you've been attacked is apparent) but set a high Repeat Action(s) threshold to avoid excessive notifications being generated.

FIGURE 26.25 The Specify The Thresholds And Intervals page

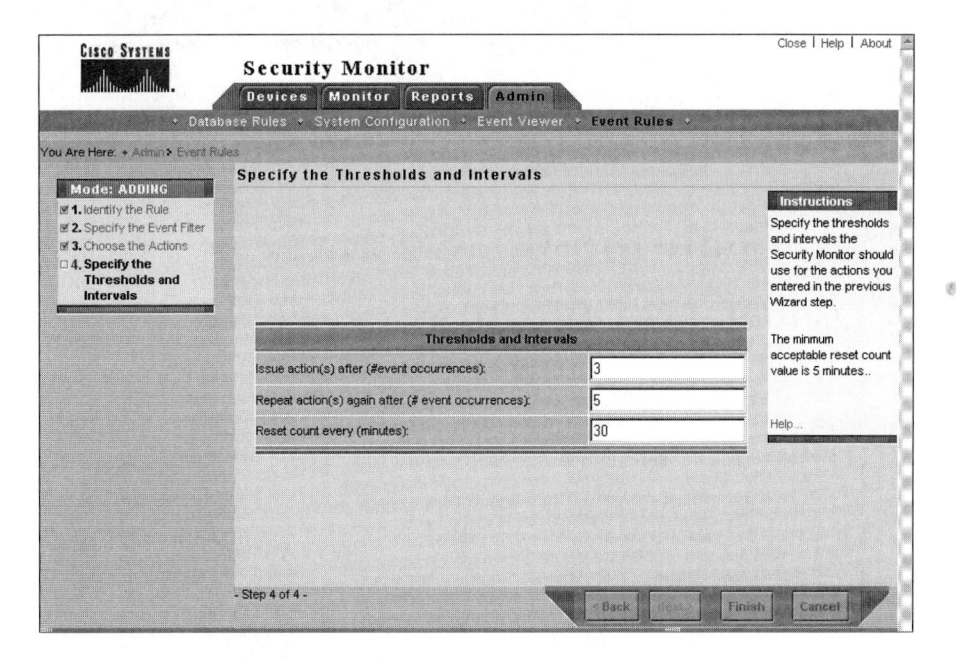

Once you've completed configuring thresholds and intervals for the event rule, click the Finish button to complete the creation of the new rule. Figure 26.26 shows the Event Rules page after a new event rule has been created.

By default, the Active column indicates the rule isn't active (disabled). To enable the rule, select the radio box next to the rule and then click the Activate button in the IDS MC for each rule.

FIGURE 26.26 The Event Rules page after adding an event rule

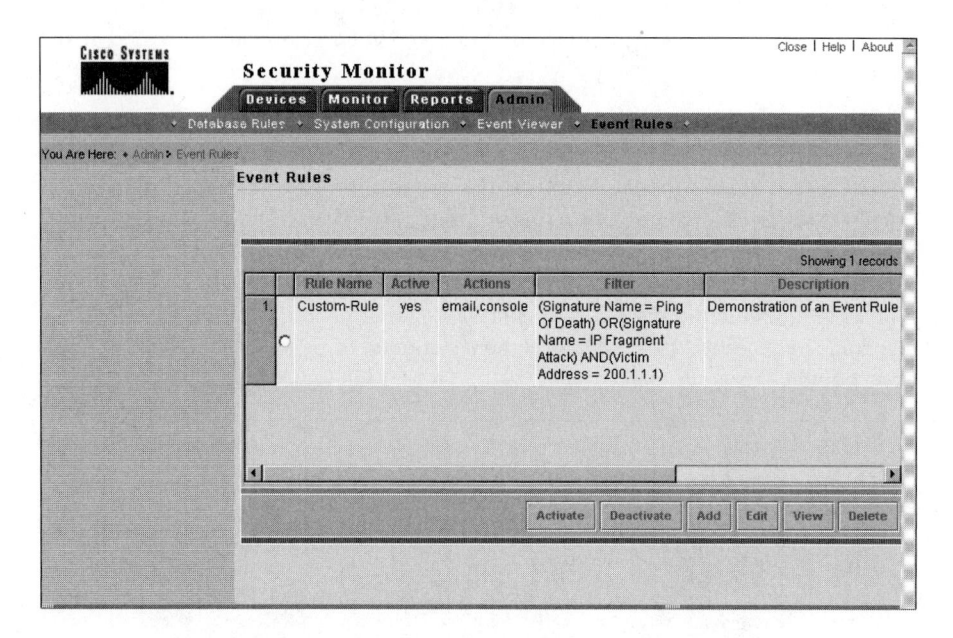

Administering the Security Monitoring Center

The Security Monitor includes a number of system configuration and report settings, which allow you to control how events are pruned from the Security Monitor database, configure a number of system-level settings, and also generate reports. Administering the Security Monitor consists of the following tasks:

- Configuring system configuration settings
- Configuring database rules
- Configuring reports

Configuring System Configuration Settings

The Security Monitor includes a number of system configuration settings, each of which defines the behavior of various aspects of the Security Monitor. To configure system configuration settings, click the Admin tab, and select the System Configuration option from the Options bar. Figure 26.27 shows the System Configuration page that is displayed:

We'll discuss each item in the System Configuration TOC next.

Defining an E-mail Server

The Security Monitor is capable of generating e-mail notifications (for example, when an event rule is triggered), providing an alternative alerting mechanism to the Event Viewer interface. Before you can configure e-mail notifications within the Security Monitor, you must configure an e-mail server, which is the IP address or name of an SMTP server. To define an e-mail server, select the E-mail server item from the Admin ≻ System Configuration TOC.

> When installed on the same server, the IDS MC and Security Monitor share a number of configuration settings, such as e-mail server and database rules. This means that if you've already configured a shared configuration item on the IDS MC, you don't need to repeat the configuration on the Security Monitor, and vice versa.

FIGURE 26.27 The System Configuration page

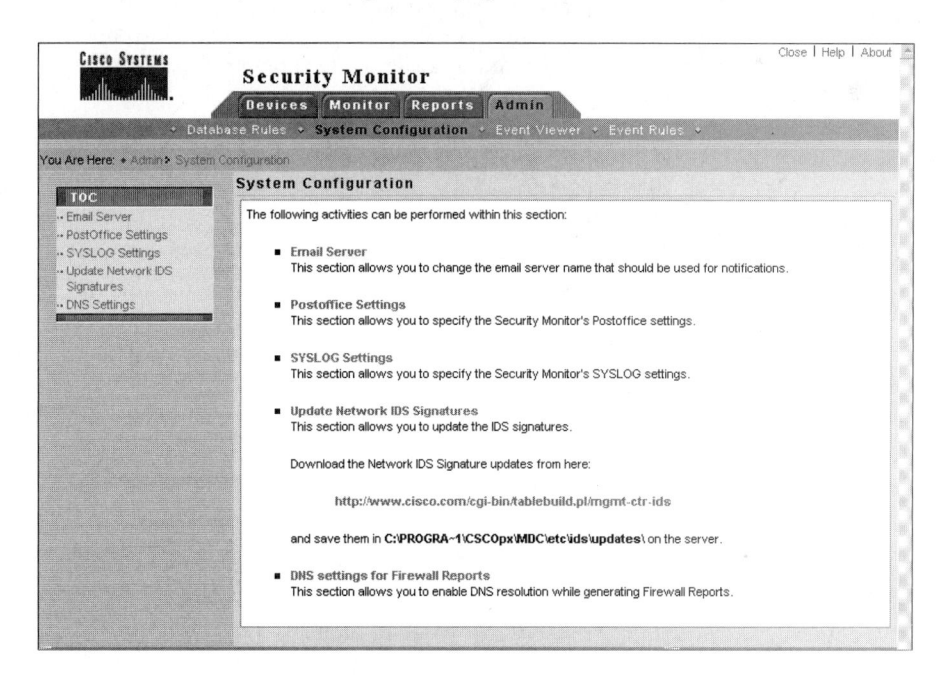

Defining PostOffice Settings

The PostOffice protocol is used by version 3.*x* sensors for communications; so, if the Security Monitor is monitoring any 3.*x* sensors, it must be configured with the appropriate PostOffice settings. To configure PostOffice settings, select the PostOffice Settings item from the Admin ➤ System Configuration TOC.

Defining Syslog Settings

The Security Monitor includes a Syslog server, which accepts security events from Syslog-enabled devices such as Cisco PIX firewalls and Cisco routers. On the Security Monitor, you can configure a number of Syslog server settings, including which UDP port the server operates on (the default is UDP port 514) and whether Syslog events should be forwarded to another server. To configure Syslog settings, select the Syslog Settings item from the Admin ➤ System Configuration TOC.

Updating Signatures

Updating signatures is an important part of maintaining any IDS deployment, because it ensures that your sensors are able to detect the latest attacks. Since the Security Monitor monitors sensors and receives alarms based on signatures, keeping the Security Monitor up-to-date is just as important as keeping your sensors up-to-date, so that the Security Monitor can interpret alarms correctly.

> **TIP** To ensure that the Security Monitor is always as up-to-date as your sensors, always update signatures on your Security Monitor before deploying signature updates to your sensors. The same rule should be applied to the IDS MC.

To update Security Monitor signatures, you follow a process similar to that for to updating signatures for the IDS MC. You must first download the signature updates from CCO and place them into the `C:\Program Files\CSCOpx\mdc\etc\ids\updates` folder. Then, select Admin ➤ System Configuration ➤ Update Network IDS Signatures in the Security Monitor interface, to open the Update Network IDS Signatures page shown in Figure 26.28.

In Figure 26.28, the drop-down list shows all update files within the Updates folder on the Security Monitor server. Once you've selected the appropriate update, click the Apply button, which displays a Summary page indicating the actions that will take place, as shown in Figure 26.29.

After you click the Continue button, the update is initiated. If you wish to view whether the update was successful, generate an Audit Log report by selecting the Audit Log report group in the Reports ➤ Generate page and selecting the Audit Log Report option. Figure 26.30 shows an audit log report generated after a signature update of the Security Monitor.

In Figure 26.30, the first two entries show the signature update being started and completed successfully.

FIGURE 26.28 The Update Network IDS Signatures page

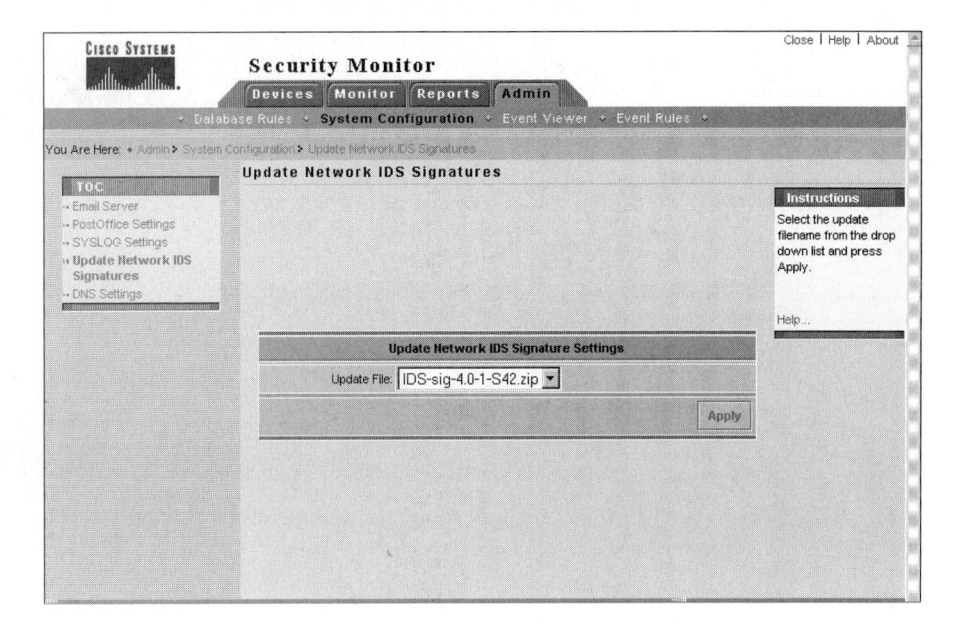

FIGURE 26.29 The Update Summary page

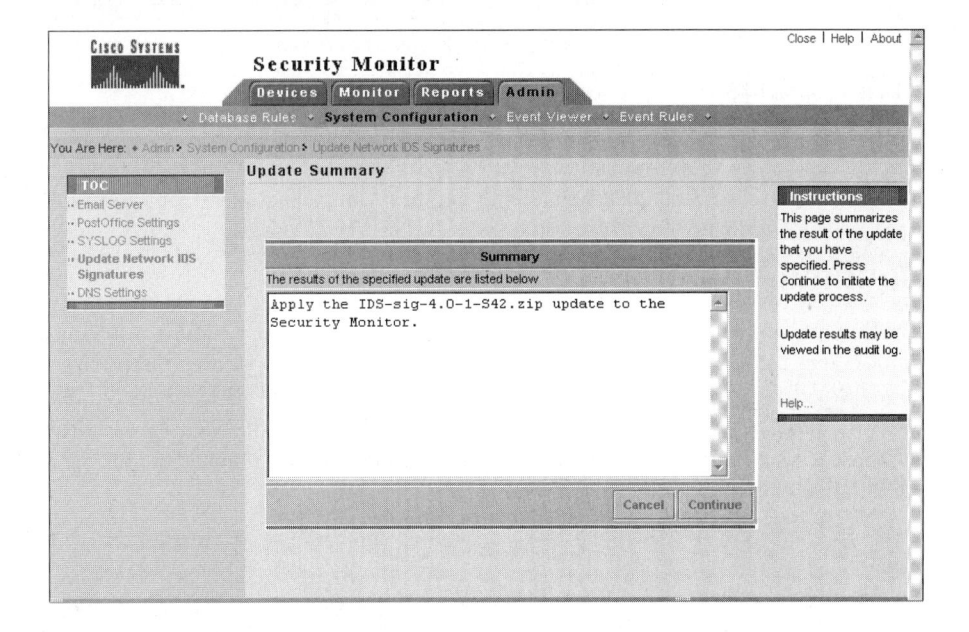

FIGURE 26.30 Verifying a signature update of the Security Monitor

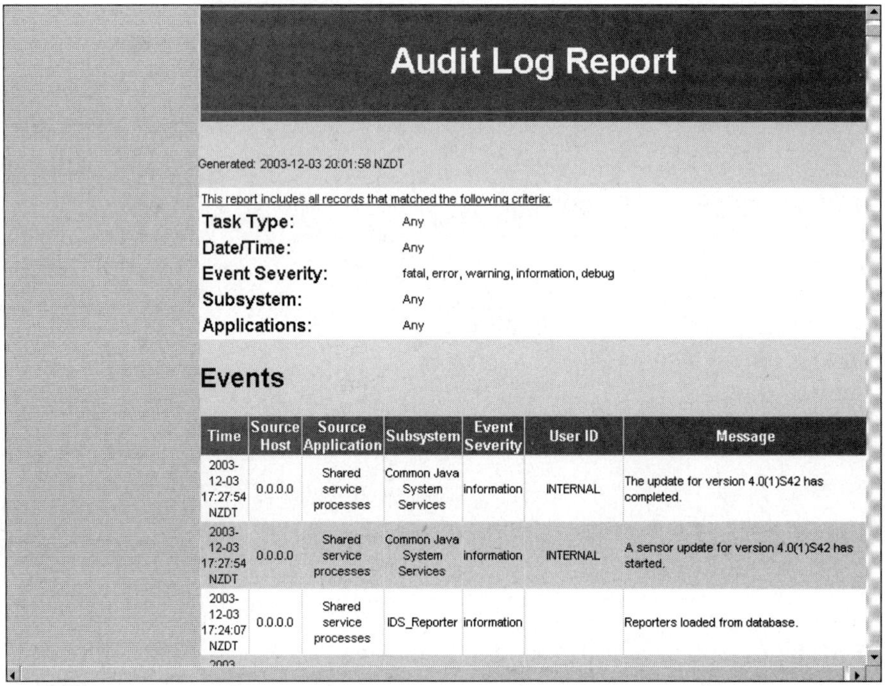

DNS Settings

The Security Monitor lets you enable/disable the DNS resolution of IP addresses associated with firewall reports (not reports related to IDS activity). By default, DNS resolution is enabled and is configurable via the DNS Settings item from the Admin ➢ System Configuration TOC.

Configuring Database Rules

The Security Monitor database is a core component of the Security Monitor, storing event information about IDS alarms, security events, and other events. Depending on the size of your sensor deployment, you'll most likely need to routinely remove events from the database to avoid low disk space and performance issues. Just like the IDS MC, the Security Monitor provides database rules, which provide the means to prune, archive, and manage events. See Chapter 25 for details on how to configure database rules.

Configuring Reports

In Chapter 25, you were introduced to the reporting features of the IDS MC. The Security Monitor also provides reports, allowing you to quickly summarize alarm information into an easy-to-read format. The Reports tab in the Security Monitor includes the same options as the IDS MC, providing the ability to generate, schedule, and view reports. Figure 26.31 shows the Select Report page, which is opened when you select Reports ➤ Generate within the Security Monitor.

Notice the Report Group drop-down list. It groups the various reports into categories that include the following:

- All
- Audit Log
- IDS Alarms
- CSA Alarms (Cisco Security Agent)
- Firewall Reports

To view a report, select the appropriate Report Group, and then choose the report that you wish to view. Click the Select button to open the Report Filtering page shown in Figure 26.32.

FIGURE 26.31 The Select Report page

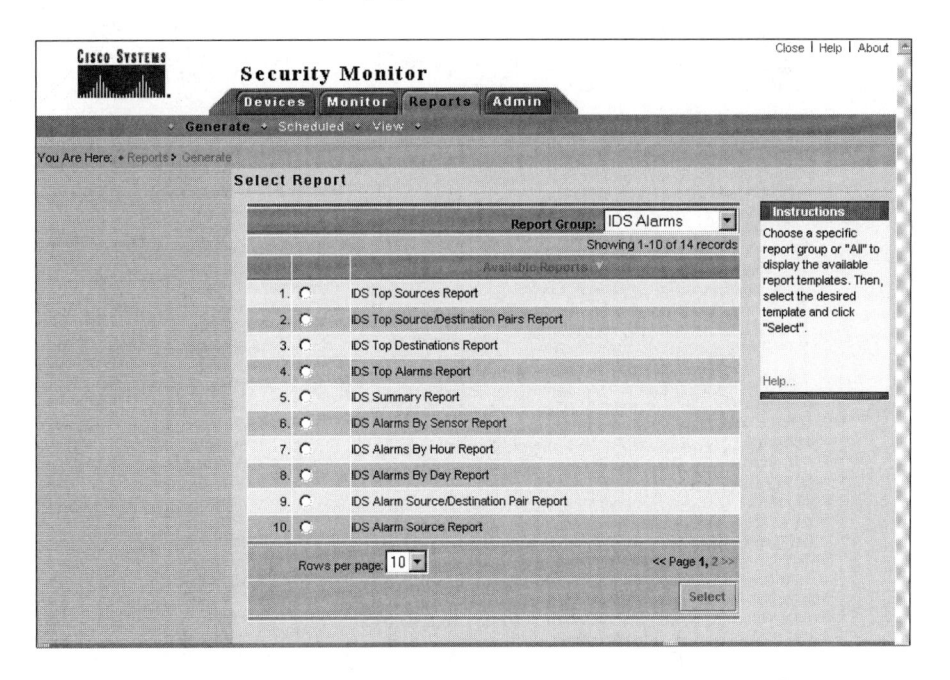

FIGURE 26.32 The Report Filtering page

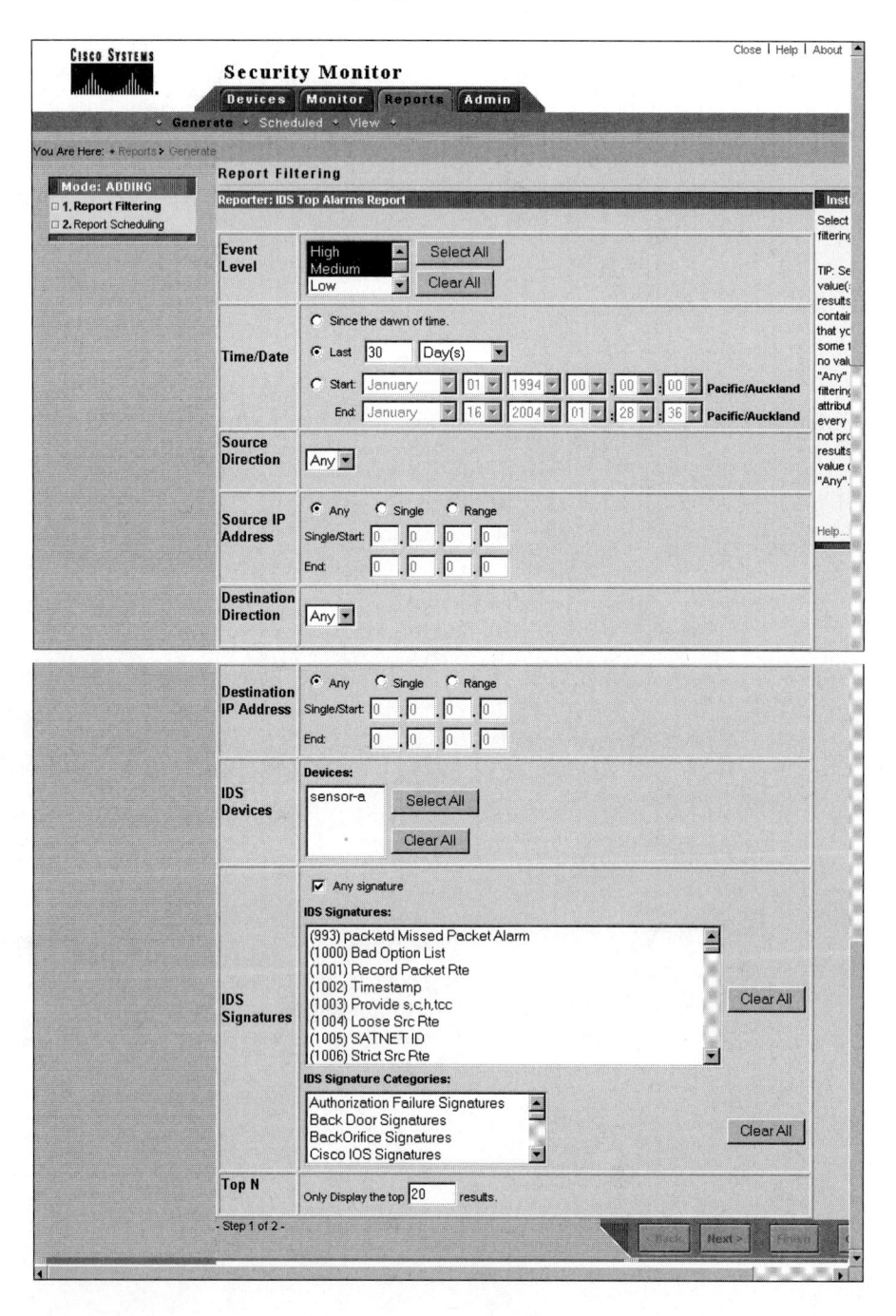

Figure 26.32 shows the Report Filtering page for the IDS Top Alarms report is shown, which lets you filter the alarm information used in the report using any of the following parameters:

- Event Severity (referred to as Event Level in Figure 26.32)
- Time/Date
- Source Direction
- Source IP Address
- Destination Direction
- Destination IP Address
- IDS sensor(s) that generated the alarm (referred to as IDS Devices in Figure 26.32)
- IDS Signatures
- Top N Results (lets you specify the number of top results displayed)

After you specify report filtering criteria and click the Next button, the Schedule Report page is displayed, as shown in Figure 26.33. Here you define the title of the report, when it should be generated, and whether it should be e-mailed to one or more recipients.

To complete the report-generation process, click the Finish button in the Schedule Report page. The Choose Completed Report page will be displayed, as shown in Figure 26.34; your report should be listed, if you've configured it to be generated immediately.

> **NOTE** Some reports may take a few minutes to generate. If your report name isn't immediately displayed, refresh the Choose Completed Report page after a few minutes by selecting Reports ➢ View.

In Figure 26.34, entry #6 (IDS Top Alarms Report) is the report generated based on the settings collected in Figures 26.31 to 26.33. To view a report, select the check box next to the appropriate report and click either the Open In Window button (opens the report in a new window) or the View button (opens the report in the same window). Figure 26.35 shows the IDS Top Alarms Report listed in Figure 26.34.

In Figure 26.35, because the default report filtering criteria have been used, only medium and high severity events are included in the report data. You can see that only a single alarm has been generated, accounting for 2.78 percent of all alarms.

FIGURE 26.33 The Schedule Report page

FIGURE 26.34 The Choose Completed Report page

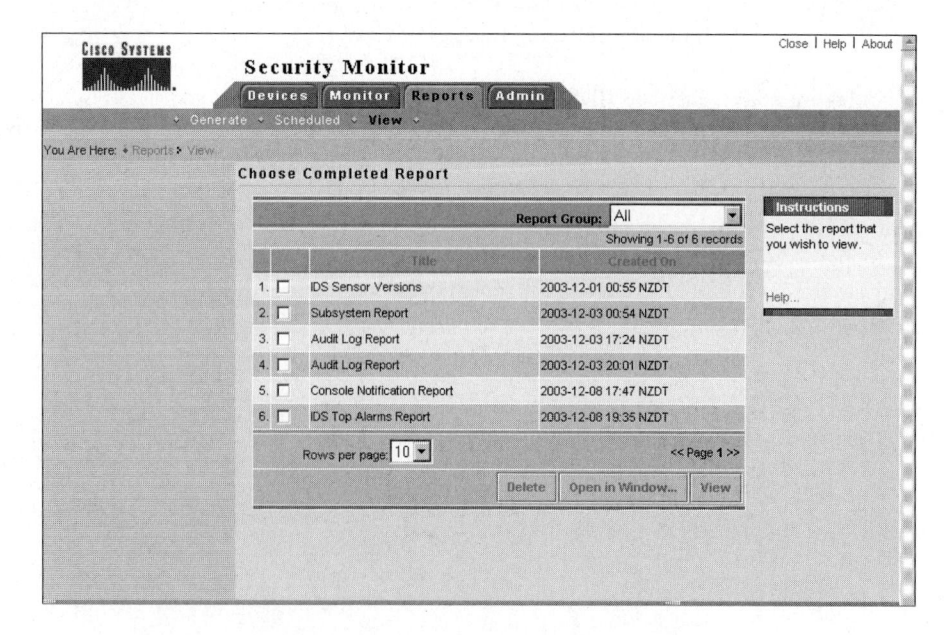

FIGURE 26.35 The IDS Top Alarms report

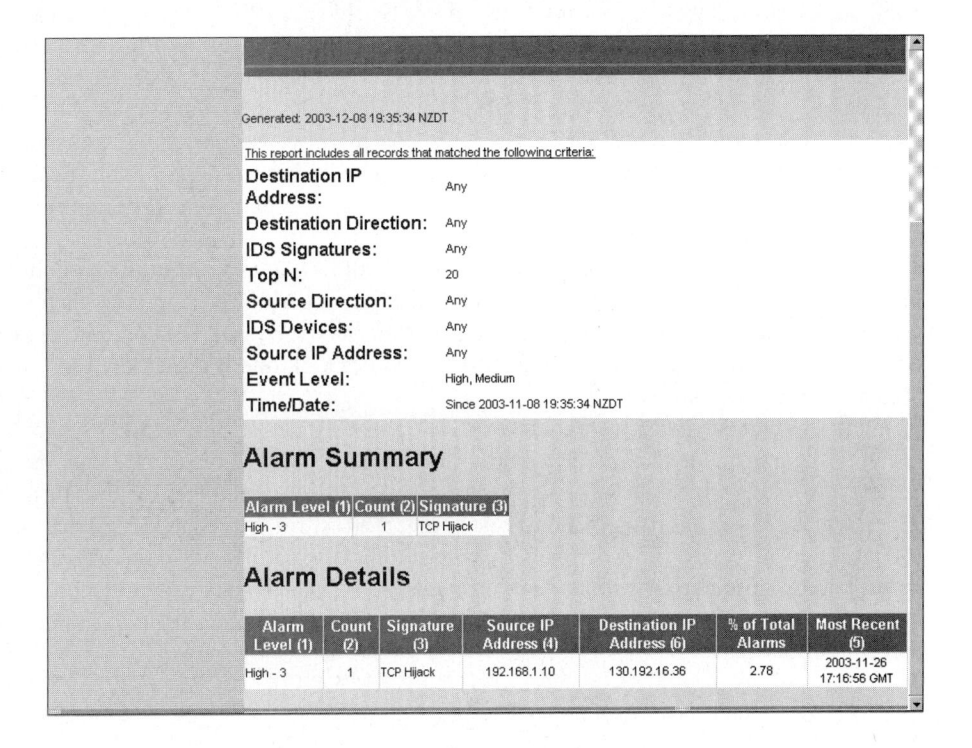

Summary

The Security Monitoring Center provides enterprise-class monitoring for medium to large deployments of up to 300 sensors. The Security Monitor can be installed as a dedicated application (along with the required CiscoWorks common services) on a dedicated server, or it can be installed alongside the IDS Management Center on the same server. To communicate with sensors, the Security Monitor uses RDEP subscriptions over HTTP or HTTP over SSL, pulling events from the event store on each sensor in the same manner as the IDS Event Viewer you learned about in Chapter 24.

When you're configuring the Security Monitor to monitor sensors, you must first add the sensor to the Security Monitor. This can be done either by manually configuring sensor identification settings required for successful communication or by importing sensor settings from the IDS MC. You must also ensure that your sensors are configured such that the Security Monitor is an allowed host. Once the Security Monitor and your sensors have established communications, you can begin to use the Security Monitor to monitor events.

The Security Monitor includes a Java-based application called Event Viewer, which provides realtime or historical views of alarms collected from each sensor. Event Viewer aggregates alarms by default, with the ability to collapse and expand branches of similar alarms. This approach lets you quickly switch between detailed views of specific alarms to a high-level summary of all current alarms.

Event Viewer offers a dashboard-style view of alarms; however, sometimes this style of event notification may not meet your requirements. You may wish for other event notification mechanisms to be triggered for specific events—for example, an e-mail notification for alarms that you want to keep a special note of.

The Security Monitor includes event rules, which allow you to execute an action based on a number of different criteria related to events in the Security Monitor database. Each event rule can generate an e-mail notification, generate an event in the console notification log, or run a custom script, and also includes a number of thresholds and timers that ensure that event rules aren't triggered excessively.

Finally, as with any product that is continually adapting to new threats, the Security Monitor requires ongoing maintenance. An important maintenance action is to update signatures on the Security Monitor, which ensures that the Security Monitor will understand the latest alarms generated by sensors. You also need to ensure that the Security Monitor database doesn't grow too large and adversely affect performance and stability, by configuring database rules that can archive events automatically if necessary. You also need to be able to generate reports that provide an overview of the security status of your network by consolidating and summarizing alarm information.

Exam Essentials

Know the features of the Security Monitor. The Security Monitor provides monitoring for up to 300 sensors and provides event display via the Event Viewer application. You can configure event rules to generate custom responses to alarms and you can generate many different reports related to security events that have occurred.

Understand how to start the Security Monitor. The Security Monitor is started from the CiscoWorks Desktop by opening the VPN/Security Management drawer in the navigation tree and selecting Monitoring Center ➤ Security Monitor.

Understand how to add sensors to the Security Monitor. Sensors can be added via the Devices tab, either manually or by importing sensor configurations from an IDS MC server.

Know how to view events using the Security Monitor. The Security Monitor includes the Event Viewer application. The Event Viewer provides either an historical or realtime view of events, with extensive alarm aggregation and correlation features.

Understand the event expansion boundary. The event expansion boundary determines the default column from which event information is aggregated in Event Viewer.

Know how to graph event information in Event Viewer. Event Viewer lets you graph event information by child (the next child node within an event branch) or by time. All graphs show event count and differentiate between the different event severity levels.

Understand event rules. Event rules allow you to create custom event notifications based on a flexible set of criteria, with the ability to generate e-mail notifications, generate console notifications, and/or execute a custom script. Event rules also include thresholds and intervals that reduce excessive firing of event rules.

Understand how to administer and maintain the Security Monitor Server. Administration and maintenance tasks include updating the signature database on the Security Monitor, configuring database rules to maintain the Security Monitor database, and generating reports.

Cisco SAFE Implementation

PART V

Chapter 27

Security Fundamentals

CISCO SAFE IMPLEMENTATION EXAM TOPICS COVERED IN THIS CHAPTER:

- ✓ Understanding the need for network security
- ✓ Understanding network attack taxonomy
- ✓ Developing a network security policy
- ✓ Understanding management protocols and functions
- ✓ Understanding the architectural overview
- ✓ Knowing the design fundamentals
- ✓ Safe axioms
- ✓ A Security Wheel

Understanding the fundamentals of any technology, whether it be security or IP telephony, is vital if you're ever going to fully understand that technology. Think of security in the same way you think of football. During preseason training, football players put numerous hours into learning and practicing their fundamentals. They do this because without a solid fundamental foundation, they wouldn't be able to perform the more advanced plays. Security is exactly the same: Without putting in ample time learning and practicing the fundamentals of security, you won't be able to learn the more advanced features of security.

Let's get started by covering the reasons and fundamentals of security.

Identifying the Need for Network Security

We hear people talking about security everywhere. When and why did security become so important? Security has always been important—it just hasn't always been given the attention it deserves. As for why it's important, that should be self-explanatory. Companies need to protect their data. We're going to look at networks of the past and networks of today so you can better understand why security is so important to companies.

Networks of the past were known as *closed networks*. A closed network is one in which there is no connection to the outside world. Telecommuters would have a dial-up connection directly into the corporate network, and remote sites would either have a connection over a packet-switched network or an ISDN connection. Since there weren't connections to the outside world, you didn't have to worry about an attack from outside the company. All you had to worry about was making sure employees didn't hack the network—and not many of them did. Figure 27.1 illustrates what one of these closed networks may have looked like.

Today, companies can't live without their Internet connections. With the emergence of e-commerce, connections to the outside world are essential to the success of a company. These new company networks are known as *open networks*. Since these networks are now open to the Internet and outside world, they're vulnerable to attack from outside the company. This means that companies now, more than ever, need security. Figure 27.2 illustrates an example of an open network.

With access available to these open networks from public networks, security threats increase dramatically. Think about it: If your house didn't have any windows or doors, no one could ever break in; but the more windows and doors you add, the more opportunities there are for a burglar. The same applies when you're opening up a closed network.

Not only have open networks increased the need for security, but so has the ease of use of hacking tools. In the past, hackers had to understand both internetworking and programming. Today, anybody with a PC and an Internet connection can download a prebuilt tool and start hacking. These tools are commonly referred to as *kiddie-scripts*. Figure 27.3 illustrates how the ease of hacking has increased security threats. As hacking tools have matured, the level of technological know-how hackers need has decreased.

FIGURE 27.1   Closed network

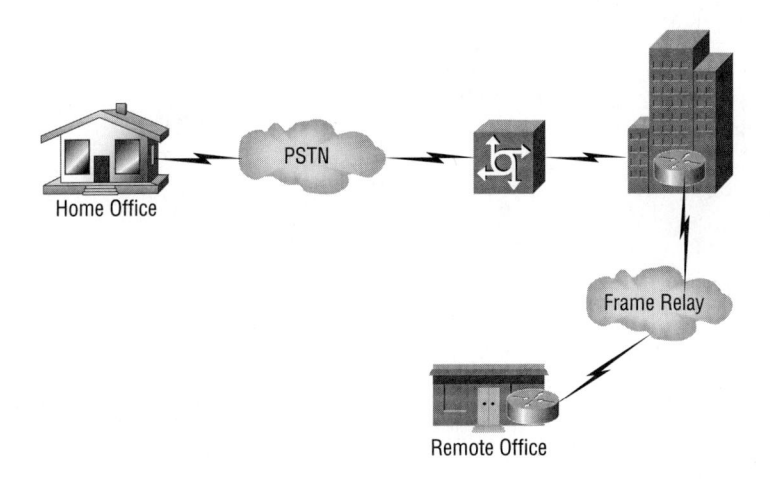

FIGURE 27.2   Open network

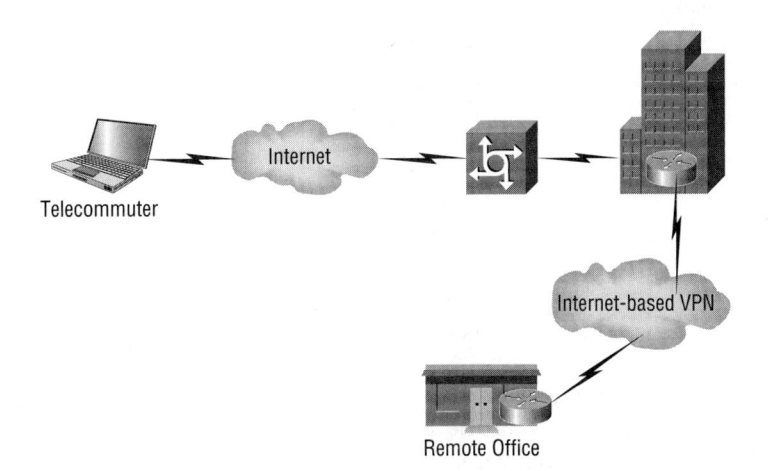

FIGURE 27.3 Hacking and security threats

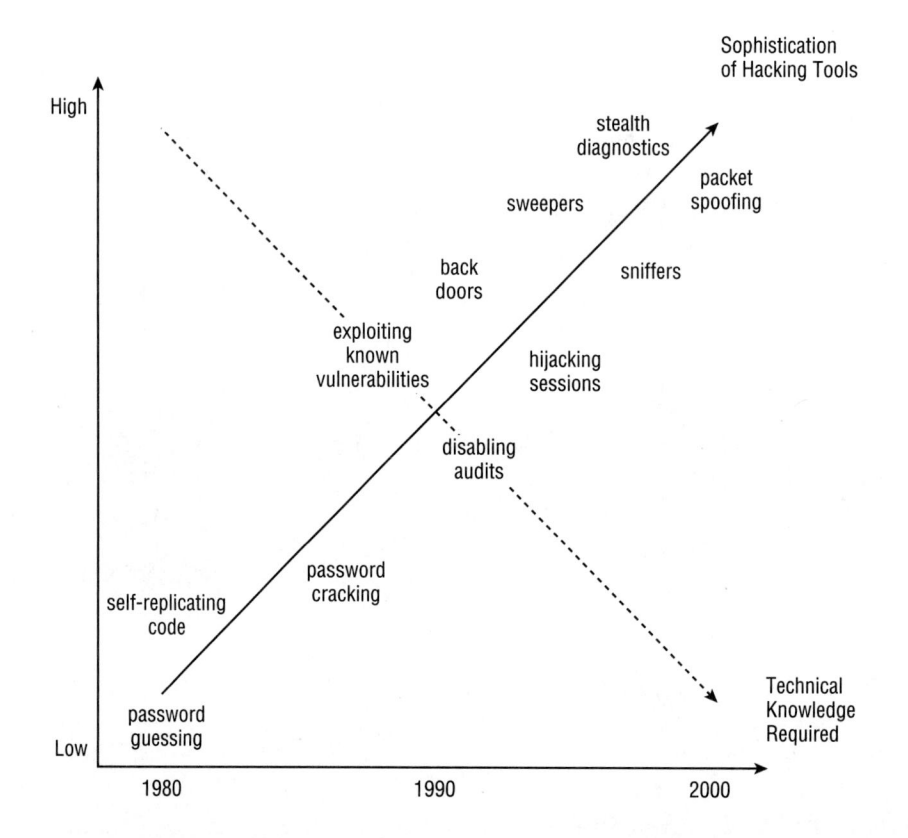

```
                                    Sophistication
                                    of Hacking Tools
        High
                                              stealth
                                              diagnostics
                                                        packet
                                    sweepers            spoofing
                            back              sniffers
                            doors
                    exploiting
                    known           hijacking
                    vulnerabilities sessions
                            disabling
                            audits

                    password
        self-replicating cracking
        code
                                              Technical
        password                              Knowledge
        Low     guessing                      Required
        1980            1990            2000
```

Everyone can see that the need for network security is increasing on a daily basis. Cisco defines the following three reasons as the main forces driving this continued increase in the need for security:

- Secure communications are required for e-business.
- Secure communications are required for communicating and doing business safely in potentially unsafe environments (the Internet).
- Networks require development and implementation of a corporate-wide security policy.

What does each of these mean? "Required for e-business" means that security is needed for e-business communications. More companies every day are using e-business for commerce. E-business requires companies to open their networks up to partners, other businesses, and customers. As you've already learned, opening a network introduces more vulnerabilities, resulting in a greater need for security.

An example of who requires security while "communicating and doing business safely in potentially unsafe environments" would be any company with an Internet connection. When connected to the Internet, vulnerability is introduced to the company's network. Security must be implemented to overcome this vulnerability.

What does "networks require development and implementation of a corporate wide security policy" mean? A security policy is used to specify the level of need of security in a company. It then specifies how the company will handle security threats.

Now we'll begin talking about security fundamentals. We'll begin with a discussion of network attacks.

Network Attack Taxonomy

Network attacks can come from many different sources, such as a disgruntled employee, a competitor who wants to steal confidential company information, or a hacker with malicious intent. No matter where attacks come from, we as security professionals need to protect against them.

There are four possible categories of network threats:

Unstructured threats An *unstructured threat* is a threat where a hacker uses common tools, such as shell scripts and password crackers, to break into a network. These types of attacks often aren't intended to be malicious, because the attacker doesn't usually exploit the vulnerabilities that are found.

Structured threats *Structured threats*, on the other hand, are often orchestrated by one or more highly skilled hackers. These hackers typically use tools they have created in order to gain access to a network for malicious reasons.

Internal threats The most overlooked type of attack is an *internal threat*. This type of threat comes from a person who has direct access to a company network. An internal threat is typically the most dangerous type of attack to a company. These attacks can and should be protected against.

External threats Remember the Code Red virus? That was an *external threat*. An external threat is any attack that occurs from outside a company. Like an internal threat, an external threat can take the form of a structured or unstructured threat.

All network attacks can be classified into one or more of these four categories. Not only is it important to understand the categories of network threats, but it's even more important to understand some of the specific attacks out there. Following are discussions of some of the most common types of network attacks:

- Application layer attacks
- Denial of service (DOS) or distributed denial of service (DDOS)
- IP weaknesses
- Man-in-the-middle attacks
- Network reconnaissance
- Packet sniffers
- Password attacks

- Port redirection
- Trojan horse
- Trust exploitation
- Unauthorized access
- Virus

All of these attacks are common, and you need to understand them if you're going to be in the security field. Let's take a closer look at each of them.

Application Layer Attacks

Application layer attacks are used to gain access to a computer in a number of different ways. One example of an application layer attack would be the exploitation of a known weakness in software on a device to gain access to that device. Trojan horses are another way to accomplish an application layer attack. In this type of attack, a hacker replaces an application with a *Trojan horse*. It looks and acts exactly like the normal application, with one exception: the Trojan horse captures the information you're inputting and sends it back to the hacker. A hacker can also exploit ports, such as HTTP, that are normally allowed through a firewall to launch an application layer attack.

Application layer attacks can never be eliminated. You can, however, reduce the likelihood of one occurring by using one or more of the following techniques:

- Keep software updated with the most recent patches.
- Join a group that publicizes software vulnerabilities.
- Use an intrusion detection system (IDS) to scan, monitor, log, and help prevent known attacks.
- Read your network and operating system logs. If you don't understand them, have them analyzed.

Denial of Service (DOS) or Distributed Denial of Service (DDOS)

Have you ever wondered what might happen if, instead of trying to gain access to your system data, a hacker just attacked the system itself? For instance, instead of gaining access to an e-mail server, they might take the e-mail server out of service. An attack that attempts to take a resource out of service instead of gaining access to the resource is known as a *denial of service (DOS) attack*.

A DOS attack is very dangerous. What would happen if a company lost its e-mail services? Serious communication issues would ensue, and the company could lose a lot of money as a result.

When a hacker launches a DOS attack, they flood a resource on a network from one system. This can occur using UDP and TCP SYN floods, Internet Control Message Protocol (ICMP) echo-request floods, and ICMP directed broadcast floods, also know as Smurf attacks. What could be more dangerous than a DOS attack? A *distributed denial of service (DDOS)* attack. In a DDOS attack, a hacker uses their system to compromise multiple other systems. These other

> ### Real World Scenario
>
> **Mitigating a DOS Attack**
>
> Bob is the network administrator for company XYZ. He was configuring the network and got tired of being bumped out of Telnet sessions due to inactivity. So, Bob, being the clever guy he is, decided to set the executive timeout on all the routers to 0 0, which means the session never times out. Bob was late getting home that day, and he forgot to reset his executive timeouts.
>
> Bob's counterpart, Rob, decided to be a jokester and log in to all the routers five times without closing any of the sessions out. By default, routers only have five VTY lines. That meant Rob locked up all the Telnet sessions.
>
> Bob came into the work the next morning and couldn't log in to any of the devices.
>
> This is a form of DOS attack. Bob could have avoided it by setting all the executive timeouts to an appropriate level. Had Bob restored the timeout settings, Rob's sessions would have timed out. But instead, a DOS attack occurred.

systems are then used to launch the attack. Think of how much you could flood a network if you had 100 systems instead of just one.

There are three methods you can use alone or together to limit DOS and DDOS attacks:

- Configure antispoofing features on your routers and firewalls. You should at a minimum use RFC 2827. This type of filtering only allows traffic originating from your network to leave and only allows traffic not originating from your network to enter.
- Configure anti-DOS features on your routers and firewalls. Doing so limits the number of half-open connections allowed.
- Configure quality of service (QoS) on your devices. Using the traffic rate–limiting feature of QoS, a device can limit the amount of bandwidth a protocol is allowed for use. For example, since ICMP is used for diagnostic purposes, it doesn't use a lot of bandwidth. However, a hacker can use ICMP to launch a Smurf attack. To reduce the possibility of this occurring, limit the amount of ICMP traffic allowed on your network.

IP Weaknesses

IP weaknesses are vulnerabilities in the TCP/IP protocol stack. One of the most widely exploited vulnerabilities is known as *IP spoofing*. IP spoofing occurs when an internal or external hacker uses an IP address that is in the range of trusted IP addresses or uses the IP address of a trusted external device. Once the hacker has spoofed the IP address, they can do one of the following:

- Inject malicious content or commands into an existing traffic stream.
- Change the routing tables to point to the spoofed IP address. This allows the hacker to receive all the network traffic that is directed at the spoofed IP address and then reply to the traffic.

You can never fully prevent IP spoofing, but you can reduce the possibility of it occurring by using the following three methods:

Access control Access control can be used to prevent IP addresses that should reside in your network from accessing your network from the outside. This mitigation technique is effective only when there aren't trusted devices outside of your network.

RFC 2827 filtering RFC 2827 filtering prevents users on your network from spoofing the IP addresses of devices on other networks. This is accomplished by only allowing traffic out of your network that has a source IP address that is part of the IP address range of your network.

Additional authentication IP spoofing can only occur when authentication is IP-based authentication. So, the best way to overcome this is to implement additional authentication, such as cryptographic authentication or strong two-way authentication utilizing one-time passwords.

Man-in-the-Middle Attacks

A *man-in-the-middle attack* requires the hacker to have access to your network. When the hacker has this access, they can use a packet sniffer or routing and transport protocols to implement the attack. Once the attack has been implemented, it can be used to perform one of the following:

- Inflict DoS
- Steal information
- Corrupt transmitted data
- Hijack an ongoing session
- Introduce new information into sessions
- Analyze traffic

The only way to protect against this type of attack is to use encrypted tunnels. If you do so, the traffic passed across the network is encrypted. The hacker will receive only cipher text instead of plain text. In other words, they won't be able to read the text.

Network Reconnaissance

Network reconnaissance can be thought of like a military reconnaissance mission. In a military reconnaissance mission, a recon unit is sent out to find out as much information about the enemy as possible, such as their location, how many enemies there are, what kinds of weapons they have, and what their daily pattern is. This information is then brought back to the commander. The commander uses the information to plan the physical attack.

In network reconnaissance, information is gathered about a network. This information can then be used to plan an actual attack against the network. Hackers perform a network reconnaissance mission by using one or more of the following:

Social engineering Hackers attempt to gain as much information as possible by talking to people who work at the company and even digging through trash.

Port scans Software can be used to determine which ports are open on a network. These ports can then be used in the future to gain access to the network.

Ping sweeps This allows the hacker to learn all active hosts and devices on a network.

Domain Name Services (DNS) queries These can be performed on the Internet. A DNS query provides information about who owns a domain and the address ranges assigned to the domain.

When all of this gathered information is put together, a hacker can then plan a more in-depth attack. You can never fully prevent this form of attack, but you can reduce them. An IDS can be used to notify an administrator when this type of attack is under way. The administrator can then be better prepared for the coming attack.

You *can* eliminate external ping sweeps. To do so, you need to disable ICMP echo requests and replies on all your edge devices.

The types of attacks discussed so far are by no means all-inclusive. You need to stay on top of all the new types of threats if you're going to be an effective security professional. But what's the use of knowing about the types of attacks if you're not sure what needs to be protected on your network? That is what we're about to explore.

Packet Sniffers

The majority of traffic in a network is sent in *clear text*. Clear text means that the data isn't encrypted. This isn't the most secure manner of transmitting traffic, especially if a hacker is able to place a *packet sniffer* on your network. A packet sniffer is a software application that uses a network interface card (NIC) to capture traffic off the physical network. This captured data can then be examined by the user through the packet-sniffer software application. In order for a packet sniffer to work, the NIC must be in promiscuous mode and must be attached to the same collision domain as the device whose traffic you wish to sniff.

As you can see, a person could use a packet sniffer to gather information they shouldn't. For instance, a packet sniffer captures some packets that are being sent across the network. When examined, the packets contain the username and password for the CFO of the company. This username and password can then be used to gain access to information that nobody but the CFO should have access to.

There are two types of sniffers:

General packet sniffers Network administrators and engineers use general packet sniffers to troubleshoot problems on a network. These packet sniffers capture all packets and may be included in an operating system.

Packet sniffers designed for attack Packet sniffers designed for attack aren't used for network troubleshooting. They are used to discover information to use in a network attack. They accomplish this by capturing the first 300 to 400 bytes of a traffic stream. They're typically used on login sessions for protocols such as FTP, rlogin, and Telnet. These types of sniffers are usually freeware or shareware.

To protect against packet sniffers, you can use four techniques:

Authentication Strong authentication can be used as a first line of defense.

Switched infrastructure By using a switched infrastructure, each port on a switch is its own collision domain. If you plug each desktop into its own port, it will be harder to place a sniffer in that collision domain.

Antisniffer tools These tools can be used to detect the use of a sniffer on a network.

Cryptography By encrypting the traffic you're sending, it will be harder for a hacker to read the intercepted traffic.

Password Attacks

Password attacks are one of the more common forms of attacks. In a password attack, a hacker attempts to gain access to a resource by learning the password of a trusted user. Password attacks can occur using any of the following methods:

- Social engineering
- Brute force
- IP spoofing
- Packet sniffers
- Trojan horses

> **NOTE** We've already discussed IP spoofing and packet sniffers; we'll cover Trojan horses in a bit.

Social engineering occurs when a hacker indirectly or directly gains information about a company's network from employees. An example would be when a hacker attempts to get a person's username and password by asking them for it. Believe it or not, quite a few people will tell others their username and password. *Brute force* is accomplished through the use of a program that continually guesses the password until the right password is found. An example of a brute force program is L0phtCrack. A good number of brute force programs can be downloaded from the Internet.

There are four ways you can reduce the risk of password attacks:

- Mandate that users can't use the same password on multiple devices.
- After a set number of failed attempts, disable the account.

- Use one-time passwords or encrypted passwords instead of plain text passwords.
- Use strong passwords. Strong passwords are at least eight characters long and must contain uppercase and lowercase letters, numbers, and special characters.

Port Redirection

Port redirection goes hand-in-hand with trust exploitation. It's actually a form of trust exploitation that uses the compromised trusted host to pass information through the firewall that normally wouldn't be allowed. A hacker compromises a trusted host in the demilitarized zone (DMZ) of the network. The hacker then redirects traffic from the trusted host to the host on the inside the firewall. By doing this, the hacker gains access to the internal network.

The best way to limit this form of attack is to use appropriate trust models. You can also use IDS to help detect this form of attack.

Trojan Horse

Another type of attack similar to a virus is a *Trojan horse*. A Trojan horse is an application that looks exactly like another application. The difference between the Trojan horse and the normal application is that the Trojan horse can forward information you enter back to the hacker. An example of a Trojan horse is one that looks like a login prompt. The user enters their username and password at the prompt; the Trojan horse returns the message "Invalid username or password." No one thinks twice about that message, because we have all seen it at one point or another. The Trojan horse shuts down, launches the actual login prompt, and then e-mails the username and password to the hacker. The end user never knows the difference.

You limit Trojan horses the same way you limit viruses: through the use of antivirus software.

Trust Exploitation

Trust exploitation occurs when a system that's trusted by other systems is compromised. The hacker can then gain access to the systems that trust the compromised system. In order for a hacker to accomplish this type of attack, they must understand the different trust models. Figure 27.4 illustrates this type of attack.

In the example, System A resides in the DMZ. However, System A is trusted by System B, which is on the other side of the firewall. The hacker compromises System A. Once System A has been compromised, the hacker can compromise System B through trust exploitation.

You can guard against trust exploitation by not allowing systems on the inside of a firewall to trust systems outside of the firewall. If trust must exist between the systems, you need to limit the trust to a protocol and require authentication other than an IP address.

FIGURE 27.4 Trust exploitation

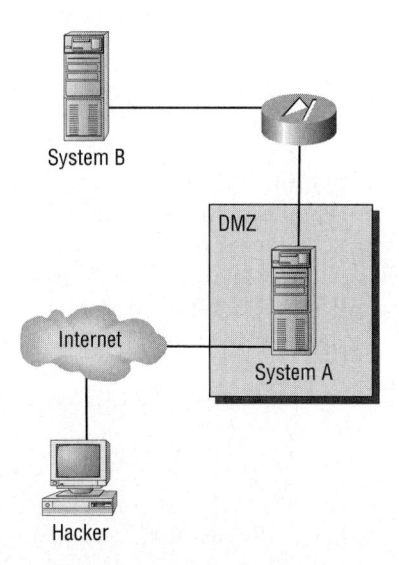

Unauthorized Access

Unauthorized access attacks are the most common type of attacks today, although they aren't really attacks in and of themselves. An unauthorized access attack occurs when a hacker receives a login prompt and then attempts to log in or launch a brute-force attack. This is known as an unauthorized attack because most login prompts say "You must have authorization to access this system." Once a user without authorization proceeds past this message, an unauthorized access attack has occurred.

Firewalls are the best form of reducing this type of attack. Also, access lists can be applied to Telnet lines of devices to prevent unauthorized users from even being able to receive the login prompt.

Virus

A *virus* is a malicious software application that is attached to another application. The virus is then used to execute unwanted functions on the end-user workstation. One of the most common viruses is used to delete files on workstations.

To prevent viruses, you must make sure you're running antivirus software, such as Norton Antivirus. You must also make sure you update the antivirus software frequently. I suggest enabling the auto-update feature of the software.

Network Security Policies

Knowing all the possible types of attacks in the world won't help if you don't have a *security policy*. RFC 2196 defines a security policy as a formal statement of the rules by which people who are given access to an organization's technology and information assets must abide. This means a security policy states what must be protected in a network and states the rules users must abide by when utilizing a company's network. Security policies can range in size from one page to hundreds of pages. It depends on how granular you want to make your policy.

Why would you want to go through the hassle of creating a security policy? For one reason, you can use it to define how to handle security incidents. You can also use it to create a baseline of your current security, define the behaviors that will be allowed and not allowed, define roles, determine procedures, and set the framework for security implementation.

A security policy isn't useful without containing certain items. A security policy should contain the following:

Statement of authority and scope   This specifies who is responsible for the policy and what areas the policy will cover.

Acceptable use policy   This specifies what a company will and won't condone regarding use of the company network.

Identification and authentication policy   This specifies the technologies and equipment used to ensure that only those who should access data can do so.

Internet access policy   This states the purposes for which the company will allow users to access the Internet.

Campus access policy   This specifies how users will use the network when on campus.

Remote access policy   This specifies how users will access and use the network from remote locations.

Incident handling procedure   This specifies how an incident-response team will be created and what procedures will be used to handle incidents.

It's important that a security policy be able to grow. As new threats increase and/or the company changes vision, the security policy must be updated to meet these new needs. A rule to keep in mind is, "If a security policy is stagnated, it's outdated!"

Management Protocols and Functions

How effective is a network if it isn't managed? The answer to that is simple—it's not. Knowing that, you need to understand that management itself is a security vulnerability. By the end of this section, you'll understand how management protocols and functions can be security vulnerabilities and what to do to reduce the risks.

Management protocols and functions can be broken down into the following five areas:

- Configuration management
- Simple Network Management Protocol (SNMP)
- Syslog
- Trivial File Transfer Protocol (TFTP)
- Network Time Protocol (NTP)

We'll now look at how each of these areas introduces security vulnerabilities. You'll also learn what you can do to reduce these vulnerabilities.

Configuration Management

Configuration management is how the configurations of a device are managed. This section mainly focuses on how you access these devices to manage them. Devices can be accessed using any of the following four protocols:

- IP Security (IPSec)
- Secure Shell (SSH)
- Secure Socket Layer (SSL)
- Telnet

Which one of these protocols do you think is the most widely used configuration management protocol and also the least secure? That's right—Telnet! Telnet sends information in clear text. That means if a hacker has a packet sniffer on your network, they can intercept and read this Telnet traffic. Telnet traffic can contain passwords and configuration information. See how this could be a problem?

No matter which protocols you use, you should create access lists on the device that only permit remote access to the device by users who need it and that log all other attempts at access. As for the problem with Telnet, you should use a more secure protocol such as IPSec, SSH, or SSL. To reduce the possibility of an outside hacker spoofing an IP address that is allowed to access the devices, use RFC 2827 filtering.

SNMP

Simple Network Management Protocol (SNMP) is a management protocol that can be used to retrieve information from a device and even change information on a device. SNMP uses TCP and UDP ports 161 and 162 for this purpose.

If you've been in networking for any period of time, more than likely you've dealt with SNMP. SNMP is used by most of the network management systems today. SNMP uses *community strings* for the purpose of managing devices. A community string can be a read-only string, which only allows you to view information on the device, or a read-write string, which lets you view and change information on a device.

SNMP has a problem: Those community strings are sent in clear text. That means anybody with a packet sniffer on your network can intercept these community strings and access your devices.

You can protect against this in two ways. First, you can create access lists on the device that only permit SNMP access to the device from hosts that need it. You can also configure read-only community strings instead of read-write community strings.

> **NOTE** SNMPv3 takes care of the community string issue by encrypting them.

Syslog

Syslog is used to log events on a device. Instead of allowing the logging to occur on a device, the logs are sent to a Syslog server. These logs are then stored and can be accessed when needed.

Syslog messages are sent in clear text on UDP port 514, and they don't have packet-level integrity checking to ensure the packets' contents haven't been altered. This creates a window of opportunity for a hacker. When attempting a network attack, the hacker can intercept the Syslog messages with a packet sniffer. The messages can then be altered to confuse the network administrator when they attempt to read them.

Because we're not hackers, we need to protect against this sort of thing. One of the best mitigation techniques is to create an IPSec tunnel between the device and the Syslog server. This way, all Syslog messages are encrypted. You can also create access lists that only allow the Syslog messages from a device to reach the management host. Finally, you can implement RFC 2827 filtering.

TFTP

Have you ever backed up a configuration file from one of your devices? If so, you probably backed it up to a Trivial File Transfer Protocol (TFTP) server. TFTP is the protocol that is used to allow the backing up of files from a device to a TFTP server. TFTP runs over UDP on port 69.

The problem with TFTP is that it sends information in clear text. Since TFTP is used to back up configuration files and sends them in clear text, anybody with a packet sniffer on that segment can intercept these files and read them. You can protect this traffic by creating an IPSec tunnel from the device to the TFTP server for the TFTP traffic. That way, if the information is intercepted, it will be cipher text and unusable by the hacker.

NTP

Network Time Protocol (NTP) is used to synchronize the clocks of devices on your network. It runs on TCP and uses port 123. Having synchronized clocks on a network is imperative for digital signatures to work and for you to be able to correctly interpret Syslog messages.

Earlier versions of NTP didn't support authentication of synchronizing devices. This left a window open for hackers to send bogus NTP information to devices. When the clocks were messed up, digital certificates wouldn't work; and when the network administrator tried to find out what had happened, the times on the Syslog messages didn't correspond. This is a form of a DOS attack.

To overcome some of the limitations of NTP, NTPv3 was released. NTPv3 supports a cryptographic authentication mechanism between devices. This means that hackers can't just start sending bogus NTP information. If you're implementing NTP, attempt to use version 3.

You can also implement NTP more securely by using your own master clock instead of one outside of your network. Finally, implement access lists that specify what devices can synchronize and that deny all others.

SAFE Architectural Overview

You may have heard the word SAFE and wondered what it was or what type of device implements it. The answer is, "It's not a device!" SAFE was created by Cisco to help designers of network security. It's not a technology or a device; it's a design philosophy that utilizes Cisco and Cisco partner products.

The SAFE approach to security is a layered one. This means that a failure at one layer won't compromise the other layers.

SAFE Small, Midsize, and Remote-User networks (SAFE SMR) takes a threat-mitigation-centric approach to security design instead of the more common device-centric design approach. What this means to a designer is that through a better understanding of the threats and the mitigations to correct them, a more secure network can be designed and deployed with fewer errors. The device-centric approach, by contrast, is more concerned with configuring and deploying devices instead of understanding why the devices need to be deployed.

The SAFE SMR architecture defines five key components:

Identity   Identity is handled through the use of authentication and digital certificates. By using these items, you can determine whether someone who is trying to talk to you is allowed to talk to you.

Perimeter security   Perimeter security is accomplished through use of access control lists (ACLs) and firewalls. This allows you to decide what is and isn't allowed inside your network.

Secure connectivity   Secure connectivity is accomplished through the use of VPN tunneling and encryption. This ensures that your traffic can't just be picked up and read by a packet sniffer.

Security monitoring   Security monitoring is accomplished through the use of IDS and scanning. This allows you to be able to detect possible security vulnerabilities.

Security management   Security management is accomplished through policy and device management. This helps you to ensure that your security policies are up-to-date and correctly implemented.

FIGURE 27.5 SAFE Enterprise modular design

The SAFE SMR architecture is a modular architecture that is built upon the modular design of the SAFE Enterprise, only smaller. Figure 27.5 illustrates the SAFE Enterprise modular design.

> **NOTE** We'll look at each of the SMR portions of the SAFE SMP Network Designs in Chapters 29 and 30.

This design allows you to design and implement security based on the module being secured.

> **NOTE** If you would like to learn more about SAFE Enterprise, you can read the blueprint on Cisco's website at www.cisco.com/en/US/netsol/ns340/ns394/ns171/ns128/networking_solutions_white_paper09186a008009c8b6.shtml.

The SAFE SMR architecture makes the following assumptions:

- That a security policy has already been created
- That you can't guarantee a secure environment
- That you've already secured your applications and operating systems

Next up are design fundamentals and architecture.

SAFE SMR Design Fundamentals

SAFE SMR has defined the following six design fundamentals that you should follow:

- Security and attack mitigation are based on policy.
- Security implementation must be throughout the infrastructure.
- Deployment must be cost-effective.
- Management and reporting must be secure.
- Users and administrators of critical network resources must be authenticated and authorized.
- Intrusion detection must be used for critical resources and subnets.

These fundamentals are essential to any SAFE SMR design. Keep in mind that these topics will be covered again and again throughout the remainder of our discussion. Now that you understand the design fundamentals behind SAFE SMR, it's time to go into more depth about the SAFE SMR architecture.

SAFE SMR Architecture

Before we get into the architecture of SAFE SMR, you must remember that SAFE SMR, unlike SAFE Enterprise, isn't resilient. By this I mean that the SAFE SMR doesn't care about redundancy.

Earlier, you learned that the SAFE SMR is a layered approach to security design. The fundamental design goals are based on the following:

- If the first line of defense is compromised, the attack must be detected and contained by the second line of defense.
- Proper security and good network functionality must be balanced.

But the decisions for the SAFE SMR architecture didn't stop there. SAFE SMR was created with the assumption that both integrated functionality and stand-alone functionality needed to be there. By integrating functionality, you decrease cost, have better interoperability, and can implement the architecture on existing devices. For example, you implement the firewall feature set on a router. You reduce the cost by only having one device, you have better interoperability since you're using one device instead of two, and the firewall feature set can be implemented on existing routers.

There's another aspect to consider: the benefits of stand-alone systems. Stand-alone systems can provide a greater depth of functionality than an integrated system. They can also provide increased performance. Knowing the importance of both methods, Cisco created SAFE SMR to support both.

Earlier, you learned that SAFE SMR uses modules. There's a reason for this. By using modules, the following benefits can be achieved:

- The architecture addresses security relationships between the various functional blocks of the network.
- Security can be implemented on a module-by-module basis instead of attempting the entire architecture in a single phase.
- Modules can and should be combined to achieve desired functionality.

FIGURE 27.6 Medium network modules

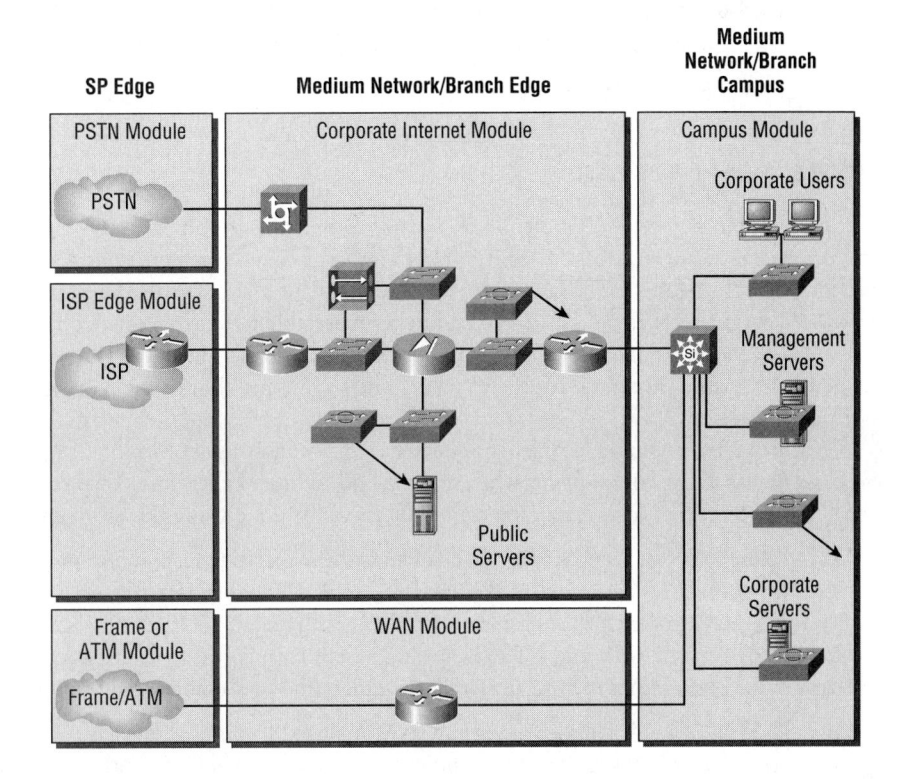

Figure 27.6 illustrates Cisco's detailed model of the SMR Medium Network Design.

It's understandable that most networks can't be broken up into exact modules. Therefore, Cisco recommends that you use a combination of the modules to implement in your network.

The next section will look at the different targets in a network and what can be done to protect them.

SAFE Axioms

SAFE SMR defines seven items, known as *axioms*, which need to be considered when you're designing a network:

- Routers are targets.
- Switches are targets.
- Hosts are targets.
- Networks are targets.

- Applications are targets.
- IDSs mitigate attacks.
- Secure management and reporting mitigate attacks.

This section will be dedicated to exploring each of these axioms.

Routers Are Targets

By this point in your career, I'm sure you know what routers do. If not: A router is used to send traffic from one network to another. Routers contain things called *routing tables*. These routing tables contain all the routes to remote destinations that a router knows. It's the router's view of the network. Imagine what could happen if a hacker were able to gain access to a router. They would have a pretty good idea of what the network looks like. Think of the devastation that could occur if they shut down the router. Hackers know this, and that's why routers are one of their prime targets.

In an attack against a router, the hacker affects the Corporate Internet Module, which controls internal user access to the company network services and to Internet services. To protect a router from hackers, you need to lock down the router. This can be done using the following methods:

Lock down Telnet   You learned earlier that Telnet is the preferred method of remote access to a device. If you're using Telnet, you need to lock it down. The most effective way of locking down Telnet is to create ACLs that limit who can access the device. Once the ACL is created, you need to apply it to all VTY and TTY lines. You need to apply the same ACL to all of those lines because when you telnet in, you don't know which line you'll be coming in on.

Lock down SNMP   You already learned that SNMP is used to manage devices. When you're using SNMP, try to use SNMPv3 if at all possible. If you can't use version 3, try to use only read-only community strings.

Control access to a router through the use of TACACS+   Instead of using normal passwords on a router, use TACACS+. TACACS+ is a protocol that is used for authentication, authorization, and accounting. By utilizing TACACS+, you can control who accesses routers and control unauthorized access.

Turn off unneeded services   Often, people forget to turn off services on a router that isn't being used. For instance, Cisco Discovery Protocol (CDP) provides layer 2 and 3 information about directly connected Cisco devices. If CDP were left on, a hacker could use it to find out device names and IP addresses. Other protocols you should turn off if they're not being used are NTP and Finger.

Log at appropriate levels   Routers support logging, so use it. Set up a Syslog server and logging on the router. Then have the router log appropriate levels of messages to a Syslog server so they can be reviewed.

Authenticate routing updates   This is probably one of the most overlooked security measures. People generally think about secure access and setting up firewalls, but they don't think to use the authentication that is included with some routing protocols. By enabling authentication with routing protocols, you can help to stop malicious attacks on your routing infrastructure.

Switches Are Targets

Routers aren't the only network devices in a network. Don't forget about your switches (layer 2 and 3). An attack against a switch will occur in the Corporate Internet Module and/or the Campus Module. The same risks that apply to routers also apply to switches.

To overcome the risks associated with switch attacks, you can use the same mechanisms used for routers, as well as the following:

- Disable all unused ports on the switch.
- A port that doesn't need to trunk needs to have trunking shut off.
- When you're using older versions of software, make sure that trunk ports use VLAN numbers not used anywhere else in the switch.
- Don't just use VLANs for securing access between subnets.
- Use private VLANs for added security.

Hosts Are Targets

Knowing something about security, what do you think is the most likely target of an attack? That's right—a host. Attacks against hosts occur in the Corporate Internet Module and/or the Campus Module.

Hosts are the mostly likely targets because they are the most visible. If you didn't work for Cisco, would you know the names of its routers? Probably not—but I bet we all know the name of its web server: `www.cisco.com`.

This causes a problem. Hosts are the most complicated devices to secure, because of the number of different hardware and software platforms, the complexity of hosts, and the different software applications, among other reasons. Given this complexity, hosts are often the most compromised systems.

To secure them, Cisco's SAFE SMR recommends you do the following:

- Pay careful attention to each of the components within the system.
- Keep any systems up-to-date with the latest patches and fixes.
- Pay attention to how these patches affect the operation of other system components.
- Evaluate all updates on test systems before you implement them in a production network.

Networks Are Targets

As with switches and hosts, a network attack can occur in the Corporate Internet Module and/or the Campus Module. A network attack takes advantage of the intrinsic characteristics of a network. For instance, an ARP attack can be used to gather hardware addresses of devices for further attack. Network attacks can also take the following forms:

- Similar to an ARP attack, a MAC-based layer 2 attack can be used to gather MAC address information.
- The use of a packet sniffer can be categorized as a network attack.
- DOS and DDOS attacks are considered network attacks.

There are several ways you can protect against a network attack. Here are a few of these preventative measures:

- Use RFC 1918 private addressing on your internal network.
- As always, use RFC 2827 filtering to prevent IP spoofing.
- Use traffic-rate limiting to specify the amount of bandwidth a specific protocol is allowed to use. This can be very effective in helping to reduce ICMP-initiated DOS attacks.
- Mark traffic that is undesirable as undesirable.

Applications Are Targets

Applications introduce interesting vulnerabilities into a network. Applications can introduce benign threats—threats that don't pose a real risk—or malign threats—threats that can cause serious problems. Hackers can take advantage of the malign threats to gather information they shouldn't have access to. An attack on an application occurs in the Corporate Internet Module and/or the Campus Module.

There are two recommendations for reducing application threats:

- Make sure that applications are up-to-date with the latest patches and fixes.
- Have a code review performed on any new applications you're going to introduce to your network. This can help in determining security risks that may be introduced by the applications.

Intrusion Detection Systems Mitigate Attacks

IDS is used to detect possible network intrusions. The IDS system can then take its own corrective actions or notify an administrator of the possible intrusion.

IDS can be either host-based or network-based. A host-based IDS works by intercepting application and operating system calls on a host. The IDS can then determine whether an attack is under way. Keep in mind that a host-based IDS only cares about a host, whereas a network IDS keeps track of potential attacks on the network as a whole. Cisco recommends a combination of both host- and network-based IDS.

When talking about IDS, there are two terms you need to be familiar with:

- *False positives* are incidents of legitimate traffic triggering an IDS alarm.
- *False negatives* are incidents of illegitimate traffic not triggering an IDS alarm.

When you're using IDS, you should first tune IDS to decrease the number of false positives received. Use TCP resets instead of shunning on TCP. If shunning must be used, it must be short and only applied to TCP traffic.

Secure Management and Reporting Mitigate Attacks

So far, we've looked at securing a network, and we've briefly looked at secure management. When you're securing a network, you need to make sure network management and reporting are secure as well.

There are two forms of managing a network: *out-of-band* and *in-band*. Although out-of-band management is by far the most secure form of network and device management, SAFE SMR doesn't recommend it. Since SAFE SMR is concerned with cost, it recommends the less secure but also less expensive alternative of in-band management.

The most common form of in-band management is Telnet. SAFE SMR recommends using the more secure IPSec, SSL, or SSH instead of Telnet whenever possible.

A needed network management function that is often overlooked is change management. *Change management* allows you to determine who made the last change to a device and when. This can be accomplished through the use of authentication, authorization, and accounting (AAA).

Accurate reporting is crucial to a network. A network administrator must be able to look at log files to track the movements of a hacker attempting to break into the network. Without proper reporting, the network administrator can't correctly put together the pieces of the puzzle.

In order to ensure that reporting is accurate, the clocks on all the devices must be synchronized. To accomplish this, you need to implement NTP. Since you're concerned with security, you should implement your own master clock and then synchronize all the other devices off of it. Doing so will help you ensure that the times on the Syslog messages are correct.

The last item we need to discuss in this chapter is the life cycle that security goes through.

Identifying the Security Wheel

Network security is an ever-evolving monster. If your network security isn't being updated, then it's no longer effective. SAFE SMR uses what's known as a *Security Wheel* to describe a security life cycle. Figure 27.7 is an illustration of the SAFE SMR Security Wheel.

As you can see from the illustration, the SAFE SMR Security Wheel rotates clockwise, with the security policy setting in the middle. This means that before anything else can occur, the security policy must be created.

FIGURE 27.7   SAFE SMR Security Wheel

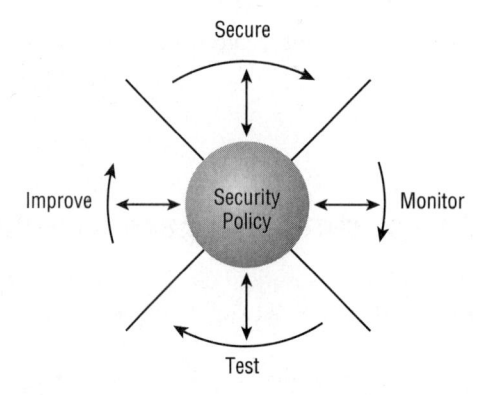

```
              Secure
                ↓
    Improve ← Security → Monitor
              Policy
                ↑
              Test
```

Once you've defined a security policy, you can begin the wheel. The rotation begins at the top of the wheel. The Security Wheel defines the following four phases:

Secure   As I said, after you've completed the security policy, you can begin with the implementation of a secure network. This portion of the Security Wheel has you implement your security policy. One method you'll use to accomplish this is authentication. Authentication requires you to determine all users and what resources they need access to. You then need to map these users to their level of authorization.

Next you'll use encryption. Encryption lets you protect your data transiting the network. Encrypting the data ensures that a hacker won't be able to intercept it with a packet sniffer and read it.

Finally, you'll incorporate firewalls and vulnerability patching. Firewalls allow you to protect the perimeter of your network, and vulnerability patching lets you patch security holes in your network.

Monitor   Once you've secured your network, you must monitor it to make sure your implementation is working and to check for any new security holes. During the monitoring phase, you can detect any violations to the security policy. Network vulnerability scanners and IDS can be used to provide you with system auditing and real-time intrusion detection. Finally, the monitoring phase validates the security implementation of the secure phase.

Test   During the test phase, you'll actually test the security implementation put in place during the secure phase. You can perform internal and/or external security audits. Doing this will make you better informed about how your network holds up against attack. You'll also learn about vulnerabilities you may not have originally thought of.

Improve   The improve phase is very important. During this phase, you'll use the information you gathered during the monitor and test phases to improve your security implementation. You can also use the information to update your security policy.

Once you've run through all the phases of the SAFE SMR Security Wheel, you'll start over. If you're not continually evaluating and adjusting your security policy and implementation, your network security will become stale. This means it will no longer be effective. The moral of the story is to stay on top of network security: That way you can reduce the risks of attacks on your network.

Summary

This chapter introduced you to the need for security. Security is necessary because networks have changed from closed to open networks. This means that vulnerabilities that were never there before have now been introduced to networks.

There are numerous attacks, such as DOS and password attacks. You may never be able to fully eliminate them, but with the proper knowledge and tools, you can reduce them.

One of the ways you can help protect your networks is through the understanding and use of Cisco's SAFE SMR design. Using the axioms discussed in this chapter will help you better understand what is at risk and how to protect it.

Network security is an ever-evolving monster that will become ineffective if you're not on top of it. In order to better protect your networks, you need to adopt the SAFE SMR Security Wheel. This Security Wheel requires you to continually update your security policies and implementations.

It's vital that you have a firm grasp on everything discussed here. If you don't, I recommend reviewing this chapter again before moving on. Remember, you're not just trying to get through a test, you're trying to become a better security professional.

Exam Essentials

Explain the need for security. You need to explain why security is needed—for instance, because company networks have moved from a closed network to an open network. Moving to an open network causes security vulnerabilities to be introduced into these networks.

Explain the common attacks and how to protect against them. You must be able to list all the common attacks discussed and what can be done to mitigate them. For example, password attacks are used to learn a user's password. Strong passwords and one-time passwords are ways of mitigating this threat.

Explain what a security policy is and why it's needed. A security policy is a formal statement that specifies a company's stand on security. It's needed in order to determine what needs to be protected and how to protect it.

Explain what management protocols and functions are and how to protect them. Configuration management, TFTP, SMTP, Syslog, and NTP are all management protocols and functions. Each has its own vulnerabilities that need to be protected against. For example, TFTP is used to back up configuration files from a device to a TFTP server. TFTP sends these configuration files across the network in clear text. One solution to overcome the clear-text vulnerability is to use IPSec tunnels.

Explain the SAFE architecture. The SAFE architecture is a modular architecture. It prevents attacks at one layer from being able to penetrate throughout a network. It defines how security should be implemented on devices in each of these modules.

Explain the SAFE axioms. SAFE SMR defines seven axioms. These axioms explain the different areas of a network that are at risk. Learn what the risks are and how you can mitigate against them.

Explain what the Security Wheel is and how it's used. The Security Wheel is made up of four phases: secure, monitor, test, and improve. At the center of the Security Wheel is the security policy. Each phase of the Security Wheel was designed to help you continually evaluate your current security policy and implementation. By continually evaluating these items, you can make sure your network is as secure as it can be.

Chapter 28

The Cisco Security Portfolio

CISCO SAFE IMPLEMENTATION EXAM TOPICS COVERED IN THIS CHAPTER:

- ✓ Understanding the Cisco security portfolio overview
- ✓ Understanding Secure connectivity—virtual private network solutions
- ✓ Understanding secure connectivity—the 3000 concentrator series
- ✓ Understanding secure connectivity—Cisco VPN optimized routers
- ✓ Understanding perimeter security firewalls—Cisco PIX and Cisco IOS firewall
- ✓ Understanding intrusion protection—IDS and Secure Scanner
- ✓ Understanding identity—access control solutions
- ✓ Understanding security management—VMS and CSPM
- ✓ Understanding Cisco AVVID

In the last chapter, you learned the theory behind SAFE SMR. This chapter will introduce you to the Cisco security portfolio for SAFE SMR. You'll learn what devices can be used for identity, perimeter security, secure connectivity, intrusion protection, and security management. We'll discuss many products in this chapter.

This chapter will wind up with an introduction to the Cisco AVVID solution. You may have heard about AVVID but never really understood what it was; well, you will by the end of this chapter. We'll also look at how SAFE can be utilized to secure an AVVID network.

Cisco Security Portfolio Overview

What good is a security policy if you don't know the devices you can use to implement it? The answer is, none. Once you have your security policy created, you need to be able to intelligently decide what products to use. Cisco has tried to make this easier with the Cisco security portfolio.

The Cisco security portfolio specifies the devices that can be used to meet the following security solutions:

Secure connectivity   You can use Cisco VPN concentrator, Cisco PIX firewall, and Cisco IOS VPN.

Perimeter security   You can use Cisco PIX firewall and Cisco IOS firewalls.

Intrusion protection   You can use Cisco network-based intrusion detection system (NIDS) sensors, Cisco host-based intrusion detection system (HIDS) sensors, Cisco IOS-based intrusion detection, Cisco Intrusion Detection System Module (IDSM), and Cisco PIX firewall-based intrusion detection.

Identity   You can use Cisco Secure Access Control Server (ACS).

Security management   You can use CiscoWorks 2000 VPN/Security Management Solution (VMS), Cisco Secure Policy Manager (CSPM), and web device managers.

In the following sections, we'll visit each of these devices in more detail.

Secure Connectivity: Virtual Private Network Solutions

When you're transiting the Internet or even a corporate intranet, it might be a wise idea to do something to keep prying eyes from looking at your data. That "something" is secure connectivity. *Secure connectivity* keeps private traffic private. It accomplishes this through encryption. Through the use of virtual private networks (VPNs), secure connectivity lets you extend the reach of your network to remote sites and users.

There are three types of VPN implementations:

- Intranet VPN
- Extranet VPN
- Remote access VPN

Each of these different implementations is required for the different situations companies encounter today with their communications. Let's take a closer look at each of these VPN implementations:

Intranet VPN   An *intranet VPN* provides secure connectivity between the corporate headquarters and remote offices. By utilizing this VPN implementation instead of a more costly wide area network (WAN) implementation, companies can dramatically reduce WAN costs and extend the functionality of the corporate network to remote offices. Figure 28.1 illustrates a simple intranet VPN implementation.

Extranet VPN   Companies today are relying more and more on direct communications with their third-party vendors and business partners. In order to achieve this business need, a company must extend elements of the corporate infrastructure to its partners. This extension must occur in a secure manner so as not to introduce new security risks. To achieve secure connectivity to partners, it's recommended that the company use an *extranet VPN* implementation. An extranet VPN is a secure connection between a company and its third-party vendors. Figure 28.2 illustrates a simple extranet VPN implementation.

FIGURE 28.1   Extranet VPN

FIGURE 28.2 Intranet VPN

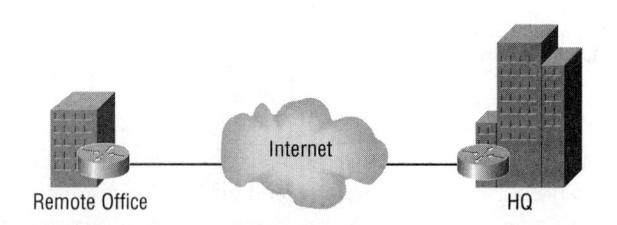

Remote Office — Internet — HQ

Remote access VPN A *remote access* VPN allows the employees who are on the road or telecommuting to securely connect into the corporate intranet. By connecting into the corporate intranet, these remote users can gain access to information just as if they were sitting at a desk in the office. Figure 28.3 illustrates a basic remote access VPN implementation.

FIGURE 28.3 Remote access VPN

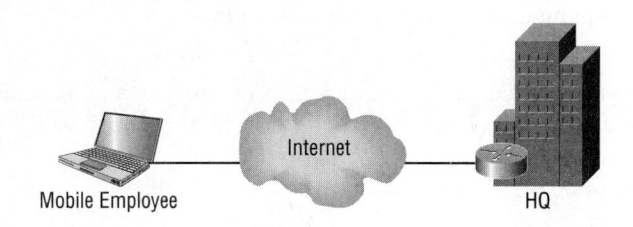

Mobile Employee — Internet — HQ

Since each implementation has its own characteristics, Cisco has created three solutions—site-to-site, remote access, and firewall-based—and corresponding product recommendations to meet these needs. The needs of your intranet, extranet, or remote access VPNs are used to determine which of the following solutions to use. Table 28.1 gives a summary of the solutions and the products that should be used.

The remainder of this section will be dedicated to a more in-depth look at each of these solutions.

> ### Real World Scenario
> #### Selecting a VPN
>
> Bob is the network administrator for company XYZ. Company XYZ is a medium-sized enterprise focusing on e-commerce. Company XYZ has numerous partners that need limited access to XYZ's network. Bob has been tasked with determining what type of VPN to implement.
>
> Bob remembers that a medium-sized enterprise should use an extranet VPN. Knowing this, Bob decides he will implement this extranet VPN using 3600 routers for the VPN connection.

TABLE 28.1 VPN Solutions

Size of Network	Site-to-Site VPN Solution	Remote Access VPN Solution	Firewall-Based VPN Solution
Service providers and/or large enterprises	7100 or 7200 Cisco routers	3060 or 3080 VPN concentrators	525 or 535 PIX firewall
Medium enterprises	7100 or 3600 Cisco routers	3030 VPN concentrator	515 PIX firewall
Remote office	3600, 2600, or 1700 Cisco routers	3015 or 3005 VPN concentrator	515 or 506 PIX firewall
SOHO	900 or 800 Cisco routers	VPN 3000 software client or VPN 3002 hardware client	506 or 501 PIX firewall

Site-to-Site VPN Solution

Site-to-site VPN solutions are used to connect remote offices into the corporate headquarters. This VPN solution is used as an alternative to the more expensive WAN services, such as Frame Relay or ATM.

Companies in the past used (and today still use) Frame Relay and ATM as their WAN service. These WAN services provide a guaranteed bandwidth and secure connections. The problem with traditional WAN services is cost. By utilizing site-to-site VPNs, you can lower the cost associated with WAN services and still provide secure connectivity.

By utilizing site-to-site VPNs, you increase the network scalability. Through the support of queuing, traffic shaping and policing, and application-aware bandwidth allocation, site-to-site VPN provides superior support of quality of service (QoS) and bandwidth allocation.

Site-to-site VPN can be supported through the use of VPN-optimized routers and/or stand-alone VPN products, providing a tremendous amount of deployment flexibility. Site-to-site VPN also has built-in support for dynamic route recovery and dynamic tunnel recovery, providing network resilience.

Now that you have an understanding of what site-to-site VPN is, let's look at some of the different solutions offered. These solutions include the following:

- Remote office to central office
- Regional office to central office
- SOHO to central office

The recommended products for each of these sites differ. So, with that in mind, let's see what products Cisco recommends.

Central Office

The central office is the site where all of these VPN connections terminate. Knowing this, you might conclude that the router to be used here is one of the higher-end ones, and you would be correct.

For a central office, Cisco recommends the use of a Cisco 7100 or 7200 series router. If the router you choose will only be used for VPN connections, you should select the Cisco 7100 series router. If you'll need to use the device for both VPN and WAN services, you should select the higher-end Cisco 7200 series router.

Both the Cisco 7100 and 7200 series of routers support VPN acceleration modules (VAMs). A VAM is used to provide IPSec processing and remove it from the main processor. This frees the main processor so it can worry about other tasks.

The features of the Cisco 7100 and 7200 series routers are as follows:

- The Cisco 7120 router can support up to 2000 simultaneous tunnels with 50Mbps of performance. It has support for two Fast Ethernet interfaces and various WAN interfaces.
- The Cisco 7140 router can support up to 2000 simultaneous tunnels with 90Mbps of performance with a single VAM, or up to 3000 simultaneous tunnels with 140Mbps of performance with dual VAMs. It has support for two Fast Ethernet interfaces and various WAN interfaces.
- The Cisco 7200 router can support up to 5000 simultaneous tunnels with 145Mbps of performance. It supports various LAN and WAN interfaces.

Time to move on to the regional office.

Regional Office

A regional office isn't as large as the central office, but it still has many users. Therefore, you don't need a router as powerful as the Cisco 7200 series, but you do need one that can support numerous users. With that in mind, Cisco recommends the use of the Cisco 2600 or 3600 series routers for regional or branch offices. The following routers are recommended:

- The Cisco 2611 router can support up to 300 simultaneous tunnels with 10Mbps of performance. It has support for two Fast Ethernet interfaces and various WAN interfaces.
- The Cisco 2621 router can support up to 300 simultaneous tunnels with 12Mbps of performance. It has support for two Fast Ethernet interfaces and various WAN interfaces.
- The Cisco 2651 router can support up to 800 simultaneous tunnels with 14Mbps of performance. It has support for two Fast Ethernet interfaces and various WAN interfaces.
- The Cisco 3620 router can support up to 800 simultaneous tunnels with 10Mbps of performance. It has support for various LAN and WAN interfaces.
- The Cisco 3640 router can support up to 1000 simultaneous tunnels with 18Mbps of performance. It has support for various LAN and WAN interfaces.
- The Cisco 3660 router can support up to 1300 simultaneous tunnels with 40Mbps of performance. It has support for 1 Fast Ethernet interface and various WAN interfaces.

What products can you use for the remote office? Let's find out.

Remote Office

A remote office is smaller than a regional or branch office, but it still isn't as small as a SOHO. Cisco recommends the Cisco 1700 series router for the job. The following 1700 series routers are recommended:

- The Cisco 1710 router can support up to 100 simultaneous tunnels with 8Mbps of performance. It has support for one Ethernet interface and one Fast Ethernet interface.
- The Cisco 1720 router can support up to 100 simultaneous tunnels with 8Mbps of performance. It has support for one Fast Ethernet interface and various WAN interfaces.
- The Cisco 1750 router can support up to 100 simultaneous tunnels with 8Mbps of performance. It has support for one Fast Ethernet interface and various WAN interfaces.

> **NOTE** You'll notice that the 1750 has the same support as the 1720.

The last office we need to look at is the SOHO.

SOHO

A SOHO is either a small office or a home office. Typically, only a couple of people are there who need access to the corporate infrastructure. The SOHO generally has an ISDN, DSL, or cable connection to the Internet. In other words, it doesn't need a powerful router. Cisco recommends the use of one of the following routers:

- The Cisco 804 router supports up to 50 simultaneous tunnels with 384Kbps of performance. It supports one ISDN interface and one Ethernet interface.
- The Cisco 806 router supports up to 50 simultaneous tunnels with 384Kbps of performance. It supports five Ethernet interfaces.
- The Cisco 807 router supports up to 50 simultaneous tunnels with 384Kbps of performance. It supports one DSL interface and one Ethernet interface.
- The Cisco 905 router supports up to 50 simultaneous tunnels with 6Kbps of performance. It supports one cable interface and four Ethernet interfaces.

Remote Access VPN Solution

Companies are using telecommuters and road warriors more today than they ever have in the past. These employees need to have access to the corporate network when they're at home or on the road. Unfortunately, they can't carry a direct connection with them to their corporate network. So, how can they access it? They are able to access their corporate network through the use of a remote access VPN solution. The remote access VPN solution allows the corporate network to scale to all users regardless of their location, as long as they have Internet access.

When you're implementing a remote access VPN solution, Cisco recommends that you utilize a VPN 3000 series concentrator at the central office. This device terminates all the remote access

VPN connections. The VPN Concentrator supports the use of RADIUS for authentication and will be placed behind the Internet access router and parallel to the PIX firewall.

The Cisco VPN 3000 series concentrator can support anywhere from 100 to 10,000 simultaneous remote access VPN connections. Table 28.2 gives a brief comparison of the VPN 3000 series concentrators.

Now that you know what you need for the central office, what about the SOHO or the single user? There are a couple of different options:

- VPN software client
- VPN 3002 hardware client

When you have an employee who is always on the road or who isn't always in the same place, your best choice for a VPN client is the VPN software client. The VPN software client can be installed on any laptop or desktop computer. This provides the users the chance to connect to the corporate network no matter where they are, as long as they have an Internet connection.

If the employee is in more of a fixed place, or if multiple employees in the same place need to connect to the corporate network, you may want to consider the VPN 3002 hardware client. This VPN hardware client is an actual device that establishes a VPN connection with the central office. Every user who is connected behind the client can then communicate with the corporate network once the hardware client has established a VPN connection.

TABLE 28.2   VPN 3000 Series Concentrators

Feature	3005	3015	3030	3060	3080
Simultaneous users	100	100	1500	5000	10,000
Performance (Mbps)	4	4	50	100	100
Encryption cards	0	0	1	2	4
Memory (Mb)	64	128	128	256	256
Upgradable	No	Yes	Yes	Yes	No
Dual power supply	No	Optional	Optional	Optional	Yes
Redundancy	No	Yes	Yes	Yes	Yes
Site-to-site tunnels	100	100	500	1000	1000

Both the software client and the hardware client utilize the *Cisco Unified Client framework*. This framework provides for the following:

- Connectivity between all clients and the central office VPN Concentrator
- Centralized push policy technology
- Implementation across all Cisco VPN Concentrators, IOS routers, and PIX firewalls

That's all of the recommended products for the remote access VPN solution. Now it's time to look at the firewall-based VPN solution and perimeter security.

Firewall-Based VPN Solution and Perimeter Security

Firewall-based VPN solutions are typically used for site-to-site VPN solutions. A PIX firewall or an IOS-based firewall can be used for this solution. These same devices are used to provide *perimeter security* as well. Perimeter security occurs at the edge of your network: It's the point where your network connects to the ISP. Perimeter security is used to aid in the protection of your internal network.

As we stated earlier, the PIX firewall or an IOS-based firewall can be used to perform these functions. Let's look at each of these products.

PIX Firewall

A PIX firewall is a hardware-based firewall, unlike a CheckPoint firewall, which is a software-based firewall. A PIX is self-contained in its own box.

PIX firewalls are primarily used to restrict access to network resources. However, they can be used to provide VPN and limited IDS services. By utilizing a PIX, you can increase the security of a network.

> **Note:** For more information on the PIX firewall and the Cisco Secure PIX Firewall Advanced exam, see Part II of this book, "Cisco Secure PIX Firewall Advanced."

A PIX can be configured through either the command-line interface (CLI) or the Cisco PIX Device Manager (PDM). The CLI looks similar to a Cisco router's CLI. The only difference is the commands that are used. The PDM is a GII-based PIX configuration tool. Through the use of wizards, the PDM can allow a novice to configure the PIX firewall.

There are five versions of the PIX firewall, each of which is suited for a different size of network. Following are the different networks and the PIX that is recommended for each:

- SOHO: PIX 501
- Remote office/branch office: PIX 501 or 506
- Small- to medium-sized business: PIX 506 or 515
- Enterprise: PIX 515, 525, or 535
- Service provider: PIX 535

To enhance the VPN support for the PIX 515, 520, 525, or 535, the VPN accelerator card (VAC) was introduced. The VAC offloads the responsibility of encryption from the main processor to itself, which helps to increase the PIX's support for VPN. In order to utilize the VAC, a PIX must be running IOS version 5.3 or greater.

IOS-Based Firewall

Any Cisco router that supports the IOS Firewall Feature Set can be used as an IOS-based firewall. The IOS Firewall Feature Set provides support for context-based access control (CBAC), authentication proxy, and limited IDS. Since all we're concerned with in this section is the IOS-based firewall, that's what we'll give attention to.

When the IOS Firewall Feature Set has been loaded onto a Cisco router, CBAC can be used. CBAC lets a Cisco router perform some of the same functions as a firewall. CBAC utilizes stateful inspection to temporarily open ports into a network. In other words, only connections that originate within the internal network can come back through the interface that is connected to the outside world.

CBAC also provides support for Java blocking, DoS prevention and detection, and realtime alerts and audit trails. With all of these features taken into consideration, CBAC can definitely increase the security of your internal network.

> **WARNING** Keep in mind that a router is made to route, so in adding these other features to a router, you're taking resources away from the true job of the router.

We'll now move on to intrusion protection.

Understanding Intrusion Protection

Intrusion protection monitors your network for anything that looks like it may be an attack. It monitors the traffic passing over your network for signatures. *Signatures* are used to match information contained in traffic to what could be an attack. Once a signature has been matched, the intrusion protection device can send an alarm, drop the packet, and/or reset the connection.

Intrusion protection can be placed in numerous locations on your network. Placing the intrusion protection device on the extranet will allow for the monitoring of traffic on the extended network. Intrusion protection can also be placed on your connection to the Internet, intranet, internal network, and remote access network to monitor the traffic on these different networks.

Intrusion protection can take the form of network-based intrusion protection or host-based intrusion protection. *Network-based intrusion protection* is used to monitor the traffic on your actual networks for the purpose of finding attacks. *Host-based intrusion protection* is used to detect and stop unauthorized activity on a host. Utilizing both together will help you to detect and stop attacks in your network. Cisco's answer to intrusion protection is its Intrusion Detection System (IDS).

IDS

When you utilize IDS, you're using what's known as an IDS sensor. An *IDS sensor* uses the Post-Office protocol to communicate with an Event Management Program. When an IDS sensor detects a signature match, it informs the Director. The Director logs this information and then tells the sensor what action to perform.

In this section, all we'll worry about is the IDS sensor. The IDS sensor can come in one of the following flavors:

> **NOTE** Part 4 of this book deals with IDS in detail.

Network sensor (NIDS) NIDS utilizes the Cisco IDS 4200 series appliances to provide network-based intrusion detection.

Host sensor (HIDS) HIDS is powered by Entercept and is used to provide host-based IDS.

Switch sensor (IDSM) Utilizing the IDSM module in a Cisco 6500 switch allows for intrusion detection on a switched environment.

Router sensor By loading the IOS Firewall Feature Set and enabling IDS on the router, the router can perform the functions of an IDS sensor.

Firewall sensor The PIX firewall can be enabled to provide limited IDS sensor functions.

Cisco recommends the use of the Cisco IDS 4200 series appliance and the IDSM module in a Cisco 6500 series switch for all of your IDS needs. Table 28.3 provides a comparison of these different IDS products.

TABLE 28.3 IDS Comparison

Feature	4210	4235	4250	IDSM
Size (U)	1	4	4	1 Slot
Processor (MHz)	566	Dual PIII-600	Dual PIII-600	Custom
RAM (MB)	256	512	512	N/A
Performance (Mbps)	45	100	100	260
Response	Reset, shun, and log	Reset, shun, and log	Reset, shun, and log	Shun
Signature coverage	Full	Full	Full	Full

Secure Scanner

You can't secure a network without first understanding what your network is vulnerable to. Cisco Secure Scanner is a vulnerability and network-mapping tool that allows for automated vulnerability scanning of your network.

Secure Scanner uses a phased approach to vulnerability scanning:

Phase 1: network mapping During this phase, Secure Scanner maps your network. It uses the list of IP addresses and ports you've specified in order to map the network. Secure Scanner performs a ping sweep of your network using the provided IP addresses. In other words, it attempts to ping all the IP addresses you have specified. Any host that responds to the ping will be considered a live host. These live hosts are then used to create an electronic map of your network.

Phase 2: data collection After mapping your network, Secure Scanner needs to gather information about your network. Secure Scanner performs a port scan on all the live hosts in your network. A port scan provides information on the ports that are currently open on a device. Once this port information has been gathered, Secure Scanner stores it in a database for later analysis.

Phase 3: data analysis During the data analysis phase, Secure Scanner first uses the information gathered previously to determine what type of a device (router, PC, and so on) a live host is. Once this has been determined, Secure Scanner consults its vulnerability database to determine the vulnerabilities of the host. The vulnerability database contains rules on the different vulnerabilities that exist.

Phase 4: vulnerability confirmation Once possible vulnerabilities have been identified, Secure Scanner probes the network to determine if any of the hosts have these vulnerabilities. In other words, Secure Scanner attempts to exploit the vulnerabilities of the hosts.

> **NOTE** Even though Secure Scanner tests vulnerabilities, it won't attempt a DoS attack against any host.

Phase 5: data presentation and navigation After all this data has been gathered, Secure Scanner needs to present it to you. Secure Scanner can do this through its grid browser, network security database (NSDB), and charts.

The grid browser lets you display all the collected data at once. If that's too much for you, you can choose to limit the amount of data presented by narrowing the scope, drilling down, or focusing on a particular vulnerability. This is known as *pivoting*.

Secure Scanner lets you further investigate a vulnerability by consulting its NSDB. The NSDB provides you with a description of the vulnerability, the level of severity, potential damage, affected systems, links to patches, and links to a comments page that lets you customize information about the vulnerability.

Finally, you can view different charts. Secure Scanner can present the data to you in any of the following chart types:

- Area charts
- Line charts
- 3D bar graphs
- Pie charts
- 2.5D column
- 3D column
- 3D horizontal row
- Stacked bar
- Stacked area

Phase 6: reporting   One of the most difficult portions of a vulnerability scan is the creation of documentation. Secure Scanner simplifies this task by providing you with a wizard-based document creation tool. These wizards allow you to create any of the following reports:

- Executive Report—A summary report of the session results. This is the report you'll present to your upper level management.
- Brief Technical Report—A short but technical summary of the session results. This report takes all the relevant information and summarizes it into a concise report.
- Full Technical Report—A full report of the session results, which includes detailed technical information.
- Custom Report—The report templates can also be customized to have the look and feel of your company.

Understanding Identity

Identity is a way of determining who someone is. Think about why you have a driver's license. You have it to drive a car, but you also use it whenever you have to write a check or check in at the airport, so they can determine whether you're who you say you are.

The same is true in the world of networking. When someone logs on to a computer, they have to enter a username and password. This is done to verify who the user is—in other words, to identify the user.

We already do this with routers when we ask a user to enter a password. As already discussed, just asking for a password isn't the most secure method of identification. So, instead we use authentication, authorization, and accounting (AAA) to determine a user's identity.

The *authentication* portion of AAA is used to determine a user's identity—in other words, who you are. The *authorization* portion of AAA determines what you have authorization for—what you can do. Accounting is used for auditing—what you did and how long you did it.

Cisco's answer to AAA is their AAA server known as Cisco Secure Access Control Server (ACS).

Cisco Secure Access Control Server (ACS)

ACS is utilized to authenticate the identity of users. It can be used to authenticate remote and dial-up users as well as internal users. ACS supports both the TACACS+ and RADIUS protocols for AAA functions.

Using an intuitive GUI-based interface, the ACS allows for simplification in configuration tasks. Figure 28.4 provides an example of the ACS GUI. ACS is supported on both the Windows and Unix platforms. The ACS interface provides an online help feature to help you when you get stuck or just want more information about its features.

ACS supports the use of LDAP, NDS, and ODBC for database services. When you're using more than one ACS for redundancy purposes, it can be configured to support data replication between all the ACSs.

FIGURE 28.4 ACS GUI

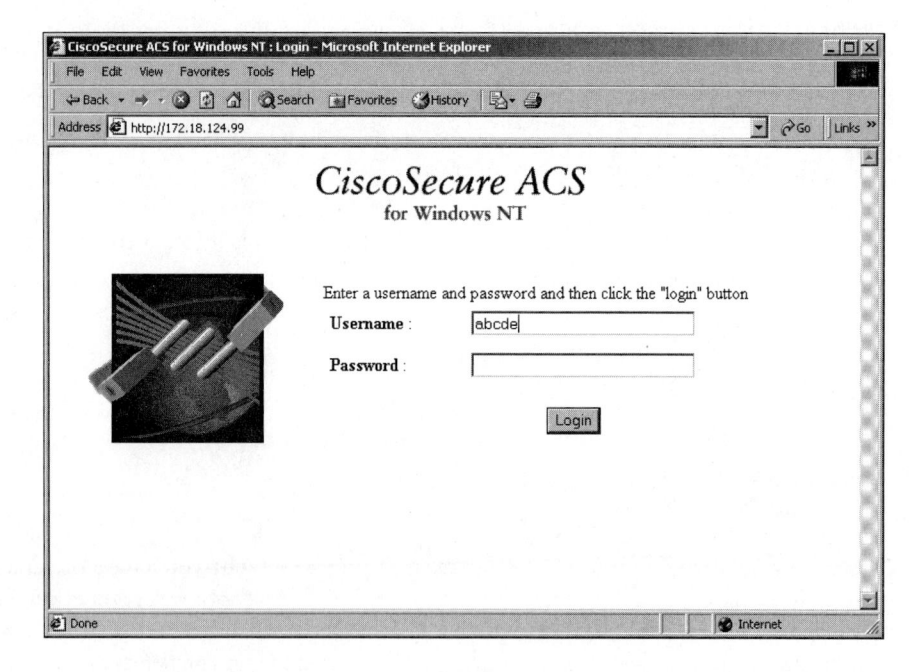

You can use the ACS to provide authentication based upon one-time passwords, static passwords, RADIUS, and TACACS+. ACS can be utilized to manage any of the following:

- Cisco routers
- Cisco switches
- VPNs
- Firewalls
- Cisco wireless solutions

- Voice over IP
- Cable access solutions
- DSL access solutions
- Network devices enabled by TACACS+ or RADIUS

AAA is one of the best solutions for identification. Identification is needed throughout your network. A centralized AAA solution, such as ACS, provides both security and ease of use.

Now that you have an idea of the products that can be utilized to provide a secure network, don't forget about a way to manage your security policies. The next section will be dedicated to secure management.

Understanding Security Management

Security management is used to enforce security policies to control access to network resources. This is done to limit the possibility of a network being hacked. These security management systems monitor users logging on to a network, which helps minimize the number of unauthorized attempts that occur.

Security management systems divide network resources into authorized areas and unauthorized areas. These areas are then used to determine who should and shouldn't have access to network resources.

Security management systems can accomplish all this by monitoring access entry points so unauthorized access is limited. They also identify network resources so they can be divided into the appropriate areas.

Cisco has two applications that can be utilized for security management. The first application, Cisco Secure Policy Manager (CSPM), is concerned with policy management. CSPM provides end-to-end policy enforcement through the support of a central policy management. CSPM also supports basic auditing tools for alerting administrators of network events.

The second application, CiscoWorks VPN/Security Management Solution (VMS), is concerned with VPN and security management. VMS can be used to configure, monitor, and troubleshoot VPNs, firewalls, NIDS, and HIDS. This is accomplished through the use of web-based applications.

When implementing security in a network, you can't forget about security management. Cisco provides the applications that can be utilized to manage a large-scale security deployment. The last section of this chapter will give you a brief introduction to Cisco's Architecture for Voice, Video and Integrated Data (AVVID).

Cisco AVVID

This section will give you only a brief introduction to AVVID. Today, more and more companies are looking to integrate their separate voice, video, and data networks into one converged network. Why would you want to do this? Because it costs too much money to have separate networks.

Knowing about this movement, Cisco created AVVID: a framework for the convergence of voice, video, and data networks.

The AVVID framework is a layered approach consisting of the following layers:

Clients   Clients are devices, such as phones and PCs, that are used to access the Internet business solutions through your network.

Network platforms   Network platforms are the equipment, such as routers and switches, used to connect users to network resources, such as an e-mail server.

Intelligent network services   Intelligent network services, such as QoS and security, are used to provide a network with the intelligence required to meet the needs of a company's business.

Internet middleware   Internet middleware joins the Internet technology layers with the Internet business solutions. This layer allows for a network to be customized to meet the needs of the applications running on it.

Internet business integrators   Through the creation of an ecosystem, a heterogeneous environment where everything works in harmony, the Cisco AVVID framework has provided a consistent set of services that allows business integrators (companies that integrate business needs within a network) to work together.

Internet business solutions   Internet business solutions let a company move its current business solutions to an e-commerce format, thus increasing its productivity and value.

AVVID brings the following benefits:

Integration   Integration allows for tools to be added to a network in order to increase productivity.

Intelligence   Through the use of QoS, a network can provide intelligence all the way up to the Application layer.

Innovation   Innovation allows companies to adapt quickly to the ever-changing world of technology.

Interoperability   Cisco developed standards-based APIs to allow integration with third-party vendors. This provides customers with choice and flexibility.

AVVID

If you would like to learn more about AVVID, you can visit the following sites:

- www.cisco.com/go/avvid
- www.cisco.com/go/avvidpartners
- www.cisco.com/go/safe
- www.cisco.com/warp/public/779/largeent/partner/esap/secvpn.html

Summary

In this chapter, you learned that secure connectivity is important in order to keep private communications private. You can use remote access VPNs to provide secure connectivity for those road warriors and telecommuters. Site-to-site VPNs can be used to reduce WAN costs and provide secure connectivity to remote offices. Finally, a firewall can be used to provide VPN connectivity.

You need to secure the perimeter of your network in order to reduce the number of external attacks. Perimeter security can be accomplished through the use of a Cisco PIX firewall or a router running the IOS Firewall Feature Set. Both the PIX and the IOS-based firewall solutions have their pros and cons.

The Cisco Secure ACS can be used to provide central authentication of internal and external users. This helps to provide identity control. By utilizing the ACS, you'll be able to reduce the number of unauthorized access attacks.

The Cisco Secure Policy Manager and the Cisco Secure VPN/Security Management solutions allow you to provide a security management solution for your secure environment. These applications provide you with security policy enforcement as well as monitoring capabilities.

It's important to remember that a secure environment can't occur without secure connectivity, perimeter security, identity, and secure management. Although you should always strive to provide a 100 percent secure environment, you'll never be able to accomplish it.

Exam Essentials

Explain the security solutions.   SAFE defines the need for secure connectivity, perimeter security, intrusion protection, identity, and security management.

List the products that provide secure connectivity.   Secure connectivity allows for secure communication over a public network, such as the Internet. You can accomplish this through the use of Cisco routers, PIX firewalls, VPN concentrators, and VPN clients.

List the different VPN solutions.   Remote access VPN solutions are used to provide secure connectivity between remote users and the corporate headquarters. Site-to-site VPN solutions are used to reduce WAN costs and to provide secure connectivity between a remote office and the corporate headquarters. A firewall-based VPN solution allows a PIX firewall or IOS-based firewall to provide a secure site-to-site connection.

List the products that provide perimeter security.   It's important to secure the perimeter of your network. This helps in limiting the number of external attacks. To accomplish perimeter security, you can use a PIX firewall or IOS-based firewall.

List the products that provide intrusion protection.   Intrusion protection is used to detect when a possible network attack is occurring. Cisco created the IDS for this very reason. The IDS can come in the form of a Cisco router, PIX firewall, or IDS 4200 series sensors.

List the products that provide identity. The Cisco Secure ACS is used to provide identity. This is accomplished through the use of AAA for authentication, authorization, and accounting of users.

List the products that provide security management. Security management can use CiscoWorks 2000 VPN/Security Management Solution (VMS), Cisco Secure Policy Manager (CSPM), and web device managers.

Chapter 29

SAFE Small and Medium Network Designs

CISCO SAFE IMPLEMENTATION EXAM TOPICS COVERED IN THIS CHAPTER:

- ✓ Understanding the SAFE Small Network Design Overview
- ✓ Understanding the small network corporate Internet module
- ✓ Understanding the small network campus module
- ✓ Understanding the medium network corporate Internet module
- ✓ Understanding the medium network corporate Internet module design guidelines
- ✓ Understanding the medium network campus module
- ✓ Understanding the medium network campus module design guidelines
- ✓ Understanding the medium network WAN module
- ✓ Implementing an ISP router
- ✓ Implementing an edge router
- ✓ Implementing an IOS Firewall
- ✓ Implementing a PIX firewall
- ✓ Implementing an NIDS
- ✓ Implementing an HIDS
- ✓ Implementing a VPN concentrator
- ✓ Implementing a layer 3 switch

Remember that in Chapter 27, "Security Fundamentals," we talked about SAFE being a design guideline. You learned that SAFE SMR is concerned with the following designs:

- Small Network Design
- Medium Network Design
- Remote Access Network Design

This chapter will focus on the SAFE SMR Small Network Design and Medium Network Design. In this chapter, you'll learn about the different modules that make up the SAFE SMR small network and medium network. Each of these modules requires certain devices and each module has its own associated risks. You'll also learn what devices to use and how to mitigate the associated risks.

Small Network Design Overview

Every design has a design layout. The SAFE SMR Small Network Design is no different. The Small Network Design is a modular-based design that consists of two modules:

- Corporate Internet module
- Campus module

Each of these modules has its key devices, associated attacks, and mitigation techniques. The reason for this modular design is the concept that a breach in one module doesn't affect the other modules. Figure 29.1 illustrates the Small Network Design modules.

Let's take a more in-depth look at each of the modules so you really understand what is going on. We'll start with the corporate Internet module.

Corporate Internet Module

The corporate Internet module provides the following services:

- Internet access
- Internet user access to the public servers
- VPN access

FIGURE 29.1 SAFE SMR Small Network Design modules

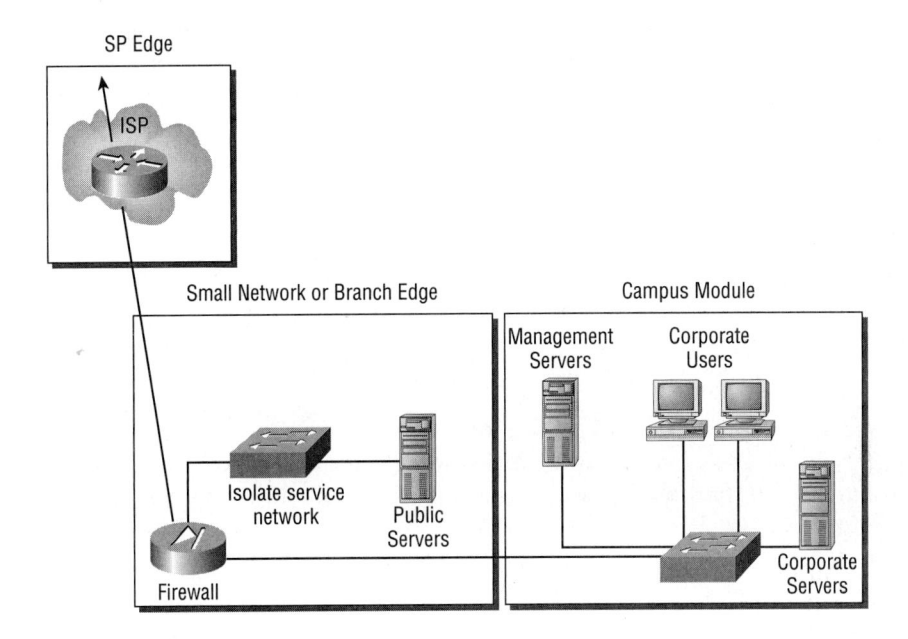

The module provides Internet access for the internal users of the network. It also terminates VPN tunnels for remote users and telecommuters. However, these employees need access to the internal network. Without the corporate Internet module, remote users wouldn't be able to securely connect into the corporate infrastructure. The module also provides access for Internet users to the company's public servers, such as the web server. Figure 29.2 illustrates the corporate Internet module.

FIGURE 29.2 Corporate Internet module

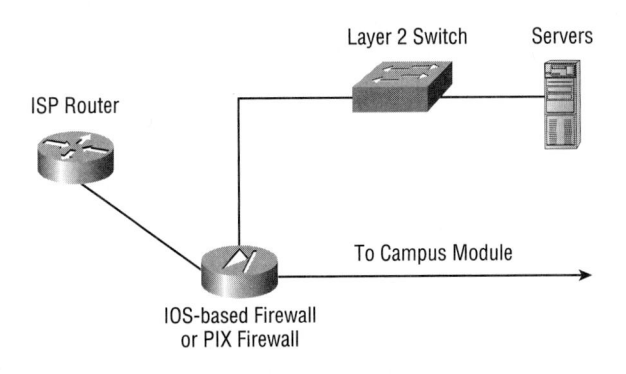

> **WARNING** The corporate Internet module of the SAFE SMR Small Network Design isn't intended for the support of e-commerce applications.

Each module of the SAFE SMR Small Network Design contains key devices. The key devices contained in the corporate Internet module are as follows:

SMTP server When an SMTP server is placed in the corporate Internet module, it acts as a relay between the internal mail servers and the Internet.

DNS server The DNS server is utilized to relay internal requests to the Internet. It's used for name resolution.

FTP or HTTP server These servers can be used to allow users on the Internet to gather information about the organization that you want to make available to the public.

Firewall or IOS-based firewall Since a VPN concentrator isn't recommended in the SAFE SMR Small Network Design, the firewall provides secure connectivity for remote users to the corporate intranet. The firewall also provides stateful filtering of traffic for protection of the corporate network.

Layer 2 switch The layer 2 switch you choose must support private VLAN. This device provides layer 2 connectivity.

Host-intrusion detection system (HIDS) HIDS provides intrusion detection services to hosts. It's used to detect an attack on the network.

Each of the devices discussed provides a form of mitigation for network threats. The ISP router provides spoof mitigation and rate-limiting. The firewall provides stateful packet filtering, basic layer 7 filtering, host DoS mitigation, and spoof mitigation. The layer 2 switch provides private VLANs. Finally, HIDS provides local attack mitigation for the devices it's utilized on, such as the public servers.

As you can see, these devices really have their work cut out for them. Not only do they have to provide their regular network services, but they also must provide threat mitigation. We've already talked about each device's mitigation role, but we haven't looked at the threats that are expected in the corporate Internet module. Following are the expected threats and what can be done to mitigate them:

> **NOTE** Each of these threats was discussed in depth in Chapter 27.

DoS To mitigate this type of attack, it's recommended that you implement committed access rate (CAR) at the ISP edge and use TCP setup controls at the firewall.

Viruses and Trojan horses To mitigate these types of attacks, use virus scanning on the hosts. Also, make sure you keep the virus-scanning software updated.

Password attacks To mitigate password attacks, use IDSs and the operating system to detect the attack. Also, use strong passwords.

Unauthorized access attacks To mitigate these types of attacks, use filtering at the firewall.

Application layer attacks HIDS implemented on public servers can mitigate this type of attack.

Packet sniffers Implementing a switched network with HIDS can be used to mitigate packet sniffer intrusions.

IP spoofing To mitigate IP spoofing attacks, RFC 2827 and 1918 filtering should be implemented at the ISP edge and the firewall.

Trust exploitation Utilizing a restrictive trust model and private VLANs can mitigate this type of attack.

Port redirection To mitigate this type of attack, use restrictive filtering and HIDS.

Network reconnaissance HIDS can be used to detect network reconnaissance and filtering can be used on protocols to limit their effectiveness.

You've now seen the recommended design for the corporate Internet module of a small network. However, not all networks exactly match this design. Knowing that, Cisco created a couple of alternatives for the design of the corporate Internet module of a small network. For instance, when WAN connectivity is required, you should use an IOS-based firewall instead of a PIX firewall. However, when WAN connectivity is performed by an xDSL or cable modem, you should use a PIX firewall. These are just a couple of alternatives to keep in mind. Any deviation you make to the SAFE SMR Small Network Design must be geared toward increasing network capacity.

Campus Module

The campus module of the SAFE SMR Small Network Design is used to provide the corporate intranet. This is the module where all the corporate servers and workstations are located. Any attack that occurs in the corporate Internet module should not affect the campus module. Figure 29.3 illustrates the campus module.

FIGURE 29.3 Campus module

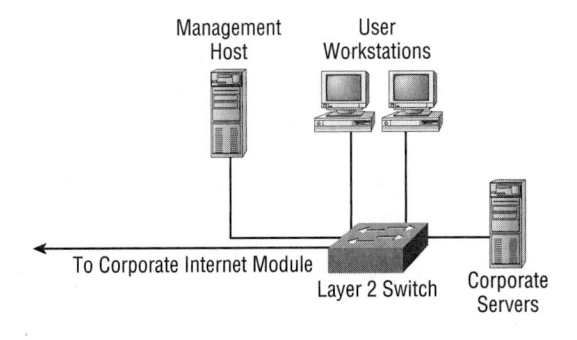

The campus module is made up of the following key devices:

SMTP or POP3 server   The SMTP or POP3 server is used to provide e-mail services to the internal users.

File and print servers   File and print servers are used to provide file and print services to the internal users.

User workstations   User workstations provide data services to internal users.

Management host   The management host (also referred to as a *management server*) provides such services as HIDS, Syslog, TACACS+ or RADIUS, and configuration management to internal users.

Layer 2 switch   The layer 2 switch you choose must support private VLANs. This device provides layer 2 connectivity to user workstations.

Each of these devices provides a form of mitigation for network threats. The user workstations provide host virus scanning. The corporate servers and the management server both provide HIDS local attack mitigation. Last but not least, the layer 2 switch provides private VLANs.

Like the key devices in the corporate Internet module, the key devices in the campus module must provide both their normal services and attack mitigation. Following are the expected threats in the campus module and what can be done to mitigate them:

Viruses and Trojan horses   To mitigate viruses and Trojan horses, use virus scanning on the hosts. Also, make sure you keep the virus scanning software updated.

Unauthorized access attacks   To mitigate unauthorized access attacks, use HIDS and application access control.

Application layer attacks   To mitigate application layer attacks, you need to keep up-to-date security fixes on operating systems, devices, and applications. You can also utilize HIDS to aid in mitigating these types of attacks.

Packet sniffers   Implementing a switched network can aid in the mitigation of packet sniffer attacks.

Trust exploitation   Utilizing a restrictive trust model and private VLANs is the best mitigation technique to reduce trust exploitation.

Port redirection   Like the mitigation technique for port redirection in the corporate Internet module, HIDS is the best mitigation technique to use in the campus module as well.

There is one alternative to the design of the campus module that you should look at. Security can be increased in the module by placing a small filtering router or firewall between the management servers and the rest of the network. By doing this, management traffic is only allowed to enter areas that the administrator feels is appropriate.

Medium Network Design Overview

The SAFE SMR Medium Network Design supports the following modules:

- Corporate Internet module
- Campus module
- WAN module

Notice something different? The SAFE SMR Medium Network Design introduces a new module: the WAN module. We still have the corporate Internet module and the campus module, with a few more devices added. Figure 29.4 illustrates the modules of the SAFE SMR Medium Network Design.

FIGURE 29.4 SAFE SMR Medium Network Design modules

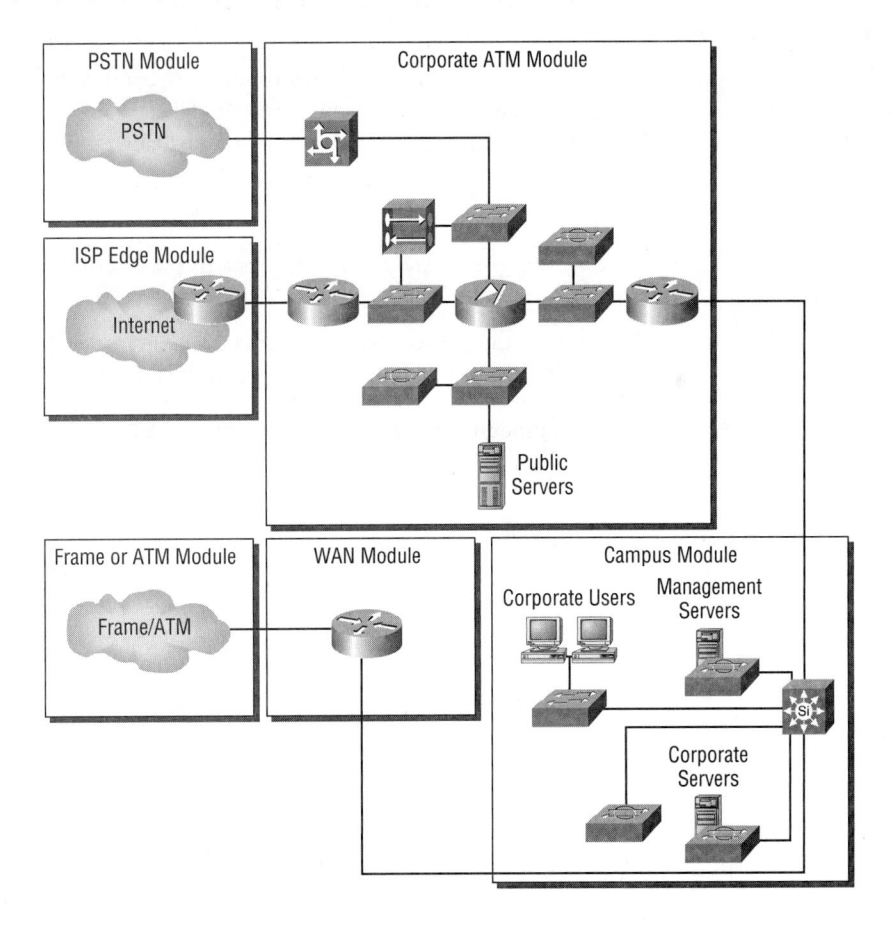

A more in-depth look at each of the modules is needed to understand the Medium Network Design. Let's start with the corporate Internet module.

Corporate Internet Module

As stated earlier, the corporate Internet module—for both the SAFE SMR Small Network Design and the SAFE SMR Medium Network Design—is responsible for the following:

- Internet access
- Internet user access to the public servers
- VPN access

Figure 29.5 illustrates the corporate Internet module for the Medium Network Design.

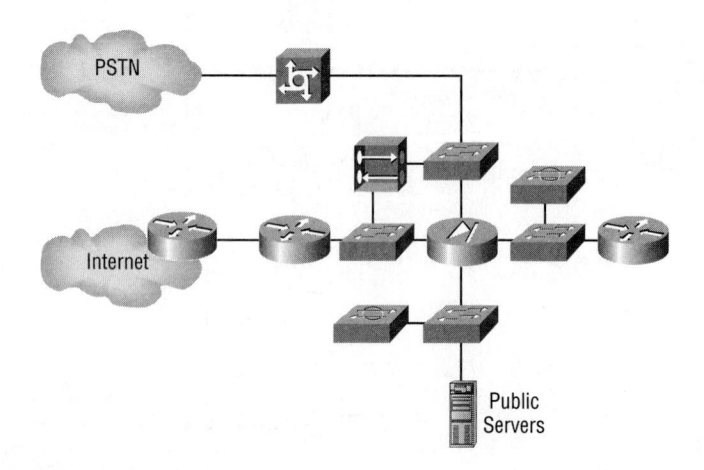

You may wonder how the corporate Internet module of the Medium Network Design differs from the one of the Small Network Design. The difference lies in the devices contained in the module. The key devices include the following:

Dial-in server Not every remote user has a DSL or cable Internet connection. Some still use an analog dial-in connection to gain access to the corporate network. To support these analog users, a dial-in server is placed in the corporate Internet module to provide authentication.

SMTP server When an SMTP server is placed in the corporate Internet module, it acts as a relay between the internal mail servers and the Internet.

DNS server The DNS server is utilized to relay internal requests to the Internet. It's used for name resolution.

FTP or HTTP server These servers can be used to allow users on the Internet to gather information about the organization that you want to make available to the public.

FIGURE 29.5 Corporate Internet module for the Medium Network Design

Firewall The firewall is the central device in the corporate Internet module. It provides by far the most security features to the module. The firewall provides stateful packet filtering, basic layer 7 filtering, and host DoS mitigation; authenticates remote sites; and terminates site-to-site IPSec tunnels.

Layer 2 switch The layer 2 switches provide layer 2 connectivity for the corporate Internet module. Through the use of private VLANs, layer 2 switches can help in the mitigation of trust exploitation attacks.

Host Intrusion Detection System (HIDS) HIDS is implemented on the public servers. It's used to provide local attack mitigation for the servers.

Network Intrusion Detection System (NIDS) NIDS is used to monitor network activity. It's used to provide layer 4 to layer 7 analysis of network traffic. This means that NIDS can detect attacks on the ports that the firewall permits through, and it provides analysis of attacks on the network.

VPN concentrator The VPN concentrator is implemented between the edge router and the firewall. It's used to provide IPSec tunnel termination and authentication for remote users.

Edge router The edge router sits on the edge of the corporate Internet module between the corporate network and the Internet, providing a demarcation point. It's responsible for spoof mitigation and basic filtering, such as RFC 1918 and 2827 filtering. When filtering, this router should be configured so it only allows expected traffic through. It also should not allow fragmented packets.

Inside router The inside router provides demarcation between the corporate Internet module and the campus module. The inside router doesn't provide any type of filtering between these two modules. However, it does provide layer 3 separation between the two modules.

Without both of these devices, the corporate Internet module wouldn't be secure. Keep in mind that these devices aren't only responsible for attack mitigation; they're also responsible for their primary jobs in the network. It's cool to learn how these different devices provide attack mitigation, but it's of no use if you don't know what they're protecting against.

The corporate Internet module has certain attacks that are prevalent. Each of these attacks can be mitigated but not eliminated. The following are the expected attacks in the corporate Internet module of the SAFE SMR Medium Network Design and how you can mitigate them (notice that this list is a bit different than the list for the Small Network Design's corporate Internet module):

Denial of service (DoS) attack To mitigate this type of attack, it's recommended that you implement committed access rate (CAR) at the ISP edge and use TCP setup controls at the firewall.

Viruses and Trojan horses To mitigate viruses and Trojan horse applications, use virus scanning on the hosts. Also, make sure you keep the virus scanning software updated.

Password attacks To mitigate password attacks, use IDSs and the operating system to detect the attack. Also, use strong passwords.

Unauthorized access attacks To mitigate these types of attacks, use filtering at the firewall.

Application layer attacks HIDS implemented on public servers can mitigate this type of attack.

Packet sniffers Implementing a switched network with HIDS can be used to mitigate packet sniffers.

IP spoofing RFC 2827 and 1918 filtering should be implemented at the ISP edge and the firewall to mitigate IP spoofing attacks.

Trust exploitation Utilizing a restrictive trust model and private VLANs can mitigate this type of attack.

Port redirection To mitigate this type of attack, use restrictive filtering and HIDS.

Network reconnaissance HIDS can be used to detect network reconnaissance and filtering can be used on protocols to limit their effectiveness.

Man-in-the-middle attack Man-in-the-middle attacks occur when a hacker is intercepting traffic and examining it as the traffic is being passed from one point to another. This form of attack is best mitigated through the use of IPSec encryption.

As you saw with the corporate Internet module of the SAFE SMR Small Network Design, there are also design alternatives for the Medium Network Design. One of these design alternatives is the removal of the inside router. If you do this, the corporate Internet module must rely on the layer 3 switch of the campus module for layer 3 services.

Another design alternative is implementation of a URL-filtering device. This device could be used to provide content filtering in addition to the content filtering of SMTP traffic. By utilizing a URL-filtering device, you can have greater control on what outside resources your employees could access.

You can also implement CBAC on your edge router to provide another layer of stateful inspection. The last design alternative introduces a NIDS onto the segment outside the firewall; this lets you receive alarms about attacks that might otherwise be dropped by the firewall.

As you've probably figured out, there isn't a huge difference between the concepts of the corporate Internet module for the SAFE SMR Small Network Design and the corporate Internet module for the SAFE SMR Medium Network Design. The difference lies in the number of devices in the modules and the responsibilities of each device. Let's move on to the campus module.

Campus Module

The campus module of the SAFE SMR Medium Network Design is used to provide the corporate intranet. This is the module where all of the corporate servers and workstations are located. Any attack that occurs in the corporate Internet module should not affect the campus module. Figure 29.6 illustrates the campus module.

The difference between the campus module of the Small Network Design and the campus module of the Medium Network Design lies in the devices involved. Following is a list of the key devices in the campus module of the Medium Network Design:

SMTP or POP3 server The SMTP or POP3 server is used to provide e-mail services to the internal users.

FIGURE 29.6 Campus module

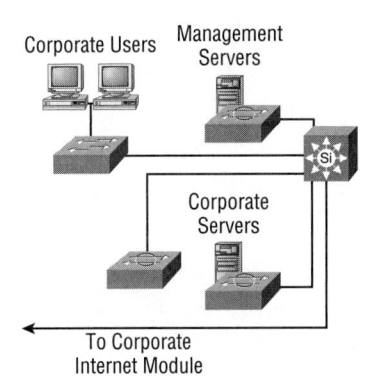

File and print servers   File and print servers are used to provide file and print services to the internal users.

User workstations   User workstations provide data services to internal users.

Management host   Management hosts provide such services as NIDS hosts for alarm aggregation; Syslog for log information aggregation of firewalls and NIDS hosts, TACACS+, or RADIUS; and configuration management for internal users.

Layer 2 switch   The layer 2 switch you choose must support private VLANs. This device provides layer 2 connectivity to user workstations.

Layer 3 switch   The layer 2 switch provides routing and switching functions to the campus module.

NIDS appliance   NIDS provides layer 4 to layer 7 monitoring of network devices. This device reports when a possible network attack is occurring.

Like the key devices in the corporate Internet module of the Medium Network Design, the key devices in the campus module must provide both their normal services and attack mitigation. Following are the expected threats in the campus module and what can be done to mitigate them (again, notice that this list of threats differs slightly from the list for the campus module for the Small Network Design):

Viruses and Trojan horses   To mitigate viruses and Trojan horses, use virus scanning on the hosts. Also, make sure you keep the virus-scanning software updated.

Unauthorized access attacks   To mitigate unauthorized access attacks, use HIDS and application access control.

Password attacks   An ACS can be used to provide strong two-factor authentication. This authentication will help in the mitigation of password attacks.

IP spoofing   IP spoofing attacks in the campus module are mitigated the same way they've been mitigated up to this point: through RFC 2827 filtering.

Application layer attacks In order to mitigate application layer attacks, you need to keep up-to-date security fixes on operating systems, devices, and applications. You can also utilize HIDS to aid in mitigating these types of attacks.

Packet sniffers Implementing a switched network can aid in the mitigation of packet sniffers.

Trust exploitation Utilizing a restrictive trust model and private VLANs is the best mitigation technique to reduce trust exploitation.

Port redirection Like the mitigation technique for port redirection in the corporate Internet module, HIDS is the best mitigation technique to use in the campus module as well.

There are a few design alternatives for the campus module of the SAFE SMR Medium Network Design. The first alternative deals with integrating the layer 2 and 3 switch functionality into the layer 3 switch. If your network is small enough, you integrate these two functions into one switch, saving the company some money.

Another design alternative requires a smaller network also. This alternative requires the replacement of the more expensive layer 3 switch with a less expensive router. However, you still need to keep a layer 2 switch for layer 2 connectivity.

The last design alternative is to replace the NIDS appliance with an integrated IDS appliance. This requires that IDS be enabled on the layer 3 switch. By integrating the IDS and layer 3 switch, the IDS will achieve higher throughput.

The next section will look at the WAN module, which is a new module introduced in the SAFE SMR Medium Network Design.

WAN Module

The WAN module of the SAFE SMR Medium Network Design is an interesting module, in that it may or may not be present in the design. The WAN module is only required when additional WAN connectivity is needed, and it can't be provided by remote VPN services. Figure 29.7 illustrates the WAN module of the SAFE SMR Medium Network Design.

The WAN module only has one key device: the IOS router. The IOS router is used to provide WAN connectivity, quality of service (QoS), access control lists (ACLs), and routing. There are two attacks you need to worry about with in this module: IP spoofing and unauthorized access. In order to mitigate IP spoofing, you need to implement RFC 2827 and layer 3 filtering on the IOS router. To mitigate unauthorized access attacks, you need to implement layer 3 filtering on the IOS router to limit the types of traffic you allow.

FIGURE 29.7 WAN module

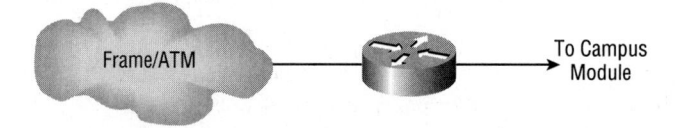

You can use a couple of design alternatives for the WAN module. The first requires the implementation of IPSec VPNs. This allows for additional privacy for your WAN connections. You can also implement an IOS firewall on the IOS router, which provides you with additional security and protection.

Implementation of Key Devices

Understanding what devices are used in a design is very useful, but without the knowledge of how to implement these devices, not much is brought to the table. This section will deal with the implementation of mitigation techniques on the following devices:

- NIDS and HIDS
- ISP router
- IOS-based firewall
- PIX firewall

NIDS and HIDS

NIDS and HIDS have already been covered in depth in this book. Therefore, we'll only discuss the initial setup steps of the NIDS sensor. If you need more in-depth knowledge of IDS, please refer to Part IV of this book, "Cisco Secure Intrusion Detection System."

Initially installing the NIDS sensor consists of the following six steps:

1. Configure the sensor's network settings.
2. Define a list of hosts that are allowed to manage the sensor.
3. Configure remote management settings.
4. Configure SSH settings.
5. Configure the sensor's date and time.
6. Change the sensor's password.

That's all there is to the initial setup of the NIDS sensor. As I said, for a more in-depth review of NIDS and HIDS, refer to Part IV of this book.

Implementing the ISP Router

The ISP is used to mitigate IP spoofing and DoS attacks. IP spoofing is mitigated through the use of RFC 2827 and RFC 1918 filtering. DoS attacks are mitigated through the use of rate limiting.

RFC 2827 filtering is used to allow only packets that originated in your network to leave your network. It's also used to allow only packets that don't have a source address from within your network to enter your network.

RFC 1918 filtering is used to prevent packets with a source address from a private range from entering your network. The private address ranges are as follows:

- 10.0.0.0–10.255.255.255
- 172.16.0.0–172.31.255.255
- 192.168.0.0–192.168.255.255

To create an access list, enter the following command in global configuration mode:

```
access-list access-list-number [dynamic dynamic-name
   [timeout minutes]] {deny | permit} protocol source-
   address source-wildcard destination-address destination-
   wildcard [precedence precedence] [tos tos] [log | log-
   input] [time-range time-range-name]
```

Once the access list has been created, you need to apply it to an interface. To apply an access list to an interface, issue the following command in interface configuration mode for the respective interface:

```
ip access-group {access-list-number | access-list-name} {in | out}
```

Following is an example of a RFC 1918 configuration:

```
!
access-list 1 deny 10.0.0.0 0.255.255.255
access-list 1 deny 172.16.0.0 0.15.255.255
access-list 1 deny 192.168.0.0 0.0.255.255
access-list 1 permit any
!
interface serial 0
  ip access-list 1 in
!
```

Committed access rate (CAR) can be used to prevent DoS attacks. This is accomplished by rate-limiting the amount of ICMP traffic on your network. The following steps must be completed in order to mitigate DoS attacks utilizing CAR:

1. Configure an extended IP access list to permit all ICMP traffic.
2. Configure CAR on the input interface, and reference the access list.
3. Configure the traffic parameters so that a normal amount of ICMP traffic is permitted but an excessive amount is denied.

The only item that should be new to you in these steps is configuring CAR. Configuring CAR is a simple task. To do it, you need to be in interface configuration mode for the respective interface and then enter the following command:

```
rate-limit {input | output} [dscp dscp-value | qos-group
 group-id | access-group acl-number | access-group rate-
 limit rate-limit-access-list-number] bps burst-normal
 burst-max conform-action action exceed-action action
```

To fully understand this command, let's walk through it step-by-step. The first step requires you to select whether CAR will be enabled for inbound or outbound traffic on an interface:

```
R1(config-if)#rate-limit ?
  input   Rate limit on input
  output  Rate limit on output
```

Next, you need to select the method for CAR to utilize for matching traffic:

```
R1(config-if)#rate-limit input ?
  <8000-2000000000>  Bits per second
  access-group       Match access list
  dscp               Match dscp value
  qos-group          Match qos-group ID
```

Not selecting a method of matching will match all IP traffic. The DifServ Code Point (DSCP) match criteria allows CAR to match traffic based on the value of its DSCP field. The QoS group match criteria allow for traffic to be matched based on the value in its QoS group field. The access group match criteria let you match traffic based upon a standard or extended IP access list.

If you specify the `access-group` keyword after the `rate-limit` keyword, CAR will allow for traffic to be matched based upon an IP precedence value, MAC address, or MPLS experimental bit, as seen here:

```
R1(config-if)#rate-limit input access-group rate-limit ?
  <0-99>     Rate-limit prec access list index
  <100-199>  Rate-limit mac access list index
  <200-299>  Rate-limit exp access list index
```

NOTE Matching on a MAC address can only occur on LAN interfaces.

Once the match criteria has been decided upon, the average rate needs to be entered:

```
R1(config-if)#rate-limit input access-group 100 ?
  <8000-2000000000>  Bits per second
```

Next, you need to enter the normal burst size in bytes:

```
R1(config-if)#rate-limit input access-group 100 16000 ?
  <1000-512000000>  Normal burst bytes
```

Now the maximum burst size must be entered in bytes:

```
R1(config-if)#rate-limit input access-group 100 16000 8000 ?
  <2000-1024000000>  Maximum burst bytes
```

The next step requires you to specify the action to perform on the traffic that conforms to the rate limit. The following actions are available:

```
R1(config-if)#$input access-group 100 16000 8000 10000 conform-action ?
  continue              scan other rate limits
  drop                  drop packet
  set-dscp-continue     set dscp, scan other rate limits
  set-dscp-transmit     set dscp and send it
  set-mpls-exp-continue set exp during imposition, scan other rate limits
  set-mpls-exp-transmit set exp during imposition and send it
  set-prec-continue     rewrite packet precedence, scan other rate limits
  set-prec-transmit     rewrite packet precedence and send it
  set-qos-continue      set qos-group, scan other rate limits
  set-qos-transmit      set qos-group and send it
  transmit              transmit packet
```

Finally, you need to specify the action to perform on traffic that exceeds the rate limit. The following actions are available:

```
R1(config-if)#$00 16000 8000 10000 conform-action transmit exceed-action ?
  continue              scan other rate limits
  drop                  drop packet
  set-dscp-continue     set dscp, scan other rate limits
  set-dscp-transmit     set dscp and send it
  set-mpls-exp-continue set exp during imposition, scan other rate limits
  set-mpls-exp-transmit set exp during imposition and send it
  set-prec-continue     rewrite packet precedence, scan other rate limits
  set-prec-transmit     rewrite packet precedence and send it
  set-qos-continue      set qos-group, scan other rate limits
  set-qos-transmit      set qos-group and send it
  transmit              transmit packet
```

> **NOTE**
>
> The only exceed options you're concerned with for rate-limiting are drop and continue. The others are primarily used for QoS.

> **NOTE**
>
> CAR is supported on inbound and outbound interfaces where up to 100 rate-limit statements can be configured per interface. When multiple rate-limit statements are configured, they're checked starting at the top and working to the bottom. If a packet doesn't match any of the rate-limit statements, the packet will be forwarded by default.

Implementing the IOS-based Firewall

When you're configuring an IOS-based firewall, you must make certain that you have the IOS Firewall Feature Set installed. Once you have it installed, you can begin configuring the IOS-based firewall.

Real World Scenario

Preventing Denial-of-Service (DoS) Attacks

John is the security administrator for company XYZ. His company's e-mail servers were recently the victims of a DoS attack. During John's investigation, he learned that the e-mail servers were flooded with ICMP packets. In replying to all the ICMP requests, the e-mail servers encountered a processor overload. John has now been tasked with ensuring that this attack won't happen again.

John recalled that CAR could be used to limit the amount of ICMP traffic allowed into a network. He decided that using CAR was worth pursuing. Through analysis, he determined that ICMP traffic should be limited to an average rate of 16,000, a normal burst of 8000, and an exceed burst of 8000. Following is the configuration that John created:

```
!
!
interface Serial 0/0
  rate-limit input access-group 110 16000 8000 8000 conform-action
    transmit exceed-action drop
!
access-list 110 permit icmp any any
!
```

The IOS-based firewall lets you provide the following mitigation techniques:

- Stateful packet filtering and basic layer 7 filtering
- IP spoof mitigation
- Host DoS mitigation
- Intrusion detection
- Authentication
- IPSec

We'll look at each of these mitigation techniques in detail, beginning with stateful packet filtering.

Stateful Packet Filtering and Basic Layer 7 Filtering

Stateful packet filtering allows for the device to temporarily open ports in an access list. You want to do this so only sessions initiated from within the internal network can be established and so sessions initiated from outside the network can't access the internal network. By providing stateful packet filtering, the firewall can protect against unauthorized access and DoS attacks.

Stateful packet filtering is accomplished through the use of context-based access control (CBAC). CBAC accomplishes stateful packet filtering through the following steps:

1. Packets entering the firewall are compared to an ACL to see if they're permitted or denied.
2. CBAC inspects the traffic that is permitted into the firewall.
3. CBAC either permits or denies TCP and UDP traffic.
4. Temporary openings are placed in the ACL.
5. A state table is maintained in order to permit the traffic that belongs to the session that was originated from within the network.

In order to configure CBAC, you need to define your inspection rules and then apply them to an interface. To create an inspection rule, enter the following command in global configuration mode:

```
ip inspect name inspection-name protocol [alert {on | off}]
    [audit-trail {on | off}] [timeout seconds]
```

CBAC supports inspection of the following protocols:

- TCP
- UDP
- CUseeMe
- FTP
- HTTP
- H323
- NetShow

- RCMD
- RealAudio
- RPC
- SMTP
- SQL*Net
- StreamWorks
- TFTP
- VDOLive

Three protocols require a bit more investigation: HTTP, SMTP, and fragments. It's recommended that when you're using CBAC, you create a rule for SMTP that permits only the following legal SMTP commands:

- DATA
- EXPN
- HELO
- HELP
- MAIL
- NOOP
- QUIT
- RCPT
- RSET
- SAML
- SEND
- SOML
- VRFY

By creating the SMTP rule, you can help prevent a hacker from using SMTP to issue illegal commands and you can also help hide mail server vulnerabilities. To create the SMTP rule, issue the following command in global configuration mode:

```
ip inspect name inspection-name smtp [alert {on | off}]
    [audit-trail {on | off}] [timeout seconds]
```

Hackers can use packet fragmentation to launch a DoS attack on your network. To prevent a fragment DoS attack, use the following CBAC rule:

```
ip inspect name inspection-name fragment max number timeout seconds
```

Java applets are very common on the Internet. However, hackers can use them to download malicious code to your PC. CBAC offers a method of specifying sites that can be trusted and sites that aren't trusted. Only Java applets from the trusted sites will be allowed to be downloaded. An important item to remember with Java blocking is that CBAC can't inspect Java applets that are wrapped or encapsulated, as is the case when the applet is contained in a ZIP file. To enable Java applet blocking, issue the following command in global configuration mode:

```
ip inspect name inspection-name http java-list acl-num
  [alert {on | off}] [audit-trail {on | off}] [timeout
   seconds]
```

Once you've created your inspection rules, you must apply the rules to an interface. Use the following command in interface configuration mode to apply the inspection rules:

```
ip inspect name inspection-name {in | out}
```

CBAC is pretty cool, and it's not that complicated to configure. It's a powerful tool that can greatly increase the security of your network.

IP Spoof Mitigation

IP spoof mitigation on the IOS-based firewall is accomplished through the use of RFC 2827 and 1918 filtering. The configuration of RFC 2827 and 1918 filtering is the same on the IOS-based router as it is on the ISP router, which we discussed in the section "Implementing the ISP Router."

Host DoS Mitigation

TCP SYN attacks are a common method of DoS attacks. In a TCP SYN attack, a hacker spoofs an IP address and then starts sending TCP SYN requests to a server on your network. The server responds to the SYN with a SYNACK and leaves the session in a half-open state. Since the hacker's machine never responds to the SYNACK, the session is left indefinitely in a half-open state.

You can use TCP intercept to mitigate TCP SYN attacks. To implement TCP intercept on the IOS-based firewall, issue the following command in global configuration mode:

```
ip tcp intercept drop-mode
```

Issuing this command protects internal TCP servers from TCP SYN attacks.

Intrusion Detection

Intrusion detection can be utilized on an IOS-based firewall to detect potential attacks. It's a good way to help mitigate unauthorized access attacks.

IDS uses signatures to detect when an attack may be occurring. When a packet matches one of these signatures, the IOS-based firewall can be configured to send an alarm to the IDS director, drop the packet, and/or reset the connection.

Authentication

Authentication, authorization, and accounting (AAA) allows for the control of remote user access to the network. Through the use of AAA, a user can be authenticated to determine who they are. Authorization is then performed on the user to determine what they can do. Accounting lets you record what the user did and how long they did it.

In order to implement AAA, you must first enable it on the router. To enable AAA, enter the following command in global configuration mode:

aaa new-model

After AAA has been enabled, you need to determine how the user will authenticate. If authentication will occur on a TACACS+ server, you must enter the following command in global configuration mode:

tacacs-server host *hostname* [port *port*] [timeout *timeout*]
  [key *string*]

Next, you need to configure authentication. To do so, enter the following command in global configuration mode:

aaa authentication login {default | *list-name*} *method1*
  [*method2*]

If authorization will be used, then you need to configure it. To do so, enter the following command in global configuration mode:

aaa authorization {network | exec | commands *level* |
  reverse-access | configuration} {default | *list-name*}
  method1 [*method2*]

The last step requires you to apply the authentication to a line or interface. To apply AAA to a line or interface, enter the following command in line or interface configuration mode:

login authentication {default | *list-name*}

IPSec

IPSec lets you create secure communications with remote devices. When you're creating an IPSec connection, you need to do the following:

1. Define interesting traffic.
2. Create a phase 1 Internet Key Exchange (IKE) policy.
3. Create a phase 2 IPSec policy.

In order to define traffic that needs to be protected, you must create an extended IP access list. It's important to remember that when you create this access list, it must be symmetric on each device. This means that the same traffic is defined as interesting. When traffic that enters the device is interesting, it's encrypted and sent across the wire. Uninteresting traffic is sent across the wire in clear text.

> ### Real World Scenario
>
> **Implementing AAA**
>
> John, who is a security administrator, has decided to implement AAA. The default group needs to attempt to authenticate to the TACACS+ server at address 10.10.10.1 with a secret key of cisco. If the TACACS+ server is unavailable, no login is required. He also wants to create a Telnet group that will authenticate against the TACACS+ server. If the server is unavailable, they should authenticate against the local database. The Telnet list should be applied to all the VTY lines. Following is a configuration that would accomplish this:
>
> ```
> !
> aaa new-model
> tacacs-server host 10.10.10.1 key cisco
> aaa authentication login default tacacs none
> aaa authentication login telnet tacacs local
> !
> line vty 0 4
>   login authentication telnet
> !
> ```
>
> If a default list is defined, it will be applied to all interfaces, by default, that don't have another authentication list applied to them.

After defining your interesting traffic, you need to create a phase 1 IKE policy. The IKE policy you create on each side must have the same encryption, hash, Diffie-Hellman group, and authentication method. To create the IKE policy, issue the following command in global configuration mode:

```
crypto isakmp policy priority
```

Once the above command has been issued, the router goes into IKE policy configuration mode. In this mode, you define the parameters of the IKE policy. The following commands are used to define the parameters:

```
authentication authentication
encryption encryption
hash hash
group dh-group
lifetime seconds
```

If the authentication used is pre-share keys, you must specify the key to share with the peer. To specify the key and peer, enter the following command in global configuration mode:

`crypto isakmp key key address peer-address`

Let's look at creating an IKE phase 1 policy. In this example, you'll need to create an IKE phase 1 policy that uses a pre-share key of cisco, a hash of MD5, and group 2. Any device that knows the pre-share key should be authenticated for phase 1. Following is a configuration that would accomplish this:

```
R1#config t
R1(config)#crypto isakmp policy 10
R1(config-isakmp)#authentication pre-share
R1(config-isakmp)#hash md5
R1(config-isakmp)#group 2
R1(config-isakmp)#exit
R1(config)#crypto isakmp key cisco address 0.0.0.0
R1(config)#
```

Now that you've defined the interesting traffic and created the phase 1 IKE policy, you need to configure the phase 2 IPSec policy. You need to create a transform set, create a crypto map, assign the parameters to the crypto map, and assign the crypto map to an interface. You're only going to concern yourself with IPSec policies that use IKE.

To create a transform set, issue the following command in global configuration mode:

`crypto ipsec transform-set name transform1 [transform2 [transform3]]`

To create a crypto map, enter the following command in global configuration mode:

`crypto map name sequence-number ipsec-isakmp`

The router now enters crypto map configuration mode. This is the mode in which you apply the parameters of the crypto map. Peers must use the same transforms in order for the IPSec tunnel to form. Following are the commands to apply parameters to a crypto map:

```
match address acl-number
set peer peer-address
set transform name
set pfs dh-group
set security-association lifetime seconds
```

Once the crypto map has been created, it must be applied to an interface. To do so, issue the following command in interface configuration mode:

`crypto-map name`

> This is a very simplified explanation of how to configure IPSec. For a more in-depth explanation, see Part I of this book, "Securing IOS Network (SECUR)."

Now that you know how to configure your transform set, create your IPSec policy, and apply it to an interface, let's look at a configuration example. In this example, you'll need to create a transform set with `esp-des`, configure your crypto map to use IKE, set your peer to 1.1.1.1, use access-list 100, and assign the crypto map to interface e0. Following is an example of a configuration that would accomplish this task:

```
R1(config)#crypto ipsec transform-set ccsp esp-des
R1(config)#crypto map cisco 10 ipsec-isakmp
R1(config-crypto-map)#match address 100
R1(config-crypto-map)#set peer 1.1.1.1
R1(config-crypto-map)#set transform ccsp
R1(config-crypto-map)#exit
R1(config)#interface e0
R1(config-if)#crypto map cisco
R1(config-if)#
```

You're now ready to start implementing security on an IOS-based firewall. I recommend practicing these different mitigation techniques in a lab before you attempt to implement them in your production network.

Next, it's time to learn a little more about the PIX firewall.

Implementing the PIX Firewall

The last device we need to look at for the SAFE SMR Small Network Design is the PIX firewall. The PIX firewall can be configured to provide the following attack mitigations:

- Stateful packet filtering
- Host DoS mitigation
- Spoof mitigation and RFC filtering
- Authentication
- IPSec

We'll only look at the configuration of host DoS mitigation, spoof mitigation, RFC filtering, authentication, and IPSec. We won't explore stateful packet filtering, because it's the default mode of the PIX firewall.

Host DoS Mitigation

Host DoS mitigation aids in the defense against DoS attacks. The PIX firewall can protect against spoofing, controlling ICMP, and utilizing frag guard.

The first method of protecting against DoS attacks is through the use of the `ip verify reverse-path interface` *int_name* command. This command performs a route lookup based upon the source address of the packet. It protects against IP spoofing attacks by providing ingress and egress filtering. Using ingress filtering, it checks each packet to make sure the packet doesn't have an IP address that belongs to the internal network. Egress filtering is used to guarantee that packets leaving the internal network were sourced from the internal network.

The PIX firewall has a command that limits the traffic that can ping an interface. Using this command, you can specify the interface that can be pinged and the address that is allowed to ping it:

`icmp permit | deny [host]` *src_address [src_mask] [type] int_name*

By controlling who is able to ping an interface, you can prevent DoS attacks, since only specified addresses can ping the interface.

The last host DoS mitigation we need to discuss is frag guard. Frag guard allows for protection against IP fragmentation attacks. IP fragmentation attacks can be used to launch a DoS attack. To prevent IP fragmentation attacks, use the `sysopt security fragguard` command.

Spoof Mitigation and RFC Filtering

By now, you're familiar with what IP spoofing attacks are and why you need to protect against them. To reiterate: IP spoofing attacks occur when someone steals an IP address. This person can then launch a DoS attack utilizing this stolen IP address.

Before we get into how the PIX firewall can protect against these types of attacks, you need a little background about how the PIX firewall functions. The PIX firewall has a concept of *security levels*. Each interface is assigned a security level, and traffic on a lower security level interface can't initiate a connection to a higher security level interface. However, a higher security level interface can initiate a connection with a lower security level interface.

You can use access control lists (ACLs) on the PIX firewall to determine what traffic is and isn't allowed through the PIX firewall. Once the ACL has been created, it needs to be applied to an interface. Not only can ACLs be used to determine traffic allowed to pass through the PIX firewall, they can also be applied to lower security level interfaces to specify traffic that is allowed to initiate a connection with a higher security level interface. In other words, ACLs on a PIX firewall are pretty powerful.

First, you need to create the ACL. To do so, issue the following command:

`access-list` *acl-ID* {deny | permit} *protocol* {*src-addr* |
   local-addr} {*src-mask* | *local-mask*} [*port*] {*destination-
   addr* | *remote-addr*} {*destination-mask* | *remote-mask*}
   [*port*]

Next, the ACL needs to be applied to an interface, using the following command:

`access-group` *acl-ID* `in interface` *interface-name*

You can also use these ACL commands to implement RFC 2827 and 1918 filtering. You only need to specify the appropriate addresses in the ACLs.

Authentication

AAA authentication on a PIX firewall works much the same as an IOS-based router. What differs is the configuration. When you're configuring AAA on a PIX firewall, you first need to specify the AAA server. To do so, issue the following commands:

```
aaa-server server-tag protocol protocol
aaa-server server-tag {if-name} host server-ip key [timeout
    seconds]
```

Once the AAA server has been specified, you must configure authentication. To do so, issue the following command:

```
aaa authentication {serial | enable | telnet | ssh | http}
    console server-tag
```

Finally, you can specify the use of a Syslog server. The Syslog server lets you store Syslog messages on it. These Syslog messages can later be used for troubleshooting purposes. To specify a Syslog server, issue the following command:

```
logging host [in-name] ip-address [protocol]
```

IPSec

Like the IOS-based firewall, IPSec on the PIX firewall lets you create secure communications with remote devices. When you're creating an IPSec on the PIX firewall, you need to follow the same steps as you did on the IOS-based firewall:

1. Define interesting traffic.
2. Create a phase 1 IKE policy.
3. Create a phase 2 IPSec policy.

In order to define traffic that will need to be protected, you need to create an ACL. It's important to remember that when you create this access list, it must be symmetric on each device. This means that the same traffic is defined as interesting. When traffic that enters the device is interesting, it's encrypted and sent across the wire. Uninteresting traffic is sent across the wire in clear text.

After defining your interesting traffic, you need to create a phase 1 IKE policy. The IKE policy you create on each side must have the same encryption, hash, Diffie-Hellman group, and authentication method. To create the IKE policy and to specify the parameters, issue the following commands:

```
isakmp policy priority encryption encryption
isakmp policy priority authentication authentication
isakmp policy priority hash hash
isakmp policy priority group dh-group
isakmp policy priority lifetime seconds
```

If the authentication used is pre-share keys, you need to specify the key to share with the peer. To specify the key and peer, enter the following command.

```
isakmp key key address peer-address
```

Let's look at creating an IKE phase 1 policy. In this example, you'll need to create an IKE phase 1 policy that uses a pre-share key of cisco, a hash of MD5, and group 2. Any device that knows the pre-share key should be authenticated for phase 1. You've already completed this example on a router, but let's look at how the configuration differs on a PIX. Following is a configuration that would accomplish this:

```
PIX#config t
PIX(config)#isakmp policy 10 authentication pre-share
PIX(config)#isakmp policy 10 hash md5
PIX(config)#isakmp policy 10 group 2
PIX(config)#isakmp key cisco address 0.0.0.0
PIX(config)#
```

Now that you've defined the interesting traffic and created the phase 1 IKE policy, you need to configure the phase 2 IPSec policy. You must create a transform set, create a crypto map, assign the parameters to the crypto map, and assign the crypto map to an interface. You're only going to concern yourself with IPSec policies that use IKE. To create a transform set, issue the following command:

```
crypto ipsec transform-set name transform1 [transform2 [transform3]]
```

To create a crypto map and specify its parameters, enter the following commands:

```
crypto map name sequence-number ipsec-isakmp
crypto map name sequence-number match address acl-ID
crypto map name sequence-number set transform-set set-name
crypto map name sequence-number set pfc dh-group
crypto map name sequence-number set security-association
    lifetime seconds seconds
crypto map name sequence-number set security-association
    lifetime kilobytes kilobytes
```

Here's yet another example for you to practice with. In this example, you need to create a transform set with esp-des, configure your crypto map to use IKE, set your peer to 1.1.1.1, use access-list 100, and assign the crypto map to outside interface. Following is an example of a configuration that would accomplish this task:

```
R1(config)#crypto ipsec transform-set ccsp esp-des
R1(config)#crypto map cisco 10 ipsec-isakmp
R1(config)#crypto map cisco 10 match address 100
```

```
R1(config)#crypto map cisco 10 set peer 1.1.1.1
R1(config)#crypto map cisco 10 set transform-set ccsp
R1(config)#crypto map cisco interface outside
R1(config)#sysopt connection permit-ipsec
```

Summary

This chapter focused on the SAFE SMR Small Network Design and Medium Network Design. The Small Network Design consists of two modules: the corporate Internet module and the campus module. Each of these modules has its own key devices that are used to perform security functions. The Medium Network Design consists of three modules: the corporate Internet module, the campus module, and the WAN module.

After we discussed the different modules and the threats associated with them, we dove into the actual implementation of the devices. First, you learned how to implement the ISP router. The ISP router can be used to mitigate IP spoof and DoS attacks. Through the use of CAR, you're able to limit the amount of ICMP traffic permitted on a network. By limiting this ICMP traffic, you can reduce the amount of ICMP DoS attacks. However, RFC 2827 and 1918 filtering can be used to aid in the prevention of IP spoof attacks.

The IOS-based firewall can be used to provide numerous mechanisms for security. For instance, CBAC can be used to provide stateful packet filtering. Stateful packet filtering permits only internal devices to initiate sessions. Also the IOS-based firewall can be used to provide IDS. IDS allows for the detection of network attacks. Based on signature matches, IDS is able to determine that a possible network attack is occurring.

Finally, we looked at the PIX firewall. The PIX firewall is a stateful firewall by default. However, it can also be used to provide IPSec termination. This means that remote users can create an IPSec encrypted tunnel to the PIX firewall, allowing for secure connectivity. The PIX can also provide RFC filtering for IP spoof mitigation.

We covered a lot in this chapter. It's very important that you fully understand this chapter if you're going to be successful on the SAFE test and as a security professional. In other words, take your time; if you need to, review this chapter before moving on.

Exam Essentials

Know the modules of the SAFE SMR Small Network Design. The SAFE SMR Small Network Design is composed of the corporate Internet module and the campus module. The corporate Internet module provides Internet access for internal users and an access point for remote users.

List the key devices of the corporate Internet module of the Small Network Design. The corporate Internet module is made up of a layer 2 switch for connectivity, public servers to provide public information about the company, and a firewall to provide protection to the Internal network.

List the expected threats in the corporate Internet module of the Small Network Design. The expected threats in the corporate Internet module are DoS, viruses and Trojan horses, password attacks, unauthorized access attacks, application layer attacks, packet sniffers, IP spoofing, trust exploitation, port redirection, and network reconnaissance.

List the key devices of the campus module of the Small Network Design. The campus module is made up of corporate servers to provide services to internal users, management servers for management services, a layer 2 switch for connectivity, and user workstations for data services.

List the expected threats in the campus module of the Small Network Design. The expected threats in the campus module are viruses and Trojan horses, unauthorized access attacks, application layer attacks, packet sniffers, trust exploitation, and port redirection.

List the modules of the SAFE SMR Medium Network Design. The SAFE SMR Medium Network Design is made up of the corporate Internet module, the campus module, and the WAN module.

List the key devices in the SAFE SMR Medium Network Design corporate Internet module. The key devices in the corporate Internet module of the SAFE SMR Medium Network Design are a dial-in server, an SMTP server, a DNS server, an FTP or HTTP server, a firewall, a layer 2 switch, HIDS, NIDS, a VPN concentrator, and an edge router.

List the key devices in the SAFE SMR Medium Network Design campus module. The key devices in the campus module of the SAFE SMR Medium Network Design are an SMTP or POP3 server, file and print servers, user workstations, a management host, a layer 2 and 3 switch, and a NIDS appliance.

List the key device in the SAFE SMR Medium Network Design WAN module. The key device in the WAN module of the SAFE SMR Medium Network Design is an IOS router.

List the threats in the SAFE SMR Medium Network Design corporate Internet module. The threats in the corporate Internet module of the SAFE SMR Medium Network Design consist of DoS, viruses and Trojan horses, password attacks, unauthorized access, application layer, packet sniffers, IP spoofing, trust exploitation, port redirection, network reconnaissance, and man-in-the-middle attacks.

List the threats in the SAFE SMR Medium Network Design campus module. The threats in the campus module of the SAFE SMR Medium Network Design consist of viruses and Trojan horses, unauthorized access attacks, password attacks, IP spoofing, application layer attacks, packet sniffers, trust exploitation, and port redirection attacks.

List the threats in the SAFE SMR Medium Network Design WAN module. The threats in the WAN module of the SAFE SMR Medium Network Design consist of IP spoofing and unauthorized access attacks.

Explain how to implement an ISP router. The ISP router can be utilized to provide DoS and IP spoof mitigation. DoS mitigation can be implemented through the use of CAR, and IP spoof mitigation can be implemented through the use of RFC 2827 and 1918 filtering.

Explain how to implement an IOS-based firewall. The IOS-based firewall can be utilized to perform numerous security functions. These functions include stateful packet filtering and basic layer 7 filtering, IP spoof mitigation, host DoS mitigation, intrusion detection, authentication, and IPSec.

Explain how to implement a PIX firewall. The PIX firewall is a stateful firewall by default. It can also be used to provide host DoS mitigation, spoof mitigation and RFC filtering, authentication, and IPSec.

Chapter 30

SAFE Remote Access Network Design

THE SAFE OBJECTIVES COVERED IN THIS CHAPTER:

- ✓ Understanding the SAFE remote-user network implementation overview
- ✓ Knowing the key devices
- ✓ Understanding the threat mitigation techniques
- ✓ Understanding the software access option
- ✓ Understanding the remote site firewall option
- ✓ Understanding the hardware VPN client option
- ✓ Understanding the remote site router option

In today's world of telecommuting and employees traveling all over the place, a drastic need has emerged for remote access to the corporate office. Not only do we need these remote connections, but we need them to be secure. You can accomplish this through the use of the Remote Access portion of the SAFE SMR Network Design, which this chapter will deal with.

You'll learn the different options available to you, the key devices involved, the attacks that Remote Access Networks are prone to, and how to defend against these attacks. The chapter will wrap up the complete SAFE SMR discussion with a look at the Remote Access Network Design.

Remote Access Network Design Overview

Who needs remote connectivity? The answer is pretty simple: any telecommuters or any mobile workers. Basically, it's anyone who will be away from the corporate office but who still requires access to the corporate office.

Back in the early days of networking, remote connectivity wasn't an issue. Everyone who worked for a company worked *at* the company. Today, more companies allow employees to work from home. The companies do this as a cost savings method by not having to pay for the office space. Great idea—however, this has put a great demand on remote connectivity and its security.

When you're looking at the Remote Access Network Design, you'll notice that the following four options are recommended for remote access connectivity:

Software access   With the *software access option*, a VPN software client with a personal firewall on the host is used to create a VPN connection to the corporate office.

Remote site firewall   When using the *remote site firewall option*, a firewall is installed at the remote location. It provides security and a VPN connection to the corporate office.

VPN hardware client   The *VPN hardware client option* allows multiple users at a remote site to use the same VPN connection to the corporate office.

Remote site router   Using the *remote site router option* lets you provide firewall security at the remote site as well as VPN connectivity to the corporate office.

To get an idea of how this works, let's look at an IPSec remote access to LAN tunnel. Figure 30.1 illustrates this concept.

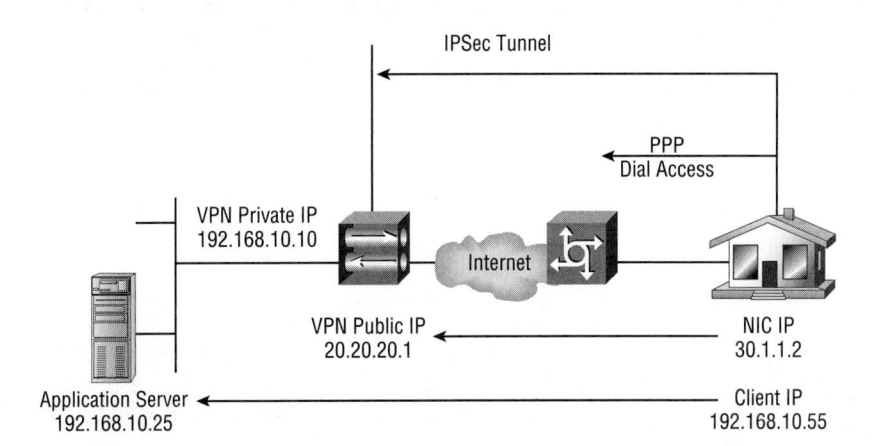

FIGURE 30.1 IPSec remote access to LAN tunnel

[Diagram: Application Server (192.168.10.25) connects to VPN Concentrator with VPN Private IP 192.168.10.10 and VPN Public IP 20.20.20.1. IPSec Tunnel traverses the Internet to a home with NIC IP 30.1.1.2 via PPP Dial Access. Client IP 192.168.10.55.]

The components that make up this tunnel are a VPN software client that resides on the user's PC and terminates one end of the tunnel, IPSec and Internet Key Exchange (IKE) that establish the secure tunnel with the VPN Concentrator, and a VPN Concentrator that terminates the tunnel and provides encryption and authentication.

Key Devices

Like all the other sections of the SAFE SMR Network Design discussed so far, the Remote Access Design has its own key devices and threat mitigations to worry about. These include the following:

Broadband access device   This device provides access to the broadband network. Examples include a DSL or cable modem.

Firewall with VPN support   This provides encrypted tunnels between remote sites and the corporate headquarters and also provides stateful packet filtering.

Layer 2 hub   This provides layer 2 connectivity at the remote site.

Personal firewall software   Personal firewall software provides device-level firewall protection for individual PCs.

Router with firewall and VPN support   This provides encrypted tunnels between remote sites and the corporate headquarters, stateful packet filtering, and advanced services such as quality of service (QoS).

VPN software client   The VPN software client is installed on individual PCs. It provides encrypted tunnels between the PC and the corporate headquarters.

VPN hardware client The VPN hardware client provides an encrypted tunnel between the remote site and the corporate headquarters. The devices at the remote site communicate with the headquarters over this connection.

The most likely attacks in a SAFE SMR Remote Access Network design are

- Unauthorized access
- Network reconnaissance
- Virus and Trojan horse attacks
- IP spoofing
- Man-in-the-middle attacks

> **NOTE** These attacks are some of the usual suspects that we've discussed elsewhere. If you need to refresh yourself on these attacks, refer to the last few chapters.

Implementing the Remote Access Devices

These attacks can be mitigated using one of the four options previously discussed. In the following sections, you'll see how to implement each of these options.

Software Access Option

The software access option is the most common remote access solution when you're dealing with mobile workers. These mobile workers are never in one place for an extended period of time. So, they need a remote access solution that is flexible and enables them to connect to the corporate office in an expedited manner. Figure 30.2 illustrates the software access option.

The software access option provides threat mitigation in three ways:

- Authentication of remote sites
- Termination of IPSec
- Use of a personal firewall and virus scanning

By authenticating the remote site, you can properly identify and verify a user or a service. Terminating the IPSec tunnel allows for the successful creation of an IPSec encrypted tunnel between the remote site and the corporate office. Finally, the use of a personal firewall and virus scanning provides local attack mitigation by reducing the possibility of virus infection.

FIGURE 30.2 Software access option

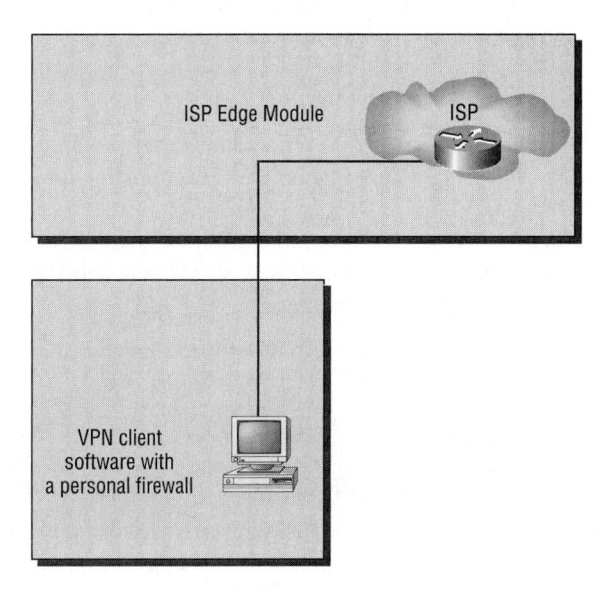

We need to introduce the concept of split tunneling here. *Split tunneling* lets you send encrypted traffic to the corporate network and clear text traffic to the Internet. Split tunneling is disabled when the VPN is operational. This means that when the VPN is operational, you access the Internet through the corporate office. When the VPN is non-operational, you access the Internet through your Internet connection.

Implementing the Software Access Option

As stated earlier, the software access option is primarily geared toward mobile workers. This means that all the user needs is a PC with a VPN software client, a personal firewall, and an Internet connection. Cisco recommends the use of VPN Client version 3.5 or higher.

The user first authenticates to the corporate office and then receives their virtual IP address. The corporate office may also decide to go ahead and provide WINS and DNS information.

If you've never installed and configured the Cisco VPN Client software, you should be pleasantly surprised: It's a simple process. When you're using the Cisco VPN Client, you first need to make sure you're running one of the following operating systems:

- Windows 95
- Windows 98
- Windows ME
- Windows NT 4
- Windows 2000

- Windows XP
- Linux
- Solaris
- Mac OS

Once you've installed the VPN Client, you can go ahead and launch it. To launch the VPN Client, you need to locate the VPN Dialer icon contained under Programs on your Windows machine. You'll see the screen in Figure 30.3.

You'll notice a couple of buttons on this screen: New and Options. Clicking the New button activates a wizard that will walk you through setting up a new VPN connection. Clicking the Options button provides you with a list of the following options:

Clone Entry   This enables you to copy a connection with all of its parameters.

Delete Entry   This lets you delete a connection.

Rename Entry   This lets you rename a connection.

Import Entry   This provides a preconfigured .pcf file that loads the VPN Client parameters.

Erase User Password   This eliminates a saved password. Erase User Password is available only when you've enabled Allow Password Storage under the Mode Configuration parameters for this VPN group.

Create Shortcut   This enables you to create a shortcut for your desktop.

Properties   This enables you to configure or change the properties of the connection.

FIGURE 30.3   Initial VPN Client screen

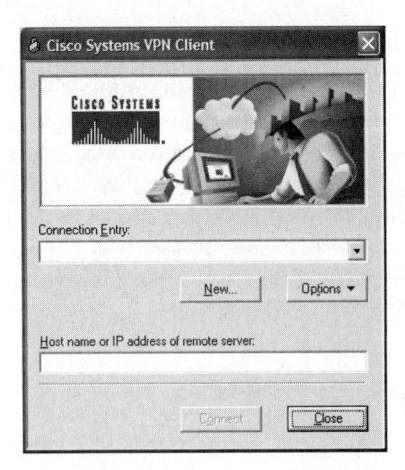

Stateful Firewall This blocks all inbound traffic that isn't related to an outbound session. After the remote user enables the stateful firewall, it's always on.

Application Launcher This enables you to launch an application before establishing a connection. This is used in conjunction with Windows Logon Properties.

Windows Logon Properties This enables the VPN Client to make the connection to the Concentrator before the user logs in.

The only option we'll examine is Properties, because it's the option you'll use all the time. When you select the Properties option, you're presented with the Properties dialog box, as seen in Figure 30.4.

The General tab lets you configure IPSec through NAT services and Microsoft network logon options.

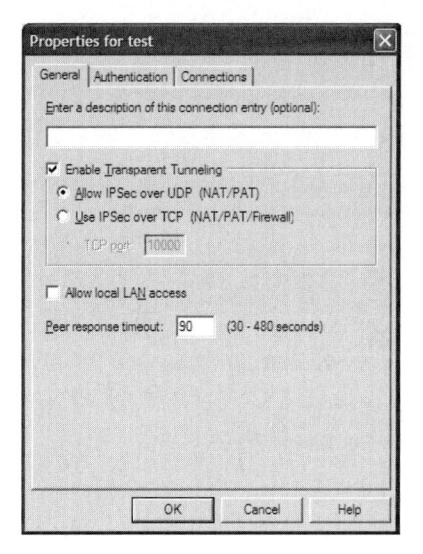

On the Authentication tab (Figure 30.5), you can choose whether you'll use digital certificates or a group name and password for authentication. You can also change your group name and/or password.

The final tab we need to look at is the Connections tab (Figure 30.6). This tab lets you specify backup networks and the method you're using to access the Internet. Using the backup networks option allows you to specify a backup VPN Concentrator to use in case your primary isn't available.

FIGURE 30.4 General tab of the Properties dialog box

FIGURE 30.5 Authentication tab

FIGURE 30.6 Connections Properties tab

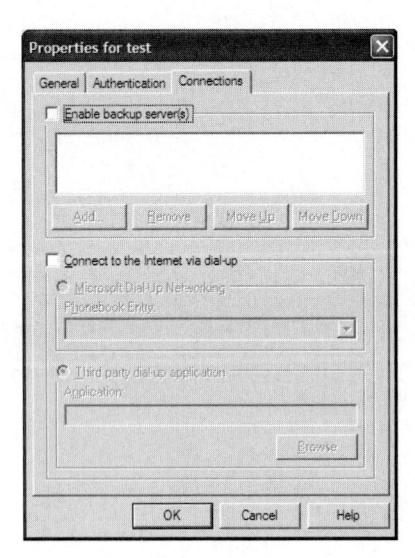

Remote Site Firewall Option

Much of the information in this section has already been covered throughout the book. So, instead of making you go through it again, we'll look more at the theory and the difference in configuration of the remote site firewall option.

The remote site firewall option for the Remote Access Design is geared toward an office in your home or a small remote site, because the firewall isn't very portable. By using the remote site firewall option, you add stateful packet filtering, basic layer 7 filtering, host DoS mitigation, authentication for remote sites, and termination of the IPSec tunnel. You'll still want to keep virus-scanning software on your PCs to provide local attack mitigation. Figure 30.7 illustrates the layout of the remote site firewall option.

Another benefit of the remote site firewall option is that the PIX firewall supports the configuration of an intrusion detection system (IDS). This provides another layer of security.

FIGURE 30.7 Remote site firewall option

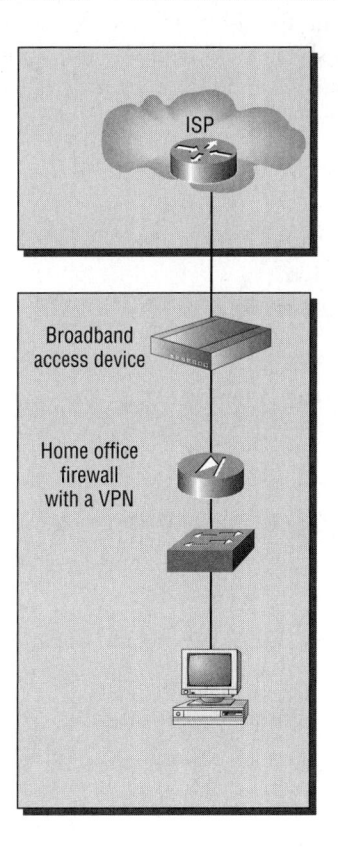

Implementing the Firewall Option

Let's look at the different mitigation roles of the remote site firewall and the commands to implement them. The PIX firewall provides stateful packet filtering by default. Therefore, there are no commands related to stateful packet filtering that we need to look at.

The PIX firewall can provide host denial of service (DoS) mitigation through the use of the following commands:

ip verify reverse-path interface   This command implements unicast RPF IP spoofing protection.

icmp   This command enables or disables pinging to an interface.

attack guard   This command is enabled by default.

static/nat   This command implements static or dynamic NAT.

Often, Internet Control Message Protocol (ICMP) is used to accomplish DoS attacks. By default, the PIX doesn't allow pinging to the outside interface. However, it does allow pinging of the inside interface. In our example, we want to limit the ability to ping the inside interface to users on the 10.10.10.0/24 network. All other users should be denied. We also want to reduce the possibility of IP spoof attacks on all interfaces, outside and inside, by making sure we can reach a source address out of the interface the packet came in on. Here is a sample configuration that will accomplish this attack:

```
PIX#conf t
PIX(conf)#ip verify reverse-path interface outside
PIX(conf)#ip verify reverse-path interface inside
PIX(conf)#icmp permit 10.10.10.0 255.255.255.0 inside
PIX(conf)#
```

The next item we'll look at is spoof mitigation and RFC filtering. These tasks can be accomplished through the use of these commands:

access-list   This command creates an access list.

access-group   This command associates the access list with an interface.

What would security be without authentication? Not much. To configure the PIX firewall to support authentication, use the following commands:

aaa-server   This command specifies an authentication, authorization, and accounting (AAA) server.

aaa authentication   This command enables or disables user authentication.

logging on   This command enables or disables Syslog and Simple Network Management Protocol (SNMP) logging.

Let's look at an example of how some of these commands fit together. You're administering a PIX. You think that anyone who uses Telnet, console access, or HTTP access to manage the PIX should be authenticated against a TACACS+ server at IP address 10.10.10.1. The server is located off the inside interface. When the PIX communicates with the server, it should use cisco as the password. Here is an example of a configuration that will accomplish this task:

PIX#**conf t**
PIX(conf)#**aaa-server TACACS+ (inside) host 10.10.10.1 cisco**
PIX(conf)#**aaa authentication serial console TACACS+**
PIX(conf)#**aaa authentication serial telnet TACACS+**
PIX(conf)#**aaa authentication serial http TACACS+**
PIX(conf)#

Finally, let's look at using the PIX to terminate an IPSec tunnel. Since we're talking about remote access, VPN termination is a key point. To configure the PIX to terminate an IPSec tunnel, use the following commands:

isakmp enable   This command enables Internet Key Exchange (IKE) on an interface.

isakmp key   This command specifies the authentication pre-share key.

isakmp policy   This command identifies the IKE policy and assigns a priority to the policy.

crypto ipsec transform-set   This command creates, modifies, views, or deletes IPSec security association (SAs), SA global lifetime values, and global transform sets.

crypto map   This command creates, modifies, views, or deletes a crypto map entry.

sysopt connection ipsec-permit   This command implicitly permits any packet that came from an IPSec tunnel.

That's all there is to the remote site firewall option. If you need a more in-depth review of the commands for the PIX, refer to one of the previous chapters. For now, let's move on to the VPN hardware client option.

VPN Hardware Client Option

The VPN hardware client option provides the same features as the remote-site firewall option with the exception of providing a firewall and IDS. This means that the user needs to have a personal firewall on their PC for protection. Figure 30.8 illustrates the VPN hardware client option.

Since the VPN hardware client option provides all the same features as the remote site firewall option (except for the firewall feature), we'll move right into implementing the VPN hardware client option.

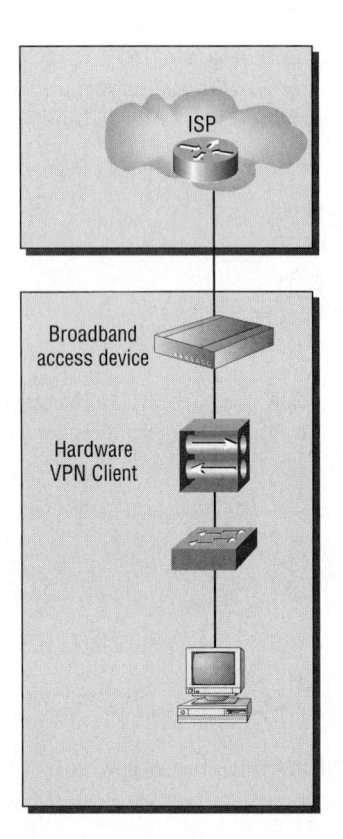

FIGURE 30.8 VPN hardware client option

Implementing the VPN Hardware Client Option

There are two methods of configuring the VPN hardware client: command-line interface (CLI) or graphical user interface (GUI). The CLI is a menu-driven method of configuring the VPN hardware client. The GUI is a graphical method of configuring the VPN hardware client. Figures 30.9 and 30.10 illustrate the two methods.

We'll only explore the use of the GUI for configuration, because this is the method you'll most encounter.

To configure the VPN hardware client using the GUI, you first need to configure your PC to communicate with the hardware client. The client has two interfaces: a public and a private interface. You'll configure the client through the use of the private interface. The private interface comes with a default IP address of 192.168.10.1 /24.

Once you've powered up the client, connected your PC to it, and configured your local IP addressing so you can speak to it, you need to ping it to make sure you can reach it. If this is successful, open a browser and type in **http://192.168.10.1**. Doing so brings up the GUI login screen.

FIGURE 30.9 VPN hardware client using CLI

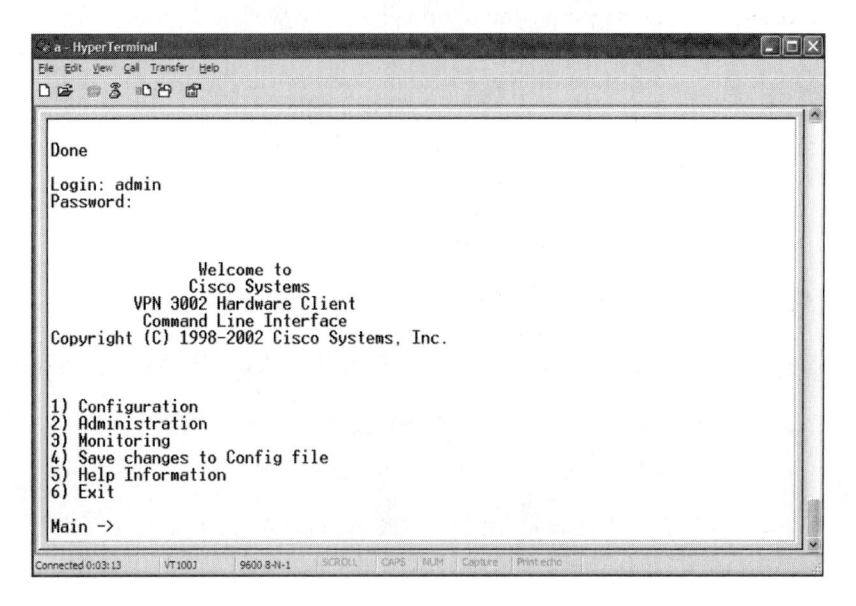

FIGURE 30.10 VPN hardware client using a GUI

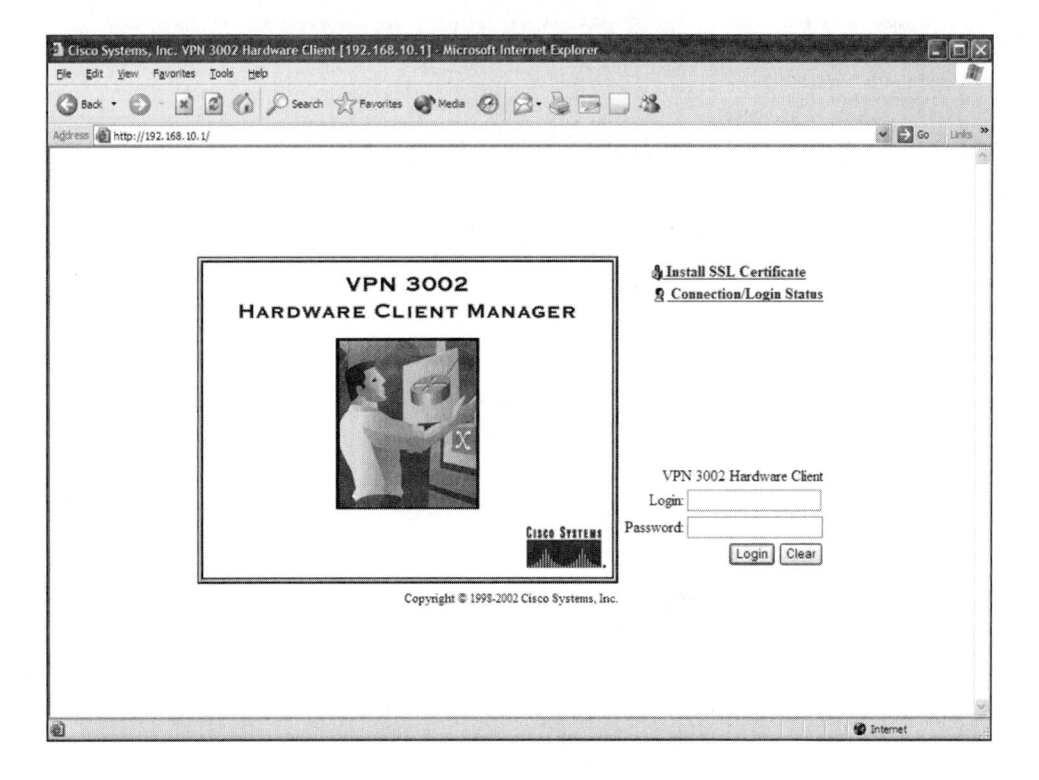

You now need to log in to the client. The default login name and password are both `admin`. Once you've successfully logged in, you're brought to the Welcome screen (Figure 30.11).

From this screen, you can select whether you want to use quick mode or main mode configuration. Quick mode configuration is a wizard that walks you through the configuration of a VPN connection. Figure 30.12 is a sample screen from this wizard. Main mode configuration requires you to go to each individual section to complete the configuration.

Finally, you can force your VPN hardware client to connect or disconnect. To accomplish this, select Monitoring from the initial VPN hardware client screen (see Figure 30.11) and then choose System Status, which brings you to the System Status screen (Figure 30.13).

FIGURE 30.11 Initial VPN hardware client screen

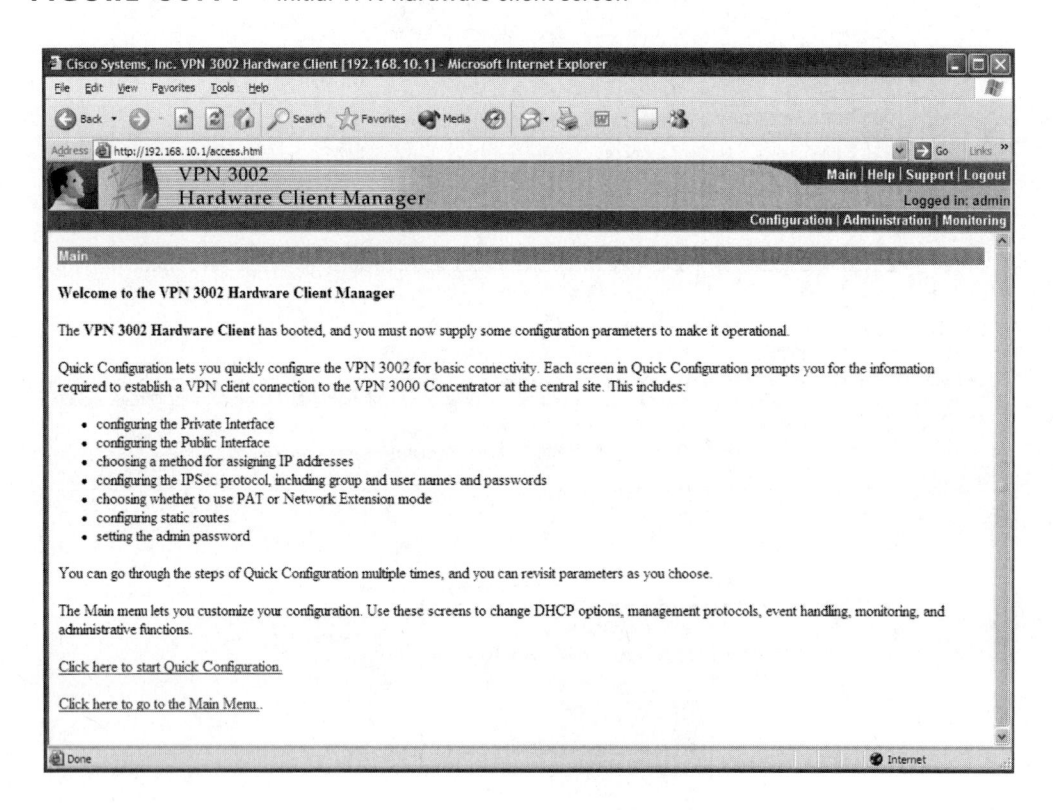

FIGURE 30.12 Initial screen in quick mode

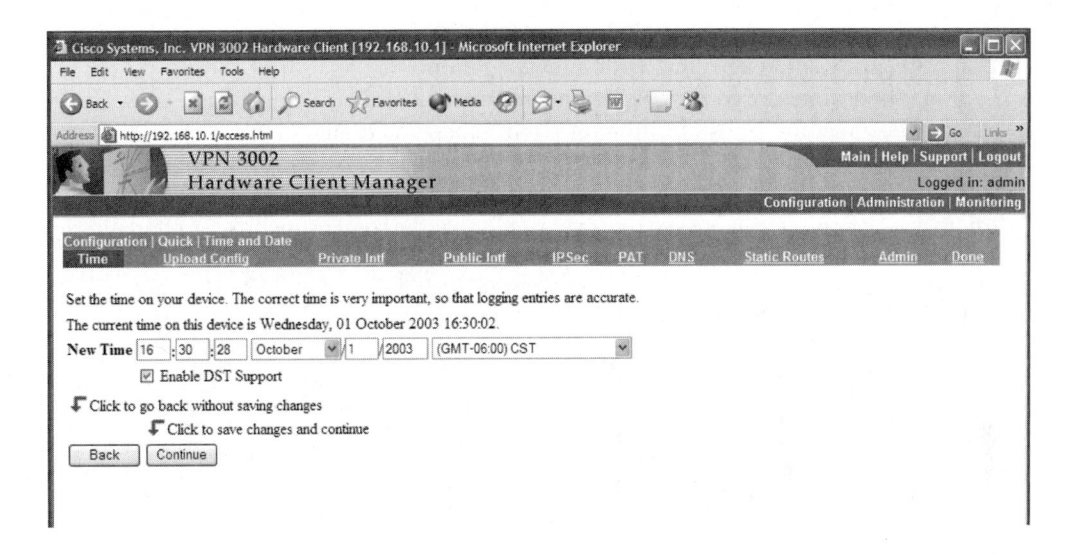

FIGURE 30.13 System Status screen

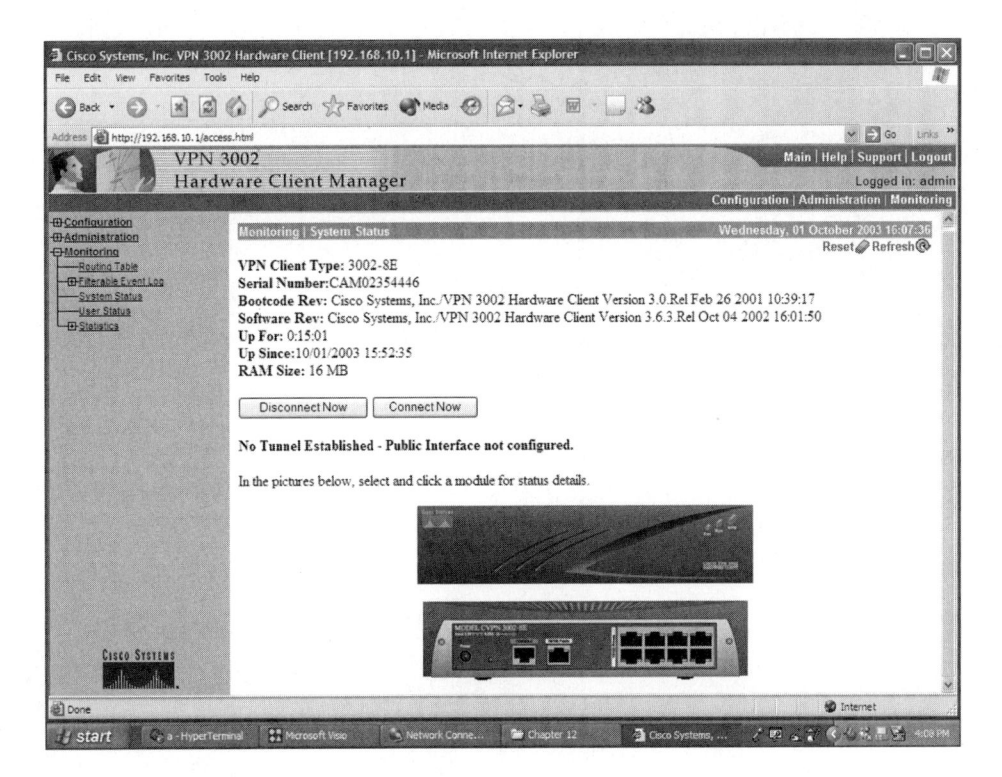

Remote Site Router Option

The remote site router option for remote access is geared toward an office in your home or a small remote site, just like the remote site firewall option.

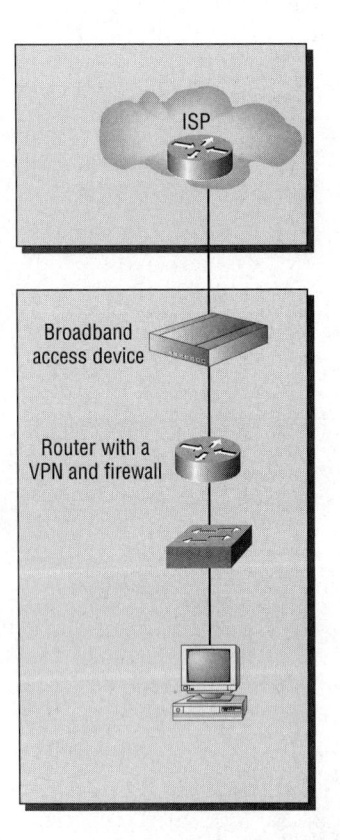

By using the remote site router option, you add stateful packet filtering, basic layer 7 filtering, host DoS mitigation, authentication for remote sites, and termination of the IPSec tunnel. You'll still want to keep virus-scanning software on your PCs to provide local attack mitigation. Figure 30.14 illustrates the layout of the remote site router option.

Another benefit of the remote site router option is that the router supports the configuration of IDS. This provides another layer of security.

FIGURE 30.14 Remote site router option

Implementing the Remote Site Router Option

Let's look at the different mitigation roles of the router and the commands to implement them. The router provides stateful packet filtering through the use of *context-based access control* (CBAC).

We'll begin by looking at spoof mitigation and RFC filtering. These tasks can be accomplished through the use of these commands:

access-list   As stated earlier, this command creates an access list.

access-group   This command associates the access list with an interface.

Next, we'll look at host DoS mitigation and basic layer 7 filtering. The commands you'll need for these tasks are as follows:

ip inspect   This command defines the application protocols to inspect.

tcp intercept   This command protects TCP servers from TCP SYN-flooding attacks.

Before we move on to configuring authentication on the router, let's take a moment to look at an example of implementing CBAC. In our example, R1 is the edge device. The E0 interface is connected to the inside network and the S0 interface is connected to the rest of the world. We want to inspect all outbound traffic and only allow traffic back into the network that belongs to a session that has been initiated from the inside network. In other words, we want to make the router act more like a PIX. Here is a sample configuration that would accomplish this task:

```
R1#conf t
R1(conf)#ip inspect name firewall tcp
R1(conf)#ip inspect name firewall udp
R1(conf)#access-list 100 deny ip any any
R1(conf)#interface e0
R1(conf-if)#ip inspect firewall in
R1(conf-if)#exit
R1(conf)#interface s0
R1(conf-if)#ip access-group 100 in
R1(conf-if)#^z
R1#
```

To configure the router to support authentication, use the following commands:

aaa new-model   To define a set of inspection rules, enter this command for each protocol that you want to inspect, using the same inspection name.

tacacs-server   This command specifies a TACACS server.

aaa authentication login   This command enables user authentication.

aaa authorization exec   This command restricts network access to a user.

aaa accounting exec   This command runs accounting for EXEC shell sessions.

logging authentication   This command specifies the name of a list of AAA authentication methods to try at login.

Let's look at configuring authentication. In this example, we need to authenticate all users telneting into R1. The users must be authenticated against a TACACS+ server at IP address 10.10.10.1. When connecting to the server, R1 needs to use the password **cisco**. If not telneting into R1, all users are required to enter the line password. Here is a sample of a configuration that would accomplish this task:

```
R1#conf t
R1(conf)#aaa new-model
R1(conf)#aaa authentication login default line
R1(conf)#aaa authentication login telnet tacacs
R1(conf)#tacacs-server host 10.10.10.1 key cisco
R1(conf)#line vty 0 4
R1(conf-line)#login authentication telnet
R1(conf-line)#^z
R1#
```

To configure the router to terminate an IPSec tunnel, use the following commands:

crypto isakmp policy   This command specifies the parameters to be used during IKE negotiation.

encryption   This command sets the algorithm to be negotiated.

authentication   This command specifies the authentication method within an IKE policy.

group   This command specifies the Diffie-Hellman group to use.

crypto isakmp key   This command configures pre-shared authentication keys.

crypto ipsec transform-set   This command sets an acceptable combination of security protocols, algorithms, and other settings to apply to IPSec protected traffic.

crypto map   This command configures filtering and classifying traffic to be protected and defines the policy to be applied to that traffic.

set peer   This command specifies an IPSec peer for a crypto map.

set transform-set   This command specifies which transform sets to include in a crypto map entry.

match-address   This command specifies an extended access list for a crypto map entry.

That's all there is to the remote site router option. If you need a more in-depth review of the commands for the router, refer to one of the previous chapters.

Summary

The SAFE SMR Remote Access Design is different than the Small and Medium Network Designs you've seen so far. Instead of having numerous different modules, you have different options for implementing one module.

The software access option requires the use of a VPN software client and a personal firewall on the end-user device. You then make a secure VPN connection into the corporate office. This option is best suited for mobile users because of its flexibility and ease of use.

The remote site firewall option and the remote site router option allow you to provide secure remote-access VPN solutions along with the added security of a firewall. This option is best suited for a remote branch. A mobile user wouldn't want to use it because of its dependency on hardware. The remote site router option has the added feature of supporting QoS.

The VPN hardware client option allows for a group of users to sit behind the client and have one secure VPN connection into the corporate office. Like the remote site firewall option, this option is best suited for a remote office. This option does require the user to have a personal firewall on their PC for added security.

Exam Essentials

Know the four remote access options available.   The SAFE SMR Remote Access Design can consist of one of four options: the software access option, the remote site firewall option, the remote site router option, and the VPN hardware client option.

Know the key devices of the Remote Access Network Design.   The key devices of the SAFE SMR Remote Access Network Design are a broadband access device, a firewall with VPN support, a layer 2 hub, personal firewall software, a router with firewall and VPN support, a VPN software client, and a VPN hardware client.

Understand the possible threats to the Remote Access Network Design.   The possible attacks in the SAFE SMR Remote Access Design are unauthorized access, network reconnaissance, virus and Trojan horse attacks, IP spoofing, and man-in-the-middle attacks.

Know how to mitigate the threats.   The different attacks can be mitigated through the use of one of the four options: the software access option, the remote site firewall option, the remote site router option, and the VPN hardware client option.

Index

Note to the Reader: Throughout this index **boldfaced** page numbers indicate primary discussions of a topic. *Italicized* page numbers indicate illustrations.

A

aaa accounting command, 44–46
aaa accounting exec command, 77
aaa accounting include command, 334
aaa accounting network command, 44–45, 76–77
aaa authentication command, 128–129, 331–333
    for IP spoofing, 1150
    in PIX Firewall, 1136
aaa authentication exec command, 76
aaa authentication login command, 1131
    for IOS Firewall, 129
    for NAS, 39–41
    for remote site routers, 1158
    for TACACS+, 76–77
aaa authentication network command, 76
aaa authentication ppp command, 41, 76
aaa authorization commands, 1131
    for IOS Firewall, 129–130
    for NAS, 42–44
    for PIX Firewall, 333–334
    for remote site routers, 1158
AAA Flood Guard, **353–354**
aaa new-model command
    for AAA enabling, 76, 128, 1131
    for remote site routers, 1157
aaa-pass command, 335
AAA security, **24–26**
    accounting, 25
        on NAS, **44–46**
        on PIX Firewall, **334**
    ACLs for, **131**
    authentication. *See* authentication
    authorization, 25
        in access control, **651**
        configuring, **129–130**
        in identity, 1105
        on NAS, **41–44**
        on PIX Firewall, **333–334**
        protocols for, **129–130**
    enabling, 38, 76, **128**, 1131
    HTTP server for, **131–132**
    implementing, **1132**
    on PIX Firewall
        accounting, **334**
        authentication, **331–333**
        authorization, **333–334**
        implementing, **330–331**
        Secure ACS for, **324–330**
    server configuration for, **125–128**, *126–127*
    TACACS+ server and key for, **130**
aaa-server command
    for IP spoofing, 1150
    in PIX Firewall, **330–332**, 1136
aaa-user command, 335
acceptable use policies, 1079
access and access control
    ACLs for. *See* ACLs (access control lists)
    in CLI, **246–247**
    in control network security, **650–652**
    IP, 1074
    to sensors, **704–708**, **715–717**
    unauthorized, **15–16**, 1078
access attacks, 11, **634–635**
    application vulnerabilities in, **640**
    authentication in, **635–636**
    back doors in, **640–641**
    configuration problems in, **640**
    physical access in, **635**
    protocol weaknesses in, **637–640**, *638–639*
    trust relationships in, **636–637**, *637*
access-class command, 823
access control entries (ACEs)
    for IDM, 813
    for VACLs, 767–768
access control lists. *See* ACLs (access control lists)

Access Control Servers. *See* ACS (Access Control Server)
access-group command
    for IP spoofing, 1150
    for ISP routers, 1125
    for perimeter routers, 87
    for PIX Firewall, 308, 310, 312, 1135
    for remote site routers, 1157
    for SNMP packets, 92
access hours for VPN Concentrators, **561**, *561*
access-list command
    for ACLs, 116–117, 131, 285
    for blocking, 822
    for IP spoofing, 1150
    for ISP routers, 1124
    for object groups, 323
    for perimeter routers, 87
    for PIX Firewall, 308–312, 1135
    for remote site routers, 1157
    for signatures, 139
    for SNMP packets, 92
    for VACLs, 771
access lists for IKE, **177**
access maps, VLAN, **771–772**
access rights, **616–619**, *617–620*
Access Rules tab, 396
Access Server Configuration screen, 62, *62*
Access Settings screen, 619, *620*
accessList command, 716, 905
accidental attacks, 14
accounting, 25
    on NAS, **44–46**
    on PIX Firewall, **334**
AccountName parameter, 881
ACEs (access control entries)
    for IDM, 813
    for VACLs, 767–768
ACK Timeouts field, 606
Acknowledged status, event filters for, 913
ACL logging, 833
AclDataSource parameter, 881
AclFilterName parameter, 881
ACLs (access control lists), 308–309
    for AAA traffic, **131**
    applying, **116–117, 310–311**
    for blocking, **820–821**, *821*

vs. CBAC, **103–105**
    configuring, 117
    converting conduits to, **311–312**
    creating, **309–310**
    for IDM, **813–814**
    for IP spoofing, 16
    for IPSec, **415**, *416*, **423–424, 491**
    for NAT, **284–286**
    for packet-filtering FTP, **347**
    for PIX Firewall, **309–312, 337–338**
    for VACLs, 771
    for VPN Concentrators, **619**, *619*
ACS (Access Control Server), **52–54**, *53–54*
    administering, **64–71**, *64–69*
    authentication in, **54–55**
    in Cisco security portfolio, **1106–1107**, *1106*
    installing, **57–64**, *58–63*, **324–330**
    new features in, **56–57**
    reports in, **70**
ACS Administration screen, 64, *64*
action buttons in IDS Management Center, 965, *965*
actions
    for audit rules, **139–141**
    for Event Viewer, 1041
    for events, **1048–1049**
    for signatures, **867–868**, 993
    for TFTP, 622
activation-key command, 236
Active-mode FTP, **346**
active monitoring, *656*
active-selection command, 840
Active Service Monitoring screen, 61, *61*, 326
active units in PIX Firewall, 380
Active Updates feature, 671
activities for Management Center, *456*
activity bars for IDM, *788*, *789*
Adaptive Security Algorithm (ASA), **239–240**
Add Address Transition Rule window, 397, *398*
Add Group page, 966, *967*
Add Host/Network? screen, 445, *445*
Add Rule window, 397, *397*
Add screen
    for ACLs, **619**, *619*
    for SNMP traps, 612, *612*

Add User page – anti-spoofing 1163

for Syslog servers, 614, *614*
for VPN Concentrators
    access hours, 561, *561*
    updates, 570, *570*
Add User page, 961, *961*
Adding page, 850, *851*
Address Assignment screen, 546–547, *546*
address-pool parameter, 429
Address Pool screen, 448, *449*
Address Translation Exemption screen, 450, *450*
addressed-key command, 191
addresses
    for blocking, 851
    event filters for, 909
    in failover, 377
    IP. *See* IP addresses
    in remote access VPNs, **427–428**
    translation. *See* NAT (Network Address Translation); PAT (Port Address Translation)
    for VPN Concentrators, 546–547, *546*
admin account for VPN Concentrators, 617
Admin Accounting reports, 70
Admin page
    in Event Viewer, 1042–1044, *1043–1044*
    in Security Monitor, 1022
Admin password
    for CLI, 504–505
    for VPN 3002 Hardware Client, 512
    for VPN Concentrators, 549, *549*
Admin Password screen, 549, *549*
Administer Sessions screen, 620
Administration Control screen, 68, *68*
administrators
    in IDC Management Center, 963, *963*
    for sensors, 719–720
    for VPN Concentrators, **616–618**, *617–618*
admission tickets in Kerberos, 29
Advanced Options screen, 60, *60*, 326
aggressive mode in IKE, 155, **487**
aging usernames and passwords, 27
AH (Authentication Header) protocol, 152, **471–473**, *472*
Alarm Aggregation table, 915, 924, **926–928**, *927–928*

Alarm Information Dialog table, **916–918**, 930, *930*
AlarmInterval parameter, 875–876
alarms
    channels
        event filters for, **810–813**, *810–812*
        sensor system variables, **797–804**, *797, 799–801*
    database management, 692
    in IDS, 136, **669**, *669*
    IEV database for, 926
        Alarm Aggregation table, **926–928**, *927–928*
        Alarm Information Dialog table, **930**, *930*
        Drill Down Dialog table, **930–931**, *931–932*
        Expanded Details Dialog table, **929**, *929*
        Realtime Dashboard, **931–935**, *933–935*
    responses to, **676**
    signature engine parameters for, **874–877**
    in signatures, 867
AlarmSeverity parameter, 874
AlarmThrottle parameter, 876–877
Alert Exclusions property, 904
alerts
    in CBAC, **108**
    in IDM, 857
All Signatures group, 884
Allow Blocking devices To Block The Sensor's IP Address property, 985
Allow Password Storage on Client property, 556
allow-sensor-shun command, 833
Allowed Hosts page, 791, 792, 830, 973, *974*
amplification in DoS attacks, 642, *642*
analysis engine statistics, 859, 907
AND operator, 1048
anomaly detection, 658
anonymous access, **651**
anti-evasive techniques, 867
anti-replay
    ESP for, 153
    IPSec for, 415, 471
anti-spoofing. *See* IP spoofing

antisniffer tools, 1076
Application Launcher option, 1147
Application layer attacks
    in campus module, 1116, 1122
        characteristics of, 18, **1072**
    in corporate Internet module, 1120
application proxies, 225, **227–229**
Application Settings window, 923–924, *924*
applications
    IEV settings for, **923–924**, *924*
    in SAFE, **1088**
    vulnerabilities in, **640**
Applications window, *959*
Apply/Cancel field, 512
applying
    ACLs, **116–117**, **310–311**
    audit rules, **142–143**
    crypto maps, **180–182**, *181*
    inspection rules, **116–117**
Approve page, 1000, *1000*
Approver in Security Monitor, 1021
architectures
    for blocking, **814–818**, *815–816*, *818*
    IDC Management Center, **963–964**, *963*
    SAFE, **1082–1085**, *1083*, *1085*
    sensor, **728–732**, *731*
archival settings for IEV, **922–923**, *922*
Archive Events Of The Following Status
    setting, 923
Are You There (AYT) feature, 587
ARP
    proxy, **94**
    weaknesses in, **638–640**, *638–639*
ArpOperation parameter, 877
ASA (Adaptive Security Algorithm), **239–240**
Assign Rules to Filter screen, 562, *563*
Assigned status, event filters for, 913
Assignments tab, 456, *457*
asterisks (*) in regular expressions, 870
asymmetric encryption, 577
ATOMIC engines
    parameters for, **877–879**
    subengines in, **868**
atomic signatures in IDS, 135–136
Attack Details window, 934, *934*
Attack group for signatures, 885
attack guard command, 1150

attack guards
    AAA Flood Guard, **353–354**
    DNS Guard, **362**
    for DoS attacks, 1150
    IP Fragmentation Guard, **359–362**, *360*
    Mail Guard, **355**, **358–359**
    SYN Flood Guard, **354–355**
attack signatures
    classes of, 362–363
    event filters for, 910
    in IDS, 136
    for sensors, 675, 992
attacks, **632–633**. *See also* network security
    access. *See* access attacks
    application layer, 18, **1072**
    custom signatures for, 889
    DDoS, 224, 645, *645*, **1072–1073**
    DoS. *See* DoS (denial of service) attacks
    eavesdropping, **12–13**, **654**
    HTML, 19
    IP spoofing. *See* IP spoofing
    man-in-the-middle, 18, **1074**
    password, 18, **1076–1077**
    reconnaissance, **10–11**, **633–634**
    repudiation, 17
    rerouting, 17, **88–90**
    session hijacking, **16–17**
    Smurf, **17–18**, 643
    Trojan horses, 19, **1077**
    viruses, 19, **1078**
    WareZ, 16
attributes for remote access VPNs, **428–429**
Attributes Pushed In Client screen, 448, *449*
Audit Log report, 1012, 1054, *1056*
audit logs, pruning, 1008
audit rules
    applying, **142–143**
    creating, **141–142**
    default actions for, **139–141**
audit trails
    in CBAC, **108**
    purpose of, 15
audits
    external, **656–657**
    in IDS, **362–368**
AUS (Auto Update Server), **456–459**, *457*, 943

authentication, 15, 25–26, 1105
  in access attacks, 635–636
  certificate authorities, 197, 412
  CHAP, 31–32
  CSNT, 328–329
  IDM, 786–787, 787
  in IKE, 161–164
  in IOS-based firewalls, 1130–1131
  for IP spoofing, 1074
  MD5, 89–90
  methods of, 26–27
  on NAS, 39–41
  for packet sniffers, 1076
  PAP, 30–31
  in PIX Firewall, 331–333, 1136
  PPP callback, 32, 34–35
  protocol configuring for, 128–129
  in SAFE, 1087
  in Secure ACS, 54–55
  in security policies, 1079
  statistics for, 859
  strong, 650–651
  user databases for, 54–55
  in VPN 3002 Hardware Client, 516–517, *516–518*
  for VPN Concentrators, 547–548, *547*, 559–560, *560*
  for VPN software clients, 521–522, *522*
  Windows, 28
authentication, authorization, and accounting (AAA) services. *See* AAA security
authentication application for IDS, 730
Authentication attribute for groups, 555
authentication command
  for IKE, 171
  for remote site routers, 1158
Authentication Data field, 473
Authentication Database Configuration screen, 58, *58*, 325
Authentication Header (AH) protocol, 152, 471–473, *472*
Authentication Proxy
  in Cisco IOS Firewall, 103
  configuring, 132–133
  for IOS Firewall, 123–124, *124–125*
Authentication screen, 547–548, *547*

Authentication tab
  in Remote Access Network Design, 1147, *1148*
  for VPNs, 521–522, *522*
authority in security policies, 1079
authorization, 25
  in access control, 651
  configuring, 129–130
  in identity, 1105
  on NAS, 41–44
  on PIX Firewall, 333–334
  protocols for, 129–130
Authorization Type attribute, 555
Authorized Keys page, 791
Auto-Config service, 93
auto-initiation of VPN software clients, 529–531, *529*
auto mode for Catalyst switches, 759
Auto Refresh Parent View On Database Modifications settings, 924
auto-update device-id command, 456, 459
Auto Update feature, 837–840, *838*
Auto Update page, 838, *838*
auto-update poll period command, 457
Auto Update Server (AUS), 456–459, *457*, 943
auto-update server command, 457, 459
Auto Update Server tab, 457–459
automatic blocking, 831
Automatic IP Logging page, 990, *990*
automatic updates
  IDM for, 837–840, *838*
  for sensors, 692
  for VPN Concentrator clients, 568–571, *569–570*
autoUpgradeParams command, 839
AUX line type, 25
availability in network security, 655
AVVID, 1107–1108
axioms, SAFE, 1085–1089
AYT (Are You There) feature, 587

B

back-channel connections, 348
back doors, 640–641

BackOrifice application, 641
backslashes (\) in regular expressions, 871
backup files for sensor configuration, 726
backup servers in VPN Hardware Client
    configuring, **563–564**, *564*
    IPSec for, **515–516**
Bandwidth Management screen, 605–607, *606*
bars (|) in regular expressions, 871
base groups for VPN Concentrators, *550*
bastion hosts, 34
Before You Begin screen, *58*, *58*, *325*
begin local command, 43
BGP (Border Gateway Protocol), 89
bin directory, **729–730**
BIOS
    for PIX Firewall, **234**
    sensor revision requirements, **694–695**
Block action for signatures, 868
blocking, 813–814
    ACLs for, **820–821**, *821*
    architectures for, **814–818**, *815–816*, *818*
    blocking devices for, **826**
        configuring, **826–829**, *828*, **835–837**, **986–988**, *987–988*
        creating, **827**, *828*
        interfaces for, **828–829**, *829*
    CLI for, **832–837**, **852–853**
    considerations for, **818–819**
    critical systems in, **824–825**, *825*
    for IDM, 814
    in IDS, **670**, *671*
    logical devices, **825–827**, *826*
    manual, **831–832**, *832*, **850–853**, *851*
    master blocking sensors for, **830–831**, *831*
    networks and hosts, **985–986**, *986*
    process, **821–823**, *822*
    properties for, **823**, *823*, **833–835**, **984–985**, *985*
    requests for, 817
    and sensors, 717, **984–990**, *989*
Blocking Devices page, 827–828, *828*, 986, 987
Blocking Direction parameter, 828
blocking forwarding sensors, 817, 988
Blocking Interface parameter, 828
Blocking Length property, 984
Blocking Properties page, 823, *823*
Boolean operators, 1048
BOOTP service, **93**
Border Gateway Protocol (BGP), 89
boundaries
    for Event Viewer, 1042
    in network security, **647–650**, *649*
breaches of integrity, firewalls for, 224
bridge tables, 739
Brief Technical report, 1105
broadband access devices, 1143
broadcast frames, 740
browsers
    for Cisco Works VMS server, 947
    for IDM, 785
    for IEV, 923
brute force attacks, 18, 636, 1076
BruteForceCount parameter, 881
Brutus tool, 636
buffer overflow, 640
built-in signatures, 867, **992–994**, *993–994*
business continuity, **9–10**
By Dst Address filter function, 909
By Sensor Name filter function, 911, *912*
By Severity filter function, 908, *909*
By Signature Name filter function, 910, *911*
By Src Address filter function, 909, *910*
By Status filter function, **913**, *913*
By UTC Time filter function, 911, *912*

C

C (Country) information for certificates, 577
ca authenticate command, 412
ca configure command, 411
ca enroll command, 412
ca generate rsa key command, 261, 411, 429
ca identity command, 411
ca save all command, 261
ca zeroize rsa command, 414
cables in failover, 377
caches for IOS Firewall, **135**
callback, PPP, **32**, **34–35**
CAM tables, 739

campus access in security policies, 1079
campus module
   medium network design, **1120–1122**, *1121*
   small network design, **1115–1116**, *1115*
capture direction, 750–751
capturing traffic, **736–737**
   for 4200 series sensors, **737–742**, *738*, *741–742*
   for IDSM, **761–764**, *762–763*, *765*
      mls ip ids command, **774–776**
      SPAN for, **765–767**, *766*
      trunk traffic in, **776–777**, *777*
      VACLs for, **767–774**
      VLANs in, **778–779**
   for NM-CIDS, **779–780**, *780*
   RSPAN configuration for, **750–761**
      on CatOS, **758–761**, *758*
      on Cisco IOS, **753–758**, *754*
      configuring, **750–753**, *751*
      trunking for, **755–756**, *759–760*
   sensors for, **690**, **722–723**
   SPAN configuration for, **743–746**
      on CatOS, **749–750**, *749*, **765–766**, *766*
      on Cisco IOS, **746–749**, *747*, **766–767**
CAR (committed access rate), 1124–1125
carets (^) in regular expressions, 871
Carrier Sense Multiple Access with Collision Detection (CSMA/CD) algorithm, 738
CAs. *See* certificate authorities (CAs)
Cat6K Blocking Interface parameter, 828–829
cat6k-devices command, 836
Catalyst 6000 IDS Module, **674**
   accessing, **705–707**
   sensors for, **700–702**, *701*
CatOS, 774
   mls ip ids command on, **775**
   RSPAN on, **758–761**, *758*
   SPAN on, **749–750**, *749*, **765–766**, *766*
   VACLs on, **767–770**
   VLANs on, **777–779**
CatOS switches for FWSM, **244**
CBAC (context-based access control), **15**, **102**, **1128**, **1157**
   and ACLs, **103–105**, **116–117**
   audit trails and alerts in, **108**
   benefits of, **104**
   configuring, **107–108**, *107*
   global timeouts and thresholds in, **108–110**
   inspection rules for, 114–117
   PAM configuration for, **110–113**
   protocol support for, **106**
   testing and verifying, 117–119
CDP (Cisco Discovery Protocol), **96**
cells in Event Viewer, **1033**, 1041
central offices, VPNs for, **1098**
central policy protection (CPP), **587–588**
centralized protection policy (CPP), **571–573**, *573*
centralized protection servers, *573*
CEP (Certificate Enrollment Protocol), 163
certificate authorities (CAs), **192**, **410**
   authenticating, **197**, **412**
   communication properties for, **411**
   declaring, **194–196**
   deleting items for, **414**
   enrolling firewalls with, **410–413**
   identifying, **411**
   in IKE, 162–163, **198**, **410–414**
   in IPSec, **480–481**
      configuring, **198–205**, *199*
      verifying, 205
   NVRAM memory management for, **194**
   in PKI, *574*, *574*
   preparing for, **410**
   root, **196**
   showing information for, **413–414**
   support for, **193**
   verifying, 198
   viewing, 580, *581*
Certificate dialog box, 585–586, *586*
Certificate Enrollment Protocol (CEP), 163
Certificate Enrollment screens, 523–525, *524–525*
Certificate Import Wizard, 785
Certificate Information window, 905, *905*
Certificate Manager window, 580, *581*
Certificate option, 792
Certificate Request Syntax (CRS), 163
certificate revocation lists (CRLs)
   downloading, **412**

obtaining, 194
support for, 163
Certificate window, 785, 786
certificates
   in IDM, 785
   in IKE, **162–163**
   PKI for, **574–575**, *574*
   requesting, **197–198**
   for VPN Concentrators
      downloading, **579–580**
      generating, **578–579**, *578–579*
      installing, **580**, *580*, **583–586**, *584–586*
      requesting, **575–578**, *576–577*, **583–586**, *584–586*
      viewing, **580–582**, *581*
   for VPN software clients, **523–526**, *524–526*
   X.509, 651
Certificates tab, **523**, *524*
Challenge Handshake Authentication Protocol (CHAP), 15, 27, **31–32**
Change Admin Password screen, 951
Change Casuser Password screen, 951, *951*
change management in SAFE, 1089–1090
channels, alarm
   event filters for, **810–813**, *810–812*
   sensor system variables, **797–804**, *797*, *799–801*
CHAP (Challenge Handshake Authentication Protocol), 15, 27, **31–32**
character-mode access
   for authentication, 25
   in NAS, 35–36
Chargen attacks, 14
chargen service, 93
ChokeThreshold parameter, 876
Choose Completed Report page, 1013, *1013*, 1059, *1060*
Choose Destination Folder screen, 949, *950*
Choose Destination Location screen, 325
Choose The Actions page, 1008, *1009*, 1048, *1049*
CIC (Cisco Integrated Client), 572
cidcli application, 730
cidDump script, 843, *843*
cidwebserver application, 730

CIPS (Cisco Intrusion Prevention System), 814
Cisco 2600/2800/3600/3700/3800 IDS network modules, **702–704**, *703*, *707–708*
Cisco Discovery Protocol (CDP), **96**
Cisco Easy VPNs, **210–211**
   clients for, **213–216**, *213–215*
   Router and Security Device Manager for, **216–217**
   servers for, **211–213**, 215
Cisco IDS Event Viewer shortcut, 901
Cisco Integrated Client (CIC), **572**
Cisco Intrusion Prevention System (CIPS), 814
Cisco IOS
   mls ip ids command on, **776**
   RSPAN on, **753–758**, *754*
   SPAN on, **746–749**, *747*, **766–767**
   traffic capture support in, **774**
   VACLs on, **771–774**
   VLANs on, **778–779**
Cisco IOS Firewall, 102, **122–123**, 1102
   AAA configuration for, **128–132**
   AAA servers for, **125–128**
   Authentication Proxy for, **103**, **123–124**, *124–125*, **132–133**
   caches for, **135**
   CBAC for. *See* CBAC (context-based access control)
   in corporate Internet module, 1114, 1119
   IDS for, **103**, **135–136**
      audit rules for, **139–143**
      initializing, 137
      signatures for, **137–139**
      stopping, **145–146**
      verifying, **143–145**
   implementing, **1127–1134**
   and PIX sensors, **675–676**
   testing and verifying, **133–135**
Cisco PIX Device Manager 2.1 window, **395**, *396*
Cisco PIX Device Manager Information window, 394, *395*
Cisco Secure ACS. *See* ACS (Access Control Server)
Cisco Secure ACS 2.3 for Unix (CSU), **70–71**

Cisco Secure ACS Service Initiation window,
327
Cisco Secure IDS (CSIDS), 667. *See also* IDS
(intrusion detection system)
alarm display and logging in, **669**, *669*
Cisco Works VMS for. *See* Cisco Works
VMS
components of, **667–668**, *668*
features of, **668**, **671–672**
host platforms for, **678–681**
intrusion response in, **669–670**, *670–671*
management platforms for, **676–678**, *677*
monitoring. *See* Security Monitor
sensor platforms in, **672–676**
sensors in. *See* sensors
Cisco Secure Policy Manager (CSPM),
452–453, *452*, **1107**
Cisco Secure User Database, **328**
populating, **329**
for RADIUS, **74**, **77–78**
Cisco Security Agent, **679**
Cisco security portfolio, **1094**
AVVID, **1107–1108**
identity in, **1105–1107**
intrusion protection, **1102–1103**
secure connectivity, **1094–1095**
for central offices, **1098**
firewall-based, **1101–1102**
for regional offices, **1098**
for remote access, **1099–1101**
types of, **150–151**, **466–467**,
1095–1097, *1095–1096*
Secure Scanner, **1104–1105**
security management in, **1107**
Cisco sequences in crypto maps, **178**
Cisco View, **943**
Cisco Works VMS, **942**
client requirements for, **947**
Common Services for, **948–952**, *949–952*
components of, **942–943**
IDS Management Center and Security
Monitor Center for, **952–956**,
953–955
licensing, **960–961**, *961–962*
server requirements for, **944–946**
starting, **956–959**, *957–959*
users in, **959–960**

CiscoSecure ACS Network Access Server
Details screen, **59**, *59*
CiscoSecure ACS Server Installation screen,
63, *63*
Classes screen, **610**, *611*
clear command, **249**
clear crypto isakmp command, **184**
clear crypto sa command, **186**
clear floodguard command, **354**
clear fragment command, **362**
clear igmp command, **305**
clear ip audit configuration command, **145**
clear ip auth-proxy command, **135**
clear shun command, **369**
clear text, **1081**
clear trunk command, **777–778**
clearing IOS Firewall caches, **135**
CLI (command-line interface)
access methods in, **246–247**
Admin password for, **504–505**
for alarm channels
event filters, **812–813**
system variables, **802–804**
for Auto Update, **839–840**
for blocking, **832–837**, **852–853**
common commands
clear, **249**
clock set, **249**
copy, **250**
debug, **250–251**
enable, **251**
enable password, **251**
passwd, **251**
perfmon, **252**
reload, **252**
show checksum, **253**
show interface, **253–254**
show tech-support, **254**
shun, **254**
who, **254**
write, **255**
editing in, **248**
for events, **858–859**
IP address configuration for, **503–504**
IPSec group configuration for, **504**
modes in, **247–248**
for sensors
IP logs, **856–857**

statistics, 860–861
updates, 847–848
for signatures, 893–898
system information configuration for, 502
tunneling protocol configuration for, 502–503
for virtual sensor system variables, 802–804
for VPN 3002 Hardware Client, 501–505
for VPN Concentrators, 536–543
Client Config tab, 555
Client Configuration Parameters page, 555, 556
Client IP Address option, 614
Client Type property, 570
Client Update screen, 569, 569
clients
in AVVID, 1108
for Cisco Easy VPNs, 216
for Cisco Works VMS, 947
VPN. *See* VPN clients
clock command, 261–262
clock set command, 249, 410
clocks
for PIX Firewall, 261–262, 410
setting, 249, 410
synchronizing, 1081–1082
Clone Entry option, 1146
closed networks, 1068, *1069*
Closed status, event filters for, 913
clusters
configuring, 566
in load balancing, 565–566
CNs (Common Names) information for certificates, 576
Code Red worm, 872–873
collapsing events, 1035
Column Set parameter, 1030
columns and column sets in IEV, 916–920, 1036–1037
command and control
for IDS, 673
for sensors, 686
command-and-control ports
in IDSM, 762–764, *762*
in VLANs, 778–779

command-line interface. *See* CLI (command-line interface)
command modes for sensors, 713–715
commands command, 42
commit security acl command, 769–770
committed access rate (CAR), 1124–1125
Common Names (CNs) information for certificates, 576
Common Services
in Cisco Works VMS, 942–943, 948–952, *949–952*
in IDC Management Center, 963
communication command, 837
communication protocols for sensors, 904
communications settings
for blocking devices, 827
for certificate authorities, 411
for sensors, 690–691, *691*, 973–975, *974–975*
community strings, 1080–1081
comparison operators, 1048
compound signatures, 135–136
Concentrator File option, 622
Concentrator screen, 623, *623*
Concentrators, VPN. *See* VPN Concentrators
conduit command, 311
conduits
converting to ACLs, 311–312
for security, 8
confidentiality
in ESP, 152–153
IPSec for, 415, 471
in network security, 654–655, *654*
config-acc prompt, 802
config account, 617
CONFIG file, 620
CONFIG.BAK file, 620–621
config users, 512
config-vsc prompt, 809
configurable thresholds, 867
configuration files
reviewing, 657
swapping, 621, *621–622*
configuration manager, 667
configuration modes
in CLI, 248
for sensors, 713–715

Configuration page
    for IDC Management Center, 965
    for IDM, 789
    for Management Center, 454, *455*
    for sensors, 971, *971*
    for system variables, 804, *805*
configuration weaknesses, **7–9**
Configure Communication Properties screen, 955, *955*
confirm-action transmit command, 1126
Conformed Rate/Volume field, 607
Connection/Login Status screen, 517, *517–518*
Connection Setting screen, 521
Connection Shun parameter, 852
connection slots in PIX Firewall, 238
connection status of sensors, 906, **1029**, *1029*
connectionless integrity, 153
connections
    for Cisco Easy VPNs, 213, *214*
    to FWSM, **244–245**
    to untrusted networks, sensors for, 688
    for VPN clients, 521, *522*
        profiles for, **437–439**
        properties for, **523**, *523*
Connections page
    in Remote Access Network Design, 1147, *1148*
    for sensors, 1029, *1029*
    for VPN clients, 523, *523*
connectivity
    in Cisco security portfolio, **1094–1102**, *1095–1096*
    in SAFE, 1082
Console line type, 25
Console Notification report, 1012
console notifications events, 1010
console ports, 704
content-based signature implementation, 933
context-based access control. *See* CBAC (context-based access control)
context-based signature implementation, 933
Context Data Buffer dialog box, 1037–1038, *1038*
context information in Event Viewer, 1037
continuity, business, **9–10**
Control/Data field, 605

control information for VPN Concentrators, 604
converting conduits to ACLs, **311–312**
cookies for IDM, 785
copy command, **250**
copy current-config backup-config command, 726–727
copy iplog command, 856
copy system command, 198
copy tftp flash command, 392
corporate Internet module
    medium network design, **1118–1120**, *1118*
    small network design, **1112–1115**, *1113*
corporate networks, configuring, **33–34**, *33*
corporate security policies, **19–20**
correlation, event, 1019
Country (C) information for certificates, 577
CPP (central policy protection), **587–588**
CPP (centralized protection policy), **571–573**, *573*
CPU Utilization graph, 401–402, *401–402*
CPUs for PIX Firewall, **232**
Crack by Alec Muffet tool, 636
Create Host/Network screen, 445, *445*
Create New VPN Connection Entry screen, 213–214, *214*, 521–522, *522*
Create Shortcut option, 1146
critical resources, sensors for, 689
critical systems in blocking
    excluding, **824–825**, *825*
    identifying, **819**
crl optional command, 195, 201–202
crl query command, 196
CRLs (certificate revocation lists)
    downloading, **412**
    obtaining, 194
    support for, 163
CRS (Certificate Request Syntax), 163
crypto ACLs for IPSec, 415, *416*
crypto ca authentication command, 197
crypto ca certificate query command, 194
crypto ca enroll command, 197
crypto ca identity command, 194, 201–202
crypto ca isakmp enable command, 203–204
crypto ca trusted-root command, 196
crypto dynamic-map command, 430

crypto ipsec security-association lifetime
    command, 176–177, 418
crypto ipsec transform-set command
    for IPSec, 176, 204–205, 1133, 1151
    for PIX Firewall, 416, 418, 430, 1137
    for remote site routers, 1158
crypto isakmp enable command, 170
crypto isakmp identity command, 171
crypto isakmp key command, 172, 1133
crypto isakmp policy command
    for IKE, 170
    for IPSec, 1132
    for remote site routers, 1158
crypto key generate rsa command, 189, 200
crypto key pubkey-chain command, 190
crypto map command
    for IKE, 179–180
    for IPSec, 186, 419, 1133, 1151
    for remote site routers, 1158
    for Xauth, 426–427
crypto maps
    applying, **180–182**, *181*
    for IKE, **177–180**
    for IPSec, **419**
cryptographic images for sensor updates, 845
cryptography for packet sniffers, 1076
cryptosystems, **164**
CSAccupdate service, 56
CSACS for Windows server, 126
CSIDS (Cisco Secure IDS). *See* Cisco Secure
    IDS (CSIDS)
CSMA/CD (Carrier Sense Multiple Access
    with Collision Detection) algorithm, 738
CSNT
    administration for, **327–328**
    authenticating, **328–329**
    features of, **329–330**
    installing, **324–330**
    system requirements for, **327**
CSPM (Cisco Secure Policy Manager),
    452–453, *452*, 1107
CSU (Cisco Secure ACS 2.3 for Unix), 70–71
CSUtil.exe utility, **55**, 329
current-config.cfg file, 727
current version for sensor software, 724
Custom Installation option
    for Common Services, 949
    for IDS Management Center and Security
        Monitor Center, 954
Custom report in Secure Scanner, 1105
custom signatures, 671
    creating, **889–893**, *889–892*, **994–996**,
        995–996
    purpose of, 867
cut-through proxies, 324

D

Data Archival tab, 921–922, *922*
data collection in Secure Scanner, 1104
data confidentiality
    in ESP, 152–153
    IPSec for, 415, 471
    in network security, **654–655**, *654*
Data Encryption Standard (DES), 152–153
data in Secure Scanner
    analysis of, 1104
    presentation and navigation of,
        1104–1105
data information for VPN Concentrators,
    604
data manipulation
    in access attacks, 634
    preventing, **86–88**
data origin authentication, 153
Data Source Information dialog box,
    925–926, *925*
data sources
    for IEV database, **925–926**, *925*
    for IEV views, 916, 920
data transfer in IPSec, 156
database rules in IDS MC, **1007–1011**, *1007*,
    1009
Database Rules page, 1007–1008, *1007*
Database section for Event Viewer, 1042
databases
    Cisco Secure User Database, **328**
        populating, **329**
        for RADIUS, **74**, **77–78**
    IEV
        administering, **924–925**
        Alarm Aggregation table, **926–928**,
            927–928

Alarm Information Dialog table, **930**, *930*
data source information for, **925–926**, *925*
Drill Down Dialog table, **930–931**, *931–932*
Expanded Details Dialog table, **929**, *929*
graphs for, **935–937**, *936–937*
Realtime Dashboard, **931–935**, *933–935*
Security Monitor, **1056**
daytime service, 93
DDoS (distributed DoS) attacks
  characteristics of, **1072–1073**
  firewalls for, 224
  operation of, **645**, *645*
debug aaa accounting command, 49
debug aaa authentication command, 47–48, 79–80
debug aaa authorization command, 48–49
debug crypto ipsec command, 426
debug crypto isakmp command, 426
debug igmp command, 305
debug ip audit command, 144–145
debug ip auth-proxy command, 134
debug mfwd command, 305
debug packet command, 250–251
debug rip command, 250, 300
debug tacacs command, 78–80
debugging IPSec, **426**
declaring certificate authorities, **194–196**
default actions for audit rules, **139–141**
Default Audit Log Pruning rule, 1008
default-domain parameter, 429
default forwarded UDP protocols, **97–98**
Default Preferences page, 1044
Default Pruning rule, 1008
default routes for PIX Firewall, **299–300**
default settings, unsecured, 8
Default Syslog Pruning rule, 1008
defense in depth protection, 229, 666
Delete Entry option, 1146
Delete Row From Database option, 928
Deleted status, event filters for, 913
deleting
  CA-related items, **414**
  Event Viewer events, **1040**

demilitarized zones (DMZs)
  dirty, 34
  for firewalls, **227–229**, *228–229*
  with NAT, **290–298**
  outbound connections from, 295
  as security zones, 648
  system variables for, **798**, *799*
denial of service attacks. *See* DoS (denial of service) attacks
deny ip any command, 116
Deobfuscate parameter, 880
deploying
  sensor configurations, **1001–1003**
  VPN clients, **433–434**
Deployment tab
  in IDC Management Center, 965
  for sensors, 998, *999*
DES (Data Encryption Standard), 152–154
description command
  for crypto maps, 179
  for object groups, 320
Description parameter, 966
design in SAFE. *See* SAFE
desirable mode for Catalyst switches, 755
DestAddrs values, 811
destination addresses
  for blocking, 851
  event filters for, 909
destination ports
  for blocking, 852
  for RSPAN, 751
  for SPAN, 743
destination sessions in RSPAN, **757–758**, 761
Details tab, **586**, *586*
device drivers as points of failure, 373
Device Manager, IDS, **676–677**, *677*
Device Manager drawer, 958
Device Properties dialog box, 903–904, *903*
Device Status dialog box, 906–907, *907*
Device Type parameter, 827
devices
  blocking, **825–827**, **986–988**, *987–988*
  for IDM, 814
  Security Monitor for, **1023–1028**
  sensor status of, **906–907**, *907*
Devices page
  in Auto Update Server, 456

in IDC Management Center, 965
in Management Center, 454
in Security Monitor, 1022, 1024, *1025*
DH (Diffie-Hellman) Key Agreement
in IKE, 155, **160–161**
in IPSec, **477–478**, *477–478*
dhcpd command, **264–265**
Diagnostics page, 841, *842*
dial-in servers, 1118
dictionary attacks, 636
Diffie, Whitfield, 477
Diffie-Hellman (DH) Key Agreement
in IKE, 155, **160–161**
in IPSec, **477–478**, *477–478*
digital certificates. *See* certificates
Direction parameter
for custom signatures, 891
for filterable event logs, 615
for signature engines, 881
Directors in IDS systems, 667
dirty DMZs, 34
Disabled Accounts reports, 70
disaster recovery plans, **10**
discard service, 93
Discards field, 606
Discover Settings option, 970
distributed denial-of-service (DDoS) attacks
characteristics of, **1072–1073**
firewalls for, 224
operation of, **645**, *645*
DMZ system variables, **798**, *799*
DMZs (demilitarized zones)
dirty, 34
for firewalls, **227–229**, *228–229*
with NAT, **290–298**
outbound connections from, **295**
as security zones, 648
system variables for, **798**, *799*
DN Field attribute, *555*
DNS (Domain Name Services) queries, 1075
DNS Guard, **362**
DNS screen, 511–512, *511*
dns-server parameter, 429
DNS servers, 1114, 1118
DNS settings
for Security Monitor, 1056

for VPN 3002 Hardware Client, **511–512**, *511–512*
dollar signs ($) in regular expressions, 871
Domain field, 511
domain-name command
for certificate authorities, 410
for PIX Firewall, 261, **263**
Domain Name Services (DNS) queries, 1075
domain names
for certificate authorities, 194
for RSA-encrypted nonces, **188–189**
DoS (denial of service) attacks, **11**, **14–15**, 641
in corporate Internet module, 1114, 1119
DDoS attacks
characteristics of, **1072–1073**
firewalls for, 224
operation of, **645**, *645*
detecting and monitoring, 15
fighting, **90–91**
firewalls for, 224
host resource starvation in, **643–644**, *644*
network resource overload in, **641–643**, *642*
out-of-bounds attacks, **644**
preventing, **652–653**, **1127**
in Remote Access Network Design, 1150
dots (.) in regular expressions, 870
down interfaces, failover for, **381–383**
downloadable ACLs, **337–338**
downloading
concentrator certificates, **579–580**
CRLs, **412**
sensor updates, **1003**
Drill Down Dialog table, 924, **930–931**, *931–932*
drops with IDS, 136
DstPort parameter, 878–880
DTP (Dynamic Trunking Protocol), 755
dual-homed gateways, **225**
Duration parameter, 848
dynamic addressing, **427–428**
dynamic NAT, **274–275**
dynamic routing for PIX Firewall, **299–300**
dynamic sequences in crypto maps, 178
Dynamic Trunking Protocol (DTP), 755

E

e-mail bonds, 15
e-mail servers, **1053**, *1053*
eavesdropping, **12–13**
    encryption for, 654
    preventing, **85–86**, *85*
echo service, **92–93**
edge routers, 1119
Edit Parameter page, 996, *997*
Edit Signature(s) page, 993, *994*
editing in CLI, **248**
egress interfaces, 180
egress ports, 743
EIGRP (Enhanced Internet Gateway Routing Protocol), 89
Empty circle icon for signatures, 887
enable-acl-logging command, 833
Enable ACL Logging property, 984
Enable Client Update screen, *569*, *569*
enable command, 48, **251**
enable default command, 41
enable password command, **251**
enable password globalnet command, 36
Enable Password option, 825
enable password routersim command, 36
Enable screen, 510, *510*
enable secret command, 77
enable secret globalnet command, 36
Enable Secret Password screen, 62, *62*
Enable Time Schedule For Archiving Events setting, 923
Enabled option
    for built-in signatures, 993
    for custom signatures, 891
    for DNS configuration, 511
    for signature engines, 874
Encapsulating Security Payload (ESP) protocol
    components of, **152–153**
    for IPSec, **473–474**, *474*
encapsulation dot1q keywords, 748
encapsulation in IPSec, **157–159**, *157–159*
encapsulation isl keywords, 748
encapsulation ppp command, 30–31
encapsulation replicate keywords, 748
encrypted nonces in IKE, **162**
encryption
    for certificates, 577
    for clusters, 566
    for eavesdropping and session replay, 86
    for IDS evasion, **664**
    in IPSec, **153–154**, **476–477**
    for passwords, **37–38**
    for PIX Firewall, 236
encryption command
    for IKE, 171
    for remote site routers, 1158
endpoints in VPNs, 654, *654*
Engine option, 993
engines for signatures
    listing, 993
    parameters for, **873–883**
    types of, **868–871**
Engines group, 884
Enhanced Internet Gateway Routing Protocol (EIGRP), 89
enrolling firewalls, **410–413**
enrollment mode command, 195
enrollment retry count command, 195
enrollment retry period command, 195
enrollment url command, 195, **201–202**
Enter Blocking Device page, 986, *987*
Enter Blocking Device Interfaces page, 986, *988*
Enter Device Information page, 1024, *1026*
Enter Filter page, 980, *981*, 983, *984*
Enter Filter Address page, 983, *983*
Enter IDS MC Server Information page, 1026, *1027*
Enter Job Properties page, 1001, *1002*
Enter Master Blocking Sensor page, 989, *989*
Enter Network Password window, 394, *395*
Enter Sensor Information page, 968, *969*
Enter Signatures page, 980, *982*
Entries screen, 570, *570*
entry points for blocking, 819
equipment weaknesses, 7
Erase User Password option, 1146
error messages for IPSec, **426**

ESP (Encapsulating Security Payload) protocol
  components of, **152–153**
  for IPSec, **473–474**, *474*
established keyword, 347
etc directory, 730
/etc/password file, 15
Ethereal utility
  for IEV, **923–924**
  for IP logs, **854–856**, *855*
Ethernet link status LED, 602
Ettercap tool, 637
evasive techniques, **664–665**
Event Class option, 614
Event Filters page, **810–812**, *810*
event horizons, 659
event manager, 667
Event retrieval option, 936
Event Rules page, 1045, *1046*, 1052, *1052*
event server statistics, 907
Event Start Time property
  for Event Viewer, 1030
  for sensors, 904
Event Statistics dialog box, 1039, *1039*
Event Stop Time parameter, 1031
Event Type parameter, 1030
Event Viewer
  columns in, **1036–1037**
  events in
    collapsing, **1035**
    deleting, **1040**
    expanding, **1034–1035**
    graphing, **1039–1040**, *1040–1041*
    viewing, **1037–1039**, *1038–1039*
  expansion boundaries in, **1035–1036**
  IDS. *See* IEV (IDS Event Viewer)
  preferences for, **1041–1044**
  realtime, 1018
  refreshing data, **1037**
  starting, **1030–1033**, *1031–1032*
  suspending and resuming, **1037**
EventAction parameter, 874
EventFilter command, 812
events
  filters for, **810–813**, *810–812*
  monitoring, **857–859**, *857–858*
  in Security Monitor
    actions for, **1048–1049**
    correlation of, 1019
    filters for, **1047–1048**, *1047*
    notification of, 1019
    reporting, 1019
    rules for, **1045**, *1046*
    thresholds and intervals for, **1050–1052**, *1051–1052*
    viewing. *See* Event Viewer
  for VPN Concentrators, **609–610**, *610*
    classes for, **610–611**, *611*
    logging, **96**
Events page, 857, *857*
Events/Page option, 615
Events screen, 609–611
EventServer statistics, 859
EventStore statistics, 859
Exception values, 811
exceptions for blocking, 819
Exclude alarms based on sensor option, 936
Exclude alerts based on severity option, 936
ExcludeDstl parameter, 879
exec mode access in NAS, **35–38**
exec-timeout command, 97
Executive report, 1105
Expanded Details Dialog table, 924, **929**, *929*
expanding events, **1034–1035**
expansion boundaries, **1035–1036**
Expansion module insertion status LED, 602
Expansion module run status LED, 602
expertise of hackers, **631**
Explanation Of Advanced Options Configuration screen, 60, *60*
Explanation Of CiscoSecure ACS Network Access Server Details screen, 59, *59*
Explanation Of Network Access Server Configuration screen, 62, *62*
explicitly deny access model, 649
explicitly permit access model, 649
exploitation
  in campus module, 1116, 1122
  in corporate Internet module, 1115, 1120
  trust, **1077**, *1078*
exploits, **632–633**

EXPN command, 358
Express Installation for Common Services, 949
expression metacharacters, **869–873**
extended authentication (Xauth)
    in IKE, 164
    in remote access VPNs, **426–427**
Extended Client Authentication screen, 448, *448*
external audits, *656–657*
external communication for IDS, 731
external networks, 799
external threats, *5*, **632**, 1071
External User Databases screen, 68–69, *68*
extranets
    as security zones, 648
    VPNs for, 151, 467, **1095**, *1095*

F

Failed Attempts reports, 70
failover
    configuring, **386–387**, *387*
    features of, 377
    licenses for, 236
    monitoring, **381–384**
    nonstateful, 388
    operation of, **378–381**, *379*
    for replication, **384–385**
    requirements for, 378
    stateful, **385**, *386*, **388**
failover command, 386–387
failover active command, 390
failover ip address command, 388
failover lan command, 381, 388–389
failover link command, 388
failover poll command, 390
failover replication command, 388
false negatives in IDSs, *659*, 1089
false positives in IDSs, *659*, 1089
Fan status LED, 602
fastEthernet router, 747
fault-tolerance, 372
    points of failure in, **372–375**
    strategies for, **376–377**

file management for VPN Concentrators, **620–622**, *621–622*
File Management screen, 620
file servers in campus module, 1116, 1121
File Transfer Protocol (FTP)
    for Auto Update, 837
    in corporate Internet module, 1114, 1118
    on PIX Firewall, 335, **345–348**
    for sensor updates, 847
file types for sensor updates, 846
FileName parameter, 881
Files screen, 620, *621*
filter activex command, 314
Filter Properties dialog box, 908, *909*
Filter Source Addresses page, 980, *982*, 983
filter url command, 313–314
Filterable Event Log, 614–615, *615*
filters
    for alarm channels, **810–813**, *810–812*
    for events, **810–813**, *810–812*, **1047–1048**, *1047*
    for IEV, **908–914**, *909–914*, 918, 920
    in IOS-based firewalls, **1128–1130**
    for IP spoofing, **819**
    in IPSec, **490**
    in PIX Firewall, **312–315**, 1135
    for sensors, 911, **980–983**, *981–984*
    URL, **312–315**
    for VPN Concentrators, **561–563**, *562–563*
Filters command, 812–813
Filters page, 980, *981*
finger command, 93
Finger utility, 634
fingerprints for sensors, 717
FireAll parameter, 876–877
FireOnce parameter, 876–877
firewall-based VPNs, **1101–1102**
firewall module command, 242
Firewall Services Module (FWSM), **241**
    CatOS switches for, 244
    configuring, **241–242**, **245–246**
    connecting to, **244–245**
    IOS switches for, **242–244**
Firewall tab, 588, *588*
firewall vlan-group command, 242

firewalls, **222**
  Cisco IOS. *See* Cisco IOS Firewall
  in corporate Internet module, 1114, 1119
  dual-homed gateways for, **225**
  for IPSec, **586–590**, *588–590*
  location of, **223**
  packet-filtering, **225–226**
  PIX. *See* PIX Firewall
  policies for, **590**, *590*
  for policy enforcement, **223**
  in Remote Access Network Design, 1143, **1149–1151**, *1149*
  sensors with, 691, *691*, 1103
  stateful, **226–229**
    for IPSec, **587**
    in Remote Access Network Design, 1147
    setting up, **571–573**, *573*
  systems for, **223**
  technology combinations for, **227–229**, *228–229*
  for threats, **224**
  trusted networks in, **223**
fixup protocol command, **344–345**
fixup protocol ftp command, **346–348**
fixup protocol h323 command, 352
fixup protocol rsh command, 348
fixup protocol rtsp command, **350–351**
fixup protocol smtp command, 359
fixup protocol sqlnet command, 349
flash file system, **232–234**
FLOOD engines
  parameters for, **879**
  subengines in, **868**
floodguard command, 354
flooding
  for IDS evasion, **664**
  SYN flood attacks, 14, 90, **643–644**, *644*
Flow field, 606
forced logins for IDM, 788
format flash string, 890, 898, 996
forwarded UDP protocols, **97–98**
forwarding sensors, **830–831**, *831*
  4200 series sensors, **673–674**, **695–696**
    accessing, **705**
    capturing traffic for, **737–742**, *738, 741–742*

4215 sensors, **696–697**, *697*
4235, 4250, and 4250-XL sensors, **698–700**, *698–699*
FQDN (Fully Qualified Domain Name) information for certificates, 577
fraggle attacks, **17–18**, 643
fragment command, 361
fragment forwarding, disabling, 653
fragment reassembly, **978–979**
fragmentation
  for IDS evasion, **664**
  IP, **807–808**, *807*
  IP Fragmentation Guard for, **359–362**, *360*
FTP (File Transfer Protocol)
  for Auto Update, 837
  in corporate Internet module, 1114, 1118
  on PIX Firewall, 335, **345–348**
  for sensor updates, 847
ftpd daemon, 345
Full circle icon for signatures, 887
full-duplex operation, 739
Full Technical report, 1105
Fully Qualified Domain Name (FQDN) information for certificates, 577
functions, one-way, 650
FWSM (Firewall Services Module), **241**
  CatOS switches for, **244**
  configuring, **241–242**, **245–246**
  connecting to, **244–245**
  IOS switches for, **242–244**

G

Gap parameter, 879
general packet sniffers, 1075
General screen, **609–610**, *610*
general statistics for VPN Concentrators, **603–607**, *604–606*
General tab
  for certificates, 585
  for Remote Access Network Design, 1147, *1147*
  for tunnels, 583
  for VPN Concentrators, **552–553**, *553*

general-usage keys, 189
Generate page, 998, 999
Generate Host Certificate page, 792–793, 793
Generate Key page, 792
Generic Routing Encapsulation (GRE) protocol
    tunnels in, 180
    for VPNs, 151
Get/Save/Clear Log option, 615
global addresses in NAT, 237, 273–274
global command
    in NAT, 278–281, 279
    in PAT, 286–287, 289–290
Global Configuration mode for sensors, 714
global profiles, 433–437
global timeouts in CBAC, 108–110
GlobalSummarize parameter, 876
graphs
    for databases, 935–937, 936–937
    in Event Viewer, 1039–1040, 1040–1041
GRE (Generic Routing Encapsulation) protocol
    tunnels in, 180
    for VPNs, 151
grid pane for Event Viewer, 1032
group command
    for IKE, 171
    for remote site routers, 1158
Group field, 607
group interfaces for sensors, 722
Group Lock attribute, 555
Group Name parameter, 966
group names
    in IDC Management Center, 966
    for VPN Concentrators, 548, 548
Group option for filterable event logs, 615
Group Setup screen
    for ACS, 65, 65
    for TACACS+, 126–127, 127
grouping styles
    for IEV views, 914–915, 918
    for sensors, 991
groups
    in ACS, 65, 65
    for Cisco Easy VPNs, 214, 214
    object, 319
        configuring, 320–323
        working with, 323–324
    signature, 884
    in TACACS+, 126–127, 127
    for VPN clients, 447
    for VPN Concentrators
        client properties for, 555–557, 556
        creating, 551, 552
        IPSec and Remote Access properties for, 553–555, 554
        names of, 548, 548
        properties for, 552–553, 553
        setting up, 550–551
Groups screen, 551, 552
GRUB boot loader, 708, 709

H

H.323 protocol, 352
hackers
    characteristics of, 631–632
    threats from, 1069, 1070
half-duplex operation, 739
Half-full circle icon for signatures, 887
hard disk requirements for Cisco Works VMS, 945–947
hardware as points of failure, 373–374
Hardware Client. See VPN 3002 Hardware Client
hardware requirements for Cisco Works VMS, 944–947
HasBadOption parameter, 878
hasBadPort parameter, 880
hashed command, 171
Hashed Message Authentication Code (HMAC), 153–154
hashing algorithms in IPSec, 153–154, 476
Hellman, Martin, 477
hello packets, 383–384
HELP command, 356, 358
Help Desk in Security Monitor, 1021
Help On IDS Event Viewer shortcut, 901

helper applications for Cisco Works VMS
 server, 945–946
heuristics in signature-based intrusion
 detection, 660
HIDS (host-intrusion detection system)
 advantages and disadvantages, **661–663**,
  662
 in corporate Internet module, 1114, 1119
 implementing, **1123**
 platforms for, **678–681**
 sensors in, 1103
High severity level, event filters for, 908
highly reliable systems, 373
hijacked sessions, **16–17**
HijackMaxOldAck parameter, 882
History page, 998, *999*
HMAC (Hashed Message Authentication
 Code), 153–154
Home drawer for Cisco Works VMS, 958
honey pots, 798
host-based intrusion protection, 1102
host.conf file, 731
host DoS mitigation
 in IOS-based firewalls, **1130**
 in PIX Firewall, **1134–1135**
host IDs, 956
host-intrusion detection system (HIDS)
 advantages and disadvantages, **661–663**,
  662
 in corporate Internet module, 1114, 1119
 implementing, **1123**
 platforms for, **678–681**
 sensors in, 1103
Host Manual Blocks page, 831, *832*, 850,
 851
host resource starvation, **643–644**, *644*
hostname command
 for certificate authorities, 410
 for PIX Firewall, 261, **263**
 for RSA, 188
 for sensors, 714
Hostname Resolution dialog box, 1038,
 1039
hostnames and hostname resolution
 for certificate authorities, 194

for Event Viewer, **1038**
for PIX Firewall, 261, **263**
for pre-shared keys, 409
for RSA, **188**
for sensors, 714
hosts
 bastion, 34
 blocking, **985–986**, *986*
 in campus module, 1116, 1121
 in corporate networks, 34
 for IDS Management Center and Security
  Monitor Center, 956
 for PIX Firewall, 397, 399, *399*
 in SAFE, **1087**
 for sensors, 666, 714–716, **973**
 signature exclusions by, **139**
 SSH, **717–719**
 statistics on, 859
Hosts/Networks tab, 397, *399*
hot spares, 564
hourFreqUpgrade command, 840
htdocs directory, 730
HTML attacks, 19
HTTP and HTTP servers
 in corporate Internet module, 1114, 1118
 disabling, **93**
 enabling, **131–132**
 on PIX Firewall, **335–337**
 for sensor updates, 847
http server enable command, 394
HTTPS, 847
hubs for 4200 series sensors, **737–739**, *738*
hw-module module command, 244

I

ICMP (Internet Control Message Protocol)
 for DoS attacks, 1150
 rate-limiting for, **652–653**
 for reconnaissance attacks, 633, 1150
 types, 321–322
 unreachable messages in, **94**
icmp command, 1150
icmp-object command, 321

icmp permit command, 1135
IcmpCode parameter, 878
IcmpID parameter, 878
IcmpSeq parameter, 878
IcmpType parameter, 878–879, 882
ID option for built-in signatures, 992
IDC Management Center, **962**
    architecture of, **963–964**, *963*
    sensors in. *See* sensors
    starting, **964–965**
identification
    certificate authorities, **411**
    critical systems for blocking, **819**
    event rules, **1045**, *1046*
    networks, **647, 976–977**, *977*
    ports, **977–978**, *978*
    in security policies, 1079
    sensor settings for, **973**, *974*
Identify The Rule page, 1045, *1046*
identity
    in Cisco security portfolio, 1094, 1105–1107
    in IKE, **171–174**, *172*
    in SAFE, 1082
identity certificates
    purpose of, *575*
    viewing, 580, *581*
identity NAT, **282–284**
Identity tab, 583
idle-time parameter, 429
IDM (IDS Device Manager), **676–677**, *677*, **784**
    accessing, **785–788**, *786–787*
    alarm channel event filters for, **810–813**, *810–812*
    for Auto Update, **837–840**, *838*
    for blocking. *See* blocking
    components and system requirements, **784–785**
    for IP logging, **848–850**, *849*
    monitoring, 854
        events, **857–859**, *857–858*
        IP logs, **854–857**, *855*
        statistics, **859–861**, *860*
    navigating, **788–789**, *788*
for sensors
    access, 704
    configuration for, **790–796**, *790, 792–796*
    system variables, **797–810**, *797, 799–801, 805–806*
    updates, **845–848**, *847*
for signatures, **796**
    configuring, **884–886**, *884–887*
    custom, **889–893**, *889–892*
    enabling and disabling, 887
    tuning, **888–889**, *889*
support information for, **841–844**, *842–844*
for system control, **853**, *854*
IDS (intrusion detection system), **135–136, 630, 658, 1102–1103**
    and attack types. *See* attacks
    in Cisco IOS Firewall, **103, 135–136**
        audit rules for, **139–143**
        initializing, 137
        signatures for, **137–139**
        stopping, **145–146**
        verifying, **143–145**
    Cisco Secure IDS
        alarm display and logging in, **669**, *669*
        Cisco Works VMS for. *See* Cisco Works VMS
        components of, **667–668**, *668*
        features of, **668, 671–672**
        host platforms for, **678–681**
        intrusion response in, **669–670**, *670–671*
        management platforms for, **676–678**, *677*
        monitoring. *See* Security Monitor
        sensor platforms in, **672–676**
        sensors in. *See* sensors
    evasive techniques, **664–665**
    Event Viewer. *See* IEV (IDS Event Viewer)
    and hacker characteristics, **631–632**
    IP audits in, **362–368**
    location of, **661–663**, *662–663*
    and network security. *See* network security

in SAFE, **1088–1089**
shunning in, **369**
signatures. *See* signatures
traffic capturing in. *See* capturing traffic
triggers, **658–661**
IDS Device Manager. *See* IDM (IDS Device Manager)
IDS Event Viewer. *See* IEV (IDS Event Viewer)
IDS Management Center, **677–678**, *679*
   for Cisco Works VMS, **952–956**, *953–955*
   database rules for, **1007–1011**, *1007*, *1009*
   reports in, **1011–1013**, *1012–1013*
   system configuration settings for, **1006–1007**, *1006*
ids-sensor interfaces, 707
IDS Sensor Versions report, 1012
ids-service-module monitoring command, 780
IDS Top Alarms report, 1059, *1061*
IDSM, **700–702**, *701*
   in Cisco security portfolio, 1103
   traffic capture for, 737–738, **761–764**, *762–763*, *765*
      mls ip ids command, **774–776**
      SPAN for, **765–767**, *766*
      trunk traffic in, **776–777**, *777*
      VACLs for, **767–774**
      VLANs in, **778–779**
IEV (IDS Event Viewer), **676–677**, *677*, **898–899**, *899*
   accessing, **901**, *902*
   application settings for, **923–924**, *924*
   data archival settings for, **922–923**, *922*
   database for
      administering, **924–925**
      Alarm Aggregation table, **926–928**, *927–928*
      Alarm Information Dialog table, **930**, *930*
      data source information for, **925–926**, *925*
      Drill Down Dialog table, **930–931**, *931–932*
      Expanded Details Dialog table, **929**, *929*

   graphs for, **935–937**, *936–937*
   Realtime Dashboard, **931–935**, *933–935*
   filters for, **908–913**, *909–914*
   installing, **900–901**, *900–901*
   refresh cycle settings for, **921–922**
   sensors for, **903–907**, *903*, *906–907*
   views for, **914–920**, *919–920*
igmp access-group command, 305
igmp forward interface command, 305
igmp join-group command, 305
igmp max-groups command, 305
igmp query-level command, 305
IKE (Internet Key Exchange), **159–160**
   access lists for, **177**
   authentication in, **161–164**
   certificate authorities for, 162–163, 198, 410–414
   configuring, **169–175**, *172*
   crypto maps for
      applying, **180–182**, *181*
      creating, **177–180**
   Diffie-Hellman Key Agreement with, **160–161**
   enabling, 170, 407
   identity in, **171–174**, *172*
   in IPSec, **478–479**
   mode configuration for, 163–164
   phase 1, **155**, 482, **486–487**
   phase 2, **156**, *156*, 483, **487–488**
   policies for
      configuring, **407–408**, *408*
      creating, **170–171**
      verifying, **174–175**, **422–423**
   pre-shared keys for, **162**, **409**
   preparing for, **169**
   for VPNs, 173–174, **407–414**, *408*
IKE Mode Config, **427–428**
IKE Peer Identity Validation attribute, 554
IKE Policy screen, 443, *443*
Images tab, 456
Import Entry option, 1146
importing sensor information, **1026–1028**, *1027–1028*
Improve phase in Security Wheel, 1090, *1091*
in-band management, 1089
in keyword for ACLs, 310

IN system variable, 798, 800–801, *801*
inbound packets in PIX Firewall, **239**
Incident handling procedures, 1079
incomplete sessions, 110
info signatures in IDS, 136
Informational severity level, event filters for, 908
informational signature class, 362–363
ingress ports for SPAN, 743
ingress vlan keywords, 748
initial contacts for Cisco Easy VPNs, 212
initializing sensors, **710–713**
initiation
   IPSec, **155**
   of VPN software clients, **529–531**, *529*
inline IDSs, 666
innovation in AVVID, 1108
input access-group command, 1126
inside global addresses, 274
inside interface for PIX Firewall, 235, 237
inside local addresses, 274
inside routers, 1119
inspection rules
   applying, **116–117**
   for CBAC, **114–117**
instructions boxes
   in IDC Management Center, 965
   in IDM, *788*, *789*
int command, 41
integration in AVVID, 1108
Integration Utility, 943
integrity
   connectionless, 153
   firewalls for, 224
   IPSec for, 415, 471
   in network security, 655
intelligence in AVVID, 1108
intelligent network services, 1108
interactive authentication, **516–517**, *516–518*
interesting traffic in IPSec, **485–486**, *485*
interface command
   for access, 87
   for Global Configuration mode, 714
   for PIX Firewall, 269–270
   for SNMP packets, 92

Interface Configuration Mode for sensors, 714
Interface Configuration screen
   for ACS, 67, *67*
   for TACACS+, 126, *126*
Interface field, 607
interface group 0 command, 723
interface keyword for PAT, 289
interface sensing command, 723
Interface Statistics screen, 600, *601*
interface vlan command, 242
interfaces
   for ACS, 67, *67*
   for blocking devices, **828–829**, *829*
   for PIX Firewall
      configuring, 267–272
      IP addresses for, 271–272
      MTUs for, **272**
      support for, **234–235**
   statistics for, 600, *601*
   for TACACS+, 126, *126*
   for VPN Concentrators, **545**, *545*
Interfaces pages, 976, *976*
internal communication for IDS, 731
internal networks
   defined, 799
   for sensors, **976–977**, *977*
internal threats, **5**, **632**, 1071
Internet access in security policies, 1079
Internet business integrators, 1108
Internet business solutions, 1108
internet connections, sensors for, 689
Internet Control Message Protocol (ICMP)
   for DoS attacks, 1150
   rate-limiting for, **652–653**
   for reconnaissance attacks, 633, 1150
   types, 321–322
   unreachable messages in, **94**
Internet Key Exchange. *See* IKE (Internet Key Exchange)
Internet middleware, 1108
Internet Security Association and Key Management Protocol (ISAKMP), 159, 409
Internet services, mismanaged, **8**
internets as security zones, 648

interoperability, 1108
intervals, event, **1050–1052**, *1051–1052*
intranets
   as security zones, 648
   sensors for, 689
   VPNs, 151, 466, **469**, 1095, *1096*
intrusion detection and protection, 630
   in Cisco security portfolio, 1094
   intrusion detection systems. *See* IDS (intrusion detection system)
   in IOS-based firewalls, 1130
   sensor settings for, **975–983**, *976–979*, *981–984*
intrusion-detection module command, 773–774, 779
intrusion-detection-module keyword, 766
IOS. *See* Cisco IOS
IOS Firewall. *See* Cisco IOS Firewall
IOS switches for FWSM, **242–244**
ip access-group command
   for ACLs, 131
   for inspection rules, 116–117
   for ISP routers, 1124
ip access list command, 117, 771
ip address command, 271–272
ip address pppoe command, 317
IP addresses
   for blocking devices, 827–829
   for CLI, 503–504
   for clusters, 566
   for IDS Management Center and Security Monitor Center, 956
   for IP logging, 848
   lack of, **88**
   for master blocking sensors, 830
   for PIX Firewall interface, **271–272**
   for sensors, 710, 904, 968
   translating. *See* NAT (Network Address Translation); PAT (Port Address Translation)
ip audit command, 139–140, 142–143
ip audit attack command, 140
ip audit attack action command, 140–141, 362–363
ip audit info command, 140, 362
ip audit interface command, 363–364
ip audit name command, 141–142, 363

ip audit notify command, 137
ip audit signature command, 138–139, 364
IP audits in IDS, **362–368**
ip auth-proxy command, 132–133
ip authentication key-chain command, 90
ip authentication mode command, 90
IP blocking. *See* blocking
ip domain-name command, 189
ip forward-protocol udp command, 97
IP fragment forwarding, 653
IP fragment reassembly, **978–979**
IP fragmentation, **807–808**, *807*
IP Fragmentation Guard, **359–362**, *360*
ip helper-address command, 97
ip host-name command, 189
ip http authentication command, 131–132
ip http server command, 93, 131
ip inspect command, 1157
ip inspect alert-off command, 108
ip inspect IOSFW command, 116
ip inspect max-incomplete command, 110
ip inspect name command, 114–115, 1128–1130
ip inspect one-minute command, 109–110
ip inspect tcp command, 109–110
ip inspect udp command, 109
ip local pool command, 427
IP logging
   IDM for, **848–850**, *849*
   in IDS, **670**
   monitoring, **854–857**, *855*
IP Logging page, 849–850, *849*
IP Logs page, 854, *855*
ip port-map command, 110–113
IP protocols
   in access attacks, 637
   weaknesses in, **1073–1074**
IP source routing, **94**
IP spoofing, **16**, 1073
   in campus module, 1121
   in corporate Internet module, 1115, 1120
   countermeasures for, **653**
   filtering for, **819**
   IOS-based firewalls for, 1130
   PIX Firewall for, **1135**
   in Remote Access Network Design, 1150
IP/TV, RTSP with, 351

ip verify reverse-path command, 1135, 1150
iplog command, 850
iplog-status command, 856
IPOption parameter, 878
IPReassembleMaxFrags system variable, 805, 810
IPSec, 150–152, 168–169, 415, 470, *470*
    ACLs for, 415, *416*, 423–424, 491
    Authentication Header protocol for, 152, 471–473, *472*
    certificate authorities in. *See* certificate authorities (CAs)
    certificates in. *See* certificates
    configuring, 175–184, *181*, 186–192
    crypto maps for, 419
    data transfer in, 156
    debugging, 426
    Diffie-Hellman key exchange in, 477–478, *477–478*
    encapsulation in, 157–159, *157–159*
    encryption in, 153–154, 476–477
    error and status messages for, 426
    ESP for, 473–474, *474*
    filtering problems in, 490
    firewall feature set for, 586–590, *588–590*
    group configuration, 504
    hashing in, 153–154, 476
    IKE in. *See* IKE (Internet Key Exchange)
    interesting traffic in, 485–486, *485*
    in IOS-based firewalls, 1131–1134
    LAN-to-LAN, 566–568, *567*
    NAT problems in, 491
    operation of, 154, 484–485
    in PIX Firewall, 1136
    pre-shared keys in, 479
    preparing for, 169
    process initiation in, 155
    RSA-encrypted nonces in, 187–192, 480
    RSA signatures in, 479–480
    on sample corporate network, 182–184
    SAs for, 176–177, 424–425, 483–484, *484*
    security protocols, 152–153
    services of, 471
    support for, 152
    task flow in, 488–489, *489*
    testing and verifying, 184–186

    traffic delay problems in, 490
    transforms, 152–154, 176, 416–418, *417*, 423–424, 481–483, *482*
    troubleshooting, 490–491
    Tunnel mode and Transport mode in, 474–476, *475*
    tunnels in, 470, *470*
        lifetime of, 418, 423–424
        in Remote Access Network Design, 1145, 1151
        termination of, 157
    verifying, 422–426
    for VPN 3002 Hardware Client, 508, *509*
    for VPN Concentrator groups, 553–555, *554*
IPSec and Remote Access Parameters page, 553–555, *554*
IPSec Group Configuration screen, 548, *548*
IPSec-isakmp sequences, 178
IPSec-manual sequences, 178
IPSec over TCP, 515–516, *515*, 594, *595*
IPSec over UDP, 592–594, *593*
IPSec over UDP attribute, 556
IPSec over UDP Port attribute, 556
IPSec SA attribute, 554, 583
IPSec screen, 515, *515*
IPSec tab, 583
IPSec Traffic Selector screen, 443–446, *444*, 446
ipsec transform-set command, 430
IPSecdlr.ini file, 526
ISAKMP (Internet Security Association and Key Management Protocol), 159, 409
isakmp client configuration address-pool local name command, 427
isakmp enable command
    for IKE, 407
    for IPSec tunnels, 1151
isakmp identity command, 409
isakmp key command
    for dynamic addressing, 427–428
    for IKE, 409
    for IPSec tunnels, 1151
    in PIX Firewall, 1137
    for remote access VPN clients, 430
isakmp peer command, 427–428

isakmp policy command, 429
    for IKE, 408
    for IPSec tunnels, 1151
    in PIX Firewall, 1136
IsBruteForce parameter, 881
isInvalidDataPacket parameter, 880
isLoki parameter, 882
isModLoki parameter, 882
isp account, 617
ISP routers, **1123–1127**
IsPASV parameter, 880
isRFCl918 parameter, 878
Issue Action(s) After threshold, 1050
IsSweep parameter, 881
IsValidPacket parameter, 881

J

Java blocking, 15
jobs for Management Center, 456

K

Kerberos authentication, **29**
key assets in networks and required access, 647
key-chain command, 90
key devices, **1123**
    IOS-based firewalls, **1127–1134**
    ISP routers, **1123–1127**
    NIDS and HIDS, **1123**
    PIX Firewall, **1134–1138**
    in Remote Access Network Design, 1143–1144
Key Size value for certificates, 577
keyboards for sensor access, 704
KeyLength parameter, 881
keys
    for certificate authorities, 194, **411**
    pre-shared
        configuring, **171–174**, *172*
        in IKE, **162**, **409**
        in IPSec, **479**
    for RSA-encrypted nonces, **188–192**
    for TACACS+, **130**

keyword substitutions
    for event actions, 1049
    for mail notification, 1008, 1010–1011
kiddie-scripts, 1069
Known Host Keys page, 792

L

L (Locality) information for certificates, 576
L0phtcrack tool, 636
L2/L3/L4 protocol signatures, 885
    event filters for, 910
    for sensors, 992
L2F (Layer 2 Forwarding) protocol, 151
L2TP (Layer 2 Tunneling Protocol), 151
LAN-based failover configuration, **388–389**
LAN Extension mode, **509–510**, *509–510*
LAN-to-LAN IPSec, **566–568**, *567*
LAN-to-LAN sessions, 607
land.c attacks, 15
Launch Event Viewer page, 1030–1031, *1031*
Layer 2 Forwarding (L2F) protocol, 151
layer 2 switches
    in campus module, 1116, 1121
    in corporate Internet module, 1114, 1119
Layer 2 Tunneling Protocol (L2TP), 151
layer 3 switches, 1121
Layer 7 filtering, **1128–1130**
LC3 tool, 636
LEAP (Lightweight and Efficient Application Protocol), 530
LED Status screen, 600, *601*
LEDs
    for IDSM-2 line cards, 701–702, *701*
    for NM-CIDS module, 703–704, *703*
    for VPN Concentrator status, **600–602**, *601*
lib directory, 730
License Information page, 961, *962*
licensing
    Cisco Works VMS, **960–961**, *961–962*
    for failover, 378
    for PIX Firewall, **236**
lifetime command, 171

lifetimes
    SA, **176–177**
    tunnel, **418**, **423–424**
Lightweight and Efficient Application
    Protocol (LEAP), 530
line authentication, **25**
line command
    in NAS, 41
    in TACACS+, 72
line con command, 26, 77
List Files access right, 618
Live Event Log, 614
load balancing
    for fault tolerance, **376**
    in VPN 3002 Hardware Client, **518–519**,
        520
    for VPN Concentrators, **564–566**
Load Balancing screen, *519*, *520*
local addresses in NAT, 237, **273–274**
local engines, parameters for, 873, **877–883**
local file systems for sensor updates, 847
local logs, **614–615**, *615*
Locality (L) information for certificates, *576*
location
    of hackers, **632**
    of IDS, **661–663**, *662–663*
Lock-and Key feature, 15
Log action for signatures, 867
log directory, 730
logApp application, 730
Logged-in User reports, 70
Logger statistics, 859
logging. *See* logs and logging
logging command, **266**
logging authentication command, 1158
logging on
    to IDM, 788
    to sensors, **708–710**, *709*
    to Syslog servers, **612**, *612*, **614**, *614*
logging on command, 1150
logging trap debugging command, 96
logging traps, **609–611**, *609–611*
Logical Device, parameter, 827
logical devices
    blocking, **825–827**, *826*
    for IDM, **835**
Logical Devices page, **825–826**, *826*

login command, 26, **39–41**, 72
login authentication command, 77
logs and logging
    ACL, 833
    events, **96**
    IDM for, **848–850**, *849*
    in IDS, **669–670**, *669*
    local, **614–615**, *615*
    monitoring, **854–857**, *855*
    in SAFE, 1086
    for sensors, **990–991**, *990*
    setting up, **613**
    Syslog servers, **612**, *612*, **614**, *614*
    viewing, **613**
Loki application, 641
longurl-deny command, 314
longurl-truncate command, 314
Low severity level, event filters for, 908

M

MAC addresses, **739–740**
Mail Guard, **355**, **358–359**
mail notifications, **1008**, **1010–1011**
main mode in IKE, 1**55**, **487**
mainApp application, 730
Maintenance Operation Protocol (MOP),
    95
malicious activity
    detecting, 659
    preventing, **86–88**
man-in-the-middle attacks, **18**
    in corporate Internet module, 1120
    damage from, **1074**
managed devices for IDM, 814
Management Center, PIX, **453–456**,
    454–455
Management Center for Cisco Security
    Agents, **678**, 943
Management Center for Firewalls, 943
Management Center for IDS Sensors, 943
Management Center for Security, 943
Management Center for VPN Routers, 943
Management Connection drawer, *958*
management hosts in campus module, **1116**,
    1121

Management Information Bases (SNMP MIBs), 609
management platforms for IDS, **676–678**, *677*
management-ports for VLANs, 779
management protocols for network security, **1079–1082**
management sessions for VPN Concentrators, 607
Management Sessions screen, 620, *620*
manual blocking, **850–853**, *851*
manual IP logging, **848–850**, *849*
mapping
    PAM, **110–113**
    in Secure Scanner, 1104
    VACLs to VLANs, 769
maps
    access, **771–772**
    crypto
        applying, **180–182**, *181*
        for IKE, **177–180**
        for IPSec, **419**
    topology, 647
Mask parameter, 879, 882
masquerade attacks, **16**
Master Blocking Sensor page, 831, *831*, **988**, *989*
master blocking sensors
    configuring, **830–831**, *831*, **988–990**, *989*
    purpose of, 817
master-blocking-sensors command, 833
master engines, parameters for, **873–877**
match address command, 179
match-address command, 1158
match ip address command, 772
MaxBytes parameter, 880
Maximum ACL Entries setting, 984
maximum events setting, 936
Maximum Number Of Archived Files setting, 923
Maximum Number Of Compressed Archived Files setting, 923
Maximum Number Of Events In setting, 923
maximum transfer units (MTUs)
    in IP fragmentation, 807–808
    for PIX Firewall interface, **272**
MaxProto parameter, 878

MaxTTL parameter, 874
MC (Management Center), PIX, **453–456**, *454–455*
MD5 authentication, 89–90
medium network design, **1117–1118**, *1117*
    campus module, **1120–1122**, *1121*
    corporate Internet module, **1118–1120**, *1118*
    WAN module, **1122–1123**, *1122*
Medium severity level, event filters for, 908
memory
    for certificate authorities, **194**
    for Cisco Works VMS, 945–947
    for IDS, 136
    for PIX Firewall, **232**
    for sensors, 694
    for VACLs, 769
Memory Utilization graph, 401–402, *401–402*
menu bars in Event Viewer, 1032
messages
    in Cisco Works VMS, 959
    in IPSec, **426**
metacharacters, **869–873**
MinHits parameter, 875–876
MinProto parameter, 878
MinUDPLength parameter, 879
mis account, 617
missing hello packets, **383–384**
misuse detection, 659
mls ip ids command, **774–776**
mode command, 176
modes
    in CLI, **247–248**
    in IKE, 163–164
    for signature engines, 880
Modify Config access right, 618
Modify screen for firewalls, 591, *591*
Monitor Center for Security, 943
Monitor mode in CLI, **247**
Monitor phase in Security Wheel, 1090, *1091*
monitor session command
    for RSPAN, 756–757
    for SPAN, 747–748
monitor session source command, 766–767
Monitor tab, 1022
monitor users, 512

monitoring
    failover, 381–384
    IDM, 854
        events, 857–859, *857–858*
        IP logs, 854–857, *855*
        statistics, 859–861, *860*
    IDS. *See* Security Monitor
    in ISDM, 764
    network security, 655–656
    security news, 657
    VPN Concentrators. *See* VPN
        Concentrators
monitoring interface
    in IDS, 673
    for sensors, 686
Monitoring tab, 399, *400*
monitors for sensor access, 704
MOP (Maintenance Operation Protocol), 95
more current-config command, 725–726,
    843
mroute command, 305
MS-CHAP authentication, 32
MSFCs (multilayer switching feature cards),
    774
mtu command, 272
MTUs (maximum transfer units)
    in IP fragmentation, 807–808
    for PIX Firewall interface, 272
multicast frames, 740
multicast interface command, 304
multicast route caching, 95
multicast routing, 304–305
multilayer switching feature cards (MSFCs),
    774
multimedia support for PIX Firewall,
    350–352
multiple interfaces, NAT on, 290–298, *292*,
    295
multiple sensors and multiple perimeter
    devices architecture, 817–818, *818*

N

Nagle TCP congestion algorithm, 95
name command
    for object groups, 321

    for PIX Firewall, 264
    for pre-shared keys, 409
named-key command, 191
nameif command, 244, 267–269
names
    domain
        for certificate authorities, 194
        for RSA-encrypted nonces, 188–189
    for logical devices, 825
    for PIX Firewall interface, 267–269
    for sensors, 710, 904, 970
    for views, 918
names command, 264
NAS (Network Access Server)
    AAA on
        accounting, 44–46
        authentication, 39–41
        authorization, 41–44
        enabling, 38–39
        troubleshooting, 47–49
    exec mode access in, 35–38
    verifying, 46–47
NAS Configuration screen, 63, *63*
NAT (Network Address Translation)
    ACLs for, 284–286
    for blocking devices, 827
    configuring, 277–278
    consequences of, 276
    global and local addresses in, 273–274
    identity, 282–284
    in IPSec, 491
    on multiple interfaces, 290–298, *292*, *295*
    nat and global commands, 278–281,
        279
    for PIX Firewall, 237–239
    RTSP with, 351
    in security, 276–277
    for sensors, 968
    static and dynamic, 274–275
    static command, 282
nat command
    in NAT, 278–281, *279*
    in PAT, 289–290
    for SYN Flood Guard, 354
NAT Transparency screen, 594, *595*
NAT-Transversal, 594, *595*
native mode software, 706

Navigation tree for Cisco Works VMS, 958, *958*
nesting object groups, 321–322
Network Access Server. *See* NAS (Network Access Server)
Network Access Server Configuration screen, 61, *61*, 326
Network Administrator, 1021
network-based intrusion detection, **662–663**, *663*
network-based intrusion protection, 1102
network command, 44–45, 89
Network Configuration screen, 66, *66*
network equipment
  misconfigured, **8–9**
  weaknesses in, 7
network ingress filtering, **819**
network-intrusion detection system (NIDS)
  in campus module, 1121
  in corporate Internet module, 1119
  implementing, **1123**
  sensors in, 1103
network media considerations for sensors, **686**
network module for IDS, **675**
network-object command, 321
network-object host command, 320
Network Operator role, 1021
Network page for IDM sensors, 791, *792*
network platforms in AVVID, 1108
network protocols for custom signatures, 889
network reconnaissance, **1074–1075**, 1115, 1120
network resource overload, **641–643**, *642*
network security, **646–647**, *646*
  access control, 650–652
  attacks in. *See* attacks
  boundaries in, **647–650**, *649*
  categories of, 1071–1072
  for confidential data, **654–655**, *654*
  configuration management, 1080
  improving, 657–658
  IP weaknesses in, **1073–1074**
  management protocols for, **1079–1082**
  monitoring, **655–656**
  need for, **1068–1071**, *1069–1070*
  network identification in, **647**
  packet sniffers, **1075–1076**
  policies for, **1079**
  port redirection, **1077**
  SAFE. *See* SAFE
  testing, **656–657**
  trust exploitation in, **1077**, *1078*
  vulnerabilities in, **653**
network security database (NSDB), 927–928, *928*, 1038
network sensors in IDS systems, 665
network snooping, **12–13**
network taps, **740–741**, *742*
Network Time Protocol (NTP)
  for IDM, **794–795**
  for PIX Firewall, **262–263**
  for synchronization, **1081–1082**
network topology maps, 647
NetworkAccess statistics, 859
networkParams command, 715–716
networks
  blocking, **985–986**, *986*
  closed and open, 1068, *1069*
  identification of, 647, **976–977**, *977*
  mapping, 1104
  in SAFE, **1088**
  signature exclusions by, **139**
  VPNs. *See* VPNs (virtual private networks)
Never Block Addresses page, 825, *825*, 985, *986*
never-shun-hosts command, 833
never-shun-networks command, 833
new-model command, 76
New status, event filters for, 913
Next Header field
  in Authentication Header, 472
  in Encapsulating Security Payload, 474
NIDS (network-intrusion detection system)
  in campus module, 1121
  in corporate Internet module, 1119
  implementing, **1123**
  sensors in, 1103
NM-CIDS module
  support for, **702–704**, *703*
  for traffic capture, 737, **779–780**, *780*
Nmap tool, 634
no access-list compiled command, 310

no ca identity command, 414
no ca save all command, 414
no cdp enable command, 96
no cdp run command, 96
no crypto isakmp enable command, 170
no failover command, 387–388
no fixup protocol command, 345
no ip audit signature command, 138, 364
no ip boot server command, 93
no ip http server command, 93
no ip inspect command, 119
no ip inspect audit-trail command, 108
no ip mroute-cache command, 95
no ip proxy-arp command, 94
no ip redirects command, 94
no ip source-route command, 94
no ip unreachables command, 94
no isakmp enable command, 407
no mop enabled command, 95
no rsa1Keys command, 719
no sensing-interface command, 723
no service config command, 93
no service finger command, 92
no service pad command, 95
no service password-encryption command, 38
no service tcp-small-servers command, 92
no service tcp-udp-servers command, 92
no shun command, 369
no snmp-server command, 96
no switchport command, 776
no tacacs-server host command, 130
noise for IDS evasion, 664
nonces, RSA-encrypted
    in IKE, **162**
    in IPSec, **187–192**, 480
    keys for, **188–192**
None access right, 618
nonrepudiation, 17
nonstateful failover, 388
NOOP command, 356–358
NOT operator, 1048
notifications
    in IDS MC, **1008, 1010–1011**
    in Security Monitor, 1019
NSDB (network security database), 927–928, 928, 1038

NSDB folder, 924
NSDB Link option, 934
Nslookup, 633
NTP (Network Time Protocol)
    for IDM, **794–795**
    for PIX Firewall, **262–263**
    for synchronization, **1081–1082**
ntp command, **262–263**
ntp trusted-key command, 263
Number of Bytes parameter, 848
Number of Packets parameter, 848
NVRAM memory management, **194**

O

O (Organizations) information for certificates, 576
OAKLEY protocol, 159
obfuscation for IDS evasion, 665
object bar in IDM, 788, 789
object-group command, 320–321, 323
object groups, **319**
    configuring, **320–323**
    working with, **323–324**
Object Selector bar, 971
Octets/Packets field, 605
oem.ini file, 216, 528
one-time passwords (OTPs), 27, 650
one-way functions, 650
open networks, 1068, 1069
Open Shortest Path First (OSPF) protocol, 89
operating systems
    CatOS. See CatOS
    for Cisco Works VMS, 944, 946–947
    IOS. See Cisco IOS
    weaknesses in, 6
operator accounts for sensors, 719
optional parameters for signature engines, 874
optionalAutoUpgrade command, 839
options bar
    in IDC Management Center, 964
    in IDM, 788, 789
OR operator, 1048
organization IDs and names for IDS Management Center and Security Monitor Center, 956

organization politics, 9
Organizational Unit (OU) information for certificates, 576
Organizations (O) information for certificates, 576
origin authentication, 415, 471
OS signatures, 885
  event filters for, 910
  for sensors, 992
OSPF (Open Shortest Path First) protocol, 89
Other events criteria, 857
OTPs (one-time passwords), 27, 650
OU (Organizational Unit) information for certificates, 576
out-of-band management, 1089
out-of-bounds attacks, **644**
OUT system variable, 798, 800
outbound connections from DMZs, **295**
outbound packets in PIX Firewall, **238–239**
outside global addresses, 274
outside interface for PIX Firewall, 235, 237
outside local addresses, 274
overengineering, 376–377
overflow, buffer, 640
oversubscription with SPAN, 743

P

packet assembler/disassembler (PAD) service, 95
packet-filtering firewalls, **225–226**, 1128–1130
packet-filtering FTP, ACLs for, **347**
packet fragmentation and reassembly, 14
packet-mode access in NAS, 35–36
packet sniffers, **12–13, 1075–1076**
  in campus module, 1116, 1122
  in corporate Internet module, 1115, 1120
packets, in PIX Firewall, **238–239, 298–299**
  dynamic, **299–300**
  multicast, **304–305**
  static, **301–304**, *301*
PAD (packet assembler/disassembler) service, 95
Pad Length field, 474

Padding field, 474
page area for IDM, *788*, 789
PAKs (Product Authorization Keys), 960–961
PAM (Port-to-Application Mapping), **110–113**
PAP (Password Authentication Protocol), 27, 30–31
paralyzing process, 681
parentheses () in regular expressions, 871
passive IDSs, 666
Passive-mode FTP, **347**
passive monitoring, 656
passwd command, 251
Password Authentication Protocol (PAP), 27, 30–31
password keyword for sensors, 720
passwordPresent parameter, 880
passwords
  attacks on, **18, 636–637, 1076–1077**
    in campus module, 1121
    in corporate Internet module, 1115, 1119
  in authentication. *See* authentication
  in CHAP, 31
  easily guessed, 7–8
  encrypting, 37–38
  for IDS Management Center and Security Monitor Center, 954
  for logical devices, 825–826
  in NAS, 36
  one-time, 27, 650
  in PAP, 30
  for PDM, 394, *395*
  for PIX Firewall, 335
  for PPPoE, 316
  in Remote Access Network Design, 1146–1147
  for sensors, 830, 904, 970
  for system accounts, **7–8**
  in TACACS+, 73
  for VPN clients, 447, 512, 517
  for VPN groups, *559*
PAT (Port Address Translation), **275–276**, 592
  configuring, **286–290**, *288*
  in security, **276–277**

verifying, **290**
for VPN 3002 Hardware Client, **509–510**, *509–510*
PAT screen, **509**, *510*
path bar
in IDC Management Center, **964**, *965*
in IDM, **788**, *789*
pattern matching, **660**
Pause function for Realtime Dashboard, **932**
payload inspection types, **889**
Payload Length field, **472**
.pcf files, **216**, **433**, **526–527**
PDM (PIX Device Manager), **390–391**
operating requirements for, **391–392**
for PIX Firewalls, **394–402**, *395–398*
preparing for, **392–394**
for VPNs, **439–440**, *440–441*
remote access, **446–450**, *447–451*
site-to-site VPNs, **441–446**, *441–446*
pdm history enable command, **394**
PDM VPN tab, **439–440**, *440–441*
Peaks parameter, **879**
Peer IP field, **605**
peers
IPSec, **155**
for pre-shared keys, **409**
Pending page, **997**, *998*
penetration in Cisco Security Agent, **680**
Perfect Forward Secrecy (PFS), **488**
perfmon command, **252**
performance
with IDS, **136**
with sensors, **685–686**, **689**
in split tunneling, **558**
perimeter problems, **84**
DoS attacks, **90–91**
eavesdropping and session replay, **85–86**, *85*
IP addresses, lack of, **88**
network services, **92–98**
rerouting attacks, **88–90**
unauthorized access, data manipulation, and malicious destruction, **86–88**
perimeter security
in Cisco security portfolio, **1094**
firewalls for, **1101–1102**
in SAFE, **1082**

periods (.) in regular expressions, **870**
permit command, **337**
permit ip any command, **127**, **822–823**
permit ip host command, **823**
permit tcp any command, **116**, **127**
permit udp command, **116**
persistence in Cisco Security Agent, **680**
personal firewalls, **222**
Personal tab, **585**
pessimistic security models, **230**
PFC memory for VACLs, **769**
PFCs (policy feature cards), **764**
PFS (Perfect Forward Secrecy), **488**
physical access in access attacks, **635**
physical interfaces for VPN Concentrators, **545**, *545*
Ping of Death attacks, **14**
Ping screen, **624**, *624*
Ping sweeps, **1075**
Ping tool, **633**
pinging devices, **624**, *624*
pivoting in Secure Scanner, **1104**
PIX (Private Internet Exchange), **34**
PIX Device Manager (PDM), **390–391**
operating requirements for, **391–392**
for PIX Firewalls, **394–402**, *395–398*
preparing for, **392–394**
for VPNs, **439–440**, *440*
remote access, **446–450**, *447–451*
site-to-site VPNs, **441–446**, *441–446*
pix-devices command, **836**
PIX Firewall, **222**, **1134–1138**
AAA services for
accounting, **334**
authentication, **331–333**
authorization, **333–334**
implementing, **330–331**
Secure ACS for, **324–330**
ACLs for
applying, **310–311**
converting conduits to, **311–312**, *312*
creating, **309–310**
downloadable, **337–338**
Adaptive Security Algorithm and security levels in, **239–240**
attack guards for
AAA Flood Guard, **353–354**

DNS Guard, 362
IP Fragmentation Guard, 359–362, *360*
Mail Guard, 355, 358–359
SYN Flood Guard, 354–355
BIOS for, 234
CLI for, 246–255
  access methods, 246–447
  commands in, 249–255
  editing in, 248
  modes, 247–248
components of, 231–232
configuration preparation for, 258–259
CPUs for, 232
failover in. *See* failover
features of, 230
Firewall Services Module. *See* Firewall Services Module (FWSM)
flash file system for, 232–234
FTP with, 335, 345–348
interfaces for
  configuring, 267–272
  IP addresses for, 271–272
  MTUs for, 272
  support for, 234–235
licensed features for, 236
multimedia support for, 350–352
NAT and PAT for. *See* NAT (Network Address Translation); PAT (Port Address Translation)
object groups for, 319–324
packet processing in, 238–239
PDM for. *See* PDM (PIX Device Manager)
points of failure in, 374
PPPoE for, 315–319
product line of, 235–236
protocol handling by, 342–345
RAM for, 232
remote access commands for, 259–266
Remote Shell with, 348
routing for, 239, 298–299
  dynamic, 299–300
  multicast, 304–305
  static, 301–304, *301*
SQL*NET with, 349
system images for, 233
URL filtering for, 312–315

virtual HTTP and telnet on, 335–337
VPNs with. *See* VPNs (virtual private networks)
PIX Management Center, 453–456, *454–455*
PKCS (Public-Key Cryptography Standards), 163
PKI (Public Key Infrastructure), 163, 574–575, *574*
playback hacking, CHAP for, 31
plus signs (+) in regular expressions, 871
Point-to-Point Protocol over Ethernet (PPPoE), 315–316
  enabling, 317–318
  usernames and passwords for, 316
  verifying, 318–319
Point-to-Point Tunneling Protocol (PPTP), 151, 604–605, *605*
points of failure, 372–375
policies, 19–20, 648
  for firewalls, 590, *590*
  for IKE
    configuring, 407–408, *408*
    creating, 170–171
    verifying, 174–175, 422–423
  for network security, 1079
  in split tunneling, 558
  weaknesses in, 9–10
policy enforcement, firewalls for, 223
policy feature cards (PFCs), 764
Policy Management screen, 509, *509*
politics, 9
poll-interval failover, 389–390
poor configuration, access attacks from, 640
POP3 servers, 1116, 1120
populating
  Cisco Secure User Database, 329
  user databases, 55–56
Port Address Translation (PAT), 275–276, 592
  configuring, 286–290, *288*
  in security, 276–277
  verifying, 290
  for VPN 3002 Hardware Client, 509–510, *509–510*
Port Mapping page, 977, *978*
port-object command, 321

port redirection, **1077**
    in campus module, 1116, 1122
    in corporate Internet module, 1115, 1120
    in PAT, 288
port scans, 1075
Port-to-Application Mapping (PAM), 110–113
PortRange parameter, 882–883
ports
    for blocking, 851–852
    for clusters, 566
    for custom signatures, 889
    for master blocking sensors, 830
    for RSPAN, 750–751
    for sensor access, 704
    for sensors, 710, 904, **977–978**, *978*
    for SPAN, 743–744, *744*
    for VLANs, **778–779**
Ports system variables, 804
PortsInclude parameter, 882
post-acl-name command, 837
Post-block ACL Name parameter, 828
post-block ACLs, 820
Post-block VACL Name parameter, 829
PostOffice protocol, 668
PostOffice settings, **1054**
power loss, failover for, 384
Power screen, 600, *601*
Power supplies LED for VPN Concentrator, 602
ppp authentication command, 30–31
ppp authentication chap command, 41, 77
PPP callback, **32, 34–35**
ppp callback accept command, 35
ppp encapsulation command, 41
PPPoE (Point-to-Point Protocol over Ethernet), **315–316**
    enabling, **317–318**
    usernames and passwords for, **316**
    verifying, **318–319**
PPTP (Point-to-Point Tunneling Protocol), 151, 604–605, *605*
pre-acl-name command, 837
Pre-block ACL Name parameter, 828
pre-block ACLs, 820
Pre-block VACL Name parameter, 829

pre-shared keys
    configuring, **171–174**, *172*
    in IKE, **162**, 409
    in IPSec, **479**
Preferences dialog box, 1041–1044, *1042*
prevention in IDS systems, 665
Primary DNS Server field, 511
primary units in PIX Firewall, 380
print servers, 1116, 1121
priority for clusters, 566
privacy violations, firewalls for, 224
private interface for VPN 3002 Hardware Client, 507, *508*
Private Interface screen, 507, *508*
Private Internet Exchange (PIX), 34
private IP addresses, 8
private keys
    for certificate authorities, 194
    for certificates, 577
    for RSA-encrypted nonces, **188–190**
private strings, 96
privilege escalation, **634–635**
privilege service keywords, 720
Privileged EXEC mode for sensors, **713**
Privileged mode in CLI, **247–248**
probing in Cisco Security Agent, 680
Product Authorization Keys (PAKs), 960–961
production licenses, 960–961
products, unsecured default settings in, 8
profile-based intrusion detection, **658–659**
profiles for VPN clients
    connection, **437–439**
    global, **433–437**
promiscuous mode, 739
propagation, 680
Properties option, 1146
protected parameters for signature engines, 873
protection suites, 407
protocol analysis, **660**
Protocol parameter
    for blocking, 852
    for custom signatures, 891
protocols
    for CBAC, **106**

IPSec, **152–153**
    PIX Firewall support for, **342–345**
    as points of failure, 374
    weaknesses in, **637–640**, *638–639*
Protocols screen, 608
proxy ARP, **94**
proxy servers, 225, **227–229**
pruning, 1008
public interface for VPN 3002 Hardware
    Client, 507, *508*
Public Interface screen, 507, *508*
Public-Key Cryptography Standards (PKCS),
    163
Public Key Infrastructure (PKI), 163,
    574–575, *574*
public keys
    for certificate authorities, 194
    for certificates, 577
    for RSA-encrypted nonces, **188–190**
public strings, 96

Q

query url command, 195
QuerySrcPortS3 parameter, 880
QueryValue parameter, 880
questions marks (?) in regular expressions,
    871
Quick Configuration Interfaces screen, 545,
    545
Quick Configuration mode for VPN
    Concentrators, **543–549**, *544–549*
Quick Configuration utility, **505–513**,
    506–514, *536–543*

R

r commands in Remote Shell, 348
RADIUS (Remote Authentication Dial-In
    User Service), **28–29**
    corporate network example, **75–77**, *75*
    database configuration for, **74**, **77–78**
    vs. TACACS+, **71**
RADIUS Accounting reports, 70

radius command, 41
radius-server key command, 77
RAM for PIX Firewall, **232**
RAs (registration authorities), 194,
    574–575
rate-limit command, 1125–1126
rate-limiting
    ICMP, **652–653**
    for ISP routers, 1125–1126
Rate parameter for signature engines, 879
RDEP (Remote Desktop Exchange Protocol),
    668
RDEP properties, 975, *975*
RDEP Properties page, 975, *975*
RDT (Real Data Transport), 350
reaction in IDS systems, 665
Read Files access right, 618
Read/Write Files access right, 618
Ready To Install The Program screen, 953
Real Data Transport (RDT), 350
real-time alerts logs, 15
Real-Time Streaming Protocol (RTSP),
    350–351
RealPlayer, RTSP with, **351**
Realtime Dashboard, **931–935**, *933–935*
Realtime Event Viewer, 1018
Realtime Graph window, 937, *937*
realtime graphs for IEV, 935, **937**, *937*
reassembly options for sensors, **978–980**,
    979
Reassembly Options page, 978–979, *979*
rebooting sensors, **727–728**
reconnaissance, 10–11, 633–634,
    1074–1075, 1115, 1120
Reconnect function, 932
redirect messages, 94
redirection, **1077**
    in campus module, 1116, 1122
    in corporate Internet module, 1115, 1120
    in PAT, 288
redundancy for fault tolerance, **376**
refresh cycle settings for IEV, **921–922**, *921*
RegexString parameter, 881, 891, 898
regional offices, **1098**
registration authorities (RAs), 194, 574–575
regular expression metacharacters, **869–873**
reload command, 252

remote access
    in NAS, 36
    in PIX Firewall, **259–266**
    in security policies, 1079
    as security zones, 648
    sensors for, 689
    VPNs for, **1099–1101**
Remote Access Client screen, 446, *447*
Remote Access Network Design, **1142–1143**, *1143*
    firewall option for, **1149–1151**, *1149*
    key devices in, **1143–1144**
    routers in, **1156–1158**, *1156*
    software access option in, **1144–1147**, *1145–1148*
    VPN hardware client in, **1152–1155**, *1152–1155*
Remote Access page, 791
Remote Access properties, **553–555**, *554*
remote-access sessions, 607
remote access VPNs, 150, **426**, **466**, **469**, 1096, *1096*
    attributes for, **428–429**
    commands for, **429–431**
    dynamic addressing in, **427–428**
    extended authentication in, **426–427**
    setting up, **446–450**, *446–450*
Remote Authentication Dial-In User Service (RADIUS), **28–29**
    corporate network example, **75–77**, *75*
    database configuration for, **74**, **77–78**
    vs. TACACS+, 71
Remote Desktop Exchange Protocol (RDEP), 668
remote offices, **1099**
remote sensors, **671**
Remote Shell (RSH), 348
remote site firewalls, 1142
Remote Site Peer screen, 441, *442*
remote site routers, 1142
remote SPAN (RSPAN), 742
    on CatOS, **758–761**, *758*
    on Cisco IOS, **753–758**, *754*
    configuring, **750–753**, *751*
    trunking for, **755–756**, **759–760**
remote-span command, 755

Rename Entry option, 1146
Repeat Action(s) After threshold, **1050**
replaying, **16–17**
replication failover, **384–385**
Report Filtering page, **1057–1059**, *1058*
Report tab, Center, 454
reports
    in ACS, **70**
    in IDS MC, **1011–1013**, *1012–1013*
    in PIX MC, 454
    in SAFE, **1089**
    in Secure Scanner, 1105
    in Security Monitor, 1019, **1057–1059**, *1057–1058*, *1060–1061*
Reports and Activity screen, 69, *69*
Reports tab
    for Auto Update Server, 456
    in Security Monitor, 1022
repudiation, 17
RequestInBalance parameter, 877
requesting certificates, **197–198**, **575–578**, *576–577*, **583–586**, *584–586*
RequestRegex parameter, 880
required access in networks, 647
required parameters for signature engines, 874
rerouting attacks, **17**, **88–90**
Reset action, 868
reset command, **727–728**
Reset Count Every threshold, **1050**
resets
    with IDS, 136
    for sensors, **727–728**, 853
    for signatures, 868
Resource Manager Essentials (RME), 943
response, intrusion, **669–670**, *670–671*
response actions in signatures, **867–868**
restoring sensor backup configuration files, 727
Restricted licenses, 236
restrictions, network access, **715–717**
Resume function for Realtime Dashboard, 932
Retries parameter, 1003
Reverse Route Injection (RRI), **514–515**
Revision property, 571

RFC filtering
    for IP spoofing, 1074
    in PIX Firewall, 1135
rip command, 299
RIPv2 (Routing Information Protocol
        version 2), 89
risk assessment for networks, 647
RME (Resource Manager Essentials), 943
role configuration for failover, 390
root CAs
    configuring, **196**
    in PKI, 574, *574*
root CEP command, 196
root PROXY command, 196
root TFTP command, 196
Rootkits, 641
Route command, 301
routed interfaces, 774
router-devices command, 836
router eigrp command, 89
Router sensor, 1103
routers
    blocking interface for, 828–829
    in IDS systems, 666
    ISP, 1123–1127
    network modules for, **675**
    in Remote Access Network Design, 1142,
        1156–1158, *1156*
    in SAFE, 1086
    for VPNs, **467–468**
Routes Details tab, 589, *589*
routes in failover, 377
Routing Blocking Device Interface page, 829,
    829
routing in PIX Firewall, **239**, **298–299**
    dynamic, 299–300
    multicast, 304–305
    static, 301–304, *301*
Routing Information Protocol version 2
        (RIPv2), 89
routing protocols as points of failure, 374
Routing Table screen, 602, *603*
routing tables for VPN Concentrators, **602**,
    603
routing updates in SAFE, 1087
RpcProgram parameter, 880
RRI (Reverse Route Injection), **514–515**

RSA-encrypted nonces
    in IKE, **162**
    in IPSec, **187–192**, 480
    keys for, **188–192**
RSA keys, 194
RSA signatures and certificates
    in IKE, **162–163**
    in IPSec, **479–480**
rsa1Keys command, 718
RSH (Remote Shell), **348**
RSPAN (remote SPAN), 742
    on CatOS, **758–761**, *758*
    on Cisco IOS, **753–758**, *754*
    configuring, **750–753**, *751*
    trunking for, **755–756**, **759–760**
RTCP (RTP Control Protocol), 350
RTSP (Real-Time Streaming Protocol),
    350–351
Rule page, 1045, *1046*
rules
    audit
        applying, **142–143**
        creating, **141–142**
        default actions for, **139–141**
    event, 1045, *1046*
    for firewall policies, 590, *590*
Rules screen, 590, *590*

S

sacrificial hosts, 34
SADs (security association databases), 156
SAFE
    architecture of, **1082–1085**, *1083*, *1085*
    axioms of, **1085–1089**
    design fundamentals in, **1084**
    IDS in, **1088–1089**
    medium network design, **1117–1118**,
        1117
        campus module, **1120–1122**, *1121*
        corporate Internet module,
            1118–1120, *1118*
        WAN module, **1122–1123**, *1122*
    Remote Access Network Design,
        1142–1143, *1143*
        firewall option for, **1149–1151**, *1149*

key devices in, **1143–1144**
routers in, **1156–1158**, *1156*
software access option in, **1144–1147**, *1145–1148*
VPN hardware client in, **1152–1155**, *1152–1155*
secure management and reporting in, **1089**
small network design, **1112**, *1113*
campus module, **1115–1116**, *1115*
corporate Internet module, **1112–1115**, *1113*
SafeNet client, **468–469**
SAs (security associations)
in IKE, **155**
in IPSec, **424–425**, **483–484**, *484*
lifetimes of, **176–177**
SATAN (Security Administrator Tool for Analyzing Networks), 634
saving sensor configurations, **997**, *998*
Scalable Encryption Processing (SEP) modules, 498
scanning tools for reconnaissance attacks, 634
SCEP (Simple Certificate Enrollment Protocol), 194
schedule command, 840
Schedule Report page, **1059**, *1060*
Scheduling parameter, 1003
scope in security policies, 1079
SCP (secure copy)
for Auto Update, **837–838**
for sensor updates, 847
screened subnets for firewalls, **227–229**, *228–229*
script kiddies, 631
scripts
for event actions, 1049
for IDS MC, **1010–1011**
SDN (Security Device Manager), **216–217**
Secondary DNS Server field, 511
Secondary sort order columns for IEV views, 915
secondary units in PIX Firewall, 380
Secure ACS. *See* ACS (Access Control Server)
secure connectivity
in Cisco security portfolio, **1094–1102**, *1095–1096*

in SAFE, 1082
secure copy (SCP)
for Auto Update, **837–838**
for sensor updates, 847
Secure phase in Security Wheel, **1090**, *1091*
Secure Scanner, **1104–1105**
Secure Shell (SSH)
for blocking devices, 827
hosts for, **717–719**
for sensors, 704, **830–831**, 970
Secure Sockets Layer (SSL)
certificates in, **580**, *581*, 785
for Cisco Works VMS, 957
in IDM, 785
secure VLAN interfaces (SVIs), 241
security. *See* network security
Security Administrator Tool for Analyzing Networks (SATAN), 634
security agents, **679**
Security Alert window, 785, *786*
security association databases (SADs), 156
security associations (SAs)
in IKE, 155
in IPSec, **424–425**, **483–484**, *484*
lifetimes of, **176–177**
Security Device Manager (SDN), **216–217**
security levels
in Cisco Works VMS, 959
in PIX Firewall, **239–240**, **267–269**, 1135
security management and administration
in Cisco security portfolio, 1094
in IDS systems, 666
in SAFE, 1082
weaknesses in, **10**
Security Monitor, **1018**, 1052
accessing, **1020–1022**, *1022–1023*
in Cisco Works VMS, 943
configuring, **1023**
database rules for, **1056**
defining devices to monitor in, **1023–1028**
DNS settings for, 1056
e-mail servers for, **1053**, *1053*
events in. *See* events
features of, **1018–1019**
PostOffice settings for, **1054**
reports for, 1019, **1057–1059**, *1057–1058*, *1060–1061*
sensors with, **1023–1028**

supported devices in, **1019–1020**
Syslog settings for, **1054**
updating signatures for, **1054**, *1054*
Security Monitoring Center, **677–678**, *679*, **952–956**, *953–955*
security monitoring in SAFE, 1082
security news, monitoring, **657**
Security Parameter Index (SPI) field, 472
Security Parameter Indexes (SPIs)
  in Authentication Header, 472
  for SAs, 156
security policies. *See* policies
security-scanner tools, **656**
security servers, authentication by, **28**
Security Wheel, 646, *646*, **1089–1091**, *1091*
security zones, **647–649**, *649*
Select CiscoWorks Syslog Port screen, *954*, *955*
Select Components screen, *950*, *951*
Select Configurations page, *1001*, *1002*
Select Database Location screen, *954*
Select Database Password screen, *954*
Select Destination Location screen, *900*, *900*
Select Device Type page, *1024*, *1025*
Select Devices page, *1026*, *1027*
Select Program Manager Group screen, *900–901*, *901*
Select Report page, *1011*, *1012*, *1057*, *1057*
Select Sensor Group page, *968*, *969*
Select Sensors To Update page, *1004*, *1005*
self-signed certificates, 785
sensing for sensors, **686**
sensing-interface command, 723
sensing interfaces
  in IDSM, **762**, *762*
  for sensors, **976**, *976*
Sensor Configuration Deployment report, 1012
Sensor Configuration Import report, 1012
Sensor page, **968**, *968*
Sensor Group page, **966**, *967*
Sensor Information page, *970*
Sensor Setup page, **790–791**, *790*
sensor-to-management platform ratio, **692**
Sensor Version Import reports, 1011
sensorApp application, 730

sensors, **684**, 1103
  access to, **704–708**, **715–717**
  adding, **1023–1025**, *1025–1026*
  administering, **724–728**
  architecture for, **728–732**, *731*
  for capturing traffic, **722–723**
  communications considerations for, **690–691**, *691*
  configurations
    approving, **1000–1001**, *1000*
    deploying, **1001–1003**
    generating, **998–1000**, *999*
    modes for, **713–715**
    saving, **997**, *998*
  connection status of, **906**, **1029**, *1029*
  filters for, **911**, **980–983**, *981–984*
  in IDC Management Center, **963**, *963*
    adding, **968–971**, *968–970*
    blocking, **984–990**
    communications settings for, **973–975**, *974–975*
    configuring, **966–968**, *967*, **971–972**, *971–972*
    internal network identification for, **976–977**, *977*
    intrusion detection settings for, **975–983**, *976–979*, *981–984*
    logging for, **990–991**, *990*
    master blocking, **988–990**, *989*
    port identification for, **977–978**, *978*
    reassembly options for, **978–980**, *979*
    sensing interfaces for, **976**, *976*
    for signatures, **991–996**, *991*, *993–996*
  IDS Device Manager for. *See* IDM (IDS Device Manager)
  in IDS systems, **665–667**, **671–676**
  for IEV, **903–907**, *903*, *906–907*
  importing information for, **1026–1028**, *1027–1028*
  initializing, **710–713**
  installing, **693**
    physical, **695–704**, *697–699*, *701*, *703*
    planning, **694–695**
  logging in to, **708–710**, *709*
  management considerations, **692**
  network access restrictions for, **715–717**
  network media considerations in, **686**

performance with, **685–686**, 689
placement considerations, **688–690**, *690*
rebooting, **727–728**
with Security Monitor, **1023–1028**
selecting, **684–688**
service accounts for, **720–721**
SSH for, **704**, **717–719**, **830–831**, **970**
system variables for
    alarm channel, **797–804**, *797*,
        799–801
    virtual sensor, **804–806**, *805–806*,
        809–810
for trunk traffic, **776–777**
trunking for, **687**
updating, 692, **845–848**, *847*,
    1003–1004, *1004–1005*
user accounts for, **719–720**
SEP (Scalable Encryption Processing)
    modules, 498
Sequence Number field, 473
sequences in crypto maps, 178
Server Certificate page, 793
Server Configuration drawer for Cisco
    Works VMS, 958
server farms, 689
servers
    ACS. *See* ACS (Access Control Server)
    backup, **515–516**, **563–564**, *564*
    for Cisco Easy VPNs, **211–213**
        configuring, **215**
        requirements, **944–946**
    dial-in, 1118
    DNS, 1114, 1118
    e-mail, **1053**, *1053*
    file, 1116, 1121
    HTTP. *See* HTTP and HTTP servers
    print, 1116, 1121
    SMTP
        in campus module, 1116, 1120
        in corporate Internet module, 1114,
            1118
        gather information from, **356–358**
    Syslog, 598, **612**, *612*, **614**, 614
    for TACACS+. *See* TACACS+ (Terminal
        Access Controller Access Control
        System) servers
    TFTP, 234, **1081**

service command, **715**
service alarm-channel-configuration
    command, 802, 812
Service Configuration mode for sensors, **715**
SERVICE engines
    parameters for, **880–881**
    subengines in, **869**
Service group, 885
service-module IDS-Sensor command, 708
service nagle command, **95**
service networkAccess command, 832
service packs, 846
service password-encryption command,
    37–38
service signatures, event filters for, 910, 992
service SshKnownHosts command, 718
service virtual-sensor-configuration
    command, 806, 893
ServicePorts parameter
    for custom signatures, 892
    for signature engines, 880
services, mismanaged, **8**
session hijacking, **16–17**
Session information for VPN Concentrators,
    604, **607–608**, *608*
session replay, **85–86**, *85*
session slot command, 244
session slot-number command, 706
Sessions field, 605
Sessions screen, 607–608, *608*
set peer command
    for crypto maps, 179
    for remote site routers, 1158
set pfs command, 179
set rspan destination command, 761
set rspan source command, 760
set security acl capture-ports command,
    769–770
set security acl ip command, 768, 770
set security acl map command, 769–770
set security-association level command, 179
set security-association lifetime command,
    179
set session-key inbound command, 187
set session-key outbound command, 187
set span command, 749–750, 766
Set Status To setting, 928

set summer-time command, 262
set transform-set command
 for crypto maps, 179
 for remote site routers, 1158
set trunk command, 759–760, 777–778
set vlan command, 244, 759, 779
setroute keyword, 272
Settings page, 971–972, *972*
Settings parameter, 966
Setup Complete screen, 63–64, *63*
Setup Type screen
 for Common Services, 949, *950*
 for IDS Management Center and Security Monitor Center, 953, *953*
setup utility
 for IDM, 790
 for PDM, 393–394
 for sensors, **710–712**
Severities option, 614
severity
 for event filters, 614, **908**, *909*
 in Event Viewer, 1042–1043, *1043*
 for signature filters, 993
Severity option, 993
shared directory, 731
Shared Profile Components screen, 66, *66*
shared secrets
 for clusters, 566
 in Diffie-Hellman key exchange, 477
shortcuts in Remote Access Network Design, 1146
show access-list command, 423
Show Attack Details option, 933
show auto-update command, 459
show ca certificate command, 413
show ca configure command, 414
show ca identity command, 414
show ca mypubkey rsa command, 413
show checksum command, **253**
show clock command, 262
Show Context option, 933
show cpu usage command, 232
show crypto ca certificates command, 198
show crypto ca roots command, 198
show crypto ipsec sa command, 185, 424

show crypto ipsec security-association lifetime command, 424
show crypto ipsec transform-set command, 184–185, 423
show crypto isakmp policy command, 174–175
show crypto isakmp sa command, 184
show crypto key command, 190–191
show crypto map command, 423
show events command, 858–859
show events error command, 859
show firewall module command, 242–243
show firewall vlan-group command, 242
show fixup command, 344
show flashfs command, 233
show floodguard command, 354
show fragment command, 362
show global command, 290
show igmp command, 305
show interface command, **253–254**, 270, 382
show interface ethernet1 command, 234
show interface vlan command, 243
show ip command, 280
show ip address outside pppoe command, 318
show ip audit command, 143–146
show ip audit count command, 364–368
show ip auth-proxy command, 133
show ip inspect config command, 117–118
show ip inspect interfaces command, 118–119
show ip inspect name command, 118
show ip port-map command, 113
show isakmp policy command, 422–423
show memory command, 232
show module command, 706
show monitor command, 758
show mroute command, 305
show nameif command, 267–268, 280
show nat command, 283–284, 290
show ntp associations command, 263
show ntp status command, 263
show route command, 302–303
show run command, 46
show settings command
 for sensors, 716, 718–719

for signatures, 896–897
for system variables, 804
show span command, 750
show static command, 290
show statistics command, 860–861
show tech-support command, **254**, 844
show tls fingerprint command, **794**, 905
show users command, 93
show version command
    for IDM, 843
    for PIX Firewall, 231–232
    for Privileged EXEC mode, 713
    for sensor software, 724
show vlan firewall-vlan command, 244
show vlan remote-span command, 755
show vpdn group command, 319
show vpdn pppinterface command, 319
show vpdn tunnel pppoe command, 318
show vpdn tunnel session command, 318
show xlate command, 238, 290
shun command, **254**, 369
shun-device-cfg command, 835, 837
shun-enable command, 833
shun-hosts command, 833, 852
shun-interfaces command, 837
shun-max-entries command, 833
shun-networks command, 833, 852
shun rules for IDM, **813–814**
shunning, 814
    in IDS, **369**
    by sensors, 717
shutdown keyword, 270
shutting down
    PIX Firewall interface, **269–271**
    sensors, 853, *854*
SIG system variables, **798**, 800
SIGID parameter
    for custom signatures, 891
    for event filters, 811
    for signature engines, 874
SigName parameter, 874
signature-based intrusion detection, **659–661**
Signature Configuration Mode page, 789, 890–892, *890–892*
signature filters, **810–813**, *810–812*

signature groups, 884
signature IDs for sensors, 991
signatures
    attack, 632
        classes of, 362–363
        filters for, 910
        in IDS, 136
        for sensors, 675, 992
    built-in, 867, **992–994**, *993–994*
    configuring, **137–138**
    custom, 671
        creating, **889–893**, *889–892*, **994–996**, *995–996*
    purpose of, 867
    disabling, **138–139**
    event filters for, **910–911**
    excluding, **139**
    in IDS, 103, **135–139**, 671, 866, 1102
        CLI for, **893–898**
        configuring, **884–886**, *884–887*
        custom, **889–893**, *889–892*
        enabling and disabling, **887–888**
        engines for, **868–871**, **873–883**
        features of, **867–868**
        tuning, **888–889**, *888*
        types of, **866–867**
    in IKE, **162–163**
    in IPSec, **479–480**
    and sensors for, 675, 846, **991–996**, *991*, *993–996*
    updating, **1054**, *1054*
signatures command, 895–896
Signatures page, 991, *991*
Signatures Configuration Mode page, 884–886, *884–887*
Signature(s) In Group page, 992, *993*, 994–995, *995*
Simple Certificate Enrollment Protocol (SCEP), 194
Simple Mail Transfer Protocol (SMTP) and SMTP servers
    in campus module, 1116, 1120
    in corporate Internet module, 1114, 1118
    gather information from, 356–358
    weaknesses in, 6

Simple Network Management Protocol
  (SNMP), 598
    blocking packets in, 92
    community strings in, 1080–1081
    configuring, 96–97
    locking down, 1086
    for VPN Concentrators, 611–612,
      611–612
    weaknesses in, 6
single destination ports for SPAN, 743
single points of failure, 373
single sensor and multiple perimeter devices
    architecture, 816–817, 816
single sensor and single perimeter device
    architecture, 815–816, 815
SinglePacketRegex parameter, 878
site-to-site VPNs, 151, 441–446, 441–446,
    1097
six interfaces, NAT on, 294–298, 295
SKEME protocol, 159
small network design, 1112, 1113
    campus module, 1115–1116, 1115
    corporate Internet module, 1112–1115,
      1113
small services, 92
SMR (Stub Multicast Routing), 304
SMTP (Simple Mail Transfer Protocol) and
    SMTP severs
    in campus module, 1116, 1120
    in corporate Internet module, 1114, 1118
    gather information from, 356–358
    weaknesses in, 6
SMTP rules in IOS-based firewalls, 1129
Smurf attacks, 17–18, 643
sniffers, 12–13, 1075–1076
    in campus module, 1116, 1122
    in corporate Internet module, 1115,
      1120
SNMP (Simple Network Management
    Protocol), 598
    blocking packets in, 92
    community strings in, 1080–1081
    configuring, 96–97
    locking down, 1086
    for VPN Concentrators, 611–612,
      611–612
    weaknesses in, 6

snmp-server community command, 97
social engineering, 1075–1076
soft tokens, 27
software, unauthorized distribution of, 16
software access in Remote Access Network
    Design, 1142, 1144–1147, 1145–1148
software client for Cisco Easy VPNs,
    213–215, 213–215
Software License Agreement screen
    for CSNT, 325
    for IDS Management Center and Security
      Monitor Center, 953
software updates for sensors, 692
software versions for sensors, 846
SOHO, VPNs for, 1099
Sort By section in Event Viewer, 1042
sort order for IEV views, 918, 920
Source Address parameter, 850
source addresses
    for blocking, 850
    event filters for, 909, 910
source ports
    for blocking, 851
    for RSPAN, 750–751
    for SPAN, 743
source sessions in RSPAN, 760–761
SP (State/Province) information for
    certificates, 577
SPAN (switch port analyzer), 740–741
    on CatOS, 749–750, 749, 765–766, 766
    on Cisco IOS, 746–749, 747, 766–767
    configuring, 743–746, 744
    for IDSM, 764–767, 766
    oversubscription with, 743
special-usage keys, 189
Specify The Event Filter page, 1047, 1047
Specify The Filter page, 1048
Specify The Thresholds And Intervals page,
    1050, 1051
Specify The Trigger Conditions page, 1008,
    1009
SPI (Security Parameter Index) field, 472
SPIs (Security Parameter Indexes)
    in Authentication Header, 472
    for SAs, 156
Split DNS Names attribute, 556
split-tunnel parameter, 429

split tunneling
    in Cisco Easy VPNs, 212
    configuring, **557–558**
    in Remote Access Network Design, 1145
Split Tunneling Network List attribute, *556*
Split Tunneling Policy attribute, *556*
spoofing, **16**, 1073
    in campus module, 1121
    in corporate Internet module, 1115, 1120
    countermeasures for, **653**
    filtering for, **819**
    IOS-based firewalls for, 1130
    PIX Firewall for, **1135**
    in Remote Access Network Design, 1150
SQL*NET, **349**
sqlUsername parameter, 880
square brackets ([]) in regular expressions, 870–871
SrcAddrs values, 811
SrcPort parameter, 878, 880
SSH (Secure Shell)
    for blocking devices, 827
    hosts for, **717–719**
    for sensors, 704, 830–831, 970
ssh command, **260–261**
ssh host-key command, 718
SSH known hosts table, 718
SSH option, 791
SSL (Secure Sockets Layer)
    certificates in, 580, *581*, 785
    for Cisco Works VMS, 957
    in IDM, 785
Stacheldraht attacks, 645
standby units in PIX Firewall, 380–381
state dependence in CBAC, 105
State/Province (SP) information for certificates, 577
STATE.STRING engine, **869**
state tables, 104
stateful failover, **385**, *386*, **388**
stateful firewalls, **226–229**
    for IPSec software client, 587
    in Remote Access Network Design, 1147
    setting up, **571–573**, *573*
stateful packet filtering, **1128–1130**
stateful pattern matching, **660**

static command
    for ACLs, 311
    in NAT, **282**
    in PAT, **288–289**
    for SYN Flood Guard, 354
static NAT, **274–275**
static/nat command, 1150
static routing
    for PIX Firewall, **301–304**, *301*
    for VPN 3002 Hardware Client, 512
Statistic Graph window, 936, *936*
statistics
    for device sensors, 907
    for events, **1039**, *1039*
    IDM, **859–861**, *860*
    IEV graphs for, **935–936**, *936*
    for IPSec software client firewalls, **588–589**, *588–589*
    for VPN Concentrators, **603–607**, *604–606*
Statistics page, 859, *860*
Statistics screen, 603–604, *604*
Stats Only access right, 618
status
    event filters for, **913**, *913*
    IPSec messages for, **426**
    sensor connection, 906, **1029**, *1029*
    VPN Concentrator, **600–602**, *601–602*
stderr traffic, 348
stdin traffic, 348
stdout traffic, 348
stealth features in reconnaissance attacks, 634
stop-stop keyword, 77
StorageKey parameter
    for custom signatures, 892
    for signature engines, **874–875**
stream reassembly for sensors, **979–980**
STRING engines
    parameters for, **881**
    subengines in, **869**
strong authentication, **650–651**
structured threats, 5, **631**, 1071
Stub Multicast Routing (SMR), 304
Subject Alternative Names for certificates, 577

Submit page, 1001, *1001*
subnet failures, **375**
subordinate CAs, **574**, *574*
subscriptions for sensors, 1029
Subsig ID option, 992
SubSig values
    for custom signatures, 891
    for event filters, 811
subsignatures, 811
Subsystem reports, 1011
Summarize parameter, 876–877
Summary screen
    for Common Services, 952, *952*
    for IDS Management Center and Security Monitor Center, 954, *954*
SummaryKey parameter
    for custom signatures, 892
    for signature engines, **875**
support protocols as points of failure, 374
SVIs (secure VLAN interfaces), 241
Swap Configuration Files screen, **621**, *621–622*
swapping configuration files, **621**, *621–622*
SWEEP engines
    parameters for, **882–883**
    subengines in, **869–870**
switch port analyzers (SPAN), **740–741**
    on CatOS, **749–750**, *749*, **765–766**, *766*
    on Cisco IOS, **746–749**, *747*, **766–767**
    configuring, **743–746**, *744*
    for IDSM, **764–767**, *766*
    oversubscription with, 743
switch sensors, 665
switched infrastructure for packet sniffers, 1076
switches
    in 4200 series sensors, **739–742**, *741–742*
    in campus module, 1116, 1121
    in corporate Internet module, 1114, 1119
    in FWSM, **242–244**
    in RSPAN, 751
    in SAFE, **1087**
switchport mode trunk command, 756
switchport trunk allowed vlans command, 244, 778
switchport trunk encapsulation command, 756
symmetric key algorithms, 153
symmetric key encryption, 478
SYN flood attacks, 14, 90, **643–644**, *644*
SYN Flood Guard, **354–355**
synchronizing clocks, **1081–1082**
SynFloodMaxEmbryonic parameter, 882
SYSLOG engine, **870**
syslog pruning, 1008
Syslog servers, 598, **612**, *612*, **614**, 614, **1081**
Syslog settings, **1054**
sysopt connection ipsec-permit command, 1151
sysopt connection permit-ipsec command, 408
sysopt security fragguard command, 361, 1135
system accounts, passwords for, **7–8**
System Administrator in Security Monitor, 1021
System Configuration page
    for IDS MC, 1006, *1006*
    for Security Monitor, 1053, *1053*
System Configuration screen, ACS, 67, *67*
system configuration settings
    for ACS, 67, *67*
    for IDS MC, **1006–1007**, *1006*
    for Security Monitor, 1053, *1053*
system control, IDM for, **853**, *854*
System Control page, 853, *853*
system images for PIX Firewall, **233**
System Info screen, 545, *546*
system information
    for CLI, **502**
    for IDM, 841, **844**
    for VPN Concentrators, 545, *546*
System Information page, 844, *844*
System LED for VPN Concentrator, 602
System Properties tab, 399, *400*
System Reboot screen, 621, *622*
system status information
    for VPN 3002 Hardware Client, 1154, *1155*
    for VPN Concentrators, **600–602**, *600–601*

System Status screen
    for VPN 3002 Hardware Client, 1154, *1155*
    for VPN Concentrators, 600, *601*
system time, 507, *507*
system variables
    alarm channel, **797–804**, *797, 799–801*
    virtual sensor, **804–806**, *805–806, 809–810*
System Variables page, 800, *800–801*
systemVariables command, 802, 804, 809–810

T

tables of contents (TOC)
    in IDC Management Center, 964, *965, 971–972, 972*
    in IDM, 788, *789*
tabs
    in IDC Management Center, 965, *965*
    in IDM, 788, *789*
TACACS+ (Terminal Access Controller Access Control System) servers, 15, **29**, **71–72**
    configuring, **72–74**
    interfaces for, 126, *126*
    in SAFE, 1086
    servers and keys for, **130**
    verifying, **78–80**
TACACS+ Accounting reports, 70
tacacs+ command, 41
tacacs-server command, 1157
tacacs-server host command, 77, 130, 1131
tacacs-server key command, 77, 130
targets
    for custom signatures, 889
    in SAFE, **1086–1088**
task flow in IPSec, **488–489**, *489*
TCP
    congestion algorithm for, 95
    fragment reassembly in, **979–980**
    incomplete sessions in, 110
TCP Intercept, **90–91**, 354
tcp intercept command, 1157

TCP/IP
    as point of failure, **374**
    subnet failures in, **375**
    weaknesses in, 6
TCP reset, 669, *670*
TCP SYN flood attacks, 14, 90, **643–644**, *644*
TCP SYN traffic, rate-limiting, **652**
tcpdump format command, 854
TCPFlags parameter, 878, 882
TCPFlags1 parameter, 882
TCPFlags2 parameter, 882
TcpInterest parameter, 882
technology weaknesses, **6–7**
telnet command, 93, **259–260**
telnet protocol
    locking down, 1086
    for network configuration, 1080
    on PIX Firewall, **335–337**
    for reconnaissance attacks, 634
    for sensors, 704, 710
Terminal Access Controller Access Control System (TACACS+) servers, 15, **29**
    configuring, **72–74**
    interfaces for, 126, *126*
    in SAFE, 1086
    servers and keys for, **130**
    verifying, **78–80**
Tertiary DNS Server field, 512
Test phase in Security Wheel, 1090, *1091*
TFN (Tribe Flood Network), 645
TFN2K attacks, 645
TFTP (Trivial File Transfer Protocol) servers
    for file transfer, **621–622**, *622*
    problems with, 234, **1081**
TFTP Server option, 622
TFTP Server File option, 622
TFTP Transfer screen, 622, *622*
threats, **630**
    attack types. *See* attacks
    firewalls for, **224**
    hacker characteristics in, **631–632**
three interfaces, NAT on, **291–294**, *292*
thresholds and intervals
    in CBAC, **108–110**
    for events, **1050–1052**, *1051–1052*
Throttled Rate/Volume field, 607

ThrottleInterval parameter, 876–877
tickets in Kerberos, 29
time
    event filters for, 911, *912*
    in IDM, 857
    for sensors, 794, *794*
    synchronizing clocks, **1081–1082**
    for VPN 3002 Hardware Client, 507, *507*
Time And Date screen, 507, *507*
Time criteria, 857
Time page, 794, *794*
Timeout parameter, 852
Timeout Period field, 512
Timeout Retries field, 512
timeouts
    in blocking, 852
    in CBAC, **108–110**
    in DNS configuration, 512
tls trusted-host ip-address command, 831
tmp directory, 732
TNS (Transparent Network Substrate), 349
TOC (tables of contents)
    in IDC Management Center, 964, *965*, 971–972, *972*
    in IDM, 788, *789*
token-card servers, 55
token cards, 27
tokens in strong authentication, 650
toolbars
    in Event Viewer, 1032
    in VPN Concentrator Manager window, 550
tools
    in IDC Management Center, 965, *965*
    in IDM, 788, *789*
top-10 sessions for VPN Concentrators, 608
topology maps, 647
traffic
    capturing. *See* capturing traffic
    delay, in IPSec, **490**
    in ESP, 153
TRAFFIC engine, **870**
Traffic Management screen, 509, *510*
TrafficFlowTimeout parameter, 882
TransactionServer statistics, 859
TransactionSource statistics, 859

transferring files with TFTP, **621–622**, *622*
Transform Set screen, 443, *444*
transforms and transform sets, **481–483**, *482*
    configuring, **416–418**, *417*
    creating, **176**
    encryption and hashing for, **153–154**
    security protocols for, **152–153**
    viewing, **423–424**
transit switches, 751
Transition Rules tab, 397, *398*
translation, address. *See* NAT (Network Address Translation); PAT (Port Address Translation)
translation slots in PIX Firewall, **238–239**
transparency, failover, 377
transparent bridging process, 739
Transparent Network Substrate (TNS), 349
Transport mode in IPSec
    encapsulation in, 157, *157–158*
    vs. Tunnel mode, 417, *417*, **474–476**, *475*
transports in access attacks, 641
transversal, NAT, 594, *595*
Trap Destinations screen, 611–612
trends, CBAC for, 105
Tribe Flood Network (TFN), 645
triggers
    for blocking, 823
    for profile-based intrusion detection, **658–659**
    for signature-based intrusion detection, **659–661**
Triple DES (3DES), 152, 154
Trivial File Transport Protocol (TFTP)
    for file transfer, **621–622**, *622*
    problems with, 234, **1081**
TROJAN engine, 870
Trojan horses, **19**, 641
    in Application layer attacks, 1072, 1077
    in campus module, 1116, 1121
    in corporate Internet module, 1114, 1119
troubleshooting
    AAA on NAS, 47–49
    IPSec, **490–491**
    LAN-to-LAN connections, **568**

trunking and trunk traffic
   for RSPAN, **755–756**, *759–760*
   and sensors, **687**, **776–777**
trust exploitation, **1077**, *1078*
   in campus module, 1116, 1122
   in corporate Internet module, 1115, 1120
trust relationships
   in access attacks, **636–637**, *637*
   eliminating, **652**
trusted computers in IP spoofing, 16
trusted hosts, 715–716, 792
Trusted Hosts page, 792
trusted networks, 223
trusted roots, **196**
TTY line type, 25
tune-alarm-channel command, 802, 812
tune-micro-engines command, 809, 893
Tune Signature page, **995**, *996*
tuned signatures, 867
Tunnel Details tab, **588–589**, *589*
Tunnel mode in IPSec
   encapsulation, **158**, *158–159*
   vs. Transport mode, 417, *417*, **474–476**, *475*
Tunnel Type attribute, 555
tunneling protocol configuration, **502–503**
tunnels, 467
   GRE, 180
   in IPSec, 470, *470*
      lifetime of, **418**, **423–424**
      in Remote Access Network Design, 1145, 1151
      termination of, **157**
   split
      in Cisco Easy VPNs, 212
      configuring, **557–558**
      in Remote Access Network Design, 1145
   for VPN Concentrators
      creating, **546**
      managing, **582–583**, *582–583*
      statistics for, **604–606**
2600/3600/3700 IDS network modules, **702–704**, *703*, **707–708**

Typical Installation option
   for Common Services, 949
   for IDS Management Center and Security Monitor Center, 954

U

UDP NAT Transparent IPSEC, 592
UDP protocols
   clusters ports, 566
   forwarded, **97–98**
   incomplete sessions in, 110
UdpInterest parameter, 882
umbrella protocols, 352
unauthorized access attacks, **15–16**, **1078**
   in campus module, 1116, 1121
   in corporate Internet module, 1115, 1120
   preventing, **86–88**
unauthorized data manipulation, 634
unauthorized distribution of software, 16
undebug all command, 78–79
unicast frames, 740
Unified client, 469
Uninstall Cisco IDS Event Viewer shortcut, 901
Unique parameter, **881–883**
UniqueTcpPorts parameter, 882
UniqueUdpPorts parameter, 882
unneeded services in SAFE, 1086
unplugged cables, failover for, 384
Unprivileged mode in CLI, **247**
unreachable messages, 94
Unrestricted licenses, 236
unsecured default settings, 8
unsecured user accounts, 7
unstructured threats, 5, **631**, 1071
untrusted network connections, 688
Update page, 846–847, *847*
Update NAT Addresses page, 1028, *1028*
Update Network IDS Signatures page, 1004, *1005*, 1054, *1055*
Update Summary page, 1054, *1055*
updates
   IDM for, **837–840**, *838*

for sensors, **692**, **845–848**, *847*, 1003–1004, *1004–1005*
signatures, **1054**, *1054*
VPN Concentrator
    automatic, **568–571**, *569–570*
    software, **623**, *623*
Updates page, 1003–1004, *1004*
upgrade command, 847
upgrading for sensors, **694–695**
UriRegex parameter, 880
url-block command, 314–315
url-cache command, 315
URL filtering, **312**
    operation of, 312–313
    PIX Firewall configuration for, **313–315**
url-server command, 313
URLs in VPN Concentrator updates, 571
usage-keys keyword, 189
Use Existing SSH Keys option, 970
user accounts. *See* users and user accounts
USER-ADDRS system variables, **798**
User Authentication screen, 124, *124*
User Datagram Protocol Network Address Translation Transparent IPSec, 592
user IDs, 970
user setup
    for ACS, **65**, *65*
    for VPN Concentrators, **559**, *559*
User Setup screen, **65**, *65*
user tunnels, **582–583**, *582–583*
user workstations, 1116, 1121
UserLength parameter, 881
username command
    in NAS, 36
    in PAP, 31
    for sensors, 720
    in TACACS+, 72
Username field, 607
usernames
    in authentication, 27
    in CHAP, 31
    for logical devices, 826
    in NAS, 31, 36
    in PAP, 30–31
    in PPPoE, **316**
    for sensors, 720, 830, 904
social engineering of, 1076
for tunnel statistics, 605
for VPN 3002 Hardware Client, 517
for VPN groups, 559
users and user accounts
    in ACS, **65**, *65*
    in Cisco Works VMS, **959–960**
    databases for
        for authentication, **54–55**
        populating, **55–56**
    for sensors, **719–720**, 970
    unsecured, 7
    for VPN 3002 Hardware Client, 512–513
    for VPN Concentrators, **559**, *559*, **561**, *561*, 617
Users page
    for Event Viewer, 1044
    for IDM, **795**, *795–796*

V

VACLs (VLAN access control lists), 740, 763–764, *765*
    for blocking devices, 829
    on CatOS, **767–770**
    on Cisco IOS, **771–774**
var directory, 732
VCA (Virtual Cluster Agent) protocol, 566
VCMs (virtual cluster masters), 518
versions
    of device sensors, 906
    for sensor updates, 846
vertical bars (|) in regular expressions, 871
View Config access right, 618
View Wizard dialog box, **918–921**, *919*
viewer accounts for sensors, 719
views for IEV, **914–920**, *919–920*
virtual alarm channels, 802
Virtual Cluster Agent (VCA) protocol, 566
virtual cluster masters (VCMs), 518
virtual HTTP, **335–337**
virtual http command, 335
virtual private dial-up networks (VPDNs), 316

virtual private networks. *See* VPNs (virtual private networks)
Virtual Router Redundancy Protocol (VRRP), 375, 518, 564
virtual sensors
　creating, 722
　system variables for, **804–806**, *805–806*, **809–810**
virtual telnet command, 336
virtualAlarm command, 812
viruses, **19**, **1078**
　in campus module, 1116, 1121
　in corporate Internet module, 1114, 1119
VLAN access control lists (VACLs), 740, **763–764**, *765*
　for blocking devices, 829
　on CatOS, **767–770**
　on Cisco IOS, **771–774**
vlan command, 242, 754
vlan access-map command, 771
vlan filter command, 772
VLAN Number parameter, 829
VLANs
　for blocking devices, 829
　on CatOS, **777–779**
　on Cisco IOS, **778–779**
　command-and-control ports for, **778–779**
　mapping VACLs to, **769**
　RSPAN, **754–755**, **759–760**
VMS. *See* Cisco Works VMS
vpdn command, 316
vpdn group command, 316
vpdn username command, 316
VPDNs (virtual private dial-up networks), 316
VPN 3000 Concentrators, **1100**
　IPSec over TCP for, **594**, *595*
　IPSec over UDP for, **592–594**, *593*
VPN 3002 Hardware Client, **500–501**, *500*
　Admin password for, 512
　CLI for, **501–505**
　configuring, **505–513**, *506–514*
　DNS configuration for, **511–512**, *511–512*
　interactive authentication in, **516–517**, *516–518*

IPSec configuration for, **508**, *509*
IPSec over TCP and backup servers in, **515–516**, *515*
load balancing in, **518–519**, *520*
managing, **513**, *513–514*
PAT and LAN Extension mode for, **509–510**, *509–510*
private interface for, 507, *508*
public interface for, 507, *508*
RRI in, **514–515**
static routing for, **512**
system time for, 507, *507*
user enabling for, **512–513**
VPN 3002 Interactive Authentication screen, 517, *517*
VPN 3005 Concentrators, **495–496**, *496*
VPN 3015-VPN 3080 Concentrators, **497–499**, *498–499*
VPN Client Group screen, 447, *447*
VPN Client Statistics screen, **588–589**, *588–589*
VPN clients, **432–433**, **468–469**, **520–521**, *521*
　authentication properties for, **521–522**, *522*
　auto-initiation of, **529–531**, *529*
　certificates for, **523–526**, *524–526*
　connections for, 521, *522*
　　profiles for, **437–439**
　　properties for, **523**, *523*
　deploying, **433–434**
　pre-configuring, **526–527**, **529**
　profiles for
　　connection, **437–439**
　　global, **433–437**
　in Remote Access Network Design, 1142, **1152–1155**, *1152–1155*
VPN Concentrator Manager window, 550, 580
VPN Concentrators, 468, **494–495**, **535–536**
　access hours for, **561**, *561*
　access rights for, **616–619**, *617–620*
　address assignments for, **546–547**, *546*
　admin password for, **549**, *549*
　administering, **616–624**, *616*

authentication for, **547–548**, *547*,
  559–560, *560*
backups for, **563–564**, *564*
certificates for
  downloading, **579–580**
  generating, **578–579**, *578–579*
  installing, **580**, *580*, **583–586**,
    584–586
  requesting, **575–578**, *576–577*,
    583–586, *584–586*
  viewing, **580–582**, *581*
CLI for, **536–543**
client support for, **499**, *499*
in corporate Internet module, 1119
file management for, **620–622**, *621–622*
filters for, **561–563**, *562–563*
firewall features for, **586–590**, *588–590*
groups in
  client properties for, **555–557**, *556*
  creating, **551**, *552*
  IPSec and Remote Access properties
    for, **553–555**, *554*
  names of, **548**, *548*
  properties for, **552–553**, *553*
  setting up, **550–551**
installing, **528**
LAN-to-LAN IPSec in, **566–568**, *567*
load balancing for, **564–566**
monitoring, **598–599**
  general statistics for, **603–607**,
    604–606
  local logs for, **614–615**, *615*
  logging traps for, **609–611**, *609–611*
  routing table information for, **602**, *603*
  session monitoring information in,
    607–608, *608*
  SNMP for, **611–612**, *611–612*
  Syslog servers for, **612**, *612*, **614**, *614*
  system status information for,
    600–602, *600–601*
physical interface configurations for, **545**,
  545
pinging devices for, **624**, *624*
stateful firewalls for, **571–573**, *573*
system information for, **545**, *546*
tunnels for
  creating, **546**

managing, **582–583**, *582–583*
statistics for, **604–606**
updating
  automatic, **568–571**, *569–570*
  software, **623**, *623*
VPN 3000, **1100**
  IPSec over TCP for, **594**, *595*
  IPSec over UDP for, **592–594**, *593*
VPN 3002. *See* VPN 3002 Hardware
  Client
VPN 3005, **495–496**, *496*
VPN 3015-VPN 3080, **497–499**,
  498–499
web Quick Configuration mode for,
  543–549, *544–549*
VPN Monitor, 943
VPN/Security Management Solutions
  drawer, 958
VPN tab, 450, *451*
VPN Wizard, **440–450**, *441–450*
vpnclient.ini file, 216, **433–437**, **526–527**,
  530–531
vpngroup command, 429
VPNs (virtual private networks), **406**, **466**,
  468
  AUS for, **456–459**, *457*
  benefits of, **469**
  for central offices, **1098**
  Cisco Easy. *See* Cisco Easy VPNs
  clients. *See* VPN clients
  Concentrators. *See* VPN Concentrators
  CSPM for, **452–453**, *452*
  endpoints in, **654**, *654*
  firewall-based, **1101–1102**
  Hardware Client for. *See* VPN 3002
    Hardware Client
  IKE for, **173–174**, **407–414**, *408*
  IPSec for. *See* IPSec
  MC for, **453–456**, *454–455*
  PDM for, **439–450**, *440–441*
    remote access, **446–450**, *447–451*
    site-to-site, **441–446**, *441–446*
  preparing for, **406–407**
  for regional offices, **1098**
  remote access. *See* remote access VPNs
  in Remote Access Network Design,
    1143–1144

for remote offices, **1099**
routers for, **467–468**
selecting, 1096
site-to-site, 151, **441–446**, *441–446*, **1097**
for SOHO, **1099**
types of, **150–151**, **466–467**, **1095–1097**, *1095–1096*
as WAN link replacements, **420–422**
VRFY command, 358
VRRP (Virtual Router Redundancy Protocol), 375, 518, 564
VSPAN, 744
VTY line type, 25
vulnerabilities and weaknesses, **6**
    configuration, **7–9**
    defined, 632
    eliminating, **653**
    IP, **1073–1074**
    policies, **9–10**
    protocols, **637–640**, *638–639*
    Secure Scanner for, 1104
    technology, **6–7**

W

wait-start keyword, 77
WAN link replacements, VPNs as, **420–422**
WAN module, **1122–1123**, *1122*
WareZ, 16
weaknesses. *See* vulnerabilities and weaknesses
Web browsers
    for Cisco Works VMS server, 947
    for IDM, 785
    for IEV, 923
web configuration for VPN Concentrators, **543–549**, *544–549*
Web servers
    for IDM, **784**
    as points of failure, 373
    for sensors, 710, 904, 907
    statistics for, 859

WEBSPORTS system variable, **804**, 806, 810
WEP (Wired Equivalent Privacy) protocol, 530
Whack-A-Mole application, 641
who command, 254
Windows, authentication in, **28**
Windows Logon Properties option, 1147
WinNuke attacks, 14
wins-server parameter, 429
Wired Equivalent Privacy (WEP) protocol, 530
workstations, 1116, 1121
worms, **19**
wrappers, TCP, 652
write command, **255**
write memory command, 385
write standby command, 385
write term command, 293

X

X.25 packet assembler/disassembler service, 95
X.509 certificates, 163
    in IKE, 164
    in PKI, 651
    in remote access VPNs, **426–427**
Xauth (extended authentication)
    in IKE, 164
    in remote access VPNs, **426–427**
xlate tables, 238

Y

Your Preferences page, 1044, *1044*

Z

ZLB (Zero Length Body) field, 605
zones, security, **647–649**, *649*

CISSP®: Certified Information Systems Security Professional Study Guide, 2nd Edition
by Ed Tittel, James Michael Stewart, Mike Chapple
ISBN 0-7821-4335-0
US $69.99

Here's the book you need to prepare for the challenging CISSP exam from (ISC)². This revised edition was developed to meet the exacting requirements of today's security certification candidates. In addition to the consistent and accessible instructional approach that earned Sybex the "Best Study Guide" designation in the 2003 CertCities Readers Choice Awards, this book provides:

- ✓ **Clear and concise information on critical security technologies and topics**
- ✓ **Practical examples and insights drawn from real-world experience**
- ✓ **Leading-edge exam preparation software, including a testing engine and electronic flashcards for your Palm**

You'll find authoritative coverage of key exam topics including:

- Access Control Systems & Methodology
- Applications & Systems Development
- Business Continuity Planning
- Cryptography
- Law, Investigation & Ethics
- Operations Security
- Physical Security
- Security Architecture & Models
- Security Management Practices
- Telecommunications, Network & Internet Security

SYBEX®
www.sybex.co

You Can Never be TOO Prepared

Extremely Affordable!

Downloadable Practice Tests from SYBEX

Sybex practice tests are a valuable way to reinforce your knowledge while preparing for your certification exam. This cutting edge testing software challenges you with questions similar to the format you will encounter on the real exams. Written by experts in the field, each practice test offers easy navigation, explanations for correct answers, and scoring by exam objective/ topic area.

Sybex Practice Tests are available for the following:
- CCNA™ (640-801)
- A+® Core Hardware (220-301)
- A+® Operating Systems Technologies (220-302)
- Network+® (N10-002)
- MCSA/MCSE Windows® XP Pro (70-270)

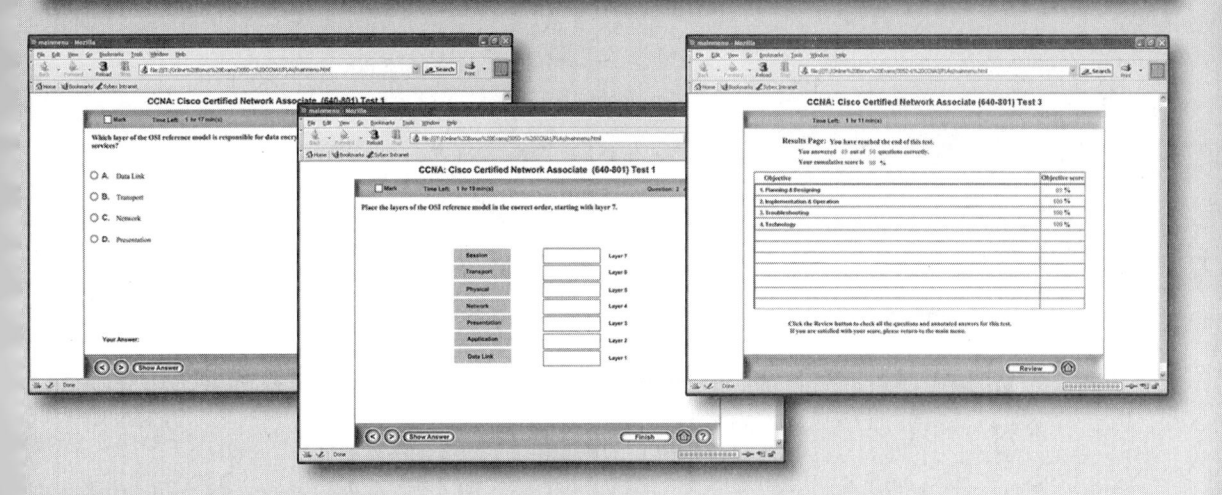

■ Detailed score reporting

■ Question formats similar to those on actual exams, including drag and drop

■ Multiple exams available for each certification

For pricing, online demos, and to purchase tests, visit www.sybex.com/practicetests

SYBEX®
www.sybex.com

TELL US WHAT YOU THINK!

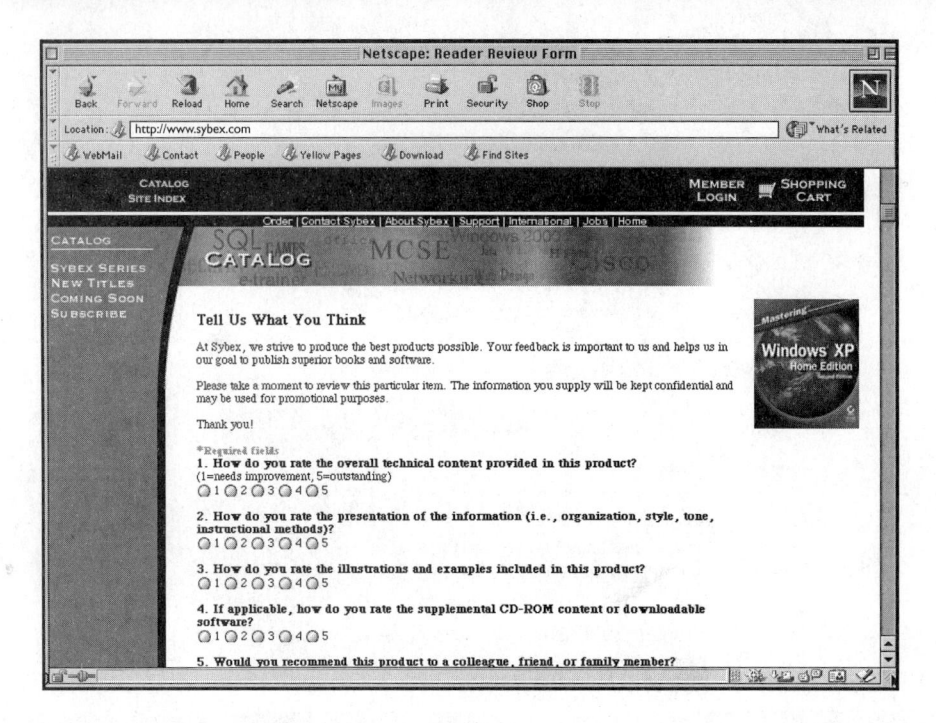

Your feedback is critical to our efforts to provide you with the best books and software on the market. Tell us what you think about the products you've purchased. It's simple:

1. Go to the Sybex website.
2. Find your book by typing the ISBN or title into the Search field.
3. Click on the book title when it appears.
4. Click **Submit a Review.**
5. Fill out the questionnaire and comments.
6. Click **Submit.**

With your feedback, we can continue to publish the highest quality computer books and software products that today's busy IT professionals deserve.

www.sybex.com

SYBEX Inc. • 1151 Marina Village Parkway, Alameda, CA 94501 • 510-523-8233